THE QUARTERLY JOURNAL OF ECONOMICS

FOUNDED 1886

VOLUME XCV

PUBLISHED FOR HARVARD UNIVERSITY
BY JOHN WILEY & SONS, NEW YORK

1980

In association with the Harvard Department of Economics and Invited Readers

Published eight times in 1980 (February, March, May, June, August, September, November and December), two volumes, four issues per volume, by John Wiley & Sons, Inc. Second class postage paid at New York, New York, and at additional mailing offices.

Subscription price (1981): $30.00 per volume. Postage and handling outside U.S.A.: $8.00 per volume. Please allow four weeks for change of address. Back volumes are available for previous years. Request price list from publisher. Claims for undelivered copies must be made no later than three months following month of publication. Missing copies will be supplied when losses have been sustained in transit and where reserve stock will permit.

Books, periodicals and manuscripts should be addressed to THE QUARTERLY JOURNAL OF ECONOMICS, Littauer Center, Cambridge, Massachusetts 02138. Two copies of manuscripts should be submitted in clear double-spaced typewritten copy. Manuscripts of more than thirty-five double-spaced typed pages in length are not ordinarily considered for publication. After publication, twenty-five complimentary reprints are sent to the author receiving proofs. This journal does not carry a page charge for contributors.

Business correspondence should be addressed to Journals Department, John Wiley & Sons, 605 Third Avenue, New York, New York 10158.

PRINTED IN UNITED STATES OF AMERICA

CONTENTS FOR VOLUME XCV

AUTHORS

PAGE

ABRAHAM, KATHARINE G., AND JAMES L. MEDOFF. Experience, Performance, and Earnings 703
ADAMS, JAMES D. Personal Wealth Transfers 159
AKERLOF, GEORGE A., AND ROSS D. MILBOURNE. Irving Fisher on his Head II: The Consequences of the Timing of Payments for the Demand for Money 145
BALLANTINE, J. GREGORY. Dividend Policy and Tax Incidence in a Growing Economy 781
BASU, KAUSHIK C. Optimal Policies in Dual Economies 187
BECKER, ROBERT A. On the Long-Run Steady State in a Simple Dynamic Model of Equilibrium with Heterogeneous Households 375
BHAGWATI, JAGDISH N., AND BALBIR S. SIHAG. Dual Markets, Rationing, and Queues 775
BHATTACHARYA, SUDIPTO. Nondissipative Signaling Structures and Dividend Policy 1
BORKAKOTI, JITENDRALAL. Generalized Findlay-Grubert Theorem 587
CALVO, GUILLERMO A., AND STANISLAW WELLISZ. Technology, Entrepreneurs, and Firm Size 663
CARLTON, DENNIS W., AND GLENN C. LOURY. The Limitations of Pigouvian Taxes as a Long-Run Remedy for Externalities 559
CHEN, CHAU-NAN, GRAHAM PYATT, AND JOHN FEI. The Distribution of Income by Factor Components 451
CLARK, KIM B. Unionization and Productivity: Micro-Econometric Evidence 613
DORNBUSCH, RUDIGER, STANLEY FISCHER, AND PAUL A. SAMUELSON. Heckscher-Ohlin Trade Theory with a Continuum of Goods 203
DRISKILL, ROBERT, AND STEPHEN MCCAFFERTY. Exchange-Rate Variability, Real and Monetary Shocks, and the Degree of Capital Mobility Under Rational Expectations 577
EATON, JONATHAN, AND HARVEY S. ROSEN. Optimal Redistributive Taxation and Uncertainty 357
ELLIOTT, J. WALTER. Wealth and Wealth Proxies in a Permanent Income Model 509
ELLIOTT, JOHN E. Marx and Schumpeter on Capitalism's Creative Destruction: A Comparative Restatement 45
FEI, JOHN, GRAHAM PYATT, AND CHAU-NAN CHEN. The Distribution of Income by Factor Components 451
FISCHER, STANLEY, RUDIGER DORNBUSCH, AND PAUL A. SAMUELSON. Heckscher-Ohlin Trade Theory with a Continuum of Goods 203
FRENKEL, JACOB A., AND BOYAN JOVANOVIC. On Transactions and Precautionary Demand for Money 25
GRETHER, DAVID M. Bayes Rule as a Descriptive Model: The Representativeness Heuristic 537
GUASCH, J. LUIS , AND ANDREW WEISS. Erratum: Adverse Selection by Markets and the Advantage of Being Late 201

PAGE

HAMERMESH, DANIEL S. Factor Market Dynamics and the Incidence of Taxes and Subsidies 751
HAURIN, DONALD R. The Regional Distribution of Population, Migration, and Climate 293
HEY, JOHN D., AND PETER J. LAMBERT. Relative Deprivation and the Gini Coefficient: Comment 567
HICKS, MICHAEL. A Model of Forced Saving Based Upon Differential Expectations 181
HOLMSTROM, BENGT. The Cost of Capital in Nonmarketed Firms 765
HURD, MICHAEL. A Compensation Measure of the Cost of Unemployment to the Unemployed 225
JOVANOVIC, BOYAN, AND JACOB A. FRENKEL. On Transactions and Precautionary Demand for Money 25
KORLIRAS, PANAYOTIS G. A Disequilibrium Macroeconomic Model: The Implications of a Correction 199
LAITNER, JOHN. "Rational" Duopoly Equilibria 641
LAMBERT, PETER J., AND JOHN D. HEY. Relative Deprivation and the Gini Coefficient: Comment 567
LEWIS, TRACY R., AND RICHARD SCHMALENSEE. On Oligopolistic Markets for Nonrenewable Natural Resources 475
LOURY, GLENN C., AND DENNIS W. CARLTON. The Limitations of Pigouvian Taxes as a Long-Run Remedy for Externalities 559
MACMINN, RICHARD D. Job Search and the Labor Dropout Problem Reconsidered 69
MANSFIELD, EDWIN, AND ANTHONY ROMEO. Technology Transfer to Overseas Subsidiaries by U. S.-Based Firms 737
MAYER, THOMAS. David Hume and Monetarism 89
MCCAFFERTY, STEPHEN, AND ROBERT DRISKILL. Exchange-Rate Variability, Real and Monetary Shocks, and the Degree of Capital Mobility Under Rational Expectations 577
MEDOFF, JAMES L., AND KATHARINE G. ABRAHAM. Experience, Performance, and Earnings 703
MILBOURNE, ROSS D., AND GEORGE A. AKERLOF. Irving Fisher on his Head II: The Consequences of the Timing of Payments for the Demand for Money 145
MILLER, JEFFREY B. A Method for Determining the Appropriateness of National Planning in a Market Economy 261
MILLER, STEPHEN M. A Disequilibrium Macroeconomic Model: A Correction 197
NEARY, J. PETER. Nontraded Goods and the Balance of Trade in a Neo-Keynesian Temporary Equilibrium 403
OFER, GUR, AND JOYCE PICKERSGILL. Soviet Household Saving: A Cross-Section Study of Soviet Emigrant Families 121
PICKERSGILL, JOYCE, AND GUR OFER. Soviet Household Saving: A Cross-Section Study of Soviet Emigrant Families 121
PLOTNICK, ROBERT. A Comment on Measuring Horizontal Equity 383
POSSEN, URI, AND STEVEN SLUTSKY. Public-Private Consumption Tradeoffs and the Balanced Budget Multiplier 679
PYATT, GRAHAM, CHAU-NAN CHEN, AND JOHN FEI. The Distribution of Income by Factor Components 451
RAM, RATI. Role of Education in Production: A Slightly New Approach 365

PAGE

RATTI, RONALD A. Bank Attitude Toward Risk, Implicit Rates of Interest, and the Behavior of an Index of Risk Aversion for Commercial Banks 309
ROBERTS, BLAINE. The Effects of Supply Contracts on the Output and Price of an Exhaustible Resource 245
ROMEO, ANTHONY, AND EDWIN MANSFIELD. Technology Transfer to Overseas Subsidiaries by U. S.-Based Firms 737
ROPER, DON E., AND STEPHEN J. TURNOVSKY. The Optimum Monetary Aggregate for Stabilization Policy 331
ROSEN, HARVEY S., AND JONATHAN EATON. Optimal Redistributive Taxation and Uncertainty 357
SAMUELSON, PAUL A., RUDIGER DORNBUSCH, AND STANLEY FISCHER. Heckscher-Ohlin Trade Theory with a Continuum of Goods 203
SAPIR, ANDRÉ. A Growth Model for a Tenured-Labor-Managed Firm 387
SCHMALENSEE, RICHARD, AND TRACY R. LEWIS. On Oligopolistic Markets for Nonrenewable Natural Resources 475
SCHMENNER, ROGER W. Choosing New Industrial Capacity: On-Site Expansion, Branching, and Relocation 103
SIHAG, BALBIR S., AND JAGDISH N. BHAGWATI. Dual Markets, Rationing, and Queues 775
SLUTSKY, STEVEN, AND URI POSSEN. Public-Private Consumption Tradeoffs and the Balanced Budget Multiplier 679
SPENCE, A. MICHAEL, Notes on Advertising, Economies of Scale, and Entry Barriers 493
STOKEY, NANCY L. Job Differentiation and Wages 431
TURNOVSKY, STEPHEN J., AND DON E. ROPER. The Optimum Monetary Aggregate for Stabilization Policy 331
WEISS, ANDREW, AND J. LUIS GUASCH. Erratum: Adverse Selection by Markets and the Advantage of Being Late 201
WEISS, LAURENCE. A Model of International Trade and Finance 277
WELLISZ, STANISLAW, AND GUILLERMO A. CALVO. Technology, Entrepreneurs, and Firm Size 663
YITZHAKI, SHLOMO. Relative Deprivation and the Gini Coefficient: Reply .. 575

TITLES

PAGE

Bank Attitude Toward Risk, Implicit Rates of Interest, and the Behavior of an Index of Risk Aversion for Commercial Banks. Ronald A. Ratti 309
Bayes Rule as a Descriptive Model: The Representativeness Heuristic. David M. Grether 537
Choosing New Industrial Capacity: On-Site Expansion, Branching, and Relocation, Roger W. Schmenner 103
A Comment on Measuring Horizontal Equity. Robert Plotnick 383
A Compensation Measure of the Cost of Unemployment to the Unemployed. Michael Hurd 225
The Cost of Capital in Nonmarketed Firms. Bengt Holmstrom 765
David Hume and Monetarism. Thomas Mayer 89
A Disequilibrium Macroeconomic Model: A Correction. Stephen M. Miller .. 197
A Disequilibrium Macroeconomic Model: The Implications of a Correction. Panayotis G. Korliras 199
The Distribution of Income by Factor Components. Graham Pyatt, Chau-nan Chen, and John Fei 451

PAGE

Dividend Policy and Tax Incidence in a Growing Economy. J. Gregory Ballentine 781
Dual Markets, Rationing, and Queues. Jagdish N. Bhagwati and Balbir S. Sihag 775
The Effects of Supply Contracts on the Output and Price of an Exhaustible Resource. Blaine Roberts 245
Erratum: Adverse Selection by Markets and the Advantage of Being Late. J. Luis Guasch and Andrew Weiss 201
Exchange-Rate Variability, Real and Monetary Shocks, and the Degree of Capital Mobility Under Rational Expectations. Robert Driskill and Stephen McCafferty 577
Experience, Performance, and Earnings. James L. Medoff and Katharine G. Abraham 703
Factor Market Dynamics and the Incidence of Taxes and Subsidies. Daniel S. Hamermesh 751
Generalized Findlay-Grubert Theorem. Jitendralal Borkakoti 587
A Growth Model for a Tenured-Labor-Managed Firm. André Sapir 387
Heckscher-Ohlin Trade Theory with a Continuum of Goods. Rudiger Dornbusch, Stanley Fischer, and Paul A. Samuelson 203
Irving Fisher on his Head II: The Consequences of the Timing of Payments for the Demand for Money. George A. Akerlof and Ross D. Milbourne 145
Job Differentiation and Wages. Nancy L. Stokey 431
Job Search and the Labor Dropout Problem Reconsidered. Richard D. MacMinn 69
The Limitations of Pigouvian Taxes as a Long-Run Remedy for Externalities. Dennis W. Carlton and Glenn C. Loury 559
On the Long-Run Steady State in a Simple Dynamic Model of Equilibrium with Heterogeneous Households. Robert A. Becker 375
Marx and Schumpeter on Capitalism's Creative Destruction: A Comparative Restatement. John E. Elliott 45
A Method for Determining the Appropriateness of National Planning in a Market Economy. Jeffrey B. Miller 261
A Model of Forced Saving Based Upon Differential Expectations. Michael Hicks 181
A Model of International Trade and Finance. Laurence Weiss 277
Nondissipative Signaling Structures and Dividend Policy. Sudipto Bhattacharya 1
Nontraded Goods and the Balance of Trade in a Neo-Keynesian Temporary Equilibrium. J. Peter Neary 403
Notes on Advertising, Economies of Scale, and Entry Barriers. A. Michael Spence 493
On Oligopolistic Markets for Nonrenewable Natural Resources. Tracy R. Lewis and Richard Schmalensee 475
Optimal Policies in Dual Economies. Kaushik C. Basu 187
Optimal Redistributive Taxation and Uncertainty. Jonathan Eaton and Harvey S. Rosen 357
The Optimum Monetary Aggregate for Stabilization Policy. Don E. Roper and Stephen J. Turnovsky 331
Personal Wealth Transfers. James D. Adams 159
Public-Private Consumption Tradeoffs and the Balanced Budget Multiplier. Uri Possen and Steven Slutsky 679

PAGE

"Rational" Duopoly Equilibria. John Laitner 641
The Regional Distribution of Population, Migration, and Climate. Donald R. Haurin 293
Relative Deprivation and the Gini Coefficient: Comment. John D. Hey and Peter J. Lambert 567
Relative Deprivation and the Gini Coefficient: Reply. Shlomo Yitzhaki 575
Role of Education in Production: A Slightly New Approach. Rati Ram 365
Soviet Household Saving: A Cross-Section Study of Soviet Emigrant Families. Gur Ofer and Joyce Pickersgill 121
Technology, Entrepreneurs, and Firm Size. Guillermo A. Calvo and Stanislaw Wellisz 663
Technology Transfer to Overseas Subsidiaries by U. S.-Based Firms. Edwin Mansfield and Anthony Romeo 737
On Transactions and Precautionary Demand for Money. Jacob A. Frenkel and Boyan Jovanovic 25
Unionization and Productivity: Micro-Econometric Evidence. Kim B. Clark . 613
Wealth and Wealth Proxies in a Permanent Income Model. J. Walter Elliott . 509

Statement of Ownership, Management and Circulation
(*Required by 39 U.S.C. 3685*)

1. Title of publication: Quarterly Journal of Economics
2. Date of filing: 1 October 1980
3. Frequency of publication: Eight times yearly
   A. Number of issues published annually: 8
   B. Annual subscription price: $50.00
4. Location of known office of publication: John Wiley & Sons, Inc., 605 Third Avenue, New York, NY 10158
5. Location of the headquarters or general business offices of the publishers: John Wiley & Sons, Inc., 605 Third Avenue, New York, NY 10158
6. Publisher: John Wiley & Sons, Inc., 605 Third Avenue, New York, NY 10158
   Board of Editors: Olivier J. Blanchard, Harvard University, Littauer 123, Cambridge, MA 02138; Robert Dorfman, Department of Economics, Harvard University, Littauer Center 325, Cambridge, MA 02138; Malcolm Gillis, HIID 1737 Cambridge St., Cambridge, MA 02138; Jerry Green, Littauer 310, Harvard University, Cambridge, MA 02138; David Hartman, Littauer 113, Harvard University, Cambridge, MA 02138; Josept P. Kalt, Littauer 211, Harvard University, Cambridge, MA 02138.
   Managing Editor: None
7. Owner: President and Fellows of Harvard College (a not-for-profit educational institution existing under the laws of the commonwealth of Massachusetts),Cambridge, MA 02138
8. Known bondholders, mortgagees, and other security holders owning or holding one percent or more of the total amount of bonds, mortgages, or other securities: None
10. Extent and nature of circulation:

	Average number of copies of each issue during preceding 12 months	Actual number of copies of single issue published nearest to filing date
A. Total number of copies printed	5275	5100
B. Paid circulation		
1. Sales through dealers and carriers, street vendors and counter sales	none	none
2. Mail subscriptions	4793	4708
C. Total paid circulation	4793	4708
D. Free distribution by mail, carrier or other means, samples, complimentary, and other free copies	71	68
E. Total distribution	4864	4776
F. Copies not distributed		
1. Office use, left over, unaccounted, spoiled after printing	411	324
2. Returns from news agents	none	none
G. Total	5275	5100

11. I certify that the statements made by me above are correct and complete.
    Allan Wittman, *Publisher*
12. For completion by publishers mailing at the regular rates: 39 U. S. C. 3626 provides in pertinent part: "No person who would have been entitled to mail matter under former section 4359 of this title shall mail such matter at the rates provided under this subsection unless he files annually with the Postal Service a written request for permission to mail matter at such rates." In accordance with the provisions of this statute, I hereby request permission to mail the publication named in Item 1 at the phased postage rates presently authorized by 39 U. S. C. 3626.
    Allan Wittman, *Publisher*

The Quarterly Journal of Economics gratefully acknowledges the help of the people listed below who refereed one or more papers in 1980.

Andrew Abel
James Adams
Walter Adams
George Akerlof
Mohiuddin Alamgir
Sidney Alexander
Elisabeth Allison
Kenneth Arrow
Roland Artle
Alan Auerbach
Costas Azariadis
Werner Baer
Martin J. Bailey
Martin N. Baily
Bela Balassa
Gregory Ballentine
P. K. Bardhan
David P. Baron
Yoram Barzel
William Baumol
Ralph Beals
Gary Becker
Barbara Bergmann
Theodore C. Bergstrom
Benjamin Bernanke
Douglas Bernheim
Sudipto Bhattacharya
Jagdish Bhagwati
John Bilson
Nancy Birdsall
Alan Blinder
Peter Bohm
Ronald Braeutigan
William Branson
Richard Brecher
Murray Brown
Edgar K. Browning
Earl Brubaker
Michael Bruno
Henry J. Bruton
John Bryant
Jeremy Bulow
Edwin Burmeister
Gerard R. Butters
Guillermo Calvo
Dennis W. Carlton
Richard Caves
Christophe Chamley
John Chipman
Kim B. Clark
Peter K. Clark
Richard Clarke
Charles Clotfelter
Robert Conrad
Peter Coughlin
Michael Crew
Leon Courville
David Dapice
Michael Darby
Ralph d'Arge
Paul David
Lance Davis
Stephen DeCanio
Padma DeSai
Peter Doeringer
David Donaldson
Rudiger Dornbusch
John Dutton
Curtis B. Eaton
Liam P. Ebrill
David Elwood
Edward Erickson
Richard Ericson
Arthur Eubank
Gershon Feder
Martin Feldstein
Gary Fields
Morris Fiorina
Stanley Fischer
Anthony C. Fisher
Franklin Fisher
Mark Flannery
David Flath
Marjorie Flavin
John Flemming
Robert Flood
Jeffrey Frankel
A. Myrick Freeman
Richard Freeman
Benjamin Friedman
James W. Friedman
Richard T. Froyen
Roman Frydman
Carl Futia
David Galenson
Peter Garber
John Geanakoplos
Nicholas Georgescu-Roegen
Richard Gilbert
Malcolm Gillis
Richard Goldman
Steven Goldman
Robert J. Gordon
L. M. Goreaux
William Gould
Henry G. Grabowski
Nils Hakansson
Robert E. Hall
Peter J. Hammond
Giora Hanoch
William Haraf
David Hartman
Richard Hartman
Robert Heilbroner
J. M. Heineke
Walter P. Heller
J. V. Henderson
Claude Henry
William Holahan
Bengt Holmstrom
Seppo Honkapohja
Thomas Horst
Robert M. Hutchens
Yuji Ijiri
Gregory Ingram
Takatoshi Ito
K. Iwai
Leif Johansen
David Johnson
George Johnson
Leroy Jones
Ronald Jones
Charles Kahn
John Kain
Nicholas Kaldor
Morton I. Kamien
Roger Kaufman
Nathan Keyfitz

Nicholas Kiefer
Benjamin Klein
William Krasker
Gene Kroch
Paul Krugman
David Landes
Donald LeCraw
Edward Lazear
William Lazonick
John Ledyard
Keith B. Leffler
Harvey Leibenstein
Dutch Leonard
Wassily Leontief
Donald Lessard
Rick Levin
David Lilien
Richard G. Lipsey
David Lipton
Robert Litterman
John Long
Millard Long
Glenn C. Loury
Robert E. Lucas
Arthur Maass
John H. Makin
Michael H. Mann
Richard C. Marston
Robert Masson
Donald Mathieson
Frank Matthewson
Richard Mattione
Stephen McCafferty
Bennett McCallum
Donald McCloskey
Rachel McCulloch
Donald McFetridge
James Medoff
Angelo Melino
Robert Merton
John Meyer
Frank Michelman
Peter Mieszkowski
Ross Milbourne
Merton H. Miller
Joseph Minarik
Jacob Mincer

Leonard Mirman
Hajime Miyazaki
William J. Moore
Knut Mork
Richard Musgrave
Thomas Nagel
D. T. Nguyen
Jurg Niehans
William Nordhaus
Walter Oi
Peter Ordeshook
Daniel Orr
Attiat Ott
Rolla E. Park
Michael Parkin
Donald O. Parsons
Peter Pashigian
James Pearce
John Pencavel
Jeffrey Perloff
James Pesando
Christopher Piro
Mitchell Polinsky
James Poterba
Walter J. Primeaux
Harvey Rosen
Gideon Rosenbluth
Marc Rosensweig
Charles Rowley
Paul H. Rubin
Mark Rubinstein
Paul Samuelson
William Samuelson
Steve Sandell
M. Satterthwaite
Frederic M. Scherer
Richard Schmalensee
Larry Selden
Eugene Seskin
Steven Shavell
John Sheahan
Eytan Sheshinski
Joel Slemrod
Dennis Smallwood
Vernon Smith
Richard Spady
David Starrett

Richard Startz
Peter O. Steiner
Stanley Stephenson
Joseph Stiglitz
Robert Stillman
James Sweeney
Moshe Syrquin
Akira Takayama
T. Takayama
John B. Taylor
Lester Taylor
Peter Temin
Irwin Tepper
Richard N. Thaler
Stavros Thomadakis
Lester Thurow
C. Peter Timmer
Robert Topel
Stephen J. Turnovsky
Harold Varian
Philip Verleger
William Vickrey
Jose Vinals
W. Kip Viscusi
George M. Von Furstenberg
C. C. Von Weizsacker
Neil Wallace
Donald Walls
Michael L. Wachter
Michael Ward
Harry Watson
Laurence Weiss
Yoram Weiss
Louis Wells
E. G. West
Frank Westhoff
John Whalley
Lawrence White
Louis Wilde
Thomas Willett
Robert Willig
Charles Wilson
Brian Wright
Pan Yotopoulos
Edward E. Zajac
Richard Zeckhauser

No. 378

THE QUARTERLY JOURNAL OF ECONOMICS

FOUNDED 1886

Vol. XCV August 1980 No. 1

ARTICLES

Nondissipative Signaling Structures and Dividend Policy .... *Sudipto Bhattacharya* 1

On Transactions and Precautionary Demand for Money .... *Jacob A. Frenkel and Boyan Jovanovic* 25

Marx and Schumpeter on Capitalism's Creative Destruction: A Comparative Restatement .... *John E. Elliott* 45

Job Search and the Labor Dropout Problem Reconsidered .... *Richard D. MacMinn* 69

David Hume and Monetarism .... *Thomas Mayer* 89

Choosing New Industrial Capacity: On-Site Expansion, Branching, and Relocation .... *Roger W. Schmenner* 103

Soviet Household Saving: A Cross-Section Study of Soviet Emigrant Families .... *Gur Ofer and Joyce Pickersgill* 121

Irving Fisher on his Head II: The Consequences of the Timing of Payments for the Demand for Money .. *George A. Akerlof and Ross D. Milbourne* 145

Personal Wealth Transfers .... *James D. Adams* 159

NOTES

A Model of Forced Saving Based Upon Differential Expectations .... *Michael Hicks* 181

Optimal Policies in Dual Economies .... *Kaushik C. Basu* 187

A Disequilibrium Macroeconomic Model:
- A Correction .... *Stephen M. Miller* 197
- The Implications of a Correction .... *Panayotis G. Korliras* 199

Erratum: Adverse Selection by Markets and the Advantage of Being Late .... *J. Luis Guasch and Andrew Weiss* 201

PUBLISHED FOR HARVARD UNIVERSITY
BY JOHN WILEY & SONS, NEW YORK

QJECAT 95(1) 1–202 (1980)
ISSN 0033-5533

The Quarterly Journal of Economics

Published eight times yearly (February, March, May, June, August, September, November and December), two volumes per year, four issues per volume, by John Wiley & Sons, Inc. Second class postage paid at New York, New York, and at additional mailing offices.

Subscription price: $50.00 per year. Postage and handling outside U.S.A.: $14.00 per year. Please allow four weeks for change of address. Back volumes are available for previous years. Request price list from publisher. Claims for undelivered copies must be made no later than three months following month of publication. Missing copies will be supplied when losses have been sustained in transit and where reserve stock will permit.

Books, periodicals and manuscripts should be addressed to THE QUARTERLY JOURNAL OF ECONOMICS, Littauer Center, Cambridge, Massachusetts 02138. Two copies of manuscripts should be submitted in clear double-spaced typewritten copy. Manuscripts of more than thirty-five double-spaced typed pages in length are not ordinarily considered for publication. After publication, twenty-five complimentary reprints are sent to the author receiving proofs. This journal does not carry a page charge for contributors.

Business correspondence should be addressed to Journals Department, John Wiley & Sons, 605 Third Avenue, New York, New York 10158.

THE

QUARTERLY JOURNAL OF ECONOMICS

Vol. XCV August 1980 No. 1

ARTICLES

Nondissipative Signaling Structures and Dividend Policy . . . . . *Sudipto Bhattacharya* 1

On Transactions and Precautionary Demand for Money . . . . . *Jacob A. Frenkel and Boyan Jovanovic* 25

Marx and Schumpeter on Capitalism's Creative Destruction: A Comparative Restatement . . . . . *John E. Elliott* 45

Job Search and the Labor Dropout Problem Reconsidered . . . . . *Richard D. MacMinn* 69

David Hume and Monetarism . . . . . *Thomas Mayer* 89

Choosing New Industrial Capacity: On-Site Expansion, Branching, and Relocation . . . . . *Roger W. Schmenner* 103

Soviet Household Saving: A Cross-Section Study of Soviet Emigrant Families . . . . . *Gur Ofer and Joyce Pickersgill* 121

Irving Fisher on his Head II: The Consequences of the Timing of Payments for the Demand for Money . . *George A. Akerlof and Ross D. Milbourne* 145

Personal Wealth Transfers . . . . . *James D. Adams* 159

NOTES

A Model of Forced Saving Based Upon Differential Expectations . . . . . *Michael Hicks* 181

Optimal Policies in Dual Economies . . . . . *Kaushik C. Basu* 187

A Disequilibrium Macroeconomic Model:
A Correction . . . . . *Stephen M. Miller* 197
The Implications of a Correction . . . . . *Panayotis G. Korliras* 199

Erratum: Adverse Selection by Markets and the Advantage of Being Late . . . . . *J. Luis Guasch and Andrew Weiss* 201

Information for Authors

The provisions of the new copyright law, which went into effect in January 1978, make it advisable for authors to transfer copyrights to publishers explicitly and in writing. Under the old copyright law the transfer implicit in submission gave adequate protection to all concerned. Accordingly, we now require that the following agreement be executed and signed by the author(s) before a manuscript is accepted for publication. The signed agreement is then to be returned to *The Quarterly Journal of Economics*.

Agreement to Transfer Copyright

Name of Article: ____

____

I submit herewith the article named above for publication in *The Quarterly Journal of Economics*. It has not been published before. If and when the article is accepted for publication, I, as the author, hereby agree to transfer (for U.S. Government employees: to the extent transferable) to the President and Fellows of Harvard College all rights under existing copyright laws except for the following, which the author specifically retains:

1. The right to make further copies of all or part of the published article for my use in classroom teaching;
2. The right to reuse all or part of this material in a compilation of my own works or in a textbook of which I am the author;
3. The right to make copies of the published work for internal distribution within the institution that employs me.

I agree that copies made under these circumstances will continue to carry the copyright notice that appeared in the original published work. I agree to inform my coauthors, if any, of the above terms.

____
Signature(s) and date(s)

____

____
Print name(s) and title(s)

____
Institutions or companies (if appropriate)

THE
QUARTERLY JOURNAL
OF ECONOMICS

Vol. XCV August 1980 No. 1

NONDISSIPATIVE SIGNALING STRUCTURES AND DIVIDEND POLICY*

SUDIPTO BHATTACHARYA

Existence conditions for signaling equilibria in which the signal is not exogenously costly are derived for the continuum of classes case. Applications to labor market models based on productivity quotas and time-profiles of wages, and an exploratory model of the "information content" of corporate dividends are discussed. The last application focuses on intertemporal consistency requirements and the role of insider trading observations.

I. INTRODUCTION

We seek to accomplish two goals in this paper. First, we develop and derive the existence conditions for a nondissipative signaling model, and examine the implications of these conditions for a class of labor market contingent contracts that serve to separate, by self-selection, a continuum of worker types with differing productivities that are not distinguishable ex ante. (The term "nondissipative," used in the spirit of the usage in Rothschild-Stiglitz [1976], or Spence's [1977] term "contingent contract" or simply "costless signal," communicates the same notion, that there is no "deadweight" loss, relative to the full information equilibrium, in the signaling equilibrium.) Second, we show that the equilibrium notion developed in the first part is relevant to the modeling of the "information content" of corporate dividends as an ex ante signal of future earnings. The appli-

*This paper is a revised and expanded version of a chapter of my Ph.D. thesis at the Sloan School of Management, Massachusetts Institute of Technology [1977]. I would like to thank Professors Stewart C. Myers, Robert C. Merton, Carliss Baldwin, George Constantinides, Stanley Fischer, David Kreps, and Stephen Ross for helpful discussions. The paper has benefited from the comments of numerous colleagues at seminars at the University of Chicago, University of British Columbia, Columbia University, and Bell Laboratories, as well as the referees and the Board of Editors of this *Journal*. I alone am responsible for remaining errors and ambiguities.

cation to the dividend-signaling problem involves an extension of our signaling model to an intertemporal setting, which gives rise to interesting questions relating to the satisfaction of fulfilled expectations criteria at more than one point in time, and the implications of that for the information content of observations of "insider trading" by managers of firms. An exploratory discussion of these issues is also provided.

The nondissipative labor market signaling equilibria that we discuss arise in situations in which workers' expected productivities are indistinguishable a priori, but some possibly imperfectly correlated or "coarse" indicator of worker productivity is observable, possibly after work. This indicator, in conjunction with some ex ante choice variable or signal whose level is chosen by the workers, is used by firms to define a contingent contract for workers that results in ex ante self-selection by the choice of the level of the signal. A part of the contribution of this paper lies in deriving the existence conditions for such contingent contract equilibria in the continuum of types case, in situations where the choice of the level of the signal per se does *not* affect the true productivity of any worker.[1] Examples of this type of signal include productivity commitments, choice among a class of tests, choice among varying time-profiles of wage payments, etc.

Both Spence [1976] and Stiglitz [1975] have alluded to the possibility of the type of equilibrium that we discuss. Salop and Salop [1976] have worked out a *two-class* example of nondissipative signaling where the two worker classes differ by quit rates and firms incur training costs that they have to recoup. They show that the use of two wage schedules with different time-profiles results in ex ante separation by self-selection. Our development of the general model for the continuum of classes case has important implications regarding the existence of an equilibrium of the Salop and Salop [1976] type. Independently of our work, Guasch and Weiss [1977] have recently obtained existence conditions that are in the spirit of our results for a specific model of a contingent contract that is based on a pass/fail test, in the case of a multiple but finite number of classes.

The second application of our model is to the problem of firms signaling expected future earnings with dividends, a problem that has

1. Spence [1977] considers existence condition for a nondissipative signaling model in which the signal *must* add to productivity, and the signaling cost to an agent is a true cost that is exogenous to both parties in the contract. Productivity is assumed to be observable ex post, and is used to determine second-period wages in a two-period model. In equilibrium, the level of investment in the signal is "efficient," i.e., the same as in the full information equilibrium. Our model may be viewed as being complementary to Spence's.

long been an important one in the finance literature. There are two major issues connected with the extent and pattern of corporate dividend payments. The first is that corporations as a whole pay much larger amounts in dividends than is justified on a strict "residual" basis, only to raise higher than necessary amounts of external financing, despite the fact that the effective tax rate on capital gains is much less than that on ordinary income for most investors.[2] The second, issue, which has received a great deal of empirical examination since the pioneering work of Lintner [1956], is the regularity of the relationship between corporate dividends and expected corporate earnings.[3] The related phenomenon of the association between unanticipated corporate dividend changes and unanticipated changes in stock prices has given rise to somewhat ill-defined hypotheses about the "information content" of dividends in "conveying" the information of corporate management about future earnings prospects. Black [1976] provides an excellent summary of these issues. Black is careful to point out that a hypothesis of information content of dividends, arising possibly from "rules of the game" followed by managers linking dividends to earnings expectations, cannot explain the payment of large amounts of dividends in spite of their tax costs, if the information contained in dividends can be obtained by investors at relatively little cost. Both of these issues invite theoretical examination using the tools of the imperfect information literature.

In this paper we provide an exploratory model of the information content hypothesis in a setting in which there are *no* exogenous costs associated with the communication of ex post earnings, through reliable accounting reports free of moral hazard or, possibly, actual cash payout. (The latter is a reliable indicator only if some conditions, discussed in Section III, are satisfied.) In such a setting, it is shown that nondissipative signaling through dividends, if they are not taxed at a higher rate than capital gains, or through earnings *forecasts,* can lead to advancement of the *timing* of information transmittal from insiders to the outside market about a firm's earnings prospects.

In a companion paper [Bhattacharya, 1979], we have analyzed a scenario in which accounting reports about earnings are completely vitiated by problems of moral hazard, *and* the personal tax disad-

2. Capital gains are taxed at roughly 40 percent of ordinary income tax rates, and capital gains taxes can be postponed by not realizing them.

In 1976, U. S. nonfinancial corporations paid approximately $31 billion in dividends, and obtained about $47 billion in new equity issues, new bond issues, and new bank credit. (These figures are from Miller and Scholes [1979].)

3. The association has often been investigated as a relationship between expected future-earnings, and "target" corporate dividends, to which actual dividends have been assumed to adjust gradually.

vantage of income received as direct cash payout from the firm in the form of dividends or regular share repurchases makes such payout costly for shareholders. We have shown therein that, under appropriate conditions, a Spence-type [1974] dissipative signaling equilibrium may emerge, with the level of dividends serving as the signal. (Tax costs *and* the costs of raising "unanticipated" new financing to fulfill dividend commitments make up the exogenous signaling costs.) If (as we believe) accounting reports are "somewhat reliable" indicators, and the reliability—as measured perhaps by the coarseness of the partitions of "true" ex-post earnings that accounting numbers convey—is capable of enhancement by the requirements of paying cash dividends that are exogenously costly for the firm, then the incorporation of such assumptions into a self-selection model would be of great importance for the information content hypothesis. This task, which would amount to a synthesis of the two types of models we have developed, is at present hampered by the absence of a sufficiently rich model of optimal costly monitoring, although the recent paper of Townsend [1979] takes some initial steps in this direction. It is hoped that the present model serves to clarify the conceptual structure of the problem.

Leland and Pyle [1977] and Ross [1977] have recently considered applications of Spence's [1974] signaling model to financial market phenomena connected with (i) incomplete diversification by entrepreneurs, and (ii) debt-equity choices by firms, respectively. In the Leland and Pyle [1977] problem of risk-sharing, only ex ante indicators or signals are relevant. Ross's [1977] model with risk-neutral agents is more directly comparable to ours. Ross obtains signaling equilibria through the use of managerial "incentive-signaling" cost structures, based on observable ex post indicators of earnings, which *do not* entail an assumption that the signaling cost structure is similar for shareholders. Our approach in this and the companion paper entails dealing with cost structures that apply to shareholders, and the nature of the equilibrium depends a great deal on assumptions made about the observability of the ex post outcome. It is our belief that extending Ross's [1977] approach to a wider scenario raises questions connected with shareholders' incentives to make disguised side payments to managers to signal falsely, since shareholders are not subject to the same cost structure. While our approach raises its own set of questions, and although the sharp distinction made here between dissipative (Spencian) and nondissipative equilibria may not carry over to richer models, we believe that a broad set of issues relating to the necessity and nature of signaling equilibria, and intertemporal consistency requirements, are raised and, where possible, addressed.[4]

This paper is organized as follows. In Section II we develop the general nondissipative signaling model with the aid of a particular labor market example, and then go on to note its implications for this type of example and the model of Salop and Salop [1976], as well as its relation to other recent models. In Section III we show the relevance of an extended intertemporal version of the model for the dividend-signaling problem, and discuss the additional considerations that arise regarding consistency, uniqueness, and the role of such auxiliary "signals" as observations of insider trading. Some brief concluding remarks in Section IV close the paper.

II. Model Formulation

II.1. A Labor Market Example

The following contingent contract example in a labor market setting serves to motivate the development of the general nondissipative signaling model. There is a continuum of worker types with differing "abilities." Expected productivity of each worker is determined by his ability and, possibly, job assignment, but *not* by the variable used as a signal per se. Actual ex post productivity, in the job assignment(s) leading to *maximal* productivity, is uniformly distributed over $[0,t]$, t (the ability variable) being different across workers. Employers cannot distinguish workers' abilities a priori. They would like to do so, through self-selection based on contingent contracts that make use of some ex post indicator of productivity, possibly because ex ante separation is useful for job assignment.[5] Initially we assume that ex post productivity is costlessly and perfectly observable over its whole range by the employer.

The labor market is assumed to be competitive. Workers and

4. Another important distinction between Ross's [1977] model and ours is that we model intertemporal—more than two-period—structures in which the original set of shareholders sells out before the end of the horizon. The motivation to realize the liquidation value makes it possible to justify signaling through financial structure variables even when the signaling incurs exogenous costs.

5. The job assignment aspect is not *explicitly* modeled, it being assumed that the productivity distribution which a worker bases his calculations on is his *maximal* productivity distribution in the appropriate job assignment(s). As long as a worker perceives that he is going to be sorted out through self-selection and optimally assigned, making his calculations conditional on maximal productivity is a "rational" expectation that is fulfilled in equilibrium. Conditional on a competitive equilibrium relative to such "conjectures," a worker cannot improve his expected payoff by signaling so as to end up in a job with less than his maximal productivity. The point is discussed further below.

firms are assumed to be risk-neutral. We are abstracting from problems of risk-sharing. Workers are assumed to know their abilities. The productivity distributions are assumed to be unaffected by wages received, i.e., no "incentive effects." For notational simplicity alone, discounting of income is not explicitly noted.

The following simple contingent contract serves to separate out workers ex ante, without any dissipative cost. A worker commits a productivity D ex ante to get a "tentative" wage commitment $W(D)$. The actual wage, which is paid after ex post productivity X is observed, is given by

$$(1) \qquad \begin{aligned} &W(D) && \text{for } X \geq D \\ &W(D) - \alpha(D - X),\ \alpha > 0 && \text{for } X < D. \end{aligned}$$

The requirement of nonnegative ex post wage, which is not a problem with narrower ranges of ex post productivity, or other contingent contracts, is ignored.

Given this, the worker of (maximal) expected productivity $t/2$ maximizes

$$(2) \qquad \max_D E(D;t) = W(D) - \int_0^D \frac{\alpha}{t}(D - X)dX = W(D) - \frac{\alpha D^2}{2t}$$

assuming that (chosen) $D < t$ which, we shall see, is true in equilibrium. The first-order condition of this maximization problem is

$$(3) \qquad E_D = W_D - \alpha D/t = 0$$

at the optimum D, conditional on t, where subscripts denote partial derivatives with respect to the appropriate variables. The competitive consistency condition is that each worker receives an ex ante expected net payment that equals his expected productivity. The equilibrium $W(D)$ schedule must be such that, along the equilibrium $D^*(t)$ schedule,

$$(4) \qquad W(D) - \alpha D^2/2t = t/2.$$

Totally differentiating equation (4), and substituting for W_D from equation (3), we show that the equilibrium $D^*(t)$ schedule is given by

$$\left(\frac{1}{2} - \frac{\alpha D^2}{2t^2}\right) \cdot \frac{dt}{dD} = 0$$

or, for a separating schedule,

(5a) $$D/t = \sqrt{1/\alpha}\,.$$

$\alpha > 1$ is needed for an interior optimum signaling equilibrium. Substituting from (5a) into (4), we note that the equilibrium $W(D)$ schedule is given by

(5b) $$W(D) = \sqrt{\alpha} * D.$$

Given this $W(D)$ schedule, it is simple to verify that the second-order condition for the maximization problem (2) is satisfied. Note that a separate equilibrium schedule corresponds to each value of the parameter α.

In the structure outlined above, wage payment equal to ex post productivity X would result in the same expected payoffs conditional on the same job assignment(s), but that would not sort out workers ex ante for optimal job assignment.[6] Our model, particularly the general model below, is just as applicable to situations in which ex post productivity as such is not observable, but a coarse or imperfectly correlated indicator is. The simplest example of such an indicator is a dichotomous one that distinguishes only "adequate" or "inadequate" performance relative to quota commitment D. If the ex post indicator is *not* a perfect monitor of ex post productivity, then a (quota-based) self-selection structure may be essential in order to have expected payoff equal expected productivity for each worker, even without job assignment needs. Wage payment $W(D)$ for adequate performance (implicitly for $X > D$) and $(W(D) - \alpha D)$ for inadequate, is an example that results in a separating equilibrium for the uniform distributions case here. In the general case, the existence conditions derived in the general model below have somewhat different implications for different contingent contracts based on ex post indicators of differing coarseness.[7]

We develop below the general nondissipative signaling model

6. In this example of self-selection being desired solely for assignment that directly manifests itself in productivity, *and* a perfect ex post monitor, it is possible to pay X and subtract a small penalty $\beta(D - X)$ for $X < D$ such that, if workers calculate taking into account the effect of chosen D on job assignment, then one may obtain corner optima (with discontinuous E_D) for $E(D,t)$ resulting in self-selection, and expected wage at least approximately equal to expected productivity. An example is $D^*(t) = t/2$, where a worker of ability t has productivity distributed uniformly with mean $\min[D,t/2]$. The question of such "anticipatory" equilibria is taken up below.

7. Specifying the coarseness of the monitor exogenously and then developing the self-selection structure is, of course, somewhat unsatisfactory. In our opinion, it should be a goal of future research to attempt to integrate this type of model with models of endogenized costly monitoring. Townsend's [1979] pioneering recent work on optimal monitoring assumes that the monitoring strategy is deterministic, and the monitor is perfect if applied. The optimal monitoring strategy can support precisely the contingent contract described earlier, i.e., X observed if it is below some D.

that this example is an illustration of, and then return to applications to this as well as other types of examples.

II.2. The General Model

It can be seen, quite transparently, that the example above is an illustration of the general structure developed below. In what follows, we have altered the notation to correspond to that of the dissipative signaling model of Spence [1974]. Let n represent an index of ability that is inherent and unalterable to an agent, and y the chosen level of a signal, or a contingent contract variable. Let

(true, expected) productivity = $S(n,y)$, $S_n > 0$, $S_y = 0$ in our model,
signaling cost to agent = $C(n,y)$, $C_y > 0$, and having other characteristics we discuss below, and
reward or wage schedule = $W(y)$.

We assume that each of these functions is twice continuously differentiable in its arguments. A major distinction between $C(n,y)$ and $W(y)$ is that $C(n,y)$ is predetermined given a contingent contract structure, whereas $W(y)$ is endogenized as part of an equilibrium model. Different from what is the case in Spence's [1974] model, $C(n,y)$ is *not* an exogenous cost to the agent whose benefit does not accrue directly to the other party in the contract. Given that, there is nothing inherently surprising about the differing existence conditions derived below.

The agent of ability n maximizes

$$\max_{y} W(y) - C(n,y), \tag{6}$$

which implies the first-order condition,

$$W_y - C_y = 0, \tag{7a}$$

and the second-order condition,

$$W_{yy} - C_{yy} < 0, \tag{7b}$$

at the maximizing y, given n. The competitive consistency condition, which reflects the fact that the signal is not exogenously costly, is given by the following equation holding along the equilibrium schedule $y^*(n)$:

$$W(y) = S(n) + C(n,y). \tag{8}$$

Equations (7a), (7b), and (8) completely specify the problem of determining the "informationally consistent" equilibrium schedules, $W(y)$ and $y^*(n)$.

Totally differentiating equation (8), we obtain

$$W_y = C_y + (S_n + C_n)\frac{dn}{dy}. \quad \text{(9a)}$$

Hence, using (7a), we get that, along the equilibrium schedule $y^*(n)$, we must have, for a separating schedule,

$$S_n + C_n = 0. \quad \text{(9b)}$$

Since $S_n > 0$, we need $C_n < 0$ for a feasible signaling equilibrium. Totally differentiating (9b), we obtain

$$\frac{dn}{dy} = -\frac{C_{ny}}{(S_{nn} + C_{nn})} \quad \text{(10)}$$

along $y^*(n)$.

Totally differentiating (7a) and substituting from (10), we obtain that, along $y^*(n)$,

$$W_{yy} - C_{yy} = C_{ny} \cdot \frac{dn}{dy} = \frac{-(C_{ny})^2}{S_{nn} + C_{nn}}. \quad \text{(11)}$$

It is readily apparent from (11) that, to satisfy the second-order condition (7b), we must have $(S_{nn} + C_{nn}) > 0$ along the equilibrium schedule.

To summarize, the existence of a separating, nondissipative, signaling equilibrium, with twice continuously differentiable reward functions satisfying the description above, requires the following basic condition to be fulfilled. There must exist a function $y^*(n)$ such that, for each n_0 in the relevant domain of n, $[S(n) + C(n, y^*(n_0))]$ attains its *unique* global minimum with respect to n at n_0. This condition implies that the equilibrium association $y^*(n)$ must be strictly monotonic (given that it is continuous), for which C_{ny} must be nonzero and of uniform sign along $y^*(n)$. (The fact that $C_{ny} \neq 0$ and is of uniform sign is not sufficient to satisfy the basic condition, of course.) These conditions differ from the existence conditions for Spence's [1974] dissipative signaling structure, which only requires that $C_{ny} < 0$ and $C_y > S_y$ for $y >$ some $y^0(n)$.[8] A somewhat more general ver-

8. The intuitive explanation is as follows. Suppose that $n_1(y_1)$ and $n_2(y_2)$ are two points on a hypothetical equilibrium schedule on which the strict minimum condition for $S(n) + C(n,y)$ is *not* satisfied. Suppose that $[S(n) + C(n,y_1)]$ attains its *maximum* with respect to n at n_1. Then

$$S(n_2) + C(n_2,y_1) < S(n_1) + C(n_1,y_1) = W(y_1).$$

But, by the definition of an equilibrium schedule,

$$W(y_2) - C(n_2,y_2) = S(n_2).$$

Hence, here the agent of ability n_2 is better off signaling y_1. Such an argument is always possible for some $n_2(y_2)$, unless $[S(n) + C(n,y_1)]$ attains its minimum with respect to n at $n_1(y_1)$ on the schedule.

sion of the model is obtained by eliminating the additivity of the reward structure above.[9]

It is useful to note explicitly the following in the context of the quota-based example discussed in Section II.1. When $S(n)$ refers to the *maximal* productivity of a worker of ability n in the appropriate job assignment(s), $[W(y) - C(n,y)]$ continues to be maximized along the same $y^*(n)$ schedule as in the above structure even if the worker explicitly considers his *lower* productivity in nonoptimal job assignments arising from indications different from $y^*(n)$ because $\partial C/\partial n < 0$ is a requirement for the equilibrium structure above. The only proviso is that productivity distributions in nonoptimal job assignments satisfy this condition. Thus, equilibria in which workers do *not* explicitly consider the effect of their signal on job assignment and resulting productivity, "simple" equilibria, are also "anticipatory" equilibria. The converse is taken up in Section II.3 below.

Two other characteristics of the nondissipative model are self-evident. First, the equilibrium schedule $y^*(n)$, for a given $C(n,y)$ resulting from a given contingent contract, is unique, as defined by (9b). There is no need for arguments of the Riley-type [1975] that determine the equilibrium $y^*(\mathbf{n})$ for the lowest $\mathbf{n}$, which are required for uniqueness in the dissipative structure of Spence [1974], which requires the specification of a boundary condition to a first-order differential equation to determine the equilibrium $y^*(n)$. Second, the informationally consistent separating equilibrium cannot be "unraveled" at the lower end by a contract that attracts more than one type by deviating from $W(y)$—i.e., the offerer of such a contract cannot make a *strictly* positive gain while keeping all the takers of the contract at least as well off as in the separating equilibrium. This is in

9. The following generalization is applicable to the model of Salop and Salop [1976], discussed below in Section II.3. Let $W(y)$ be the explicit payoff schedule as a function of the signal y. The resulting effective expected payoff to a worker is given by $R(W(y),y,n)$. True expected productivity is $S(n)$ as before. The worker maximizes

$$\max_{y} R(W(y),y,n),$$

which has the first-order condition,

$$R_W W_y + R_y = 0.$$

The competitive consistency condition implies that the equality,

$$R(W(y^*(n)),y^*(n),n) = S(n),$$

holds along the equilibrium schedule $y^*(n)$. Totally differentiating the consistency condition and substituting from the first-order condition, we obtain

$$(S_n - R_n) = 0$$

along the equilibrium schedule. The second-order condition for the maximization problem is satisfied if and only if $(S_{nn} - R_{nn}) > 0$ along the equilibrium schedule.

contrast to Spence's model, where such unraveling is possible, as Riley [1979] proves. The basic reason is very simple and hardly needs formalizing. Any possible unraveling contract must, in our model, have a net (expected) payoff of at least $S(n)$ *from the offerer to the taker*, regardless of the choice of the signal.[10]

On the other hand, equilibrium in our nondissipative model is non-unique in a broader sense because $C(n,y)$ is not technologically given, but defined by a set of contingent contracts, though each agent's expected net payoff is the same in all such equilibria corresponding to alternative feasible contingent contract structures and parameter values. We shall have more to say below about this in the context of specific models.

II.3. Further Applications of the Model

Consider first the quota-based self-selection structure of our example in Section II.1 above, in the context of a wider class of distribution functions for ex post productivity. As the first example, we look at the truncated linear penalty function contingent contract $(W(D) - \alpha \max(D - X,0))$, both for its easy tractability, as well as the existence of some theoretical support for this form for an optimal monitoring policy, if the ex post outcome is costly to monitor [Townsend, 1979]. Let $F_M(X)$, $f_M(X)$ denote the distribution and density functions of ex post productivity X, assumed to be distributed over [0,1] without loss of generality for bounded random variables, where the subscript M denotes the mean productivity. In the cross section of workers, there is assumed to be a one-to-one correspondence between M and $\{F,f\}$.

Given the above description, the signaling cost $C(D,m)$, or the expected deduction from $W(D)$, for the worker with mean productivity M can be written as

$$\text{(12a)} \quad C(D,M) = \alpha \int_0^D (D - X) f_M(X) dX = \alpha \int_0^D F_M(X) dX.$$

$C(D,M)$ is negatively related to M if in the cross section the $F(X)$ functions satisfy the same Rothschild-Stiglitz [1970] "increasing risk" ordering for all X, *without* preserving the same mean. Marginal signaling cost $\partial C/\partial D$ is negatively related to M at all D below the upper endpoint of the distribution if cross sectionally the $F(X)$ function values

10. For a proof and a resolution in terms of an "anticipatory" (non-Nash) equilibrium concept, see Riley [1979]. Rothschild and Stiglitz [1976] have also discussed problems of nonexistence of equilibria in dissipative signaling models. In Spence's [1974] model, the unraveling arises essentially because, in equilibrium, there is "overinvestment" in the signal relative to a full-information equilibrium and thus C_y is strictly greater than S_y at all but the lowest end-point of the equilibrium schedule.

are ordered in the same ordering for all X, and the ordering is possibly weak only where $F(X) = 1$. However, these conditions do *not* guarantee that $[M + C(D,M)]$ will, for a given D, attain a unique interior minimum in M. For a simple counterexample, consider the following "family" of distribution functions:

$$F(X) = X - \gamma \sin(\pi X),\ X \epsilon [0,1],\ 0 \leqq \gamma \leq 1/\pi \tag{12b}$$

with γ varying across the cross section, for which $C(D,M)$ as defined in (12a) and M are linear in γ, although both $C(D,M)$ and $\partial C/\partial D$ are negatively related to M.

Consider next the dichotomous reward structure given by $W(D)$ if $X \geq D$, $(W(D) - \alpha(D))$ if $X < D$. The corresponding $C(D,M)$ is given by

$$C(D,M) = \alpha(D) F_M(D). \tag{12c}$$

It is clear that the distribution function "family" of (12b) provides a case in which $[M + C(D,M)]$ does *not* attain unique interior minima in M for given levels of D for this contingent contract. Furthermore, for dichotomous structures the marginal signaling cost is given by

$$\frac{\delta C}{\delta D} = \frac{\delta \alpha}{\delta D} F_M(D) + \alpha(D) f_M(D),$$

and this will be negatively related to M for "families" of $\{F(X)\}$ satisfying the unique ordering criterion discussed above only if the curvature of the $\alpha(D)$ function is "sufficient" to make the $F_M(D)$ term "dominate," except in the case of uniform distributions for which both $F_M(D)$ and $f_M(D)$ are negatively related to M.

The nonexistence of (separating) equilibrium problems detailed above carry over to an application of the general model of Section II.2 to the Salop and Salop [1976] model of labor market turnover. In the Salop and Salop model, n is an exogenously given quit-probability attribute of a worker that is unobservable to firms. Workers' productivities on the job are exogenously given, unaffected by any income-leisure tradeoff, and equal across workers. A firm incurs training-orientation costs T per new worker. Workers and firms are risk-neutral. If a firm pays a worker the wage y in the first period, and $W(y)$ in each period thereafter, the worker's discounted expected value of anticipated wages during tenure in the firm is given by $R(W(y),y,n)$. The discounted expected productivity during tenure less training cost of the worker is given by $S(n)$. Salop and Salop [1976] show in a two-class model that two different $\{y, W(y)\}$ profiles can be provided such that workers of different quit probability n will separate themselves by self-selection—choosing different y's to maximize $R(W(y),y,n)$—and, given the optimizing choices, $R(W(y), y,n)$ would equal $S(n)$ for each chosen $\{y,W(y),n\}$ triple.

Our general model, specifically the version in note 8, can easily be used to prove the following about the Salop and Salop [1976] structure. Given their assumptions, particularly that all wages are "vested," i.e., the contracted wage for a particular period must be paid regardless of whether or not the worker quits at the end of the period, *there is no separating equilibrium in the continuum of classes case.* A separating equilibrium would require there to be two functions, $\{y^*(n),W(y)\}$, such that for each n_0, $[S(n) - R(W(y^*(n_0)),y^*(n_0),n)]$ attains a unique global minimum in the variable n at n_0. However, under the conditions outlined, the effect of n on $S(\cdot)$ and $R(\cdot)$ is exactly "symmetric" and such interior minima are not possible. More precisely, if n and P represent per period quit-probability and productivity, respectively, π is the discount rate, and T is the training cost, then

$$R(W(y),y,n) = \frac{y}{(1+\pi)} + \sum_{i=2}^{\infty} \frac{W(y)(1-n)^{i-1}}{(1+\pi)^i}$$

$$S(n) = \sum_{i=1}^{\infty} \frac{P(1-n)^{i-1}}{(1+\pi)^i} - \frac{T}{(1+\pi)}$$

for which there is only a nonseparating equilibrium with $y = (P - T)$ and $W(y) = P$.

The above-mentioned difficulties with the existence of separating equilibria have to be viewed in the following perspective. First, in problems in which there is no particular gain from a separating equilibrium per se, a nonseparating equilibrium with $\{y^*,W(y^*)\}$ such that $S(n)$ equals $[W(y^*) - C(n,y^*)]$ or $R(W(y^*),y^*,n)$ *for each n* is sometimes feasible. This is clearly the case with the Salop and Salop [1976] model, as well as for the dichotomous indicator quota-based self-selection model with distribution functions given by equation (12b), when there is no job assignment aspect to the problem. While this is a partial resolution, self-selection structures that are embedded within models with an endogenized degree of moral hazard in communication or effort or both, appear to provide rich problems for future research. Examples of such research would include endogenized optimal monitoring in the quota-based model, as well as the recent conjecture of Shavell and Weiss [1979] regarding the incorporation of Salop and Salop-type [1976] self-selection structures in problems involving time-profiles of unemployment insurance payments, in a scenario of moral hazard with respect to the unobservable intensity of job search.

As a second point, it should be noted that in the quota-based self-selection structure *with* job assignment benefits from ex ante separation, it has been assumed that workers do not (or cannot precisely) explicitly take into account the effect of different quota choices on job assignment and thus productivity. If a separating equilibrium exists with such simple "conjectures," then it is also an equilibrium for a more complex structure in which workers do explicitly take job assignment into account, as we showed in Section II.2. The converse is less generally true because workers' reward functions need *not* be continuously differentiable with such anticipatory conjectures, and counterexamples exist as noted in note 6. In the Appendix we discuss this issue in more detail, and note reasonable sufficient conditions that result in the existence conditions being essentially the same for separating equilibria with simple versus anticipatory conjectures by workers.

Before going on to further applications of the quota-based signaling structure, the following should also be noted. First, structures, in which the ex post indicator has at least *three* partitions, are likely to have a separating equilibrium even when structures with dichotomous indicators do not. This is suggested by the fact that when the ex post outcome X is fully observable, reward structures that are concave in X often provide separating equilibria. Of course, concavity of the reward structure is difficult to define with coarse indicators when the distribution of X differs in the cross section, and a full characterization of structures that result in separating equilibria has *not* been developed in this paper. Second, as we noted before, separating equilibria are non-unique and dependent on the functional form and parameter values of the contingent contract. There is, however, some justification for "unbiased" structures in which $C(D,M)$, the expected adjustment to the "tentative" $W(D)$, is zero *in equilibrium.* In the labor market context, such justification may arise from X being viewed as productivity over many periods with effort being adversely affected by non-uniform expected wages over time. In the intertemporal dividend-signaling problem of Section III, there is a more precise and interesting justification. As an example that is used further below, consider the concave structure

$$W(D) + \alpha(\sqrt{XD} - D). \tag{13}$$

With X having a degenerate distribution concentrated at M, the separating equilibrium is given by

$$D^*(M) = 4M/\alpha^2, \tag{14}$$

which is "unbiased" for $\alpha = 2$. Similar examples exist when X is uniformly distributed. However, separating equilibria that are also "unbiased" need *not* exist, as when X is distributed with $F(X) = X^a$, $X \epsilon [0,1]$, $a > 0$ and differing across workers, where in a separating equilibrium with the reward structure (13),

$$C\left(D, M = \frac{a}{a+1}\right) = \frac{2(a+1/2)}{(a+1)^4}\left[(a^3 + 2a^2 + a) - \frac{2}{\alpha}\left(a^3 + \frac{3}{2}a^2 + \frac{3}{4}a + \frac{1}{8}\right)\right]$$

which cannot be made to equal zero for each a by the choice of α.

It is also instructive to compare the quota-based contingent contract structure of our examples above with a test-based self-selection model that has been independently developed by Guasch and Weiss [1977]. Both models, it can be argued, constitute explicitly worked out examples of performance-based contingent contract structures for self-selection that were alluded to in Spence [1976] and Stiglitz [1975]. Our comparison focuses on an important issue connected with the time structure of events in the two models.

In the Guasch and Weiss [1977] model, firms administer a given pass/fail test to workers that the more able and productive workers have a higher probability of passing. The self-selection aspect results from workers choosing among different versions of the test (administered by different firms), having differing discrepancies between the payoffs conditional on success versus failure. Since wages are determined before ("real") work begins, their model has to satisfy the requirement that even payoff conditional on failure at least equals true self-selected productivity, so that other firms do not have an incentive to lure workers away. As a result, a "testing fee" larger than the cost of the test is required, in equilibrium. This feature clearly creates an incentive for firms to start "hiring and firing," of some fraction of unsuccessful as well as successful workers for appearance's sake, and that is detrimental to the survival of the equilibrium structure. If quits are costly to the worker, because of firm-specific human capital, for example, then these problems are mitigated because wage conditional on failure can be set lower than the self-selected marginal product. Our quota-based structure, in which we assume payment of wages after productivity is observed, does not share a similar feature. On the other hand, the descriptive superiority of the Guasch and Weiss [1977] model vis à vis the "apprenticeship" market that they allude to is quite evident.

However, as the argument above illustrates, it is difficult to specify consistent multiperiod versions of these performance-based self-selection models in which testing ends at some point, and future wages are determined by prior indicators, if the indicator of future expected productivity is "noisy." In the next section we consider an application of the quota-based self-selection model to a problem of firms signaling their future earnings prospects with dividends. This application of the model in an intertemporal setting raises issues relating to the compatibility of the reward structure with agents' incentives, which are similar in nature to those mentioned immediately above, as well as other issues connected with the presence of a self-selected reward-price at multiple points in time.

III. Dividends as Signals

III.1. The Basic Model

In this section we apply the quota-based signaling model of our preceding examples to a problem of signaling in the capital market. The model developed below relates to a setting in which a costless indicator of ex post profitability, which is also free of moral hazard, is available. The use of dividends or earnings forecasts as signals by firms helps to advance the timing of the communication of firms' future earnings prospects to the outside market.

A primary characteristic of our dividend-signaling models, here and in our companion paper, is that they are "intertemporal," involving at least *three* or more time points. There are two reasons for this. First, we assume here that the elements of the perceived contingent contract structure that gives rise to signaling all relate to market-based valuations for shareholders and not to some other postulated cost function for some agent. To have this happen, we must have a relevant nonzero market value, hence remaining cash flows beyond the "horizon" point of the contingent contract perceived by current shareholders. The second reason is that current shareholder horizons that are shorter than the full horizon of the model are essential for any kind of exogenously costly dividend-signaling equilibrium to come about, as is the case in our companion paper [Bhattacharya, 1979], which is developed in a setting in which accounting reports are vitiated by moral hazard, and communication of ex post earnings through cash payout is costly because of a lower tax on capital gains.[11] In this paper we develop the model in the simplest three-time-point ("snapshot") version to illustrate some basic considerations relating to existence and rational expectations over time in the nondissipative dividend-signaling model. We believe that progress toward the harder problem of synthesizing the nondissipative and dissipative (exogenously costly) approaches to the dividend-signaling problem, through the modeling of "less than complete" moral hazard in accounting reports, has to be preceded by an understanding of the basic issues with respect to these two types of models.

Consider a three-time-point model, $t = 0,1,2$, in which there is a cross section of firms holding assets with differing payoffs $\{X_t\}$ at $t = 1$ and $t = 2$. The current generation of shareholders plans to sell out to a new generation at $t = 1$. The spirit of this assumption is that of a life cycle model in which, say, agents work, consume, and save in one period and then hold shares and consume the proceeds from selling the shares in the next period. It will be assumed for simplicity that assets held by different firms are similar in the intertemporal stochastic process of cash flows—all intertemporally independently distributed, for example—and that the market is aware of this pattern. It will also be assumed that cash flows at $t = 1$ can be communicated costlessly and without moral hazard, either because accounting reports are inherently honest or because actual cash payout (dividend) is not disadvantageously taxed.[12] Given the assumptions above, the market has sufficient information at $t = 1$ to arrive at a liquidation value schedule for $t = 1$ based on the ex post outcome that results in "fair," competitive market values, in terms of the ex ante expected liquidation values perceived by current shareholders of firms at $t = 0$. However, the market is not able to distinguish firms a priori at $t = 0$.

In the stylized, simple structure described above, it is shown

11. In a recent paper Miller and Scholes [1979] have argued that the direct tax disadvantage of dividends may not matter because investors can (i) borrow to generate interest deductions equaling dividends received, *and* (ii) invest the borrowing proceeds in such "effectively" tax-exempt means of accumulation as life insurance contracts and retirement accounts. Both the empirical reasonableness of this argument at large scales of operation, and the reconciliation of this approach with other tax-based models of financial structure like that of Miller [1977], are as yet unresolved problems.

12. The market "knowing" the intertemporal stochastic process of cash flows should be interpreted in the sense of the market coming to be aware, over time, of a cross-sectional uniformity. With preferential taxation of capital gains, cash payout is not costless, since the cash could have been reinvested in new projects instead, especially in say an infinite-horizon model. Cash payout can be a fully reliable, *direct* indicator of earnings only if all investment expenditures are strictly separable from current expenses in a timing sense, i.e., expenses have to be currently paid for, and timing of investment expenditure is completely flexible. In a many-period setting we must also assume an exogenous time-structure of cash flows from investment.

below that a contingent contract structure that is based on a "market-accepted" adjustment of the liquidation value at $t = 1$, based on the discrepancy between some ex ante ($t = 0$) signal and the actual cash flow at $t = 1$, can serve to sort out firms by self-selection at $t = 0$. This serves the cause of informationally efficient market valuation at $t = 0$, which leads to efficient allocation of investment, and fair selling prices to any small proportion of current shareholders who deviate from the normal life cycle pattern and wish to sell at $t = 0$. For simplicity, we consider the case of risk-neutral current and future investors with one-period horizons.[13]

If the $t = 1$ cash flows of firms can be accurately disclosed by accounting reports, then earnings forecasts by firms can serve as ex ante signals. If in addition the payment of dividends is costless from a tax point of view, then dividends paid at $t = 0$ can also serve as signals. When we speak of dividends paid at $t = 0$, we really have in mind a longer, possibly infinite horizon model that started before $t = 0$, of which the three-period abstraction dealt with here is a "snapshot." Alternatively, even if accounting reports are not free of moral hazard, if cash payment is costless from the tax point of view, it may be able to serve as the reliable indicator of ex post cash flows. In this case we may envisage an ex ante "promised" (at $t = 0$) dividend being the signal. In this case, even in a longer horizon model, the distinction between "promised" and actual dividends needs to be maintained, since the actual dividend variable cannot necessarily serve the roles of both ex post indicator and ex ante signal.

Our nondissipative dividend-signaling structure is very similar to the quota-based labor market signaling structure of the last section. We assume shareholders to be risk-neutral and signaling decisions being made by "insiders" or managers of firms who know the true cash flow distributions and who are serving in the interests of current shareholders, possibly because their incentive compensation is tied to shareholder returns. We ignore discounting for notational simplicity. It is assumed that insiders perceive a "market accepted" contingent contract having the two elements of (i) a *liquidation* ($t = 1$) value schedule as a function of the ex ante signal D, $W(D)$, and (ii) a function relating the adjustment in liquidation value to the dis-

13. If agents were risk-averse, then endogenizing the extent of desired trading in shares at $t = 0$ for diversification purposes, and the information content of this variable (discussed in Leland and Pyle [1977]), would become important additional problems, in general. See note 15 for a scenario in which these problems are minimized. Note that if the $t = 1$ valuation is perceived to be based just on the $t = 1$ earnings indicator, then there is a clear incentive to exaggerate in the signal at $t = 0$ to increase the selling price for *any* small extent of selling by shareholders at $t = 0$.

crepancy between D and first-period earnings X. The adjustment function generates an expected signaling cost function $C(D,M)$ as a function of D and the mean first-period cash flow M, in a setting in which each cash flow distribution function corresponds to a separate mean. Each firm's "insiders" or managers maximize the objective function,

$$\max_{D} W(D) + M - C(D,M). \tag{15}$$

The M in (15) arises from the fact that current shareholders obtain the gains from cash flows at $t = 1$.

A competitive consistency condition is that, at least on average as perceived at $t = 0$, the adjusted liquidation value at $t = 1$ must equal the fair, competitive market value of the $t = 2$ cash flows along the equilibrium schedule, and this is where the "trend" part of the intertemporal pattern between first- and second-period cash flows becomes important. Assuming intertemporally independently identically distributed cash flows for each firm, this consistency condition implies that, along the equilibrium schedule $D^*(M)$,

$$W(D) - C(D,M) = M. \tag{16}$$

Obtaining the "equilibrium" $W(D)$ and $D^*(M)$ schedules satisfying the maximization and consistency conditions is identical to that for the quota-based equilibrium of Section II. Conditions for existence of equilibrium are identical to those discussed in Section II.2 above. We consider below some important additional consistency criteria that arise in this intertemporal model.

III.2. Rational Expectations and Insider Trading

The structure outlined above cannot really accommodate generalized uncertainty in true cash flows X. The reason is very simple. The consistency condition, equation (16), ensures consistent valuation only at $t = 1$ *on average*. However, if the signaling structure is assumed to serve to sort out firms by ex ante cash flow expectations at $t = 0$, given the contingent contract, then if the realization of X is such that the adjusted liquidation value is different from M, individual outside investors have an incentive to deviate from the "market accepted" liquidation value adjustment rule. If we relax the assumption that the two cash flows of an asset are i.i.d., we *approach* resolution of this problem with "ex post rational expectations" in a limiting case of parameter values, if the cash flows follow random walks over time.[14]

We envisage the following implications of this difficulty for our model and potential extensions. First, one type of uncertainty in cash flows can always be accommodated. This is when cash flows next period are certain, conditional on a set of state variables that change randomly, but whose values insiders know currently, i.e., when setting the value of the ex ante signal. In such a scenario, our model can easily be made to be consistent with risk-averse shareholders.[15] Second, solving the above ex post rational expectations (or "incentive compatibility") problem for more general stochastic processes would probably require solving the difficult problem of integrating the dissipative and nondissipative dividend-signaling models, with an endogenized degree of reliability or coarseness in the ex post indicator at $t = 1$.[16] It is possible, however, that this difficult integration need not be required for a dynamically consistent model in some special circumstances. A "promising" scenario for further research is one where cash flows or earnings follow continuous-time diffusion processes (so that differences between local means and realizations are "small"), shareholders are risk-averse, and there is imperfect information regarding the drift-rate function of the diffusion process. Clearly, much remains to be done in this area.

In the intertemporal dividend-signaling problem, the signaling

14. Consider cash flows uniformly distributed over $[0,t]$ and following a random walk, and let the adjustment rule be $-\alpha(D - X)$ for $X < D$, i.e., "truncated." Equations (5a) and (5b) give us that, in equilibrium,

$$D^*(t) = \sqrt{1/\alpha} \cdot t, \quad W(D) = \sqrt{\alpha} \cdot D, \qquad \text{so that} \qquad W(D^*(t)) = t.$$

Revised liquidation value is, therefore,

$$\begin{aligned} &= t - \alpha(D - X) \qquad \text{for } X < D, t \text{ otherwise} \\ &= (1 - \sqrt{\alpha})t + \alpha X, \end{aligned}$$

which approaches consistency as $\alpha \to 1$.

15. Consider the following scenario. At $t = 0^-$ current shareholders have bought across firms in desired proportions from the previous generation with their savings. At $t = 0^+$ the insiders of firms learn the values of the state variables that modify next period expected cash flows. The firms then signal, subject to the perceived contingent contracts, and get revalued. If there is no residual uncertainty about $t = 1$ cash flows conditional on this intra-horizon revision of expectations, then there is no modified diversification demand for reallocations of shareholdings across firms ("rebalancing").

16. It should be noted that no such difficulty with ex post rational expectations arises in the dissipative signaling model of Bhattacharya [1979], since there is no direct expectations revision conditional on X. If the contingent contract that results in signaling were to apply to managers only, and the money involved was large enough to rule out the profitability of side-payments to managers by shareholders who gain from the signaled value at $t = 0$, then again this problem would not arise. These are strong assumptions, however, and it appears to be more promising to focus on imperfect observability of the ex post outcome in future research.

of anticipated cash flows would lead to an informationally consistent *current* value at $t = 0$ (as a function of the ex ante signal) schedule $V(D)$. In equilibrium, under the assumption that the $t = 1$ and $t = 2$ cash flows expected at $t = 0$ are the same for any given firm, the equilibrium $V(D)$ and $W(D)$ schedules are related by the transformation

$$V(D) = 2[W(D) + \text{anticipated adjustment to liquidation value at } t = 1]. \tag{17}$$

The second term on the right-hand side of (17) is clearly dependent on the precise perceived contingent contract structure, as well as the equilibrium $D^*(M)$ association. In equilibrium, $D^*(M)$ is definitionally known, as reflected in the consistency condition (16). In addition, there is an interesting, if heuristic, convergence to equilibrium argument that one can build around this scenario. Trading by insiders at $t = 0$ in response to the valuation schedules plays an important part in this story.

In our model the insiders or managers of firms are assumed to solve the one-period (liquidation at $t = 1$) problem to maximize the shareholders' objective function, possibly because they are compensated for shareholders' returns. Consider a scenario in which the insiders choose the optimal D^0 by this criterion, conditional on a possibly nonequilibrium $W(D)$ schedule and, in addition, decide to buy or sell shares on their own account—in amounts that are small relative to their incentive compensation—depending on whether or not the corresponding $V(D^0)$ results in under- or overvaluation of the cash flow stream. In that case, observations of insider trading, if it is public information, can provide the market with a basis for convergence to the equilibrium $W(D)$ schedule, particularly if the consistent transformation between the $W(D)$ and $V(D)$ schedules is a simple one, in that it does not involve any computation of the optimizing $D^0(M)$ response to the $W(D)$ schedule and the perceived adjustment structure.

However, the consistent transformation between $W(D)$ and $V(D)$ schedules is simple in the above sense only if the anticipated $t = 1$ adjustment to (the equilibrium) $W(D)$ is zero in equilibrium. That is the case only for particular parameter values of the anticipated adjustment rule; e.g., $\alpha = 2$ for the contingent contract of equations (13) and (14) of Section II, where it is assumed that X has a degenerate distribution concentrated at M. There is some reason, then, to expect the parameter values of the market adjustment rules to "evolve" so that this simplifying condition is satisfied. Although it is very heuristic, we do find this description of the "information content" of insider trading, which has its basis in the intertemporal nature of the model, to be intuitively appealing and worthy of further exploration in richer models of dividend-signaling. Inquiries along these lines, as well as those connected with the ex post rational expectations problem above, seem needed to determine the functional form and parameter values of contingent contracts as a part of the model.

IV. Concluding Remarks

We have derived and discussed the implications of the existence conditions for a class of nondissipative signaling models. We have also discussed some simple exploratory applications to the modeling of the "information content" of corporate dividends as signals of future earnings prospects. The results obtained and the questions raised suggest that further research on models with an endogenized degree of moral hazard (in communicating ex post outcomes, for example) is needed to provide richer and more robust structures in which these self-selection models can be embedded. Significant questions that arise in intertemporal applications of these self-selection models also need to be addressed.

It is hoped that the discussion here will help provide an impetus to further research on imperfect information models of dividend policy. In an important paper on this topic, Black [1976] conjectured that the inability of excellent empirical methods to discriminate well among different hypotheses about the effect of dividend payout on risk-adjusted expected returns, may help "explain" similar ignorance on the part of economic agents regarding the effect of dividends on firm values. An assumption that economic agents are as dependent on estimates derived from past returns data as empirical researchers—as opposed to their knowing the stochastic processes for future cash flows and prices, as well as current values conditional on policies—does *not* constitute a perfect-information assumption. If recourse to such as assumption appears necessary to justify the empirical behavior of dividends, *explicitly* exploring the implications of imperfect information models for the "dividend puzzle" appears to us to be a worthwhile endeavor.

Appendix

When separating equilibria are desired for job assignment reasons, and workers make calculations taking explicit account of their lower expected productivity in nonoptimal job assignments, the structure of the general model in Section II.2 is modified *only* as follows. *Conditional* on a (hypothesized) equilibrium schedule $y^*(n)$, we define a function $n'(n,y) \leqq n$, such that $S(n') \leqq S(n)$ is the (perceived) expected productivity of the worker of ability n who indicates $y \neq y^*(n)$. The worker now maximizes

$$\max_y W(y) - C(n'(n,y),y). \tag{A1}$$

Note that the competitive consistency condition, equation (8), remains unaltered.

It is now possible that the maximum in (A1) is attained at a $y^*(n)$ where $(Wy - Cy) \neq 0$, even if the $W(\cdot)$ and $C(\cdot)$ functions are continuously differentiable in the arguments y and n', *if* $n'(n,y)$ is *not* continuously differentiable in y. An example is where $n'(n,y) = \min[n,n^+(y)]$, where $n^+(y)$ is the inverse function of $y^*(n)$, i.e., productivity is completely determined by job assignment provided the job "capacity" does not exceed ability, and solely by ability otherwise.

If $n'(n,y)$ is not continuously differentiable in y, it is no longer possible, in general, to derive the existence conditions as in Section II.2. The intuitive reason for these conditions given in note 8 is no longer compelling with $n'(n,y) \neq n$, since even if for $y_1(n_1)$, $y_2(n_2)$ on $y^*(n)$

$$S(n_2) + C(n_2 y_1) < S(n_1) + C(n_1,y_1) = W(y_1). \tag{A2}$$

The person of ability n_2 may *not* prefer to signal y_1 if

$$S(n_2) + C(n'(n_2,y_1),y_1) > W(y_1). \tag{A3}$$

It is easy to write down a sufficient condition that makes this difference between anticipatory and nonanticipatory conjectures by workers unimportant. The spirit of the condition is that (at least in his perception) a worker loses negligibly little productivity in job assignments that are close to those in which he has maximal productivity, in the sense that

$$\operatorname*{limit}_{y \to y^*(n)} \frac{n'(n,y) - n}{y - y^*(n)} = 0 \tag{A4}$$

for both right and left limits for all n. Given this, we have on differentiating (A1) that

$$\begin{aligned} \frac{\partial}{\partial y}[W(y) - C(n'(n,y),y)]_{y=y^*(n)} &= \left[W_y - C_y - C_{n'}\frac{\partial n'}{\partial y}\right]_{y=y^*(n)} \\ &= (W_y - C_y)_{y=y^*(n)}. \end{aligned} \tag{A5}$$

Using equation (A5), one can proceed exactly as in Section II.2 to derive the following necessary condition for the existence of a separating equilibrium. There must exist a strictly monotonic, differentiable function $y^*(n)$ such that, for each n_0 in the relevant domain, $[S(n) + C(n,y^*(n_o))]$ attains a *local* minimum with respect to n at n_0.

STANFORD UNIVERSITY

REFERENCES

Bhattacharya, S., Ph.D. thesis, M.I.T., 1977.
——, "Imperfect Information, Dividend Policy, and the 'Bird in the Hand Fallacy,'" *Bell Journal of Economics,* X (Spring 1979), 259–70.
Black, F., "The Dividend Puzzle," *Journal of Portfolio Management,* II (Winter 1976), 5–8, reprinted in S. C. Myers, *Modern Developments in Financial Management* (New York: Praeger, 1976).
Guasch, J. L., and A. Weiss, "Prices as a Sorting Mechanism in Competitive Markets with Asymmetric Information," Discussion Paper, Bell Laboratories, 1977.
Leland, H., and D. H. Pyle, "Informational Asymmetries, Financial Structure, and Financial Intermediation," *Journal of Finance,* XXXII (May 1977), 371–88.
Lintner, J., "Distribution of Incomes of Corporations among Dividends, Retained Earnings, and Taxes," *American Economic Review,* XLVI (May 1956), 97–113.
Miller, M. H., "Debt and Taxes," *Journal of Finance,* XXXII (May 1977), 261–76.
——, and M. Scholes, "Dividends and Taxes," *Journal of Financial Economics,* VI (Dec. 1978), 333–64.
Riley, J., "Competitive Signaling," *Journal of Economic Theory,* X (April 1975), 174–86.
——, "Informational Equilibrium," *Econometrica,* XLVII (March 1979), 331–60.
Ross, S. A., "The Determination of Financial Structure: The Incentive-Signaling Approach," *Bell Journal of Economics,* VII (Spring 1977), 23–40.
Rothschild, M., and J. E. Stiglitz, "Increasing Risk I: A Definition," *Journal of Economic Theory,* II (Sept. 1970), 225–43.
——, and ——, "Equilibrium in Competitive Insurance Markets: An Essay on the Economics of Imperfect Information," this *Journal,* XC (Nov. 1976), 628–50.
Salop, J., and S. Salop, "Self-Selection and Turnover in the Labor Market," this *Journal,* XC (Nov. 1976), 619–28.
Shavell, S., and L. Weiss, "The Optimal Payment of Unemployment Insurance Benefits over Time," *Journal of Political Economy,* LXXXVII (Dec. 1979), 1347–62.
Spence, A. M., "Competitive and Optimal Responses to Signals: An Analysis of Efficiency and Distribution," *Journal of Economic Theory,* VIII (March 1974), 296–332.
——, "Competition in Salaries, Credentials, and Signaling Prerequisites for Jobs," this *Journal,* XC (Feb. 1976), 51–74.
——, "Signals, Contingent Contracts, and the Divergence of Earnings from Productivity: Survey and Extensions," Discussion Paper No. 540, Harvard Institute of Economic Research, 1977.
Stiglitz, J., "The Theory of 'Screening,' Education and Distribution of Income," *American Economic Review,* LXV (June 1975), 283–300.
Townsend, R. M., "Optimal Contracts and Competitive Markets with Costly State Verification," *Journal of Economic Theory,* XXI (Oct. 1979), 265–93.

ON TRANSACTIONS AND PRECAUTIONARY DEMAND FOR MONEY*

JACOB A. FRENKEL AND BOYAN JOVANOVIC

This paper develops a stochastic framework for determining transactions and precautionary demand for money. Through application of the principles of inventory management, the analysis integrates and extends the work of Baumol, Tobin, and Miller and Orr. Optimal money holdings are shown to depend on the rate of interest, on the mean and the variance of net disbursements and on the cost of portfolio adjustment. The properties of the distribution of the payment period are analyzed. The optimal solution is obtained by minimizing net present value of cost. This solution is compared with the one obtained by the conventional method of minimizing the steady-state cost.

I. INTRODUCTION

In this paper, we develop a model of the demand for money that incorporates transactions and precautionary motives. The analytical framework is based on the principles of inventory management that have been applied by Baumol [1952] and Tobin [1956] to study the transactions demand for money. The key feature of our model is its stochastic characteristics that lead to the need for precautionary reserves. We analyze the determinants of optimal money holdings when net disbursements are governed by a stochastic process. In this context we adopt some aspect of the analytical framework that has been developed by Miller and Orr [1966], and provide closed-form solutions that include variance and trend.

Section II contains the analytical framework of the model and the formal derivation of optimal money holdings. In this context we analyze the determinants of the various elasticities of the demand for money. In Section III we analyze the properties of the distribution of the optimal payments period (the time spacing consecutive adjustments of money holdings), as well as the determinants of the probability that adjustment will be necessary during a given period. In Sections II and III optimal behavior is determined by minimizing

* We are indebted to Robert J. Barro, William A. Brock, Stanley Fischer, Benjamin M. Friedman, and Merton H. Miller for comments and suggestions. J. A. Frenkel acknowledges financial support from a National Science Foundation grant, SOC 78-14480. The research reported here is part of the NBER's research program in International Studies. Any opinions expressed are those of the authors and not those of NBER.

The Quarterly Journal of Economics, August 1980 0033-5533/80/0095-0025$01.90

the net present value of cost. In Section IV we analyze the optimal behavior from the perspective of minimizing steady-state cost. We provide a complete characterization of the steady-state distribution, and we show that optimal holdings as determined by the steady-state approach may differ significantly from the optimum obtained by minimizing the net present value of cost. Concluding remarks are contained in Section V.

II. A Model of the Optimum Holdings of Money

In this section, we outline the analytical framework that is used for the derivation of the optimum holdings of money. The analytical framework integrates transactions and precautionary motives underlying the demand for money. We start with a formal derivation.

A. A Formal Derivation of the Demand for Money

Earlier studies of the transactions demand for money emphasized the lack of synchronization between payments and receipts as the prime reason for holding an inventory of money. To highlight the transactions motive for holding money, the early formulations of Baumol [1952] and Tobin [1956] have assumed that transactions occur in a steady stream that is perfectly foreseen. In contrast with the completely deterministic nature of these models, studies of the precautionary demand for money adopted a different formulation emphasizing the stochastic nature of transactions. One of the most significant contributions along these lines was made by Miller and Orr [1966], who highlighted the stochastic elements underlying the demand for money by adopting the opposite extreme assumption that net cash flows are completely stochastic.[1] In what follows, we analyze the determinants of optimal money holdings by incorporating various aspects of these two formulations.

We assume that changes in money holdings can be characterized by the following stochastic equation:

$$(1) \qquad dM(t) = -\mu dt + \sigma dW(t); \quad M(0) = M_0, \quad \mu \geq 0,$$

where $W(t) \sim N(0,t)$ is the standard Wiener process that is distributed normally with mean zero and with variance t, and is temporally

1. Other studies that emphasized the stochastic nature of transactions include Olivera [1971], Orr [1970], Patinkin [1965, Ch. VI], Tsiang [1969], and Whalen [1966].

independent.[2] In equation (1), M_0 denotes the optimal initial money holdings, and μ denotes the deterministic part of net expenditures. Thus, at each point in time, the distribution of money holdings $M(t)$ is characterized by

$$M(t) = M_0 - \mu t + \sigma W(t) \tag{2}$$

and

$$M(t) \sim N(M_0 - \mu t, \sigma^2 t).$$

In analyzing the determinants of optimal money holdings, M_0, individuals (or firms) consider two types of cost; the first being forgone earnings on inventory holdings; and the second being the cost of adjustment that has to take place once inventories have reached an undesirable lower bound. Money holders could reduce the probability of having to adjust by holding a sufficiently large stock of money. The costs of acquiring the higher level of security are the forgone earnings on the large inventories of money which could have been invested in interest-bearing assets. On the other hand, money holders could reduce forgone earnings by holding a smaller stock of money, thereby raising the probability of more frequently incurring the cost of adjusting the monetary stock to the optimal level M_0. The optimal level is determined by minimizing the cost of financial management where both sources of cost are taken into account. As indicated above, the two sources of cost are (i) forgone earnings that depend on the rate of interest r and on money holdings $M(t)$, and (ii) the cost of adjustments, which is assumed to depend on the frequency of adjustment and on the fixed cost C per adjustment (e.g., "broker's fee").

It is assumed that an adjustment of the money stock is necessary whenever, due to the stochastic nature of net disbursement, money holdings reach a lower bound. Without loss of generality we shall set

2. The Weiner process (a white noise Brownian motion) is distributed normally over any interval and is the natural limiting process for the simple random walk with independent increments. In a discrete time form, equation (1) can be written as (1′)$M(t + h) - M(t) = -\mu h + \sigma y(t)\sqrt{h}$, where $y(t)$ is a normal random variable with zero mean and serially uncorrelated unit variance. The limit of (1′) as $h \to 0$ can be written as equation (1) in the text where $dW(t) \equiv y(t)\sqrt{dt}$. Thus, for the Weiner process the change in $M(t)$ in a small time interval dt is a normal variate with mean $-\mu dt$ and variance $\sigma^2 dt$, and is independent of $M(t)$ and of the change in any other small interval. Miller and Orr [1966] have assumed a Bernoulli process; at the limit when the increments and the time interval between increments approach zero, one obtains the Weiner process for continuous time. This process is rather general, and all diffusion processes (i.e., processes whose paths are continuous with probability one) can be represented as a functional transformation of the Weiner process. For details on the properties of the process, see Cox and Miller [1965], and for a simple exposition and an application see Fischer [1975].

this lower bound at zero.[3] Forgone earnings and the number of times that the "broker's fee" is being paid (i.e., the frequency of adjustments) are both random, since as is indicated in equation (2), at each point in time money holdings are random. It is assumed, therefore, that asset holders determine the optimal size of the money stock M_0 by minimizing the *expected* cost of financial management.

For analytical convenience, it is useful to separate the expected cost into the part that is incurred prior to the period of the first adjustment and the part that is incurred thereafter. Consider first the expected forgone earnings during the period up to the date of the first adjustment. At period t, the instantaneous forgone earnings are $rM(t)$, and their present value is

$$rM(t)e^{-rt}.$$

Let $h(M,t|M_0,0)$ be the probability that money holdings $M(t)$, which at period zero were at the optimal level M_0, have *not* reached zero (the lower bound) prior to period t at which money holdings are M. Thus, the present value of expected forgone earnings up to the first adjustment is

$$(3) \qquad J_1(M_0) = r \int_0^{\infty} e^{-rt} \left\{ \int_{M=0}^{\infty} Mh(M,t|M_0,0)dM \right\} dt.$$

It is shown in part A of the Appendix that expected forgone earnings may be written as

$$(3') \qquad J_1(M_0) = M_0 - (1 - \alpha)(\mu/r),$$

where

$$\alpha = \exp\{-(M_0/\sigma^2)[(\mu^2 + 2r\sigma^2)^{1/2} - \mu]\} \equiv \exp\{-kM_0\},$$

and as may be seen, α depends on the various parameters of the model as well as on the optimal money holdings M_0.

3. Miller and Orr [1966] adopted a two-parameter control-limit policy by assuming that adjustment is necessary when money holdings reach a lower bound (zero), as well as when they reach an upper bound. Since their analysis is based on the steady-state distributions, and since they assume that the stochastic process is without a drift, the two bounds are necessary for the existence of the steady-state distribution. In the Appendix, Miller and Orr derive a steady-state formula for the case of a nonzero drift but, in the authors' words [p. 427], the results "turn out to be extremely cumbersome and hard to interpret." Our assumption that adjustment is necessary only when money holdings reach a lower bound is basically due to computational difficulties in obtaining closed-form solutions for the more general case. The upper bound is probably more significant, the smaller is the rate of downward drift relative to the variance, and the smaller is the cost of downward adjustment. Obviously, the upper bound would not be important if the variance is zero, and its neglect would be optimal when the cost of downward adjustment tends to infinity.

We turn now to the derivation of the second component of the expected cost—the part that is incurred following the first adjustment. Let the present value of total expected cost be denoted by $G(M_0)$. Clearly, $G(M_0)$ is independent of time.[4] The period at which money holdings reach zero and adjustment becomes necessary is random. Let $f(M_0,t)$ be the probability that money holdings, which at period zero were at the optimal level M_0, reached zero (the lower bound) at period t. Thus, the present value of the expected cost following the first adjustment is

$$(4) \qquad J_2(M_0) = \int_0^\infty e^{-rt}[C + G(M_0)]f(M_0,t)dt,$$

and it can be shown that[5]

$$(4') \qquad J_2(M_0) = \alpha[C + G(M_0)].$$

Combining the two components of the cost, $J_1(M_0)$ and $J_2(M_0)$, yields $G(M_0)$, the present value of total expected cost:

$$(5) \qquad G(M_0) = M_0 - (1 - \alpha)(\mu/r) + \alpha[C + G(M_0)],$$

or equivalently,

$$(5') \qquad G(M_0) = \frac{M_0 + \alpha C}{1 - \alpha} - \frac{\mu}{r}.$$

Minimizing the expected cost of financial management amounts to minimizing $G(M_0)$ with respect to the optimal money stock M_0.[6] Carrying out the minimization yields equation (6) as the necessary condition for optimality:[7]

$$(6) \qquad (1 - \alpha) + (M_0 + C)\frac{\partial \alpha}{\partial M_0} = 0.$$

Expanding the necessary condition (6) in Taylor series (around M_0),

4. The $G(M_0)$ function, which excludes the current "broker's fee" that is associated with acquiring M_0, plays the role of the value function of dynamic programming. It is independent of time due to the infinite horizon and the constant discount rate.

5. Cox and Miller [1965, Ch. 5.7] show that α is the Laplace transform of the first passage probability of a Weiner process through a linear boundary, that is

$$\alpha = \int_0^\infty e^{-rt}f(M_0,t)dt.$$

6. It may be noted that $G(M_0)$ is a U-shape with cost approaching infinity as M_0 approaches zero or infinity.

7. Since $\alpha = \exp\{-kM_0\}$, it is clear that the optimality condition (6) is consistent with the homogeneity postulate, in that an equiproportionate change in the quantity of money and the price level reduces k (by raising σ, C, and μ) by the same proportion and does not disturb the equilibrium.

ignoring terms of third and higher order and solving for M_0, yields equation (7) as the optimal money holding:[8]

$$(7)\qquad M_0 = \left[\frac{2C\sigma^2}{(\mu^2 + 2r\sigma^2)^{1/2} - \mu}\right]^{1/2} = \left(\frac{2C}{k}\right)^{1/2}.$$

As is evident, equation (7) satisfies the homogeneity postulate; a rise in the price level that raises σ, C, and μ by a given proportion results in an equiproportional rise in M_0.

B. Two Special Cases

Equation (7) encompasses the various strands in the literature of optimal money holdings. It contains elements of the pure transactions motive that have been emphasized in the Baumol-Tobin models (summarized by the deterministic drift μ), along with elements of the precautionary motive arising from the stochastic nature of net disbursements that have been emphasized in the Miller-Orr [1966] and Whalen [1966] models (summarized by σ). In view of these contributions, it is of interest to examine the implications of two special cases. In the first case, corresponding to the Baumol-Tobin framework, it is assumed that the process governing net disbursements is deterministic, that is, $\sigma^2 = 0$. In the second case, corresponding to the Miller-Orr and Whalen framework, it is assumed that the process governing net disbursements is stochastic without any drift, that is, $\mu = 0$.

To examine the first case, we expand the bracketed term in the denominator of equation (7) around $\sigma^2 = 0$:

$$(\mu^2 + 2r\sigma^2)^{1/2} = \mu + (1/2)\mu^{-1}2r\sigma^2 + 0(\sigma^4),$$

where $0(\sigma^4)$ denotes terms of order σ^4 and higher. Substituting in equation (7) yields

$$(8)\qquad M_0 = \left[\frac{2C\sigma^2}{\mu^{-1}r\sigma^2 + 0(\sigma^4)}\right]^{1/2}.$$

Taking the limit of (8) as σ^2 approaches zero yields

$$(9)\qquad \lim_{\sigma^2 \to 0} M_0 = \left(\frac{2C\mu}{r}\right)^{1/2}.$$

8. It is shown in Part B of the Appendix that the error that is introduced by the approximation involved in neglecting terms of third- and higher order is negligible. Here, and in what follows, we refer to M_0 as the optimal money holdings. Strictly speaking, M_0 denotes the *initial* optimal money holdings; i.e., it denotes the magnitude of the adjustment in money holdings. If the adjustment is affected by withdrawing cash from the bank, then M_0 denotes the size of the withdrawal.

As is evident, equation (9) is identical to the Baumol-Tobin formulation of optimal transaction balances. In this case, when net disbursements are deterministic, the time profile of money balance has the familiar "saw-tooth" form, and the minimum cost of financial management yields the familiar "square-root rule."

To examine the second special case in which $\mu = 0$, we evaluate equation (7) at $\mu = 0$ obtaining

$$M_0 = \left[\frac{2C\sigma^2}{(2r\sigma^2)^{1/2}}\right]^{1/2}, \tag{10}$$

which can be written as

$$M_0 = 2^{1/4}C^{1/2}\sigma^{1/2}r^{-1/4}. \tag{10'}$$

In this case, the elasticities of the demand for money with respect to the cost of transactions C and with respect to the standard deviation of net disbursements are ½, and the elasticity with respect to the rate of interest is −¼. In the Miller-Orr model (with lower and upper bounds) and in Whalen's model, the elasticity of the demand with respect to the cost of transactions is ⅓, the elasticity with respect to the standard deviation is ⅔, and the elasticity with respect to the rate of interest is −⅓. We turn now to a more detailed analysis of the various elasticities for the general case.

C. The Elasticities of Optimal Money Holdings

From equation (7) it can be seen that the transactions elasticity of optimal money holdings ($\eta_{M_0\mu}$) is

$$\eta_{M_0\mu} = \tfrac{1}{2}(1 + 2r\sigma^2/\mu^2)^{-1/2}. \tag{11}$$

Thus, in general, the transactions elasticity is positive and smaller than ½; it increases with the volume of transactions μ, and it decreases with the rate of interest r and with the standard deviation of net disbursements σ.[9] It is also evident from equation (11) that, in the special case for which $\sigma^2 = 0$, the transactions elasticity is ½—the Baumol-Tobin case.

Likewise, from equation (7), the interest elasticity of optimal money holdings (η_{M_0r}) is

9. It might be noted that the transactions elasticity approaches zero as the ratio $r\sigma^2/\mu^2$ approaches infinity. Thus, the range of the transactions elasticity is between zero and ½. For attempts to introduce flexibility into the implications of the Baumol-Tobin model, see Barro [1970], Karni [1973], and Buiter and Armstrong [1978], where the latter allow for random returns but assume that the process governing net disbursements is deterministic.

$$(12) \qquad \eta_{M_0r} = -\tfrac{1}{2}\{r\sigma^2/[\mu^2 + 2r\sigma^2 - \mu(\mu^2 + 2r\sigma^2)^{1/2}]\},$$

and as may be seen, the interest elasticity is negative and is smaller than ½ (in absolute value). It may also be seen that it approaches $-\frac{1}{2}$ as σ^2 approaches zero—the Baumol-Tobin case.[10] For a positive σ^2, the interest elasticity varies with the volume of transactions μ. It approaches $-\frac{1}{2}$ when μ approaches infinity, and as shown in equation (10′), it approaches $-\frac{1}{4}$ as μ approaches zero.[11]

It can be shown that the elasticity of optimal money holdings with respect to the standard deviation of net disbursements ($\eta_{M_0\sigma}$) is related to the corresponding elasticity with respect to the rate of interest according to

$$(13) \qquad \eta_{M_0\sigma} = 1 + 2\eta_{M_0r}.$$

The relationship between the two elasticities in equation (13) seems to be robust. For example, it is also satisfied in the Miller-Orr and Whalen models of optimal money holdings.

III. THE PAYMENTS PERIOD AND THE PROBABILITY OF ADJUSTMENT

In this section we analyze (i) the determinants of the payments period—the length of time intervals between consecutive adjustments, and (ii) the determinants of the probability that money holdings reach the lower bound and thereby make adjustment necessary.

In a fully deterministic model of the Baumol-Tobin variety, the length of the payments period is M_0/μ—the ratio of the optimal money stock to the steady flow of expenditures per unit of time.[12] In a stochastic framework, the length of the payments period is characterized by a distribution whose mean is equal, by definition, to the ratio of M_0 to the mean flow of net disbursements. Since in our case the mean flow of net disbursements is μ, it follows that the mean payments period is M_0/μ. We turn now to a more detailed analysis of the distribution of the payments period.

In Section IIA we denoted the probability that money holdings,

10. This can be seen by expanding $(\mu^2 + 2r\sigma^2)^{1/2}$ around $\sigma^2 = 0$ and ignoring terms of order σ^6 and higher; alternatively, expanding around $r = 0$ and ignoring terms of r^3 and higher yields the same result.

11. The specification in equation (7), and the implied transactions and interest elasticities, include σ^2 as one of the parameters whose omission in empirical estimation may lead to a specification bias. For example, to the extent that income (and thus transactions) and σ^2 are positively correlated, estimates of the demand for money will result in upward biased estimates of the transactions elasticity.

12. For an interesting analysis of the optimal payments period, see Barro [1970].

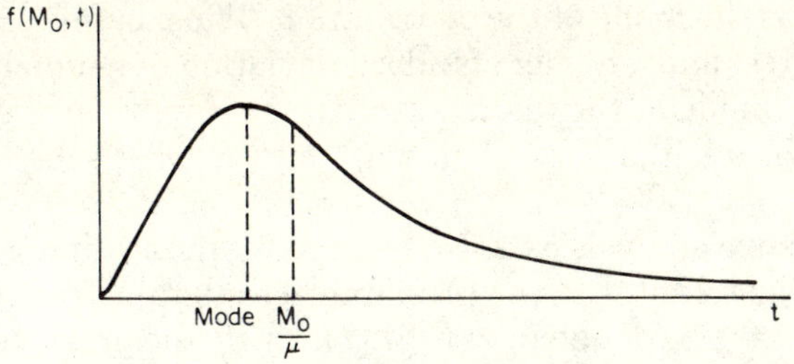

FIGURE I
The Distribution of the Payments Period

which at period zero were at the optimal level, reached zero at period t, by $f(M_0,t)$. It is clear that the distribution of the length of the payments period is governed by the function $f(M_0,t)$. It is shown in Cox and Miller [1965, Ch. 5.7] that the density (known as the inverse Gaussian; see Tweedie [1957]) is

$$(14) \qquad f(M_0,t) = [M_0/\sqrt{2\pi}\sigma t^{3/2}] \exp\{-(M_0 - \mu t)^2/2\sigma^2 t\},$$

with a mean M_0/μ and a variance $M_0\sigma^2/2\mu^3$. To find the mode of the distribution, we differentiate equation (14) with respect to time, equate to zero, and solve for the mode. The resulting (unique) mode is

$$(15) \qquad [M_0/\mu]\{[1 + (3\sigma^2/2M_0\mu)^2]^{1/2} - 3\sigma^2/2M_0\mu\}.$$

As may be seen, the mode of the distribution is smaller than the mean,[13] and it coincides with the mean when $\sigma = 0$ (the Baumol-Tobin case). These properties of the distribution of the payments period are summarized in Figure I.

In the special case for which μ approaches zero, it can be shown, using equation (15), that the mode of the distribution of the payments period is $M_0{}^2/3\sigma^2$.[14] Substituting equation (10) for M_0 yields

13. This can be verified from equation (15) by noticing that $(1 + x^2)^{1/2} - x < 1$.

14. This can be shown by rewriting equation (15) as

$$(\tfrac{1}{2}\mu^2)[-x + (x^2 + 4\mu^2 M_0^2)^{1/2}],$$

where $x \equiv 3\sigma^2$. Expanding $(x^2 + 4\mu^2 M_0^2)^{1/2}$ in a Taylor series yields

$$x + (\tfrac{1}{2})x^{-1}4M_0^2\mu^2 + 0(\mu^4),$$

where $0(\mu^4)$ denotes terms in μ^4 and higher. Substituting back yields

$$(\tfrac{1}{2}\mu^2)[x^{-1}2M_0^2\mu^2 + 0(\mu^4)].$$

By taking the limit as μ^2 approaches zero, we obtain $M_0{}^2/3\sigma^2$ as the value of the mode.

$C\sqrt{2/r}/3\sigma$ as the mode of the distribution. Thus, in this case a higher rate of interest and a higher standard deviation of net disbursements reduce the (mode of the distribution of the) length of the payments period, while a higher cost of adjustment ("broker's fee") raises the mode.

The above analysis can also be used for determining the probability of adjustment. Let the probability that adjustment will occur prior to period t be denoted by $F(M_0,t)$. Using the previous notations, we see that

$$(16) \qquad F(M_0,t) = \int_0^t f(M_0,s)ds,$$

and as is shown in Cox and Miller [1965, Ch. 5.7], this probability can be written explicitly as

$$(17) \quad F(M_0,t) = 1 - N\left[\frac{M_0 - \mu t}{\sigma t^{1/2}}\right] + N\left[\frac{-M_0 - \mu t}{\sigma t^{1/2}}\right] \exp\left[\frac{2\mu M_0}{\sigma^2}\right].$$

In the special case for which $\mu = 0$, equation (17) becomes

$$(18) \qquad F(M_0,t) = 2(1 - N[M_0/\sigma t^{1/2}]),$$

where

$$N(x) = \frac{1}{\sqrt{2\pi}} \int_{-\infty}^{x} e^{-x^2/2}\, dx.$$

As is clear,

$$\lim_{t\to\infty} F(M_0,t) = 1, \quad \text{since } N(0) = 1/2.$$

To analyze the determinants of the probability of adjustment in this case, we substitute equation (10) for M_0 in equation (18) to yield

$$(19) \qquad F(M_0,t) = 2(1 - N[(C\sqrt{2}\,/r^{1/2}\sigma t)^{1/2}]).$$

Thus, higher values of r, σ, and t increase the probability that adjustment will be necessary, while a higher cost of adjustment decreases that probability. The effect of σ is of some interest because a higher value of σ raises optimal money holdings that operate to reduce the probability of adjustment (since from equation (18) $\partial F(\cdot)/\partial M_0 < 0$). Equation (19) reveals that the induced rise in the optimal money stock will not completely offset the direct effect of the rise in σ on the probability of adjustment.

IV. The Steady-State Distribution and a Steady-State Approach

In this section we derive the steady-state distribution of money holdings and provide a complete characterization of this distribution. We then adopt a steady-state approach and use these results for an alternative derivation of optimal money holdings.

A. The Steady-State Distribution

In deriving the steady-state distribution, we start with some notation. Let the steady-state probability density of money holdings be denoted by the function $\phi(M)$. In Section IIA we denoted by $h(M,t|M_0,0)$ the probability that money holdings, which at period zero were at the optimal level M_0, had not reached zero prior to period t, at which money holdings were M. In what follows, it will be convenient to simplify the notation and denote this probability by $\theta(M|t)$. We further denote the probability that adjustment took place exactly t periods ago by $g(t)$. In Section III we saw that the mean of the length of the payments period is M_0/μ. As is known from renewal theory, in the steady state the probability $g(t)$ approaches a constant g^*, which is equal to the inverse of the mean of the payments period:[15]

$$g^* = \mu/M_0. \tag{20}$$

Finally, let $\psi(t|M)$ be the probability that the previous adjustment occurred exactly t periods ago, given that current money holdings are M. Using Bayes's Theorem, the steady-state distribution can be expressed as

$$\phi(M) = \frac{\theta(M|t)g^*}{\psi(t|M)}, \tag{21}$$

and substituting equation (20) for g^* yields

$$\phi(M) = \frac{\mu}{M_0}\frac{\theta(M|t)}{\psi(t|M)}. \tag{22}$$

The function $\phi(M)$ pertains to the steady state, and thus it is independent of time. It follows that the ratio $\theta(M|t)/\psi(t|M)$ in equation (22) must also be independent of time, and therefore we can use in (22) the ratio of the integrals of $\theta(\cdot)$ and $\psi(\cdot)$ with respect to time:

15. See, for example, Feller [1971, Ch. XI]. In this context $[g^*dt]$ can be interpreted as the probability that the process (which has been in existence forever) will cross the zero boundary during the time interval $[t,t + dt]$.

$$\phi(M) = \frac{\mu}{M_0}\frac{\int_0^\infty \theta(M|t)dt}{\int_0^\infty \psi(t|M)dt}. \tag{22'}$$

We note, however, that the probability that the previous adjustment occurred *more* than t periods ago approaches zero as t approaches infinity, and therefore

$$\int_0^\infty \psi(t|M)dt = 1.$$

Using this fact in (22′) yields the expression for the steady-state distribution:

$$\phi(M) = \frac{\mu}{M_0}\int_0^\infty \theta(M|t)dt. \tag{23}$$

By integrating the right-hand side of equation (23) (using some of the expressions from Part A of the Appendix), the steady-state distribution can be written as[16]

$$\phi(M) = \begin{cases} [1/M_0][1 - \exp(-2M\mu/\sigma^2)] & \text{for } 0 \leq M \leq M_0 \\ [1/M_0][\exp(-2(M - M_0)\mu/\sigma^2) - \exp(-2M\mu/\sigma^2)] & \text{for } M > M_0. \end{cases} \tag{24}$$

It can be verified that average money holdings in the steady state are

$$E(M) \equiv \int_0^\infty M\phi(M)dM = \frac{1}{2}\left(M_0 + \frac{\sigma^2}{\mu}\right), \tag{25}$$

and the variance of money holdings in the steady state is

$$\text{var}(M) \equiv M_0^2/12 + \sigma^4/4\mu^2. \tag{26}$$

These derivations of the steady-state distribution are exact, since equations (24)–(26) hold for any arbitrary positive M_0. In the special case for which $\sigma = 0$, the constant flow of expenditures is μ, and the mean of the distribution of steady-state money holdings is $M_0/2$ (the Baumol-Tobin case). Finally, it should be noted that in the special case for which $\mu = 0$ the steady-state distribution does not exist.[17] The various characteristics of the steady-state probability density of

16. It can be verified that $\int_0^\infty \phi(M)dM = 1$, as it should.

17. As indicated in note 3, the steady-state distribution in the Miller-Orr model exists, since they assume lower and upper bounds.

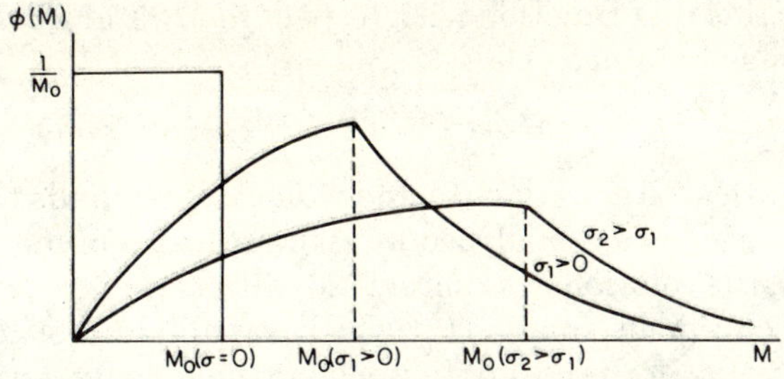

FIGURE II
The Steady-State Probability Density of Money Holdings for Alternative Values of σ

money holdings for alternative values of σ are described in Figure II; as may be seen, in the special case for which $\sigma = 0$, the distribution becomes uniform.

B. An Alternative Derivation: The Steady-State Approach

In deriving the optimal money holdings M_0, we followed the procedure of minimizing the present value of financial management. In contrast, an alternative methodology which has been adopted by Miller and Orr [1966] and investigated by Arrow, Karlin, and Scarf [1958], is to compute the optimum from the solution obtained by minimizing the steady-state cost function. Arrow *et al.* indicated that the two alternative approaches may not yield identical results, and that the justification for the use of the approximation involved in minimizing the steady-state cost function is on the grounds of simplicity. In order to compare the two alternative methods, we turn to the steady-state approach and derive the optimal money holdings that are implied by minimizing the steady-state cost function.

The expected cost of financial management per unit of time in the steady state is composed of the expected "broker's fee" and the expected forgone earnings per unit of time. The expected number of adjustments per unit of time in the steady state is g^* (the steady-state renewal density), which, from equation (20), equals μ/M_0—the inverse of the mean payments period. Thus, the expected steady-state "broker's fee" per unit of time is Cg^*. In addition, average money holdings in the steady state are $E(M)$, and forgone earnings per unit of time are $rE(M)$. Thus, given equations (20) and (25), total costs per unit of time in the steady state are

$$Cg^* + rE(M) = C\mu/M_0 + (r/2)(M_0 + \sigma^2/\mu). \tag{27}$$

Minimizing this cost function with respect to M_0 and solving for the optimal money holdings yields

$$M_0 = (2C\mu/r)^{1/2}, \tag{28}$$

which is identical to equation (9) and which corresponds to the solution for the special case analyzed by Baumol and Tobin.

Clearly, the solution in equation (28) differs fundamentally from the general solution in equation (7), which was obtained by minimizing the present value of the cost of financial management. The most important difference is that the solution obtained by the steady-state approach does not depend on the value of the variance σ^2, which, in turn, plays a key role in the general solution. It seems that, in this case, the adoption of a steady-state approach results in an elimination of the effects of the stochastic characteristics of the process governing money holdings. Thus, following the steady-state approach results in a fundamentally different interpretation of the determinants of optimal money holdings. While the solution in equation (7) may be interpreted as containing elements that pertain to both transactions and precautionary motives for holding money, the solution in equation (28) contains only the deterministic transaction motive. Obviously, in the special case for which $\sigma = 0$, the two solutions coincide.[18]

The comparison of the two solutions in equations (7) and (28) also raises a methodological question concerning the appropriateness of approximating optimal adjustment policies by using a steady-state approach. The steady-state approach is, of course, much simpler, but unless one knows the true solution (as in our case), the cost of obtaining simplicity cannot be assessed.

V. Concluding Remarks

In this paper we developed a stochastic framework for the analysis of transactions and precautionary demand for money, and we

18. As is indicated by Arrow *et al.* [1958, p. 35], the two methods yield identical results when the rate of interest is zero. It implies that the difference between the two methods arises due to the discounting involved in the present value computation. A comparison of equation (8) and (24) with a zero rate of interest illustrates the point. Analyzing the deterministic case and performing numerical computations for "reasonable" values of the parameters, Hadley [1964] found that the steady-state solution did not differ greatly from the optimal solution obtained by minimizing the present value of net cost. Our analysis suggests that in a stochastic framework the difference may not be negligible, and that it will rise with the value of σ. It may be noted that the difference between the solutions obtained by the two approaches may not be attributed to our assumption that adjustment is necessary only when money holdings reach a lower bound, since, as we indicated above, when the cost of downward adjustment tends to infinity, the neglect of the upper bound is indeed optimal.

attempted to integrate some aspects of previous contributions by Baumol [1952], Tobin [1956], and Miller and Orr [1966]. We formally derived the closed-form solution for optimal money holdings as a function of the rate of interest, the mean rate of net disbursements, the cost of portfolio adjustment, and the variance of the stochastic process governing net disbursements. We also analyzed the determinants of the optimal length of time elapsing between two consecutive portfolio adjustments. We then followed the more traditional approach and analyzed the steady-state distribution of money holdings, and derived the optimal money stock that is implied by the steady-state approach. A comparison of the two solutions illustrated that the two approaches may yield solutions which differ significantly from each other. This comparison led to the methodological question concerning the appropriateness of approximating optimal adjustment policies by following the steady-state approach.

APPENDIX: MATHEMATICAL DERIVATIONS

In Part A of this Appendix we derive equation (3′) in the text, and in Part B we show that the approximation involved in the derivation of equation (7) introduces a negligible error.

Part A

We have assumed that money holdings are governed by the stochastic equation:

(A.1) $$dM(t) = -\mu dt + \sigma dW(t); \quad M(0) = M_0.$$

In order to correspond to Cox and Miller's framework [1965, Ch. 5.7], in which the first passage is for a process that starts at zero and goes through a positive boundary, we perform the following transformations. Define

(A.2) $$d\hat{M}(t) = \mu dt - \sigma dW(t); \quad M(0) = -M_0.$$

and

(A.3) $$dx(t) = \mu dt - \sigma dW(t); \quad x(0) = 0.$$

Thus, $\hat{M}(t)$ is the mirror image of $M(t)$ in the negative half-plane, and $x(t) = \hat{M}(t) + M_0$.

Let $\hat{h}(M,t| - M_0,0)$ be the probability that $\hat{M}(t)$ (defined by equation (A.2)) will not reach zero before period t, *and* that $\hat{M}(t) = M$. Then equation (3) in the text becomes

(A.4) $$J_1(M_0) = -r \int_0^\infty e^{-rt} \left\{ \int_{-\infty}^0 M\hat{h}(M,t| - M_0,0)dM \right\} dt.$$

Analogously, in order to shift the origin to conform with Cox and

Miller's framework, let $h^*(x,t|0,M_0)$ be the probability that $x(t)$ will not reach the boundary M_0 before t, *and* that $x(t) = x$. Since $x(t) = \hat{M}(t) + M_0$, the relationship between $h^*(\cdot)$ and $\tilde{h}(\cdot)$ is

$$h^*(x,t|0,M_0) = \tilde{h}(x - M_0,t| - M_0,0). \tag{A.5}$$

In order to use the function $h^*(\cdot)$, we change the variables in (A.4) by substituting $x = M + M_0$:

$$J_1(M_0) = -r\int_0^\infty e^{-rt}\left\{\int_{-\infty}^{M_0}(x - M_0)\tilde{h}(x - M_0,t|- M_0,0)dx\right\}dt, \tag{A.6}$$

and using (A.5) in (A.6) results in

$$J_1(M_0) = -r\int_0^\infty e^{-rt}\left\{\int_{-\infty}^{M_0}(x - M_0)\,h^*(x,t|0,M_0)dx\right\}dt. \tag{A.7}$$

Decomposing (A.7) into expressions that involve M_0 and expressions that involve x yields

$$J_1(M_0) = rM_0\int_0^\infty e^{-rt}\left\{\int_{-\infty}^{M_0}h^*(x,t|0,M_0)dx\right\}dt - r\int_0^\infty e^{-rt}\left\{\int_{-\infty}^{M_0}xh^*(x,t|0,M_0)dx\right\}dt. \tag{A.8}$$

Let $f(M_0,t)$ be the probability that $x(t)$ will reach M_0 for the first time at t. To simplify the notation, we shall refer to this probability as $f(t)$. Thus, $f(t)$ is also the probability that $M(t)$ reaches zero for the first time at t; therefore, the probability that the process will reach zero prior to t is

$$F(t) \equiv \int_0^t f(s)ds.$$

It follows that the probability of *not* reaching zero prior to period t is

$$\int_{-\infty}^{M_0}h^*(x,t|0,M_0)dx = 1 - F(t).$$

Using this result to evaluate the first integral in (A.8) yields

$$\int_0^\infty re^{-rt}[1 - F(t)]dt = [-e^{-rt}(1 - F(t))]_0^\infty - \int_0^\infty e^{-rt}f(t)dt. \tag{A.8.i}$$

Cox and Miller [1965, Ch. 5.7] show that

$$\int_0^\infty e^{-rt}(f)dt = \alpha,$$

where

$$\alpha = \exp\{-(M_0/\sigma^2)[(\mu^2 + 2r\sigma^2)^{1/2} - \mu]\};$$

substituting in (A.8.i) yields

$$\text{(A.8.ii)} \qquad \int_0^\infty re^{-rt}\left\{\int_{-\infty}^{M_0} h^*(x,t\,|\,0,M_0)dx\right\}dt = 1-\alpha.$$

We turn now to evaluate the second integral in (A.8). Cox and Miller [1965, Ch. 5.7] show that

$$h^*(x,t\,|\,0,M_0) = \frac{1}{\sqrt{2\pi}\sigma t^{1/2}}\left[\exp\left\{\frac{-(x-\mu t)^2}{2\sigma^2 t}\right\} - \exp\left\{\frac{2\mu M_0}{\sigma^2} - \frac{(x-2M_0-\mu t)^2}{2\sigma^2 t}\right\}\right].$$

Substituting into (A.8) and integrating by parts yields

$$\text{(A.9)} \qquad J_1(M_0) = M_0 + \mu\int_0^\infty e^{-rt}D(t)dt,$$

where

$$D(t) = N\left[\frac{-M_0-\mu t}{\sigma t^{1/2}}\right]\exp\left\{\frac{2\mu M_0}{\sigma^2}\right\} - N\left[\frac{M_0-\mu t}{\sigma t^{1/2}}\right]$$

and where

$$N(x) \equiv \int_{-\infty}^{x} (2\pi)^{-1} e^{-z^2/2}dz.$$

Integrating by parts yields equation (3′) in the text.

Part B

The necessary condition for optimization is

$$\text{(B.1)} \qquad (1-\alpha) + (M_0 + C)\frac{\partial\alpha}{\partial M_0} = 0.$$

When (B.1) is multiplied through by $\beta \equiv 1/\alpha$, and noting that $\partial\alpha/\partial M_0 = -k\alpha$, where α is defined by equation (3′) in the text and where $k = (1/\sigma^2)[(\mu^2 + 2r\sigma^2)^{1/2} - \mu] > 0$, it becomes

$$\text{(B.1′)} \qquad -k(M_0 + C) + \beta - 1 = 0.$$

Taylor's Theorem with remainder implies that, for some constant $\lambda(0 \leq \lambda \leq 1)$, the term β in (B.1′) can be expanded as

$$\text{(B.2)} \quad \beta = \beta(0) + \frac{\partial\beta(0)}{\partial M_0}M_0 + \frac{1}{2}\frac{\partial^2\beta(0)}{\partial {M_0}^2}M^2 + \frac{1}{6}\frac{\partial^3\beta(\lambda M_0)}{\partial M_0^3}M_0^3.$$

Substituting a quadratic expansion of β (without the third-order term) into (B.1′) yields

$$\text{(B.3)} \qquad -k(M_0 + C) + \frac{\partial\beta(0)}{\partial M_0}M_0 + \frac{1}{2}\frac{\partial^2\beta(0)}{\partial M_0^2}M_0^2 = 0$$

(since $\beta(0) = 1$), and the solution for M_0 is given in equation (7) in the text. Using (B.1′) and (B.2), we find that the true solution for M_0, which is denoted by $\overline{M}$, satisfies equation (B.4):

$$\text{(B.4)}\quad -k(\overline{M}+C)+\frac{\partial\beta(0)}{\partial M_0}\overline{M}+\frac{1}{2}\frac{\partial^2\beta(0)}{\partial M_0^2}\overline{M}^2+\frac{1}{6}\frac{\partial^3\beta(\lambda\overline{M})}{\partial M_0^3}\overline{M}^3=0.$$

To determine the extent of the error involved in the approximation, we subtract (B.2) from (B.4) and cancel terms to obtain

$$\text{(B.5)}\qquad (1/2)(\overline{M}^2-M_0^2)+(1/6)k\exp\{\lambda\overline{M}k\}\overline{M}^3=0,$$

since

$$\frac{\partial\beta(0)}{\partial M_0}=k,\quad \frac{\partial^2\beta(0)}{\partial M_0^2}=k^2,\quad\text{and}\quad \frac{\partial^3\beta(\lambda\overline{M})}{\partial M_0^3}=k^3\exp\{\lambda\overline{M}k\}.$$

Equation (B.5) implies that

$$(M_0^2-\overline{M}^2)/\overline{M}^2=(k/3)\exp\{\lambda\overline{M}k\}\overline{M}\geq 0,$$

and therefore the approximate solution M_0 exceeds the true solution $\overline{M}$. Substituting M_0 for $\overline{M}$ yields the following inequalities:

$$\text{(B.6)}\quad 0\leq(M_0^2-\overline{M}^2)/\overline{M}^2\leq(k/3)\exp\{\lambda M_0k\}M_0\leq k/3\,e^{M_0k}M_0,$$

where the last inequality follows, since $0\leq\lambda\leq 1$. Since equation (7) in the text states that

$$M_0=(2C)^{1/2}k^{-1/2},$$

(B.6) becomes

$$\text{(B.6}'\text{)}\qquad 0\leq(M_0^2-\overline{M}^2)/\overline{M}^2\leq[(2kC)^{1/2}/3]\exp\{(2kC)^{1/2}\}.$$

Thus, the relative error is negligible if kC is negligible. From equation (7) in the text, $k=2C/M_0^2$, and therefore

$$kC=2(C/M_0)^2\leq 2(C/\overline{M})^2,$$

where $C/\overline{M}$ is the "broker's fee" divided by the true optimum $\overline{M}$. As a practical matter, for any reasonable order of magnitude the ratio $C/\overline{M}$ must be a very small fraction; its square must be negligible; and so is kC. Thus, the solution for the optimum that is given by equation (7) is a good approximation to the true solution.

University of Chicago and National Bureau of Economic Research
Bell Laboratories and Columbia University

References

Arrow, Kenneth J. Samuel Karlin, and Herbert Scarf, *Studies in the Mathematical Theory of Inventory and Production* (Stanford: Stanford University Press, 1958).

Barro, Robert J., "Inflation, the Payment Period and the Demand for Money," *Journal of Political Economy,* LXXVIII, no. 6 (Nov./Dec. 1970), 1228–63.

Baumol, William J., "The Transactions Demand for Cash: An Inventory Theoretical Approach," this *Journal,* LXVI (Nov. 1952), 545–56.

Buiter, Willem H., and Clive A. Armstrong, "A Didactic Note on the Transactions Demand for Money and Behavior Towards Risk," *Journal of Money, Credit and Banking,* X, 4 (Nov. 1978), 529–38.
Cox, R. D., and H. D. Miller, *The Theory of Stochastic Processes* (London: Methuen Ltd., 1965).
Feller, W., *An Introduction to Probability and Its Application,* Vol. II, 2nd ed. (New York: Wiley, 1971).
Fischer, Stanley, "The Demand for Index Bonds," *Journal of Political Economy,* LXXXIII, no. 3 (June 1975), 509–34.
Hadley, George, "A Comparison of Order Quantities Computed Using the Average Annual Cost and the Discounted Cost," *Management Science,* X, 3 (April 1964), 472–76.
Karni, Edi, "The Transactions Demand for Cash: Incorporating the Value of Time into the Inventory Approach," *Journal of Political Economy,* LXXXI (Sept./Oct. 1973), 1216–25.
Miller, Merton H., and Daniel, Orr, "A Model of the Demand for Money by Firms," this *Journal,* LXXX (Aug. 1966), 413–35.
Olivera, Julio H., "The Square-Root Law of Precautionary Reserves," *Journal of Political Economy,* LXXIX (Sept./Oct. 1971), 1095–1104.
Orr, Daniel, *Cash Management and the Demand for Money* (New York: Praeger, 1970).
Patinkin, Don, *Money Interest and Prices,* 2nd ed. (New York: Harper & Row, 1965).
Tobin, James, "The Interest-Elasticity of Transactions Demand for Cash," *Review of Economics and Statistics,* XXXVIII (Aug. 1956), 241–47.
Tsiang, S. C., "The Precautionary Demand for Money: An Inventory Theoretical Analysis," *Journal of Political Economy,* LXXVII (Jan./Feb. 1969), 99–117.
Tweedie, M. C. K. "Statistical Properties of Inverse Gaussian Distributions I," *Annals of Mathematical Statistics,* XXVIII (1957), 362–77.
Whalen, Edward L., "A Rationalization of the Precautionary Demand for Cash," this *Journal,* LXXX (May 1966), 314–24.

MARX AND SCHUMPETER ON CAPITALISM'S CREATIVE DESTRUCTION: A COMPARATIVE RESTATEMENT*

JOHN E. ELLIOTT

Despite well-known differences, the respective visions of capitalism's future by Marx and Schumpeter show striking and neglected similarities. This is illustrated, first, by their strong focus upon capitalism's progressive and creative properties; second, by their analyses of capitalism's dysfunctional properties; and third, by their respective analyses of the creatively destructive character of institutional and attitudinal change in advanced capitalism.

It is well-known that Schumpeter postulated an "inevitable decomposition of capitalist society" [1950, p. xiii]. "Can capitalism survive?" he asked pointedly. "No, I do not think it can" [1950, p. 61]. Capitalism's prospective demise is not perceived to emanate from "its breaking down under the weight of economic failure. . . ." Instead, "its very success undermines the social institutions which protect it, and 'inevitably' creates conditions in which it will not be able to live and which strongly point to socialism as the heir apparent" [1950, p. 61]. In short, the "paradoxical conclusion" is not the result, but the process: "capitalism is being killed by its achievements" [1950, p. xiv].

How does Schumpeter's vision of capitalism's future prospects compare and contrast with that of Marx who, by fascinating coincidence, died during the year of Schumpeter's birth (1883)? Since Schumpeter's *Capitalism, Socialism and Democracy,* greater emphasis has been placed on the contrasts than on the parallels. Popular expositions generally present a sharp dichotomy between the themes of Marxian contradiction ("capitalism cannot survive because of economic failure") and Schumpeterian paradox ("capitalism is being destroyed because of its very creative success").

No doubt there are differences between the two men, some quite striking, in ideological commitment, economic analysis, and social vision. But there are important parallels as well. A comparative restatement of these two perspectives, focusing on important similarities, is overdue. There is more "Schumpeter" in Marx's writings than

* The author would like to thank Professors Horst Betz and Richard Schenning, and two anonymous referees for helpful comments on an earlier draft on this paper.

The Quarterly Journal of Economics, August 1980 0033-5533/80/0095-0045$02.40

many Marxists are willing to accept,[1] and more "Marx" in Schumpeter's analysis than even Schumpeter was willing to recognize.[2] On the specific subject of "capitalism's creative destruction," the two respective theories seem closer to each other than either is to any other prominent vision of capitalism's future. At the very least, they are much closer than has been popularly supposed. The prima facie evidence supporting this interpretation is reinforced by Marx's recently published *Grundrisse,* which also incorporates a process of creative destruction and supercession. As the present author has noted elsewhere: "Socialism is conceived and nurtured in capitalism's womb, and is its product, not merely its heir apparent. It emerges on the basis of capitalism's development and creativity as well as emanates from its conflicts and contradictions. Capitalism's very success stimulates changes which both portend and facilitate the process of movement toward socialism" [Elliott, 1978–79].

This paper compares the Marx-Schumpeter visions of capitalism's creative destruction, with emphasis on three major themes: (i) capitalism as a revolutionary economic system; (ii) capitalism's economic dysfunctioning from a creative destruction perspective; and (iii) capitalism's transformation and socialization.

CREATIVE DESTRUCTION I: CAPITALISM AS A REVOLUTIONARY ECONOMIC SYSTEM

The "essential point to grasp" about capitalism, according to Schumpeter, is that it is an "evolutionary process," as "was long ago emphasized by Karl Marx." Capitalism is "by nature a form or method of economic change and not only never is but never can be stationary" [1950, p. 82]. This evolutionary dynamic of capitalist development has three salient characteristics: It comes from *within* the economic system and is not merely an adaptation to exogenous changes. It occurs *discontinuously* rather than smoothly. It brings *qualitative* changes or "revolutions," which fundamentally displace old equilibria and create radically new conditions. Economic development is accompanied by growth, i.e., sustained increases in national income. But

1. Schumpeter described the *Communist Manifesto* as "an account nothing short of glowing of achievements of capitalism; and even in pronouncing *pro futuro* death sentence on it, he never failed to recognize its historical necessity. This attitude, of course, *implies quite a lot of things Marx himself would have been unwilling to accept*" [1950, p. 7, italics added].

2. Schumpeter frequently cited "similarities in results" between his analysis of capitalism and that of Marx, but felt that they were "not only obliterated by a very wide difference in general outlook, but also reached by such different methods, that stressing parallelisms would be highly unsatisfactory to Marxians" [1951, p. 161].

mere quantitative growth does not constitute development per se. "Add successively as many mail coaches as you please, you will never get a railway thereby" [1961, p. 64n]. The immediate stimulus to development emanating "in the sphere of industrial and commercial life, not in the sphere of the wants of the consumers of final products," is "innovation," i.e., the new product, method of production, market, source of supply, or form of industrial organization [1961, pp. 65–66]. The innovational process "incessantly revolutionizes the economic structure *from within*, incessantly destroying the old one, incessantly creating a new one. This process of Creative Destruction is the essential fact about capitalism" [1950, p. 83].

Interestingly, Schumpeter virtually identified his own position on creative destruction *in this sense* with that of Marx. As Marx expressed it in the *Communist Manifesto,* the bourgeoisie "has played a most revolutionary role in history." Inter alia,

> It cannot exist without constantly revolutionising the instrument of production, and thereby the relations of production, and with them the whole relations of society. The need of a constantly expanding market for its product chases the bourgeoisie over the whole surface of the globe. The bourgeoisie, by the rapid improvement of all instruments of production, by the immensely facilitated means of communication, draws all nations, even the most barbarian, into civilisation. The bourgeoisie, during its rule of scarce one hundred years, has created more massive and more colossal productive forces than have all preceding generations together [Marx and Engels, 1976, pp. 487–89].

The key point of Schumpeter's commentary on these famous passages is not their description as a "panegyric upon bourgeois achievement that has no equal in economic literature" [1949, in Hamilton *et al.*, 1962, p. 354], or even his observation that "all of the achievements referred to are attributed *to the bourgeoisie alone* which is more than many thoroughly bourgeois economists would claim" [1950, p. 7n]. What is noteworthy is the strong Schumpeterian cast given to his description of Marx's analysis of capitalism's revolutionary role as

> "constant revolutionizing of production," creation that spells the obsolescence and consequent destruction of any industrial structure of production that exists at any moment: capitalism is a process, stationary capitalism would be a *contradictio in adjecto.* But this process does not simply consist in increase of capital by saving—as the classics had it. It does not consist in adding mailcoaches to the existing stock of mailcoaches, but in their elimination by railroads. Increase of physical capital is an incident in this process, but it is not its propeller [1949, in Hamilton *et al.*, 1962, p. 355].

Finally, Schumpeter concludes, "not more than that (i.e., Marx's analysis in the *Manifesto*) is implied in anything I shall say about the performance of capitalism" [1950, p. 7n].

Marx's emphasis on capitalism's creative propensities is reinforced by the *Grundrisse.* Capitalism, Marx argues in this work, destroys the old pre-capitalist economy "and constantly revolutionizes it, tearing down all the barriers which hem in the development of the forces of production, the expansion of needs, the all-sided development of production, and the exploitation and exchange of natural and mental forces" [1973, p. 410]. Capitalism's "universalizing tendency," both technologically and geographically, radically distinguishes it from all previous societies. Capitalism contains an "endless and limitless drive to go beyond its limiting barrier. Every limit appears as a barrier to be overcome" [1973, pp. 334, 408]. The extended analysis of the *Grundrisse,* combined with the earlier commentary in the *Manifesto* and the brief, but pointed, designations in *Capital* of development of technological and economic preconditions for socialism as the "historical mission" of capitalism, undergirds the conclusion that Marx's descriptions of capitalism's creatively destructive proclivities were not mere verbal fluff, but were instead a strategic component of his analytic program.

Beyond the general theme of capitalism's revolutionizing propensities are other parallels between the two. Marx, no less than Schumpeter, perceived capital accumulation to occur irregularly, in bursts, with cyclical consequences [Marx, 1906, pp. 672, 693–94]. Similarly, the perception of change as emanating from within the economic system, notably from the sphere of production rather than consumption, mentioned above as one of several prominent elements in Schumpeter's definition of economic development, is of course vintage Marx. Even their respective analyses of the process of innovation-competition-reduction of innovative profits contain similar elements.[3]

Turning from similarities to differences, it has often and appropriately been observed that Marx's discussions of capitalism's creative properties are usually accompanied by identification of its

3. "The capitalist continually tries to get the better of competition by incessantly introducing new machines, . . . producing more cheaply, and new division of labour in place of the old. . . . If, now, by a greater division of labor, by the utilisation of new machines and their improvement, by more profitable and extensive exploitation of natural forces, one capitalist [increases productivity and creates extraordinary profits], [his] *privileged position*. . . is not of long duration; other competing capitalists introduce the same machines, the same division of labor. . . . On the basis of [the] new [lower] cost of production [and associated lower prices], the same game begins again. . . . We see how in this way the mode of production and the means of production are continually transformed, revolutionised. . ." [Marx, *Wage Labor and Capital,* in Elliott, 1980, Ch. 2].

contradictory features and prognoses of its future demise.[4] This is certainly true, although whether this sharply separates the analyses of Marx and Schumpeter is open to question. for economic contradictions take on a different cast when examined from a creative destruction perspective (see the following section).

More important here than differing perspectives on capitalism's performance are alternative perceptions of its social relations. The difference is not primarily that of the classificatory schema itself, i.e., that Schumpeter writes of "entrepreneurs," while Marx writes about "capitalists." A resurrected Marx could easily agree that not all capitalists are equally adept in the exercise of the entrepreneurial-innovative function and that "a man without wealth, but with energy, solidity, ability and business sense" *may* become a capitalist, bringing "an unwelcome number of new soldiers of fortune into the field and into competition with the already existing individual capitalists," expanding capitalism's social base, and enabling it to "recruit ever new forces for itself out of the lower layers of society," thereby solidifying its rule [cited in Balinky, 1970, p. 89, italics added]. On his part, Schumpeter made it clear that successful entrepreneurs *become* capitalists (or landowners), while unsuccessful ones presumably become workers or managers [Schumpeter, 1961, pp. 78–79]. Similarly, Marxian capitalists and Schumpeterian entrepreneurs share important elements of conduct and motive. The successful Marxian capitalist, like his Schumpeterian entrepreneurial counterpart, presumably embodies a significant "will to found a private kingdom," a "will to conquer," and a "joy of creating" [Schumpeter, 1961, p. 93]. The Schumpeterian entrepreneur presumably embodies a passionate drive for enlargement of profits and power that closely rivals that of the Marxian capitalist. Certainly, *neither* is perceived as a hedonistic maximizer of utility from consumption goods.[5]

4. Marx and Engels "sang a veritable hymn of praise to the glory of capitalism in their *Communist Manifesto,* which nevertheless sounded its knell. . . . [Their] poetic description of the achievements of the capitalist mode of production serves only to underline still more strikingly the contradictions which it at the same time engenders. . . . Marx sees no contradiction between acknowledging and emphasizing this 'historically necessary mission' of capitalism and constantly pillorying whatever is exploitative, inhuman, and oppressive in it. Marx keeps in view all the time the[se] two *contradictory aspects* of capitalist historical reality. . ." [Mandel, 1971, pp. 56–57, 110].

5. Schumpeter: "[I]n no sense is his characteristic motivation of the hedonist kind [i.e.,] capable of being satisfied by the consumption of goods. . . . Hedonistically, . . . the conduct which we usually observe in [entrepreneurs] would be irrational" [1961, p. 92]. Marx: "Use-values must therefore never be looked upon as the real aim of the capitalist. . . . The restless never-ending process of profit-making alone is what he aims at . . . [the] boundless greed after riches, [the] passionate chase after exchange value . . ." [1906, pp. 170–71].

The key difference between Schumpeter and Marx may best be described as follows:[6] Each begins with a simple model of exchange economy. Although the institutional details are different, each is characterized by private property, market exchange, and competition, but in each the perceived *essential properties of capitalism are missing.*[7] The first stage of the analysis specifies the economic behavior of such a simple exchange economy. The second stage incorporates the perceived essential properties of capitalism and inquires into the prospective effects on economic behavior of this capitalist modification of the institutional structure. (A third stage, examined below, analyzes the transformation and socialization of capitalism's institutions, e.g., from competition to monopoly.)

In Marx's version of the (pre-capitalist) exchange economy, there are no separate classes of capitalists and landowners. Work and ownership coalesce. The artisans, merchants, and independent peasants, who own their own means of production and work for themselves, exchange their commodities, but do not employ the labor power of a separate, propertyless proletariat. The absence of a capital-labor class division precludes the creation of surplus values from the employment of labor power in production, while competitive pressures conduce to the elimination of pure economic profits in exchange. In Schumpeter's simple model of exchange economy, broadly similar conclusions are reached, but through a different institutional structure. A capital-labor relation exists, but the capitalist-employer is "capitalist" in name only, for he is devoid of or precluded from exercising crucial capitalist-entrepreneurial functions. Pure competition distributes wages and rents to workers and landowners on the basis of the value of the marginal product of labor and land, respectively. Perfect competition operates with a vengeance. "Everyone has equal access to 'capital.' Under these circumstances, clearly, no surpluses can accrue to employers of labor; for if they did, the laborers would themselves turn employers and compete the surplus away" [Sweezy,

6. Succeeding discussion extends and applies to a comparison of Marx and Schumpeter a mode of exposition developed most effectively by Meek in an earlier discussion of Marx [1967, pp. 99 ff].

7. More precisely, for Marx, "simple commodity production" is perceived as a distinctly different, pre-capitalist mode of production from capitalist economy. Although similar, in embryonic form, to capitalism in certain respects, it is perceived to lack fundamental defining properties of capitalism, as described in the next paragraph [see Elliott, 1978]. Schumpeter's simple model of the exchange economy is nominally capitalist (in Marxist terms) in its institutional structure, but lacks certain properties crucial to its real-world, dynamic character. Although a useful methodological device for each—Meek aptly called it a "mythodology" [1967, p. 98]—the distinction for Marx also held important historical significance.

1953, p. 277; and Schumpeter, 1961, pp. 30 ff.]. The "how" of production is a simple matter of production technology and resource prices; the "what" follows readily from adaptation to market demands.

What are the differentiating properties of capitalism, and how is the model of the behavior of the exchange economy modified by incorporating those properties? For Schumpeter, the "*differentia specifica*" of capitalist economy is provision of credit by banker capitalists to entrepreneurs to finance innovative investment [1961, pp. 69–70]. This enables entrepreneurs to bid resources away from other uses to new, innovative activities. By incorporating new technologies, sources of supply, etc., innovations create surpluses of revenues over costs. Competition tends to eliminate these surplus values, but innovation re-creates them.[8]

For Marx, surplus profits are certainly generated (prior to their elimination through competition) by the process of innovation, as is described pointedly in *Wage-Labour and Capital* [see footnote 3]. But capitalism's surplus values are fundamentally created and sustained through the class division between capitalist employers and workers and the accompanying capitalist "class monopoly" of the means of production, with the resulting differential, generated within *production* itself, between the value of labor power and the value of output [Medio, in Hunt and Schwartz, 1972]. Why doesn't *competitive exchange* eliminate these differentials? First, the real wage is kept below the level of the value of the output by the pressure of the reserve army of the unemployment, which alternately rises during cyclical depressions, falls during cyclical expansions, and rises again with labor-saving inventions stimulated by rising wages during booms. Second, competition rages within the capitalist class itself, generating strong pressure (not merely enticement) to innovate, thereby decreasing costs and raising national income above the value of labor power. But competition does not extend easily to the process of *becoming* a capitalist. It is easy for capitalists and small businessmen to become workers. Millions do so through the process of bankruptcy, especially during depressions. But, because both technology and credit availability favor the large, established firm, it is difficult for workers to become businessmen, much less major capitalists. Consequently,

8. Thus, Schumpeter defends Marx's conclusion (and his own) under dynamic conditions: "Surplus values may be impossible in perfect equilibrium but can be ever present because that equilibrium is never allowed to establish itself. They may always *tend* to vanish and yet be always there because they are constantly recreated" [1950, p. 28].

although competition tends to adjust commodity prices (other than labor power) so as to equalize profit rates among different sectors, it is not sufficient to eliminate aggregate surplus values.[9] As was already noted, this would require "equal access to 'capital'" and perfectly free inter*class* (not merely interindustry) mobility—conditions inconsistent with Marx's perception of capitalism's fundamental institutional structure and behavior.

CAPITALISM'S ECONOMIC DYSFUNCTIONS FROM A CREATIVE DESTRUCTION PERSPECTIVE

Many who might otherwise accept broad similarities between the Marxian and Schumpeterian visions of capitalism's creatively destructive properties balk at the thought of drawing parallels between their respective analyses of capitalism's dysfunctional properties. After all, did not Marx sharply delineate contradictory and dehumanizing features of the capitalist system, and incorporate these features as strategic elements in the impending drama of capitalism's prospective demise and supercession? And did not Schumpeter, on his part, explicitly reject the hypothesis of capitalism's "breaking down under the weight of economic failure"?

The answer to these questions is, most assuredly, "yes." And yet, the popular conclusion of a virtual Marx-Schumpeter dichotomy is unpersuasive, because it is countervailed by other powerful similarities that emerge more clearly when capitalism's dysfunctional propensities are assessed *from a perspective of creative destruction.* Differences between Marx and Schumpeter concerning capitalism's dysfunctions take on a different hue when "bathed in [creative destruction's] penetrating light." The net conclusion is that differences between the two are substantially less than is popularly supposed. Although by no means identical, their respective views on this subject on balance are closer to one another than that of either was to any other prominent system of socioeconomic thought.

As for Marx, his analyses of capitalism's dysfunctions never blinded him to its "positive" aspects, as summarized tautly in his 1847 draft outline subsequently published as *Wage Labour and Capital*:

9. In the third stage of their analyses, differences between Schumpeter and Marx on the generation of surplus values decrease. For Schumpeter, the shift to "trustified capitalism" makes it increasingly difficult for workers to become capitalists. Thus, competition does not work as smoothly to eliminate surplus values. For Marx, increasing barriers (e.g., factory legislation) are placed on expanding "absolute surplus values" by increasing working hours, stimulating greater emphasis on expanding "relative surplus values" through innovation and technological improvements.

> If one says "positive aspect of wage labor" one says "positive aspect of capital," of large-scale industry, of free competition, of the world market. . . without these production relations neither the means of production—the material means for the emancipation of the proletariat and the foundation of a new society—would have been created, nor would the proletariat itself have taken to the unification and development through which it is really capable of revolutionising the old society and itself [Marx and Engels, 1976, p. 436].

Indeed, capitalism's dysfunctional features themselves serve as cause as well as effect of its development process, and certainly do not repudiate its creative success. Alienation of the worker from his product, the work process, and his tools and means of production, although brought to a peak under capitalist auspices, establishes and reinforces capitalists' dominion over labor and production, and gives them the power and incentives to expand their own wealth and thereby to develop society's productive forces. Exploitation of surplus values from workers, although systemic to capitalism and a "miserable foundation" for wealth [Marx, 1973, p. 705], "is capitalism's means of creating an economic surplus, distributing the surplus to a politico-economic elite, and investing the surplus and generating economic growth" [Elliott, 1978–79, p. 6]. Recurrent capitalist depressions are the "most striking form in which advice is given [capitalism] to be gone and to give room to a higher state of social production." Still, by annihilating a large part of existing capital values, they "violently" lead capitalism back to the point where it is able to go on "fully employing its productive powers without committing suicide" [Marx, 1973, p. 750]. Monopoly and centralization of capital, although reinforcing and intensifying capitalism's proclivities toward alienation, exploitation, and cyclical depression, (i) enable rapid expansion in the scale of operations and, thereby, dramatic large-scale investment projects (e.g., railroadization) which would be impossible through mere growth of existing enterprises; (ii) by "accelerating and intensifying the effects of accumulation" hasten "revolutions in the technical composition of capital" [Marx, 1906, pp. 688–89].

Although capitalism's dysfunctions contribute significantly to its eventual demise, they are insufficient, either as preconditions for or as transition to the new society. Other elements, notably economic development and working class solidarity and resolve to build the new society, are also necessary. Further, Marx's vision of growing economic contradictions should not be characterized as simply another (radical) diagnosis of failure in capitalism's "economic engine." We may agree with Schumpeter that Marx visualized an impending period of system decay, i.e., a "more or less prolonged historical period. . .[in which] capitalism would begin to work with increasing friction and display the symptoms of fatal illness" [1950, p. 41]. Still, Marx did not suggest either secular stagnation or a stationary state. "In a real sense it can be said that Marx's entire theoretical system constitutes a denial of the possibility of indefinite capitalist expansion and an affirmation of the inevitability of the socialist revolution. But nowhere in his work is there to be found a doctrine of the specifically economic breakdown of capitalist production" [Sweezy, 1956, pp. 191–92]. Advanced capitalism à la Marx would certainly be a less creative and more tense society to live in. Still, despite Marx's occasional apocalyptic statements [1906, pp. 534, 836–37; and 1973, pp. 749–50], it is discordant with his overall view to ascribe capitalism's impending demise as emanating uniquely or specifically from some imminent moment of final "economic breakdown" per se. Capitalism's death and socialism's birth, in Marx's perspective, is pushed by the class struggle and pulled by institutional change as well as propelled by more strictly (and increasingly severe) socioeconomic contradictions [Elliott, 1976, 1978–79, and 1980, Chs. 7–8].

Turning to Schumpeter, the most direct starting point is to observe that, although he differed from Marx on details (notably concerning such long-run tendencies as increasing cyclical intensity and increasing "immiserization" of labor), he never denied the existence of any of Marx's *major* dysfunctional features of capitalism. Alienation, class struggle, surplus values, cyclical crises, depressions, unemployment, inequality in wealth, power, and income, and monopoly and centralization of capital are all woven into Schumpeter's analysis. Thus, Schumpeter's rationale for capitalism is not burdened by the need to disprove the broad contours of Marx's critique. Nor is it constrained by a perspective that admits the practical relevance of some dysfunctional properties (e.g., exploitation, unemployment, monopoly), but insists that "in principle" they would not exist in ideally functioning, perfectly competitive markets.

Instead, Schumpeter confronts Marx directly. First, whatever its dysfunctional proclivities, capitalism has been an immense success. Second, dysfunctional propensities actually perform a creative function in industrialization. Third, capitalism shows no likelihood of imminent breakdown "under the weight of economic failure." To illustrate, consider cyclical depressions, inequality and surplus values, and monopoly [1950, pp. 63–106].

In Schumpeter's analysis, cyclical fluctuations are no barrier to economic growth. Indeed, growth results from a cyclical development process, in which depressions are, largely, a "normal" and healthy period of absorption of the bunching of innovations during the preceding prosperity. Further, contractions eliminate inefficient, non-innovating businesses, as new products and methods replace the old in a "perennial gale of creative destruction" [1950, p. 85]. Similarly, surplus values are the normal result of innovations. Because of tremendous uncertainties involved, i.e., the possibility of failure and the likelihood of competitive encroachment in the event of success, the lure and occasional realization of extraordinary profits may well be the price society pays for the evolutionary contributions of its entrepreneurial leaders. Further, in practice capitalism reduces inequality: by increasing opportunities for entry into the ruling strata relative to earlier, more class-bound societies; by the creation of mass-produced products that especially benefit working masses; and by philanthropy and social legislation underwritten by capitalist growth. As for monopoly, innovation does create a monopoly position for the innovating firm. But because of the tendency for innovations to spread, by imitation and extension to allied fields, the industrial pioneer's monopoly position is only temporary. The possibility of temporary retention of above-normal innovative profits may well stimulate greater technological improvement, and practices that protect these temporary monopoly positions may be the price for technological progressivity and higher growth rates. In short, although the content and emphases are different, the analyses of capitalism's dysfunctional properties in Marx and Schumpeter share important common elements. For both, capitalism is tremendously creative and successful. Its dysfunctional propensities actually serve as cause as well as effect of its development process. And whatever its tendencies toward system-decay, it is not in danger of imminent economic collapse.

Creative Destruction II:

Capitalism's Transformation and Socialization

Thus far, "creative destruction" has referred to the revolutionizing process whereby the new product or method displaces the old. But Schumpeter describes a broader process for which the expression also seems appropriate, namely one wherein capitalism, through its creative success, leads on to its own destruction and prepares the way for a socialist economic system to supercede it. In this broader sense, "creative destruction" is also common to both Marx and Schumpeter. Differences, as well as similarities, between the two visions may be conveniently summarized by interweaving commentary on Marx into Schumpeter's organizational format.[10]

Obsolescence of the Entrepreneurial Function

In entrepreneurial capitalism, innovations are embodied in new firms. But in "trustified capitalism," the "competitive economy is broken up by the growth of great combines. . . and the carrying out of new combinations must become in ever greater measure the internal concern of one and the same economic body. The difference so made is great enough to serve as the water-shed between two epochs in the social history of capitalism" [Schumpeter, 1961, p. 67]. The large corporation, with its research departments, automatizes economic progress, making the social function of the entrepreneur, as the innovative outsider, increasingly obsolete. Consequently, the positions and incomes of the active entrepreneurs and those portions of the "entire bourgeois stratum" dependent upon them evaporate. Because capitalist enterprise, "by its very achievements, tends to automatize progress, we conclude that it tends to make itself superfluous—to break to pieces under the pressure of its own success." In the end, the giant corporation "ousts the entrepreneur and expropriates the bourgeoisie as a class. . ." [1950, p. 134].

For Marx, capitalism is characterized by a de facto class monopoly of the means of production even under competitive conditions. It is difficult (though not impossible) for workers to become capitalists, whether infused with heroic entrepreneurial spirit or not. However, as Marx turns to the stage of corporate, big business capitalism, a Marxian counterpart to Schumpeter's point emerges, and the differences between the two perspectives subside. Schumpeter's basic point is not that entrepreneurship becomes obsolete, but that, as innovation becomes increasingly automatized, entry of new blood into the mainstream of business activity, much less circulation into the ruling circles of society, becomes increasingly difficult. Although a resurrected Marx would insist that this is difficult enough to begin with, he would presumably agree that it becomes much more so as production and innovation become more concentrated and centralized. In short, for both Marx and Schumpeter the large corporation, a product of capitalist development and technology, renders the economic and social position of the small-scale, competitive firm and its associated small bourgeoisie increasingly obsolete. Consequently,

10. For a fuller examination of Marx's analysis of creative destruction, per se, in contrast to those aspects particularly relevant to comparisons between Marx and Schumpeter, see Elliott [1976, 1978–79].

economic power and social position become more heavily concentrated and centralized in the hands of the established capitalist and corporate elite, and the small capitalist (Marx)-entrepreneurial (Schumpeter) escape routes from working class life are increasingly closed off, reducing the solidity of capitalist rule.

Destruction of the Institutional Framework

For Schumpeter, capitalism's very economic success undermines its institutions though the development of the large corporation, notably atomistic competition and private property. As for competition, the argument that monopoly power reduces economic performance, quite apart from its accuracy, "misses the salient point." Even if large-scale firms were managed with angelic perfection, the elimination of small-scale producers and consequently their "dependents, henchmen, and connections" profoundly affects the political structure and reduces political support for capitalism [1950, p. 140]. "Here of course," Schumpeter observes, "Marx scores" [1950, p. 140]. "He not only predicted the emergence of big business; he visualized industrial concentration as part of the logic as well as the factual pattern of the accumulation process" [1950, p. 34]. In short, Marx, like Schumpeter, did not perceive the "concentration and centralization of capital" as perversion of an ideally competitive state, but as the logical consequence of competition itself in the industrialization process. Further, for Marx no less than for Schumpeter, some of the most profound consequences of big business, corporate capitalism were socio-political, and monopoly was perceived to play a strategic role in capitalism's creative destruction and prospective demise [Marx, 1906, pp. 836–37].[11]

As for private property, here the intellectual distance between the two is quite small. According to Schumpeter, the "separation of ownership and management" in the large-scale corporation has resulted in the disappearance of the "specifically proprietary interest" and the "evaporation" of the "material substance" of property–its "visible and touchable reality"—and, thereby, the evaporation of "moral allegiance" for industrial private property. Eventually, nobody is left who really supports capitalism as did the small-scale owner-

11. The sociopolitical implications of monopoly are described in even more pointed terms in the writings of the later Engels who argues, for example, in *Socialism: Utopian and Scientific,* that because of trends toward monopoly and the large scale corporation, exploitation is becoming "so palpable that it must break down. No nation will put up with production conducted by trusts, with so barefaced an exploitation of the community by a small band of dividend-managers" [in Elliott, 1980, Ch. 7].

managers of the nineteenth century. "Thus the modern corporation, although the product of the capitalist process, socializes the bourgeois mind. . ." [1950, p. 156]. Moreover, the "bureaucratization of economic life"—an "inevitable complement" to both democracy and modern economic development—is stimulated by and within the large-scale corporation [1950, p. 206]. This immensely simplifies the the transition to a socialist "bureaucratic apparatus" by establishing new modes of managerial responsibility and executive selection that are "not without an appreciable measure of rationality" and that "could no doubt be reproduced in a socialist society" [1950, pp. 206–07].

In Marx's roughly comparable interpretation, the (emerging) industrial corporation is itself a product of capitalist development. Its growing economic role emanates from capitalism's enlarging appetite for investment funds with large-scale production and accumulation. But the corporation has profound effects on the capitalist property system, notably a "transformation of the actually functioning capitalist into a mere manager. . . and of the owners of capital into mere owners. . ." and an "abolition of the capitalist mode of production within capitalist production itself, a self-destructive contradiction, which represents. . . a necessary transition to . . . social property outright. . ." [Marx, 1909, pp. 516–517, 519]. Thus for Marx, like Schumpeter, bureaucratized corporate capitalism is a "phase of transition to a new form of production." It aims at the "expropriation" of small-scale, individual production, although it appears as the centralization of capital and "appropriation of social property by a few. . ." [Marx, 1909, p. 520]. Moreover, it "establishes a monopoly in certain spheres and thereby challenges the interference of the state. It reproduces a new aristocracy of finance, a new sort of parasites in the shape of promoters, speculators and merely nominal directors; a whole system of swindling and cheating by means of corporation juggling, stock jobbing, and stock speculation. It is private production without the control of private property" [Marx, 1909, p. 519].

Marx supplements his analysis of corporations with a parallel description of worker cooperative factories, which are perceived to evolve out of capitalist industrialization, are facilitated by the development of the credit system, and, like corporations, are a form of "transition from the capitalist mode of production to the associated one, . . ." [Marx, 1909, p. 521]. Thus, the credit system, itself effect as well as cause of capital accumulation and capitalist development, generates a transformation and socialization of capitalist property relations eventually "turning over into communism" [cited by Nicolaus in "Introduction" to Marx, 1973, p. 55].

Destruction of the Protecting Strata

Both Marx and Schumpeter perceive capitalism in the dominant Western European model as emerging out of feudalism, and the surge to dominance of the industrial bourgeoisie as emanating from the creatively destructive impact of an industrializing capitalism on pre-capitalist values, institutions, and class positions. Adapting Marx's classic analysis of the nineteenth century British Constitution,[12] Schumpeter further argues that the industrialist, outside the economic arena, is "rationalist and unheroic." He lacks the "mystic glamour" that "counts in the ruling of men" [1950, p. 137].[13] He requires an aristocratic class to protect him, to manage the affairs of church and state and leave him "unfettered" to carry out his revolutionary economic leadership. For Schumpeter, the landowning aristocrats were "partners of the capitalist stratum, symbiosis with whom was an essential element of the capitalist schema" [1950, p. 139]. Thus, capitalism's very success in removing pre-capitalist institutions and classes leaves the bourgeoisie "politically helpless" and unable "to take care of its particular class interest. . ." [1950, p. 138]. Although Marx would no doubt disagree that capitalists are "politically helpless," he would presumably agree that the "romantic glory" of the aristocracy, which to some degree lingers on as a residual ideological vestige as its economic base is transformed by industrialization, may facilitate capitalism's consolidation, and yet that the "necessary victory of the capitalist. . . [and] the final ruin of the old aristocracy . . ." [Marx, 1964, pp. 113, 143] removes yet another barrier in the historical process of movement toward post-capitalist society. Still, Marx believed that the working class was able to exploit conflicts between capitalists and landlords, as illustrated by developments in the 1840s. Manufacturers had courted working class support for repeal

12. Marx described the British Constitution as "an antiquated and obsolete compromise made between the bourgeoisie, which rules in actual practice, although *not officially,* in all the decisive spheres of bourgeois society, and the landed aristocracy, which forms the *official government*." Through the Reform Bill of 1831, the bourgeoisie "gained general *political* recognition as the *ruling class,* but only on the condition that "the whole business of government. . . remained the guaranteed domain of the landed aristocracy" [Marx, 1974, p. 282]. The agents of this compromise are the Whigs, who function as the "*aristocratic representatives* of the bourgeoisie. . . ." In exchange for a "monopoly of government and the exclusive possession of office," they assist the industrial and commercial middle class in conquering those concessions to its class interest which have become "*unavoidable* and *undelayable*" [Marx, 1974, p. 250].

13. Marx writes of "the *aristocratic* condition of land-ownership which reflects a romantic glory upon its lord. . . and puts the workers on the estates. . . in directly political. . . relations of respect, subordination and duty" to the lord [1964, pp. 114–15].

of the Corn Laws. With the repeal, the working class "found allies (e.g., for new social and factory legislation) in the Tories panting for revenge" [1906, p. 311].

Growing Hostility and Social Classes

According to Schumpeter, although Marx analyzed capitalism in economic terms by a "bold stroke of analytic strategy," he defined it sociologically, in terms of the class dominance of capitalists. Thus, by an "ingenious tautology," the full realization of working class interests requires the supercession of capitalism, and socialism in turn is perceived as an economic society dominated by the working class [1950, p. 19]. Schumpeter rejected this interpretation of the relations between social classes and economic systems partly because, like Lenin, he believed that working class interests, *if* left alone to develop spontaneously, tend more to trade unionist and petty bourgeois aspirations. The Schumpeterian worker aspires not to overthrow the capitalist, but to extract more from him through shrewd bargaining or to escape from him through small-scale entrepreneurial or business activity. However, (i) workers are not left alone to develop class interests spontaneously, and (ii) other factors, emanating from the capitalist evolutionary process, stimulate class struggles and growing hostility toward capitalism. As to (i), capitalist evolution "produces a labor movement" and "the rise of the labor interest to a position of political power and sometimes of responsibility" [1950, p. 153; and 1939, II, p. 697]. In conjunction with corporations, labor unions have collectivized the labor market, thus socializing capitalism's institutional structure. Also, intellectuals have often invaded labor organizations and labor politics, providing "theories and slogans" (e.g., class war), and radicalizing the labor movement, "eventually imparting a revolutionary bias to the most bourgeois trade-union practices . . ." [1950, p. 154].

Marx's different but related commentary on these points would be that capitalist development contributes directly to working class organization and solidarity. Capitalist power, cyclical crises, and monopoly stimulate the establishment of labor unions as protective devices in the economic struggle to keep wage rates up, while improvements in transportation and communication centralize the class struggle, making it increasingly political in character. Indeed, the "real fruit" of the class struggle lies in the increasing political unity and organization of the working class rather than in specific wage negotiations [Marx and Engels, 1976, p. 493; and 1974b, pp. 224–29]. The socialist intelligentsia, Marx would presumably agree, thrive on criticism and are given wide opportunities to "nibble at the foundations of capitalist society" through freedom of public discussion as well as improved means of communication [Schumpeter, 1950, p. 151], and play a guiding and educative role in the development of working class organization. However, Marx was committed to a view of the working class "as the decisive force charged with the social transformation of society" [Leonhard, 1974, p. 87]. For Marx, no amount of theorizing or organizing by an intelligentsia (or body of professional revolutionaries) can substitute for working class solidarity and resolve to "effect its interests in a general form" [Marx to Bolte, cited in Padover, 1971, p. 61].

As to (ii), Schumpeter's basic point is that capitalism, by its own evolution, stimulates hostility and class struggles beyond those emanating from capital-labor relations. Some examples are capitalism's self-destruction, noted earlier, of its own institutional framework; the fact that although capitalism's basic rationale (economic progress) rests on long-run considerations, "[f]or the masses, it is the short-run view that counts," and in the short run, inequalities, surplus values, and unemployment "dominate the picture" [1950, p. 145]; and capitalism's creation of a "New Middle Class," which, together with farmers and small businessmen, may constitute a majority of the population, and whose interests and attitudes, though often different from those of the working class more narrowly conceived, are generally just "as hostile to the interests of the bigger and big bourgeoisie" [1939, pp. 697–99].

For Marx, the *basic* class struggle of advanced capitalism is, of course, that between the large bourgeoisie and the working class. Given this fundamental conflict, there are related conflicts, problems, or sources of disenchantment, several already enumerated. As for short-run problems versus long-run rationale, one suspects that if Marx could directly confront Schumpeter, he would contend that the cat had been let out of the bag, for what is the long-run rationale if it is not capitalism's "positive" or creative properties, and what are short-run problems of depression, etc., if not capitalism's dysfunctional properties?

Public Policy and Social Change

When Marx and Schumpeter turn to public policy and social change their respective arguments show striking parallels, despite important differences of emphasis and perspective. First, each believed that the capitalist state, under the pressure of "social reformers" (Schumpeter) or the class struggle (Marx), may engage in social legislation and reform, provided that such policies do not constitute "*significant interference with the capitalist process*" [Schumpeter, 1950, p. 69], or, phrased negatively, that the consequences of not providing concessions to the working class "are sufficiently dangerous to the stability and functioning of the system as a whole" [Sweezy, 1956, p. 249].

For Marx, the best single example was a bundle of reforms comprised of "factory legislation," i.e., restriction of working hours, sanitation regulation, child labor laws, and education. These reforms, which were as much the product of nineteenth century capitalist development as its technology and industry,[14] constitute genuine concessions to working class interests; departures from a laissez-faire, market-oriented economy and movements toward as well as portents of the socialist society to come; and a practical school for the political education of the working class [Marx, 1906, Ch. 10]. To this list Schumpeter added ample unemployment compensation, care for the aged and the sick, public health, collective goods of various kinds, and limited public ownership. In the United States, Schumpeter observed, the "better part of the task could even now be accomplished *without undue strain on the system*" [1950, p. 70, italics added].

Second, however, none of these reforms constitutes a social revolution or radical transformation of the capitalist system. Both Marx and Schumpeter expected this to happen. For Schumpeter the transformation of, plus hostility toward, "trustified" capitalism combine to give birth to public policies incompatible with it, "policies which do not allow it to function" [1939, p. 1038], either through the imposition of injurious financial burdens on the capitalist-enterpreneurial sector or the alteration of the institutional environment so as to excessively constrain industrialists' power and autonomy. As illustrations, Schumpeter cited developments during the New Deal, notably burdensome income, corporation and estate taxes, labor legislation, public utility regulation, and anti-monopoly policies. The injurious effects of these programs on private investment and innovation were heightened by the rapidity, hostility, and anti-business spirit with which they were enacted, and the overzealous, tactless

14. According to Marx, factory legislation partly constituted concessions to curb social tensions and working class fervor "that daily grew more threatening. . ." [1906, p. 263]. More significantly, they represented increasing recognition by capitalists of a class interest in collective action to sustain the labor force and its capacity to produce and reproduce itself, that is, to prevent intensity of unregulated exploitation by individual capitalist employers, the collective effect of which could potentially unduly sap the health and life of workers and thereby threaten the viability and continuity of the capitalist system itself [Marx, 1906, Ch. X, esp. pp. 310–30].

manner in which they were administered [1939, pp. 1038 ff.]. "Faced by the increasing hostility of the environment and by the legislative, administrative and judicial practice born of that hostility, entrepreneurs and capitalists—in fact the whole stratum that accepts the bourgeois scheme of life—will eventually cease to function" [1950, p. 156].

Although from a Marxian perspective the reference to the New Deal would appear premature and misplaced, the *general character* of the Schumpeterian vision of the role of public action under late-stage capitalism has a strong counterpart in the *Communist Manifesto.* There, Marx and Engels present a three-stage model for social revolution and transition to socialism. The first step is for the proletariat to "win the battle of democracy" and achieve political supremacy. In advanced democracies such as the United Kingdom and the United States, this follows essentially, though not automatically, from genuine universal suffrage. The second step is to engage in measures that in themselves appear "economically insufficient and untenable" (most of which, indeed, have been implemented in modern industrial societies) but that make "despotic inroads on the rights of property," and that, "in the course of the movement, outstrip themselves, necessitate further inroads upon the old social order, and are unavoidable as a means of entirely revolutionising the mode of production" [Marx and Engels, 1976, p. 504].[15] The third is to transfer the physical means of production, by degrees, to worker-state control.

Although brief, this strategy is sophisticated. It satisfies Schumpeter's interpretation of Marx's revolution as differing "entirely, in nature and in function, from the revolutions both of the bourgeois radical and of the socialist conspirator. It is essentially "revolution in the fullness of time" [1950, p. 58]. It also bears a striking resemblance to Schumpeter's vision of capitalism's final death-knell. The "moment" of the revolution is a dynamic *period* of transition in which socialization of the means of production occurs fairly late in the process. "Private industry will be allowed to continue to exist surrounded by such a climate of economic and political arrangements that it will slowly. . . have to transform itself." Public measures which challenge capitalist-corporate autonomy and wealth "will slowly ease private industry out. . . by gradually creating the economic conditions

15. For a contemporary application of this kind of strategy, see Gorz's distinction between "reformist" and "nonreformist" reforms [1967].

which will make the further existence of private industry economically unviable" [Avineri, 1968, p. 206].

Capitalist Transformation and Socialization

Capitalism's "tendency toward self-destruction" [Schumpeter, 1950, p. 162], which, for Marx, is associated with tendencies toward system-decay and, for Schumpeter, "may well assert itself in the form of a tendency toward retardation of progress" [1950, p. 162], embodies for both a process of transformation and socialization. For Schumpeter, the various factors discussed earlier—"objective and subjective, economic and extra-economic. . . reinforcing each other in imposing accord. . . [—] make not only for the destruction of the capitalist but for the emergence of a socialist civilization. . . . The capitalist process not only destroys its own institutional framework but it also creates the conditions for another" [1950, p. 162].

But "transformation," Schumpeter adds, may be a better word than "destruction." Capitalism, he suggests in a 1928 article, is "in so obvious a process of transformation into something else, that it is not the fact, but only the interpretation of this fact, about which it is possible to disagree. . . . Capitalism. . . creates, by rationalizing the human mind, a mentality and a style of life. . ." which is not only "incompatible with its own fundamental conditions, motives and social institutions," but which provides the preconditions for a socialist future [1951, pp. 71–72]. Capitalism's self-destruction does not simply provide a "void" in which virtually anything might happen. Instead, "things and souls are transformed in such a way as to become increasingly amenable to the socialist form of life." In short, the capitalist "economic process tends to socialize *itself*—and also the human soul" in that "the technological, organizational, commercial, administrative, and psychological prerequisites of socialism tend to be fulfilled more and more" [1950, pp. 168, 219]. The same factors that explain capitalism's coming demise also "strongly point to socialism as the heir apparent" [1950, p. 61].

On this overall theme of capitalism's transformation and socialization, there are strong parallels in Marx's writings. Beyond specific examples already cited, notably corporations, workers' cooperatives, labor unions and labor politics, and factory legislation, the following passages from the *Grundrisse* are illustrative:

> [T]he *material and mental conditions* of the negation of wage labour and of capital, themselves already the negation of earlier forms of unfree social production, *are themselves results of its* [*capitalism's*] *productive process* [p. 749]. [The capitalist

> mode of production] is itself fleeting, and *produces the real conditions of its own suspension* [pp. 541–42]. [Capitalism's "historic destiny" is fulfilled] when the severe *discipline of capital*, acting on succeeding generations, has *developed general industriousness* as the general property of the new species—and, finally, when the development of the productive powers of labour, which capital incessantly whips onward with its unlimited mania for wealth, . . . have flourished to the stage where. . . wealth require[s] a lesser labour time of society as a whole, and where the labouring society relates scientifically to the process of its progressive reproduction. . . [p. 325]. [The] universalist tendency of capital [will, at a] certain stage of its development, *allow itself to be recognized* as being itself the greatest barrier to this tendency and hence will drive towards its own suspension [p. 410]. (Italics and material in brackets added.)

Similarly, in the often-cited "expropriators are expropriated" passage of *Capital*, socioeconomic dysfunction and system-decay provide the rhetoric and revolutionary class struggle the drama, but the bulk of the analytic thrust of the argument is comprised of a twofold model of capitalist transformation and socialization. First centralization of capital, "accomplished by the action of the imminent laws of capitalistic production itself," stimulates technological, social, organizational, and administrative preconditions of socialism, notably:

> The co-operative form of the labour-process, the conscious technical application of science, the methodical cultivation of the soil, the transformation of the instruments of labour into instruments of labour only usable in common, the economising of all means of production by their use as the means of production of combined, socialised labour, the entanglement of all peoples in the net of the world-market, and this, the international character of the capitalistic regime [1906, p. 836].

Second, along with monopoly, misery, and exploitation "grows the revolt of the working-class, a class always increasing in numbers, and disciplined, united, organised by the *very mechanism of the process of capitalist production itself*" [1906, pp. 836–37, italics added], thus providing organizational and psychological bases for working class solidarity and action in making the transition to and building the new society.

Certainly, there are important specific differences between the two visions, especially concerning this second aspect of Marx's analysis. As noted, Marx makes the working class the agent of social transformation, whereas Schumpeter explicitly disconnects Marx's linkage between socialism and the labor movement.[16] Throughout this section, we have noted other particular differences. In addition,

16. According to Schumpeter, "the labor movement, though often allied with socialism, has remained distinct from it to this day. . . the labor movement is not essentially socialist, just as socialism is not necessarily laborite or proletarian" [1950, p. 310].

Marx, in the *Grundrisse,* delves more deeply and specifically than Schumpeter into the prospective transformative effects of science, technology, and automation upon productivity, leisure, the composition of labor, and the character of work [Marx, 1973, pp. 705 ff.; and Elliott, 1978–79]. On the overall theme of capitalism's future, however, the parallels are again quite striking. Marx's vision is far from one of simple economic failure, while Schumpeter's analysis, no less than Marx's, is one of transformation and socialization as well as destruction based on economic success. At one point, Schumpeter revealingly recognizes the broad similarity with Marx's analysis, indeed minimizes the differences between the two perspectives. "In both these respects [transformation and socialization] Marx's vision was right. We can also agree with him in linking the particular social transformation that goes on under our eyes with an economic process as its prime mover." Further, in the end "there is not so much difference as one might think between saying that the decay of capitalism is due to its success and saying that it is due to its failure" [1950, p. 162]. At the very least, parallels and similarities are sufficient to temper significantly the popular myth of a sharp dichotomy and unbridgeable gulf between these two heroic perspectives on the internal dynamic of modern capitalist society.

In closing, we should note two final overall parallels and one major caveat. First of the overall similarities is that Schumpeter's analysis of capitalism's prospects is "not pure economics, of course," but economics "seen in a wide context and with a broad historical horizon." The combination of economic theory, politics, sociology, and history, which is Schumpeter's "major characteristic" [Stolper, 1979, pp. 69, 64], is strikingly similar to Marx's endeavor "to unite economic history, sociology and economics in a kind of ménage à trois. . ." [Meek, 1967, p. 101]. Second, Schumpeter's vision, like Marx's, contains no timetable. Its constituent elements, "while everywhere discernible, have as yet nowhere fully revealed themselves." Superficial "temporary reverses" on the "surface" may easily mask "the tendency toward another civilization that slowly works deep down below." The Schumpeterian outlook, no less than the Marxian one, is a *long-run* vision in an accounting system in which "a century is a 'short-run' . . ." [1950, p. 163].

The major caveat, of course, is that the comparative commentary in this paper has focused exclusively on the vision(s) of capitalism's creatively destructive properties and preparation for socialism, where parallels between Marx and Schumpeter are strongest. In ideological commitment, in the details of their respective technical analyses of the behavior of the capitalist economy, and in their perceptions of the socialist future, differences in perspective are both clear and significant.[17]

UNIVERSITY OF SOUTHERN CALIFORNIA

17. Brus [1975, p. 17] summarizes this latter point, deserving of a separate paper in its own right, aptly as follows: "Whilst in its understanding of socialism as a product of historical development Schumpeter's conception displays a number of points of resemblance to the Marxist position as most generally understood, in its actual definition of socialism and the problems connected with it there is a clear difference to be seen. . . . The resemblance concerns the aspect of continuity (of socialism in relation to capitalism) whereas the differences relate to the *aspect of negation;* in Schumpeter this aspect barely exists, whereas in the Marxist conception it is at least of equal importance."

REFERENCES

Avineri, Shlomo, *The Social and Political Thought of Karl Marx* (Cambridge: Cambridge University Press, 1968).

Balinky, Alexander, *Marx's Economics* (Lexington: Heath, 1970).

Brus, Wlodzimierz, *Socialist Ownership and Political Systems,* translated by R. A. Clarke (Boston: Routledge and Kegan Paul, 1975).

Elliott, John E., "Marx Resurrected: The Transformation and Socialization of Capitalism," *Bulletin of the Association for Comparative Economic Studies,* XVIII (Summer 1976), 53–69.

——, "Marx's Socialism in the Context of his Typology of Economic Systems," *Journal of Comparative Economics,* II (March 1978), 25–41.

——, "Marx's *Grundrisse:* Vision of Capitalism's Creative Destruction," *Journal of Post Keynesian Economics,* I (Winter 1978–79), 148–69.

Engels, Frederick, in John E. Elliott, *Marx and Engels on Economy, Society, and Politics* (Santa Monica: Goodyear, 1980).

Gorz, André, *A Strategy for Labor* (Boston: Beacon, 1967).

Leonhard, Wolfgang, *Three Faces of Marxism* (New York: Holt, Rinehart and Winston, 1974).

Mandel, Ernest, *The Formation of the Economic Thought of Karl Marx* (New York: Monthly Review, 1971).

Medio, Alfredo, "Profits and Surplus-Value: Appearance and Reality in Capitalist Production," in *A Critique of Economic Theory,* E. K. Hunt and Jesse G. Schwartz, eds. (London: Penguin, 1972).

Meek, Ronald L., *Economics and Ideology and Other Essays* (London: Chapman and Hall, 1967).

Marx, Karl, *Capital,* Vol. I (New York: Modern Library, n.d. Originally published by Charles H. Kerr, Chicago, 1906).

——, *Capital,* Vol. III (Chicago: Kerr, 1909).

——, *Early Writings,* translated by T. B. Bottomore, ed. (New York: McGraw-Hill, 1964).

——, *Letter to Friedrich Bolte,* in Saul K. Padover, ed., *Karl Marx on Revolution* (New York: McGraw-Hill, 1971).

——, *Grundrisse* (*Introduction to the Critique of Political Economy*), translated, with a Foreward by Martin Nicolaus (New York: Vintage, 1973).

——, *Surveys from Exile: Political Writings,* Volume II, introduced by David Fernback, ed. (New York: Random House, 1974a).

——, *Wages, Prices and Profit,* in *Karl Marx—Frederick Engels, Selected Works* (New York: International Publishers, 1974b).
——, *Wages,* in *Karl Marx–Frederick Engels, Collected Works,* Vol. 6 (New York: International Publishers, 1976).
——, *Wage Labour and Capital,* in John E. Elliott, *Marx and Engels on Economy, Society, and Politics* (Santa Monica: Goodyear, 1980).
——, and Frederick Engels, *The Communist Manifesto,* in *Karl Marx—Frederick Engels, Collected Works,* Vol. 6 (New York: International Publishers, 1976).
Schumpeter, Joseph A., *Business Cycles,* Vol. II (New York: McGraw-Hill, 1939).
——, *Capitalism, Socialism and Democracy* (New York: Harper, 1950).
——, *Essays,* Richard V. Clemence, ed. (Cambridge: Addison-Wesley, 1951).
——, *The Theory of Economic Development* (New York: Oxford, 1961).
——, "The Communist Manifesto in Sociology and Economics," *Journal of Political Economy,* LVII (June 1949), 199–212; in Earl Hamilton, Albert Rees, and Harry Johnson, *Landmarks in Political Economy,* Vol. 2 (Chicago: University of Chicago Press, 1962).
Stolper, Wolfgang, "Joseph Alois Schumpeter—A Personal Memoir," *Challenge,* XXI (Jan./Feb. 1979), 64–69.
Sweezy, Paul M., *The Present as History* (New York: Monthly Review, 1953).
——, *The Theory of Capitalist Development* (New York: Monthly Review, 1956).

JOB SEARCH AND THE LABOR DROPOUT PROBLEM RECONSIDERED*

RICHARD D. MACMINN

This paper establishes the existence of an equilibrium wage distribution for a labor market in which job seekers search sequentially. The search model shows why some workers will drop out of the market. Previous analysis of policies designed to reduce the number of dropouts was partial because wage distributions were exogenously given. Through the use of the equilibrium wage distribution implied by each policy, the analysis here shows that subsidizing search or imposing a minimum wage will reduce the number of dropouts, while a job training program or a reduction in unemployment compensation may either increase or decrease the number of dropouts.

I

In his article, "Economics of Information and Job Search" [1970], John McCall proposed a sequential search process that job seekers could use to screen the market for information. McCall's model provided an intuitive explanation of why some workers decide to drop out of the labor market and several policies designed to reverse the dropout decision. However, the policy implications of the model have been subject to skepticism because, like other search models in the literature, the behavior of employers is not modeled, the wage distribution is not endogenously determined, and therefore the persistence of wage dispersion, which motivates the dropout decision, is not guaranteed. Even if wage dispersion is not transitory, the effect each policy has on the number of discouraged workers cannot be ensured without considering its effect on employer behavior. The purpose of this paper is to reconsider the policies in the context of a complete market.

The first step is the construction of a market model that sustains a nondegenerate equilibrium distribution of wages. Two modifications of a model originally proposed by Wilde [1975] are made. First, job seekers have different search costs and the set of search costs is not bounded below by a positive constant. Second, employers have different technologies. These assumptions differentiate this model from others in the literature, which generate equilibrium price distributions

* I wish to thank Richard Kihlstrom, Andrew Postlewaite, and Leonard Mirman for their constructive criticism of earlier drafts of this paper. I would also like to thank the referees for valuable comments.

The Quarterly Journal of Economics, August 1980 0033-5533/80/0095-0069$01.90

(e.g., see Butters [1977], Stiglitz [1974], and Wilde [1977]). The assumptions are made here to allow the dropout decision of employers and job seekers to be analyzed. Then the model determines the number of employers and job seekers who are active in the labor market. The assumption that there is no lower bound on the set of search costs is made to handle the well-known problem with sequential search in an equilibrium setting.[1]

The market model is constructed in Section II, which establishes the existence of an equilibrium wage distribution and provides its summary statistics. The following policies are considered in Section III: subsidizing search, reducing the expected return from unemployment, job training, and a minimum wage. The effect each policy has on the number of dropouts is determined using the equilibrium wage distribution implied by the policy. The analysis shows that subsidizing search or imposing a minimum wage will reduce the number of labor dropouts, but that the other policies may either increase or decrease the number of dropouts. A condition sufficient to guarantee the effectiveness of each of these policies is established. Section IV contains some concluding remarks.

II

This section presents the basic labor market model in which homogeneous labor services are traded for money. The operation of the market may be summarized briefly as follows: job seekers enter the market and search for employment. Each individual makes the decision to continue searching or to accept employment after each observed wage offer. Employers set wages and accept all job applicants at their respective wage offers. The set of wage offers determines the wage distribution and is a Nash equilibrium if no employer, taking the behavior of others as given, can increase his expected profit by selecting another wage.

The construction of the model is accomplished in two steps. First, McCall's sequential search model is reconstructed and used to derive the expected labor supply function for the market. Second, the employer's expected labor supply function is derived; employer behavior is explained by supposing that employers maximize expected profit. Then each market participant has an optimal decision-making rule, allowing a proposition on the existence of a market equilibrium to be established.

1. See the papers by Green [1976] and Reinganum [1978] for discussions of the case in which consumers' search costs are bounded below by a positive constant.

Job Search

Consider the behavior of a job seeker with search cost c who supplies one unit of labor. The distribution of wages $F(w)$ is known but not the wage offers of particular employers, so the individual searches. The wage observations are independent and identically distributed random variables. After each observation, the job seeker decides to continue searching or to accept employment at his highest wage observation. The cost of search limits the number of observations. Under these conditions, the job seeker will adopt a search policy that specifies a reservation wage ε. For any wage observation $w \geq \varepsilon$, the job seeker will decide to stop searching and to accept employment, while for $w < \varepsilon$, he will continue to search.

The method used to determine the job seeker's reservation wage is well-known (e.g., see McCall [1970], and Kohn and Shavell [1974]). The reservation wage is the value of ε such that

$$c = \int_{\varepsilon}^{\infty} (w - \varepsilon)dF(w) \equiv g(\varepsilon).$$

The left-hand side is the cost of generating one more job offer, while the right-hand side is the expected increase in payoff from another search. The function g is decreasing, continuous, convex, and differentiable almost everywhere. Clearly $g'(\varepsilon) = -P\{W \geq \varepsilon\}$ where it exists.

The sequential search model has been used to distinguish the discouraged worker or dropout from the frictionally unemployed (see McCall [1970]). The dropout is the individual who decides not to search, while the frictionally unemployed worker is the individual who is searching but has not found a job offer that satisfies his optimal policy, i.e., $w \geq \varepsilon$.

Consider the decision to drop out. For a given distribution of wages, the decision is based on a comparison of the individual's maximum expected payoff from searching and his expected return from remaining unemployed. Let ε^0 be the expected return from remaining unemployed, and let c^0 be the search cost that yields a maximum expected payoff from searching of ε^0. Let μ_W denote the mean wage offer. Then, since g is a decreasing function, all individuals with search costs,[2]

$$c \geq c^0 = g(\varepsilon^0) = \mu_W - \varepsilon^0,$$

2. Since no worker will accept employment at a wage of ε° or below, all wage offers satisfy the relation $w > \varepsilon^\circ$.

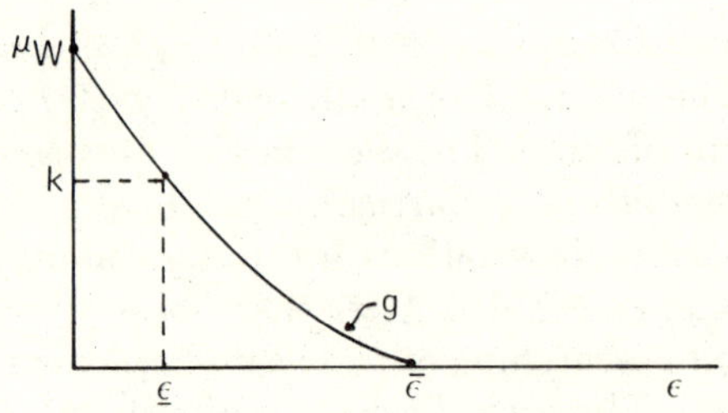

FIGURE I

will decide to drop out of the labor market because the expected gain from search is no greater than the cost of search. Equivalently, for $c \geq c^0, \varepsilon^0 \geq \mu_W - c$, and so the expected return from remaining unemployed is at least as great as the expected payoff from searching.

To complete the specification of the job search model, let [0,1] denote the set of job seekers and $(0,k]$ the set of search costs. The set of search costs determines a set of reservation wages, i.e., $g^{-1}((0,k]) = [\underline{\varepsilon}, \bar{\varepsilon})$, as shown in Figure I. Let Ω be the distribution function for search costs and $\omega = \Omega'$ be its density function. Then $\Omega(c)$ is the number of job seekers with search costs no greater than c. Hence the number of labor dropouts is $1 - \Omega(c^0)$. In the analysis that follows, it will be assumed that $\varepsilon^0 > \underline{\varepsilon}$ so that $1 - \Omega(c^0) > 0$. The case $\varepsilon^0 \leq \underline{\varepsilon}$ is considered in the Appendix, since it is also of some interest and is needed to put bounds on the parameters ε^0 and k, which guarantee a positive number of dropouts.

Next, consider the expected labor supply function implied by the sequential search process. Since wage observations are identically and independently distributed random variables and the job seeker accepts the first wage offer that satisfies his optimal policy, $F(w \mid W \geq \varepsilon)$ is the probability that the job seeker with reservation wage ε accepts a wage offer no greater than w. The worker supplies one unit of labor if he accepts employment and zero units otherwise. Hence, $F(w \mid W \geq \varepsilon)$ is the job seeker's expected supply at a wage no greater than w. The next proposition derives the expected market supply function by noting that it is the sum of the workers' expected supply functions.

PROPOSITION 1. Let Ω be the uniform distribution on $(0,k]$ and let $S(w)$ be the expected labor supply at w. Then

$$S(w) = \frac{1}{k} \int_{g(w)}^{g(\varepsilon^0)} \frac{f(w)}{P(W \geq g^{-1}(c))} dc,$$

where $g^{-1}(c) = \varepsilon$.

Proof. By hypothesis $\omega(c) = 1/k$, $c \in (0,k]$, is the number of job seekers with search cost c. All workers with a search cost $c \leq g(\varepsilon^0)$ will seek employment. Hence the expected market supply at a wage no greater than w is

$$\frac{1}{k}\int_0^{g(\varepsilon^0)} F(w \mid W \geq g^{-1}(c))\,dc = \frac{1}{k}\int_{g(w)}^{g(\varepsilon^0)} \frac{F(w)}{P(W \geq g^{-1}(c))}\,dc$$

and differentiating with respect to w yields the desired result.

The next result provides an equivalent characterization of the expected supply function.

COROLLARY 1. $S(w) = f(w)\,(1/k)(w - \varepsilon^0)$, $w \geq \varepsilon^0$, and zero otherwise.

Proof. Note that $c = g(\varepsilon)$. Hence applying the Change of Variable Theorem from the calculus yields

$$\frac{1}{k}\int_{g(w)}^{g(\varepsilon^0)} \frac{f(w)}{P(W \geq g^{-1}(c))}\,dc$$

$$= \frac{1}{k}\int_{w}^{\varepsilon^0} \frac{f(w)}{P(W \geq \varepsilon)}\, g'(\varepsilon)d\varepsilon = f(w)\frac{1}{k}(w - \varepsilon^0),$$

since $g'(\varepsilon) = -P(W \geq \varepsilon)$.

Since each worker in the market supplies one unit of labor, the supply of labor at all wages is equal to the number of workers with a search cost $c \leq c^0 = g(\varepsilon^0)$, i.e.,

$$\Omega(c^0) = (1/k)g(\varepsilon^0) = (1/k)(\mu_W - \varepsilon^0),$$

equivalently

$$\int_{\varepsilon^0}^{\infty} S(w)dw = \frac{1}{k}(\mu_W - \varepsilon^0).$$

The number of labor dropouts is $1 - (1/k)(\mu_W - \varepsilon^0)$.

Employer Behavior

To complete the market model, the employer's optimal decision-making model must be specified. The employer produces at a constant average productivity y and sells the output at a fixed price normalized to one. The imperfect information allows the employer to maintain some monopsony power in determining an optimal wage offer, since a reduction in his wage offer will not cause his expected supply to go to zero. Let $s(w)$ denote the employer's expected labor supply function. Then the employer selects an optimal wage offer by maximizing his expected profit $\pi(w) = (y - w)\,s(w)$.

Let [0,1] be the set of employers, and suppose that each is equally likely to be observed on any search. Suppose that employers have different technologies. Let Y be a continuous random variable, denoting average productivity, defined on the interval $I = [\mathbf{y}^*, \bar{y}]$. Let H be the distribution function and h be the probability density function of Y. Then $H(y) = P\{Y \leq y\}$ or, equivalently, the number of firms with productivity no greater than y. Clearly $s(w) = 0$ for $w \leq \varepsilon^0$, so it will be assumed that employers with productivity $y \leq \varepsilon^0$ drop out of the labor market. $H(\varepsilon^0)$ is the total number of employers who drop out. Although job seekers do not observe the employer's productivity, the expected profit maximization by employers specifies a one-to-one mapping Φ from productivities to wage offers. Then $W = \Phi(Y)$, and the distribution of W may be derived as shown in the following remark.

REMARK 1. Let $I^0 = [\max\{\mathbf{y},\varepsilon^0\}, \bar{y}]$, i.e., the set of productivities for employers in the market. Let Φ be a strictly increasing function from I^0 to R, with inverse ϕ. Then since $P(W \geq \varepsilon^0) = 1$, and

$$\begin{aligned} F(w) &= P\{W \leq w \,|\, W \geq \varepsilon^0\} = P\{\Phi(Y) \leq w \,|\, \Phi(Y) \geq \varepsilon^0\} \\ &= P\{Y \leq \varphi\ (w) \,|\, Y \geq \varepsilon^0\} = H(\phi(w) \,|\, Y \geq \varepsilon^0). \end{aligned}$$

The density function is

$$f(w) = \begin{cases} \dfrac{h(\phi(w))\phi'(w)}{P(Y \geq \varepsilon^0)}, & w \in \Phi(I^0) \\ 0 & \text{otherwise.} \end{cases}$$

Now deriving the employer's expected supply is a relatively simple matter. The expected supply of labor at w is equal to the employer's expected supply of labor at w times the number of employers offering w. From Remark 1, $h(\phi(w))\phi'(w)$ is the number of employers offering w. Thus, $S(w) = h(\phi(w))\phi'(w)\, s(w)$, and the next proposition follows immediately from Corollary 1 and Remark 1.

PROPOSITION 2.

$$s(w) = \frac{1}{P(Y \geq \varepsilon^0)} \frac{1}{k} (w - \varepsilon^0),$$

if $w \geq \varepsilon^0$ and zero otherwise.

The employer's expected supply function is obviously continuous and increasing. Each employer has a maximization problem similar to that found in monopsony models. The next proposition establishes the existence of an equilibrium wage distribution.

PROPOSITION 3. An equilibrium wage distribution exists and is fully characterized by its density function

$$f(w) = \begin{cases} \dfrac{2h(2w - \varepsilon^0)}{P(Y \geq \varepsilon^0)}, & w \in \Phi(I^0) \\ 0 & \text{elsewhere,} \end{cases}$$

where $\Phi(I^0) = [\max\{\tfrac{1}{2}(y + \varepsilon^0), \varepsilon^0\}, \tfrac{1}{2}(\bar{y} + \varepsilon)]$.

Proof. The employer with productivity y has an expected profit of $\pi(w) = (y - w)\,s(w)$. Using proposition 2, the first-order condition for a maximum is $(y - w) - (w - \varepsilon^0) = 0$. Hence

$$\Phi(y) = \tfrac{1}{2}(y + \varepsilon^0),\ y \in I^0,$$

and so[3]

$$\phi(w) = 2w - \varepsilon^0, w \in \phi(I^0).$$

Then the distribution is $F(w) = H(2w - \varepsilon^0 | Y \geq \varepsilon^0), w \in \Phi(I^0)$, by Remark 1, and differentiating F yields the desired result.

REMARK 2. The summary statistics of the wage distribution are easily derived using Φ:

$$\mu_W \equiv EW = E(\Phi(Y)|Y \geq \varepsilon^0) = \tfrac{1}{2}[E(Y|Y \geq \varepsilon^0) + \varepsilon^0].$$

Let σ_W^2 denote the variance of the wage distribution. Then

$$\sigma_W^2 \equiv \text{var } W = \text{var}(\Phi(Y)|Y \geq \varepsilon^0) = \tfrac{1}{4}\,\text{var}(Y|Y \geq \varepsilon^0).$$

Since $E(Y|Y \geq \varepsilon^0)$ is a nondecreasing function of ε^0, the mean wage offer is an increasing function of ε^0. The variance of the wage distribution may increase or decrease given an increase in ε^0, but clearly $\sigma_W^2 \to 0$ as $\varepsilon^0 \to \bar{y}$.

III

Several policies are available that may reduce the number of discouraged workers. McCall [1970] considered three policies. However, the policy implications of the McCall model have been subject to skepticism because the wage distributions used in the analysis are

3. Let $\eta(w)$ be the elasticity of the expected labor supply function. Then it may be noted that $\phi(w) = w(1 + 1/\eta(w))$ and the Lerner Index of monopsony power is $1/\eta(w)$.

exogenous. Since each policy may affect the wage distribution, the comparative statics on the number of discouraged workers will be derived here using the equilibrium distribution implied by the policy.

Before considering each policy instrument, recall that the number of discouraged workers is $1 - (1/k)\,(\mu_W - \varepsilon^0)$, or equivalently, $1 - (1/2k)(E(Y|Y \geq \varepsilon^0)$ by Remark 2. The number of discouraged workers is positive if the parameters k and ε^0 are in the set $D \equiv \{(k,\varepsilon^0):\frac{1}{2}(\mu_Y - y) < k < \frac{1}{2}\mu_Y, \mu_Y - 2k < \varepsilon^0 < \bar{y}\}$, as shown in the Appendix. Let $\psi : D \rightarrow R$, where $\psi\,(k,\varepsilon^0) \equiv 1 - (1/2k)(E(Y|Y \geq \varepsilon^0))$. The function ψ maps the parameter values into the number of labor dropouts. Let $D_1\psi$ and $D_2\psi$ be the partial derivatives of ψ with respect to k and ε^0, respectively. The first two policies to be considered here may be evaluated by determining the sign of the partial derivatives.

Suppose that a policy of reducing search costs (or equivalently a policy of subsidizing job search) is implemented. In the context of this model a subsidy may be interpreted as a reduction in k, i.e., a reduction in the search cost of every job seeker. The wage distribution in Proposition 3 is not affected by this program; however, it will reduce the number of dropouts, since it increases job seekers' reservation wages. Equivalently, using ψ, it is obvious that a reduction in k will reduce the number of dropouts, since $D_1\psi > 0$. The effect of this program is summarized in Proposition 4.

PROPOSITION 4. $\psi(k,\varepsilon^0)$ is increasing in k.

McCall did not consider changes in the expected return from unemployment, but if ε^0 is interpreted as a government welfare payment, then the number of dropouts can be adjusted using ε^0. Proposition 3 shows that the wage distribution will be affected by a change in the welfare payment, and Remark 2 shows that a decrease (increase) in ε^0 will not increase (decrease) the mean wage offer. In general, a policy of reducing the welfare payment may either increase or decrease the number of discouraged workers. Since job seekers with a search cost $c \geq \mu_W - \varepsilon^0$ drop out, this policy will decrease (increase) the number of discouraged workers if a reduction in ε^0 increases (decreases) $\mu_W - \varepsilon^0$, or equivalently as $D_2\psi > 0$ ($D_2\psi < 0$). The next proposition specifies a sufficient condition on the distribution of employers' productivities for a reduction in the welfare payment to decrease the number of dropouts.

PROPOSITION 5. Suppose that h is monotone increasing. Then $\psi(k,\varepsilon^0)$ is monotone increasing in ε^0.

Proof. Differentiating ψ with respect to ε^0 gives

$$D_2\psi(k,\varepsilon^0) = \frac{1}{2k}\left\{1 - \frac{h(\varepsilon^0)\int_{\varepsilon^0}^{\bar{y}} yh(y)dy}{\int_{\varepsilon^0}^{\bar{y}} h(y)dy}\right\}$$

$$\geq \frac{1}{2k}\left\{1 - \frac{h(\varepsilon^0)\,(\bar{y} - \varepsilon^0)}{\int_{\varepsilon^0}^{\bar{y}} h(y)dy}\right\}.$$

By the Mean Value Theorem, there exists a $y^0 \in (\varepsilon^0,\bar{y})$ such that

$$\int_{\varepsilon^0}^{\bar{y}} h(y)dy = h(y^0)(\bar{y} - \varepsilon^0).$$

Hence,

$$D_2\psi\,(k,\varepsilon^0) \geq \frac{1}{2k}\left\{1 - \frac{h(\varepsilon^0)}{h(y^0)}\right\} \geq 0,$$

since $h(y^0) \geq h(\varepsilon^0)$ by hypothesis.

Proposition 5 demonstrates a condition that makes the policy of reducing ε^0 effective for all ε^0 in D. One could also consider a stronger condition. If $\varepsilon^0 \leq \mathbf{y}$, then $D_2\psi > 0$, independent of h. This observation suggests that a decrease in the welfare payment may increase the number of dropouts if the entry of less productive employers into the market decreases the mean wage offer by more than the welfare payment. Consider the density h, which yields $D_2\psi < 0$ for some $\varepsilon^0 \in [\mathbf{y},\bar{y})$. Since $\psi(k,\bar{y}) = 1$, $D_2\psi > 0$ in a neighborhood of $\bar{y}$. Hence a reduction in ε^0 will reduce the number of dropouts if ε^0 is sufficiently close to $\bar{y}$. However, in this case there is a welfare payment z such that $\psi(k,z) \leq \psi(k,\varepsilon^0)$ for all $z,\varepsilon^0 \in (\mathbf{y},\bar{y})$, and so any decrease in ε^0 that makes $\mathbf{y} < \varepsilon^0 < z$ will increase the number of dropouts and make the policy ineffective.

A reinterpretation of the model will also allow the effects of a job training program to be considered. Suppose that each laborer has productivity θ and that employers differ in their ability to use that raw productivity effectively; let $y = a\theta$, where $a > 0$ is not the same for all employers. Let $a \in [\mathbf{a},\bar{a}]$ so that $I \equiv [\mathbf{y},\bar{y}] = [\mathbf{a}\theta,\bar{a}\theta]$. A training program that increases θ will increase all y and may be treated as a linear transformation of the distribution of productivities. One may expect the job training program to decrease the number of dropouts and increase the mean wage offer. However, the results depend upon the distribution of productivities. To show this, let $[\mathbf{y},\bar{y}]$ be the set of productivities before the program is instituted and $[\mathbf{y}+\delta,\bar{y}+\delta]$, $\delta > 0$, be the set of productivities after the program is completed. Let $K(\delta)$ denote the number of labor dropouts and $M(\delta)$ denote the mean wage offer. Then using the mean wage in Remark 2 and a linear transformation of productivities yields

$$M(\delta) = \frac{1}{2}\frac{\int_{\varepsilon^0}^{\bar{y}+\delta} (y+\varepsilon^0)\, dH(y-\delta)}{\int_{\varepsilon^0}^{\bar{y}+\delta} dH(y-\delta)},$$

and

$$K(\delta) = 1 - (1/k)(M(\delta) - \varepsilon^0).$$

It is apparent that if $M(\delta)$ increases (decreases) with δ, then $K(\delta)$ decreases (increases) with δ. Thus, it is sufficient to determine how $M(\delta)$ changes with δ. The next proposition gives a sufficient condition for the mean wage offer to increase (at least initially) as a result of the training program.

PROPOSITION 6. Suppose that h is monotone increasing. Then $M'(0) > 0$, and $K'(0) < 0$.

Proof. Let $t = y - \delta$ and $dH(y) = h(y)dy$.

Then

$$\frac{\int_{\varepsilon^0}^{\bar{y}+\delta} (y+\varepsilon^0)\, dH(y-\delta)}{\int_{\varepsilon^0}^{\bar{y}+\delta} dH(y-\delta)} = \frac{\int_{\varepsilon^0-\delta}^{\bar{y}} (t+\varepsilon^0+\delta)dH(t)}{\int_{\varepsilon^0-\delta}^{\bar{y}} dH(t)}$$

$$= \frac{\int_{\varepsilon^0-\delta}^{\bar{y}} (y+\varepsilon^0+\delta)\, h(y)dy}{\int_{\varepsilon^0-\delta}^{\bar{y}} h(y)dy},$$

and

$$M(\delta) = \tfrac{1}{2}\frac{\int_{\varepsilon^0-\delta}^{\bar{y}} (y+\varepsilon^0)h(y)dy + \delta \int_{\varepsilon^0-\delta}^{\bar{y}} h(y)dy}{\int_{\varepsilon^0-\delta}^{\bar{y}} h(y)dy}.$$

The derivative of $M(\delta)$ at $\delta = 0$ is

$$M'(0) = \frac{\left[2\varepsilon^0 h(\varepsilon^0) + \int_{\varepsilon^0}^{\bar{y}} h(y)dy\right] \int_{\varepsilon^0}^{\bar{y}} h(y)dy - h(\varepsilon^0) \int_{\varepsilon^0}^{\bar{y}} (y + \varepsilon^0)h(y)dy}{2\left[\int_{\varepsilon^0}^{\bar{y}} h(y)dy\right]^2}.$$

The sign of the derivative is the same as the sign of the numerator. Let N denote the numerator. If h is increasing, then $N > 0$, since

$$\begin{aligned} N &= \left[2\varepsilon^0 h(\varepsilon^0) + \int_{\varepsilon^0}^{\bar{y}} h(y)dy\right] \int_{\varepsilon^0}^{\bar{y}} h(y)dy - h(\varepsilon^0) \\ &\quad \times \int_{\varepsilon^0}^{\bar{y}} (y + \varepsilon^0)\, h(y)dy \\ &= \int_{\varepsilon^0}^{\bar{y}} \left[2\varepsilon^0 h(\varepsilon^0) + \int_{\varepsilon^0}^{y} h(t)dt - (y - \varepsilon^0)\, h(\varepsilon^0)\right] h(y)dy \\ &= \int_{\varepsilon^0}^{\bar{y}} \left[\int_{\varepsilon^0}^{\bar{y}} h(t)dt - (y - \varepsilon^0)h(\varepsilon^0)\right] h(y)dy \\ &> \int_{\varepsilon^0}^{\bar{y}} \left[\int_{\varepsilon^0}^{y} h(t)dt - (y - \varepsilon^0)h(\varepsilon^0)\right] h(y)dy \\ &\geq \int_{\varepsilon^0}^{\bar{y}} \left[\int_{\varepsilon^0}^{y} h(\varepsilon^0)dt - (y - \varepsilon^0)h(\varepsilon^0)\right] h(y)dy \\ &= 0. \end{aligned}$$

Proposition 6 shows that if h is monotone increasing, a job training program will increase the mean wage offer and decrease the number of discouraged workers (at least initially). The training program may have the opposite effect if it allows a sufficient number of the least productive employers to enter the market and so decrease the mean wage offer; h monotone increasing prevents this possibility. Of course, if $\mathbf{y} + \delta > \varepsilon^0$, then the mean wage offer is $\frac{1}{2}(\mu_Y + \delta + \varepsilon^0)$, and so the job training program will be effective given any h.

The choice of an optimal policy for reducing the number of discouraged workers depends upon the expected costs and benefits of each program. Determining the optimal policy goes beyond the scope of this paper, but we do discuss the effect each policy has on the market participants. In an equilibrium setting, we have verified McCall's conclusion that a reduction in search costs decreases the number of dropouts; in addition, we have shown that this policy will not change the wage distribution. This policy increases each job seeker's reservation wage. Since it also reduces the number of dropouts, this policy will increase the expected aggregate wage bill. The analysis also allows us to determine the effect of this policy on the employer's expected profit. Employers with a productivity $y > \varepsilon^0$ have a maximum expected profit of

$$\pi(\Phi(y)) = \frac{1}{P(Y \geq \varepsilon^0)} \frac{1}{4k} (y - \varepsilon^0)^2.$$

Then it is obvious that a reduction in k increases the employer's expected profit. Since a profits' tax would not change employers' wage offers, the government could consider such a tax to help finance a reduction in workers' search costs.

The government may also change its welfare payment. We have shown in Remark 2 that the mean wage offer is an increasing function of ε^0. If the productivity density is an increasing function, then by Proposition 5 a decrease in ε^0 will reduce the number of labor dropouts. If $\varepsilon^0 > \mathbf{y}$, then a decrease in ε^0 will increase the number of employers in the market. However, since this policy causes a lower mean wage offer, it reduces the expected payoff of job seekers in the market prior to the reduction in the welfare payment. Similarly, $\pi \circ \Phi$ may be differentiated with respect to the parameter ε^0. Then it is easily shown that the policy will reduce the expected profit of employers in the market prior to the reduction in ε^0. Hence this policy benefits only market entrants.

Finally, we have established a modified version of McCall's conclusion that a job training program reduces the number of discouraged workers. Since McCall did not specify employer behavior, he reached the conclusion by assuming that the trained worker searched a wage distribution with a larger mean. In the completed market model presented here, we have specified a condition that is sufficient to guarantee that McCall's assumption holds. If h is increasing, then the job training program will increase the mean wage offer, all workers' reservation wages, and the number of workers in the market. Thus, the policy benefits workers and increases the expected wage bill. The program increases the employer's productivity from y to $y + \delta$, and so his optimal wage offer from $\Phi(y) = \frac{1}{2}(y + \varepsilon^0)$ to $\Phi(y + \delta) = \frac{1}{2}(y + \delta + \varepsilon^0)$ if $y > \varepsilon^0$ or allows the employer with $y < \varepsilon^0 < y + \delta$ to enter the market with a wage offer of $\Phi(y + \delta)$. At the optimal wage offer, the employer's expected profit is

$$\pi(\Phi(y + \delta)) = (y + \delta - \varepsilon^0)^2/(4kP(Y \geq \varepsilon^0 - \delta)),$$

which is greater for $\delta > 0$ if h is increasing. Hence the expected profits of all employers with $y + \delta > \varepsilon^0$ increase. A profits tax here may also be an effective tool to help finance the job training program.

The effects of a minimum wage law on the number of discouraged workers can also be interpreted within the framework of this model. McCall argues correctly that if the minimum wage is less than ε^0, then it will not influence the discouraged worker's decision. This case is obvious, since a minimum wage no greater than ε^0 will not change the wage distribution and so will not change the decisions made by any employer or job seeker. However, McCall also argues that a minimum wage greater than ε^0 will not change the dropout decision because it is beyond the range of alternatives that the discouraged worker considers. The argument is appealing, but we claim that it is incomplete for two reasons. First, it considers the effect of the law only on individuals who have already made the dropout decision; it does not allow for the possibility that the law may discourage (encourage) more workers. Second, the argument does not depend upon the changed wage distribution implied by the law.

Consider the form of the wage distribution implied by the minimum wage law. Let $\hat{\varepsilon}$ denote the minimum wage, and let $\hat{\varepsilon} > \varepsilon^0$. Since no employer with a productivity $y \leq \hat{\varepsilon}$ will remain in the market, $P(Y > \hat{\varepsilon})$ is the number of employers in the market, and each has an expected supply function $\hat{s}(w)$, where

$$\hat{s}(w) = 1/(kP(Y \geq \hat{\varepsilon}))\,(w - \varepsilon^0).$$

The next proposition establishes the existence of the equilibrium wage distribution.

PROPOSITION 7. Given a minimum wage $\hat{\varepsilon} > \hat{\varepsilon}^0$, an equilibrium wage distribution exists and is fully characterized by its density function:

$$\hat{f}(w) = \begin{cases} H(2\hat{\varepsilon} - \varepsilon^0 | Y > \hat{\varepsilon}), & w = \hat{\varepsilon} \\ 2h(2w - \varepsilon^0 | Y > \hat{\varepsilon}), & \hat{\varepsilon} < w \leq (\bar{y} + \varepsilon^0)/2 \\ 0, & \text{elsewhere.} \end{cases}$$

Proof. Each employer with a productivity $y > \hat{\varepsilon}$ maximizes $\hat{\pi}(w) = (y - w)\,\hat{s}(w)$ subject to the constraint $w \geq \hat{\varepsilon}$. The employer's optimal wage offer is $\frac{1}{2}(y + \varepsilon^0)$ if the constraint is not binding; otherwise the optimal wage offer is $\hat{\varepsilon}$, since $\hat{\pi}$ is decreasing on the interval $(\frac{1}{2}(y + \varepsilon^0), y]$. Hence

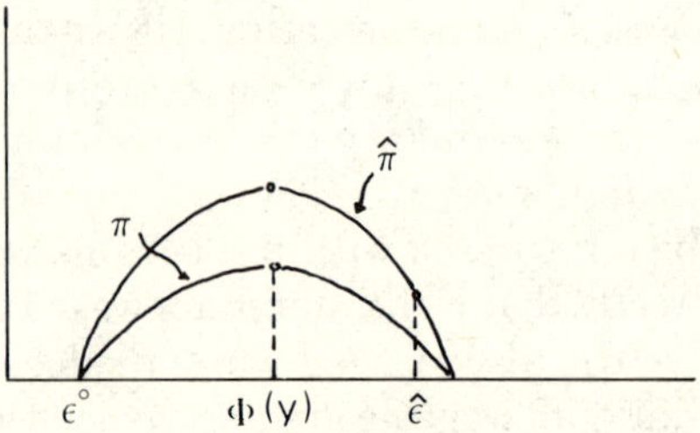

FIGURE II

$$\begin{aligned}\hat{\Phi}(y) &= \max\{\hat{\varepsilon}, \tfrac{1}{2}(y+\varepsilon^0)\} \\ &= \begin{cases}\hat{\varepsilon}, & \hat{\varepsilon} < y < 2\hat{\varepsilon} - \varepsilon^0 \\ \tfrac{1}{2}(y+\varepsilon^0), & 2\hat{\varepsilon} - \varepsilon^0 \le y \le \bar{y}.\end{cases}\end{aligned}$$

Thus, $H(2\hat{\varepsilon} - \varepsilon^0 | Y \ge \hat{\varepsilon})$ is the probability of observing $\hat{\varepsilon}$, and

$$\hat{F}(w) = \begin{cases} 0, & w < \hat{\varepsilon} \\ H(2w - \varepsilon^0 | Y \ge \hat{\varepsilon}), & \hat{\varepsilon} \le w \le \tfrac{1}{2}(\bar{y}+\varepsilon^0) \\ 1 & w \ge \tfrac{1}{2}(\bar{y}+\varepsilon^0) \end{cases}$$

is the wage distribution. Then the density $\hat{f}$ is obtained by noting that there is a mass point at $\hat{\varepsilon}$ and differentiating $\hat{F}$ at $w > \hat{\varepsilon}$.

As noted above, the minimum wage is a binding constraint if $\hat{\varepsilon} > \varepsilon^0$, and Proposition 7 shows that $\hat{\varepsilon}$ must be less than $\tfrac{1}{2}(\bar{y}+\varepsilon^0)$ to obtain a nondegenerate wage distribution. Let $M{:}[\varepsilon^0, \tfrac{1}{2}(\bar{y}+\varepsilon^0)) \to R$ be the function that maps the minimum wage into the mean wage offer. Then by Proposition 7,

$$M(\hat{\varepsilon}) \equiv \frac{\int_{\hat{\varepsilon}}^{2\hat{\varepsilon}-\varepsilon^0} \hat{\varepsilon} h(y)dy + \int_{2\varepsilon-\varepsilon^0}^{\bar{y}} \tfrac{1}{2}(y+\varepsilon^0)\, h(y)dy}{\int_{\hat{\varepsilon}}^{\bar{y}} h(y)dy}.$$

Now it is possible to return to our consideration of the number of labor dropouts. Let $K(\hat{\varepsilon})$ denote the number of dropouts as a function of $\hat{\varepsilon}$. Then $K(\hat{\varepsilon}) = 1 - (1/k)(M(\hat{\varepsilon}) - \varepsilon^0)$. Since the number of dropouts is $1 - (1/k)(\mu_W - \varepsilon^0)$ for $\hat{\varepsilon} \le \varepsilon^0$ (where μ_W is the mean wage from Remark 2), the number of discouraged workers decreases if and only if $M(\hat{\varepsilon}) > M(\varepsilon^0) \equiv \mu_W$. The next proposition establishes this result.

PROPOSITION 8. M is an increasing function of $\hat{\varepsilon}$ on its domain $(\varepsilon^0, \frac{1}{2}(\bar{y} + \varepsilon^0))$. It follows that K is a decreasing function of $\hat{\varepsilon}$ on $(\varepsilon^0, \frac{1}{2}(\bar{y} + \varepsilon^0))$.

Proof. Since $M(\varepsilon^0) = \mu_W$, it suffices to show that $M'(\hat{\varepsilon}) > 0$. Differentiating M yields

$$M'(\hat{\varepsilon}) = \left(\int_{\hat{\varepsilon}}^{\bar{y}} h(y)dy \left[-\hat{\varepsilon}h(\hat{\varepsilon}) + \int_{\hat{\varepsilon}}^{2\hat{\varepsilon}-\varepsilon^0} h(y)dy\right] + h(\hat{\varepsilon}) \times \left[\int_{\hat{\varepsilon}}^{2\hat{\varepsilon}-\hat{\varepsilon}^0} \hat{\varepsilon}h(y)dy + \int_{2\hat{\varepsilon}-\varepsilon^0}^{\bar{y}} \frac{y+\varepsilon^0}{2} h(y)dy\right]\right) \Big/ \left[\int_{\hat{\varepsilon}}^{\bar{y}} h(y)dy\right]^2$$

$$= \left(\int_{\hat{\varepsilon}}^{\bar{y}} h(y)dy \left[\int_{\hat{\varepsilon}}^{2\hat{\varepsilon}-\varepsilon^0} h(y)dy\right] + h(\hat{\varepsilon}) \times \left[\int_{2\hat{\varepsilon}-\varepsilon^0}^{\bar{y}} (\tfrac{1}{2}(\bar{y}+\varepsilon^0) - \hat{\varepsilon})\, h(y)dy\right]\right) \Big/ \left[\int_{\hat{\varepsilon}}^{\bar{y}} h(y)dy\right]^2$$

$$> 0.$$

This proposition shows that the introduction of a minimum wage will decrease the number of dropouts. It contradicts McCall's claim that the minimum wage will not affect the dropout decision. By increasing the mean wage, the law increases the number of workers in the market, the expected payoff of each worker, and the expected wage bill. Hence a minimum wage $\hat{\varepsilon} > \varepsilon^0$ will be supported by job seekers. The employer's optimal profit is $(\hat{\pi}\circ\hat{\Phi})(y)$. For $\varepsilon^0 < \hat{\varepsilon} < \mathbf{y}$, it is obvious that $\pi = \hat{\pi}$ for all employers. In this case $(\hat{\pi}\circ\hat{\Phi})(y) < (\pi\circ\Phi)(y)$ if the minimum wage constraint is binding, otherwise $(\hat{\pi}\circ\hat{\Phi})(y) = (\pi\circ\Phi)(y)$. For $\hat{\varepsilon} > \varepsilon^0 > \mathbf{y}$, $\hat{\pi} \geq \pi$ for all employers as shown in Figure II. In this case $(\hat{\pi}\circ\hat{\Phi})(y) > (\pi\circ\Phi)(y)$ if the constraint is not binding. However, if the constraint is binding the employer's expected profit may either increase or decrease. Figure II displays the case in which expected profit is lower. It is clear that employers with productivity y sufficiently close to $\hat{\varepsilon}$ will have a smaller expected profit. Thus, the minimum wage will not be supported by all employers.

IV

This paper shows that the choice of a policy to reduce the number of discouraged workers is important because it will affect the behavior of market participants. Subsidizing job search decreases the number of labor dropouts, increases workers' reservation wages, and increases the expected labor supply and employers' expected profits; this policy does not change the number of employers participating in the market. If the density of productivities is an increasing function, then a decrease in the welfare payment will decrease the number of discouraged workers and increase the number of employers participating in the market. However, this policy benefits market entrants at the expense of other participants. A job training program will always be effective in reducing the number of dropouts if the density of productivities is increasing. In addition, when the job training program is effective, it increases the mean wage offer, workers' reservation wages, the number of employers in the market, and employers' expected profits. Finally, if the minimum wage is greater than the expected return from unemployment, then it will reduce the number of discouraged workers and increase the mean wage offer and workers' reservation wages, but it will decrease the number of employers in the market and the expected profits of some of the employers.

A few comments on the assumptions of the model are necessary, since they are not found in most other market models of search. The assumption that firms have different technologies seems natural because employers may be producing different products. The productivity may also be interpreted as marginal value produce, since employers may be selling their output at different prices. The assumption of different search costs seems natural here, but it is also crucial in explaining why some job seekers search more than others, and why some individuals drop out of the market. Finally, the assumption that the set of search costs is not bounded below by a positive constant is very strong but necessary, since otherwise the highest wage firm may decrease its wage offer without a decrease in expected supply. It may be possible to eliminate the last assumption if workers are assumed to have elastic labor supply functions. Of course, as long as the optimal stopping rule is myopic, it will be necessary to assume that workers have different search costs in order to explain why some workers search more than once.

This model, like others on equilibrium distributions, assumes a particular mechanism for the collection of information. Optimally, the mechanism(s) used for the collection or dissemination of information should be endogenous to the model. For job seekers the sequential search process will dominate nonsequential search, because no job seeker observing the highest wage offer on his first random draw from the wage distribution will have an incentive to continue searching. However, there are other information-generating mechanisms available. Any market participant may choose to advertise. The employer behavior assumed here is passive, but if an employer can increase the probability that his wage offer is observed and increases his expected supply and profit, then the advertising mechanism will be used. Hence the optimal choice of mechanism(s) remains an important question in the economics of information.

APPENDIX

Consider the labor market in which there are no discouraged workers, i.e., $0 < \varepsilon^0 \leq \boldsymbol{\varepsilon}$. The following propositions correspond to the same numbered propositions in the text. Proofs are omitted when they are the same.

PROPOSITION 1′.

$$S(w) = \frac{1}{k} \int_{g(w)}^{g(\boldsymbol{\varepsilon})} \frac{f(w)}{P(W \geq g^{-1}(c))} dc.$$

COROLLARY 1′.

$$S(w) = f(w)\,(1 - (1/k)\,\mu_W + (1/k)w).$$

Proof. $S(w) = f(w)\,(1/k)(w - \boldsymbol{\varepsilon})$ by the Change of Variable Theorem. Then

$$k = g(\boldsymbol{\varepsilon}) = \int_{\boldsymbol{\varepsilon}}^{\infty} (w - \boldsymbol{\varepsilon})dF(w) = \mu_W - \boldsymbol{\varepsilon}.$$

Hence $\boldsymbol{\varepsilon} = \mu_W - k$ and substitution yields the result.

PROPOSITION 2′.

$$s(w) = \frac{1}{P(Y \geq \boldsymbol{\varepsilon})}\left(1 - \frac{1}{k}\mu_W + \frac{1}{k}w\right)$$

if $w \geq \mu_W - k$ and zero otherwise.

Notice that the price intercept on the employer's expected supply function is $\mu_W - k$. This suggests the possibility of $\mathbf{y} < \mu_W - k$ for sufficiently small k. It is possible to specify the conditions under which a decrease in k causes a decrease in the number of employers in the market (i.e., employers drop out when their productivity is less than the minimum reservation wage $\boldsymbol{\varepsilon} = \mu_W - k$). However, if $\varepsilon^0 > \boldsymbol{\varepsilon} = \mu_W - k$ holds, as assumed in the text, no decrease in k for which this inequality remains valid will cause a reduction in the number of employers in the market. Hence, for our purpose there is no loss in generality and greater simplicity in assuming $\mathbf{y} > \mu_W - k > 0$. Then the next proposition follows easily.

PROPOSITION 3′. Suppose that $\mathbf{y} > \mu_Y - 2k > 0$. Then an equilibrium distribution exists and is fully characterized by its density function:

$$f(w) = \begin{cases} 2h(2w - \mu_W + 2k), & w \in \Phi(I) \\ 0, & \text{elsewhere,} \end{cases}$$

where $\Phi(I) = [\tfrac{1}{2}(\mu_Y - 2k + \mathbf{y}), \tfrac{1}{2}(\mu_Y - 2k + \bar{y})]$.

Proof. The employer with productivity y has an expected profit function $\pi(w) = (y - w)\, s(w)$, where $s(w)$ is given in Proposition 2′. The first-order condition for expected profit maximization is

$$(1/k)(y - w) - (1 - (1/k)\mu_W - (1/k)w) = 0.$$

Hence

$$\Phi(y) = \tfrac{1}{2}(\mu_W - k + y).$$

If all employers remain in the market, the mean wage offer is found by noting that

$$\mu_W \equiv EW = E\Phi(y) = \tfrac{1}{2}(\mu_W - k + \mu_Y).$$

Then $\mu_W = \mu_Y - k$. By hypothesis $\mathbf{y} > \mu_W - k = \mu_Y - 2k > 0$. It follows that $\mathbf{y} > \Phi(\mathbf{y}) = \tfrac{1}{2}(\mu_Y - 2k + \mathbf{y}) > \mu_Y - 2k > 0$ and $\pi(\Phi(y)) > 0$ for all $y \in I$. Hence all employers remain in the market. Finally, since $\phi(w) = 2w - \mu_W + k = 2w - \mu_Y + 2k$, the equilibrium price distribution is $F(w) = H(2w - \mu_Y + 2k)$ for $w \in \Phi(I) = [\tfrac{1}{2}(\mu_Y - 2k + \mathbf{y}), \tfrac{1}{2}(\mu_Y - 2k + \bar{y})]$ and $f(w) = F'(w)$.

By using Proposition 3′, it is possible to define the set of parameter values k and ε° for which a positive number of workers decide to drop out of the labor market. By hypothesis $\mathbf{y} > \mu_Y - 2k > 0$, or equivalently $\tfrac{1}{2}(\mu_Y - \mathbf{y}) < k < \tfrac{1}{2}\mu_Y$. For these values of k there will be a positive number of dropouts if $\varepsilon^\circ > \varepsilon = \mu_Y - 2k$. Clearly $\varepsilon^\circ < \bar{y}$ must be satisifed for the market to exist. Then collecting results, we obtain the set

$$D = \{(k,\varepsilon^\circ): \tfrac{1}{2}(\mu_Y - \mathbf{y}) < k < \tfrac{1}{2}\mu_Y, \mu_Y - 2k < \varepsilon^\circ < \bar{y}\}$$

for which $c^\circ = \mu_W - \varepsilon^\circ < k$ and so $1 - \Omega(c^\circ) > 0$.

STATE UNIVERSITY OF NEW YORK, BINGHAMTON

REFERENCES

Butters, Gerard R., "Equilibrium Price Distributions and the Economics of Information," *Review of Economic Studies*, XLIV (1977), 465–91.

Green, Edward, "Equilibrium in a Market Where Consumers Search," unpublished paper, Carnegie-Mellon University, 1976.

Kohn, M. G., and S. Shavell, "The Theory of Search," *Journal of Economic Theory,* IX (1974), 93–123.
McCall, John J., "Economics of Information and Job Search," this *Journal*, LXXXIV (1970), 113–26.
Reinganum, Jennifer, "A Simple Model of Equilibrium Price Dispersion," unpublished paper, Northwestern University, 1978.
Rothschild, Michael, "Models of Market Organization with Incomplete Information: A Survey," *Journal of Political Economy,* LXXXI (1973), 1283–1308.
Stiglitz, Joseph E., "Equilibrium Wage Distributions," Institute for Mathematical Studies in the Social Sciences, Technical Report No. 154, November 1974.
Wilde, Louis L., "Labor Market Equilibrium Under Sequential Search," unpublished paper, California Institute of Technology, June 1975.
——, "Labor Market Equilibrium Under Nonsequential Search," *Journal of Economic Theory*, XVI (1977), 373–93.

DAVID HUME AND MONETARISM*

THOMAS MAYER

Of the twelve characteristics of modern monetarism, five are explicit in Hume's writings: the quantity theory, the Chicago transmission process, private sector stability, the vertical Phillips curve, which Hume originated, and preference for free markets. Two others, irrelevance of allocative detail and focus on the price level as a unit, are implicit. Preference for reduced-form models fits Hume's theory of causation. Preference for stable money growth fits the whole tenor of Hume's discussion. Two propositions on targets and indicators were irrelevant in Hume's day, but Hume rejected the monetarists' strong opposition to inflation.

As current economic theories change, so should our evaluation of previous economists. This paper, therefore, suggests that David Hume's reputation, which has declined since the nineteenth century, should now be rising again because in 1752, long before Ricardo, he anticipated modern monetarism on an amazing number of issues.[1] To see how Hume did this, one must first set out the characteristics of monetarism. Elsewhere [Mayer, 1975] I characterized it by twelve interrelated propositions and characteristics.[2] They are as follows:

A. Core Propositions and Characteristics:

1. Changes in the money stock lead to predictable changes in money income, and these changes in the money stock are the predominant variable determining money income. This is the quantity theory.

2. A specific approach to the transmission process, which focuses on the money stock rather than on interest rates, and on a relatively large number of channels.

* The author is indebted for helpful comments to Peter Berman, Robert Blewett, Phillip Cagan, Dietrich Fausten, Gillian Garcia, Robert Hetzel, Thomas Humphrey, David Laidler, Charles Lieberman, Raymond Lombra, Will Mason, Hans Palmer, Don Patinkin, T. Y. Shen, and Alan Stockman. Earlier versions of this paper were presented at a seminar at UCLA and at the 1978 Western Economic Association meetings.

1. For Hume's position in economics see Feilbogen [1890], pp. 699–700; Johnson [1937], p. 163; Vickers [1968], p. 218; O'Brien [1975], pp. 7, 17; and Arkin [1956], p. 217. With respect to monetary theory von Hayek [1976, p. 23] wrote that "Richard Cantillion and David Hume began the development of modern monetary theory," while Friedman [1975, pp. 176–77], in discussing the rediscovery of money in the last twenty-five years, wrote: "We have advanced beyond Hume in two respects only: first, we now have a more secure grasp on the quantitative magnitudes involved; second, we have gone one derivative beyond Hume." The latter is due to the fact that whereas Hume could take stable prices as a norm, nowadays we must focus on the change in the inflation rate.

2. This list does not include the monetarist theory of the balance of payments, since it is not clear whether or not it is part of monetarism per se. (See Laidler [1978], and Fausten [1978].) Moreover, it is also open to dispute whether Hume should be considered its ancestor. (See Fausten [1979], Frenkel [1976], Keleher [1978], and Parkin [1977].) The rational expectations approach is also excluded from the list, since many monetarists do not accept it.

The Quarterly Journal of Economics, August 1980 0033-5533/80/0095-0089$01.30

3. Belief in the inherent stability of the private sector.

B. Method:

4. Irrelevance of allocative detail for the explanation of short-run changes in money income, and belief in a fluid capital market.

5. Focus on the price level as a unit rather than on individual prices, in the sense of not attributing inflation to supply pressures in those sectors in which relative prices are rising.

6. Reliance on small, rather than large, econometric models.

C. Monetary Policy:

7. Use of the reserve base or related measures as the indicator of monetary policy.

8. Use of the money stock as the target of monetary policy.

9. Acceptance of a stable money growth rate rule, or a similar rule.

D. General Macro Policy:

10. Rejection of an unemployment-inflation tradeoff.

11. Relatively greater concern about inflation than about unemployment.

12. Support of free markets rather than government intervention.

Most of these propositions can be traced to a general tendency of monetarists to emphasize the long run much more than Keynesians do. (See Fellner [1977], Gordon [1976], pp. 55–57, and Modigliani [1977], p. 20.)

One difficulty that arises in trying to find these, or any other current ideas in an earlier writer, is that it is so easy to read them into his work by focusing on isolated passages and obiter dicta. But as Patinkin [1972, p. 139] has remarked: "isolated passages do not a theory make." To show that this is not a problem with Hume's monetarism, after discussing whether Hume had each of these propositions, I reverse field and take up the points that were central to Hume, to see whether they are important components of modern monetarism as well. Another seeming difficulty is that modern monetarism should be seen in the context of a reaction to Keynesianism. But Hume too was reacting to the mercantilists who shared a number of ideas with Keynes.

THE QUANTITY THEORY AND INTEREST RATE THEORY

Hume certainly could not claim to be the *originator* of the quantity theory in the sense of being the first to attribute inflation to an increase in the quantity of money; in 1694 Brisco had already written out an equation of exchange, though omitting velocity

[Schumpeter, 1954, p. 314]. Moreover, Hume has been accused by von Hayek [1935, p. 9] of plagiarizing from Cantillion, and by Marx and Engels of plagiarizing from Vanderlint [Sekine, 1973, p. 274]. But other economists have defended Hume against these charges. (See Humphrey [1932], p. 237, Sekine [1973], pp. 274–75, and Stadlin [1954], pp. 24–25.) Schumpeter [1954, p. 316] credited Hume with being the first to show "clearly and explicitly" that, on an abstract level, there is no unique quantity of nominal money that a country needs. He thus understood the distinction, so much emphasized by modern monetarists, between the real and the nominal quantity of money. Hegeland [1951, p. 34] described Hume's discussion as the "most elucidating account" of the essence of the original quantity theory. And O'Brien [1975, p. 144] attributed to Hume, Cantillion, and Harris the first published "clear formulation" of the quantity theory. Here is Hume's own exposition [1955, pp. 33, 41, and 48]:

> If we consider any one kingdom by itself, it is evident, that the greater or less plenty of money is of no consequence; since the prices of commodities are always proportioned to the plenty of money . . . . It is a maxim almost self-evident, that the prices of everything depend on the proportion between commodities and money, and that any considerable alteration on either has the same effect, either of heightening or lowering the price . . . . All augmentation [of gold and silver] has no other effect than to heighten the price of labor and commodities . . . .

Hume recognized that the money stock and prices need not always move proportionately. Transactions could vary. "It is the proportion between the circulating money, and the commodities in the market, which determines the prices" [Hume, 1955, p. 43]. Hume was much less explicit about velocity. He surely learned about it by reading Locke, who had a highly developed analysis of velocity, including its relation to the interest rate [Leigh, 1974]. Perhaps Hume was less explicit about velocity because, at the time, the "quickness of circulation" was included in the concept of the quantity of money [Blaugh, 1968, p. 20; and Stadlin, 1954, p. 30.][3]

3. Hume did make a few references to velocity. In one [p. 42] he wrote that coin "locked up in chests . . . is the same thing with regard to prices as if they were annihilated." In addition, he recognized the importance of money substitutes, writing:

"Banks, funds and paper credit . . . render paper equivalent to money, circulate it throughout the whole state, make it supply the place of gold and silver, raise proportionably the price of labor and commodities . . . . Public securities are with us become a kind of money, and pass as readily at the current price as gold or silver" [Hume, 1955, pp. 67–68].

Hume then went on to say that these money substitutes lower the cost of holding working-capital, and hence, by reducing cost of production, lower prices [p. 93]. This is a strange argument. One possible explanation is that Hume here forgot his own theory that prices are determined by the quantity of money. The second possibility is that he was thinking of relative prices. The former interpretation seems somewhat more plausible.

An important characteristic of Hume's quantity theory is that, instead of stating it only as a truistic, comparative statics proposition as Locke did, Hume presented it as a causal theory of price determination. Blaugh [1968, p. 20] and Hegeland [1951, p. 168] attributed this to confusion, but monetarists are more likely to praise Hume for it. Another characteristic of Hume's quantity theory is that, like present day international monetarism, it applies to the whole world rather than to any single country, since a country's money stock is not exogenous, but is determined by the specie-flow mechanism [Keleher, 1978]. Hence, for a single country causation can run from prices to money, as well as from money to prices. Hume's emphasis on the interrelation of monetary economics and the balance of payments theory became an important strand of thought in British monetary analysis until the 1930s.

Like modern quantity theorists, Hume had a real theory of the interest rate. A high stock of money does not mean a low interest rate:

> Lowness of interest is generally ascribed to plenty of money. But money, however plentiful, has no other effect, *if fixed,* than to raise the price of labour. Interest in BATAVIA and JAMAICA is at 10 *percent,* in Portugal at 6; though these places, as we may learn from the price of everything, abound more in gold and silver than either LONDON or AMSTERDAM [Hume, 1955, p. 47].

Compare this to Friedman's 1968 [pp. 6–7] statement:

> . . . high and rising nominal interest rates have been associated with rapid growth in the quantity of money, as in Brazil or Chile or in the United States in recent years, and . . . low and falling interest rates have been associated with slow growth in the quantity of money, as in Switzerland now, or in the United States from 1929 to 1933.

The only differences are that Hume, unlike Friedman, did not have the "Fisher effect" available, and also talked about a high stock of money instead of a high growth rate.

Hume believed that an increase in the money stock may sometimes lower the interest rate temporarily, depending upon where the money is injected. If it is concentrated in a few hands, then it will initially be offered on the loan market, and thus lower the rate of interest *temporarily.* But this is not so if the additional money enters the economy gradually and is widely spread among many people. Even then, however, like in our growth models, it can have *some* long-run effect on the rate of interest by temporarily stimulating output, which raises the stock of accumulated savings, and thus lowers interest rates. (See Lowe [1954], p. 125.)

THE TRANSMISSION PROCESS

The modern monetarist transmission process has several characteristics. According to its critics, one is its use of a "black box," despite the fact that Brunner and Meltzer [1976a] give a detailed and complex analysis of the transmission process. Other characteristics are that it is formulated in terms of money rather than interest rates, and that money directly affects consumption as well as "investment." Finally, the Brunner-Meltzer version has a relative price and a wealth interpretation of the transmission process.

The seeming "black box" approach of the Chicago school fits well into Hume's theory of causation, which is a salient contribution to philosophy. He treated cause and effect as being fundamentally nothing but correlation; if event A always occurs in connection with—and before—event B, then A is the cause of B (see Blake, Ducasse, and Madden [1960], Ch. 4).[4] In his own discussion of the specie flow mechanism, Hume explicitly used "black box" reasoning, writing [p. 77]:

> . . . Money always finds its way back again by a hundred canals, of which we have not notion or suspicion . . . . For above a thousand years, the money of EUROPE has been flowing to ROME, by an open and sensible current; but it has been emptied by many secret and insensible canals.

In his treatment of the quantity theory, Hume also did not discuss the transmission channels in any detail. There is only a single passage in which he pointed out that money can affect prices only by changing aggregate demand [Sekine, 1973, pp. 275–76], though Patinkin [1965, p. 530] has suggested that Hume may simply not have bothered to state what was obvious.

Moreover, he focused on changes in the money stock, and not on the resulting changes in interest rates, since in his model a rise in the money stock need not lower the interest rate even temporarily, except for the "growth model" effect previously mentioned. Hume's discussion of the difference between the effects of concentrated and widely dispersed increases in the money supply also shows that Hume agreed with modern monetarists that a change in the money supply can affect consumption as well as investment. Admittedly, Hume did not have the sophisticated relative price and wealth analysis of

4. This did not prevent Hume from sometimes describing the causal chain involved. And indeed, Hume's theory may require correlation between variables that are finely detailed. But in his own discussion of the quantity theory, he showed no concern about using a black box.

Brunner and Meltzer, but in any case this analysis is by no means accepted by all modern monetarists. There is also some debate as to whether it is actually monetarist [see Brunner and Meltzer, 1976b; and Dornbusch, 1976, pp. 123–24].

Stability of the Private Sector

Hume's discussion of the stability of the private sector dealt with whether mercantilist policies are needed to preserve a country's supply of specie; to this Hume's answer was clear. Though he was not the first to point out that the supply of specie could, and should, be left to look after itself, he was by far the most influential proponent of this view in his day.

Unemployment was a serious problem in Hume's day, though it may well have been more regional and structural than cyclical. Mercantilist writers advocated full employment policies, arguing, for example, that a worker has a right to a job [Furniss, 1920, Chs. 3 and 4]. But not so Hume. Although at least at one point he implied that involuntary unemployment existed [see Vickers, 1957, p. 230; and O'Brien, 1975, p. 163], he had very little to say about it. Moreover, he believed that prices are highly flexible, which goes a long way to ensure the stability of the private sector:

> Nor is it probable, that the diminution of circulating money was ever sensibly felt by the people, or ever did them any prejudice. The sinking of the prices of all commodities would *immediately* replace it, by giving England the advantage in its commerce with the neighboring kingdoms [Hume, 1955, p. 73, emphasis added].

Stability of the private sector not only implies the absence of severe unemployment, but also that the private sector does not itself generate inflation. Unless there is a large increase in the world supply of specie or paper money, this condition is implicit in Hume's quantity theory. And further, in his discussion of taxes Hume [p. 87] argued that sales taxes cannot start a cost-push, thus supporting the monetarist rejection of cost-push inflation.[5]

Three Methodological Propositions

The first proposition is that one should deemphasize allocative

5. However, in listing the disadvantages of "exhorbitant" taxes [p. 85], Hume mentioned that they raise wages. *Perhaps* the explanation of the apparent contradiction is that "exhorbitant" taxes have to be passed on, since the worker can lower his living standard only to a limited extent.

details in macroeconomics. Aggregate demand is determined "from the top down" by the stock of money, rather than built up by adding up demands in various sectors. The second is that one should think of the price level as a single unit. Hume did not discuss these two propositions explicitly, but this is more or less true of modern monetarists, too. Both of them are definitely implied in Hume's espousal of the quantity theory.[6]

Then there is the monetarist's preference for small reduced-form models. Obviously, Hume did not discuss econometric techniques, but one of the issues involved here is the "black box" argument. On this issue, Hume was on the side of the monetarists.

MONETARY POLICY

The next three monetarist propositions would have had little meaning for Hume, since monetary policy, in the current sense of the term, did not exist in his day. For Hume the quantity of money was determined by the specie flow mechanism, and the issue was whether it should be allowed to operate freely or whether the government should aim for a positive balance of trade. Hence, the question of what the targets and indicators of monetary policy should be was totally meaningless for Hume.

The next monetarist proposition is adherence to a monetary rule. Hume obviously could not advocate a policy of stable money growth, but he did share some of the underlying conceptions that dispose monetarists to favor it. He showed a great deal of skepticism regarding the efficiency of discretionary policy in his criticism of mercantilism, and his discussions of deficit spending and paper money. After pointing out the advantage of paper money, he nonetheless opposed it because of its inherent riskiness [Hume, 1955, p. 68 n]. He did not mention the possibility that the government might issue paper money and maintain its soundness.

Moreover, Hume, unlike modern monetarists, did not have to advocate a stable money growth rule to eliminate discretionary policy; the specie flow mechanism operates with even less discretion than does a money growth rate rule.[7]

6. Furthermore, Hume assumed that prices are highly flexible. If so, then price behavior in a particular industry has little effect on the overall price level; if steel prices rise because of increased monopoly, other prices are forced down due to the decline in real balances.

7. Friedman [1962, pp. 221–22] argued that if it were feasible, an automatic commodity standard would be an "excellent solution."

General Macro Policy

Monetarists believe that an increased money growth rate raises employment for only a quite limited time, and after that just raises prices. This point was discovered by Hume, who "perhaps for the first time in economics" [Taylor, 1965, p. 77] drew a sharp distinction between the short run and the long run when he wrote:

Though the high price of commodities be a necessary consequence of the encrease of gold and silver, yet it follows not immediately upon that encrease; but some time is required before the money circulates through the whole state, and makes its effect be felt on all ranks of people. At first, no alteration is perceived; by degrees the price rises, first of one commodity, then of another; till the whole at last reaches a just proportion with the new quantity of specie which is in the kingdom. In my opinion, it is only in this interval or intermediate situation, between the acquisition of money and rise of prices, that the encreasing quantity of gold and silver is favourable to industry . . . . Here are a set of manufacturers or merchants . . . . who have received returns of gold and silver for goods which they sent to CADIZ. They are thereby enabled to employ more workmen than formerly, who never dream of demanding higher wages, but are glad of employment for such good paymasters. If workmen become scarce, the manufacturer gives higher wages, but at first requires an encrease of labor . . . . it is easy to trace the money in its progress through the whole commonwealth; where we shall find, that it must first quicken the diligence of every individual, before it encreases the price of labor [Hume, 1955, pp. 37–38].

It would therefore be fitting to call the prominent principle in current literature that an increased money growth rate raises output only temporarily the "Hume effect," to honor one of the greatest minds who ever wrote on economics, even though Hume did not discuss workers being temporarily fooled by inflation, and did not allow for the development of inflationary expectations.

The next monetarist characteristic is relatively greater concern about inflation than about unemployment and deflation. Hume was *not* a monetarist in this respect. He did not mention any losses resulting from inflation, and in this respect is similar to the mercantilists [Stadlin, 1954, p. 26]. In part, this may be due to the fact that, since he did not allow for the development of inflationary expectations, he did not appreciate that the temporary rise in output resulting from an increased money growth rate has to be paid for eventually. Another part of the explanation may be that Hume, like the mercantilists, did not treat full employment output as a given. Dealing as he was with an underdeveloped economy, he believed that there was a potential for rapid economic growth through stimulating production for the market rather than only for personal consumption (see Rotwein's introduction in Hume [1955], pp. LXI–LXVI). An increase in the money supply, by helping to monetize the economy, was therefore, desirable. Hence, he wrote:

The good policy of the magistrate consists only in keeping . . . money, if possible still encreasing; because, by that means, he keeps alive a spirit of industry in the nation, and encreases the stock of labour . . . . A nation whose money decreases, is actually, at that time, weaker and more miserable than another nation, which possesses no more money, but is on an encreasing hand [Hume, 1955, pp. 39–40].

The final monetarist proposition is the superiority of the free market over government intervention. In the contemporaneous context Hume, with his criticism of mercantilism, is obviously in the monetarist camp on this score, even though Viner warned us that "in Hume's economic writings the laissez-faire doctrine is to be found only by implication if at all" [Viner, 1937, p. 99]. An example of Hume's distrust of government intervention is his rejection of the "Keynesian" argument of some of his contemporaries that a large public debt is harmless because "we owe it to ourselves." In Hume's view:

The practice, therefore, of contracting debt will almost infallibly be abused, in every government. It would scarcely be more imprudent to give a prodigal son a credit in every banker's shop in London, than to impower a statesman to draw bills, in this manner, upon posterity [Hume, 1955, p. 92].

An underlying hallmark of monetarism is emphasis on the long run. This too, was shared by Hume. According to Keynes [1936, p. 343 n.]:

Hume began the practice amongst economists of stressing the importance of the equilibrium position as compared with the ever-shifting transition towards it, though he was still enough of a mercantilist not to overlook the fact that it is in the transition that we actually have our being.

In addition Hume, like modern monetarists, emphasized empirical testing. While of course he did not run regressions, he did—like Friedman and Schwartz—make much use of that other great source of empirical tests, history. Hume, after all, was the author of a massive and pioneering history of England. His writings are replete with references to the experience of both classical civilization and contemporary Europe. Moreover, like monetarists and unlike many Keynesians, he showed sympathy for businessmen whom he compared favorably to professionals [Hume, 1955, pp. 53–54]. Finally, on a much more detailed level, Hume [1955, p. 36] advocated 100 percent reserve banking.

NONMONETARIST ASPECTS OF HUME'S THOUGHT

Hume also held some views that are not monetarist. The most important one—explained by the time he lived in—was his great emphasis on economic development through monetizing the economy and his preference for rising prices. Hume also treated government debt as a close substitute for money, even calling it [p. 95] "a kind of paper credit" that tends to replace gold and silver in large transactions and to raise prices.

Moreover, Hume believed that, in moderation, taxation is desirable, since it stimulates effort.[8] In addition, Hume remained a mild protectionist [O'Brien, 1975, p. 36], and was concerned with increasing the strength and power of the British state relative to other states.[9]

Finally, Hume was a person who always saw both sides of any issue, and tried to make as good a case as he could for his opponents. He was too much of a skeptic to take unequivocal positions. [See Feilbogen, 1890, pp. 709–12.] This is hardly a salient characteristic of modern monetarism.

THE ROLE OF MODERN MONETARISTS' PROPOSITIONS IN HUME'S THOUGHT

Were Hume's monetarist ideas significant components of his thought, or mere casual asides? The quantity theory was obviously central to Hume's economics. In the transmission process, the Chicago monetarist's deemphasis of the channels of causation fits well into a dominating aspect of Hume's thought, his theory of causation. The focus on the money stock rather than the interest rate, as well as the proposition that money affects not only investment, but also consumption, are both required by Hume's theory of interest, which is an important component of his economics. The stability of the private sector received little explicit discussion by Hume, but that very fact suggests by implication that it was an important proposition for him. Hume was a man of wide social sympathy, and had he thought that unemployment was an important problem, he would, in all probability, have discussed it at length.

The next two monetarist propositions, the unimportance of allocative detail, and the treatment of the price level as a whole are not discussed by Hume, and can be read into his work only by implication.

8. See O'Brien [1975], p. 242. Many of his contemporaries went much farther than Hume and considered high taxes on workers to be desirable since this forces them to work harder. Hume, on the other hand, tempered his advocacy of taxes.He considered it a useful attribute of a tax that there was a natural limit beyond which it could not be expanded [Humphrey 1932, p. 286].

9. Johnson [1937, p. 177] argued that "although Hume's essays postulated that the happiness of individuals should be the purpose of policy, the greatness of the state should always be regarded as an even more important goal." But this may be an overstatement.

But then the same is true of most modern monetarist writings. Moreover, these propositions, despite being implicit, were important for Hume, since they are necessary implications of the quantity theory. But a preference for reduced-form models is relevant only in a very indirect way, since it relates to Hume's theory of causation.

The monetarist views of policy targets and indicators were, of course, not applicable in Hume's time, but on the issue of a monetary rule we have Hume's strong distrust of government intervention and his specie-flow mechanism, both of which were far from being mere asides. The absence of a long-run tradeoff between unemployment and inflation was also central to Hume because, if such a tradeoff exists, it weakens the specie-flow mechanism and the quantity theory, since prices then do not rise in proportion to the increase in the quantity of money. Mercantilist policies of reducing unemployment by improving the balance of trade might then succeed.

Another way to see whether monetarism played a significant, and not just a peripheral, role in Hume's thought is to reverse field, and ask whether the three basic themes running through Hume's monetary analysis are also important for modern monetarists. They are the quantity theory of money, the specie-flow mechanism, and the benefits of increased monetization of the economy. The first of these is obviously central to modern monetarism; the second is connected with certain propositions about the international distribution of (convertible) money that are basic to a close relative of modern monetarism, the monetary theory of the balance of payments. Only the third one, increased monetization—no longer a relevant issue in developed countries—is not part of modern monetarism.[10]

Stepping outside the confines of monetary theory, we meet two other ideas that were of great importance to Hume, and fit in well with modern monetarism. They are his distrust of government intervention and his theory of causation.

CONCLUSIONS

This paper discussed Hume's positions on twelve propositions of modern monetarism. On five of them he was explicitly in the monetarist camp. They are the following: the quantity theory, the Chicago school's transmission process, the stability of the private sector, the temporary effect of inflation on output, and a preference

10. The degree of monetization is, however, of great concern to one prominent economist who is, at least partially, a monetarist. See Shaw [1973].

for private market process. Two other monetarist propositions, the irrelevance of allocative detail and the focus on the price level as a unit rather than on individual prices, are clearly implied by the quantity theory, and hence Hume was implicitly a monetarist on these two issues also. Moreover, the use of a reduced-form model instead of a structural model fits in well with Hume's theory of causation. Further, while Hume did not advocate a stable money growth rate rule, such a rule follows naturally in the spirit of his writings, much better than a Keynesian belief in discretionary policy does. Two other characteristics of monetarism, using a reserve base measure as the monetary policy indicator and using the money stock as the target of monetary policy, were not relevant issues in Hume's day. The only monetarist characteristic Hume rejected is the monetarist's strong opposition to inflation.

UNIVERSITY OF CALIFORNIA, DAVIS

REFERENCES

Arkin, Marcus, "The Economic Writings of David Hume: A Reassessment," *South African Journal of Economics,* XXIV (1956), 204–20.

Blaugh, M., *Economic Theory in Retrospect* (Homewood, IL: Irwin, 1968).

Blake, Ralph, Curt Ducasse, and Edward Madden, *Theories of Scientific Method, The Renaissance Through the Nineteenth Century* (Seattle: University of Washington Press, 1960).

Brunner, Karl, and Allan Meltzer, "An Aggregative Theory for a Closed Economy," in Jerome Stein, ed., *Monetarism* (Amsterdam: North-Holland Publishing Co., 1976a), pp. 69–113.

——, "Reply—Monetarism: The Principal Issues, Areas of Agreement and the Work Remaining," in Jerome Stein, ed., *Monetarism* (Amsterdam: North-Holland Publishing Co., 1976b) pp. 150–82.

Dornbusch, Rudiger, "Comments" in Jerome Stein, ed., *Monetarism* (Amsterdam: North-Holland Publishing Co., 1976), pp. 104–25.

Fausten, Dietrich, "Beyond the Analytics of the Monetary Approach to the Balance of Payments: Methodology, Innovation and Monetarism," unpublished manuscript, 1978.

——, "On the Humean Origins of the Contemporary Monetary Approach to the Balance of Payments," this *Journal,* XCIII (Nov. 1979), 655–74.

Feilbogen, Sigmund, "Smith und Hume," *Zeitschrift fur die Gesamte Staatswissenschaft,* XLVI (1890), 695–716.

Fellner, William, "Schools of Thought in the Mainstream of American Economics," *Acta Oekonomica,* XVIII (1977), 247–62.

Frenkel, Jacob, "Adjustment Mechanisms and the Monetary Approach to the Balance of Payments: A Doctrinal Perspective," in E. Claasen and P. Salin, eds., *Recent Issues in International Monetary Economics* (Amsterdam: North-Holland Publishing Co., 1976), pp. 29–48.

Friedman, Milton, "Should There Be an Independent Monetary Authority?" in Leland Yeager, *In Search of a Monetary Constitution* (Cambridge, MA: Harvard University Press, 1962), pp. 219–43.

——, "The Role of Monetary Policy," *American Economic Review,* LVIII (1968), 1–17.

——, "25 Years After the Rediscovery of Money: What Have We Learned?: Discussion," *American Economic Review,* LXV (May 1975), 176–79.

Furniss, Edgar, *The Position of Labor in a System of Nationalism* (Boston: Houghton Mifflin, 1920).
Gordon, Robert J., "Comments," in Jerome Stein, *Monetarism* (Amsterdam: North-Holland Publishing Co., 1976), pp. 52–66.
Hegeland, Hugo, *The Quantity Theory of Money* (Gotenborg, Sweden: Elanders Boktryckeri, 1951).
Hume, David, *Writings on Economics,* E. Rotwein, ed. (London: Nelson, 1955).
Humphrey, Don, "David Hume: Economist," Ph.D. thesis, University of California, Berkeley, 1932.
Johnson, E. A. J., *Predecessors of Adam Smith* (London: P. S. King and Son, 1937).
Keleher, Robert, "Of Money and Prices: Some Historical Perspectives," unpublished manuscript, 1978.
Keynes, John Maynard, *The General Theory of Employment, Interest and Money* (New York: Harcourt-Brace, 1936).
Laidler, David, "Mayer on Monetarism: Comments from a Britist Point of View," in Thomas Mayer *et al., The Structure of Monetarism* (New York: W. W. Norton, 1978), pp. 133–144.
Leigh, Arthur, "John Locke and the Quantity Theory of Money," *History of Political Economy,* VI (1974), 200–19.
Lowe, J. M., "The Rate of Interest: British Monetary Opinion in the Eighteenth Century," *Manchester School,* XXII (May 1954), 115–38.
Mayer, Thomas, "The Structure of Monetarism," *Kredit und Kapital,* VIII (1975), 191–215, and 293–313; reprinted in T. Mayer *et al., The Structure of Monetarism* (New York: W. W. Norton, 1978).
Modigliani, Franco, "The Monetarist Controversy, or Should We Forsake Stabilization Policies?" Federal Reserve Bank of San Francisco, *Economic Review, Supplement* (Spring 1977).
O'Brien, D. P., *The Classical Economists* (Oxford: Clarendon Press, 1975).
Parkin, Michael, "A 'Monetarist' Analysis of the Generation and Transmission of World Inflation: 1958–71," American Economic Association, *Papers and Proceedings,* LXVII (1977), 164–71.
Patinkin, Don, *Money, Interest and Prices* (New York: Harper and Row, 1965).
——, "Keynesian Monetary Theory and the Cambridge School," Banca Nazionale del Lavoro, *Quarterly Review* (June 1972), 138–58.
Schumpeter, Joseph, *A History of Economic Analysis* (New York: Oxford University Press, 1954).
Sekine, Thomas, "The Discovery of International Monetary Equilibrium by Vanderlint, Cantillion, Gervais and Hume," *Economia Internazionale,* XXVI (May 1973), 262–82.
Shaw, Edward, *Financial Deepening in Economic Development* (New York: Oxford University Press, 1973).
Stadlin, Alois, *Die Entwicklung der Quantitatstheorie* (Winterthur, Germany: P. G. Keller, 1954).
Taylor, W. L., *Francis Hutcheson and David Hume as Predecessors of Adam Smith* (Durham, NC: Duke University Press, 1965).
Vickers, Douglas, "Method and Analysis in David Hume's Economic Essays," *Economica,* XXIV (Aug. 1957), 225–34.
——, *Studies in the Theory of Money 1690–1776* (New York: Augustus Kelley, 1968).
Viner, Jacob, *Studies in the Theory of International Trade* (New York: Harper and Row, 1937).
von Hayek, Friedrich, *Prices and Production* (London: George Routledge and Sons, 1935).
——, "Choice in Currency," Institute of Economic Affairs, London, Occasional Paper #48, 1976.

CHOOSING NEW INDUSTRIAL CAPACITY: ON-SITE EXPANSION, BRANCHING, AND RELOCATION*

ROGER W. SCHMENNER

A manufacturing firm can increase its capacity through expansion at existing sites, opening new plants, or relocating to new, larger space. These options are in fact not very good substitutes for one another. This paper argues why one might be preferred to the others and supports its view of the capacity choice with detailed evidence from over 400 plants in New England.

Evidence of the decentralizing of U. S. manufacturing activity continues to mount. Not only are cities losing plants and employment to suburban and rural areas, but the industry-rich North is losing plants and employment to the so-called Sunbelt. An important and traditional explanation for this decentralization is that factor cost differences work to spread economic activity to less-developed areas. And it is true that wage levels, land prices, and taxes have been lower in both suburban-rural and Sunbelt locales and that energy costs have been lower in the South and Southwest.

Technological change, particularly in the realm of transportation and communication, has made it easier for manufacturing plants to thrive apart from the traditional industrial enclaves of the Northern cities. The interstate highway system, for example, has certainly been a boon to both suburban and Sunbelt manufacturing. Plants' increased ability to flourish away from the old manufacturing centers has, in addition, spurred the exploitation of advances in plant design, particularly the land-extensive, single-story factory.

Further, as the Sunbelt has grown in population and income, it makes more sense for manufacturers to locate there simply to supply that market with goods it previously imported from elsewhere. Within metropolitan areas, the dispersion of industry has been aided by the concomitant decentralization of population.

Without at all diminishing the importance of these explanations of industrial decentralization, I would like to suggest in this paper that some managerial considerations also exist that can act independently

* This paper is derived from a broader study of industrial location funded by grants from the Office of Economic Research, Economic Development Administration, the U. S. Department of Commerce to the Harvard-MIT Joint Center for Urban Studies, and from the Associates of the Harvard Business School. I wish to thank John Hekman, John R. Meyer, Clint Oster, Raymond Struyk, and a referee for comments on previous drafts.

The Quarterly Journal of Economics, August 1980 0033-5533/80/0095-0103$01.70

to spread out economic activity. These considerations deal fundamentally with how manufacturers cope with the diseconomies of scale that develop in their plants and what geographic portfolio of plants these manufacturers view themselves supporting.

I. On-Site Plant Expansion: Its Attractions, Its Perils, and Their Remedies

On-site plant expansion is by far the most popular means of adding industrial capacity. My data suggest that between 6 and 9 percent of all plants actually expand on-site during any one year [Schmenner, 1978]. It is generally the cheapest way to add capacity, the least disruptive to current operations, and often the quickest way to expand.

Although frequently attractive, on-site plant expansion can usher in a host of diseconomies as well, particularly if it has been a repeated practice. For example, as more production space is added on-site, a plant's layout typically becomes less optimal, since only a few portions of the plant get shifted around at any one time. Over time departments, once close together, become separated. Materials handling and storage become more difficult, with more delays and errors. Managers find themselves isolated from one another, or from the work groups they oversee, or both. In short, intra-plant transportation and communication become strained, with detrimental consequences for product delivery and quality.

Staying at the same site often postpones the introduction of new process technology as well. Old equipment is kept in use, old methods are followed, and the advantages of new equipment and techniques are forgone with consequences for both future costs and product innovation.

Continued on-site expansion means that more workers, and often more products, must be managed. Such a layering of expanded responsibilities creates real complexities for managers at all levels. The existing cadre of managers may be asked to supervise more than they are readily capable of, thus lessening the attention certain problems should receive. With more products and output from the same plant, decisions on the levels, composition, and uses of inventories become more difficult. Decisions on production control—what and when to produce, how to sequence it through the factory—become vastly more complex as well, just as the cost accounting system is becoming more arbitrary and thus less helpful. With more products in the plant, management runs the risk not only of complicating supervision, inventory, and production control systems, but also of placing demands on managers, workers, and systems that are incompatible.

The addition of more workers to an existing site is also apt to require an increasingly formal workforce-management relationship. The workforce is less apt to identify strongly with the company, and labor relations within the plant may become strained. Old management concessions to the workforce may come back to haunt operations, especially new ones. With increasing size as well, the plant is more likely to become a target for unionization, if it is not already organized.

For these reasons, continued on-site expansion becomes less and less desirable. The alternatives, branching and relocation, can avoid many of these long-term and frequently subtle pitfalls of on-site expansion, although their abilities to surmount certain of them differ.

New branch establishment, for example, is at a relative advantage if the plant's problems run more to product proliferation, workforce size, or meeting expected future growth. By branching, a company can avoid overloading one plant with too many products or workers. At the same time, a new branch can exploit the latest production technology and the most sensible plant design. The operating policies of the branch can also be meshed carefully with the product(s) chosen for manufacture and with the competitive priorities (e.g., cost, delivery) attached to them.

Plant relocation, on the other hand, is at a relative advantage if the plant's problems are more involved with plant layout, materials handling and storage, new process technology, production and inventory control, or a perceived shortage of managers capable of operating independently in separate plants. Relocation can readily scrap old capital, technology, and policies for new. Thus, relocation gains in standing when the plant's problems are less related to large size and more to process technology and control.

Given this background of diseconomies of plant scale and the relative advantages of branching and relocation, one should expect the growing firm to view on-site expansion, branching, and relocation not so much as substitutes, but as distinct choices. Only for larger plants would all three alternatives be considered, since those plants would be much more likely to suffer from several problems at once.

II. The Empirical Evidence

The empirical evidence rewards this expectation as well as the characterizations of branch establishment and plant relocation. The

TABLE I

DATA SOUGHT BY PLANT SURVEYS

I. Company Identity

- Company name
- Street address of plant
- Status as headquarters plant, branch plant, or subsidiary operation
- Name of headquarters or parent company (if applicable)
- Street address of headquarters or parent company (if applicable)
- Chief executive officer of parent company (if applicable)
- Year of company founding
- Year plant was first occupied by this company
- Whether plant's founder lived in Cincinnati or New England prior to founding plant there
- How true it is that plant was located to offer the chief executive officer(s) a short commute

II. Nature of Plant

- Major products manufactured at plant
- Number of products produced
- Number of product lines
- Extent of new product development
- Presence of selected business functions at plant (e.g., personnel, purchasing, marketing, etc.)
- General type of production process employed (e.g., job shop, line flow)
- Character of plant space required (e.g., loft space, single story, special construction)
- Acreage of plant site and square footage of plant itself
- Extent of room for expansion
- Past 10-year history of expansion on-site (year and area added)
- Number of structures on site
- How those structures were acquired (e.g., built, bought, leased)
- Nature of major structure on site (e.g., multistory, single story)
- Whether plant is sole occupant of site
- Nature of site's previous use
- Skill level of labor employed
- Average employment over past year
- Maximum employment over last 5 years
- Number of shifts run at plant
- Whether workers are unionized
- Sites of any warehousing
- Plant's use of water
- Plant's use of various public utilities
- Any disappointment with present site

III. Concerns for Transportation and Proximity

- Distance to nearest expressway interchange
- Use of any railroad siding
- Percent of plant's output shipped by various transportation modes
- Percent of plant's inputs shipped by various transportation modes
- Perceived importance of transportation costs to business

TABLE I (*continued*)

	Perceived value of proximity to labor, suppliers, customers, financial institutions, special services, railroad reciprocal switching limits, commercial truck zone
IV.	Rough Statistics
	Plant's latest annual sales
	Materials costs, as a percent of sales
	Labor costs (including fringe benefits), as a percent of sales
	Annual rent, or value of land and buildings
	Value of plant's equipment and inventories
V.	Character of Plant's Market and Suppliers
	Recent average annual rate of growth
	Character of market for plant—percent of output to various classes of buyers (e.g., wholesalers)—percent of output to various geographic areas (e.g., Midwest, nationally)
	Change in any categories in preceding question over past 10 years
	Character of plant's suppliers—percent of inputs from various geographic areas
	Change in any categories in preceding question over past 10 years
	Whether suppliers have remained the same over time
VI.	General Changes over the Past 10 Years
	Change in nature of products produced
	Change in extent of product lines
	Nature of sales (e.g., cyclical, steadily growing)
	Change in reliance on truck transportation
	Transport costs, as a percent of sales
	Changes in production technology over past 10 years
	Changes, as a percent of sales, to labor costs, materials costs, and profit rates
VII.	Choice of Branching or Relocation
	(*Asked Only of Stationary Plants*)
	Whether plant seriously considered relocating since 1970
	Whether plant considered establishing a branch operation
	Whether, in fact, a branch plant was established
	Whether plant expanded on site as an alternative
	Whether plant has absorbed operations from other plants since shut down
	(*Asked of Relocating Plants*)
	Had a new branch operation been considered as alternative

data for this study were derived from questionnaires sent to manufacturing plants in New England. The questionnaire asked about a plant's present operations and recent history, and about its production, marketing, purchasing, and financial character. A list of the data asked of each plant is given in Table I.

The sample included plants that had relocated since 1970, as well as those that had remained at their present locations.[1] For both types of plants it is also known whether they had spun off new branch plants. More than this, it is known whether relocating plants had "considered establishing a branch operation rather than relocating," and for plants remaining at the same location it is known whether their companies had "seriously contemplated" a relocation or a new branch operation. Thus, the data identify those plants that had thought seriously of relocation or branching as well as those that had actually carried through with relocations or branch establishments in New England.[2]

The sample numbers 407 plants, of which 141 relocated during the time period 1970–1976. All of the plants employed at least 20 workers, and 209 were unambiguously part of a multi-plant corporation. The sample is thus richer in larger plants, relocated plants, and branch plants than is the entire population of manufacturing establishments.

The results of the analysis of these surveys are presented below in three subsections: a. considering the choices, b. the decision to branch, and c. the decision to relocate.

a. Considering the Choices

The extent to which plants contemplate one or the other option is reflected in Figure I, which is a Venn diagram indicating the sets of responding stationary plants in New England that (i) expanded on-site, (ii) thought seriously of relocating their plant, or (iii) thought seriously of or actually established a new branch plant. Accompanying the plant counts in the diagram are average employment levels for the plants in each subset.

The data reveal a good deal of overlap in considering capacity and location. Of those plants that either thought seriously of moving or branching or that actually expanded on-site, 45 percent considered more than one alternative, although only 5 percent thought or acted on all three. Yet, the fact remains that a clear majority of plants seriously considered or acted on only a single choice, if they considered any choices at all. On-site expansion, branching, and plant relocation do appear to be allied but not perfectly substitutable means of aug-

1. Data for relocated plants included information about their previous sites and operations as well.

2. Tracking down plants that moved from New England was next to impossible, and only a few such movers were confirmed. None provided usable data. Evidence from the study indicates that interregional moves are rare occurrences; far more important are moves within a region, and, indeed, within twenty miles of the initial location.

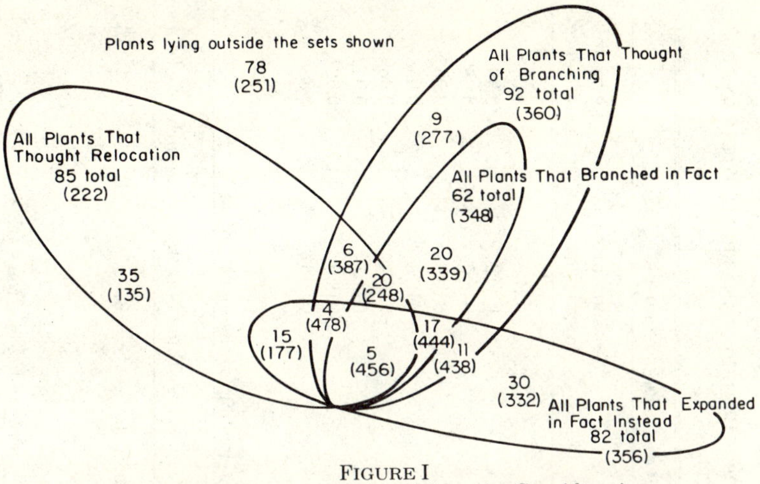

FIGURE I
New England Stationary Plants' Capacity Considerations
Venn Diagram

All Stationary Plants in diagram total 250 in number.

Note: Figures shown in parentheses are average employment figures.

menting capacity.

The confirmation of expectations is reinforced by the employment data in the diagram. Those plants contemplating more than one means of augmenting capacity are, on average, larger than the plants that consider only one or the other. Size definitely complicates the scope of the decision. Furthermore, as expected, those plants contemplating a new branch are, on the average, larger than those plants contemplating relocation.

b. The Decision to Branch

The character of the branching decision has been investigated further using probit analysis. Two probit analyses have been performed. The first, Table II, estimates how the probability of contemplating new branch establishment is influenced by a variety of plant-specific characteristics. The dependent variable is a 0–1 dummy variable that takes the value 1 if the plant thought seriously of branching and is 0 otherwise. Only those influencing variables whose estimated coefficients are significantly different from zero are listed in the table. The coefficients listed are the so-called C-standardized coefficients that represent the rate of change of the probability, P, evaluated at $p = 0.5$, for a change of one standard deviation in the value of the independent variable in question when all other independent variables are held fixed. This coefficient, then, can be in-

TABLE II

DIFFERENTIATING PLANTS THAT THOUGHT SERIOUSLY ABOUT ESTABLISHING A NEW BRANCH PLANT FROM OTHER PLANTS THAT HAVE REMAINED AT THE SAME LOCATION

Summary of Probit Analysis for New England (only significant coefficients retained)

Variables (in order of importance)	C-standardized coefficient	Level of significance
Multi-plant status (0 = single-plant company, 1 = multi-plant)	0.163	1.000
Product line change over 10 years (high value = more products)	0.118	0.999
New product development (high value = all the time)	0.090	0.987
Kind of labor (low value = high skilled)	0.089	0.987
Importance of transportation (high value = slight importance)	−0.076	0.968
Built-bought-leased (high value = leased)	−0.074	0.969
Sales growth rate over last 5–10 years	0.061	0.942
Percent of inputs purchased nationally outside New England	−0.059	0.921
Change in labor costs/sales over past 10 years (low value = increase, high value = decline)	0.048	0.882

Goodness of fit: $R^2 = 0.275$ Number of observations = 192

Splitting at $P = 0.5$: Predicted

True	Did not think branch	Thought branch	Totals
Did not think branch	96	20	116
Thought branch	27	49	76
Totals	123	69	192

Probability of error = 0.245

Peeling off the top: Predicted

True	Did not think branch	Thought branch	Totals
Did not think branch	91	25	116
Thought branch	25	51	76
Totals	116	76	192

Probability of error = 0.260

terpreted as the loss of explanatory power that would result if the particular variable in question were dropped from the model. Thus, the larger this C-standardized coefficient, the more important, in some sense, the variable is to our ability to differentiate between the types of plants. The table lists the variables in descending order of importance.

Table II differentiates those stationary plants thinking of establishing a new branch plant from other stationary plants. The results confirm in large measure the relative advantages outlined above for new branch plants. To put these results in broad, interpretive terms, the base plant contemplating the opening of a new branch plant tends to be an already well-established but rapidly growing plant of a multi-plant operation, well-established in the sense that it enjoys a facility built expressly for its particular operation and also in the sense that it has been devoted to reducing labor costs. These facts suggest that the products produced are nonspecialized, and this, in turn, is supported by the sensitivity the plants shows toward transportation costs. The plant feels compromised by transport costs from competing in some geographic markets, and even its inputs tend more to be purchased within the region, perhaps because they are nonspecialized as well. The base plant's rapid growth may be accounted for by a geographic market expansion that makes the plant's management feel uncomfortable. The rapid growth, however, may also be accounted for by product line expansions. In that case, the plant's discomfort may be caused by a proliferation of products. These findings, then, are totally in concert with the expectations one derives from the relative advantages branching enjoys vis à vis on-site expansion and relocation.

The success of the model in classifying plants can be gauged by how much better it does relative to the simple decision rule of classifying every plant as one that followed the rule of the majority. In this case, three-fifths of the sample did not think of branching, so under the simple decision rule, the two-fifths of the sample that did think of branching would have been misclassified. In contrast, the model misclassifies only a quarter of the plants, which is a definite improvement.

A similar probit analysis has been performed for those stationary plants that actually opened new branches. The findings from these two probit analyses can be compared, and conclusions can be reached as to what factors actually tip a plant's management from simply considering the issue to taking action on it.

Table III displays the results of this second probit analysis. The

TABLE III

DIFFERENTIATING PLANTS THAT HAVE OPENED BRANCH PLANTS FROM OTHER PLANTS THAT HAVE REMAINED AT THE SAME LOCATION

Summary of Probit Analysis for New England
(only significant coefficients retained)

Variables (in order of importance)	*C*-standardized coefficient	Level of significance
Multi-plant status (0 = single-plant company, 1 = multi-plant)	0.293	0.998
Capital-to-labor ratio	0.165	0.919
Change in sales (low value = steadily increasing sales)	−0.146	0.990
New product development (high value = all the time)	0.130	0.974
Employment	0.123	0.987
Number of products produced at plant	−0.121	0.964
Self-sufficiency (high value = more corporate functions performed at plant)	0.114	0.962
Value of proximity to suppliers (low value = proximity valued)	0.099	0.958
Kind of labor (low value = high skilled)	0.083	0.926

Goodness of fit: $R^2 = 0.339$ Number of observations = 115

Splitting at $P = 0.5$: Predicted

True	No branching	Branched	Totals
No branching	78	5	83
Branched	15	17	32
Totals	93	22	115

Probability of error = 0.174

Peeling off the top: Predicted

True	No branching	Branched	Totals
No branching	73	10	83
Branched	10	22	32
Totals	83	32	115

Probability of error = 0.174

error rate of this probit model is less than that of the one introduced above. Plants that actually branch are apparently more easily differentiated than plants that only think about it. The error rate falls to 17.4 percent, which lies below the error rate implied by the simple decision rule of classifying all plants as nonbranching, namely 27.8 percent. The model thus appears to be a significant improvement in distinguishing plants that actually establish a new branch from others.

Broadly interpreted, the results suggest that the base plant which opens a new branch is very much like the plant which considered a new branch. This, of course, is not surprising, since so many of those plants considering a new branch actually go ahead with it, 69 percent using the New England data. In general, plants of multi-plant operations with rapid growth, lots of new product development, and a low labor skill, high capital investment process technology are more likely both to consider and actually to open a new branch facility. But those plants that do open new branches share some other, important differentiating characteristics that do not surface in Table II's probit analysis.

The base plant that actually branches is not only growing, but is already big. Further, it is largely self-sufficient, and thereby an ideal base plant for spinning off branch or satellite plants producing more well-established products that can be supported from the base plant. Nevertheless, despite its size the base plant manufactures a relatively low number of products. This is an important consideration. Despite a strong tradition of new product development, the base plant spinning off a branch appears devoted to a narrow product line itself and a capital-intensive, low labor skill production process. One other variable is conspicuous by its absence: apparently the extent of room for expansion on-site has no bearing on a plant's branching. New branches are established even when sufficient space exists for on-site expansion. As we shall see, this is not the case for relocating plants.

An underlying theme suggested by these results and corroborated by company interviews is the company's pursuit of a specific multi-plant manufacturing strategy. By this I mean a predetermined view of how each plant's output fits together to serve the company's market. The probit analyses suggest two distinct multi-plant strategies, one of placing different products in separate plants, and one of separating plants geographically into market areas. The former strategy is supported by evidence of new product development coupled with narrow product lines at the base plant. The latter is supported by the revealed importance of transportation to markets and the revealed

TABLE IV

DIFFERENTIATING PLANTS THAT THOUGHT SERIOUSLY OF MOVING, BUT DID NOT, FROM OTHER PLANTS THAT HAVE REMAINED AT THE SAME LOCATION

Summary of Probit Analysis for New England
(only significant coefficients retained)

Variables (in order of importance)	C-standardized coefficient	Level of significance
Percent of output sold direct or through retailers	−0.138	1.000
Multi-plant status (0 = single-plant company, 1 = multi-plant)	0.086	0.979
Sole occupant of site (1 = yes, 2 = no)	0.082	0.976
Percent of inputs delivered by truck	0.082	0.970
Change in labor costs/sales over last 10 years (low value = increase, high value = decline)	−0.072	0.949
Value of proximity to labor (low value = proximity valued)	0.068	0.947
Percent of costs attributable to materials	0.068	0.945
Kind of labor (low value = skilled)	−0.061	0.924

Goodness of fit: $R^2 = 0.144$ Number of observations = 159

Splitting at $P = 0.5$: Predicted

True	Did not think move	Thought move	Totals
Did not think move	86	15	101
Thought move	36	22	58
Totals	122	37	159

Probability of error = 0.321

Peeling off the top: Predicted

True	Did not think move	Thought move	Totals
Did not think move	74	27	101
Thought move	27	31	58
Totals	101	58	159

Probability of error = 0.340

unimportance of locating close to suppliers. New branch dependence on markets and not suppliers buttresses the observation of continuing decentralization for manufacturing.

The corroborating interview evidence, as well as other survey evidence from the larger study, suggests five different multi-plant manufacturing strategies:[3] (1) a product plant strategy, where distinct products or product lines are manufactured in separate plants, each plant serving the company's entire domestic market area; (2) a market area plant strategy where plants are designated to serve particular sub-national market areas, manufacturing all or most of the corporation's product line; (3) a product-market plant strategy, found in corporations so large that market area plants can be assigned within a product division organization; (4) a process plant strategy where, rather than separate their products into individual plants some companies, notably those with complex products, separate their production process into various plants that are often viewed as feeders to one or more final assembly plants; and (5) a general purpose plant strategy where no specific plant charters exist, but where flexibility in adapting to constantly changing product needs (e.g., defense contracting) is prized.

The probit analysis results are certainly consistent with the view expressed in most of the company interviews that manufacturers are deeply concerned with the melding of a new branch plant into an existing multi-plant strategy. And, to the extent that such a strategy clearly dictates the geographic dispersion of manufacturing (e.g., market area and product-market plants), the decentralization of manufacturing activity is assured.

Even under other strategies, it is not likely that all of a company's manufacturing will be concentrated into just a few local jurisdictions. Most companies want to give their product plants or divisions considerable autonomy. Often this means a geographic separation of division headquarters as well as of manufacturing plants. To the extent, also, that plants or divisions may have been acquired by merger or purchase, geographic decentralization is likely to persist.

c. The Decision to Relocate

Two other probit analyses have been performed. Table IV's analysis differentiates plants that seriously thought of relocating, but did not, from other plants that remained stationary. The plant that

3. For more detail see Schmenner [1979] and [1978].

TABLE V

DIFFERENTIATING MOVER FROM STATIONARY PLANTS

Summary of Probit Analysis for New England
(only significant coefficients retained)

Variables (in order of importance)	C-standardized coefficient	Level of significance
Room to expand, before move (high value = none)	0.216	1.000
Employment	−0.141	0.978
Percent of output sold nationally outside New England	0.111	0.997
Square feet of plant per worker, before move	−0.095	0.996
Multi-plant status (0 = single-plant company, 1 = multi-plant)	−0.095	0.993
10-year change in materials as percent of sales (high value = decreasing percent)	0.090	0.991
Labor as percent of sales	−0.084	0.984
Degree of product change (low value = no change)	−0.074	0.970
Percent of input value bought nationally outside New England	0.069	0.964
Growth rate of sales over last 5–10 years	0.055	0.926
Degree of warehousing off-site (low value = none off-site)	−0.068	0.956

Goodness of fit: $R^2 = 0.408$ Number of observations = 253

Splitting at $P = 0.5$: Predicted

True	Stationary plant	Mover plant	Totals
Stationary plant	135	21	156
Mover plant	27	70	97
Totals	162	91	253

Probability of error = 0.190

Peeling off the top: Predicted

True	Stationary plant	Mover plant	Totals
Stationary plant	131	25	156
Mover plant	25	72	97
Totals	156	97	253

Probability of error = 0.198

contemplated relocation, but did not follow through, is conspicuously different from the plant that seriously considered branching.

In broad terms, the plant that remained stationary over the period, but that thought seriously of relocating, is largely one that does not feel itself tied down geographically in its sales, its materials, or its labor. Its sales channels appear to be well established, its multiplant status no doubt contributing to this feeling. The plant itself is one that combines high-skilled labor with high-valued inputs that appear readily delivered anywhere by truck. The plant pulls its skilled labor force from a large area, and thus places low value on close proximity to labor. There are indications, too, that the plant may be feeling uneasy about its present location because labor costs have been rising there; the plant may thus be thinking of a relocation as a means of escape.

This probit formulation performs less well than the others. Not only is the error rate higher, but the difference between the error rate estimated, about a third, and the error rate implied by the simple decision rule of classifying all plants as not contemplating relocation, 36.5 percent, is small.

Plants that actually relocate are markedly different from plants that only think about it. The mover plant tends to be small, in need of increased production space, independent of other plants, growing, but tied to an unsophisticated logistics system. These general characteristics are evident from the results depicted in Table V.

The fundamental impact of the need for additional space is demonstrated by the importance of the "room to expand" and "square feet of plant per worker" variable coefficients. That mover plants are generally smaller than others is signaled by the employment variable and its high rank in the variable list.

The independent nature of mover plants and thus their ability to be footloose in their locations is confirmed in several ways. For one, the more the plant engages in sales or purchases outside New England, the more likely it is to be a mover plant. Plants with lower labor costs as a percent of sales and plants that have experienced declines in materials costs as a percent of sales over the last ten years, both signs of independence, are more likely to relocate. Single-plant companies, typically more independent than branch plants, emerge, too, as more likely movers, as do plants that have not pursued radical changes in their product offerings.

The immaturity of the logistics systems for mover plants is evident by the result that the more complex and geographically dispersed the warehousing, the less likely the plant is to relocate. Finally, the positive and significant coefficient for the growth rate variable confirms that mover plants are those that are typically growing more rapidly than stationary plants, in many instances, no doubt, forcing space problems on the firm.

This probit model seems able to halve the error rate implied for a simple look at the relative magnitudes of movers and stationary plants in the sample; from 38 percent, the error rate is reduced to between 19 and 20 percent.

Table V refers to plants that have actually moved and differentiates between them and plants that have remained stationary. The probit analysis reported in Table IV differentiated between those stationary plants that seriously considered relocation but did not relocate, and those that did not even consider relocation. The influences showing up there as important to the plant considering relocation evoke notions of escape and the corresponding ability to do so, but they do not carry with them the urgency and independence of the actual mover. Only one variable coefficient, that of multi-plant status, turns up as significantly different from zero in both those probit analyses, but it carries a different sign in each. Whereas actual movers are associated more with single-plant companies, plants that only considered relocation are associated more with multi-plant companies. For actual movers concerns for space, growth, independence, and simplicity emerge as key discriminating factors. On the other hand, with stationary plants that considered relocation but did not act, the key differentiating factors are the sales and logistics freedom of the plant, its relatively loose ties to particular sites and to a particular labor force, and its concern over increasing labor costs. Any indication of the space needs, growth, and independent simplicity of the actual mover plant is missing.

What is striking about this result is that the typical mover plant is so much characterized by managerial considerations and not by more factor-related items such as rising labor costs or transportation costs. Moreover, that space problems and not product change loom so large for the mover plant is confirmation of some of the relative advantages of relocation versus branching or on-site expansion. The importance of space, of independence, and of simple logistics all argue as well for the decentralization of manufacturing. Most mover plant destinations are within twenty miles of their origins (see Schmenner [1978]) anyway, but the footlooseness of such plants frees them for new, decentralized locations, and the importance of space acts to make vacant suburban and rural sites relatively more attractive to the relocating plant than sites within an already developed central city.

This paper has presented evidence for adding some explicitly managerial considerations to the traditional and powerful explanations for the decentralization of manufacturing. These managerial considerations derive largely from consideration of the ways that the diseconomies which accompany increasingly centralized manufacturing can be avoided. Some argue for branching and some for relocation. In any event, they complement forces such as factor price differentials, technological change, and regional import substitution in explaining the decentralization of manufacturing, and moreover, they serve to explain much of the character of that decentralization as well.

JOINT CENTER FOR URBAN STUDIES OF THE
MASSACHUSETTS INSTITUTE OF TECHNOLOGY AND HARVARD UNIVERSITY

REFERENCES

Schmenner, Roger W., *The Manufacturing Location Decision: Evidence from Cincinnati and New England,* report to the Economic Development Administration, U.S. Department of Commerce, March 1978.

—— "Look Beyond the Obvious in Plant Location," *Harvard Business Review,* LVII (Jan.–Feb. 1979), 126–32.

SOVIET HOUSEHOLD SAVING: A CROSS-SECTION STUDY OF SOVIET EMIGRANT FAMILIES*

GUR OFER AND JOYCE PICKERSGILL

This study examines the saving patterns of Soviet households by developing a saving function based on cross-section data derived from a family budget survey of Soviet emigrants. The results are very similar to those of Western studies. While saving is a positive function of current income, the average rate of saving rises only relatively mildly with income, indicating that current income from the public sector is much more "permanent" than in market economies. The proportion of income earned from the private sector that is saved is much higher—indicating that it is highly transitory and risky. The long-run saving rate is, by international comparison, rather low.

I. INTRODUCTION

According to the conventional theory of Soviet planning, the level of investment is unrelated to the level of household saving. The amount of resources designated for investment purposes is acquired, as are all other public funds, from the household sector in the form of taxes and from the production sector in the form of taxes and profits. With a few minor exceptions, households are not permitted to invest in productive assets directly. For these reasons, private savings have not been considered to be an important element influencing the level and composition of Soviet output. In fact, when private saving started to grow during the latter part of the 1950s and 1960s, many students of the Soviet economy explained the phenomenon mainly as "forced saving," a manifestation of repressed inflation, since there seemed to be no reason for Soviet households to save [Bronson and Severin, 1970, 1973; Keizer, 1971; and Bush, 1973].

Recent work by Pickersgill [1976, 1977] and Millar and Pickersgill [1977], employing both a time-series analysis of Soviet household saving and an aggregate model of the Soviet economy, cast doubt on the forced saving hypothesis and the consequent separation of the planners' decisions on the level of investment from the households' decisions on the level of their saving. The purpose of this paper is to extend the analysis of Soviet household saving, by developing a saving function based on cross-section data derived from a family budget survey of Soviet emigrants.

* An earlier version of this paper was prepared at the Rand Corporation, where Gur Ofer spent a year on leave. The paper benefited from the comments of Khan A. Mohabbat, Bill Butz, Jim Hosek, and Chuck Phelps, as well the participants in a session at the Western Economic Association meetings in Hawaii in June, 1978, and in a seminar held at Rand. We would also like to thank Avi Timkin for his research assistance and Aron Vinokur for his helpful comments on the revised draft.

The Quarterly Journal of Economics, August 1980 0033-5533/80/0095-0121$02.40

First of all, we propose to use Western theories of household saving behavior to explain similar behavior in the Soviet Union. Although the Soviet economy is characterized as a planned economy, not all resources are centrally allocated. Despite the planned allocation of natural resources and intermediate goods by the central planners, the supply of labor, the demand for consumer goods, and the allocation of household income between consumption and saving is not directly determined by the planners. To influence household choices in these three areas, the planners must alter the costs and benefits of household decisions, and thus, indirectly, their choices.

Soviet households, like their Western counterparts, make choices with respect to the education, occupation, and employment of the various family members, all of which affect their lifetime income. Soviet workers allocate their time between leisure activities, public employment, and within certain constraints, private employment.[1] Despite the labor controls used by the central planners, workers can supplement income from their official place of employment through moonlighting in the public sector or engaging in legal, quasi-legal, or illegal activity in the private sector. In addition, each Soviet household may allocate the income it earns to the purchase of a variety of consumer goods from the public and private sectors and may save a portion of its income for future comsumption.

Given that there is wide room for choice, we proceed by assuming that Soviet households, like Western ones, behave in ways consistent with utility maximization and that neoclassical theories of consumer behavior such as those of Becker and Lancaster are applicable also in the Soviet Union. In particular, we expect to observe behavior similar to that in the West with respect to saving; for example, positive saving when current income is high relative to lifetime income, and zero or negative saving when current income is relatively low.[2] We would expect Soviet household saving patterns to differ from Western patterns to the extent that differences in the respective economic systems influence income patterns and the opportunities for and the constraints on the use of this income.

In the next section of the paper, we consider the nature of the opportunities and constraints that may influence Soviet household saving behavior and discuss probable Soviet savings patterns. Section

1. Although the vast majority of the adult Soviet population is in the labor force and has jobs in the public sector, an individual still has some choice with respect to overtime, date of entry into the labor force, and retirement.

2. For a survey of Western studies on saving and consumption see Mayer [1972], and Mikesell and Zinser [1973].

III is devoted to a description of the data base and the variables, and in Section IV the empirical results are presented.

II. Variables Influencing Soviet Household Saving

In this section we outline Soviet income and expenditure patterns and investment opportunities. Differences between Soviet and Western institutions and practices that may affect saving behavior are discussed, using the approach of the permanent income and life cycle theories of saving and consumption.

A. *Income Patterns*

The pattern of income derived from the public sector in the Soviet Union differs in two major respects from income earned in a market economy. First, Soviet income shows less variation over the life cycle than commonly observed in market economies, and short-run income variations around the long-run trend are narrower. Since one of the major motives for saving is to transfer income from high- to low-income periods, the rate of saving out of public income in the Soviet Union should be lower than that found in market economies. These statements do not relate to income from private sources, which may vary as much or even more than incomes in market economies in both the long and the short run. For this reason, we treat public and private sources of income separately.

1. *The Soviet Life Cycle Income.* The reduced income variation is in part due to the fact that the overwhelming proportion of Soviet personal income is derived from wages and salaries, the most stable element in total income. In addition, wage differentials among occupations, and according to skill levels and seniority within occupations, are narrower than in most Western economies [Chapman, 1977; and McAuley, 1977]. Moreover, these wage differentials have been declining in the Soviet Union since the 1950s. Further, the income of the Soviet household at retirement is cushioned by a mandatory pension system, which, despite a rising trend, is still substantially below the worker's pre-retirement income. Finally, both pre-retirement income and, more importantly, retirement income, are supplemented by substantial transfers-in-kind in the form of free education and medical care, low-cost housing and transportation, and the subsidization of some other basic items, all of which contribute to a smoother income trend over the life cycle.

2. *Variations in Current Income Around the Life Cycle Trend.* Many of the major sources of short-run income instability in the West

are absent or sharply reduced in the Soviet Union. First, labor income is, in the the short run, more stable than entrepreneurial income, and its dominance in Soviet personal income thus dampens short-run income variations. Second, short-run wage variations are narrower mainly because of the much lower incidence of open (and unpaid) unemployment in the Soviet Union. This is due to smaller cyclical variations in the level of economic activity and to the fact that Soviet enterprises are not motivated to lay off workers but rather find it in their interest to retain extra workers as a buffer. To the extent that cyclical variations do exist, they affect mainly the quantity and quality of consumer goods, and since prices remain constant, also the level of *real* income.[3] The effect on saving of this last phenomenon is discussed below.

A possible source of income variation over the short run is the supplementary wage or bonus. In 1974 various bonus payments amounted to 11 percent of the wage bill. Bonuses and premiums that are paid as rewards for fulfillment and overfulfillment of targets for sales, profits, labor productivity, etc. are paid on a monthly basis to managerial and technical personnel and at year end to all workers. For the first group, bonuses amount to 30 or even 75 percent of their annual salaries, and this may cause significant income variations. However, in many cases the bonus is used as a more or less permanent addition to a wage rate that is out of equilibrium in periods between wage reforms and in such cases forms a part of anticipated income.

The most important source of household entrepreneurial income in the Soviet Union is the proceeds from the sale of produce grown by farmers and others on legal, private agricultural plots. The probable high variation in these incomes as well as the investment opportunity that the private plot provides (see below) probably causes the Soviet farmer to save more than he would have on the basis of the much more stable income stream he gets from the collective farm. But since our sample is entirely urban, there is no way to test hypotheses on rural saving habits.

3. *Private Urban Incomes.* There is a good deal of evidence that many urban families in the Soviet Union supplement their incomes from the public sector with private income; in addition to a small number of private plots and some renting of rooms or dachas, people earn money by a whole range of activities from the provision of medical services on private account to the pilferage of goods from the

3. From recent econometric work, we know that cyclical variations in Soviet output are largely connected with the fate of the harvest; see Green and Higgins [1977].

main place of work. In our sample more than 40 percent of all families reported having some private income. For all families private income averages around 12–15 percent of official income [Ofer, Vinokur, and Bar-Chaim, 1979]. One would certainly expect much greater variation in this unofficial income than in income earned at the main place of work. Also, such incomes are in many cases less than fully legal and thus highly risky. High variance and high risk are the two major characteristics of entrepreneurial earnings in market economies, and the two major reasons that high proportions of such earnings are saved. We should thus expect high rates of savings from private income also in the Soviet Union.

B. Expenditure Patterns

In addition to the level and pattern of variation of Soviet household incomes, the propensity to save may be affected by the unique characteristics of Soviet capital and consumer goods markets. These characteristics include a restricted set of portfolio choices facing the typical Soviet household, the lack of consumer credit, the state provision of a variety of "free" goods and services, the stochastic nature of the availability of consumer goods, the absence of inheritance taxes, and the taste for inconspicuous behavior. In the section below we shall outline these characteristics and their implications for Soviet saving.

1. Portfolio Choices. In a market economy households may select a wide variety of real and financial assets, varying with respect to risk, yield, and liquidity. By contrast, Soviet households are not allowed to acquire or hold productive assets (or claims to them), and as mentioned above, investment, financed from the budget of the public sector, is divorced from household savings. They may hold currency, savings deposits, 3 percent lottery bonds, consumer durables, and jewelry. The interest paid on savings deposits ranges from 2 to 3 percent. Although this rate is comparable to or even higher than the real rate paid on savings deposits in the United States today, the lack of higher yield, higher risk assets, such as common stocks or direct investment in productive capital, must result in a significant reduction of the proportion of permanent income saved in the Soviet Union.[4]

Perhaps one of the most important assets held by Soviet households is human capital. Given the relative ease with which people may add to their stock of human capital and the relatively high yield in the form of higher status and lifetime income, one would expect to observe

4. Less opportunity for direct investment may also be the reason one commonly observes lower saving rates out of labor income; see Houthakker [1965].

Soviet households holding a large part of their wealth in this form. Milton Friedman has suggested that the rate of saving is positively affected by the ratio of human to nonhuman wealth. Given the extent of education in the Soviet Union and the difficulty of accumulating wealth in nonhuman form, one would expect to observe the Soviets saving a higher proportion of their permanent income in order to increase the liquidity of their portfolio [Friedman, 1957].

2. *Consumer Credit.* The use of consumer credit to purchase goods on the installment plan is extremely limited in the Soviet economy. Consumers must be prepared to pay in cash for nearly all purchases, including automobiles. One expects that the limited supply of consumer credit will increase the proportion of income saved. The limited availability of credit also makes it more difficult for young Soviet households to transfer income from high to low earning years through the use of installment credit. Thus, households can only dissave if they have previously accumulated positive savings or if they can receive financial assistance or borrow privately (from their parents). One would expect to observe a low incidence of dissaving and a higher average propensity to save throughout the life cycle.

3. *State Provision of Consumer Goods and Services.* The supply of "free" education and medical care and low-rent housing in the Soviet Union reduces the demand for savings compared to market economies. Home buying, sending children to college, and creating reserves as security in case of health hardships are among the main motives for household savings in many market economies. While a small proportion of Soviet households do plan on buying a cooperative apartment or a dacha, and while better medical treatment or even better education may be obtained through side or private payments, the overall burden of these purchases on Soviet households is much lighter, and the demand for savings on their account much smaller.

4. *The Availability of Consumer Goods.* Many writers have argued that shortages of consumer goods have been the primary cause of Soviet saving, and thus that most Soviet saving is "forced" simply because there is an excess demand for goods at the current set of prices.[5] In addition, if official prices are rigid and consistently below the equilibrium level, households can reduce their cash holdings by reducing their labor supply. There have been substantial year-to-year variations in the marginal propensity to save and recent time series evidence does indicate higher saving rates in the post-1965 period.[6]

5. See Bronson and Severin [1973], Bush [1974], and Schroeder [1975].
6. See Pickersgill [1976, 1980].

If forced saving does occur, the level of saving will of course be higher.

Whether or not saving may be increased by repressed inflation, it is certainly affected by the perennial uncertainty and irregularity of the availability of consumer goods, including food items, clothing, and consumer durables. Not only does this uncertainty of supply affect Soviet real income as discussed in the previous section, but it provides a motive for increased liquidity. One would expect the average propensity to save to be higher, since the Soviet household must have liquid assets to take advantage of unexpected opportunities. As the level of income goes up, so must the incremental additions to this precautionary stock of cash.

5. *Inheritance.* Since 1943 there has been no inheritance or gift tax in the Soviet Union [Diachenko, 1964]. This fact should increase the proportion of lifetime income saved. On the other hand, the absence of the opportunity to invest productively must reduce the incentive to accumulate for future generations as well as the average size of inheritances.

6. *The Political and Social Environment.* Finally, we should mention the rather unique political and social environment of Soviet households, which may affect their saving behavior. It is difficult to assess the impact of the currency reform of 1947 on saving behavior today. In 1947 the Soviet authorities traded old rubles for new rubles at a rate of exchange that was particularly disadvantageous for holders of cash and large saving deposits. The fear of future confiscations still lingers. In addition, the political authorities look upon the accumulation of private wealth with suspicion, and Soviet citizens have learned to avoid conspicuous behavior.

C. *Soviet Savings Patterns: A Summary*

Can we sum together the disparate effects on Soviet saving and deduce anything about the nature of the saving function we expect to observe? Our remarks on both the nature of income over the life cycle and transitory shocks throughout the life cycle lead us to believe that the variation in current income around expected lifetime income in the Soviet Union is narrower than in the market economies of the West. Tests of both the life cycle and permanent income hypothesis support the view that the high proportion of transitory income in the West is responsible for the gap between the long-run saving rate and the much higher marginal propensity to save (MPS) observed in Western cross-section studies [Mayer, 1972, p. 350]. If our arguments about the nature of Soviet public income patterns are correct, the

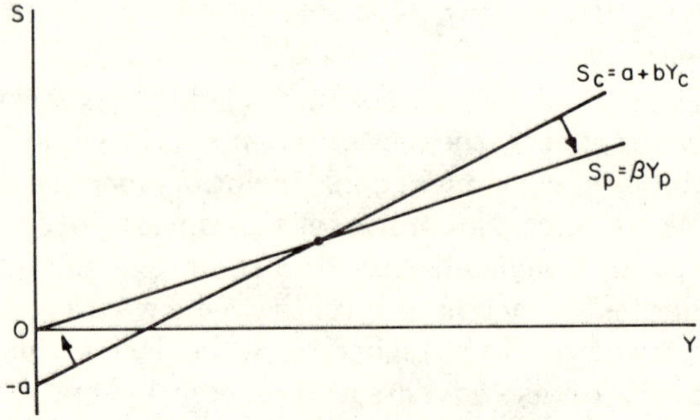

FIGURE I
Saving Out of Current and Permanent Income

MPS estimated from Soviet cross-section data will not be much higher than the average saving rate, and the corresponding average rate of saving (APS) will not rise as much, if at all. Rather, the estimated APS will approach the MPS and both will closely correspond to the long-run or permanent saving rate. Figure I illustrates the classical saving function estimated using cross-section and long-run time series data for a market economy. For a given *permanent* saving function, we expect the Soviet *current* saving function to rotate clockwise toward the permanent function. The impact of income earned from private sources will partially offset this tendency. The rotating effect should thus be best observed when "private" income is excluded from the analysis.

The influences on the proportion of permanent income saved are more difficult to summarize, since they point in different directions. On the one hand, the lack of investment opportunities, the access to free education, medical services, and low-rent housing, and the avoidance of conspicuous behavior would tend to reduce the proportion of permanent income saved. On the other hand, the uncertainty of supplies, the lack of credit, the absence of inheritance taxes, the ratio of human to nonhuman wealth, and the possibility of repressed inflation would have the opposite effect. A judgment of the net impact will have to depend upon actual results, but it is our strong feeling that the factors that reduce saving tip the balance to bring the saving rate below normal market economy rates.

III. The Data and Variables

The data used in this study come from returns of a retrospective family budget survey of 1,016 Jewish families who emigrated from the

Soviet Union during the mid-1970s. The families reported, in great detail, on their earnings and income by sources, and on their expenditures during the last year of normal life in the Soviet Union, that is the year before they decided to emigrate or applied for an exit visa. The interviews were performed during the second half of 1976 and the reports are distributed roughly evenly between 1972, 1973, and 1974; only a small number of them refer to earlier or later years. An obvious weakness of the data is that they are made up of recollections of roughly three years back. However, since economic matters are high on the minds of Soviet citizens, and since the economic realities (incomes, prices) are fairly constant over time, this may not be as large a handicap as may be assumed by outsiders who base their judgments on personal experience.

The sample was limited to urban residents only (few emigrants come from rural areas) and to families of European origin. It was further limited to include only full, two-parent families whose male head was still active in the labor force during the normal year. The sample was not selected randomly and was not pre-structured except that an attempt was made to obtain an occupational structure that is closer to that of the Soviet urban population. As it turned out, the sample population overrepresents the Baltic and Western republics of the Soviet Union and underrepresents the RSFSR, and it overrepresents larger cities as opposed to smaller ones [Ofer, Vinokur, and Bar-Chaim, 1979]. Demographically, the sample is similar to the Soviet urban population, but is very different with respect to its economic characteristics. The sample is made up of roughly two-thirds white collar workers and one-third blue collar workers, almost exactly the opposite of the target Soviet population. Likewise, the average levels of education, earnings, and family incomes are considerably higher.

All of the above intentional and unintentional nonrepresentiveness on the part of the sample of the Soviet non-Asiatic urban population may cause biases in any deduction about the economic behavior of the latter based on the sample returns. Some of these biases can be reduced or eliminated by reweighting the sample data with the structural weights of the target population. In some forms of analysis the structural biases may not have a significant distorting effect. An example is regression analysis in the absence of heteroskedasticity. In other cases, there is no way to account for possible biases other than with the help of outside information, if available. The best examples here are the possibility of a specified Jewish or emigrant bias. Analyses that were carried out so far in a number of directions on the basis of these data produce a general impression of a high level of reliability.

The study of Soviet household saving behavior on the basis of the survey data suffers from a number of general and specific limitations and biases. First, all we can study directly are saving habits of the urban working Soviet population (of European descent) and even this only for complete families. All the excluded groups may have somewhat lower tendencies to save, so that our findings may be biased upward. Since we were not able to discover statistically significant differences in saving habits between groups classified by geographic location, level of education, occupation, or even age, for a given income, structural differences between the sample and the target population with respect to these criteria should not affect the results of our analysis. There are, of course, differences in the saving behavior of families with different levels and structures of earnings, income, and wealth, as well as demographic variables. We hope that the use of regression analysis helps to minimize the effect of the rather wide sample to population differences that do exist with respect to many of these variables. For reasons that are explained below, we believe that the variances of savings among people at the lower and upper ends of the income range are not much higher than those with incomes in between, so that biases resulting from a combination of nonrepresentiveness of the sample and heteroskedasticity of savings along the income range should not be serious.

The specific data on saving as well as those on income are, however, subject to a number of more significant limitations and shortcomings. Let us discuss these together with a general description of the variables used in the analysis.

Saving. The data on saving (S) used in this paper are made up of two elements: first, direct saving in the form of additions during the normal year to various saving accounts or to bond and cash holdings, as reported by the respondents. Second, saving includes mortgage payments on apartments. While in principle the respondents could have reported negative saving, no one did so. We conclude that negative saving was not reported because the respondents did not understand that they could report it, not because it did not exist. A broader definition of saving includes credit payments net of purchases on credit. Since credit purchases are rather limited in the Soviet Union, the results using the more inclusive definition were very close to our reported results. The quality of the data on credit activity was not good enough to justify its inclusion. An alternative definition of saving—the difference between total income and total expenditure on consumption—had to be ruled out at this point, since such a residual contains many errors and inconsistencies and is not sufficiently reliable.

The most serious deficiency of our definition of saving is that it overstates saving because of the absence of negative savers. This is in addition to the bias in the same direction created by the total exclusion from the sample of groups like pensioners, student families, and one-parent families, among whom negative savings should be more common. In addition to overstating the level of saving, this shortcoming may also affect the slope of the saving function with respect to income and wealth variables. However, under Soviet conditions, discussed in the last section, these biases may be less serious than in a market economy. Due to the absence of credit and the resulting necessity to accumulate prior to dissaving, the unknown dissavers may be more evenly distributed along the entire income range, and not overconcentrated among low-income families, as is usually the case. In addition, since savings are used more often to bridge over uneven *expenditure* streams than to bridge over variations in lifetime income, fewer low-income families (compared to a typical Western sample) are temporarily in such a situation, and thus able to afford dissaving on the basis of their long-range, permanent income.[7]

Of the 1,014 families included, 526 reported on positive direct saving and an additional 80 families with no direct saving were paying on mortgages. Among the nonsavers, only 86 had at the end of the normal year a stock of savings of 300 rubles or more. Nonreporting dissavers most likely belong to this group.

In addition to the absence of dissavers, there is also a possibility that some nonsavers did indeed save but failed to report it. While the interviewers were instructed to insist on getting a definite answer, they may have failed to do so in some cases. The bias created is opposite to that discussed above, but should be considered of smaller significance, since we do find a rather wide and highly significant income difference between the group of savers and nonsavers.

Income. Total income (Y) is defined as disposable family monthly income (in cash and in kind) and is divided into the following:

YO = net earnings from all places of public employment
YWP = net earnings from private employment

7. Pensioners may constitute an exceptional group with respect to this proposition.

YPO = net incomes from unspecified private economic activities (including proceeds from renting rooms or apartments)
YF = net incomes from private agricultural plots
YT = government transfer payments (pensions, educational stipends, social security-type payments)
YG = cash gifts (or loans) from private people
YDIF = the difference between our estimate of *Y* and the sum of all income elements as reported by the families. This sum was revised on the basis of answers to other questions that were inconsistent with the sum. We have strong support for the supposition that much of *YDIF* are incomes from private sources that the respondents did not care to report on.[8]

We also define $YP = YWP + YPO + YF + YDIF$—the sum of all income earned from private sources.

Finally, in order to test the hypothesis that saving behavior may vary according to the proportion of private income (*YP*) in total income, the empirical analysis is also carried out using dummy variables for two subgroups. The two subgroups are (a) families for which *YP* is 10 percent of their income or less—$DYP = 0$ and (b) families for which *YP* is in excess of 10 percent—$DYP = 1$. *DYP* is the dummy variable for the two groups, respectively.[9]

IV. Empirical Results

A. *Average Saving Rates and the Permanent Income Hypothesis*

As reported in Table I, the average saving rate for the entire sample is estimated at 7 percent. This rate of household saving falls within the range found in other studies of this type, although it is closer to the average rate for less developed countries. In his work on international comparisons of saving rates, Houthakker found that the weighted average ratio of personal saving to personal income for developed countries was 9 percent, while for underdeveloped countries it was 5 percent [Houthakker, 1965]. In his study of personal saving in Asian countries, Williamson estimated the long-run MPS at 16 percent [Williamson, 1968]. Both studies found a significantly higher saving rate from nonlabor income, and the saving rate from labor income varied between 0 and 10 percent.[10] The mean household

8. For more details on the derivation of the revised *Y*, see Ofer, Vinokur, Bar-Chaim [1979].

9. The choice of "10" percent as the dividing line was made on the basis of experimentation with other rates. The sensitivity of the results to the rate chosen is small.

10. Saving rates lower out of labor income than out of nonlabor income were also found by Johnson [1968], Friend [1968], and Mikesell [1973].

TABLE I

SAVING RATES BY EDUCATIONAL AND OCCUPATIONAL GROUPS

Classification	Monthly income (rubles)	Saving rate (percent)	Number of obs's.
A. *Education of household head*			
Entire population	397.5	7.00	1,014
University degree	438.8	7.11	426
Professional secondary	388.7	6.86	187
University uncompleted	375.6	6.29	36
General secondary	370.3	6.67	174
7–9 years of school	354.8	7.68	115
Less than 7 years of school	325.2	6.88	76
B. *Occupation of head of household*			
Entire population*	397.9	7.02	1,009
Managers	463.9	8.18	258
Professionals	396.4	6.22	324
Technicians	384.3	7.85	56
White collar employees	352.0	4.19	14
Service workers	377.7	10.12	80
Skilled production workers	378.4	5.87	123
Semiskilled production workers	327.5	6.14	122
Low skilled production workers	318.6	5.56	32

* Not including five families whose heads did not work.

saving rate was calculated for a number of developed and less developed countries for the period 1955–1968 and varied from a rate of 1.6 percent for Korea to 14.6 percent for Italy [Lluch, 1977]. The Soviet rate is below all the developed countries except the United Kingdom, which averaged 6.5 percent, but not significantly below saving rates out of labor income. It seems that some of the "less developed" characteristics of the consumer sector in the Soviet Union as well as the other dampening factors discussed in the previous sections manage to keep the saving rate low. It should, however, be remembered that this is a net result and thus no judgments on the importance of individual factors, especially those that could have raised the rate, can be made here. The APS estimated from our sample is almost identical to the long-run MPS derived from macro time series data by Pickersgill for the period 1955 to 1971, although below the rate found for the more recent period 1965–1977 [Pickersgill, 1980].

The average rate of saving for families with a high proportion of private income (there are 249 such families) is 13.36 percent, much higher than the 5.86 percent rate for those with little or no YP (765 families). This finding is clearly in line with our hypothesis, and we shall discuss it in greater detail below.

TABLE II

REGRESSION COEFFICIENTS OF ESTIMATED SAVING FUNCTIONS*

A.	Intercept	Y	DYP	$YDYP$	FS	$FS.DYP$				R^2
(1) S	−36.7850	0.1744								0.3246
	(−10.7944)	(22.0892)								
(2) S	−18.5053	0.1154	−47.9865	0.1413						0.3814
	(−4.7921)	(11.8825)	(−5.8625)	(8.3703)						
(3) S	−4.5208	0.1282	−20.3723	0.1453	−5.5480	−8.8972				0.4056
	(−0.7959)	(12.4738)	(−1.7463)	(8.4228)	(−3.3025)	(−2.9164)				
B.	Intercept	YO	YPW	YPO	YF	$YDIF$	YT	YG	FS	$\bar{R}^2$
All (1,014 observations):										
(4) S	−23.8380	0.1295	0.2903	0.1355	0.1132	0.3960	0.0819	0.0199		0.4289
	(−7.1135)	(14.5055)	(14.5670)	(4.2441)	(1.1527)	(18.0738)	(2.0921)	(0.3827)		
(5) S	−4.5547	0.1439	0.2921	0.1414	0.1668	0.3912	0.1416	−0.0184	−7.3205	0.4426
	(−0.9047)	(15.5346)	(14.8339)	(4.4818)	(1.7089)	(18.0575)	(3.5021)	(−0.3554)	(−5.0836)	
$DPY = 0$ (765 observations):										
(6) S	−19.4885	0.1256	−0.2731	−0.1919	0.3810	0.1791	0.0111	0.0131		0.2592
	(−6.5248)	(15.5042)	(−1.2599)	(−0.9608)	(1.8736)	(1.0142)	(0.3130)	(0.2750)		
(7) S	−3.5763	0.1369	−0.3091	−0.1126	0.4788	0.1628	0.0612	−0.0185	−6.0433	0.2777
	(−0.7774)	(16.3296)	(−1.4430)	(−0.5686)	(2.3704)	(0.9332)	(1.6698)	(−0.3877)	(−4.5071)	
$DPY = 1$ (249 observations):										
(8) S	−41.2773	0.1497	0.3259	0.1833	0.1174	0.4255	0.2835	0.0698		0.4607
	(−3.7428)	(5.0644)	(8.8344)	(3.4079)	(0.7199)	(11.8607)	(2.4665)	(0.4670)		
(9) S	−12.7810	0.1705	0.3216	0.1816	0.1626	0.4144	0.3629	0.0138	−10.3405	0.4733
	(−0.8274)	(5.6568)	(8.8116)	(3.4175)	(1.0030)	(11.6048)	(3.0861)	(0.0925)	(2.6031)	

* Figures in parentheses are t values.

Following a method commonly used in Western studies, we have classified households by two variables correlated with permanent income—education and occupation.[11] Households are grouped into seven educational and eight occupational classifications, and the mean income and the mean saving rate for households in each group are calculated. These are reported in Table I.

If the mean income of each group contains no transitory elements, then the differences in mean income between groups represents the differences in permanent income. If the permanent income hypothesis is correct, one would expect to observe no significant difference between the saving patterns of the various groups. Turning to the calculations reported in Table I, we see that with only a few exceptions the saving rate for each group is clustered around the mean ratio of 7.0 percent, and does not vary positively with income.[12]

Our results provide stronger support for the permanent income hypothesis than do many Western studies using similar classifications [Mayer, 1972]. As was mentioned in a previous section, this may be due to the relatively limited amount of variation in the income of Soviet households. Support for the permanent income hypothesis is provided also by the failure to obtain significant coefficients for the ratio of saving to income with respect to income in a number of regression equations.

B. Estimating the Saving Function

In line 1 of panel A of Table II, we display estimates of a simple saving function of the form,

$$S = a + bY + E, \tag{1}$$

where S and Y are the monthly saving and disposable income of the ith household and E is the error term. In line 2 we reestimate the equation adding the dummy term (DYP) discussed above and a product term ($YDYP$). The new equation to be estimated is

$$S = a + bY + a'(DPY) + b'(YDYP) + E. \tag{2}$$

The data for the entire population for the two subgroups are presented in Table II. When the entire population is undifferentiated (line 1), we obtain a very high (and significant) negative intercept and an es-

11. For a summary of the results of these tests using Western data, see Mayer [1972].

12. The somewhat more bumpy pattern of rates among the occupational groups—especially the high rate of saving of service workers—is due to different concentrations of private income families in the various occupations.

timated MPS of 0.1744. This last rate is lower than the range of rates of 0.20 to 0.40, which are estimated from United States cross-section data but higher than those derived from time series; the MPS estimated in time series for the United States ranges between 0.11 and 0.13. The estimated Soviet MPS is also significantly higher than the average rate of saving (estimated *from the equation* as 8.2 percent for the average income of 391.5 rubles per month) and from the long-run MPS's of 7 and 10 percent estimated from time series [Pickersgill 1980]. Thus, even if the cross-section MPS reflects the stability elements discussed in Section II above, it does so only to a limited extent. The stability hypothesis is, however, upheld when we separate families with regular public incomes from those with significant proportions of private incomes. As can be seen from line 2 of Table II, when only families with little or no private income are included, the MPS falls to 0.1154; much closer to its time series counterpart or that of the United States, and the intercept—while still significantly different from zero—is much closer to it.[13] Similarly, while in equation (1) the APS varies from 1.4 percent for income one standard deviation below average to 11 percent for income one standard deviation above it, in equation (2) when only families with little private income are included, the APS varies over the same income range from 3 to 8 percent. The other side of the same picture is observed in equation (2) for families with private incomes: the estimated intercept $(a + DYP)$ is equal to -66.49 and the MPS $(Y + DYP)$ is equal to 0.2667. Both coefficients are highly significant. This is indeed a very steep function, not different from regular cross-section equations in market economies. The estimated intercepts and slopes for all three groups are presented in Figure II, where the differences are clearly demonstrated.

That saving rates vary with different types of income can also be observed from the equations estimated in Part B of Table II. Total income is broken into its components, which differ by the size of the transitory element as well as by other characteristics. The equation to be estimated is

$$S = a + B(YO) + cY(PW) + d(YF) + e(YDIF) + f(YT) + g(YG) + E. \tag{3}$$

The results for the entire population are shown in line 4 of Table II, and those for the two separate groups of families in lines 6 $(DYP = 0)$ and 8 $(DYP = 1)$.

13. In this way a and b are the intercept and MPS for families with little private income, and $(a + a')$ and $(b + b')$ are the corresponding coefficients for families with more private income.

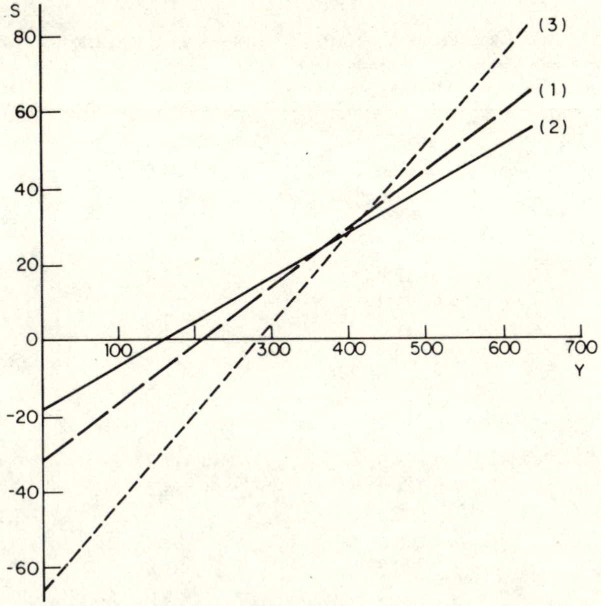

FIGURE II
Saving Functions
(1) Entire sample (1014 observations): $S = -36.78 + 0.174Y$
(2) No private income (765 observations): $S = -18.51 + 0.115Y$
(3) With private income (249 observations): $S = -66.49 + 0.257Y$

The most interesting result is that the MPS from components of private income are in most cases significantly higher than for earnings derived from public jobs. The MPS's for *YPW* and *YDIF* are between 30 and 40 percent as compared with 13–15 percent for *YO*.[14] The MPS for *YPO*, while only 13.5 percent in equation (4), goes up to 18.3 percent in equation (8). Only the MPS out of private plot incomes remains relatively low and insignificant in both equations (4) and (8). One thus observes very clearly not only the expected results due to the large transitory element in *YP* and its components but also an element of insurance against the risk involved in acquiring these incomes as well as a tendency to avoid conspicuous consumption.

These results support the view that the higher saving rates found for high private income families do not result merely from their higher incomes. Although, as shown in Table III, such families have an av-

14. We did not find differences between the MPS of components of *YO*, i.e., between earnings from the main job and from extra public jobs.

TABLE III

AVERAGE LEVELS OF VARIABLES USED IN THE REGRESSIONS*

	All families	DYP = 0	DYP = 1
No. of obs's	1014	765	249
S	32.6	24.0	59.1
Y	397.6	367.9	488.6
YO	334.3	342.8	308.2
YPW	18.6	0.8	73.3
YPO	8.8	1.0	32.5
YF	2.4	0.7	7.5
YDIF	12.5	1.8	45.6
YT	13.8	13.6	14.2
YG	7.2	7.2	7.3
YP	42.3	4.3	158.9
FS	3.39	3.37	3.45
W	3,115.9	2,514.8	5,149.7
SS	2,034.2	1,524.2	3,607.5
APV	828.9	730.9	1,131.5
CAR	208.5	163.5	347.0
GARDEN	36.9	31.6	53.3
DACHA	7.4	6.5	10.1

* All variables measured in current rubles. Flow variables measured in current rubles per month.

erage income of 488.6 rubles per month as compared with only 367.9 rubles for low private income families, the MPS's out of public earnings (*YO*) for the two groups of families are not significantly different: 0.1256 for the low *YP* and 0.1497 for high *YP* families.

We find very low and insignificant MPS's out of private transfers (*YG*), as should be expected, and low or average MPS out of government transfers (*YT*). While the first result is stable for all groups, high *YP* families save a lot from *YT*, while low *YP* families save very little out of that source. This dichotomy may be due to the fact that on the one hand *YT* is temporary (thus transitory), and on the other hand is made up of welfare payments for poor families.

Finally, it should be pointed out that equation (4) has a coefficient of determination ($\bar{R}^2$) of 0.43, which is higher than those of equations (1) or (2) in Part A of Table II, and is rather high for cross-section saving functions.

Theory and empirical studies have established relationships between demographic variables and the proportion of income saved. According to the life cycle hypothesis, saving and age are related because the young and the old should dissave from income saved during mid-life years. Family size should affect saving through its effect on real per capita income. The absence of credit and the exclusion from our data of households headed by pensioners may explain our failure to establish the expected negative relation between age and saving. However, we did establish the expected negative relation between family size (*FS*) and saving as can be observed from lines 3, 5,7, and 9 in Table II.[15] In all the equations the coefficients of *FS* are negative and significant. In all cases adding *FS* into the equations significantly raises the MPS out of private plot incomes and out of government transfers. In both cases there is a positive correlation between *FS* and the income component, and the somewhat surprising low MPS's from these sources can now be attributed to the biases created by omitting *FS* from the equations.

We also examined the effect of the reporting year (1972, 1973, or 1974) and of the location of the family, but found no relationship with saving.

The results presented above support our hypotheses discussed in the summary of Section II. However, a word of caution on the direction of possible biases and errors is warranted. Two groups of observations have been included in the analysis that may bias the results. For thirty-four families the estimated level of saving was substantially below the actual level of saving. Eighteen additional families reported saving 50 percent or more of their income. In all these cases total expenditures (including saving) were significantly higher than income, and in most of them we had a good reason to suspect (on the basis of occupation) that they could have additional private sources of income. With one exception, these families also had large accumulations of savings to justify their high saving rates. In these cases we decided to include the observations but to use total expenditures as the measure of income. Both groups, fifty-two cases altogether, are characterized by high accumulations of saving, high saving rates, high incomes, and high proportions of private income. To the extent that the error is not in the reported level of income (as we assume) but in the level of saving, the inclusion of these observations biases the results by raising the average saving rate, and raising the slope (MPS) and the (negative) intercept of the saving functions. These results are indeed manifested in equations that exclude the fifty-two observations. For example, the average saving rate falls from 7 to 6 percent; the MPS estimated in line (1) of Table II falls from 0.1744 to 0.1090; the coefficient for *YDYP* (line 3) falls from 0.1453 to 0.0369, and the coefficient for *YDIF* (line 4) from 0.3960 to 0.2057. In all cases the coeffi-

15. *FS* may also have captured part of the age effect, since small families concentrate in low and high aged families.

TABLE IV

REGRESSION COEFFICIENTS OF ESTIMATED SAVING FUNCTIONS INCLUDING WEALTH*

Dependent variable A.	Intercept	*W*	W^2	*Y*	*FS*	*DYP*	*WDYP*	$W^2.DYP$	*Y.DYP*	*FS.DYP*	$\bar{R}^2$
(1) *S*	13.6787	0.0066	-0.0052×10^{-6}								0.2355
	(7.2482)	(12.6471)	(−3.4668)								
(2) *S*	−32.3427	0.0037	-0.0020×10^{-6}	0.1358							0.3948
	(−9.8615)	(7.4228)	(−1.4339)	(16.3355)							
(3) *S*	−10.4177	0.0036	-0.0021×10^{-6}	0.1527	−8.3207						0.4150
	(−2.1343)	(7.2907)	(−1.5897)	(17.6576)	(−5.9832)						
(4) *S*	−7.9096	0.0065	-0.0022×10^{-5}	0.0951	−4.5016	−18.2487	−0.0040	0.0021×10^{-5}	0.1433	−8.1652	0.4662
	(−1.4557)	(8.4009)	(−5.2302)	(8.9788)	(−2.8183)	(−1.6313)	(−3.7051)	(4.6948)	(8.0211)	(−2.7992)	

B.	Intercept	*SS*	*APV*	*CAR*	*GAR*	*DACHA*	*Y*	*FS*	$\bar{R}^2$
S(All)	−10.0700	0.0041	0.0006	−0.0011	0.0007	−0.0160	0.1509	−7.6633	0.4354
	(−2.0936)	(12.1875)	(1.0514)	(−0.7643)	(0.1888)	(−1.6375)	(17.8055)	(−5.5902)	
S(*DPY* = 0)	−3.7907	0.0043	0.0022	0.0003	0.0030	−0.0196	0.0967	4.7492	0.3508
	(−0.9255)	(9.5759)	(3.7233)	(0.2518)	(0.9088)	(−2.1550)	(11.9874)	(−3.9317)	
S(*DPY* = 1)	−26.6843	0.0033	−0.0016	−0.0024	0.0001	−0.0099	0.2307	−10.5005	0.4616
	(−1.7844)	(5.3460)	(−1.0663)	(−0.6948)	(−0.0110)	(−0.3944)	(10.5178)	(−2.7930)	

* Figures in parentheses are *t* values.

cients of determination for equations including all observations are much higher than those without the fifty-two observations.

C. Saving and Wealth

According to the permanent income hypothesis, consumption and wealth should be positively related. An increase in wealth, holding current income constant, will result in an increase in consumption and thus an increase in the proportion of income consumed. The empirical evidence on this proposition, derived from Western budget studies, has been mixed, many studies showing no or negative relationships between consumption and wealth [Mayer, 1972; and Evans, 1969].

These mixed results may be explained by the confounding of the consumption-wealth relationship by a taste variable. Some of the households with larger amounts of wealth are those who have saved in the past, and thus have a "taste" for saving. For them wealth is a result of high saving rates (and lower consumption rates) and wealth and saving are positively related. A negative relation may exist when wealth comes in as a windfall (inheritance, capital gains, and the like).

In the Soviet Union at the present time, the primary source of household wealth is still past saving. As mentioned earlier, present households received little or nothing by way of inheritance, and the nature of Soviet real and financial assets precludes significant capital gains. One would then expect to observe, at least up to a certain wealth level, a negative relationship between consumption and wealth or a positive wealth coefficient when wealth is substituted for or added to income in the savings function.

However, as wealth increases and some of the assets for which liquid wealth is accumulated are purchased, the positive relationship between saving and wealth may weaken or even turn negative. This hypothesized nonlinear relationship is tested in Part A of Table IV by estimating a saving function of the following form:

$$\begin{aligned}(4) \qquad S &= a + bW + cW^2 + dY + eFS \\ &\quad + DYP(a' + b'W + c'W^2 + d'Y + e'FS) + E.\end{aligned}$$

Wealth (W) is defined as

$$W = APV + SS + CAR + GAR + DACHA,$$

where

W = total wealth
APV = value of the equity in an apartment

SS = savings deposits + currency + 3 percent bonds at end of year
CAR = value of car (depreciated)
GAR = value of garden
$DACHA$ = value of dacha.

W^2 is introduced to test for the nonlinearity in the relationship between S and W. We also add the dummy variable to test for differences between families with high and low proportions of private income.

We find a positive relationship between saving and wealth that is declining slightly as wealth grows. See equations (1)–(4) in Table IV. When wealth is included, the MPS out of income drops slightly.

Separating the population into high and low YP families does not produce different coefficients with respect to wealth—the coefficients of both $W{\cdot}DYP$ and W^2DYP are very small. The results of including family size are similar to those reported in Table II.

In Part B of Table IV we substitute the components of wealth—as listed above—for the total, and estimate the equation for the entire population as well as its two subgroups. Of all the wealth components, only liquid savings retains a positive (and highly significant) coefficient in the three equations. The coefficients for the material components of wealth are in some cases negative, in others positive, and in most cases not statistically significant. This result is consistent with the nonlinearity hypothesis presented above: first, part of the accumulation of liquid assets is earmarked for the future purchase of a material asset—like an apartment or car. When the goal is reached, the saving stream declines. Second, the owners of material assets are also those with larger holdings of wealth, and the positive effects of wealth on consumption may be stronger.

It is interesting to note that despite the fact that mortgage payments are included in saving and that only apartment owners pay them, the coefficient of the apartment value for the entire population is not significantly different from zero. It is positive and significant only for those with low private incomes (line 16), where mortgage payments are an important element in total savings.[16]

Finally, the exclusion of the fifty-two observations discussed

16. When savings are defined to exclude mortgage payments, the coefficient for apartment ownership becomes negative throughout.

above reduces the wealth coefficients, but otherwise the results are unchanged.

V. Conclusions

The empirical evidence does support our hypothesis that Soviet saving behavior can be explained using the same variables found to be significant in Western studies based on the permanent income and life cycle theories of saving. Saving is a positive function of current income, and the APS is positively related to income—the situation found in nearly all Western cross-section studies. The proportion of transitory income saved is significantly higher than the proportion of permanent income saved. Finally, as in Western studies, family size and saving are negatively related.

The nature of Soviet conditions, however, affected the shape and pattern of the saving function in particular ways: the average saving rate seems to be lower than normal by international comparisons judged by the Soviet level of economic development. If only public sources of income, or families with mostly public income are considered, then the Soviet cross-section saving function is found to be much flatter than ordinary Western ones; that is, the short-run MPS is low by international comparison and much closer to the short-run APS and the long-run saving rate. But the Soviet Union has its own group of high savers in the form of earners of income from private sources whose saving behavior is very similar to that of the self-employed or entrepreneurs elsewhere. Furthermore, if their weight in the Soviet urban sector is similar to that found in our sample, then the saving behavior of the entire urban sector is closer to the Western pattern than the observed behavior of those families earning only public incomes.

Finally, we also find a positive relation between wealth and saving, which is not surprising given that wealth mostly represents the accumulation of past saving by the families in the sample.

In conclusion, the proportion of income saved found in this budget study is consistent with that found in time series studies and does not support the proposition that Soviet households save inordinately large amounts of their income for lack of consumer goods and services to purchase. The analysis is not complete enough, however, to exclude the possibility that some saving does represent a response to repressed inflation.

Hebrew University
California State University, Fullerton

References

Bronson, D. W., and B. S. Severin, "Recent Trends in Consumption and Disposable Money Income in the U.S.S.R.," in U. S. Congress, Joint Economic Committee, *New Directions in the Soviet Economy,* Part II-B (Washington, DC: U. S. Government Printing Office, 1966).

——, and ——, "Soviet Consumer Welfare: The Brezhnev Era," in U. S. Congress, Joint Economic Committee, *Soviet Economic Prospects for the Seventies* (Washington, DC: U. S. Government Printing Office, 1973).

Bush, K., "Soviet Inflation," in Yves Laulan, ed., *Banking, Money and Credit in Eastern Europe* (Brussels: NATO, 1973).

Chapman, J., "Recent Trends in the Soviet Industrial Wage Structure," paper presented at the Conference on Problems of Industrial Labor in the U.S.S.R., Kennan Institute for Advanced Russian Studies, Washington, DC, 1977.

Diachenko, V. P., *et al.,* eds., *Finan Sovokredit nyi Slovori Finan uy* (Moscow, 1964), Vol. II, p. 70.

Evans, Michael K., *Macroeconomic Activity* (New York: Harper and Row, 1969).

Friedman, M., *A Theory of the Consumption Function* (Princeton: Princeton University Press, 1957).

Friend, I., and P. Taubman, "The Aggregate Propensity to Save: Some Concepts and Their Application to International Data," *Review of Economics and Statistics,* XLVIII (May 1968), 113–23.

Green, H. S., and C. I. Higgins, *Sovmod I* (New York: Crane, Russak Co., Inc., 1977).

Houthakker, H. S., "On Some Determinants of Saving in Developed and Underdeveloped Countries," in E. A. G. Robinson, ed., *Problems in Economic Development* (London: Macmillan & Co., 1965), 212–24.

Johnson, D. W., and J. Chiu, "The Saving-Income Relation in Underdeveloped Countries," *Economic Journal,* LXXVIII (June 1968), 321–33.

Keizer, W., *The Soviet Quest for Economic Rationality* (Rotterdam: Rotterdam University Press, 1971).

Lluch, C., *et al., Patterns in Household Demand and Saving* (New York: Oxford University Press, 1977).

Mayer, T., *Permanent Income, Wealth and Consumption* (Berkeley: University of California Press, 1972).

McAuley, A., "The Distribution of Earnings as Income in the Soviet Union," *Soviet Studies,* XXIX (April 1977), 225–26.

Mikesell, R. F., and R. E. Zinser, "The Nature of the Savings Function in Developing Countries: A Survey of the Theoretical and Empirical Literature," *Journal of Economic Literature,* II (March 1973), 1–26.

Millar, James R., and Joyce Pickersgill, "Aggregate Economic Problems in Soviet-Type Economies," *ACES Bulletin,* XIX, No. 1 (Spring 1977).

Ofer, G., and A. Vinokur, "The Extent of Private Economic Activity in the Urban Sector in the Soviet Union," unpublished manuscript.

Ofer, G., A. Vinokur, and Y. Bar-Chaim, "Family Budget Survey of Soviet Emigrants in the Soviet Union," RAND Corporation (P-6015), 1979.

Pickersgill, Joyce, "Soviet Household Saving Behavior," *Review of Economics and Statistics,* LVIII (May 1976), 139–47.

——, "Soviet Inflation: Causes and Consequences," *Soviet Union,* IV, No. 2 (1977).

——, "Recent Evidence on Soviet Household Saving Behavior," *Review of Economics and Statistics, LXII* (Nov. 1980), forthcoming.

Schroeder, G., "Consumer Goods Availability and Repressed Inflation in the Soviet Union," in *Economic Aspects of Life in the USSR* (Brussels: NATO, 1975).

Williamson, J. G., "Personal Savings in Developing Nations: An Intertemporal Cross-Section from Asia," *Economic Record,* XLIV (June 1968), 194–210.

IRVING FISHER ON HIS HEAD II: THE CONSEQUENCES OF THE TIMING OF PAYMENTS FOR THE DEMAND FOR MONEY*

GEORGE A. AKERLOF AND ROSS D. MILBOURNE

This paper explores the consequences of the timing of payments for the demand for money. It is found that if payments are the minimum of the money in the bank account or bills due, the demand for money will respond slowly to changes in income. This prediction disagrees with some formulations of the short-run demand for money (e.g., Irving Fisher's) but agrees with empirical estimates. The demand for money is adjusted to supply by changes in quantities (i.e., payments flows) rather than by changes in prices or interest rates.

I. INTRODUCTION

According to the old-style (pre-Milton Friedman, pre-Patinkin) quantity theory, velocity, which is defined variously as the ratio of total nominal transactions to the money supply or as the ratio of nominal income to the money supply, is constant. According to a more general interpretation of the quantity theory, which is in the spirit of Fisher's *Purchasing Power of Money* [1911], the transactions demand for money responds quickly to changes in income but only slowly to changes in other variables, including the rate of interest.

The logic behind the latter proposition can be stated as follows: payments habits are such that outflows from bank accounts follow inflows into bank accounts with a constant average lag. An increase in nominal income is associated with proportionately greater inflows into bank accounts. Hence, money held will be responsive to changes in money income and unresponsive to changes in the rate of interest, in the short run in which these habits are fixed.[1]

* The authors would like to thank Olivier Blanchard, Richard Lipsey, Thomas Mayer, Hajime Miyazaki, Janet Yellen, and two anonymous referees for valuable comments and suggestions. They would also like to thank the Board of Governors of the Federal Reserve System and the National Science Foundation (grant number SOC 79-05562 administered by the Institute for Business and Economic Research, University of California, Berkeley) for generous financial support.

1. According to Fisher, transactions velocity is the weighted average of individual money holders' rates of turnover of money holdings; these rates in turn are dependent on "the habits of the individual (as to thrift and hoarding, as to book credit and as to the use of checks), the systems of payments of the community (as to the frequency of receipts and disbursements, as to regularity of receipts and disbursements, [and] as to the correspondence between times and amounts of receipts and disbursements) and general causes (such as density of population [and] rapidity of transportation" [Fisher, 1911, p. 79]. Since none of the above factors can be expected to change in the short run, transactions velocity should be expected to be constant in turn. A fixed relation between transactions and income then implies the constancy of income velocity. Although there

The Quarterly Journal of Economics, August 1980 0033-5533/80/0095-0145$01.30

A previous paper [Akerlof, 1979] showed, with logic isomorphic to that of Irving Fisher, that if bank accounts are monitored by the "habit" of a constant target-threshold policy rather than the habit of a constant lag of outflow following inflow, velocity is proportional to income and not constant. This paper demonstrates the same result with a second type of fixed habit.

The spirit of Irving Fisher, as opposed to optimization in the fashion of Baumol [1952] and Tobin [1956], is that habits of payment are fixed in the short run because persons are a bit slow (or lazy) about changing their payment and money-holding habits in response to changes in income and the rate of interest. That same spirit underlies our model. In our model, persons who have to pay their bills and have insufficient funds in their bank accounts take the easiest response—they delay their payments by the use of credit cards for example, or by the temporary nonpayment of their bills (the taking of trade credit).[2] Payment is completed at times when the cash balance is more liquid. This is equivalent to a payments rationing procedure at times of illiquidity. In addition to this mode of behavior regarding payment of bills, persons also monitor their bank accounts periodically, setting their bank balances at a fixed target at these times of monitoring, so as to insure that bank balances do not become too small on the one hand or too large on the other hand.

With this preceding description of payments habits, there is a zero aggregate income elasticity of the demand for money as long as the targets to which bank accounts are periodically adjusted are constant. Since there is no reason why these targets should adjust faster to changes in income than to changes in interest, there can be no presumption, contrary to Irving Fisher, that the slow adjustment of habits of payment and money holding produces a transactions demand for money that responds quickly to changes in income but slowly to changes in interest. In this sense, going from habits of con-

is some possibility of ambiguous interpretation of *The Purchasing Power of Money* (since Irving Fisher also discusses a "transitional period" and aggregate income is a later concept), Keynes has stated the position quite clearly:

"There is, of course, no reason for supposing that V [the ratio of money income to the transactions demand for money] is constant. Its value will depend on the character of banking and industrial organization, on social habits, on the distribution of income between different classes, and on the effective cost of holding idle cash. Nevertheless, if we have a short period of time in view and can safely assume no material change in any of these factors, we can treat V as nearly enough constant" [Keynes, 1936, p. 201].

2. For the viewpoint most similar to this paper, see Brechling and Lipsey [1936] on why trade credit "frustrates" the effects of monetary contraction and expansion. Our paper shows in a formal model that limited quantities of money with variable trade credit will not "frustrate" the effects of expansionary or contractionary fiscal policy.

stant lag of outflow following inflow to the habit of delayed payment turns Irving Fisher on his head.

II. Discussion of the Model

The result of zero income elasticity can be explained in two different ways, first by an analogy to rationing equilibrium models, second by an analogy to a poker game, as shall be explained presently.

A. Explanation of Low Short-Run Income Elasticity

The fundamental equation regarding payments is the following. Let λ be the date at which a person attempts to pay his/her bills. Let $b(\lambda)$, $m(\lambda)$, $p(\lambda)$ be, respectively, the bills, money, and payments of this person at the date λ. According to our hypothesis,

$$p(\lambda) = \min(m(\lambda), b(\lambda)). \tag{1}$$

The passivity of velocity, which is a consequence of our model, results because changes in the timing of payments constitute a way—other than the usual changes in income and interest—whereby the demand for money adjusts to the supply. This possibility should not be surprising to those familiar with the recent work on equilibrium in rationed markets obtained by quantity adjustments. In such markets, quantity adjustments cause either demand to equal a rationed supply or supply to equal a rationed demand. In our model, payments flows, even for given expenditures may be rationed. Equations similar to (1) describe the mathematics of quantity adjustment in the works of Grossman [1971], Barro and Grossman [1971], Benassy [1975], and others, and describe the way in which quantity flows ration supply (demand) to a fixed demand (supply). In a similar fashion in our model, the timing of payments flows, rather than changes in income and interest, cause the demand for money to adjust to its supply.

The second analogy that explains the zero income elasticity of the demand for money in our model is that of a poker game. Consider a group of friendly gamblers who play a weekly poker game. Each player decides each week how much money to bring to the game. At some point, however, during one of the weekly games, the stakes are increased. A quantity-theoretic story would have each player recruit money from alternative sources after the stakes are raised, and if insufficient money is available, the players will go home early. According to the parable of our model, the initial (i.e., the short-run) response to the increase in stakes is that the winners will give credit to the losers and the game will continue otherwise unaltered by the limits imposed by the amount of money brought to the game. Of course, if the stakes are increased permanently, after some interval of time, the money brought to the game will increase proportionately with the stakes, but this will be a long-run rather than a short-run response.

B. Relation of Our Model to Optimization Models

As shall be discussed, we believe that payments habits described here are similar to those that would be derived in a complete optimization model of money holding. As a first degree of approximation, optimal rules such as those proposed by Clower and Howitt [1978] or Miller and Orr [1966] (or even more simply by Baumol and Tobin) are suggestive of how people select longer run monitoring rules and targets and thus implicitly select average money holdings. However, in the short run, we believe that the use of credit cards and the taking of trade credit constitute the least costly response to short-run and perhaps unexpected fluctuations in expenditures and receipts.

This is because the transactions costs involved in the use of credit cards or delayed payments are typically much lower than alternative means of financing shortfalls of cash, such as arranging transfers from other assets or arranging for short-term credit. Using credit cards involves almost negligible transactions costs, and on average six weeks to pay without penalty.[3] Similarly, there are many bills on which payment can be delayed for short periods of time without prior arrangement for which there may or may not be an interest charge. A delayed payment of $100 at 10 percent per annum costs 83 cents for a delay of up to one month. This may be less than the transactions costs of making switches between bonds or securities and money. Thus, for temporary shortfalls, it may be less costly to vary the timing of payments than to engage in transactions in bonds or securities, so that behavior may be closely approximated by equation (1). It is precisely because of these relative cost differences that we believe the timing of payments belongs in an optimizing model of money holding.

It might be argued that trade credit should always be taken to its maximum and not just used at times of cash shortfall. This is false for at least three reasons. In the first place, the taking of trade credit, or the use of credit cards, involves lower transactions costs, but generally higher rates of interest, than other credit sources. Consequently,

3. On average, payments are made during the middle of one billing period (typically a month) and are payable without penalty up until the end of the next month.

it is only optimal to use these methods to finance small or short-term cash shortfalls, as use of trade credit involves penalties. Second, the low transactions costs–high interest rates make the flexibility of trade credit and credit cards optimal for short periods and small amounts. Third, continual heavy use of trade credit in general causes poor credit ratings and the possible curtailment of services, which entail great disadvantages.

Some trade credit is negotiated, as in very large sales, in which the payments schedule is contractually specified. In this case, the welfare of both parties can be improved by a payments schedule that economizes on the borrowing from third parties and therefore conforms to the liquidity of the two sides involved in the contract.

C. Implications Concerning Deficiency in Optimization Models of Money Holdings

Our model with variable timing of payments behavior is suggestive of important deficiencies in the standard inventory-theoretic models in which money holdings are optimally derived. According to these models, autonomous payments flows depend only upon income. (For the definition of *autonomous,* see Akerlof [1979].) As income changes, these flows change and, consequently, so do optimal money balances (even after taking account of the reaction of money holders to the greater returns at higher income of monitoring their bank account with greater frequency). Further, as interest rates increase, the opportunity cost of holding money increases; thus, people tend to monitor their bank accounts more frequently, and this greater care in monitoring will cause the demand for money to decline. However, these models leave out the possibility of a third form of optimal adjustment of the demand for money, namely the variable timing of payments.[4]

Finally, by way of introduction we should mention that our theory, at least in some respects conforms to the facts. First, velocity is observed to vary in the short run with income; it is not constant, as Irving Fisher would probably have predicted. Also, there is considerable variation in trade credit over the business cycle. As will be reported below for the United States in recent years, variation in the growth of trade credit around trend has been greater in absolute magnitude than variation in money holdings.

The following section gives a simple "textbook"-style example

4. See Chow [1966], Friedman [1959], Goldfeld [1973, 1976], and Laidler [1966].

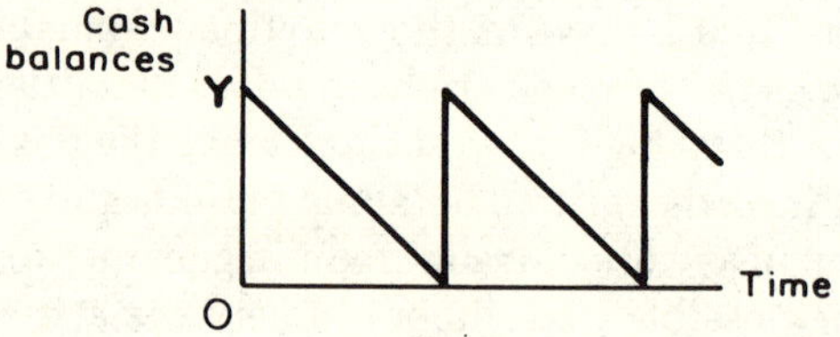

FIGURE I

that conveys the structure of the model and contrasts our result with that of Irving Fisher. Section IV formalizes the analysis and demonstrates the short-run passivity of velocity. We also examine the empirical relevance of our theory.

III. A Simple Example

Consider the simple textbook version of the quantity theory. A consumer receives income Y in a lump sum and spends it at a constant rate, as shown in Figure I. Average money balances are

$$M^d = Y/2,$$

so that an increase in income to the consumer results in a proportional increase in average money holdings. Therefore, the income elasticity of the demand for money is unity.

However, such a simple model is only one-half of the story. If consumers have cash balances as shown in Figure I, firms must have cash balances that are complementary. The simplest economy with one consumer and one firm is shown in Figure II. The firm pays factor payments to the consumer of Y dollars; the consumer spends his income at a constant rate, paying money to the firm as this income is spent. When the firm pays the consumer Y dollars, the cash balance of the firm is reduced to zero, and the cash balance of the consumer increases from zero to Y. Aggregate demand for money remains constant at Y dollars, the average money demand of both the consumer and the firm being $Y/2$ dollars.

However, an increase in income now has a different effect on money holdings from that of the simple model given in Figure I. Increases in payments to the consumer must come from the firm, and vice versa. In particular, in the model illustrated in Figure II, consider an increase in income resulting from increased spending by the consumer from time $t = 1$. Suppose that during the period the consumer spends $Y + \Delta Y$ at a constant rate, instead of Y, and the firm pays Y

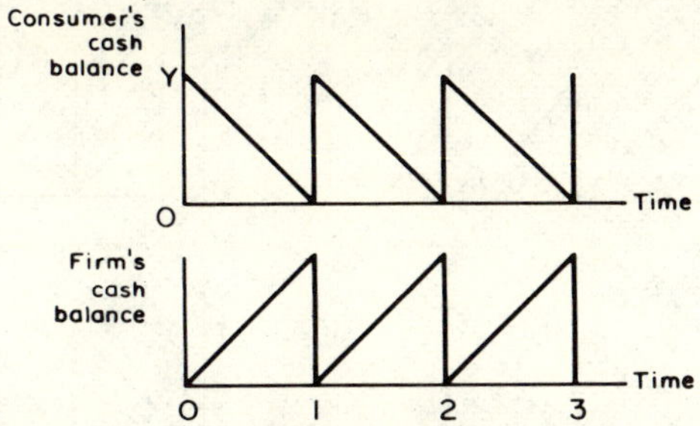

FIGURE II

$+ \Delta Y$ in factor payments at the next payment date, which is time $t = 2$.

These changes are displayed in Figure III. If the consumer's bank account is at Y dollars at time $t = 1$, then spending $Y + \Delta Y$ at a constant rate during the next period means that the consumer will fall short of cash before his receipt of income from the firm. In particular, the consumer will exhaust his cash balances by time $t_0 = 1 + Y/(Y + \Delta Y)$ shown in Figures IIIa and IIIb. Figures IIIa and IIIb exhibit two different types of behavior on the part of the consumer at time t_0. In Figure IIIa the consumer decides to sell an asset, so that he can continue to pay for his purchases. In Figure IIIb the consumer delays his payment to the firm until he receives his next inflow of cash, whereupon he pays the bill.

Consider each of these in turn. In Figure IIIa the consumer needs to sell ΔY dollars worth of other assets in order to continue paying for purchases from the firm, since he is buying $Y + \Delta Y$ during the period and he has already paid out Y dollars. If he does this, his cash balance rises to ΔY at time $t = t_0$, falling at a constant rate back to zero at time $t = 2$. The cash balance of the firm continues to rise at a constant rate to $Y + \Delta Y$ at time $t = 2$, the amount received from the consumer. Thus, at time $t = t_0$, aggregate money holdings rise from Y to $Y + \Delta Y$. At time $t = 2$, the firm pays the consumer $Y + \Delta Y$ in factor payments; the consumer's cash balance rises to $Y + \Delta Y$, the firm's cash balance falls to zero. Aggregate demand for money remains at $Y + \Delta Y$. Consequently, the effect of an increase in income beginning at time $t = 1$ is an increase in the demand for money at time $t = t_0$. When income was Y, aggregate demand for money was Y; when income rises to $Y + \Delta Y$, aggregate demand for money rises to $Y + \Delta Y$. The demand for money is proportional to income, and hence the income elasticity of the demand for money is unity.

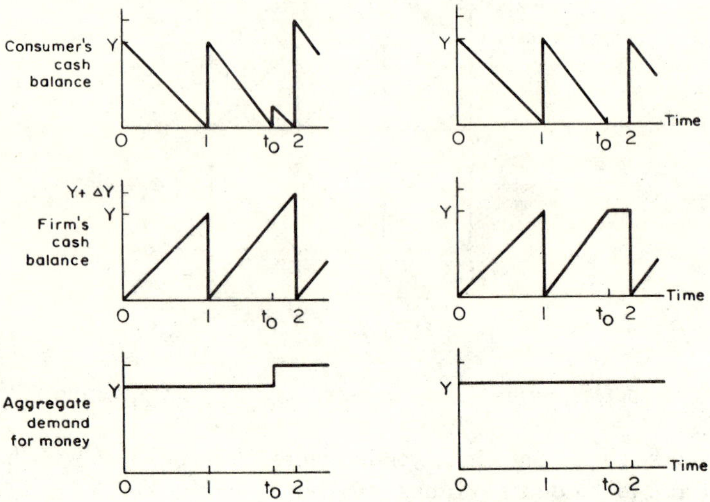

FIGURE IIIa
"Irving Fisher"

FIGURE IIIb
"Irving Fisher on His Head"

On the contrary, Figure IIIb yields the opposite result. If at time t_0 the consumer refrains from paying for his purchases immediately, his cash balances remain at zero. Correspondingly, the cash balance of the firm remains at Y (instead of rising to $Y + \Delta Y$ as in IIIa). The aggregate demand for money remains at Y. When the firm pays factor payments of $Y + \Delta Y$ to the consumer at $t = 2$, the consumer immediately hands back to the firm ΔY in delayed payments; that is, the firm pays a net Y dollars to the consumer, and the bill has been paid. Thus, the cash balance of the consumer rises to Y, and the cash balance of the firm falls to zero. Aggregate demand for money under this behavior is Y. Hence, an increase in income from Y to $Y + \Delta Y$ is accompanied by no increase in the demand for money. Rather than being unity, the income elasticity of the demand for money is zero.

Figure IIIa with the consumer selling assets when temporarily short of cash leads to the simple quantity theory of Irving Fisher. However, when the consumer changes the timing of his payments, money demand is unchanged and velocity varies proportionately with income. The difference in assumption regarding agents' behavior when they are temporarily cash short yields a great difference in terms of the short-run income elasticity of the demand for money. In the next section, we formalize this idea in an economy with many agents, each with different monitoring rules and different payments flows.

IV. The Generalization

The model presented in this section is a generalization of the example of the last section, and differs from the usual models of money holdings, in which payments depend only upon expenditures. The model exactly corresponds to the earlier story of the poker game. Periodically, at the start of a new game, the players bring a fixed-target amount of money to the game. In the course of the game, between those points at which bank accounts are monitored, in our terminology, those without sufficient cash to cover their debts delay payments to their creditors.

Payments at time $t = \lambda$ are defined by (1), reproduced from above:

$$p(\lambda) = \min(m(\lambda), b(\lambda)). \tag{1}$$

Payments made at time λ are rationed by the available cash balances if the individual is cash short. If the individual is not cash short, all bills are paid.

Assuming continuous time, the equation for the change in money holdings is given by the difference between inpayments and outpayments:

$$\dot{m}(\lambda) = y(\lambda) - p(\lambda), \tag{2}$$

where $y(\lambda)$ refers to cash inflows at time $t = \lambda$. Similarly, the differential equation for the change in accumulated bills is given by

$$\dot{b}(\lambda) = e(\lambda) - p(\lambda), \tag{3}$$

where $e(\lambda)$ refers to expenditures made at time $t = \lambda$. Thus, payments and expenditures are not inextricably linked; it is possible at particular times for individuals to make expenditures without making simultaneous monetary payments, and vice versa.

The economy can be considered as composed of a continuum of agents (households, firms, etc.) each having different payments and receipts patterns. The typical agent is denoted ω in the set Ω of all agents. Each agent makes his expenditures and pays his bills according to his own rules, except that he follows the payments rationing scheme when he is temporarily short. In addition, each agent has a monitoring habit. Since target-threshold type monitoring has been dealt with elsewhere, we deal here with the more Fisherian assumption of periodic monitoring, that is, where each agent monitors his bank account at regular intervals with periodicity l. At these monitoring times, agent ω adjusts his cash balance to $\overline{m}_\omega$ (determined by some long-run optimizing procedure) by either purchases or sales of assets. Each agent is taken to monitor his account at times $t = 0, l, 2l, \ldots$ (an assumption that can be shown to generalize (footnote 5)).

For each agent ω at time λ when he wishes to make payments, these payments are defined by

$$p_\omega(\lambda) = \min(m_\omega(\lambda), b_\omega(\lambda)). \tag{4}$$

Let $\mu_{\nu\omega}(t)$ represent the proportion of payment made at time t by agent ν to agent ω, so that at time t agent ω receives $\mu_{\nu\omega}(t)p_\nu(t)$ from agent ν. Since all payments by agent ν at time t go to some agent,

$$\int_{\omega\in\Omega} \mu_{\nu\omega}(t)d\omega = 1 \quad \text{for all } \nu \text{ and } t. \tag{5}$$

Except at times at which the bank account is monitored, all inflows to agent ω consist of all payments coming from other agents, so that we may write

$$y_\omega(t) = \int_{\nu\in\Omega} \mu_{\nu\omega}(t)p_\nu(t)d\nu. \tag{6}$$

Suppose that the cash balance was last monitored at time $t = kl$ whereupon agent ω set his cash balance at $\overline{m}_\omega$. The cash balance of ω at time $t = \tau$ is then equal to

$$m_\omega(\tau) = \overline{m}_\omega + \int_{t=kl}^{t=\tau} \dot{m}_\omega(t)dt. \tag{7}$$

Summing over all agents, desired aggregate money demand at time $t = \tau$ is

$$\begin{aligned} M(\tau) &= \int_{\omega\in\Omega} m_\omega(\tau) \\ &= \int_{\omega\in\Omega} \overline{m}_\omega + \int_{\omega\in\Omega}\int_{t=kl}^{t=\tau} \dot{m}_\omega(t)dt\,d\omega \\ &= \int_{\omega\in\Omega} \overline{m}_\omega + \int_{t=kl}^{t=\tau}\left(\int_{\omega\in\Omega} \dot{m}_\omega(t)d\omega\right)dt \\ &= \int_{\omega\in\Omega} \overline{m}_\omega + \int_{t=kl}^{t=\tau}\left(\int_{\omega\in\Omega} (y_\omega(t) - p_\omega(t))d\omega\right)dt \end{aligned} \tag{8}$$

by use of (2). Summing (6) across all agents,

$$\begin{aligned} \int_{\omega\in\Omega} y_\omega(t)d\omega &= \int_{\omega\in\Omega}\int_{\nu\in\Omega} \mu_{\nu\omega}(t)p_\nu(t)d\nu\,d\omega \\ &= \int_{\nu\in\Omega} p_\nu(t)\int_{\omega\in\Omega} \mu_{\nu\omega}(t)d\omega\,d\nu \\ &= \int_{\nu\in\Omega} p_\nu(t)d\nu \end{aligned}$$

using (5). Consequently,

$$\int_{\omega\epsilon\Omega} (y_\omega(t) - p_\omega(t))d\omega = 0,$$

so that in equation (8)

$$M(\tau) = \int_{\omega\epsilon\Omega} \overline{m}_\omega + \int_{t=kl}^{t=\tau} 0\, dt \qquad (9)$$

$$= \int_{\omega\epsilon\Omega} \overline{m}_\omega.$$

Thus, at any time τ, desired *aggregate* money holdings are independent of τ and of expenditure and income flows, and depend only on the monitoring rule. While individual money holdings will be dependent upon expenditure and income flows, aggregate money holdings will not. This will occur insofar as the monitoring rule and the payments behavior, as given by (1), do not change.

But this is precisely our point. Only insofar as these habits change will desired aggregate money holdings change in response to changes in aggregate income. Consequently, as these habits are slow to change, so will desired money holdings be slow to change, and so the income elasticity of the demand for money, and not just the interest elasticity, will be low. This, of course, occurs in the short run, which is defined as the time period in which habits are constant. The longer run, in which time period habits adjust to changes in the rate of interest, will also be a time period in which habits adjust to changes in income. This adjustment of habits is represented in this model by changes in the target levels $\overline{m}_\omega$.[5]

5. This model can be generalized to allow for agents having different monitoring intervals. Each agent is then represented by a pair (ω,l), where ω represents the agents' inpayments and outpayments, and l represents the monitoring rule. Each agent is then a member of an economic system described by $\Omega \times L$, when $\omega\epsilon\Omega$, $l\epsilon L$. In particular, assume that the distribution of ω is independent of l; that is, there is an identically distributed population of agents for each monitoring rule l. A simple example shows why this assumption is necessary to obtain a zero income elasticity. Suppose an increase in income results in agent A's gaining cash balances at the expense of agents B, C, and D, so that at their next monitoring periods, agents B, C, and D decrease, and agent A increases their net demand for other assets or securities. If agent A monitors his account at time t_1 and agents B, C, and D monitor at time t_2, then at time t_1 there exists an excess demand for securities and, at time t_2, an excess supply. Over the period including t_1 and t_2, net demand for securities is zero or, equivalently, aggregate money demand is constant (so that the stock equilibrium is preserved), but at times t_1 and t_2, the flow equilibrium is not preserved. The independence of ω and l eliminates this problem, since, at each point in time, sets of identically distributed people are monitoring their bank balances. It then follows that (9) holds at each point in time.

V. Variability of Trade Credit and Money

This section considers the empirical relevance of our theory of short-run changes in the timing of payments as reflected partially in changes in trade credit. Laffer [1970] has claimed that *changes* in trade credit are of such a small order of magnitude relative to the money *stock* that theoretical calculations regarding trade credit cannot possibly be empirically important. In our model, a more appropriate comparison, contrary to Laffer, would be *changes* in trade credit relative to *changes* in the money stock.

Empirically, the growth and variability of trade credit, both in absolute and percentage terms, has been greater than that of M_1. Figures for the period 1946–1975 show that aggregate trade credit has risen more than tenfold during this period (from \$21 billion to \$273 billion), whereas M_1 has risen approximately threefold (from \$113 billion to \$344 billion).[6] Moreover, trade credit shows a greater relative cyclical variation. While total cyclical variation in absolute figures during 1946–1975 is somewhat meaningless because of the very different rates of growth, computing variation in (detrended) percentage growth rates reveals that changes in trade credit are of a higher order of magnitude than the money stock. The standard deviation of the percentage annual growth rate of trade credit from 1946 to 1975 was 5.8 percent, compared to a comparable figure for M_1 of 2.5 percent. In terms of 1975 levels, this means that the standard deviation of trade credit is \$15.9 billion, compared to \$7.7 billion for M_1. That is, the absolute cyclical variation for trade credit is more than twice that for M_1, which is certainly *not* a smaller order of magnitude.

Further consideration shows that this trade credit may be even more important than those figures indicate. In our model, trade credit replaces the use of money on a dollar-for-dollar basis at the time of peak need for liquidity—i.e., on the "monthly" day of payment. To have an extra dollar of money on this day, it would be necessary to hold an extra dollar for the whole month. On the other hand, the trade credit may be paid back quickly, as pictured in our simple model of Section III. Thus, it will take less than \$1 average trade credit over the month to give an extra \$1 of liquidity on the day of peak need. For this reason, changes in trade credit can offset the effects of much larger changes in the money supply.

6. Board of Governors of the Federal Reserve System [1976]: pp. 134–36 (money stock); 158–60 (trade credit).

VI. Conclusion

The models given above demonstrate that the timing of payments is an important and overlooked consideration in the short-run demand for money. There seems little doubt that it is relatively simple for the individual to vary the timing of payments to overcome temporary shortages in money balances. Consequently, the timing of payments is an important mechanism whereby the demand for money adjusts to the supply in the short run. This implies that even though the rate of interest may be slow to adjust the demand for money to the supply in the short run, velocity will vary proportionately with income; that is, the short-run income elasticity of the demand for money will be quite low.

University of California, Berkeley, and London School of Economics
Queen's University, Canada

References

Akerlof, G. A., "Irving Fisher on His Head: The Consequences of Constant Threshold-Target Monitoring of Money Holdings," this *Journal*, XCIII (1979), 169–87.
Barro, R. J., and H. I. Grossman, "A General Disequilibrium Model of Income and Employment," *American Economic Review*, LX (1971), 82–93.
Baumol, W. J., "The Transactions Demand for Cash: An Inventory Theoretic Approach," this *Journal*, LXVI (1952), 545–56.
Benassy, J. P., "Neo-Keynesian Disequilibrium in a Monetary Economy," *Review of Economic Studies*, XLII (1975), 503–23.
Board of Governors of the Federal Reserve System, *Flow of Funds Accounts 1946–1975*, December 1976.
Brechling, F. P. R., and R. G. Lipsey, "Trade Credit and Monetary Policy," *Economic Journal*, LXX (1963), 618–41.
Chow, G. C., "On the Long-Run and Short-Run Demand for Money," *Journal of Political Economy*, LXXIV (1966), 111–31.
Clower, R. W., and P. W. Howitt, "The Transactions Theory of the Demand for Money: A Reconsideration," *Journal of Political Economy*, LXXXIII (1978), 449–66.
Fisher, I., *The Purchasing Power of Money* (New York: Macmillan, 1911).
Friedman, M., "The Demand for Money: Some Theoretical and Empirical Results," *Journal of Political Economy*, LXVII (1959), 327–51.
Goldfeld, S. M., "The Demand for Money Revisited," *Brookings Papers on Economic Activity*, 3 (1973), 577–638.
——, "The Case of The Missing Money," *Brookings Papers on Economic Activity*, 3 (1976), 683–730.
Grossman, H. I., "Money, Interest and Prices in Market Disequilibrium," *Journal of Political Economy*, LXXIX (1971), 943–61.
Keynes, J. M., *The General Theory of Employment, Interest and Money* (New York: Macmillan, 1936).
Laffer, A. B., "Trade Credit and the Money Market," *Journal of Political Economy*, LXXVIII (1970), 239–67.
Laidler, D., "The Rate of Interest and the Demand for Money: Some Empirical Evidence," *Journal of Political Economy*, LXXIV (1966), 543–55.
Miller, M. H., and D. Orr, "A Model of the Demand for Money by Firms," this *Journal*, LXXX (1966), 413–35.
Tobin, J., "The Interest Elasticity of the Transactions Demand for Cash," *Review of Economics and Statistics*, XXXVIII (1956), 241–47.

PERSONAL WEALTH TRANSFERS*

JAMES D. ADAMS

A theory of personal wealth transfers is developed which implies that components given to a recipient, such as education and bequests, are perfect substitutes. Therefore, components whose marginal cost rises more rapidly than average reveal wealth elasticities that are smaller than average. For related reasons, time series elasticities are expected to fall short of cross-sectional elasticities. An empirical investigation estimates cross-sectional wealth elasticities of gifts and bequests and time series wealth elasticities of bequest. The estimates are ranked in the order that is anticipated from the theory.

I. INTRODUCTION

The mechanism of personal wealth transfers, or the means by which wealth is passed from one generation to the next, has stimulated persistent interest among economists. Yet despite the interest, particularly with respect to inheritance, comparatively little work has been done to develop an approach based on the economist's theory of consumer choice. Principal exceptions appear to be Becker [1974], Blinder [1974], Ishikawa [1975], and Parsons [1974, 1975].

Under the broadest interpretation, the problem deals with nothing less than the economic and institutional continuity of society, making its scope impossibly wide. This paper is limited to the study of human and material transfers, particularly education and bequests.

While there is little doubt concerning the link between education and income, whatever its cause, it may seem that bequests are an insignificant part of wealth. Since the distribution of bequests is concentrated among upper income groups, this is surely true for most persons. Nevertheless, the absolute magnitude of bequests is substantial; in 1963, for example, 17 billion dollars alone were left by the small fraction of decedents included in the federal estate tax sample

* I would like to thank the members of my thesis committee, Gary S. Becker, T. W. Schultz, and Gilbert R. Ghez, for helpful advice and criticism that materially improved the content of this paper, an outgrowth of my dissertation [1976] research at the University of Chicago. Margaret G. Reid and Larry Kenny also made useful suggestions. I am indebted to Marvin Sussman and Judith Cates for permission to use their inheritance data. Any remaining errors are of course my own. Support provided by the Ford Foundation and the National Institute of Mental Health is gratefully acknowledged. The National Science Foundation supported work on the Sussman data under grant number SOC 76-84304.

The Quarterly Journal of Economics, August 1980 0033-5533/80/0095-0159$02.10

[Pechman, 1966, p. 292], and under reasonable assumptions the annual flow of bequests is approximately 6 percent of GNP.[1]

This paper addresses a wide range of empirical questions. What is the comparative effect of a rise in family income on educational attainment of children as opposed to bequests? Why might bequests and other asset transfers rise more sharply than income in the cross section, while they may have fallen relative to income over time even as income has risen? What is the role of educational attainment of parents in the educational attainment of children versus material inheritance? Why has the estate tax rate regularly exceeded the gift tax rate?

Moreover, some of the empirical findings reported below have interesting macroeconomic consequences. If the permanent income elasticity of bequests exceeds (or is less than) unity, then the lifetime savings ratio, or average propensity to save, rises (or falls) with income, through the usual average-marginal relation [Blinder, 1976]. Time series estimates of the income elasticity of bequests contained in this paper are typically less than unity. These estimates therefore suggest a slightly declining savings ratio as income increases over time.

The theory and empirical results are also relevant to the issue of whether or not Social Security decreases private savings. Since transfer components are perfect substitutes according to our theory, and educational transfers occur at lower wealth even while material bequests are equal to zero, then a considerable fraction of the population leaves positive intergenerational transfers. Thus, a much greater number of persons than simply those leaving financial inheritances take notice of the forced Social Security transfer from young to old, and private savings are less likely to decrease because of Social Security payments.

The remainder of the paper is divided into three sections. Section II presents the theoretical model, and compares it to an alternative. Section III presents empirical estimates of parental demand functions for educational attainment based on cross-section data, and similar equations for bequests based on both cross-section and time series

1. If death samples randomly among asset holders, a 1 percent death rate implies that 1 percent of physical wealth is transferred annually through bequest. According to estimates by Schultz [1971, p. 71], 60 percent of all wealth is physical wealth, so that 0.6 percent of all wealth would pass annually through bequests. Since, on the assumption of a 10 percent rate of return income is $1/10$ of wealth, a 0.6 percent transfer of wealth is equivalent to 6 percent of income. The figure may be biased upward by attributing too large a share to physical wealth, and downward by assuming that death samples asset holders randomly. It may also be biased upward because donors decumulate assets so that bequests are less than average net worth.

data. Section IV concludes the paper and suggests directions for additional research.

II. Theoretical Analysis

A. Introductory Discussion

The basic hypothesis of this paper asserts that persons who transfer wealth (hereafter, donors) are motivated by altruism. By this it is meant that donors seek only to raise the utility of their recipients and do not attempt to control the manner in which recipients consume. The donor's intertemporal utility therefore depends on his own consumption and the utility of his recipients.[2] Looked at differently, the donor consumes bundles of commodities, where the bundles are the consumption of the donor and each recipient. These assumptions imply a separable utility function in the consumption of the different persons.

For simplicity, the analysis that follows treats the case of a single recipient. The multiple-recipient case involves an extension of the list of arguments and the attachment of subscripts, with little analytical gain. Assuming prior maximization with respect to individual commodities at fixed prices, we obtain the donor's indirect utility function,

$$U = U\,[V_D(P_C,C_D) + V_R\,(P_R,C_R^*)], \tag{1}$$

where V_D is a function bundling the donor's consumption that depends on P_D, the price vector of goods the donor consumes, and on C_D, the present value of his lifetime consumption. Similarly, V_R is the recipient's utility function that bundles his consumption, P_R the price vector of goods the recipient consumes, and C_R^* the present value of his total expenditures, comprised of his own consumption and transfers that the recipient makes to others.[3] Since goods prices are

2. Several kinds of interdependent utility functions are discussed in Becker [1974]; the utility function of this paper is separably interdependent. See Strotz [1957, 1959] and Gorman [1959] for a technical discussion of their properties. Separable utility functions display the general form $U = U[G_1(\cdot), G_2(\cdot), \ldots, G_k(\cdot)]$, where G_i are branch utilities, known as specific satisfaction functions, into which only quantities of commodity group i enter. The commodity groups are defined by persons in this paper.

3. Thus, $C_R^* = C_R + T_{G,R}$, where $T_{G,R}$ = gross transfers given by recipients. The functions V_D and V_R are the result of maximizing the original specific satisfaction functions subject to fixed expenditure levels C_D and C_R^*, respectively. The optimal individual quantities consumed by the donor and recipient are written as functions of their respective prices and expenditures, and these functions are substituted into the original specific satisfaction functions.

The expenditure levels are lifetime present values because they encompass all the consumption of the donor and recipients. Notice also that the price vectors include discount factors, which are assumed constant.

fixed, the problem reduces to the choice between present values of expenditures C_D and C_R^*.

Budget constraints and transfer identities complete the statement of the problem. The donor's wealth constraint is

$$W_D^* = C_D + T_D, \tag{2}$$

where W_D^* is his total wealth, his endowment and transfers received by him, C_D is his consumption, and T_G the gross transfer, or the total amount spent on the recipient. The recipient's wealth constraint, which relates the net transfer to his total expenditure, is

$$W_R + T_R = C_R^*, \tag{3}$$

where W_R is the recipient's endowed wealth, T_R the net transfer, or the amount received, and C_R^* the recipient's total expenditure.[4] The distinction between gross and net transfers is central to the model. We make the reasonable assumption that it costs more than a dollar to transfer a dollar received, so the gross transfer is the larger of the two magnitudes.

The net transfer itself is the present value of components distinguished by date and form (examples of form are educational contributions, land, stock, and so forth). In symbols the net transfer is

$$T_R = \sum_i \sum_k T_{ik} \frac{1}{(1+r)^i}, \tag{4}$$

where i stands for the date and k for the form of transfer. Gross amounts generally exceed net amounts because of transfer costs, which are represented as follows. If net amounts are scaled in units worth one dollar, then T_{ik} units are worth T_{ik} dollars to the recipient, but cost the donor $P_{ik}T_{ik}$ dollars, where $P_{ik} \geq 1$, reflecting the transfer costs. Thus, the gross component exceeds the net, or $P_{ik}T_{ik} \geq T_{ik}$. The gross transfer is the present value of the gross components, or

$$T_D = \sum_i \sum_k P_{ik}T_{ik} \frac{1}{(1+r)^i}, \tag{5}$$

and clearly $T_D \geq T_R$. Note that P_{ik} may depend on the net amounts T_{ik}.

Maximizing the donor's utility subject to the constraints and identities, we obtain the first-order conditions:

4. The endowed wealth of recipients derives from genetic inheritance and other donors, such as governmental subsidies. For an analysis of the latter, see Barro [1974].

(6)
$$\frac{\partial U}{\partial V_R}\frac{\partial V_R}{\partial C_R}\frac{1}{(1+r)^i} - \lambda MC_{ik}\frac{1}{(1+r)^i} \leq 0$$
$$k = 1 \ldots n$$
$$i = 1 \ldots m$$

(7)
$$\frac{\partial U}{\partial V_D}\frac{\partial V_D}{\partial C_D} - \lambda = 0$$

(8)
$$W_D = C_D + T_D,$$

where we assume a positive solution for total transfers, and MC_{ik} is the nondiminishing marginal cost of the ikth transfer.[5] It follows from (6) that $MC_{ik} = (\partial U/\partial V_R \cdot \partial V_R/\partial C_R)/\lambda$, for all i and k involving positive components. Therefore, individual marginal costs are equated to a common value, or

(9)
$$MC_{ik} = MC$$

(10)
$$dMC_{ik} = dMC, \qquad T_{ik} > 0,$$

where d is the differential operator, and (10) follows from (9) because equality also holds for changes. This equalization result has important implications for transfer behavior. For example, it implies that true tax rates on gifts and bequests are equalized.

The model developed in this paper also provides a rigorous explanation for the frequently observed combination of zero material inheritances and positive educational contributions, especially among parents with ordinary incomes. First, the inequality in (6) implies that transfers whose marginal cost exceeds the common value are set at zero, since components are perfect substitutes. Second, the human capital literature suggests that marginal costs of educational transfers rise with the acquisition of training, since abilities of the individual are held constant and are a cause of diminishing returns. Therefore, if education were cheaper to transfer than assets at low levels of each, only education would be given by persons with lesser wealth and lesser total transfers.

The situation is depicted in Figure I. The curved loci labeled T_iT_i' are constant expenditure curves. Higher curves represent larger transfers, while concavity in each case is due to rising marginal costs of the transfers. From the origin to point A, the marginal cost of education is less than the marginal cost of inheritance or gifts, and no

5. In writing equations (6), $\partial CR/\partial T_{ik} = [1/(1+r)^i]$, from equations (2) and (3). But $MC_{ik} = P_{ik} + T_{ik} \cdot dP_{ik}/dT_{ik}$, from equations (4) and (5), where the MC_{ik} are marginal prices.

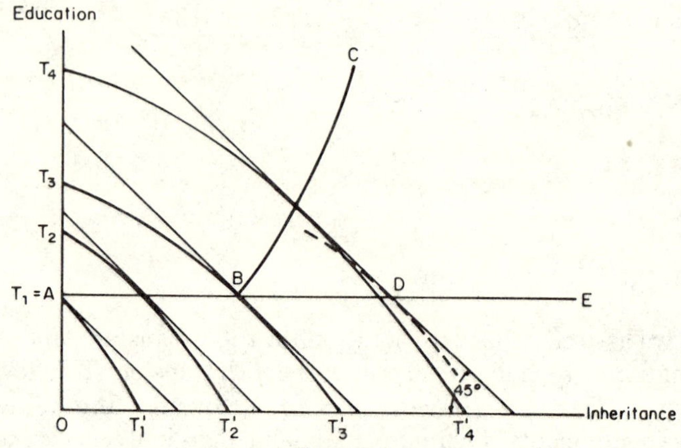

FIGURE I
Locus of Cost-Minimizing Points, Education, and Inheritance

inheritances or gifts are made. To the right of point A, it is assumed that marginal costs of the asset transfers are constant, assuming zero taxation within the limits of the exemptions. Since marginal costs of educational transfers rise continuously, no more wealth is given through schooling, unless marginal costs of the assets begin to rise. If estate and gift taxation become progressive, marginal costs of inheritance rise, and educational transfers resume their increase, as on the segment BC. Otherwise the expansion path is the horizontal line BDE. Notice that interior solutions involve equality of marginal costs, indicated by tangencies with 45° lines.

The issue of marginal cost equalization provides a convenient point of comparison between this approach and others. The main competitor is probably some version of an Enforcement Hypothesis, which assumes that the transfers are devices the donor uses to obtain services or to encourage consumption of merit goods. In this view, the donor values specific actions recipients take or goods they consume as opposed to valuing the actions or commodities the way recipients themselves would, as altruism assumes. The specific actions are assumed to depend on the present value of net transfer components T_{ik} through enforcement functions; the actions depend on the present value because dollars in the future are valued less highly than dollars today; they depend on the net amounts, because these are the amounts received and supply the incentives. In addition, the actions depend primarily on future transfers and the probabilities of loss.[6]

6. We say primarily, because the receipt of past transfers can affect behavior if recipients regard them as an addition to wealth, even though there is no deterrent effect that channels behavior. We disregard the wealth effects on the grounds that the transfers are anticipated and not windfalls.

The Enforcement Hypothesis suggests that transfer components are unlikely to be perfect substitutes, and that marginal costs are unlikely to be equal. If transfers exert little influence on the actions after they are made, later transfers affect later actions more than earlier transfers do; furthermore, the farther in the future transfers are, the less their effect on any of the actions, because of discounting. Since the transfers vary in their effects on the actions, they also vary in their effects on the donor's utility, and their marginal costs are likely to differ.[7]

For example, the marginal estate tax rate exceeds the marginal gift tax rate, if bequests are a more effective enforcement device. This is the explanation given in Shoup [1966] for the persistently higher estate tax rate. In a separate paper [Adams, 1978], little difference is found in the rates once they are appropriately calculated. On the basis of this supporting evidence, we develop additional implications of the Altruistic Hypothesis.

B. *Comparative Statics*

The preceding discussion has made it clear that the composition of the net transfer is governed by a cost-minimization criterion; namely the minimization of the gross transfer for any given size of net transfer. Assuming that the optimal composition has been established, the first-order conditions show that net and gross transfers are determined by the schedule of marginal cost, the donor's wealth, and the recipient's endowed wealth. Moreover, the net transfer is the more

7. To illustrate, let the donor's utility depend on a vector of own consumption goods X_D and a vector of the recipient's actions X_L, assumed for simplicity to be a single action recurring through time. Then the donor's utility function is

$$U = U(X_D, X_L). \tag{a}$$

The actions themselves depend positively on the present discounted value of future net transfers and the probabilities of losing them ρ_{ik}, through the enforcement functions, which are

$$X_{jL} = X_{jL}\left(\rho_{ik}, T_{ik}\left[1/(1+r)^{i-j}\right]\right) \quad i \geq j. \tag{b}$$

The restriction to future transfers and probabilities of loss is indicated by the time subscript. Maximizing (a) subject to the enforcement functions (b), the donor's wealth constraint and definitions of net and gross transfers (equations (2), (4), and (5)) yield the first-order conditions,

$$\sum_j \sum_L \frac{\partial U}{\partial X_{jL}} \frac{\partial X_{jL}}{\partial T_{ik}} - \lambda\, MC_{ik} = 0. \tag{c}$$

Clearly, since the weighted sums of the utilities are not identical across transfer components, neither are the marginal costs MC_{ik}.

It should be emphasized that this is not a full solution to the enforcement problem. It is assumed that the transfers have an effect on the actions, but the effect is not determined in the model. For two recent enforcement schemes in different contexts, see Becker and Stigler [1974], and Tideman and Tullock [1976].

fundamental concept because it is the donor's contribution to the recipient. It is the difference between the recipient's consumption desired by the donor and endowed wealth. Transfer demand is an excess demand.

In this part, implications of the theory are drawn for shifts in the donor's wealth.[8] A natural way for an economist to express the relation between the net transfer (or its components) and the donor's wealth is through the use of wealth elasticities. They conveniently express percentage movements in transfers relative to percentage movements in wealth.

We first consider the net transfer wealth elasticity. Because it has been shown that the level of the net transfer depends on marginal costs, donor's wealth, and recipient's wealth, the wealth elasticity depends on percentage changes in marginal costs, recipient's consumption, and recipient's wealth set in motion by a given percentage change in the donor's wealth. Moreover, since the net transfer demand is an excess demand, the elasticity is the usual difference of two terms. The first term reflects rising demand for recipient's consumption; the second term reflects the correlated increase in recipient's wealth, and the rising supply of recipient's consumption.

In symbols, the exact formula for the net transfer wealth elasticity is

$$\text{(11)} \qquad \eta_{T_R W_D} = \beta(1 + [\gamma/(1-\gamma)]\,\sigma)\eta_{C_R W_D} - (\beta - 1)(1 + \beta E \eta^{S}_{C_R C_R})\sigma,$$

where β (> 1) is the ratio of recipient consumption to the transfer, γ the share of recipient's endowed wealth in combined wealth, $\eta_{C_R W_D}$ the wealth elasticity of recipient's consumption, σ (> 0) the wealth correlation factor (the percentage increase in recipient's wealth per 1 percent increase in the donor's wealth), E the elasticity of marginal cost with respect to the transfer, and $\eta^{S}_{C_R C_R}$ (< 0) is the compensated price elasticity of recipient's consumption.[9] The derivations of (11) and equations to follow are found in the Appendix; there it is also

8. Shifts in wealth are observable; shifts in transfer prices much less so.

9. Under a certain condition, the wealth elasticity of total transfers $\eta_{T_R W_D}$ will exceed the wealth elasticity of recipient consumption $\eta_{C_R W_D}$. In symbols,

$$\eta_{T_R W_D} > \eta_{C_R W_D}$$

if

$$\eta_{C_R W_D} > \frac{\mu}{1 + [((1-\sigma)/\sigma + \beta/(\beta-1)\gamma/(1-\gamma))]},$$

where $\mu = 1 + \beta E \eta_{C_R C_R}$. Since the numerator is less than one and the denominator greater than one, the critical value that $\eta_{C_R W_D}$ must exceed is less than one; if $\eta_{C_R W_D} = 1$, then $\eta_{T_R W_D} > 1$, since $0 < \sigma < 1$, $0 < \gamma < 1$, and $\beta > 1$.

TABLE I

DEFINITIONS OF SYMBOLS USED IN THE MODEL OF ALTRUISM

$\eta_{T_R W_D}$ =	observed net transfer wealth elasticity
$\eta_{T_{ik} W_D}$ =	observed wealth elasticity of ik component
$\eta_{T_{jK} W_D}$ =	observed wealth elasticity of jK component
σ =	$\partial(\ln W_R)/\partial(\ln W_D)$, the relative percentage movement of recipients' with donor's wealth or wealth correlation factor
E_{ik} =	$d(\ln MC_{ik})/d(\ln T_{ik})$[a]
E_{jK} =	$d(\ln MC_{jK})/d(\ln T_{jK})$, elasticities of component marginal cost with respect to the component[a]
E =	$d(\ln MC)/d(\ln T_r)$, (mean) elasticity of common marginal cost on all transfers[a]
β =	ratio of recipients' consumption to all transfers (greater than 1)
$\beta - 1$ =	ratio of recipients' (endowed) wealth to all transfers
γ =	share of recipients' wealth in the donor's social wealth[b]
$1 - \gamma$ =	share of donor's wealth in his social wealth
$\eta_{C_R W_D}$ =	wealth elasticity of recipient consumption
$\eta^S_{C_R C_R}$ =	compensated own price elasticity of demand for recipients' consumption

a. These elasticities are assumed nonnegative throughout.

b. The donor's social wealth is the sum of his own wealth and endowed wealth of recipients valued at the marginal transfer price.

shown that $1 + \beta \acute{E} \eta^S_{C_R C_R}$ exceeds zero, because the effect of a shift in recipient's wealth on the transfer cannot be eliminated by the changes in marginal cost that it sets in motion. The signs of the other factors comprising the terms are self-evident. Table I defines these symbols at length.

A useful approximation to (11) assumes the recipient's endowed wealth to be small relative to combined wealth, or $\gamma/(1-\gamma) \cong 0$.

Therefore,

$$\eta_{T_R W_D} \cong \beta \eta_{C_R W_D} - (\beta - 1)(\beta E \eta^S_{C_R C_R})\sigma. \quad (11')$$

The justification for this approximation is that most wealth is generated through family transfers, so that endowed wealth is unimportant. According to (11′), transfers are more wealth elastic, the greater the wealth elasticity of recipient consumption ($\eta_{C_R W_D}$) is, and the smaller the elasticity of marginal cost is with respect to the transfer (E). An increase in the wealth correlation factor (σ) decreases the wealth elasticity of the net transfer, essentially because it lowers the percentage growth in excess demand for the recipient's consumption as donor's wealth rises.[10]

10. Differentiate (11′) to prove each of these statements.

Of these factors, we would expect σ to be larger in time series than cross section data, because the assocation between wealth of entire generations over time is stronger than the association for individual families in a cross section. Therefore, we expect a smaller time series elasticity, and the time series elasticity could be less than unity even while the cross-section elasticity was greater than unity. Put differently, transfers need not be increasingly important relative to wealth as wealth rises over time, even though this may hold as wealth rises in a cross-section of individuals.

Since total transfers are not observed, it is useful to develop wealth elasticities for components, which are observable. The wealth elasticity of the *ik*th component is linked to the wealth elasticity of the net transfer. To see this, note that equalization of marginal costs implies that a component, whose marginal cost rises more slowly than the net transfer, must increase at a faster rate to maintain equality of marginal costs. For example, if the marginal cost of the net transfer rises 5 percent more rapidly than the marginal cost of the *ik*th component, the *ik*th component must rise at a 5 percent faster rate. Reflecting this consideration, the equation linking the wealth elasticities is

$$\eta_{T_{ik}W_D} = (E/E_{ik})\, \eta_{T_R W_D}, \tag{12}$$

where $\eta_{T_{ik}W_D}$ is the *ik*th wealth elasticity, and E_{ik} measures the elasticity of marginal cost for the *ik*th component. Thus, if E/E_{ik} = 1.05, as in the above example, (12) implies that $\eta_{T_{ik}W_D}/\eta_{T_R W_D}$ = 1.05.

Since the theory also implies that the *ik*th and *lm*th marginal costs are equated, their wealth elasticities are linked by a similar relation:

$$\eta_{T_{ik}W_D} = (E_{lm}/E_{ik})\, \eta_{T_{lm}W_D}. \tag{13}$$

Thus, when $E_{lm} \gtreqless E_{ik}$, $\eta_{T_{ik}W_D} \gtreqless \eta_{T_{lm}W_D}$, just as in the preceding discussion.[11]

Equation (12) is an important linking equation for empirical research: other things being equal, the implication that the overall wealth elasticity is smaller on time series data applies to any component. Equation (13) is also useful. It implies that components whose marginal costs rise less rapidly are more wealth elastic than human

11. Another way of expressing the result is to say that the wealth elasticities are inversely proportional to the elasticities of their marginal costs; hence the relative wealth elasticities of gifts and bequests are inversely proportional to the relative progressivity of their taxes; similarly for education and bequests.

TABLE II

TOBIT ESTIMATES OF CROSS-SECTIONAL INHERITANCE EQUATIONS[a]

Variable or statistic	2.1	2.2	2.3	2.4	2.5
Mean family income[b]	1.556	1.358		1.030	1.517
	(0.321)[c]	(0.307)		(0.349)	(0.360)
Donor's age	−0.044	0.005	0.012	−0.004	−0.015
	(0.009)	(0.010)	(0.007)	(0.011)	(0.011)
Donor's marital status	−2.112	−2.318	−2.348	−2.005	
	(0.191)	(0.183)	(0.186)	(0.180)	
Number of siblings or kin[d]	−0.198	−0.227	−0.249	−0.241	−0.180
	(0.053)	(0.073)	(0.074)	(0.083)	(0.077)
Mean education of recipients			0.135		
			(0.040)		
Mean number of labor force participants	−0.245	−0.507	−0.187	−0.262	−0.611
	(0.207)	(0.207)	(0.196)	(0.239)	(0.240)
Percent of recipients married				−0.798	
				(0.571)	
Intercept	−2.861	−4.753	1.322	−2.303	−6.634
Standard error	1.504	1.356	1.386	1.056	1.122
N	440	410	410	277	164

a. Dependent variable is zero if the inheritance equals zero, the logarithm of the inheritance if the inheritance exceeds zero.

b. See text for a discussion of this variable.

c. Asymptotic standard errors are in parentheses.

d. Number of next of kin is entered in equation (2.1); number of siblings is entered in all other equations.

capital transfers [Becker, 1967, pp. 35–37]. If so, transfer behavior helps to explain why there is greater inequality in asset holdings than in the holding of human wealth.

III. EMPIRICAL ANALYSIS

Part A of this section reports estimates of demand functions for inheritance based on cross section and time series evidence. In particular, these estimates permit us to test whether the cross-section wealth elasticity (for sons and daughters, and others) is larger, as the discussion in IIB suggests. Part B uses the same body of cross-section data to study the determinants of educational attainment of sons and daughters. A comparison can then be made between the wealth elasticity of education and inheritance for the same persons.

A. Demand Functions for Inheritance

Table II reports findings from an analysis of the Sussman data, a 5 percent random sample of estates submitted to probate in

Cleveland, Ohio, during 1965.[12] These data contain a unique combination of variables pertaining to at least two generations of the same families. In particular, they contain education of donors and recipients, family income of recipients, and material inheritance. Moreover, the estates are representative in size; few are subject to tax, and most of the inheritances assume a value of zero or one thousand dollars.[13] The dependent variable is assigned a value of zero if the inheritance is zero, or the logarithm of inheritance otherwise.[14] Since the majority of the observations take on values of zero, the equation residual has a truncated normal distribution, and Tobit is the appropriate estimation technique.[15]

Let us turn to the results found in Table II.[16] Mean family income in logarithms is used to approximate parental resources. It is an average across recipients of predicted income based upon their characteristics.[17] Recipient income is originally recorded on a monthly basis and contains a sizable transitory error component, which makes it unsuitable for the purpose at hand, estimation of permanent income effects on the transfers. Note that estimated family income consistently outperformed mean recorded family income in test regressions, suggesting the validity of the transient error component interpretation.

Equation (2.1) examines the determinants of inheritance for a combined sample of spouses and sons and daughters. This equation reveals a dominance of three variables that is prevalent throughout: mean family income, the donor's marital status, and the number of kin (or siblings). The coefficient of income is the estimated income

12. The data are described in Sussman, Cates, and Smith [1970].

13. For example, 247 of 410 sons and daughters received inheritances at or below one thousand dollars.

14. Original coding of the inheritances is in thousands of dollars; a tie between zero and one thousand dollars amounts is therefore necessary if all observations are to be kept and the logarithmic form is to be used, which in preliminary tests was better fitting than some alternatives.

15. See Tobin [1958] and Amemiya [1973] for discussions of this technique.

16. All samples require that recipients be between the ages of 25 and 64, that the source of their income be known (whether from wages, salaries, etc.), that someone in their family be currently working, that the principal wage earner be either themselves or their spouses, that the education of recipients be known, and that sex of the principal wage earner be male. These restrictions increase the permanent component in income.

17. The procedure followed actually had three steps. A Pareto regression was used to estimate the mean of the uppermost, open interval (see Bowley, [1920], pp. 462–63, for derivations), and midpoints assigned otherwise. Recoded income in logarithms was then regressed on recipient's education, age, marital status, number of labor force participants, quality of residence, and religion for the entire group of recipients. Predicted values obtained from this regression were then averaged by families.

elasticity of inheritance. Not only equation (2.1), but also the others based on smaller samples reveal an elasticity above unity; clustering about a central value of 1.3 is evident. Wherever it is entered, donor's marital status has a powerful negative effect; the interpretation is that married decedents leave most of the estate to surviving spouses who are largely omitted from the sample. The spouse contributes income to the marriage and owns much of the net worth at the partner's death.

Equation (2.1) also shows a powerful negative effect of the number of next of kin, an effect that can be given a quantity-quality interpretation; as the number of kin increases, the implicit cost of giving to any one recipient increases. The donor's age lowers inheritance. This finding can be interpreted either as a vintage effect, where wealth of parents diminishes the older the cohort, or else as a planned life cycle decumulation of assets. However, the effect fails to carry over to the other equations. Mean number of labor force participants among recipients is entered to control for bias in mean family income, which may show an increase as more persons join the work force, even though per capita income declines.

Let us turn to the other equations. Notice first (2.2) and (2.3), which are restricted to sons and daughters alone. Equation (2.2) enters nearly the same variables as (2.1), permitting evaluation of the effects of the sample restriction. The comparison shows a smaller income elasticity, and a larger impact of donor's marital state. The smaller income elasticity indicates a downward bias, if any, in the estimated income elasticity of inheritance. Incomes of spouses are largely omitted from the restricted sample, since they enter primarily in single recipient cases; but income of the spouse more closely approximates ideal parental income. Remaining incomes thus measure ideal income with an even larger error. The negative effect of donor's marital state is consistent with the interpretation that surviving spouses receive the bulk of the estate, given their omission from the sample. Donor's age is not significant in (2.2).

Mean family income is omitted from (2.3), and mean education of recipients is entered in its place as a predictor of inheritance. Mean family income, which alone can provide an income elasticity estimate, also seems to provide the better fit, judged by the standard errors of the two equations.

Equations (2.4) and (2.5) split the sample still further; in (2.4) the number of siblings in each family exceeds one. Percent of recipients married is introduced to test whether marriage is an indicator of recipients' wealth position, thereby shifting transfers away from them.[18] The final equation takes the role of the spouse into acount by omitting married decedents; this raises the mean inheritance received and lowers the fraction of zero inheritances in the sample.[19] The coefficients on this sample show a rise in absolute value, although they are otherwise similar to the other estimates.

Time series regressions are presented in Table III. Annual data on deflated mean estate from the Federal Estate tax sample are available for most years from 1922 to 1949; these data represent the uppermost fraction of 1 percent of wealth-holders. Mean estate in logarithms is entered as the dependent variable.[20]

The income measure used is the log of deflated per capita income of the fractional upper 1 percent of the population represented by top wealth-leavers. The ratio of property to wage income, again for the upper 1 percent, is entered as a shift factor.[21] The argument is that, as the ratio increases, the wealth-correlation factor declines between the generations. Income from property presumably involves more luck and greater Galtonian regression toward the mean than earnings, so the latter have greater inheritability. Since nominal exemption, tax rates, and the price level varied over the course of this period, real exemption dummies (*RDi*) were also included. The numerator of these variables assumes the value 1 for periods in which a particular version of the estate tax laws was in effect, and 0 otherwise; the denominator is the Consumer Price Index.[22] Changes in nominal exemptions are reflected in the numerator, while changes in the price level and the real exemptions are reflected in the denominator. As the CPI rises or falls, a given nominal exemption corresponds to a lower or higher real exemption. In case changes in tax rates affect the wealth

18. The original coding of recipient's marital status is 0 if not married, 1 if married.

19. The mean inheritance in logarithms rises from 0.613 in the full sample of sons and daughters to 1.214 in the decedent unmarried sample, or from $1,846 to $3,367 in antilogs. Similarly, there are only 39 zero observations in the restricted sample or 24 percent as opposed to 247 or 60 percent in the full sample.

20. Data are missing for 1945. The dependent variable is mean disposable estate, defined as gross estate minus debts, expenses, and taxes per return.

21. It would be desirable to adjust the property-wage income ratio to match the appropriate fractional 1 percent, as was done for the income measure, but it is not obvious how to make the correction. In the case of income per capita, the adjustment amounted to linearization of the Lorenz curve for income over the top 1 percent. The simplicity of that adjustment and its minor violation of the facts do not apply to the ratio variable.

22. Changing the exemption amounts to truncating the sample at a different point and changing the applicable level of mean income. Therefore, omitting the real exemption variables implies that real income enters less significantly. This can be seen by a direct comparison of equation (3.1) with equation (3.3). The income elasticity may be biased downward in Table III because of transitory components of income. However, this point applies at least equally well to the cross-sectional estimates.

TABLE III

TIME SERIES BEQUEST REGRESSIONS

Variable or statistic	3.1	3.2[a]	3.3	3.4
*RD*1				0.2400
				(0.2133)[b]
*RD*2				0.5745
				(0.2060)
*RD*3				0.4737
				(0.1733)
*RD*4				0.2244
				(0.1643)
*RSL*1			0.1274	
			(0.0906)	
*RSL*2			0.2680	
			(0.0886)	
*RSL*3			0.2189	
			(0.0739)	
*RSL*4			0.1123	
			(0.0690)	
Property/wage	1.2449		0.5619	0.6593
income	(0.1757)		(0.1962)	(0.1841)
Log of upper	0.7332	0.6295	0.8522	1.1398
1% income	(0.3278)	(0.3128)	(0.2359)	(0.2552)
Intercept	2.8700	3.9284	2.5051	1.8115
R^2	0.6879	0.8710	0.9277	0.9257
F-statistic	25.3450	148.4910	40.6325	39.4342
D.W. statistic	0.5749	1.3591	2.2407	2.2267
N	26	24	26	26

a. Regression used Cochrane-Orcutt method of calculating first-order autoregressive transformation; ρ was 0.9575 at the final step.

b. Standard errors are in parentheses.

Note. Definitions of the variables are as follows. The dependent variable is the logarithm of mean disposable estate. *RD*1 = 1/*CPI*, if year 1922–1925, 0 otherwise; *RD*2 = 1/*CPI*, if year 1926–1932, 0 otherwise; *RD*3 = 1/*CPI*, if year 1933–1935, 0 otherwise; *RD*4 = 1/*CPI*, if year 1936–1948, 0 otherwise. The *RSLi* = *RDi* log of income, *i* = (1, 2, 3, 4), and *CPI* = Consumer Price Index of BLS.

Sources for these variables are the following. The arithmetic form of the dependent variable is found in Lampman [1962, p. 30]. The 0–1 dummy variables, divided by *CPI* to obtain the RD1, stand for periods of time in which estate exemptions and tax rates differed: these periods are defined in U. S. Treasury Department [1945, pp. 328–31]. The *CPI* series is found in U. S. Bureau of the Census [1960, pp. 125–26]. The ratio variable is taken directly from Kuznets [1953, p. 668]. The arithmetic form of log income is the product of the following: the share of the upper 1 percent of population in income [Kuznets 1953, p. 582]; the fraction of donors, defined as the number of estate tax returns [Lampman 1962, p. 30] divided by a death rate applicable to wealthy persons [Lampman 1962, p. 54] and population [U. S. Bureau of the Census, 1960, p. 8]; and personal income [U. S. Bureau of the Census, 1960, p. 139].

elasticity (see equation (12)), interactions of the exemption dummies with income are entered as an alternative form (*RSLi*). Results are mostly as expected. In three of four equations the income elasticity lies below unity, and the income ratio variable increases bequests.

Estimates of the income elasticity cluster about 0.8 or 0.9, certainly lower than the mean of the cross-sectional estimates, though clearly there is overlap. Prior to entry of the real exemption variables, significant autocorrelation is present; in moving from (3.1) to (3.2), we have corrected for first-order autocorrelation. The transformation causes log income and the income ratio to become highly collinear, and the latter is therefore dropped from (3.2). In (3.3) and (3.4) different forms of the real exemption variables are introduced. This eliminates autocorrelation, increases the significance of the income variable, and raises R^2.

B. Educational Attainment Regressions

Let us now turn to the equations determining education attainment. These are also based upon the Sussman data. According to the development of Section II, we expect a lower income elasticity of education than of inheritance. The only additional variable entered is donor's education, which was not significant in the inheritance equations and was therefore omitted from them.

Before discussing the results, notice that the income elasticity is likely to be biased upward by the estimation procedure. The reason is that mean family income depends on the recipient's education. There is automatic positive correlation between the dependent variable and income. Multiple recipient samples are chosen in (4.2), (4.3), and (4.5) to break this correlation, though the adjustment turns out to be unimportant. Given that the income elasticity of inheritance is probably biased downward (see the discussion of equations (2.1) and (2.2)), the difference in the two elasticities is conservatively estimated in this paper.

Two forms of equation are shown in Table IV. The first uses the log of parents' and children's schooling, the second arithmetic forms of both variables. Since mean family income is logarithmic, (4.1) and (4.2) provide a direct estimate of the income elasticity.

Results agree with expectations. Income elasticities of education are approximately 0.35 in (4.1) and (4.2), and nearly identical at the mean in (4.4) and (4.5). Equation (4.3) enters the mean number of labor force participants to control for the bias in income discussed in relation to Table II; even here the income elasticity is only 0.44. These estimates are clearly far less than the corresponding elasticities in Table II (for example, equation (2.2)).

There are other important findings in Table IV. First, donor's age significantly lowers educational attainment. Given the insignificant effect of his age on the inheritance of sons and daughters, this result indicates an interesting shift in the composition of intergen-

TABLE IV

EDUCATIONAL ATTAINMENT REGRESSIONS

Variable or statistic	Logarithmic[a]			Arithmetic[b]	
	4.1[c]	4.2[d]	4.3[d]	4.4[c]	4.5[d]
Mean family income[e]	0.357	0.436	0.342	4.422	4.105
	(0.027)[f]	(0.041)	(0.039)	(0.328)	(0.476)
Donor's age	−0.003	−0.003	−0.003	−0.036	−0.034
	(0.001)	(0.001)	(0.001)	(0.012)	(0.017)
Donor's education				0.161	0.174
				(0.026)	(0.035)
Log of donor's education	0.093	0.073	0.100		
	(0.017)	(0.020)	(0.023)		
Number of siblings	0.004	0.014	0.013	0.018	0.100
	(0.006)	(0.009)	(0.009)	(0.073)	(0.111)
Mean number of labor force participants		−0.153			
		(0.028)			
Intercept	0.177	−0.174	0.224	−15.495	−13.960
R^2	0.477	0.441	0.375	0.502	0.396
F-statistic	88.246	40.984	39.151	97.487	42.793
Standard error	0.143	0.146	0.154	1.748	1.843
N	392	266	266	392	266

a. Dependent variable is the log of recipient's education in years.
b. Dependent variable is the recipient's education in years.
c. Sample of Sons and Daughters.
d. Sample of Sons and Daughters, number of siblings greater than 1.
e. See the text for a discussion of this variable.
f. Standard errors are in parentheses.

erational transfers. Donor's age seems to behave as a vintage effect: educational attainment (in (4.1) and (4.2)) drifts upward by a third of a percent annually as families move forward in time, while material inheritance remains the same. Transfers favor human wealth for more recent cohorts, presumably reflecting a decline in their price, relative to that of assets.

Second, donor's education significantly increases the education of sons and daughters in every equation. We are inclined to think this finding indicates an efficiency effect. More educated parents are more efficient in the transfer of human wealth, since donor's education does not appear to influence material inheritance. Therefore, parental education does not seem to measure wealth effects, but efficiency of transmission.

IV. SUMMARY

In this paper, a model of interdependent preferences has been developed that seeks to explain the behavior of personal wealth transfers. Two major implications of this model were tested, pertaining to income effects; both were supported by the available evidence, First, cross-sectional estimates of the income elasticity of inheritance were predicted to exceed time series estimates. A comparison, though necessarily informal, suggests that this is in fact the case. Although some overlap exists, there is clear evidence of clustering in the expected directions. Second, cross-sectional estimates of the inheritance income elasticity for sons and daughters were expected to exceed the corresponding income elasticity for education. This prediction was also supported. A third prediction, that true or comprehensive gift and estate tax rates would be equalized, has been documented elsewhere [Adams, 1978].

The analysis is incomplete in several ways. It is important to investigate the determinants of inheritance shares, although that is beyond the scope of the present paper. This topic will be explored in later work. Second, while at various points the substitution between human and financial transfers has been stressed, there are important alternatives to both. These are transfers of position or privilege. As an alternative to human capital transfers that may be complementary to them, privilege by implication assumes greater importance when financial transfers are heavily taxed or forbidden. If adequate measures of privilege were to be devised, the present analysis could prove a key to understanding its prevalence, and therefore limitations on opportunity.

Appendix: Derivation of the Altruistic Model

The theoretical results of Section II are proved in this Appendix. Space is devoted only to the one recipient case, since the extension to handle multiple recipients is straightforward. First-order conditions of the text reduce to three equations:

$$\begin{aligned} &U_R V_R^R - \lambda MC = 0 \\ \text{(A.1)} \qquad &U_R V_D^D - \lambda = 0 \\ &W_D = C_D + T_G, \end{aligned}$$

where $U_R = \partial U/\partial V_R$, $V_R^R = \partial V_R/\partial C_R$, etc. Note that since marginal cost MC is rising, utility is maximized under a nonlinear constraint. Following the discussion in Allen [1938, pp. 498–500], the bordered determinants that alternate in sign for a maximum are of the form,

$$\text{(A.2)} \qquad \left| \begin{array}{c|c} F_{ij} - \lambda \phi_{ij} & \phi_i \\ \hline \phi_i & 0 \end{array} \right|,$$

where F is the function to be maximized, ϕ is the (nonlinear) constraint, subscript i indicates a first partial derivative, and subscripts

ij indicate that a second partial derivative has been taken. The displacement system of (A.1) is therefore

$$\begin{bmatrix} U_{RR}V_R^{R2} + U_R V_{RR}^R - \lambda \dfrac{dMC}{dT_R} & U_{RD}V_R^R V_D^D & -MC \\ U_{RD}V_R^R V_D^D & U_{DD}V_D^{D2} + U_D V_{DD}^D & -1 \\ -MC & -1 & 0 \end{bmatrix} \cdot$$

(A.3)

$$\begin{bmatrix} dC_R \\ dC_D \\ d\lambda \end{bmatrix} = \begin{bmatrix} \left(-\dfrac{\partial MC}{\partial T_R} dW_R + \sum_1 \sum_m \dfrac{\partial MC}{\partial P_{1m}} dP_{1m}\right) \\ 0 \\ -dW_D - MCdW_R + \sum_1 \sum_m T_{1m} dP_{1m} \end{bmatrix},$$

since in the present case all $\phi_{ij} = 0$, except for the leading element in the left-hand matrix. If the determinant of this matrix is called D, and its RSth cofactor D_{RS}, the second-order conditions (A.2) imply that D_{RR} and D are opposite in sign.

Let $dP_{1m} = 0$, all 1 and m in (A.3). Taking the determinant of the left-hand matrix, and using Cramer's Rule to solve for the derivative of recipient consumption with respect to donor's wealth,

$$\text{(A.4)} \qquad \frac{\partial C_R}{\partial W_D} = \frac{-D_{31}}{D}\left(1 + MC\frac{\partial W_R}{\partial W_D}\right) - \frac{\lambda D_{11}}{D}\frac{dMC}{dT_R}\frac{\partial W_R}{\partial W_D}.$$

Given that $\lambda D_{11}/D = \partial C_R^S/\partial MC$, and $-D_{31}/D = \partial C_R/\partial W_D$, and also that

$$\text{(A.5)} \qquad \frac{\partial T_R}{\partial W_D} = \frac{\partial C_R}{\partial W_D} - \frac{\partial W_R}{\partial W_D},$$

upon substituting (A.4) into (A.5), it is found that

$$\text{(A.6)} \qquad \frac{\partial T_R}{\partial W_D} = \left(1 + MC\frac{\partial W_R}{\partial W_D}\right)\frac{\partial C_R}{\partial W_D} - \left(\frac{\partial C_R^S}{\partial MC}\frac{dMC}{dT_R} + 1\right)\frac{\partial W_R}{\partial W_D}.$$

In each of equations (A.4), (A.5), and (A.6), it is assumed that recipient's and donor's wealth are positively correlated, so $\partial W_R/\partial W_D > 0$. Equation (A.6) written in elasticity form is (11) of the article. The sign of the second term of (A.6) is found as follows.

Let an increase in recipient's wealth be compensated by a decrease in the donor's wealth, so that $dW_D = -MCdW_R$ in (A.3), and let $dP_{lm} = 0$ all l and m. Solving this gives the (compensated) change in recipient consumption as a function of their wealth,

$$\text{(A.7)} \qquad \frac{\partial C_R^S}{\partial W_R} = -\frac{\partial C_R^S}{\partial MC}\frac{dMC}{dT_R},$$

while the change in the transfer is

$$\text{(A.8)} \qquad \frac{\partial T_R^S}{\partial W_R} = \frac{\partial C_R^S}{\partial W_R} - 1 = \frac{-\partial C_R^S}{\partial MC}\frac{dMC}{dT_R} - 1.$$

The elasticity transformation of (A.8) is $-(1+\beta E\eta^S_{C_R C_R})$. The sign of (A.8) must be negative, and so must the transformation, according to the following reasoning. The solution to the first-order conditions implies a demand function for recipient consumption of the form $C_R = f(MC, W_D + P_R W_R)$, where P_R is the average cost of transfers. Inverting this function and solving for MC as a function of combined wealth $W_D + P_R W_R$ and recipient consumption C_R gives

$$g(W_D + P_R W_R, C_R) = MC. \tag{A.9}$$

Writing marginal cost as a function h of the transfers gives the analogue of the supply function:

$$h(T_R) = MC. \tag{A.10}$$

Differentiating (A.9) and (A.10) totally with respect to W_R, noticing that $C_R = W_R + T_R$, and holding social wealth constant, one obtains the compensated change in transfers:

$$\frac{\partial T^S_R}{\partial W_R} = -\frac{\partial g}{\partial C_R}\bigg/\frac{\partial g}{\partial C_R} - \frac{dh}{dT_R} < 0, \tag{A.11}$$

since

$$\frac{\partial g}{\partial C_R} = 1\bigg/\frac{\partial C^S_R}{\partial MC} < 0,$$

and

$$\frac{dh}{dT_R} = \frac{dMC}{dT_R} > 0.$$

To obtain relations for components, we have by equality of marginal costs that

$$\frac{dMC_{ik}}{dT_{ik}}\frac{\partial T_{ik}}{\partial W_D} = \frac{dMC}{dT_R}\frac{\partial T_R}{\partial W_D}\frac{dMC_{lm}}{dT_{lm}}\frac{\partial T_{lm}}{\partial W_D}, \tag{A.12}$$

from which equations (12) and (13) are derived by rewriting in elasticities.

UNIVERSITY OF FLORIDA

REFERENCES

Adams, J. D., "A Theory of Intergenerational Transfers," Ph.D. thesis, University of Chicago, 1976.

——, "Equalization of True Gift and Estate Tax Rates," *Journal of Public Economics,* IX (March 1978), 59–71.

Allen, R. G. D., *Mathematical Analysis for Economists* (London: Macmillian, 1938).

Amemiya, T., "Regression Analysis When the Dependent Variable Is Truncated Normal," *Econometrica,* XLI (Nov. 1973), 997–1016.

Barro, R. J., "Are Government Bonds Net Wealth?" *Journal of Political Economy,* LXXXII (Nov./Dec. 1974), 1095–1119.

Becker, G. S., *Human Capital and the Personal Distribution of Income: An Analytical Approach* (Ann Arbor, MI: Institute for Public Administration, University of Michigan Press, 1967).

——, "A Theory of Social Interactions," *Journal of Political Economy,* LXXXII (Nov./Dec. 1974), 1063–93.

——, and G. J. Stigler, "Law Enforcement, Malfeasance, and Compensation of Enforcers," *Journal of Legal Studies,* III (Jan. 1974), 1–18.

Blinder, A. S., *Towards an Economic Theory of Income Distribution* (Cambridge: Massachusetts Institute of Technology Press, 1974).

——, "Intergenerational Transfers and Life Cycle Consumption," *American Economic Review,* LXVI (May 1976), 87–93.

Bowley, A. L., *Elements of Statistics* (London: P. S. King and Sons, 1920).

Gorman, W. M., "Separable Utility and Aggregation," *Econometrica,* XXVII (July 1959), 469–81.

Ishikawa, T., "Family Structure and Family Values in the Theory of Income Distribution," *Journal of Political Economy,* LXXXIII (Oct. 1975), 987–1008.

Kuznets, S., *Shares of Upper Income Groups in Income and Savings* (New York: National Bureau of Economic Research, 1953).

Lampman, R. J., *The Share of Top Wealth Holders in National Wealth, 1922–1956* (New York: National Bureau of Economic Research, 1962).

Parsons, D. O., "On the Economics of Intergenerational Relations," unpublished manuscript, Ohio State University, 1974.

——, "Intergenerational Transfers and the Educational Decisions of Male Youth," this *Journal,* LXXXIX (Nov. 1975), 603–17.

Pechman, J. A., *Federal Tax Policy* (Washington, D. C.: Brookings Institution, 1966).

Schultz, T. W., *Investment in Human Capital* (New York: Free Press, 1971).

Shoup, C. S., *Federal Estate and Gift Taxes* (Washington, D.C.: Brookings Institution, 1966).

Strotz, R. H., "The Empirical Implications of the Utility Tree," *Econometrica,* XXV (April 1957), 269–80.

——, "The Utility Tree: A Correction and Further Appraisal," *Econometrica,* XXVII (July 1959), 482–88.

Sussman, M., J. N., Cates, and D. T. Smith, *Inheritance and the Family* (New York: Russell Sage, 1970).

Tideman, T. N., and G. Tullock, "A New and Superior Process for Making Social Choices," *Journal of Political Economy,* LXXXIV (Dec. 1976), 1145–60.

Tobin, J., "Estimation of Relationships for Limited Dependent Variables," *Econometrica,* XXVI (Jan. 1958), 24–36.

U. S. Bureau of the Census, *Historical Statistics of the United States: Colonial Times to 1957* (Washington, D.C.: U. S. Government Printing Office, 1960).

U. S. Treasury Department, *Statistics of Income for 1942,* Part I (Washington, D.C.: U. S. Government Printing Office, 1945).

A MODEL OF FORCED SAVING BASED UPON DIFFERENTIAL EXPECTATIONS

MICHAEL HICKS

I

An unanticipated inflation transfers wealth from creditors to debtors. If the marginal propensity of debtors to save is greater than the marginal propensity of creditors to save, this transfer will in itself slow the inflation. In this paper a state preference model of the allocation of risk is considered. There is no aggregate risk. Creditors hold a safe claim to future output. Debtors are individuals who have borrowed to speculate in particular assets. It is shown under what conditions debtors' marginal propensity to save is greater than that of creditors.

Intuitively the argument is as follows. A speculator considers that the rate of return is higher than what other people consider it to be, hence he saves more. On the other hand, he thinks that he is going to be rich; therefore he saves less. The first effect is more important if the elasticity of demand for future consumption is greater than one. The second effect is more important if this elasticity is less than one.

In Section II the model is described, and in Section III the proof is provided.

II

A list of symbols is provided first.

$q1,q2$	= first- and second-period output
$U(q1,q2)$	= the universal utility function for certain quantities of first- and second-period output
Ai,Bi	= the events that the ith asset yields high and low second-period output, respectively
vi	= the probability attached to high output for the ith asset by a diversifier
v^*i	= the probability attached to high output for the ith asset by an individual who speculates in the ith asset
Q	= (qA,qB) = a vector of second-period outputs contingent upon events A and B

The Quarterly Journal of Economics, August 1980 0033-5533/80/0095-0181$01.00

$P = (pA,pB)$ = a vector of implicit prices of second-period outputs contingent upon events A and B in terms of first-period output

E = the elasticity of demand for second-period output with respect to its price

t = a parameter that runs from zero to one.

Consumption takes place in two periods. First-period output provides first-period consumption. Assets provide second-period output, which is consumed in the second period. In this model there are many kinds of assets and no production. The total quantity of first-period output that exists and the total quantity of each kind of asset that exists are fixed. An asset provides either a high or a low quantity of second-period output. Monetary debt is a promise to pay money in the second period. No inflation is expected, so that a promise to pay a fixed quantity of dollars is considered to be a promise to pay a fixed quantity of second-period output.

Prior to the first period an allocation is reached. Each individual owns some quantity of first-period output and some claims to second-period output in the form of real assets or debts. Some individuals owe debts. An individual's wealth is the total value in terms of first-period output of an individual's first-period output and his claims to second-period output. An individual's marginal propensity to consume is the increase in his purchases of first-period output divided by the increase in his wealth. An individual's marginal propensity to save is the increase, measured in terms of first-period output, in his purchases of claims to second-period output, divided by the increase in his wealth.

Prior to the first period, but after the initial allocation has been reached, the price of second-period output in terms of dollars that the public expects to prevail changes by a definite amount. This question is asked: If the rate at which a certain claim to second-period output is discounted in terms of first-period output is held constant, would the transfers brought on by inflation cause the aggregate demand for first-period output to fall or to rise? If the aggregate demand for first-period output falls, then these transfers will reduce the inflation. If the aggregate demand rises, these transfers will increase the inflation. Aggregate demand will fall if and only if the debtors' marginal propensity to consume is lower than that of the creditors'. This will be the case if and only if the debtors' marginal propensity to save is higher than that of the creditors'.

All individuals have the same homothetic utility function $U(q1,q2)$ for certain quantities of first- and second-period output $q1$,

$q2$. Individuals differ in the probabilities they attach to high and low outputs for various assets. According to the conventional evaluation, the ith asset will have high output with probability vi and low output with probability $1 - vi$. A diversifier is an individual who accepts the conventional evaluation for every asset. A speculator is an individual who accepts the conventional evaluation for every asset but the ith asset. He thinks that the ith asset will have high output with probability v^*i, where v^*i is greater than vi. Different kinds of speculators speculate in different assets. In this model all speculation is long. Since the short sale of most assets is essentially impossible, short speculation and the probability beliefs that would support it have not been considered.

All individuals consider that the return from each asset is distributed independently of the return from every other asset. Each asset is a small part of the total; hence all individuals consider that, in the aggregate, assets provide a safe claim to second-period output. For an individual, claims to second-period output may be greater or less than real assets held depending on whether he is a creditor or debtor. In the aggregate the value of claims to second-period output equals the value of real assets. It is assumed that diversifiers own a substantial fraction of total claims to second-period output. Thus, in the aggregate, diversifier holdings are considered to be a certain claim to second-period output. Since all diversifiers are alike, they will all hold the same portfolio except for scale, and each individual diversifier will hold what he and others consider to be a safe claim to second-period output. An individual who takes no risk is willing to purchase or sell small risks at their expected value. Diversifiers are willing to buy or sell a particular asset at what they consider to be its expected value. The only exception to this would occur if diversifiers sold the entire quantity of an asset to speculators, and it is assumed that this does not occur.

A speculator in the ith asset thinks that this asset has been undervalued by the market, and he purchases a large quantity of this asset in exchange for safe claims. A speculator holds a risky portfolio. A speculator who purchases the ith asset in exchange for safe claims to second-period output is, in effect, purchasing second-period output, contingent upon the event that the ith asset yields high output in exchange for second-period output, contingent upon the event that the ith asset yields low output. The market price for this exchange is given by (1):

$$pAi/pBi = vi/(1 - vi). \tag{1}$$

A speculator holds a large quantity of his favorite asset plus either a positive or a negative quantity of certain claims to second-period output. The speculator who holds a positive quantity of certain claims to second-period output may be either a borrower or a lender and is not considered further. The speculator who holds a negative quantity of certain claims to second-period output is necessarily a borrower, and it is this sort of speculator who is considered in the remainder of this paper.

For an ordinary commodity, the elasticity of demand with respect to price is the percentage change in quantity divided by the percentage change in price, multiplied by minus one. Provided that the changes considered are very small, this definition can easily be extended to a bundle of commodities. Consider the speculator in the ith asset, and let the subscript i be dropped. He owns a quantity $q1$ of first-period output and a bundle $Q = (qA,qB)$ of second-period outputs in events A and B. The price, in terms of first-period output of second-period outputs contingent upon events A and B, is given by the vector $P = (pA,pB)$. The percentage change in the quantity of second-period output is PdQ/PQ. The percentage change in the price of second-period output is QdP/PQ. The elasticity of demand for second-period output with respect to its price is defined by the equation $E = -PdQ/QdP$. It is assumed that the speculator's wealth is held constant, while the price changes. Equation (2) asserts that the change in the speculator's

$$d(PQ) = (1 - E)QdP \tag{2}$$

total expenditure on second-period output equals one minus the elasticity and then multiplied by the change in price times the initial quantity.

III

Let P be indexed by the parameter t so that the conditions of (3) hold. $P(1)$ is the actual equilibrium price:

$$\begin{gathered} pA(0)/pB(0) = v^*/(1 - v^*) \\ pA(1)/pB(1) = v/(1 - v) \\ pA(t) + pB(t) = pA(1) + pB(1) \quad \text{for all } t \\ \frac{dpA(t)}{dt} < 0. \end{gathered} \tag{3}$$

If prices $P(0)$ held, the speculator would hold a safe claim to second-period output. The price of a safe claim at $P(0)$ is the same as the price of a safe claim at $P(1)$. Since all individuals have the same utility function for safe claims, the speculator would hold at prices $P(0)$ exactly the same quantity of second-period output as a diversifier of equal wealth holds at prices $P(1)$. Let the speculator's wealth be held constant. The speculator saves more than the diversifier if his expenditures on second-period output are higher for prices $P(1)$ than for prices $P(0)$.

The difference between a speculator's expenditure on second-period output at prices $P(1)$ and at prices $P(0)$ is given by (4):

$$(4) \qquad P(1)Q(1) - P(0)Q(0) = \int_0^1 \left[\frac{d(PQ)}{dt}\right] dt.$$

Equation (5) follows from (2) and (4):

$$(5) \qquad P(1)Q(1) - P(0)Q(0) = \int_0^1 \left[\frac{(1-E)QdP}{dt}\right] dt.$$

Since qA is greater than qB, then from (3) QdP/dt is negative. Hence the speculator saves more than a diversifier of equal wealth if and only if E is greater than one. With homothetic utility functions, marginal propensities equal average propensities so that the speculator's marginal propensity to save exceeds the diversifier's marginal propensity to save if and only if E is greater than one.

OPTIMAL POLICIES IN DUAL ECONOMIES*

KAUSHIK C. BASU

I. INTRODUCTION

A dual economy is typically characterized as one that has an urban industrialized sector with institutionally fixed wages and a rural sector [Lewis, 1954]. Such economies and their optimal shadow wages have been analyzed a great deal (see, e.g., Sen [1968]). But more recently, Todaro [1969] and Harris and Todaro [1970] have given a new dimension to the problem with the introduction of a migration equilibrium condition (see also Fields [1975], and Mazumdar [1976]). Harris and Todaro (HT) argued that in a migration model, such as theirs, no single wage subsidy can ensure optimality. But Bhagwati and Srinivasan [1974] have elegantly demonstrated that there does exist a wage subsidy S^*, which, if given to all sectors, leads the economy to optimality.

A serious problem with the Bhagwati-Srinivasan (BS) optimal subsidy is that a particular component of their subsidy formula is the marginal product of labor *in the optimal situation.* To suppose that this will be known to the government at the time when the subsidy is given (i.e., prior to attaining the optimum) is an extremely strong informational assumption.[1]

Fortunately, however, the BS result can be substantially generalized. I shall argue that in the HT model there is a whole interval of optimal subsidies, and S^* is only one element in this interval. While S^* guarantees optimality, so does any other subsidy in this interval. It is then shown that the prevailing urban market wage is an element of this interval. Hence, the government can now give a subsidy which ensures optimality, the value of which is easily determined. Similar results hold for the HT second-best subsidy.

The next two sections outline the HT model and develop a simple diagram that illustrates the complete migration equilibrium. The diagram is an extremely useful aid for the analysis of economic policy.

* I thank T. N. Srinivasan and R. K. Das for helpful comments. I also benefited from a seminar at the Indian Statistical Institute, Calcutta.

1. In fact, recent studies of decentralized iterative planning are largely motivated by the need to avoid such strong informational assumptions. Another way of avoiding this is to assume a partial-equilibrium model where the sector that the government can control is relatively small (e.g., Sen[1968]).

The Quarterly Journal of Economics, August 1980 0033-5533/80/0095-0187$01.00

II. The Harris-Todaro Model

There are two sectors: the rural (R) and the urban or modern (M). They produce X_R and X_M units of output and employ L_R and L_M units of labor. The output in each sector is a function of labor.[2]

$$X_R = f_R(L_R); \quad f'_R > 0, f''_R < 0 \tag{1}$$

$$X_M = f_M(L_M); \quad f'_M > 0, f''_M < 0. \tag{2}$$

Labor availability is fixed and, by assumption, equal to unity. Hence,

$$L_R + L_M \leq 1; \quad L_R, L_M \geq 0. \tag{3}$$

I shall assume, for simplicity, that both sectors produce the same good (though by different techniques). This leaves all the major HT and BS results unaltered. This assumption can be viewed in an alternative manner. We could think of X_R and X_M as different commodities in an open economy. Then, assuming constant world prices, we may redefine the units of X_R and X_M such that both their prices are equal to unity.

As in the HT model, we assume that the social welfare function is $U = U(X_R, X_M)$, $U_1 > 0$, $U_2 > 0$. But since in the present model X_R and X_M refer to the same commodity, the social welfare function may be simply written as $U = U(X_R + X_M)$, $U' > 0$; and given that welfare is ordinal, this may be expressed as

$$U = X_R + X_M. \tag{4}$$

Maximization of this utility subject to (1)–(3) entails distributing labor such that

$$L_R + L_M = 1, \text{ and } f'_M(L_M) = f'_R(L_R). \tag{5}$$

Let the amount of labor, output, and utility in this *optimum* condition be written as $[L^*_R, L^*_M, X^*_R, X^*_M, U^*] = E^*$.

The optimum condition E^*, however, is unattainable in an HT economy. In the HT economy the wage paid in the urban sector has an institutional lower bound at $\bar{w}$. Hence,

$$w \geq \bar{w}, \tag{6}$$

where w is the urban market wage and is expressed in units of output. In the HT model $\bar{w}$ is above the laissez-faire equilibrium wage $f'_M(L^*_M)$.

2. This should be treated as a short-run model with fixed capital endowment in each sector.

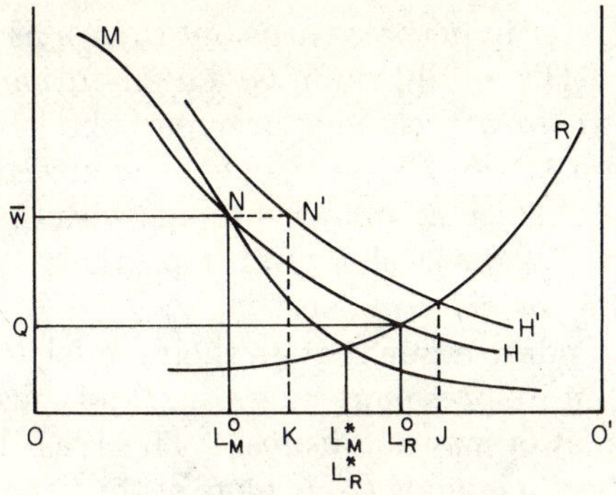

FIGURE I

Hence, w settles at $\bar{w}$. The urban sector maximizes profits, implying that

(7) $$f'_M = \bar{w}.$$

Laborers maximize expected earnings. The rural sector is run along competitive lines, and everybody is provided with employment. The probability of getting a job in the urban sector is given by the rate of urban employment: $L_M/(1 - L_R)$. Hence, migration equilibrium is attained when

(8) $$f'_R = \bar{w}\, L_M/(1 - L_R).$$

Solving (1), (2), (7), and (8), we get the values of L_R, L_M, X_R and X_M. Using (4), we can determine social welfare. These values, denoted by $[L^0_R, L^0_M, X^0_R, X^0_M, U^0] = E^0$, represent the HT equilibrium. Given $\bar{w} > f'_M(L^*_M)$, this equilibrium implies the existence of urban unemployment and sub-optimal production.

A simple diagram can be developed to depict the HT model. In Figure I, let M and R be the marginal product of labor curves with 0 and 0′ as origins, respectively. The optimum condition (i.e., maximum output) involves employing $0L^*_M$ and $0'L^*_R$ in the urban and rural sectors.

Given an institutional wage of $\bar{w}$, the urban sector employs $0L^0_M$ labor. What is the level of rural employment? For that we have to draw a rectangular hyperbola H, through $N = (L^0_M, \bar{w})$. The point of intersection between H and R gives the rural equilibrium. $0'L^0_R$ is the level of rural employment. This is so because $(\bar{w})(0L^0_M) = (0Q)(0L^0_R)$, since H is a rectangular hyperbola. This implies that $(\bar{w})(0L^0_M)/(0L^0_R) = 0Q$. This is the same as (8), and hence L^0_M and L^0_R in Figure I represent the HT equilibrium. Urban unemployment consists of $L^0_M\, L^0_R$.

The rectangular hyperbola turns out to be a handy instrument for describing an HT equilibrium. Given any urban wage and employment level, we draw a rectangular hyperbola through the "urban wage-employment" point (N, in the above analysis), and the point of intersection of this rectangular hyperbola with the rural marginal product curve gives us the level of rural employment. The explanation is the same as the one given above.

Harris and Todaro argue that, in their model, the generation of urban employment induces more migration, and consequently urban unemployment may or may not decrease. This is easily seen in Figure I. Let the urban sector employ $L_M^0 K$ more at the fixed wage $\overline{w}$ because of governmental pressure. Then the relevant rectangular hyperbola is the one through N'. This is labeled H' in the diagram. It is obvious that rural employment drops by $L_R^0 J$. Hence urban unemployment, instead of dropping by $L_M^0 K$, drops by $L_M^0 K - L_R^0 J$. This can be positive or negative, and hence unemployment could decrease or increase.

III. Standard Policy Prescriptions

The Harris-Todaro Prescription

In the earlier models of the dual economy, such as that of Marglin [1967], the level of unemployment could be decreased by lowering the shadow wage (i.e., increasing wage subsidy) in the urban sector. In the HT model this need not happen. While a subsidy of S would increase urban employment, that in turn would induce further migration, and net unemployment may rise or fall. However, if the subsidy in the urban sector is raised to $\overline{S}$, where $\overline{S}$ is defined as follows:

$$\overline{S} = \overline{w} - f'_M(1 - \overline{L}_R), \tag{9}$$

where $\overline{L}_R$ is such that $f'_R(\overline{L}_R) = \overline{w}$,[3] then full employment is attained. This has been proved by Srinivasan and Bhagwati [1975].

THEOREM 1. There exists a unique equilibrium corresponding to each wage subsidy S to the manufacturing sector in the interval $[0,\overline{S}]$. At $\overline{S}$ full employment is reached.

The proof of this is obvious, once we analyze this diagrammatically as done below. I shall refer to $\overline{S}$ (as defined in equation (9)) as

3. The existence of such an L_R is guaranteed by introducing the BS assumption that $\lim_{L_R \to 0} f'_R(L_R) = \infty$ and $\lim_{L_M \to 0} f'_M(L_M) = \infty$. This rules out corner solutions.

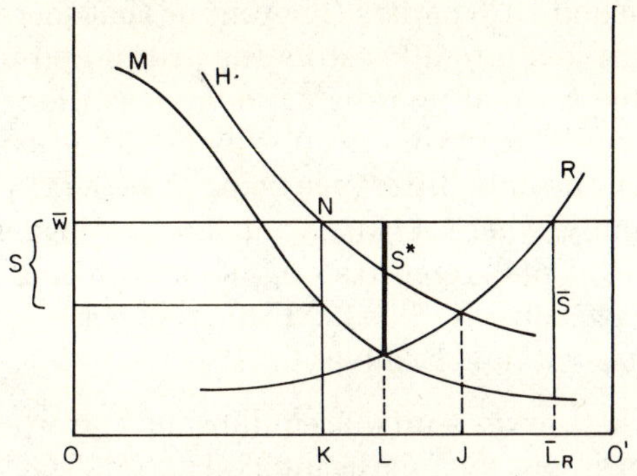

FIGURE II

the HT second-best wage subsidy. Note that this subsidy takes the economy to a full employment situation but not to E^*.

But what if we want to attain the first-best equilibrium E^*? Then Harris and Todaro concluded that we must give a subsidy,

$$S^* = \overline{w} - f'_M(L^*_M), \tag{10}$$

where L^*_M is defined as above, and this, with a complete migration restriction, ensures the attainment of E^*. This led to the well-known HT conclusion that no single policy measure can lead the economy to E^*.

The effect of a subsidy to the urban sector may be analyzed diagrammatically. In Figure II, M is the urban sector's marginal product of labor schedule. Given a subsidy S to the urban sector, the level of urban employment is $0K$. Drawing a rectangular hyperbola through $(K,\overline{w}) = N$, we see that rural employment is $0'J$.

$\overline{L}_R$, defined as that L_R for which $f'_R = \overline{w}$, is shown in Figure II. It is obvious that a subsidy of $\overline{S}$ as defined in equation (9) and depicted in Figure II removes unemployment completely. If a subsidy of S^* is given, then urban employment is at $0L$, and if migration is prohibited, rural employment is at $0'L$. This is the optimum distribution of labor.[4]

The Bhagwati-Srinivasan Prescription

It was Bhagwati and Srinivasan's disagreement with the HT claim that no *single* policy could lead the economy to the optimum, which

4. An alternative way of diagrammatically representing a subsidy is to construct an *effective* marginal product curve by vertically raising the actual marginal product curve by the amount of the subsidy. This method is useful for understanding the effect of large subsidies, e.g., those greater than $\overline{w}$.

led to their 1974 and 1975 papers. They argue that there exists a wage subsidy which, if given to all sectors (i.e., rural and urban) and financed by "some form of non-distortionary taxation," leads to the optimum, i.e., E^*. This optimum subsidy S^* is the same as defined in equation (10); the only difference being that the BS subsidy is for the entire economy, whereas Harris and Todaro suggested it for the urban sector only. I shall refer to a wage subsidy meant for all sectors as a *uniform* wage subsidy. The next theorem is the important contribution of Bhagwati and Srinivasan [1974].

THEOREM 2. There exists a unique equilibrium corresponding to each uniform wage subsidy S in the interval $[0,S^*]$. At S^* the optimum is reached.

The Information Problem

There is, however, a serious information problem with the BS optimal subsidy $S^* = \overline{w} - f'_M(L^*_M)$. While $\overline{w}$ is immediately observable, $f'_M(L^*_M)$ is not. The latter represents the marginal product of labor *when labor is optimally distributed.* Hence, while the BS result is comforting in that it assures us that an optimal subsidy exists, it is not really useful in practice because the value of this optimal subsidy will in general not be known. The same problem arises with the HT second-best subsidy $\overline{S}$. This requires knowledge of $f'_M(1 - \overline{L}_R)$, which again is not an observable.[5]

Fortunately, the situation is not so hopeless as it seems. This is because the BS result can be greatly generalized. While their S^* does lead to E^*, S^* is not the only subsidy that does this. There is a large class of subsidies that lead to optimality.

IV. A CLASS OF OPTIMAL SUBSIDIES

This section proves certain theorems rigorously. Consequently, we need to restate formally some HT conditions in the case where there is a wage subsidy S to both sectors. The urban sector is supposed to maximize profits. This implies two conditions:

(11) $$w > \overline{w} \rightarrow L_R + L_M = 1$$

(12) $$f'_M(L_M) = w - S.$$

The migration equilibrium condition is now restated as

(13) $$f'_R(L_R) + S = w\, L_M/(1 - L_R).$$

5. This problem is not peculiar to the HT model. All general equilibrium models of dual economies, e.g., Dixit [1971] share this information problem.

While (12) and (13) are familiar conditions (see BS [1974]), (11) needs a word of explanation. It simply says that, given profit maximization, if there is unemployment, then wages cannot be above the institutional minimum. This is obvious enough and is implicitly there in both HT and BS formulations, but there it is not significant because they never consider a case where $w > \bar{w}$. Such cases will arise in our analysis below, and that also accounts for the reason we have w instead of $\bar{w}$ in (12) and (13).

The next theorem generalizes the BS result.

THEOREM 3. (a) If a wage subsidy of $S \geq S^*$ is given to all sectors, then the equilibrium reached is the optimum E^*.

(b) This equilibrium is unique.

Proof. (a) An equilibrium is attained if there exist L_R, L_M, and w that satisfy (3), (6), (11), (12), and (13).

Consider that $L_R = L_R^*$ and $L_M = L_M^*$(L_R^* and L_M^* are as defined above). From (5), we know that $L_R^* + L_M^* = 1$. Hence, (11) and (3) are satisfied. From (12), $w = f'_M(L_M^*) + S$. Since $S \geq S^* = \bar{w} - f'_M(L_M^*)$, hence $w \geq \bar{w}$, thereby satisfying (6). From (12), and given that $f'_M(L_M^*) = f'_R(L_R^*)$ (see (5)), we get $f'_R(L_R^*) + S = w$. This can be written as $f'_R(L_R^*) + S = w\, L_M^*/(1 - L_R^*)$, since $L_M^* + L_R^* = 1$. Therefore, L_R^* and L_M^* satisfy (13). Hence $[L_R^*, L_M^*]$ is an equilibrium commensurate with (3), (6), (11), (12), and (13). Given L_R^* and L_M^*, the amounts of output and utility are X_R^*, X_M^*, and U^*. Hence $S \epsilon [S^*, \infty)$ leads to E^*.

(b) Now we have to show that if $S \geq S^*$, then no distribution of labor other than $[L_M^*, L_R^*]$ comprises an equilibrium. Consider a distribution of labor $[L_M, \bar{\bar{L}}_R]$, such that $\bar{\bar{L}}_M + \bar{\bar{L}}_R \leq 1$ and $\bar{\bar{L}}_M \neq L_M^*$. Now either (i) $\bar{\bar{L}}_R = 1 - \bar{\bar{L}}_M$, or (ii) $\bar{\bar{L}}_R < 1 - \bar{\bar{L}}_M$. If (i), then from (12) and (13), $f'_R(\bar{\bar{L}}_R) = f'_M(\bar{\bar{L}}_M)$. Since $f''_R, f''_M < 0$, hence $f'_R = f'_M$ and $L_R + L_M = 1$ can be true at some unique L_R and L_M. Since $f'_R(L_R^*) = f'_M(L_M^*)$, we have a contradiction. If (ii), then $\bar{\bar{L}}_M/(1 - \bar{\bar{L}}_R) < 1$ and by (12) and (13) $f'_M(\bar{\bar{L}}_M) > f'_R(\bar{\bar{L}}_R)$. This, which can easily be checked, implies that $f'_M(\bar{\bar{L}}_M) > f'_M(L_M^*)$. Hence, $w = f'_M(L_M) + S > f'_M(L_M^*) + S \geq \bar{w}$, since $S \geq S^*$. This implies that $w > \bar{w}$ and $L_R + \bar{\bar{L}}_M < 1$. This contradicts (11). Hence $\bar{\bar{L}}_M = L_M^*$. It is easily seen that this implies $\bar{\bar{L}}_R = L_R^*$.

This theorem shows that, for all subsidies equal to or greater than S^*, we obtain E^*. If S is raised above S^*, then the only variable that changes is w. In fact, w is a function of S. For all $S \geq S^*$, $w = f'_M(L_M^*) + S$. If $S \leq S^*$, then $w = \bar{w}$. ‖

This theorem implies that we no longer need to know the exact value of S^*. The government can always make sure of reaching E^*, by choosing a sufficiently large S. The next theorem shows that the government's problem is actually even simpler.

THEOREM 4. If a wage subsidy of $S = \overline{w}$ is given to all sectors, then E^* is reached.

Proof. By definition, $S^* = \overline{w} - f'_M(L^*_M)$. Hence, $\overline{w} > S^*$, since by assumption $f'_M > 0$, for all L_M. Consequently, by Theorem 3, a subsidy of $\overline{w}$ guarantees that we reach E^*. ||

Thus, the government need not give an arbitrarily high subsidy to make sure of reaching E^*. A subsidy equal to $\overline{w}$, which is an observable parameter of the economy, suffices. The problem of having information on variables at the optimal situation is, therefore, totally bypassed.

From Theorem 3 we know that for all uniform subsidies above S^*, social welfare remains at the maximum. What happens to social welfare for subsidies in the range 0 to S^*? Srinivasan and Bhagwati [1975] studied the effects of an *urban* wage subsidy on social welfare, and concluded that U does not always increase as the urban wage subsidy S increases. Indeed, U may even fall over certain ranges. Fortunately, for a *uniform* subsidy, monotonicity always holds.

THEOREM 5. If S is a wage subsidy given to both sectors and $S \epsilon [0,S^*]$, then as S increases, social welfare U also increases.

Proof. $U = X_M + X_R = f_M(L_M) + f_R(L_R)$.

It is clear from (11), (12), and (13) that L_M and L_R depend on S.

Hence,

$$\frac{dU}{dS} = f'_M \frac{dL_M}{dS} + f'_R \frac{dL_R}{dS}. \tag{14}$$

From (12),

$$f''_M \frac{dL_M}{dS} = -1; \quad \text{i.e.,} \quad \frac{dL_M}{dS} = \frac{-1}{f''_M}.$$

From (13),

$$f'_R + S - L_R f'_R - SL_R - \overline{w} L_M = 0.$$

By differentiating with respect to S:

$$f''_R \frac{dL_R}{dS} + 1 - L_R f''_R \frac{dL_R}{dS} - \frac{dL_R}{dS} f'_R - S\frac{dL_R}{dS} - L_R - \overline{w}\frac{dL_M}{dS} = 0.$$

By grouping and substituting for dL_M/dS, we get

$$\frac{dL_R}{dS} = \frac{\{L_R - 1 - \overline{w}/f''_M\}}{\{(1 - L_R) f''_R - f'_R - S\}}.$$

By substituting for dL_M/dS and dL_R/dS into (14), we get

$$\frac{dU}{dS} = -\frac{f'_M}{f''_M} + \frac{f'_R\{L_R - 1 - \overline{w}/f''_M\}}{(1 - L_R) f''_R - f'_R - S}$$

$$= \frac{-f'_M (1 - L_R) f''_R + L_R f'_R f''_M - f'_R f''_M + f'_R (f'_M - \overline{w}) + S f'_M}{f''_M \{(1 - L_R) f''_R - f'_R - S\}}$$

$$= \frac{(L_R - 1) f''_R f'_M + (L_R - 1) f'_R f''_M + S(f'_M - f'_R)}{f''_M\{(1 - L_R) f''_R - f'_R - S\}},$$

since

$$f'_M - \overline{w} = -S,$$

by (12). Noting that $L_R + L_M \leq 1, f'_i > 0, f''_i < 0, i \in \{R,M\}$, and $f'_M > f'_R$ (this is easily checked), we know that $dU/dS > 0$. ‖

Results, similar to those derived for uniform subsidies above, hold for the HT type sector-specific subsidies. Theorem 1 states that a wage subsidy of $\overline{S}$ to the urban sector removes unemployment. It can be shown that for all urban wage subsidy $S \in [\overline{S}, \infty)$, unemployment is removed. This result, however, is not so useful as Theorem 3 because it is easily checked that as S rises above $\overline{S}$, social welfare U, drops.

In conclusion, we may recall that the BS and HT models assume that the subsidy is financed by "some form of nondistortionary tax." This problem demands further investigation. When doling out large economy-wide subsidies, there is always the danger of inflation and of the savings rate dropping. In fact, research into subsidy finance may reveal that no completely "nondistortionary tax" exists, and in reality we have to be reconciled to a smaller "second-best" subsidy.

DELHI SCHOOL OF ECONOMICS

REFERENCES

Bhagwati, J. N., and T. N. Srinivasan, "On Reanalyzing the Harris-Todaro Model: Policy Rankings in the case of Sector-Specific Sticky Wages," *American Economic Review,* LXIV (1974), 502–08.

Dixit, A., "Short-Run Equilibrium and Shadow Prices in the Dual Economy," *Oxford Economic Papers,* XXIII (1971), 384–400.

Fields, G., "Rural-Urban Migration, Urban Unemployment and Under-Employment, and Job-search Activity in LDCs," *Journal of Development Economics,* II (1975), 165–87.

Harris, J. R., and M. P. Todaro, "Migration, Unemployment and Development: A Two-Sector Analysis," *American Economic Review,* LX (1970), 126–42.

Lewis, W. A., "Economic Development with Unlimited Supplies of Labour," *Manchester School of Economic and Social Studies,* XXII (1954), 139–91.

Marglin, S. A., *Public Investment Criteria* (London: Unwin, 1967).

Mazumdar, D., "The Rural-Urban Wage Gap, Migration and the Shadow Wage," *Oxford Economic Papers,* XXVIII (1976), 406–25.
Sen, A. K., *Choice of Techniques,* 3rd ed. (Oxford: Blackwell, 1968).
Srinivasan, T. N., and J. N. Bhagwati, "Alternative Policy Rankings in a Large, Open Economy with Sector-Specific, Minimum Wages," *Journal of Economic Theory,* XI (1975), 356–71.
Todaro, M. P., "A Model of Labor Migration and Urban Unemployment in Less Developed Countries," *American Economic Review,"* LIX (1969), 138–48.

A DISEQUILIBRIUM MACROECONOMIC MODEL: A CORRECTION

STEPHEN M. MILLER

In a recent issue of this *Journal,* P. G. Korliras [1975] developed a disequilibrium macroeconomic model. One of his objectives was to formulate a model that allowed one to investigate dynamic adjustment and stability. Unfortunately, in presenting the results, Korliras overlooked important constraints implicit in the system, and consequently, most of his phase diagrams are erroneous.

In discussing the phase diagrams, Korliras remarks that "Not only the slopes of the $w^* = 0$ and $r^* = 0$ loci, but also their positions in the (w,r) plane, are crucial. We do not have enough information about what determines their position" [p. 73]. In fact, additional information is contained in the following equations (equation numbers correspond to the original article):

$$w^* = W^* - P^*, \tag{32}$$

$$W^* = \lambda_N E_N(w), \tag{33}$$

and

$$P^* = \lambda_y E_y(w,r), \tag{34}$$

where asterisks signify relative rates of change and λ's are constant positive and finite speeds of adjustment. The nominal wage (W) adjusts with excess demand in the labor market ($N^d - N^s$), while the price level (P) adjusts with excess demand in the goods market ($Y^d - Y^s$). Clearly, if both W^* and P^* are zero (i.e., both labor and goods markets clear), then w^* is zero. Consequently, in (w,r) space, the w^* equal to zero locus should pass through the intersection of the w equal w_f and Y^d equal Y^s loci that represent labor and goods market equilibria. In Korliras' paper, only Figures VII, VIII, IX, and X satisfy this requirement.

From equation (32), note that w^* also equals zero when W^* equals P^*. In the phase diagrams, the w^* equal to zero locus must pass through regions for which W^* and P^* have the same sign. Focusing on Figure I in Korliras, one can see that this occurs when (i) w exceeds w_f and Y^d is less than Y^s or (ii) w is less than w_f and Y^d exceeds Y^s. This further restriction eliminates Figures VII, VIII, and X. Therefore, only Figure IX is correct. This greatly simplifies the analysis of

The Quarterly Journal of Economics, August 1980 0033-5533/80/0095-0197$01.00

potential equilibria and their stability which is a large part of Korliras' paper.

UNIVERSITY OF CONNECTICUT

REFERENCE

Korliras, P. G., "A Disequilibrium Macroeconomic Model," this *Journal*, LXXXIX (Feb. 1975), 56–80.

A DISEQUILIBRIUM MACROECONOMIC MODEL: THE IMPLICATIONS OF A CORRECTION

PANAYOTIS G. KORLIRAS

In the comment on my paper [1975], Miller suggests that an important constraint on the constant real wage ($w^* = 0$) locus has been overlooked. This is correct, and as a result, some of the original phase diagrams are redundant. Indeed, the $w^* = 0$ locus must bear a specific relationship with both the constant price level ($P^* = 0$) and the constant money wage ($W^* = 0$) loci. The constant price level locus is shown in Figure I [1975, p. 66] as the kinked curve dividing the (w,r) space into two half-planes, with E_y positive to the left and E_y negative to the right of that locus. The constant money wage locus coincides with the horizontal line at w_f, again dividing the space into an E_N negative half-plane above it, and an E_N positive one below it. As a consequence, the constant real wage locus must have the following properties:

For any w greater than w_f, it must be below the $E_y = 0$ line, with both output and labor markets in excess supply, and be positively sloped; for any w smaller than w_f, it must be to the left of the $E_y = 0$ line, with both output and labor markets in excess demand, but with its slope not exactly determined (see equations (38a) and (38b)); for $w = w_f$, the constant real wage locus must pass through the intersection of the $E_y = 0$ and the $E_N = 0$ loci, with both markets cleared.

While the above restrictions on the real wage locus do simplify the analysis of the short-run equilibrium, it must be noted that we still face several possibilities:

(A) At the excess supply half-plane, there can be a quasi equilibrium that is a stable focus;

(B) At the excess demand half-plane, the following can be seen: 1. if the $w^* = 0$ locus is negatively sloped, we have a quasi equilibrium that is a stable node, when the $r^* = 0$ locus intersects the $w^* = 0$ locus from above; 2. if the $w^* = 0$ locus is negatively sloped, we have a quasi equilibrium that is a saddle point, when the $r^* = 0$ locus intersects the $w^* = 0$ locus from below; 3. if the $w^* = 0$ locus is vertical, we have again a saddle point quasi equilibrium; 4. if the $w^* = 0$ locus is positively sloped, we have a quasi equilibrium that is a stable focus. There exists one possibility of multiple quasi equilibria, since cases (A) and (B1) can coexist. Otherwise, we have a unique quasi equilibrium. Finally, the extreme case of a full-market-clearing general equilibrium continues to be described by "Case 3" [p. 72].

The Quarterly Journal of Economics, August 1980 0033-5533/80/0095-0199$01.00

In conclusion, we see that taking into account the restrictions on the position of the constant real wage locus does eliminate several improbable cases of short-run quasi equilibrium. It remains true, however, that even so there exist a multiplicity of types of short-run quasi equilibrium, whose uniqueness and stability cannot be a priori settled. This is, of course, the essential argument and character of a disequilibrium macroeconomic model, and the suggested restrictions on the position of the constant real wage locus do not alter the argument and character of the model.

ATHENS SCHOOL OF ECONOMICS AND BUSINESS SCIENCE

REFERENCE

Korliras, P. G., "A Disequilibrium Macroeconomic Model," this *Journal,* LXXXIX (Feb. 1975), 56–80.

ERRATUM: ADVERSE SELECTION BY MARKETS AND THE ADVANTAGE OF BEING LATE

J. LUIS GUASCH AND ANDREW WEISS

A reference was inadvertently omitted from the above paper. The proof of the existence of a symmetric Nash Equilibrium in mixed strategies which appears on pages 461 and 462 is due to Charles Wilson. A complete characterization of equilibria in models of this sort appears in "When to Move: A Game Theoretic Analysis of Strikes, Price Wars and Market Entry," by A. Weiss and C. Wilson.

REFERENCE

Guasch, J. Luis, and Andrew Weiss, "Adverse Selection by Markets and the Advantage of Being Late," this *Journal,* XCIV (1980), 453–466.

No. 379

THE QUARTERLY JOURNAL OF ECONOMICS

FOUNDED 1886

Vol. XCV September 1980 No. 2

ARTICLES

Heckscher-Ohlin Trade Theory with a Continuum of Goods .... *Rudiger Dornbusch, Stanley Fischer, and Paul A. Samuelson* 203

A Compensation Measure of the Cost of Unemployment to the Unemployed .... *Michael Hurd* 225

The Effects of Supply Contracts on the Output and Price of an Exhaustible Resource .... *Blaine Roberts* 245

A Method for Determining the Appropriateness of National Planning in a Market Economy .... *Jeffrey B. Miller* 261

A Model of International Trade and Finance .... *Laurence Weiss* 277

The Regional Distribution of Population, Migration, and Climate .... *Donald R. Haurin* 293

Bank Attitude Toward Risk, Implicit Rates of Interest, and the Behavior of an Index of Risk Aversion for Commercial Banks .... *Ronald A. Ratti* 309

The Optimum Monetary Aggregate for Stabilization Policy .... *Don E. Roper and Stephen J. Turnovsky* 331

NOTES

Optimal Redistributive Taxation and Uncertainty .... *Jonathan Eaton and Harvey S. Rosen* 357

Role of Education in Production: A Slightly New Approach .... *Rati Ram* 365

On the Long-Run Steady State in a Simple Dynamic Model of Equilibrium with Heterogeneous Households .... *Robert A. Becker* 375

A Comment on Measuring Horizontal Equity .... *Robert Plotnick* 383

PUBLISHED FOR HARVARD UNIVERSITY
BY JOHN WILEY & SONS, NEW YORK

QJECAT 95(2) 203–386 (1980)
ISSN 0033-5533

The Quarterly Journal of Economics

Published eight times in 1980 (February, March, May, June, August, September, November and December), two volumes, four issues per volume, by John Wiley & Sons, Inc.

Second class postage paid at New York, New York, and at additional mailing offices.

Subscription price (1981): $30.00 per volume. Postage and handling outside U.S.A.: $8.00 per volume. Please allow four weeks for change of address. Back volumes are available for previous years. Request price list from publisher. Claims for undelivered copies must be made no later than three months following month of publication. Missing copies will be supplied when losses have been sustained in transit and where reserve stock will permit.

Books, periodicals and manuscripts should be addressed to THE QUARTERLY JOURNAL OF ECONOMICS, Littauer Center, Cambridge, Massachusetts 02138. Two copies of manuscripts should be submitted in clear double-spaced typewritten copy. Manuscripts of more than thirty-five double-spaced typed pages in length are not ordinarily considered for publication. After publication, twenty-five complimentary reprints are sent to the author receiving proofs. This journal does not carry a page charge for contributors.

Business correspondence should be addressed to Journals Department, John Wiley & Sons, 605 Third Avenue, New York, New York 10158.

THE
QUARTERLY JOURNAL OF ECONOMICS

Vol. XCV September 1980 No. 2

ARTICLES

Heckscher-Ohlin Trade Theory with a Continuum of Goods
.... *Rudiger Dornbusch, Stanley Fischer, and Paul A. Samuelson* 203

A Compensation Measure of the Cost of Unemployment to the Unemployed
.... *Michael Hurd* 225

The Effects of Supply Contracts on the Output and Price of an Exhaustible Resource .... *Blaine Roberts* 245

A Method for Determining the Appropriateness of National Planning in a Market Economy .... *Jeffrey B. Miller* 261

A Model of International Trade and Finance .... *Laurence Weiss* 277

The Regional Distribution of Population, Migration, and Climate
.... *Donald R. Haurin* 293

Bank Attitude Toward Risk, Implicit Rates of Interest, and the Behavior of an Index of Risk Aversion for Commercial Banks .... *Ronald A. Ratti* 309

The Optimum Monetary Aggregate for Stabilization Policy
.... *Don E. Roper and Stephen J. Turnovsky* 331

NOTES

Optimal Redistributive Taxation and Uncertainty
.... *Jonathan Eaton and Harvey S. Rosen* 357

Role of Education in Production: A Slightly New Approach .... *Rati Ram* 365

On the Long-Run Steady State in a Simple Dynamic Model of Equilibrium with Heterogeneous Households .... *Robert A. Becker* 375

A Comment on Measuring Horizontal Equity .... *Robert Plotnick* 383

Information for Authors

Dear Author(s):

The provisions of the new copyright law, which went into effect in January 1978, make it advisable for authors to transfer copyrights to publishers explicitly and in writing. Under the old copyright law the transfer implicit in submission gave adequate protection to all concerned. Accordingly, we now require that the following agreement be executed and signed by the author(s) before a manuscript is accepted for publication. The signed agreement is then to be returned to *The Quarterly Journal of Economics.*

Agreement to Transfer Copyright

Name of Article: ____

____

I submit herewith the article named above for publication in *The Quarterly Journal of Economics*. It has not been published before. If and when the article is accepted for publication, I, as the author, hereby agree to transfer (for U.S. Government employees: to the extent transferable) to the President and Fellows of Harvard College all rights under existing copyright laws except for the following, which the author specifically retains:

1. The right to make further copies of all or part of the published article for my use in classroom teaching;
2. The right to reuse all or part of this material in a compilation of my own works or in a textbook of which I am the author;
3. The right to make copies of the published work for internal distribution within the institution that employs me.

I agree that copies made under these circumstances will continue to carry the copyright notice that appeared in the original published work. I agree to inform my coauthors, if any, of the above terms.

____

Signature(s) and date(s)

____

____

Print name(s) and title(s)

____

Institutions or companies (if appropriate)

THE
QUARTERLY JOURNAL
OF ECONOMICS

Vol. XCV September 1980 No. 2

HECKSCHER-OHLIN TRADE THEORY WITH A CONTINUUM OF GOODS

RUDIGER DORNBUSCH
STANLEY FISCHER
PAUL A. SAMUELSON

This paper studies trade theory for the case of a continuum of goods, two factors, two countries, and Cobb-Douglas demand functions. If factor endowments are similar, factor price equalization obtains and geographic patterns of production are indeterminate; nonetheless the effects of changes in factor endowments on prices and welfare in each country are well defined. Factor price equalization does not obtain if factor endowments are far apart, and the geographic pattern of specialization is then determinate. The effects of changes in endowments on the range of goods produced in each country and on prices of goods and factors are analyzed for this case, and the elasticity of substitution in production is shown to play an important role in determining comparative static outcomes.

I. INTRODUCTION

This paper studies Heckscher-Ohlin trade theory in a model with a continuum of goods. In earlier work [Dornbusch, Fischer, and Samuelson, 1977] we formulated a continuum model for the case of Ricardian technology—constant unit labor requirements and labor as the only factor—and showed that the continuum assumption offers great convenience in analyzing standard questions in trade theory. In this paper we report on some applications of the continuum model to the more complicated case of two factors of production.

Section II introduces the model and shows the derivation of the closed-economy equilibrium. Here it is shown that the equilibrium wage-rental ratio fully characterizes the equilibrium of our economy,

* Financial support was provided by grants from the National Science Foundation. We are indebted to an anonymous referee for a speedy and careful report.

even though there is an infinity of goods. In Section III we proceed to an open economy with equalized factor prices. The familiar result that the world economy under factor price equalization is like a single economy is shown, as is the fact that there is no determinate trade pattern. There are nevertheless interesting results relating to growth, world income distribution, and welfare that can be demonstrated for this case.

Section IV develops the analysis of equilibrium in the world economy when factor prices differ internationally, as they will when factor endowments are sufficiently far apart. We show first the determination of equilibrium specialization patterns, and then derive the relationship between relative factor prices and the various regional endowments of factors of production. There is now the possibility—not present in the two-commodity model—of some ambiguity about the effects of growth on relative factor and commodity prices and trade patterns. There is also the fact that specialization will always extend to a range of goods rather than to a single commodity and that accordingly, as we shall show, relative factor prices may move in opposite directions in the two countries.

To pave the way for analysis of the Heckscher-Ohlin continuum model, we recapitulate known results for the case of n goods and m factors. In particular, the case of $n > m$ is of most interest here, since the continuum model involves n as an uncountably infinite number. The exposition simplifies when we assume the following: (1) uniform (strongly quasi-concave) homothetic tastes;[1] and (2) each country has the same concave, first-degree-homogeneous production functions, of the smooth neoclassical type. In the two-factor case ($m = 2$, corresponding to capital and labor), the exposition simplifies when out of any pair of goods, one is always definitely more capital-intensive than the other at *every* factor-price ratio.

One can verify the following results:

For any pattern of factor endowments, a unique pattern of goods and factor pricing is determined. Also, there is a unique equilibrium pattern of world and regional consumptions, with consumption ratios the same in every country when transport costs of goods are literally zero.

If all countries have identical factor-endowment ratios, the pricing and consumption pattern prevailing in every country is what

1. Much of our continuum analysis will be carried out under the further simplifying assumption that uniform homothetic tastes are of the Millian or Cobb-Douglas form: regardless of prices and incomes, every region always spends a fixed function of its income on each respective good. See Samuelson [forthcoming], Wan [1977], and Wilson [forthcoming] for more general models.

would prevail in each and every country under autarky. Real factor returns are, of course, equalized (with or without goods' trade).

However, if there are more goods than factors, it need *not* be the case that each region produces its own autarky-quantum of consumption goods, although that is an admissible pattern of geographical specialization. But, with $n > m$, there will be an $(n - m)$-fold infinity of geographical patterns or production specialization.[2] The indeterminacy is inessential when transport costs are zero.[3]

With $n = m$, the geographical pattern will almost always be unique.

Now let the two countries differ slightly in factor-endowment ratios. Then factor returns will stay equalized, and uniform world pricing and consuming patterns are uniquely determined. Again, with $n > m$, the pattern of production specialization is not geographically determined in a unique way. There will still be an $(n - m)$-fold infinity of indifferent admissible patterns. However, the region with excess labor endowment on average produces goods that are of higher labor intensity than goods produced abroad.

Finally, let the two countries differ more and more in factor-endowment ratios. With n finite, eventually the country with the greater relative capital endowment will find its real rental rate (in terms of every good) falling below that of the other country; as the real rental rate r falls here and the wage-rental ratio w/r rises, the real wage also rises here; and w^*/r^*, w^*, and $1/r^*$ all move in the same direction.[4]

Here is a brief account of Heckscher-Ohlin specialization patterns in the two-factor case. Under our strong assumption, we can rank the goods in order of decreasing relative capital intensity:

$$1, 2, \ldots, j, j + 1, \ldots, n.$$

Good 1 will certainly be produced at home if ours is the capital-rich region with higher w/r. Good n will certainly be produced abroad and be imported by us. As in the analysis of Ricardian comparative advantage, from technology alone, one cannot deduce which other goods

2. See Meade [1950] for discussion of the algebra of the $n = 3 > m = 2$ case. Geometrically, when $n > m$, the production-possibility frontier of any region has straight lines or planes on it; so the tangency between two regions' frontiers, needed to define the world production-possibility frontier, can be along an infinity of points belonging to both regions' flat facets. See also Melvin [1968].

3. When transport costs are positive, the invisible hand of competitive arbitrage will solve the problem that minimizes deadweight loss from cross haulage or non-optimal specialization.

4. An increase in capital in our region, other things equal, lowers both real r and, at least initially, r^*; it raises both real w and initially real w^*; how it ultimately affects r/r^* does not seem to be uniformly predictable.

2, . . . , j the home region must also produce, and which goods $j, \ldots, n$ we definitely have to import. Where j falls between 1 and n must depend on the full general-equilibrium conditions of reciprocal demand.

In the discrete many-goods case, there are two possible types of equilibria: one in which *no* good is produced by *both* countries; and the other "limbo" case in which the borderline good *is* produced in both countries. The continuum case that we consider in this paper is special in that there is only one type of equilibrium, which we may think of as involving the joint production of the borderline commodity. We proceed now to the closed-economy continuum model.

II. The Closed Economy

There is a continuum of goods, indexed by z (z runs from zero to one), and two factors of production, capital and labor. Supplies of the two factors are fixed exogenously at levels K and N, respectively. Production functions for each of the goods are regularly neoclassical, satisfying the Inada conditions. The goods are indexed in order of decreasing capital intensity of production; there are no factor intensity reversals so that, for instance, good zero is the most capital-intensive in production at all wage-rental ratios.

We assume *uniform* homothetic demand. Our earlier paper's assumption of Millian or Cobb-Douglas demand is again postulated: C-D demand means that the function of income spent on good z, $b(z)$, is the same at all prices and in both countries. The integral over $b(z)$ on the interval $0 \leq z \leq 1$ is thus unity, as all income is spent.

1. *The Equilibrium*

We now examine the existence and properties of the equilibrium of this economy. For every good, the condition of equality of supply and demand is

$$P(z)Q(z) = b(z)(wN + rK), \tag{1}$$

where $Q(z)$ is the output of good z, $P(z)$ is the price, w is the wage rate, r is the rental rate on capital.

Full employment is assumed, so that total income is equal to the bracketed expression on the right-hand side of (1). By virtue of the assumed constant returns to scale, the value of output of commodity z is equal to $[wN(z) + rK(z)]$, where $N(z)$ and $K(z)$ are the quantities of labor and capital employed in the production of z. Simple manipulation results in (2) as an equivalent statement of the equilibrium condition in market z:

$$x(z) \equiv \frac{N(z)}{N} = \frac{b(z)(\sigma + k)}{\sigma + k(\sigma;z)}, \tag{2}$$

where $\sigma \equiv w/r$ is the wage-rental ratio, k is the aggregate capital-labor ratio, and $k(\sigma;z)$ is the capital-labor ratio in industry z, a function of σ, the wage-rental ratio.[5]

Labor and capital must be fully employed in equilibrium. This fact implies, for labor, that

$$\int_0^1 N(z)dz = N \tag{3}$$

or

$$\int_0^1 x(z)dz = 1 = \int_0^1 \frac{b(z)\,(\sigma + k)}{\sigma + k(z)}\,dz. \tag{4}$$

The full-employment condition for capital is, analogously,

$$\int_0^1 x(z)k(z)dz = k = \int_0^1 \frac{b(z)k(z)(\sigma + k)}{\sigma + k(z)}\,dz. \tag{5}$$

Combining (4) and (5), we obtain the fundamental equilibrium condition for the closed economy:

$$\phi(\sigma;k) \equiv \int_0^1 \frac{b(z)(\sigma + k)}{\sigma + k(z)}\,[k(z) - k]dz = 0. \tag{6}$$

To demonstrate the existence of a unique equilibrium, we consider first the case of Cobb-Douglas production functions. With such production functions distributive shares are constant, and we can substitute in (4) the constant ratios of income shares $\Psi(z) \equiv k(z)/\sigma$ to obtain

$$1 = \int_0^1 b(z)\,\frac{1 + k/\sigma}{1 + \Psi(z)}\,dz \equiv \xi\left(\frac{k}{\sigma}\right). \tag{4$'$}$$

It is immediately apparent that the right-hand side is a uniformly decreasing function of the wage-rental ratio that runs the gamut from $+\infty$ to a number less than one, and that accordingly there exists a unique $\bar{\sigma}$ that solves (4)′ as shown in Figure I.

For the more general case of production functions not restricted to unit elasticities of substitution, it is convenient to look at (6). That at least one equilibrium for this economy exists is established by ob-

5. In what follows, we shall simplify notation and write $k(z)$ instead of $k(\sigma,z)$.

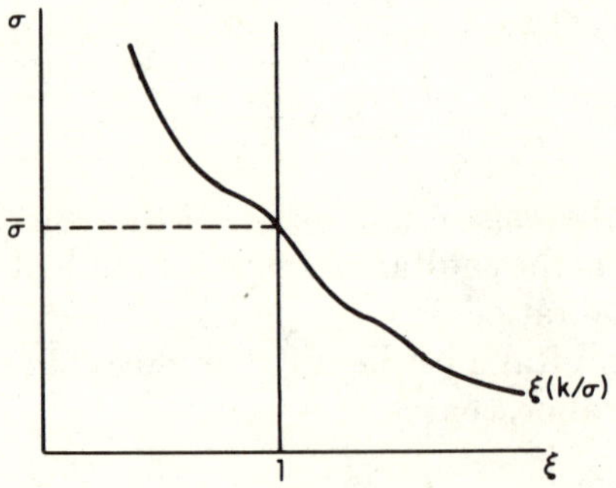

FIGURE I

serving first that, by virtue of the assumption that the production functions are neoclassical, $\phi(\ )$ is continuous in σ; and second, that because each production function satisfies the Inada conditions, there are values of σ such that $k(z)$ is greater than k for all z, and hence that $\phi(\sigma,k)$ is positive at those values of σ, and similarly, that there are values of σ at which $k(z)$ is less than k for all z, so that $\phi(\ )$ is negative at those values of σ. Given that $\phi(\sigma,k)$ is continuous in σ, there is some $\bar{\sigma}$ such that $\phi(\ )$ is equal to zero; $\bar{\sigma}$ is an equilibrium wage-rental ratio.

At such a wage-rental ratio there is full employment of both factors, and the production of each good can be determined from (2) and (3). The equilibrium is in fact unique. To show this, we establish that the derivative of $\phi(\ )$ with respect to σ is positive. Differentiating (6) yields

$$(7)\quad \frac{\partial \phi}{\partial \sigma} = \int_0^1 \frac{b(z)}{[\sigma + k(z)]^2}\left[(k(z) - k)^2 + (\sigma + k)^2 \frac{\partial k(z)}{\partial \sigma}\right] dz > 0.$$

The existence of a unique equilibrium $\bar{\sigma}$ under our strong assumptions is thus established. Given the wage-rental ratio, the rental rate in terms of any good can be determined from the production functions. The relative price structure and the level of income are accordingly determined, as is the demand for each good. We next examine relative price behavior in more detail.

Defining the relative price of commodity z in terms of commodity z', we have

$$\frac{P(z)}{P(z')} = \frac{a(z)w + c(z)r}{a(z')w + c(z')r} = \frac{a(z)[\sigma + k(z)]}{a(z')[\sigma + k(z')]},$$

where $a(z)$ is the unit labor requirement and $c(z)$ the unit capital requirement for commodity z. Taking logs and differentiating, we obtain the familiar result,

$$\frac{d\ \ln[P(z)/P(z')]}{d\sigma} = \frac{[k(z') - k(z)]}{[\sigma + k(z)][\sigma + k(z')]},$$

so that an increase in the wage-rental ratio lowers the relative price of the capital-intensive good.

Real factor returns are also determined by the wage-rental ratio. An increase in the wage-rental ratio raises the real wage in terms of all commodities and lowers the real rental on capital in terms of all goods.[6]

2. *Comparative Statics*

The equilibrium condition and the relative price structure can now be used to discuss questions of comparative statics. We consider here two applications, changes in the factor endowments, and changes in tastes.

Endowment Changes. We would expect an increase in the capital-labor ratio to reduce the relative return to capital. That result can be demonstrated by differentiating the equilibrium condition in (6), noting that

$$\left.\frac{\partial\phi}{\partial k}\right|_{\phi=0} = -(\sigma + k)\int_0^1 \frac{b(z)}{\sigma + k(z)}\,dz = -1$$

and hence

$$\frac{d\bar{\sigma}}{dk} = 1 \Big/ \frac{\partial\phi}{\partial\sigma} > 0.$$

The increase in the equilibrium wage-rental ratio induced by a higher capital-labor ratio implies changes in relative prices, real factor returns, and resource allocation.[7] The relative price of labor-intensive goods will rise, and the real wage will increase in terms of all com-

6. Defining the real wage and the real rental in terms of commodity z yields

$$\frac{w}{P(z)} = \frac{w}{wa(z) + rc(z)} = \frac{\sigma/a(z)}{\sigma + k(z)}; \quad \frac{r}{P(z)} = \frac{1/a(z)}{\sigma + k(z)}.$$

The elasticities of the real factor prices with respect to the wage-rental ratio are

$$\frac{d\ \ln(w/P(z))}{d\ \ln\sigma} = \frac{k(z)}{\sigma + k(z)}\ \text{and}\ \frac{d\ \ln[r/P(z)]}{d\ \ln\sigma} = -\frac{\sigma}{\sigma + k(z)}.$$

7. For the special case of Cobb-Douglas demand *and* production functions, it can be shown that the elasticity of σ with respect to k is unity. This is directly apparent from (4)′.

modities, while the real return to the more plentiful capital declines in terms of all commodities.

Next we ask how an increase in the capital stock affects the output of each good. The output of good z (per capita) is given by

$$q(z)=\frac{b(z)(w+rk)}{P(z)}=\frac{b(z)(\sigma+k)f(k(z))}{\sigma+k(z)}. \tag{8}$$

The effect of an increased k therefore is

$$\frac{dq(z)}{dk}=\frac{b(z)f(k(z))}{\sigma+k(z)}\left[1+\frac{d\sigma}{dk}\frac{k(z)-k}{\sigma+k(z)}\right]. \tag{9}$$

For all low z industries, for which $k(z)>k$, an increase in the aggregate capital stock unambiguously increases physical production. However, it is possible that output in high z industries falls.[8] Note from (9) that if output for any industry falls, it also falls for all those with lower capital intensity. These results simply reflect the income and price effects induced by an expansion in the capital-labor ratio. The income effect raises demand for all goods. The induced increase in the wage-rental ratio lowers the relative price of capital-intensive goods—goods where $k(z)>k$—and thus adds to the demand for those commodities, while reducing demand for relatively labor-intensive goods.

Given that $d\sigma/dk>0$, capital intensity of production rises in every industry when the overall capital-labor ratio rises. Accordingly, an increase in k must mean that labor is withdrawn in absolute quantity from those high z industries (if any) whose output falls. But it is not necessarily true that labor input is increased for *all* low z industries; that depends on the derivative $\partial k(z)/\partial\sigma$. The more the industry's capital-output ratio responds to a change in the wage-rental ratio (i.e., the higher the elasticity of substitution at that point), the less likely is it that labor is shifted into a particular low z industry. But, on average, labor is shifted into low z industries.

Shifts in Tastes. We ask next about a shift in tastes toward the low z industries. Since we are increasing the demand for capital-intensive goods, we should expect the wage-rental ratio to fall. We conveniently parameterize the change in tastes by adding to each $b(z)$ an amount $\lambda\Delta b(z)$, where λ is a positive scalar, $\int\Delta b(z)dz=0$, and $\Delta b(z)>0$ for $0\le z\le\hat{z}$; and $\Delta b(z)<0$ for $\hat{z}\le z\le 1$, where $k(\hat{z})=k$.

8. Of course, it is possible that the output of *all* goods rises. That *must* happen with Cobb-Douglas production functions for every good: in that case a rise in K can be shown to leave real income measured in wage units unchanged. Hence costs, measured in wage units, fall for every good and output increases.

Then

$$\frac{\partial \phi}{\partial \lambda} = \int_0^1 \frac{\Delta b(z)(\sigma + k)(k(z) - k)}{\sigma + k(z)} dz > 0,$$

and accordingly

$$\frac{d\sigma}{d\lambda} < 0.$$

An interesting implication of the shift in demand, and a perhaps surprising one, is that the net effect is not necessarily to raise equilibrium output of all the goods toward which demand shifts. The reason again is the relative price effect, which in this instance implies an increase in the relative price of capital-intensive goods. Since the relative price increases with capital intensity, the substitution effect works against increases in the output of highly capital-intensive commodities and thus for the most capital-intensive goods potentially offsets the shift in demand.

We shall not pursue the properties of the closed-economy equilibrium further because our main interest in it is as a prelude to the open-economy model, to which we now turn.

III. Trading Equilibrium with Equalized Factor Prices

We now put the closed economy of Section II together with another such economy, which differs only in its factor supplies: the foreign capital-labor ratio k^* is smaller than ours. Their labor force is of size N^*.

Initially assume that after the opening of the economies to trade, factor price equalization obtains. The costs of production of all goods will accordingly be identical in both countries after trade opens. Any particular good z can be produced as well (cheaply) in one country as in the other. Given zero transport costs, prices of goods are the same in both countries. Patterns of production are not, however, totally indeterminate, since full employment of both factors requires us, on balance, to produce more capital-intensive goods.

We leave to the Appendix the demonstration that the equilibrium conditions for the world economy are precisely those of the closed economy except that now the capital-labor ratio is $\hat{k} \equiv \pi k + (1 - \pi)k^*$, that is, the respective country's capital-labor ratios weighted by the shares in the world labor force, $\pi \equiv N/(N + N^*)$. The opening of trade with the resulting establishment of a common wage-rental ratio implies, using the result $d\sigma/dk > 0$ of the previous part, that in the capital poor country the wage-rental ratio will rise, while at home it will decline. Prices will be equalized and in the home country the relative price of labor-intensive goods will fall by comparison with autarky, while abroad it will rise.

Production patterns will be indeterminate except in one important respect. Only in a probabilistic sense are we, the capital-rich country, exporters of a *particular* capital-intensive commodity. On *average,* however, we do export capital-intensive commodities, while foreigners export labor-intensive commodities. Equivalently, we are *net* exporters of capital services and *net* importers of labor services. It is this fact that is used now to discuss the effects of endowment changes on income distribution and welfare.

Consider first the benefits from the opening of trade. We noted above that the opening of trade will equalize wage-rental ratios, lowering the relative price of labor in the capital-rich country and increasing the relative price of labor in the capital-poor country. Now we want to show that the opening of trade raises "welfare" for both countries.

We define the welfare function corresponding to our Cobb-Douglas tastes:

$$U = \int_0^1 b(z)[\ln D(z)]dz, \tag{10}$$

where $D(z)$ denotes per capita consumption of commodity z. Substituting for $D(z)$, we have the indirect utility function:

$$U = \int_0^1 b(z)\left[\ln b(z)\frac{\sigma + k}{\sigma + k(z)} f(k(z))\right] dz = U(\sigma,k). \tag{10'}$$

The opening of trade will reduce our wage-rental ratio, since by assumption, we are the capital-rich country. To assess the effect on welfare, we take the derivative of (10′) with respect to σ to obtain

$$\frac{dU}{d\sigma} = \int_0^1 b(z)\left[\frac{1}{\sigma + k} - \frac{1}{\sigma + k(z)}\right] dz. \tag{11}$$

Using (6), with k replaced by $\hat{k}$, and noting that $\int_0^1 b(z)\,dz = 1$, we have

$$\frac{dU}{d\sigma} = \frac{\hat{k} - k}{(\sigma + k)(\sigma + \hat{k})}. \tag{11'}$$

For the home country, $\hat{k} < k$, and σ falls on the opening of trade; thus (11′) shows that the opening of trade makes us better off. For the foreigners, an expression similar to (11′), but with k replaced by k^*, applies. For them, $\hat{k} > k^*$, and σ rises on the opening of trade, which also makes them better off. The magnitude of the gain will depend on the extent of the differences in factor endowments.

We turn next to the income distribution and welfare effects of changes in factor endowments. Consider first the distribution of income. Our share in world income is equal to

$$\frac{wN + rK}{wN + rK + wN^* + rK^*} = \pi \frac{\sigma + k}{\sigma + \hat{k}}. \tag{12}$$

A change in factor endowments would therefore change the international distribution of income. First, a larger labor force would raise the capital-rich country's share in world income. Second, an increase in the foreign capital-labor ratio raises the world capital-labor ratio and thus the wage-rental ratio. Income, therefore, is redistributed away from capital and toward labor. That redistribution must benefit the capital-poor country.

What are the welfare effects of a change in our own capital-labor ratio? Again using the indirect utility function and taking the derivative with respect to k, noting that $\sigma = \sigma(\hat{k})$, we have

$$\frac{\partial U}{\partial k} = \frac{1}{\sigma + k} + \pi \frac{\hat{k} - k}{(\sigma + k)(\sigma + \hat{k})} \frac{d\sigma}{d\hat{k}}. \tag{13}$$

The first term measures the welfare gain of an increase in capital in the closed economy and is of course positive. The second term is negative for the capital-rich country and arises from the international redistribution of income toward the capital-poor country. An increase in the world capital-labor ratio worsens the terms of trade of capital and may do so sufficiently to more than offset the gains from increased productive resources. It can be shown, though, that this possibility cannot arise with elasticities of substitution in production of unity or more.[9]

In summary, the home country, being capital rich and therefore being a net exporter of capital services and importer of labor services, will benefit from a rise in the world wage-rental ratio due to demand shifts or foreign endowment changes. The foreign country, being labor rich, will benefit if the home country accumulates capital or experiences balanced growth or if demand shifts raise the equilibrium wage-rental ratio.

The interesting conclusion of the model with factor price equalization is that, the absence of a determinate production pattern notwithstanding, we can make judgments about welfare effects of

9. Proof of this proposition is omitted for brevity. However, examination of (13) suggests that if $d\sigma/dk$ is low, the second term is less likely to dominate. And $d\sigma/dk$ is inversely related to individual elasticities of substitution in production.

growth or demand changes. The welfare effects are determinate because there is no ambiguity about the fact that the home country is a *net* exporter of capital services and importer of labor services and there is a unique relation between endowments and relative factor and commodity prices.

IV. Trade with Complete Specialization

Now we consider the case where endowments differ sufficiently to give rise to complete specialization. Assuming, as before, that the foreign capital-labor ratio falls short of ours ($k^* < k$), the equilibrium is one where we produce in the capital-intensive range of goods, while foreigners specialize, without overlap, in the range of labor-intensive commodities. The borderline $\bar{z}$ is one of the variables determined as part of the equilibrium along with the two wage-rental ratios. In the equilibrium, we shall produce goods z, $0 \leq z \leq \bar{z}$, and foreigners produce those z in the interval $\bar{z} \leq z \leq 1$.

1. The Equilibrium

The equilibrium is determined by the conditions of trade balance equilibrium and factor market equilibrium in each country. In addition, the cost of production of the borderline commodity $\bar{z}$ is equalized between the two countries. Cost and price equalization at the margin requires that

$$(14) \qquad P(\bar{z}) = wa(\bar{z}) + rc(\bar{z}) = P^*(\bar{z}) = w^*a^*(\bar{z}) + r^*c^*(\bar{z})$$

or

$$(14') \qquad \frac{r}{r^*} = \frac{a^*(\bar{z})}{a(\bar{z})} \frac{\sigma^* + k^*(\bar{z})}{\sigma + k(\bar{z})}.$$

Since the wage-rental ratios differ, with $\sigma > \sigma^*$, the borderline commodity will be produced with a more capital-intensive technique at home compared to that used abroad.

Next we examine the condition of trade balance: the value of our imports is equal to the value of our exports. Our total income is $wN + rK$, and we import all those goods we do not produce, i.e., goods lying in the interval $\bar{z} \leq z \leq 1$. Similarly, foreigners import goods in the range $0 \leq z \leq \bar{z}$. The condition of trade balance is therefore[10]

10. After a little manipulation, (15) can be written in the form

$$\frac{w}{w^*} = \frac{N^*}{N} \frac{(1 + k^*/\sigma^*)}{(1 + k/\sigma)} B(\bar{z}),$$

which is similar to (10′) in our 1977 Ricardian paper.

$$(15)\quad (wN + rK)\int_{\bar{z}}^{1} b(z)dz = (w^*N^* + r^*K^*)\int_{0}^{\bar{z}} b(z)dz.$$

Using (14)′, we can rewrite the trade balance condition as

$$(16)\quad \mathrm{B}(\hat{z}) \equiv \frac{\int_0^{\bar{z}} b(z)dz}{\int_{\bar{z}}^{1} b(z)dz} = \frac{\pi}{1-\pi}\left(\frac{\sigma + k}{\sigma^* + k^*}\right)\left(\frac{a^*(\bar{z})}{a(\bar{z})}\right)\left(\frac{\sigma^* + k^*(\bar{z})}{\sigma + k(\bar{z})}\right).$$

The equilibrium conditions are completed by the requirement of factor market equilibrium in each country:[11]

$$(17)\qquad 0 = \int_0^{\bar{z}} \frac{b(z)}{\sigma + k(z)}\,[k(z) - k]dz,$$

and

$$(18)\qquad 0 = \int_{\bar{z}}^{1} \frac{b(z)}{\sigma^* + k^*(z)}\,[k^*(z) - k^*]\,dz.$$

It goes almost without saying that prices of goods are equal in the two countries in the assumed absence of transport costs, and that the costs of production of goods that we do not produce would be higher here than they are abroad.

The equilibrium conditions in (16) to (18) determine the equilibrium wage-rental ratios in each country, $\bar{\sigma}$ and $\bar{\sigma}^*$, and the equilibrium competitive margin $\bar{z}$. The relative price structure, incomes, commodity demands, and factor allocation are associated with the equilibrium relative factor prices. The relative prices and the competitive margin determine trade patterns.

That there is a unique equilibrium of equations (16), (17), and (18), with its implied pricing relationships that we have not written out explicitly, can be established by considering the normative problem that is satisfied by, and only by, the competitive solution. This is shown in Appendix 1.

11. To obtain (17), start from the labor market equilibrium condition,

$$N = \int_0^{\bar{z}} [a(z)b(z)(wN + rK) + (w^*N^* + r^*K^*)]/P(z)\,dz,$$

use (15), and obtain

$$\theta = \int_0^{\bar{z}} \frac{b(z)(\sigma + k)}{\sigma + k(z)}\,dz,$$

where $\theta \equiv \int_0^{\bar{z}} b(z)dz$. Similar manipulation, starting from the full employment condition for capital shows that

$$\theta k = \int_0^{\bar{z}} \frac{b(z)(\sigma + k)}{\sigma + k(z)}\,k(z)dz.$$

Equation (17) follows.

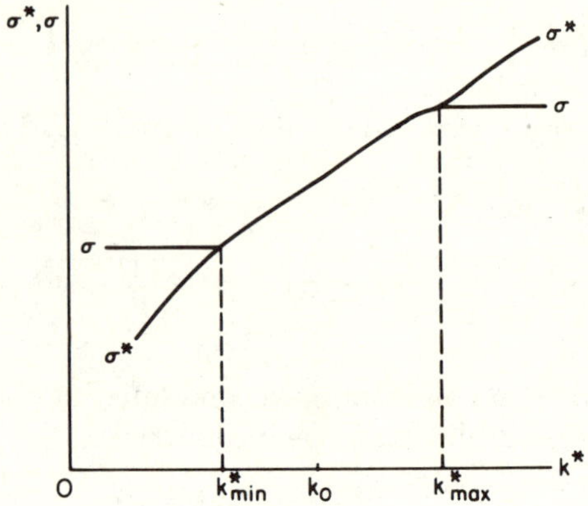

FIGURE II

2. *Comparative Statics*

We turn now to questions of comparative statics. Specifically we want to establish the effect of endowment changes on relative factor and commodity prices and on trade patterns. In our 1977 paper we showed how growth in one country changes the *equilibrium* dividing line $\bar{z}$ with the growing country increasing the range of goods produced but experiencing a decline in the equilibrium relative wage and terms of trade. In the present model there is a broader range of questions, since in addition to labor growth we can consider balanced growth or growth in the capital-labor ratio. As we shall see presently, there is ambiguity in the effect of growth on factor and commodity prices and in the effect of growth on trade patterns.

Before establishing these results, it is worth asking what the effects of growth are in the standard two-commodity Heckscher-Ohlin model. Figure II summarizes these results in plotting the equilibrium wage-rental ratios as a function of the foreign capital-labor ratio, given our capital stock k_0. The range of factor price equalization is $k^*_{\min}$ to $k^*_{\max}$. For that range of their capital-labor ratio, relative commodity and hence factor prices are such that we are nonspecialized.

A rise in their capital-labor ratio at constant relative prices of goods would, via the Rybczynski effect, create a world excess supply of the capital-intensive good and hence lower its equilibrium relative price and therefore raise the common equilibrium wage-rental ratio. As foreign k^* goes outside the range ($k^*_{\min} \leq k^* \leq k^*_{\max}$), we become completely specialized in one sector, and consequently our wage-rental ratio is determined by the relative marginal productivities in the producing sector. For the foreign country, though, the wage-rental

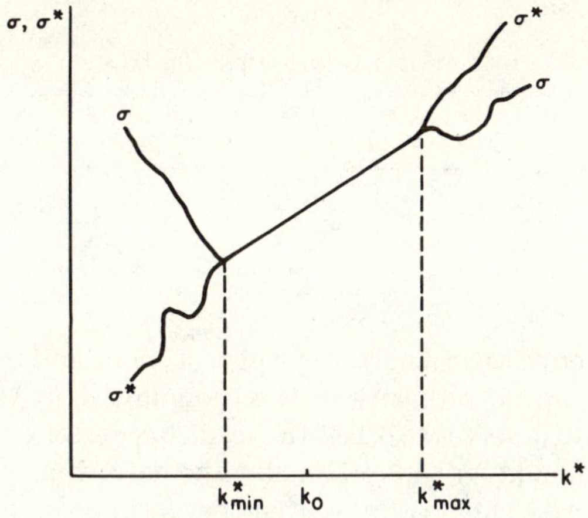

FIGURE III

ratio would continue to be an increasing function of the capital-labor ratio.[12]

One important difference in a multi-commodity model, and in particular in our continuum model, is the fact that we never achieve complete specialization in one single good and that accordingly the relation between relative factor prices and endowments will differ from that in Figure II.[13] The comparative static results of the continuum case are laid out in Table I and are illustrated in Figure III, which is to be compared with Figure II.

Consider first the case where our capital-labor ratio is larger than that abroad, $k^* < k_{\min}$, and where we have complete specialization and unequalized factor returns. A rise in the foreign capital-labor ratio, as Figure III shows, will reduce our wage-rental ratio but will have an ambiguous effect abroad. The interpretation of this result is that at constant relative factor and commodity prices, and hence a given $\bar{z}$, the increased foreign income leads to increased spending on all goods with production concentrated on only the range $\bar{z} \leq z \leq 1$. There will accordingly be excess demand for our goods and an excess supply of foreign goods. In the home country the adjustment takes the form of a decline in the wage-rental ratio and therefore an increase in the relative price of our goods that are capital-intensive. The decline in the wage-rental ratio also leads to the use of more labor-intensive techniques. This adjustment is appropriate since, as Table I shows,

12. For an exposition of these relations see Johnson [1957].
13. On the multi-commodity model see Jones [1974].

TABLE I

COMPARATIVE STATIC RESULTS ($k > k^*$)

		Change in		
		k	k^*	π
Effect on	σ	+	−	+
	σ^*	?	?	+
	$\bar{z}$	?	−	+

we shall concentrate on a narrower range of goods and therefore raise the average capital intensity in the economy. The decline in the wage-rental ratio serves to offset the resulting excess supply of labor and excess demand for capital. Finally, the narrowing of the range of goods produced at home implies that there will be increased output levels so that, in conjunction with the increased relative price, there will be an adjustment to higher foreign real income and spending on our goods.

Consider next the foreign country. Real income has increased, and therefore demand has risen for foreign-produced goods. The increased supply of capital raises potential output, but there is now an excess demand for labor. Suppose for a moment that the elasticity of substitution in production were zero. Then the foreign adjustment could take the form of a shift in the competitive margin, thus increasing capital use, and of a rise in the wage-rental ratio so as to raise the relative price of labor-intensive goods and thus reduce labor demand. It can indeed be shown that for low elasticities of substitution these conclusions hold. If elasticities of substitution are larger than one, though, it becomes possible that an increase in the wage-rental ratio creates an excess demand for capital, as substitution of capital for labor becomes important. This is the source of the ambiguity in the effect of foreign capital growth on their equilibrium wage-rental ratio.

We look now at the case where foreigners are the capital-rich country and experience further growth in their capital-labor ratio. Note that now they produce in the range $0 < z < \bar{z}$, i.e., they produce the relatively capital-intensive goods. Now the foreign wage-rental ratio will rise, but there is uncertainty about our wage-rental ratio and about the change in trade patterns. Abroad, the increase in the wage-rental ratio induces more capital-using techniques, and it lowers the relative price of relatively capital-intensive goods. Both effects operate to absorb the increased capital, but they leave us uncertain about the demand for labor. With no substitutability labor demand would decline, and we would find the foreign country expanding its range of production to encompass more labor-intensive goods. With high substitutability, by contrast, there may be an excess demand for labor requiring a narrowing of the production range. The uncertainty about the effects on trade patterns also leaves us uncertain about the change in the equilibrium wage-rental ratio at home. Again, if substitution elasticities are small, abroad we expect an expansion in the foreign production range, and therefore at home an increase in the wage-rental ratio in order to accommodate ourselves to a more labor-intensive range of products.

Consider finally a balanced increase in our own endowment. This leads to a rise in both countries' wage-rental ratios and to an expansion in the range of goods we produce. The increased range of goods production leaves us with more labor-intensive production that we offset through a rise in the wage-rental ratio. Abroad where the production range shrinks to devote resources more intensively to meet the increased world demand, the more labor-intensive output mix requires a rise in the wage-rental ratio to retain factor market equilibrium.

In the case of balanced growth, analysis of terms-of-trade effects is straight-forward. Here the goods we produce fall in price relative to the borderline commodity, which is the most labor intensive. Abroad all commodities rise in price relative to the borderline commodity, which is the least labor intensive abroad. Accordingly, our terms of trade unambiguously deteriorate.

3. The Borderline Case: Complete Specialization with Factor Price Equalization

We now briefly investigate the borderline case where both countries are completely specialized but factor prices remain equalized. This is the dividing line between the case of overlapping production ranges when endowments are close together and the case of the previous section. The relevant equations are (16) simplified to take account of the common wage-rental ratio and thus the common choice of technique:

$$B(\bar{z}) = \frac{\pi}{1-\pi}\frac{\sigma + k}{\sigma^* + k^*}, \tag{16'}$$

as well as the conditions of factor market equilibrium in (17) and (18) with $\sigma^* = \sigma$.

What can be said of the relationship between k and k^* such that we remain on the borderline? The natural conjecture is that an increase in our capital-labor ratio requires an accompanying increase in the foreign relative supply of capital so as to preserve factor price equalization. Perhaps surprisingly that result cannot be demonstrated in general.

It is true that if all production functions are Cobb-Douglas, the borderline has a positive slope. However, an ambiguity arises when elasticities of substitution at home are small and those abroad are large. In such a case an increase in the domestic capital stock may tend to result in a larger increase in σ^* than in σ, requiring a *fall* in k^* to maintain factor price equilibrium (see the discussion of Section IV above).

V. Concluding Remarks

This paper has extended our Ricardian continuum model to the case of two-factor Heckscher-Ohlin trade theory. The extension is rewarding because it introduces, in a still manageable fashion, the scope for relative price changes within a country rather than only changes in relative wages and the terms of trade of the Ricardian composite commodities that emerged in our earlier analysis.

The changes in relative factor and commodity prices induced by such disturbances as demand shifts or endowment changes cannot be determined without ambiguity outside the range of factor price equalization. This ambiguity arises because changes in relative factor supplies can be accommodated either by a shifting of the competitive margin toward more or less capital-intensive goods or by a change in relative factor prices and hence commodity prices. Even under our strong demand assumptions we cannot be certain about the distribution—or even direction—of adjustment between relative factor price changes and changes in trade patterns. Hence the elasticity of substitution in production plays an important role. With elasticities of substitution that are low (equal to or less than unity) the increase in a country's capital-labor ratio will raise the wage-rental ratio, as would be true in the two-commodity model, a closed economy, or under factor price equalization. With high elasticities of substitution, that regularity is no longer assured.

Under factor price equalization the model shows the well-known indeterminacy of geographic specialization. But we can make use of the fact that the capital-rich country is a net exporter of capital services to derive results concerning income distribution and welfare as they are affected by the opening of trade or changes in factor endowments.

The Heckscher-Ohlin variant of our continuum model remains manageable under our demand assumptions because, the multiplicity of goods notwithstanding, the equilibrium can be reduced to three variables—wage-rental ratios in each country and the equilibrium competitive margin. The Stolper-Samuelson theorem ensures that the single wage-rental ratio in each country determines the entire price structure for goods produced in that country, a result only slightly more complex than the Ricardian model.

APPENDIX 1: THE EXISTENCE OF EQUILIBRIUM

The normative problem that is solved by the competitive equilibrium is

$$\text{(A.1)}\quad \Phi(K,N,K^*,N^*) = \max_{\{K(z),N(z),K^*(z),N^*(z)\}} \int_0^1 b(z)\log\{F[K(z),N(z)] + F[K^*(z),N^*(z)]\},$$

subject to

$$\left[\int_0^1 K(z)dz,\ \int_0^1 N(z)dz,\ \int_0^1 K^*(z)dz,\ \int_0^1 N^*(z)dz\right] = [K,N,K^*,N^*] = [y_1,\ldots,y_4] = y.$$

Denoting partial derivatives by numerical subscripts,

$$\frac{\partial\Phi(y_1,y_2,y_3,y_4)}{\partial y_i} = \Phi_i(y), \quad (i = 1,\ldots,4).$$

we can express our equilibrium unknowns by

$$\text{(A.2)}\quad \omega = w/w^* = \Phi_2(y)/\Phi_4(y)$$
$$\sigma = w/r = \Phi_2(y)/\Phi_1(y)$$
$$\sigma^* = w^*/r^* = \Phi_4(y)/\Phi_3(y).$$

$\bar{z}$ is the root for z in

$$\omega = \left(a^*(z) + \frac{c^*(z)}{\sigma^*}\right)\Big/\left(a(z) + \frac{c(z)}{\sigma}\right).$$

The Kuhn-Tucker conditions, necessary and sufficient for the maximum and the equilibrium, can be expressed compactly with the help of the following notations:

$$[K(z),N(z),K^*(z),N^*(z)] \equiv [y_1(z),\ldots,y_4(z)] = y(z)$$
$$F(y_1(z),y_2(z)) + F(y_3(z),y_4(z)) \equiv F(y(z))$$
$$\frac{\partial F[y_1(z),\ldots,y_4(z)]}{\partial y_i(z)} \equiv F_i(y(z)), \qquad i = 1,\ldots,4.$$

Then (A.1) implies that

$$\text{(A.3)}\quad \bar{L}[y(z);\mu] = \frac{b(z)F_i[y(z)]}{F[y(z)]} - \mu_i \geq 0 \qquad (i = 1,\ldots,4)$$

$$L_{4+i}[y(z);\mu] = y_i - \int_0^1 y_i(z)dz \geq 0; \quad \mu \geq 0, \quad y(z) \geq 0$$

$$\sum_1^4 L_i[y(z);\mu]y_i - \sum_1^4 L_{4+j}\,[y(z);\mu]\mu_j = 0.$$

The μ's are dual variables, proportional to real factor prices of (K,N,K^*,N^*), respectively.

Appendix 2: The Equilibrium with Factor Price Equalization

Let $\alpha(z) \geq 0$ denote the fraction of the world output of good z that we produce; $(1 - \alpha(z))$ is produced by foreigners. Denote our proportion of the world labor force, $N/(N + N^*)$, by π. Equilibrium requires that trade balances. The condition for trade balance is that our income be equal to the value of our production:

$$\text{(A.4)} \quad wN + rK = \int_0^1 \alpha(z)P(z)[Q(z) + Q^*(z)]dz$$
$$= \int_0^1 \alpha(z)b(z)[(wN + rK) + (wN^* + rK^*)]dz.$$

Rearranging terms, and recalling that $\int_0^1 b(z)dz = 1$, we may write the trade balance as

$$\int_0^1 b(z)(1 - \alpha(z))(\sigma + k)dz = \frac{N^*}{N}\int_0^1 \alpha(z)b(z)(\sigma + k^*)dz$$
$$\text{(A.5)} \quad = \frac{1 - \pi}{\pi}\int_0^1 \alpha(z)b(z)(\sigma + k^*)dz.$$

The remaining equilibrium conditions are those for the factor markets in the two countries:

$$\text{(A.6)} \quad \int_0^1 \frac{k(z)b(z)\alpha(z)[\sigma + \pi k + (1 - \pi)k^*]}{\sigma + k(z)}dz = \pi k$$

and

$$\int_0^1 \frac{k(z)b(z)(1 - \alpha(z))[\sigma + \pi k + (1 - \pi)k^*]}{\sigma + k(z)}dz = (1 - \pi)k^*.$$
(A.7)

The world capital stock per capita is

$$\text{(A.8)} \quad \hat{k} \equiv \frac{K + K^*}{N + N^*} = \pi k + (1 - \pi)k^*.$$

Adding (A.6) and (A.7), we can summarize the two capital market equilibrium conditions by

$$\text{(A.9)} \quad \int_0^1 \frac{k(z)b(z)[\sigma + \hat{k}]}{\sigma + k(z)}dz = \hat{k}.$$

Similarly, the two labor market equilibrium conditions reduce to

$$\text{(A.10)} \quad \int_0^1 \frac{b(z)[\sigma + \hat{k}]}{\sigma + k(z)}dz = 1.$$

Now these are precisely the same equilibrium conditions as equations (5) and (6). A unique equilibrium σ therefore exists. Because

$k > k > k^*$ and we showed earlier that $d\sigma/dk > 0$, we conclude that the wage-rental ratio after the opening of trade is between the two closed economy wage-rental ratios. Furthermore, an increase in the capital stock in either country will increase the equilibrium σ, as long as factor-price equalization continues to obtain.

APPENDIX 3: COMPARATIVE STATICS UNDER COMPLETE SPECIALIZATION

This appendix sketches the derivation of comparative static results for the case of complete specialization without factor price equalization. The equilibrium conditions, repeated here for convenience, are those for balanced trade and equilibrium in factor markets:

$$B(\bar{z}) = \frac{\pi}{1-\pi}\left(\frac{\sigma + k}{\sigma^* + k^*}\right)\left(\frac{a^*(\bar{z})}{a(\bar{z})}\right)\left(\frac{\sigma^* + k^*(\bar{z})}{\sigma + k(\bar{z})}\right) \tag{A.11}$$

$$0 = \int_0^{\bar{z}} \frac{b(z)}{\sigma + k(z)}[k(z) - k]dz \tag{A.12}$$

$$0 = \int_{\bar{z}}^{1} \frac{b(z)}{\sigma^* + k^*(z)}[k^*(z) - k^*]\, dz. \tag{A.13}$$

Differentiating (A.11)–(A.13) yields the following system:

$$[A]\begin{bmatrix} d\bar{z} \\ d\sigma \\ d\sigma^* \end{bmatrix} = [B]\begin{bmatrix} dk \\ dk^* \\ d\pi \end{bmatrix}, \tag{A.14}$$

where $[A]$ and $[B]$ are each 3×3 matrices, with elements a_{ij}, b_{ij}, respectively.

The elements are given by

$$a_{11} = \frac{B'(\bar{z})}{B(\bar{z})} = \frac{b(\bar{z})}{[\int_{\bar{z}}^{1} b(z)dz]^2} > 0; \quad a_{12} = \frac{k - k(\bar{z})}{(\sigma + k)(\sigma + k(\bar{z}))} > 0;$$

$$a_{13} = \frac{k^*(\bar{z}) - k^*}{(\sigma^* + k^*)(\sigma^* + k^*(\bar{z}))} > 0;$$

$$a_{21} = \frac{b(\bar{z})}{\sigma + k(\bar{z})}[k(\bar{z}) - k] < 0;$$

$$a_{22} = \int_0^{\bar{z}} \frac{b(z)}{[\sigma + k(z)]^2}\left[\frac{\partial k(z)}{\partial \sigma}(\sigma + k) - (k(z) - k)\right]dz > 0;$$

$$a_{23} = 0;$$

$$a_{31} = \frac{-b(\bar{z})}{\sigma^* + k^*(\bar{z})}[k^*(\bar{z}) - k^*] < 0; \quad a_{32} = 0;$$

$$a_{33} = \int_{\bar{z}}^{1} \frac{b(z)}{[\sigma^* + k^*(z)]^2} \cdot \left[\frac{\partial k^*(z)}{\partial \sigma^*}(\sigma^* + k^*) - (k^*(z) - k^*)\right] dz > 0;$$

$$b_{11} = \frac{1}{\sigma + k} > 0; \quad b_{12} = -\frac{1}{\sigma^* + k^*} < 0; \quad b_{13} = \frac{1}{\pi(1 - \pi)} > 0;$$

$$b_{21} = \int_{0}^{\bar{z}} \frac{b(z)}{\sigma + k(z)} dz > 0; \quad b_{22} = 0 = b_{23};$$

$$b_{31} = 0; \quad b_{32} = \int_{\bar{z}}^{1} \frac{b(z)}{\sigma^* + k^*(z)} dz > 0; \quad b_{33} = 0.$$

Now, substituting the elements a_{ij} and b_{ij} into (A.4) makes it possible to derive the results shown in Table I of the text.

MASSACHUSETTS INSTITUTE OF TECHNOLOGY

REFERENCES

Dornbusch, R., S. Fischer, and P. A. Samuelson, "Comparative Advantage, Trade and Payments in a Ricardian Model with a Continuum of Goods," *American Economic Review,* LXVII (Dec. 1977), 823–29.
Johnson, H. G., "Factor Endowments, International Trade and Factor Prices," *The Manchester School,* XXV, No. 3 (Sept. 1957), 270–83.
Jones, R. W., "The Small Country in a Many-Commodity World," *Australian Economic Papers,* XXXVII (Dec. 1974), 225–36.
Meade, J., "The Equalization of Factor Prices: The Two-Country, Two-Factor, Three-Product Case," *Metroeconomica,* II (Dec. 1950), 129–33.
Melvin, J. R., "Production and Trade with Two Factors and Three Goods," *American Economic Review,* LVIII (Dec. 1968), 1249–68.
Samuelson, P. A., "Two Country Ricardian Analysis for Discrete Goods and for a Continuum of Goods," *Journal of International Economics,* forthcoming.
Wan, H. Y., Jr., "Three Variations on a Theme of Samuelson," mimeo, Cornell University, 1977.
Wilson, C., "On the General Structure of Ricardian Models with a Continuum of Goods: Applications to Growth, Tariff Theory and Technical Change," *Econometrica,* forthcoming.

A COMPENSATION MEASURE OF THE COST OF UNEMPLOYMENT TO THE UNEMPLOYED*

MICHAEL HURD

Under the assumption that unemployment is the result of job rationing, Hicks's compensating variation measures the payment that would make a worker indifferent between employment at his desired annual hours and rationed employment. This theory is applied at the individual level to find the compensation for the rationing. It varies according to the position of the compensated labor supply function, the wage rate, and the duration of unemployment. The individual measures are aggregated for each year from 1967 through 1975. The aggregate measure varies sharply with the level of unemployment; but it is small when compared with more conventional measures such as the difference between actual GNP and potential GNP.

I. INTRODUCTION

Most of the social concern about unemployment, as reflected in government programs, is with the damage done to the unemployed individual. Most of the work economists have done on the cost of unemployment is based on Okun's Law, which calculates an aggregate loss of output associated with the unemployment rate. The cost from the point of view of the unemployed and the cost from the point of view of Okun's Law are very different both in conception and measurement. In particular, Okun's Law includes losses of output due to idled or underutilized capital as well as lost labor income.[1] The purpose of this paper is to study the cost to the unemployed individual.

I calculate the cost of unemployment to an individual by measuring his welfare loss under the assumption that unemployment is caused by job rationing: the individual is forced to accept fewer hours of work than he would prefer given his wage rate. This welfare loss, Hicks's compensating variation, is the money compensation necessary to make the unemployed person as well off as he would have been in the absence of unemployment.

* This research was supported by Labor Department Grant #J9-M5-060 and a contract between the states of Washington and Colorado, and Stanford Research Institute, through a subcontract between SRI and Stanford University. I should like to thank Mordecai Kurz for his encouragement and support of this work and David Starrett for a discussion of the theory of compensation.

1. R. J. Gordon [1973] has corrected Okun's law to account for the value of leisure when there are small changes in unemployment. His work is very different from what I do here because the total cost to the unemployed is critically dependent on the duration of unemployment, and that dependence changes the direction of the work.

The Quarterly Journal of Economics, September 1980 0033-5533/80/0095-0225$01.90

The compensating variation is very sensitive to the elasticity of labor supply and to the duration of unemployment. Using labor supply functions that have been estimated with cross-section data, I form the compensated labor supply functions and calculate the average cost of unemployment in each of the years 1966 through 1975 by race, family position, and duration of unemployment. Using data from the Bureau of Labor Statistics, I estimate the number of people who were unemployed in each of those years by race, family position, and duration of unemployment. Measures of the total welfare loss or the total compensating variation are calculated by aggregating in each year. These are the basic empirical results of the paper.

I find that the welfare loss due to unemployment increases sharply with the duration of unemployment; and because high unemployment rates result mainly from long spells of unemployment rather than from a large increase in the number of people ever unemployed, the aggregate loss increases sharply with the unemployment rate. A social welfare function will guard against very high unemployment rates but will not insist on very low rates. The welfare loss was substantial in 1975, about $25 billion. This is much above the losses of a decade ago; if the losses are converted to constant dollars, they somewhat more than tripled. These losses are, of course, substantially less than what would be measured by the lost income of the unemployed, because the value of leisure is not zero according to the compensated supply functions.

II. Compensation for Unemployment

I assume that unemployment is the result of job rationing: people have a normal wage rate; when they are unemployed, they are unable to get a job at that wage rate. If they lower their wage rate, they will not increase their probability of getting a job. This assumption, of course, ignores a very large body of theoretical work on search unemployment. Although modifying my assumption about unemployment to include search unemployment would be desirable, the way to do this is not at all obvious in view of our limited empirical knowledge of labor market dynamics. Furthermore, as we shall see, most of the loss from the point of view of the unemployed is incurred by the long-term unemployed, those unemployed more than fifteen weeks. Even if all short-term unemployment were due to workers searching for the best paying job, the basic results would not be too different, provided that long-term unemployment is the result of job rationing. At the individual level I define the loss due to unemploy-

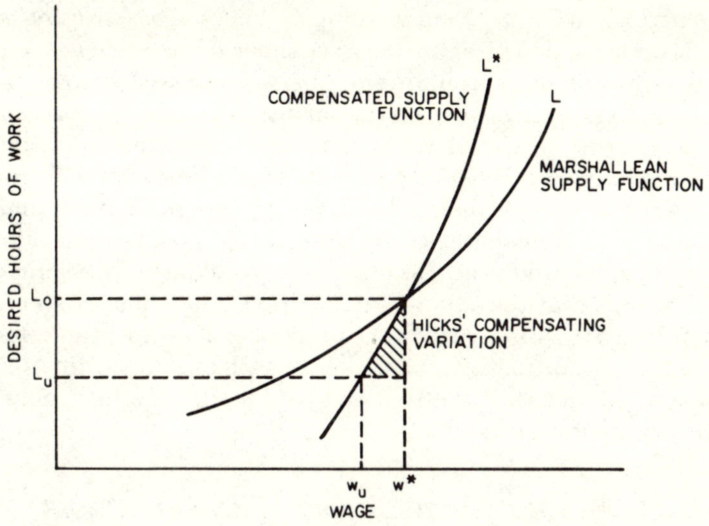

FIGURE I
Compensating Variation

ment as the payment required to make the unemployed indifferent between being unemployed and being employed at his normal wage rate, in the absence of unemployment compensation or other offsetting payments. This clearly is a gross measure of the loss, and can be compared with the offsetting payments to give an estimate of the adequacy of those payments. The presence of these payments does not complicate the estimation or interpretation of the loss.[2]

If unemployment is due to job rationing, and the labor supply function reflects the strength of the desire for leisure of the unemployed, well-known results from price theory can be used to show that a worker with a normal wage of w^* will be indifferent between working L_0 hours in a certain time period, and working L_u hours at the wage w^*, with the additional compensation given by the area under the compensated supply function as shown in Figure I. That this is the correct compensation when hours of work are rationed can be seen as follows. As is well-known, an individual is indifferent between

2. This is true if the rules for determining eligibility for unemployment compensation are strictly applied. Eligible people enter unemployment involuntarily and leave when a job becomes available; duration is not under individual control. It is in the spirit of this paper to make that assumption, but if it is not true, the losses reported here will be somewhat too large. The error is not likely to be substantial because short-term unemployment will be most affected, yet most of the loss occurs from long-term unemployment.

working L_0 hours at w^*, and working L_u hours at w_u with the additional compensation given by the area under L^* between w_u and w^*. That is, the individual is indifferent between L_0 with income L_0w^*, and L_u with income L_uw^* plus the shaded area. But L_uw^* is exactly the income the individual would receive if he were involuntarily unemployed for $L_0 - L_u$ hours during the relevant time period; therefore, the shaded area is the appropriate compensation. I have estimated this area for the unemployed by race, family position, duration of unemployment, and year. Because these results will be useful only to the extent that the compensated supply functions are well estimated, I turn to a discussion of the properties of compensated supply functions, the difficulties of estimating them, an outline of the methods that underlie the estimates I have used, and a brief summary of the supply functions.

III. Compensated Labor Supply Functions

As is well-known, the Slutsky substitution effect,

$$\frac{\partial L^*}{\partial w} = \frac{\partial L}{\partial w} - L(w^*,I^*)\frac{\partial L}{\partial I}, \tag{1}$$

(where w is the wage rate and I is nonlabor income), is the slope of the compensated supply function at the point w^*,I^*, and it must be positive if the supply function is the result of utility maximization.

Because the duration of unemployment is substantial for some of the unemployed, the compensated supply function must be evaluated at wage rates far from the normal wage rate; therefore, it is desirable to have compensated supply functions based on the recognition that equation (1) is only locally approximate. This rules out estimating conventional linear or log linear supply functions, or using the ones that are already available.

By a Taylor expansion about w_0 and I_0,

$$\begin{aligned} L(w,I) &= L_0 + \left.\frac{\partial L}{\partial w}\right|_0 \left(w - w_0\right) + \left.\frac{\partial L}{\partial I}\right|_0 \left(I - I_0\right) + R \\ &= L_0 + \left.\frac{\partial L^*}{\partial w}\right|_0 \left(w - w_0\right) + \left.\frac{\partial L}{\partial I}\right|_0 \\ &\quad \times \left[I - I_0 + L_0\left(w - w_0\right)\right] + R. \end{aligned} \tag{2}$$

One could estimate L_0, $(\partial L^*/\partial w)_0$, and $(\partial L/\partial I)_0$, and have some confidence in the results, provided that $w - w_0$ and $I - I_0$ were small.[3] If a very large number of observations were available so that one could restrict the variation in w and I to be arbitrarily small, good estimates of the three parameters could be obtained in some circumstances by ordinary least squares. This is essentially the approach I take, although other estimation problems require a more complicated estimation technique.

I have specified and estimated labor supply functions of the form,

$$L_i = \alpha_j + \beta_j w_i + \gamma_j I_i + X'_i \delta_j + u_{ij}, \tag{3}$$

when $\bar{w}_{j-1} < w_i \leq \bar{w}_j$, where L_i is annual hours of labor supply of the ith observation; w_i is the real marginal after-tax wage rate; I_i is nonlabor income adjusted for taxes; X_i is a vector of exogenous variables, which may include the spouse's wage rate and certain demographic variables depending on family position; u_{ij} is a disturbance term with an $N(0,\sigma_j^2)$ distribution; and $\bar{w}_{j-1}$ and $\bar{w}_j$ are wage boundaries.[4] This is a piecewise linear functional form that allows all the parameters in each wage interval to be different from the parameters in the other wage intervals. This labor supply function may be rearranged to the form of equation (2).[5]

Using the 1967 Survey of Economic Opportunity (SEO) data, I estimated supply functions of white husbands, wives, male single heads of households, female single heads of households, male dependents, and female dependents.[6] The theoretical left-hand variable was desired annual hours of employment in 1966. The variable used was annual hours worked plus an estimate of hours unemployed. The number of wage intervals varied according to family position from three for single male heads to eight for wives. In each interval, coefficients were estimated on variables that included the own wage, nonlabor income, the spouse's wage, earnings of other family members, three age indicators, three children indicators, a welfare indicator, and an indicator called for by the special nature of the SEO sample. For example, 112 parameters were estimated to describe the supply function of wives, and 98 parameters were estimated for the

3. This is a modification of the approach of Ashenfelter and Heckman [1974]. The main difference is that they assume that $\partial L^*/\partial w$ and $\partial L/\partial I$ are constant over the entire range of their data. However, no $L(w,I)$ exists that satisfies that assumption.

4. The estimation methods and results are given in Hurd [1976a].

5. To keep the number of parameters manageable, the labor supply function was restricted to be linear in nonlabor income in each wage interval rather than piecewise linear in nonlabor income.

6. This is a survey made in March 1967 of about 38,000 households. See Hall [1973] for a description of the data.

supply function of husbands. Over all the groups, 381 parameters were estimated.

A serious problem in the estimation of supply functions is that many people in the sample do not work, and most of them would not work even if the wage rate offered them were raised. An equivalent way to put this is that at the going wage some people have negative desired hours of work. In the estimation one would like to know desired hours for the entire sample, but they are known only for those who actually work. This truncation problem requires estimators other than ordinary least squares. A similar problem is that the wage rate is observed only for those who work; this problem also must be attacked by nonlinear methods. The supply functions I estimate thus lead to special difficulties, because one does not know in which wage interval to classify observations without a wage rate. A final problem is that the utility maximization framework behind the use of the compensated supply function to estimate the compensating variation requires that the wage rate be the real marginal after-tax wage rate. Because the income tax schedules are nonlinear, it is not straightforward to deal with this econometrically.

The maximum likelihood estimation method I developed and applied accounts for all these problems. I do not report these voluminous results here; rather, in Table I, I give the slopes of the conditional compensated supply functions of whites. The unconditional supply function of the ith observation is $E(L_i) = \mu_i$, and because desired hours may be negative, μ_i may be negative. In fact, μ_i is negative in some of the wage intervals, reflecting low labor force participation rates in those intervals. However, μ_i does not relate to anything that is observable. Labor supply of a worker is given by the conditional labor supply function,

$$E(L_i | L_i > 0) = \mu_i + \left[\frac{\phi(\mu_i/\sigma_j)}{\Phi(\mu_i/\sigma_j)}\right] \sigma_j,$$

where σ_j is the standard error of u_{ij} in (3), and ϕ and Φ are the standard normal density and distribution, respectively. Even within an interval, this function is nonlinear in the wage rate and nonlabor income; hence, $\partial E(L_i | L_i > 0)/\partial w$ is not constant. It is this slope and the corresponding income derivative that tell how workers vary labor supply when the wage and nonlabor income vary. The slope of the compensated supply function of a worker is

$$\beta_i^* = \frac{\partial E(L_i | L_i > 0)}{\partial w} - E(L_i | L_i > 0) \left[\frac{\partial E(L_i | L_i > 0)}{\partial I}\right].$$

In Table I the averages of the β_i^* in each interval are given, where the

TABLE I

CONDITIONAL COMPENSATED SLOPES OF WHITE WORKERS

Family position	Wage intervals/Slopes							
Husbands	0.50–1.50	1.50–2.00	2.00–2.50	2.50–3.00	3.00–3.50	3.50–4.50	4.50–20.00	
	−754	165	168	533	474	125	−190	
Wives	0.50–1.00	1.00–1.25	1.25–1.50	1.50–1.75	1.75–2.00	2.00–2.25	2.25–2.50	2.50–4.50
	356	1,179	1,251	1,654	1,414	639	373	−17
Single male heads	0.50–1.75	1.75–2.50	2.50–4.50					
	297	−334	−105					
Single female heads	0.50–1.25	1.25–1.75	1.75–2.50	2.50–4.50				
	980	1,287	805	227				
Male dependents	0.50–1.25	1.25–1.75	1.75–2.50	2.50–4.50				
	476	582	14	−98				
Female dependents	0.50–1.25	1.25–1.75	1.75–2.25	2.25–4.50				
	1,192	1,045	870	−120				

averages are taken over workers only. I take these to be good approximations to the slopes of the compensated supply functions of the unemployed because they have indicated that their desired hours are positive: they are in the labor force.

I also calculated, but do not report, conditional compensated slopes for nonwhites by forming similar averages over the conditional slopes and hours of nonwhites. The supply functions of whites evaluated at the right-hand variables of the nonwhites were used for these calculations.

IV. Compensating Variation

Table I gives the slopes of the conditional compensated supply functions, which I shall refer to simply as the compensated functions. The compensated function of a worker can be found by integration. I find the constants of integration from the requirements that the compensated function intersect the uncompensated function at the observed wage and expected hours of work, and that the compensated function be continuous at the wage boundaries. In constructing the compensated functions, I put the negative slopes to zero. It would have been better to do this in the estimation, but that would have beeen very costly. As a practical matter, the only constraint that affects the overall results much is the one on the first wage interval for husbands. However, it is necessary that the inverse function $w = w^*(L)$ be defined in order to find the compensation. A typical compensated function and the method of calculating the compensating variation are shown in Figure II. The conditional supply functions give desired annual hours of work of people who want to work; therefore, someone with unemployment in 1966 would have desired to work $E(L_i|L_i > 0)$ hours on average, where L_i is evaluated at his real marginal after-tax wage rate (his imputed wage rate if his wage is not observed), his nonlabor income, and his actual values of the other right-hand variable. In this work no distinction is made between part-year, full-time work and full-year, part-time work; therefore, someone who was unemployed for μ weeks is estimated to have been unemployed for $(\mu/52)$. $E(L_i|L_i > 0)$ hours during the year. Although this estimate may be considerably in error for a particular observation, it will be correct on average provided that the supply functions of the unemployed are the same on average as the supply functions of the employed. In Figure II a person with real marginal after-tax wage w has desired hours L_d, where L_d is found by evaluating the supply function appropriate for his family position and wage interval. From his esti-

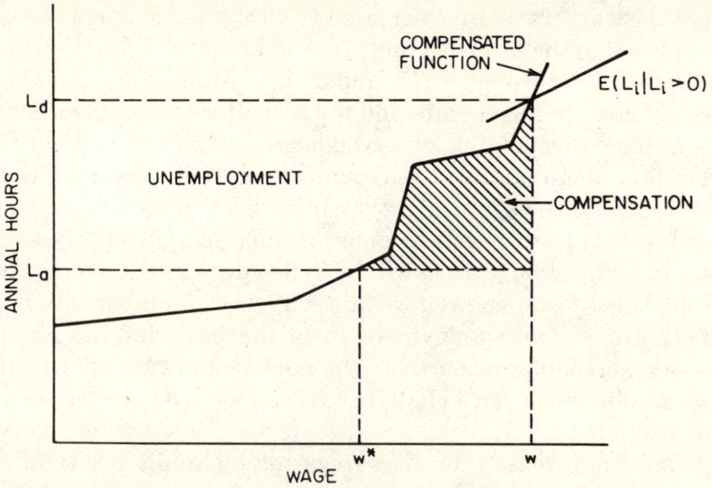

FIGURE II
Compensated Supply Function and the Compensation for Unemployment

mated hours of unemployment and L_d, actual employment L_a is calculated. The wage w^* is the rate that would just induce him to work L_a annual hours if he were compensated for the fall in the wage rate. The area C is the amount that would make him indifferent between working L_d at wage w and working L_a at wage w. Under these assumptions, area C is therefore the welfare loss of this observation caused by unemployment.[7]

The preceding description gives the method of finding the welfare loss due to unemployment of an individual of given family position, race, and duration of unemployment in 1966.[8] I calculated this loss for each person who was unemployed in 1966 and formed the weighted average loss by family position, race, and duration, where the weights account for the special sampling scheme in the SEO.[9] This is different from a weighted average loss over the entire sample of workers to the extent that the unemployed have different characteristics from the

7. In the SEO actual weeks of unemployment are not reported; rather one of seven intervals is given. I estimated the mean of each interval and used the means rather than the midpoint of the intervals. See an earlier and longer version of this paper [Hurd, 1976b].

8. In husband-wife families, there is a complication that I ignore: the substitution between the leisure of the wife and of the husband. This causes the loss from the unemployment of husbands to be overstated. I discuss that issue in the earlier version of this paper and conclude that the error is not large.

9. About half the sample in the SEO comes from intensive sampling in geographical areas with a small portion of whites. One can construct a national average by assigning weights to the observations according to the probability of sampling.

rest of the workers. I also calculated the weighted average loss of the unemployed in the SEO by family position, race, and duration in each year from 1966 through 1975, under the assumptions that the real marginal after-tax wage rates and the real after-tax nonlabor incomes grew at the corresponding observed aggregate growth rates.[10] To the extent that marginal tax rates remained constant because of tax cuts since 1966 and the aggregate growth rates are representative of the growth rates of wages and incomes of the unemployed, the average losses in 1967 through 1975 will be as accurate as the average losses in 1966. These average welfare losses by year, family position, race, and duration of unemployment form the basis for the aggregate time-series results presented in the next section. Before turning to those results, however, I shall discuss some of the properties of the averages in the SEO.

One major reason for disaggregating by family position, which is also a disaggregation by sex because of the way family position is defined, is that the supply functions of wives are generally found to be considerably more elastic than the supply functions of husbands (see Table I, for example). Figure II shows that the compensation depends critically on the slope of the compensated function: if the function is inelastic, the compensation approaches the income lost because little value is put on leisure; if the function is very elastic, the compensation is small because the person is almost indifferent between working and not working. Another reason for disaggregating by family position is that the compensation also depends on the wage rate, and men generally have higher wage rates that women. In Table II, I give average losses due to unemployment, by worker characteristics and duration of unemployment. Because the wage is a real after-tax wage, the compensations are also real, after-tax compensations. As expected, there is great variation in the loss by family position. Not all of the variation is due to differences in wages and the compensated functions: wives have a smaller average loss partly because they are unemployed for shorter periods than husbands; nonwhites have higher unemployment losses than whites despite their smaller wage rates because they are unemployed for longer periods. In the bottom part of the table, the strong dependence of the measure of loss on the duration of unemployment stands out clearly. Roughly, the increase in loss for a one-week increase in unemployment begins at about $6 at two weeks of unemployment, rises to $50 at about six-

10. The data on growth rates of wages come from Table B-28 of the 1976 *Economic Report of the President*. Growth rates of nonlabor income were calculated from the growth in national income less compensation of employees.

TABLE II

AVERAGE REAL AFTER-TAX LOSS DUE TO UNEMPLOYMENT IN 1966: SEO DATA

Whites	$296
Nonwhites	352
Husbands	539
Wives	92
Single male heads	715
Single female heads	124
Male dependents	234
Female dependents	62
Duration of unemployment	
1–2 weeks	21
1–4 weeks	27
5–10 weeks	183
11–14 weeks	406
15–26 weeks	765
27–39 weeks	1,279
40 or more weeks	1,474

teen weeks of employment, and then begins to decline. This happens because the loss is quadratic in the duration of unemployment for small increases in duration. If the duration is long enough to drive w^* in Figure II to zero, the loss becomes linear in duration because the area is not calculated under the part of the compensated function where the wage is negative. Whether w^* goes to zero depends on the slope and position of the compensated function, but for some observations that surely happens. For durations of medium length, the loss is neither quadratic nor linear in duration because the boundary between wage intervals is reached. Most of the compensated functions have the **S**-shaped appearance of Figure II; that shape leads to larger increases in the loss as the duration of unemployment increases. This empirical property illustrates the necessity of allowing the compensated function to be very general in the estimation.

V. AGGREGATE RESULTS

The discussion of the last section outlined how the average loss due to unemployment was calculated by family position, race, duration of unemployment, and year. To find the aggregate loss, it is necessary to know the number of people in each of these categories in each year since 1966; specifically, the number of different people by family position and race who had unemployment of a certain length in each of those years. There are two difficulties in discovering this information. First, important changes in the distribution of the unemployment duration take place continually, so that taking the year to be the appropriate unit of time is purely arbitrary. This difficulty is easily and reasonably solved not by finding the actual unemployment loss in a year, which will depend on the time-path of unemployment during the year, but by finding the steady-state loss, the yearly loss if the flows into and out of unemployment remain constant long enough for the stocks of unemployed to reach their permanent levels. All the results to follow should be interpreted in this way. The second difficulty is that there are no official data that give the desired numbers directly. The most useful data for this purpose come from the Special Labor Force Reports, which are summarized in the *Employment and Training Report of the President, 1976.* These tables on the extent of unemployment are derived from supplementary questions in the Current Population Survey. People were asked how many weeks they were unemployed during the preceding year, and the tables give the numbers who fell in each duration of unemployment category. These data, which seem to be precisely what is needed, do not give good estimates of the steady-state numbers in each duration category because people whose unemployment spanned the beginning or end of the year would tend to be classified in a shorter-duration category. One would expect, therefore, that the numbers reported in the tables would underestimate the true extent of unemployment in the longest-duration category, and overestimate the true extent in the shorter-duration categories. In a longer version of this paper, I discuss a probability model to determine the extent of unemployment, and compare the results of applying that model with the tables. The basic strategy is to estimate the steady-state weekly flows into unemployment of different durations. For example, I estimate the number of people who enter unemployment weekly and who will be unemployed for five–ten weeks. In a static economy, the annual number of different people who would have left unemployment after a duration of five–ten weeks would be this flow multiplied by fifty-two. This procedure corrects for counting people twice if their period of unemployment lasted over the end of a year, for misclassifying people into categories of lower duration, and for the fact that unemployment may be divided into several periods. It appears that fewer different people are actually unemployed during the year than the tables report, but in the highest-duration category there are considerably more.

There are other problems in using these data, the main one being the lack of detail. All that needs to be said here is that, in calculating the aggregate loss, the estimates of the total number of people ever unemployed during a year are consistent with the official data and the probability model. When detail was absent in the official data, I estimated the detail by finding the distributions in the SEO and applying them to the official data.

Table III presents the aggregate results for each year. The column titled "Ever Unemployed" is my estimate of the steady-state number of different people who were unemployed in each year, taking care not to count the same person in both of two adjacent years. These entries were considerably below those in the official data: for example, in 1969 the Employment and Training Report gives 11.7 million ever unemployed, and in 1971 it gives 15.9 million. These numbers are, respectively, 19 and 31 percent greater than what I estimate; the difference is due to misclassification in the official data. The misclassification is the greatest when the unemployment rate and, hence, the duration of unemployment are high: in 1975 the difference was 35 percent. The next column of Table III gives the total real after-tax compensating variation, as calculated by aggregating the loss by year, race, family position, and duration of unemployment according to the estimated ever-unemployed by those categories. To calculate the numbers in the column labeled "Nominal After-Tax," I recalculated the loss of each of the unemployed in the SEO and converted each loss to a before-tax loss using the estimated marginal tax rate of each observation; these losses were converted to nominal losses each year by inflating with the Consumer Price Index. Finally, averages by year, race, family position, and duration were formed as before, and the aggregate loss was again calculated using the estimated ever-unemployed by year, race, family position, and duration. The use of the marginal tax rate may overstate the before-tax loss slightly, but this seemed preferable to adjusting by the average tax rate. The average marginal rate over the unemployed is about 13 percent. The last two columns give the real after-tax loss and the nominal before-tax loss per person ever unemployed.

I suppose that the most surprising results are the very sharp rise in total loss over the last ten years, and the small size of the loss compared with aggregate measures of income such as personal income. In 1966, for example, the loss was about 0.84 percent of personal income; even in 1975, when the unemployment rate was 8.5 percent, the loss was only 2.04 percent of personal income. The increase in total loss was due partly to increases in the wage rate, partly to increases in the unemployment rate, and partly to changes in the composition of the unemployed.

TABLE III

NUMBER UNEMPLOYED AND UNEMPLOYMENT LOSS, 1966–1975

Year	Unemployment rate (percent)	Ever unemployed (millions)	Total loss: Real after tax 1966 dollars (billions of dollars)	Total loss: Nominal before-tax (billions of dollars)	Real loss per unemployed (dollars)	Nominal loss per unemployed (dollars)
1966	3.8	9.4	4.3	4.9	461	520
1967	3.8	9.6	4.3	5.0	449	522
1968	3.6	9.5	3.8	4.6	401	486
1969	3.5	9.8	4.2	5.4	429	548
1970	4.9	11.5	7.4	10.0	647	870
1971	5.9	12.1	9.5	13.2	781	1,090
1972	5.6	11.9	8.4	12.2	710	1,025
1973	4.9	11.6	6.7	10.3	578	890
1974	5.6	14.5	9.5	16.3	659	1,123
1975	8.5	15.0	13.7	25.4	918	1,698

Because the unemployment rate is calculated by counting the stock of unemployed during a month, it will increase with average duration even if the number of ever-unemployed remains constant. For example, even though the unemployment rate more than doubled between 1966 and 1975, the number of ever-unemployed increased by only about 60 percent, despite the growth in the labor force. In fact, the average number of unemployed increased by 272 percent over that period. The fact that the unemployment rate rises mainly as a result of an increase in the duration of unemployment implies that the average loss per ever-unemployed increases sharply as the unemployment rate increases. This is illustrated in Figure III. I calculated average loss per ever-unemployed husband, holding wage rates at the 1966 level. These are plotted against the unemployment rate to hold constant changes in the composition of the unemployed by family position and changes in real wages as the unemployment rate changed. This is, therefore, a pure unemployment rate effect. I roughly estimate that a 1 percent increase in the unemployment rate increases the loss per ever-unemployed husband by about $200 in 1966 after-tax dollars. Similar results could be obtained for the other family positions.

It is often said that a higher unemployment rate can be tolerated now than, say, ten years ago because the composition of the stock of unemployed has changed. This change consists of the presence of more "secondary" workers, workers with a weak attachment to the labor force, who will not suffer as great a loss if unemployed as will primary workers. Secondary workers are generally wives and teenagers, and primary workers are mature males. This belief is not reflected in my estimates of the unemployment loss. I calculated the average loss in 1975 using the family position weights of 1966 and found the loss almost exactly the same. It is true that wives are estimated to have much smaller losses on average than husbands, and that relatively more wives than husbands were ever unemployed in 1975 than in 1966. Over the same period, however, the fraction of the ever-unemployed who were single male heads increased substantially, enough so that the total weight on husbands and single male heads together remained almost the same.

In Table IV, I give the unemployment loss of whites as a percent of total loss. Because whites comprise about 89 percent of the labor force, these entries would be about 89 percent if the wage rates and the duration of unemployment were the same for whites and nonwhites. This is far from the case: nonwhites have a much greater duration of unemployment and lower wage rates. There seems to be neither any trend in this ratio nor any correlation with the unem-

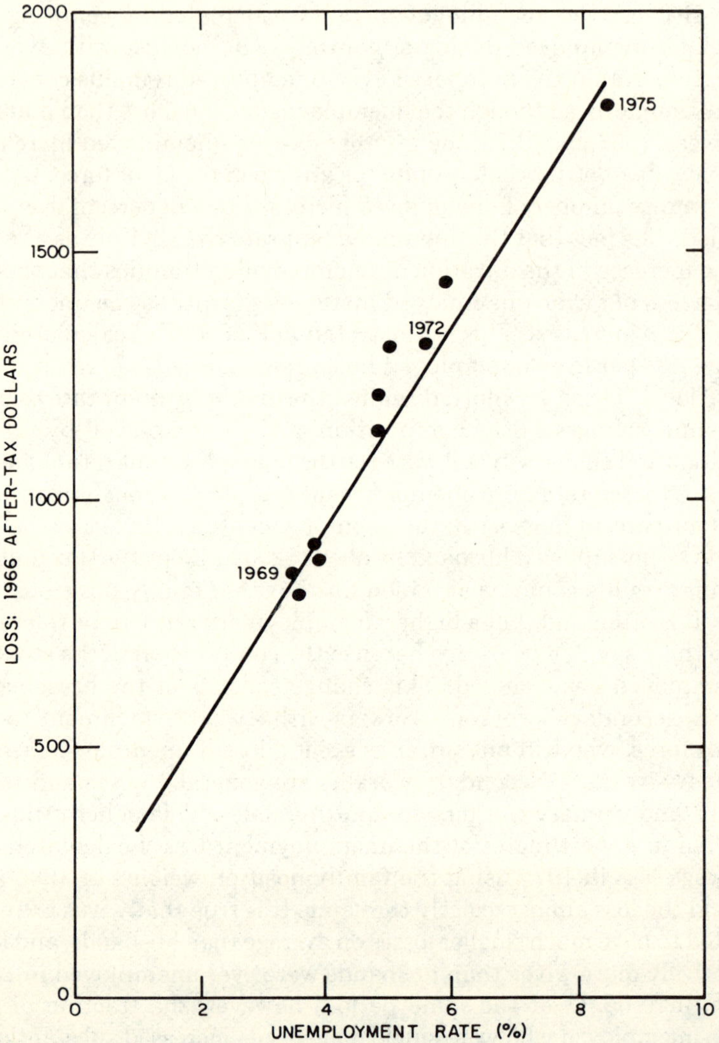

FIGURE III
Loss per Husband ever Unemployed with No Wage Growth

ployment rate. Apparently, when the unemployment rate rises, there is no differential increase in the duration.

I mentioned in Section II that the basic results on the aggregate loss would not change by much if the short-term unemployed are excluded from the calculations. In Table V the fraction of the loss incurred by those with more than fifteen weeks of unemployment is

TABLE IV

PERCENT OF TOTAL UNEMPLOYMENT LOSS INCURRED BY WHITES

Year	Unemployment rate	Percent of total loss
1966	3.8	81
1967	3.8	82
1968	3.6	82
1969	3.5	83
1970	4.9	84
1971	5.9	84
1972	5.6	83
1973	4.9	82
1974	5.6	82
1975	8.5	83

given. Although the fraction is not constant, but varies directly with the unemployment rate, it is clear that the order of magnitude of the unemployment loss is not changed by excluding the loss of those unemployed less than fifteen weeks. I take this to be good evidence that ignoring search unemployment in this study has not caused a serious misestimation of the results.

VI. CONCLUSION

If the basic labor supply functions accurately describe the behavior of the unemployed, and if unemployment can be characterized as job rationing, then the entries in Table III are good estimates of the total compensation that would have made the unemployed as well off

TABLE V

PERCENT OF UNEMPLOYMENT LOSS DUE TO LONG-TERM UNEMPLOYMENT

Year	Percent of loss
1966	80
1967	80
1968	78
1969	78
1970	84
1971	89
1972	88
1973	84
1974	87
1975	93

with the unemployment they experienced as they would have been if they had been steadily employed at their normal wage and normal hours of work. The totals are small compared with the magnitudes derived from Okun's Law. For example, Okun's Law attaches a \$48-billion loss to a 1 percent increase in unemployment in 1975; whereas I calculate the total compensation for all the unemployment to be about \$25 billion in 1975. Of course, these two measures are concerned with very different issues; however, if one is concerned with unemployment loss from the point of view of the unemployed, it is clear that Okun's Law is not a good guide to the order of magnitude.

The aggregate loss is not large compared with the amount paid in unemployment compensation. In 1971, for example, about \$6.2 billion were paid in benefits. This is after-tax income because unemployment compensation is not taxed. The nominal after-tax loss in 1971 was estimated to have been \$11.5 billion by deflating the appropriate entry in Table III by the 13 percent average marginal tax rate in the SEO. These averages, of course, do not reveal some important details. On the one side, only about 52 percent of the average stock of unemployed received the unemployment compensation benefits. If the recipients were representative of all the unemployed, they were better off under unemployment than they would have been if they had been employed. On the other side, the covered unemployed tend to come from high-wage industries that have a high concentration of workers with fairly inelastic supply functions. The average required compensation of the covered unemployed was therefore probably higher than the overall average.

One sensible quality of the compensating variation as a measure of the loss due to unemployment is that the loss increases sharply with the duration of unemployment. This accords with the common observation that for many workers a layoff of a week or two is not at all undesirable, as that is considered to be like an extension of vacation. The aggregate loss thus increases rapidly with the unemployment rate, due to the strong dependence of the unemployment rate on the average duration of unemployment. Duration of unemployment, rather than the increase in the number of people who experience unemployment during the year, is the source of most of the aggregate loss increase. High unemployment rates should therefore be avoided by policy makers, not because more people are out of work but because some people have very long spells of unemployment. Unfortunately, the unemployment compensation system is designed on almost exactly the reverse principle, which is incorrect if the purpose is to provide a minimum level of welfare for the unemployed. Rather than providing support for the long-term unemployed, who are the unemployed with the largest welfare losses, compensation begins very soon after unemployment begins and stops after thirty-nine weeks of unemployment. The short-term unemployed receive enough compensation to make them prefer unemployment; the long-term unemployed receive none. Surely a better system would be one in which the amount of compensation followed the welfare loss: the compensation would begin at a low level after a few weeks of unemployment and increase with the duration. This approach would remedy two defects in the present unemployment compensation program, which have been pointed out by a number of economists, particularly Feldstein. First, if unemployment is actually leisure, payments larger than the compensating variation encourage unemployment on the part of the worker. Second, on the side of management, high unemployment obtains because, to the extent that the unemployment compensation payments are not fully paid by the company through the rating system, an organization of production with frequent layoffs and callbacks is encouraged, so that part of the workers' vacations is paid for by the unemployment compensation system.

STATE UNIVERSITY OF NEW YORK AT STONY BROOK

REFERENCES

Ashenfelter, O., and J. Heckman, "The Estimation of Income and Substitution Effects in a Model of Family Labor Supply," *Econometrica,* XLII (Jan. 1974), 73–85.

Gordon, R. J., "The Welfare Cost of Higher Unemployment," *Brookings Papers on Economic Activity,* IV (1973), 133–95.

Hall, R. E., "Wages, Income, and Hours of Work in the U. S. Labor Force," in *Income Maintenance and Labor Supply,* G. Cain and H. Watts, eds. (Chicago: Rand McNally, 1973), 102–62.

Hurd, M., "The Estimation of Nonlinear Labor Supply Functions with Taxes from a Truncated Sample," Technical Report No. 217, Economics Series, Institute for Mathematical Studies in the Social Sciences, Stanford University (October 1976a).

——, "The Welfare Implication of the Unemployment Rate," Research Memorandum 37, Center for the Study of Welfare Policy, Stanford Research Institute (Nov. 1976b).

THE EFFECTS OF SUPPLY CONTRACTS ON THE OUTPUT AND PRICE OF AN EXHAUSTIBLE RESOURCE*

BLAINE ROBERTS

This paper analyzes the effects of contracts for exhaustible resources. The conclusions are as follows: (1) for a single mine, with increased risk production for the spot market falls, long-term contracting increases, total output falls, contract length generally decreases, equilibrium spot prices increase, and contract prices may rise or fall; (2) with changing economies because of past production, output (spot prices) rises (fall) and then falls (rise), and this scalloped pattern remains with entry and storage included; and (3) contracting permits pairwise gains, may create losses for others, and prices are "fuzzy" signals as they may change for several different reasons.

I. INTRODUCTION

Anthony Scott [1967] has analyzed the output of the mine under certainty based on the early pioneering work of Gray [1914] and Hotelling [1931], and several recent papers have contained an analysis of the equilibrium price of an exhaustible resource over time under different market structures and the social efficiency of this price. Examples are contained in the 1974 symposium in the *Review of Economic Studies,* Solow [1974], Dasgupta and Stiglitz [1976], and Kamien and Schwartz [1978]. These papers generally have ignored the possibility of contractual arrangements among suppliers and purchasers of the exhaustible resource. Given the empirical significance of long-term contracting associated with exhaustible resources, the purpose of this paper is to fill that gap.[1]

There are a number of conclusions developed in this paper that can be separated into three categories. First, with respect to the output of a single mine, an increase in perceived risk or risk aversion by mine

* Valuable comments from Michael Connolly, G. S. Maddala, Yoram Peles, and a referee are gratefully acknowledged. Any shortcomings and errors are solely the author's responsibility. A previous version of this paper was presented at the European Meetings of the Econometric Society, Geneva, September, 1978.

1. In the theoretical literature of the firm, there is relatively little discussion of contracts per se. However, contracts are related in some ways to: (1) future markets and speculation [Keynes, 1930; Hicks, 1946; Working, 1953, 1962; Muth, 1961; and Hirshleifer, 1975, 1977], since the purchaser and the seller have the option of buying in the future on the spot market; (2) insurance markets (e.g., Rothschild and Stiglitz [1976] and Shavell [1979]), since long-term contracting generally reallocates risk among the parties of the contract; (3) share tenancy (e.g., Cheung [1969], Stiglitz [1974], Newberry [1974], Bell and Zusman [1976], Hammond [1977], and Reid [1977]), since many long-term contracts are joint ventures in part or in whole; and (4) vertical integration (e.g., Blair and Kasserman [1978]), since long-term contracts can have the effect of vertically integrating the supplier and the purchaser.

The Quarterly Journal of Economics, September 1980 0033-5533/80/0095-0245$01.60

managers, ceteris paribus, has the following effects: (a) production for the spot market falls; (b) the optimal amount under long-term contracts increases; (c) total production falls; (d) the optimal length of the contract may increase but, generally, it decreases; (e) equilibrium spot market prices rise; and (f) contract prices may rise or fall.

With respect to equilibrium market prices, the existence of "open-up economies" in the early phases of a mine and "mined-out diseconomies" in the latter phases of a mine: (a) causes production to rise and then fall over time, holding prices and costs constant; (b) in turn, the equilibrium spot market price falls and then rises over time with the number of mines constant and no storage by purchasers possible; and (c) the equilibrium spot market price will retain a scalloped pattern even when entry of new mines and storage by purchasers is permitted.

Third, with respect to the social efficiency of spot prices and contracting: (a) although contracting is a consequence of incomplete markets and the market system is inefficient, contracting permits pairwise expected utility improvements for some, but (b) may create welfare losses for others if the variance of market prices increases, which is likely; and (c) the market price, taken alone, is a "fuzzy" signal, since it can rise or fall for several different reasons.

Section II contains the development of a dynamic model of the firm under uncertainty[2] with intertemporal cost relations and the potential for contracts. In Section III the implications for market prices over time are explored. Summary and conclusions follow in Section IV.

II. The Model

The following incentives for forming long-term contracts have been pointed out in the literature:[3] (1) to pool risk; (2) to eliminate moral hazard; (3) to transfer risk; (4) to take advantage of differing expectations; (5) to coordinate complementary factors of production; (6) to extend monopoly power to downstream markets; and (7) to reduce costs.

Given the incentives to form a long-term contract and holding constant "bargaining abilities," the consequences of contracting po-

2. This portion of the model builds on the wide body of literature of the theory of the firm under uncertainty, of which Baron [1970], Sandmo [1971], Leland [1972], and Holthausen [1976] are representative. These models under uncertainty are static models, whereas the model developed here is dynamic.

3. See the references in note 1.

tential will be analyzed as if the risk averse mine manager faced a schedule of potential contracts into which it could enter, and as if the relation between contract price and the quantity supplied per year is nonpositive.

The amount under contract q^c will be assumed to be constant for the period of the contract. This assumption greatly simplifies the exposition, but does not affect the results of the model in a major way for the following reasons. The major purpose of this paper is to analyze how the existence of contracts affects the market price of the resource and the comparative static properties of changes in risk or risk aversion. Although in many cases mines are contracted for the total amount produced, what is observed in total is that part of production is under contract and part is traded on the spot market.

Further, because the model is one of choice under uncertainty, future contracting can be ignored without much harm. Thus, the expected present value of the spot price, the alternative to selling under contract, can be interpreted as the expected value of average net revenue from any source: the spot market or future contracts.

Although it is not clear that there would always be a nonpositive and continuous relation between contract price and quantity, there are some reasons why it may be a close approximation. If the output of the mine is large relative to the demand by individual buyers, and if each buyer is charged the same amount for delivered resources, spatial transportation costs would result in a declining net price to the mine as greater amounts were placed under contract.

It will also be assumed that an increase in the number of years of the contract requires the mine to accept a lower price. This seems reasonable from a bargaining point of view that, when a mine manager is risk-averse, to obtain concessions of a higher quantity under contract and a greater length of time for the contract, the mine manager would have to accept a lower price.[4]

The assumption that all contracts entered into are for the same amount of time T is restrictive, and a more general formulation would include the option of entering into contracts with different lengths. However, imposing the restriction, a common period for all contracts, greatly simplifies the algebra and does not change the essential effect

4. The menu of choices faced by the mine manager would clearly depend upon the risk preferences and expectations of the potential purchasers, and there may be situations where the increase in quantity or length of the contract would be associated with increased contract prices. Such situations cannot produce an interior solution; that is, a solution where some output is sold under contract, and some is sold on the spot market, and where the length of the contract is less than the economic life of the mine.

of long-term contracts on the output and price of an exhaustible resource demonstrated in this paper.

Another principal feature of the model to be developed here is the intertemporal relationship among costs. Most industrial processes have a significant variation in average costs over time, as in the case of "learning by doing" [Arrow, 1962]. In the case of a mine, for a given rate of extraction average costs of extraction are relatively high initially as the mine is being developed. These average costs fall as more is mined until a substantial amount of the total reserves of the mine has been extracted. Then, to obtain more from the mine, higher operating costs must be incurred. Average costs continue to increase until, depending upon economic factors, the mine is "mined out."[5]

This intertemporal relation among costs will cause the rate of production to vary over time, holding prices and factor costs constant. Initially it will pay to increase the rate of production to obtain the lower costs associated with having the mine "opened up." In the later stages, the rate of production will fall over time as further production raises costs.

A final simplifying assumption is that the sole random variable is the spot price of the resource. Making other factors random in the model would only add more covariance terms and expected values but would not change the major conclusions.

The mine manager is assumed to maximize the expected utility of the present value of profits from the mine.[6] Formally,

$$\max E\{U(\pi)\}, \tag{1}$$

where E is the expectation operator;.

$$\pi = \int_0^T p^c q^c e^{-\rho t} dt + \int_0^\infty e^{-\rho t} \{p_t^s q_t^s - C(q_t, m_t)\} dt,$$

where ρ is the instantaneous rate of discount;

$p^c = p^c(q^c, T) =$ the contract price, a function of [7]

5. The mine is "mined out" when the variable costs of extraction exceed the total net revenues in a static, no uncertainty case. When uncertainty exists, "close down," "open up," and maintenance costs modify this condition somewhat.

6. This assumes the existence of a perfect capital market where a unique, constant rate of discount ρ translates any future certain earnings into the present. In addition, it assumes that the owner is indifferent between equally risky prospects in the future according to the discount rate ρ.

7. In Section III the contact price is also a function of the present value of the spot price as follows:

$$p_t^c = p^c\left(q^c, T; \int_0^T e^{-\rho t} E(p_t^s) dt\right).$$

The mine is assumed to be a price taker on the spot market.

q^c, the constant amount supplied per year, and
T = the number of years of the contract.

where

$$\frac{\partial p^c}{\partial q^c} < 0 \quad \text{and} \quad \frac{\partial p^c}{\partial T < 0},$$

$p_t^s = p^s(x_t, \epsilon_t)$ = the spot market price at time t, which depends upon aggregate economic factors, x_t and a random element ϵ_t;
q_t^s = the amount sold on the spot market at time t;
q_t = the total amount produced at t;
$C(q_t, m_t)$ is the cost function and is a function of q_t, and
$m_t = \int_0^t q_\tau d\tau$, the total amount that has been mined by time t.

The integral in (1) is to be interpreted as a Stieltjes integral. Thus, the results that follow apply to discrete or continuous decisions. Clearly, however, mine managers have to formulate a plan for extraction that cannot be varied on a minute-to-minute basis.

Consistent with the discussion of intertemporal costs, the derivatives of the cost function are postulated to have the following signs (the t subscript is omitted when unnecessary for clarity):[8] $C_q > 0$; $C_{qq} > 0$;

$$C_m \lesseqgtr 0 \quad \text{as} \quad m \lesseqgtr m^*$$

$$C_{mm} \lesseqgtr 0 \quad \text{as} \quad m \lesseqgtr m_1.$$

If the optimal solution is where some amount is sold on contract and some on the spot market, it is necessary that conditions (2) through (4) hold:

$$\text{(2)} \quad E\left\{U'\left(\frac{\partial \pi}{\partial q^c}\right)\right\} = E\left\{U'\left(\left(p^c + \frac{\partial p^c}{\partial q^c} q^c\right) \int_0^T e^{-\rho t} dt - \int_0^T e^{-\rho t} \left(C_q + \int_t^\infty e^{-\rho(\tau - t)} C_m d\tau\right) dt\right)\right\} = 0.$$

8. An example of a cost function that might describe the variable costs for a mine operation would be

$$C_t = w_1 q_t^\alpha + q_t \left(d - \int_0^t q_\tau d\tau\right)^\beta w_2.$$

The first term on the right-hand side is operation costs at the drilling point and a function of unit labor costs w_1 and α, which is greater than one. The second term on the right-hand side is transportation costs that depend upon the total amount mined and unit transportation costs per mile w_2.

$$(3)\quad E\left\{U'\left(\frac{\partial \pi}{\partial q_t^s}\right)\right\} = E\left\{U'\left(e^{-\rho t}(p_t^s - C_q) - \int_t^{\infty} e^{-\rho\tau} C_m d\tau\right)\right\} = 0$$

for all t.

$$(4)\quad E\left\{U'\left(\frac{\partial \pi}{\partial T}\right)\right\} = E\left\{U'\left(p^c q^c e^{-\rho T} + \frac{\partial p^c}{\partial T} q^c \int_0^T e^{-\rho t} dt\right)\right\} = 0.$$

And, condition (3) can be rewritten as (5):

$$(5)\quad E(p_t^s) + \frac{\text{cov}(p_t^s, U')}{E(U')} = C_q + \int_t^{\infty} e^{-\rho(\tau - t)} C_m d\tau$$

for all $t \geq 0$ if $q_t^s > 0$.

Combining (2) and (5) gives (6):

$$(6)\quad \left(p^c + \frac{\partial p^c}{\partial q^c} q^c\right) \int_0^T e^{-\rho t} dt = \int_0^T e^{-\rho t} \left\{E(p_t^s) + \frac{\text{cov}(U', p_t^s)}{E(U')}\right\} dt.$$

Condition (6) says that the mine should equate the present value of marginal revenue from the contract for T years to the present value of the expected spot price plus the discount for risk aversion for the same T years. Condition (4) can be simplified to (7), then (6) and (7) can be solved simultaneously for the optimal contract price and length of the contract. The solution where $\partial p^c / \partial q^c$ is negative is illustrated in Figure I, where $PV(\cdot)$ indicates present value:

$$(7)\quad p^c = \frac{\partial p^c}{\partial T} \frac{(1 - e^{\rho T})}{\rho}.$$

Figure I illustrates three major conclusions. First, if $\partial p^c / \partial q^c$ is negative, the optimal contract price may be above or below the expected spot price, depending on the magnitude of the present value of the covariance term. If $\partial p^c / \partial q^c = 0$, then the contract price will be strictly less than the expected spot price if some output is sold in the spot market. Given the assumption of risk aversion of the mine manager, if p^c is constant and greater than or equal to $E(p^s)$, then all output, or as much as is possible, will be put under contract. Second, an increase in uncertainty or risk aversion on the part of the mine, defined as $d\ \text{cov}(U', p^s) < 0$ and $E(p^s)$ constant,[9] will reduce the optimal contract price and more output per year will be under contract.

9. While other definitions are possible, this is in accord with the usual ones. See Rothschild and Stiglitz [1970].

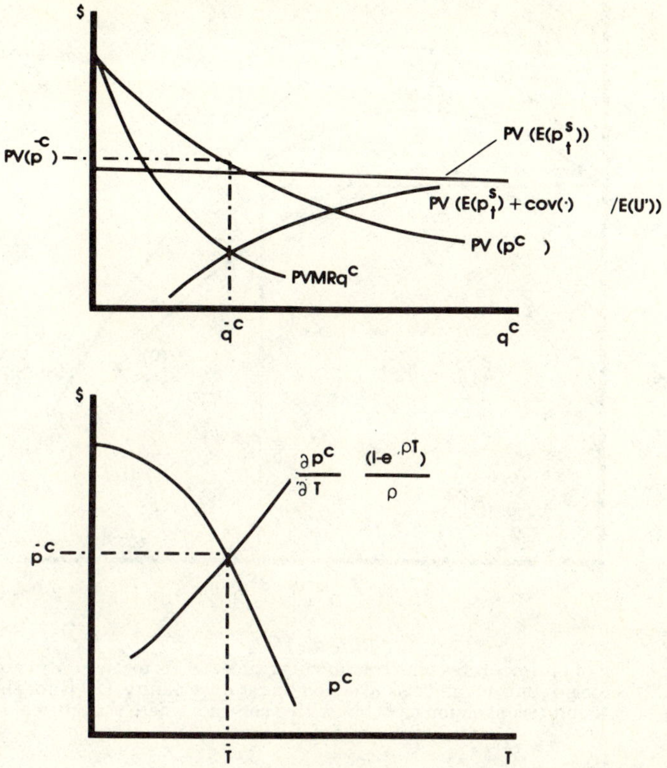

FIGURE I
Illustration of the optimal solution for a mine selling on contract an amount q^c for T years. *PV* indicates present value.

Third, if a change in the contract price does not affect the tradeoff between the length of the contract and the price, then the contract length will be shorter. These propositions are formally derived in the Appendix.

Figure II illustrates this solution in terms of the total amount mined and the rate of extraction over time. (For simplicity of the graph, continuously variable production is illustrated in the figure.) If C_m is sufficiently negative, which would occur at the early stages of mining, then output would be set at a rate where marginal cost was greater than the spot price. If $\int_t^\infty e^{-\rho(\tau-t)}C_m d\tau$ becomes more negative as t increases, then the rate of production would increase. At some point, the rate of production falls over time.

Curve *A* is the general shape of the solution path of the optimal

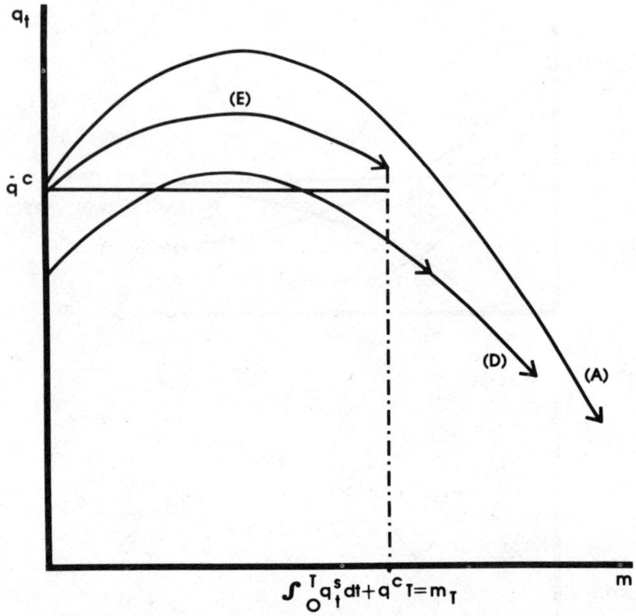

FIGURE II
Comparison of optimal rates of extraction over time. (A) is for no contract and no risk. (D) is for no contract and risk aversion under uncertainty. (E) is for the same degree of risk and risk aversion as D but with a contract where the optimal solution is for q^c for T years.

rate of production over time with no risk and no contract when the "open-up economies" are significant. If the "open-up economies" are not significant, and if marginal costs rise over time because of depletion, then the rate of production would simply fall over time. For higher prices or lower costs, the optimal production path over time would be similar to A, but higher with more being produced at each point in time and the total amount mined over the life of the mine greater.

Referring to equation (5), for Curve A the covariance term is zero. Curve D is the optimal rate of extraction over time for a risk-averse mine under uncertainty with no contract, since if the firm is risk-averse, the covariance term in condition (5) will be negative because[10]

$$\frac{\partial U'}{\partial \epsilon_t} < 0 \quad \text{and} \quad \frac{\partial(\rho p_t - \dot{p}_t)}{\partial \epsilon_t} > 0.$$

10. By definition $\partial p_t / \partial \epsilon_t > 0$, and since $E(\dot{p}_t) = (\partial p / \partial x)\dot{x}_t$ and the errors are uncorrelated over time, $\partial \dot{p}_t / \partial \epsilon_t < 0$.

This means that risk aversion will reduce the planned rate of extraction over time. Given the assumption that ϵ_t is uncorrelated over time and has a constant variance, the difference between a risk neutral (expected profit-maximizing) production plan and a risk-averse production plan will be greater initially and diminish for planned production rates far into the future. In other words, under these conditions the effect of a variation from expected price has a greater effect on the present value of profit if it occurs sooner rather than later.

Curve E is the total production solution for a risk-averse mine under uncertainty with a contract for q^c for T years. At the expiration of the contract, with no further contract potential, the rate of extraction would follow curve D. If T does not affect the contract price, then the mine would set T at the maximum, where q^c intersected the continuation of curve E in Figure II.

III. The Implications for Market Prices

The foregoing analysis has concentrated on the output of a single existing mine. To determine the consequences of contracting on the spot market price, additional assumptions are needed about demand, the number of mines, and under what conditions these open up and close down. Furthermore, attention will be focused on the equilibrium spot market price. Thus, the random component of demand will now be eliminated, and market price will be determined by the intersection of the amount supplied and the demand function.

To start, the number of mines will be taken as fixed and just opening. Demand for the resource with no contracts will be taken as a fixed function of the current spot price; that is, no storage by purchasers is possible. Further, mine managers will be assumed to have rational expectations (in the sense of Muth [1961]), in that actual market prices turn out as expected.

Under these conditions, with "open-up economies" sufficient to generate the humped Curve A in Figure II, which assumes the market price is constant, the market price will first fall and then rise. The price cannot be constant because if it were, output of the mines will be rising and then falling. With a fixed demand curve, this will cause prices to fall, then rise. However, the basic humped shape of production, as illustrated by Curve A in Figure II, will be retained. This is so because in the initial stages, for output of the mine to remain constant, price must be falling; but with demand fixed and output constant, price will be constant.

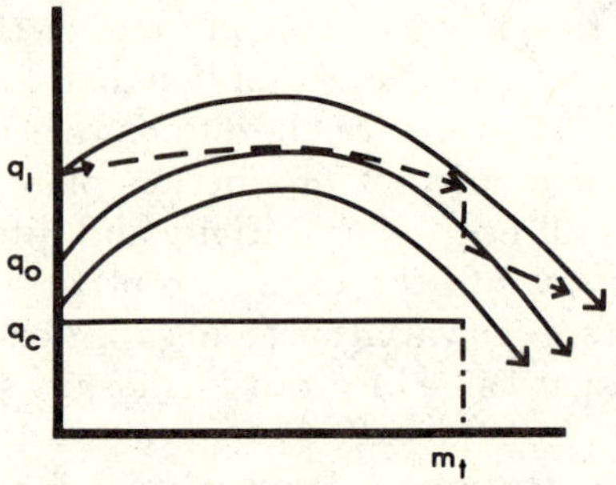

FIGURE III
Production path for a typical mine with a contract T years is given by the dashed line, with market equilibrium determined by a fixed number of mines that open simultaneously and remain open.

Allowing contracting reduces risk to the mine and increases total output for the length of the contract. To illustrate, suppose that each mine contracts for a portion of its production with a buyer for T years. The market price and the typical production path for each mine with contracting is now illustrated in Figures III and IV.

The contacts will mean that the expected demand curve is shifted in for the spot market and probably becomes more elastic for two reasons: (1) ceteris paribus, the more inelastic the demand, the greater the incentive for contracting under risk aversion; and (2) total output (contract plus spot production) is greater. If spot market demand is more elastic with contracting than without contracting, then both the percentage change in price and the change in price over time are less in absolute terms then they would be without contracting, except perhaps, at the point T, where the production plan returns to the no contract plan. For the same reasons, it seems likely that the demand would now have a greater variance.

As for the contract price, it seems reasonable that it would also be positively related to expectations of future spot prices as indicated in note 7 and as stated in (8). Thus, with "rational expectations" and with contracting,

$$(8) \qquad p_t^c = p^c\left(q^c, T; \int_0^T e^{-\rho t} E(p_t^s)dt\right),$$

where

$$\frac{\partial p_t^c}{\partial E(p_\tau^s)} > 0,$$

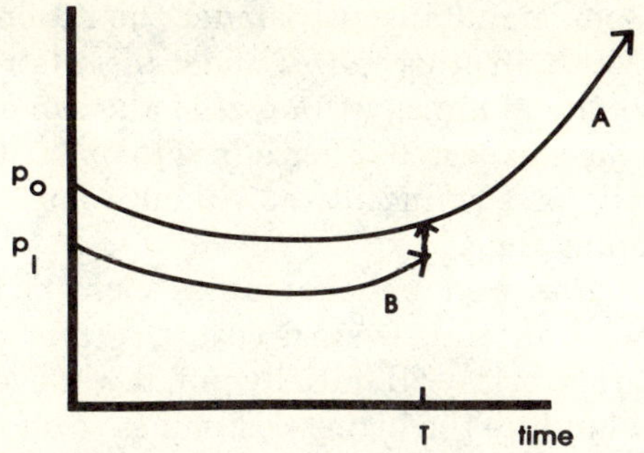

FIGURE IV
Price path over time. *A* is with no contracting and *B* is with contracts that all expire at *T* years.

the expected spot price, is lower. The contract price is indirectly proportional to the amount put under contract because of two effects: (1) the direct effect of $\partial p^c/\partial q^c \leq 0$, and (2) the indirect effect that lowers the expected spot price. Increasing the amount under contract reduces risk to the mine and increases total output. This is true because the mine will put output under contract only if it increases the expected utility of profits.

Next, to allow the timing of a mine's opening to differ from others, let R_t represent expected net revenues from all sources at time t. Then market equilibrium requires that expected profits be positive for each firm with more risk-averse firms requiring higher expected profits. If we let t_i be the opening time of the ith firm and $\pi_i{}^*$ the maximum expected present value of profits, then market equilibrium requires that

$$(9) \qquad \int_{t_i}^{\infty} \{R_t - C(q,m)\}e^{-\rho t}dt = \pi_i{}^*$$

$$(10) \qquad \frac{d\pi_i{}^*}{dt_i} = 0.$$

In turn, (10) can be interpreted as requiring that the profit rate at time t_i be just equal to the present value of the gain in profits to the firm from waiting as shown in (11).

$$(11) \qquad R_{t_i} - C(q_{t_i},0) = \int_{t_i}^{\infty} \frac{d\{R_t - C(q,m)\}}{dt_i} e^{-\rho(t-t_i)}dt.$$

From this, one can conclude that in terms of costs, identical mines with identical contracting potential and with identical degrees of risk aversion will open simultaneously under the rational expectations hypothesis of Muth. In other words, under these (strong) conditions, all perfectly identical mines will open at the same time. All mine managers will have expected other mines to open at the same time, and no mine will have an incentive, without some sort of collusion, to alter its opening time.

Suppose there are a number of mines open and a number of potential mines with differing average costs that are not opened. Even though the market price will initially fall, it will eventually rise. As it rises, this will induce the higher cost mines to open. Suppose that the expectations of new mines are sufficiently accurate, or that close-down and open-up costs are sufficiently great that once a mine is opened it never closes. This addition to supply from the new mines with a fixed demand curve will retard the price increase or cause the spot price to fall, depending upon the amount of the new supply relative to the market and the magnitude of the response of the existing mines to lower price increases or lower prices. In either case, the price path will now be scalloped as shown in Figure V.

Relaxation of many of the foregoing assumptions will smooth the scallops in Figure V. If the degree of risk aversion differs among otherwise identical mines, the degree of smoothing will depend upon the distribution of attitudes toward risk over types of mines. If storage by purchasers is possible, the degree will depend upon the cost of storage.

While many of the assumptions maintained above are strong, in many cases the effects of relaxing them are not significant, and they are consistent with a definition of market equilibrium.

IV. CONCLUSIONS

The preceding analysis has a number of implications for the elasticity of the supply of an exhaustible resource. With the price rising at the same percentage as unit costs from factor prices and productivity, the supply of the resource will be increasing for "young" mines and declining for "old" mines. The rate of change in supply from each mine will depend upon the economies or diseconomies of the age of the mine.

If prices are rising faster than cost increases for a given level of output, then the response of output from an existing mine will depend upon the rate at which prices are increasing. When prices are outpacing costs at an increasing rate, then the rate of extraction should fall. When prices are rising over costs at a decreasing rate, the rate of

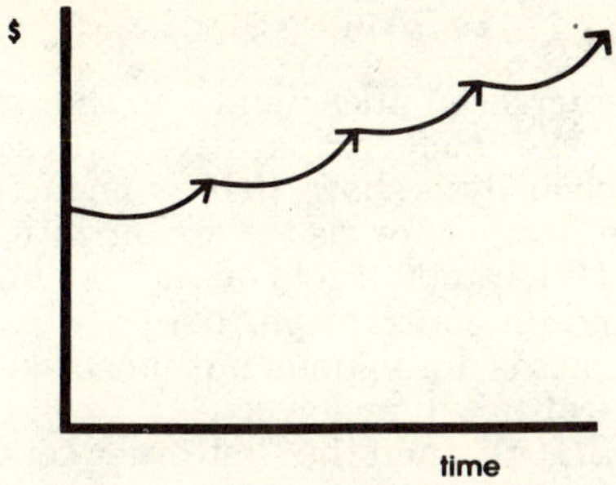

FIGURE V
Price path with new mines opening.

extraction will rise above what it would have been without the rise in prices over costs.

If there is no change in expectations by purchasers but an increase in perceived risk or risk aversion by mine managers, output for the spot market will fall. However, this will increase the incentive to contract. Thus, the amount placed under contract should increase. The effect on total output of a mine will be negative.

Therefore, the equilibrium spot market price should rise. The effect on contract prices is ambiguous: putting more under contract requires a lower contract price, but rising market prices would offset this.[11]

Any time there are incomplete markets, which is the case when there is risk, the market system is inefficient. Contracts permit pairwise expected utility improvement for some, but may create welfare losses for others if the spot market becomes thinner and the variance of market price increases. However, this would tend to be offset by the fact that total output will be greater.

The assumptions employed to illustrate the equilibrium spot market price over time were used for exposition only. The equilibrium price could take a number of paths depending upon the parameters that have been pointed out. What is clear, however, is that the spot market price is a "fuzzy" signal, in that it could be rising or falling for several different reasons. Consequently, to understand the meaning of movements of the spot price, an empirical model is necessary.

A final point is that the assumptions involved in obtaining an equilibrium in the spot market are quite restrictive. So restrictive, in fact, that they suggest that it is quite unlikely that the spot market would ever be in equilibrium in the traditional sense.

11. All of these consequences are derived holding purchasers' perceived risk or risk aversion constant.

APPENDIX

The effect of increased uncertainty on the variables q^c, q^s, and T can be shown by the usual comparative statics procedure. In particular, the following analysis shows that for an increase in uncertainty for the risk-averse firm, or for risk aversion with the expected spot price unchanged: (1) the amount sold on the spot market will decrease; (2) the amount sold on contract per period will be higher; (3) the length of the contract is ambiguous but most likely will be shorter; and (4) expected profits will be lower.

Letting $\phi = E\{U(\pi)\}$, then the first-order conditions are derived from $d\phi = 0$. The second-order conditions require that $d^2\phi < 0$ or that

$$E\{U''(\pi_{q^c}\,dq^c + \pi_{q_t^s}\,dq_t^s + \pi_T\,dT) + U'(Q)\} < 0,$$

where

$$Q = \sum_{i,j=q^c,q^s,T} \sum \pi_{ij} di dj.$$

This in turn requires that

$$(12) \qquad E\left\{U'\begin{bmatrix} \pi_{q^cq^c} & \pi_{q^cq_t^s} & \pi_{q^cT} \\ \cdot & \pi_{q_t^sq_t^s} & \pi_{q_t^sT} \\ \cdot & \cdot & \pi_{TT} \end{bmatrix}\right\} = E\{U'[H]\}$$

be negative definite. Furthermore, since $\pi_{q_t^sq_t^s}$ must be negative, $\pi_{q^cq_t^s}$ is also negative, since $\pi_{q^cq_t^s} = \pi_{q_t^sq_t^s}$. Also, $\pi_{q_t^sT} = 0$ by inspection of (4).

The technique used here is to rewrite the first-order conditions (2), (3), and (4) as (2′), (3′), and (4′):

$$(2') \qquad E(\pi_{q^c}) = 0$$

$$(3') \qquad E(\pi_{q_t^s}) = -\text{cov}(U',p_t^s)/E(U')$$

$$(4') \qquad E(\pi_T) = 0.$$

An increase in uncertainty is then defined as $d\ \text{cov}(U',p_t^s) < 0$, and $E(p_t^s)$ is assumed to remain constant.

Differentiation of the first-order conditions (2′), (3′), and (4′), along with the definition of $E(\pi)$, yields the following system of equations expressed in matrix form (the expectations operator E, where unnecessary, has been dropped for clarity):

$$(13) \qquad \begin{bmatrix} \pi_{q^cq^c} & \pi_{q^cq^s} & \pi_{q^cT} & 0 \\ \pi_{q_t^sq^c} & \pi_{q_t^sq_t^s} & 0 & \dfrac{-\text{cov}(p^s,U')E(U'')}{E(U')^2} \\ \pi_{Tq^c} & 0 & \pi_{TT} & 0 \\ 0 & \dfrac{\text{cov}(p^s,U')}{E(U')} & 0 & 1 \end{bmatrix}$$

$$\times \begin{bmatrix} \dfrac{dq^c}{d\,\mathrm{cov}(\cdot)} \\ \dfrac{dq^s_t}{d\,\mathrm{cov}(\cdot)} \\ \dfrac{dT}{d\,\mathrm{cov}(\cdot)} \\ \dfrac{d\pi}{d\,\mathrm{cov}(\cdot)} \end{bmatrix} = \begin{bmatrix} 0 \\ \dfrac{-1}{E(U')} \\ 0 \\ 0 \end{bmatrix}.$$

The determinant of the left-hand matrix in (13), $|\overline{H}|$, is

$$(14)\quad |\overline{H}| = |H| - \frac{\mathrm{cov}(p^s_t,U')E(U'')}{E(U')^2} \begin{vmatrix} \pi_{q^cq^c} & \pi_{q^cq^s_t} & \pi_{q^cT} \\ \pi_{Tq^c} & 0 & \pi_{TT} \\ 0 & \dfrac{\mathrm{cov}(\cdot)}{E(U')} & 0 \end{vmatrix},$$

where $|H|$ is the determinant of H as defined in (12).

From the second-order conditions the last determinant in (14) is positive, and since $\mathrm{cov}(p^s_t,U')$ and U'' are both negative by assumption, $|\overline{H}|$ is negative.

Solving (13) then gives

$$(15)\quad \frac{d\pi}{d\,\mathrm{cov}(\cdot)} = \frac{\mathrm{cov}(p^s_t,U')}{E(U')^2} \begin{vmatrix} \pi_{q^cq^c} & \pi_{q^cT} \\ \pi_{Tq^c} & \pi_{TT} \end{vmatrix} \Big/ |\overline{H}| = \frac{-\,+}{-} > 0$$

$$(16)\quad \frac{dq^c}{d\,\mathrm{cov}(\cdot)} = \frac{1}{E(U')}\, \pi_{q^cq^s_t}\, \pi_{TT} \Big/ |\overline{H}| = \frac{+\,-\,-}{-} < 0$$

$$(17)\quad \frac{dq^s_t}{d\,\mathrm{cov}(\cdot)} = -\frac{1}{E(U')} \begin{vmatrix} \pi_{q^cq^c} & \pi_{q^cT} \\ \pi_{q^cT} & \pi_{TT} \end{vmatrix} \Big/ |\overline{H}| = \frac{-\,+\,+}{-} > 0$$

$$(18)\quad \frac{dT}{d\,\mathrm{cov}(\cdot)} = \frac{-\,(1/E(U'))\,\pi_{q^cq^s}\,\pi_{Tq^c}}{|\overline{H}|}$$

$$= \frac{-\,+\,-\,?}{-} \gtreqless 0 \quad \text{as} \quad \pi_{q^cT} \lesseqgtr 0.$$

Since

$$\mathrm{sign}(\pi_{q^cT}) = \mathrm{sign}\left(\frac{\partial p^c}{\partial q^c}\, q^c e^{-\rho T} + \frac{\partial^2 p^c}{\partial q^c \partial T}\, q^c\, \frac{(1 - e^{-\rho T})}{\rho}\right),$$

then if $\partial^2 p^c/\partial q^c \partial T \leq 0$, which seems to be more likely, the length of the contract would be shorter for an increase in uncertainty or risk aversion (a decrease in $\mathrm{cov}(U',p^s_t)$).

UNIVERSITY OF SOUTH CAROLINA

REFERENCES

Akerlof, G., "The Market for Lemons: Qualitative Uncertainty and the Market Mechanism," this *Journal,* LXXIV (Aug. 1970), 488–500.

Arrow, K. J., "The Economic Implications of Learning by Doing," *Review of Economic Studies,* XXIX (1962), 152–73.

Baron, D., "Demand Uncertainty in Imperfect Competition," *International Economic Review,* XI (Oct. 1970), 463–80.

Bell, C., and P. Zusman, "A Bargaining Theoretic Approach to Cropsharing Contracts," *American Economic Review,* LXVI (Sept. 1976), 578–88.

Blair, R., and D. Kasserman, "Uncertainty and the Incentive for Vertical Integration," *Southern Economic Journal,* XLV (July 1978), 266–72.

Cheung, S. N. S., *The Theory of Share Tenancy* (Chicago: University of Chicago Press, 1969).

Dasgupta, P., and J. E. Stiglitz, "Uncertainty and the Rate of Extraction Under Alternative Institutional Arrangements," Technical Report No. 179, March 1976, Institute for Mathematical Studies, Stanford University.

Gray, L. C., "Rent Under the Assumption of Exhaustibility," *Quarterly Review of Economics,* XXVIII (May 1914), 464–89.

Hammond, P. J., "On the Irrelevance of Share Contracts," Working Paper, University of Essex (Oct. 1977).

Hicks, J. R., *Value and Capital,* 2nd ed. (London: Oxford University Press, 1946).

Hirshleifer, J., "Speculation and Equilibrium: Information, Risk, and Markets," this *Journal,* LXXXIX (Nov. 1975), 519–42.

——, "The Theory of Speculation Under Alternative Regimes of Markets," *Journal of Finance,* XXXII (Sept. 1977), 975–99.

Holthausen, D., "Input Choices and Uncertain Demand," *American Economic Review,* LXVI (March 1976), 94–103.

Hotelling, H., "The Economics of Exhaustible Resources," *Journal of Political Economy,* XXXIX (April 1931), 137–75.

Kamien, M., and N. Schwartz, "Optimal Exhaustible Resource Depletion With Endogenous Technical Change," *Review of Economic Studies,* XLV (Feb. 1978), 179–96.

Keynes, J. M., *A Treatise on Money* (New York: Macmillian, 1930).

Leland, H. E., "Theory of the Firm Facing Uncertain Demand," *American Economic Review,* LXII (June 1972), 278–91.

Muth, J. F., "Rational Expectations and the Theory of Price Movements," *Econometrica* (July 1961), reprinted in David Cass and L. W. McKenzie, eds., *Selected Readings in Macroeconomics and Capital Theory From Econometrica,* Vol. 3 (Cambridge, MA: M.I.T. Press, 1974).

Newberry, D. M. G., "Cropsharing Tenancy in Agriculture: Comment," *American Economic Review,* LXIV (Dec. 1974), 1060–66.

Reid, J. D., "The Theory of Share Tenancy Revisited—Again," *Journal of Political Economy,* LXXXV (April 1977), 403–07.

Rothschild, M., and J. Stiglitz, "Increasing Risk: I. A Definition," *Journal of Economic Theory,* II (Sept. 1970), 225–43.

——, and ——, "Equilibrium in Competitive Insurance Markets: An Essay on the Economics of Imperfect Information," this *Journal,* XC (Nov. 1976), 629–49.

Sandmo, A., "On the Theory of the Competitive Firm Under Uncertainty," *American Economic Review,* LXI (March 1971), 65–73.

Scott, A., "The Theory of the Mine Under Conditions of Certainty," in Mason Gaffney, ed., *Extractive Resources and Taxation* (Milwaukee: University of Wisconsin Press, 1967), 25–62.

Shavell, S., "On Moral Hazard and Insurance," this *Journal,* XCIII (Nov. 1979), 541–62.

Solow, R. M., "The Economics of Resources and the Resources of Economics," *American Economic Review,* LXIV (May 1974), 1–14.

Stiglitz, J. E., "Growth with the Exhaustible Resources: Efficient and Optimal Growth Paths," *Review of Economic Studies,* Symposium on the Economics of Exhaustible Resources, XLI (Feb. 1974), 123–38.

——, "Incentives and Risk Sharing in Sharecropping," *Review of Economic Studies,* XLI (April 1974), 219–55.

Working, H., "Future Trading and Hedging," *American Economic Review,* XLIII (June 1953), 314–43.

——, "New Concepts Concerning Future Markets and Prices," *American Economic Review,* LII (June 1962), 431–59.

A METHOD FOR DETERMINING THE APPROPRIATENESS OF NATIONAL PLANNING IN A MARKET ECONOMY*

JEFFREY B. MILLER

Meade demonstrates how, in the absence of futures markets for many commodities, indicative planning can supply economic agents with the requisite information about future market conditions. An incentive scheme designed to encourage agents to relay accurate information to central planners is introduced into Meade's model. It is then shown how the Groves and Loeb voting procedure can be used to determine whether an indicative planning program would be beneficial.

I. INTRODUCTION

Indicative planning in a market economy is designed to improve economic decision making by providing economic agents with additional information. A theoretical justification for such planning is that spot markets by themselves provide insufficient information. Meade [1970] demonstrates how, in the absence of futures markets for many commodities, indicative planning can supply economic agents with the requisite information about future market conditions. Grossman [1976, 1977] and Grossman and Stiglitz [1976] show that there may be underinvestment in futures markets because they create a positive externality when information is passed from informed to uninformed agents.

While these arguments suggest that governmentally sponsored indicative planning might be beneficial, the cost of an indicative planning program may exceed the benefits. One way of evaluating the merits of indicative planning is to let economic agents participating in the construction of the plan decide. Since the information provided by an indicative plan can be used by firms to improve production decisions, this information is a public input,[1] and the voting procedure suggested by Groves and Loeb [1975] can be used to determine whether an indicative planning program would be beneficial.

The benefits and costs of indicative planning may vary with the extensiveness of the planning effort. Demands for more information will increase the costs of collection. Because the projections developed

* I would like to thank Michael Marrese, Peter Murrell, James Thornton, and an anonymous referee for their comments on an earlier version of this paper.

1. A commodity is a public input when "the total quantity is available to all firms and the use of it by one firm does not diminish its availability to the other firms" [Groves and Loeb, 1975, p. 213].

The Quarterly Journal of Economics, September 1980 0033-5533/80/0095-0261$ 01.60

in the plan are a public input and are based on information provided by economic agents, there must be appropriate incentives to encourage agents to bear the costs of becoming informed and relaying this information to the planners.[2] By adjusting the incentives, the information obtained will vary. Thus, evaluation of different degrees of indicative planning requires finding the optimal level of planning and then comparing this to the choice of no planning at all.

In this paper we introduce into Meade's model of indicative planning an incentive scheme designed to encourage agents to relay accurate information to central planners. We then use the Groves and Loeb voting procedure to determine how extensive the planning effort should be. In the next section Meade's model is described, and the associated difficulties of inducing agents to provide accurate information are analyzed. We then suggest how incorporating an appropriate incentive mechanism can resolve these difficulties. In Section III a simple example is presented to illustrate how such a planning arrangement might function. Section IV concludes the paper.

II. The Planning System

Meade presents a model of indicative planning where agents indicate through a pseudo-market process what their actions would be under different sets of circumstances or environmental paths. An iterative procedure eventually yields the equilibrium price vector. This model is very similar to the general equilibrium models of Arrow-Debreu. The fundamental distinction is the mechanism through which the equilibrium price vector is obtained. In an Arrow-Debreu world agents make binding contracts in futures markets. In Meade's scheme they simply indicate their future intentions, and payments are made at the time of delivery.

Although allowing payments to occur in every period creates some problems that do not explicitly arise in the Arrow-Debreu formulation, Meade shows that prices in the two systems are algebraically equivalent if all interest rates and insurance premiums as well as commodity prices are known. Instead of signing contracts in conditional forward markets, representatives of all buyers and sellers in effect meet at a huge convention and bargain for what they would want to buy or sell under different environmental circumstances.[3] Thus, the agents merely "indicate" what they would do when an actual

2. For a discussion of the problem of truthful reporting of their future intentions by economic agents, see Albin [1971].

3. Meade calls this meeting a giant "higgle-haggle."

spot market comes into existence, at some future date. The vector of commodity prices, interest rates, and insurance premiums that emerge from this convention constitutes the indicative plan.[4]

The accuracy of the plan thus depends on the accuracy of the output projections announced by the individual agents. For example, if a particular environmental path occurs and a larger quantity of a good is in fact offered for sale than had been originally indicated, the actual commodity price vector will diverge from the indicated one. Since either intentional misrepresentation of future actions or poorly conceived forecasts (due to the cost of preparing accurate projections) will create inaccurate forecasts from the planning process, it is desirable that agents be encouraged to reveal their intentions accurately.[5]

Although each manager might assemble much of the information sought by the planners even if there were no planning process (since doing so would improve the efficacy of the resulting decisions), participation in the planning process is likely to create demands for additional information and therefore create additional information costs. Whether or not agents will voluntarily bear these additional information costs depends on whether the resulting benefits accruing to the firm warrant these additional expenditures. Unfortunately, important externalities are associated with the additional information produced by a Meade-type indicative plan. As Grossman and Stiglitz [1976] point out when discussing the information generated by futures markets, the benefits derived from the price information accrue to all agents, even to those who do not participate. Similarly, all agents benefit from the prices established by the indicative planning process. Although the benefits derived from the indicative plan may be considerable, the benefits that an individual agent derives from his contribution to the construction of the plan may appear to be quite small. Thus, while additional expenditures by an agent may appreciably improve the accuracy of the plan and thereby benefit every agent, these expenditures will not be made. As is typically the case, positive externalities lead to underinvestment of resources.

If the government could create an incentive system that rewards

4. The equilibrium concept developed here by Meade is similar to Radner's [1972, 1976] "rational expectations" equilibrium: "an equilibrium in which traders have models of market price determination that are imperfect, or imprecise, but that are consistent with observations of the market during the process of model revision or 'learning' " [1976, p. 2]. While Hart [1975] has shown that such an equilibrium may not necessarily be Pareto optimal, Grossman [1977] has proved that the equilibrium will satisfy a condition that he terms a "Social Nash Optimum."

5. Misrepresentation may also arise in competitive situations as well. For an analysis of some of these problems, see Hurwicz [1972, 1977].

honest disclosure of accurately planned future activity and penalizes agents whose actions diverge from those stipulated during the construction of the plan, more accurate information would be obtained during the plan construction process. Such a system would not only reduce intentional misrepresentation, it would also provide agents with incentives to obtain costly information.

Bonin [1976] and Weitzman [1976] have analyzed incentive mechanisms of this type.[6] They show that in situations where future output is uncertain, the targets agents report will depend on the relative size of the overfulfillment and underfulfillment penalties. For example, in the case where agents are risk-neutral and the overfulfillment and underfulfillment penalties are equal, the agent will choose a target equal to the median of the distribution of uncertain output.[7]

The penalties associated with choosing an incorrect target may be reduced by collecting more information and thereby improve the accuracy of the target. A plan that utilizes this type of incentive mechanism will provide a greater incentive for investing in information than a plan that does not. Furthermore, the greater the penalties for divergence, the larger the investment made in information will be. By adjusting the severity of the penalties, a tradeoff can be made between more accurate planning and less costly, less accurate planning. Higher penalties will mean more accurate plan projections, but this will come at the expense of greater expenditures on information.

Each firm benefits from the plan, since the information contained in the plan increases expected profits. But the plan is also costly to a firm, since it requires additional expenditures on information acquisition and possible penalties for divergence from its target. Furthermore, there are the administrative costs of operating the plan. To pay these expenses, taxes must be imposed to generate sufficient revenues. The divergence penalties will cover some, if not all, of these costs. If the plan is to be self-sufficient and the revenues raised by the

6. The Bonin-Weitzman mechanism has the following form:

$$B = \begin{matrix} aX - b(X - T) & X \geq T \\ aX - c(T - X) & X < T, \end{matrix}$$

where $a > b > 0$, $a > c > 0$ and B is a bonus payment. X is actual output, and T is the output target selected by the economic agent. a is the marginal bonus for an extra unit of output; b and c are the divergence penalties.

Stigler [1975] has suggested a similar system of penalties. For example, under his scheme the firm would be taxed 1/300 of 1 percent of receipts for every 1 percent difference between the announced output and the actual output.

7. The agent will set the target so that the probability that output exceeds the target is $P(X \geq T) = b/(c + b)$.

divergence penalties are inadequate, the participants will have to share whatever additional costs may be incurred. If the revenues raised by the divergence penalties are expected to more than cover the administrative expense, then the firm can share this surplus.

By subtracting new expected costs from the new expected revenues, the firm can determine whether it will benefit from the plan and what the expected gains or losses might be. This calculation can be carried out for different values of the divergence penalties.[8] The locus of points derived from these calculations represents a willingness-to-pay function.[9]

Normally, if a firm had a positive demand for an input, it could simply purchase it in a private market. Planning information, however, is a public input. To determine the appropriate level of planning, these demands must be revealed and properly aggregated. This can be done by using the demand-revealing process developed by Groves [1973], Clarke [1971], and Vickrey [1961] and applied to the problem of public inputs by Groves and Loeb [1975].

These demand-revealing processes encourage economic agents to reveal their true preferences by imposing taxes in such a manner that, regardless of how other agents vote, it is in the best interest of

8. Incorporating the Bonin-Weitzman-type incentive mechanism as part of the plan will alter future behavior. Since divergences from previously announced targets are penalized, if firms have some discretion over their future output they will attempt to produce closer to target levels than they otherwise would have. As a result, some unanticipated opportunities for expansion are less likely to be undertaken. On the other hand, greater expenditures will also be made to overcome unanticipated future difficulties.

The Bonin-Weitzman mechanism, therefore, tends to place restrictions on agent behavior. At the same time, since firms are encouraged to produce near target levels, their activities are likely to be better coordinated than they would have been otherwise. Thus, there are tradeoffs to be considered here as well.

While we assume (as do Weitzman and Bonin) in the example in Section III that the firm cannot adjust its output to future uncertainties in this way, the same principles apply in determining the willingness-to-pay function. The difference is that, in calculating the willingness-to-pay function, the agent will want to compare the situation without planning, where his actions will not be affected by divergence penalties, to the situation with planning, where he will be better informed but will have to bear the costs of plan participation, i.e., divergence penalties, information collection costs, and adjustment costs.

For a discussion of the Bonin-Weitzman mechanism in an environment where managers can adjust output by increasing or decreasing their level of effort, see Miller and Thornton [1978].

9. A possible criticism of this approach is that the firms might have inadequate information about the impact of higher divergence penalties to make rational choices. As Radner [1968] points out, this is a problem of "infinite regression" and is common to much of the literature on the value of information in economic systems. It arises from the fact that, in deciding whether or not to collect additional information (or to collect information in order to decide whether or not to collect additional information), the agent may have insufficient information for rational decision making. In these circumstances it may sometimes be necessary to use a "rule of thumb" in making final choices if the process becomes too complex.

the agent to tell the truth. By having agents vote on the basis of their willingness-to-pay, the government can determine the kind of planning program that should be developed.

III. An Example

The following example may clarify how an indicative planning scheme of the Meade-type might work when an incentive mechanism penalizing divergence from projected targets is included as part of the planning machinery. While the purpose of indicative planning is to improve overall social welfare, to keep the illustration simple, we consider how the plan might affect short-run production efficiency only in a single industry in a two-period context. The problem facing the individual firms in the industry is choosing a level of inputs (i.e., labor) that will maximize profits. What makes this decision difficult is that the firm knows neither its production function nor the sales price of its output with certainty.

The primary function of the indicative plan is to reduce price uncertainty. The planners do this by making price forecasts based on output projections of individual firms. Since the prices in the plan depend upon information provided by firms, the accuracy of the price projections will depend upon how well firms can predict their future output levels. How much firms know about their future output depends upon how much firms are willing to invest in information. The more information firms collect, therefore, the smaller the expected divergence associated with price forecasts made in the plan. By penalizing poor output forecasts, firms are encouraged to collect more information. Higher levels of Ψ, the penalty rate for inaccurate forecasts, will bring about more information collection. Thus, Ψ determines the accuracy of the price forecasts contained in the plan. We propose that Ψ be set by having each firm weigh the benefits and costs of collecting additional information and then, using the Groves and Loeb procedure, voting for the Ψ which establishes a level of information collection that will maximize profits.

For purposes of the example, we assume that firms are price-takers in both output and factor markets. Furthermore, we assume that the uncertainty faced by each firm is localized. In other words, the information that a firm collects about its own production function will not reduce the uncertainty associated with the production function of other firms. The production function for each of the n firms is a special case of the constant elasticity of substitution production function where the substitution parameter $\rho = -1/2$, and the returns-to-scale parameter $v = \frac{1}{2}$. Thus,

$$\tilde{x}_i = \gamma L_i{}^{1/2} + (1 - \gamma)K^{1/2}\left(\sum_{j=1}^{t} \tilde{\theta}_{ij}\right), \tag{1}$$

where L_i is the amount of labor input purchased by firm i and K is the amount of capital that we assume is equal for all firms. The advantage of using this production function is that, in the short run, it yields a linear supply curve. There are t different $\tilde{\theta}$ (the tilde indicates a random variable), each of which is an independent uniformly distributed random variable over the interval $(1 - 1/10t, 1 + 1/10t)$. This says, in effect, that without any information about the $\tilde{\theta}_{ij}$'s, the firm does not know exactly how productive its capital inputs will be. The productivity of capital could vary anywhere from 10 percent below to 10 percent above its expected value.[10]

The relationship between information and the cost of its collection is assumed to be extremely simple. By spending c_{ij}, firm i can learn the value of $\tilde{\theta}_{ij}$, thereby reducing the uncertainty associated with its production. Furthermore, we assume that these costs are the same across firms and these costs increase as more information is gathered. Thus,

$$c_{kj} = c_{ij} \qquad \text{for any firms } k \text{ and } i$$

and

$$c_{iu} < c_{iv} \qquad \text{if } u < v.$$

In addition, we assume that the cost of collecting this information is high enough that, even though knowledge of its own $\tilde{\theta}_{ij}$ will enable the firm to improve its price forecasts, these benefits will not be sufficient to warrant the expenditure on more information. Thus, unless there are additional benefits to information collection (e.g., a reduction in expected divergence penalties when $\Psi > 0$), firms will not choose to collect information on the $\tilde{\theta}_{ij}$'s.[11]

10. The uncertainty described here is related to local problems. For example, the productivity of a new piece of machinery may not be known with certainty. There is no environmental uncertainty. In a more complex model, environmental uncertainty could be analyzed by, say, making $\tilde{\theta}_{ij}$ the same for all firms. Under these circumstances, the information passed through the plan might include more than price projections. The plan might also be a mechanism through which firms that knew the value of $\tilde{\theta}_{ij}$ passed this information to those firms that did not.

11. This assumption greatly simplifies the mathematics and does not fundamentally affect our results as to how Ψ, the penalty for inaccurate forecasts, is determined. See footnotes 14 and 16 for a further elaboration of this point.

Assume that the demand curve for total output X is a linear function of the price p so that

$$(2)\qquad \tilde{p} = \frac{1}{\beta}(\alpha - \tilde{X}) = \frac{1}{\beta}\left(\alpha - \sum_{i=1}^{n} \tilde{x}_i\right), \qquad \alpha > 0, \qquad \beta > 0.$$

With planning the firm may obtain better price information, but there will also be additional costs. These fall into two categories. First, there are payments made to the government. These take the form of divergence penalties to encourage more accurate information collection and taxes to pay the administrative cost of the planning program. These payments should be sufficient to cover the administrative cost of the program. If the administrative cost exceeds the size of the divergence penalties and is independent of the penalties, the expected total government collections for the planning program (i.e., the sum of divergence penalties and taxes) will not change even if the divergence penalties are altered. In addition, since the production functions and cost of information gathering are similar for every firm, the expected payments for each firm will be the same.

The second cost of planning is the cost of additional informational gathering. This cost will vary with changes in the divergence penalties. The higher the penalty, the greater the possible loss due to inaccurate prediction. It is, therefore, in the best interests of the firm to invest in information when the marginal expected loss exceeds the cost of gathering additional information. If the central planners set penalties for over- and underfulfillment in the Bonin-Weitzman incentive scheme equal to each other, risk-neutral agents will set their output projection or target T_i equal to the median value of $\tilde{x}_i$ which because of our assumptions about the distribution of the $\tilde{\theta}_{ij}$, is also the mean.

If the first q of the $\tilde{\theta}_{ij}$ becomes known to the firm through information gathering, then the firm's target would be

$$T_i = \gamma L_i^{1/2} + (1 - \gamma)K^{1/2}\left[\sum_{j=1}^{q} \theta_{ij} + (t - q)\right].$$

The θ_{ij}'s are the true values of the $\tilde{\theta}_{ij}$. If Ψ is the divergence penalty,[12] then the penalty will be

$$\Psi\,|x_i - T_i|.$$

12. The optimal value of Ψ is determined by the voting procedure.

At the margin the expected savings from investing the amount c_{iq} to learn the value of $\tilde{\theta}_{iq}$ will be

$$(3) \quad E\left[\Psi\left|(1-\gamma)K^{1/2}\left(\sum_{j=q}^{t}\tilde{\theta}_{ij}-(t-q+1)\right)\right| - \Psi\left|(1-\gamma)K^{1/2}\left(\sum_{j=q+1}^{t}\tilde{\theta}_{ij}-(t-q)\right)\right|\right]$$

$$= \Psi(1-\gamma)K^{1/2}\left\{E\left[\left|\sum_{j=q}^{t}\tilde{\theta}_{ij}-(t-q+1)\right|\right] - E\left[\left|\sum_{j=q+1}^{t}\tilde{\theta}_{ij}-(t-q)\right|\right]\right\}.$$

This reduces to[13]

$$\Psi(1-\gamma)K^{1/2}(1+1/20t).$$

When $\Psi(1-\gamma)K^{1/2}(1+1/20t) \geq c_{iq}$, it will be profitable for the firm to invest in more information. Since the cost of information gathering is the same for every firm, each firm will choose to invest in more information at the same point.

Firms benefit from the establishment of indicative planning if the planning process results in an increase in profits (net of these two costs of planning). Even if the plan's price projections are based on information supplied when $\Psi = 0$, the firms may nonetheless benefit. In measuring the overall value of plan information for the firm, these benefits should be added to those that accrue to firms from further observation of the $\tilde{\theta}_{ij}$'s. Let B be the expected gain to the firm from using plan information, where $\Psi = 0$. Then the firm's willingness-to-pay at any level of planning will be the expected improvement in profits or B plus the expected increase in profits that may result from an adjustment of Ψ.

The firm's actual profits under planning will be equal to revenues

13. When X is uniformly distributed over the interval (s,r) and $\overline{X}$ is the mean of the distribution,

$$E[|X-\overline{X}|] = 2\int_{\overline{X}}^{r}\frac{X}{r-s}\,dX = \frac{r^2-\overline{X}^2}{r-s} = \tfrac{1}{2}(r+\overline{X}).$$

Applying this result to equation (3), we have

$$E\left[\left|\sum_{j=q}^{t}\tilde{\theta}_{ij}-(t-q+1)\right|\right] = t-q+1+\frac{t-q+1}{20t}.$$

Similarly,

$$E\left[\left|\sum_{j=a+1}^{t}\tilde{\theta}_{ij}-(t-q)\right|\right] = t-q+\frac{t-q}{20t}.$$

minus factor costs, information costs, and government payments, or

$$\tilde{\pi}_{iq} = \tilde{p}_q \tilde{x}_i - wL_i - rK - \sum_{j=1}^{q} c_{ij} - G, \tag{4}$$

where w is the price of the input L, r is the price of input K, $\tilde{p}_q$ is the random price in equation (2), where the value of the first q of the $\tilde{\theta}_{ij}$ is known by each firm, and G is the total payment made to the government and is independent of Ψ.

In a long-run context the information provided by the plan could be used by firms to make decisions regarding both capital and labor inputs. In the short run, however, where the stock of capital is fixed, the problem facing the firm is that, with only limited information about the market price and its production function, the firm will want to choose a level of input L_i that will maximize its expected profits $E(\tilde{\pi}_i)$. If we assume that the firm is a price-taker, then differentiating $E(\tilde{\pi}_i)$ with respect to L_i yields

$$\hat{L}_{iq} = \left[\frac{\gamma E(\tilde{p}_q)}{2w}\right]^2, \tag{5}$$

where $\hat{L}_{iq}$ is the optimum level for a given predetermined amount of information gathering q. From (2) the equation for $E(\tilde{p}_q)$ is

$$E(\tilde{p}_q) = \frac{1}{\beta}\left(\alpha - \left\{\gamma \sum_{i=1}^{n} \hat{L}_{iq}{}^{1/2} + (1-\gamma)K^{1/2}\left[\sum_{i=1}^{n}\sum_{j=1}^{q} \theta_{ij} + n(t-q)\right]\right\}\right). \tag{6}$$

Substituting expression (5) for $\hat{L}_{iq}$ and rearranging terms yields

$$E(\tilde{p}_q) = \frac{2w}{2w\beta + \gamma^2 n} \times \left[\alpha - (1-\gamma)K^{1/2}\left(\sum_{i=1}^{n}\sum_{j=1}^{q} \theta_{ij} + n(t-q)\right)\right]. \tag{7}$$

The expected gain from planning will be the increase in expected profits due to the additional information now available to firms. The profits to be earned at any level of q can be found by substituting (1) and (5) into (4):

$$\tilde{\pi}_{iq} = \tilde{p}_q\left[\frac{\gamma^2 E(\tilde{p}_q)}{2w} + (1-\gamma)K^{1/2}\sum_{j=1}^{t} \tilde{\theta}_{ij}\right] - w\left[\frac{\gamma E(\tilde{p}_q)}{2w}\right]^2 - rK - \sum_{j=1}^{q} c_{ij} - G. \tag{8}$$

Then the expected overall gains will be the expected value of the difference between profits with no planning and profits with q information gathering plus the net benefits of doing any planning at all (i.e., $B - G$).

Define π_{i0} as the level of profit and $\tilde{p}_0$ as the price with planning when $\Psi = 0$, which in this example means that $q = 0$ also.[14] The expected gain for any q will be

$$(9)\quad E(\tilde{\pi}_{ip} - \tilde{\pi}_{i0} + B - G) = E\left\{\tilde{p}_q\left(\frac{\gamma^2 E(\tilde{p}_q)}{2w}\right) - \tilde{p}_0\left(\frac{\gamma^2 E(\tilde{p}_0)}{2w}\right) + (\tilde{p}_q - \tilde{p}_0)(1-\gamma)K^{1/2}\left(\sum_{j=1}^{t}\tilde{\theta}_{ij}\right) - w\left[\left(\frac{\gamma E(\tilde{p}_q)}{2w}\right)^2 - \left(\frac{\gamma E(\tilde{p}_0)}{2w}\right)^2\right] - \sum_{j=1}^{q} c_{ij} + B - G\right\}.$$

Since $(\tilde{p}_q - \tilde{p}_0)$ is not a random variable,[15] (9) reduces to

$$(10)\quad E(\tilde{\pi}_{iq} - \tilde{\pi}_{i0} + B - G) = \frac{\gamma^2}{4w}\left[(E(\tilde{p}_q))^2 - (E(\tilde{p}_0))^2\right] - \sum_{j=1}^{q} c_{ij} + B - G.$$

Substituting (7) for $E(\tilde{p}_q)$ and $E(\tilde{p}_0)$ as appropriate yields

14. It should be noted here again that the $\tilde{\theta}_{ij}$ are independent across firms. In this example there are two important reasons why $q = 0$. The first is due to the assumption that, while collecting information on the $\tilde{\theta}_{ij}$ will help the firm in forecasting the price, the expected gain will not be sufficient to compensate the firm for additional expenditures on information collection. The second reason is related to the structure of the production function. As it stands, the choice of labor inputs depends on the expected price, the wage rate, and γ. In other circumstances, where the marginal physical product of labor is not known with certainty, information about the production function might be collected even without planning. When information is gathered for this reason, the price projection made by the planners even when $\Psi = 0$ will reflect this information.

15.

$$\tilde{p}_q = \frac{1}{\beta}\left[\alpha - \sum_{i=1}^{n}\left(\frac{\gamma^2 E(\tilde{p}_q)}{2w} + (1-\gamma)K_i^{1/2}\sum_{j=1}^{t}\tilde{\theta}_{ij}\right)\right]$$

and

$$\tilde{p}_0 = \frac{1}{\beta}\left[\alpha - \sum_{i=1}^{n}\left(\frac{\gamma^2 E(\tilde{p}_0)}{2w} + (1-\gamma)K_i^{1/2}\sum_{j=1}^{t}\tilde{\theta}_{ij}\right)\right].$$

Therefore,

$$\tilde{p}_q - \tilde{p}_0 = -\frac{1}{\beta}\left[\sum_{i=1}^{n}\frac{\gamma^2 E(\tilde{p}_q)}{2w} - \sum_{i=1}^{n}\frac{\gamma^2 E(\tilde{p}_0)}{2w}\right] = -\frac{n\gamma^2}{2w\beta}\left[E(\tilde{p}_q) - E(\tilde{p}_0)\right].$$

$$(11)\quad E(\tilde{\pi}_{iq} - \tilde{\pi}_{i0} + B - G) = \frac{w\gamma^2}{(2w\beta + \gamma^2 n)^2}\Bigg\{-2\alpha(1-\gamma)K^{1/2}\sum_{i=1}^{n}\sum_{j=1}^{q}(\theta_{ij} - 1) + (1-\gamma)^2 K\left(\sum_{i=1}^{n}\sum_{j=1}^{q}(\theta_{ij} - 1)\right)^2 + 2(1-\gamma)^2 tnK\left(\sum_{i=1}^{n}\sum_{j=1}^{q}(\theta_{ij} - 1)\right)\Bigg\} - \sum_{j=1}^{q} c_{ij} + B - G.$$

Since the firm has no knowledge of the θ_{ij} when the decision must be made as to how much planning would be appropriate, the expected gain cannot be known with certainty. However, the expected value of the expected gain can be calculated:

$$(12)\quad E(E(\tilde{\pi}_{iq} - \tilde{\pi}_{i0} + B - G)) = \frac{\gamma^2(1-\gamma)^2 wnq\sigma^2 K}{(2w\beta + \gamma^2 n)^2} - \sum_{j=1}^{q} c_{ij} + B - G,$$

where σ^2 is the variance of any $\tilde{\theta}_{ij}$. Finding the optimal plan is a matter of determining the q, which maximizes the expected gain. Any change in q will create both gains and losses for the firm. An increase in q by one unit, which is equivalent to voting for a higher Ψ and more restrictive planning program, will reduce the variance in the price and increase the expected gain from planning by

$$\frac{\gamma^2(1-\gamma)^2 w\sigma^2 nK}{(2w\beta + n\gamma^2)^2}.$$

This is the principal advantage of the planning program. By giving each firm the incentive to gather more information, all firms can produce with less uncertainty. Losses are reflected in the second term. An increase in Ψ will bring about greater expenditures on information.[16]

16. In this example it has been assumed that, because of the high cost of information, firms will not collect information unless given additional incentives in the plan. It is possible to relax this assumption, however, without fundamentally altering the analysis.

To demonstrate this, the level of information collection when $\Psi = 0$ must first be determined. Under these conditions, the firm will weigh only the impact of its own information collection on the expected price. Thus, in contrast to equation (7), the expected value of the price $\tilde{p}_s^k$, projected by the plan when the nth firm chooses to collect information on k of the θ_{ij} and each of the other firms collect information on s of their θ_{ij}, will be

$$(a)\qquad E(\tilde{p}_s^k) = \frac{2w}{(2w\beta + \gamma^2 n)}\left[\alpha - (1-\gamma)K^{1/2}\left(\sum_{i=1}^{n-1}\sum_{j=1}^{s}\theta_{ij} + (n-1)(t-s) + \sum_{j=1}^{k}\theta_{nj} + (t-k)\right)\right]$$

If there is an advantage to collecting information, the gain from planning will be maximized for the firm when

$$(13) \qquad c_{iq+1} > \frac{\gamma^2(1-\gamma)^2 w\sigma^2 nK}{(2w\beta + n\gamma^2)^2} \geq c_{iq}.$$

This, together with the fact that firms will invest in information as long as $\Psi(1-\gamma)K^{1/2}(1 + 1/20t) \geq c_{iq}$, suggests, assuming equalities throughout, that the formula for determining the level of Ψ, where the optimal amount of information (with recognition of the positive externalities) will be collected, is[17]

$$(14) \qquad \Psi = \frac{(1-\gamma)\gamma^2 w\sigma^2 nK^{1/2}}{(2w\beta + n\gamma^2)^2}\left(\frac{20t}{20t+1}\right).$$

Since $\sigma^2 = 1/300t^2$, this reduces to

$$(15) \qquad \Psi = \frac{(1-\gamma)\gamma^2 wnK^{1/2}}{(2w\beta + n\gamma^2)^2(300t^2 + 15t)}.$$

If K is larger or β is smaller, the variance in the price will be larger, the value of more information search will increase, and the optimal value of Ψ will rise.[18] A change in t will also affect Ψ. The larger the value of t, the smaller the reduction in uncertainty when

By following the same basic procedure described above, it can then be shown that the net gain from collecting information on the kth θ_{ij} is

$$(b) \qquad \frac{\gamma^2(1-\gamma)^2 w\sigma^2 K}{(2w\beta + n\gamma^2)^2} - c_{ik}.$$

The first term in this expression does not vary as k changes, but c_{ij} increases as more information is collected. The firm will, therefore, collect information on the θ_{ij}'s up to the point where this expression becomes negative.

If equation (b) is positive for some values of c_{ij}, firms will collect information on the θ_{ij}, even when $\Psi = 0$. The benefits associated with $\Psi > 0$ will then be reflected in the additional information that firms will choose to collect. Expression (12) will then become

$$(12') \qquad E(E(\tilde{\pi}_{iq} - \tilde{\pi}_{ik} + B - G)) = \frac{\gamma^2(1-\gamma)^2 wn(q-k)\sigma^2 K}{(2w\beta + \gamma^2 n)^2} - \sum_{j=k+1}^{q} c_{ij} + B - G.$$

Relevant q's will always be at least as great as k, since the determination of Ψ reflects a recognition that there are positive externalities associated with information collection. Thus, under these circumstances a higher Ψ, which leads to a one unit increase in q, will still create an expected gain of

$$\frac{\gamma^2(1-\gamma)^2 wn\sigma^2 K}{(2w\beta + n\gamma^2)^2}.$$

17. In circumstances where the costs of information gathering for each firm are different or where the amount of capital varies across firms, the optimal Ψ will not be the same for all firms. The optimal Ψ for the economy will then be the one for which the aggregate overall gain in profits is greatest.

18. The variance of $\tilde{p}_q$ can be derived from expression (7) and is equal to

$$\operatorname{var}(\tilde{p}_q) = \frac{4w^2(1-\gamma)^2 Kn(t-q)\sigma^2}{(2w\beta + n\gamma^2)^2}.$$

an investment is made in learning the value of one more θ_{ij}. Thus, when t is larger, it becomes more costly to become more informed, and Ψ will fall.

The effect on Ψ of changes in γ and w is more complicated. While an increase in w will increase the variance in the price, it will also reduce the expected level of output, since less labor will be hired. These two changes have opposite effects on the variance of profits. The determination of which effect dominates depends on the relationship between the slope of the demand curve $1/\beta$, and the slope of the supply curve $2w/n\gamma^2$.[19] If $2w/n\gamma^2 < 1/\beta$, then an increase in w will cause Ψ to rise, and more information will be collected.[20]

The impact of γ is even more complicated, since a change in γ not only will affect the variance in the price and the level of output but also will reduce the size of the divergence penalties. The effect of a change in γ is determinate, however, when $\gamma \geq 2/3$ or $2w/n\gamma^2 < 1/\beta$. Under these circumstances, increasing γ reduces Ψ and the amount of information collected.[21]

The Groves and Loeb demand-revealing process can now be used to determine what value of Ψ is optimal and whether planning should be adopted at all. Equation (12) describes how much each firm will benefit from a given level of planning. Through the demand-revealing process each firm indicates its willingness-to-pay for the plan. From this vote, the optimal value of Ψ is determined. Since in this instance all the firms are similar, if there is a positive expected gain from planning for each firm at the optimal Ψ, the plan should be adopted. Thus, in this way policy makers can determine whether the establishment of a plan is appropriate, and if it is, how severe the divergence penalties should be.

IV. CONCLUSION

Indicative planning improves economic decision making by providing additional information to economic agents. One type of

19. From equations (1) and (5) and the fact that $X = \Sigma_{i=1}^{n} x_i$, the level of total output when no information is collected will be

$$X = \frac{n\gamma^2}{2w} E(\tilde{p}_0) + (1-\gamma)K^{1/2} \sum_{i=1}^{n} \sum_{j=1}^{t} \tilde{\theta}_{ij}.$$

20.

$$\frac{d\Psi}{dw} = \frac{(1-\gamma)\gamma^2 n K^{1/2}}{(2w\beta + n\gamma^2)^3 (300t^2 + 15t)} (n\gamma^2 - 2w\beta).$$

21.

$$\frac{d\Psi}{d\gamma} = \frac{wnK^{1/2}\gamma}{(2w\beta + n\gamma^2)^3 (300t^2 + 15t)} [2(2w\beta - n\gamma^2) - \gamma(6w\beta - n\gamma^2)].$$

indicative planning program, designed to compensate for the absence of futures markets, is a process where the planning information comes from querying individual agents about their future intentions. Because the needs of the planning system and the needs of individual agents do not coincide, individual agents will have little incentive to collect voluntarily the information needed by the central planner.

The government can encourage more information collection by establishing penalties for divergence from announced intentions. However, too much control can be just as damaging as too little information. One way of determining an appropriate degree of control is to let economic agents themselves decide. Even though the information supplied by an indicative plan is a public input, the demand-revealing process developed by Clark, Vickrey, and Groves and Loeb provides a method for determining whether a planning program would be beneficial, and if a program is established, how restrictive it should be.

UNIVERSITY OF DELAWARE

REFERENCES

Albin, Peter, "Uncertainty, Information Exchange and the Theory of Indicative Planning," *Economic Journal,* LXXXI (March 1971), 61–90.

Bonin, John, "On the Design of Managerial Incentive Structures in a Decentralized Planning Environment," *American Economic Review,* LXVI (Sept. 1976), 682–87.

Clarke, Edward H., "Multipart Pricing of Public Goods," *Public Choice,* XI (Fall 1971), 17–33.

Grossman, Sanford, "On the Efficiency of Competitive Stock Markets Where Traders Have Diverse Information," *Journal of Finance,* XXXI (May 1976), 573–85.

——, "A Characterization of the Optimality of Equilibrium in Incomplete Markets," *Journal of Economic Theory,* XV (June 1977), 1–15.

——, and Joseph E. Stiglitz, "Information and Competitive Pricing Systems," *American Economic Review,* LXVI (May 1976), 246–53.

Groves, Theodore, "Incentives in Teams," *Econometrica,* XLI (July 1973), 617–31.

——, and Martin Loeb, "Incentives and Public Inputs," *Journal of Public Economics,* IV (Aug. 1975), 211–26.

Hart, O., "On the Optimality of Equilibrium When Markets Are Incomplete," *Journal of Economic Theory,* XI (Dec. 1975), 418–43.

Hurwicz, Leonid, "On Informationally Decentralized Systems," in *Decisions and Organization: A Volume in Honor of Jacob Marschak,* pp. 297–336, C. B. McGuire and Roy Radner, eds. (Amsterdam: North-Holland Publishing Co., 1972).

——, "Pareto Optimality of the (Manipulation) Nash Equilibria for Prescribed Adjustment Rules," unpublished paper, University of California at Berkeley, April 1977.

Meade, James E., *The Theory of Indicative Planning* (Manchester: Manchester University Press, 1970).

Miller, Jeffrey, and James Thornton, "Effort, Uncertainty, and the New Soviet Incentive System," *Southern Economic Journal,* XLV (Oct. 1978), 432–46.

Radner, Roy, "Competitive Equilibrium Under Uncertainty," *Econometrica,* XXXVI (Jan. 1968), 31–58.

——, "Existence of Equilibrium of Plans, Prices and Price Expectation in a Sequence of Markets," *Econometrica,* XL (March 1972), 289–304.
——, "Rational Expectations Equilibrium with Price Information," unpublished paper, University of California, Berkeley, 1976.
Stigler, George, "Comments on Politics and Planning," unpublished paper presented at the Liberty Fund, Inc. Conference on Economic Planning and the American Constitutional System, December, 1975.
Vickrey, William, "Counterspeculation, Auctions, and Competitive Sealed Tenders," *Journal of Finance,* XVI (May 1961), 8–37.
Weitzman, Martin, "The New Soviet Incentive Model," *Bell Journal of Economics,* VII (Spring 1976), 251–57.

A MODEL OF INTERNATIONAL TRADE AND FINANCE*

LAURENCE WEISS

An equilibrium model of international trade, payments, and financial asset flows is developed with implications for the relationship between asset returns and changes in the relative prices of consumption goods of different countries. The model focuses on international trade as enlarging the opportunity for intertemporal exchange. The main source of uncertainty in the model is revisions of investors' expectations of the profitability of country-specific capital. The model is extended to include money to demonstrate how international monetary agreements may affect individual portfolio decisions.

The justification for a distinct theory of international capital asset price formation and portfolio composition rests upon a systematic relationship between asset returns and changes in the relative prices of consumption goods of investors of different countries.[1] Otherwise, the theory would be a simple extension of the single country model by modifying the original choice set to include foreign assets. On purely theoretical grounds, the relevant price index might vary among heterogeneous investors within a country as well as among investors of different countries. In order to explain observed asset holdings, it is necessary to make identifying restrictions on the sources of exogenous uncertainty, which influence aggregate returns and relative price changes.

In this paper an equilibrium model of international trade, payments, and financial asset flows is presented. The model lays no claim to generality; it has several special features that may prove useful to explain observed relationships. The basic characteristics of the model are the specification of consumer tastes, money demand, production technology, and the sources of exogenous uncertainty. The latter are taken to be revisions of expectations concerning the future productivity of capital, what Keynes called "the state of long term expectations." It will be shown that international trade and capital flows, variations in relative prices and exchange rates, and the return to alternative capital assets may all be explained as arising from unexpected changes in the state of long-term expectations in one country relative to those in its trading partner. I have examined elsewhere

* Financial support from NSF Grant SOC78-07299 is gratefully acknowledged. I wish to thank William Brainard, Carlos Diaz-Alejandro, Paul Krugman, and Albert Fishlow for their many helpful discussions and comments.

1. For example Solnik's [1974] international capital asset pricing model assumes that residents of each country consume a different good that is only produced domestically. This relationship precludes, however, trade in both commodities and financial assets.

The Quarterly Journal of Economics, September 1980 0033-5533/80/0095-0277$01.60

[Weiss, 1980a,b] the implications of this type of shock for closed economies. Those papers suggest that observed business cycles may arise from sudden, imperfectly perceived, changes in investor expectations. The ultimate source of this variability and the rationality of these beliefs, though important concerns, are largely irrelevant for analysis of their implications for current resource allocation. To capture the idea that expectations change suddenly, it is simplest to treat the yield to capital as if it were exogenously determined by the technology and to treat the pace of embodied technological progress as random.

The model assumes a particular structure of international trade that enlarges opportunities for intertemporal exchange. There is trade neither in physical capital goods, nor in some collection of domestically consumed goods. Potential exports are perfect consumption substitutes for potential importables, so that at any time merchandise trade flows in only one direction in return for financial assets. The model does not incorporate information lags that may be responsible for real effects associated with monetary phenomena. The model does suggest, however, an informational role for asset prices and exchange rates as disseminating structural information.[2] These factors may prove useful for explaining variations in utilization in open economies.

An important factor in explaining asset holdings is shown to be the time horizon of investors' prospective consumption streams. For those investors with relatively longer economic horizons, foreign assets will be held as a risk avoidance strategy, while myopic investors will find domestic assets to provide for more nearly certain consumption.

The paper is organized as follows: Section I describes the nonmonetary (Walrasian) model in the hope of integrating financial equilibrium relationships with international trade theory. This section examines the theoretical justification for asset preferences to depend upon both the country of residence and the relevant time horizon of investors. Section II introduces money in a somewhat ad hoc, but conventional manner, by postulating plausible money demand functions. This is analyzed both under the assumptions of country-specific money with an endogenous (flexible) exchange rate, and under the assumption of world money, equivalent to a regime of fixed exchange rates. Section III contains some interpretations of the results and the testable implications of the model.

2. Harris and Purvis [1979] developed a model in which the exchange rate was useful to infer the contemporaneous price level.

I. The Model

There are two symmetric countries, and three periods. There exist three distinct consumption commodities in periods 2 and 3; a good that is traded internationally and is consumed by residents of either country (T) and two other goods that are nontraded, the quantity of which in the home country is denoted by N, and in the foreign country by N'. The second period permits the production of country-specific capital goods (I_2 and I_2', respectively), which are not physically traded internationally, although financial claims to their output are exchanged.

In the home country the ordinal preferences of each agent may be described by a Cobb-Douglas utility function,

$$U = \log N_2 + \log T_2 + \log N_3 + \log T_3 \tag{1}$$

(subscripts refer to time periods).

The aggregate production opportunities in the home country are described by the following relationship:

$$N_2^2 + T_2^2 + I_2^2 = K_2^2 \tag{2}$$

$$K_3 = I_2 \tag{3}$$

$$N_3^2 + T_3^2 = \tilde{x}K_3^2, \tag{4}$$

where $\tilde{x}$ is an index of productivity of period 3 capital specific to the home country, a random variable that is realized costlessly and publicly prior to period 2 trade. Thus, $\tilde{x}$ is an indication of the profitability of investment, corresponding to the state of long-term expectations. Note that the aggregate production opportunities for the four domestically produced consumables, given by

$$N_2^2 + T_2^2 + \frac{1}{x}N_3^2 + \frac{1}{x}T_3^2 = K_2^2, \tag{5}$$

are homogeneous of degree one, so that factor payments, which accrue exclusively to the holders of period 2 capital, exhaust the value of output. The tastes and production opportunities in the foreign country are identical. The index of productivity of period 3 foreign capital will be denoted by x'. All expectations of period 3 prices are held with certainty during period 2 trade. The revelation of the state of expectations is the only source of uncertainty in the model.[3]

3. The model does not consider the possibility of exchange controls or other uncertain government policies that may explain a relative preference for domestic assets.

The only economic activity that occurs in the first period is trade in claims to the capital stock. The valuation of these claims will depend upon relative goods prices, which are in turn influenced by asset holding patterns. The simultaneous determination of asset and goods prices will be aided considerably by assuming that initial endowments of capital are symmetric between the two countries, and that expectations of x and x' are homogeneous and symmetric. The x's will be assumed to be independently and identically distributed. By imposing symmetry on the resulting equilibrium, it may be assumed that the relative price of claims to the two kinds of first-period capital is one. The outcome of period one trade may be summarized by a scalar α ($0 \leq \alpha \leq 1$), which denotes the fraction of capital in each country that is owned by residents.[4] Given a particular value of α, the equilibrium prices of the six economically distinct final goods may be determined for each realization of x and x' by assuming competitive behavior. This will generate a joint probability distribution for asset returns and relative prices. The period 1 equilibrium must be such that each investor, taking as given this probability distribution and relative asset prices, is content to allocate a fraction α of his wealth to domestic assets. The particular α that emerges will be shown to depend upon attitudes toward risk as expressed by monotonic transformations at the specified ordinal preference ranking, and the relevant time horizon of investors.

Normalizing the price of second-period traded goods at one yields the five relative price relations (see Appendix I):

$$P_{N_2} = \frac{1}{2}(\alpha r^2 + 4(1-\alpha))^{1/2}, \qquad P_{N2}' = \frac{1}{2}(\alpha r'^2 + 4(1-\alpha))^{1/2},$$

$$P_{N_3} = \frac{1}{2}((\alpha r^2 + 4(1-\alpha))/x)^{1/2},$$

$$P_{N3}' = \frac{1}{2}((\alpha r'^2 + 4(1-\alpha))/x')^{1/2},$$

$$P_{T_2} = ((r + r')/(xr' + x'r))^{1/2},$$

where r and r' are the aggregate returns to capital at home and abroad. For the home country this number (in units of T_2) is given by

$$(6) \quad r^2 = \left(\frac{3-2\alpha}{2-\alpha}\right)\left(1 - \frac{x}{x'}\right) + \left[\left(\frac{3-2\alpha}{2-\alpha}\right)^2\left(\frac{x}{x'} - 1\right)^2 + 16\frac{x}{x'}\right]^{1/2}$$

For the foreign country x and x' are interchanged.

4. The possibility of short sales is not considered. I have not been able to find conditions that make this constraint binding.

It will prove useful to approximate the value of r by its first-order expansion about $x = x' = 1$. This is given by

$$r^2 \cong 4 + \frac{1}{(2-\alpha)}(dx - dx') \tag{7}$$

or

$$r \cong 2 + \frac{1}{4(2-\alpha)}(dx - dx'). \tag{7'}$$

Qualitatively, the equilibrium may be described in the following manner. A rise in productivity of investment in one country increases both the value of that country's capital stock (equal to current period GNP) and the fraction of resources used for investment, with an opposite and equal effect in its trading partner. In order to acquire capital in the now more productive country, residents of the now less productive country will be net exporters of current period consumables. This will raise the price of period 2 nontradeables in the importing country relative to traded goods, and lower the relative price of nontradeables in the exporting country. This is equivalent to saying that price of a representative basket of consumables in the importing country rises relative to the price of the equivalent basket of period 2 consumables in the exporting country. Thus, each country's capital stock maintains a more constant purchasing power over a typical second-period basket of domestic consumption than would claims to foreign capital.

More precisely, the second-period price of nontraded home goods in terms of traded goods is given by the first-order approximation,

$$P_{N_2} \cong 1 + \frac{\alpha}{8(2-\alpha)}(dx - dx'), \tag{8}$$

which rises with domestic productivity as long as some capital is domestically owned ($\alpha > 0$). The balance of trade for the home country in period 2 is the difference between production of tradeables and consumption of tradeables, given by

$$T_2^S - T_2^D = \frac{1}{r} - \frac{\alpha r + (1-\alpha)r'}{4}, \tag{9}$$

which is approximately equal to $-(\alpha/4(2-\alpha))(dx - dx')$. A rise in relative productivity implies a deficit in the second-period current account and, necessarily in this Walrasian nonmonetary equilibrium, a surplus on the capital account.

Thus, the competitive equilibrium (the determination of all prices and quantities for each realization of x and x') is completely described by the share of capital domestically owned and the ordinal preferences of each agent. However, to predict the value of α, which emerges from first-period maximizing behavior requires knowledge of attitudes toward risk as represented by the von Neumann-Morgenstern (cardinal) utility function, and the relevant[5] price index for each investor.

If investors, whether through lack of foresight or in contemplation of mortality, are concerned only with period 2 consumption,[6] the relevant domestic price index would be $P_{T_2}^{1/2}P_{N_2}^{1/2}$. Thus, the ratio of the price index for consumers in the home country to consumers in the foreign country would be $P_{T_2}^{1/2}P_{N_2}^{1/2}/P_{T_2}^{1/2}P_{N'_2}^{1/2}$, which has a first-order approximation of $1 + [\alpha/4(2-\alpha)](dx - dx')$. Consumers of goods in the country with bullish expectations require more wealth (evaluated in units of T_2, the numeraire) to achieve the same utility as consumers in the bearish country.

However, this relationship is reversed if agents have two-period time horizons. The increased productivity of period 3 capital raises the supply of period 3 nontraded consumption goods and thus lowers their relative price. The ratio of period 3 consumption goods prices between the two countries is $P_{N_3}P_{T_3}/P_{N'_3}$ which has a first-order approximation of $1 - [(3\alpha + 8)/4(2-\alpha)](dx - dx')$, which declines with a relative increase in home country capital productivity. The relevant price index for agents who contemplate consumption in both periods is, for the stated ordinal preferences, the geometric mean of each period's price index. The ratio of this index between the home and foreign country falls with an increase in relative productivity:

$$\text{(10)} \qquad \frac{P_{N_2}^{1/4}P_{T_2}^{1/4}P_{N_3}^{1/4}P_{T_3}^{1/4}}{P_{N'_2}^{1/4}P_{T_2}^{1/4}P_{N'_3}^{1/4}P_{T_3}} = \left[\frac{\alpha r^2 + 4(1-\alpha)}{\alpha r'^2 + 4(1-\alpha)}\right]^{1/4}\left[\frac{x'}{x}\right]^{1/8}$$

$$\cong 1 - \frac{1-\alpha}{8(2-\alpha)}(dx - dx').$$

Ordinal utility may be described as an increasing function of nominal wealth deflated by the correct price index. To characterize how agents trade wealth across states requires knowledge of cardinal preferences, unique up to a positive linear transformation. For ex-

5. The price index depends only upon ordinal preferences. Grauer, Litzenburger, and Stehle [1976] used a similar index in their international capital market paper. However, the index was identical across countries.

6. The case of myopic investors requires the introduction of new period 2 agents in both countries endowed with labor services who can substitute consumption between periods 2 and 3. This modification would not change the qualitative equilibrium properties.

ample, it is well-known that if the cardinal utility function is additive in the logarithms of the quantities consumed, then the indirect utility function is

(11) $$\log W - \log \prod_i P_i^{\alpha_i},$$

where W = nominal wealth, α_i = fraction of income spent upon good i, and P_i = price of the ith good. In this case the indirect utility function is separable in income and prices, and each investor would seek to maximize the expected logarithm of nominal wealth, independent of his particular price index. Because of the assumed symmetry of the initial situation, the outcome of period 1 trading would be that $\alpha = 1/2$, so that each investor would have an identical portfolio with half of his wealth invested at home and half invested in foreign assets.[7]

However, suppose that cardinal utility is expressed by

(12) $$U(X) = F\left(\sum_i \alpha_i \log x_i\right), \quad F' > 0.$$

Then the indirect utility function is

(13) $$V(W, P) = F\left(\log W - \log \prod_i P_i^{\alpha_i}\right),$$

and the marginal utility of wealth is given by

(14) $$\frac{\partial V}{\partial W} = \frac{1}{W} F'\left(\log W - \log \prod_i P_i^{\alpha_i}\right).$$

A rise in the price index will raise the marginal utility of nominal wealth if

(15) $$\frac{\partial^2 V}{\partial W \partial \left(\prod_i P_i^{\alpha_i}\right)} = -\frac{1}{W\left(\prod_i P_i^{\alpha_i}\right)} F''\left(\log W - \log \prod_i P_i^{\alpha_i}\right)$$

7. The problem of each agent in period 1 may be defined as selecting the α that maximizes

$$E\left[\log \alpha r + (1-\alpha)r' - \log \prod_i P^{\alpha_i}\right].$$

The necessary first-order condition for this problem is

$$E\frac{r - r'}{\alpha r + (1-\alpha)r'} = 0,$$

which at $\alpha = 1/2$ equals $E[(r - r')/(1/2 r + 1/2 r')]$, which by symmetry equals 0, establishing that $\alpha = 1/2$ is the unique equilibrium.

is positive, which occurs if $F'' < 0$, or when investors are more risk-averse than the logarithm.[8]

In the present analysis, this implies that, if agents have two-period consumption horizons, domestic assets will comprise the dominant share of each portfolio ($\alpha > 1/2$) when investors are less risk-averse than the logarithm, and favor foreign assets in the opposite case (see Appendix II). However, if investors are concerned only with the utility of period 2 consumption, the qualitative results of equilibrium portfolio composition are reversed, with domestic assets affording relatively safer consumption streams. In this way investors guarantee for themselves high nominal returns when the marginal utility of wealth, for any fixed level of nominal wealth is relatively high.

II. An Ad Hoc Monetary Model

In this section money is added to the model with the hope of integrating the determinants of exchange rate movements, inflation, and balance of payments phenomena with the real sector of the economy. This will be done first under the assumption that the relative price of currencies is endogenous, corresponding to a case of national currencies and freely floating exchange rates. This extension will be assumed to have no effect on the Walrasian equilibrium previously described. Its purpose is to try to show why domestic currency might be relatively safer in terms of domestic consumption than foreign currency, or equivalently why exchange rate flexibility is a partial substitute for money price flexibility. The analysis then considers a world of fixed exchange rates, which is modeled by assuming that there is world money. In this case foreign trade and capital accumulation may be financed by running down real cash balances that may affect relative prices.

In both situations, the approach taken is consistent with what has been called "the monetary approach to the balance of payments."[9] This views the determinant of the exchange rate under flexible exchange rates, and the balance of payments under fixed rates, to be the relative demands for real money balances in the two countries. The supplies of nominal monies are fixed; the model does

8. An agent with a utility function $U(\quad)$ is said to be more risk-averse than an agent with a utility function $V(\quad)$ if and only if there exists a concave, increasing function $F(\quad)$ such that $U = F(V(\quad))$.

9. This analysis of exchange rate and determination may be found in Hahn [1959], Dornbusch [1973a and b], Frenkel and Rodriguez [1976], and Kouri and Porter [1975].

not analyze the effects of either anticipated or unanticipated changes in money supply.

A. Flexible Exchange Rates

The ratio of final period real money balances between the two countries is assumed to be influenced primarily by the division of real output. Thus,

$$\left(\frac{M}{P}\right)_3^D \Big/ \left(\frac{M}{P'}\right)_3^D = 1 + K_1\left(\frac{Y_3}{Y_3'} - 1\right), \qquad K_1 > 0, \tag{16}$$

where Y_3/Y_3' is the ratio of third-period production in the home country relative to its trading partner. The justification for this money demand function is that money is basically used to facilitate domestic transactions, the values of which are proportional to the value of production. Since both countries have access to the same international capital market, the influence of interest rates on relative money demand is neglected. P and P' are the domestic and foreign money price indexes of the *same* basket of world consumption. The exchange rate, defined as e units of foreign currency per unit of domestic currency may be defined as equal to P'/P, so that variations in the exchange rate equilibrates the relative demands for real money balances.

The ratio of third-period production between the two countries is

$$\begin{aligned}\frac{P_{N_3}N_3 + P_{T_3}T_3^S}{P_{N_3'}N_3' + P_{T_3}T_3^{S\prime}} &= \left[\frac{4-\alpha}{4}r + \frac{\alpha-2}{r}\right] \Big/ \left[\frac{4-\alpha}{4}r' + \frac{\alpha-2}{r'}\right] \\ &\cong 1 + \frac{3-\alpha}{4(2-\alpha)}(dx - dx').\end{aligned} \tag{17}$$

The nominal supply of each type of national currency is taken to be one unit. Initial money endowments are exclusively in the domestic currency, and there is no forward market in currency. Money market equilibrium implies that

$$e \equiv \frac{1}{P_3} \Big/ \left(\frac{1}{P_3}\right)' = 1 + k_1\left(\frac{3-\alpha}{4(2-\alpha)}(dx - dx')\right). \tag{18}$$

An increase in domestic productivity ($dx > 0$) can be seen to induce higher real domestic income, the need for relatively greater real cash balances, and an appreciation of the exchange rate.

Second-period money demand is modified to the extent that inflationary expectations differ between the two countries. Suppose that

$$\left(\frac{M}{P_2}\right)^D \Big/ \left(\frac{M'}{P_2}\right)^D = 1 + k_2\left(\frac{Y_2}{Y_2'} - 1\right) - k_2\left(\frac{\pi}{\pi'} - 1\right)^{\text{expected}}, \tag{19}$$

where $\pi = (P_3/P_2)^{\text{expected}}$, and $\pi' = (P_3'/P_2')^{\text{expected}}$, equal to one plus the expected inflation rate. The demand for real balances increases with real income, and decreases with expected inflation. Since π/π' equals e_2/e_3, the term $(\pi/\pi') - 1$ will be approximated by its first-order expansion $e_2 - e_3$. Substitute the ratio of relative real second-period real income between the two countries,

$$\frac{r}{r'} \cong 2 + \frac{1}{4(2-\alpha)}(dx - dx'), \tag{20}$$

and assume that agents have correct ("rational") point expectations of future inflation rates. Therefore, second-period equilibrium in the money market implies that

$$\begin{aligned} e_2 &\equiv \frac{1}{P_2} \Big/ \left(\frac{1}{P_2}\right)' \\ &= 1 + k_1\left(\left(1 + (2-\alpha)\frac{k_2}{1+k_2}\right) \Big/ 4(2-\alpha)\right)(dx - dx') \end{aligned} \tag{21}$$

and

$$(e_2 - e_3) = \frac{-1}{4(1+k_2)}(dx - dx'). \tag{22}$$

The exchange rate movement in the second period is greater than what could be explained solely by changes in current period real income. The excess represents anticipation of future differential inflation and exchange rate movements. The relative discrepancy in period 3 production is $(3 - \alpha)$ times as great as the percentage disparity in period 2 production. This is because all investors seek to acquire capital in the country with the higher productivity. The movement in the real value of each currency will be qualitatively similar to the movement in the relative price of that country's non-traded good. Each national currency will maintain a more constant period 2 purchasing power over a representative domestic consumption bundle than would foreign currency.[10] This does not arise

10. This theoretical conclusion has received empirical support. Kouri and de Macedo [1978] report that domestic currency will dominate the portfolios of minimum variance real purchasing power in the case of Germany, the United Kingdom, and the United States, but not for France or Japan.

from the failure of prices to reach their market clearing values instantaneously, but is the solution to an admittedly simplified and somewhat ad hoc general equilibrium system.

Flexibility of exchange rates serves to lessen the burden of adjustment in relative prices borne by changes in money prices, since the relative price of nontraded goods and the value of domestic currency are affected similarly by revisions in the long-term state. It would be possible for the domestic money price of nontraded goods to be invariant to changes in the expected productivity of capital and to leave the burden of adjustment in relative prices to the exchange rate and the money price of traded goods.

The theory presented is an explicit alternative to the purchasing power parity theory of exchange rate determination. Those shocks that cause an increase in the value of that country's currency also raise the equilibrium value of that country's nontraded good, and hence the price of all consumables. Hence, the purchasing power of an appreciating currency over a basket of domestic consumption will be less than the purchasing power of a depreciating currency over its domestic counterpart. Over time, however, the relative price of consumables will fall in the appreciating country because of superior productivity, and the once overvalued currency will appear undervalued by the purchasing power criterion.

B. *Fixed Exchange Rates*

Under fixed exchange rates a country can finance the acquisition of capital or goods by running down real cash balances. The transfer of real resources effected by exporting money can affect relative prices.

Let Z be the size of the transfer of real resources to the home country financed by exporting money. Positive Z implies a balance of payments deficit for the home country. This will be spent like any other income, which will alter relative prices and factor rewards. The return to domestic capital will increase by $Z/4 - 2\alpha$ (see Appendix III), and the aggregate return to foreign capital will decrease by the same amount.

Suppose that the relative demand for money in each country in the third period is dependent upon the ratio of the value of aggregate production:

$$(23)\quad \left(\frac{M}{P}\right)_3^D \Big/ \frac{M}{P}^{\prime D=1+k_1}\left(\frac{Y_3}{Y_3'}-1\right)=k_1\left[\frac{P_{T_3}T_3^S+P_{N_3}N_3}{P_{T_3}T_3^{S'}+P_{N_3}'N_3'-1}\right],$$

which equals[11]

$$(24)\qquad 1 + k_1\left[\left(\frac{3-\alpha}{4(2-\alpha)}\right)(dx - dx') + \left(\frac{5-2\alpha}{2(2-\alpha)}\right)Z\right].$$

Since the exchange rate is assumed to be fixed, the demand and supply of money between the two countries is equilibriated by a flow of Z percent of the value of currency from the home to the foreign country. Equilibrium implies that

$$(25)\qquad \frac{1-Z}{1+Z} = \left(\frac{M}{P}\right)_3^D \Big/ \left(\frac{M}{P}\right)_3^{\prime D}$$

or[12]

$$Z = -\left[\frac{3-\alpha}{26-12\alpha}\right](dx - dx').$$

Thus, the flow of real resources from the country with high productivity to the other country reduces the decline in income for any size exogenous shock. In each country there will be less variability in the return to capital than under flexible exchange rates, since the transfer of real resources is opposite in sign from the random disturbance and accrues partly to the holders of capital.

It would be erroneous, however, to conclude that monetary integration achieves something that could not be duplicated through private channels. If a market for forward delivery of currency existed, then the private economy could duplicate the transfer of resources effected by fixed exchange rates by agreeing to deliver forward a fixed quantity of domestic currency in return for foreign currency at a specified price. In this way each agent insures himself against a decline in the value of his own portfolio induced by the relative decline in the productivity of investment in his home country.

11. Third-period production in the home country is equal to

$$P_{N_3}N_3 + P_{T_3}T_3^S,$$

which is equal to $(4 - \alpha/4)r + (\alpha - 2/r) + Z/4$. The first-order approximation at $Z = 0, r = 2$ is given by

$$1 + (3-\alpha)/2\, dr + \tfrac{1}{4}dZ,$$

where $dr = [1/4(2-\alpha)]\,(dx - dx') + [1/2(2-\alpha)]dZ$ so that third-period production is

$$1 + \frac{3-\alpha}{8(2-\alpha)}(dx - dx') + \frac{5-2\alpha}{4(2-\alpha)}dZ.$$

For the foreign country, the change in production is of opposite sign and of the same magnitude, so that the percentage discrepancy is doubled, yielding expression (23) in the text.

12. Approximating expression (24) by $1 - 2Z$.

III. Conclusion

This paper has set forth a model of international trade and capital flows in which asset preferences depend upon investors' relevant consumption sets. These differ across investors of different countries because some consumption goods are not traded internationally. Within a country the relevant consumption sets might vary among agents with different consumption time horizons.

The principal result is that bullish expectations in one country raise not only the proportion of resources devoted to capital formation, but also the return to existing capital and the relative price of nontraded goods in this country. Over time, the greater productivity of domestic capital will increase the supply of nontraded goods and make them cheaper relative to their foreign counterparts.

Although the treatment of money in the model is not wholly satisfactory,[13] the explicit characterization of sources of aggregate uncertainty may help to explain the co-movements between exchange rates and relative price changes. The model confirms a widely held proposition among international trade theorists that internal price stability may be inconsistent with exchange rate stability. Those shocks that cause an appreciation in the value of the domestic country also raise the relative price of nontraded goods. Thus, part of the adjustment in relative prices is borne by exchange rate movements, which leaves a smaller burden of adjustment in the domestic money price of nontraded goods. If, because of factors not included in the model, downward price adjustments are accompanied by low rates of utilization,[14] flexible exchange rates may avoid undesirable fluctuations in aggregate income that would occur under fixed rates.

The model also illustrates the types of private portfolio adjustments that could be expected to accompany a switch from fixed to flexible exchange rates. The use of the forward market to hedge against unexpected changes in exchange rates is well-known. However, because the return to domestic capital moves in the same direction as the external value of domestic currency, the model predicts that ownership in claims to foreign capital can substitute, at least partially, for hedging in the forward market in foreign exchange. In this way the private economy will share those risks that were implicitly borne by agreeing to accept each other's currency at a fixed exchange rate.

13. A more complete analysis would integrate money holdings with claims to private capital as a way of intermediating intertemporal exchange.

14. One factor that could explain aggregate fluctuations in aggregate output is the limited information transmitted by observation of money price signals. This idea was suggested by Lucas [1972].

Private international financial relationships can substitute for international monetary cooperation.

Perhaps the most important feature of the model is its emphasis on the role of expectations of the profitability of new investment for determination of exchange rates and investment flows. This view leads to the conclusion that exchange rate movements will be of the same direction as domestic capital values. Thus, the model stands in contrast to previous monetarist approaches to the balance of payments that have primarily examined the responses to unanticipated changes in the supply of nominal balances [Frenkel and Rodriguez, 1976]. Such monetary shocks could be expected to cause divergent movements between the external value of domestic currency and the money price of claims to real capital assets.

APPENDIX

I

In the home country firms seek to

$$\text{maximize } P_{N_2}N_2 + T_2 + P_{N_3}N_3 + P_{T_3}T_3$$

$$\text{subject to } N_2^2 + T_2^2 + \frac{1}{x}N_3^2 + \frac{1}{x}T_3^2 = K_2^2,$$

to which the optimal solution is

$$N_2^S = \frac{P_{N_2}}{r}, \quad T_2^S = \frac{1}{r}, \quad T_3^S = \frac{xP_{T_2}}{r}, \quad N_3^S = \frac{xP_{N_3}}{r},$$

where r equals the shadow price on a unit of domestic capital.

Let $W = \alpha r + (1-\alpha)r'$ be the income accruing to domestic residents, and W' be the income to foreigners. Then demand for the nontraded goods is given by $N_2^D = (W/4P_{N_2})$ and $N_3^D = (W/4P_{N_3})$ so that $P_{N_2} = (rW/4)^{1/2}$ and $P_{N_3} = (rW/4x)^{1/2}$.

The world demand for traded goods is given by

$$T_2^D + T_2^{D'} = \frac{r+r'}{4}, \qquad T_3^D + T_3^{D'} = \frac{r+r'}{4P_{T_3}},$$

which must equal world supply

$$T_2^S + T_2^{S'} = \frac{1}{r} + \frac{1}{r'}, \quad T_3^S + T_3^{S'} = xP_{T_3}\left(\frac{1}{r} + \frac{1}{r'}\right).$$

yielding the equilibrium price relationships $rr' = 4$ and $P_{T_3} = ((r+r')/(xr'+rx'))$.

II

The necessary first-order conditions for a competitive equilibrium are that in the home country

$$\frac{\partial EU}{\partial \alpha} = E\left[\frac{r-r'}{W} F'\left(\log W - \log \prod_i P_i^{\alpha}\right)\right] = 0$$

and in the foreign country

$$\frac{\partial EU'}{\partial \alpha} = E\left[\frac{r'-r}{W'} F'\left(\log W' - \log \prod_i P_i^{\alpha'}\right)\right] = 0,$$

which at $\alpha = \frac{1}{2}$ imply that

$$\frac{\partial EU}{\partial \alpha} + \frac{\partial EU'}{\partial \alpha} = E\left[\left(\frac{r-r'}{r/2+r'/2}\right)\left(F'\left(\log W - \log \prod_i P_i^{\alpha}\right) - F'\left(\log W - \log \prod_i P_i^{\alpha'}\right)\right)\right].$$

The first term in the expression is increasing in (x/x'). It has been demonstrated that $\log \Pi_i P_i^{\alpha i} - \log \Pi_i P_i^{\alpha' i}$ is decreasing in x/x' so that if F' is increasing $(F'' > 0)$, the term in the second parentheses $[F'(\log(r/2 + r'/2) - \log \Pi_i P_i^{\alpha i}) - F'(\log(r/2 + r'/2) - \log \Pi_i P_i^{\alpha' i})]$ is increasing in (x/x'), and decreasing if $F'' < 0$. Thus, the expression is positive, negative, 0, as F'' is positive, negative, 0. This implies that the sum of expected utility will increase with an increase in α at $\alpha = \frac{1}{2}$ if $F'' > 0$, which by symmetry implies that both agents' expected utility will increase.

III

Because of the particular pattern of trade, a transfer will not affect nominal demand for tradeables. In the home (receiving) country the demand for nontradeables becomes $N_2^D = (Y+Z)/4P_{N_2}$ and $N_3^D = (Y+Z)/4P_{N_3}$. Market clearing implies that

$$r^2 = \left(\frac{rY}{2} + 1 + \frac{Z}{2} + \frac{r^2+4}{r^2(x'/x)+4}\right),$$

which, after some manipulation becomes

$$r^2 = \left(\frac{3-2\alpha}{2-\alpha}\right)\left(1-\frac{x}{x'}\right) + \frac{Z}{2-\alpha} + \left[\left(\left(\frac{3-2\alpha}{2-\alpha}\right)\left(\frac{x}{x'}-1\right) - \frac{2}{4-2\alpha}\right)^2 + 16\frac{x}{x'} - \frac{4Z}{2-\alpha}\frac{x}{x'}\right]^{1/2}$$

so that

$$\left.\frac{\partial r^2}{\partial Z}\right|_{T=0} = \frac{1}{2-\alpha} - \frac{4/(2-\alpha)}{2\sqrt{16}} = \frac{1}{2(2-\alpha)}.$$

YALE UNIVERSITY

REFERENCES

Dornbusch, R., "Currency Depreciation, Hoarding and Relative Prices," *Journal of Political Economy*, LXXI (July/Aug. 1973a), 893–915.

——, "Devaluation, Money and Non-Traded Goods," *American Economic Review,* LXIII (Dec. 1973b), 871–80.
Frenkel, J. A., and C. H. Rodriguez, "Portfolio Equilibrium and the Balance of Payments: A Monetary Approach," *American Economic Review,* LXVI (May 1976), 163–70.
Grauer, F. L. A., R. H. Litzenburger, and R. E. Stehle, "Sharing Rules and Equilibrium in an International Capital Market under Uncertainty," *Journal of Financial Economics,* III (June 1976), 233–57.
Hahn, F., "The Balance of Payments in a Monetary Economy," *Review of Economic Studies,* XXVI (Feb. 1959), 110–25.
Harris, R. G., and D. Purvis, "Diverse Information and Market Efficiency in a Monetary Model of the Exchange Rate," Queens University, unpublished, 1979.
Kouri, P. J. K., and M. G. Porter, "International Capital Flows and Portfolio Equilibrium," *Journal of Political Economy,* LXXXII (May/June 1974), 443–46.
Kouri, P. J. K., and J. B. de Macedo, "Exchange Rates and the International Adjustment Process," *Brookings Papers on Economic Activity* (1978:1), 111–51.
Lucas, R. E., "Expectations and the Neutrality of Money," *Journal of Economic Theory,* IV (April 1972), 103–24.
Solnik, B., "An Equilibrium Model of the International Capital Market," *Journal of Economic Theory,* VIII (Aug. 1974), 500–24.
Weiss, L., "The Role for Active Monetary Policy in a Rational Expectations Model," *Journal of Political Economy,* LXXXVIII (April 1980a), 221–34.
——, "The Effects of Money Supply on Economic Welfare in the Steady State," *Econometrica,* XLVIII (April 1980b), 565–77.

THE REGIONAL DISTRIBUTION OF POPULATION, MIGRATION, AND CLIMATE*

DONALD R. HAURIN

Regional migration is analyzed utilizing a model that develops a system of urban areas. The areas differ in their endowment of a site-specific factor—climate is used as the example. The effects of differences in tax rates and technology are determined in a model where the price of housing is endogenous. Compensation for an inferior climate occurs through regional differences in income levels or the price of housing, dependent on the manner in which climate affects production or consumption. The market distribution of households is found to be suboptimal in cases where utility is derived directly from the consumption of climate.

The locational choice of households is determined by a variety of factors. Recent contributions concentrating on climatic variations are Graves [1979], Graves and Linneman [1979], and Izraeli [1973]. A problem with the migration literature has been the lack of specification of a model that contains a system of urbanized areas. The model should determine the equilibrium size of urban areas. The migration flow results from the adjustment of the stock of population to changes in exogenous variables.

In the model developed, households are assumed to choose a location such that utility levels are equalized across the economy. Climatic differences take the form of a nontraded and nonproducible public good.[1] In general, one would expect this site-specific factor to enter both production and consumption decisions. Some form of compensation must occur across urban areas through wage or price of housing differentials. One goal of the model is to distinguish when a certain form of compensation will predominate. After establishing an initial equilibrium, a series of parametric variations are analyzed to determine the change in the spatial distribution of population. The direction of migration and changes in the forms of compensation are presented. Of special interest is a test of the Mieszkowski [1972] hypothesis that property taxes can be separated into a uniform national tax and local differentials.

The regional distribution of households is investigated, and the efficiency of the market allocation is also considered. In other works

* I wish to thank William Oakland and other members of the public finance seminar at Ohio State for their comments on this work.

1. The general class of public goods is excluded, since public goods can be produced at any location. To obtain higher levels of a local public good, the community could increase quantity supplied. However, to change quantities of the site-specific factor, migration must occur.

The Quarterly Journal of Economics, September 1980 0033-5533/80/0095-0293$01.60

by Flatters, Henderson, and Mieszkowski [1974], and Buchanan and Goetz [1972], the efficiency of regional allocation was studied in a world composed of nonspatial urban areas. Their work is extended with the incorporation of an urban housing sector with an endogenous and spatially variant price of housing. This model is more restricted in terms of the type of public good analyzed.

I. The Market Allocation of Population

In this model a system of cities based on the existence of site-specific factors is analyzed.[2] The site-specific factor compensates for the additional costs of urban living compared with those in rural areas. The model can generate a complete system of cities.

However, to obtain results relevant for migration: only two areas are required. Initially, the cities are assumed identical in production technology except for the level of the site-specific factor. Households are homogeneous and fully mobile. The model allocates a fixed total population between areas determining the equalized utility level.

The following model is developed with the assumptions of specific functional forms. This restriction allows for the solution of the endogenous price of housing and utility levels. The areas of study are assumed to specialize in the production of a traded good X. The production function is

$$X_i = (Q_i C_i)^{\delta} L_{x_i}^{1-\delta} \qquad 0 < \delta < 1, \tag{1}$$

where

C_i = index of climate in area i

Q_i = index of site-specific technology

L_{x_i} = labor utilized in export good production.

It is assumed that a good climate has a positive effect on the production of the exported good. Given competition, the wage rate is[3]

$$w_i = p_x(1-\delta) Q_i^{\delta} C_i^{\delta} L_{x_i}^{-\delta}. \tag{2}$$

Since X is sold in a national market, p_x is assumed constant across urban areas. The difference between revenues in the export sector and its labor costs accrues to the site-specific factor in the form of land rentals.

Households derive utility from the consumption of two traded goods, (x,y), a locally produced but nontraded good (h, housing ser-

2. This form of model was first developed by Charles Upton [1976]. An alternative model would be one based on economies of scale in production [Henderson, 1977].

3. Wages are per year as are expenditures on consumption goods.

vices), and directly from a beneficial climate. Climate is assumed to increase utility as a consumption good, perhaps the ideal being a year-round temperature of 72°–74°F. The assumption is made that the characteristics of climate relevant for production are also relevant for consumption. Thus, the same index can be utilized:

$$U_i = x_i^{\alpha 1} y_i^{\alpha 2} h_i^{\alpha 3} C_i^{\theta}, \tag{3}$$

where $\alpha_1 + \alpha_2 + \alpha_3 = 1$ and $\theta \geq 0$. The household's budget constraint is

$$p_x x_i + p_y y_i + p_{h_i} h_i = w_i + z_i, \tag{4}$$

where $z_i > 0$ represents a neutral return of land rentals to city residents. If $z_i = 0$, then workers are renters of housing with land rentals paid to nonresident landlords. The other extreme assumes all land rentals are paid to a city land bank [Henderson, 1977] with an equal per capita return made to households. It will be demonstrated that the market allocation of households is in many cases independent of the value of z. The distinction will become important when the optimal distribution of households is considered.

The demand equations for the three purchased goods derived from utility maximization are[4]

$$p_x x_i = \alpha_1 (w_i + z_i) \tag{5}$$

$$p_y y_i = \alpha_2 (w_i + z_i) \tag{6}$$

$$p_{h_i} h_i = \alpha_3 (w_i + z_i). \tag{7}$$

Substitution of (5)–(7) into (3) and (4) yields an indirect utility function:

$$\begin{aligned} U_i &= K_0 C_i^{\theta} p_{h_i}^{-\alpha 3} (w_i + z_i) \\ K_0 &= \alpha_1^{\alpha 1} \alpha_2^{\alpha 2} \alpha_3^{\alpha 3} p_x^{-\alpha 1} p_y^{-\alpha 2}. \end{aligned} \tag{8}$$

The model's housing sector appears nonspatial in nature, but it reacts with the characteristics of a spatial housing market aggregated across the urban area. The production function for housing in area i is

$$H_i = (A_i C_i)^{\sigma} L_{h_i}^{1-\sigma} \quad 0 < \sigma < 1, \tag{9}$$

where L_{h_i} = labor used in the production of housing and A_i is a con-

4. The relative price of the traded goods is determined by considering the trade between cities specializing in the production of X, those specializing in the production of Y, and the landowners.

stant. A beneficial climate is assumed to be a positive input to housing production; for example, construction is more efficient in a warm dry climate. In competition, the price of housing can be determined from the marginal product of labor and the constraint that all urban labor be paid a uniform wage (no skill differences are assumed):

$$p_{h_i} = w_i\left(\frac{\partial L_{h_i}}{\partial H_i}\right) = \frac{w_i}{1-\sigma} L_{h_i} H_i^{-1}. \tag{10}$$

The difference between housing revenues and the payment to labor is interpreted as land rentals. If households are landowners, their return is determined from total land rentals in the export and local production sectors:

$$z_i = (\delta(1-\delta)^{-1} w_i L_{x_i} + \sigma(1-\sigma)^{-1} w_i L_{h_i}) L_i^{-1}. \tag{11}$$

The value of z_i can be specified once the division of labor between sectors is known.

Aggregate housing demand is

$$H_i^d = L_i h_i = \alpha_3(w_i + z_i) L_i p_{h_i}^{-1}, \tag{12}$$

where L_i is the total population of area i. Equating (12) and (10) yields the allocation of labor in production:

$$L_{h_i} = \alpha_3(1-\sigma)(1+\psi_i)L_i; \tag{13}$$

and

$$L_{x_i} = (1 - \alpha_3(1-\sigma)(1+\psi_i))L_i, \tag{14}$$

where $\psi_i = z_i/w_i$ and $\psi_i = 0$ represents nonresident landowners. The value of ψ_i is found by substituting (13) and (14) into (11) and simplifying:

$$\psi_i = \frac{\delta - \delta\alpha_3 + \sigma\alpha_3}{1 - \delta + \delta\alpha_3 - \sigma\alpha_3} > 0. \tag{15}$$

Note that if the parameter values in (15) are identical between urban areas, then ψ will not vary regionally.

The endogenous price of housing in area i is obtained by substituting (9) and (13) into (12):

$$p_{h_i} = \alpha_3^{\sigma}(1-\sigma)^{\sigma-1} A^{-\sigma}(1+\psi_i)^{\sigma} w_i L_i^{\sigma} C_i^{-\sigma}. \tag{16}$$

The cost of living in the city increases with the total population size of the city holding constant the wage rate, a result characteristic of urban areas.

The level of utility is derived from (2), (8), and (16):

$$(17) \qquad U_i = K_1 Q_i^{\delta(1-\alpha_3)} C_i^{\theta + K_2} L_i^{-K_2}$$

$$K_1 = K_0(\alpha_3^{\sigma}(1-\sigma)^{\sigma-1}A^{-\sigma})^{-\alpha_3}(p_x(1-\delta))^{1-\alpha_3} \times (1-\alpha_3(1-\sigma)(1+\psi_i))^{-\delta(1-\alpha_3)}(1+\psi_i)^{1-\alpha_3\sigma}$$

$$K_2 = \delta(1-\alpha_3) + \alpha_3\sigma \qquad 1 > K_2 > 0.$$

The two areas of study are assumed to be related such that region 1 has been endowed with a better climate, $C_1 > C_2$. Since labor is mobile, equilibrium is attained when $U_1 = U_2$. The relative sizes of population, wages, and the price of housing are determined from (2), (16), and (17). The presentation of the results will separate the effect of climate on production from that on consumption and then indicate the composite result.

A. Climate Affects Export Good Production Only

The solutions are presented in logarithmic form, first comparing the relative size of the two areas, if $\psi_1 = \psi_2$:

$$(18) \qquad \ln\left(\frac{L_1}{L_2}\right) = \frac{\delta(1-\alpha_3)}{K_2} \ln\left(\frac{C_1}{C_2}\right).$$

Inspection of (18) indicates that $L_1 > L_2$; the city with the better climate is larger. Labor is drawn to this region due to higher wages in the export sector. Equilibrium is reestablished, as the price of housing increases and the additional population lowers the marginal productivity of labor. Specifically,

$$(19) \qquad \ln(w_1/w_2) = (\delta\alpha_3\sigma/K_2)\ln(C_1/C_2),$$

and

$$(20) \qquad \ln(p_{h_1}/p_{h_2}) = (\sigma\delta/K_2)\ln(C_1/C_2).$$

Thus, $w_1 > w_2$, and $p_{h_1} > p_{h_2}$. The compensation for the inferior climate occurs through the lowered price of housing in the smaller city in region 2. Related results are that $h_1 < h_2$ and $p_{h_1}h_1 > p_{h_2}h_2$. A smaller quantity of housing is consumed in the city with good climate, but expenditures are greater.

B. Climate Affects Consumption Only

In this case, $L_1 > L_2$, since the beneficial climate attracts households. This effect is dependent on θ, a parameter that indicates the degree to which climate affects household's utility:

$$(21) \qquad \ln(L_1/L_2) = (\theta/K_2)\ln(C_1/C_2).$$

With no difference in production technology, the relatively larger number of workers in area 1 decreases wage rates, $w_1 < w_2$:

(22) $$\ln(w_1/w_2) = -(\delta\theta/K_2)\ln(C_1/C_2).$$

This result, dependent on diseconomies of scale in city size, tends to offset the effect of climate on the export sector. The compensation for an inferior climate is partially through a higher wage level in that area, and there may be reinforcing differences in the price of housing.

(23) $$\ln(p_{h_1}/p_{h_2}) = (\theta/K_2)(\sigma - \delta)\ln(C_1/C_2).$$

In general $p_{h_1} \gtreqless p_{h_2}$ as $1 - \sigma \lesseqgtr 1 - \delta$, the parameters indicating the shares of labor production of housing and the export good. The price of housing is determined by both the productivity of labor in the housing sector and the wage level, determined in the export sector. If $1 - \sigma = 1 - \delta$, then there is an exact offset, and the price of housing does not change with variations in city size. In this case, the full compensation for climatic variation occurs through variations in the level of income. Other results are $h_1 < h_2$ and $p_{h_1}h_1 < p_{h_2}h_2$. This case reinforces the preceding one in that region 1 consumes a smaller quantity of housing per household, but expenditures are lower in this case.

C. Climate Affects Housing Production

If climate affects the productivity of labor in housing, then the market distribution of population results in the area with the good climate being larger:

(24) $$\ln(L_1/L_2) = \alpha_3\sigma/K_2\ln(C_1/C_2).$$

In response, the productivity of labor in the export sector falls, and wages are lower in the larger area:

(25) $$\ln(w_1/w_2) = -(\delta\alpha_3\sigma/K_2)\ln(C_1/C_2).$$

The decrease in wages is of exactly the same magnitude as the increase that results from considering the effect of climate on export good production. The combined production effects offset, and no differential in wages between areas would be expected. A similar result occurs for the price of housing:

(26) $$\ln(p_{h_1}/p_{h_2}) = -(\sigma\delta/K_2)\ln(C_1/C_2).$$

There are three effects on housing: a lowering of production costs due to the climatic advantage of region 1; the lowered cost of housing due to a smaller wage rate paid to labor utilized in housing; and the offsetting increase in costs due to the larger population. The net result is that the price of housing is lower in region 1, again an exactly offsetting quantity compared to the effect of climate on export good production. In this case, compensation for the variation in climate occurs through variations in the regional wage rate. The comparison of the three hypothesized effects of climate indicates that the form of compensation between regions depends on the manner in which climate affects production or consumption.

Aggregating the various influences of climate on the distribution of population results in

$$\ln(L_1/L_2) = ((\theta + K_2)/K_2)\ln(C_1/C_2). \tag{27}$$

Thus, $L_1 > L_2$. The separate effects of climate upon production and consumption all contribute to the relatively larger population size in region 1. It should be noted that this result is independent of the value of ψ if $\psi_1 = \psi_2$. If regional differences were solely climatic, the market allocation of population is independent of workers being renters or owners of housing. The wage rate and price of housing ratios (not levels) are also independent of ψ. The difference in wage rates results from the consumption effect. Thus, equation (22) describes the relative difference, $w_1 < w_2$. The region better endowed will have lower wage rates. The net effect upon the price of housing is given in equation (23); that is, it is dependent on a parameter's values. The observation of identical housing prices in the two regions[5] does not indicate a lack of independent effects of climate on housing, but rather that the interactions are offsetting. If the cities were of equal size, the price of housing would be cheaper in the area with the better climate. The change in the distribution of population and the response of wage rates tends to offset the climatic advantage. Related results are that housing consumption and housing expenditures are both lower in the region with the better climate.

II. Comparative Statics

A series of exogenous changes will be presented to determine when and in what direction migration would occur.[6] The first change is very direct—an increase in the difference in climates. From (27),

5. It is important to remember that the cities of comparison are not of the same population size.

6. The analysis will not extend to determination of changes in the terms of trade between cities.

if C_1/C_2 increases, L_1/L_2 will also. Thus, a relative increase in the climatic differential would induce migration toward the improved area. The change in climate could occur directly (long-term drought) but an alternative explanation not included in the formal model would be a change in the relative price of providing goods related to climate. For example, a fall in the relative price of air conditioning or an increase in heating costs would improve the relevant climate in southern states and would lead to migration to the south. The immigration to the area of improved climate necessarily leads to increased compensation in the other area. From (22), $E(w_1/w_2) < 0$, the relative wage differential increases, where the symbol E represents the percentage change in the variable. The relative price of housing falls in the area with the inferior climate if $1 - \sigma < 1 - \delta$, the share of labor in production of the export good is greater than that in housing.

The next change is to impose a differentially high and uncompensated tax on labor in area 2. An equal rate tax on labor in all areas has no effect on the distribution of population in this model, even though regional tax yields differ in absolute amounts. Similarly, a system of grants (based on income) neutral with respect to the allocation of population would be one with an equal rate applied to all regions. Thus, the region with higher wages (with the inferior climate) would receive a larger grant per capita.

Since the price of X is constant, labor bears the burden of the differential tax. The net wage is $(1 - t)w_2$, where w_2 is given in equation (2). Differentiating the solution to the model results in[7] $E(L_1/L_2)/Et > 0$. An increase in the differential tax rate in area 2 leads to L_1/L_2 increasing, a migration toward the fiscally efficient area resulting in a fall in wages in region 1. The migration also leads to a relative increase in the gross of tax wage in area 2 compared to the post-tax wage in area 1.

The third experiment is a technological change in production in a single location, modeled as Q_1/Q_2, increases. A realistic interpretation of this change would be that new capital investment occurs in region 1, while older, in place capital is in region 2. The reaction to this change is that migration toward region 1 will occur as shown in (28):

$$(28) \qquad E\left(\frac{L_1}{L_2}\right) = \frac{\delta(1 - \alpha_3)}{K_2} E\left(\frac{Q_1}{Q_2}\right) > 0.$$

7. $\frac{E(L_1/L_2)}{Et} = \frac{t(1 - \delta)}{K_2(1 - t + \delta t)}\left[1 - \alpha_3\sigma + \frac{\delta(1 - \alpha_3)(1 - \sigma)(1 + \psi_2 - t)}{1 - \alpha_3(1 - \sigma)(1 + \psi_2 - t)}\right].$

The change in the wage ratio is

$$E(w_1/w_2) = (\alpha_3\delta\sigma/K_2)E(Q_1/Q_2) > 0. \tag{29}$$

There are two effects on wages in the region benefiting from technological change. The direct improvement in technology increases wage rates, but the resultant immigration lowers wages. Equation (29) indicates that the net result is an increase in w_1/w_2. The value of $w_1 - w_2$ depends on the relative strength of climatic and technological differences. It is possible to observe an equilibrium, where $C_1 > C_2$ and $w_1 > w_2$, but the lower price of housing compensates households in area 2.

A related experiment is to raise both Q_1 and Q_2, a nationwide technological improvement. In this model wage rates increase; and utility increases; but if $E(Q_1/Q_2) = 0$, then $E(L_1/L_2) = 0$. No migration between regions results from this specific increase in aggregate income. In an alternative specification that considered the two cities to be small relative to the rest of the country, an improvement in the technology of producing X would lead to immigration to both regions. The numerical difference in population between regions would increase, but the percentage change would be equal.

The next change investigates the reaction of households to local residential property taxation. With local property taxes at rate t_i, the budget constraint is now

$$p_x x_i + p_y y_i + p_{h_i} h_i(1 + t_i) = w_i + z_i, \tag{4'}$$

where p_{h_i} is the net price of housing. The demand for housing is now

$$p_{h_i} h_i(1 + t_i) = \alpha_3(w_i + z_i). \tag{7'}$$

In equilibrium, the price of housing is

$$p_{h_i} = \alpha_3^\sigma(1 - \sigma)^{\sigma-1}A_i^{-\sigma}w_i L_i^\sigma C_i^{-\sigma}(1 + t_i)^{-\sigma}(1 + \psi_i)^\sigma, \tag{16'}$$

and the level of utility is

$$U_i = K_1' C_1^{\theta+K_2} L_i^{-K_2}(1 + t_i)^{\alpha_3(\sigma-1)}(1 + \psi_i)^{1-\alpha_3\sigma} \times (1 - \alpha_3(1 - \sigma)(1 + \psi_i)(1 + t_i))^{-1}$$

$$K_1' = K_1 Q_i^{\delta(1-\alpha_3)}(1 - \alpha_3(1 - \sigma)(1 + \psi_i))^{\delta(1-\alpha_3)} \tag{17'}$$

$$\psi_i = \frac{\delta(1 + t_i) - \delta\alpha_3(1 - \sigma) + \sigma\alpha_3(1 - \delta)}{(1 - \delta)(1 + t_i) + \delta\alpha_3(1 - \sigma) - \sigma\alpha_3(1 - \delta)}.$$

There are two interesting problems: the levying of an equal rate property tax in all areas, or levying a differentially high property tax in one area. Mieszkowski has hypothesized that property taxes can be separated into two components—a national tax and local differentials.[8] In this model if $t_1 = t_2$, the hypothesis suggests that there should be no allocational effect on population, which can be confirmed by utilizing (17′). Thus, a uniform tax on residential property does not change L_1/L_2 or the wage ratio. The hypothesis also suggests that distributional effects are due to local differentials in property tax rates defined as $t_i^* = t_i - \bar{t}$ where $\bar{t} = (t_1 + t_2)/2$. Utilizing (17′) permits comparison of the modeled distribution based on t_1^*, t_2^*. The hypothesis is not confirmed; however, the separation is approximately correct. Thus, the statement that the locational effects of property taxes are derived from local tax differentials can be supported. The same result would hold if $\bar{t}$ were the minimum of observed tax rates, and t_i^* were the positive differentials. One possible error would be to predict that an equal percentage tax rate increase would be locationally neutral. From (17′), $E(L_1/L_2) \neq 0$ if $Et_1 = Et_2$, unless $t_1 = t_2$ originally.

To analyze the effects of property tax differentials, assume that $t_1 = 0$ and $t_2 > 0$. If workers are renters ($\psi = 0$), then households migrate toward the region without the differentially high and uncompensated tax:

$$E\left(\frac{L_1}{L_2}\right) = \frac{t_2\alpha_3(1-\sigma)}{(1+t_2)K_2}\left[1 + \frac{\delta(1-\alpha_3)}{1+t_2-\alpha_3(1-\sigma)}\right] Et_2 > 0.$$

The increase in population in region 1 results in a fall in the productivity of labor. Thus, relative wages rise in the highly taxed region:

$$E\left(\frac{w_1}{w_2}\right) = \frac{-\delta t_2\alpha_3(1-\sigma)(1+t_2-\alpha_3)}{(1+t_2)K_2(1+t_2-\alpha_3(1-\sigma))} ET_2 < 0.$$

The change in the price of housing in each area depends on the shares of labor in housing and the production of the export good. If they are equal, $1 - \sigma = 1 - \delta$, then

$$Ep_{h_1} = 0, \quad Ep_{h2}^g > 0, \quad Ep_{h2}^n < 0,$$

where the g and n refer to the gross and net of tax prices of housing, respectively. In this case the immigration to the nontaxed region creates two exactly offsetting forces, increased population bids up the price of housing and a decreased wage lowers household's demands. In the taxed region the gross price of housing increases, while the net price falls due to the relative strength of the decline in population compared to the wage increase.

8. See Courant [1977] for an alternative view of this issue.

For the cases where the shares of labor are unequal,

$$1 - \sigma > 1 - \delta, \quad Ep_{h_1} < 0, \quad E\left(\frac{p^g_{h2}}{p_{h_1}}\right) > 0, \quad E\left(\frac{p^n_{h2}}{p_{h_1}}\right) \gtreqless 0,$$

and

$$1 - \sigma < 1 - \delta, \quad Ep_{h_1} > 0, \; E\left(\frac{p^g_{h}}{p_{h_1}}\right) \gtreqless 0, \; E\left(\frac{p^n_{h2}}{p_{h_1}}\right) < 0.$$

This result is not unexpected, since the relative level of the pre-tax price of housing between regions is ambiguous (see equation (23)). If labor's share of revenues in housing is greater than in the production of X, then the price of housing falls in the nontaxed area. The relative price falls compared to the gross price in region 2, but the change relative to the net price in region 2 depends on specific parameter values. For the other case where labor's share of revenues in housing is less than in the export good, the price of housing increases in the nontaxed region due to the immigration of households. The relative price net of taxes falls in the taxed region, but the relative change in the gross price is not determinate.

If workers are landowners, then the determination of the direction of migration is more complex. If $\sigma \geq \delta$, which appears likely, given parameter estimates, then migration is toward the region with lower property tax rates. However, if $\delta > \sigma$, then per capita landbank returns can increase in the highly taxed area, mitigating migration. The reason is that although uncompensated property taxation directly lowers the per capita return from the landbank, it also changes the allocation of labor between sectors. The ratio L_x/L_h increases in the taxed region. Thus, if the share of land in total output is greater in that sector ($\delta > \sigma$), then total land rentals per capita could increase, raising ψ.

The model presented indicates some of the factors that will account for migration between urbanized areas. Relatively high rates of growth would be created for an area if its climate improved relative to the other area. Other factors accounting for migration away from an area are uncompensated increases in labor or property taxes. An increase in income in one area due to a technological improvement results in migration to that area. However, a nationwide increase in aggregate income does not result in a redistribution of population in this model.

The final comment in this section is directed at empirical work in the field. Equation (2) could be utilized to determine the effect of wage rate increases on migration:

$$EL_i = \beta_0 + \beta_1 Ew_i.$$

The presumed reason for this form is that technological change in area i is not directly measurable; therefore the wage increase is used as a proxy with the expectation that $\beta_1 > 0$. However, a number of alternative situations have been explored indicating that wage rates will vary due to a variety of exogenous changes. Thus, there is no prior on the sign of β_1, and there is no single appropriate interpretation of β_1 in previous works that relate migration to changes in average wage levels, unless the changes in tax rates or other parameters between regions have been allowed for.

A similar point can be made concerning wage differentials. They will exist in equilibrium if there are differences in site-specific factors between regions. Hence migration is not necessarily expected if $w_1 \neq w_2$. Deflating wages by a local price index does not solve the problem, since the influence of climate on utility is left out. Thus, w_i/P_i (where P_i is an expenditure weighted price index) is not equalized across regions. Utilizing (22) and (23), the following ratio is equalized:

$$w_i/p_{hi}^{\delta/(\delta-\sigma)}.$$

Only if $\sigma = 0$, would the price of housing (or a price index for local goods) be the appropriate deflator. This occurs if local production is not affected by climate.

IV. The Optimal Allocation of Population

The question addressed in this section is whether the market distribution of households is optimal. The first problem allows a planner to allocate households between regions, but no control over consumption activity is assumed. The interest in this case, which is not realistic to implement, is derived from the solution.

Maximize the summation of regional utilities:

$$\overline{U} = \sum_i L_i U_i,$$

subject to

$$\overline{L} = \sum_i L_i$$

$$U_i = K_1 Q_i^{\delta(1-\alpha_3)} C_i^{\theta+K_2} L_i^{-K_2}:$$

the solution is

$$L_1/L_2 = (C_1/C_2)^{(\theta+K_2)/K_2}.$$

This distribution of population is identical to the market allocation. Thus, given this limited form of control, no population redistribution policy is appropriate.[9]

The planner will now be allowed to reallocate the export good between regions, but no direct control on migration is assumed. Housing is viewed as a local industry, and each city must be self-sufficient in this sector.

In this problem it is possible to increase household's welfare at the expense of nonresident landlords. Thus, the only case investigated is when workers are owners. A preliminary problem is to maximize the level of utility in a single city for a given population L. The planner selects x, y, h, L_x, and L_h, maximizing utility subject to the constraint that housing is locally produced.

Formally, maximize

$$U(x,y,h,C) + \lambda_1[H - hL] + \lambda_2[L - L_x - L_h] + \lambda_3[X - L(x + y(p_y/p_x))].$$

The third constraint indicates that the value of exported goods must be sufficient to pay for imports. The results are

$$U_x/U_y = p_x/p_y \tag{30}$$

$$U_x/U_h = H'/X', \tag{31}$$

where $H' = \partial H/\partial L_h$ and $X' = \partial X/\partial L_x$. Equation (31) indicates that labor should be allocated between sectors so that the ratio of marginal products of labor equals the inverse of the ratio of marginal utilities.

To compare this solution to the competitive allocation, multiply (31) by p_h/p_x. The right-hand side is the ratio of value of marginal products of labor, and both equal the area's wage rate. The left-hand side is also unity in the market solution, since $p_h U_x/p_x U_h = 1$ is a result of a household's utility maximization. For a single urban area, the competitive allocation in production and consumption is optimal.

9. Nonresident landlords could attempt to control the distribution of population ($\psi = 0$), and therefore increase aggregate land rentals. This would require cooperation between landowners of different regions, a condition that makes this hypothesis unlikely. Maximize total land rentals: $\sum_i(\delta p_x X_i + \sigma p_{h_i} H_i)$, choosing, L_1, L_2 subject to $L_1 + L_2 = \bar{L}$ yields $L_1/L_2 = C_1/C_2$. At this allocation (with fewer residents in the region with the good climate), the marginal product of labor is equalized between regions. Given the fixed price of export good, the maximization of total product implies revenue maximization resulting in the largest gain to landlords. Total household income is maximized at the allocation $L_1/L_2 = C_1/C_2$ and aggregate housing expenditures are largest at this distribution. Landlords' income is maximized, since their share of housing expenditures is constant. In summary, total landowner income would be increased if they could restrict migration from the region with the inferior climate.

The final problem discussed is the allocation of households among regions. It is assumed that direct population control is not possible, and thus, utility levels are equated between regions. In the market solution each city was self-sufficient in both housing and the composite bundle of other goods. The planner now has the choice of reallocating production and consumption in an attempt to increase the equalized level of welfare. Thus, one region could produce relatively more X and ship it to the other region for consumption. Since marginal products are not equalized in the market allocation if climate directly affects utility,[10] it may be possible that the market solution is not Pareto optimal.

Formally, the planner maximizes utility in region 1:

$$\begin{aligned} &U_1(x_1,y_1,h_1,C_1) + \lambda_1(U_1 - U_2) + \lambda_2(L_1h_1 - H_1) \\ &\quad + \lambda_3(L_2h_2 - H_2) + \lambda_4(\overline{L}_1 - L_1 - L_2) + \lambda_5(L_1 - L_{x_1} - L_{h_1}) \\ &\qquad + \lambda_6(L_2 - L_{x_2} - L_{h_2}) + \lambda_7(X_1 + X_2 \\ &\qquad\quad - L_1(x_1 + y_1(p_y/p_x)) - L_2(x_2 + y_2(p_y/p_x))). \end{aligned}$$

The constraints are that utility must be equalized regionally, housing is locally produced in each region, the total population allocated is $\overline{L}$, and households must live in the city where they work. The last constraint is the combined budget for the exported and imported goods. This formulation allows $X_1 \gtreqless L_1(x_1 + y_1(p_y/p_x))$. If equal, then the result is identical to the maximization of utility in a single area, implying that the market solution is efficient. The solution indicates that

$$U_{x_i}/U_{y_i} = p_x/p_y \tag{32}$$

$$U_{x_i}/U_{h_i} = H_i'/X_i' \tag{33}$$

$$\frac{U_{h_i}}{U_{x_i}}(H_1' - h_1) - x_1 - \frac{p_y}{p_x}y_1 = \frac{U_{h2}}{U_{x2}}(H_2' - h_2) - x_2 - \frac{p_y}{p_x}y_2. \tag{34}$$

The market solution satisfies (32) and (33), but, in general, (34) is not fulfilled. Substituting the market condition $U_{h_i}/U_{x_i} = p_{h_i}/p_x$ into (34) and simplifying yields

$$\begin{aligned} p_{h_1}H_1' - (p_{h_1}h_1 + p_xx_1 + p_yy_1) \\ = p_{h_2}H_2' - (p_hh_2 + p_xx_2 + p_yy_2). \end{aligned} \tag{35}$$

10. If $\theta = 0$, then $L_1/L_2 = C_1/C_2$ in the market solution, the distribution where marginal products are equated.

Since $w_i = p_{h_i} H'_i$, (35) is equivalent to a market solution where wages minus expenditures were equal in both regions. In a city with nonresident landlords, equation (35) is satisfied in the market allocation, since wages equal expenditures in each city. If residents were landowners, expenditures per household equal $w_i(1 + \psi)$, but only if $w_1 = w_2$ is equation (35) met. Regional wage rates are equated in the market if $X'_1 = X'_2$, that is, equal marginal productivities of labor among regions. This occurs only if climate does not directly enter the utility function, $\theta = 0$. If household location is directly dependent on the site-specific factor, the distribution of population is not Pareto optimal.

The market solution implies that as θ increases, more labor resides in the better endowed region. Thus, if $\theta > 0$, the market distribution of population results in too many households residing in the region with the good climate compared to the optimal allocation of resources. It should be emphasized that in this problem the planner cannot control the allocation of population directly, only the distribution of resources.

V. Summary

In equilibrium, average wage rates will vary among regions and compensate for differences in endowments of location-specific attributes. Compensation can also occur through differences in the price of housing, and this result is dependent on the parameters of the model and the manner in which the site-specific factor affects production and consumption. The model also indicated the difficulty in establishing a local price deflator, if attempting to determine real wages in each area.

It was found that a system of taxes or grants, neutral with respect to the distribution of population, is one with an equal rate applied to all areas. This can be interpreted to mean that cost of living differences should be allowed for. A system of equal-sized grants would induce households to migrate toward the area with the lower income (superior climate). The Mieszkowski hypothesis that the allocative effects of property taxes arise from spatial differentials was confirmed—the portion of the tax at the national average rate was spatially neutral. The market allocation with full mobility of landowning workers leads to overconsumption of the region better endowed with the site-specific factor.

Ohio State University

References

Buchanan, J., and Goetz, C. J., "Efficiency Limits of Fiscal Mobility: An Assessment of the Tiebout Model," *Journal of Public Economics,* I (1972), 25–43.

Courant, P. W., "A General Equilibrium Model of Heterogeneous Property Taxes," *Journal of Public Economics,* VIII (1977), 313–27.

Flatters, F., J. V. Henderson, and P. Mieszkowski, "Public Goods, Efficiency, and Regional Fiscal Equalization," *Journal of Public Economics,* III (1974), 99–112.

Graves, P. E., "A Life-Cycle Empirical Analysis of Net Migration and Climate by Race," *Journal of Urban Economics,* VI (1979), 135–47.

——, and P. D. Linneman, "Household Migration: Theoretical and Empirical Results," *Journal of Urban Economics,* VI (1979), 383–404.

Henderson, J. V., *Economic Theory and the Cities* (New York: Academic Press, 1977).

Izraeli, Oded, "Differentials in Nominal Incomes and Prices Between Cities," Ph.D. thesis, University of Chicago, 1973.

Mieszkowski, P., "The Property Tax: An Excise or a Profits Tax?" *Journal of Public Economics,* I (1972), 73–96.

Upton, C., "An Equilibrium Model of City Size," unpublished manuscript, 1976.

BANK ATTITUDE TOWARD RISK, IMPLICIT RATES OF INTEREST, AND THE BEHAVIOR OF AN INDEX OF RISK AVERSION FOR COMMERCIAL BANKS*

RONALD A. RATTI

This paper presents an analysis of a quasi-risk-averse bank facing uncertainty with respect to demand deposit flows and default risk on loans. On the basis of a formal model, testable hypotheses of bank attitude toward risk and the qualitative behavior of the index of relative risk aversion for commercial banks are developed. Through the use of data on the member banks of the Tenth Federal Reserve District, the empirical tests that were conducted indicated that banks are strongly risk-averse and that their index of relative risk aversion is increasing in profits. These results suggest that favorable (unfavorable) environmenzal changes will generate income effects that will result in proportionately less (more) risk taking by banks.

I. INTRODUCTION

Although decision makers at commercial banks constitute one of the single most important groups of portfolio managers in the entire financial sector, no formal empirical work has yet appeared that explicitly investigates their collective attitude toward risk taking and uncertainty. This lacuna has become all the more serious given the large number of policy proposals currently being considered that would significantly alter the banking environment, and possibly result in major portfolio adjustment. Without information regarding bank attitude toward the assumption of risk following a favorable or unfavorable environmental change, it is not possible to predict the consequences of any of the proposed changes. The purpose of this paper is to develop testable hypotheses regarding (a) bank attitude toward risk and (b) the qualitative behavior of bank indices of risk aversion; and then, by using recent data on the member banks of the Tenth Federal Reserve District, to test these hypotheses.

The work concerning bank attitude toward risk will involve simultaneous estimation of the marginal interest rates on both bank assets and liabilities as they appear in consolidated reports of condition. The formal model of bank behavior presented in the paper will provide a theoretical basis for interpreting coefficients obtained by regressing bank income on asset (excluding reserves) and liability

* The author is grateful to Josef Hadar for valuable discussion on the content of this study, and to an anonymous referee for a constructive critique of an earlier version of the paper. The work was completed while the author was a visiting scholar at the Federal Reserve Bank of Kansas City.

The Quarterly Journal of Economics, September 1980 0033-5533/80/0095-0309$02.30

items as marginal returns and costs. It is shown that statistically significant negative (positive) coefficients on liability items and statistically significant positive (negative) coefficients on asset items imply aversion (attraction) toward risk. The empirical results turn out to be consistent with the view that banks are risk-averse.

The other focus of the paper concerns the behavior of what will be referred to as the Arrow [1964]-Pratt [1964] index of relative risk aversion for commercial banks. This work involves three stages. First, the comparative static effects of variation in a tax parameter are signed by appeal to the qualitative behavior of the index. Second, empirical evidence on the qualitative nature of the comparative static result is obtained and presented. Third, this evidence is juxtaposed with the tax paradigm and used to deduce the most likely behavior of the index. These exercises suggest that the index of relative risk aversion is increasing in profits.

The following section presents the formal model of a commercial bank operating under conditions of uncertainty. This model is in some ways more general than many of those that have hitherto appeared in the literature in that it contains a broader spectrum of assets and liabilities, sources of uncertainty, market structures, and attitudes toward risk. In the third section a criterion is developed and used to deduce bank attitude toward risk. In Section IV the relationship between the index of relative risk aversion and bank behavior is developed, and empirical results presented. At the outset of this study, it needs to be emphasized that the conclusions arrived at are tentative and merely suggestive. In the concluding section the restrictive nature of the assumptions and procedures under which results are obtained is emphasized.

II. The Model

A commercial bank operating subject to a minimum reserve constraint faces uncertainty with regard to demand deposit withdrawals. The liabilities of the bank consist of bank capital W, demand deposits D, and time deposits T, with assets consisting of cash reserves R, government securities G, and private loans L. The bank confronts the problem of how it should adjust these quantities in order to maximize the expected value of a quasi-concave function of final wealth, given that these quantities, once chosen, may undergo change owing to the stochastic nature of deposit flows.[1] For want of a better name, this quasi-concave objective function shall be referred to as the utility function.

The rate of interest on time deposits is given by $r_T = r_T(T)$, with $r'_T \geq 0$ according as the bank is a monopsonist or a pure competitor.

The return on loans is defined to be αr_L, where α is a random variable defined on the interval [0, 1] with cumulative density function $V(\alpha)$, and r_L is the contract rate of interest. When $\alpha < 1$, the bank has a loss on loans; and when $\alpha = 1$, the bank earns the contracted rate of interest, and there is no default. It will be assumed that the contract rate of interest is a decreasing function of the amount lent; i.e., $r_L = r_L(L)$, with $r'_L \leq 0$ according as the bank is a monopolist or pure competitor.[2]

In the market for government securities the bank is a pure competitor and is able to trade without affecting the rate of interest r_G paid on government securities.

It is assumed that the level of demand deposits and cash reserves changes during the period of analysis due to unforeseen cash deposits and withdrawals by the public, deposit of checks drawn on other banks, etc. The net change in deposits y is assumed to be treated by the bank as a random variable with a subjectively perceived probability density function $f(\cdot)$ and cumulative density function $F(\cdot)$. Demand deposits at the end of the period of analysis will be given by $D + y$, a positive value for y indicating a gain in deposits. Reserves at the end of the period, $R + y$, will be legally sufficient if they are greater than or equal to the level of required reserves as determined by the level of deposits at the start of the period. Required reserves equal $k_D D + k_T T$, where k_D and k_T are the reserve requirements on demand and time deposits, respectively, so that if

$$(1) \qquad y \geq b, \quad \text{where} \quad b = k_D D + k_T T - R,$$

the bank will end the period with excess reserves. If $y < b$, the bank has insufficient reserves and must borrow at the penalty rate r_P in order to make up the deficiency.

1. The implicit assumptions here are the following: (1) stockholders do not exercise close enough control to impose their preferences on a myopic management, or stockholders are myopic, or both; (2) it is possible to construct a quasi-concave function of final wealth that represents the collective preferences of whatever decision-making group emerges from (1). Examples of authors who have presented formal models of banks operating under conditions of uncertainty who have implicitly adopted these assumptions would be Morrison [1966], Poole [1968], and Frost [1971], who were concerned with bank demand for cash; Orr-Mellon [1961], Grossman [1965], Cooper [1971], and Ratti [1979], who were concerned with the effects of uncertainty on the traditional analysis of credit expansion; Porter [1961], Scott [1957], and Kane-Malkiel [1965], who were concerned with optimal loan-security choice; Klein [1971], who attempted to analyze the effects of market structure on bank behavior; and Parkin [1970], who investigated debt selection by the U. K. discount houses. The paper by Kane-Malkiel [1965] adopted a mean variance analysis, the paper by Parkin [1970] worked with an exponential utility function, the paper by Ratti [1979] worked with a general utility function, and the other authors operated with expected profit objective functions. For a discussion of the problems involved when working with an objective function based on a single period, see Fama and Miller [1972, pp. 67–75].

2. Given this formulation of default risk, the expected return on loans is a decreasing function of the amount lent. It is similar to the treatments by Klein [1970] and Taggart-Greenbaum [1978].

Bank revenues consist of interest earned on loans and securities, while bank costs consist of interest payments on demand and time deposits, and the possible costs of meeting a reserve deficiency. Bank income π is defined as follows:[3]

$$(2)\quad \pi_1 = \alpha L r_L + G r_G - T r_T - D r_D - (b - y) r_P, \quad \text{when } y < b;$$

$$(3)\quad \pi_2 = \alpha L r_L + G r_G - T r_T - D r_D, \quad \text{when } y \geq b,$$

where r_D represents the average cost of servicing demand deposits net of charges.

In these expressions for bank income, the rates of interest on loans, and securities are defined to be net of operating or administration costs, while the rates on borrowed funds and deposits are defined to be gross of operating costs.

Define U to be a single argument thrice differentiable von Neuman-Morgenstern utility function on the real line with $U' > 0$ and $U'' \leq 0$, and suppose that y is defined on the real interval $[a, c]$. Then, let E represent the expectation operator and give expected utility by

$$(4)\quad E[U] = \int_0^1 \left\{ \int_a^b U[\pi_1] dF(y) + \int_b^c U[\pi_2] dF(y) \right\} dV(\alpha).$$

It is assumed that the bank attempts to maximize $E[U]$ by choosing $T, L, G,$ and R. These decision variables are linked by the accounting identity

$$(5)\quad L + G + R = W + D + T$$

at all times. Eliminating R from equation (4) by using equation (5), making note of the definitions of π_1, π_2, and b, and differentiating equation (4) with respect to T, L, and G, respectively, yields the following first-order conditions:

$$(6)\quad \frac{\partial E[U]}{\partial T} = \int_0^1 \{(-MC_T + (1 - k_T) r_P) I_1 - MC_T I_2\} dV = 0;$$

$$(7)\quad \frac{\partial E[U]}{\partial G} = \int_0^1 \{(r_G - r_P) I_1 + r_G I_2\} dV = 0;$$

$$(8)\quad \frac{\partial E[U]}{\partial L} = \int_0^1 \{(\alpha MR_L - r_P) I_1 + \alpha MR_L I_2\} dV = 0;$$

3. π_2 could be redefined to include interest earned on excess reserves by lending in the federal funds market, say at rate $r_p{}^*$. However, as long as $r_p{}^* < r_p$, the results that are derived in what follows hold true even when $r_p{}^* \neq 0$. Given that borrowing rates are defined to be inclusive of operating or administration costs, and lending rates are net of these costs, it is reasonable to conclude that $r_p{}^* < r_p$. For the purpose of simplifying the presentation, it is assumed without loss of generality that $r_p{}^* = 0$.

where

$$I_1 \equiv \int_a^b U'[\pi_1]dF(y), \qquad I_2 \equiv \int_b^c U'[\pi_2]dF(y),$$

$$MC_T = \frac{\partial Tr_T(T)}{\partial T}, \quad \text{and} \quad MR_L = \frac{\partial Lr_L(L)}{\partial L}.$$

In the next section these equations are used to generate testable hypotheses regarding bank attitude toward risk.

III. Attitude Toward Risk and Marginal Interest Rates

The Theory

In this section the implications of the efficiency conditions for the qualitative sign of coefficients obtained by regressing measures of bank income on asset and liability levels are derived. Net income, a random variable, is defined in equations (2) and (3). If $\overline{\alpha}$ is the expected value of α, expected income is given by

$$\text{(9)} \quad E(\pi) = \int_a^b [\overline{\alpha}Lr_L + Gr_G - Tr_T - Dr_D - (b - y)r_P]dF(y) + \int_b^c [\overline{\alpha}Lr_L + Gr_G - Tr_T - Dr_D]dF(y).$$

The effect on expected income of varying T, G, or L by simultaneously varying R can be obtained by substituting for b from equation (1), eliminating R by the accounting identity in equation (5), and differentiating $E(\pi)$ with respect to T, G, and L. If p_1 is the probability of borrowing (and $p_2 = 1 - p_1$ is the probability of excess reserves), this procedure yields the following:[4]

$$\text{(10)} \quad \frac{\partial E(\pi)}{\partial T} \equiv a_T = -MC_T + (1 - k_T)r_P p_1(T,G,L)$$

$$\text{(11)} \quad \frac{\partial E(\pi)}{\partial G} \equiv a_G = r_G - r_P p_1(T,G,L)$$

$$\text{(12)} \quad \frac{\partial E(\pi)}{\partial L} \equiv a_L = \overline{\alpha}MR_L - r_P p_1(T,G,L).$$

These expressions are readily explained. For example, if time deposits are expanded by \$1, excess reserves are increased by \$(1 − k_T). This results in an increase in the cost of time deposits of value

4. By definition, $p_1 = \int_a^b dF(y)$. Note that since $b = k_D D + k_T T - R$, any action that raises R lowers the probability of borrowing. By the accounting identity such actions would be declines in loans or securities, or an increase in deposits.

MC_T, and a reduction in the expected cost of a reserve deficiency of value \$$(1 - k_T)r_P p_1$. The impact on expected income is the difference between the latter and the former as given by a_T. If government securities are increased by \$1, expected revenues increase by r_G, but since reserves have been reduced by \$1, the expected cost of borrowing has increased by $r_P p_1$. The net effect on expected income is given by a_G.

The a_i ($i = T,G,L$) can be interpreted in terms of the risk premium of the bank decision maker(s). The risk premium θ is defined to be the amount by which $E(\pi)$ needs to be adjusted to make the decision maker indifferent between the random income π, and the certain income $E(\pi) - \theta$. That is, θ is defined by the condition,

$$E[U(\pi)] = U[E(\pi) - \theta]. \tag{13}$$

Differentiating with respect to T, G, and L yields, at the point of equilibrium[5]

$$a_T = \frac{\partial \theta}{\partial T}, \quad a_G = \frac{\partial \theta}{\partial G}, \quad \text{and} \quad a_L = \frac{\partial \theta}{\partial L}. \tag{14}$$

This is, a_T, a_G, and a_L are the rates of change of the risk premium with respect to T, G, and L.

The optimal values for T, G, and L are obtained from the efficiency conditions given in equations (6), (7), and (8). These values can then be used to determine the values of a_T, a_G, and a_L. It is quite obvious that for the risk-neutral bank, T, G, and L are chosen to set, via the probability of borrowing (p_1), $a_T = a_G = a_L = 0$. In Appendix A it is demonstrated, by comparing equations (6), (7), and (8) with equations (10), (11), and (12), that the risk-averse bank sets p_1, by choosing T, G, and L to make a_T negative, and a_G and a_L positive, and that the risk-attracted bank does the opposite; i.e.,

$$-a_T, a_G, a_L \gtreqless 0 \quad \text{according as} \quad U'' \gtreqless 0. \tag{15}$$

The risk-averse bank does not trade reserves for other assets up to the point at which the expected income gain from further trading is zero. It halts the process at an earlier stage, for which the expected interest income from a further increase in L or G is greater than the expected loss resulting from an anticipated increase in borrowing. The risk-averse bank will be in equilibrium at such a point by definition,

5. For example, differentiating equation (13) with respect to T yields $\partial E[U(\pi)]/\partial T = U'[\partial E(\pi)/\partial T - \partial\theta/\partial T]$. Since the assumption of expected utility maximization requires that the left-hand side of this expression be zero, the result in equation (14) follows.

because the additional utility to it of an extra dollar in income is less than the loss in utility that would result from a fall in income of one dollar. The result for loans is illustrated in Figures Ia and Ib. In these diagrams $\bar{L}$ is the optimal value of loans for the risk-averse bank, L^* is the optimal value of L for the risk-neutral bank, and $\tilde{L}$ is the optimal value of L for the risk-attracted bank. The value of a_L has been indicated for the risk-averse bank and is therefore shown to be positive. The value of a_L is varied by altering $p_1(T,G,L)$.

With regard to deposits, the risk-averse bank does not contract deposits and reserves back to the point at which a further contraction yields no change in expected income. For at such a point, the reduction in the interest and maintenance expense of deposits is equal to the increase in the expected costs of borrowing from having fewer reserves, and since $U'' < 0$, the marginal utility gained from the former is less than the marginal utility lost due to the latter. Therefore, the risk-averse bank expands deposits beyond the point at which their increase forces expected income to zero.

Some Empirical Results

The relationship between expected bank income and liability and asset items is given in equation (9). The a_i show the change in expected income as the ith asset or liability changes, given that reserves also change in order to satisfy the accounting identity. In a linear regression of bank income on liability and asset items (excluding reserves), the estimated coefficients can be interpreted as linear approximations of the a_i.[6] The above discussion implies that if, in this regression, the coefficients on the liability items are statistically significant and negative (positive), and the coefficients on the asset items are statistically significant and positive (negative), then the banks in the sample are averse (attracted) to risk, while coefficients statistically insignificant from zero would imply that they are risk-neutral.[7]

In order to shed empirical light on this question of bank attitude toward risk, call and income report data were collected for the member

6. The regression equation that is being visualized is a linear version of equation (9): that is,

$$E(y) = \text{intercept} + \Sigma b_i \text{ asset}(i) + \Sigma c_i \text{ liability}(i) + \text{error term},$$

where the b_i and c_i are linear estimates of the a_i defined in equations (10), (11), and (12), and cash due does not appear as one of the assets.

7. The claim about insignificance is of course partly conditional on the absence of lump sum transactions costs. However, these costs made a given asset or liability item (at the margin) too small for some banks and too large for other banks. This effect tends to be washed out overall.

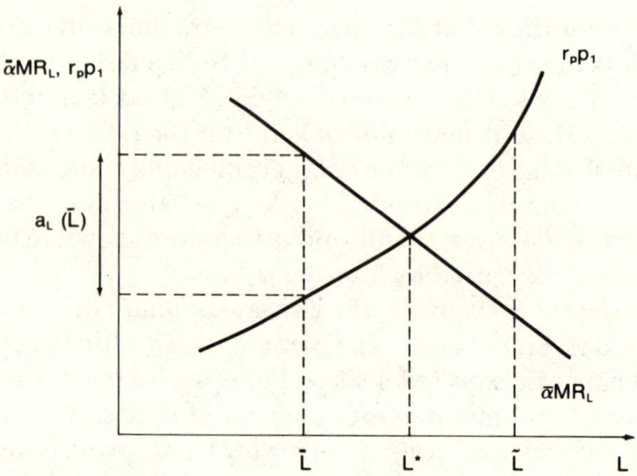

FIGURE Ia

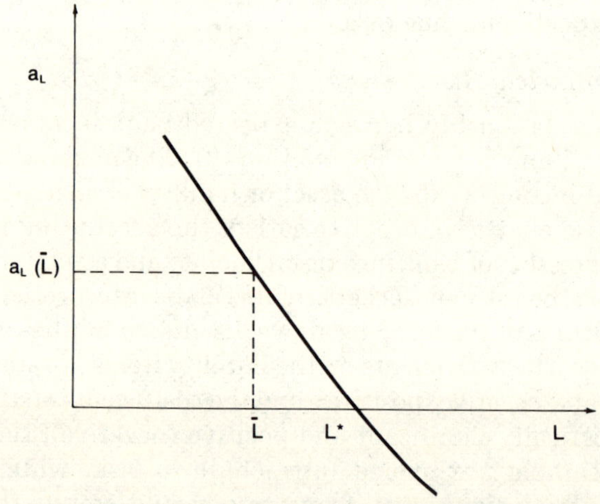

FIGURE Ib

banks of the Tenth Federal Reserve District for 1976 and 1977.[8] Three alternative measures of income—net operating income, income before

8. There are several reasons for choosing these years. First, beginning with the March 1976 call, data are available on securities by remaining maturity, on savings deposits separate from time deposits, and on time deposits divided into large time certificates of deposit, other large time deposits, and time deposits, in denominations of $100,000 or less. Second, for the period September 1963 through September 1975, the March and September calls were shorter and not as complete as the June and December calls, implying that detailed analysis of data for recent periods prior to 1976 would have to be based on just two calls.

taxes, and net income after taxes[9]—were regressed in turn on asset (excluding reserves) and liability items drawn from consolidated reports of condition.[10]

All asset items, liability items, and net income measures were deflated by total assets, and all regressions include a constant term and a scale variable given by the reciprocal of total assets. The estimated equations have the form,

$$\text{(16)} \quad \frac{\text{profit}}{TA} = \text{intercept} + \sum_{i, i \neq k} b_i \frac{\text{asset}(i)}{TA} + \sum_i c_i \frac{\text{liability}(i)}{TA} + \frac{1}{TA} + w,$$

where k represents cash due and w is the random error term.

Attempts to improve the explanatory power of the regression equations by the appropriate disaggregation of the asset and liability categories eventually resulted in the regressions reported in Table I.[11] The data for 1976 and 1977 were pooled, since an analysis of the error sum of squares of regressions for the years separately and combined had revealed that the data were very similar. In each regression the coefficients of the six liability variables are negative and statistically significant at least at the 1 percent level. Twenty-four out of the twenty-seven coefficients on the asset variables are positive and for the most part are statistically significant at least at the 5 percent level (the three exceptions are statistically insignificant at the 5 per-

9. Net operating income is essentially the value of services sold minus operating costs exclusive of loan loss provision. From the Consolidated Report of Income forms for 1976 and 1977, it would be given by "income before taxes and securities gains or losses" plus "provision for possible loan losses." Net income before taxes is calculated by adding "securities gains (losses), gross" to "income before taxes and securities gains or losses." Net income after taxes equals net income before taxes minus taxes.

10. The numbers on assets and liabilities for 1976 were obtained by giving a weight of three-eighths to the March call, weights of one-fourth each to the June and September calls, and a weight of one-eighth to the December call. For 1977 a weight of one-eighth was given to the December 1976 call, weights of one-fourth each to the March, June, and September calls, and a weight of one-eighth to the December 1977 call.

11. The statistical test employed for determining whether more than two regressions have the same coefficient is described in Goldberger [1964, p. 175, theorem (7.19)]. It was found that the five loan categories had significantly (at the 5 percent level) different coefficients from each other and that the components of time deposits also had significantly different coefficients. The hypothesis that the coefficients of the demand deposits of individuals, partnerships, and corporations, of the U. S. Government, and other demand deposits were significantly different at the 5 percent level was rejected. The same conclusion was arrived at when time deposits and savings deposits were divided in the same way. The hypothesis that the coefficients of U. S. securities and the securities of U. S. agencies and corporations were different was also rejected. A breakdown of the different government securities by remaining maturity also did not significantly increase the explanatory power of the regression equations.

TABLE I

RATES OF CHANGE OF RISK PREMIUM EXPRESSED AS PERCENTAGE OF TOTAL ASSETS FOR POOLED 1976 AND 1977 DATA

	Net operating income	Net income before taxes	Net income after taxes
Intercept	8.176	5.106	2.216
	(9.11)	(4.05)	(2.20)
Demand balances at other banks	−1.311	−0.288	5.217
	(−1.83)	(−0.29)	(0.65)
United States securities	1.082	2.782	2.280
	(1.96)	(3.59)	(3.69)
State and local securities	2.131	4.443	5.236
	(3.77)	(5.59)	(3.26)
Real estate loans	1.971	2.783	2.269
	(3.34)	(3.36)	(3.34)
Commercial and industrial loans	1.730	2.244	1.870
	(2.93)	(2.71)	(2.82)
Loans to consumers	1.908	2.235	1.856
	(3.21)	(2.68)	(2.79)
Loans to farmers	2.341	3.378	2.553
	(4.31)	(4.43)	(4.49)
Other loans	0.000	0.470	1.408
	(0.00)	(0.31)	(1.16)
Other noncash assets	−0.806	0.519	0.974
	(−1.29)	(0.59)	(1.40)
Demand deposits	−7.285	−4.980	−2.653
	(−9.00)	(−4.38)	(−2.92)
Small time deposits	−9.449	−7.614	−4.179
	(−12.70)	(−7.29)	(−5.01)
Large time certificates of deposit	−9.594	−8.260	−4.653
	(−12.36)	(−7.58)	(−5.35)
Other large time deposits	−9.505	−8.828	−5.376
	(−10.32)	(−6.83)	(−5.21)
Savings deposits	−9.524	−7.494	−4.306
	(−12.40)	(−6.95)	(−5.00)
Other liabilities	−9.622	−6.807	−3.668
	(−11.22)	(−5.66)	(−3.82)
Reciprocal of total assets	−1.201	−2.017	−0.894
	(−6.03)	(−7.21)	(−4.00)
R^2	0.298	0.224	0.239
F	38.79	26.41	28.69
N	1,480	1,480	1,480

cent level).[12] These regression results are consistent with the view that banks or their regulators or both are risk-averse.

IV. Index of Relative Risk Aversion

The purpose of this section is to present some evidence on the behavior of the Arrow-Pratt Index of Relative Risk Aversion. This will be accomplished by introducing a tax parameter into the above model and signing comparative static expressions resulting from its variation by appealing to the behavior of the index. Empirical evidence is then obtained on the qualitative nature of the comparative static results and used to deduce the most likely behavior of the index of relative risk aversion.

Unfortunately, determinate solutions for the comparative static results following variation in the tax rate cannot be obtained for the level of generality of the model presented in Section I, i.e., for two sources of uncertainty appearing simultaneously. However, results are signed for the sources of uncertainty introduced one at a time and are presented below.

Stochastic Reserve and Deposit Flows

The special case of no default risk on loans can be analyzed using the general framework developed above by treating α as nonstochastic and letting it take its expected value $\bar{\alpha}$. If t is defined as the rate of tax on profits, the relevant first-order conditions will be given by the product of $(1 - t)$ and the expressions in equations (6), (7), and (8). It can be shown that differentiating the first-order conditions with

12. Regression coefficients such as those appearing in Table I have been interpreted "as the marginal interest rates that the average sample bank could earn if it could substitute a dollar of asset or liability for a dollar of vault cash" [Hester and Pierce, 1975, p. 216]. This interpretation is not correct. If, for example, an asset item rises, the effect on profit is not simply the marginal return on that item. Since the level of vault cash is now reduced, the regression coefficient is an estimate of a linear approximation of the marginal return adjusted by the marginal cost and probability of short-term borrowing. Nor will the assumption of risk neutrality, implicitly made by Hester and Pierce [1975], alter the validity of this claim as an examination of equation (9) makes clear. The basic problem with the Hester-Pierce interpretation is that there is no theoretical base for the derivation of their conclusions. A procedure for obtaining estimates of the marginal returns and costs of asset and liability items would be the following. Equation (9) can be written as

$$E(\pi) = \bar{\alpha} r_L L + r_G G - r_T T - r_D D - r_p \mu(b),$$

where $\mu(b)$ is the expected absolute value of the reserve deficiency given that reserves will be deficient. An estimate of $\mu(b)$ from the weekly report of deposits for each bank for each of the two years 1976 and 1977 is given by

$$\hat{\mu}(b) = -\frac{\text{sum of negative value of basic reserves}}{\text{\# of Wednesdays basic reserves is negative}}.$$

In regressions of each of the three net income measures on the variables listed in Table I and $\hat{\mu}(b)$, the coefficient on $\hat{\mu}(b)$ was found to be of the appropriate sign in all three regressions, and statistically significant at the 5 percent confidence level in two of the regressions.

respect to t yields the following:[13]

(17) $$\frac{\partial T}{\partial t} = 0,$$

(18) $$\frac{\partial G}{\partial t} = \frac{-\bar{\alpha} MC'_T MR'_L (I_1 + I_2)^2 H(G)}{D},$$

(19) $$\frac{\partial L}{\partial t} = 0,$$

and

(20) $$\frac{\partial R}{\partial t} = \frac{\bar{\alpha} MC'_T MR'_L (I_1 + I_2)^2 H(G)}{D},$$

where

(21) $$H(G) = (r_G - r_P) \int_a^b \pi_1 U''[(1-t)\pi_1] dF + r_G \int_b^c \pi_2 U''[(1-t)\pi_2] dF.$$

It is shown in Appendix B that

$$H(G) \lesseqqgtr 0 \quad \text{according as} \quad R_R' \gtreqqless 0,$$

where R_R is the Arrow-Pratt Index of Relative Risk Aversion. Therefore, since $MR'_L < 0$, $MC'_T > 0$, and $D < 0$ (by the second-order conditions),

(22) $$\frac{\partial G}{\partial t} \gtreqqless 0 \quad \text{according as} \quad R_R' \gtreqqless 0,$$

13. Differentiation of equations (6), (7), and (8) yields the following system:

$$\begin{vmatrix} e(TT) & e(TG) & e(TL) \\ e(GT) & e(GG) & e(GL) \\ e(LT) & e(LG) & e(LL) \end{vmatrix} \cdot \begin{vmatrix} \partial T/\partial t \\ \partial G/\partial t \\ \partial L/\partial t \end{vmatrix} = \begin{vmatrix} H(T) \\ H(G) \\ H(L) \end{vmatrix},$$

where $e(IJ) = \partial^2 E[U]/\partial i \partial j$; $i,j = T,G,L$, and (for example)

$$H(G) = (r_G - r_P) \int_a^b \pi_1 U''[(1-t)\pi_1] dF + r_G \int_b^c \pi_2 U''[(1-t)\pi_2] dF.$$

An examination of equations (6) and (7) will reveal that time deposits are expanded up to the point at which $MC_T = (1 - k_T) r_G$ and for nonstochastic α an examination of equations (7) and (8) will show that loans are expanded up to the point at which $\bar{\alpha} MR_L = r_G$. By inspection these results reveal that $H(T) = -(1 - k_T) H(G)$ and $H(L) = H(G)$. A comparison of the written expressions for the $e(ij)$ will show that

$$e(TT) = -MC'_T (I_1 + I_2) + (1 - k_T)^2 e(GG), \quad e(TG) = e(TL) = -(1 - k_T) e(GG),$$

$$e(GL) = e(GG), \qquad \text{and} \qquad e(LL) = \bar{\alpha} MR'_L (I_1 + I_2) + e(GG).$$

These relationships allow equations (17), (18), and (19) to be derived. The expression for $\partial R/\partial t$ in equation (20) is obtained by differentiating the accounting identity in equation (5) and using equations (17), (18), and (19).

and

$$\frac{\partial R}{\partial t} \lesseqqgtr 0 \quad \text{according as} \quad R_R' \gtreqqless 0. \tag{23}$$

The meaning of these results will be better understood if a parallel is established between this model and Arrow's [1964] portfolio model. Arrow, taking an expected utility approach to a simple portfolio model, found that as the decision maker became worse off, the proportion of the portfolio in the "risky" asset increased (decreased) if the index of relative risk aversion was increasing (decreasing). In the absence of default risk there is no "risky" asset, but risk taking does increase if the expected level of borrowing (relative to portfolio size) rises. The expected level of borrowing, of course, will rise if the level of reserves is reduced. Formally, the expected level of borrowing is given by

$$E[\text{borrowing}] = \int_a^b (b - y)dF(y). \tag{24}$$

Noting the definition of b in equation (1), the rate of change in the expected level of borrowing (as a fraction of total assets TA) with respect to t can be shown to be[14]

$$\frac{\partial(E[\text{borrowing}]/TA)}{\partial t} = -\frac{\partial R}{\partial t}\frac{F(b)}{TA} \gtreqqless 0 \quad \text{according as} \quad R_R' \gtreqqless 0. \tag{25}$$

This result is in accord with the Arrow result in that as the tax rate increases and the bank becomes worse off, the expected level of borrowing (and hence risk taking) rises (falls) if relative risk aversion is increasing (decreasing).

Default Risk on Loans

When reserve and deposit flows are nonstochastic, before-tax profit is no longer broken on the real line at b and is instead given by

$$\pi = (1 - t)[\alpha r_L L + r_G G - r_T T - r_D D]. \tag{26}$$

The problem is now one of varying T, G, and L to maximize the expected utility of after-tax profit, subject to the accounting identity in equation (5) and the constraint that reserves equal required reserves $k_D D + k_T T$. If this procedure is followed, it can be shown that

14. The accounting identity defines $TA = W + D + T$. By the result in equation (17), $\partial TA/\partial t = 0$. Therefore, $\partial(E[\text{borrowing}]/TA)/\partial t = (\partial b/\partial t)F(b)/TA$. The required result follows from noting the definition of b in equation (1).

$$\frac{\partial T}{\partial t} = 0, \tag{17'}$$

$$\frac{\partial G}{\partial t} = \frac{-\left[(1-t)\int_0^1 (\alpha MR_L - r_G)\pi U''[(1-t)\pi]dV(\alpha)\right]}{D}, \tag{18'}$$

$$\frac{\partial L}{\partial t} = \frac{\left[(1-t)\int_0^1 (\alpha MR_L - r_G)\pi U''[(1-t)\pi]dV(\alpha)\right]}{D}, \tag{19'}$$

and

$$\frac{\partial R}{\partial t} = 0. \tag{20'}$$

In Appendix C it is shown that

$$\int_0^1 (\alpha MR_L - r_G)\pi U''[(1-t)\pi]dV(\alpha) \lesseqgtr 0 \quad \text{according as} \quad R_R' \gtreqless 0. \tag{27}$$

This result implies that (by the second-order conditions $D < 0$)[15]

$$\frac{\partial G}{\partial t} \gtreqless 0 \quad \text{according as} \quad R_R' \gtreqless 0, \tag{28}$$

and

$$\frac{\partial L}{\partial t} \gtreqless 0 \quad \text{according as} \quad R_R' \gtreqless 0. \tag{29}$$

These results are also in accord with those obtained by Arrow [1964]; i.e., as the decision maker becomes worse off (i.e., t rises), the proportion of the portfolio in the "risky" asset (which will be loans in the presence of default risk) increases (decreases) if the index of relative aversion is increasing (declining).

The comparative static results of the preceding two subsections are given in Table II. In the first column the effects of raising tax rates, when there is default risk (and nonstochastic deposit flows), are

15. The denominator is given by

$$D = (1-t)^2 \int_0^1 (\alpha MR_L - r_G)^2\, U''[(1-t)\pi]dV + (1-t)\int_0^1 \alpha MR_L' U'[(1-t)\pi]dv < 0,$$

since $MR_L' < 0$ and $U'' < 0$.

TABLE II

COMPARATIVE STATIC RESULTS GIVEN ALTERNATIVE SOURCES OF UNCERTAINTY

	Default risk	Stochastic reserve and deposit flows	Both sources of uncertainty
$\frac{\partial L}{\partial t}$	$\gtreqless 0$ as $R_R' \gtreqless 0$	0	$\gtreqless 0$ as $R_R' \gtreqless 0$
$\frac{\partial G}{\partial t}$	$\lesseqgtr 0$ as $R_R' \gtreqless 0$	$\gtreqless 0$ as $R_R' \gtreqless 0$	?
$\frac{\partial R}{\partial t}$	0	$\lesseqgtr 0$ as $R_R' \gtreqless 0$	$\lesseqgtr 0$ as $R_R' \gtreqless 0$
$\frac{\partial E[\text{borrowing}]}{\partial t}$	0	$\gtreqless 0$ as $R_R' \gtreqless 0$	$\gtreqless 0$ as $R_R' \gtreqless 0$

presented, and in the second column the effects when there are stochastic deposit flows (but no default risk) are presented. The third column presents the combined results. It will be noticed that the effect of higher tax rates on holdings of government securities is of opposite sign in columns one and two, yielding an indeterminate result in column three.

The reasons for this are as follows. If relative risk aversion is increasing and taxes are raised, Arrow's [1964] work would suggest that the bank portfolio should become proportionately more risky. When default risk on loans is the only source of uncertainty, this occurs if the proportion of the portfolio in loans increases. In this case, since reserves are mechanically determined by the level of deposits, this means that government securities decline. However, when stochastic deposit flows are the only source of uncertainty, the portfolio will become proportionately more risky, following the increase in t, if reserves fall and other assets increase; i.e., if holdings of government securities rise. When both sources of uncertainty appear simultaneously, it is no longer clear what the effect on G will be. The net effect will probably depend upon which source of uncertainty is in some sense the greater.

For the purposes of conducting empirical work, the tax rate was defined as[16]

$$t \equiv \text{taxes/before tax income.} \tag{30}$$

Loans, U. S. securities, and borrowings from the Federal Reserve (all deflated by total assets) were regressed in turn on t, and then on t and

16. In a different context, Harberger [1962, 1966] has employed a similar definition of the effective rate of tax for the purpose of conducting empirical work.

other variables.[17] The regression results are presented in Table III.[18]

It will be noted that the coefficients on the tax parameter in the loan and federal borrowing regression equations are positive and significant (at least at the 10 percent level). A look at the comparative static results in the final column of Table II indicates that the regression results are consistent with the hypothesis that the index of relative risk aversion is increasing for commercial banks.[19] In the same equation for U. S. securities, the tax parameter is insignificant. The result is consistent with the assumption that the two sources of uncertainty in the model are of approximately "equal size." The major qualifications that need to be emphasized when evaluating these results are taken up in the concluding section.

V. Conclusion

The work in this paper culminated in the previous section with the presentation of empirical results that were claimed to be consistent with the hypothesis that the index of relative risk aversion is increasing in profits. The further step of concluding that the empirical results imply that the index is increasing has not been taken. The major reason for this caution turns on the issue of the monotonicity of R_R. If R_R is not monotone, then the conclusion that $R_R' > 0$ does not follow from the empirical work. Further, since there are many "satisfactory" utility functions for which R_R is nonmonotone, this possibility cannot be dismissed out of hand.[20]

Additional reasons for regarding the conclusion of the preceding sections as suggestive rather than definitive would be the following.

17. The data on loans, U. S. securities, and total assets were obtained from the call reports. The data on borrowing from the Fed were obtained from weekly reports of deposit data by summing borrowings in each week for each bank in order to get a yearly total. Presumably this annual total is a reasonable estimate of E[borrowing]. The regression including the other variables (essentially deposit proportions) was included to ensure that the link between loans and t, and borrowing and t, was robust.

18. A regression involving reserves was not included, since reserve requirements are not uniform across banks and the model does not allow for this (i.e., in the model reserve requirements are not functionally dependent upon the level of deposits).

19. The value of the R^2 in these regression equations will strike the reader as being small. However, in the type of empirical work that attempts to say something about the behavior of indices of risk aversion, they are in the "normal" range. For example, see the work of Graves [1976]. He investigates the behavior of R_R using data on the demand for money.

20. The issue of monotonicity, however, must also be placed in the context of the existence of a vast theoretical literature that routinely signs comparative static expressions by appealing to the behavior of a monotone index of relative or absolute risk aversion.

TABLE III

EMPIRICAL RELATIONSHIP BETWEEN LOANS, U.S. SECURITIES, FEDERAL BORROWING, AND THE EFFECTIVE RATE OF TAX

	Loans		U.S. securities		Federal reserve borrowing	
Intercept	0.523	1.164	0.164	−0.587	0.035	0.502
	(139.25)	(10.60)	(47.46)	(−5.91)	(7.13)	(4.49)
t	0.157	0.108	−0.009	0.006	0.030	0.027
	(4.54)	(5.78)	(−0.81)	(0.34)	(1.82)	(1.68)
Time deposits over total deposits		−0.110		0.196		0.138
		(−2.15)		(4.26)		(2.60)
Demand deposits over total deposits		−0.363		0.087		−0.002
		(−6.08)		(1.61)		(−0.03)
Total deposits over total assets		−0.502		0.670		0.070
		(−4.57)		(6.78)		(1.60)
Inverse of total assets		−0.143		0.334		0.588
		(−3.91)		(10.14)		(−5.49)
R^2	0.104	0.122	0.000	0.148	0.002	0.031
F	20.57	30.63	0.66	38.51	3.33	9.27
N	1,480	1,480	1,480	1,480	1,480	1,480

First, the tax rate introduced in the previous section is not really a parameter, but is an endogenous variable, determined in large measure by the proportion of its portfolio that a bank decides to maintain in the form of nontaxable securities.[21] Second, the comparative static results were not derived for both sources of uncertainty appearing simultaneously.[22] Third, all the theoretical results of the paper have been obtained under the assumption that banks maximize the expected value of a monotone-increasing function of after-tax profits.

These are undoubtedly powerful criticisms of the assumptions and methodology adopted in this paper. However, given the absence of formal empirical work on the subject of bank attitude toward risk and the potential importance of such a study, a theoretical framework that possessed empirical content was constructed and tested.[23]

Appendix A

The purpose of this Appendix is to show that

$$\frac{-\partial E(\pi)}{\partial T}, \frac{\partial E(\pi)}{\partial G}, \frac{\partial E(\pi)}{\partial L} \lesseqqgtr 0 \quad \text{according as} \quad U'' \lesseqqgtr 0.$$

Since the result concerning $\partial E(\pi)/\partial L$ is the most difficult of the three to establish and the proofs of the results concerning $\partial E(\pi)/\partial T$ and $\partial E(\pi)/\partial G$ follow by similar means, it is the only one proved here.

Proof

Equation (8) can be rewritten as

$$\text{(A-1)} \quad \underset{\alpha}{E}(\alpha MR_L - r_P)\underset{\alpha}{E}(I_1) + \underset{\alpha}{E}(\alpha MR_L)\underset{\alpha}{E}(I_2) + \underset{\alpha}{\text{cov}}[\alpha MR_L - r_P; I_1] + \underset{\alpha}{\text{cov}}[\alpha MR_L; I_2] = 0.$$

Now, since $\partial I_1/\partial\alpha$, $\partial I_2/\partial\alpha \lesseqqgtr 0$ according as $U'' \lesseqqgtr 0$, then

21. t does measure the effective rate of tax on a bank, and has the precedent of having been used extensively in the public finance area as a measure of the effective rate of tax on a firm for the purpose of conducting empirical work (for example, see Harberger [1962, 1966]).

22. This point draws attention to the general problem of the difficulty of obtaining determinate comparative static results when there is more than one source of uncertainty. The vast bulk of the literature in the area of the economics of uncertainty does not treat more than one source, and the remainder that does, either does not have the degree of institutional complexity of the model in this paper or works with a specific utility function.

23. The potential importance of the results of any such study can be gauged by looking at the one recent controversy: that concerning the effects of the removal of the prohibition of explicit interest payments on demand deposits by Gambs [1975, 1977], Caperaa-Eeckhoudt [1977], and Quick [1977]. Here the results of the different authors turned on the assumptions (sometimes implicit) made regarding the qualitative behavior of bank indices of risk aversion.

$$\text{(A-2)}\quad \underset{\alpha}{\mathrm{cov}}[\alpha MR_L - r_P;I_1] + \underset{\alpha}{\mathrm{cov}}[\alpha MR_L;I_2] \lesseqgtr 0$$

$$\text{according as} \quad U'' \lesseqgtr 0.$$

This result in (A-2), together with (A-1), implies that

$$\text{(A-3)}\quad \underset{\alpha}{E}(\alpha MR_L - r_P)E(I_1) + \underset{\alpha}{E}(\alpha MR_L)\underset{\alpha}{E}(I_2) \lesseqgtr 0$$

$$\text{according as} \quad U'' \lesseqgtr 0.$$

Risk-Averse Case

Note that for $U'' < 0$,

$$\text{(A-4)}\quad \underset{\alpha}{E}[I_1] = \underset{\alpha}{E}\left[\int_a^b U'[\pi_1]dF(y)\right]$$

$$= \underset{\alpha}{E}\left[U'[\pi|y=b]\int_a^b \frac{U'[\pi_1]}{U'[\pi|y=b]}dF(y)\right]$$

$$> \underset{\alpha}{E}\left[U'[\pi|y=b]\int_a^b dF(y)\right] = p_1\underset{\alpha}{E}U'[\pi|y=b],$$

and that

$$\text{(A-5)}\quad \underset{\alpha}{E}[I_2] = \underset{\alpha}{E}\left[\int_b^c U'[\pi_2]dF(y)\right]$$

$$= \underset{\alpha}{E}\left[U'[\pi|y=b]\int_b^c \frac{U'[\pi_2]}{U'[\pi|y=b]}dF(y)\right]$$

$$< \underset{\alpha}{E}\left[U'[\pi|y=b]\int_b^c dF(y)\right] = p_2\underset{\alpha}{E}U'[\pi|y=b].$$

An examination of the efficiency condition in equation (8) reveals that in order to obtain an interior solution, the bank will set $\bar{\alpha}MR_L - r_p < 0$. This condition on $\bar{\alpha}MJ_L$ and the results in (A-4) and (A-5) imply that for risk-averse banks

$$\text{(A-6)}\quad (\bar{\alpha}MR_L - r_P)p_1\underset{\alpha}{E}U'[\pi|y=b] + \bar{\alpha}MR_Lp_2\underset{\alpha}{E}U'[\pi|y=b]$$

$$> (\bar{\alpha}MR_L - r_P)\underset{\alpha}{E}(I_1) + \bar{\alpha}MR_L\underset{\alpha}{E}(I_2).$$

The right-hand side of this inequality is the expression appearing in (A-3) and is positive for the case we are considering; i.e., for $U'' < 0$. It follows, therefore, that

$$(\overline{\alpha}MR_L - r_P)p_1\underset{\alpha}{E}U'[\pi|y = b] + \overline{\alpha}MR_Lp_2\underset{\alpha}{E}U'[\pi|y = b]$$

$$= a_L\underset{\alpha}{E}U'[\pi|y = b] > 0 \quad \text{for } U'' < 0.$$

This gives the result that $a_L > 0$ for $U'' < 0$. The required results for $U'' > 0$ and $U'' = 0$ follow by similar arguments.

Appendix B

In what follows, we shall make extensive use of the Pratt-Arrow measure of relative risk aversion:

$$R_R[\text{after-tax profits}] = -[\text{after-tax profits}]\,\frac{U''[\text{after-tax profits}]}{U'[\text{after-tax profits}]}.$$

PROPOSITION.

$$H(G) = (r_G - r_P)\int_a^b \pi_1 U''[(1-t)\pi_1]dF + r_G \times \int_b^c \pi_2 U''[(1-t)\pi_2]dF \lesseqgtr 0$$

$$\text{according as} \quad R_R' \gtreqless 0.$$

Proof

Take $R_R' > 0$,
For $y < b$,

$$-(1-t)\pi_1\frac{U''[(1-t)\pi_1]}{U'[(1-t)\pi_1]} < R_R[(1-t)\pi|y = b].$$

Multiplying through by the negative number $(r_G - r_P)U'[(1-t)\pi_1]$ yields

$$-(1-t)(r_G - r_P)\pi_1 U''[(1-t)\pi_1] > (r_G - r_P)\,U'[(1-t)\pi_1]R_R[(1-t)\pi_1|y = b].$$

Taking expectations over y gives

$$\text{(B-1)} \quad -(1-t)(r_G - r_P)\int_a^b \pi_1 U''[(1-t)\pi_1]dF(y) > \left[(r_G - r_P)\int_a^b U'[(1-t)\pi_1]dF(y)\right]R_R[(1-t)\pi_1|y = b].$$

For $y > b$,

$$-(1-t)\pi_2\frac{U''[(1-t)\pi_2]}{U'[(1-t)\pi_2]} > R_R[(1-t)\pi|y = b].$$

Multiplying through by $r_G U'[(1-t)\pi_2]$ yields

$$-(1-t)r_G\pi_2 U''[(1-t)\pi_2] > r_G U'[(1-t)\pi_2]\,R_R[(1-t)\pi|y = b].$$

Taking expectations over y gives

$$\text{(B-2)}\quad -(1-t)r_G \int_b^c \pi_2 U''[(1-t)\pi_2]dF(y) > \left[r_G \int_b^c U'[(1-t)\pi_2]dF(y)\right] R_R[(1-t)\pi | y = b].$$

Adding (B-1) and (B-2) yields

$$\text{(B-3)}\quad -(1-t)\left[(r_G - r_P)\int_a^b \pi_1 U''[(1-t)\pi_1]dF + r_G \int_b^c \pi_2 U''[(1-t)\pi_2]dF\right] > \left[(r_G - r_P)\int_a^b U'[(1-t)\pi_1]dF + r_G \int_b^c U'[(1-t)\pi_2]dF\right] R_R[(1-t)\pi | y = b] = 0$$

by equation (7).
The results implied by the proposition when $R_R' \lesseqgtr 0$ follow by similar means.

Appendix C

If $(1-t)\pi$ is the level of after-tax profits, the Arrow-Pratt measure of relative risk aversion is given by

$$R_R[(1-t)\pi] = -(1-t)\pi \frac{U''[(1-t)\pi]}{U'[(1-t)\pi]}.$$

PROPOSITION.

$$\int_0^1 (\alpha MR_L - r_G)\pi U''[(1-t)\pi]dV(\alpha) \lesseqgtr 0 \quad \text{according as} \quad R_R' \lesseqgtr 0.$$

Proof

Take $R_R' > 0$.
For $\alpha < r_G/MR_L$,

$$-(1-t)\pi \frac{U''[(1-t)\pi]}{U'[(1-t)\pi]} < R_R\left[(1-t)\pi | \alpha = \frac{r_G}{MR_L}\right].$$

Multiplying throughout by the positive number $-(\alpha MR_L - r_G)U'[(1-t)\pi]$ yields

$$\text{(C-1)}\quad (1-t)\pi(\alpha MR_L - r_G)U''[(1-t)\pi] < -(\alpha MR_L - r_G)U'[(1-t)\pi]R_R[(1-t)\pi | \alpha = r_G/MR_L].$$

For $\alpha > r_G/MR_L$,

$$-(1-t)\pi \frac{U''[(1-t)\pi]}{U'[(1-t)\pi]} > R_R\left[(1-t)\pi | \alpha = \frac{r_G}{MR_L}\right].$$

Multiplying throughout by the negative number $-(\alpha MR_L - r_G)U'[(1-t)\pi]$ also yields

(C-2) $$(1-t)\pi(\alpha MR_L - r_G)U''[(1-t)\pi] < -(\alpha MR_L - r_G)U'[(1-t)\pi]R_R[(1-t)\pi|\alpha = r_G/MR_L].$$

Integrating (C-1) over $\alpha < r_G/MR_L$ and (C-2) over $\alpha > r_G/MR_L$, and adding together yields

(C-3) $$(1-t)\int_0^1 (\alpha MR_L - r_G)\pi U'' dV < -\left[\int_0^1 (\alpha MR_L - r_G)U' dV\right] R_R[(1-t)\pi|\alpha = r_G/MR_L].$$

Subtracting equation (7) from equation (8) in the text above yields the first term on the right-hand side of the inequality in (C-3). This term in equilibrium is zero. The required result in the proposition is therefore established for $R_R' > 0$. Results for the other cases of R_R' $\leq$ follow by similar means.

UNIVERSITY OF MISSOURI, COLUMBIA

REFERENCES

Arrow, K. J., *Aspects of the Theory of Risk Bearing* (Helsinki: Yrjo Jahnsonin Saatio, 1964).

Caperaa, Philippe, and Louis Eeckhoudt, "Interest Bearing Demand Deposits and Bank Portfolio Behavior: Comment," *Southern Economic Journal,* XLIV (1977), 395–98.

Cooper, J. Phillip, "Stochastic Reserve Losses and Expansion of Bank Credit: Note," *American Economic Review,* LXI (1971), 741–45.

Fama, Eugene F., and Merton H. Miller, *The Theory of Finance* (New York: Holt Rinehart and Winston, Inc., 1972).

Frost, P. A., "Bank's Demand for Excess Reserves," *Journal of Political Economy,* LXXIX (1971), 805–25.

Gambs, Carl M., "Interest Bearing Demand Deposits and Bank Portfolio Behavior," *Southern Economic Journal,* XLII (1975), 79–82.

——, "Interest Bearing Demand Deposits and Bank Portfolio Behavior: Reply," *Southern Economic Journal,* XLIV (1977), 403–05.

Goldberger, Arthur S., *Econometric Theory* (New York, London, Sydney: John Wiley & Sons, Inc., 1964).

Graves, Philip E., "Wealth and Cash Asset Proportions," *Journal of Money, Credit and Banking,* VIII (1976), 487–96.

Grossman, Herschel I., "A Stochastic Model of Commercial Bank Behavior," *The American Economist,* IX (1965), 27–34.

Harberger, Arnold C., "The Incidence of the Corporation Income Tax," *Journal of Political Economy,* LXX (1962), 215–40.

——, "Efficiency Effects of Taxes on Income from Capital," in *Effects of Corporation Income Tax,* M. Krzyzaniak, ed. (Detroit: Wayne State University Press, 1966).

Hester, Donald D., and James L. Pierce, *Bank Management and Portfolio Behavior* (New Haven and London: Yale University Press, 1975).

Kane, Edward J., and Burton G. Malkiel, "Bank Portfolio Allocation, Deposit Variability, and the Availability Doctrine," this *Journal,* LXXIX (1965), 113–34.

Klein, Michael A., "Imperfect Asset Elasticity and Portfolio Theory," *American Economic Review,* LX (1970), 491–94.

——, "A Theory of a Banking Firm," *Journal of Money, Credit and Banking,* III (1971), 205–18.

Morrison, George R., *Liquidity Preferences of Commercial Banks* (Chicago: University of Chicago Press, 1966).

Orr, D., and W. G. Mellon, "Stochastic Reserve Losses and Expansion of Bank Credit," *American Economic Review,* LI (1961), 614–23.

Parkin, M., "Discount House Portfolio and Debt Selection," *Review of Economic Studies,* XXXVII (1970), 469–98.
Poole W., "Commercial Bank Reserve Management in a Stochastic Model: Implications for Monetary Policy," *Journal of Finance,* XXIII (1968), 769–91.
Porter, Richard C., "A Model of Bank Portfolio Selection," *Yale Economic Essays,* I (1960), 232–59.
Pratt, J. W., "Risk Aversion in the Small and in the Large," *Econometrica,* XXXII (1964), 122–36.
Quick, Perry D., "Interest Bearing Demand Deposits and Bank Portfolio Behavior: Comment," *Southern Economic Journal,* XLIV (1977), 399–402.
Ratti, Ronald A., "Stochastic Reserve Losses and Bank Credit Expansion," *Journal of Monetary Economics,* V (1979), 283–94.
Scott, I. O., "The Availability Doctrine: Theoretical Underpinnings," *Review of Economic Studies,* XXV (1957), 41–48.
Taggart, Robert A., and Stuart I. Greenbaum, "Bank Capital and Public Regulation," *Journal of Money, Credit and Banking,* X (1978), 158–69.

THE OPTIMUM MONETARY AGGREGATE FOR STABILIZATION POLICY*

DON E. ROPER AND STEPHEN J. TURNOVSKY

This paper presents a procedure for determining the optimal monetary aggregate for stabilization policy. To illustrate the procedure, a simple stochastic IS-LM model is used, and how, in general, stabilizing an aggregate consisting of both money and interest bearing government debt will provide superior stabilization for output is shown. The relative weight given to the two components in the aggregate may vary widely, depending upon the source of random disturbances in the economy. Also, for a specific weight, stabilizing the aggregate is equivalent to stabilizing the interest rate. Finally, we show how stabilizing the aggregate is equivalent to other forms of optimal monetary policy proposed by Poole, and Kareken, Muench, and Wallace.

I. INTRODUCTION

The implication of most theoretical literature is that, except under extreme assumptions, it is generally suboptimal to stabilize a monetary aggregate. If the demand for money has, as most economists agree, some sensitivity to interest rates, and if interest rates and bank deposits are observable on a fairly current basis, then the money supply should *not* be held constant even if the demand for money is perfectly stable (i.e., all shocks are in other sectors of the economy). This point is found in the combination policy developed by Poole [1970] and in the recent exposition by LeRoy and Lindsey [1978]. It has also been emphasized in the studies by Kareken, Muench, and Wallace [1973] (hereinafter referred to as KMW) and B. Friedman [1977].[1]

The purpose of this paper is to argue that this well-entrenched theoretical proposition rests on the use of conventional or suboptimal aggregates. By directly relating the definition of "money" to the goal(s) of stabilization policy, the role of a constant (rate of growth of) money may indeed be optimal. Within the context of the standard IS-LM model used in most investigations of this subject, stabilization of the appropriately chosen aggregate is, as will be shown below, always optimal.

* The authors have benefited from comments by Lance Girton, John Judd, Dale Henderson, Larry Kotlikoff, John Scadding, Staffan Viotti, Roger Waud, and the referees on earlier drafts of this paper.

1. This proposition in no way conflicts with the view frequently expressed by monetarists and proponents of rational expectations that it is optimal to maintain the money supply at some present level. This argument rests on the assumption that the options available to the monetary authorities are to adjust the money supply on the basis of alternative feedback rules, embodying only *past* information.

The Quarterly Journal of Economics, September 1980 0033-5533/80/0095-0333$02.30

Any monetary aggregate can be interpreted as a particular case of a weighted average of available financial instruments. Conventional aggregates usually employ weights of ones and zeros. The criterion developed in this paper for determining the optimal weights and, thereby, the optimal aggregate, is obtained by maximizing the objective function of the policymaker in a stochastic environment, with our chosen objective being the stabilization of income.

The monetary policy necessary to stabilize the aggregate found through this optimizing procedure is analytically equivalent to the open market strategy derived by Poole [1970] and by KMW [1973]. This equivalence is another way of looking at the point mentioned earlier, viz., that the demonstrations of the suboptimality of stabilizing an aggregate rest on the use of a conventional suboptimal aggregate. Once the optimum aggregate is chosen for monetary policy, the operations necessary to stabilize this aggregate will—by virtue of the optimizing procedure used to obtain the aggregate—be optimal.

Various criteria have been suggested for defining "money." As Mason [1963] has pointed out, "money" was once used to refer to gold or silver (which were thought to determine the price level) and "currency" referred to the broader aggregate, the medium of exchange. Although Friedman and Schwartz [1970] question the medium-of-exchange criterion for defining money, the popularity of M1 over other aggregates is undoubtedly related to its close proximity to the medium of exchange. With new regulatory changes authorizing NOW (negotiable order of withdrawal) accounts and ATS (automatic transfers from savings to demand deposits), a revised measure of M1 has been proposed [Simpson, 1979] which corresponds more closely to the medium of exchange. A somewhat more general criterion for defining "money" is to weight various items according to their turnover rates. And, perhaps an even more general criterion is the concept of liquidity which was emphasized in the Radcliffe Report [1959] and by Gurley and Shaw [1960]. While there is an intuitive appeal with each of these criteria, the precise reason why an aggregate constructed using such criteria would be best for stabilization policy is unclear.

In other studies the criteria for defining money has focused on the degree of substitution among various liabilities of banking and thrift institutions [Scadding, 1979; and Barnett, 1980] and on the stability of the demand for money. Beginning with early work in the 1950s by Milton Friedman and his students, the stability of money-demand continues to be a cornerstone of the monetarist argument for stable money growth. Any evidence that the historical relationship between money, income, and interest rates is less stable than it was before is regarded as a serious threat to the use of money as an intermediate target. According to Enzler, Johnson, and Paulus [1976] and

Goldfeld [1976], the most popular aggregate M1, has fallen below the values predicted by standard money-demand equations since mid-1974. Another possible downward shift beginning in late 1978 has been discussed by Porter, Simpson, and Mauskopf [1979]. Further money-demand studies of the stability of money-demand by Hamburger [1977], Cargill and Meyer [1979], Garcia and Pak [1979], Lieberman [1979], and Wenninger and Sivesind [1979] indicate the widespread importance currently attached to this issue. The questionable stability of the demand for M1 has caused some observers [Froewiss, Judd, Keran, and Scadding, 1979] to advocate the adoption of M2 over M1. The argument of this paper is that the choice of aggregate should be expanded to a much wider range of aggregates (as Barnett [1980] has also argued), and that the choice of aggregate should be explicitly related to the policymakers' objective(s). The stability of money-demand will, other things being the same, enhance stabilization policy. But this is not the sole characteristic on which the argument for a money growth target rests, since it is not the only characteristic of the optimal aggregate.

The remainder of the paper is organized as follows: In Section II the IS-LM model is used to determine the optimal weights between the two assets (bank liabilities and government bonds) using the variance of real output as the objective function. In Section III various characteristics of the optimal aggregate are studied, and the underlying monetary policy required for stabilizing the optimum aggregate is discussed. Not only does focusing on this simplified model have the advantage of enabling us to obtain an analytical solution to the optimal aggregate problem, but also it makes it possible to relate our approach to Poole's combination policy and the monetary strategy recommended by KMW. This relationship is discussed in Section IV. A brief final section summarizes the conclusions and indicates some qualifications to our work.

II. THE STABILIZATION OF A MONETARY AGGREGATE IN A TWO-ASSET MODEL

A general monetary aggregate can be defined as the sum of the money values of various assets, each with an individual weight. If there are n assets in existence, with A_{it} denoting the stock of asset i at time t, and P_{it} the price of asset i at time t, expressed in terms of the numeraire, money, then a general expression that encompasses all monetary aggregates is given by

$$\Phi_t = \sum_{i=1}^{n} v_i P_{it} A_{it}, \tag{1}$$

where ν_i = weight assigned to the ith asset.[2] It is intuitively clear and will be demonstrated below that the policy of stabilizing an aggregate is invariant with respect to the *scale* of the set of ν_i's. Accordingly, the interesting problem of the *relative* weights of the components can be distinguished from the inconsequential question of scale by rewriting the aggregate formula as

$$\Phi_t = \mu \sum_{i=1}^{n} \lambda_i P_{it} A_{it}, \tag{1'}$$

where

$$\sum_{i=1}^{n} \lambda_i = 1$$

and μ is an arbitrary scale parameter. The problem of determining the optimal aggregate can in general be treated as the problem of finding the $(n-1)$ relative weights to attach to the n assets. We find no reason for imposing nonnegative restrictions on the λ_i's. Indeed, as will be demonstrated below, there are conditions under which the optimum weight on a financial asset can be negative.

In the context of a two-asset IS-LM model (where there is only one relative weight λ to be determined), it seems most useful to focus on the determination of the optimum aggregate in terms of determining the weight to be given to the liabilities of the banking system, relative to the weight given to the interest-bearing liabilities of the government. In other words, while it is ultimately desirable to examine the more detailed problem of how much weight should be attached to demand deposits versus time deposits (of various kinds) versus currency, it seems more appropriate as an initial analysis to address the basic question of bank liabilities versus interest-bearing government debt.

For expositional simplicity, it is convenient to abstract from a commercial banking sector, so that the bank liabilities component, which we shall rather loosely refer to as "money," is in fact equivalent to the monetary base in our aggregate. We shall allow the optimizing procedure to determine to what extent this component of the aggregate should be augmented to include interest-bearing government debt as well. Subsequently, we shall briefly indicate how our results would be altered by the introduction of a simple commercial banking

2. Since we are constructing an aggregate from a number of components, the relative prices of which may vary, we must define the numeraire in terms of one of these components. Following the example of most macro literature, the numeraire commodity will be referred to as "money."

sector, in which total demand deposits are taken to be a simple multiple of the monetary base.

We now embed the aggregate defined in (1′) (with $n = 2$) into a simple IS-LM model, similar to that used by Poole [1970]. Since all constants have been removed, the system is to be interpreted as being measured in *deviation* form about some steady-state equilibrium. The model consists of the following relationships:

$$y_t = ap_t + u_t \qquad a > 0 \tag{2a}$$

$$m_t = b_1 y_t + b_2 p_t + v_t \qquad b_1 > 0, b_2 > 0 \tag{2b}$$

$$\phi_t = \mu[\lambda m_t + (1 - \lambda)[\overline{P} b_t + \overline{B} p_t]] \tag{2c}$$

$$m_t - m_{t-1} + \overline{P}(b_t - b_{t-1}) = 0, \tag{2d}$$

where

y_t = (real) income at time t
b_t = number of government bonds outstanding
p_t = price of government bonds
$\overline{P}$ = steady-state equilibrium price level of government bonds
$\overline{B}$ = steady-state equilibrium number of government bonds outstanding
m_t = money, taken to be high-powered or base money
ϕ_t = monetary aggregate
u_t = stochastic disturbance in the demand for output, assumed to be additive
v_t = stochastic disturbance in the demand for money, assumed to be additive.

Two general features of this model merit comment. First, the price of output is assumed to be fixed. It would be possible to apply our procedure to a context where prices are determined endogenously. In this case, if price expectations are formed rationally, it may be more appropriate to focus on the stabilization of prices rather than income.[3] However, our concentration on the fixed price case facilitates the

3. We are referring here, of course, to the increasingly familiar proposition that, under rational expectations, the variance of real output may be invariant with respect to the choice of a fixed monetary stabilization rule: see e.g., Sargent and Wallace [1975]. However, as shown in Section IV below, our procedure for stabilizing an optimal monetary aggregate is equivalent to an optimal Poole [1970] combination policy. As shown recently by Woglom [1979], such a combination policy *can* succeed in reducing the variance of real income, implying that the stabilization of real income may indeed remain an appropriate objective (along with the stabilization of prices) in our context.

comparison with the alternative approaches to optimal monetary policy, discussed in Section IV below, which are also based on this assumption. Second, an apparent difference between the above model and the conventional specification of an IS-LM model is the introduction of the bond price, rather than the interest rate into the demand functions of the system. This is done primarily to facilitate the linearization process that is necessary to obtain an explicit solution to the optimization procedure.[4] But the use of the bond price or its associated interest rate is strictly equivalent if rates and prices are uniquely and inversely related, as will be the case in all but extreme and perverse circumstances.[5]

We now turn to the equations of the model: (2a) describes the IS curve, solved explicitly for output, while (2b) is the LM curve. Both of these relationships are subject to random disturbances, the properties of which are outlined below. Equations (2c) and (2d) are linear approximations to the expression for the monetary aggregate and the government budget constraint, respectively. From (1), the general expression for a monetary aggregate consisting of a weighted average of money and government bonds is given by

$$\Phi_t = \mu[\lambda M_t + (1 - \lambda)P_t B_t], \tag{2c$'$}$$

where Φ_t, M_t, B_t, P_t denote levels of the monetary aggregate, the stock of money, stock of bonds, and price of bonds respectively. Note that B_t and M_t are not dimensionally equivalent; consequently, the aggregate must be defined as the weighted average of $P_t B_t + M_t$, or as the weighted average of $B_t + M_t/P_t$. We have chosen the former, since it makes the exposition more intuitive, without altering the results. Subtracting this expression from the corresponding steady-state

4. The introduction of asset prices into the demand functions is analogous to the use of the "Tobin q" being increasingly adopted in theoretical specifications of investment functions; see Tobin [1969].

5. The usual rate of return r_t introduced into discrete-time macromodels is the one-period rate of return. In general, this is related to the corresponding asset price p_t by the following relationship:

$$r_t = \frac{\bar{d}}{P_t} + \frac{P^*_{t+1,t} - P_t}{P_t},$$

where $\bar{d}$ is the coupon rate and $P^*_{t+1,t}$ is the expectation of the asset price for time t + 1, formed at time t. Differentiating this relationship yields

$$\frac{\partial r_t}{\partial P_t} = \frac{-\bar{d}}{P_t^2} + \frac{P^*_{t+1,t}}{P_t}\left(\frac{\partial P^*_{t+1,t}}{\partial P_t}\frac{P_t}{P^*_{t+1,t}} - 1\right).$$

A mild sufficient condition which ensures that $\partial r_t/\partial P_t < 0$ is that the elasticity of expectations, with respect to the current price level, not exceed unity.

values $\overline{\Phi}$, $\overline{M}$, $\overline{B}$, $\overline{P}$, we have[6]

$$\Phi_t - \overline{\Phi} = \mu[\lambda(M_t - \overline{M}) + (1 - \lambda)(P_t B_t - \overline{PB})],$$

and using the linear approximation,

$$P_t B_t - \overline{PB} \doteq \overline{P}(B_t - \overline{B}) + \overline{B}(P_t - \overline{P}) \equiv \overline{P} b_t + \overline{B} p_t$$

yields (2c). Throughout the analysis we shall assume that the government continually adjusts its taxes to maintain a balanced budget. This continually balanced budget is justified on the grounds that monetary policy is not mixed with fiscal policy, and in general implies a government budget constraint of the form,

$$M_t - M_{t-1} + P_t(B_t - B_{t-1}) = 0. \tag{2d'}$$

Subtracting this from the steady state and linearizing similarly leads to (2d), in deviation form.

The monetary authorities are assumed to be able to control B_t and M_t through open market operations. However, this does not mean that the aggregate itself is controllable. In fact, for certain weights open market purchases of m_t against b_t will leave the aggregate unchanged. This possibility is fortunately ruled out in the optimization process, as will be explained in footnote 11 below.

The stochastic disturbances, u_t and v_t, are assumed to have zero means, a finite variance-covariance matrix, and to be independently distributed over time. Thus, we have

$$E(u_t) = E(v_t) = 0 \tag{3a}$$

$$E(u_t^2) = \sigma_u^2; E(v_t^2) = \sigma_v^2; E(u_t v_t) = \sigma_{uv} = \sigma_u \sigma_v \rho, \tag{3b}$$

where ρ denotes the correlation coefficient between the two disturbances. Moreover, because of the aggregate budget constraint in the economy, which imposes a linear dependence in discrete time between the output, money, and bond markets (enabling us to eliminate the bond market as we have done), it follows that the sum of the random demand for output u'_t, demand for money v_t, and the random demand for bonds w_t satisfy the "adding up" condition[7]

6. These steady-state values are obtained by writing down the system in original levels form, and setting all stochastic terms identically to zero. Because of the balanced budget condition, the dynamics of the system become singular, so that the steady-state to which the system converges depends upon the initial conditions from which it starts. The precise details of this equilibrium, however, are now required for our analysis.

7. As is well-known, in continuous-time models the "adding up" conditions extend over the set of asset demands. For a discussion of the relationship between the adding up conditions for discrete-time and continuous-time models, see Turnovsky [1977, Ch. 3].

(3c) $$u'_t + v_t + w_t = 0.$$

With the IS solved as in (1a), u_t and u'_t are related by

$$u_t = u'_t/s_t,$$

where s denotes the marginal propensity to save[8] so that with the model as expressed above, the adding up condition becomes

(3c′) $$su_t + v_t + w_t = 0.$$

Equations (3c) and (3c′) assert that the stochastic shifts in demand cannot be independent; a random shift in one market will be reflected in at least one other. This constraint imposes severe restrictions on the variances and covariances of the disturbances. For instance, multiplying (3c) through by u_t, v_t, and w_t, in turn, and taking expected values, one can express the covariances in terms of the variances. Thus, for instance, one can establish

(4) $$2s\sigma_{uv} = \sigma_w^2 - s^2\sigma_u^2 - \sigma_v^2,$$

where σ_w^2 denotes $E(w_t^2)$. Equation (4) turns out to be convenient for the other covariances if they should be required. The normal case (see, e.g., Poole [1970]) is where $\rho < 0$, so that an unexpected increase in the demand for output is reflected in a reduction in the demand for money. But it is possible that $\rho > 0$, and this will arise if w_t is sufficiently negatively correlated with both u_t and v_t. From (4) this is equivalent to requiring that $\sigma_w^2 > s^2\sigma_u^2 + \sigma_v^2$.

The four equations (2a)–(2d) determine the four variables y_t, p_t, m_t, and b_t in terms of the pegged monetary aggregate ϕ_t, the lagged values b_{t-1}, m_{t-1}, and the stochastic disturbances u_t, v_t. In particular, it is clear that pegging the aggregate will in general involve continually accommodating adjustments in the other financial variables m_t, b_t, and p_t. Before proceeding further, it is instructive to consider this aspect briefly, by interpreting the aggregate ϕ_t for different values of the weights λ, and by discussing the implications of different λ's for the rates-versus-aggregates tradeoff mentioned in the introduction.

It is immediately seen from (2c′) that setting $\lambda = 1$ is equivalent

8. The relationship between u'_t and u_t is obtained as follows. With u'_t representing the additive disturbance in output demand, the IS curve can be written as

$$y_t = cy_t + ip_t + u'_t, \qquad \text{where } 0 < c < 1, i > 0.$$

Solving for y_t yields

$$y_t = (i/s)p_t + u'_t/s \equiv ap_t + u_t, \qquad \text{where } s = 1 - c.$$

The modified form of the adding-up condition given in (3c′) asserts, in effect, that any random disturbance in savings $(-su_t)$ must be reflected in either a random increase in the demand for money (v_t) or in the demand for bonds (w_t).

to pegging (within each period) the level of money, or equivalently the monetary base, and setting $\lambda = 0$ involves pegging the value of government bonds. On the other hand, we see that when $\lambda = 1/2$, (2c′) becomes

$$\Phi_t = (\mu/2)[M_t + B_t P_t],$$

so that the aggregate being pegged is total government debt (interest-bearing plus non-interest-bearing). Taking first differences of (2c′), and combining with (2d), we obtain

$$\Delta\Phi_t/\mu = (1 - 2\lambda)\Delta M_t + (1 - \lambda)B_t\Delta P_t \tag{5}$$

so that pegging Φ_t (i.e., $\Delta\Phi_t = 0$) implies the relationship

$$-(1 - 2\lambda)\Delta M_t + (1 - \lambda)B_t\Delta P_t = 0 \tag{5′}$$

or equivalently

$$-\gamma(\lambda)\Delta M_t + B_t\Delta P_t = 0, \tag{5″}$$

where

$$\gamma(\lambda) = (1 - 2\lambda)/(1 - \lambda).$$

These equations emphasize the constraint imposed by pegging the aggregate Φ_t on the accommodating adjustment in deposits and bond prices (interest rates). In particular, γ/B is the weight given to changes in M_t relative to changes in the bond price or interest rate. Note that if $\lambda = 1/2$, so that the aggregate being pegged is the total government debt, then $\gamma = 0$ so that $\Delta P_t = 0$. In other words, pegging the total government debt is equivalent to pegging the price of bonds, or equivalently an interest rate policy. For other values of λ and γ, (5″) indicates the tradeoffs between ΔM and ΔP. If $1 > \lambda > 1/2$, M_t and P_t must move in opposite directions for the aggregate to remain fixed. That is, in response to an unexpected fall in demand for bonds, say, the monetary authority should let both the interest rate and deposits increase together. On the other hand, for $\lambda < 1/2$ or $\lambda > 1$, γ will be positive, and the adjustment of M_t and P_t will be in the same direction. This will be considered further in the context of specific stochastic disturbances in Section III.

Returning to the complete model (2a)–(2d), we shall assume that the monetary authority wishes to stabilize income (in the sense of minimizing its asymptotic variance) about its steady-state level, by holding the aggregate ϕ_t at some optimal value over each unit time period. It is because we are concerned with the stability of the system relative to some equilibrium that makes it convenient to consider it in deviation form as we have done. In order to calculate the asymptotic variance of y_t, we must first solve (2a)–(2d) for y_t. This procedure yields the expression,

$$
(6) \qquad y_t = \frac{\begin{vmatrix} u_t & -a & 0 & 0 \\ -v_t & b_2 & -1 & 0 \\ \phi_t & \mu(1-\lambda)\overline{B} & \mu\lambda & \mu(1-\lambda)\overline{P} \\ m_{t-1} + \overline{P}b_{t-1} & 0 & 1 & \overline{P} \end{vmatrix}}{\begin{vmatrix} 1 & -a & 0 & 0 \\ b_1 & b_2 & -1 & 0 \\ 0 & \mu(1-\lambda)\overline{B} & \mu\lambda & \mu(1-\lambda)\overline{P} \\ 0 & 0 & 1 & \overline{P} \end{vmatrix}}.
$$

At this point, further consideration must be given to our choice of time unit. It will be noted that all demand functions are specified in terms of current variables. Thus, the unit time interval in this model is defined by the interval over which the government finances its deficits and which we take to be sufficiently long for the lags in demand to have worked themselves through. Over this period, the monetary aggregate ϕ_t remains pegged at its predetermined level.

But at the beginning of each time interval, which for practical purposes we might view as being on the order of six months, the monetary aggregate is adjusted optimally, so as to minimize the asymptotic variance of y_t, σ_y^2. Assuming that b_{t-1}, m_{t-1} are known at time t and that ϕ_t is costless to adjust, it is a standard proposition from linear control theory that σ_y^2 will be minimized by eliminating the autoregressive structure of the system, which can only compound the asymptotic variance.[9] Resetting the value of the aggregate at the beginning of each time interval in this way yields the following linear control law:[10]

9. See, e.g., Turnovsky [1975]. This general approach is used in another stabilization context by Currie [1976].

10. This rule is obtained as follows. First, split in two the determinant appearing in the numerator of (6), writing the equation in the form,

$$
\Omega y_t = \begin{vmatrix} u_t & -a & 0 & 0 \\ -v_t & b_2 & -1 & 0 \\ 0 & \mu(1-\lambda)\overline{B} & \mu\lambda & \mu(1-\lambda)\overline{P} \\ 0 & 0 & 1 & \overline{P} \end{vmatrix} + \begin{vmatrix} 0 & -a & 0 & 0 \\ 0 & b_2 & -1 & 0 \\ \phi_t & \mu(1-\lambda)\overline{B} & \mu\lambda & \mu(1-\lambda)\overline{P} \\ \overline{P}b_{t-1} + m_{t-1} & 0 & 1 & \overline{P} \end{vmatrix},
$$

where Ω denotes the denominator of (6). Now use the fact that the asymptotic variance of y_t will be minimized by choosing ϕ_t so as to annihilate the autoregressive structure of the system. This involves setting ϕ_t so that the second of these two determinants is zero. Equation (7) is the resulting solution for ϕ_t to that equation.

(7) $$\phi_t = \mu(1 - \lambda)(\overline{P}b_{t-1} + m_{t-1}).$$

That is, the monetary aggregate is adjusted in response to lagged values of m_{t-1} and b_{t-1} with the scale parameter μ entering as a constant of proportionality.

By substituting the adjustment rule (7) into (6), the dynamic, or autoreggressive, structure of the system is eliminated, such that the (irreducible) fluctuations in y_t are due only to random drawings of the current stochastic terms u_t, v_t. Hence y_t is now given by

(8) $$y_t = \frac{\begin{vmatrix} u_t & -a & 0 & 0 \\ -v_t & b_2 & -1 & 0 \\ 0 & (1-\lambda)\overline{B} & \lambda & 1-\lambda \\ 0 & 0 & 1 & 1 \end{vmatrix}}{\begin{vmatrix} 1 & -a & 0 & 0 \\ b_1 & b_2 & -1 & 0 \\ 0 & (1-\lambda)\overline{B} & \lambda & 1-\lambda \\ 0 & 0 & 1 & 1 \end{vmatrix}}.$$

Squaring (8) and taking expected values, the asymptotic variance of y_t is given by

(9) $$\sigma_y^2 = \frac{\omega_1^2\sigma_u^2 + \omega_2^2\sigma_v^2 + 2\omega_1\omega_2\omega_{uv}}{\delta^2},$$

where

(10a) $$\omega_1 = (1 - 2\lambda)b_2 - \overline{B}(1 - \lambda)$$

(10b) $$\omega_2 = -a(1 - 2\lambda)$$

(10c) $$\delta = (1 - 2\lambda)(b_2 + ab_1) - (1 - \lambda)\overline{B}.$$

The expression given in (9) is a function of the composition λ of the aggregate, but is independent of the scale parameter μ. If $\lambda = 1$, (9) simplifies to an expression (not reported here) that is identical to the variance obtained by Poole [1970, equation (11)] for the case in which the money supply is stabilized.

The remaining task is to choose the optimal aggregate by minimizing σ_y^2 with respect to λ. The details of this operation are extremely tedious and are not reported here. The end product of the calculations is the expression,

(11) $$\hat{\lambda} = \frac{b_1(\overline{B} - b_2)\sigma_u^2 + a\sigma_v^2 + (ab_1 + \overline{B} - b_2)\sigma_{uv}}{b_1(\overline{B} - 2b_2)\sigma_u^2 + 2a\sigma_v^2 + (2ab_1 + \overline{B} - 2b_2)\sigma_{uv}},$$

where a caret denotes the optimum.[11] Using (4), one can eliminate the covariance σ_{uv} from (11) and express $\hat{\lambda}$ equivalently in terms of the three variances $\sigma_u^2, \sigma_v^2, \sigma_w^2$. The corresponding minimized variance of income is

$$\hat{\sigma}_y^2 = \frac{\sigma_u^2 \sigma_v^2 (1 - \rho^2)}{b_1^2 \sigma_u^2 + \sigma_v^2 + 2b_1 \sigma_{uv}}. \tag{12}$$

Before discussing (11) in more detail, two further points should be noted. First, the assumption that all demand lags are worked through within our chosen unit time period is made only for convenience. The method would remain the same if such lags persisted beyond the period. In this case, the adjustment rule for the monetary aggregate would need to take them into account and annihilate them from the lag structure as well. Although the resulting control law would be somewhat complicated, the resulting behavior of y_t would remain essentially unaltered, and nothing of substance would be changed. The critical assumption we are making is that the period the monetary aggregate be pegged coincides with our chosen unit time period, but this does not seem an unreasonable assumption to make. Second, the variance given by (9) is also equal to the first-period variance, in a situation where ϕ_t is pegged at a fixed value for a period longer than our chosen unit interval. The determination of the asymptotic variance in this case becomes utterly intractable, and we do not attempt either to calculate or to optimize it.

III. Properties of the Optimal Aggregate and Associated Monetary Policy

In this section we discuss the properties of $\hat{\lambda}$, and the associated monetary policies involved in the stabilization of ϕ for various values of $\hat{\lambda}$.

It will be observed that $\hat{\lambda}$ depends upon $\bar{B} - b_2$, $\bar{B} - 2b_2$, both of which are indeterminate in sign. In order to analyze $\hat{\lambda}$, it is convenient to impose sign restrictions on these quantities, and specifically, we shall assume that

$$\bar{B} - 2b_2 > 0 \qquad \text{(and hence } \bar{B} - b_2 > 0\text{)}. \tag{13}$$

The empirical justification for these restrictions requires careful consideration of the monetary magnitudes involved. It will be recalled that for notational and expositional simplicity we have abstracted

11. One of the roots of the equation $\partial \sigma_y^2 / \partial \lambda = 0$ is $\delta = 0$. But this root produces a maximum rather than a minimum, as its presence in the denominator of equation (9) suggests. Although the explanation is too detailed to report here, $\delta \neq 0$ is a necessary and sufficient condition for the authorities to be able to control ϕ_t through open market operations.

from a commercial banking sector, so that m_t refers to high-powered money. If we were to impose a simple banking system and assume that the total money supply (deposits) m_t and the monetary base h_t were linked by a simple stable multiplier relationship,

$$m_t = kh_t, \tag{14}$$

where k denotes the money multiplier, then it can be shown that the analogous restrictions to (13) would become

$$\bar{B}k - (1 + k)b_2 > 0 \qquad \text{(and hence } \bar{B}k - b_2 > 0). \tag{13'}$$

The inequality (13′) may be rewritten as

$$(P\bar{B}/M)k - (1 + k)\eta > 0,$$

where η = elasticity of the demand for money (deposits) with respect to the price of bonds, which for perpetual bonds is simply minus the elasticity with respect to the interest rate. For the length of time period envisaged here, this may be taken to be around 0.2. Given the fairly broad nature of our aggregate, it would seem reasonable to assume that the ratio of government interest-bearing debt to deposits is around 1.0, while $k = 7$ would appear plausible. Parameter values chosen in these neighborhoods will ensure that (13′) is met. Accordingly, since (13) is in effect a simplification of (13′), it too is required to hold.

While the expression (11) for $\hat{\lambda}$ is rather complex, a number of definite conclusions can nevertheless be drawn. First, $\hat{\lambda}$ need not lie between 0 and 1. As we shall illustrate for special cases below, it is sometimes optimal to assign a negative weight to either M_t or P_tB_t. Second, as discussed in Section II, pegging the money supply ($\lambda = 1$), and pegging the interest rate ($\lambda = \frac{1}{2}$) are special cases of pegging the optimal aggregate. Except in special cases noted below, these are nonoptimal policies, and are dominated by some more general intermediate target. Third, if $\sigma_{uv} \geqq 0$, so that u_t and v_t are nonnegatively correlated, $\hat{\lambda} \geqq \frac{1}{2}$. It is worth noting that, in the more general case where the money supply and monetary base are linked by the money multiplier (14), the critical value $\hat{\lambda} = \frac{1}{2}$ is now replaced by $\hat{\lambda} = 1/(1 + k)$. Thus, for example, setting $\lambda = 1/(1 + k)$ will now result in the pegging of the nominal interest rate.

The partial derivatives of $\hat{\lambda}$ with respect to the variance σ_u^2, σ_v^2, and σ_w^2 (recalling (4)) have signs determined by the following relations:

$$\operatorname{sgn}\left(\frac{\partial\hat{\lambda}}{\partial\sigma_u^2}\right) = \operatorname{sgn}\left(-\frac{\sigma_v^2}{b_1^2} + \frac{\sigma_w^2}{(b_1 - s)^2}\right) \tag{15a}$$

(15b) $$\operatorname{sgn}\left(\frac{\partial\hat{\lambda}}{\partial\sigma_v^2}\right) = \operatorname{sgn}\left(\sigma_u^2 - \frac{\sigma_w^2}{(b_1 - s)^2}\right)$$

(15c) $$\operatorname{sgn}\left(\frac{\partial\hat{\lambda}}{\partial\sigma_w^2}\right) = \operatorname{sgn}\left(\frac{\sigma_v^2}{b_1^2} - \sigma_u^2\right).$$

There are various combinations of three terms on the right-hand side, all of which can be given a precise interpretation. The term σ_u^2, for instance, is the variance of income that would be necessary to clear the IS-equation if p_t were constant. Similarly, the term σ_v^2/b_1^2 is the variance of income that would be necessary to clear the LM-equation if p_t were constant. The same interpretation holds for $\sigma_w^2/(b_1 - s)^2$ and the bond equation. By dividing the variances σ_u^2, σ_v^2, and σ_w^2 by their respective income parameters, we have comparable measures of variance in terms of the power of the stochastic terms to affect y. We can refer to σ_u^2, σ_v^2/b_1^2 and $\sigma_w^2/(b_1 - s)^2$ as the "income variances" in the goods, deposits, and bond markets. Thus, whether an increase in σ_u^2 implies that more or less weight should be given to deposits versus bonds is determined by whether the income variance in the deposit market is greater or less than the income variance in the bond market as shown by equation (15a). Similar interpretations can be given for the other two equations.

To give some idea of the intuition underlying the signs given by (15), let us consider (15b) in conjunction with

(4′) $$2\sigma_{vw} = s^2\sigma_u^2 - \sigma_v^2 - \sigma_w^2.$$

Suppose that (15b) is negative, so that σ_u^2 is small relative to σ_w^2. Then for reasonable parameter values (15b) and (4′) imply that v_t and w_t will be negatively correlated. Moreover, with σ_u^2, σ_w^2 held constant, an increase in σ_v^2 will increase the degree of negative correlation. Thus, for example, any random increase in the demand for money that will lead to a lower p_t will typically be accompanied by a random fall in the demand for bonds, thereby making p_t fall even further. This fall in bond price will induce a fall in output demand and consequently a random fall in income. By reducing the weight λ in the aggregate as (15b) asserts, we find from the tradeoff relationship (5′) that the fall in p_t (or increase in the interest rate) will be accommodated by a larger increase in deposits. This will tend to offset the random fall in income associated with the fall in p_t, thereby reducing the variance of income. The other cases can be analyzed similarly.

Further insight can be gained by focusing on special cases. When there is no disturbance in the goods market ($u_t \equiv 0$), equation (11) reduces to the simple expression $\hat{\lambda} = \frac{1}{2}$. That is, the optimal aggregate to stabilize is total government debt which, as we have seen, is equivalent to stabilizing the interest rate. This result is consistent with

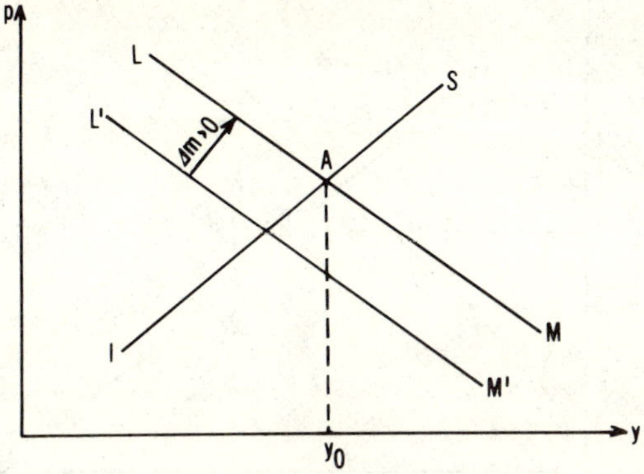

FIGURE I
Positive Disturbance in Deposits Market Matched by Negative Disturbance in Bond Market (i.e., $u_t \equiv 0$)

Poole [1970], who shows that with no disturbances in the goods market the optimal monetary policy is to peg the interest rate. Moreover, as in his analysis, this case implies that the variance of output is reduced to zero (i.e., perfect stabilization), as can be seen by setting $\sigma_u = 0$ in the minimal variance (12).

Thus, we have a case in which the stabilization of an aggregate chosen in an optimal manner is equivalent to stabilizing the interest rate. The fact that we are considering the optimal composition of such a broad aggregate makes this result possible. This suggests that some of the disagreement between the monetarist advocacy of aggregate stabilization and the nonmonetarist advocacy of interest rate stabilization might be reconcilable if the aggregate were broadened to include the money value of government interest-bearing debt.

A graphical illustration of this case is given in terms of familiar IS-LM analysis in Figure I. Note that since we have plotted these figures in $y - p$ space (rather than $y - r$ space), the slopes of the IS and LM curves are reversed. A random upward shift in the demand for money (reflected entirely in the bond market) will shift the LM curve down to L′M′. By engaging in an open market purchase of bonds, the monetary authorities can shift the curve back up, thereby stabilizing both y and p simultaneously at their initial levels.

As a second special case, assume the money market is free of stochastic disturbances, so that $v_t \equiv 0$. The optimal weight then simplifies to

$$(16) \qquad \hat{\lambda} = (\overline{B} - b_2)/(\overline{B} - 2b_2) > 1,$$

with the inequality following from the restrictions (13). This implies that, in the optimal aggregate, the weight on deposits should exceed

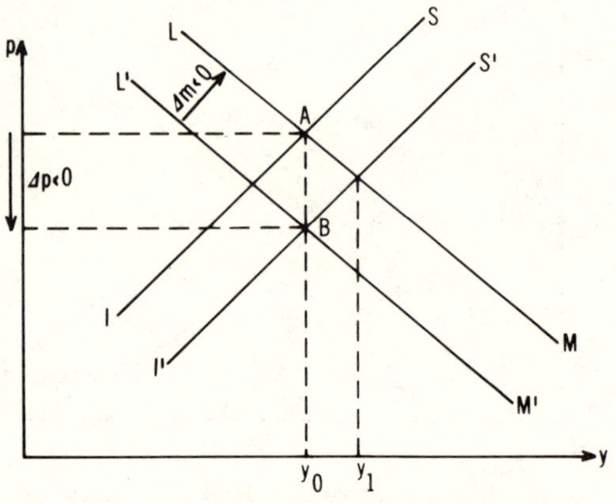

FIGURE II
Positive Disturbance in Goods Market Matched by Negative Disturbance in Bond Market (i.e., $v_t \equiv 0$)

unity, with a corresponding negative weight being applied to government bonds.

To understand the monetary policy underlying this result, it is helpful to consider Figure II, in which an unanticipated increase in the demand for goods, $u_t > 0$ (matched by a corresponding reduction in the demand for bonds), causes the IS curve to shift downward to I′S′. If m_t remains unchanged (i.e., $\lambda = 1$), the LM curve will remain fixed so that income will increase to y_1, with bond prices falling. By now introducing a contractionary monetary policy, p_t can be reduced further, thereby lowering y_t and offsetting the previous expansion. Indeed, by selling sufficient bonds to shift the LM curve to L′M′, the monetary authority is able to stabilize y_t (but not p_t) at its initial level. Note that in moving from equilibrium at A to equilibrium at B, we shall observe a reduction in bond price being accompanied by a fall in m_t. From our earlier remarks on the tradeoff relationship between these two quantities, this may certainly be achieved by setting $\lambda > 1$.

As a third example, suppose that the bond market is free of stochastic disturbances, so that $w_t \equiv 0$. In this case the optimal weight becomes

$$(17) \qquad \hat{\lambda} = [\overline{B} - (b_2 + as)]/[\overline{B} - 2(b_2 + as)] \cdot$$

Unfortunately, (17) cannot be signed unambiguously on the basis of our previous restrictions. By comparing it to (16), we can show that, provided a_1 or s is sufficiently small, (17) exceeds (16), in which case $\hat{\lambda} > 1$; or as a_1 or s becomes larger, $\hat{\lambda} < 1/2$.

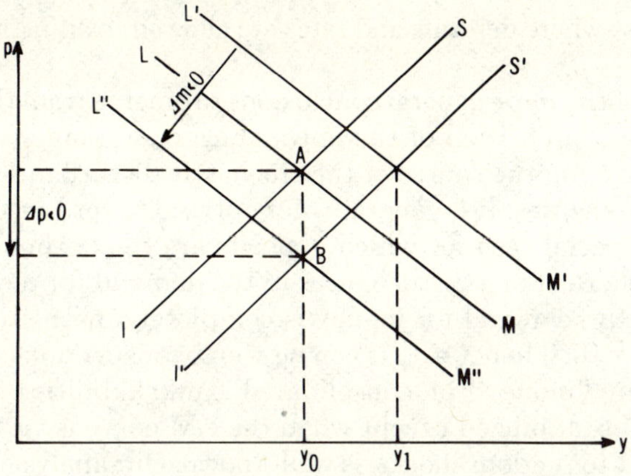

FIGURE III
Positive Disturbance in Goods Market Matched by Negative Disturbance in Deposit Market (i.e., $w_t \equiv 0$)

In Figure III we illustrate this case by considering a positive disturbance in the goods market, matched by an equal reduction in the demand for money. The IS curve moves downward to I′S′, with the LM curve moving outward by an equal amount to L′M′. In the absence of any active policy, this combination of disturbances will induce a substantial shift in y_t, causing it to increase from y_0 to y_1. By selling sufficient bonds to shift the LM curve back to L″M″, the monetary authority is able to stabilize y_t at its initial level. In this case an operation larger than what was in our previous example is required. Again, comparing A to B, we shall observe both m_t and p_t being reduced together. From (5′) this requires either that $\lambda > 1$ or that $\lambda < 1/2$, consistent with the restrictions we have derived for (17).

These three special cases are all extreme, in the sense that the stabilization of the optimal aggregate will reduce the variance of income to zero. They are also extreme in the sense that they require deposits and interest rates to adjust in opposite directions to accommodate the stabilization of the aggregate. For more realistic cases, where stochastic disturbances occur simultaneously in all three markets, both of these aspects tend to disappear. The minimized variance of income is almost certainly nonzero.[12] Moreover, in many cases the optimal λ will lie in the range (1/2, 1), yielding the more

12. From equation (12) it is seen that the three conditions for $\sigma_y^2 = 0$ are $\sigma_u^2 = 0$, $\sigma_v^2 = 0$ and $\rho^2 = 1$. Using (4), it can be seen that $\rho^2 = 1$ if and only if $s^4\sigma_u^4 + \sigma_v^4 + \sigma_w^4 - 2(s^2\sigma_u^2\sigma_v^2 + s^2\sigma_u^2\sigma_w^2 + \sigma_v^2\sigma_w^2) = 0$. While this condition will be met if $\sigma_w^2 = 0$ (our third case), it may conceivably also be met if all three variances are nonzero. This, however, would be an extremely unlikely situation.

normal case where deposits and rates are allowed to adjust in the same direction.

One of the more general conclusions to emerge from this exercise is that the composition of the optimal aggregate may vary widely, depending upon the source of the stochastic disturbances and their relative intensities. It is generally not optimal to set $\lambda = 1$. However, one very special case for which deposits are the optimal aggregate occurs if there are no disturbances in the demand for deposits ($v_t \equiv 0$), and if the demand for money is completely insensitive to bond prices ($b_2 = 0$). Then $\hat{\lambda} = 1$, as can be seen by inspection of (16). This result, that "money" or consolidated bank liabilities should not generally be stabilized except when the LM curve is vertical and is not subject to random shocks, is well-known. Our analysis shows how this result can also be established when the problem is approached from the viewpoint of searching for the optimal aggregate. But this new perspective produces a further conclusion in addition to the familiar result above. That is, the optimal aggregate must generally be constructed by assigning some nonzero weight to government interest-bearing debt.

IV. Relationship to Alternative Approaches

Stabilization of the optimum monetary aggregate can require a very active monetary policy. Since the optimal weights were chosen by our procedure to minimize the variance of income, we would expect that the policy required to stabilize the optimum aggregate would be related to other forms of optimal monetary policy, namely Poole [1970] and KMW [1973], based on income stabilization. Indeed, in the context of a linear IS-LM model the monetary policy required to stabilize the optimum aggregate proves to be equivalent to their optimal monetary policies, despite the dissimilarity in the approaches.

Using the IS-LM model with income stabilization as the objective, LeRoy and Waud [1977] have already shown the equivalence between Poole's combination policy and the policy implied by KMW. Consequently, it is only necessary to demonstrate the equivalence of the monetary policies implied by our approach to either of these two, to establish the equivalence of all three approaches. We have chosen the latter because we have a simplified procedure for presenting the essence of the KMW analysis, which may be of interest in its own right.

The KMW research shows that the policy of retaining a preset monetary aggregate is suboptimal because it fails to utilize important current information. According to their approach, the monetary aggregate—or deposits in our terminology—is important because its observation, along with observations on interest rates, contain information about the source of stochastic disturbances in the economy. This information can be exploited in the stabilization of a less frequently observed target variable (real income) if the authorities relinquish their intermediate targeted value of deposits.

Thus, in keeping with this informational approach, we now take explicit account of the fact that p_t and m_t are observable, whereas Y_t is unobservable, in the short term. The period of time for which this assumption is most applicable would be a month, since (in the United States) income is observed only quarterly and weekly money figures have considerable noise.[13] This section deviates from much of the new literature by abstracting from problems of autocorrelation, consistent with our previous assumptions.[14]

An important consequence of the observability of m_t and p_t is that it implies the observability of a composite disturbance, even though the separate components are not known. This can be shown in the following manner. First, recall the IS-LM equations:

$$y_t = ap_t + u_t \tag{2a}$$

$$m_t = b_1 y_t + b_2 p_t + v_t. \tag{2b}$$

Then solve equations (2a) and (2b) to eliminate the unobservable income variable to obtain the reduced-form relation between p_t and m_t:

$$m_t = (b_1 a + b_2) p_t + e_t, \tag{18}$$

where $e_t = b_1 u_t + v_t$. Since p_t and m_t are observable, it follows from (18) that the composite stochastic disturbance, e_t (but not its separate elements u_t and v_t) is also known.

We now assume that the monetary authority engaged in active stabilization by adjusting m_t and p_t in response to the observed composite disturbance e_t. These adjustments cannot be made independently, but must be constrained by the reduced-form equation (18). It is most convenient to specify the adjustment in p_t by

$$p_t = \phi e_t = \phi(b_1 u_t + v_t), \tag{19}$$

where ϕ is constant, with the implied adjustment in m_t being obtained

13. The sharp distinction drawn between the perfectly observable aggregate, m and the completely unobservable income variable y is overdrawn, since money is observed with measurement errors and since other indicators provide some evidence of short-run income movements. LeRoy and Waud [1975] have shown that the unobservability is just an extreme case of measurement error, and have extended the procedure of weighted regression to include observable variables.

14. A main idea behind the Kareken-Muench-Wallace approach (namely, using observable variables like monetary aggregates to acquire information) has been developed for a static model by LeRoy [1975] using a maximum likelihood procedure.

by substituting (19) in (18). The behavior of income corresponding to the policy rule (19) is given by

$$y_t = (1 + ab_1\phi)u_t + a\phi v_t, \tag{20}$$

implying a variance

$$\sigma_y^2 = (1 + ab_1\phi)^2\sigma_u^2 + a^2\phi^2\sigma_v^2 + 2a\phi(1 + ab_1\phi)\sigma_{uv}. \tag{21}$$

The optimal exploitation of information on e_t requires that ϕ be chosen to minimize (21). Carrying out this calculation yields

$$\hat{\phi} = \frac{-(b_1\sigma_u^2 + \sigma_{uv})}{a[b_1^2\sigma_u^2 + \sigma_v^2 + 2b_1\sigma_{uv}]}. \tag{22}$$

The tradeoff in the adjustment of m_t and p_t in the KMW approach is found by substituting the general policy rule (19) into the linear constraint (18), yielding

$$-\phi m_t + [1 + \phi(ab_1 + b_2)]p_t = 0. \tag{23}$$

Substituting the solution (22) for $\hat{\phi}$ into (23), we obtain the optimal tradeoff given by the KMW approach:

$$(b_1\sigma_u^2 + \sigma_{uv})m_t + [-b_1b_2\sigma_u^2 + a\sigma_v^2 + (ab_1 - b_2)\sigma_{uv}]p_t = 0. \tag{24}$$

By taking first differences, this is seen to be equivalent to the tradeoff between m_t and p_t implied by the stabilization of the optimal aggregate, and obtained by substituting (11) into (5′). All of the special properties associated with a particular value of $\hat{\phi}$ have their counterpart in particular values of $\hat{\lambda}$. When, for instance, $\hat{\lambda} = 1/2$, $\hat{\phi} = 0$, which means that the interest rate on government bonds is being stabilized. All other special cases hold as well. Moreover, since the stabilization of the optimum aggregate on the one hand, and the optimal exploitation of information on the other, are being conducted within the same IS-LM model, using the same objective function and subject to equivalent linear constraints, (5′) and (23), respectively, one would expect the performance of the two procedures to be identical. This indeed turns out to be the case. The minimized variance of income, obtained by substituting $\hat{\phi}$ into (21), reduces simply to (12).

The equivalence of the monetary policies implied by the KMW approach and our approach shows that the KMW conclusion that it is generally suboptimal to stabilize money (deposits) is contingent on their choosing a suboptimal aggregate to stabilize. But it should be emphasized that the equivalence between the monetary policies involved in stabilizing the optimum aggregate, the Poole's combination approach, or the KMW approach has been established only for a very special linear IS-LM model.[15] The equivalence, or otherwise, of the monetary policies implied by these three approaches in a more general model remains an open question.[16]

V. Conclusions

The primary objective of this paper has been to present a procedure for determining the optimum monetary aggregate for stabilization policy. This procedure stands in marked contrast to efforts to find the aggregate that yields the most stable demand for money function and with efforts to construct an aggregate with weights based on liquidity or turnover ratios. To make the procedure operational for policy analysis would require the introduction of several complications. The objective function would need to be expanded to incorporate multiple goals; the range of financial assets would need to be extended; the banking sector would have to be developed in detail; and the problem of controlling the aggregate would have to be included in the optimizing framework.

We have followed this procedure to address the question of the extent to which government interest-bearing debt should be included in the optimum aggregate. Except for one very special case, we found that the inclusion of government debt in the aggregate unambiguously improved stabilization. The weight given to such debt, relative to that attached to, say, bank deposits, may vary widely depending on the sources of random disturbances in the economy. It is also possible for the relative weights to be such that stabilizing the aggregate is equivalent to stabilizing the interest rate. Thus, by broadening the aggregate along the lines we are proposing, some reconciliation is possible between the monetarist advocacy of aggregate stabilization

15. A further intuitive explanation of the equivalence between our procedure and Poole's combination policy and therefore the KMW approach, suggested to us by a referee, is as follows. The IS-LM model contains only one nonmonetary asset. The Poole combination policy determines optimal policy in terms of an optimal combination relating the quantity of money and the price of (interest rate on) the nonmoney asset. Our procedure focuses instead on the optimal combination relating the quantity of money and the quantity of the nonmoney asset. Assuming that the price and quantity of the nonmonetary-asset are uniquely related, there is a one-to-one relationship between these two approaches.

16. Intuitively it would seem that the equivalence we have obtained between our approach and the KMW approach will continue to hold in a multi-asset world, as long as the number of securities in the aggregate equals the number of securities the stocks and associated interest rates of which can be observed. If the number of securities so observed exceeds the number included in the aggregate, one would expect the informational approach to prove superior to stabilizing an aggregate, and vice versa. We hasten to add that these are tentative comments, requiring further detailed analysis.

and the nonmonetarist advocacy of interest rate stabilization. They can both be viewed as special cases of stabilizing the optimum aggregate. Finally, we have shown how, at least for the simple IS-LM model we consider, our procedure of stabilizing an optimal aggregate turns out to be equivalent to the approaches of Poole and Kareken, Muench, and Wallace for determining optimal monetary policy.

TULANE UNIVERSITY
AUSTRALIAN NATIONAL UNIVERSITY

REFERENCES

Barnett, W. A., *Consumer Demand and Labor Supply: Goods, Monetary Assets, and Time* (Amsterdam: North-Holland, 1980).
Cargill, T. F., and R. A. Meyer, "Stability of the Demand for Money: An Unresolved Issue," *Papers and Proceedings of the A.E.A.*, LXIX (1979), 318–23.
Currie, D. A., "Optimal Stabilization Policies and the Government Budget Constraint," *Economica*, XLIII (1976), 159–67.
Enzler, J. L., L. Johnson, and J. Paulus, "Some Problems of Money Demand," *Brookings Papers on Economic Activity*, 1 (1979), 123–229.
Friedman, B. M., "The Inefficiency of Short-Run Monetary Targets for Monetary Policy," *Brookings Papers on Economic Activity*, 2 (1977), 293–347.
Friedman, M., and A. Schwartz, *Monetary Statistics of the United States* (New York: National Bureau of Economic Research, 1970).
Froewiss, K. C., J. P. Judd, M. W. Keran, and J. L. Scadding, "Comments on Redefining the Monetary Aggregates," Discussion Paper, Federal Reserve Bank of San Francisco, 1979.
Garcia, G., and S. Pak, "Some Clues in the Case of the Missing Money," *Papers and Proceedings of the AEA*, LXIX (1979), 330–34.
Goldfeld, S. M., "The Case of the Missing Money," *Brookings Paper on Economic Activity*, 3 (1976), 683–739.
Gurley, J., and E. Shaw, *Money in a Theory of Finance* (Washington: Brookings Institution, 1960).
Hamburger, M. J., "The Behavior of the Money Stock: Is There a Puzzle?" *Journal of Monetary Economics*, III (1977), 265–88.
Kareken, J. H., "The Optimum Monetary Instrument Variable: A Comment," *Journal of Money, Credit and Banking*, II (1970), 385–90.
——, T. Muench, and N. Wallace, "Optimal Open Market Strategy: The Use of Information Variables," *American Economic Review*, LXIII (1973), 156–72.
LeRoy, S. F., "Efficient Use of Current Information in Short-Run Monetary Control," Special Studies Paper No. 66, Federal Reserve Board, 1975.
——, and D. E. Lindsey, "Determining the Monetary Instrument: A Diagrammatic Exposition," *American Economic Review*, LXVIII (1978), 929–35.
——, and R. N. Waud, "Observability, Measurement Error, and the Optimal Use of Information for Monetary Policy," Special Studies Paper No. 72, Federal Reserve Board, 1975.
——, and ——, "Application of the Kalman Filter in Short-Run Monetary Control," *International Economic Review*, XVIII (1977), 195–207.
Lieberman, C., "Structural and Technological Change in Money Demand," *Papers and Proceedings of the AEA*, LXIX (1979), 324–29.
Mason, W. E., *Clarification of the Monetary Standard* (University Park: Pennsylvania State University Press, 1963).
Poole, W., "Optimal Choice of Monetary Policy Instruments in a Simple Stochastic Macro Model," this *Journal*, LXXXIV (1970), 197–216.
Porter, R. D., T. D. Simpson, and E. Mauskopf, "Financial Innovation and the Monetary Aggregates," *Brookings Papers on Economic Activity*, 1 (1979), 123–229.

Radcliffe Committee, *Report on the Working of the Monetary System* (Her Majesty's Stationery Office, 1959).
Sargent, T. J., and N. Wallace, "Rational Expectations, the Optimal Monetary Instrument, and the Optimal Money Supply Rule," *Journal of Political Economy,* LXXXIII (1975), 241–54.
Scadding, J. L., "Are Currency and Demand Deposits Substitutes?" Discussion Paper, Federal Reserve Bank of San Francisco, 1979.
Simpson, T. D., "A Proposal for Redefining the Monetary Aggregates," *Federal Reserve Bulletin,* LXV (1979), 13–42.
Tobin, J., "A General Equilibrium Approach to Monetary Theory," *Journal of Money, Credit and Banking,* I (1969), 15–20.
Turnovsky, S. J., "Optimal Choice of Monetary Instrument in a Linear Economic Model with Stochastic Coefficients," *Journal of Money, Credit and Banking,* VII (1975), 51–80.
——, *Macroeconomic Analysis and Stabilization Policy* (Cambridge, U. K.: Cambridge University Press, 1977).
Wenninger, J., and C. Sivesind, "Changing the M1 Definition; an Empirical Investigation," Discussion Paper, Federal Reserve Bank of New York, 1979.
Woglom, G., "Rational Expectations and Monetary Policy in a Simple Stochastic Macroeconomic Model," this *Journal,* XCIII (1979), 91–105.

OPTIMAL REDISTRIBUTIVE TAXATION AND UNCERTAINTY*

JONATHAN EATON AND HARVEY S. ROSEN

The literature on optimal taxation has provided useful principles for guiding thought about both efficient commodity taxation and optimal redistributive taxation.[1] However, most contributions to optimal tax theory have assumed that all prices, including that of leisure, are known with certainty at the time that resources are allocated. Although there have been a few discussions of the impact of uncertainty on optimal taxation [Diamond *et al.,* 1978; Mayshar, 1977], for the most part uncertainty appears to have had little influence upon optimal tax research. The purpose of this paper is to analyze optimal redistributive taxation when workers have imperfect information about their wages at the time they choose their labor supplies. The results are contrasted with those of the certainty case.

Throughout this paper, we assume that the market fails to provide insurance against the vagaries of wage rates. Problems of moral hazard associated with insurance in general are especially pervasive in the insurance of the returns to human capital.[2] The private insurer, unable to distinguish clearly between external events and the endogenous behavior of the insured party, would provide an incentive for an insured worker to work less hard, spend less time seeking a higher paying job, or otherwise earn an income below potential. In such a situation the market is unlikely to provide insurance.

It is useful to begin by examining how the presence of uncertainty changes the optimal tax problem when there is no redistributive issue; i.e., when all individuals are identical. Under certainty, a lump sum tax is efficient because it does not break the equality between the marginal rate of substitution in consumption and the marginal rate of transformation in production. In the presence of uncertainty, however, a lump sum tax is generally inefficient. To develop an intuition for this result,[3] consider an individual whose wage is uncertain. In the face of uncertainty, the individual's welfare will increase if he

* We are grateful to Alan Blinder, Peter Diamond, Yoram Weiss, and a referee for useful suggestions. Part of Rosen's work was supported by NSF grant no. SOC-7907847.

1. Sandmo [1976] discusses many of the important optimal taxation results.
2. Arrow [1970] discusses problems of moral hazard as they arise in insurance markets.
3. A complete proof is provided in Eaton and Rosen [1979].

The Quarterly Journal of Economics, September 1980 0033-5533/80/0095-0357$01.00

can obtain insurance. But a proportional earnings tax in effect acts as insurance—it lowers risk because the government shares in both losses and gains. Indeed, if labor supply were completely exogenous, the individual would desire a 100 percent earnings tax, with the expected value of earnings returned as a lump sum.[4]

This extreme result is a consequence of the unrealistic assumption that the individual's gross earnings stream is exogenous. When labor supply is endogenous, a tax rate between zero and unity will generally be required for efficient taxation. The efficient tax rate falls short of 100 percent, because taxation distorts the leisure-income choice as well as providing insurance. This proposition is similar (but not identical) to theorems in the insurance literature, which state that the optimal coinsurance rate lies between zero and one. (See, e.g., Shavell [1979].)

We now turn our attention to the more interesting case, in which individuals are not identical. When people differ according to their abilities and in their endowments of nonhuman wealth, both utilitarian and Rawlsian principles of social justice suggest that society impose taxes to redistribute income. To the extent that taxes impose distortions, optimal redistribution does not require equal post-tax incomes for all. Redistribution continues only as long as the incremental gains from more equality exceed the incremental excess burdens. Analyses of optimal income taxation under certainty indicate that, when labor supply is endogenous, the optimal degree of progressivity of the income tax may indeed be quite low.[5] In view of the fact just noted that under uncertainty a positive earnings tax is optimal even when all workers are identical ex ante, one might suppose that when individuals differ in terms of their expected productivities, uncertainty in wages raises the optimal progressivity of the income tax.

Unfortunately, general conditions under which this conjecture is true are difficult to obtain. Just as is the case in the literature on optimal income taxation in certainty models, it appears necessary to make fairly specific assumptions in order to obtain many interesting results. In this section we develop a model in which two classes of individuals with random wages must allocate their time between labor and leisure and the decisions are made ex ante.[6] Some numerical re-

4. This result parallels that of Mayshar [1977], who considers the effects of uncertainty on optimal subsidization.

5. See Stern [1976] for a review of these results.

6. For the case in which the labor supply decision occurs ex post, wage uncertainty and wage inequality are formally identical: increased wage uncertainty is equivalent to increased wage inequality.

sults suggest that the presence of uncertainty may have a substantial impact on optimal marginal tax rates. Overall, the analysis implies that because previous studies ignored uncertainty, they may have generated incorrect estimates of optimal tax rates.

In our model, workers must determine their labor supplies on the basis of the subjective probability distributions of their wages. Inequality represents differences in wage *distributions* that workers *do* know at the time they make their labor supply decisions. In an economy with equality and uncertainty, all workers choose their labor supplies with the same expectations about their realized earnings. Conversely, in an economy with inequality and no uncertainty, workers know exactly what their wages are at the time they choose their labor effort. This is the case typically analyzed in the optimal income tax literature. The same distribution of wages may be observed in both situations, but the allocation of labor effort and optimal tax policy may differ substantially in the two situations. In the presence of pure wage uncertainty, for instance, if workers' tastes are homogeneous, then we should observe the same effort on the part of all workers. This is not the case in the presence of inequality.

To derive the optimal linear wage tax in the presence of both inequality and wage uncertainty, we first consider the individual's optimization problem. The worker has a smooth concave utility function $u(c,L)$, where c is consumption ($\partial u/\partial c > 0$) and L is hours of work ($\partial u/\partial L < 0$). The worker pays a proportional earnings tax at rate $(1 - \theta)$, and receives from the government a (positive or negative) lump sum transfer T. Nonlabor income ω is assumed for simplicity to be the same for all workers. An individual in class i has a random wage w^i with probability distribution function $f^i(w^i)$. (Risks across workers are assumed to be independent.) Thus, he chooses L^i to maximize

$$E[u(\theta w^i L^i + T + \omega, L^i)]. \tag{1}$$

Let L^{i*} denote the value of L^i that maximizes (1). Expected social welfare is then given by

$$\int E[u(\theta w^i L^{i*} + T + \omega, L^{i*})] g(i) di, \tag{2}$$

where $g(i)$ gives the relative number of members of class i.

Revenue from the earnings tax T_y is

$$T_y \equiv \int (1 - \theta) E(w^i) L^{i*} g(i) di,$$

which, under our assumption that risks are independent, is nonrandom. The optimal tax problem is then to choose θ to maximize (2) and satisfy

$$T_y - T - G \geq 0,$$

where G denotes government revenue requirements.

A number of interesting questions arise in this context: Does introducing uncertainty in wages increase the optimal progressivity of the income tax? To what extent do revenue requirements affect this result? Given the ex post wage distribution, is the optimal progressivity of the tax necessarily greater when uncertainty, rather than inequality, is generating the observed wage distribution? As is the case with optimal taxation problems under certainty, a fruitful approach toward answering these questions is to consider specific numerical examples.

We consider an economy consisting of two classes, one and two, each with different wage distributions. Members of each class have constant elasticity of substitution utility functions,

$$u^i = 1/\gamma[\alpha(c^i)^{-\mu} + (1 - L^i)^{-\mu}]^{-\gamma/\mu},$$

where γ determines the degree of relative risk aversion with respect to consumption, R ($R = 1 - \gamma$), μ determines the elasticity of substitution between consumption and leisure ($\sigma = 1/(1 + \mu)$), and α determines in part the distribution of full income between consumption and leisure.

We compute the linear income tax that maximizes $E(u^1) + E(u^2)$ under several alternative assumptions about wage distributions and parameter values.[7] For all the calculations we set $\mu = 1.45$, a value that Stern [1976] has shown is implied by a number of econometric studies of labor supply. The share parameter α was set at 0.33.

Four sets of simulations were done, which we now discuss in turn.

1. Effects of Changing Risk Aversion

The purpose of these simulations is to determine how uncertainty and risk aversion change optimal tax rates. We assume at the outset that members of class one receive a wage of 0.5 or 1.5, each with probability ½, while members of class two receive a wage of 1.0 or 3.0, again each with probability ½. In order to focus on the effects of uncertainty per se, it is assumed that both revenue requirements and nonwage income are zero. We then compute optimal tax rates con-

7. The computations were performed using *GQOPT*, a numerical optimization package. See Goldfeld and Quandt [1971] for details. Optimal marginal tax rates were found on the basis of a grid search between zero and one in intervals of 0.01.

TABLE I

RISK AVERSION AND OPTIMAL TAX RATES

	$\gamma = -2.5$	$\gamma = -1.5$ $(G = 0)$	$\gamma = -0.5$	$\gamma = 0.5$
Uncertainty	0.57	0.55	0.52	0.47
Certainty	0.41	0.37	0.31	0.23

TABLE II

REVENUE REQUIREMENTS AND OPTIMAL TAX RATES

	$G = -0.2$	$G = -0.1$ $(\gamma = -1.5)$	$G = 0.1$	$G = 0.2$
Uncertainty	0.47	0.51	0.59	0.63
Certainty	0.30	0.33	0.41	0.46

ditional on various values of γ. The results are shown in the first row of Table I. The rates increase as γ decreases. Thus, as individuals become more risk-averse, they value more highly the insurance aspects of wage taxation, and higher tax rates become appropriate.

It is of some interest to determine how optimal tax rates change if the wage is known with certainty. We therefore compute optimal tax rates when each individual receives his mean wage with probability of one. These results are exhibited in the second row of Table I. In every case, uncertainty leads to higher tax rates than those associated with certainty.[8] The differences are most pronounced when the degree of risk aversion is low.

2. *Effects of Changing Revenue Requirements*

We now investigate the impact of different revenue requirements upon optimal tax rates. We set $\gamma = -1.5$, a figure consistent with recent empirical evidence. (See Friend and Blume [1975], p. 919.) Negative values of G, of course, are algebraically equivalent to positive unearned income.

The results for both the certainty and uncertainty cases are shown in Table II. For both cases, positive revenue requirements raise optimal tax rates. This result parallels one found by Feldstein [1973] in the context of a certainty model.

8. The tax rates vary with γ even with certainty because γ affects the marginal social benefit of redistribution. Indeed, it is impossible to disentangle the role of γ as a risk aversion parameter from its role as a distributional weight.

TABLE III

UNCERTAINTY, INEQUALITY, AND OPTIMAL TAX RATES

	$\gamma = -2.5$	$\gamma = -1.5$ $(G = 0)$	$\gamma = -0.5$	$\gamma = 0.5$
Uncertainty-equality	0.54	0.52	0.49	0.44
Certainty-inequality	0.60	0.57	0..52	0.42

3. Effects of Inequality Versus Uncertainty

If there were neither inequality nor uncertainty, optimal tax rates would be zero. Either inequality or uncertainty is sufficient to generate positive tax rates, but how important is each effect? To answer this question, we first assume that our two individuals are identical, but that they both face an uncertain wage: 0.5 with a probability of ½ and 1.5 with a probability of ½. The associated optimal tax rates for $G = 0$ and various values of γ are shown in the first row of Table III.

These rates are then contrasted with those that emerge when individuals one and two have wages of 0.5 and 1.5, respectively, with certainty. (See the second row of Table III.) For most cases, the certainty-inequality case yields higher marginal tax rates, although the difference diminishes as γ increases, and the relationship is actually turned around when $\gamma = 0.5$.

An alternative interpretation of the results of Table III is useful. The first row shows the optimal tax rates when labor supply decisions are made ex ante, and the second when they are made ex post. The table suggests that even if individuals must make their decisions before the wage is known, it does not necessarily increase the progressivity of the optimal linear earnings tax. The outcome depends upon the degree of risk aversion, and for a wide range of values uncertainty leads to *less* progressivity.

4. Effects of Alternative Loci of Uncertainty

Casual observation suggests that not all individuals face equal amounts of uncertainty. We therefore study how optimal tax rates depend upon who is bearing the risk. To begin, we first compute the optimal tax rate when there is equality (in the sense that both individuals have the same expected wage), but only one person faces uncertainty. More specifically, assume that individual one faces a wage of 0.5 or 1.5, each with probability ½; and individual two faces a wage

TABLE IV

LOCUS OF INEQUALITY AND OPTIMAL TAX RATES

Uncertainty for "poor"	Uncertainty for "rich"
($\gamma = -1.5, G = 0$)	
0.52	0.46

of 1.0 with certainty. (For this set of simulations, $\gamma = -1.5$, and $G = 0$.) The optimal tax rate is 0.44. This is a striking result when it is recalled that if both individuals face certainty, the optimal tax rate is zero, while if both individuals face uncertainty, it is 0.52 (from the second column of Table III). When one-half the population faces uncertainty, the optimal rate is much closer to the one that prevails if all face uncertainty than if none faces uncertainty.

We now examine a situation in which only one individual faces uncertainty, and there is also inequality. Consider first a case in which individual one faces a wage of 0.5 or 1.5, each with probability of $1/2$, and individual two faces a wage of 2.0 with certainty. Then imagine giving individual one a wage of 1.0 with certainty, but individual two a wage of 1.0 or 3.0, each with probability of $1/2$. The results are recorded in Table IV. When the "poor" individual's income is uncertain, a more progressive tax structure emerges than when the "rich" man is the risk-bearer. This is true even though the ratio of the variance of the wage to its mean is the same for both uncertainty cases.

Comparison of these results with those of the third column of Table I is also quite useful. When *either* individual faces uncertainty, the optimal tax rate is considerably above the certainty rate, and when the poor person's income is the source of the uncertainty, the result is strikingly close to the value of 0.55, which occurs when *both* individuals face uncertainty. We are led to conjecture that even if a relatively small fraction of the population experiences wage uncertainty, there may be a significant impact on optimal tax rates.

As stressed above, since these results are based on a simple and unrealistic model, we do not claim that they reflect actual optimal marginal tax rates for any real economy. The analysis does show, however, the complex ways in which uncertainty and inequality interact in the optimal taxation problem.

In this paper we have focused on the distinction between wage differences that are known at the time labor supply is determined and those that do not arise until after the work decision is made. Our perspective has been a utilitarian one in that we have viewed all wage differences in terms of their impact on individuals' expected utility. It is not obvious, however, that society does in fact view income differences arising from different sources equivalently. Even egalitarians may view those income differentials that are systematically related to race and sex as worse than those arising from purely random occurrences. Defining an appropriate social objective function in a world with uncertainty is worth further investigation.

PRINCETON UNIVERSITY

REFERENCES

Arrow, K. J., *Essays in the Theory of Risk Bearing* (Amsterdam: North-Holland, 1970).

Diamond, P., J. Helms, and J. Mirrlees, "Optimal Taxation in a Stochastic Economy: A Cobb-Douglas Example," mimeo, MIT, 1978.

Eaton, J., and H. S. Rosen, "Notes on Optimal Wage Taxation and Uncertainty," N.B.E.R. Working Paper No. 388, 1979.

Feldstein, M. S., "On the Optimal Progressivity of the Income Tax," *Journal of Public Economics,* II (Nov. 1973), 357–76.

Friend, I., and M. E. Blume, "The Demand for Risky Assets," *American Economic Review,* LXV (Dec. 1975), 900–22.

Goldfeld, S. M., and R. E. Quandt, *Nonlinear Methods in Econometrics* (New York: North-Holland Publishing Company, 1971).

Mayshar, J., "Should Government Subsidize Risky Private Projects?" *American Economic Review,* LXVII (March 1977), 20–28.

Sandmo, A., "Optimal Taxation—An Introduction to the Literature," *Journal of Public Economics,* VI (July/Aug. 1976), 37–54.

Shavell, S., "On Moral Hazard and Insurance," this *Journal,* XCIII (Nov. 1979), 541–62.

Stern, N. H., "On the Specification of Models of Optimum Income Taxation," *Journal of Public Economics,* V (July/Aug. 1976), 123–62.

ROLE OF EDUCATION IN PRODUCTION: A SLIGHTLY NEW APPROACH*

RATI RAM*

INTRODUCTION

Questions about the role of education in productive activities are important. They help one understand what, if anything, education in general does to enhance the productivity of people. Thus, they assist one in learning what the nature of this "human capital" is, and also whether the demand for such capital in the market arises from its skill-increasing character or is based primarily on any "screening" or "signaling" function that schooling might perform. Obviously, therefore, such questions and the answers to them have a bearing on some of the most important issues relating to education in both the high-income countries and the developing world.[1]

The work reported in this paper is an effort toward identifying and understanding the role of education in production. It is in the "tradition" of, and in some respects similar to, the research done by Zvi Griliches, Finis Welch, George Fane, and Wallace Huffman toward defining and quantifying the "allocative" function of schooling, particularly in agricultural production in the United States.[2] The present work may, however, be regarded as original in several ways. First, it offers a slight refinement of the "allocative role" hypothesis in regard to the productivity effect of schooling, and suggests an implication in terms of *different* effects of the schooling of two categories of workers. Second, its empirical setting is a major developing agriculture of recent years. Third, it is hoped that the design of the empirical part captures, at least approximately, the impact of schooling

* This work is based on a part of my doctoral dissertation [Ram, 1976] at the University of Chicago. I wish to thank the members of my dissertation committee, especially Professors M. J. Bowman and D. Gale Johnson. The conceptual approach that is briefly outlined in this paper became explicit during my early discussions with Professor Gary S. Becker, to whom I am grateful. My debt to Professor Zvi Griliches is obvious, since it was he who pioneered the use of production function estimation for analysis of the role of education. Professors T. W. Schultz, Finis Welch, and Glenn Blomquist read an earlier version and made useful comments. An anonymous referee of this *Journal* brought an important point to my attention. The responsibility for the remaining errors and deficiencies is, of course, entirely mine.

1. For a flavor of some of these issues, see Blaug [1976]. Note that in this paper the terms "education" and "schooling" are used interchangeably.
2. See, for example, Griliches [1970], Welch [1970], Fane [1975], and Huffman [1977].

The Quarterly Journal of Economics, September 1980 0033-5533/80/0095-0365$01.00

not merely on the degree of optimality in the use of inputs, but also efficiency in product-mix. The main finding is that not only does schooling seem to have an efficiency-raising effect, but also, perhaps more importantly, the observed *differential* in the effect of the schooling of two classes of agricultural workers supports the basic conceptual framework.

Elements of a Theory

A primary postulate of the "allocative hypothesis" is that education enhances the productive capabilities of persons by helping them choose more optimal bundles of factors, more efficient output-mix, and a more appropriate scale; in short, by increasing their allocative efficiency in the production of whatever they are producing. The framework stresses the role of information in allocative decisions, and mentions the possible usefulness of schooling in relation to receiving and "decoding" information. However, an explicit postulate relating education, information, allocative efficiency, and productivity seems to be lacking.

We propose the following modest extension of the allocative hypothesis: Education generally has the effect of lowering the (marginal) costs of acquiring production-related information, and of raising the (marginal) benefits of such information. Such lowering of marginal costs may occur for a variety of reasons, including the improved communication skills of more educated persons, and the possible superiority of their "contacts." The rise of marginal benefits could similarly be rationalized through the consideration that higher schooling probably sharpens the judgmental faculties of persons and increases their capability to process and apply the received information. Thus, by lowering marginal costs and raising marginal benefits, schooling is likely to increase the rate of acquisition of useful information by producers, and such an increase in information-acquisition is likely to constitute a major source of higher allocative and productive efficiency among more educated producers.

Even at the simple level stated above, the postulated role of information as an intermediary between schooling and allocative efficiency appears plausible and useful. It can throw light on the role of schooling in such diverse "production" situations as fertility and contraception, agricultural efficiency, and household and market production in general.

One straightforward implication of the suggested framework merits some elaboration. Since it is proposed that the major effect of schooling operates through increased information, the value of schooling would be related to the value of information. To the extent that information is more valuable in an economic setting, schooling is likely to have a larger payoff. Thus, by identifying situations in which information may be expected to be more valuable, one can locate the circumstances that make education more worthwhile. For instance, information and thus schooling might have greater value in "dynamic" production situations than in "static" environments, a theme propounded by Schultz and Welch.[3] Another example, more directly relevant to this paper, is of the possible difference between the value of information to farm *operators* and to farm hands hired for performing specific, routine tasks. It seems likely that production-related information is more valuable to farm operators who take the relevant input-output decisions than to hired hands: the former have allocative functions to perform, while the latter typically do not. We should thus expect the schooling of farm operators to have a larger payoff (value) than that of hired farm laborers. The implication suggested is quite similar to that mentioned by Griliches, with reference to the Nelson-Phelps [1966] hypothesis, when he said,

> Data from the 1964 Census of Agriculture may allow a test of the Nelson-Phelps hypothesis. These data provide separate information on the education of the farm *operator* as distinct from that of the rest of the farm labor force. The Nelson-Phelps hypothesis implies that the education of entrepreneurs is a more crucial, in some sense, determinant of productivity than the education of the rest of the labor force [1970, p. 85 ff].[4]

The Empirical Setting and the Model

The implication outlined above in regard to higher payoff from the schooling of farm operators (relative to that of hired workers) is the principal basis of the empirical work reported here, which pertains to India's agriculture. To avoid basing the analysis on just one period, two samples were taken, one each for the years 1961 and 1971. The basic sample size is 149 for 1961 and 151 for 1971. The unit of observation is a district that is somewhat comparable to a U.S. county. Although not random, the sample is large and includes about 40 percent of India's districts and an even larger fraction of the overall crop operations, and the units are reasonably well distributed throughout the country.[5] The two groups of workers for which the

3. See in particular Schultz [1964, 1975] and Welch [1970, 1978].

4. Note that the implication mentioned by Griliches can also be derived indirectly from the "allocative hypothesis," and it follows directly from the education-information-productivity nexus postulated here.

5. There are about 400 districts in India. The sample selection was based primarily on data availability for 1971.

productivity effect of schooling is compared are "cultivators" and "agricultural laborers." Broadly speaking, the term "cultivators" includes those persons who take all or most of the allocative and management decisions in regard to farm operations, while "agricultural laborers" are hired hands who usually perform the routine tasks assigned to them by cultivators.[6] Following the reasoning given in the last section, we expect the schooling of cultivators to have a higher effect on agricultural productivity than the schooling of agricultural laborers. The major statistical technique used is production function estimation with aggregate district level data on crop output and the various inputs. The production function is postulated to be of the Cobb-Douglas variety:

$$Q = \beta_0 \prod_{i=1}^{10} X_i^{\beta_i} \exp\left(\sum_{j=1}^{5} \delta_j D_j + v\right), \tag{1}$$

where Q is a weighted sum of the output of twenty-four principal crops; X_i's are the ten major inputs, namely, land, irrigation, agricultural capital, chemical fertilizer, extension intensity, number of cultivators, number of agricultural laborers, schooling of cultivators, schooling of agricultural laborers, and rainfall;[7] the D_j's are the dummy "shifters" that permit the constant term to vary across the different states in which the sample districts are located; and v is a stochastic disturbance term conforming to the standard assumptions of a linear regression model.

As a production function of the Cobb-Douglas type, (1) has the following well-known characteristics: (a) the exponents of X's are the elasticities of output with respect to the relevant inputs; (b) it is easy to calculate the marginal value products of each input implicit in the elasticity estimate; and (c) divergence between the marginal value product of an input and its price provides one measure of the degree of inefficiency in the use of that input.[8] These properties of the production function parameters and the prediction concerning the relative effects of the schooling of cultivators and agricultural laborers

6. The category of "cultivators" also includes family workers who may not be performing the role of operators. However, presumably even they have *some* management assignments. At any rate, the degree of allocative role is clearly higher in the cultivator group than in the class of agricultural laborers.

7. Details relating to computation of the variable values may be obtained from the author, or may be seen in Appendix III of Ram [1976].

Note that we are overlooking the problems related to aggregation and the possible "simultaneous equations" bias. Our justification in these respects is indeed the same as that of almost every other worker in this area. See (among others) Huffman [1977] for various arguments in support of the procedure. In regard to the aggregation question, it may be useful to point out that the pattern of the results, which are reported in Table I, is not altered when variable values "per cultivating household," rather than the aggregate values, are used.

8. See Fane [1975, especially p. 455], who shows that the inefficiency criterion (which in his framework is the divergence between the optimal and actual cost shares) can be used for any subset of variable factors as well as for all of them.

are used in conducting the empirical tests.

Before our empirical tests are stated, a brief mention is made of two studies that, out of the many investigations in this area, come closest to ours. Fane [1975] used county level data from the U. S. Agricultural Censuses of 1959 and 1964 to estimate a production function and to test the hypothesis that education of farm workers reduces inefficiency in input-use as indexed by the difference between the optimal (cost-minimizing) share of a variable input (or a set of inputs) in the cost and the actual share of that input (set). Through a somewhat similar procedure, Huffman [1977] showed that schooling enhanced the speed at which farmers adjusted to an increase in the optimal usage of nitrogenous fertilizer caused by a fall in its price between 1959 and 1964. Although our data are not as good as those used by Fane and Huffman, it is possible to show that with a given input bundle, increased schooling of agricultural workers implies increased value of crop output, and also that such increase in schooling implies a more optimal use of the major inputs. However, as our brief discussion of the theoretical framework would suggest, we make an effort to go beyond gauging an undifferentiated effect of schooling on the value of output or on the degree of efficiency in the use of a major variable input like fertilizer. The procedure followed in this paper is of focusing on the *differential* effects of the schooling of cultivators (or farm operators) on the one hand and hired agricultural laborers on the other. The differential is investigated along three dimensions: (a) Comparison of the elasticities of output with respect to the schooling of cultivators and agricultural laborers, such elasticities being taken as general proxies for the "impact" of schooling; (b) comparison of marginal value products of the schooling of these groups, as implied by the elasticity estimates and evaluated at the sample means; and (c) comparison of the effect of schooling of the two groups on one measure of the degree of inefficiency in the use of chemical fertilizer.

In regard to (a) above, the production function mentioned in (1) is slightly modified to let the "value added" by factors other than chemical fertilizer become the output variable.[9] Thus, we have

9. See Welch [1970], who ranks various estimations for evaluating the effect of schooling in a production function framework. The broad idea is that if schooling is included as a regressor along with other inputs, the efficiency effect of schooling is understated in the estimated coefficient of schooling, because an important part of the effect of schooling operates via efficient allocation of inputs for given output levels. In our formulation, effect of schooling on the output-mix is also captured, since the output variable is a weighted sum of the production of twenty-four crops. Still, at least in Welch's framework, the impact of schooling is likely to be sharpened if an important purchased input like chemical fertilizer is not included as a regressor along with schooling, and the output measure is a sort of "value added" by factors other than chemical fertilizer. Hence, we have the slight reformulation in (2). Actually, the pattern of the estimates for (1) and (2) is similar.

$$Q' = \beta'_0 \prod_{i=1}^{9} X_i^{\beta'_i} \exp\left(\sum_{j=1}^{5} \delta'_j D_j + v'\right), \tag{2}$$

where Q' is a measure of output net of the value of the chemical fertilizer used, and X_i's now do not include fertilizer. The elasticities of output with respect to the schooling of cultivators and agricultural laborers in (2) are compared.

For (b), the marginal value products of the schooling of cultivators and agricultural laborers are obtained (at the sample means) by the simple relation:

$$MP_K = \hat{\beta}_K \cdot \overline{Q}'/\overline{X}_K, \tag{3}$$

where MP_K is the marginal value product, $\hat{\beta}_K$ is the estimated elasticity, $\overline{X}_K$ is the mean value of the schooling of group K (cultivator or agricultural laborer), and $\overline{Q}'$ is the mean value of Q'.[10]

For the comparison mentioned at (c), first the elasticity of output with respect to fertilizer is obtained by estimating (1), and then the implicit marginal value product of fertilizer is calculated for each observation by using an expression similar to (3); i.e.,

$$MP_F^t = \hat{\beta}_F Q_t / X_F^t, \tag{4}$$

where the superscript t now refers to the unit of observation and the subscript F merely indicates that the values relate to the fertilizer input. The implied marginal value product is then compared with fertilizer price and the (absolute) difference between the two is taken as an index of the degree of inefficiency in the use of chemical fertilizer. That measure of "inefficiency" is then treated as a function of the schooling of cultivators and agricultural laborers, and extension. The estimated relation is[11]

$$ABS[P_F^t - MP_F^t] = \alpha_0 + \alpha_1 X_1^t + \alpha_2 X_2^t + \alpha_3 X_3^t + \sum_{j=1}^{5} \gamma_j D_j^t + \epsilon^t, \tag{5}$$

where P_F is the price of fertilizer and X_1, X_2, X_3 refer, respectively,

10. The rationale for equation (3) is obvious since Marginal Product = Elasticity × Average Product. The left-hand side can be regarded as an estimate of the marginal value product because the weights used to aggregate the elements of Q' are prices, and thus Q' becomes essentially a measure of the value of output.

11. The dependent variable in (5), namely, $ABS[P_F^t - MP_F^t]$ is *not* a measure of the loss of profit due to inefficient fertilizer use. It is the divergence between the market price and the marginal value product of fertilizer, and therefore, it is an index of the degree of inefficiency in the use of chemical fertilizer. Given the nature of the data, it is not easy to calculate loss of profit with any reasonable degree of precision. However, estimation of (5) with a rather crude measure of loss suggests a pattern of coefficients very similar to that reported in Table I.

TABLE I

COMPARISON OF THE EFFECTS OF SCHOOLING OF CULTIVATORS AND AGRICULTURAL LABORERS ON PRODUCTIVITY AND EFFICIENCY IN INDIA'S AGRICULTURE: 1961 AND 1971

(t-statistics are in parentheses)

	Cultivator schooling	Schooling of agricultural laborers
A. Elasticities of output (net of fertilizer cost) (based on estimation of equation (2) of the text)		
1961	0.164	0.016
(N = 149)	(2.26)	(0.31)
1971	0.243	−0.068
(N = 151)	(2.31)	(−0.82)
B. Mean marginal value products (in Rupees) implied by elasticities in Section A (see equation (3) in the text)		
1961	152	95
1971	264	0 (actually a negative figure)
C. Effect on the degree of inefficiency in the use of chemical fertilizer (see equation (5) in the text)		
1961	−282.2	−9.64
(N = 141)	(−2.32)	(−0.04)
1971	−50.64	−1.38
(N = 144)	(−3.29)	(−0.06)

Full regression results on which sections A, B, and C are based may be obtained from the author. The estimates appear plausible. R^2's for the estimates corresponding to section A are 0.89 and 0.88, respectively, for 1961 and 1971. R^2's for section C are roughly 0.40 and 0.37 for the two years.

The number of observations in section C is somewhat smaller because units having fertilizer usage of zero or close to zero are excluded. Note that a negative sign on the coefficients is expected, since the dependent variable is a measure of inefficiency.

to the schooling of cultivators and of agricultural laborers, and to extension. The superscripts refer to the observations, ϵ is a random stochastic term, and D_j's are the intercept shifters as in (1) and (2).

The predictions, of course, are that in (2) $\hat{\beta}_j$ for cultivator schooling is larger than that for the schooling of agricultural laborers; similarly in (3), MP_K for cultivator schooling is larger; and in (5) absolute value of the coefficient of X_1 is larger than that of X_2.

RESULTS AND A BRIEF DISCUSSION

Table I contains a summary of the main results. The position reveals considerable conformity to the predictions. For each year, the elasticity of output with respect to cultivator schooling is substantial and "significantly" positive, while that relative to the schooling of agricultural laborers is close to zero. The situation with respect to the marginal products has a similar pattern for 1971 especially. In Section C also, the efficiency-raising effect of the schooling of the two groups on fertilizer use has the expected structure for both years. Thus, while the analysis is based on a relatively straightforward methodology and has a data base of modest quality, the results seem to encourage one to have confidence in the broad pattern revealed here.

A brief discussion of some of the implications of the results may be in order. Aside from extending to a major less developed region some of the analyses conducted for the United States, the primary value of the exercise probably lies in the evidence it provides in support of the thesis that, while general schooling may not impart any direct "skill," its usefulness lies in the advantage it generates with regard to increased acquisition of production-related information; and that, therefore, payoff from schooling is likely to depend on the value of information or, in a slightly more conventional terminology, on the allocative context. Indirectly, however, the analysis seems to bear on some other important issues also. In particular, neither the conceptual framework that underlies the exercise nor the results suggest that schooling does not have a direct productivity-raising effect. The observed differences in the payoff to the schooling of the two groups of agricultural workers are large. It appears unlikely that these differences reflect a process of selection through schooling in terms of "ability" or some other innate worker characteristic, for it seems implausible to believe that the population of agricultural laborers on the whole is less "intelligent" or less "able" than the population of cultivators.[12] It seems more likely that the differences reflect one consequence of what may be called a structural feature of the situation, namely, the almost total lack of allocative role for a large segment of the agricultural work force. A little more reflection leads one to another point. The debates on "land reform" typically focus on the wealth equity issue or on the output effects of land redistribution in the context of economies or diseconomies of scale. The present analysis may reasonably be interpreted to add another significant dimension to the "land reform" question. It suggests that a movement toward a wider diffusion of land ownership and hence of allocative functions in agriculture may substantially raise the payoff

12. The levels of schooling of both groups are rather low. However, note that it is unlikely that the low t-statistics for the coefficients of the schooling of agricultural laborers are due to smaller variance in their (low) schooling levels. In fact, the coefficient of variation ($\sigma_S/\bar{S}$) for the schooling of agricultural laborers is *higher* than that for the schooling of cultivators.

to the schooling of a large number of agricultural workers. Such a change should thus improve the overall return to schooling, and should also provide a stronger schooling incentive to a large fraction of the populace, especially among those whose low education levels may be of particular concern to the policy-makers.

WASHINGTON STATE UNIVERSITY

REFERENCES

Blaug, Mark, "The Empirical Status of Human Capital Theory: A Slightly Jaundiced Survey," *Journal of Economic Literature,* XIV (Sept. 1976), 827–55.

Fane, George, "Education and the Managerial Efficiency of Farmers," *Review of Economics and Statistics,* LVII (Nov. 1975), 452–61.

Griliches, Zvi, "Notes on the Role of Education in Production Functions and Growth Accounting," in W. Lee Hansen, ed., *Education, Income and Human Capital* (New York: National Bureau of Economic Research, 1970), pp. 71–115.

Huffman, Wallace, "Allocative Efficiency: The Role of Human Capital," this *Journal,* XCI (Feb. 1977), 59–79.

Nelson, R. R., and E. S. Phelps, "Investment in Humans, Technological Diffusion, and Economic Growth," *American Economic Review* LVI (May 1966), 69–75.

Ram, Rati, "Education As a Quasi Factor of Production: The Case of India's Agriculture," Ph.D. thesis, University of Chicago, 1976.

Schultz, Theodore W., *Transforming Traditional Agriculture* (New Haven: Yale University Press, 1964).

——, "The Value of the Ability to Deal with Disequilibria," *Journal of Economic Literature,* XIII (Sept. 1975), 827–46.

Welch, F., "Education in Production," *Journal of Political Economy,* LXXVIII (Jan.–Feb. 1970), 35–59.

——, "The Role of Investments in Human Capital in Agriculture," in Theodore W. Schultz, ed., *Distortions of Agricultural Incentives* (Bloomington: Indiana University Press, 1978), pp. 259–81.

ON THE LONG-RUN STEADY STATE IN A SIMPLE DYNAMIC MODEL OF EQUILIBRIUM WITH HETEROGENEOUS HOUSEHOLDS*

ROBERT A. BECKER

This paper examines the long-run behavior of a one-good model of dynamic equilibrium with heterogeneous households.[1] The main result is a characterization of the long-run steady state that verifies a conjecture of Ramsey [1928].[2] If an agent's lifetime utility function over an infinite horizon is represented by a stationary, additive, discounted function with a constant pure rate of time preference, then the income distribution is shown in the long-run steady state to be determined by the lowest discount rate. The household with the lowest rate of discount owns all the capital and earns a wage income; all other households receive a wage income. If discount rates are equal between households, than the steady state distribution of income is indeterminate.

Rader [1979] shows the emergence of a dominant consumer in the long run for a model without an explicit capital accumulation structure. The dominant consumer has the lowest pure rate of time preference in the economy. Advantages of our work over Rader's presentation are that the analysis is related to the theory of economic growth and the mathematics is elementary.

One difference from the Rader result is that nondominant consumers have positive steady state consumption. Normally, those with high discount rates would want to contract to trade future labor for present consumption. These agents would then incur a debt equal to the discounted value of their wage income.

Rader's result admits intertemporal trades of future labor for current consumption in a loan market extending into the indefinite future. Each consumer's budget constraint requires total assets to be

* This note is a revision of Chapter V of my Ph.D. dissertation. I would like to thank Professors Lionel McKenzie and Lawrence Benveniste, the members of my dissertation committee at the University of Rochester, for their suggestions and comments. Thanks also are due to Professors William Brock, Michael Magill, and Trout Rader for additional helpful discussions. The suggestions of the referee were also useful.

1. The steady state theory is a special case of the model presented in Becker [1978].

2. Brock [1973] states a conjecture of this result in a continuous time framework with many capital goods. Brock argues that for the case of normal utility there will be at most one steady state equilibrium.

The Quarterly Journal of Economics, September 1980 0033-5533/80/0095-0375$01.00

nonnegative asymptotically.[3] Therefore, high discount rate individuals may borrow against future wage income to increase their current consumption. If the total assets of a high discount rate individual consist only of a discounted wage income, then these individuals have zero consumption asymptotically. The market structure of our model requires capital assests to be nonnegative at each moment of time and that agents without capital are not admitted to the loan market; for high discount rate consumers with zero initial capital stocks, this implies that the wage income is consumed at each time. Therefore, the present model constrains the possibilities for intertemporal trade so that the resulting competitive equilibrium distribution of income is a constrained Pareto optimum with respect to all possible intertemporal trades.

Time is taken in discrete intervals, $t = 1, 2, \ldots$. There are $H \geq 1$ households indexed by $h = 1, 2, \ldots, H$. There is a single commodity called "schmoos" or "goods" available for consumption or investment at each time. Households are endowed with stocks $k_0^h \geqq 0$ at time 0.

Let $(1 + r)$ be a given interest factor; w is a given wage rate. Assume that each household supplies one unit of labor inelastically at each time. Then h solves

$$P_h^c(1 + r, w; k_0^h): \max \sum_{t=1}^{\infty} \delta_h^{t-1} u_h(c_t^h)$$

by choice of $\{c_t^h\}_{t=1}^{\infty}$ such that

$$c_t^h + x_t^h = w + (1 + r)x_{t-1}^h \quad t = 1, 2, \ldots, \tag{1}$$

$$x_t^h, c_t^h \geq 0, \quad \text{all } t; x_0^h = k_0^h,$$

where $0 < \delta_h < 1$ is a discount factor, u_h is the instantaneous utility function, c_t^h is consumption at time t, and x_t^h is capital stocks held by h at time t for earning rentals at time $t + 1$.

ASSUMPTION I. $u_h \in C^{(2)}(R_+, R)$, strictly concave, $u_h' > 0$, $u_h'' < 0$ for all $c^h \geq 0$, and $\text{limit}_{c^h \to 0} u_h'(c^h) = +\infty$, $h = 1, 2, \ldots, H$.

Let $\{x_{t-1}^h(1 + r, w)\}_{t=1}^{\infty}$ and $\{c_t^h(1 + r, w)\}_{t=1}^{\infty}$ denote the solution to P_h^c above.

3. Total assets of household h at time t, A_t^h, are defined as

$$A_t^h = x_t^h + w/r,$$

where x_t^h is the household's stock of capital at time t.

The production sector problem is for given $(1 + r)$,

$$P^F(1 + r)\colon \max_{x \geq 0} f(x) - (1 + r)x,$$

where f is a production function satisfying

ASSUMPTION II. $f \in C^{(2)}(R_+,R_+)$, strictly concave, $f' > 0$, $f'' < 0$, $\text{limit}_{x\to 0} f'(x) = +\infty$, $\text{limit}_{x\to +\infty} f'(x) = 0$, $f(0) = 0$.

P^F can be thought of as myopic wage (profit) maximization.

REMARK (a). $\bar{x} > 0$ solves $P^F(1 + r)$ iff $f'(\bar{x}) = (1 + r)$. (b) Let $G(1 + r) = (f')^{-1}(1 + r)$.

Now define $w = \phi(1 + r)$ according to

$$w = (1/H)[f(G(1 + r)) - (1 + r)G(1 + r)]. \tag{2}$$

DEFINITION. We say that $(1 + \bar{r},\bar{w};\bar{k}_0{}^1, \ldots, \bar{k}_0^H)$ is *A Stationary Perfect Foresight Competitive Equilibrium* (S.P.F.C.E.) if it is a Perfect Foresight Competitive Equilibrium that exhibits the following special properties:

$$1 + \bar{r},\bar{w} \text{ are constant over time with } \bar{w} = \phi(1 + \bar{r});^4 \tag{3}$$

$$x_{t-1}^h(1 + \bar{r},\phi(1 + r)) = \bar{k}_0^h, \quad t = 1, 2, \ldots, H; \tag{4}$$

$$\sum_{h=1}^{H} \bar{k}_0^h = \bar{k}; \tag{5}$$

where $\bar{k}$ is the unique solution to $(1 + \bar{r}) = f'(\bar{k})$.[5]

THEOREM. Let $0 < \delta_H < \delta_{H-1} < \cdots < \delta_1 < 1$. Let Assumptions I and II be satisfied. Then there is a unique S.P.F.C.E. given by

$$(1 + \bar{r}) = \delta_1^{-1}; \quad \bar{w} = \phi(\delta_1^{-1}); \tag{6}$$

$$\bar{k}_1^0 = k^{\delta_1}, \tag{7}$$

4. $\bar{w} = \phi(1 + \bar{r})$ requires $(\bar{r},\bar{w})$ to be on the factor-price frontier defined by the function ϕ for all time.

5. A *perfect foresight competitive equilibrium* is a pair of sequences $\{\bar{r}_t\}_{t=1}^{\infty},\{\bar{w}_t\}_{t=1}^{\infty}$ such that, whenever $(\bar{r}_t,\bar{w}_t)$ replace (r,w) in (1) at each time t, then the solution to $P_h^c(\{1 + \bar{r}_t\},\{\bar{w}_t\})$ given by $\{(\bar{c}_t^h,\bar{x}_{t-1}^h)\}_{t=1}^{\infty}$ $(h = 1,\ldots, H)$ satisfies

$$(1 + \bar{r}_t) = f'\left(\sum_{h=1}^{H} \bar{x}_{t-1}^h\right); \tag{a}$$

$$\bar{w}_t = \phi(1 + \bar{r}_t). \tag{b}$$

Conditions (a) and (b) imply

$$\sum_{h=1}^{H} \bar{x}_{t-1}^h$$

maximizes myopic profits $P_F(1 + \bar{r}_t)$ for each t.

where k^{δ_1} is the unique solution to $f'(k^{\delta_1}) = \delta_1^{-1}$;

(8) $$\bar{k}_h^0 = 0 \quad \text{for} \quad h = 2, \ldots, H;$$

(9) $$\bar{c}^1(1+\bar{r}) \equiv \bar{c}^1 = \phi(\delta_1^{-1}) + \delta_1^{-1}k^{\delta_1};$$

(10) $$\bar{c}^h(1+\bar{r}) \equiv \bar{c}^h = \phi(\delta_1^{-1}) \quad \text{for } h = 2, \ldots, H.$$

The proof will be carried out in a sequence of lemmas. We begin by conjecturing that $(1+\bar{r}) = \delta_1^{-1}, \bar{w} = \phi(\delta_1^{-1})$ hold for all t, and given (7) and (8), consider that

$$P_h^c(\delta_1^{-1},\phi(\delta_1^{-1});\bar{k}_0^h) \begin{cases} k_0^h = k^{\delta_1} & \text{if } h = 1; \\ k_0^h = 0 & \text{if } h \geq 2. \end{cases}$$

LEMMA (1). For $h = 1, P_1^c(\delta_1^{-1},\phi(\delta_1^{-1});k^{\delta_1})$ has the unique optimal solution (7), (9) where $x_{t-1}^1(\delta_1^{-1},\phi(\delta_1^{-1})) = k^{\delta_1}$ for $t = 1, 2, \ldots.$

Proof. The path defined by (7), (9) may be certified as satisfying the usual Euler Difference Equation necessary for optimality. Since $0 < \delta_1 < 1$ and the path is constant, the transversality condition $\lim_{t\to\infty} \delta_1^t u'(\bar{c}^1)k^{\delta_1} = 0$ holds. It is now a standard exercise to use strict concavity of u_1 to show that the conjectured path is in fact optimal for $P_1^c(\delta_1^{-1},\phi(\delta_1^{-1});k^{\delta_1})$.

Q.E.D.

LEMMA (2). Consider $h = 2, \ldots, H$; fix $k_0^h = 0$, then $P_h^c(\delta_1^{-1}\phi(\delta_1^{-1});0)$ has the unique optimal solution,

$$\bar{c}_t^h = \phi(\delta_1^{-1}) \qquad \text{for all } t;$$
$$x_{t-1}^h(\delta_1^{-1},\phi(\delta_1^{-1})) = 0 \qquad \text{for } t = 1, 2, \ldots.$$

Proof. To ease typing, drop all superscripts referring to h and let $0 < \delta < \delta_1$. Let $\{c_t\}_{t=1}^{\infty}$ be a feasible policy starting from $k_0 = 0$ that is *good*, i.e.,

$$\sum_{t=1}^{\infty} \delta^{t-1}u(c_t) > -\infty.$$

For construction of a comparison path, we need look only at these good paths.

Let $\bar{c} = \bar{w} \equiv \phi(\delta_1)$; then (11) must be verified:

(11) $$\sum_{t=1}^{\infty} \delta^{t-1}[u(\bar{w}) - u(c_t)] > 0,$$

where $\{c_t\}_{t=1}^{\infty}$ is any feasible path that is good and $c_t \neq \bar{w}$ for some t.

By strict concavity of u,

(a) $$u(\overline{w}) - u'(\overline{w})\overline{w} \geq u(c_t) - u'(\overline{w})c_t$$

for all $c_t \geq 0, t = 1, 2, \ldots$; for $c_t \neq \overline{w}$, (a) holds as a strict inequality. So rearranging (a) for $c_t \neq \overline{w}$ implies that

(b) $$u(\overline{w}) - u(c_t) > u'(\overline{w})(\overline{w} - c_t).$$

Therefore, if $c_t \neq \overline{w}$ for some t, then

(c) $$\sum_{t=1}^{\infty} \delta^{t-1}[u(\overline{w}) - u(c_t)] > \sum_{t=1}^{\infty} \delta^{t-1}u'(\overline{w})(\overline{w} - c_t).$$

Feasibility of the comparison path $\{c_t\}_{t=1}^{\infty}$ requires that

(d) $$c_t = \overline{w} + \delta_1^{-1}x_{t-1} - x_t, \quad x_0 = 0.$$

Therefore, the right-hand side of (c) becomes

(e) $$\sum_{t=1}^{\infty} \delta^{-1}u'(\overline{w})[x_t - \delta_1^{-1}x_{t-1}], \quad x_0 = 0.$$

Let $\rho_1 > 0$ and $\delta_1^{-1} = 1 + \rho_1$, thus ρ_1 is household one's pure rate of time preference. Therefore, (e) can be written as

$$u'(\overline{w}) \sum_{t=1}^{\infty} \delta^{t-1}[\Delta x_{t-1} - \rho_1 x_{t-1}], \quad \Delta x_{t-1} = x_t - x_{t-1}.$$

We may change the indices on (e) to run from $t = 0, 1, \ldots$ and using the formula for summation by parts [Hardy, 1949, p. 51] write (e) as

(f) $$u'(\overline{w}) \lim_{T\to\infty} \left\{ \sum_{t=0}^{T-1} (\delta^t - \delta^{t+1}) \sum_{s=0}^{t} \Delta x_s + \delta^T \sum_{t=0}^{T} \Delta x_s - \sum_{t=0}^{T} \delta^t \rho_1 x_t \right\},$$

where

$$\Delta x_s = x_{s+1} - x_s, x_0 = 0, \quad \sum_{s=0}^{t} \Delta x_s = x_{t+1} - x_0 = x_{t+1}.$$

Define $\delta = (1 + \rho)^{-1}$ and rewrite (f) as

(g) $$u'(\overline{w}) \lim_{T\to\infty} \left\{ \sum_{t=0}^{T-1} \delta^{t+1}\rho x_{t+1} - \sum_{t=0}^{T} \delta^t \rho_1 x_t + \delta^T x_{T+1} \right\}$$

$$= u'(\overline{w}) \lim_{T\to\infty} \left\{ (\rho - \rho_1) \sum_{t=1}^{T} \delta^t x_t - \delta^0 \rho_1 x_0 + \delta^T x_{T+1} \right\} \geqq 0,$$

since

$$(\rho - \rho_1) > 0 \quad \text{iff} \quad 0 < \delta < \delta_1, \quad x_0 = 0, \quad x_t \geq 0 \quad \text{all } t,$$

and

$$\lim_{T\to\infty} \delta^T x_{T+1} \geqq 0.$$

Therefore (11) obtains.

Q.E.D.

LEMMA (3). There is a unique k^{δ_1}, $0 < k^{\delta_1} < +\infty$, such that $f'(k^{\delta_1}) = \delta_1^{-1}$, hence k^{δ_1} solves

$$\max_{x\geq 0} \delta_1 f(x) - x. \tag{12}$$

Proof. Existence of k^{δ_1} follows from the usual Inada conditions and the intermediate value theorem; uniqueness stems from $f'' < 0$. Equation (12) follows from strict concavity of f.

Q.E.D.

REMARK. Gale [1970] showed that (12) holds for the case $H = 1$ and that (12) gives a complete characterization of the stationary state in that case. Thus, for the case of heterogeneous households, (12) holds as in Gale but for an appropriate choice of δ.

COROLLARY. $\{\delta_1^{-1},\phi(\delta_1^{-1});k_0^1 = k^{\delta_1},k_0^h = 0 \text{ for } h = 2, \ldots, H\}_{t=1}^{\infty}$ is a S.P.F.C.E.

LEMMA (4). The S.P.F.C.E. of Corollary (1) is the only S.P.F.C.E.

Proof. In any other candidate S.P.F.C.E., either $(1 + \bar{r}) > \delta_1^{-1}$ or $(1 + \bar{r}) < \delta_1^{-1}$ must hold.

If $(1 + \bar{r}) > \delta_1^{-1}$, then household one has a feasible policy of ever increasing accumulation and consumption yielding arbitrarily large stocks; by diminishing returns this cannot be a S.P.F.C.E.

If $(1 + r) < \delta^{-1} < \delta_1^{-1} < \delta_h^{-1}$ for $h = 2, \ldots, H$, then for any initial distribution of capital, it can be shown to be optimal for each household to decumulate from its initial stocks to zero in finite time. Thus, $\Sigma_h x_{t-1}^h(1 + \bar{r}) \to 0$ was $t \to +\infty$, hence $f'(\Sigma_h x_{t-1}^h(1 + \bar{r})) \to +\infty$, thereby violating the condition of stationarity for a S.P.F.C.E.

Q.E.D.

Lemmas (1)–(4) prove the Theorem.

The Theorem is our version of Ramsey's conjecture and gives the first formal proof of that conjecture. There is no difficulty in rewriting our arguments to satisfy a continuous time model as in the original Ramsey paper.

In contrast to his detailed and explicit model of optimal growth,

Ramsey left a model of equilibrium undeveloped. The development of his model was the subject of Becker [1978]. The long-run equilibrium structure is consistent with both perfect foresight and static expectations hypotheses. The choice of an expectations hypothesis for an equlibrium model is important in the analysis of short-run dynamics. Becker used long-run perfect foresight for an expectations structure on the short-run dynamics (see Magill [1977] for the distinction between short- and long-run dynamics).

An interesting property of long-run equilibrium is that $\phi(\delta_1^{-1})$ depends only upon δ_1^{-1} and ϕ is the maximized present value of wages valued at the present value prices $(\delta_1,1)$; note that myopic wage maximization iff wage maximization over the infinite horizon occurs at k^{δ_1}. As noted in equation (12) and the following Remark, this is similar to the case of optimal growth where the planner discounts future utilities by the factor δ_1. In the present model, $\phi(\delta_1^{-1})$ is determined by a decentralized economy in long-run competitive equilibrium. This decentralization works to select a particular δ and corresponding $\phi(\delta^{-1})$; given that $\delta_1^{-1} < \delta_h^{-1}$ for all $h \geqq 2$, then $\phi(\delta_1^{-1})$ is the largest wage bill that could be attained if present value prices are restricted to be chosen from $(\delta_h,1)$ and applied to (12). Thus,

$$\delta_1 f(k^{\delta_1}) - k^{\delta_1} = \max_{\delta_h} \max_{x \geq 0} \delta_h f(x) - x. \tag{13}$$

Following in the tradition of general equilibrium theory, the equilibrium presented in the Theorem is Pareto optimal.[6] It is well-known that such a Pareto optimum may not be pleasing when viewed within the context of other value judgments.

Let us now consider the case where each household discounts future utilities at the same constant rate $\rho > 0$, or if $\delta = (1+\rho)^{-1}$, then $\delta = \delta_h$ for all h. Let $f'(k^\delta) = \delta^{-1}$, and define an $(H-1)$ dimensional k^δ – unit simplex by

$$S = \left\{(k_1,\ldots,k_H) \,\middle|\, \sum_{h=1}^{H} k_h = k^\delta \quad \text{and} \quad k_h \geqq 0, \quad h = 1,2,\ldots,H\right\}.$$

Let $\overset{0}{S}$ be the subset of S with $k_h > 0$ for all h; $\overset{0}{S}$ represents the possible distributions of capital stocks in a S.P.F.C.E. under the assumption of a common discount factor across households. In particular, for this case, the distribution of capital in a S.P.F.C.E. is *indeterminate.* Long-run equilibrium is consistent with any distribution

6. As noted in the introductory paragraphs, this Pareto optimum is a constrained one as compared to the Pareto optimum in Rader [1979].

of capital in $\overset{0}{S}$ by Lemma (1). Under the common δ assumption, each household may hold positive stocks in a long-run equilibrium, but there may be an unequal distribution of capital and hence income, with income identified with consumption.

If u_h is replaced by $V_h(x^h_{t-1},x^h_t), V_h$ strictly concave, $C^{(2)}$, etc., then even for $H = 1$, it is known that there may be multiple stationary states. This case may merit further examination when households differ across δ's. One might also follow Beals and Koopmans [1969], Iwai [1972], and Boyer [1975] and study the case of stationary nonadditive utility functions that generalize the properties of our utility sums. In these cases, one expects the extreme distribution of capital in the Theorem to change.

INDIANA UNIVERSITY, BLOOMINGTON

REFERENCES

Beals, R., and T. C. Koopmans, "Maximizing Stationary Utility in a Constant Technology," *Society for Industrial and Applied Mathematics Journal of Applied Mathematics,* XVII (1969), 1001–15.
Becker, R., "The Existence of a Perfect Foresight Competitive Equilibrium in a Simple Dynamic Model of Capital Accumulation with Heterogeneous Households," Ch. IV, Ph.D. thesis, University of Rochester, 1978.
Boyer, M., "An Optimal Growth Model with Stationary Non-Additive Utilities," *Canadian Journal of Economics,* VIII (1975), 215–37.
Brock, W., "Intertemporal General Equilibrium Theory—Notes," unpublished lecture notes, 1973.
Gale, D., "Nonlinear Duality and Qualitative Properties of Optimal Growth," in J. Abadie, ed., *Integer and Nonlinear Programming* (Amsterdam: North-Holland, 1970), Ch. 13, pp. 309–19.
Hardy, G. H., *Divergent Series* (Oxford: Oxford Press, 1949).
Iwai, K., "Optimal Economic Growth and Stationary Ordinal Utility—A Fisherian Approach," *Journal of Economic Theory,* V (1972), 121–51.
Magill, M. J. P., "Some New Results on the Local Stability of the Process of Capital Accumulation," *Journal of Economic Theory,* XV (1977), 174–210.
Rader, T., "Utility Over Time: The Homothetic Case," working paper, Department of Economics, Washington University (St. Louis), 1979.
Ramsey, F., "A Mathematical Theory of Saving," *Economic Journal,* XXXVIII (1928), 543–59.

A COMMENT ON MEASURING HORIZONTAL EQUITY

ROBERT PLOTNICK

I. INTRODUCTION

Harvey Rosen [1978] recently presented an interesting empirical analysis of a notion of horizontal equity that is framed in terms of utility rather than income or some other standard measure of economic well-being. While carefully qualifying his methodology and results, he does suggest that "for those features of the tax system that have been studied [the federal income and payroll tax], there do not seem to be major departures from horizontal equity. . . . "

This comment addresses neither the conceptual problem of measuring and comparing utilities, nor Rosen's empirical estimates of utility functions. It takes issue with his two measures of departure from horizontal equity. The first is Spearman's rank correlation. The second is a related correlation coefficient. The latter is defective on conceptual grounds because it may indicate that a perfectly horizontally equitable tax exhibits departures from horizontal equity. The former suffers because its benchmark value for a "grossly inequitable" tax depends in an undesirable way on certain specific characteristics of the sample under study. Thus, Rosen's conclusion, while quite possibly valid, cannot be inferred from his empirical work.

II. SPEARMAN'S RANK CORRELATION AS A MEASURE OF HORIZONTAL INEQUITY

Rosen suggests that, given an indicator of horizontal inequity, one's judgment of the seriousness of the horizontal inequities of a tax depends strongly on a comparison of a benchmark value for a grossly inequitable tax to the observed value for the tax being analyzed. Such a benchmark should be independent of specific characteristics of the data set being studied, except for its pretax distribution of income.

Rosen's grossly inequitable tax is equal to twice the average observed tax payment and levied randomly with a probability of one half. Given the average tax, the expected value of Spearman's rank correlation (r_s) for such a tax regime varies with the size of the sample. For example, assuming that the average tax equals 25 percent of mean income and applying the benchmark tax to a random sample of 5,000 drawn from a normal distribution of income gave $r_s = 0.5873$. For a

The Quarterly Journal of Economics, September 1980 0033-5533/80/0095-0383$01.00

subsample of 1,000 randomly selected from these 5,000, r_s was 0.5315. Other samples and average taxes yielded parallel results.[1]

Conclusions about horizontal equity should not depend on sample size. Thus, r_s has limited use as a measure of horizontal inequity, unless a more satisfactory standard of gross inequity can be developed or preferably, until, as Rosen notes, a plausible social welfare function that incorporates the extent of horizontal inequity using r_s can be specified.

III. A Difficulty with the Second Measure of Inequity

Rosen's alternative measure attempts to take into account "closeness" in the pre-and posttax distribution. To calculate it, one randomly orders the units and computes

$$DU_{b,i} = | U_{b,i} - U_{b,i-1} |$$

and

$$DU_{a,i} = | U_{a,i} - U_{a,i-1} |,$$

where U_b is before-tax utility and U_a after-tax utility. The simple correlation between DU_b and DU_a, ρ, is the measure of departures from horizontal equity. Of two tax regimes, the one with ρ closer to one is judged the less inequitable. Rosen points out that this measure is invariant only for linear monotonic transformation of U.

Even if we ignore this problem, this measure is seriously defective. It will only equal one for tax schemes in which $U_{a,i}$ is a linear function of $U_{b,i}$. If $U_{a,i} = s + tU_{b,i}$, then

$$|U_{a,i} - U_{a,i-1}| = |t(U_{b,i} - U_{b,i-1})| = t|U_{b,i} - U_{b,i-1}|.$$

Hence, $\rho = 1$. Such a tax does indeed treat equals equally and leave rank order unchanged.

Suppose, though, that $U_{a,i} = U_{b,i}{}^t$. Such a tax also satisfies the two criteria of horizontal equity (and is quite progressive), but $\rho \neq 1$. For example, this tax rule was used to calculate ρ for 100 units whose pretax incomes assumed the values 1, 2, . . . 100. For $t = 0.9$, $\rho = 0.9986$; for $t = 0.8$, $\rho = 0.9942$. With this measure, one would conclude that the real world income and payroll taxes analyzed by Rosen are less inequitable than this perfectly equitable tax if $t = 0.8$! There is no compelling reason to accept a measure such as ρ that does not yield

1. A formal proof of the effect of sample size and further details on the example are available upon request to the author.

a consistent value for all perfectly horizontally equitable taxes, regardless of their specific functional form.

IV. Conclusion

Rosen has contributed a useful analysis of horizontal equity. The task of deriving conceptually sound and empirically workable measures of horizontal inequity remains before us, however.

Dartmouth College

Reference

Rosen, H. S., "Income, Utility and Horizontal Equity," this *Journal,* XCII (May 1978), 307–22.

No. 380

THE QUARTERLY JOURNAL OF ECONOMICS

FOUNDED 1886

Vol. XCV November 1980 No. 3

ARTICLES

A Growth Model for a Tenured-Labor-Managed Firm .... *André Sapir* 387
Nontraded Goods and the Balance of Trade in a Neo-Keynesian Temporary Equilibrium .... *J. Peter Neary* 403
Job Differentiation and Wages .... *Nancy L. Stokey* 431
The Distribution of Income by Factor Components .... *Graham Pyatt, Chau-nan Chen, and John Fei* 451
On Oligopolistic Markets for Nonrenewable Natural Resources .... *Tracy R. Lewis and Richard Schmalensee* 475
Notes on Advertising, Economies of Scale, and Entry Barriers .... *A. Michael Spence* 493
Wealth and Wealth Proxies in a Permanent Income Model .... *J. Walter Elliott* 509
Bayes Rule as a Descriptive Model: The Representativeness Heuristic .... *David M. Grether* 537

NOTES

The Limitations of Pigouvian Taxes as a Long-Run Remedy for Externalities .... *Dennis W. Carlton and Glenn C. Loury* 559
Relative Deprivation and the Gini Coefficient:
Comment .... *John D. Hey and Peter J. Lambert* 567
Reply .... *Shlomo Yitzhaki* 575
Exchange-Rate Variability, Real and Monetary Shocks, and the Degree of Capital Mobility Under Rational Expectations .... *Robert Driskill and Stephen McCafferty* 577

PUBLISHED FOR HARVARD UNIVERSITY
BY JOHN WILEY & SONS, NEW YORK

QJECAT 95(3) 387–586 (1980)
ISSN 0033-5533

The Quarterly Journal of Economics

Published eight times in 1980 (February, March, May, June, August, September, November and December), two volumes, four issues per volume, by John Wiley & Sons, Inc.

Second class postage paid at New York, New York, and at additional mailing offices.

Subscription price (1981): $30.00 per volume. Postage and handling outside U.S.A.: $8.00 per volume. Please allow four weeks for change of address. Back volumes are available for previous years. Request price list from publisher. Claims for undelivered copies must be made no later than three months following month of publication. Missing copies will be supplied when losses have been sustained in transit and where reserve stock will permit.

Books, periodicals and manuscripts should be addressed to THE QUARTERLY JOURNAL OF ECONOMICS, Littauer Center, Cambridge, Massachusetts 02138. Two copies of manuscripts should be submitted in clear double-spaced typewritten copy. Manuscripts of more than thirty-five double-spaced typed pages in length are not ordinarily considered for publication. After publication, twenty-five complimentary reprints are sent to the author receiving proofs. This journal does not carry a page charge for contributors.

Business correspondence should be addressed to Journals Department, John Wiley & Sons, 605 Third Avenue, New York, New York 10158.

THE

QUARTERLY JOURNAL OF ECONOMICS

Vol. XCV November 1980 No. 3

ARTICLES

A Growth Model for a Tenured-Labor-Managed Firm .... *André Sapir* 387

Nontraded Goods and the Balance of Trade in a Neo-Keynesian Temporary Equilibrium .... *J. Peter Neary* 403

Job Differentiation and Wages .... *Nancy L. Stokey* 431

The Distribution of Income by Factor Components .... *Graham Pyatt, Chau-nan Chen, and John Fei* 451

On Oligopolistic Markets for Nonrenewable Natural Resources .... *Tracy R. Lewis and Richard Schmalensee* 475

Notes on Advertising, Economies of Scale, and Entry Barriers .... *A. Michael Spence* 493

Wealth and Wealth Proxies in a Permanent Income Model .... *J. Walter Elliott* 509

Bayes Rule as a Descriptive Model: The Representativeness Heuristic .... *David M. Grether* 537

NOTES

The Limitations of Pigouvian Taxes as a Long-Run Remedy for Externalities .... *Dennis W. Carlton and Glenn C. Loury* 559

Relative Deprivation and the Gini Coefficient:
Comment .... *John D. Hey and Peter J. Lambert* 567
Reply .... *Shlomo Yitzhaki* 575

Exchange-Rate Variability, Real and Monetary Shocks, and the Degree of Capital Mobility Under Rational Expectations .... *Robert Driskill and Stephen McCafferty* 577

THE
QUARTERLY JOURNAL
OF ECONOMICS

Vol. XCV November 1980 No. 3

A GROWTH MODEL FOR A TENURED-LABOR-MANAGED FIRM*

ANDRÉ SAPIR

The theory of the labor-managed firm is a recent addition to the economic literature on organization. Analyses of the behavior of workers' self-managed firms have produced two versions of the theory. The present paper is primarily concerned with the employment decisions of labor-managed firms, which are analyzed within the framework of a new model drawing upon both versions of the existing theory. We present a growth model for a firm characterized by the division of labor between tenured and nontenured workers, whose aim is the intertemporal maximization of the net income per tenured worker. Using Pontryagin's Maximum Principle, we obtain the optimality conditions, the transition path, and the steady state for the model. We also analyze a series of policy alternatives. Some references are made to the Yugoslav economy.

I. INTRODUCTION

The theory of the labor-managed firm constitutes a relatively recent addition to the literature on economic organization. Analyses of the behavior of workers' self-managed firms have produced two versions of the theory: the pure-theory version, and the realistic-theory version. The first version corresponds to the Ward [1958]-Domar [1966]-Vanek [1970]-Meade [1972] model, which postulates that the firm's objective is simply to maximize income per worker. The realistic-theory version departs from the previous one in seeking to specify the institutional environment within which the firm operates. In particular, Furubotn has challenged the income-per-worker cri-

* Part of the work on this paper was done while the author was funded by the Belgian National Foundation for Scientific Research. I am grateful to William Brock, Charles Wilson, and the referees for their comments, and to Jerry Green for his encouragement.

terion by insisting that "an adequate theory of the self-managed firm must consider the preferences and wealth increasing opportunities of those individuals actually making economic decisions" [1976, p. 104]. Instead, he has proposed a model that emphasizes the role of the "original" members of the collective. One of the results Furubotn derives from his model is that "because of the pressure of internal politics and concern for the firm's environment, there will be reluctance on the part of the original majority to increase the labor force" [1976, p. 122].

The one country where worker management is a reality on a large scale is Yugoslavia. Furubotn's conclusion seems relevant to the recent situation in this country, where a slowdown in job creation has occurred since 1965. This has coincided with an important economic reform that allowed Yugoslav firms to become truly labor-managed. Thus, the average annual growth rate for man-hours in the labor-managed manufacturing sector dropped from 6.6 percent for 1956–1965 to 2.2 percent for 1966–1974 [Sapir, 1980].

The present paper attempts to analyze employment decisions of a labor-managed firm by presenting yet another model, which draws upon both versions of the existing theory. Our focus is primarily theoretical. Although some brief reference to the Yugoslav situation will be made when appropriate, the paper should be viewed as a contribution to the behavioral theory of the labor-managed firm rather than as an explanation of macro phenomena in Yugoslavia for which a micro model is obviously ill-suited. Section II discusses the assumptions of the model. The model itself is described in Section III, where the optimality conditions are also derived. Section IV analyzes the transition path, and the convergence toward the steady state. Section V examines the steady state, and presents some comparative-static results. Finally, Section VI summarizes the analysis.

II. Notation and Assumptions of the Model

The conventional Ward-Domar-Vanek-Meade model postulates a one-period maximization of the income per homogeneous worker. We depart from it in two respects. (1) We assume that labor is heterogenous, in the sense that some workers are tenured (the so-called "members"), while the others are not (the "nonmembers").[1] (2) We postulate an intertemporal maximization of the income per member, i.e., we make the assumption that the firm's objective is to maximize the discounted present value of dividends.[2]

We divide the workers of the labor-managed firm into two groups, the "members" (T) and the "nonmembers" (E). Workers belonging to the latter group are employees, in the sense that they receive a wage payment (w)[3] and that they can freely[4] be hired and laid off. Also, these workers are assumed to be unskilled. Workers belonging to the former group are tenured, in the sense that they cannot be laid off. They form—alone—the management committee of the firm. These workers are skilled: each member is k ($k > 1$) times as productive as a nonmember.

We borrow from Ehrenberg [1971] the notion of "internal labor market." The firm starts with a given stock of members, and the only way to increase this stock is through hiring employees, training them, and giving them tenure when they have become skilled:[5]

> The amount of training required is assumed to be fixed, since [k] is assumed constant. However, the length of the training period may be varied. The shorter the training period, the more intensive the training must be within the period, and hence the greater the instantaneous marginal cost of training each new employee per period. In fact, it is probably reasonable to assume that this cost increases at an increasing rate. If we let $1/\theta$ be the average period that [unskilled] workers must spend in training before [becoming skilled], then θ will be the average proportion of [nonmembers] to achieve [membership] at each moment in time [Ehrenberg, 1971, p. 88].

The training cost can therefore be written as

$$c(\theta)E, \quad c' \geq 0, \quad c'' > 0, \quad c''' = 0. \tag{1}$$

As for the change in the stock of members, we have

$$\dot{T} = \theta E - qT, \tag{2}$$

1. Ward had already mentioned that it is possible "to hire workers who would agree to work for the contractual wage rate for unskilled workers and renounce their right to profit" [Ward, 1958, p. 584]. In the context of their Yugoslav model, Adelman and D'Andrea Tyson also note that "some workers may be hired on a temporary basis at a fixed wage. These workers have no influence on the decision-making process of the firm, and thus they receive no weight in its objective function. Temporary workers are to be understood as those workers who the firm can freely lay off during a production period. Permanent workers or "members of the firm" are distinguished from the so-called temporary workers by the fact that they cannot be disemployed by the firm during a production period without their consent" [Adelman and D'Andrea Tyson, 1973, pp. 4–5].

2. Intertemporal optimization in labor-managed firms is also analyzed by Atkinson [1973], Bonin [1975], Litt, Steinherr, and Thisse [1975], and Furubotn [1976].

3. w is the minimum wage set by the authorities. It applies to all firms.

4. It is assumed that firms operate in an environment of unlimited supply of unskilled workers. This assumption ensures that unskilled workers are all paid the minimum wage—regardless of the firm that employs them. Therefore, we avoid Salop's problem of wage differentials in a given labor market, and of having quits related to the relative wage rate. See Salop [1973].

5. The brackets in the quotation indicate the adaptation of Ehrenberg's text to our own purpose.

where q is the retirement rate for the tenured workers. Note that, like Ehrenberg, we limit ourselves to consideration of on-the-job training. Thus, we totally disregard the possibility of the existence of a market for skilled wage labor. New hires occur only at the unskilled level. Similarly, only unskilled workers can be laid off.

It is assumed that the firm's technology can be described by the production function $X = F(K,L)$, where X is the single output produced by the quantity of capital K, and by the flow of labor services L, measured in efficiency units:

$$L = E + kT. \tag{3}$$

Moreover, the production function is assumed to possess positive marginal products and to be strictly concave, i.e.,

$$F_K, F_L > 0 \tag{4a}$$

$$F_{KK}, F_{LL} < 0 \tag{4b}$$

$$F_{KK}F_{LL} - F_{KL}^2 > 0 \tag{4c}$$

$$F_{KL} = F_{LK} > 0. \tag{4d}$$

Following Drèze, we call a labor-managed economy "an economy where production is carried out in firms organized by workers who get together and form collectives or partnerships. These firms hire nonlabor inputs, including capital, and sell outputs, under the assumed objective of maximizing the welfare of the members . . . . The capital can be either publicly or privately owned" [1976, p. 1125]. On this latter point, Vanek insists that "it is of truly fundamental importance that the basis of the cooperative worker-managed firm be the work in common and not ownership in common" [1973, p. 144]. In contrast, Furubotn [1974 and 1976] and Furubotn and Pejovich [1970] have recently analyzed the behavior of a labor-managed firm where productive assets are what they call "nonowned assets" from the point of view of its workers. In their model, investment is generated by means of self-financing, and the workers belonging to the firm possess only the usufruct of the stock of physical capital that is owned by society at large. "Having neither permanent nor transferable claims on the assets of the labor-managed firm, decision makers operate with relatively short planning horizons" [Furubotn, 1976, p. 116].

In this paper, we accept Vanek's argument that there is nothing inherent in labor management about self-financing and collective (society) ownership of productive assets. We postulate that capital goods are rented at a given price (ρ) in a competitive market at each point of time.[6] It is assumed to be a completely variable factor, in the sense that it bears no adjustment costs. In addition, we assume that the firm is a price taker in the market of its output and that the price per unit of output is p. Therefore, its so-called "Residual Enterprise Income" ($R.E.I$) can be written as

$$R.E.I. = pF(K,L) - wE - c(\theta)E - \rho K. \tag{5}$$

Since capital is entirely rented, there are no retained earnings, and the residual enterprise income is simply divided among the members of the collective:

$$R.E.I. = dT, \tag{6}$$

where d is the dividend paid to each tenured worker of the firm. For simplicity, along with the assumption of outside financing, we postulate an infinite planning horizon. As Furubotn and Pejovich have shown, this postulate would not make sense in the context of self-financing and nonowned assets, where one expects the planning horizon to be relatively short.

It is worth pointing out that, in view of the various assumptions we have imposed, our labor-managed firm might resemble less a Yugoslav industrial concern than a law firm in the United States.[7] Indeed, think of a law firm owned by partners, and employing young lawyers on a temporary basis. The employee-lawyer's income is presumably mainly a wage, while for the partner-lawyer it is mainly a share in the firm's residual income. With time and training, young lawyers might be granted partnership. Also, this type of firm generally tends to rent rather than to buy its capital equipment. Nonetheless, the dichotomy between members and nonmembers is a reality in Yugoslavia today. For obvious ideological reasons, it is hard to find written evidence on the existence of nonmembers, but several specialists have definitely confirmed it in personal communications.[8] The extent of this phenomenon however, is uncertain, but presumably limited.

6. For a further discussion on the effect of various modes of financing on the behavior of labor-managed economies, see Schlicht and von Weizsäcker [1977], who note that "the actual Yugoslav system has characteristics of some similarity to the leasing system" [p. 58].

7. For a discussion of law firms and other professional partnerships as labor-managed firms, see the very interesting paper by Jensen and Meckling [1979].

8. However, a Yugoslav publication has recently pointed to the existence of a new practice that allows "thousands of workers" to be employed by labor-managed firms on a temporary basis. See *Politika,* November 14, 1979. I am grateful to Professor Sirc of the University of Glasgow for providing me with this source.

III. The Model and Optimality Conditions

The problem of the tenured-labor-managed firm is, at each moment of time, to choose a stock of capital (K), a stock of hired workers (E), and a promotion ratio (θ) in such a way as to maximize

$$\int_0^\infty \frac{pF(K,E+kT) - wE - c(\theta)E - \rho K}{T} e^{-\rho t} dt \tag{7}$$

subject to the constraints

$$\begin{aligned} &\dot{T} = \theta E - qT, \quad T(0) \text{ given;} \\ &\theta, E, T, K \geq 0. \end{aligned} \tag{8}$$

Letting π denote the value—in terms of dividend per member—of increases in the membership, and using Pontryagin's Maximum Principle, define the Hamiltonian:

$$H = \frac{pF(K,E+kT) - wE - c(\theta)E - \rho K}{T} + \pi(\theta E - qT). \tag{9}$$

The following first-order conditions must hold along the optimal path:

$$K \geq 0, \quad (pF_K - \rho)/T \leq 0, \tag{10}$$

and

$$K(pF_K - \rho)/T = 0;$$

$$E \geq 0, \quad (pF_L - w - c)/T + \pi\theta \leq 0, \tag{11}$$

and

$$E[(pF_L - w - c)/T + \pi\theta] = 0;$$

$$\theta \geq 0, \quad -c'E/T + \pi E \leq 0 \tag{12}$$

and

$$\theta[-c'E/T + \pi E] = 0.$$

Equation (10) specifies that, since capital is a perfectly variable input in this model, optimality requires that the firm choose its capital stock so as to bring its marginal product into equality with its rental price.

Equation (11) states that the firm should continue to hire unskilled workers until the net marginal value of doing so becomes zero. That is, if E is raised by one unit, direct costs for each member rise by $(w + c)/T$; but the revenue increases by pF_L and the number of skilled workers increases by θ units, with each of these workers being valued by the tenured workers at π.

Equation (12) tells us that the promotion rate (θ) should be increased up to the point where the value of an additional skilled worker equals the marginal training cost attached to this worker.

The transition equations are given by

$$\dot{T} = \theta E - qT; \tag{13}$$

$$\dot{\pi} = \pi(\rho + q) + (pF - wE - cE - \rho K)/T^2 - kpF_L/T. \tag{14}$$

For an interior solution ($K > 0, E > 0, \theta > 0$), conditions (10), (11), and (12) can be written as

$$pF_K(K,E + kT) - \rho = 0, \tag{15}$$

and

$$(pF_L - w - c)/T + \pi\theta = -c' + \pi T = 0 \tag{16}$$

$$\therefore pF_L(K,E + kT) - w - c(\theta) + \theta c'(\theta) = 0.$$

Equations (15) and (16) can be interpreted as a system of two equations in the two unknowns K and E. This system can be written as

$$K = K(T,k,p,\rho,w,\theta), \tag{17a}$$

and

$$E = E(T,k,p,\rho,w,\theta). \tag{17b}$$

Equation (17b) can be viewed as an equation relating E and θ along the optimal path, for given T, k, p, ρ, w, and θ. It can easily be seen that

$$\frac{\partial E}{\partial \theta} = -\frac{c'' pF_{KK}}{\Delta} > 0, \tag{18}$$

where

$$\Delta = p^2(F_{KK}F_{LL} - F_{KL}^2),$$

and that

$$\frac{\partial^2 E}{\partial \theta^2} = -\frac{1}{\Delta^2}\left[c'' pF_{KK}\Delta + c''\theta p^3 \frac{\partial E}{\partial \theta}\frac{1}{F_{KK}}\left(3F_{KK}^2 F_{KL}F_{LLK} - 3F_{KL}^2 F_{KK}F_{KKL} + F_{KL}^3 F_{KKK} - F_{KK}^3 F_{LLL}\right)\right] > 0 \tag{19}$$

if the term in parentheses is ≥ 0.[9]

9. Note that the convexity of E in θ has no bearing on the rest of the analysis of this problem.

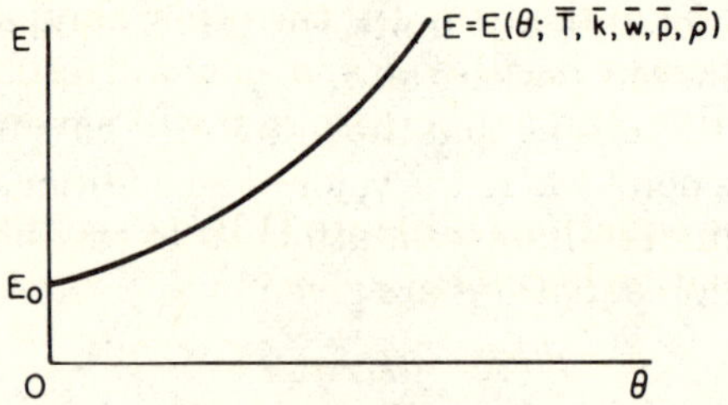

FIGURE I

Also,

(20a) $$\frac{\partial E}{\partial T} = -k < 0;$$

(20b) $$\frac{\partial E}{\partial k} = -T < 0;$$

(20c) $$\frac{\partial E}{\partial p} = \frac{p(F_K F_{LK} - F_L F_{KK})}{\Delta} > 0;$$

(20d) $$\frac{\partial E}{\partial \rho} = -\frac{pF_{LK}}{\Delta} < 0;$$

(20e) $$\frac{\partial E}{\partial w} = \frac{pF_{KK}}{\Delta} < 0.$$

And,

(21a) $$\frac{\partial K}{\partial T} = \frac{\partial K}{\partial k} = 0;$$

(21b) $$\frac{\partial K}{\partial p} = \frac{p(F_L F_{KL} - F_K F_{LL})}{\Delta} > 0;$$

(21c) $$\frac{\partial K}{\partial \rho} = \frac{pF_{LL}}{\Delta} < 0;$$

(21d) $$\frac{\partial K}{\partial w} = -\frac{pF_{KL}}{\Delta} < 0;$$

(21e) $$\frac{\partial K}{\partial \theta} = \frac{c''\theta pF_{KL}}{\Delta} > 0.$$

Defining E_0 as the solution of equation (17b) for $\theta = 0$, and using the results from (18) and (19), we have graphed the relationship between E and θ in Figure I. We observe that an increase in the promotion ratio must be accompanied by an increase in the number of employees working in the firm. On the other hand, as indicated by system (20), an increase in either T, k, ρ, or w will result in a downward shift of the E-curve, and an increase in p will have the opposite effect.

Substituting equation (17b) into (13), we see that the change in membership equation becomes

$$\dot{T} = \theta E(\theta, T, k, p, \rho, w) - qT. \tag{22}$$

As for equation (14), the other dynamic equation in our model, we can use the necessary condition (12)—i.e., $\pi T = c'(\theta)$—to transform it into an equation giving the change of the promotion ratio. Indeed, combining (12) and (13), we find that

$$\dot{\pi} T^2 + c'\theta E - c'qT = c''T\dot{\theta}, \tag{23}$$

and substituting (14) into (23), we derive

$$\dot{\theta} = (c'T\rho + pF - wE - cE - \rho k - kTpF_L + c'\theta E)/c''T. \tag{24}$$

Note that the system of differential equations defined by (13) and (24) is autonomous, in the sense that time t does not enter explicitly into these equations. As Arrow has indicated, great interest is attached to the stationary point of an autonomous system. Indeed, he has shown that in this case a path which satisfies the condition for optimality and converges to a stationary point constitutes an optimal path. And thus this stationary point is optimal.[10]

The stationary state equilibrium $(T^*, \theta^*, E^*, K^*)$ for this model is defined by the values of T and θ such that $\dot{T} = \dot{\theta} = 0$ in (13) and (24), and by the values of E and K for which (15) and (16) hold. Hence, $(T^*, \theta^*, E^*, K^*)$ is the solution to the system:

$$\theta E - qT = 0 \tag{25a}$$

$$c'T\rho + pF - wE - cE - \rho K - kTpF_L + c'\theta E = 0 \tag{25b}$$

$$pF_L - w - c + \theta c' = 0 \tag{25c}$$

$$pF_K - \rho = 0. \tag{25d}$$

Equations (25c) and (25d) are demand equations for unskilled workers and capital, respectively. Equation (25a) is a supply equation for skilled workers:

$$T = \theta E/q. \tag{26}$$

10. See Arrow [1968, pp. 96–7]. The reader is also directed to this reference for arguments relevant to the discussion in Section IV with respect to the transition path.

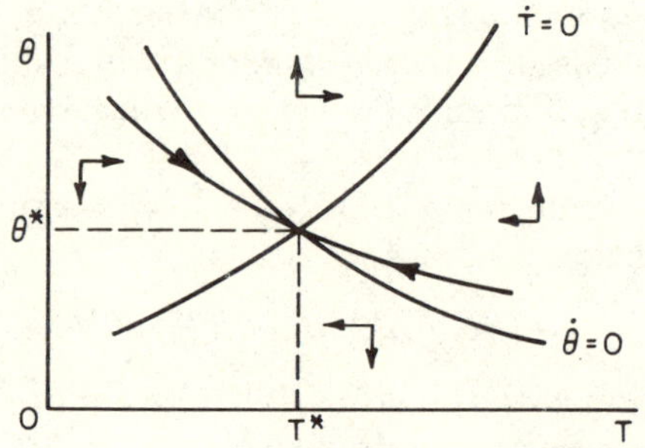

FIGURE II

As for equation (25b), it resembles the usual labor demand curve for workers' managed firms. In that sense, it is a demand equation for skilled workers indicating that, in equilibrium, the value of the marginal product of labor must equal the average net earnings per member, corrected for training costs:

$$kpF_L = (pF - wE - cE - \rho K)/T + c'(\rho + \theta E/T). \tag{27}$$

IV. Transition Path

Having obtained the steady state solution of the model, we now study the question of convergence toward the steady state from arbitrary initial conditions.

Making use of (17), we can rewrite the transition equations as

$$\dot{T} = \theta E(T,k,p,\rho,w,\theta) - qT, \tag{28}$$

and

$$\begin{aligned}\dot{\theta} = \{&c'(\theta)T\rho + pF[K(T,k,p,\rho,w,\theta),E(T,k,p,\rho,w,\theta) + kT] \\ &+ [c'(\theta)\theta - w - c(\theta)]E(T,k,p,\rho,w,\theta) - \rho K(T,k,p,\rho,w,\theta) \\ &-kTpF_L[K(T,k,p,\rho,w,\theta),E(T,k,p,\rho,w,\theta) + kT]\}/c''(\theta)T.\end{aligned} \tag{29}$$

The properties of this system can be conveniently seen by means of the phase diagram constructed in Figure II. In order to study the slopes of the $\dot{T} = 0$ and $\dot{\theta} = 0$ loci, we define

$$N(\theta,T) \equiv \dot{T} = 0, \tag{30}$$

and

$$M(\theta,T) \equiv \dot{\theta} = 0. \tag{31}$$

Considering first (30) and (28), we have

(32a) $$N_\theta = E + \theta\left(\frac{\partial E}{\partial \theta}\right) > 0,$$

and

(32b) $$N_T = \theta\left(\frac{\partial E}{\partial T}\right) - q < 0,$$

and therefore,

(32c) $$\left.\frac{d\theta}{dT}\right|_{\dot{T}=0} = -\frac{N_T}{N_\theta} > 0.$$

Thus, the locus $N(\theta,T)$ is upward sloping in the (T,θ) phase plane. For fixed levels of $\theta, \dot{T}$ is a decreasing function of the membership. This can be seen from (32b). Therefore, $\dot{T} < 0$ to the right of $\dot{T} = 0$, and $\dot{T} > 0$ to the left. The reason for this slope is that an increase in θ increases E above E^*, so that an increase in T is required to restore this value. (See equations (18) and (20a).)

Now considering (31) and (29), we have

(33a) $$M_\theta = c''(T\rho + \theta E + \theta kT) > 0,$$

(33b) $$M_T = c'\rho > 0,$$

and therefore

(33c) $$\left.\frac{d\theta}{dT}\right|_{\dot{\theta}=0} = -\frac{M_T}{M_\theta} < 0.$$

The $\dot{\theta} = 0$ curve is the downward sloping line in the phase diagram. For constant $T, \dot{\theta}$ is an increasing function of the promotion ratio. This is indicated by (33b). Therefore $\dot{\theta} > 0$ above $\dot{\theta} = 0$, and $\dot{\theta} < 0$ below.

In order to characterize the equilibrium point, we take the linear approximation to the dynamic system (28) and (29) in the neighborhood of (θ^*, T^*):

(34a) $$\dot{T} = N_T(T - T^*) + N_\theta(\theta - \theta^*),$$

(34b) $$\dot{\theta} = M_T(T - T^*) + M_\theta(\theta - \theta^*).$$

It can easily be verified that the corresponding characteristic equation,

(35) $$\lambda^2 - (N_T + M_\theta)\lambda + (N_T M_\theta - M_T N_\theta) = 0,$$

admits two real roots, with different signs. Therefore, the equilibrium point is a saddle point, the stable branches of which correspond to the negative root and constitute the optimal path. The optimal trajectory is graphed in Figure II.

The optimal path may be interpreted as a decision rule in which, given the membership of the firm at the beginning of the plan, it is optimal for the firm to choose its promotion rate at the level dictated by this path and proceed to equilibrium. Thus, when the membership is below the level T^*, the tenured-workers' management chooses a high promotion ratio and decreases it as the membership increases. On the other hand, when the stock of members is above T^*, the management sets θ at a low level and increases it as this stock decreases toward its equilibrium level. Note that the system is not stable, in the sense that it does not converge toward the steady state from any initial point. The management must therefore select the proper level of θ, given the initial T, in order to converge toward the equilibrium position. However, this instability in the (T,θ) phase plane does not preclude stability in the (T,t) plane. Given $T(0)$, there exists a unique $\theta(0)$, which puts the firm on a stable arm of the saddle point taking it to (T^*,θ^*).

Once the value of θ corresponding to the initial membership has been assigned on the optimal path, the choice of the instruments K and E is determined through equations (17). The smaller the initial membership, the larger the promotion ratio, or the larger both the capital stock and the number of unskilled workers. If we start below T^*, K and E will have to be decreased along the optimal path in order to converge toward the steady state: see inequalities (18), (20a), (21a), and (21e).

Note that along any path which satisfies the necessary conditions—and, in particular, along the optimal path—equation (20a) implies that if T increases by one unit, E must decrease by $k > 1$ units, and therefore $(E + T)$ must unambiguously fall. Thus, if the original membership is below T^*, it will be optimal from the viewpoint of criterion (7) to increase the number of tenured workers in the firm while at the same time reducing the total number of workers.

V. Comparative Statics

This section investigates the impact and long-run effects of variation in the parameters. The initial position will, in all cases, be taken as the steady state point (θ^*,T^*). Taking the total differential of system (25) and solving it, we obtain the effects of changes in the parameters of the model on the equilibrium values as shown in Table I.

TABLE I

	∂q	∂w	∂k	$\partial \rho$	∂p
∂T	−	?	−	−,−,?*	?
$\partial \theta$	+	+	+	?,+,+*	−
∂E	+	−	−	?	?
∂K	+	−	?	?	?

* For $(K - c'T) <, =, > 0$.

An increase in the retirement rate (q) shifts the $\dot{T} = 0$ schedule upward, while leaving the $\dot{\theta} = 0$ schedule unchanged, so that θ^* rises, and T^* falls. The elasticity of T with respect to q being larger than unity, the number of retiring members increases in the long run, and therefore the number of promoted nonmembers must increase as well. This increase results from a simultaneous rise in the number of nonmembers employed in the firm and in the promotion ratio.

A higher wage rate (w) shifts both the $\dot{T} = 0$ and $\dot{\theta} = 0$ schedules upward. It follows that θ^* rises, while the effect on T^* is ambiguous. A simple condition eliminating this indetermination could not be formulated. However, the number of employees working in the firm clearly declines as the wage rate increases. In the short run, the stock of capital falls as w increases—equation (21d)—under the assumption that $F_{KL} > 0$; in the long run, this assumption guarantees an increase in the stock of capital via the rise in θ^*—equation (21e).

An increase in the productivity coefficient (k) has a similar effect on the $\dot{T} = 0$ and $\dot{\theta} = 0$ schedules as an increase in the retirement rate. However, in this case the number of members retiring decreases as T^* falls, and the number of promoted employees decreases accordingly. This decrease occurs through a fall in the number of employees in the long run. Interestingly, in the short run for given T^* and θ^*, and for given costs of labor and capital, the increase in the productivity of skilled workers implies a reduction in the stock of unskilled workers. However, in the long run, as T^* falls and θ^* rises, this stock tends to rise, but this tendency is more than offset by the direct effect of k.

An increment in the interest rate (ρ) shifts the $\dot{T} = 0$ schedule upward, but has an ambiguous effect on the $\dot{\theta} = 0$ schedule. Three cases can be distinguished according to the size of K relative to that of $c'T$, i.e., according to which of the interest payments on capital by each member and of the forgone interest on the marginal training cost is larger. If $K = c'T$, the $\dot{\theta} = 0$ schedule remains unchanged, so that θ^* rises and T^* falls. If $K < c'T$, the schedule shifts downward, and

T^* falls while the change in θ^* is ambiguous. Finally, if $K > c'T$, $\dot{\theta} = 0$ shifts upward, so that θ^* rises, while the effect on T^* is ambiguous. Thus, so long as K is not strictly larger than $c'T$, an increase in ρ—i.e., a tendency for the tenured-workers' management to maximize present versus future dividends—implies a reduction in the membership of the firm. When the interest payment on capital becomes relatively large, this result might not hold anymore, since it might pay for each member to have more tenured workers in the firm sharing the cost of capital.

An increase in the output price (p) shifts both the $\dot{T} = 0$ and $\dot{\theta} = 0$ schedules downward. Therefore, θ^* must decline, but the effect on T^* is ambiguous. Again, the algebraic expression gave no simple condition eliminating the indetermination.

What policy could the authorities devise in order to increase the level of employment in the tenured-labor-managed firm? Assuming that the authorities control the retirement rate (q), the wage rate (w), the level of education—and therefore the productivity premium (k)—and the rate of interest (ρ), our results indicate the following policies for increasing the employment of nonmembers: increase the retirement rate, lower the wage rate, or narrow the productivity differential between skilled and unskilled workers. Some simple calculations indicate that an increase in the retirement rate or a decrease in the wage rate will also result in an increase in employment measured in natural units ($E + T$). A similar effect can be obtained by narrowing the productivity differential. Economically, early retirement and lower minimum wage are both feasible. However, the possibility of reducing the productivity gap is not entirely realistic in this model where skill is acquired through on-the-job training. It is unfortunate that we are unable to make any prediction about the effect of changes in the interest rate on the level of employment, since this policy is probably more relevant than the other three to the Yugoslav case.

VI. Conclusions

We have presented a growth model for a labor-managed firm characterized by the division of labor between skilled members and unskilled nonmembers. We have examined the employment behavior of the firm as well as policies aimed at affecting it, under the assumed objective of intertemporal maximization of income per member. The main results obtained in this paper can be summarized as follows:

1. There is no natural tendency for the tenured-labor-managed firm to converge toward a steady state equilibrium. Appropriate

planning by the tenured workers' management is therefore required to reach equilibrium.

2. In a situation where the original membership of the firm is below the optimal level, the management chooses to initiate its operation with a relatively large number of nonmembers and a high promotion ratio. Proceeding along the optimal path, both magnitudes will have to be decreased in order to reach the steady state, and simultaneously, the membership will progressively increase. Compared to the initial situation, the size of the firm's total labor force (members plus nonmembers) will be smaller in the steady state.

3. For a firm operating in the steady state, the authorities can induce a long-run increase in the hiring of workers by lowering their wage rate, increasing the retirement rate, or narrowing the productivity gap between skilled and unskilled workers. In the case of Yugoslavia where the slowdown in job creation after 1965 was partially solved by sending workers to Germany (and some other Western European countries), there might therefore be hopeful prospects for returning migrant workers seeking employment in the labor-managed sector, provided that they have acquired relevant skills in Germany.[11] Policies that result in a long-run increase in the hiring of workers also imply a long-run increase in the total labor force of the firm.

To conclude, we discuss several avenues open for further research. The issue of investment financing and property rights is an important one. An exploration of various modes of financing within the context of a model allowing for the heterogeneous nature of labor would be an obvious step forward. Also, more work needs to be done to extend the analysis to the macro level and to gain more relevance.[12] In this context, it is perhaps time for researchers interested in worker management, including this author, to seek to bridge the gap between the real Yugoslavia and the planet too often labeled "Yugoslavia."

UNIVERSITY OF WISCONSIN—MADISON

REFERENCES

Adelman, I., and L. D'Andrea Tyson, "A Regional Micro-Economic Model of Yugoslavia: Factors Affecting the Distribution of Income in the Short Run," Report for the IBRD, mimeographed, 1972.

11. Implicitly, we are assuming that migrant workers were originally unskilled and therefore nonmembers. This follows from the fact that, in our model, skills can be acquired only through on-the-job training. Obviously, the model would really need to be reformulated to address this issue properly.

12. Recent work on the macroeconomics of labor management includes Vanek [1970], Pierce [1977], and Meade [1979].

Arrow, K. J., "Applications of Control Theory to Economic Growth," *Lectures in Applied Mathematics,* XII (Mathematics of the Decision Sciences—Part 2), 1968, 85–119.

Atkinson, A. B., "Worker Management and the Modern Industrial Enterprise," this *Journal,* LXXXVII (Aug. 1973), 375–92.

Bonin, J. P., "Unemployment in the Labor-Managed Economy: Can Macroeconomic Policy Help?" Discussion Paper #75-8, University of California, San Diego, mimeographed, 1975.

Domar, E., "The Soviet Collective Farm as a Producer Cooperative," *American Economic Review,* LVI (Sept. 1966), 734–57.

Drèze, J. H., "Some Theory of Labor Management and Participation," *Econometrica,* XLIV (Nov. 1976), 1125–39.

Ehrenberg, R. G., "Heterogenous Labor, the Internal Labor Market, and the Dynamics of Employment-Hours Decision," *Journal of Economic Theory,* III (March 1971), 85–104.

Furubotn, E. G., "Bank Credit and the Labor-Managed Firm: The Yugoslav Case," in E. G. Furubotn and S. Pejovich, eds., *The Economics of Property Rights* (Cambridge, MA: Ballinger, 1974), pp. 257–76.

——, "The Long-Run Analysis of the Labor-Managed Firm: An Alternative Interpretation," *American Economic Review,* LXVI (March 1976), 104–23.

——, and S. Pejovich, "Property Rights and the Behavior of the Firm in a Socialist State: The Example of Yugoslavia," *Zeitschrift fur Nationalokonomie,* XXX (Dec. 1970), 431–54.

Jensen, M. C., and W. H. Meckling, "Rights and Production Functions: An Application to Labor-Managed Firms and Codetermination," *Journal of Business,* XLII (Nov. 1979), 469–506.

Litt, F. X., A. Steinherr, and J. F. Thisse, "Investment Decisions in Profit-Maximizing and Labor-Managed Enterprises: A Dynamic Comparative Analysis," Paper Prepared for the Second Conference on Self-Management, Ithaca, mimeographed, 1975.

Meade, J. E., "The Theory of Labour-Managed Firms and of Profit Sharing," *Economic Journal,* LXXXII (March 1972), 402–28.

——, "The Adjustment Processes of Labour Co-operatives with Constant Returns to Scale and Perfect Competition," *Economic Journal,* LXXXIX (Dec. 1979), 781–88.

Pearce, I. F., "Participation and Income Distribution," in D. F. Heathfield, ed., *The Economics of Co-Determination* (London: Macmillan, 1977), pp. 26–35.

Salop, S. C., "Wage Differentials in a Dynamic Theory of the Firm," *Journal of Economic Theory,* VI (Aug. 1973), 321–44.

Sapir, A., "Economic Growth and Factor Substitution: What Happened to the Yugoslav Miracle?" *Economic Journal,* XC (1980), forthcoming.

Schlicht, E., and C. C. von Weizsäcker, "Risk Financing in Labour-Managed Economies: The Commitment Problem," *Zeitschrift für die Gesamte Staatswissenschaft,* CXXXIII (1977, Special Issue), 53–65.

Vanek, J., *The General Theory of Labor-Managed Market Economies* (Ithaca: Cornell University Press, 1970).

——, "Some Fundamental Considerations on Financing and the Form of Ownership Under Labor Management," in H. C. Bos, H. Linnemand, and P. de Wolff, eds., *Economic Structure and Development* (Amsterdam: North-Holland, 1973), pp. 139–52.

Ward, B., "The Firm in Illyria: Market Syndicalism," *American Economic Review,* XLVIII (Sept. 1958), 566–89.

NONTRADED GOODS AND THE BALANCE OF TRADE IN A NEO-KEYNESIAN TEMPORARY EQUILIBRIUM*

J. PETER NEARY

This paper explores the implications for international monetary economics of recent work on macroeconomic models of temporary equilibrium with rationing. A model of a small open economy is presented, which, though fully consistent in the long run with the monetary approach to the balance of payments, behaves very differently in the short run when the wage and the price of nontradeables are sticky. Among the comparative statics properties of the model are the following: a devaluation may not improve the trade balance; a wage cut may not increase employment; and technological progress has different effects, depending on the sector in which it occurs.

> What we need for balance-of-payments theory is a marriage of the Keynesian and the Hicksian type of analysis; and our model constitutes such an attempt.
>
> J. E. Meade, *The Balance of Payments: Mathematical Supplement*, p. 2.

I. INTRODUCTION

This paper explores the implications for international monetary economics of an approach that is rapidly gaining attention as one of the more promising escape routes from the current "crisis in Keynesian economics." This approach examines situations of *temporary equilibrium* in the sense of Hicks [1946, Ch. 10] rather than of Walrasian general equilibrium, meaning by the former an equilibrium at a point in time where there is genuine uncertainty about the future, and where complete markets for future goods may not exist. Hence agents base their current demands and supplies on their expectations of prices in future periods, and no mechanism exists to ensure that these expectations are shared by different individuals. The only good that can be carried forward (in the simplest formulations) is money, and therefore it plays the essential role of transferring purchasing power between periods.

In addition, and by contrast with Hicks's own version, the present paper considers a *neo-Keynesian*[1] temporary equilibrium in the sense

* This paper was written while I was Heyworth Research Fellow at Nuffield College, Oxford. I am very grateful to Nick Stern for encouragement in writing it and for his careful reading of earlier drafts. Helpful comments and suggestions were also received from Avinash Dixit, Kevin Roberts, Peter Sinclair and Joe Stiglitz, and from participants in seminars at Concordia (Montreal), Oxford, Reading, Southampton and Warwick. All remaining errors of omission and commission are my own responsibility.

1. Despite its potential ambiguity and its doubtful fidelity to Keynes's own views, we follow Benassy [1975] in using the term "neo-Keynesian," since it serves as a convenient contrast with "neoclassical" (in the sense of "neoclassical synthesis"). Grandmont [1977] and Dixit [1978] use the more precise term "temporary equilibrium with rationing."

The Quarterly Journal of Economics, November 1980 0033-5533/80/0095-0403$02.70

that current markets clear by quantity rather than by price adjustments. This means, since only voluntary exchange is assumed to take place, that agents on the long side of each market are rationed, and this in turn forces them to recalculate their demands and supplies in other markets. These recalculated or "effective" demands and supplies—which reflect the "dual decision hypothesis" of Clower [1965]—need not satisfy Walras' Law, and hence the tendency to return to full (i.e., "Walrasian") equilibrium may be rather weak (even if tâtonnement-type price adjustment is assumed to take place eventually).

All of these issues have been extensively studied by general-equilibrium theorists (see the literature surveyed by Grandmont [1977]), and their implications for macroeconomics are becoming widely known through the work of Barro and Grossman [1971], Malinvaud [1977], and Muellbauer and Portes [1978], among others. To date, however, only Gordon [1977][2] and Dixit [1978] have formally explored their implications for macroeconomic theory in an open economy. The model of the present paper and the approach adopted to analyze it owe a great deal to Dixit, but the model differs from his in explicitly incorporating a nontraded good whose price is sticky in the short run. This permits a reconciliation between the very different conclusions obtained by Malinvaud and Dixit. From the standpoint of international monetary economics, it also permits an examination of some of the issues raised by the seminal work of Salter [1959]. Salter was the first to use a diagram in the space of traded and nontraded goods, and noting that full equilibrium would take place only at the "kissing-point of tangency" between a production possibilities curve and a social indifference curve in this space, he added that all other points in his diagram are "ex ante disequilibrium positions in which the economy is always in the process of movement: overseas reserves are either decreasing or increasing; there is a rising or falling domestic price level; and either over- or under-full employment." Writing in the 1950s, Salter may be forgiven for assuming that disequilibrium in the nontraded good market would necessarily give rise to immediate price adjustment; in all other respects this passage is an excellent description of the possible disequilibrium characteristics of a small open economy. But while writers on the "monetary approach to the balance of payments" (e.g., Frenkel and Johnson [1976]) have paid

2. Gordon's model is similar to that of the present paper, except that he assumes a fixed supply of labor. However, he does not explicitly discuss the relationship between different regimes, and he considers the comparative statics response to only a single exogenous change (namely, an increase in foreign prices).

considerable attention to the process of reserve changes, neither Salter nor subsequent writers have explicitly analyzed disequilibria in the labor or nontraded good markets. It is one of the objects of this paper to remedy this oversight.

The plan of the paper is as follows. Section II introduces the model, and Section III examines its behavior when wages and prices are flexible. Section IV shows that when the wage rate and the price of the nontraded good are sticky, the economy may exhibit any one of a number of possible disequilibrium regimes, each of which is characterized by a different pattern of rationing of firms and households. Section V shows how changes in exogenous variables may lead to shifts *between* regimes, while Sections VI and VII outline the comparative static properties of the model *within* different regimes, looking at the determinants of employment and the trade balance, respectively. Finally, Section VIII summarizes the principal results and notes some directions for future research.

II. The Model

In this section we examine in turn the behavior of each of the three types of agent in the economy: households, firms, and the government.

A. Households

For simplicity we ignore distributional effects, and assume that aggregate household behavior may be represented by the maximization of a single utility function, defined over consumption of nontradeables x_1 and tradeables x_2, leisure (i.e., labor endowment less hours worked) $H - l$, and end-of-period holdings of money balances m:

$$U = u(x_1, x_2, H - l, m). \tag{1}$$

Since (1) is an indirect utility function, representing in compressed form the utility derived from consumption and leisure in both present and future periods, it depends on expectations of future prices, as well as on expectations concerning the extent of unemployment and goods rationing in the future. In a complete analysis the dependence of utility on these expectations should be explicitly considered (for partial attempts to do this, see Benassy [1975], Section 7, and Muellbauer and Portes [1978]); however, in the present paper we abstract from this issue and thus implicitly assume that expectations are completely exogenous.

Households receive wage income related to the amount of labor they supply l as well as a lump-sum income I, consisting of money balances carried over from the previous period $\overline{m}$, plus transfer payments received from the government t, plus dividend payments, being the amount of last period's profits $\overline{\pi}$. Note that, following other writers in this literature, we assume, rather arbitrarily, that profits are redistributed to consumers in the next period, and hence do not directly affect current consumption decisions. (Their indirect effect, through expectations of future dividend payments, has already been assumed to be exogenous.) This assumption greatly simplifies the algebra and, except in some cases to be noted in Section VI, makes no significant difference to the results. The household's decision problem is therefore to maximize (1) subject to the budget constraint:

$$p_1x_1 + p_2x_2 + m \leq wl + I \tag{2}$$

or

$$p_1x_1 + p_2x_2 + m \leq wl + \overline{m} + t + \overline{\pi}. \tag{3}$$

This yields unconstrained or "notional" demand functions for each good, a labor supply function, and a flow demand function for savings:

$$x_i = x_i(p_1,p_2,w,I) \qquad i = 1,2 \tag{4}$$

$$l = l(p_1,p_2,w,I) \tag{5}$$

$$m - \overline{m} = \Delta m(p_1,p_2,w,I). \tag{6}$$

We assume throughout that all commodities are normal (including leisure, so $\partial l/\partial I$ is negative), that all own-price elasticities of demand are negative, and that labor supply is an increasing function of the wage rate. In addition, it is convenient for diagrammatic purposes to assume that all commodities are gross substitutes; this assumption will be adopted henceforth except when otherwise stated.

When prices and wages do not change to clear markets, households may face constraints additional to (2), in which case their decision problem must be recalculated. Thus, if households are involuntarily unemployed, they face a constraint on the number of hours of labor they may supply, $\overline{l} < l(p_1,p_2,w,I)$, which leads to recalculated or "effective" demand functions that depend explicitly on the level of the constraint:[3]

3. We adopt the following notational convention: a bar over a variable (e.g., $\overline{m}$) indicates that, from the point of view of the agent under consideration, its value is predetermined in the current period; a tilde (e.g., $\tilde{x}_1$) indicates a function or parameter arising from household behavior in the face of a labor-market constraint; a circumflex (e.g., $\hat{l}$) corresponds to behavior in the face of a goods-market constraint; and a double tilde (e.g., $\tilde{\tilde{x}}_2$) to behavior in the face of constraints in both markets.

(7) $$\tilde{x}_i(\bar{l};p_1,p_2,w,I) \qquad i = 1,2$$

(8) $$\Delta\tilde{m}(\bar{l};p_1,p_2,w,I).$$

The functions in equation (7) are essentially disaggregated Keynesian consumption functions, though with an explicitly choice-theoretic basis. Alternatively, households may face a purchasing constraint in the nontraded good market, $\bar{x}_1 < x_1(p_1,p_2,w,I)$ in which case their effective demand and supply functions are

(9) $$\hat{x}_2(\bar{x}_1;p_1,p_2,w,I)$$

(10) $$\hat{l}(\bar{x}_1;p_1,p_2,w,I)$$

(11) $$\Delta\hat{m}(\bar{x}_1;p_1,p_2,w,I).$$

Finally, households may face both of these constraints simultaneously, leading to a set of doubly constrained demand functions:

(12) $$\tilde{\tilde{x}}_2(\bar{l},\bar{x}_1;p_1,p_2,w,I)$$

(13) $$\Delta\tilde{\tilde{m}}(\bar{l},\bar{x}_1;p_1,p_2,w,I).$$

The properties of these functions may be established by making use of the results of rationing theory, first systematically derived by Tobin and Houthakker [1950–51] and extended by Neary and Roberts [1980]. In particular, these results imply that, if all commodities are net substitutes, *or* if the utility loss imposed on the household by the rationing constraint(s) is relatively large, then the derivatives of the effective functions (7)–(13) may be unambiguously signed with respect to the constraint levels, with the exception of the effect of a change in a goods constraint on the demand for other commodities. For later use, we write these derivatives in terms of the corresponding marginal propensities to consume

(14) $$\tilde{c}_i' = \frac{p_i}{w}\frac{\partial \tilde{x}_i}{\partial \bar{l}} \geq 0 \qquad i = 1,2$$

(15) $$\hat{c}_l' = \frac{w}{p_1}\frac{\partial \hat{l}}{\partial \bar{x}_1} \gtrless 0$$

(16) $$\hat{c}_2' = -\frac{p_2}{p_1}\frac{\partial \hat{x}_2}{\partial \bar{x}_1} \gtrless 0$$

(17) $$\tilde{\tilde{c}}_2' = \frac{p_2}{w}\frac{\partial \tilde{\tilde{x}}_2}{\partial \bar{l}} \geq 0.$$

In addition, we assume that all these marginal propensities are less than unity, which amounts to assuming that the marginal propensity to save is always positive. Note finally that these marginal propensities to consume following changes in constraint levels are written with a prime (′) to distinguish them from the corresponding marginal propensities to consume out of lump-sum income (e.g., $\tilde{c}_1 = p_1 \partial \tilde{x}_1 / \partial I$), since in general the two are not equal. (See Neary and Roberts [1980].)

B. Firms

All firms are assumed to be profit maximizers and price takers in both input and output markets, and to face diminishing returns to the only variable input, labor. Hence the behavior of each sector may be characterized as if it were choosing employment levels e_1 and e_2 to maximize profits subject to the production functions:

$$y_1 = F(e_1,h) \qquad \text{and} \qquad y_2 = G(e_2,k), \tag{18}$$

where h and k are exogenous parameters representing the state of technology. This yields unconstrained output supply and labor demand functions for each sector:

$$y_1 = y_1(p_1,w,h) \qquad y_2 = y_2(p_2,w,k) \tag{19}$$

$$e_1 = e_1(p_1,w,h) \qquad e_2 = e_2(p_2,w,k). \tag{20}$$

Clearly, an increase in output price or a fall in the nominal wage raises output supply and employment demand. In addition, technological progress (an increase in h or k) must raise output in the progressing sector at a given real wage, but it need not raise the sector's demand for labor, if the technological progress is predominantly labor-saving and if the sector's price elasticity of supply is less than unity (see Neary [1980]). For simplicity, we rule out this paradoxical case henceforth. Finally, when firms are constrained in either the output or input market, their behavior in the other market is completely determined by their production function, and so the notional supply and demand functions, (19) and (20), do not apply.

C. Government

The government may make transfer payments t to households, or it may purchase quantities of either good, the volume of such purchases being g_1 and g_2, respectively. All such transactions are financed by printing money. However, the government does not engage in production, it does not intervene in the labor market, and its activities do not directly affect household utility. Also, though purchases of goods by the government will be referred to throughout as "fiscal policy," they do not correspond to "pure," or bond-financed, fiscal policy, since the present paper does not incorporate an explicit monetary sector.[4]

D. Accounting Relationships

Certain accounting relationships must hold ex post in this model, for both notional and effective demands and supplies, i.e., irrespective of whether market clearing is brought about by price or quantity adjustment. Thus, since neither good can be stored for use in future periods, the market for the nontraded good must clear, and any domestic excess supply of the traded good must equal the balance of trade surplus s:

$$y_1 = x_1 + g_1 \tag{21}$$

$$s = y_2 - x_2 - g_2. \tag{22}$$

In addition, the labor market must clear in an ex post sense (though of course this does not rule out the possibility of involuntary unemployment):

$$l = e_1 + e_2. \tag{23}$$

Substituting from (21), (22), and (23) into (2), and writing π for total profits in the current period gives, after a little manipulation,

$$(\pi - \overline{\pi}) + (m - \overline{m}) = (p_1 g_1 + p_2 g_2 + t) + p_2 s. \tag{24}$$

The left-hand side of (24) is the net acquisition of money balances by the private sector, made up of those acquired by firms (i.e., the excess of this period's over last period's profits) and those acquired by households; this must equal total money creation, which is the sum of the government's budget deficit and the trade surplus. Equation (24) has been the focus of much of the writings on the monetary approach to the balance of payments; but while it must play a crucial role in any dynamization of the model, it is of less importance in a short-run analysis such as that of the present paper, because over a short time horizon (especially when prices are sticky) the acquisition of money balances by both firms and households is likely to be involuntary (a point stressed by Tsiang [1977]).

4. See Hool [1978] for a model similar to the present one that incorporates a bond market with a flexible interest rate.

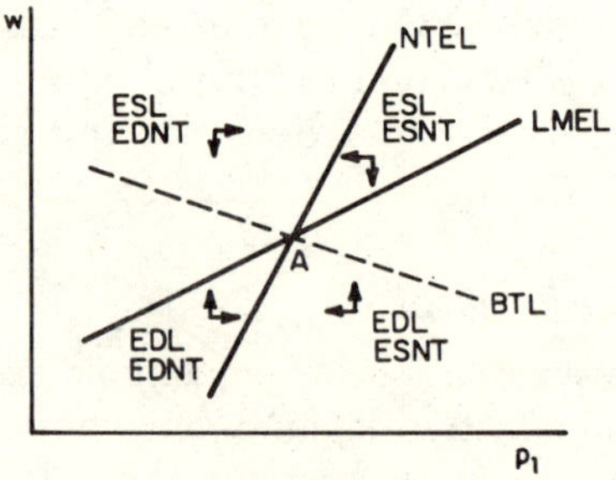

FIGURE I

III. Notional Equilibrium under Fixed Exchange Rates

In this section we analyze the model under the Walrasian assumptions that the wage rate and the price of the nontraded good change instantaneously to equate supply and demand, so that rationing does not take place in any market. For a given exchange rate (i.e., a fixed p_2), the equilibrium wage and nontraded good price are therefore determined by the intersection of the notional labor market equilibrium locus (LMEL) and the notional nontraded good market equilibrium locus (NTEL):

LMEL:

$$l(p_1,p_2,w,I) = e_1(p_1,w,h) + e_2(p_2,w,k) \tag{25}$$

NTEL:

$$y_1(p_1,w,h) = x_1(p_1,p_2,w,I) + g_1. \tag{26}$$

It is easily seen that, with gross substitutability in demand, both of these loci must be upward-sloping in (w,p_1) space; for example, starting from a point of labor market equilibrium, an increase in the wage will lead to excess supply of labor, requiring an increase in p_1 to restore equilibrium. Concerning the relative slopes of the two loci, two separate arguments, both due to Dixit [1978], suggest that the NTEL should be more steeply sloped than the LMEL, as in Figure I: first, the equilibrium at A will then be stable if w and p_1 adjust according to tâtonnement-type processes (cf. the directions of the arrows in the diagram); and second, consideration of real-balance effects would suggest that the region of excess demand in both markets should correspond to low rather than high values of w and p_1.

Some of the standard conclusions of the monetary approach to the balance of payments may be illustrated by combining (25) and (26) with the expression for the notional trade balance:

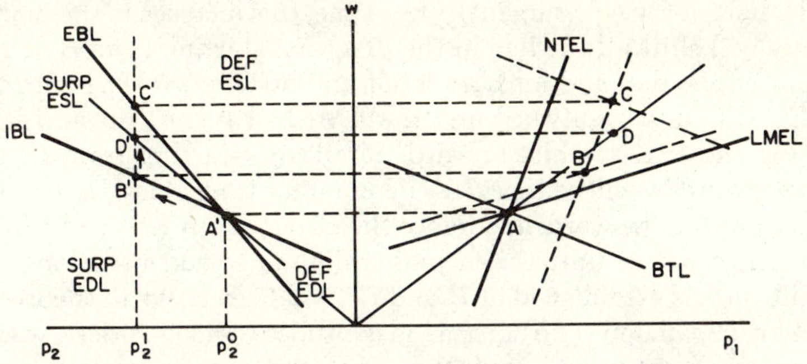

FIGURE II

$$s = y_2(p_2,w,k) - x_2(p_1,p_2,w,I) - g_2. \tag{27}$$

Assuming gross substitutability, (27) with s equal to zero gives a downward-sloping balance of trade locus (BTL) in Figure I. As drawn, the locus passes through A, indicating that A is a point of both internal and external balance; all points above the locus correspond to a trade deficit, and points below to a trade surplus.

Consider now the effects of a devaluation (i.e., an increase in the home price of tradeables from p_2^0 to p_2^1). At the initial wage and nontraded good price, this leads (assuming gross substitutability) to excess demand for both labor and nontradeables; hence the LMEL shifts upward and the NTEL shifts rightward, leading to a new short-run equilibrium at B in the right-hand panel of Figure II. The move from A to B is matched by the move from A' to B' in (p_2,w) space, the left-hand panel of Figure II, which therefore traces out an internal balance locus (IBL) in the latter panel. At the same time, the BTL is shifted upward in the right-hand panel, intersecting the new NTEL at C, which lies above B, on the assumption that the devaluation improves the trade balance. Corresponding to the move from A to C is the move from A' to C' in the left-hand panel, which therefore traces out an external balance locus (EBL) contingent on instantaneous clearing of the nontraded good market. As indicated in the diagram, the IBL and EBL divide the left-hand panel into four "zones of economic unhappiness" similar to those of Swan [1963].[5] Since the balance of trade is in surplus at the new short-run equilibrium, the domestic money supply will be increased (assuming no offsetting actions

5. The left-hand panel of Figure II is identical to Figure I of Dixit [1978]. In this and in other respects, the addition of a *flex*-price nontraded good to Dixit's model makes no qualitative difference to the model's behavior, except for the inevitable complications that follow from the addition of an extra commodity (most of these complications can be avoided in any case by the assumption of gross substitutability).

on the part of the government). Over time, this increase in the money supply will shift all the loci in the diagram: starting from B, it will induce excess demand for both labor and nontradeables; hence the NTEL will shift rightward and the LMEL will shift upward, also causing the IBL to shift upward. Similarly, starting from C, the monetary inflow will cause excess demand for tradeables, leading the BTL to shift downward, and hence the EBL to shift leftward. These shifts will continue until the surplus is eliminated and a new long-run equilibrium is established at D and D', where, relative to the initial equilibrium, all domestic nominal magnitudes (namely, prices, wages, and the money supply) have increased by the same proportion as the devaluation, and so all real magnitudes return to their initial values: the devaluation has no real effect in the long run.[6]

A similar analysis may be carried out for the effects of a domestic monetary expansion under fixed exchange rates. Finally, although the short-run characteristics of the adjustment paths in this example are necessarily valid only if gross substitutability is assumed, some equivalences between different short-run effects may be established without any assumptions other than zero degree homogeneity of all demand and supply functions. For example, the result of Krueger [1974], that a devaluation will worsen the trade balance if and only if a domestic monetary expansion will improve it, may be shown to hold in the present model when wages and prices are flexible[7] (though not, as we shall see in Section VII, when they are sticky).

IV. Effective Equilibria under Fixed Exchange Rates

We now turn to consider the model's properties when w and p_1 are assumed to be completely fixed within the current period. This extreme assumption might be justified by invoking trade-union strength, oligopolistic pricing, fixed-term contracts, or informational inadequacies. But probably the most satisfactory justifications are empirical plausibility and analytical tractability, combined with the need to redress the balance of attention that has hitherto favored the widely studied case of perfectly flexible wages and prices.

The immediate effect of this change of assumptions is that any

6. This result may be proved by totally differentiating (25), (26), and (27), setting ds equal to zero, and solving for dp_1, dw and dI in terms of dp_2, invoking the homogeneity of the excess demand functions.

7. To prove this, totally differentiate (25), (26), and (27), and solve for ds in terms of dI/I and dp_2/p_2.

point in Figure I, not just A, is now a potential short-run, or temporary, equilibrium. But at all points other than A, at least one market is cleared by quantity rationing, and this affects decisions on other markets, according to Clower's dual decision hypothesis. In particular, the two equilibrium loci, and hence the partitioning of (w,p_1) space into different regions, are affected. Consider the NTEL: when there is excess supply of labor but a rigid money wage (i.e., at all points above the LMEL in Figure I), and when the nontraded good market is in equilibrium, nontraded good firms are not rationed on any market; hence their effective supply function remains their notional one. However, households are constrained to supply less labor than they would wish; their notional demand function for nontradeables $x_1(.)$ must therefore be replaced by a constrained demand function $\tilde{x}_1(\bar{l};.)$, and so the NTEL becomes[8]

NTEL (ESL):

$$y_1(p_1,w,h) = \tilde{x}_1\{\bar{l}(.);p_1,p_2,w,I\} + g_1, \tag{28}$$

where $\bar{l}(.)$, the labor supply constraint facing households, is the unconstrained demand for labor by the two sectors combined:

$$\bar{l}(.) = e_1(p_1,w,h) + e_2(p_2,w,k). \tag{29}$$

Since $\bar{l}(.)$ is less than $l(.)$, and since the marginal propensity to consume nontradeables has been assumed to be positive, it follows that $\tilde{x}_1(.)$ must be less than $x_1(.)$ for a given set of values of the exogenous variables. Thus, a wage-price combination that yields notional equilibrium in the nontraded good market must yield excess supply of nontradeables when excess supply of labor prevails, and so the region of generalized excess supply in Figure I expands when we move from considering notional to considering effective equilibria.

Turning next to the NTEL under excess demand for labor, we find it necessary to make some assumption about how the available labor force is allocated between the two sectors.[9] In a properly specified dynamic analysis, this allocation would be determined by the past evolution of the economy; in the present one-period analysis, however, the only satisfactory approach is to consider two extreme cases, where one or another of the sectors gets priority and so is not

8. We assume throughout that the government is a priority purchaser, and hence is never rationed on any market.

9. Even with only one sector a similar problem of how the labor force is allocated between firms under excess demand for labor must be faced. Malinvaud [1977, p. 50] assumes that more efficient firms get priority, but though this is a convenient and perhaps essential simplification, it is clearly an unsatisfactory assumption for a decentralized economy.

rationed on the labor market.[10] In the first case, which we designate EDL(a), the traded good sector gets priority, and so the effective labor demand by the nontraded good sector is the total available labor supply less the traded good sector's notional labor demand. The NTEL therefore becomes

NTEL (EDL,a):

$$(30) \quad F\{l(p_1,p_2,w,I) - e_2(p_2,w,k);h\} = x_1(p_1,p_2,w,I) + g_1.$$

The left-hand side of (30) is the nontraded sector's employment-constrained supply function, and since this is less than its notional supply, $y_1(.)$, for given values of w and p_1, the effective NTEL under excess demand for labor of type (a) must shift to the right in Figure I, thus enlarging the region of EDL and EDNT. As for the alternative assumption about how the labor force is allocated, EDL(b), namely that the nontraded sector is unrationed, the NTEL in this case is simply the notional locus, (26).

Similar arguments may be used to determine the location of the effective LMEL under different regimes in the nontraded good market. Thus, when there is an excess supply of the nontraded good, households are unconstrained but firms must produce less than their notional supply of nontradeables. Their effective demand for labor is therefore given by the inverse of the production function $F(.)$, and so the LMEL becomes

LMEL (ESNT):

$$(31) \quad l(p_1,p_2,w,I) = F^{-1}\{x_1(p_1,p_2,w,I) + g_1;h\} + e_2(p_2,w,k).$$

Since constrained demand must be less than notional demand, the region of excess supply in both markets must again expand. But more than this can be said about the location of (31), for inspection confirms that it is actually identical with (30). The region of ESNT and EDL therefore vanishes when assumption (a) is made about labor-market rationing under excess demand for labor. This reflects the fact that when stocks cannot be carried over to the next period, and so firms' decisions are essentially of a one-period kind, it does not make sense to consider a state where nontraded good firms are rationed on both markets, simultaneously unable to hire as many workers as they wish and unable to sell as much output as they wish. As shown by Malinvaud [1977, Appendix] and Muellbauer and Portes [1978], this con-

10. We assume throughout that the excess demand for labor is never so severe that the notional demand for labor by a single sector exceeds the total available labor supply.

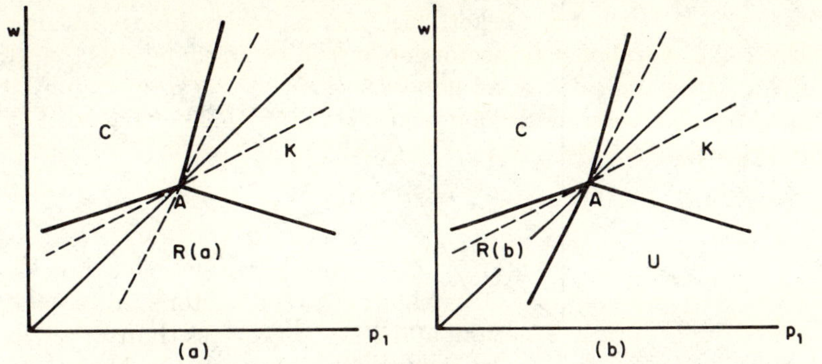

FIGURE III

clusion must be modified when firms are allowed to have a two- or more period horizon.

Finally, under excess demand for nontradeables, firms in both sectors are unconstrained, but households are unable to obtain as many nontradeables as they wish, and so they adjust their labor supply, taking the goods market constraint into account. The LMEL therefore becomes

LMEL (EDNT):

(32) $$\hat{l}\{\bar{x}_1(.);p_1,p_2,w,I\} = e_1(p_1,w,h) + e_2(p_2,w,k),$$

where the constrained consumption of nontradeables is simply what is left over after the government makes its priority purchases:

(33) $$\bar{x}_1(.) = y_1(p_1,w,h) - g_1.$$

On the plausible assumption that (15) is positive, (32) must lie above the notional locus, (25), in the region of EDNT.

Figure III summarizes the effects of considering the interrelationships between constraints in different markets on the taxonomy of disequilibrium regimes. Panel (a) shows that if traded good firms are assumed to be given priority in labor allocation when there is a general excess demand for labor, only three regimes are possible. Following Malinvaud, these are labeled *C*, for Classical Unemployment (households are rationed in both labor and nontraded good markets); *K*, for Keynesian Unemployment (or generalized excess supply: households are rationed in the labor market, nontraded good firms in the output market); and *R*, for Repressed Inflation (or generalized excess demand: households are rationed in the nontraded

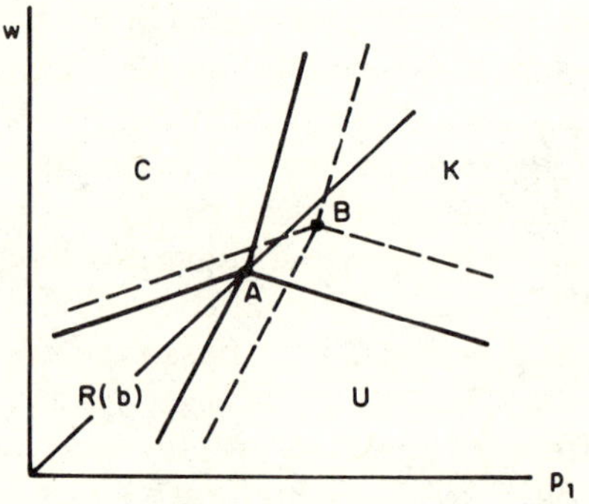

FIGURE IV

good market, and firms in the labor market). Panel (b) shows that, even with an atemporal theory of the firm, a fourth regime is possible if traded good firms are rationed under conditions of excess labor demand. Following Muellbauer and Portes [1978], we label this regime U, for underconsumption; in this regime, households are unconstrained in all markets, nontraded good firms are unconstrained in the labor market but rationed in the goods market, and traded good firms are unconstrained in the goods market (as always, because of the small country assumption) but rationed in the labor market.

V. Comparative Statics: Shifts Between Regimes

In this section we consider the effects of exogenous changes on the location of the equilibrium loci in Figure IIIb, beginning with the effects of a monetary expansion. Inspection of the expressions for the equilibrium loci in Section IV shows that in all cases an increase in lump-sum income I leads to excess demand in both labor and output markets. Therefore the effect of a monetary expansion is as shown in Figure IV: region $R(b)$ expands, and region K contracts, with corresponding changes in the other two regions. Thus, if the economy is at point A, which initially represents a point of Walrasian equilibrium, an increase in I will shift it into region R, irrespective of which assumption is made about the allocation of the labor force between sectors under excess demand for labor. Conversely, if at point B the economy is in initial Walrasian equilibrium and the money supply is reduced, a situation of Keynesian unemployment will ensue. These findings are identical to those of Malinvaud, and insofar as the "normal" evolution of contemporary capitalist economies may be viewed as characterized by fluctuations in the level of aggregate demand in the neighborhood of a full employment growth path, they provide one of his arguments as to why regions K and R are likely to be the ones most frequently observed in practice.

Turning to the effects of fiscal policy, we see clearly that government purchases of traded goods have no direct effect on the location of the equilibrium loci; instead they effectively bypass the domestic economy and lead to a *pari passu* deterioration of the trade balance. Hereinafter, in discussing fiscal policy, we confine our attention to the effects of government purchases of nontraded goods. Such purchases have the same qualitative effect on the diagram as a monetary expansion, but because they operate directly on the demand for nontradeables, they have a greater impact than monetary policy on all the equilibrium loci, with the exception of the LMEL under excess demand for nontradeables, (32). This means that a balanced budget expansion, in the sense of a government purchase of nontraded goods financed by a lump-sum tax on households' initial money balances ($p_1 dg_1 = -dI$), will affect the diagram in a fashion similar to that of a monetary expansion as depicted in Figure IV, except that the locus separating regions C and $R(b)$ is not affected. Therefore, if we start from a Walrasian equilibrium, such a policy leads to excess demand for nontradeables, though the labor market equilibrium is not disturbed. Conversely, a contractionary balanced budget shifts the economy from Walrasian equilibrium into the region of Keynesian unemployment.

Turning next to the effects of a devaluation, we see that it has the direct effect of raising profitability in the traded good sector. This tends to expand the regions of excess labor demand, and by relaxing the labor supply constraint facing households and tightening the employment constraint facing nontraded good firms (in region $R(a)$), it tends to expand the regions of excess demand for nontradeables. Therefore, as far as these direct effects are concerned, a devaluation has the same qualitative effects on the diagram as the monetary expansion depicted in Figure IV. However, a devaluation also has indirect cross-price effects, and these reinforce the direct effects only if the assumption of gross substitutability is made. For example, if traded and nontraded goods are complementary in demand, a devaluation in a situation of Walrasian equilibrium may shift the economy into region U rather than region R, while a revaluation could lead to Classical, rather than Keynesian, unemployment.

Finally, it is necessary to consider the effects on the diagram of technological progress and regress (where one possible interpretation

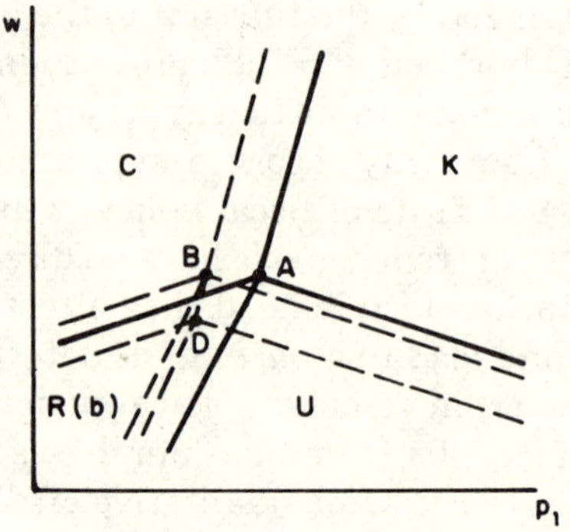

FIGURE V

of the latter is, following Malinvaud, a rise in the price of an intermediate input). As we would expect, the effects of such a change differ greatly depending on whether it is assumed to take place in the traded or the nontraded good sector.[11] In the former case, the effect on the diagram is similar to that of monetary expansion as in Figure IV, except that the locus separating regions $R(b)$ and U is not affected. Starting at Walrasian equilibrium therefore, we see that technological progress in the traded good sector leads to excess demand for labor, but does not impinge on the nontraded good sector, provided that assumption (b) about labor force allocation is made. Conversely, technological regress leads to Keynesian unemployment.

By contrast, technological progress in the nontraded sector has a very different effect, resembling what it has in the closed economy model of Malinvaud. Since the technological progress raises the output of nontradeables at given wages and prices, the regions of excess supply of nontradeables expand, as illustrated in Figure V. In addition, since the labor required to produce a given amount of nontraded goods necessarily falls, the region of excess supply in both labor and nontraded good markets (region K) must expand at the expense of region U. This means that, starting at Walrasian equilibrium, technological progress in the nontraded sector leads to Keynesian unemployment, which is the Ricardian result of Malinvaud. However, the effect of technological progress on the location of equation (32) (which separates regions C and $R(b)$) is not so clear-cut: differen-

11. Its effects also depend on whether, as was implicitly assumed by both Malinvaud and Dixit, technological progress increases the demand for labor in the progressing sector at a given wage and price (and conversely for technological regress). As noted in Section II.B, this outcome may not occur, in which case the conclusions of this paragraph must be amended.

tiating that equation, it emerges that technological progress in nontradeables (i.e., an increase in h), by raising the output of nontradeables, relaxes the purchases constraint faced by households and therefore raises their labor supply, and so tends to expand region C; but in addition, it raises the demand for labor by the nontraded sector and so tends to expand region $R(b)$:

$$\frac{\partial}{\partial h}\{\text{ESL (EDNT)}\} = \frac{\partial \hat{l}}{\partial \bar{x}_1}\frac{\partial y_1}{\partial h} - \frac{\partial e_1}{\partial h}. \tag{34}$$

There is no presumption as to which of these two effects will dominate (even when utility and production functions are of the Cobb-Douglas form, as was pointed out by Malinvaud [1977, p. 91, fn. 4]). If the first (positive) term dominates, technological progress shifts the point of Walrasian equilibrium in Figure V from A to D; in this case, the model predicts that technological regress in the nontraded sector will lead to repressed inflation. Whereas, if the second term in (34) is negative and dominates the first, the relevant points are A and B, and so technological regress in the nontraded sector will shift the economy from a state of Walrasian equilibrium into one of Classical unemployment. It is clear that the latter outcome, which underlies Malinvaud's explanation of the effects of the 1973 oil price rise on the economies of Western Europe [1977, pp. 107ff.], is guaranteed only if labor supply is relatively inelastic or if the technological regress is accompanied by a sufficiently large increase in the real wage.

VI. Comparative Statics: Determinants of Classical and Keynesian Unemployment

We now turn to examine the comparative statics properties of the different regimes, keeping in mind the crucial assumption that the state of expectations is given, and also that the analysis only applies strictly to infinitesimally small changes in the exogenous variables, not merely for the usual reason that the linearization implicit in taking derivatives may be invalid for large changes, but also because large changes may shift the economy from one region into another. For convenient reference, all the results are summarized in the Appendix.

In region C all firms are unconstrained, and so the level of employment is determined by the notional demand for labor, (29). This has unambiguously "classical" properties: a fall in the real wage, whether brought about by a nominal wage cut, a reduction in the price of nontradeables, or a devaluation, increases employment; fiscal and monetary policy do not affect employment (although monetary expansion reduces labor supply and thus lowers true unemployment); and technological progress in either sector raises employment.

The situation in region K is very different. At any point in the interior of this region, employment is demand-constrained, but the demand for labor on the part of nontraded good firms depends on the sales constraint that they face, and this sales constraint in turn depends on the employment constraint facing households. The level of employment $\bar{l}$ is therefore given by the solution (which we assume to be unique) of equation (35):

$$\bar{l} = F^{-1}\{\tilde{x}_1(\bar{l};p_1,p_2,w,I) + g_1;h\} + e_2(p_2,w,k). \tag{35}$$

The presence of $\bar{l}$ on both sides of this equation implies that any exogenous change has a multiplier effect. For example, consider the effects of fiscal and monetary policy. Differentiating (35) yields

$$\frac{\partial \bar{l}}{\partial I} = \frac{\tilde{c}_1}{p_1}\frac{\partial \bar{l}}{\partial g_1} = \frac{1}{w}\frac{M}{1-M'}, \tag{36}$$

where

$$M \equiv \frac{w}{p_1 F_e}\tilde{c}_1 \quad \text{and} \quad M' \equiv \frac{w}{p_1 F_e}\tilde{c}_1'. \tag{37}$$

Equation (36) is a familiar multiplier-type expression, with the only novel feature being that the denominator is not one minus the marginal propensity to consume nontradeables, but one minus the latter times the ratio of the wage rate to the value marginal product of labor in the nontraded sector. This ratio may be interpreted heuristically as the "shadow price" of the output constraint facing nontraded good firms, since it equals unity if these firms are unconstrained and so operate on their notional labor demand schedules; whereas it is less than unity whenever there is excess supply of the nontraded good. Hence (36) shows that the greater the extent of excess supply of nontraded goods, the *lower* the multiplier is relative to the usual textbook formula. However, this result arises from the assumption that profits are not consumed in the current period; when this is relaxed, the denominator of (36) reduces to one minus a weighted average of $\tilde{c}_1$ and $\tilde{c}_1'$ (i.e., of the marginal propensities to consume nontradeables out of profits and wages), and it therefore equals the textbook formula when $\tilde{c}_1$ and $\tilde{c}_1'$ are equal. Equation (36) also shows, since $\tilde{c}_1$ is less than unity, that a given monetary expansion has a smaller effect on employment and output than an equal-value government purchase of nontraded goods, because some of the first round of the monetary expansion leaks into increased saving and increased spending on traded goods.

However, the major difference in the determinants of employment between the Classical and Keynesian regions lies in the effects of a fall in the real wage. Consider first the effect of a change in the price of nontradeables. As in region c, an increase in p_1 raises the profitability of producing, and hence the notional supply of, nontradeables. However, in region K this increase in notional supply cannot become effective, because the demand for nontradeables by households is reduced by the price increase. Thus, total employment falls following this change:

$$\frac{\partial \bar{l}}{\partial p_1} = \frac{1}{F_e} \frac{1}{1 - M'} \frac{\partial \tilde{x}_1}{\partial p_1} < 0. \tag{38}$$

As for a change in the real wage brought about by a devaluation, this has the direct effect of increasing profitability in the traded good sector, and since that sector is unconstrained in the output market, this tends to raise employment. In addition, the devaluation has an indirect effect on the demand for nontradeables, thus affecting the output constraint faced by nontraded good firms. If tradeables and nontradeables are gross substitutes, this effect is also expansionary, and so both effects of the devaluation tend to raise employment:

$$\frac{\partial \bar{l}}{\partial p_2} = \frac{1}{1 - M'} \left\{ \frac{1}{F_e} \frac{\partial \tilde{x}_1}{\partial p_2} + \frac{\partial e_2}{\partial p_2} \right\}. \tag{39}$$

Finally, what of a direct cut in the nominal wage? The analyses of Malinvaud and Dixit gave very different predictions concerning its effects on employment: in the closed-economy model of Malinvaud, a wage cut in region K unambiguously reduced employment through its depressing effect on aggregate demand, whereas in Dixit's open-economy model firms were never constrained on the output market, and so a wage cut always increased output and employment. In the present model, both of these effects are present, the former applying to the nontraded good sector, and the latter to the traded good sector. The net effect of a wage cut therefore depends on the relative strengths of these two effects, though since the multiplier applies to *both*, there is no presumption that the "Keynesian" effect is likely to dominate:

$$\frac{w}{\bar{l}} \frac{\partial \bar{l}}{\partial w} = \frac{1}{1 - M'} \left\{ M + \lambda \frac{w}{e_2} \frac{\partial e_2}{\partial w} \right\}, \tag{40}$$

where λ is the proportion of $\bar{l}$ employed in the traded good sector.

Finally, it should be noted that the prediction that a wage cut will lower aggregate demand and so tend to reduce employment depends in this model (and in Malinvaud's) on the assumption that profits are not consumed in the current period. It can be shown that if this assumption is dropped and profits are assumed to be consumed instantaneously, then a wage cut will have no direct effect on employment in the nontraded good sector.

The only remaining determinant of employment to be considered is technological progress. Here again, the present model yields results that are midway between those of Malinvaud and Dixit. Technological progress in the traded good sector raises employment, as in Dixit's model; whereas technological progress in the nontraded good sector has, as in Malinvaud's model, an unambiguously depressive effect on employment: although notional supply of nontradeables rises, aggregate demand, and so the demand constraint facing nontradeable firms, is not affected, and so the only effect of the technological improvement is to reduce the employment required to produce the given constrained level of output.

In summary, it is clear that the behavior of employment in region K is very different from that in region C: expansionary policies, especially direct purchases of nontraded goods, have a multiplied expansionary effect on employment; a change in the real wage has different effects, depending on whether it is brought about by a higher price of nontradeables (which definitely reduces employment), a devaluation (which probably increases it), or a nominal wage cut (which is more likely to raise employment the smaller the multiplier, the smaller the proportion of those employed who work in the nontraded good sector, and the higher the propensity to consume out of current profits); and technological progress will raise or lower employment depending on whether it occurs in the traded or nontraded good sectors.

VII. Comparative Statics: Determinants of the Trade Balance

Turning next to the determinants of the trade surplus, and in particular to the effects of a devaluation, we consider these first in region C, where the surplus equals the difference between the notional supply of traded good firms and the effective demand by households, who are constrained in both the labor and the nontraded good markets, the constraint levels being determined by (29) and (33):

$$s = y_2(p_2,w,k) - \tilde{\tilde{x}}_2\{\bar{l}(.);\bar{x}_1(.);p_1,p_2,w,I\} - g_2. \tag{41}$$

A devaluation has both a price (or "elasticities") effect, tending to improve the surplus by increasing home supply of and reducing home demand for tradeables, and an income (or "absorption") effect, tending to reduce the surplus:

$$\frac{\partial s}{\partial p_2} = \frac{\partial y_2}{\partial p_2} - \frac{\partial \tilde{\tilde{x}}_2}{\partial p_2} - \frac{\partial \tilde{\tilde{x}}_2}{\partial \bar{l}} \frac{\partial \bar{l}}{\partial p_2} \tag{42}$$

$$= \frac{\partial y_2}{\partial p_2}\{1 - \tilde{\tilde{c}}_2'\} - \frac{\partial \tilde{\tilde{x}}_2}{\partial p_2} > 0. \tag{43}$$

This shows that a devaluation must improve the trade balance in region C, and also that, as noted by Dornbusch [1975], a necessary condition for the elasticities approach to give a complete answer to the effects of a devaluation is that $\tilde{\tilde{c}}_2'$, the marginal propensity to consume tradeables in this region, must be zero.

In region K, traded good firms are also unconstrained in both markets, and households are constrained in the labor market only. Hence the expression for the trade surplus is

$$s = y_2(p_2,w,k) - \tilde{x}_2\{\bar{l}(.);p_1,p_2,w,I\} - g_2, \tag{44}$$

where $\bar{l}(.)$ is the solution to (35). In this region the effect of a devaluation is

$$\frac{\partial s}{\partial p_2} = \frac{\partial y_2}{\partial p_2} - \frac{\partial \tilde{x}_2}{\partial p_2} - \frac{\partial \tilde{x}_2}{\partial \bar{l}} \frac{\partial \bar{l}}{\partial p_2} \tag{45}$$

$$= \frac{\partial y_2}{\partial p_2}\frac{1 - M' - \tilde{c}_2'}{1 - M'} - \frac{\partial \tilde{x}_2}{\partial p_2} - \frac{w}{p_2 F_e}\frac{\tilde{c}_2'}{1 - M'}\frac{\partial \tilde{x}_1}{\partial p_2}, \tag{46}$$

making use of (39). The first and second terms in (46) are unambiguously positive, reflecting the direct (price) effects of the devaluation in increasing supply of and reducing home demand for tradeables, respectively (although as in (43) the former is damped by the tendency for the increased employment induced by the devaluation to lead to greater consumption of tradeables). The third term represents an additional effect of the devaluation that could lead it to worsen the trade balance in precisely that case which has so far yielded conventional prediction, i.e., when tradeables and nontradeables are gross substitutes. In this case, the devaluation increases the demand for nontradeables, so relaxing the goods market constraint facing nontraded sector firms. The resulting expansion in employment, and so in income, could lead to a sufficiently large increase in spending on tradeables to offset the first two terms in (46) and so to worsen the trade balance. Of course, this outcome is impossible if tradeables and nontradeables are independent in demand, which is another of the conditions given by Dornbusch [1975] as necessary for the simple elasticities approach to be valid. It may be noted that in both (43) and (46) (i.e., in both regions C and K), the improvement in the surplus is greater, the greater the supply elasticity in the traded good sector is (or equivalently, the greater its elasticity of demand for labor), and the smaller is the home marginal propensity to consume tradeables. Both of these conditions directly contradict the results of Helpman [1977].[12]

Next we consider the trade balance in region R, under assumption (a) concerning the allocation of labor between the two sectors: that traded good firms get priority, and hence are not rationed on any market. Since households are constrained in the amount of nontradeables they can purchase, the expression for the trade balance is

$$s = y_2(p_2,w,k) - \hat{x}_2\{\overline{x}_1(.);p_1,p_2,w,I\} - g_2. \tag{47}$$

The level of nontraded good production $\overline{x}_1$ is in turn determined by equation (48):

$$\overline{x}_1 = F\{\hat{l}(\overline{x}_1;p_1,p_2,w,I) - e_2(p_2,w,k);h\} - g_1. \tag{48}$$

As in the case of $\overline{l}$ in equation (25), the appearance of $\overline{x}_1$ on both sides of (48) suggests the presence of a multiplier, in this case the "supply multiplier" of Barro and Grossman [1974]. Thus, an increase in government purchases of nontraded goods in region $R(a)$ has a direct "first-round" effect of reducing the quantity of nontradeables available for household consumption, and faced with a tighter constraint in the nontraded good market, households respond by adjusting their labor supply. From (15), the response implied is ambiguous in sign, but it is most likely to take the form of a reduction in households' labor supply, which exacerbates the excess demand for labor, and so leads to a sequence of further falls in output and consumption of nontradeables. The total effect is given by the multiplier,

12. This is all the more surprising, since in the neoclassical literature, Helpman's model is the one that most resembles that of the present paper. The source of the difference in results appears to be not that his model assumes a Keynesian consumption function rather than deriving it as the outcome of constrained maximizing behavior, nor his assumption of a flexible price of nontradeables, but rather that he does not allow any acquisition of financial assets by the private sector. From (24), this implies that the trade deficit equals the government's budget deficit, whence a devaluation (with unchanged government policies) cannot eliminate a deficit, but may only reduce it if it reduces the foreign-currency value of the government's deficit. This in turn requires (since government spending is fixed in real terms) that the price of nontradeables must fall relative to the price of tradeables as a result of a devaluation.

(49)
$$\frac{\partial \bar{x}_1}{\partial g_1} = -\frac{1}{1-N}$$

where

(50)
$$N = \frac{p_1 F_e}{w} \hat{c}_l',$$

and we assume that N is less than unity.[13] The effect of a devaluation on the trade balance may now be established by differentiating both (47) and (48): in addition to the usual direct price effects, the devaluation changes the employment constraint facing nontraded good firms, and hence the nontraded purchases constraint facing households, in two ways: first, by changing the total available labor supply, and second, by raising the profitability of traded good production, and so leaving less labor available for nontraded sector firms:

(51)
$$\frac{\partial s}{\partial p_2} = \frac{\partial y_2}{\partial p_2} - \frac{\partial \hat{x}_2}{\partial p_2} - \frac{\partial \hat{x}_2}{\partial \bar{x}_1}\frac{\partial \bar{x}_1}{\partial p_2}$$

(52)
$$= \frac{\partial y_2}{\partial p_2}\frac{1}{1-N}\left\{1 - \frac{p_1 F_e}{w}(\hat{c}_l' + \hat{c}_2')\right\} - \frac{\partial \hat{x}_2}{\partial p_2} + \frac{p_1}{p_2}\hat{c}_2' \frac{F_e}{1-N}\frac{\partial \hat{l}}{\partial p_2}.$$

The first term in (52), representing the supply effect of the devaluation, is positive, except (possibly) when the initial excess demand for labor is sufficiently large that the term p_1F_e/w is considerably greater than unity; the second, demand, term is always positive. However, the final term, representing the induced change in labor supply, is likely to be negative when leisure and traded goods are gross substitutes. Hence the presumption that a devaluation must improve the trade balance is no stronger in this region than it is under conditions of Keynesian unemployment.[14]

Finally, what of the effects of a devaluation under assumption (b) about the labor market under excess demand, that nontraded good firms get priority? In region $R(b)$, with consumers constrained in the nontraded good market and traded good firms constrained in the labor market, the trade balance is given by

(53)
$$s = G[\hat{l}\{\bar{x}_1(.);p_1,p_2,w,I\} - e_1(p_1,w,h);k] - \hat{x}_2\{\bar{x}_1(.);p_1,p_2,w,I\} - g_2,$$

13. As with equation (36), the slightly unconventional form of equation (49) is a consequence of the assumption that profits are not redistributed instantaneously. If this assumption is relaxed, N becomes a weighted average of $\hat{c}_l$ and $\hat{c}_l'$ (the marginal propensities to consume leisure following changes in lump-sum income and in the constraint level $\bar{x}_1$, respectively). Hence, when these propensities are equal, (49) reduces to the usual formula for the supply multiplier.

14. The assumption that profits are redistributed instantaneously increases the likelihood that a devaluation will worsen the trade balance in region $R(a)$, since it implies an additional income effect that raises the demand for tradeables.

where the demand constraint facing households $\bar{x}_1$ is given by (33). As for region U, in which traded good firms are constrained in the labor market and nontraded firms in the output market, the corresponding equation is

$$(54) \qquad s = G[l(p_1,p_2,w,I) - F^{-1}\{x_1(p_1,p_2,w,I) + g_1;h\};k] - x_2(p_1,p_2,w,I) - g_2.$$

These two equations have a number of common features. In particular, neither of them implies a multiplier effect, since in these two regions there is no good for which the corresponding labor and output markets are both subject to constraints. Moreover, the cross-price effects of a devaluation tend to worsen the trade balance in both regions, under the assumption of gross substitutability. For example, in region U a devaluation reduces labor supply and increases demand for nontradeables if gross substitutability is assumed, tending on both counts to tighten the labor market constraint faced by traded good firms and so to worsen the trade balance:

$$(55) \qquad \frac{\partial s}{\partial p_2} = G_e \left\{ \frac{\partial l}{\partial p_2} - \frac{1}{F_e} \frac{\partial x_1}{\partial p_2} \right\} - \frac{\partial x_2}{\partial p_2}.$$

A similar analysis applies in region $R(b)$, except that the second term inside the brackets in (55) does not appear.

In summary, therefore, and contrary to the implication of the elasticities approach that a devaluation must improve the trade balance of a small open economy,[15] the effect of a devaluation on the trade balance is ambiguous in all regions, except that of classical unemployment. By contrast, however, it may easily be seen that expansionary fiscal and monetary policies almost always worsen the trade balance, although the chains of causation are very different in different regions. (The only exception to this rule is the effect on the trade balance in region C of government purchases of nontradeables, which depends on the effect of their reduced availability on household demand for tradeables, and so, as noted in (16), is indeterminate.) Taken in conjunction with the findings of Section VI that devaluation affects employment in regions C and K more predictably than do fiscal and monetary policy, this would appear to favor the assignment of policy instruments to targets associated with the "New Cambridge" (U. K.) school—fiscal policy for external balance, exchange rate policy for internal balance—rather than the more conventional assignment

15. This may be seen by considering the special case appropriate to a small open economy of the general Bickerdike-Robinson-Metzler criterion for a devaluation to improve the trade balance. See Dornbusch [1975], equation 20′.

assumed in most discussions of policy choice in a small open economy.[16]

VIII. Summary and Conclusion

This paper has presented a model of a small open economy under fixed exchange rates that, though fully consistent in the long run with the monetary approach to the balance of payments, exhibits very different properties in the short run when the wage rate and the price of the nontraded good are sticky. In many respects, the model behaves rather like a hybrid of the single-traded-good model of Dixit [1978] and the closed-economy model of Malinvaud [1977]: for example, the comparative statics effects of technological progress and of government purchases depend on the sector in which they take place: if in the traded good sector, they have effects similar to those in Dixit's model, whereas if they occur in the nontraded good sector, their effects resemble those found in Malinvaud. In addition, the greater complexity of the model was found to lead to a richer set of properties. While some of these additional properties could be ruled out by assuming that all commodities were gross substitutes, this was not true of all: for example, it was found that a devaluation under conditions of Keynesian unemployment can worsen the trade balance (and that the conditions under which this outcome is more likely are precisely the opposite of those presented in Helpman [1977]); also, it was shown that even with an atemporal theory of the firm, a region of "Underconsumption" in the sense of Muellbauer and Portes [1978] is possible, where households are unconstrained and firms are constrained on both labor and goods markets (although no single firm is subject to both constraints). Finally, while the dangers of placing too much reliance on comparative statics derivatives were stressed, it was noted that the model gives some support to the unorthodox policy assignment associated with the "New Cambridge" school: taking all possible regimes together, exchange rate policy was found to exert a more predictable influence on the level of employment than fiscal or monetary policy, whereas the reverse was true of the influence of these two sets of instruments on the trade balance.

From the perspective of international monetary economics, the model of this paper may be seen as providing a consistent microeconomic foundation for the traded-nontraded goods model of Salter

16. For discussion of the New Cambridge approach, see Cripps and Godley [1976] and Spraos [1977]. The New Cambridge assignment is also supported by Helpman [1977].

[1959]. By comparison with many recent contributions to the literature on international monetary economics, the model is in some respects relatively unsophisticated: exchange rate expectations and international capital movements are completely ignored, while other issues that have attracted recent interest such as the financing of the government's budget deficit and the effects of trade-imbalance-induced changes in the domestic money stock are given only sketchy treatment. On the other hand, the model provides a more secure foundation than any existing treatments for the discussion of the impact effects of policy changes in a small open economy. While the paper has raised more questions than it has answered (especially concerning the dynamic evolution of the model, and the effects of explicitly incorporating expectations), it is to be hoped that the novel properties of the model, as well as the light it throws on matters of traditional interest to international monetary economists, will be taken to justify its study.

APPENDIX

Each entry in the table gives the sign of the partial derivative of the endogenous variable in the region indicated with respect to the relevant exogenous variable.

Region	Endogenous variable (with equation number in parentheses)	Exogenous variable							
		w	p_1	p_2	h	k	I	g_1	g_2
C	$\bar{l}$ (29)	–	+	+	+[a]	+[a]	0	0	0
K	$\bar{l}$ (35)	?	–	+[b]	–	+[a]	+	+	0
C	s (41)	?	?	+	?	+	–	?	–
K	s (44)	–[b]	?	?	+	+	–	–	–
$R(a)$	s (47)	–[b]	–	?	–	+	–	–	–
$R(b)$	s (53)	?	?	?	?	+	–	–	–
U	s (54)	–[b]	?	?	+	+	–	–	–

a. This sign is reversed if the technological progress shifts the labor demand schedule of the progressing sector inward. A necessary and sufficient condition for this outcome is given in Neary [1980].

b. Gross substitutability is sufficient but not necessary for this sign.

TRINITY COLLEGE, DUBLIN

REFERENCES

Barro, R. J., and H. I. Grossman, "A General Disequilibrium Model of Income and Employment," *American Economic Review,* LXI (1971), 82–93.

——, and ——, "Suppressed Inflation and the Supply Multiplier," *Review of Economic Studies,* XLI (1974), 87–104.

Benassy, J. P., "Neo-Keynesian Disequilibrium in a Monetary Economy," *Review of Economic Studies,* XLII (1975), 503–23.

Clower, R. W., "The Keynesian Counter-Revolution: A Theoretical Appraisal," in F. H. Hahn and F. Brechling, eds., *The Theory of Interest Rates* (London: Macmillan, 1965).

Cripps, F., and W. Godley, "A Formal Analysis of the Cambridge Economic Policy Group Model," *Economica,* XLII (1976), 335–48.

Dixit, A., "The Balance of Trade in a Model of Temporary Equilibrium with Rationing," *Review of Economic Studies,* XLV (1978), 393–404.

Dornbusch, R., "Exchange Rates and Fiscal Policy in a Popular Model of International Trade," *American Economic Review,* LXV (1975), 859–71.

Frenkel, J. A., and H. G. Johnson, eds., *The Monetary Approach to the Balance of Payments* (London: Allen and Unwin, 1976).

Gordon, R. J., "Interrelationships Between Domestic and International Theories of Inflation," in R. Z. Aliber, ed., *The Political Economy of Monetary Reform* (London: Macmillan, 1977).

Grandmont, J. M., "Temporary General Equilibrium Theory," *Econometrica,* XLV (1977), 535–73.

Helpman, E., "Nontraded Goods and Macroeconomic Policy Under a Fixed Exchange Rate," this *Journal*, XCI (1977), 469–80.

Hicks, J. R., *Value and Capital,* 2nd ed. (Oxford: Clarendon Press, 1946).

Hool, B., "Monetary and Fiscal Policies in Equilibria with Rationing," mimeo, University of Wisconsin, Madison, 1977.

Krueger, A. O., "The Role of Home Goods and Money in Exchange Rate Adjustment," in W. Sellekaerts, ed., *International Trade and Finance: Essays in Honour of Jan Tinbergen* (London: Macmillan, 1974).

Malinvaud, E., *The Theory of Unemployment Reconsidered* (Oxford: Basil Blackwell, 1977).

Muellbauer, J., and R. Portes, "Macroeconomic Models with Quantity Rationing," *Economic Journal,* LXXXVIII (1978), 393–404.

Neary, J. P., "On the Short-Run Effects of Technological Progress," *Oxford Economic Papers,* XXXII (1980), forthcoming.

——, and K. W. S. Roberts, "The Theory of Household Behaviour Under Rationing," *European Economic Review,* XIII (1980), 25–42.

Salter, W. E. G., "Internal and External Balance: The Role of Price and Expenditure Effects," *Economic Record,* XXXV (1959), 226–38.

Spraos, J., "New Cambridge Macroeconomics, Assignment Rules and Interdependence," in R. Z. Aliber, ed., *The Political Economy of Monetary Reform* (London: Macmillan, 1977).

Swan, T. W., "Longer-Run Problems of the Balance of Payments," in H. W. Arndt and W. M. Corden, eds., *The Australian Economy: A Volume of Readings* (Melbourne: Cheshire Press, 1963); reprinted in R. E. Caves and H. G. Johnson, eds., *Readings in International Economics* (London: George Allen and Unwin, 1968).

Tobin, J., and H. S. Houthakker, "The Effects of Rationing on Demand Elasticities," *Review of Economic Studies,* XVIII (1950–51), 140–53.

Tsiang, S. C., "The Monetary Theoretic Foundation of the Modern Monetary Approach to the Balance of Payments," *Oxford Economic Papers,* XXIX (1977), 319–38.

JOB DIFFERENTIATION AND WAGES*

NANCY L. STOKEY

The determination of wage rates and skill requirements for jobs is studied in a model where workers, who vary in ability, acquire skill through (costly) training. If firms' skill requirements are fixed, there exists a unique Nash equilibrium in wage rates, but the resulting allocation of labor is inefficient. The Nash equilibrium wage rates and allocation of labor approach the competitive equilibrium if and only if the number of job types increases on every skill range and no firm remains a monopsonist on any skill range. If firms choose both skill requirements and wage rates, no Nash equilibrium in pure strategies exists.

I. INTRODUCTION

During the industrial revolution the introduction of interchangeable parts made mass production possible, bringing with it enormous increases in productivity. The use of interchangeable parts is not confined to manufactured goods, however. In many instances, labor, too, is highly standardized. Looking inside a firm, one typically finds many workers performing identical tasks—assembly line workers, clerks, telephone operators, etc. Any such group within a firm can also be viewed as a set of "interchangeable parts."

Organizing work in this way has the advantage that both supervision of the work process and comparison of performance among workers are easier when there are such groups of "homogeneous labor." However, it has the disadvantage that fully utilizing the talents and skills of individual workers is more difficult. Hence, we may expect the pressure toward standardization to be stronger for larger firms, where organizational problems are more severe and the degree of specialization of labor is greater, and weaker in smaller firms, where the reverse is true.

If work is standardized within each firm, a "job" can be thought of as a certain set of tasks. We may ask, then, what determines the types of jobs and the corresponding wage rates firms offer.

A model of imperfect competition in the labor market will be used here to examine how job descriptions and wages are determined. For simplicity, a job description will consist of a single parameter, which can be thought of as a level of skill.

Workers acquire skill through training, which is assumed to have

* I am grateful to the participants in the 1978 I.M.S.S.S. seminar at Stanford University, and particularly to Eric Maskin, for many helpful comments. This research was partially supported by N.S.F. Grant No. SER76-17502.

The Quarterly Journal of Economics, November 1980 0033-5533/80/0095-0431$01.90

a positive cost. In order to hold a particular job, a worker must have attained a skill level at least as high as the one specified for that job, and if he takes the job, he is paid the corresponding wage rate. It is assumed that any worker can acquire any level of skill, and hence can hold any job, but that training costs differ among workers. Skill is assumed to be nonfirm-specific, so that the worker bears his own cost of training.

Given the menu of skill-wage offers made by all firms, each worker selects the job that maximizes his wage net of training costs. Since training costs differ among workers, job choices differ as well. Consequently, although workers differ from each other ex ante, ex post, any two workers who hold the same job are equally skilled (since no worker will choose to acquire skill above the minimum required for the job he selects) and receive equal wages.

The problem facing each firm is to select a skill level and wage rate. These two parameters determine, given the actions of other firms, how many workers it will attract and, consequently, its profit level.

The behavior of firms in such a world is examined below. First, competition in wages alone is discussed, under the assumption that each employer's skill level is exogenously fixed. Then competition in both wages and skills is discussed. It is shown that for any number of profit-maximizing firms, if skill levels are fixed, there is a unique Nash equilibrium in pure wage strategies. However, if firms choose both skill levels and wage rates, there is no Nash equilibrium in pure strategies.

II. The Model

A. Production Technology

The production technologies of all firms are assumed to be identical, and to be linear in labor input. Thus, by choosing units appropriately, "skill" and "productivity" can be taken as identical, so that "s" is the marginal (and average) product of individuals with skill level s. The difference between the skill level and the wage rate set by a firm is its profit margin per worker. A job offer will be called *viable* if it specifies a wage rate no greater than the associated skill level, i.e., if it specifies a nonnegative profit margin.

Initially, it will be assumed that each firm can make only one job offer. Since the firm's total profit is linear in the number of workers, it hires all workers seeking a job who have the required qualifications.

B. Workers

There is a continuum of workers, with each characterized by a parameter $z \in [0,Z]$ that reflects his training costs. The parameter is defined so that costs are decreasing in z. Costs might vary among individuals because of differences in ability, access to capital markets, etc.

The cost to a z-worker of acquiring skill level s is given by $f(z)c(s)$ satisfying

$$f(z) > 0, \quad f'(z) < 0, \quad 0 \le z \le Z, \tag{1}$$

$$c(s) > 0, \quad c'(s) > 0, \quad c''(s) > 0, \quad 0 < s, \tag{2a}$$

$$c(0) = 0, \quad c'(0)f(Z) < 1. \tag{2b}$$

Therefore, the productivity net of training costs of a z-worker at skill level s is $s - f(z)c(s)$. Assumption (2b) is sufficient to guarantee that at least some individuals have a positive net product over some ranges of skills.

Furthermore, since costs are strictly convex in skill, each worker's net product is strictly concave in skill. Let $\sigma(z)$, defined by

$$f(z)c'[\sigma(z)] = 1, \quad \text{if } f(z)c'(0) \le 1$$

$$\sigma(z) = 0, \quad \text{if } f(z)c'(0) \ge 1,$$

denote a z-worker's most productive skill level. The interval $[\sigma(0), \sigma(Z)]$ will be called the *efficient range* of skills, since at any skill level outside this range all workers' net productivities could be raised either by increasing the required skill to $\sigma(0)$ or by decreasing it to $\sigma(Z)$.

C. The Allocation of Labor

Suppose that there are n firms, indexed by $i = 1, \ldots, n$, making skill-wage offers $[(s^i,w^i), i = 1, \ldots, n]$. Assume that the firms are indexed so that s^i is increasing in i. Each worker chooses the job for which his wage, net of training costs, is maximized (see Figure I). If $w^i \le w^j$ for any $j < i$, then obviously firm i will attract no workers. Hence we may assume that w^i is also increasing in i.

First, it can be established that under the assumptions in (1) and (2), workers' choices increase monotonically in z. For suppose that $j < i$, and that z chooses firm j and z' chooses firm i. Then

$$f(z)[c(s^i) - c(s^j)] > w^i - w^j > f(z')[c(s^i) - c(s^j)]. \tag{3}$$

The higher wage offered by firm i compensates z', but not z, for the higher training costs. From (3) we see that $f(z) > f(z')$, which implies that $z' > z$.

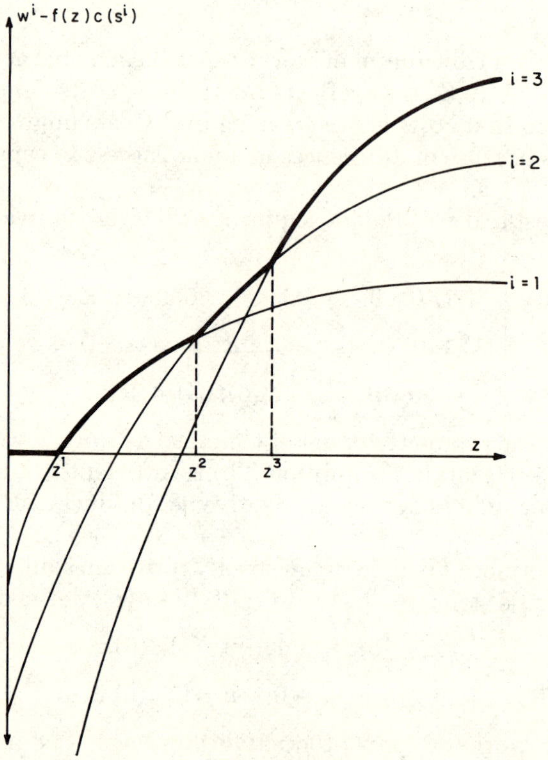

FIGURE I

Next, we shall show that, even if wage offers increase with skill requirements, some firms may attract no workers. However, if we impose the restriction that each s^i lies in the efficient range, then for any viable wage rates offered by its competitors each firm can make a viable wage offer that is high enough to attract some workers.

First, consider any pair of firms k and j, with $s^k < s^j$ and $w^k < w^j$. From the argument above, we know that if any worker chooses firm j over firm k, then worker Z also chooses j. Hence, if

$$f(Z)[c(s^j) - c(s^k)] > w^j - w^k,$$

then all workers prefer k to j, and firm j attracts no workers. However, if s^j in the efficient range, since $w^k \leq s^k$,

$$f[\sigma^{-1}(s^j)]\,[c(s^j) - c(s^k)] < s^j - s^k \leq s^j - w^k.$$

By offering a wage of $s^j - \epsilon$, for ϵ sufficiently small firm j can attract

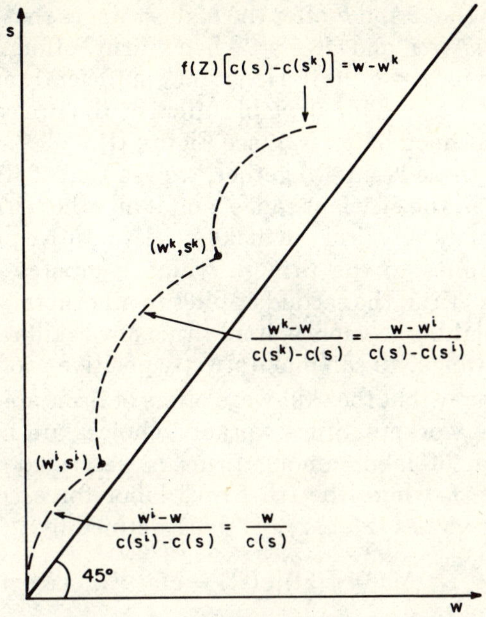

FIGURE II

workers with z-paramter in a neighborhood of $\sigma^{-1}(s^j)$ (see Figure II).

Next, consider any three firms i, j, and k, all requiring skills in the efficient range, and all making viable wage offers (or unemployment, $s^i = w^i = 0$, may be one "offer").

$$\sigma(0) \leq s^i < s^j < s^k \leq \sigma(Z),$$
$$w^i < w^j < w^k,$$
$$w^\alpha \leq s^\alpha, \quad \alpha = i, j, k.$$

Those workers satisfying

$$w^i - f(z)c(s^i) < w^j - f(z)c(s^j)$$

and

$$w^k - f(z)c(s^k) < w^j - f(z)c(s^j)$$

choose firm j. Rearranging terms shows that this is equivalent to

$$\frac{w^k - w^j}{c(s^k) - c(s^j)} < f(z) < \frac{w^j - w^i}{c(s^j) - c(s^i)}. \tag{4}$$

Now suppose that i and k offer the highest wages that are viable, i.e., suppose that $w^i = s^i$ and $w^k = s^k$. Then if firm i offers a wage $w^j = s^j$, (4) is satisfied for $z = \sigma^{-1}(s^j)$. Hence for ϵ sufficiently small, (4) is also satisfied if $w^j = s^j - \epsilon$, for all viable offers by the two competitors, for z in a neighborhood of $\sigma^{-1}(s^j)$ (see Figure II).

Putting these results together, we see that if its own skill requirement is in the efficient range, and if all other firms are making viable wage offers, any firm can make strictly positive profits. The first argument applies to the firm n, which competes with only one "neighboring" firm; the second applies to all others, which compete with two "neighbors." Hence, if all firms have skill requirements in the efficient range, all can make strictly positive profits.

Assume now that the skill-wage offers of firms are such that each attracts some workers. Since workers' choices are monotone in z, the allocation of labor among firms is described by the vector $(z^1, z^2, \ldots, z^n)$, where the ith firm's labor force consists of $z \in (z^i, z^{i+1})$. The values $(z^1, \ldots, z^{n+1})$ are defined by

$$w^i - w^{i-1} \equiv \Delta w^i = f(z^i)[c(s^i) - c(s^{i-1})], \quad i = 1, \ldots, n,$$

$$s^0 \equiv w^0 \equiv 0,$$

$$z^{n+1} \equiv Z.$$

III. Wage Competition

Consider first the situation in a market with n firms, each with a predesignated skill requirement, competing by making wage offers. Given $(s^1, \ldots, s^n)$, let $\alpha(\cdot)$ be the function relating z^i to $w^i - w^{i-1}$:

$$\Delta w^i \equiv f[\alpha^i(\Delta w^i)][c(s^i) - c(s^{i-1})], \tag{5}$$

and let

$$\alpha_1^i \equiv \left.\frac{d\alpha(\Delta w)}{d(\Delta w)}\right|_{\Delta w^i} = \frac{1}{f'(\alpha^i)[c(s^i) - c(s^{i-1})]} < 0,$$

$$\alpha_{11}^i \equiv \left.\frac{d^2\alpha(\Delta w)}{d(\Delta w)^2}\right|_{\Delta w^i} = \frac{-f''(\alpha^i)(\alpha_1^i)^2}{f'(\alpha^i)}.$$

Furthermore, let $m(\cdot)$ be the density function for z in the population, and recall that the parameter z is an artificial index, so that the choice of scale is arbitrary. Hence when training costs have the form in (1)–(2), it can be assumed without loss of generality that z is scaled so that

$$m'(z)f'(z) - m(z)f''(z) = 0, \quad 0 \leq z. \tag{6}$$

(The proof is in the Appendix.)

The reaction function of firm i, if it makes the Nash assumption of no response by its competitors, is defined as the solution of

$$\max_{w^i} \Pi^i(w^{i-1},w^i,w^{i+1}) = (s^i - w^i) \int_{\alpha^i}^{\alpha^{i+1}} m(z)dz. \tag{7}$$

Note that firm i's response depends only on the actions of its near neighbors. Differentiating (7) gives the condition for a maximum:

$$\frac{\partial \pi^i}{\partial w^i} = -\int_{\alpha^i}^{\alpha^{i+1}} m(z)dz - (s^i - w^i)[m(\alpha^{i+1})\alpha_i^{i+1} + m(\alpha^i)\alpha_1^i] = 0, \tag{8}$$

and since, using (6) gives

$$\frac{\partial^2 \pi^i}{(\partial w^i)^2} = 2[m(\alpha^{i+1})\alpha_1^{i+1} + m(\alpha^i)\alpha_1^i] < 0, \quad w^{i-1} \leq w^i \leq w^{i+1},$$

the solution in (8) is unique.

Totally differentiating (8), we find firm i's response to wage changes by its neighbors to be

$$dw^i = \frac{m(\alpha^{i+1})\alpha_1^{i+1}dw^{i+1} + m(\alpha^i)\alpha_1^i dw^{i-1}}{2[m(\alpha^{i+1})\alpha_1^{i+1} + m(\alpha^i)\alpha_1^i]}. \tag{9}$$

Hence, equal wage changes by both of firm i's near competitors induce a reaction in the same direction, but only one-half as large, in firm i's wage.

Using these results about reaction functions, we can prove the existence and uniqueness of a Nash equilibrium in pure wage strategies.

THEOREM 1. Given n firms, requiring skill levels $s^1, \ldots, s^n$, with $\sigma(0) \leq s^1 < s^2 < \cdots < s^{n-1} < s^n \leq \sigma(Z)$, there exists a Nash equilibrium in pure wage strategies.

Proof. A Nash equilibrium can be constructed as follows. Let $\mathbf{w}(0) = \mathbf{0}$, and let $w^i(t)$ be firm i's best response against $\mathbf{w}(t-1)_{/i}$, for

$t = 1,2,\ldots$ The sequence of wage vectors $\{\mathbf{w}(t), t = 0,1,2,\ldots\}$ is strictly increasing. To see this, note that at step $t = 0$ each firm makes zero profit, since all workers will prefer to remain unemployed. At step $t = 1$ each firm will offer a positive wage, expecting to attract some workers and to make a positive profit. Hence all wage rates increase at step $t = 1$. Inspecting (9), we see that at step $t = 2$, since each firm is reacting against strictly higher wage offers by its competitors, its own response is also higher. By induction, then, each firm's response also increases at every later step. Since the sequence $\{\mathbf{w}(t)\}$ is increasing and is obviously bounded above by $\mathbf{s}$, it converges.

It is also obvious that each firm's reaction function is continuous. Therefore, since $\lim_{t\to\infty} [\mathbf{w}(t) - \mathbf{w}(t-1)] = \mathbf{0}$, $\lim_{t\to\infty} \mathbf{w}(t)$ is a Nash equilibrium.

Q.E.D.

THEOREM 2. The Nash equilibrium of Theorem I is unique.

Proof. Suppose that there are two Nash equilibrium wage vectors, $\mathbf{w}$ and $\hat{\mathbf{w}}$. Consider

$$\max_i |w^i - \hat{w}^i|,$$

i.e., the firm (or any one of the firms), call it m, whose wage offers differ by the greatest amount between the two equilibria. At any equilibrium all firms attract some workers, so that w^m depends only on w^{m-1} and w^{m+1}. (If $m = 1$, w^m depends only on w^2, and if $m = n$, only on w^{n-1}. In these cases the obvious modifications in the argument must be made.) But, from (9) we see that

$$|w^m - \hat{w}^m| < 1/2 \max \{|w^{m-1} - \hat{w}^{m-1}|, |w^{m+1} - \hat{w}^{m+1}|\},$$

contradicting the selection of m.

Q.E.D.

From (9) it is easy to see that the entry of a new firm has the expected effect on the equilibrium wage offers of all firms. The wage rates of the two closest neighbors of the entrant are increased by the direct effect of competition from the new firm, and there is then a ripple effect on all other firms, with the wage increases becoming more and more damped for more distant firms.

Suppose now that each firm makes several job offers. Let there be G firms, indexed by $g = 1, \ldots, G$, offering a total of $n \geq G$ jobs, indexed by $i = 1, \ldots, n$. As before, assume that $\sigma(0) \leq s^1 \leq s^2 \leq \cdots \leq s^n$. Let I^g denote the index set for jobs offered by firm g. Clearly,

$$I^g \cap I^{g'} = \varnothing \qquad \forall_{g \neq g'}$$

$$\bigcup_{g=1}^{G} I^g = \{1,2,3, \ldots, n\}.$$

Given the wage rates offered by all other firms, firm g chooses $(w^i, i \in I^g)$ as the solution of

$$\max_{(w^i, i \in I^g)} \Pi^g = \sum_{i \in I^g} (s^i - w^i) \int_{\alpha^i}^{\alpha^{i+1}} m(z)dz,$$

where the α^i's are, as before, determined by (5). The conditions for a maximum are

$$\text{(10)} \quad \Pi_i^g \equiv \frac{\partial \Pi^g}{\partial w^i} = -\int_{\alpha^i}^{\alpha^{i+1}} m(z)dz + m(\alpha^{i+1})\alpha_1^{i+1}[X_g^{i+1}e^{i+1} - e^i]$$
$$-m(\alpha^i)\alpha_1^i(e^i - X_g^{i-1}e^{i-1}) = 0, \quad i \in I^g$$

where

$$X_g^j \equiv \begin{cases} 1 \text{ if } j \in I^g \\ 0 \text{ if } j \notin I^g \end{cases}, \quad i = 1, \ldots, n; g = 1, \ldots, G,$$

and

$$e^i \equiv s^i - w^i, \quad i = 1, \ldots, n.$$

Since $[\Pi_{ij}^g]$ is negative definite, the solution is unique, and each firm's reaction function is single-valued. The existence and uniqueness of a Nash equilibrium in pure strategies can be shown using the same arguments as above.

Furthermore, some qualitative remarks can be made about the nature of the equilibrium as the number of firms or the pattern of offers (the index sets I^g) is varied.

It is clear from (10) that only actions by adjacent competitors affect a firm's optimal wage offers. Hence, if there are two firms making multiple skill-wage offers, but their skill levels alternate at every step; i.e., if $I^1 = \{1,3,5, \ldots, n-1 \text{ or } n\}$ and $I^2 = \{2,4,6, \ldots, n-1 \text{ or } n\}$, then the Nash equilibrium vector of wage offers is exactly the same as if there were n different firms. Only if a firm offers jobs at two or more adjacent skill levels can it exercise an extra degree of monopsony power.

In fact, the Nash equilibrium wage vector depends only on the pattern of competition in the following sense. Let **v** be the $(n-1)$-dimensional vector defined as follows:

$$v_i = \begin{cases} 0 \text{ if } \{i, i+1\} \subset I^g, & \text{for some } g \\ 1 & \text{otherwise} \end{cases}$$

$$i = 1, \ldots, n-1.$$

Thus $v_i = 0$ if the same firm controls skill levels i and $i+1$, and $v_i = 1$ if different firms control them. Clearly the equilibrium wage vector depends only on the vector **v**, and thus only indirectly on the number of firms or the index sets I^g. That is, **v** conveys complete information about the "degree of competition" in the market.

For any fixed set of skill levels $(s^1, \ldots, s^n)$, changing the index sets I^g or the number of firms G, increases (decreases) all wage rates if competition among adjacent neighbors is unambiguously increased (decreased). I.e., the Nash equilibrium wage rates associated with the market described by the sets $\hat{I}^g$ are all higher than those in the market described by the sets I^g $(\hat{\mathbf{w}} > \mathbf{w})$, if $\hat{\mathbf{v}} > \mathbf{v}$.

It can also be shown that the firm's ability to exploit workers (to pay them less than their marginal product) is greater for skill levels that are more insulated from outside competition. For suppose that firm g offers jobs at skill levels $s^i, s^{i+1}, \ldots, s^j$. From (10) we see that the conditions for profit maximization include

$$\text{(11)} \qquad \Pi_k^g = -\int_{\alpha^k}^{\alpha^{k+1}} m(z)dz + m(\alpha^{k+1})\alpha_1^{k+1}(e^{k+1} - e^k) - m(\alpha^k)\alpha_1^k(e^k - e^{k-1}) = 0$$

$$k = i+1, \ldots, j-1.$$

Suppose that the firm's profit margin per worker were lower for skill level k than at both adjacent skill levels; i.e., that

$$\text{(12)} \qquad e^{k-1} > e^k < e^{k+1}, \quad \text{for some } k = i+1, \ldots, j-1.$$

Then, from (11) we see that every term of Π_k^g would be negative, and the necessary condition for an optimum could not be satisfied. Hence (12) cannot hold for an optimal set of wage offers. For a single monopsonist making n job offers, the same argument implies that $e^1 < e^2 < \cdots < e^n$.

Next, let us consider the efficiency properties of the equilibrium. It is easy to show that given any fixed set of skill requirements, assuming that there is a free labor market governed by private incentives, the allocation of labor among jobs is efficient if and only if for each job the wage rate is equal to the marginal product of labor.

THEOREM 3. Given $\mathbf{s} = (s^1, s^2, \ldots, s^n)$, the skill levels required for each of n types of jobs, the allocation of labor is efficient if and only if

$$w^i = s^i, \quad i = 1, \ldots, n.$$

Proof. For any given $\mathbf{s}$ and $\mathbf{w}$, the net output of the economy is

$$Y = \sum_{i=1}^{n} \int_{\alpha^i}^{\alpha^{i+1}} [s^i - f(z)c(s^i)]m(z)dz,$$

where $(\alpha^1, \ldots, \alpha^{n+1})$ are, as before, defined by (5). Differentiating Y with respect to $\mathbf{w}$, the conditions for a maximum are

$$(13) \quad \frac{\partial \gamma}{\partial w^i} = [s^{i+1} - s^i - f(\alpha^{i+1})[c(s^{i+1}) - c(s^i)]] \frac{\partial \alpha^{i+1}}{\partial(\Delta w^{i+1})}$$

$$- [s^i - s^{i-1} - f(\alpha^i)[c(s^i) - c(s^{i-1})]] \frac{\partial \alpha^i}{\partial(\Delta w^i)} = 0$$

$$i = 1, \ldots, n-1,$$

$$\frac{\partial \gamma}{\partial w^n} = - [s^n - s^{n-1} - f(\alpha^n)[c(s^n) - c(s^{n-1})]] \frac{\partial \alpha^n}{\partial(\Delta w^n)} = 0.$$

Using the last equation above together with the last equation in (5), we find that

$$s^n - s^{n-1} = f(\alpha^n)[c(s^n) - c(s^{n-1})] = w^n - w^{n-1}.$$

Using this result together with the $(n-1)$st equations in (5) and (13) then gives

$$s^{n-1} - s^{n-2} = f(\alpha^{n-1})[c(s^{n-1}) - c(s^{n-2})] = w^{n-1} - w^{n-2}.$$

Continuing by induction,

$$(14) \quad s^i - s^{i-1} = w^i - w^{i-1}, \quad i = 1, \ldots, n.$$

Since $w^0 = s^0 = 0$, the first equation in (14) implies that $w^1 = s^1$, and by induction,

$$w^i = s^i, \quad i = 1, \ldots, n.$$

Q.E.D.[1]

Not surprisingly, the Nash equilibrium wage vector is, in general, inefficient. What is perhaps less obvious is the degree of competition required to achieve efficiency. Consider firm i, with fixed skill requirement s^i. For a given sequence of viable actions by its closest competitors, i.e., a sequence

$$(s^{i-1}(t),w^{k-1}(t)),(s^{i+1}(t),w^{i+1}(t)), \quad t = 1,2, \ldots,$$

satisfying

$$s^{i-1}(t) < s^i < s^{i+1}(t),$$

$$w^{i-1}(t) \leq s^{i-1}(t), \; w^{i+1}(t) \leq s^{i+1}(t), \quad t = 1,2, \ldots,$$

let $[w^i(t),t = 1,2, \ldots]$ be firm i's sequence of optimal responses. Suppose that $w^i(t)$ converges, and that $\lim_{t \to \infty} w^i(t) = s^i$. What can be said about the sequence $[(s^{i-1},w^{i-1}),(s^{i+1},w^{i+1})]$? The answer is given by

THEOREM 4. The optimal wage of firm i approaches the efficient (competitive) level, $\lim_{t \to \infty} w^i(t) = s^i$, if and only if

1. the wage offers of both neighboring competitors approach their competitive levels; *and*
2. the skill requirements of both neighboring competitors approach s^i, i.e., if and only if

$$\lim_{t \to \infty} w^{i-1}(t) = \lim_{t \to \infty} s^{i-1}(t) = s^i,$$

and

$$\lim_{t \to \infty} w^{i+1}(t) = \lim_{t \to \infty} s^{i+1}(t) = s^i.$$

Proof. Consider any sequence of skill-wage offers by firms

1. This assumes that some workers choose to remain unemployed. If all workers are employed, any wage schedule satisfying

$$s^i - s^{i-1} = w^i - w^{i-1}, \quad i = 2, \ldots, n$$

leads to an efficient allocation of labor.

$i - 1$ and $i + 1$, and assume that the sequence of optimal responses by firm i satisfies

$$\lim_{t\to\infty} w^i(t) = s^i.$$

From (8), this implies that

$$\lim_{t\to\infty} \frac{\partial \pi^i}{\partial w^i} = - \lim_{t\to\infty} \int_{\alpha^i}^{\alpha^{i+1}} m(z)dz = 0$$

$$\Rightarrow \lim_{t\to\infty} \alpha^i(t) = \lim_{t\to\infty} \alpha^{i+1}(t) = \sigma^{-1}(s^i),$$

where the last equality follows from the fact that workers with $z = \sigma^{-1}(s^i)$ prefer the offer $(s = s^i, w = s^i)$ to any other viable offer.

Using (5) and the definition of $\sigma(z)$, we see this in turn implies that

$$\text{(15)} \qquad \lim_{t\to\infty} \frac{c(s^i) - c[s^{i-1}(t)]}{s^i - w^{i-1}(t)} = \lim_{t\to\infty} \frac{c[s^{i+1}(t) - c(s^i)]}{w^{i+1}(t) - s^i}$$
$$= \frac{1}{f[\sigma^{-1}(s^i)]} = \frac{1}{c'(s^i)}.$$

Furthermore, the restriction

$$w^{i-1}(t) \leq s^{i-1}(t) < s^i, \quad t = 1,2,\ldots$$

implies that

$$\frac{c(s^i) - c[s^{i-1}(t)]}{s^i - w^{i-1}(t)} \leq \frac{c(s^i) - c[s^{i-1}(t)]}{s^i - s^{i-1}(t)} < \frac{1}{c'(s^i)},$$
$$t = 1,2,\ldots.$$

Hence (15) is satisfied if and only if

$$\lim_{t\to\infty} s^{i-1}(t) = \lim_{t\to\infty} w^{i-1}(t) = s^i.$$

An exactly analogous argument with the inequalities reversed establishes that

$$\lim_{t\to\infty} s^{i+1}(t) = \lim_{t\to\infty} w^{i+1}(t) = s^i.$$

Q.E.D.

Given Theorem 4, the conditions under which the Nash equilibrium approaches the competitive equilibrium ($\mathbf{w} = \mathbf{s}$) are clear.

THEOREM 5. The Nash equilibrium vector of wage offers approaches the competitive equilibrium if and only if

1. the number of job types increases on every sub-interval of $[\sigma(0),\sigma(Z)]$; *and*
2. no single firm retains control of all job types in any sub-interval of $[\sigma(0),\sigma(Z)]$.

Theorem 5 points out a rather fundamental inefficiency under a competitive market. Wage rates converge to their efficient levels only as the number of job types gets larger (and even then, only if competition among closest neighbors is maintained). On the other hand, if there are fixed costs associated with maintaining different types of jobs—organizational costs, costs of supervision, etc.—then the efficient number of job types may be rather small. The inefficiency arising from noncompetitive wages is eliminated only by adding more job types, a change that—past a point—creates inefficiencies of its own.

The problem would be especially severe in a "thin" labor market, like a small, geographically isolated town, where the range of worker types would be wide relative to the total number of workers. Stated the other way around, a "thick" market has two advantages: the efficient number of job types is larger, so that on the average jobs and workers could be more closely matched; and wage rates will be bid up toward their competitive levels, so that workers will, in fact, select jobs for which they are better suited.

IV. WAGE-SKILL COMPETITION

Suppose now that firms may choose both skill requirements and wage rates. Then it is easy to show that there is no Nash equilibrium in pure strategies.

THEOREM 6. For any $n \geq 2$ firms choosing both skill requirements and wage rates, no Nash equilibrium in pure strategies exists.

Proof. The proof will be given for $n = 2$; the extension for a larger number of firms will be obvious.

Let $\Pi(s,w,\hat{s},\hat{w})$ denote the profit of a firm offering (s,w) when its competitor offers $(\hat{s},\hat{w})$. Suppose that $[(\bar{s}^1,\bar{w}^1),(\bar{s}^2,\bar{w}^2)]$ is a Nash equilibrium. Then by assumption

$$\Pi(\bar{s}^1,\bar{w}^1,\bar{s}^2,\bar{w}^2) \geq \Pi(\bar{s}^2 - \epsilon,\bar{w}^2 + \epsilon,\bar{s}^2,\bar{w}^2),\ \forall\, \epsilon$$

and

$$\Pi(\bar{s}^1,\bar{w}^2,\bar{s}^1,\bar{w}^1) \geq \Pi(\bar{s}^1 - \epsilon,\bar{w}^1 + \epsilon,\bar{s}^1,\bar{w}^1), \forall \epsilon.$$

Since every worker prefers a job that requires less skill and pays a higher wage, a firm making such an offer will attract all workers who choose to take a job. Hence

$$\Pi(\bar{s}^2 - \epsilon,\bar{w}^2 + \epsilon,\bar{s}^2,\bar{w}^2) = \Pi(\bar{s}^2 - \epsilon,\bar{w}^2 + \epsilon,0,0), \quad \forall \epsilon > 0,$$

and

$$\Pi(\bar{s} - \epsilon,\bar{w}^1 + \epsilon,\bar{s}^1,\bar{w}^1) = \Pi(\bar{s}^1 - \epsilon,\bar{w}^1 + \epsilon,0,0), \quad \forall \epsilon > 0.$$

Consequently, since the profit function $\Pi(s,w,s^1,w^1)$ is continuous except where $s = s^1$ and $w = w^1$,

$$\begin{aligned}\lim_{\epsilon+\to 0} \Pi(\bar{s}^2 - \epsilon,\bar{w}^2 + \epsilon,\bar{s}^2,\bar{w}^2) &= \lim_{\epsilon+\to 0} \Pi(\bar{s}^2 - \epsilon,\bar{w}^2 + \epsilon,0,0) \\ &= \Pi(\bar{s}^2,\bar{w}^2,0,0) \geq \Pi(\bar{s}^2,\bar{w}^2,\bar{s}^1,\bar{w}^1).\end{aligned}$$

Similarly,

$$\begin{aligned}\lim_{\epsilon+\to 0} (\bar{s}^1 - \epsilon,\bar{w}^1 - \epsilon,\bar{s}^1,\bar{w}^1) &= \lim_{\epsilon+\to 0} \Pi(\bar{s}^1 - \epsilon,\bar{w}^1 + \epsilon,0,0) \\ &= \Pi(\bar{s}^1,\bar{w}^1,0,0) \geq \Pi(\bar{s}^1,\bar{w}^1,\bar{s}^2,\bar{w}^2).\end{aligned}$$

Putting the inequalities together gives

$$\begin{aligned}\Pi(\bar{s}^1,\bar{w}^1,\bar{s}^2,\bar{w}^2) &\geq \Pi(\bar{s}^2,\bar{w}^2,0,0) \geq \Pi(\bar{s}^2,\bar{w}^2,\bar{s}^1,\bar{w}^1) \\ &\geq \Pi(\bar{s}^1,\bar{w}^1,0,0) \geq \Pi(\bar{s}^1,\bar{w}^1,\bar{s}^2,\bar{w}^2).\end{aligned}$$

The second (fourth) inequality must be strict if firm 2 (firm 1) loses some workers when its competitor makes its Nash equilibrium offer instead of a zero offer. Hence the second (fourth) inequality must be strict if $\bar{s}^2 \leq \bar{s}^1 (\bar{s}^1 \leq \bar{s}^2)$. In either case we obtain a contradiction.

Q.E.D.

Intuitively, the proof says that for any pair of competing (neighboring) firms, located at different points in $s - w$ space, at least one will be able to increase its profit by abandoning its own position and instead undercutting its competitor by the smallest possible amount.

V. Conclusions

The model examined above shares several features with the signaling model developed by Spence [1976 and 1974]. Here, as in

Spence's models firms offer wage schedules, with wage rates dependent on "skill" or "education."[2] Then, given the menu of alternatives offered by firms, heterogeneous workers choose how much "skill" to acquire.

However, the model here differs from Spence's in several respects. It is assumed here that a worker's productivity depends only on the level of skill he attains, and not on his personal characteristic (z-parameter). A job can be thought of as being so highly regimented that there is no room for performing it "better" or "worse." Rather, the alternatives are only "successful" or "unsuccessful" completion of the tasks. Furthermore, adequate performance is certain if the worker possesses the required level of skill, and inadequate performance is certain if he does not. Consequently, the signaling function of educational attainment disappears: since the z-parameter (ability, family background, or whatever) does not affect productivity directly, firms have no interest in acquiring information about that parameter. Only the worker's "education" (which should be thought of as "highest level of training completed" rather than "years of training") affects his productivity, and that is directly and perfectly observable. Hence, the problem of adverse selection that arises under differential information does not arise here.

The structure of competition, on the other hand, is more richly spelled out here. While Spence considers only perfect competition, the emphasis here has been to study the properties of equilibria when the number of firms is small, so that each exercises some degree of monopsony power.

Consequently some of the conclusions reached here are quite different. Spence found that, at the competitive equilibrium, either each worker receives a wage equal to his marginal product, or else all indistinguishable members of a group receive a wage equal to the average marginal product of that group's members. However, because of the signaling function of education, there is a tendency toward overinvestment in it, so that the competitive outcome may be inefficient.

In the model examined here, given the skill requirements of firms, setting a wage equal to the marginal product for each skill level would be efficient. Since the inefficiency in Spence's model arises because of the signaling function of education, this is not surprising. However,

2. Spence's [1976] step-function wage schedules are exactly equivalent to the "point" offers in the model here, since only left-hand end-points of the "steps" are ever chosen by workers.

the wage rate offered for a particular skill level s^i approaches the marginal product for that skill level if and only if *both* neighboring competitors offer jobs with skill requirements approaching s^i and wage rates approaching the competitive levels. If all jobs' skill requirements differ significantly from each other, all wage rates will fall short of the corresponding marginal products. Hence the equilibrium wage configuration in this model reflects the use of monopsony power to depress wages.

Furthermore, a basic inefficiency in monopolistically competitive markets is revealed. Inefficiencies in the allocation of labor are eliminated only if wage rates are bid up to their competitive levels. However, this occurs only if the number of competing job offers increases. Hence, if there are fixed costs in the underlying technology, increasing the number of job offers may also be inefficient. This problem would be most severe in a "thin" market.

In Section IV it was shown that if firms compete in both wages and skills, then there is no Nash equilibrium. This result is similar to a nonexistence proposition of Spence [1976, Proposition 8]. Using a model where there are only two types of workers, he showed that if firms can carry on production using only one "type" of worker, then an equilibrium wage configuration may not exist. Nonexistence occurs whenever there is a "one-step" wage contract (i.e., a contract that leads to equal education and equal wages for both "types") that both types of workers prefer to the efficient contract (i.e., the contract that leads to the efficient level of training for each group, and sets the wage equal to the marginal product for each group). Here it was shown that if there is a continuum of "types" of workers, and if firms are limited to making a finite number of job offers, an equilibrium *never* exists. The nonexistence theorem in Section IV eliminates from further consideration one potential explanation of how the constellation of job offers found in the market is determined.

Finally, note that the results here can be extended in a straightforward way to a situation of imperfect competition among firms selling a differentiated product. The product should be thought of as one of which a consumer purchases one and only one unit of. Let s^i denote the quality (equal to cost of production) of firm i's product and p^i the price charged by firm i. Let $g(z)v(s)$ denote a z-consumer's valuation of a product of quality s. Each consumer chooses the product i for which his net surplus is greatest:

$$\max_i [g(z)v(s^i) - p^i].$$

For $g(\cdot)$ and $v(\cdot)$ satisfying

$$v(s) > 0, \quad v'(s) < 0, \quad v''(s) < 0, \quad s \geq 0;$$
$$g(z) > 0, \quad g'(z) > 0, \qquad z \geq 0,$$

theorems 1–6 remain valid.

Appendix

Given

$$m(z) > 0, \quad f(z) > 0, \quad f'(z) < 0, \quad 0 \leq z \leq Z,$$

let $\gamma(z)$ be the solution of the differential equation:

$$\gamma'(z) = af'(z)/m(z)$$
$$\gamma(0) = 0,$$

where $a < 0$ is an arbitrary constant. Thus, $\gamma(\cdot)$ is merely a rescaling of z, with $\gamma' > 0$. Straightforward calculation shows that

$$\gamma''/\gamma' = f''/f' = m'/m.$$

Next, define $\varphi(\cdot)$ and $\mu(\cdot)$ as the cost and density functions for the rescaled parameter:

$$\varphi(x) \equiv f[\gamma^{-1}(x)],$$
$$\mu(x) \equiv m[\gamma^{-1}(x)], \quad 0 \leq x \leq \gamma(Z),$$

with

$$\varphi'[\gamma(z)] = f'(z)/\gamma'(z),$$
$$\varphi'[\gamma(z)] = \frac{1}{[\gamma'(z)]^2}\left[f''(z) - f'(z)\frac{\gamma''(z)}{\gamma'(z)}\right],$$
$$\mu''[\gamma(z)] = \frac{m'(z)}{\gamma'(z)}, \quad 0 \leq z \leq Z.$$

It is easily verified that the cost and density functions associated with the rescaled parameter γ satisfy (6):

$$\mu'[\gamma(z)]\varphi'[\gamma(z)] - \mu[\gamma(z)]\varphi''[\gamma(z)]$$
$$= \frac{m'f'}{(\gamma')^2} - \frac{m}{(\gamma')^2}\left[f'' - f\frac{'\gamma''}{\gamma'}\right]$$
$$= \frac{1}{(\gamma')^2}\left[m'f' - mf'' + mf'\left(\frac{f''}{f'} - \frac{m'}{'m}\right)\right] = 0.$$

Consequently the assumption in (6) involves no loss of generality.

Northwestern University

References

Spence, Michael, *Market Signaling: Information Transfer in Hiring-Related Processes* (Cambridge: Harvard University Press, 1973).

——, "Competitive and Optimal Responses to Signals: An Analysis of Efficiency and Distribution," *Journal of Economic Theory,* VIII (March 1974), 296–332.

——, "Competition in Salaries, Credentials, and Signaling Prerequisites for Jobs," this *Journal,* XC (Feb. 1976), 51–74.

THE DISTRIBUTION OF INCOME BY FACTOR COMPONENTS*

GRAHAM PYATT
CHAU-NAN CHEN
JOHN FEI

The paper provides a rigorous and exact formulation of the relationship between the Gini measure of inequality in total income across families, and corresponding measures of inequality in such components of total income as wages, transfer income, etc. It is shown that serious problems of bias arise when individual family data are not available and when data on averages for families grouped by the size of total income are used instead. These problems are illustrated with reference to data for Taiwan, 1964 to 1976.

I. INTRODUCTION

In a recent paper, "Growth and the Family Distribution of Income by Factor Components," John Fei, Gustav Ranis, and Shirley Kuo [1978] set out a methodology for the statistical decomposition of family income inequality in terms of such components of family incomes as wages, income from agricultural activities, property income, etc. Their analysis translates the statistical decomposition of income inequality into meaningful economic components of growth and inequality, to yield a mapping from the statistical magnitudes into the conceptual framework of economic theory. A methodology that allows this to be done is clearly of great interest for any attempt to understand the process of economic development. The Fei, Ranis, and Kuo (F-R-K) paper also provides a numerical illustration of the methodology with reference to Taiwan for the period 1964 to 1972.

The measure of inequality used is the Gini coefficient. Links with the Lorenz curve make this coefficient an attractive statistic for the purpose at hand, and recent contributions to the literature on the Gini coefficient have added to our understanding of its properties and characteristics. The present paper is directed toward furthering this understanding in the context of the F-R-K application, with particular emphasis on the issues that arise when data for individual families are not available and the decomposition of family income has to be

* We are indebted to Gustav Ranis and John H. Duloy for comments on an early draft and for their contributions to a dialogue, over an extended period, which have led to the present paper. We are also grateful to T. W. Tsao for his most valuable contribution in preparing the data reported in this paper. It is to be noted that the views expressed in this paper do not necessarily reflect those of the World Bank or its affiliates.

The Quarterly Journal of Economics, November 1980 0033-5533/80/0095-0451$02.30

based on grouped data of the type that are readily accessible in published form.

An aspect of the problems raised by grouped data has previously been discussed in the literature. Specifically, Gastwirth [1972] analyzed the errors involved when a Gini coefficient is calculated from grouped data as opposed to individual observations. The present analysis shows that this problem is only a minor facet of the issues that arise when grouped data are used as a basis for the decomposition of total income into additive factor components. The nature of the broader issues has been the subject of exchanges between the present authors for some time. Using results in an early round of these exchanges, Gary Fields [1979] examined the problems using some 1967–1968 data for Colombia.[1] He writes: "[The evidence] suggests that for this particular decomposition problem with this particular type of grouped data, the option of doing nothing at all rather than using what imperfect data we have deserves serious consideration." [2] This is a strong conclusion, which requires a perspective. This paper attempts to provide one, first from a conceptual point of view, and then in terms of empirical results for Taiwan, using data for individual families that have recently become available.

In discussing the problems that arise when a Gini coefficient is decomposed into additive factor components, the present analysis builds on a statistic known as the concentration ratio. Some authors, especially in the statistical literature, use the term "concentration ratio" synonymously with that of a Gini coefficient. However, in the definition of the former, set out in Section II below, the concentration ratio is a more general concept, with respect to which the Gini coefficient is a special case. So, too, is the pseudo-Gini coefficient, which plays such an important part in the F-R-K methodology. However, true Ginis and pseudo-Ginis are not the same thing, and a clarification of the difference is central to the present discussion.[3]

The next section (Section II) of this paper provides a definition of the concentration ratio for a variable z with respect to some other variable t, when both z and t are observed for each household. The Gini coefficient for z is then defined as the concentration ratio of z with respect to itself. Based on this we are able to show that, for both grouped data and for individual family data when available, the Gini coefficient of inequality for total family incomes can be decomposed

1. It is stated incorrectly in Fields [1979] that the fundamental result, which is given as equation (36) below, is derived in Fei, Ranis, and Kuo [1978]. See Fields [1979], footnote 2, p. 328.
2. Fields [1979], p. 334.
3. See Section III below.

exactly as a sum over all types of factor incomes, of the cross products of two terms, namely, (i) the share of each factor in total income, and (ii) the concentration ratio for the distribution of each type of factor income with respect to that for total income. Moreover, when individual family data are available, the concentration ratio for each type of factor income can be expressed as the product of (a) a correlation effect depending on the respective rankings of households according to total income and income of the given factor type; and (b) the Gini coefficient for the distribution of the particular type of factor income. Hence, with individual family data, we get an exact decomposition of the Gini coefficient for income inequality into factor shares, correlation effects, and the Gini coefficient for each factor. This decomposition is illustrated for Taiwan (1964 to 1976) in Section VI below.

In the absence of individual family data, it is still possible to obtain an exact decomposition of the Gini coefficient for total income (based on grouped data) into a weighted average of the concentration ratios for each type of factor income with respect to total income. In the F-R-K paper these concentration ratios were interpreted as being (approximately) equal to the factor Gini coefficients. However, using the individual family data now available, we show in the numerical results in Section V that Gini coefficients and concentration ratios can be markedly different both in level (by a factor of 2) and trends over time (including turning points). Accordingly, our results show that, in general, it is not safe to interpret the concentration ratios for factor components of income as if they were Gini coefficients, since the factor components also depend on correlation effects. We therefore conclude that the decomposition of the total income Gini adopted by F-R-K is legitimate, but their interpretation of its components is not.

Before presenting our numerical results in Sections V and VI, a conceptual basis is established in Sections II to IV. As previously noted, the concentration ratio is defined in Section II, and exact decomposition by additive factor components is explored for the case where individual data are available. Section III then presents the exact decomposition applicable to grouped data. Problems of accuracy and interpretation are then discussed in Section IV. It is shown that the accuracy problem discussed in Gastwirth [1972] is essentially irrelevant to the main issue, which is the extent to which factor concentration ratios can be interpreted as Gini coefficients. The theoretical discussion is then completed: first by showing that the concentration ratios always underestimate the corresponding factor Ginis, and then by deriving necessary and sufficient conditions for this bias to be zero.

The results on exact decomposition that are obtained in this paper are largely anticipated by the work of Rao [1969], which, in turn, has antecedents in the literature. It seems, however, that the earlier statistical literature has not focused on the problems of empirical analysis, and especially those which arise from grouped data and the use of secondary source material. Insofar as the pioneering work of Fei, Ranis, and Kuo is being reproduced in contemporary studies,[4] the analysis and results that are presented here may caution other investigators about the limitations that are inherent in working with secondary, as opposed to primary, data sources. In addition, our results show that translation from the exact Rao decomposition of the Gini for total income into the framework of economic theory is less straightforward than Fei, Ranis, and Kuo have assumed.

II. Gini Coefficients and Concentration Ratios

Before coming to the problems that arise when only grouped data are available, and since the new results in Section VI below are based on individual family data, it is useful to start our discussion with general definitions of Gini coefficients and concentration ratios that can be applied in the various situations to be encountered subsequently.

The starting point is to assume that there are n families and that two variables, z_i and t_i, are observed for each ($i = 1,2,\ldots,n$). Families are to be ranked according to t_i: the ranking of the ith family will be denoted $r(t_i)$ with the convention that $r(t_i) = 1$ for the family for which t_i is smallest, and $r(t_i) = n$ for the family for which t_i is largest. If two or more families have the same value for t_i, they are each to be given the average of the ranks that they would get if there were an infinitesimal difference between them. With these conventions the average of all ranks $r(t_i)$ is given by

$$(1) \qquad \bar{r}(t_i) = \frac{1}{n}\sum_{i=1}^{n} r(t_i) = \frac{(n+1)}{2} = \bar{r}.$$

The average rank is therefore independent of the ranking criterion t_i, which is adopted.

Next, it is assumed that the average value of z_i is positive, i.e.,

4. See, for example, Ayub [1977] and Mangahas and Gamboa [1976].

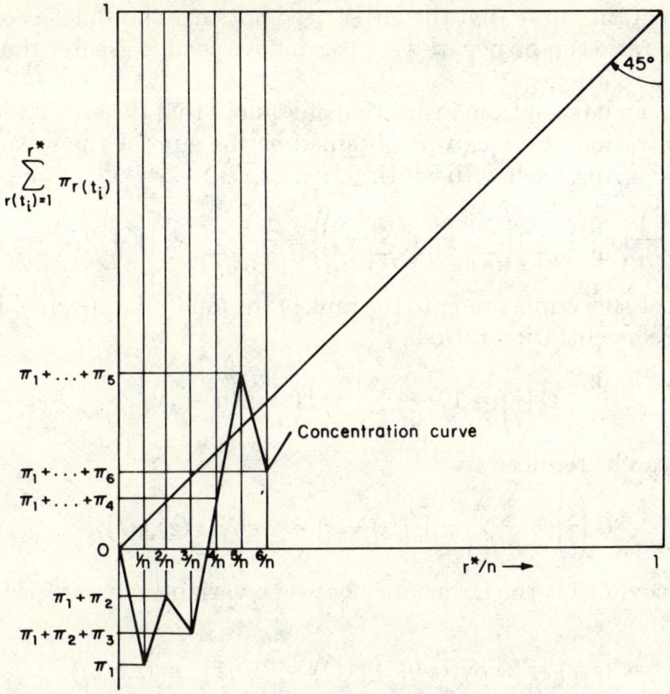

FIGURE I
Schematic Construction of a Concentration Curve

(2)
$$\bar{z} = \frac{1}{n} \sum_{i=1}^{n} z_i \geq 0.$$

It can be noted that this does not require that z_i be positive for all i.

Given $\bar{z}$, we can also define

(3)
$$\pi_i(z) = z_i/n\bar{z}$$

for each household. From (2) and (3) it is apparent that the sum over i of π_i is unity.

The concentration ratio of z_i with respect to t_i is obtained from a concentration curve. This curve graphs cumulative values of π_i against actual values of $r(t_i)/n$, when the cumulative sums are formed by taking families in the order indicated by $r(t_i)$. Figure I illustrates a concentration curve. The concentration ratio of z with respect to t, denoted as $C(z/t)$, is now defined as one *minus* twice the area under the concentration curve. It can be noted from the figure and the definition of the curve that the latter need not be monotonic: a concentration ratio can be negative, or it can have a value greater than one if some z's are negative.

It can be seen from inspection of Figure I that the area under the concentration curve can be obtained as the sum of the areas of n vertical strips, each with width $(1/n)$, i.e., as[5]

$$(4)\qquad \frac{1}{2}\frac{1}{n}\left(\pi_1 + \sum_{j=z}^{n}\left(\sum_{l=1}^{j-1}\pi_l + \sum_{l=1}^{j}\pi_l\right)\right) = \frac{1}{2}\frac{1}{n}\sum_{j=1}^{n}\pi_j\,\{1 + 2(n-j)\},$$

where the subscripts i refer to the rank of the family, i.e., to $r(t_i)$. From (4) the concentration ratio is

$$(5)\qquad C\left(\frac{z}{t}\right) = 1 - \frac{1}{n}\sum_{j=1}^{n}\pi_j\,\{1 + 2(n-j)\},$$

which can be reduced to

$$(6)\qquad C\left(\frac{z}{t}\right) = \frac{2}{n}\sum_{i=1}^{n}\pi_i\{r(t_i) - \bar{r}\} = 2\,\mathrm{cov}(\pi(z),r(t)),$$

where cov(a,b) is the covariance between variables a and b. Hence, from (3),

$$(7)\qquad C(z/t) = 2\,\mathrm{cov}((z/n\bar{z}),r(t)) = (2/n\bar{z})\,\mathrm{cov}(z,r(t)).$$

In this framework a Gini coefficient is the concentration ratio of a variable with respect to itself, since in this case the concentration curve in Figure I is now the Lorenz curve. If y_i is the total income of the ith family, the Gini coefficient for family incomes is

$$(8)\qquad G(y) = C(y/y) = (2/n\bar{y})\,\mathrm{cov}(y,r(y)).$$

The F-R-K study is concerned with the decomposition of $G(y)$ in terms of the factor components of y_i. If x_{ik} is the contribution of factor component k (e.g., wages) to the total income of the family y_i, then

$$(9)\qquad y_i = \sum_{k=1}^{m} x_{ik} \quad \text{for } i = 1,\ldots,n,$$

where total income is made up of m factor components (k = $1,\ldots,m$); and

$$(10)\qquad \bar{y} = \sum_{k=1}^{m}\bar{x}_k,$$

5. When the concentration curve falls below the abscissa (i.e., is negative), then the area under the curve is also negative.

where $\overline{x}_k$ is the average, over all families, of x_{ik}.

Substituting (9) in (8) now gives

$$(11)\qquad G(y) = \left(\frac{2}{n\overline{y}}\right) \operatorname{cov}\left[\sum_k x_{ik}, r(y)\right] = \sum_{k=1}^{m} \phi_k C\left(\frac{x_k}{y}\right),$$

where

$$(12)\qquad \phi_k = \overline{x}_k/\overline{y}.$$

From (10) and (12) it follows that the sum, over k, of ϕ_k is unity, so that result (11) expresses the Gini coefficient for total income y_i as the weighted average of the concentration ratios for factor incomes with respect to total incomes.

Result (11) is due to Rao [1969]. It provides an exact decomposition of $G(y)$, in which the weights ϕ_k are the shares of each factor type in total incomes. Condition (2) implies that these weights are nonnegative. However, the concentration ratios that appear in (11) can be negative as previously noted.

To examine the difference between factor concentration ratios and factor Ginis, it follows from (8) that the latter are given by

$$(13)\qquad G(x_k) = (2/n\overline{x}_k) \operatorname{cov}(x_k, r(x_k)).$$

Using (7), this gives

$$(14)\qquad \frac{C(x_k/y)}{G(x_k)} = \frac{\operatorname{cov}(x_k, r(y))}{\operatorname{cov}(x_k, r(x_k))} = R(y, x_k).$$

The ratio $R(y,x_k)$ will be referred to as a rank correlation ratio. It is not a rank correlation coefficient, but inspection of (14) suggests that this ratio will be unity only if

$$(15)\qquad r(y) = r(x_k),$$

i.e., only if families have the same ranking with respect to factor income k as they have with respect to total income.

It can also be shown that unity is an upper bound for $R(y,x_k)$. This can be argued with respect to concentration curves. To obtain $G(x_k)$, families are ranked by the size of x_{ik}. Hence the rth point on the concentration curve depends on the r families for which x_{ik} is smallest. Some other ordering is involved in obtaining $C(x_k/y)$, namely, the ordering of families according to the size of y_i. The sum of x_{ik} cannot be smaller for the first r families according to this other ordering. Hence the concentration curve that yields $C(x_k/y)$ cannot lie below what yields $G(x_k)$, and therefore

(16) $$C(x_k/y)/G(x_k) = R(x_k,y) \leq 1.$$

More generally, the argument implies that the concentration ratio of a variable cannot exceed its Gini coefficient, and hence that

(17) $$\mathrm{cov}(z,r(z)) \geq \mathrm{cov}(z,r(t)) \quad \text{for all } t.$$

III. Grouped Data

For present purposes the discussion of grouped data can be restricted to instances where grouping results in an equal number of families in each group, irrespective of the grouping criterion that is used. This covers two special cases of interest, namely, the decile grouping of families as employed in F-R-K, and the case of only one family in each group, i.e., the ungrouped data case.

If families are grouped by size of income, then information is restricted to the average income within each group. Notation $\hat{y}_i$ will be used for the average income in the group within which y_i falls. Thus, $\hat{y}_i$ is defined for each family and can be used to define $r(\hat{y}_i)$ in each case.[6] Obviously $\hat{y}_i$ and $r(\hat{y}_i)$ will be the same for all families within a given group. Thus, if there are s groups of families, the concentration curve will be a connected series of s linear segments.[7] It will yield the Gini coefficient for grouped income data:

(18) $$G(\hat{y}) = C(\hat{y}/\hat{y}) = (2/n\bar{y})\,\mathrm{cov}(\hat{y},r(\hat{y})).$$

We can now note that[8]

(19) $$\mathrm{cov}(\hat{y},r(\hat{y})) = \mathrm{cov}(y,r(\hat{y}_i)).$$

Hence, from (18),

$$\mathrm{cov}(\hat{y},r(\hat{y})) \leqslant \mathrm{cov}(y,r(y))$$

or

(20) $$G(\hat{y}) \leqslant G(y),$$

6. Recall that in our earlier definition of $r(t_i)$ we adopted the convention that, if t_i is the same for two or more families, then for each of these families $r(t_i)$ takes on the average of the values it would have if there was an infinitesimal difference in t_i between the families.

7. This is equivalent to saying that the concentration curve is obtained by joining the origin and s of the n successive points on the concentration curve by straight lines. In the notation of Figure I, these s points correspond to the actual points at which $r^* = n/s, 2n/s, \ldots, (s-1)n/s, n$.

8. This follows directly from $\mathrm{cov}(y,r(\hat{y})) = \mathrm{cov}(\hat{y},r(\hat{y})) + \mathrm{cov}(y-\hat{y},r(\hat{y}))$ and from noting that the second term on the right-hand side must be zero. This is because this second term depends on covariances within groups for which one of the variables, viz. $r(\hat{y}_i)$, is in fact constant.

i.e., the Gini coefficient calculated from grouped data must always underestimate the true Gini.

The size of this underestimation has been explored by Gastwirth [1972], among others. His analysis and our own empirical results suggest that it is of marginal importance. It is obviously an element in the accuracy of the F-R-K statistics and is attributable to the use in that investigation of grouped data. However, our main concerns here are with problems that arise from the interaction of decomposition methods and grouped data. From this perspective the bias implied by (20) is not essential, as we shall show in Section IV.

When information is restricted to data for families grouped by size of total income, we may also know the average value of each factor income within each of the total income groupings. Let $\tilde{x}_{ik}$ denote the average value of type k income for households in the total income group that includes household i. A typical element of $\tilde{x}_{ik}$ is therefore the average wage income of families that fall in, say, the third size group according to total income. Then the sum over k of $\tilde{x}_{ik}$ is the average of the combined income from all sources of families in a particular size group for total income, i.e.,

$$\hat{y}_i = \sum_{k=1}^{m} \tilde{x}_{ik}. \tag{21}$$

Making this substitution in (19) yields

$$G(\hat{y}) = \sum_{k=1}^{m} \phi_k C\left(\frac{\tilde{x}_k}{\hat{y}}\right). \tag{22}$$

This is an exact decomposition of the Gini coefficient for incomes $\hat{y}_i$, which is analogous to that previously obtained for ungrouped data as equation (11). Since (22) corresponds to the case where the only data available are grouped by income levels y_i, it follows that such grouping, of itself, does not preclude an exact decomposition.

Result (22) is the basic decomposition equation employed by F-R-K.[9] The concentration ratios $C(\tilde{x}_k/\hat{y})$, which appear in it, are referred to in their analysis as pseudo-Ginis. However, we prefer to use here the longer but more precise name of "factor concentration ratios for data grouped by total income level."

IV. Problems of Accuracy and Interpretation

Result (22) in the previous section provides an exact decomposition of the Gini coefficient for total income when data are grouped

9. See Fei, Ranis, and Kuo [1978], Appendix equation (A2.11).

into size classes defined by the level of total income. This can be written as

$$(23) \qquad G(y) = \sum_{k=1}^{m} \phi_k C\left(\frac{\tilde{x}_k}{\hat{y}}\right) + \{G(y) - G(\hat{y})\},$$

where the term in braces on the right-hand side of (23) must be positive in view of the inequality (20). We have previously suggested that this term, which is discussed by Gastwirth [1972], is not large and has limited relevance to the problems that concern us. The next step in the present argument is to justify this position, given that our main concern is the extent to which it is legitimate to interpret the concentration ratios $C(\tilde{x}_k/\hat{y})$ as Gini coefficients for factor incomes.

To develop the argument, let $G(x_k)$ be the Gini coefficient of inequality among individual families for the kth type of factor income, e.g., property income. Clearly, if individual family data on property income were available, we could group families (into deciles, for example) according to the size of their property income. The individual data could now be discarded, and a Gini coefficient $G(\hat{x}_k)$ could be calculated from the grouped data, on the assumption that each family has an amount of property income equal to the average property income among families that fall within the same size class (decile) according to the level of property income. Separate calculations for each type of factor income ($k = 1,2, \ldots, m$) would now yield a series of statistics $G(x_k)$ and $G(\hat{x}_k)$, which, in view of result (20), would have the property

$$(24) \qquad G(\hat{x}_k) \leq G(x_k) \quad \text{for } k = 1, \ldots, m.$$

It should be noted that calculating each $G(\hat{x}_k)$ requires a reranking of households according to the size of x_{ik}, and then grouping of the ranked data. These groupings will imply that for a given k there are no overlaps in the size of x_{ik} between groups. To compute the set of statistics $G(\hat{x}_k)$ for $k = 1,2, \ldots, m$ requires m distinct rerankings of the individual data. Clearly, such rerankings are impossible if individual data are not available. Hence, access to primary family data is necessary if the statistics $G(\hat{x}_k)$ are to be computed.

Simple manipulation of equation (23) yields the result

$$(25) \qquad G(y) = \sum_{k=1}^{m} \phi_k G(x_k) + \sum_{k=1}^{m} \phi_k \epsilon_k + e,$$

where

$$(26) \qquad \epsilon_k = C(\tilde{x}_k/\hat{y}) - G(\hat{x}_k) \quad \text{for } k = 1, \ldots, m$$

and

$$e = \{G(y) - G(\hat{y})\} - \sum_{k=1}^{m} \phi_k \{G(x_k) - G(\hat{x}_k)\}. \tag{27}$$

Hence, from (25), there are two types of error involved in assuming that the Gini coefficient for total income can be expressed as a weighted sum of the Gini coefficients for the separate types of factor income. The first type of error, ϵ_k for $k = 1, \ldots, m$, is the major source of error and is discussed in detail below. The second type of error e is less important for three reasons.

Components of the error e arise from using grouped data to calculate Gini coefficients. If the size of a variable z is the criterion used to group families, then the error in calculating the Gini coefficient for z from grouped data can be expressed as[10]

$$G(z) - G(\hat{z}) = \sum_{\upsilon=1}^{s} p_\upsilon \pi_\upsilon g_\upsilon, \tag{28}$$

where it is assumed that the population has been divided into s groups; p_υ is the population proportion in the υth group; π_υ is the share of group υ in the total of z for the whole population; and g_υ is the Gini coefficient of inequality for the distribution of z within group υ. Hence, if the population is grouped into deciles according to the size of z, we have $s = 10$ and $p_\upsilon = 1/10$ for all υ. Similarly, in this example, π_υ will have an average value of $1/10$ while g_υ will be bounded between 0 and 1 if z is a nonnegative variable. Hence the error term (28) has an order of magnitude of $1/10$. In fact, Gastwirth [1972] is able to impose much tighter bounds on this error term. These provide the first reason for regarding the term e in (27) as negligible.

The second reason for regarding e as negligible is that its determination as in (27) involves compensating errors. Each of the terms in braces in (27) must be positive, while the sum of the weights ϕ_k is unity. Hence, if decile grouping is always employed, the error e is the difference between two nonnegative terms each of the same order of magnitude. Hence it may be quite reasonable to ignore e in numerical work.

A third reason for ignoring e is that the problem we are interested in can be explored without reference to it. If available data are restricted to a grouped distribution according to total family income, then $G(y)$ is unknown, and analysis must necessarily be restricted to the decomposition of $G(\hat{y})$. Hence, taking (22) as the starting point, we can easily show that

10. See, for example, Pyatt [1976].

(29) $$G(\hat{y}) = \sum_{k=1}^{m} \phi_k G(\hat{x}_k) + \sum_{k=1}^{m} \phi_k \epsilon_k,$$

i.e., a decomposition of $G(\hat{y})$ that does not involve errors of the type discussed by Gastwirth.

Our analysis in Section V will be based on equation (29). In terms of it, the interpretation problem using the F-R-K methodology is whether the concentration ratios $C(\tilde{x}_k/\hat{y})$ are good approximations of the Gini coefficients $G(\hat{x}_k)$, i.e., whether the error terms ϵ_k are negligible. To explore this, we shall find it useful to express each ϵ_k as the sum of two terms, both of which are nonpositive. Beyond this, necessary and sufficient conditions can be obtained for each component of ϵ_k to be zero. Hence we can obtain conditions under which there is no interpretation problem.

At this stage our analysis requires a new concept, denoted $G(\tilde{x}_k)$, which can be called a quasi-factor Gini. Given this, we want to prove that

(30) $$C(\tilde{x}_k/\hat{y}) \leqslant G(\tilde{x}_k) \leqslant G(\hat{x}_k),$$

i.e. that the quasi-factor Gini lies between the concentration ratio $C(\tilde{x}_k/\hat{y})$ and the Gini coefficient $G(\hat{x}_k)$. If (30) is valid, then it follows that

(31) $$\epsilon_k = \epsilon_{1k} + \epsilon_{2k},$$

where

(32) $$\epsilon_{1k} = C(\tilde{x}_k/\hat{y}) - G(\tilde{x}_k) \leqslant 0$$

and

(33) $$\epsilon_{2k} = G(\tilde{x}_k) - G(\overline{x}_k) \leqslant 0.$$

The variables $\tilde{x}_{ik}$ have already been defined in Section II. They are defined for each k by grouping households according to the size of total income y_i, and then calculating the average value of x_{ik} within each of these groups. The groupings are therefore independent of k. They are the same grouping or clustering of families as is involved in computing the $\hat{y}_i$'s i.e., the average values of total income among groups of families defined with respect to the size of their total income. However, there is no reason why $r(\tilde{x}_{ik})$ and $r(\hat{y}_i)$ should be the same: there is no reason, for example, why average transfer income should increase monotonically as we move upward between groups defined with respect to the size of y_i. Hence the rankings $r(\tilde{x}_{ik})$ and $r(\hat{y}_i)$ are not necessarily the same, and results (17) and (18) are sufficient to establish the inequality (32).

This discussion of the difference between $r(\tilde{x}_{ik})$ and $r(\hat{y}_i)$ suggests the following condition:

FIRST INTERPRETATION CONDITION. A necessary and sufficient condition for $\epsilon_{1k} = 0$ is that the graph of $r(\hat{y}_i)$ *versus* $r(\tilde{x}_{ik})$ is monotonic nondecreasing.

To establish this first interpretation condition, we can argue as follows. The concentration curve that yields the pseudo-Gini $G(\tilde{x}_k)$ ranks families according to $r(\tilde{x}_{ik})$, i.e., according to the average level of x_{ik} for groups that result from the stratification of families by income levels. As previously noted, this must imply the same clustering or grouping as $r(\hat{y}_i)$. The only difference that can arise between $C(\tilde{x}/\hat{y})$ and $G(\tilde{x}_k) = C(\tilde{x}_k/\tilde{x}_k)$ is therefore in the ordering of these groups in the derivation of the concentration curve. The ordering for $G(\tilde{x}_k)$ is the one that minimizes the ordinate of the concentration curve for each value of the abscissa. Either any other ordering must result in a larger value of the ordinate, or $\tilde{x}_{ik}$ must have the same value for at least two groups. But if this latter possibility maintains, then, for two such groups, $r(\tilde{x}_{ik})$ is also the same. Hence the condition is not violated. Under the former possibility, the condition is violated and the concentration coefficient $C(\tilde{x}_k/\hat{y}_i)$ will be strictly less than the pseudo-Gini $G(\tilde{x}_k)$.[11]

To establish inequality (33), we can note that both $G(\tilde{x}_k)$ and $G(\hat{x}_k)$ are Gini coefficients calculated from grouped data. The difference between them must therefore lie in the grouping criterion, given that we assume an equal number of groups in all cases, and an equal number of households in each group. For $\tilde{x}_{ik}$, the grouping criterion is the size of y_i; while for $\hat{x}_{ik}$ the criterion is the size of x_{ik}. Hence the grouping criterion for computing $\hat{x}_{ik}$ is the one that minimizes the ordinate of the concentration curve (i.e., the Lorenz curve in this instance) for each value of the abscissa. Hence the concentration (Lorenz) curve that yields $G(\tilde{x}_k)$ can never lie below what yields $G(\hat{x}_k)$. From this, inequality (33) follows directly.

This argument leads to our second interpretation condition.

SECOND INTERPRETATION CONDITION. A necessary and sufficient condition for $\epsilon_{2k} = 0$ is that $r(\tilde{x}_{ik}) = r(\hat{x}_{ik})$ for all i.

This condition is clearly necessary, since if there is any difference in the weak ordering of families given by $r(\tilde{x}_{ik})$ and $r(\hat{x}_{ik})$, then the

11. It can be noted that, since $\tilde{x}_{ik}$ derives from groups defined by common values of $\hat{y}_i$, it is impossible to have the same value of $r(\hat{y}_i)$ for two groups which have different values of $r(\tilde{x}_{ik})$.

concentration curve for $G(\tilde{x}_k)$ must be above that for $G(\hat{x}_k)$ at at least one point. Since the latter concentration curve is invariably a lower bound for the former, it follows that $\epsilon_{2k} = 0$ only if there is no divergence in these weak orderings. Beyond this, if there is no difference in the weak orderings, then there will be no difference in $G(\tilde{x}_k)$ and $G(\hat{x}_k)$. Hence sufficiency is established.

The two interpretation conditions given above can be combined to yield necessary and sufficient conditions for the interpretation of the concentration ratios $C(\tilde{x}_k/\hat{y})$ (the F-R-K pseudo-Ginis), as Gini coefficients of form $G(\hat{x}_k)$. These are

Necessary: the graph of $r(\hat{y}_i)$ versus $r(\hat{x}_{ik})$ is monotonic nondecreasing

Sufficient: $r(\hat{y}_i) = r(\hat{x}_{ik})$ for all i.

Neither condition is as strong as the one that F-R-K discuss, namely, that the relationship between $\hat{x}_{ik}$ and $\hat{y}_i$ should be linear and have a positive slope: nonlinearity does not necessarily violate the sufficient condition.

V. The Interpretation Problem: Some Empirical Results

Given data grouped by size of total income y_i, the variables $\tilde{x}_{ik}$ can be calculated, but the variables $\hat{x}_{ik}$ cannot. Hence F-R-K were able to examine the first interpretation condition—that on ϵ_{1k}—but not the second. Generally, they found ϵ_{1k} to be small. However, there should be no presumption that this implies small or negligible values for ϵ_{2k}. To illustrate this point, some 1974 data for Taiwan have been analyzed with the results set out in Table I.

Table I shows that there is no interpretation problem of the first type for this data set, which refers to wage incomes. The average family wage incomes $\tilde{x}_{iw}$ increase in strict monotonic fashion as we move through deciles of the total income distribution. Hence the first interpretation condition is satisfied entirely. However, the second interpretation condition is far from satisfied. If it were satisfied, then ranking into deciles by wage income level x_{iw} and total income level y_i would place all families on the main diagonal of Table I. In fact, 924 out of 5,256 families (17.6 percent) at most are to be found there. The reason why this figure has to be given as an upper limit, rather than an exact number, is because 201 families in the first two income deciles belong to the 18.1 percent of all families that have zero wage income. Whether all these 201 families should be assumed to lie on the diagonal is ambiguous. But meanwhile the fact that 18.1 percent of all

TABLE I

DISTRIBUTION OF FAMILIES AND AVERAGE WAGE INCOMES BY DECILES OF THE WAGE INCOME AND TOTAL INCOME DISTRIBUTIONS

TAIWAN: 1974

Deciles of the distribution of total income y_i	Deciles of the distribution of wage income x_{iw}: 1st and 2nd: Families with zero wage income	1st and 2nd: Other families in the 2nd decile	3rd	4th	5th	6th	7th	8th	9th	10th	Total[a]	Average wage Income $\tilde{x}_{iw}$ [b]
1st	121	35	194	159	9						518	21.8
2nd	80	10	86	124	213	16					529	35.2
3rd	86	10	60	61	119	186	5				527	41.2
4th	109	16	45	35	44	129	146				524	44.0
5th	94	7	29	36	40	72	157	92			527	52.2
6th	81	5	37	27	30	49	96	169	19		513	57.4
7th	89	2	23	24	28	35	50	147	140		538	65.3
8th	108	5	24	20	16	19	37	61	207	29	526	69.8
9th	92	4	17	15	16	16	20	30	121	194	525	87.5
10th	91	2	11	13	17	9	15	24	40	307	529	135.8
Total[a]	951	96	526	514	532	531	526	523	527	530	5256	
Average wage income $\hat{x}_{iw}$ [b]	zero	7.0	23.1	39.4	50.9	61.6	71.8	83.8	103.9	173.5		61.1

a. Totals vary between deciles because all families with the same (wage) income have been placed in the same cell of the table.
b. Units: thousands of won.

TABLE II

EXACT DECOMPOSITION OF TOTAL INCOME INEQUALITY USING FACTOR SHARES AND CONCENTRATION RATIOS, AND FACTOR GINI COEFFICIENTS FOR TAIWAN, 1964 TO 1976, BASED ON DATA GROUPED BY DECILES

	Wage income			Profit income			Agricultural income			All other income				
	Factor share ϕ_W	Concentration ratio $C(\tilde{x}_W/\hat{y})$	Gini coefficient $G(\hat{x}_W)$	Factor share ϕ_π	Concentration ratio $C(\tilde{x}_\pi/\hat{y})$	Gini coefficient $G(\hat{x}_\pi)$	Factor share ϕ_A	Concentration ratio $C(\tilde{x}_A/\hat{y})$	Gini coefficient $G(\hat{x}_A)$	Factor share ϕ_X	Concentration ratio $C(\tilde{x}_X/\hat{y})$	Gini coefficient $G(\tilde{x}_X/\hat{y})$	$G(\hat{y}) = \sum_k \phi_k \times C(\tilde{x}_k/\hat{y})$	$\sum_k \phi_k \times G(\tilde{x}_k)$
							Agricultural families							
1964	0.230	0.120	0.523	0.063	0.263	0.451	0.635	0.413	0.469	0.072	0.532	0.984	0.345	0.517
1966	0.207	0.189	0.590	0.070	0.270	0.424	0.651	0.336	0.400	0.073	0.486	0.891	0.311	0.484
1968	0.300	0.249	0.583	0.080	0.241	0.419	0.495	0.277	0.434	0.125	0.538	0.852	0.298	0.530
1970	0.355	0.270	0.538	0.079	0.281	0.442	0.451	0.238	0.427	0.116	0.486	0.853	0.282	0.517
1972	0.416	0.269	0.497	0.077	0.257	0.434	0.395	0.235	0.456	0.112	0.497	0.858	0.280	0.516
1974	0.395	0.247	0.503	0.074	0.271	0.455	0.431	0.268	0.467	0.100	0.416	0.879	0.275	0.522
1976	0.389	0.248	0.503	0.087	0.281	0.439	0.388	0.258	0.461	0.137	0.364	0.816	0.271	0.525

						Nonagricultural families								
1964	0.514	0.259	0.479	0.107	0.446	0.678	0.021	0.077	0.823	0.358	0.431	0.705	0.337	0.588
1966	0.585	0.260	0.472	0.093	0.500	0.755	0.013	−0.312	0.874	0.309	0.424	0.705	0.326	0.576
1968	0.567	0.240	0.454	0.111	0.531	0.725	0.008	−0.194	0.878	0.314	0.425	0.730	0.327	0.574
1970	0.631	0.233	0.417	0.088	0.439	0.681	0.006	−0.071	0.880	0.275	0.382	0.746	0.290	0.534
1972	0.709	0.277	0.384	0.118	0.471	0.692	0.005	−0.007	0.902	0.168	0.281	0.803	0.299	0.493
1974	0.655	0.262	0.412	0.122	0.487	0.682	0.008	−0.025	0.900	0.215	0.346	0.767	0.305	0.525
1976	0.648	0.243	0.402	0.112	0.424	0.631	0.008	0.068	0.900	0.232	0.325	0.742	0.281	0.511
							All families							
1964	0.332	0.171	0.534	0.079	0.340	0.576	0.415	0.454	0.651	0.174	0.418	0.847	0.345	0.640
1966	0.443	0.235	0.541	0.084	0.429	0.679	0.251	0.350	0.755	0.221	0.420	0.788	0.321	0.660
1968	0.491	0.260	0.510	0.102	0.466	0.675	0.148	0.167	0.786	0.260	0.465	0.772	0.320	0.636
1970	0.535	0.268	0.486	0.085	0.390	0.620	0.161	0.121	0.752	0.220	0.433	0.792	0.291	0.608
1972	0.644	0.295	0.430	0.109	0.447	0.670	0.092	0.079	0.826	0.156	0.336	0.819	0.299	0.554
1974	0.605	0.273	0.446	0.113	0.469	0.668	0.089	0.129	0.854	0.193	0.372	0.790	0.302	0.574
1976	0.591	0.264	0.445	0.107	0.407	0.610	0.091	0.095	0.831	0.211	0.354	0.762	0.283	0.565

families have zero wage income is quite lost when families are grouped by income level. More generally, the data in Table I imply a concentration ratio (or pseudo-Gini) of 26.4 percent. The true Gini for wages using decile groups is 44.3 percent.[12] Therefore there is a major problem in interpreting pseudo-Ginis as true Ginis even when there is no interpretation problem of the first type.

Since both types of interpretation problem generally can arise, it follows that the gap between $C(\tilde{x}_k/\hat{y})$ and $G(\hat{x}_k)$ must be the only measure of reliability of the F-R-K methodology in the sense that, if this gap is large, then the decomposition

$$G(\hat{y}) \doteqdot \sum_{k=1}^{m} \phi_k G(\hat{x}_k) \tag{34}$$

must be subject to substantial errors. Table II sets out some results for the period 1964 to 1976 on the size of the gap.

Numerically, the results in Table II are not strictly comparable to those presented in Fei, Ranis, and Kuo [1978]. There are two reasons for this. First, F-R-K used published survey results. The data in Table II use individual family survey results. Not all the original questionnaires could be recaptured for our purposes, so that results for the earlier years especially are open to doubt.[13] Second, the surveys used by F-R-K and here have changed in coverage over the years, notably in the representation of Taipei city from 1970 onward when the sample size was doubled. An adjustment for this has been made by F-R-K, while the present results refer to original, unadjusted data.

With these reservations, Table II shows some interesting and significant gaps. Since the concentration ratios $C(\tilde{x}_k/\hat{y})$ must always be smaller than $G(\hat{x}_k)$ ($\epsilon_k \leq 0$), it follows that

$$G(\hat{y}_i) = \sum_k \phi_k C\left(\frac{\tilde{x}_k}{\hat{y}}\right) \leq \sum_k \phi_k G(\hat{x}_k). \tag{35}$$

The final columns of Table II show the difference between the exact decomposition (22) and the decomposition (34), which is implied by interpreting concentration ratios as Gini coefficients. The gap is substantial, so that the F-R-K interpretation of concentration ratios (pseudo-Ginis) as true Ginis is hardly appropriate.

12. It can be noted that these numbers differ slightly from those in Tables II and III below, because the Table I data are taken from a tape that excludes certain families, because data for them are incomplete in respects that do not concern the issues under discussion here. We are indebted to Pravin Visaria for the Table I tabulation.

13. The sample recovery fractions are as follows:

1964	1966	1968	1970	1972	1974	1976
41.6%	80.6%	99.7%	98.0%	99.6%	98.6%	100.0%

Table II illustrates the fact that concentration ratios can be negative. Such an observation implies an inverse relationship between a factor income of a given type and total income: the concentration ratio is zero for a factor if all income groups receive an equal amount of income of the given factor type. Table II also illustrates the possibility that trends in concentration ratios can be quite different from those for Gini coefficients. Two extreme examples are provided by the data on wages and agricultural incomes for all families. With respect to agricultural income, the concentration ratio falls from 0.45 to 0.10 over the period (with a minor break in monotonicity for 1972). In contrast, the Gini coefficient rises from 0.65 to 0.83 (again with minor breaks in monotonicity). Similarly, the Gini coefficient trend for wages is **U**-shaped with a minimum of 0.43 in 1972: the trend of the concentration ratio has an inverse **U**-shape with a maximum in 1972 of 0.30. It is apparent from these examples that the level and trend of the concentration ratio $C(\tilde{x}_k/\hat{y})$ may be misleading as a guide to the level and trend of the factor Gini $G(\hat{x}_k)$.

It is not difficult to provide an explanation of such results. A high value for the Gini coefficient $G(\hat{x}_k)$ is a necessary but insufficient reason for having a high value of $C(\tilde{x}_k,\hat{y})$. Suppose, for example, that there is a high Gini for agricultural income, mainly due to the fact that many families have zero agricultural incomes, so that such income is concentrated among a few farm families. Then if average income levels among farm families are similar to those among nonfarm families, the importance of agricultural income as an element of total family income will be largely independent of the size of total income, irrespective of inequality among farm families. Hence the concentration ratio will be small: the size of total income gives little or no guide to the size of agricultural income in a mixed population of farm and nonfarm families in this case.

VI. Exact Decomposition Using Individual Family Data

When individual family data are available, the results in Section II above can be used to obtain an exact decomposition. This is based on the results in equations (11) and (14), which combine to give

$$G(y) = \sum_k \phi_k R(y,x_k) G(x_k), \tag{36}$$

i.e., an exact decomposition of the Gini coefficient for total income $G(y_i)$ into separate components for each type of factor income. The component of the decomposition corresponding to each type of factor

TABLE III

EXACT DECOMPOSITION OF TOTAL INCOME GINI AND OF CONCENTRATION RATIOS INTO RANK CORRELATION EFFECTS AND FACTOR GINI EFFECTS USING INDIVIDUAL FAMILY DATA, TAIWAN, 1964 TO 1976

	Wage income			Profit income			Agricultural income			All other income			Total income Gini
	Concentration ratio $C(x_W/y)$	Rank correlation ratio $R(y,x_W)$	Gini coefficient $G(x_W)$	Concentration ratio $C(x_\pi/y)$	Rank correlation ratio $R(y,x_\pi)$	Gini coefficient $G(x_\pi)$	Concentration ratio $C(x_A/y)$	Rank correlation ratio $R(y,x_A)$	Gini coefficient $G(x_A)$	Concentration ratio $C(x_X/y)$	Rank correlation ratio $R(y,x_X)$	Gini coefficient $G(x_X)$	$G(y) = \sum \phi_k \times R(y,x_k) \times G(x_k)$
							Agricultural families						
1964	0.122	0.229	0.532	0.270	0.583	0.463	0.420	0.879	0.478	0.553	0.538	1.028[a]	0.351
1966	0.191	0.318	0.601	0.277	0.632	0.438	0.344	0.843	0.408	0.494	0.533	0.926	0.319
1968	0.250	0.423	0.591	0.245	0.568	0.431	0.283	0.640	0.442	0.562	0.635	0.885	0.305
1970	0.276	0.504	0.548	0.288	0.632	0.456	0.241	0.554	0.435	0.504	0.570	0.884	0.287
1972	0.275	0.545	0.505	0.264	0.589	0.448	0.240	0.515	0.466	0.509	0.574	0.887	0.280
1974	0.252	0.493	0.511	0.279	0.592	0.471	0.273	0.572	0.477	0.426	0.469	0.908	0.286
1976	0.253	0.495	0.511	0.288	0.634	0.454	0.262	0.555	0.472	0.376	0.448	0.840	0.276

						Nonagricultural families							
1964	0.264	0.542	0.487	0.462	0.665	0.695	0.084	0.100	0.846	0.452	0.619	0.730	0.348
1966	0.263	0.548	0.480	0.511	0.658	0.777	−0.306	−0.337	0.908	0.437	0.580	0.753	0.333
1968	0.244	0.529	0.461	0.545	0.726	0.751	−0.195	−0.213	0.916	0.438	0.585	0.749	0.335
1970	0.236	0.557	0.424	0.449	0.641	0.700	−0.077	−0.084	0.919	0.394	0.516	0.764	0.297
1972	0.283	0.722	0.392	0.480	0.676	0.710	−0.023	−0.024	0.971	0.288	0.350	0.824	0.306
1974	0.268	0.638	0.420	0.502	0.715	0.702	−0.008	−0.008	0.985	0.354	0.450	0.786	0.313
1976	0.247	0.604	0.409	0.436	0.672	0.649	0.064	0.065	0.987	0.334	0.440	0.759	0.287
						All families							
1964	0.174	0.320	0.543	0.348	0.587	0.593	0.462	0.696	0.664	0.438	0.498	0.879	0.354
1966	0.238	0.432	0.551	0.439	0.626	0.701	0.360	0.466	0.773	0.430	0.531	0.810	0.328
1968	0.264	0.509	0.519	0.483	0.691	0.699	0.175	0.217	0.806	0.477	0.601	0.794	0.329
1970	0.273	0.553	0.494	0.399	0.625	0.638	0.121	0.158	0.767	0.447	0.550	0.813	0.297
1972	0.301	0.686	0.439	0.457	0.664	0.688	0.085	0.100	0.850	0.343	0.407	0.842	0.305
1974	0.280	0.615	0.455	0.484	0.702	0.689	0.133	0.151	0.880	0.379	0.467	0.811	0.309
1976	0.269	0.595	0.452	0.418	0.667	0.627	0.097	0.113	0.857	0.362	0.464	0.780	0.289

a. $G(x_k)$ calculated via cov $(x_k, r(x_k))$ can exceed unity if some values of x_k are negative.

income is the product of three terms: (i) the share of the factor in total income; (ii) a rank correlation ratio as defined in equation (14); and (iii) the Gini coefficient for the distribution of income of the given factor type. Table III sets out this exact decomposition using the same data source as Table II.[14] (Values for ϕ_k are the same as in Table II and therefore are not repeated in Table III.)

Apart from the modifications of concentration ratios and Gini coefficients that arise from the use of individual as opposed to grouped family data, the new information in Table III concerns the rank correlation ratios $R(y,x_k)$. These ratios show some interesting trends, notably the decline among all families and among agricultural families in the rank correlation ratio for total income *versus* agricultural income. The implication of these results is that the ranking of families by agricultural income has declined in importance as a determinant of ranking by total income. This is perhaps what one would expect, given the declining importance of agricultural income as a share of total income, which can be seen from Table II. It can also be noted that the Gini coefficient for agricultural income among agricultural families has tended to increase since the late sixties. This would be consistent with a greater tendency to move toward other forms of remunerative activity (e.g., wage employment) by members of those families that are at the lower end of the agricultural income distribution.

From the point of view of statistical decomposition, the results in Table III tell a complete story of the trends in total income Gini coefficients in terms of factor components. However, the mapping from the statistical magnitudes to the concepts of economic theory is not straightforward. Such a mapping is provided in F-R-K, but under the assumption that the correlation effects $R(x_k,y)$ are stable over time and approximately unity. Our new results show that this is too restrictive, and point to the need for an interpretation of the correlation effects in terms of economic concepts. We have no such interpretation to offer at this juncture. At best, we can suggest that the correlation effects are potentially associated with some dynamic aspects of development, not least with migration out of the farm sector and into wage employment. This would be consistent with the observation that wages grow in importance as an explanation of (i.e., in their correlation with) total income; and with a narrowing of the differential in incomes between farm and nonfarm families, which tends

14. It can be noted that one of the Gini coefficients in Table III exceeds unity. This is possible, given that our definitions do not exclude the computation of a Gini coefficient for a variable that takes on negative values for some families.

to reduce the correlation between total income and income from agriculture. Such phenomena are consistent with our observations and sensible from a theoretical perspective. In going beyond them, it may be that a marriage of the statistical approach in this paper and the interpretation of Gini coefficients in Pyatt [1976] would take us further toward a sound theoretical interpretation for the correlation effects. But such developments must wait for the future; for the present we leave these questions open.

DEVELOPMENT RESEARCH CENTER, WORLD BANK
THE INSTITUTE OF THE THREE PRINCIPLES OF THE PEOPLE,
ACADEMIA SINICA, TAIPEI
YALE UNIVERSITY

REFERENCES

Ayub, M., "Income Inequality in a Growth-Theoretic Context: The Case of Pakistan," Ph.D. thesis, Yale University, 1977.
Fei, J. C. H., G. Ranis, and S. W. Y. Kuo, "Growth and the Family Distribution of Income by Factor Components," this *Journal,* XCII (Feb. 1978), 17–53.
Fields, G. S., "Income Inequality in Urban Colombia: A Decomposition Analysis," *Review of Income and Wealth,* Series 25, No. 3 (Sept. 1979).
Gastwirth, J. L., "The Estimation of the Lorenz Curve and Gini Index," *Review of Economics and Statistics,* LIV (Aug. 1972), 306–16.
Mangahas, M., and E. Gamboa, "A Note on Decomposition of the Gini Ratio by Family and by Type of Income," *Philippine Review of Business and Economics,* XIII (Dec. 1976), 97–130.
Pyatt, G., "On the Interpretation and Disaggregation of Gini Coefficients," *Economic Journal,* LXXXVI (June 1976), 243–55.
Rao, V. M., "Two Decompositions of Concentration Ratio," *Journal of the Royal Statistical Society,* Series A, CXXXII, Part 3 (1969), 418–25.

ON OLIGOPOLISTIC MARKETS FOR NONRENEWABLE NATURAL RESOURCES*

TRACY R. LEWIS AND RICHARD SCHMALENSEE

Noncooperative oligopoly behavior in nonrenewable resource markets is analyzed under stationary conditions assuming perfect information. The existence of Cournot-Nash equilibria in output paths is established under standard cost and demand assumptions, and a number of comparative dynamic results are obtained. If all suppliers have the same costs, for instance, and total reserves are fixed, either increasing the number of suppliers or equalizing their reserve holdings causes more rapid resource use. If suppliers' costs differ, it is shown that equilibrium involves inefficient production; high-cost reserves may even be exhausted before low-cost reserves.

Considerable effort has been devoted to the theoretical analysis of the effects of supply-side market structure on the pattern of exploitation of nonrenewable resources. Weinstein and Zeckhauser [1975], Stiglitz [1976], and Sweeney [1977] have compared competitive and monopolistic exploitation policies, while Salant [1976], Lewis and Schmalensee [1978, 1979], and Gilbert [1978] have considered markets in which a cartel faces price-taking buyers and competitive fringe suppliers. The theoretical literature on oligopolistic markets for nonrenewable resources, markets with "few" important suppliers, is much thinner. It seems to consist of some remarks by Salant [1976, Appendix B], a preliminary comparative dynamic exercise by Lewis and Schmalensee [1979, Section 4], and an analysis of existence and uniqueness of equilibrium by Salant [1979].[1] This relative neglect cannot be defended by arguing that such market structures have little empirical importance. All markets considered by Pindyck [1977b, 1978a], for instance, are either actually or potentially (with cartel breakdown) oligopolistic.

The present essay derives some of the basic properties of noncooperative equilibria (described more fully below) in oligopolistic markets for nonrenewable natural resources under simplifying assumptions. The stationary model analyzed here seems the most natural intertemporal extension of the standard static Cournot model of oligopoly equilibrium: output level choice in the static framework is replaced here by choice of an output *path* over time. Neither the

* We wish to thank Robert S. Pindyck and a referee for useful suggestions. Since completing this paper, we have learned about a very interesting analysis of natural resource production under oligopolistic conditions developed independently by Loury [1980].

1. The report in which Salant [1979] is embedded provides a most interesting simulation analysis of an oligopolistic resource market.

The Quarterly Journal of Economics, November 1980 0033-5533/80/0095-0475$01.70

Cournot model nor the noncooperative model of this paper can be defended as universally descriptive. But both are tractable representations of oligopoly situations, both have at least a degree of coherence and plausibility, and both may yield useful insights and intuitions. Given the state of static oligopoly theory, we see no defensible, tractable alternative to the Cournot-Nash cooperative approach taken here, but we would not argue that this approach should be taken as the last word. In light of these considerations, it may or may not be reassuring that the general message of our analysis seems to be that natural analogs of many of the properties of the static Cournot model hold in the dynamic situation considered here.

We begin by presenting our assumptions and notation, describing some general properties of equilibria, and establishing the existence of equilibria. Section II provides some comparative dynamic properties of equilibria in which all sellers have the same costs. We show there, among other things, that increases in the number of sellers or equalization of their reserve holdings (total reserves constant) tends to speed up resource use. Section III deals with the case of unequal costs. Equilibria are characterized in somewhat more detail, and it is shown that the industry equilibrium output path is produced inefficiently. It is demonstrated by example that noncooperative equilibrium may entail the exhaustion of high-cost deposits of a resource before the exhaustion of low-cost deposits.

I. Existence and Properties of Equilibrium

In order to see with some clarity how different oligopoly structures interact with the dynamics inherent in natural resource markets, we follow the papers cited above and make the sort of simplifying assumptions common in the literature begun by Hotelling [1931].[2] First, exploration does not occur in the world of this model, and all reserve stocks are known. There exist N "firms," which may be ordinary firms, nations, cartels, or other resource owners, with firm i's reserves at time zero equal to I_i. Let I be the sum of the I_i. Second, each firm i can extract its reserves (and transport them to market) at a constant unit cost $C_i \geq 0$; there are neither depletion effects nor capacity constraints. Let $q_i(t)$ be firm i's rate of production at time t, and let $Q(t)$ be the sum of the $q_i(t)$.

2. Most of the assumptions that follow have been relaxed somewhere in the literature, though usually only one at a time and never in the context of an oligopoly model. In addition to the papers cited thus far, see Schmalensee [1976a], Loury [1978], Pindyck [1978b], Arrow [1979], and the references they cite.

Third, the model is partial equilibrium and stationary; consumers are passive price-takers and their behavior can be summarized by the smooth inverse demand function $P(t) = P[Q(t)]$, with $P' < 0$. There is a single, constant discount rate, r. Following Salant [1976] and others, the inverse demand curve is assumed to satisfy the following:

(D.1) $P(0) = F$, a finite constant greater than the largest of the C_i;

(D.2) Demand elasticity, $E = -(1/P')(P/Q)$, is strictly decreasing in Q (or increasing in P);

(D.3) There exists a price $\mathbf{P}$ such that $\mathbf{P}\{1 - [1/NE(\mathbf{P})]\}$ equals the smallest of the C_i.

The "choke price" F may be thought of as determined by the cost and other properties of some sort of backstop, with demand declining smoothly to zero as the price of the resource becomes high enough. If F does not exceed the largest of the C_i, the set of firms must be redefined, since price can never rise above F. Assumption (D.2) is sufficient but not necessary for industry marginal revenue to be declining in Q whenever it is positive; it is thus a strong convexity assumption. Assumption (D.3) plays much the same role here as Salant's [1976] assumption of a point of unit elasticity; it serves to rule out pathological and technically troublesome behavior of P and E as Q becomes large. It is a bounding assumption and is applied by the plausible assumption that demand is finite at zero price.

Finally, the nature of equilibrium must be clarified. We shall be concerned with solutions to a noncooperative game with full information, in which each firm chooses its time-path of output, $q_i(t)$, to maximize its net wealth subject to the reserve constraint, taking as fixed the output plans of all other producers. An equilibrium exists when no $q_i(t)$ can profitably be changed. The presumption of noncooperative behavior is strong, as is the assumption that firms know each other's output paths in advance. The latter comes close to the assumption of complete futures markets.[3] This sort of equilibrium has been explored widely enough in the natural resources context and elsewhere, however, to make our application of it here of some interest, if not to establish its descriptive value.

3. The validity of this equilibrium concept under conditions of incomplete futures markets with a dominant firm has been explored by Lewis and Schmalensee [1978,1979]. Under that structure, the ability to accurately estimate the current output of the dominant firm may serve to support an equilibrium of this basic type. It is worth noting that, in the terminology used by Pindyck [1977a], ours is an "open-loop" equilibrium in output paths, rather than a "closed-loop" equilibrium in reaction functions. The latter concept seems intractable in this model.

Under these assumptions, we can partially characterize an equilibrium reasonably simply, relying on the fact that each firm basically faces a relatively simple constrained maximization problem. Let $a(P) = -dP/dQ$, the absolute value of the slope of the market demand curve. Then at equilibrium there must exist a set of constants λ_i and functions $q_i(t)$ such that for $i = , \ldots , N$ and $t \geq 0$

$$\text{(1a)} \qquad e^{-rt}\{P(t) - q_i(t)a[P(t)] - C_i\} = \lambda_i, \quad \text{if } q_i(t) > 0;$$

$$\text{(1b)} \qquad e^{-rt}\{P(t) - C_i\} \geq \lambda_i, \quad \text{if } q_i(t) = 0,$$

and

$$\text{(1c)} \quad \lambda_i \geq 0, \quad I_i \geq \int_0^\infty q_i(t)dt, \quad \lambda_i\left[I_i - \int_0^\infty q_i(t)dt\right] = 0,$$

where $P(t)$ satisfies the demand constraint.

The second inequality in (1c) is the reserve constraint. The left-hand side of (1a) is the discounted net marginal revenue of firm i when $q_i(t)$ is positive and the other firms' outputs are taken as fixed. Demand assumption (D.2) implies that this is a decreasing function of $q_i(t)$, all else constant. It then follows from first principles that, unless firm i's discounted net marginal revenue is equal at each instant when it is producing (and nonnegative at all such instants), wealth can be increased by redistributing total production over time (or by reducing total production). The constant λ_i is then the marginal value of additional reserves, in units of wealth at time zero. Condition (1b) simply says that, if any firm rationally elects not to produce at any instant, discounted net marginal revenue at that instant with $q = 0$ cannot exceed discounted net marginal revenue at times when production optimally occurs. The third part of condition (1c) is a standard complementary slackness statement: reserves will be exhausted unless the marginal value of additional reserves is zero.

Suppose that at some instant m firms are producing, with $1 \leq m \leq N$. Differentiation of (1a) totally with respect to time and addition across producing firms yields an equation employed frequently in what follows:[4]

$$\text{(2)} \qquad \dot{P} = \frac{r[P(mE - 1) - \overline{C}(mE)]}{E[(m + 1) - Qa']},$$

where $\overline{C}$ is the average of the C_i for producing firms. The assumption that E rises with P can be seen to imply that

$$\text{(3)} \qquad Qa' < (E + 1)/E,$$

4. Dots denote time derivatives.

from which it follows that the denominator on the right side of (2) is positive as long as $Em > 1$. For given P, $\dot{P}$ is easily seen to be decreasing in C and increasing in m.

Using assumptions that resemble (ii) and (iii) above, Frank and Quandt [1963] establish the existence of equilibrium in a static Cournot oligopoly model. The work of Roberts and Sonnenshein [1976] indicates that assumptions of this sort are almost necessary for existence, in the sense that equilibria apparently exist only by chance or in very special cases if they are violated. Since our model is related to the Cournot model studied by these authors, worries about nonexistence of equilibria would seem to have more than usual force here. If our assumption did not suffice to establish existence, one might suspect them of either inconsistency or incompleteness. If equilibria cannot be shown to exist, it is hard to take the study of their properties very seriously.

As it happens, the assumptions made above suffice to ensure existence. Let T be the time at which all production of the resource ceases. Then the Appendix establishes[5]

PROPOSITION 1. A noncooperative equilibrium satisfying conditions (1) exists and involves (a) $Q(t) > 0$ for $0 \leq t < T$, (b) $\lambda_i > 0$ for $i = 1, \ldots, N$, (c) T finite, (d) $I_i = \int_0^\infty q_i(t)\, dt$ for $i = 1, \ldots, N$, (e) $P(t)$ continuous for $0 \leq t \leq T$, and (f) $P(t) \geq \mathbf{P}$ for $0 \leq t \leq T$.

From part (a) of the Proposition, some firms are operating at all times. Adding condition (1a) across the operating firms, the numerator on the right of (2) is seen to equal $rm\bar{\lambda}Ee^{rt}$, where $\bar{\lambda}$ is the average of the λ_i of the m operating firms. By (b) of Proposition 1, this means that the numerator on the right of (2) is always positive. This in turn directly implies that $mE > 1$ at all times, which along with (3), implies that the denominator on the right of (2) is positive also. Thus, P is always strictly increasing. Price starts out at some level not below $\mathbf{P}$ and rises continuously and monotonically until it reaches F in finite time, whereupon demand and the resource market vanish forever as the last remaining reserves are exhausted. Total output is positive and decreasing at all times, and it follows from (e) of Proposition 1 that $Q(t)$ declines smoothly to zero as t approaches T.

Let us define market marginal revenue in the usual fashion:

5. Salant [1979] had independently developed a fixed-point argument similar to that used in the Appendix, and employed it both to study the existence of equilibrium when marginal cost is increasing in current output and to compute equilibrium paths for a variety of particular structures.

$$MR = P - aQ. \tag{4}$$

The arguments of the preceding paragraphs, along with (1a), (2), and (3) above, then serve to establish

PROPOSITION 2. In equilibrium with m firms producing, (a) $0 < \dot{P} \leq r(P - \overline{C})$, with strict inequality for finite m, and (b) $\dot{MR} \geq r(MR - \overline{C})$, with strict inequality for $m > 1$.

Hotelling [1931] established that (price-marginal cost) grows at the rate of interest under competition in models of this sort, while (marginal revenue-marginal cost) grows at the same rate under monopoly. Proposition 2 indicates, as one might expect, that noncooperative oligopoly equilibria are intermediate between these polar cases in this dimension.

II. EQUAL COSTS

In this section, we make the simplifying assumption that $C_i = C$ for all i. Proposition 2 implies that $(P - C)$ is always growing at a rate less than r in this case. This, along with conditions (1a) and (1b), implies that all firms with positive reserves will produce at time zero. As long as net marginal revenue when $q = 0$, $(P - C)$ grows at a rate less than the rate of interest, so that discounted net marginal revenue declines, it does not pay to postpone the start of production. On the other hand, some firms may exhaust their reserves and cease producing before P reaches F. From these remarks and Proposition 1, it follows that equilibrium in the equal costs case can be characterized by a set of positive, finite exhaustion times $\{T_i\}$ and shadow values of reserves $\{\lambda_i\}$, such that for $i = 1, \ldots, N$,

$$e^{-rt}\{P(t) - q_i(t)a[P(t)] - C\} = \lambda_i, \quad 0 \leq t \leq T_i, \tag{5a}$$

$$q_i(t) = 0, \quad t > T_i, \tag{5b}$$

and

$$\int_0^{T_i} q_i(t)dt = I_i. \tag{5c}$$

From Proposition 1, $P(t)$ is continuous. It is then apparent that for (5a) and (5b) to hold, the $q_i(t)$ must also be continuous at all times. If not, some firm's net marginal revenue would change discontinuously at some instant, and this cannot happen in equilibrium. (Such changes imply the desirability of shifting production either before or after the discontinuity until the jump is eliminated.) Each of the $q_i(t)$ must thus decline smoothly to zero as t approaches T_i.

It follows from (5a) that, if firms i and j are producing at any instant, and if $\lambda_i < \lambda_j$, then $q_i > q_j$. This holds even in the limit as $q_j \rightarrow 0$, so it must be that $T_i > T_j$. But it is then clear that firm i's total production exceeds firm j's, so that $I_i > I_j$. If firms have unequal reserves, it must be that the firm with the larger reserves has the smaller value of λ, produces more at each instant, and exhausts later.[6] The first of these suggests that firms with smaller reserves have greater exploration incentives, all else equal.

The preceding paragraph also indicates that if $I_i = I/N$ for all i, it must be that $\lambda_i = \lambda$ for all i. If firms have equal reserves in addition to equal costs, equilibrium is thus unique and is described by (5) with all i subscripts removed.[7] For this symmetric case, a large number of comparative dynamic results can be established:

PROPOSITION 3. If $C_i = C$, and $I_i = I/N$ for $i = 1, \ldots, N$, the noncooperative equilibrium is unique. Holding I constant, increases in N (a) increase $\dot{P}(P)$, (b) lower T, (c) reduce price at every level of reserves encountered, thus lowering $P(0)$ and leading to more rapid resource use, (d) raise λ, the marginal value of reserves to each firm, (e) lower the present value of total industry profits, and (f) raise discounted producer's plus consumers' surplus.

These comparative dynamic results are proved in Lewis and Schmalensee [1979, Section 4] for the case $C = 0$, and only trivial modifications are required to generalize that proof.[8] In the symmetric case, Proposition 3 indicates that increases in N tend to make the market more nearly competitive, as in the standard static Cournot model.[9] Increases in N serve to speed up resource use, in the sense that the total time to exhaustion is reduced and total production is larger at any level of reserves. The latter assertion follows directly from a proof that, with I constant, increases in N lower the initial price.

6. Salant [1976, Appendix B] notes the latter two points in a special case of this model with only two firm types.

7. In fact, we have been able to demonstrate uniqueness without the assumption of equal reserves (but using the assumption of equal costs by using the same sort of proof by contradiction employed to show uniqueness in a dominant extractor model in Lewis and Schmalensee [1979]). As the proof is somewhat tedious and the result neither very surprising nor useful for any of our comparative statements, we do not report it. Salant [1979] offers a proof of uniqueness when demand is linear and marginal cost is increasing in current output.

8. By setting $q_i = Q/N$, conditions (5) can be defined for non-integer N. The proof of (e) and (f) in Lewis and Schmalensee [1979] relies on demand being sufficiently smooth that $Q(t)$ is a differentiable function of N for all t.

9. On the relations between competition and monopoly in natural resource markets under these demand assumptions, see Weinstein and Zeckhauser [1975], Stiglitz [1976], and Sweeney [1977]. On the effects of changing N in static Cournot models, see Okuguchi [1973].

Because reserves are drawn down faster with more firms, though, such increases will always make the price higher than it otherwise would have been at some future *times*. Part (d) of Proposition 3 indicates that more intense rivalry, even though it reduces prices and profits, may enhance exploration incentives. Parts (e) and (f) of that Proposition support the standard intuition that when rivalry intensifies, consumers' gains outweight producers' losses.

We now want to consider the implications of unequal reserves, still assuming cost equality. Let $P^s(t)$ and T^s be the price path and exhaustion time, respectively, in the symmetric case. Consider another market with the same demand curve and the same values of r, C, I, and N, but in which $I_i \neq I_j$ for some i and j. Let the price path and exhaustion date in this asymmetric case be $P^a(t)$ and T^a, respectively. We now show that $P^s(0) < P^a(0)$ and $T^s < T^a$.

From the discussion above, $T_i \neq T_j$ in the asymmetric case, so that the number of firms operating decreases over time; an instant before T^a, fewer than N firms are operating. In contrast, all N firms operate until T^s in the symmetric case. Let T_1^a be the time at which the first firm (the one with the smallest of the I_i) runs out of reserves in the asymmetric case.

Suppose that $P^s(0) \geq P^a(0)$. Since the motion of price until time T_1^a in both cases is given by equation (2), with $m = N$ and $\overline{C} = C$, it must be that $P^s(T_1^a) \geq P^a(T_1^a)$. But after T_1^a, fewer firms are operating in the asymmetric case, so that equation (2) implies $\dot{P}^s(P) > \dot{P}^a(P)$ for all relevant values of P. (Recall that the right-hand side of (2) is increasing in m, all else fixed.) It follows that $P^s(t) > P^a(t)$ for all $t > T_1^a$. Since $P^a(T^a) = P^s(T^s) = F$ and prices are monotone-increasing, $T^s < T^a$. But this implies that total production in the asymmetric case exceeds that in the symmetric case and this is impossible. The supposition at the start of the paragraph must therefore be false. Thus, $P^s(0) < P^a(0)$. It the price paths never cross, equality of total production will be violated. It follows from the arguments just above that they can cross only after T_1^a and that they can cross only once. After the crossing, $P^s(t) > P^a(t)$, so that $T^s < T^a$, as was to be shown. We have thus completed the proof of

PROPOSITION 4. If $C_i = C$ for $i = 1, \ldots, N$, and $I_i > I_j$ for some i and j, then (a) firm i produces more at each instant than firm j and ceases production later, and (b) $P(0)$ and T are greater than if the I_i were all equal, so that resource use is less rapid.

There are many measures of concentration in the industrial organization literature, the most appealing of which have the property that they increase as the number of firms falls and as some measure of the inequality of firm size rises.[10] Propositions 3 and 4 taken together indicate that, if firm size is defined as total reserves, changes of both these sorts tend to produce higher initial prices and thus higher prices at any given level of total reserves. These results are thus consistent with the usual notion that increases in concentration worsen market performance, with the problem here being excessive conservation of the resource.

Both of these Propositions depend on the equal cost assumption, under which the level of reserves provides a natural, exogenous measure of firm size. The association between concentration and market performance in the static Cournot theory is of a rather different sort. Rader [1972, pp. 270–73], for instance, shows that the H index of concentration (equal to the sum of squared market shares) relates market demand elasticity to the percentage markup over (an average across the firms of) marginal cost. But in that model, market shares are endogenously determined as a function of marginal costs; H is thus logically endogenous. If all firms have equal costs in the Cournot structure, all will have equal market shares. In natural resource markets, even with equal costs, market shares vary over time if reserve holdings are unequal, so that reserve holdings provide the only reasonable basis for judgments about concentration. If costs differ, however, it seems apparent that any measure of concentration that relates to pricing behavior must reflect both costs and reserve holdings, but it is not yet clear to us how any such measure might be constructed.

III. Unequal Costs

We now allow both costs and reserve levels to differ among firms. Let us order firms so that $C_1 \leq C_2 \leq \cdots \leq C_N$, with at least one of the inequalities strict. We first investigate whether or not firms with different C_i produce simultaneously in equilibrium.

If production were efficient, in the sense that the discounted cost of producing the actual total output stream $Q(t)$ were minimized, this could not occur. Suppose, for simplicity, that the C_i are all different. Then it is reasonably well-known that, as long as the rate of interest is positive, efficiency requires exploiting only firm 1's reserves until they are exhausted at time T_1, then exploiting only firms 2's reserves until some later time T_2, and so on. It is never efficient to produce from any but the lowest cost reserves that are currently available; see

10. See, for instance, Hart [1975] and the references he cites.

Solow [1974] for a discussion. To see what drives this, suppose that extraction of a small amount dq of I_1 were postponed from t_1 to t_2, where $t_1 < T_1 < t_2$, with the same amount of I_2 extracted at t_1 rather than at t_2. The change in the present value of cost is then

$$(6)\quad dq\{\exp(-rt_1)(C_2 - C_1) + \exp(-rt_2)(C_1 - C_2)\}$$
$$= dq\{\exp(-rt_1)(C_2 - C_1)[1 - \exp(-r(t_2 - t_1))]\} > 0.$$

Under monopoly, with all reserves in the hands of a single firm, discounted costs are minimized, and reserves with different costs are not simultaneously exploited. Under competition, with many small firms operating at each cost level, production is also efficient.

But under oligopoly, efficient exploitation is impossible because equilibrium *must* involve periods during which reserves with different costs are simultaneously exploited. To show this, let us first note that the $q_i(t)$ are continuous in any oligopoly equilibrium along with (from Proposition 1) $P(t)$ and $Q(t)$. Given continuity of $P(t)$, continuity of the $q_i(t)$ follows directly from conditions (1a) and (1b). Now assume the contrary: suppose oligopoly equilibrium output path $Q(t)$ is produced efficiently. Suppose that there are N_1 firms with unit cost equal to C_1, and N_2 firms with unit cost equal to C_2. By the assumption of efficiency, there must be a time T_1 such that all firms in the first group cease production at T_1 and all firms in the second group start at that time. By the continuity of the $q_i(t)$, however, this must mean that $Q(t)$ approaches zero as t approaches T_1 from either above or below. This means that price falls after T_1, and that is impossible. The only way that $Q(t)$ can be kept smooth at T_1 with a shift of all production from firms in the low-cost group to those in the next higher cost group would be for some of the $q_i(t)$ to be discontinuous. But, given the continuity of $P(t)$, conditions (1) rule out the discontinuous change in discounted marginal revenue that would result. We have thus established

PROPOSITION 5. If $C_i \neq C_j$ for some i and j, the discounted cost of producing the equilibrium total output stream, $Q(t)$, is not minimized, because firms with different costs are simultaneously producing at some times.

This inefficiency result is the intertemporal analog of the standard finding of inefficiency in asymmetric static Cournot oligopoly; see Schmalensee [1976b] for a simple example. In that context, efficiency requires equating marginal costs of all plants operated at any time, but only in symmetric cases does noncooperative behavior produce this result. These inefficiency results indicate that to think of oligopolistic markets as intermediate between monopoly and competition in all respects is to overlook potentially important qualitative differences.

A number of important properties of equilibria when costs are unequal are given by Propositions 1 and 2. It turns out to be difficult to say much more. In particular, many of the properties of equilibria with equal costs do not generalize. In order to illustrate the variety of possible outcomes when costs differ, the rest of this section is devoted to establishing and discussing

PROPOSITION 6. If $C_i > C_j$ for some i and j, then in noncooperative equilibrium it is *possible* that (a) some firms do not begin production at time zero, (b) firm i's output is greater than firm j's at some times and less at others, and (c) production inefficiency is sufficiently severe that firm i's reserves are exhausted before firm j's.

We argue for the first possibility in general terms; the second and third are illustrated by a simple example.

Suppose that there is initially only one firm on the market: firm 1 with unit cost C_1 and reserves I_1. Acting as a monopolist, that firm would choose price path $P^m(t)$. Now add a second firm to the market, with cost C_2 between $P^m(0)$ and F and reserves I_2 less than I_1. Let $P^d(t)$ be the noncooperative duopoly equilibrium price trajectory. It is clear that by making C_2 sufficiently close to F and I_2 sufficiently small relative to I_1, $P^d(0)$ can be made to be below C_2. But this means that firm 2 must wait until price has risen (a finite distance) above C_2 before it begins production. (Recall that $q_2(t)$ must then rise continuously from zero; it cannot jump to a positive value.) There is nothing pathological about such behavior, of course. Inefficiency arises only because both firms produce for some time, not because firm 2 waits.

At any instant, conditions (1a) and (1b) describe a Cournot equilibrium in the q_i, based on unit costs equal to $(C_i + \lambda_i e^{rt}) \equiv C_i'$. It follows from condition (1a) that $q_i > q_j$ if and only if $C_i' < C_j'$. When the C_i are all equal, the rankings of the C_i' cannot switch over time, and as Proposition 4 establishes, the rankings of the q_i cannot change either. But if the C_i are not equal, it would appear possible for $(C_i' - C_j')$, and thus $(q_i - q_j)$, to switch sign once before T for some i and j. To show that appearances are not deceiving in this case and to establish part (c) of Proposition 6, we turn to an example.

Suppose that $N = 2$, $0 < C_1 < C_2 < F$, and demand is linear with $P(Q) = F - aQ$. With this demand structure, $\mathbf{P} = (F + 2C_1)/3$. Let

$P_0 = (F - C_1)/2$, and assume that $C_2 < C_1 + P_0$. Then it is straightforward to show from conditions (1) that if $P \geq P_0$ and firm 1 (firm 2) is acting as a monopolist, $(P - C_2)[(P - C_1)]$ is growing at a rate less than r. This means that if $P_0 \leq P \leq F$ and either firm is producing, the other will rationally elect to produce also. If $F < 7C_1$, it follows that $P_0 < \mathbf{P}$, so that both firms will begin production at time zero because P will always exceed P_0 in equilibrium (from Proposition 1).[11]

At any time when both firms are producing, conditions (1a) can be written as

$$d_1 \equiv F - C_1 = \lambda_1 e^{rt} + 2aq_1 + aq_2,$$

$$d_2 \equiv F - C_2 = \lambda_2 e^{rt} + aq_1 + 2aq_2. \tag{7}$$

Let $s_2 = q_2/Q$ be the high-cost firm's share of total output. By solving the two equations above for s_2, differentiating, and manipulating the result, one obtains

$$\dot{s}_2 = [r(d_1 + d_2)/3aQ][s_2 - s_2^*], \tag{8a}$$

where

$$s_2^* = (2d_2 - d_1)/(d_1 + d_2). \tag{8b}$$

It is clear that $s_2 = s_2^*$ is an unstable node of (8a). If s_2 begins above s_2^*, s_2 increases and reaches unity in finite time; if $s_2(0) < s_2^*$, s_2 declines with time and reaches zero in finite time. With C_1 fixed, s_2^* is a decreasing function of C_2; it is easy to show that $C_2 > C_1$ implies $s_2^* < 1/2$.

In order to establish part (b) of Proposition 6, it must be shown that equilibria exist in which $s_2(t)$ takes on values greater than and less than $1/2$. Suppose that we have $s_2^* < I_2/I < 1/2$. Then if $s_2(0) \leq s_2^*$, firm 2's share of production at each instant will be less than its share of total reserves. Similarly, if $s_2(0) \geq 1/2$, q_2/Q exceeds I_2/I at all times. Thus, in order to meet the reserve constraint, $s_2(0)$ must be between s_2^* and $1/2$, so that $s_2(t)$ is below $1/2$ for a finite time and above $1/2$ thereafter, and the proof is complete.

This example illustrates the difficulty, discussed at the end of Section II, of measuring concentration in a sensible way in this sort of market. In the preceding paragraph, firm 2 has higher costs and lower reserves than firm 1 does, but after a finite period of time its output comes to exceed that of firm 1. Indeed, since s_2 goes to unity,

11. This illustrates, in an inverse fashion, the discussion just below Proposition 6: if cost differences are minor, there is a presumption that all firms will begin production at the same time.

firm 2 is a monopolist for the latter part of the resource market's existence.

Part (c) of Proposition 6 is established by showing that equilibrium may involve $s_2^* > s_2(0)$, since then s_2 goes to zero in finite time, and this means that firm 2 exhausts its reserves, while firm 1 is still producing at a positive rate. (We noted above that if this happens and if C_1 and C_2 are close enough together, condition (1b) is satisfied thereafter for firm 2.) Suppose that $0 < I_2/I < s_2^*$. If $s_2(0)$ exceeds s_2^*, it follows that q_2/Q always exceeds I_2/I. But this is impossible, so that $s_2(0)$ must be less than s_2^* (and greater than I_2/I). Firm 2, the high-cost firm, then exhausts first, and the proof of Proposition 6 is complete.

Notice that in this example, as in general, the patterns described by (b) and (c) of that Proposition cannot occur when $C_1 = C_2$. Then $s_2^* = 1/2$, (b) is impossible because I_2/I cannot be between s_2^* and $1/2$, and (c) is impossible because there is no high-cost firm. The example explored here suggests that these patterns are, at least, more likely when the higher cost firm has the smaller reserves. Moreover, (b) may be more likely when reserve differences are moderate relative to cost differences, while (c) may require reserve differences that are substantial relative to cost differences. Whether these features of this example hold in general is not known, however.

IV. Conclusions

Our results indicate that many of the central features of static Cournot oligopoly models are present in approximately generalized form in Cournot-Nash models of nonrenewable resource markets. The generalizations involved raise some interesting questions, however, as the discussion above of concentration measures indicates. Further, a number of the results obtained here depend crucially on the inherent dynamics of resource markets: the form of inefficiency discussed in Proposition 5 is the best example.

There are, of course, a number of directions in which the analysis here might be extended. Some of the demand and cost assumptions in Section I might be relaxed, for instance, or stability of equilibrium might be analyzed. Some of the conjectures above in connection with Proposition 6 might be explored. We would repeat the caveat at the start of this essay, however: the value of all of this depends critically on the value of the Cournot-Nash assumption of noncooperative equilibrium in output paths. Other equilibrium concepts should be explored.

Appendix: Proof of Proposition 1

It will first be shown that conditions (1) imply (a)–(d) directly. A fixed-point argument using the λ_i is then used to establish the existence of equilibrium, and (e) and (f) are proved in the course of that demonstration.

To prove (a), suppose the contrary. First, suppose that $Q(t)$ jumps to zero at some t'. From (1a) and (1b) in the text, this would involve a discontinuous increase in the net marginal revenue of all firms. In the face of such a jump, all firms operating just before t' would have an incentive to delay some production. Thus, $Q(t)$ cannot jump to zero in equilibrium. Second, suppose that $Q(t)$ declines smoothly to zero at some time t' before T. This means that $Q(t'')$ is positive for some $t'' > t'$. Thus, for at least one firm conditions (1) imply that

$$e^{-rt'}[F - C_1] \leq \lambda_i = e^{-rt''}[P - aq_i - C_i].$$

But since $t'' > t'$, and $(P - aq_i) < F$, this is clearly not possible. Thus, $Q(t)$ cannot decline to zero before T. It follows that $Q(t) > 0$ for $0 \leq t < T$, as was to be shown, and that $Q(t)$ declines smoothly to zero as t approaches T.

It follows also that equation (2) holds until time T, since $m \geq 1$. Adding conditions (1a) for operating firms, we may easily see that the numerator on the right of (2) equals $rmE\bar{\lambda}e^{rt}$, where $\bar{\lambda}$ is the average of the λ_i for the operating firms. If $\bar{\lambda} = 0$ at any instant, price will be constant forever afterwards, as (1b) makes it clear that no entry will ever occur. But total production must then eventually come to exceed total reserves for all operating firms, so this is impossible. It is clear from (1b) that if $(C_i + \lambda_i e^{rt})$ exceeds F, firm i will not produce. If $\lambda_i > 0$, this must occur in finite time. If any of the λ_i are zero, it then follows that the corresponding firms will be alone in the market after finite time. But we just showed that this implied that those firms would produce constant q_i forever after, violating (1c), so that λ_i cannot be zero for any i in equilibrium, establishing (b) of the Proposition. The argument just above then establishes (c), and (d) follows from (1c) in the text.

Let λ be a vector of the $N \lambda_i$, and let Λ be the set of all λ such that $0 \leq \lambda_i \leq (F - C_i)$. This set is clearly compact and convex. We construct a continuous function γ mapping Λ into itself. By the Brouwer fixed point theorem, this function must have a fixed point, a vector $\lambda*$ such that $\lambda* = \gamma(\lambda*)$. The function γ is defined so that any such fixed point corresponds to an equilibrium satisfying conditions (1).

The first step is to obtain the path $P(t)$ satisfying (1a) and (1b) for any $\lambda \epsilon \Lambda$. Let us define

$$\text{(A1)} \quad Z_i(P,\lambda_i e^{rt}) = \max[0, P - C_i - \lambda_i e^{rt}], \quad i = 1, \ldots, N.$$

These functions are continuous, but not differentiable when $P = C_i + \lambda_i e^{rt} \equiv P_i^c(t)$. Next define the continuous function $\phi(P,\lambda e^{rt})$:

$$\text{(A2)} \quad \phi(P,\lambda e^{rt}) = \sum_{i=1}^{N} Z_i(P,\lambda_i e^{rt}) - a(P)Q(P).$$

It is apparent that ϕ is continuous everywhere, though it is not differentiable when $P = P_i^c$ for any i. Comparison of equations (1) in the text shows it is clear that Z_i is positive in equilibrium if and only if firm i is producing, and $\phi[P(t),\lambda e^{rt}] = 0$ for all t.

For given λ, P, and t, let m be the number of positive Z_i. If $P = F$, $Q(F) = 0$ implies that, no matter what m is, $\phi(F,\lambda e^{rt}) \geq 0$. Now suppose that $P = \mathbf{P}$, defined in assumption (D.3) in the text. If $m = 0$ at this price, $\phi = -aQ \leq 0$. If $m > 0$, (A1) and (A2) imply that

$$\text{(A3)} \qquad \phi(P,\lambda e^{rt}) = m\{P[1 - (1/mE)] - \overline{C} - \overline{\lambda} e^{rt}\},$$

where $\overline{C}$ and $\overline{\lambda}$ are the averages of the C_i and λ_i, respectively, for firms with positive Z_i. When $P = \mathbf{P}$,

$$P[1 - (1/mE)] \leq \mathbf{P}\{1 - [1/NE(\mathbf{P})]\} = \min_i C_i \leq \overline{C},$$

so that $\phi(\mathbf{P},\lambda e^{rt}) \leq 0$ by (A3). Because ϕ is continuous, there thus exists a scalar $P^e \epsilon [\mathbf{P},F]$ such that $\phi[P^e,\lambda e^{rt}] = 0$.

Now let us show that P^e thus defined is unique. As long as $P \neq P_i^c$ for all i, the derivative $\partial\phi/\partial P$ exists and satisfies

$$\text{(A4)} \qquad \frac{\partial\phi}{\partial P} = m + 1 - a'Q > m\left[1 - \left(\frac{1}{mE}\right)\right] = \frac{[\phi + \overline{C} + \overline{\lambda} e^{rt}]}{P},$$

from (3) in the text and (A3) above. It follows that if $\phi[P_i^c,\lambda e^{rt}] \neq 0$, $i = 1, \ldots, N$, then $\partial\phi/\partial P$ is positive whenever $\phi = 0$, and P^e is unique. Suppose, then that $\phi[P_i^c,\lambda e^{rt}] = 0$ for some i. From the first equality in (A4), this means that $\partial\phi/\partial P$ increases discontinuously at a point where $\phi = 0$ as m increases by one. If this derivative is positive in the limits as P approaches P_i^c from above and below, the continuity of ϕ establishes that ϕ is increasing for all P in a neighborhood of P^e, and uniqueness still holds. But $(\partial\phi/\partial P)$ cannot be negative in the limit as P approaches P_i^c from below, since (A4) indicates that ϕ cannot decline to zero as P increases. Since $(\partial\phi/\partial P)$ increases at P_i^c, it cannot be negative in the limit as P approaches P_i^c from above either, so it must be positive in both limits. Thus there is one and only one P that solves $\phi(P,\lambda e^{rt}) = 0$ for any $\lambda \epsilon \Lambda$ and $t \geq 0$. This equation thus defines an implicit function $P^e(\lambda e^{rt})$, with range contained in the interval $[\mathbf{P},F]$.

Next we must demonstrate that this function is continuous. Suppose the contrary: suppose that there exist sequences $\{t^i\}$ and $\{\lambda^i\}$, such that $t^i \geq 0$ and $\lambda^i \epsilon \Lambda$ for all i, and such that the sequence $\{\lambda^i e^{rt^i}\}$ approaches $\lambda^0 e^{rt^0}$, with $\lim P^3[\lambda^i e^{rt^i}] = P^e[\lambda^0 e^{rt^0}] + K$, where $K \neq 0$. By construction, $\phi[P^e(\lambda^i e^{rt^i}),\lambda^i e^{rt^i}] = 0$ for all i, so that by the continuity of ϕ,

$$\lim \phi[P^e(\lambda^i e^{rt^i}),\lambda^i e^{rt^i}] = \phi[P^e(\lambda^0 e^{rt^0}) + K,\ \lambda^0 e^{rt^0}] = 0.$$

But this implies that there are two P's that solve $\phi[P,\lambda^0 e^{rt^0}] = 0$, and we showed above that this could not occur. The continuity of P^e is thus established by contradiction. Since P^e depends on λe^{rt}, it follows that in equilibrium $P(t)$ is continuous, establishing part (e) of the Proposition.

We can now define the function γ on which the existence proof turns. Pick a vector $\lambda \epsilon \Lambda$. For all $t \geq 0$, compute $\hat{P}(t) = P^e(\lambda e^{rt})$. Then use (1a) in the text and (A1) to obtain for all i and t

$$\hat{q}_i(t;\lambda) = Z_i[\hat{P}(t),\lambda_i e^{rt}]/a[\hat{P}(t)].$$

Integration then yields total resource production for each firm implied by λ and conditions (1a) and (1b):

$$\hat{I}_i(\lambda) = \int_0^\infty \hat{q}_i(t;\lambda)dt, \quad i = 1,\ldots,N.$$

It follows from the continuity of P^e that the $\hat{I}_i$ are continuous. Next, define

(A5) $$D_i(\lambda = \max[\hat{I}_i(\lambda) - I_i,0], \text{ and } E_i(\lambda) = \max[I_i - \hat{I}_\infty(\lambda),0], \quad i = 1,\ldots,N.$$

The components of the vector-valued function γ are then given by

(A6) $$\gamma_i(\lambda) = \lambda_i + (F - C_i - \lambda_i)\{1 - \exp[-D_i(\lambda)]\} - (\lambda_i)\{1 - \exp[-E_i(\lambda)]\}, \quad i = 1,\ldots,N.$$

This continuous function takes points in the compact, convex set Λ into points in that same set, so by the Brouwer theorem it has at least one fixed point, one vector $\lambda * \epsilon \Lambda$ such that $\gamma_i(\lambda *) = \lambda_i^*$ for $i = 1,\ldots,N$.

By construction, conditions (1a) and (1b) are satisfied by the $\hat{q}_i(t;\lambda *)$. To prove that fixed points of γ are equilibria, it remains only to show that conditions (1c) are satisfied. The first inequalities in (1c) are satisfied by the definition of Λ. Suppose that $D_i > 0$ at a fixed point for some i, so that $\hat{I}_i$ exceeds I_i and the inequality constraint on total production in (1c) is violated. Since E_i must then be zero for that i by (A5), it follows that $\lambda_i^* = F - C_i$. But since P can never exceed F, it follows from (A1) that Z_i is never positive, thus $\hat{q}_i$ is never positive, $\hat{I}_i$ is zero, and $\hat{I}_i$ cannot exceed I_i. This contradicts the assumption that $D_i > 0$, so D_i must equal zero at a fixed point and the reserve inequality constraints in (1c) are satisfied at fixed points of γ. Now suppose that $E_i > 0$ at a fixed point. As above, this implies that total production falls short of total reserves for firm i with $\lambda_i^* = 0$. This would not violate (1c). But the argument for (b) of the Proposition shows that if $\lambda_i = 0$, firm i's total production as given by (1a) and (1b) in the text is infinite. Thus, E_i cannot be positive at a fixed point. At such points, as at equilibria, $E_i = D_i = 0$; initial reserves are exactly used up by all firms. The proof of Proposition 1 is complete.

UNIVERSITY OF BRITISH COLUMBIA
MASSACHUSETTS INSTITUTE OF TECHNOLOGY

References

Arrow, K. J., "Optimal Pricing, Use and Exploration of an Uncertain Natural Resource Stock," in P. T. Liu, ed., *Dynamic Optimization and Applications to Economics* (New York: Plenum Press, 1979).
Frank, C., and R. E. Quandt, "On the Existence of the Cournot Equilibrium," *International Economic Review,* IV (Jan. 1963), 92–96.
Gilbert, R. J., "Dominant Firm Pricing Policy in a Market for an Exhaustible Resource," *Bell Journal of Economics,* IX (Autumn 1978), 385–96.
Hart, P. E., "Moment Distributions in Economics: An Exposition," *Journal of the Royal Statistical Society, Series A,* XXXVIII (1975), 423–34.
Hotelling, H., "The Economics of Exhaustible Resources," *Journal of Political Economy,* XXXIX (April 1931), 137–75.
Lewis, T. R., and R. Schmalensee, "Cartel Deception in Nonrenewable Resource Markets," Working Paper 1010-78, Sloan School of Management, M.I.T., July 1978.
——, and ——, "Cartel and Oligopoly Pricing of Nonrenewable Natural Resources," in P. T. Liu, ed., *Dynamic Optimization and Applications to Economics* (New York: Plenum Press, 1979).
Loury, G. C., "The Optimal Exploitation of an Unknown Reserve," *Review of Economic Studies,* XLV (Oct. 1978), 621–36.
——, "A Theory of 'Oil'igopoly: Cournot Equilibrium in Exhaustible Resource Markets with Fixed Supplies," mimeo, University of Michigan, 1980.
Okuguchi, K., "Quasi-Competitiveness and Cournot Oligopoly," *Review of Economic Studies,* XL (Jan. 1973), 145–48.
Pindyck, R. S., "Optimal Economic Stabilization Policies under Decentralized Control and Conflicting Objectives," *IEEE Transactions on Automatic Control,* AC-22 (Aug. 1977a), 517–30.
——, "Cartel Pricing and the Structure of the World Bauxite Market," *Bell Journal of Economics,* VIII (Autumn 1977b), 343–60.
——, "Gains to Producers from the Cartelization of Exhaustible Resources," *Review of Economics and Statistics,* LX (May 1978a), 238–51.
——, "The Optimal Exploration and Production of Nonrenewable Resources," *Journal of Political Economy,* LXXXVI (Oct. 1978b), 841–62.
Rader, T., *Theory of Microeconomics* (New York: Academic Press, 1972).
Roberts, J., and H. Sonnenschein, "On the Existence of Cournot Equilibrium Without Concave Profit Functions," *Journal of Economic Theory,* XIII (1976), 112–17.
Salant, S. W., "Exhaustible Resources and Industrial Structure: A Nash-Cournot Approach to the World Oil Market," *Journal of Political Economy,* LXXXIV (Oct. 1976), 1079–93.
——, "Existence and Uniqueness of Equilibrium and Convergence of Algorithms," Appendices 1 and 2 in S. W. Salant, *et al.,* "Imperfect Competition in the International Energy Market: A Computerized Nash-Cournot Model," Report Submitted to the Office of Policy and Evaluation, Department of Energy, Washington, ICF Incorporated, May 1979.
Schmalensee, R., "Resource Exploitation Theory and the Behavior of the Oil Cartel," *European Economic Review,* VII (April 1976a), 257–79.
——, "Is More Competition Necessarily Good?" *Industrial Organization Review,* IV (1976b), 120–21.
Solow, R. M., "The Economics of Resources and the Resources of Economics," *American Economics Review,* LXIV (May 1974), 1–14.
Stiglitz, J. E., "Monopoly and the Rate of Extraction of Exhaustible Resources," *American Economic Review,* LXVI (Sept. 1976), 655–61.
Sweeney, J., "Economics of Depletable Resources: Market Forces and Intertemporal Bias," *Review of Economic Studies,* XLIV (Feb. 1977), 125–42.
Weinstein, M., and R. J. Zeckhauser, "The Optimal Consumption of Depletable Natural Resources," this *Journal,* LXXXIX (Aug. 1975), 371–92.

NOTES ON ADVERTISING, ECONOMIES OF SCALE, AND ENTRY BARRIERS*

A. MICHAEL SPENCE

The paper discusses how advertising and economies of scale in production interact to produce economies of scale. The latter are defined to occur when costs per dollar of revenues decline with revenues. It is argued that, in an industry with differentiated products and advertising, it is the declining costs per collar of revenues rather than declining production costs per unit of output that directly affects entry barriers and the profitability of established firms.

I. INTRODUCTION

In the industrial organization literature, advertising is claimed to be an entry barrier or to reflect some aspect of structure that creates an entry barrier. There is considerable empirical literature exploring the relationship between advertising and profitability.[1] In it, several observations of a theoretical kind are made in defense of the view that advertising has an entry-deterring effect. It is sometimes said that advertising has the character of a fixed cost, and therefore, if advertising is required to sell the good, it has the effect of creating economies of scale. It is also asserted that there are threshold effects in advertising, creating regions of increasing returns to scale. In addition, the technology and markets for producing and distributing advertising "messages" may exhibit declining average costs. And finally, if a certain amount of advertising is "needed," and if it is expensive, then it may contribute to risk or to absolute capital requirements barriers. As the reader will see, I agree that advertising can contribute to entry barriers by augmenting the extent to which profitability increases with firm size.

The problem with the propositions above is not that they are untrue, but rather that they are incomplete. They are clearly relevant to the issue of the relation of advertising to entry barriers. While advertising may have something of the character of fixed costs, it also influences demand by making it possible to sell a higher volume at a fixed price, or the same volume at a higher price, or some combination of these. Thus, the fact that costs per unit of physical volume

* This research was supported by the National Science Foundation, Grant No. SOC-78-21016. The author would like to thank an anonymous referee for numerous helpful comments.

1. See, for example, Comanor and Wilson [1974], Porter [1976], and Telser [1964].

The Quarterly Journal of Economics, November 1980 0033-5533/80/0095-0493$01.50

may decline with output does not imply the conclusion that operating at relatively small scales is impossible. Similarly to say that a certain amount of advertising is "needed" to counteract rivals' advertising, or to establish a market position, begs the question or assumes the conclusion.

Because advertising is designed to influence demand and therefore prices, it cannot be discussed entirely in terms of economies of scale or cost advantages in the normal sense. Yet scale economies, or advantages of size, are clearly relevant to the entry barrier problem. But demand and prices are affected by advertising so that the relevant measure of scale economies is to be found in the relation between the firm's revenues and its costs per dollar of revenue, rather than in the relation between costs and output in physical units. The purpose of this short paper, therefore, is to explore the circumstances under which advertising plays a role in causing costs per dollar of revenues to decline. The paper argues that advertising can contribute to the entry barriers by influencing the extent of economies of scale when measured properly.

In examining the relation between costs and revenues, we will hold industry revenues constant. In so doing, we shall be examining the relative profitability of firms of varying sizes in an industry with a given total dollar sales volume.

From a modeling standpoint, my strategy is simply to reduce the problem with advertising to an "equivalent" problem that involves only economies of scale and a homogeneous good. Once this is done, various models of entry and entry deterrence can be applied. I would prefer to postpone the discussion of the entry-deterring effects of advertising to a later section, after the simple model has been set forth.

II. THE MODEL

This model has some special features, but it is useful for illustrating the determinants of the economies of scale and the role of advertising in erecting entry barriers. Its qualitative predictions, I think, are not misleading in these areas.

The market has several sellers, each selling differentiated products. The sales in physical units of product i (by firm i) are x_i. The advertising expenditures of firm i are a_i. The inverse demand for the ith product is

$$p_i = B(m)(A(a_i)x_i^{\alpha-1}),$$

where

$$m = \sum_{j=1}^{n} \frac{A(a_j)x_j^{\alpha}}{\alpha},$$

and where $A(a_j)$ is a function of the advertising level of firm j, $j = 1, \ldots, n$, and $B(m)$ is a scalar function that declines as m increases.[2] Note that there are no income effects in these inverse demand functions.

Given these assumptions, the revenues of the ith firm are

$$R_i = p_i x_i = B(m)A(a_i)x_i^{\alpha}.$$

Assume that the production costs of the ith firm are $c(x_i)$, and that the advertising expenditures in dollars are a_i, so that total costs are $c(x_i) + a_i$. This permits us to write the profits of the ith firm as

$$\Pi_i = B(m)A(a_i)x_i^{\alpha} - (c(x_i) + a_i).$$

The transformation that turns this into a problem that looks like a homogeneous good problem is straightforward. It is $y_i = A(a_i)x_i^{\alpha}$, $i = 1, \ldots, n$. With this set of new variables,

$$\Pi_i = B(m)y_i - h(y_i,a_i),$$

where

$$m = \frac{1}{\alpha} \sum_{j=1}^{m} y_i,$$

and the costs are

$$h(y_i,a_i) = c\left(\left(\frac{y_i}{A(a_i)}\right)^{1/\alpha}\right) - a_i.$$

With that transformation, it is as if there were a single homogeneous good, where y_i is the output of firm i and the industry inverse demand is $B(m)$. With or without that interpretation, the advertising variable appears only in the cost function. Other firms' advertising affects a particular firm's revenues and hence profits, but only through the effect on the y_i's. And the y_i's are determined not only by advertising, but also by output (or, equivalently, price). The firm's decision can be thought of then as selecting revenues, that is, y_i, and then minimizing costs per dollar of revenues with respect to advertising.

2. The inverse demands derive from a consumer benefit function of the form $V(m) = \int_0^m B(s)ds$. Inverse demands are (in the absence of income effects),

$$\frac{\partial V}{\partial x_i} = B(m)A(a_i)x_i^{\alpha-1}.$$

Define

$$\phi(y) = \min_a \left[c\left(\left(\frac{y}{A(a)}\right)^{1/\alpha}\right) + a \right].$$

The questions that we are interested in, and the questions of most direct relevance to the presence or absence of entry barriers are whether, when, and to what extent do costs per dollar of revenue decline with revenue, or when is $\phi(y)/y$ declining in y. However, note that $R_i = B(m)y_i$. The question posed above about costs per dollar of revenues assumes that m, and therefore industry revenues, are held constant.[3] I want to emphasize here that no assumption is being made as yet about competitive interaction. There is, I am *not* assuming that when firm i raises y_i, other firms contract so that m, and hence industry revenues, are constant. What we are doing is asking how the costs per dollar of revenues vary with market share. Allowing y_i to vary with m held fixed is equivalent to allowing $s_i = y_i/m$, the firms' share, to vary. There are obviously a whole variety of models or hypotheses about how market shares are determined interactively. But they are not the subject of the present discussion.

To gain some insight into the factors influencing returns to scale in the revenue sense, let us consider the following example. Suppose that $A(a) = ba^{1/\gamma}$ or $a = \phi A^{\gamma}$, and that $c(x) = cx^{\beta}$. Here $1/\gamma$ is the elasticity of the firm's inverse demand with respect to advertising, and β is the elasticity of costs with respect to output. If $\gamma < 1$, there are "increasing returns" to advertising expenditures, and if $\beta < 1$, there are declining average production costs. The parameter α is related to the price elasticity of demand in a manner that will be discussed shortly.

The inverse demand for the ith firm's product is

$$p_i = B'(m)ba_i^{1/\gamma} x_i^{\alpha-1}.$$

Hence $1/\gamma$ can be interpreted as the advertising elasticity of the inverse demand. With m fixed, we can invert to get the direct demand:

$$x_i = (bB'(m))^{1/(1-\alpha)} a_i^{1/\gamma(1-\alpha)} p_i^{-1/(1-\alpha)}.$$

Thus, the advertising elasticity of demand with m fixed is $1/\gamma(1-\alpha)$, and the price elasticity is $1/(1-\alpha)$.

With these assumptions, the costs can be written as

$$h(y,a) = cy^{\beta/\alpha}A^{-\beta/\alpha} + \phi A^{\gamma}.$$

3. In this model, industry revenues are $B(m)m\alpha$. Thus, if m is held constant, industry revenues are constant.

The cost-minimizing level of advertising corresponds to the following value for A:

$$A = \left(\frac{\beta c}{\alpha\phi\gamma}\right)^{\alpha/(\beta+\alpha\gamma)} y^{\beta/(\beta+\alpha\gamma)}.$$

As a result, $\phi(y)$, the minimized costs, are

$$\phi(y) = ky^{\theta}, \tag{1}$$

where $\theta = \beta\gamma/(\beta + \alpha\gamma)$, and k is a constant.[4]

Formula (1) contains the information we need concerning economies of scale. The costs per dollar of revenues (holding industry revenues fixed at any level) will decline if $\theta < 1$, and conversely.

Using the formula for θ, one finds that $\theta < 1$ if $1/\gamma + \alpha/\beta > 1$, or $1/\gamma > 1 - \alpha/\beta$. If $\alpha > \beta$, this inequality will always hold. I shall interpret this case below, but it is not the one of greatest interest to us. If $\alpha < \beta$, then there are economies of scale in the revenue sense if $\gamma < \beta/(\beta - \alpha)$. Recall that there are "increasing returns to scale" in advertising if $\gamma < 1$. It is *not* necessary for $\gamma < 1$ for the condition $1/\gamma > (\beta - \alpha)/\beta$ to hold, because the right-hand side of this inequality is less than one. It is sufficient for there to be declining costs per dollar of revenue, that there be returns to scale in advertising, but it is not necessary to have returns to scale in the partial effect of advertising.

We have seen that $\theta < 1$ if $1/\gamma > (\beta - \alpha)/\beta$. Multiplying both sides of this inequality by $1/(1 - \alpha)$, we have

$$1/\gamma(1 - \alpha) > (\beta - \alpha)/(\beta - \beta\alpha).$$

The left-hand side is the advertising elasticity of direct (as opposed to inverse) demand. This elasticity also need not be greater than one for there to be revenue returns to scale unless $\beta \geqq 1$, which means that there are constant or diminishing returns to scale in production. This may be the most straightforward way of seeing the tradeoff between advertising elasticities of demand and output elasticities of costs in achieving revenue returns to scale.

As we saw earlier, $1/\gamma$ is the elasticity of inverse demand with respect to advertising, and β is the elasticity of costs with respect to

4. In fact, k can be calculated easily. It is

$$k = \frac{1}{\theta}(\gamma\phi)^{\theta/\gamma}\left(\frac{c\beta}{\alpha}\right)^{\alpha\theta/\beta}.$$

output. The parameter $1 - \alpha$ is the quantity elasticity of the inverse demand with m held constant. Thus, because of the structure of the model, $1/(1 - \alpha)$ is the price elasticity of demand with m constant. Formally, let $\eta_a = 1/\gamma(1 - \alpha)$, the advertising elasticity of demand, and $\eta_p = 1/(1 - \alpha)$, the elasticity of demand with respect to price. With these definitions, the condition required for costs per dollar of revenues to decline with revenues (so that there are economies of scale in this sense) becomes

$$\eta_a > \eta_p - (\eta_p - 1)/\beta. \tag{2}$$

It should be noted that in this model, with a constant price elasticity of demand, $\eta_p \leq 1$. I should also note that the reason price elasticities enter this formula is because we are studying the relation between costs and revenues, rather than that between costs and output.

From formula (2) one can see that there are a variety of circumstances under which there are advantages to size. To begin with the familiar ones, if β is small, there will be substantial economies of scale in production. That will cause the right-hand side of (2) to decline and reduce the advertising elasticity required to achieve declining costs of revenues. In particular, if $\beta < 1 - 1/\eta_p$, then economies of scale in production will outweigh the declining returns from extra output due to product differentiation. In this case, even if $\eta_a = 0$ (i.e., advertising has no impact), there will be returns to scale in generating revenues. This is the case $\beta < \alpha$, which I referred to earlier.

Provided that $\beta < 1$, the effect of an increase in η_p is to lower the right-hand side of (2), and thus to increase the likelihood of declining costs of revenues. This means that, as the products become naturally closer substitutes, there is more likely to be an advantage to size.[5] In fact, raising η_p (equivalent to raising α) has the same effect as lowering β. Recall that the costs expressed in terms of y and A are $cA^{-\beta/\alpha}y^{\beta/\alpha} + \phi A^{\gamma}$. Proportional changes in α and β clearly have no effect.

If $\eta_a > \eta_p$, that will ensure an advantage to size, regardless of the presence or absence of production economies or diseconomies. Now $\eta_a > \eta_p$ when $\gamma < 1$, or the advertising elasticity of inverse demand is greater than one. In this sense, scale economies in the production

5. In this model, the parameter α is related to the cross elasticities of demand. To see this, we can calculate the cross elasticity of p_i with respect to x_j. It is

$$\frac{x_j}{p_i}\frac{\partial p_i}{\partial x_i} = \alpha\frac{mB'(m)}{m}s_j,$$

where s_j is the market share of firm j. Thus, for a given m and s_j, the larger α is, the larger the cross elasticity will be.

or impact of advertising messages may be said to be strongly related to declining costs of revenues and therefore to entry barriers. They are sufficient to generate revenue returns to scale, independent of production or the other elasticities.

Formula (2) can be thought of as a generalization of some cases that are familiar. If $\eta_a = 0$, then we have costs declining with market share if economies of scale outweight the diminishing returns associated with the product differentiation effect ($\alpha < 1$). If $\eta_p = \infty$ (or $\alpha = 1$) so that there is no product differentiation effect, and $\eta_a = 0$, then unit costs of revenues decline with share if $\beta < 1$, i.e., there are production economies of scale.

III. An Alternative Derivation of the Economies of Scale Proposition

There is an alternative method of deriving the economies of scale proposition that is akin to the familiar theory of production and cost. Earlier, we defined $y = Ax^{\alpha}$. Noting that $A = ba^{1/\gamma}$, and defining $z = x^{\beta}$, we can express the profits of the representative firm as follows:

$$\Pi = B(m)ba^{1/\gamma}z^{\alpha/\beta} - (cz + a).$$

If one were to minimize costs for a given level of revenue, then one would minimize $cz + a$ subject to $B(m)ba^{1/\gamma}z^{\alpha/\beta} \gtrless R$, for some R. This is the analogue of the problem of minimizing costs with a Cobb-Douglas production function. We know the average costs will decline with R if the "production function" exhibits economies of scale, i.e., $1/\gamma + \alpha/\beta > 1$. This is precisely the condition we derived earlier. Here it is clear that advertising and output are combined to generate revenues. If we rescale output so that costs are linear in output as well as in advertising, then there will be economies of size if there are increasing returns to scale in the production function that generates revenues from the good itself and advertising. Built into that production function are (1) the technology and costs for producing advertising messages, (2) the impact of advertising messages on consumers (threshold effects, for example), (3) the production technology for the good itself, and (4) the degree of substitutability of the goods (captured by α in this model).

Therefore there is no unambiguous answer to the question of whether advertising erects entry barriers. It sometimes works in conjunction with scale economies and inherent diseconomies associated with differentiated products to cause costs per dollar of revenues to decline with revenues. It is possible, of course, that the elasticities are such that the inequality (2) is reversed, in which case the unit cost of revenues rises with revenues.

The preceding model does provide some guidance concerning the circumstances under which advertising is likely to contribute significantly to returns to scale in producing revenues. First, as noted earlier, economies of scale in the relation between demand and advertising expenditures are sufficient to cause costs per dollar of revenue to decline as revenue or market share increases.[6] The greater the revenue returns to scale are, the lower is the inherent product differentiation ($1 - \alpha$ in this model). And, of course, production economies and advertising economies are complements in the production of revenue returns to scale. It is worth noting that there can be revenue returns to scale even if there are diminishing returns to both physical volume and advertising, taken separately.

IV. Entry Barriers: An Example

This particular model, because it can be transformed into one that looks like a homogeneous goods model, lends itself to any one of a variety of models that are available for analyzing entry barriers in the presence of economies of scale. In this section the analogue of the limit price, or more accurately, the limit quantity model, is used to determine the entry-deterring levels of industry revenues. We then explore the relations among market shares, price cost margins, and advertising to sales ratios.

In carrying out these calculations, it is assumed that $B(m) = qm^{-\epsilon}$. As before, costs are given by $cx_i^\beta + a_i$. In addition, $y_i = A_i x_i^\alpha$ and $A_i = ba_i^{1/\gamma}$.

The minimized costs for a given level of y_i are ky_i^θ, where

$$\theta = \left(\frac{1}{1/\gamma + \alpha/\beta}\right),$$

as in the previous section.[7] The assumption about entry is that in response to entry, established firms maintain both their output and

6. These economies can result from economies in either production or from the impact of advertising messages, or from a combination of the two.

7. In this model, we assume that $\theta + \epsilon - 1 > 0$, which ensures that the industry inverse demand lies below average costs at very high levels of output.

TABLE I

$f_1 = 1 - Ds_i^{\theta-1}$	Price-cost margin of firm
$f = 1 - D \sum_{j=1}^{n} s_j^{\theta}$	Industry price-cost margin
$r_i = \theta/\gamma D s_i^{\theta-1}$	Advertising to sales ratio of firm
$r = \frac{\theta}{\gamma} D \sum_{j=1}^{n} s_j^{\theta}$	Industry advertising to sales ratio
$f_i = 1 - \gamma/\theta r_i$	Relation between price-cost margin and advertising to sales ratio for firm
$f = 1 - \gamma/\theta r$	Relation between price-cost margin and advertising to sales ratio for the industry

advertising levels at the pre-entry levels.[8] We then look for the entry-deterring level of m, call it $\overline{m}$. The entry-deterring level $\overline{m}$ is the solution to

$$\max_{y} \, [q(\overline{m} + y)^{-\epsilon} y - k y^{\theta}] = 0.$$

The entry-deterring level of $\overline{m}$ (and hence industry revenues) is given by

$$\overline{m}^{\theta+\epsilon-1} = q/k(\epsilon + \theta - 1)^{\epsilon+\theta-1}\epsilon^{-\epsilon}(1 - \theta)^{1-\theta}.$$

Intra-Industry Profitability and Advertising Behavior

Given the entry-deterring level of revenue, the profits of established firms are determined by market shares. I shall not attempt to explain what determines those shares. In a real world case, the shares would be determined by the evolutionary phase of the industry before it reached its mature phase.[9]

The relations among shares, margins, and advertising to sales ratios are of interest because they correspond to observable variables

8. This is the analogue in this world of the limit price, or more accurately, limit quantity model for homogeneous products.

9. For a discussion of some of the features of that process, see Spence [1979]. Because of such considerations as the inversibility of investment in capacity, I do not want simply to assume that there is either a monopoly or a number of identical firms.

that appear in the empirical literature. Let s_i be the share of firm i, f_i be the price cost margin for firm i (revenues minus costs, divided by revenues), and r_i be the advertising to sales ratio. Similarly, let f be the industry price cost margin and r the industry advertising to sales ratio. Define D in terms of $\overline{m}$ as follows:

$$D = \frac{k}{q}\overline{m}^{\epsilon+\theta-1} = (\epsilon + \theta - 1)^{\epsilon+\theta-1}\epsilon^{-\epsilon}(1-\theta)^{1-\theta}. \tag{3}$$

The results of solving the model for price-cost margins and advertising to sales ratios are summarized in Table I. In all of what follows, $m = \overline{m}$, the entry deterring level of m.

Let me briefly indicate the derivation of these formulae. The profits of the ith firm are

$$\Pi_i^\epsilon = q\overline{m}^{-\epsilon}y_i - ky_i^\theta.$$

Letting $s_i = y_i/\overline{m}$, and noting that revenues for firm i are $R_i = q\overline{m}^{-\epsilon}y_i$, One finds that the price cost margin f_i is

$$f_i = \frac{\Pi^i}{R_i} = 1 - \frac{k}{q}\overline{m}^{\epsilon+\theta-1}s_j^{\theta-1}.$$

The definition of D from (3) above gives

$$f_i = 1 - Ds_i^{\theta-1}.$$

For the industry

$$f = \sum_{j=1}^{n} s_j f_j = 1 - D\sum_{j=1}^{n} s_j^\theta.$$

If one calculates the minimum costs for a given level y_i, one finds that

$$\text{cost} = ky_i^\theta$$

and that

$$\text{cost} = (\gamma/\theta)a_i.$$

Thus, the optimal level of advertising, given y_i, is

$$a_i = (\theta/\gamma)ky_i^\theta.$$

Since revenues are $q\overline{m}^{-\epsilon}y_i$, the advertising to sales ratio is

$$r_i = \frac{a_i}{R_i} = \frac{\theta}{\gamma}\frac{k}{q}\overline{m}^{\epsilon}y_i^{\theta-1}.$$

Since $s_i = y_i/\overline{m}$,

$$r_i = \theta/\gamma D s_i^{\theta-1}.$$

This is the formula reported in Table I. For the industry

$$r = \sum_{j=1}^{n} s_j r_j = \frac{\theta}{\gamma} D \sum_{j=1}^{n} s_j^{\theta}.$$

For the remainder of this paper, I shall assume that $\theta < 1$ so that there are declining costs of revenues in the sense described earlier. Built into these formulae is a measure of concentration.[10] Define

$$C = \left[\sum_{j=1}^{n} s_j^{\theta-1}\right].$$

If there were just one firm, then $C = 1$. If there are n firms of equal size, $C = n^{\theta-1}$. This declines toward zero as n increases. The industry price cost margins and advertising to sales ratio depend directly on concentration, measured in this way:

$$f = 1 - \frac{D}{C}$$

$$r = \frac{\theta}{\gamma}\frac{D}{C}.$$

The price-cost margin rises with concentration, while the advertising to sales ratio falls.

To interpret these formulae, we begin with the parameter D. D is determined by the parameters θ and ϵ and is a summary of the effects of entry barriers. That is to say, D determines rates of return and price-cost margins. Therefore, whatever factors affect D can be thought of as entry barriers. The parameter θ is the elasticity of costs with respect to market share. We have already seen that θ depends upon α, β, and γ, as discussed earlier. The parameter ϵ is an aggregate or industry elasticity. It is the elasticity of the general price level with respect to m. From (3)

$$D(\theta,\epsilon) = (\theta + \epsilon - 1)^{\theta+\epsilon-1}\epsilon^{-\epsilon}(1-\theta)^{1-\theta}.$$

As a function of ϵ, D is declining. That means that effective entry barriers increase as ϵ rises. As a function of θ, D has a minimum at $\theta = 1 - \epsilon/2 > 1 - \epsilon > 0$. Figure I shows lines of constant D in $\theta - \epsilon$ space.

10. Note that the relevant definition of concentration depends upon the parameter θ, which determines the extent of cost advantage associated with size.

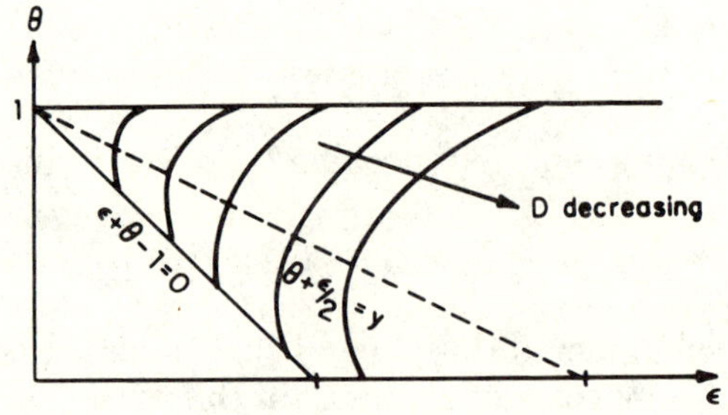

FIGURE I

It is interesting to note that the effective entry barriers as measured by D are not monotonic in θ. Rather, for a given θ, entry barriers are maximized at an intermediate level of θ; $\theta = 1 - \epsilon/2$. As ϵ rises, the optimal (from the standpoint of erecting entry barriers) degree of returns to scale increases (i.e., θ falls).

Let us return to the price-cost margins and advertising to sales ratios. Fixing the parameters, if we look across firms within an industry with these characteristics, price-cost margins and market shares will move together, while advertising to sales ratios and shares move in the opposite direction. Eliminating shares, price-cost margins and advertising to sales ratios to move in opposite directions. It is important to emphasize that this applies to firms within a market, and not across industries.

The industry price-cost margin increases with entry barriers and increases with concentration. The industry advertising to sales ratio increases with concentration, but declines with entry barriers as measured by D. However, both firm and industry advertising to sales ratios increase with θ and $1/\gamma$, which are the elasticity of costs with respect to share and the elasticity of inverse demand with respect to advertising expenditures, respectively.

Interindustry Comparisons

It is well-known that industries with high advertising to sales ratios tend to be profitable. Regressions of profitability on advertising to sales ratios and concentration generally yield positive and significant coefficients for the advertising to sales ratio variable. Of course there is some controversy about the interpretation of this type of regression result.

The model presented in the preceding pages implies, among other things, that with the parameters that determine entry barriers held constant, profitability and advertising will move in opposite directions. The question naturally arises whether that is consistent with the regression results, or whether it contradicts them.

These observations are not inconsistent. While profitability and advertising move in opposite directions when only concentration varies, if the entry barrier parameters vary as they will across industries, then advertising and profitability may move together in cross section.

To take a simple example, in the previous model let $\alpha = \beta = \epsilon = 1$. In this case, with $\phi = 1/\gamma$,

$$D = 1/(1 + \phi)\phi^{\phi/(1+\phi)}.$$

It is easy to verify that for $\phi < 1$, D is declining in ϕ, so that f rises as ϕ increases. On the other hand, $r = \phi/1 + \phi\, D/C$. For $\phi \geqslant 0.8$ roughly, r is increasing in ϕ as well. Thus, for ϕ in the range [0.8,1.0], profits and advertising move together.

This example does not dispose of the issue, but it illustrates the general point that, in a cross-industry sample, it is not unreasonable to expect profits and advertising to be positively correlated, when the advertising elasticity is near one.

The subject of what is contained in the cross-industry studies, and how it relates to formal models of single markets or industries, is too extensive to permit a full treatment here. It will be the subject of a subsequent paper.

V. Conclusions

By using a simple model, I have tried to indicate that there is something like a production function for a firm, the output of which is revenues, the inputs, the product in physical units, and advertising expenditures. If that production function is characterized by increasing returns to scale, then a firm's cost per dollar of revenue generated will decline with market share. Those increasing returns to scale will then have a role in creating entry barriers analogous to the role of ordinary returns to scale in the case of a homogeneous, undifferentiated product.

When we look inside the relation between revenues and costs, we find that output and advertising are used to generate revenues in combinations that are determined by the elasticities that characterize the response of prices to output and to advertising expenditures, and by the elasticity of average production costs with respect to physical volume. It is the combination of these elasticities and not the magnitude of any one taken separately that determines the extent to which costs per dollar of revenues decline with revenues. It is quite possible to have diminishing returns to advertising alone, limited (or no) production economies, and considerable inherent differentiation, and still have overall economies of scale in the relevant sense. Just as in production theory, it is the sum of the response elasticities to the inputs that determines the extent of the returns to scale.

Finally, when there are activities such as advertising that influence prices and demand it is useful, where possible, to discuss returns to scale in terms of the relation of costs to revenues or market share, and not in terms of physical units. The latter can be misleading with respect to entry barriers and the relevant advantages to size.

The technique for assessing the impact of advertising on economies of scale employed here can be used in a more general setting. It is not necessary to reduce the problem to a homogeneous good model, for example. To illustrate, let $\phi_i(x_i,a_i) = A_i(a_i)x_i^{\alpha_i} = y_i$. If perceived consumer benefits are a function $B(y_i, \ldots, y_n) = B(y)$, then the revenues of firm i are

$$R_i(y) = \alpha_i B_i(y) y_i.$$

The costs, expressed in terms of y_i and a_i, are

$$c_i((y_i/A_i)^{1/\alpha_i} + a_i).$$

As in the earlier analysis, advertising appears in the costs. Advertising is set to minimize costs, given y_i. Once that is done, what remains is a differentiated product model, the equilibrium of which depends upon the structure of $B(y)$.[11]

The point that I want to make is that it is simply not necessary that the model be reducible to a homogeneous product problem for this technique for understanding the role of advertising to be useful.

HARVARD UNIVERSITY

11. For analyses, see Spence [1976] and Dixit and Stiglitz [1977]. It is perhaps worth noting in passing that the model in the paper, even without advertising, can be reduced to a homogeneous good model with the substitution $y_i = Ax_i^{\alpha}$. If $c(x_i) = cx_i^{\beta}$, then costs in terms of y_i are $c(y_i/A)^{\beta/\alpha}$. Average costs decline with y_i if $\beta/\alpha < 1$, which is a special case of the model in the text with a zero advertising elasticity. Note that β/α is declining in α. This means that inherent differentiation (i.e., small α) tends to offset product scale economies, as one would intuitively expect.

References

Comanor, W., and T. Wilson, *Advertising and Market Power* (Cambridge: Harvard University Press, 1974).

Dixit, A., and J. E. Stiglitz, "Monopolistic Competition and Optimum Product Diversity," *American Economic Review,* XXXIV (1944), 297–308.

Porter, M. E., *Interbrand Choice, Strategy, and Bilateral Market Power* (Cambridge: Harvard University Press, 1976).

Spence, M., "Product Selection, Fixed Costs, and Monopolistic Competition," *Review of Economic Studies,* XLIII (1976), 217–35.

——, "Investment, Strategy, and Growth in a New Market," *Bell Journal of Economics,* X (1979), 1–19.

Telser, L., "Advertising and Competition," *Journal of Political Economy,* LXXII (1964), 537–62.

WEALTH AND WEALTH PROXIES IN A PERMANENT INCOME MODEL

J. WALTER ELLIOTT

This paper formulates a permanent income model of consumer expenditures. Through use of this model, measures of permanent income are examined that are alternatively based on (a) measured income patterns, (b) stocks of consumer liquid assets, (c) stocks of consumer financial assets, and (d) stocks of consumer real and financial assets. Using assets in permanent income measures is found to improve upon using measured income patterns in explaining consumer expenditure. Consumer assets are further found not to be treated as one homogeneous stock by consumers. Money and risky financial assets contribute significantly to explaining consumer spending, while savings and real assets are of no value. Finally, asset effects on consumption are found to be inelastic but statistically significant.

This paper examines the value of new measures of the stock of consumer wealth in explaining U. S. consumer expenditures over 1960–1977. Measures of permanent income that rely upon current consumer income and upon the stock of consumer wealth are developed. These measures are alternatively used in a permanent income model, producing results that bear upon whether wealth-based or income-based surrogates for permanent income better explain consumer expenditures. The results suggest that unique information may be contained in explicit measures of consumer wealth, and that not all components of wealth are treated by households as homogeneous.

I. INTRODUCTION

The period from the publication of Keynes's *General Theory* to the appearance of the permanent income and life cycle theories of Friedman [1957] and Ando and Modigliani [1963] is marked by a primary concern with current income flow as the budget constraint or scale variable in most macroeconomic models of consumer spending. Permanent income models produced renewed if not new interest in the role of the stock of wealth in consumer expenditures, since permanent income is defined as an expected yield on the stock of total wealth. Scattered empirical tests of asset effects on consumption in the United States and the United Kingdom made in the mid-1960s and early 1970s produced mixed results, and were generally

The Quarterly Journal of Economics, November 1980 0033-5533/80/0095-0509$02.70

characterized by inadequate data on household asset stocks.[1] The most explicit continuing attention to asset effects on consumption during this period is undoubtedly associated with studies by Modigliani [1971], in conjunction with development of the MPS model.

However, the bulk of the empirical time series work done on the permanent income hypothesis in the late 1960s and 1970s sidesteps the direct use of wealth measures by taking permanent income to be some type of a smoothed function of measured consumer income, rather than inferring values of permanent income from a measure of the stock of wealth. Representative of this flow of work are papers by Zellner and Geisel [1970], Laumas and Mohabbat [1972], Darby [1974, 1975], and Holbrook and Stafford [1971].

The prevalent approach thus associates fluctuations in permanent income with patterns of change in measured income, instead of relying upon fluctuations in the measured stock of wealth to indicate fluctuations in permanent income.

Until recently, little a priori reason has existed for exploring alternatives to the prevalent approach to approximating permanent income. Time series data on consumer wealth stocks have been available only in fragments, while data on consumer income have been relatively complete and well understood. However, with the development by the Federal Reserve Board of data on consumer wealth stocks, the base is laid for deriving a reasonably reliable time series on the stock of nonhuman wealth owned by consumers. This development renews interest in the question of whether explicit use of measures of nonhuman wealth in permanent income formulations produces a surrogate more or less sensitive for this purpose than permanent income measures based on current income. It also renews interest in the broader questions of the empirical role of wealth in consumption spending, and in the most empirically useful definition of wealth itself.

These questions are of more than technical interest. Fluctuations in the value of consumer wealth holdings occur when stocks or bonds

1. Ando and Modigliani [1963] found statistically significant asset effects on consumption. Later studies, such as those of Bhatia [1972], Feldstein [1973], and Feldstein and Fane [1973] conducted empirical experiments with measures of asset stocks, with the general conclusion that asset effects on consumption are small in magnitude and not always statistically significant. However, studies done in conjunction with the MIT-PENN-SSRC [1973] model are contrary to this pattern, by finding sufficient evidence of asset effects to warrant giving emphasis to wealth effects as an important channel of influence upon consumer spending. For a recent example of this view, see Modigliani [1971]. Cross-sectional studies by Friend and Lieberman [1975] show significant asset effects on consumption from this perspective.

change in price, or when the stock of money held by consumers changes. Consumers' perceived stock of wealth may also change when residential structures appreciate or depreciate in market value. The use of explicit wealth measures in permanent income explanations of consumption associates these types of wealth changes with changes in consumer expenditures. In contrast, permanent income measures based on the prevalent approach of smoothing current consumer disposable income implicitly assume that changes in stock or bond prices, money holdings, or in the market value of real assets will not have a systematic current impact upon consumer spending. Whether this is in fact the case is an open question.

We examine these issues by first formulating a permanent income model into which we can alternatively place measures of permanent income based on wealth and upon current income. Several measures of consumer wealth are derived, reflecting successively broader definitions of effective wealth, along with a standard definition of permanent income based on current income. Experiments are then run on these wealth and income models using quarterly data from 1960–1977.

II. The Permanent Income Model

The permanent income model used here is a variation on a frequently used framework, recent examples of which can be found in papers by Poole [1972] and Darby [1974, 1975]. Pure consumption c_t^f is defined as a service flow. Besides consumption expenditures on pure services, c_t^f includes what Friedman [1957] called the use value of durables. This is similar to a rental value and can be expressed as the product of a rental price times the stock of durables. The rental price includes recovery of depreciation plus a real return. In this form, c_t^f does not correspond to the definition of consumer expenditure given in the National Income Accounts (NIA), due to the intermingling of assets and services in several NIA categories. However, the value of c_t^f can be approximated as follows:

$$c_t^f = c_t^n + (R + \delta)d_{t-1}, \tag{1}$$

where c_t^n is actual real GNP-type expenditures on consumer nondurables and services, d_{t-1} is the real stock of consumer durables at the end of period $t - 1$ (or start of period t), R is the expected real rate of interest appropriate to durables, and δ is the rate of depreciation in the durables stock.

We follow Darby and the empirical results of Fama [1975] in treating R as approximately constant over our sample. Fama's somewhat controversial results suggest that the real return expected on short-term financial assets in the United States has been approximately constant over the postwar period. The expression $(R + \delta)$ is the rate per real dollar of the durables stock.

Real expenditures on newly produced consumer durables, denoted as c_t^d, are made for replacement and to change the durables stock, i.e.,

$$c_t^d = \Delta d_t + \delta d_{t-1}, \tag{2}$$

where Δd_t is the change in the durables stock over time period t. With total NIA consumer expenditures c_t^x, defined as

$$c_t^x = c_t^n + c_t^d, \tag{3}$$

we can combine (1), (2), and (3) to obtain

$$c_t^x = c_t^f + \Delta d_t - R d_{t-1}. \tag{4}$$

The permanent income hypothesis asserts that

$$c_t^f = k y_{p,t} \qquad 0 < k < 1, \tag{5}$$

where $y_{p,t}$ is the flow of permanent real income and k is a coefficient whose value is assumed stable through time.

Explaining the change in the durables stock has been the subject of recent work by Juster and Wachtel [1972], as well as by Darby [1975] and others. In the present analysis the focus of attention is not upon obtaining a detailed structuring of the durables sector, but only to represent it sufficiently to free our income versus wealth comparisons from any serious specification error. Accordingly, the view we take here is that additions to durables stocks are fundamentally an allocation of saving flows to acquiring durables, and thus are part of an equilibrating process that involves other wealth components. Wealth consists of financial assets and real assets (durables). Accordingly, the allocation of saving flows to these asset categories is influenced by the rates of return on each category. Besides these price-theoretic terms, we follow Darby and others in presuming transitory income to be the principal budget constraint on the acquisition of durables. Representing in part the return on financial assets by a short-term interest rate r_t, the return on durables by the rental value of durables $(R + \delta)$, and transitory income by $y_{T,t}$, we have[2]

(6) $$\Delta d_t = f[y_{T,t}, r_t, (R + \delta)] \qquad f_2, f_3 < 0 \qquad f_1 > 0.$$

Treating the relationship generalized by (6) to be linear in the parameters $\lambda_1 \ldots \lambda_3$, we combine the model for Δd_t with expressions (4) and (5) to obtain a testable structure for consumer expenditures:

(7) $$c_t^x = ky_{p,t} + \lambda_1 y_{T,t} + \lambda_2 r_t + \lambda_3 (R + \delta) - Rd_{t-1} \qquad k, \lambda_1 > 0 \qquad \lambda_2, \lambda_3 < 0.$$

III. Alternative Measures of Permanent Income

The two formulations of permanent income we examine rely alternatively upon measured income and the stock of wealth. The first of these approaches follows a procedure frequently seen in recent years, starting with the following discrete-time variant of Friedman's original formulation:

(8) $$y_{p,t} = \beta y_t + (1 - \beta)(1 + g) y_{p,t-1},$$

where β is the weight of current income in permanent income and g is the growth rate of permanent income. We follow Darby's [1974, 1975] method of estimating g and $y_{p,0}$, where the latter is an initial value of y_p. Thus, the following equation is estimated over the sample period:

(9) $$\log(y_t) = a_0 + a_1 t,$$

where t is a quarterly index of time, beginning with a value of zero at the start of the sample period. Then, the estimated value of g is a_1 and the estimated value of $y_{p,0}$ is $\exp(a_0)$.[3] In his work with expression (8), Darby experimented with a range of values of β. This experimentation

2. This is somewhat similar to Darby's model for Δd_t, but much simpler. The present model does not contain the relative price ratios between durable and nondurable goods, the money supply, or permanent income. Darby found that the relative price ratio produced unsatisfactory results. In some preliminary exploration, I found the same thing. One possible reason for this is that the allocation of income between consumption and wealth additions is largely governed by permanent income, as Darby's model hypothesizes. The decision regarding the form of adding wealth (i.e., durables, securities, money) thus logically has little to do with relative prices between consumption goods and assets, but instead is related more fundamentally to the relative yields in the asset categories, as expression (6) reflects. I also followed Darby's use of an excess money balance term, and found it to be of no significance in either version of the present model.

3. The present estimate of expression (9) covers 1959.1 to 1978.1, and produces $g = 0.00911$ and $y_{p,0}$ for 1959.1 of 123.6 billions of 1972 dollars.

led to the conclusion that a quarterly value of 0.025 gave the best results in explaining consumption expenditures. In initial tests of the present model, we used Darby's results to narrow the range of possible β to three points: 0.025, 0.050, 0.075. Fits of the consumption model using $y_{p,t}$ based on these various β leads to the conclusion that $\beta = 0.025$ is the best of the three, as Darby found. Accordingly, the results we report below for the current income approach are based on a measure of $y_{p,t}$ calculated from expression (8) with $\beta = 0.025$. Transitory income is then $y_t - y_{p,t}$.

The measured income (y_t) series used in formulating permanent income is equal to real disposable income plus real undistributed corporate profits, where the latter is intended to be a surrogate for capital gains by households. Darby found this measure somewhat superior to other alternatives in explaining consumer expenditures.

The permanent income estimate based on explicit measures of the stock of consumer or household wealth treats the t-period expectation of permanent income as the expected income yield during t from the stock of wealth at the beginning of period t. Thus,

$$y_{p,t} = \gamma_1 \frac{A_{h,t-1}}{P_t} + \gamma_2 \frac{A_{n,t-1}}{P_t}, \tag{10}$$

where $A_{h,t-1}$ and $A_{n,t-1}$ are, respectively, household stocks of human and nonhuman wealth at the end of period $t-1$ or at the start of period t or both, and P_t is an index of consumer prices. γ_1 and γ_2 are the expected long-run rates of return on human and nonhuman wealth, respectively. They can be viewed as the geometric means of vectors of quarterly rates of return expected by households over the remainder of their permanent income cycle. If actual rates of return have a mean-reverting tendency and expectations are not biased, then γ_1 and γ_2 will tend to show only minor fluctuation over time, even though short-run fluctuations in short-run expected rates of return may be substantial. Thus, even though short-term fluctuations in prices of financial assets may cause a substantial change in the value of A, it is reasonable to suppose that the expected long-run rates of return per unit of human and nonhuman wealth will fluctuate by only a minor amount. As an approximation, we take both γ_1 and γ_2 as constant over our sample period.

The observable portion of wealth is A_n. To approximate the unobservable portion, we rewrite this portion of (10) as follows:

$$\frac{A_{h,t-1}}{P_t} = \frac{y^w_{p,t}}{\gamma_1}, \tag{11}$$

where $y^w_{p,t}$ is real permanent labor income expected during t from the yield on the stock of human capital at the start of t. Thus, (10) can be re-expressed as

$$y_{p,t} = y^w_{p,t} + \gamma_2 A_{n,t-1}/p_t. \tag{12}$$

The value of $y^w_{p,t}$ is estimated by the same procedure as the earlier estimate of $y_{p,t}$.[4] Thus, a version of expression (9) is estimated as having the log of measured real labor income as the dependent variable, and time as the independent variable. This established the values of g and $y^w_{p,0}$. β is assumed to be 0.025 as indicated by Darby's and our own earlier results. With these parameters, $y^w_{p,t}$ is then calculated from an expression analogous to (8).

Under this approach, transitory income is the sum of transitory labor income $y^w_{T,t}$ and transitory nonhuman income $y^A_{T,t}$. The first of these is given by subtracting permanent labor income from actual labor income, the latter denoted by y^t_w, i.e., $y^w_{T,t} = y^w_t - y^w_{p,t}$. Transitory nonhuman income is approximated by subtracting permanent nonhuman income from actual total real earnings accrued from nonhuman wealth, y^A_t. We represent y^A_t by the deflated after-tax sum of personal interest, dividend, and rental income received by households F_t, plus a measure of capital gains income G_t; i.e., $y^A_t = (F_t + G_t)/P_t$. Thus,

$$y^A_{T,t} = (F_t + G_t)/P_t - \gamma_2 A_{n,t-1}/P_t, \tag{13}$$

and total transitory income is

$$y_{T,t} = y^w_{T,t} + (F_t + G_t)/P_t - \gamma_2 A_{n,t-1}/P_t. \tag{14}$$

To approximate G_t, we follow Darby in using the real value of undistributed corporate profits, adjusted for taxes. Specific definitions of all variables used in the analysis are given in Appendix A.

IV. Measures of Household Nonhuman Wealth

The permanent income estimate given by expression (12) is completed by directly estimating A_n, the stock of household nonhu-

4. The estimates of this variant of expression (9) are for 1959.1 to 1978.1. The value of g is 0.01047, while $y^w_{p,0}$ for 1959.1 is 98.2 billions of 1972 dollars.

man wealth. From an accounting standpoint, consumer wealth includes (a) stocks of money and near money financial assets held by households, holdings of private and public bonds, equity, and other securities by households, and (c) net holdings of durable good and other real assets by households.

From a behavioral standpoint, it is not clear that all of these components of "accounting wealth" are effective influences upon A_n, and thus upon consumer perceptions of permanent income. Fundamentally, the household wealth stock enables consumption to be rearranged intertemporally. To be effective in this function, components of wealth must be viewed as candidates for liquidation when the motivation arises to raise purchasing power, and should be candidates for wealth additions when the motivation arises to store more purchasing power. It is the components of accounting wealth that households stand ready to "cash in" that are capable of producing a wealth or permanent income effect or both upon consumer expenditures.

Viewed in this way, the most appropriate definition of effective aggregate household wealth is an empirical question. Households may in fact respond only to fluctuations in real money holdings, as suggested by the real balance effect. Or, it is plausible to suggest that households treat all highly liquid assets as wealth, viewing less liquid components of accounting wealth as not being a part of realizable purchasing power.[5] Alternatively, households may behave as if even the most illiquid of their assets are a part of realizable purchasing power, and involve all components of accounting wealth in the formulation of permanent income.

The suggestion that effective wealth differs from accounting wealth finds some support in past empirical studies. Measures of consumer liquid assets have frequently been found to relate to consumer spending.[6] Concerning less liquid assets, fluctuations in stock prices have been found to relate to consumer spending with increasing

5. Such households would never consider selling the house, the car, or the refrigerator as a way to adjust purchasing power, and would not feel more or less "wealthy" when these assets appreciated or depreciated in unit market value. Although a second mortgage on the house would be a way to make capital gains on housing available for consumption, the opposite income effect produces ambiguous results on consumption.

6. For examples, see the analysis by Suits and Sparks in Duesenberry, *et al.* [1965, p. 208], and Patinkin's [1965, pp. 656–57] analysis, in which he reports on the results of twelve consumption function studies, of which ten find support for measures of liquid assets. A less frequent example of a negative finding on the role of liquid assets in consumption models is contained in an analysis by Evans and Klein [1968].

TABLE I

HOUSEHOLD WEALTH DEFINITIONS

$A_{1,t}$ =	Demand Deposits plus Currency ($M1_t$)
	+ Time and Savings Accounts at Commercial Banks and Savings & Loans ($M3_t$)
	+ U. S. Savings Bonds (Series E)
	+ Open Market Paper and Money Market Fund Shares
$A_{2,t}$ =	A_1
	+ U. S. Government Bonds[a]
	+ State and Local Bonds[a]
	+ Corporate & Foreign Bonds[a]
	+ Mortgages
	+ Corporate Equity at Market Value
	+ Life Insurance & Pension Fund Reserves
	+ Security Credit & Other Financial Assets
$A_{3,t}$ =	A_2
	+ Value of Consumer Durables[b]
	+ Value of Residential Property[b]
	− Mortgage Debt
	− Consumer Installment & Other Debt

Note. These data are as given in the FRB *Sector Statements of Financial Assets and Liabilities,* except where noted.

a. Converted to market value by the procedure given in Appendix.

b. Estimated directly by the procedure described in Appendix.

frequency.[7] However, overall wealth measures that contain stocks of real assets as well as liquid assets have not fared as well, producing a mixture of results.[8] These studies are roughly consistent with the idea that households may not treat all of their accounting wealth as effective wealth in their expenditure decisions.

The effective wealth question is first examined by constructing two measures of household real balances and three successively broader measures of household nonhuman wealth. These measures are based largely upon the Federal Reserve Board's *Sector Statements of Financial Assets and Liabilities for Households,* with appropriate modifications made to adjust between book and market value. Table I shows specific definitions for the real balance and effective wealth measures used. The two real balance measures $M1_t$ and $M3_t$ correspond to the Federal Reserve money definitions of the same

7. For examples of this, see papers by Bhatia [1972] and Friend and Lieberman [1975].

8. The strongest continuing case for overall wealth measures is represented by the flow of work on the FMP model. See, for example, the report by de Leeuw and Gramlich [1969].

name, and are the household portion of these money stocks. The first wealth measure, $A_{1,t}$, includes only household holdings of money and near-monies having fixed capital values. Accordingly, $A_{1,t}$ directly reflects household liquidity. $A_{2,t}$ adds to $A_{1,t}$ the market value of household holdings of government and corporate bonds, mortgages, and household holdings of equities and other financial assets. $A_{2,t}$ thus combines household liquid assets with household risky financial assets. $A_{3,t}$ is a complete measure of accounting net wealth by including the net value of consumer real assets in addition to the components of $A_{2,t}$. The net value of consumer real assets is the market value of the stock of consumer durables plus the market value of residential property, less mortgage and consumer debt. The calculation of all of these measures, except those taken directly from the FRB sector data, is described in Appendix A. With $A_{n,t}$ now empirically represented alternatively by $M1_t$, $M3_t$, $A_{1,t}$, $A_{2,t}$, or $A_{3,t}$, we have two permanent income frameworks subject to testing. The first form of the model using the measure of permanent income that is based on current income is given by expression (7). The final form of the model that results from substituting expressions (12) and (14) into (7) for each of the alternative measures of nonhuman household wealth is

$$(15) \quad c_t^x = ky_{p,t}^w + \gamma_2(k - \lambda_1)A_{i,t-1}/P_t + \lambda_1[y_{T,t}^w + (F_t + G_t)/P_t] + \lambda_2 r_t + \lambda_3(R + \delta) - Rd_{t-1} \qquad \text{for } i = 1, 2, 3; \quad k, \lambda_1, \gamma_2 > 0; \quad \lambda_2, \lambda_3 < 0,$$

where M1 and M3 replace A_i in the real balances version of (13), and where G_t is equal to zero for the M1, M3, and $w1$ versions because no changes in capital values are considered in these definitions.

V. Empirical Results

These models are estimated on a quarterly basis using data from 1960.2 to 1977.2. This is a particularly interesting period for study of the wealth variables, since real wealth, as measured by either A_2 or A_3, fluctuated substantially over this period, due primarily to stock market gyrations and to the persistent and sometimes severe U. S. inflation of the 1970s. By contrast, neither of the usual permanent income measures, M1, M3, or A_1, shows the deep cyclical fluctuations present in A_2 and A_3. Thus, the empirical tests should help establish whether these cyclical patterns in A_2 and A_3 systematically relate to consumer expenditures, or whether they essentially add noise to the equation.

Initial experiments with both the income and wealth versions of the permanent income model suggest its formulation presents an empirical problem. A high degree of intercorrelation among the independent variables is present, especially due to the d_{t-1} and $y_{p,t}$ or $y^w_{p,t}$ terms. This is undoubtedly the result of the presence of strong time trends in both the durables stock and the permanent income terms. Because this may lead to somewhat unstable coefficient estimates, and unreasonably large error variances, we assume rather than estimate a value for R, the real rate of return on money invested in the stock of durables. This allows the real dollar return on durables Rd_{t-1} to be calculated and combined with c^x_t, thus removing this term from the left-hand side of the equation and greatly reducing the intercorrelation involved. Experimentation with quarterly values of R that compound to 2 percent, 3 percent, and 4 percent per year showed that very small differences in estimated coefficients and goodness of fit resulted in substituting one for another. Thus, we chose an annual rate of 4 percent, or a quarterly rate of 0.74 percent for R. In the empirical results, we thus redefine the left-hand side of (7) and (15) as

$$c^{xd}_t = c^x_t + 0.0074d_{t-1}, \tag{16}$$

and estimate the following:

$$c^{xd}_t = ky_{p,t} + \lambda_1 y_{T,t} + \lambda_2 r_t + \lambda_3(R + \delta) \tag{7a}$$

$$\begin{aligned} c^{xd}_t = {} & dy^w_{p,t} + \gamma_2(k - \lambda_1)A_{i,t-1}/P_t \\ & + \lambda_1[y^w_{T,t} + (F_t + G_t)/P_t] + \lambda_2 r_t + \lambda_3(R + \delta). \end{aligned} \tag{15a}$$

GLS procedures are used with a first-order autoregressive structure due to high autocorrelation. These results are shown in the first six rows of Table II. The value of the interest rate coefficient λ_2 is found to be essentially zero in all six cases examined, with the t-statistic for the hypothesis $\lambda_2 = 0$ never higher in absolute value than 0.42. This indicates that we make no significant specification error by dropping this term from both (7a) and (15a). In the lower six rows of Table II, the equations are reestimated with $\lambda_2 = 0$. The results are almost identical with the upper six rows.

In either case we find that the A_2 and A_3 definitions of wealth lead to the lowest standard errors, followed closely by M3 and A_1. The

TABLE II

STATISTICS FOR PERMANENT INCOME ESTIMATES

$$c_t^{xd} = ky_{p,t} + \lambda_1 y_{\tau,t} + \lambda_2 r_t + \lambda_3(R + \delta)$$
$$c_t^{xd} = ky_{p,t}^w + \gamma_2(k - \lambda_1)A_{i,t-1}/P_t + \lambda_1[ty_{\tau,t}^w + (F_t + G_t)/P_t] + \lambda_2 r_t + \lambda_3(R + \delta)$$

Definition of wealth (income)	k	$\gamma_2(k - \lambda_1)$	λ_1	λ_2	$\lambda_3(R + \delta)$	R^2	*SEE*	*D.W.*	γ_2
M1	0.9573	0.0820	0.4380	−4.589	−2.601	0.956	1.064	1.76	0.1580
	(28.97)	(2.58)	(6.47)	(0.04)	(0.54)				
M3	0.6016	0.0832	0.3493	−33.71	18.13	0.978	0.977	1.93	0.3299
	(6.88)	(4.49)	(5.56)	(0.39)	(3.92)				
A_1	0.5993	0.0855	0.3395	−36.08	12.31	0.976	0.983	1.91	0.3290
	(6.58)	(4.34)	(5.30)	(0.42)	(3.14)				
A_2	0.9309	0 0084	0.1625	30.25	−3.317	0.984	0.965	2.03	0.0109
	(42.22)	(4.99)	(5.15)	(0.35)	(1.11)				
A_3	0.9306	0.0081	0.1616	23.31	−7.067	0.986	0.964	2.03	0.0106
	(44.56)	(5.27)	(5.16)	(0.28)	(2.21)				
y_p	0.8692	—	0.3902	−6.947	3.767	0.964	1.042	2.06	—
	(40.33)		(6.91)	(0.07)	(0.97)				
M1	0.9483	0.0781	0.4644	—	−1.539	0.979	1.068	1.65	0.1614
	(37.72)	(2.47)	(7.20)		(0.44)				
M3	0.6051	0.0817	0.3527	—	17.19	0.982	0.973	1.89	0.3237
	(7.18)	(4.58)	(5.67)		(4.17)				
A_1	0.6051	0.0833	0.3455	—	12.13	0.982	0.973	1.85	0.3208
	(6.95)	(4.43)	(5.45)		(3.49)				
A_2	0.9344	0.0082	0.1733	—	−3.229	0.983	0.970	2.05	0.0107
	(39.87)	(5.02)	(5.04)		(2.14)				
A_3	0.9349	0.0077	0.1717	—	−6.639	0.982	0.972	2.07	0.0101
	(43.24)	(4.88)	(5.35)		(1.94)				
y_p	0.8680	—	0.4136	—	3.875	0.979	1.040	1.98	—
	(55.99)		(7.57)		(1.35)				

Note. Numbers in parentheses are absolute values of t-statistics. GLS is used in these results with $\rho = 0.8$.

highest standard errors are produced by using either M1 or the income version of the model. The differences in fit are not large among any of the M3, A_1, A_2, or A_3 versions of the model. The difference between either the A_2 or A_3 versions of the wealth equation and the income equation are more noticeable. The standard error of the estimate of consumer spending rises by about 7–8% percent when income is used rather than A_2 or A_3 wealth. This difference in fit is not dramatic, but it does suggest rather clearly that the considerably more cyclical patterns of A_2 or A_3 compared to y_p are not just additional "noise" but have a positive net effect in explaining consumer expenditures.

The signs of the measured coefficients in Table II generally coincide with our expectations. Exceptions are the value of $\lambda_3(R + \delta)$, which is hypothesized to be negative and measured to be positive and significant when either M3 or A_1 is used, and positive but insignificant when y_p is used. Also, in two cases where the interest rate is used, its effect is found to be positive but insignificant.

We find that some important differences are present among the income and wealth models concerning the size of permanent and transitory income effects, as indicated by the size of k relative to λ_1. For the income version of the model and for M1, M3, and A_1, permanent income effects on consumer expenditures are found to be between about 1.7 to 2.2 times as great as transitory income effects. This is consistent with a substantial amount of past work. However, for the A_2 and A_3 wealth versions of the model, permanent income effects are found to be about 5.7 times as great as transitory income effects. We thus find that the use of the market value of the broader A_2 or A_3 measures of household wealth produces a clearly larger permanent income effect and a smaller transitory income effect than using either current income or liquid balances to infer permanent income. Since the values of A_2 and A_3 are affected by changes in the prices of financial assets—whereas the values of A_1, M1, M3, and y_p are not—it is logical to interpret the larger permanent income effect as being the result of the difference. One view of the A_2 and A_3 results is that they show the effects of a correction of an error of omission in the other specifications and in much prior work. The theory of permanent income clearly indicates that, when the market value of the stock of real wealth rises, permanent income and consumption should also rise. The larger value of k relative to λ_1 we observe in the case of A_2 or A_3 thus may largely reflect differences associated with incorporating rather than ignoring the impact upon permanent income of market revaluations of the price of financial wealth.

The value of the long-run expected rate of return on financial wealth γ_2 is implied by the results of the first three columns of Table II. It is calculated in the last column of the table. As a quarterly rate of return, the implied values of γ_2 for the M1, M3, and A_1 versions of the model are clearly unreasonable. However, for A_2 and A_3 the values compound to annual long-run expected returns on financial wealth in the 4.1 percent–4.4 percent range that corresponds well with a priori expectations. This result lends support to the theoretical interpretation of the coefficients in the case of A_2 and A_3, and raises questions about the interpretation of the coefficients in the case of M1, M3, and A_1. We examine possible reasons for the M1, M3, and A_1 results in further analysis below.

The estimates in Table II are subject to a bias of unknown magnitude due to the simultaneous nature of either the (7a) or (15a) version of the consumption function. In particular, for the model that excludes interest rates consumption expenditures and transitory income are clearly both endogenous products of a larger macrosystem. We explore the effect of this bias by using probable instruments from a representative underlying macrosystem to reestimate (7a) and (15a) with $\lambda_2 = 0$ by two-stage least squares. Table III shows these results.

The only substantive differences we observe are with respect to the λ_1 coefficient. In the income version of the model, the transitory income coefficient rises from 0.4136 to 0.4964, while the permanent income coefficient remains about the same. The opposite movement occurs for A_2 and A_3. In these cases λ_1 falls from 0.1733 to 0.0772 and from 0.1717 to 0.0683, respectively, while the permanent income effect increases slightly in each case. Thus, taking simultaneity into account leads to an even larger distinction between permanent and transitory effects when wealth rather than measured income is used to approximate permanent income. Indeed, in the 2SLS results using wealth rather than income supports the conclusion that transitory income effects are zero, i.e., for both A_2 and A_3 the t-statistics for λ_1 allow acceptance of the hypothesis that $\lambda_1 = 0$, and thus that transitory effects are insignificant. This supports the original Friedman version of the permanent income hypothesis. However, it should be kept in mind that error variances are expected to be larger for 2SLS estimates than for comparable OLS estimates. I prefer to interpret the results in Table III as adding reliability to the previous contention that using explicit wealth measures instead of income measures produces larger permanent income effects and smaller transitory income effects than

TABLE III

TWO-STAGE-LEAST-SQUARES RESULTS

$$c_t^{xd} = ky_{p,t} + \lambda_1 y_{\tau,t} + \lambda_3(R + \delta)$$
$$c_t^{xd} = ky_{p,t}^w + \gamma_2(k - \lambda_1)A_{i,t-1}/P_t + \lambda_1[y_{\tau,t}^w + (F_t + G_t)/P_t] + \lambda_3(R + \delta)$$

	k	$\gamma_2(k - \lambda_1)$	λ_1	$\lambda_3(R + \delta)$	R^2	*SEE*	*D.W.*	λ_2
M1	0.9486	0.0577	0.4565	1.074	0.978	1.089	1.67	0.1172
	(32.40)	(1.78)	(4.66)	(0.29)				
M3	0.5281	0.1003	0.2676	21.63	0.981	0.994	1.82	0.3849
	(6.17)	(5.39)	(2.79)	(4.98)				
A_1	0.5156	0.1050	0.2583	14.79	0.981	1.002	1.77	0.4081
	(5.86)	(5.39)	(2.66)	(4.19)				
A_2	0.9536	0.0103	0.0772	−5.228	0.980	1.044	1.96	0.0117
	(34.46)	(5.43)	(1.45)	(1.43)				
A_3	0.9566	0.0099	0.0683	−9.916	0.979	1.051	1.98	0.0111
	(34.44)	(5.45)	(1.26)	(2.38)				
y_p	0.8749	—	0.4964	2.453	0.977	1.074	2.20	—
	(52.85)		(4.88)	(0.79)				

Note. Numbers in parentheses are absolute values of standard errors. 2SLS is used in these estimations. Instruments used are current and one-lagged values of both the monetary base and high-employment government spending, and one and two-lagged values of consumer spending. GLS is also used in the second stage with $\rho = 0.8$ throughout.

using either measured income or less encompassing measures of liquidity.

We reach the same conclusions about γ_2 from Table III as from Table II; i.e., we observe reasonable values for γ_2 using A_2 or A_3, but not with other wealth measures. We also find the explanation of consumer expenditures is improved by using A_2 or A_3 over y_p, but the difference is smaller than what we observed using OLS. Also, the best fit in this case is provided by M3 rather than A_2.

VI. Identifying Effective Wealth

We have now examined measures of wealth that range from money holdings to holdings of all components of financial and real net worth. In Table II we find that the explanation of consumer spending is not improved by broadening the measure of wealth beyond financial assets, thus implying that real wealth adds no explanatory power beyond financial wealth. To explore this question further, we examine the main components of wealth separately to see whether we can exclude some components and distill a measure of wealth that is of clearest influence upon consumer spending. To do this, we generalize (15a) as follows:

$$\begin{aligned}(17)\qquad c_t^{xd} = {} & ky_{p,t}^w + \gamma_{2,1}(k - \lambda_1)A_{1,t-1}/P_t \\ & + \gamma_{2,2}(k - \lambda_1)(A_{2,t-1} - A_{1,t-1})/P_t \\ & + \gamma_{2,3}(k - \lambda_1)(A_{3,t-1} - A_{2,t-1})/P_t \\ & + \lambda_1[y_{\tau,t}^w + (F_t + G_t)/P_t] + \lambda_3(R + \delta).\end{aligned}$$

If the wealth components unique to A_2 are indistinguishable from those unique to A_3 and also indistinguishable from those in A_1, then $\gamma_{2,1} \cong \gamma_{2,2} \cong A_{2,3}$, and (17) collapses to (15a). On the other hand, if we observe some of the $\gamma_{2,j}$ to be close to zero, we may conclude that the associated wealth component has no important explanatory power in expression (15a). We test these questions by first estimating (17). Based on the 2SLS experiment, it appears that we shall make no substantive error in our conclusions by using single equation estimating techniques. We use GLS in the work that follows. This estimate is shown in row (a) of Table IV. We now assume $\gamma_{2,3} = 0$, and rerun the modified expression (17). This result, shown in row (b) of Table IV, allows computation of an F-statistic for the hypothesis that the restriction $\gamma_{2,3} = 0$ characterizes the data. We obtain $F = 0.30$, which allows acceptance of the hypothesis that $\gamma_{2,3} = 0$ at the 1 per-

TABLE IV

TESTS OF WEALTH COMPONENTS

$$c_t^{xd} = ky_{p,t}^w + \gamma_{2,1}(k-\lambda_1)A_{1,t-1}/P_t + \gamma_{2,2}(k-\lambda_1)(A_{2,t-1} - A_{1,t-1})/P_t + \gamma_{2,3}(k-\lambda_1)(A_{3,t-1} - A_{2,t-1})/P_t + \lambda_1[ty_{\tau,t}^w + (F_t + G_t)/P_t] + \lambda_3(R+\delta)$$

	k	$\gamma_{2,1}(k-\lambda_1)$	$\gamma_{2,2}(k-\lambda_1)$	$\gamma_{2,3}(k-\lambda_1)$	λ_1	$\lambda_3(R+\delta)$	R^2	*SEE*	*D.W.*
(a)	0.7738	0.0442	0.0059	0.0101	0.1497	2.078	0.983	0.967	1.95
	(7.86)	(2.01)	(2.69)	(0.55)	(4.34)	(0.22)			
(b)	0.7747	0.0444	0.0065	—	0.1519	2.300	0.983	0.962	1.92
	(7.91)	(2.04)	(3.41)		(4.46)	(0.51)			

$$c_t^{xd} = ky_{p,t}^w + \gamma_{21.1}(k-\lambda_1)\mathrm{M1}_{t-1}/P_t + \gamma_{21.2}(k-\lambda_1)(A_{1,t-1} - \mathrm{M1}_{t-1})/P_t + \gamma_{2,2}(k-\lambda_1)(A_{2,t-1} - A_{1,t-1})/P_t + \lambda_1[y_{\tau,t}^w + (F_t + G_t)/P_t] + \lambda_3(R+\delta)$$

	k	$\gamma_{21.2}(k-\lambda_1)$	$\gamma_{21.2}(k-\lambda_1)$	$\gamma_{22}(k-\lambda_1)$	λ_1	$\lambda_3(R+\delta)$	R^2	*SEE*	*D.W.*
(c)	0.8290	0.0643	0.0287	0.0068	0.1670	−1.588	0.983	0.962	1.90
	(7.40)	(2.18)	(1.07)	(3.51)	(4.48)	(0.27)			
(d)	0.9462	0.0578	—	0.0077	0.1882	−6.797	0.983	0.963	1.91
	(40.32)	(2.00)		(4.39)	(5.95)	(2.00)			

Note. Numbers in parentheses are absolute values of t-statistics. All equations are estimated with GLS using a first-order autoregressive structure with $\rho = 0.8$.

cent level.[9] This result supports the conclusion that fluctuations in the net (of debt) value of household stocks of durable goods and real estate do not systematically influence consumer spending. Presumably, these assets are not treated by households as wealth in forming permanent income perceptions.

In the regression shown in row (b) of Table IV, we observe a value of $\gamma_{2,2}$ that is quite similar to those obtained in Table II for A_2, but a value for $\gamma_{2,1}$ that is somewhat large if γ_2 is to be interpreted as a long-run expected quarterly return. Note that $\gamma_{2,1}$ associates with money and risk-free near-money assets, while $\gamma_{2,2}$ associates only with risky financial assets. How is it that we observe a higher long-run expected return on the former than on the latter? One interpretation is that the closeness of money and near-money assets to realizable purchasing power creates a real-balance effect on spending in addition to the theoretical effect associated with γ_2. However, before pursuing this notion further it is useful to examine whether or not the differences we observe between $\gamma_{2,1}$ and $\gamma_{2,2}$ are of significance. To do this, we compare the modified expression (17) with expression (15a) for A_2, the latter of which results from restricting $\gamma_{2,1} = \gamma_{2,2} = \gamma_2$. We obtain $F = 2.79\ (1,64)$ for a test of this restriction, which also is insignificant at 5 percent but significant at 10 percent. We conclude that, while there is a suspicious difference between the two coefficients, it is not of clear statistical significance. The data thus hesitatingly support the suggestion that the components of liquid and risky financial wealth are treated largely the same by households in forming permanent income expectations.

We can pursue our examination of the role of near money assets by further dividing A_1 into money balances and near money assets. This sheds light on the possibility that we are observing a type of real balance effect. To explore this, we define

$$
\begin{aligned}
(18)\qquad c_t^{xd} = {} & k y_{p,t}^{w} + \gamma_{21.1}(k - \lambda_1) \cdot \mathrm{M1}_{t-1}/P_t \\
& + \gamma_{21.2}(k - \lambda_1)(A_{1,t-1} - \mathrm{M1}_{t-1})/P_t \\
& + \gamma_{2,2}(k - \lambda_1)(A_{2,t-1} - A_{1,t-1})/P_t \\
& + \lambda_1[y_{\tau,t}^{w} + (F_t + G_t)/P_t] + \lambda_3(R + \delta).
\end{aligned}
$$

If consumers treat holdings of currency and demand deposits (M1) indistinguishably from holdings of savings accounts, open market paper, and money market funds (A_1 − M1), then we shall

9. Indeed, the standard error of the equation actually falls when the $\gamma_{2,3}$ term is deleted.

observe $\gamma_{21.1} = \gamma_{21.2}$. If $\gamma_{21.2} = 0$, then we can conclude that the observed significance of our A_1 wealth measure is due to a real balance effect. If $\gamma_{21.1} = 0$, then we may conclude that the data support no real balance effect, but instead support the interpretation that liquid interest-bearing wealth has a unique influence on consumer spending. Row (c) of Table IV shows the result of estimating (18). We find that all of the coefficients are significantly nonzero except $\gamma_{21.2}$. An F-statistic is formed by eliminating the $(A_1 - \mathrm{M1})$ term from the equation. The F-value of 1.00 shows that no significant increase in residual variation occurs at the 1 percent level when $\gamma_{21.2}$ is set to zero. The resulting equation is shown in row (d) of Table IV. This result suggests that money holdings play a clearly significant role in consumer spending, but that holdings of savings accounts and other interest-bearing near money assets do not.[10] Notice that the coefficients on the money term, $\gamma_{21.1}(k - \lambda_1)$ in rows (c) and (d), are even larger than the coefficients in row (a) or (b). This gives more support to a real-balance effect, since in its absence dropping out all of the interest-bearing components of A_1 would be expected to lower the long-run expected financial return. But in our case, $\gamma_{21.1}$ cannot be interpreted as a pure long-run expected financial return, as can $\gamma_{2,2}$. Rather, it more generally reflects the translation of holdings of immediate purchasing power into permanent income perceptions and consumer expenditure.[11]

Two consumer wealth components, net real assets and savings accounts, have now been separately identified by our tests as being ineffective in explaining consumer spending. We can confirm this by testing the joint hypotheses that $\gamma_{2,3} = \gamma_{21.2} = 0$, i.e., that the joint influence of real asset stocks and liquid savings accounts upon consumption is zero.[12] We obtain $F = 0.92$, which allows the clear acceptance of this joint hypothesis.

An additional avenue of inquiry concerning the components of

10. A further subdivision was also made, that of M1, (M3 − M1), and $(A_1 - \mathrm{M3})$, which separates out savings accounts from other short-term liquid assets. When we run tests of this expanded version of (18), we find t-statistics of 1.06 and 0.35 for (M3 − M1) and $(A_1 - \mathrm{M3})$, respectively. We obtain $F = 0.57$ for the hypothesis that the effects of (M3 − M1) and $(A_1 - \mathrm{M3})$ are jointly zero. Thus, this further disaggregation produces the same conclusion as that shown in Table IV.

11. The hypothesis that $\gamma_{21.2} = \gamma_{22}$, i.e., that the observed differences in these coefficients in row (d) of Table IV are just stochastic, can be tested by an F-statistic, $F = 2.95$, which is not significant at the 5 percent level but which is significant at the 10 percent level. Thus, we obtain only suspicious evidence that the effects of money and of financial assets on consumption are not the same.

12. The appropriate F-statistic is formed from the residual sums of squares from the equation estimated in row (d) of Table IV and equation (15a) using the A_3 definition of wealth.

effective wealth is whether the main components of household risky assets, $(A_2 - A_1)$, are treated indistinguishably by households. Although (as Table I shows) household risky assets include government and corporate bonds, mortgages, life insurance and pension reserves, and equities, holdings of equities comprise about half of the total. Equities are also the most volatile category of consumer risky assets, and the most closely followed category by the news media. To explore the possibility that equity holdings are the effective component of risky assets, we decompose $(A_2 - A_1)$ into holdings of equity A_s, and holdings of all other risky assets $(A_2 - A_1 - A_s)$, and reexamine this further modification of expression (18). We find we can clearly accept the hypothesis that the influence of the value of equities upon consumption is indistinguishable from that of all other risky assets on an F-test. We obtain $F = 0.90$ on a test of the restriction that the coefficients on the A_s term and the coefficient on the $(A_2 - A_1 - A_s)$ term are the same.[13] This evidence suggests that households treat holdings of all risky assets pretty much the same as far as their consumer spending behavior is concerned.

From these tests we conclude that the measure of wealth that is effective in influencing consumer spending has two components. The first is holdings of M1 money by households, the influence of which suggests a real balance effect. The second component of effective wealth is the market value of consumer risky assets, including stocks, bonds, life insurance claims, and pension funds claims. Other assets, most notably savings accounts and real assets, are found to have no significant influence on consumer spending. The savings account result suggests that these assets may be held for largely precautionary reasons and may not be so close to purchasing power as intuition could suggest. The real asset result suggests that houses, automobiles, furniture, and appliances may be treated more as part of the environment by households than as a part of realizable purchasing power.

VII. Stock Prices and Consumer Spending

One asset effect that has been the subject of considerable prior attention and work is the effect of stock prices upon consumer spending. From row (d) of Table IV, we calculate the partial elasticity of consumer spending with respect to stock prices. We find that this

13. We also find we can reject at the 5 percent level the hypothesis that the coefficient on the "all other" term is zero ($F = 4.08$), and that we can reject beyond 1 percent the hypothesis that the coefficient on the equity term is zero ($F = 10.70$).

elasticity varies between 0.016 and 0.041 over the sample. Put differently, in 1977.2 a 10 percent increase in stock prices, ceteris paribus, is associated with a rise in consumer spending of a seasonally adjusted annual rate of about 2.1 billion. During the same time period, a one dollar capital gain in the value of household equities is associated with an increase in consumer spending of \$0.030. This capital gains effect is very similar to the range of \$0.02 to \$0.04 measured cross-sectionally by Friend and Lieberman [1975]. It is somewhat higher than the corresponding time series estimates of Arena [1964, 1965], Bhatia [1972], and Feldstein and Fane [1973]. Our results also find this asset effect on consumption to be statistically significant, as indicated by the t-statistic on the $(A_2 - A_1)$ term in Table IV. In general this is contrary to the findings of Arena, Bhatia, and Feldstein and Fane. The significance of asset effects in the present study may be attributed to our improved wealth series and to our use of a fully developed permanent income structure.[14]

Although interesting, the partial elasticity associated with stock price movements understates the actual association of consumer spending with stock price movements. This is because other risky assets held by households also tend to change in value as stock prices change. If we assume that all other risky assets change in proportion to stock prices, the stock price elasticity rises from the 0.016–0.041 range to the 0.043–0.065 range, and the expenditure effect of a dollar in capital gains during 1977.2 rises from \$0.030 to \$0.073.[15] Because both this "proportional" assumption and the earlier ceteris paribus assumption are extreme, we feel that the true expenditure elasticity of stock prices lies between the values given above.

VIII. Conclusions

We have found that permanent income measures based explicitly on stocks of household wealth give an improved explanation of consumer spending compared to measures based on current realized income. Among various wealth measures, those that take into account the sometimes sharp cyclical variation in prices of stocks and bonds generally explain consumer spending better than wealth measures

14. The present asset effects are lower than the 0.04 to 0.08 values reported in a recent version of the MPS model [1973].

15. A 10 percent increase in all asset values in 1977.2 is associated with an increase in consumer expenditure of an annual rate of 5.0 billion.

that do not include these fluctuations. This suggests that some net gain in explaining consumer spending is associated with cyclical movements in the market value of household wealth, as compared to the much less cyclical movement of standard permanent income measures. Our results support the idea that consumer expenditures react systematically and positively to market revaluations in the stock of household wealth.

We find that using wealth stocks to measure permanent income leads to a clearly higher marginal propensity to consume permanent income, and a lower marginal propensity to consume transitory income than using measured income to measure permanent income. This difference is a direct product of including the effects of market revaluations in the household stock of wealth, and suggests stronger support for a more Friedman-like version of permanent income theory than is typical of results that have used income to approximate permanent income.

When we further examine the influence of individual components of wealth by testing for both the equivalence of and lack of significance of various wealth measures, we find that fluctuations in the net value of household holdings of consumer durables and real estate do not associate significantly with fluctuations in consumer spending. We also find that fluctuations in the value of consumer savings accounts do not contribute significantly to explaining fluctuations in consumer spending.

The components of wealth we find to be of clear importance in explaining consumer spending are (1) stocks of real money balances and (2) holdings of equities, bonds, and other risky financial assets. We find these two asset groups to have somewhat separable effects upon spending, with the former presumably including a real balance effect and the latter presumably being more of a pure measure of long-run perceptions of permanent nonhuman income.

Our results also imply values of the expenditure elasticity of stock price changes with mean values in the 0.030–0.055 range, which are consistent with those obtained in prior work done on capital gains effects.

APPENDIX

Variables involved in the empirical tests are defined below. All expenditure variables are expressed as quarterly totals rather than annual rates, and interest rates are quarterly rates.

c_t^x = total constant dollar consumer expenditures as given in the National Income Accounts (NIA) and published by the Department of Commerce in the *Survey of Current Business*.

y_t = realized consumer real income, measured as the sum of real Disposable Personal Income and Undistributed Corporate Profits deflated by the Implicit Price Deflator for consumer goods. All three series are from the NIA data of the Department of Commerce.

$y_{p,t}$ = permanent real income, calculated by using y_t and expression (8) as described in the text.

$y_{\tau,t}$ = real transitory income, given by $y_t - y_{p,t}$ for the income model, and given by expression (14) for the wealth models.

r_t = the rate of interest on 4–6 month prime commercial paper. Quarterly values are obtained by averaging the three monthly values. Monthly data are from the Federal Reserve Board's *Federal Reserve Bulletin*.

d_t = the real stock of household durable goods, defined as the value of the stock of durables (as defined below) deflated by the Implicit Price Deflator for Durable Goods as calculated by the Department of Commerce.

P_t = price of consumer goods, measured by the Implicit Price Deflator for all Consumer Goods calculated by the Department of Commerce.

y_t^w = disposable labor income, defined as real Disposable Income less real after-tax income from rents, dividends, and interest. Definitions of each component are as given in the NIA accounts by the Department of Commerce.

$y_{p,t}^w$ = permanent real labor income, calculated by using y_t^w and expression (8) as described in the text.

$y_{\tau,t}^w$ = transitory real labor income, given as $y_t^w - y_{p,t}^w$.

F_t = current dollar payments on nonhuman wealth, defined as the after-tax sum of personal interest income, personal rental income, and personal dividend income.

G_t = realized real capital gains, approximated as the value of undistributed corporate profits.

y_T^A = realized real income from nonhuman capital, defined as $(F_t + G_t)/P_t$.

c_t^{xd} = the sum of observable real NIA consumer expenditures plus the estimated value of the real return on the stock of durables, as approximated by expression (16).

A_s = market value of household holdings of equity securities, as given by the Federal Reserve Board in their *Sector Statements of Financial Assets and Liabilities: Households*.

M1, M3, A_1, A_2, A_3. The construction of these liquidity and wealth measures is defined in Table I. Most of the statistical series identified there are taken directly from the Federal Reserve Board's Sector Statements. The exceptions are noted in Table I and described in more detail here.

1. Market Value of Government Bonds

The market value of government bonds held by households is estimated by multiplying the FRB series on the book value of government bonds by the ratio of market to book value for government bonds, which we designate as P/R. The ratio P/R is found by transforming the standard expression for the price or yield on a bond. This expression is

$$C\left[\frac{(1-r)^n-1}{r(1+r)^n}\right]+\frac{R}{(1+r)^n}=P, \tag{A-1}$$

where C is coupon, R is book or par value, P is market value, r is yield to maturity, and n is maturity. This expression is divided through by R to obtain an expression giving the desired ratio:

$$\frac{C}{R}\left[\frac{(1+r)^n-1}{r(1+r)^n}\right]+\frac{1}{(1+r)^n}=\frac{P}{R}. \tag{A-2}$$

To apply this expression to the Federal bonds, C is defined as the total coupon payments on Federal debt; R is the book value of Federal debts; and r is estimated by weighting market yields on securities of less than one year to maturity, three to five years to maturity, and over five years by their relative book value composition in the maturity structure of the Federal debt. The result is a time series on average r. Similarly, n is the average maturity of the Federal debt. Yields, weights, and maturities are from the U. S. Treasury's *Treasury Bulletin.*

The state and local ratio of market book value is estimated in the same way as the Federal ratio. Interest Payments come from the Department of Commerce's *Survey of Current Business*. Average yields and maturities come from *The Weekly Bond Buyer*. The maturity is fixed at the midpoint of the maturities included in the sample. Thus, the Bond Buyer sample is taken to be representative of state and local bonds in general. From expression (A-2), these data enable calculations of P/R for both state and local and Federal bonds. This way of estimating market value has the advantage of being free of the bias associated with assuming the debt to be perpetual and using the expression C/r to approximate P.

2. Market Value of Corporate and Foreign Bonds

The market value of this class of bonds held by households is also calculated as the product of the FRB series on household holdings at book value and the ratio of market to book value. This ratio is calculated in the same way as for Federal, state, and local bond price ratios in (1) above. However, it is impossible to separate corporate bond interest payments from bank and other interest payments. Therefore, C/R for corporations is found by dividing total nonfinancial business interest payments (assuming that bank bonds are a negligible portion of total outstanding bonds) by the sum of outstanding business and commercial loans plus the outstanding book value of publicly issued corporate bonds and notes. Coupon payments are from the Department of Commerce's *Survey of Current Business*. Until 1969, the value of R is obtained from the U. S. Department of Census, *Bicentennial Statistical Supplement*. Thereafter, the series is completed by adding the net new issues of corporate bonds and notes from FRB *Federal Reserve Bulletin*. r is estimated as the average yield on corporate bonds from Moody's Corporation *Moody's Bond Survey*. n is the midpoint of the maturity structure of the bonds in Moody's sample, assuming them to represent all corporate bonds.

3. The Value of Consumer Durables

A quarterly series on the value of consumer durables is calculated by first taking benchmark values for the stock of durables from the U. S Census Bureau's *Bicentennial Statistical Supplement* [U. S. Bureau of Census, 1976] for 1960.4 (14.8 billion) and 1968.4 (233.8 billion). Using the GNP series on durables expenditures over this period, an implied depreciation rate β is calculated from the following expression:

(A-3) $$K_t = E_t + (1 - \beta)K_{t-1},$$

where K_t is the stock of durables and E_t is the quarterly expenditure level. This is done by solving the following polynomial for β:

(A-4) $$K_t = E_t + (1 - \beta)E_{t-1} + (1 - \beta)^2E_{t-2} + \cdots + (1 - \beta)^{32}K_{t-32},$$

This gives $\beta = 0.06838$ per quarter, or a depreciation rate of slightly more than 25 percent per year in the stock of consumer durables. Using 1960 as a starting point, the calculated β is used, along with quarterly values of E_t, to calculate K_t quarterly from 1960–1977 according to expression (A-3).

4. The Value of Residential Property

This value is estimated by first decomposing the series into structures and land. The stock of structures is estimated exactly the same way as the stock of consumer durables described in (3) above. Benchmarks, obtained from the same source as (3), are 433.1 billion for 1960.4 and 682.7 billion for 1968.4. The quarterly value of β obtained by evaluating expression (A-4) is -0.000695, indicating that price appreciation in residential housing more than offset physical depletion, leading to a negative depreciation rate in nominal terms. The last few years in the sample probably saw greater rates of appreciation in structures than estimated by the benchmarks, but there was no way to estimate this effect reliably.

The value of residential land is obtained by fitting a log-linear curve through benchmarks over 1960 to 1968. The stock of structures is calculated by using the estimated β and the GNP series on residential structures to evaluate (A-3) at quarterly intervals. Land and structures are then added together to obtain the quarterly series on value of residential property.

The indicated rate of appreciation in residential land from this estimate is 7.14 percent per year. Combining the two appreciation rates together by market value weights indicates that the average appreciation in residential structures and land over the sample period is about 3 percent per year on the existing stock of assets.

UNIVERSITY OF WISCONSIN

REFERENCES

Ando, Albert, and Franco Modigliani, "The Life Cycle Hypothesis of Saving: Aggregate Implications and Tests," *American Economic Review*, LIII (March 1963), 55–84.

Arena, John J., "Capital Gains and the 'Life Cycle' Hypothesis of Saving," *American Economic Review*, LIV (March 1964), 107–11.

——, "Postwar Stock Market Changes and Consumption," *Review of Economics and Statistics*, XLVII (Nov. 1965), 379–91.

Bhatia, Kul, "Capital Gains and the Aggregate Consumption Function," *American Economic Review*, LXII (Dec. 1972), 866–79.

Darby, Michael R., "The Permanent Income Theory of Consumption—A Restatement," this *Journal*, LXXXVIII (May 1974), 228–50.

——, "Postwar U. S. Consumption, Consumer Expenditures, and Saving," *American Economic Review*, LXV (May 1975), 217–22.

deLeeuw, F., and E. Gramlich, "Channels of Monetary Policy," *Federal Reserve Bulletin* (June 1969), 472–91.

Duesenberry, James S., G. Fromm, L. R. Klein, and E. Kuh, *The Brookings Quarterly Econometric Model of the United States* (Chicago: Rand McNally, 1965).

Evans, Michael R., and L. R. Klein, *The Wharton Econometric Forecasting Model*, 2nd enlarged edition (Philadelphia: Wharton School of Finance and Commerce, University of Pennsylvania, 1968).

Fama, Eugene, "Short-Term Interest Rates as Predictors of Inflation," *American Economic Review*, LV (June 1975), 269–82.

Feldstein, Martin, "Tax Incentives, Corporate Saving, and Capital Accumulation in the United States," *Journal of Public Economics*, II (April 1973), 159–71.

——, and George Fane, "Taxes, Corporate Dividend Policy, and Personal Savings: The British Postwar Experience," *Review of Economics and Statistics*, LV (Nov. 1973), 399–411.

Friedman, Milton, *Theory of the Consumption Function* (Princeton: NBER, Princeton University Press, 1957).

Friend, Irwin, and Charles Lieberman, "Short-Run Asset Effects on Household Saving and Consumption: The Cross-Section Evidence," *American Economic Review*, LXV (Sept. 1975), 624–33.

Holbrook, R., and F. Stafford, "The Propensity to Consume Separate Types of Income: A Generalized Permanent Income Hypothesis," *Econometrica*, XXXIX (Jan. 1971), 1–21.

Juster, F. T., and P. Wachtel, "Anticipatory and Objective Models of Durables Goods Demand," *American Economic Review*, LXII (Sept. 1972), 564–79.

Laumas, Prem S., and R. A. Mohabbat, "The Permanent Income Hypothesis: Evidence from Time Series Data," *American Economic Review*, LXII (Sept. 1972), 730–34.

MIT-PENN-SSRC Econometric Model of the United States, mimeo (Jan. 1973). Wharton Econometric Forecasting Associates.

Modigliani, Franco, "Monetary Policy and Consumption," in *Consumer Spending and Monetary Policy: The Linkages,* Federal Reserve Bank of Boston, Monetary Conference Series, 5, Boston (June 1971), 9–85.

Patinkin, Don, *Money, Interest, and Prices,* 2nd ed. (New York: Harper and Row, 1965).

Poole, William, "The Role of Interest Rates and Inflation in the Consumption Function," *Brookings Papers on Economic Activity,* 1 (1972), 211–19.

Zellner, Arnold, and M. S. Geisel, "Analysis of Distributed Lag Models with Applications to Consumption Function Estimation," *Econometrica,* XXXVIII (Nov. 1970), 865–88.

BAYES RULE AS A DESCRIPTIVE MODEL: THE REPRESENTATIVENESS HEURISTIC*

DAVID M. GRETHER

Results of experiments designed to test the claim of psychologists that expected utility theory does not provide a good descriptive model are reported. The deviation from tested theory is that, in revising beliefs, individuals ignore prior or base-rate information contrary to Bayes rule. Flaws in the evidence in the psychological literature are noted, an experiment avoiding these difficulties is designed and carried out, and the psychologists' predictions are stated in terms of a more general model. The psychologists' predictions are confirmed for inexperienced or financially unmotivated subjects, but for others the evidence is less clear.

There are a number of areas of economic research for which the nature of individual decision processes is important. In addition, there are some substantive areas to which economic theory has been applied in which market forces cannot be relied upon to "discipline" the behavior of economic agents. Recently economists have begun to study the sensitivity of market equilibria to imperfect information. These studies have considered labor markets [Mortensen, 1976, and Wilde, 1977] and consumer products market [Salop and Stiglitz, 1977, and Wilde and Schwartz, 1979]. One of the conclusions which has emerged from this literature is that the properties of market equilibria are sensitive to the search strategies used by individual consumers or workers. For example, consider Salop and Stiglitz [1977] versus Wilde and Schwartz [1979]. Knowledge about individual behavior under uncertainty can also be of importance in several policy areas. Examples are interventions in markets where information is incomplete [Schwartz and Wilde, 1979], the provision of insurance against natural disasters [Slovic *et al.*, 1977b], a variety of "truth in lending" or labeling-type issues, etc. Also, note the use of economic theory in nonmarket settings, e.g., the analysis of voting [Riker and Ordeshook, 1973], and legislative behavior [Fiorina, 1974]. In addition, there are situations to which economic theory of individual behavior has been applied in which no trades or arbitrage is possible, e.g., such areas as crime [Becker, 1968, and Erlich, 1975], suicide [Hamermesh and Soss, 1974], marriage [Becker, 1973, 1974], and extramarital affairs [Fair, 1978].

* Financial support by the National Aeronautics and Space Administration is gratefully acknowledged. I would like to thank my colleagues, Forrest D. Nelson, Charles R. Plott, and Louis L. Wilde for their many helpful suggestions and comments, and Steven Matthews, Brian Binger, Elizabeth Hoffman, and Gerhard Befeld for their research assistance.

In a series of papers [Kahneman and Tversky (K and T), 1972, 1973; and Tversky and Kahneman (T and K), 1971, 1973, 1974], D. Kahneman and A. Tversky have suggested that individuals use certain heuristics in making decisions under uncertainty. When adopted, these heuristics (which are called availability, representativeness, and anchoring) lead to certain predictable and consistent biases in individual judgments concerning the likelihood of uncertain events. In their experiments people simply do not behave as predicted by economic theory. K and T present detailed and persuasive experimental evidence which supports their view that, in some circumstances, individuals adopt the simple rules of thumb that K and T have characterized. Their experiments, of course, were not designed for an economics audience, and it is not clear from the evidence they present whether or not the behavior they find could be expected to be an important factor in an economic setting. The purpose of this paper is to report the results of a series of experiments designed to test, in a way relevant to economics, one of the heuristics; namely, representativeness.

The plan of the paper is as follows. The heuristic and the nature of the evidence concerning it is discussed in Section I. The experimental design is presented in Section II, and the results are presented in Section III. The discussion of the results and the conclusions of the paper are given in Section IV.

The final conclusion reached is that the representativeness heuristic, as interpreted here, is a good descriptive model of behavior under uncertainty for untutored and unmotivated (or at least not financially motivated) individuals. There is some evidence that with increasing experience and financial motivation individuals rely less on the rule of thumb and act more like Bayesians, but the evidence for this latter position is far from conclusive.

I

K and T provide evidence concerning the representativeness heuristic in three papers [T and K, 1971, 1973; K and T, 1972]. "A person who follows this heuristic evaluates the probability of an uncertain event, or a sample, by the degree to which it is (i) similar in essential properties to its parent population and (ii) reflects the salient features of the process by which it is generated" [K and T, 1972, p. 431].

An example of the representativeness heuristic is given by the following experiment reported in K and T [1973] and T and K [1974].

Eighty-five subjects were given the following instructions.

A panel of psychologists have interviewed and administered personality tests to 30 engineers and 70 lawyers, all successful in their fields. On the basis of this information, thumbnail descriptions of the 30 engineers and 70 lawyers have been written. You will find on your forms five descriptions chosen at random from the 100 available. For each description, please indicate your probability that the person described is an engineer on a scale of 0 to 100 [K and T, 1973, p. 241].

Another group of 86 subjects was given identical instructions, except that the number of lawyers was changed to thirty and the number of engineers to seventy. Both groups were given the same five descriptions, one of which was the following:

Jack is a forty-five year old man. He is married and has four children. He is generally conservative, careful, and ambitious. He shows no interest in political and social issues and spends most of his free time on his many hobbies which include carpentry, sailing, and mathematical puzzles. The probability that Jack is one of the 30 [70] engineers in the sample of 100 is ——% [1973, p. 241].

In addition the two groups were asked the following question:

Suppose now that you are given no information whatsoever about an individual chosen at random from the sample. The probability that this man is one of the 30 [70] engineers in the sample of 100 is ——% [1973, p. 241].

Both groups of subjects gave nearly the same posterior probabilities for each of the five descriptions in spite of the substantial change in the priors. Some of the descriptions were intended to sound very much like lawyers, and others very much like engineers, so that a subject using the representativeness heuristic is expected to assign a high probability that a description is of, say, a lawyer, even though the prior probability is small. For one of the five descriptions the median estimate of the probability that the man chosen was an engineer was around 0.05 for both groups of subjects, and another of the descriptions was around 0.95. Both groups made the "correct" response to the question quoted above. Perhaps the most interesting result reported was the response to the following:

Dick is a thirty-year old man. He is married with no children. A man of high ability and high motivation he promises to be quite successful in his field. He is well liked by his colleagues [1973, p. 242].

This description was intended to be neutral, and apparently was judged so by both subjects. For both groups the median estimate was 0.50. Thus, these subjects evaluated useless information and no information quite differently.

The results of K and T certainly do support the hypothesis that individuals judge by something like representativeness and ignore prior probabilities. The responses to the vacuous description and the fact that the subjects were reminded of the prior odds after each description was given are especially convincing. Nevertheless, this experiment has features that make the applicability of the findings to economic decisions doubtful. First, there is the difficulty of controlling the information given when verbal descriptions or situations are presented. This problem is well illustrated by the results reported by Hammerton [1973], who demonstrated that rewording mathematically equivalent problems could lead subjects to provide different answers. (For a more detailed discussion see Grether [1978].)

A second potential source of difficulty is that, as is often the case in experiments, the subjects are not told the truth about the random process being examined. Clearly, the thumbnail descriptions were not a random sample from the alleged population. The subjects' responses would agree with Bayes rule only if they either "played the game" or believed the experimental instructions and thereby badly misperceived what was going on. Also, the use of the word "probability" in the instructions raises questions about the results. After all, the proper definition of the term has been the subject of a major debate among statisticians for years.

Finally, there is the question of incentives; it is not clear that K and T's subjects had a positive incentive to give "correct" answers. The instructions included the following statement:

> The same task has been performed by a panel of experts, who are highly accurate in assigning probability to the various descriptions. You will be paid a bonus to the extent that your estimates come close to those of the expert panel [1973, p. 241].

Thus, there was an incentive to behave as the "experts," which may or may not be interpreted as attempting to give the right answer.

K and T present additional evidence in favor of the representativeness hypothesis and some evidence that many truths of mathematical statistics are not intuitive concepts even to individuals trained in them (see also T and K [1971]). In particular, regression effects (e.g., sampling based upon the value of the dependent variable) and sampling variability are often misunderstood. Also, it should be noted that judgment by representativeness has other implications, e.g., insensitivity to sample size and certain misconceptions concerning randomness. Consider a sample drawn from a binomial distribution.

> The most salient property of a binomial sample is, clearly, the sample proportion. Hence we expect, at least in the aggregate case, that the subjective posterior probability will depend primarily on the proportion of red chips, say, in the sample with little or no regard to the size of the sample or to the difference between the proportion of red chips in the two symmetric populations [K and T, 1972, p. 446].

II

In order to test the representativeness hypothesis, a series of experiments were conducted using students from Pasadena City College, Occidental College, University of Southern California, California State University Los Angeles, California State University Northridge, and University of California at Los Angeles as subjects. These experiments (not counting a pilot experiment run at California Institute of Technology) involved a total of 341 subjects.

Students were recruited from a variety of classes. They were told that an "economics experiment" was to be held and were given the time and place of the experiment. They were guaranteed that the experiment would last no more than one hour and that they would be paid at least five dollars for participating. They were given no other prior information concerning the nature of the experiment. When the subjects arrived, they were randomly sent to two different rooms. The only difference in practice between the rooms was the method of payment.

Instructions were passed out, and after obtaining the participants' names and social security numbers, the first three paragraphs of the instructions were read aloud to the subjects (see Appendix).

At this time the subjects elected one of themselves to be a monitor. The monitor was allowed to inspect all equipment, and more importantly, to observe all procedures during this experiment. It was stated in the instructions that the monitor "should check the truthfulness of what the experimenter says, but other than that may not communicate any information to you in any way. If the monitor communicates any other information, he or she will be asked to leave without payment." It appeared that this solved the credibility problem, and most monitors were quite conscientious and occasionally even officious.

After the monitor was elected, the remainder of the instructions were read, and subjects' questions were answered. Once it appeared that subjects understood what their tasks were, the procedures were gone through (i.e., a dry run so to speak) to make sure that the subjects fully understood the mechanics of the experiment.

The equipment used consisted of three bingo cages and an opaque screen. One of the cages designated Cage X contained balls numbered one through six. The second cage (Cage A) contained four balls marked with an "N" and two balls marked with a "G," and the third cage (Cage B) also contained six balls, three marked with an "N" and three with a "G." All balls were the same color and it was not possible to distinguish between cages except by close inspection.

The experiment proceeded as follows: Cages A and B were put behind the screen, and the rule used to determine which of them was to be chosen was announced; Cage X served as the "prior." The rules were of the form "if one of the numbers one through *k* is drawn from Cage X, we shall choose Cage A; otherwise we shall choose Cage B." *k* was varied between two and four, thereby generating prior odds ratios for Cage A of one-half, one, and two. Next, a ball was drawn from Cage X (the subjects could not see the number on the ball) and, depending upon that number, either Cage A or Cage B was chosen and a sample of size six was drawn (with replacement) from it. After each draw the result ("N" or "G") was announced, written on a blackboard, and also recorded by the subjects on forms provided. After the six draws were completed, subjects were asked to indicate on their forms "the one (cage) you think the balls came from." Subjects were allowed to take as long as they wished, and when all were ready, the procedure was repeated again (with possibly a different prior).

The sample size of six and sample proportions were picked so that the probability of picking a sample that "looked like" one of the parent populations (four N's and two G's or three N's and three G's) was large; the idea being that if the representativeness hypothesis is correct, subjects would tend to think that such samples came from the population they "looked like," even though the actual posterior odds favored the other cage, considering the prior odds.

Notice that, although designed to test hypotheses about the forming of subjective probabilities, everything was handled operationally, so that one does not need to speculate about how the words "odds" or "probabilities" are interpreted. In addition, the subjects actually are observing the results of the random process described to them, rather than being shown a series of nonrandom data and asked to believe that (counterfactually) the data were generated by a particular random process. Though the data are generated as described, this does not assure that the subjects believe that they are, and the use of the monitor was intended to provide additional credibility. By asking for judgments about bingo cages and the numbers one through six, the problem of accidentally "importing" information when problems are presented in story form is avoided.

Table I gives the posterior probabilities for each outcome-prior combination, and Table II shows the posterior odds in favor of the most likely alternative. Notice that the experiment has been designed so that several outcome-prior combinations have the same (or nearly the same) posterior odds.

Two cells with the same posterior odds might be thought of as

TABLE I

POSTERIOR PROBABILITIES OF CAGE A

Prior probability		Number of N's						
		0	1	2	3	4	5	6
for	2/3	0.149	0.260	0.413	0.584	0.737	0.849	0.918
A	1/2	0.081	0.149	0.260	0.413	0.584	0.737	0.849
	1/3	0.042	0.081	0.149	0.260	0.413	0.584	0.737

TABLE II

POSTERIOR ODDS FOR MOST LIKELY ALTERNATIVES

Prior probability		Number of N's: 0	1	2	3	4	5	6
for	2/3	5.70:1	2.85:1	1.42:1	1.40:1	2.81:1	5.62:1	11.24:1
A	1/2	11.39:1	5.70:1	2.85:1	1.42:1	1.40:1	2.81:1	5.62:1
	1/3	22.78:1	11.39:1	5.70:1	2.85:1	1.42:1	1.40:1	2.81:1

representing equally difficult problems for the subjects. Thus, all six situations in which the odds favoring the most likely alternatives are 1.4:1 may represent equally difficult choices. Note that in two of these cases the observed data are three N's, and in two cases the data are four N's. As interpreted here, the representativeness hypothesis predicts that when subjects observe four (three) N's, they will tend to believe that the sample came from the population it is representative of—Cage A (Cage B). From Tables I and II, one can see that of the six cases with posterior odds of 1.4:1 (or 1:1.4) a subject using the representativeness heuristic would be led to make the correct response in two cases, the incorrect response in two cases, and be uninfluenced in two cases.

Finally, in order to provide subjects with an incentive to give correct answers, and to measure the effect of the incentive, subjects were paid in two different ways. In one room all subjects were told that they would be paid \$7 at the end of the experiment. In the other room the subjects were told that at the end of the experiment one of their decisions would be chosen (again by drawing numbers from a bingo cage), and if the event that the subject had indicated was the most likely occurred, they would receive \$15; otherwise they would be paid \$5. The only exception was the last experiment that was run using two sections of an introductory logic course at California State University at Northridge. For this experiment both groups were under monetary incentives for accuracy.

III

Table III shows the proportion correct for the several situations for which the posterior odds favoring the most likely alternatives are 1.4 to 1, by school and method of payment. Note that in almost every case the assumption that some of the subjects are using a heuristic similar to representativeness would explain the pattern found. Also, it is apparent that reliance on the heuristic is not markedly affected by the use of monetary incentives.

Analysis of the contingency tables underlying Table III supports the conclusion just mentioned. There are significant differences among the proportions correct across the three types of events shown in the table ($\chi^2(2) = 154$). The Northridge data are omitted in all the significance tests. On the other hand, there does not appear to be a systematic effect of the monetary incentive. Subjects paid for accuracy were more frequently correct for events of type A ($\chi^2(1) = 7$), less often correct for events of type B ($\chi^2(1) = 14$), and more often correct

TABLE III

EFFECTS OF REPRESENTATIVENESS PERCENT CORRECT WITH POSTERIOR ODDS OF 1.4:1

School	With monetary incentives			Without monetary incentives		
	A[a]	B[b]	C[c]	A[a]	B[b]	C[c]
Pasadena City College	55	86	86	43	76	83
Occidental College	59	72	88	55	76	79
University of Southern California	64	95	88	58	87	100
California State University, Los Angeles	67	76	84	51	60	70
University of California, Los Angeles	60	70	81	62	71	86
California State University, Northridge 1	56	90	63			
California State University, Northridge 2	69	69	88			

a. A = Representativeness favors wrong choice.
b. B = No representativeness data.
c. C = Representativeness favors right choice.

though not significantly so ($\chi^2(1) = 1$) for events of type C. Pooling across the three types of events, one finds that those paid for accuracy were correct 73 percent of the time compared with 70 percent for the others. This difference, while in the direction an economist would predict, is rather modest and statistically insignificant ($\chi^2(1) = 3.0$).

From Tables I and II one can see that there are two remaining cases in which the representativeness heuristic is available (three N's prior 1:2 and four N's prior 2:1), and four other cases with the same or nearly the same posterior probabilities. For the cases for which the representativeness heuristic applies, the subjects were correct 91 percent of the time compared with 88 percent correct in other ones. This difference, while in the direction predicted of the use of the representativeness heuristic, is statistically insignificant.

As discussed in the previous section, one of the implications of the representativeness hypothesis is that individuals judging likelihood of representativeness should tend to ignore prior probabilities. Consider the case when the representativeness heuristic is available. That is, the cases when $N = 3$ or $N = 4$ so that the sample "looks like" one of the parent population. Table IV shows that even for these cases

TABLE IV

PERCENT STATING "A" MOST LIKELY (posterior odds 1.4:1 or 1:1.4)

School	With monetary incentives, Prior Odds for A 2:1	1:1	1:2	Without monetary incentives, Prior Odds for A 2:1	1:1	1:2
			Data N = 3			
Pasadena City College	50	11	16	48	—	—
Occidental College	72	12	10	55	19	12
University of Southern California	68	5	0	60	0	—
California State University, Los Angeles	35	15	12	53	—	15
University of California, Los Angeles	—	—	8	64	—	6
California State University, Northridge 1	58	23	3			
California State University, Northridge 2	65	8	0			
			Data N = 4			
Pasadena City College	76	—	35	91	83	59
Occidental College	92	88	68	87	77	45
University of Southern California	95	73	55	93	—	43
California State University, Los Angeles	81	82	18	90	70	50
University of California, Los Angeles	94	80	30	96	86	40
California State University, Northridge 1	—	55	48			
California State University, Northridge 2	85	87	29			

the prior odds clearly affected the choices made by the subjects. As before, the effects are statistically significant and hold independently of the use of monetary incentives.

Thus, it appears that something like the representativeness heuristic is being employed by the subjects, but some consideration is also being given to the prior probabilities. Thus, while the representativeness heuristic may partially explain the subjects' behavior, a more general model is required to characterize what is going on even in this simple situation. Let Y^*_{it} be the subjective log odds in favor of Cage A of subject i at time t, i.e., $e^{Y^*_{it}}$ is the ith subject's posterior odds in favor of A. Consider the following model:

$$e^{Y^*_{it}} \equiv \left(\frac{P_A}{1-P_A}\right)_{it} = e^{\alpha}[LR(A)]_t^{\beta_1}\left[\frac{\hat{P}_A}{1-\hat{P}_A}\right]_t^{\beta_2} e^{u_{it}}, \qquad (1)$$

where $(P_A/(1-P_A))$ is the subjects' posterior odds, $LR(A) = L(X|A)/L(X|B)$ is the likelihood ratio for A, $\hat{P}_A/(1-\hat{P}_A)$ is the prior odds in favor of A, and u_i is a random variable with mean zero and finite variance. Of course, if subject i correctly follows Bayes rule, then $\alpha = 0$, $\beta_1 = \beta_2 = 1$, and $u_{it} \equiv 0$.

In the experiments reported here, direct observations on Y^*_{it} are not available, but from the subjects' choice behavior we can observe the variable Y_{it}, where

$$\begin{aligned} Y_{it} &= 1 \qquad \text{if } Y^*_{it} \geq 0 \\ &= 0 \qquad \text{otherwise.} \end{aligned} \qquad (2)$$

Taking logarithms of (1) gives

$$Y^*_{it} = \alpha + \beta_1 \ln LR(A)_t + \beta_2 \ln\left(\frac{\hat{P}_A}{1-\hat{P}_A}\right)_t + u_{it}, \qquad (3)$$

which is suitable for estimating by logit, probit analysis, or other similar methods [McFadden, 1976; Amemiya, 1975; Maddala, 1977, Ch. 9; and Dhrymes, 1978, Ch. 7]. It should be pointed out that the model presented here is different from, and not completely consistent with, the representativeness heuristic if generalized to other situations. This is because opinions formed according to (1) will, of course, be sensitive to sample size through the likelihood ratio. All of the experiments reported here used a single sample size, so this was not of concern.

Since Y^*_{it} is not observed, the parameters of (3) can be estimated only up to an unknown scale parameter. Nevertheless, one can formalize the various polar hypotheses to be tested.

Bayes Rule $\alpha = 0, \beta_1 = \beta_2 > 0$.

Representativeness Hypothesis $\beta_1 > \beta_2 \geq 0$.

Thus, the interpretation of K and T's representativeness heuristic suggested here is that individuals place greater weight on the likelihood ratio than on the prior odds and consider both factors when making decisions. An alternative formulation is the following:

$$\begin{aligned} Y^*_{it} = \alpha &+ \beta_1 \ln LR(A)_t + \beta_2 \ln\left(\frac{P_A}{1-P_A}\right)_t \\ &+ \beta_3 D_{3t} + \beta_4 D_{4t} + u_{it}, \end{aligned} \qquad (4)$$

where

$$\begin{aligned} D_{3t} &= 1 \qquad \text{if } N_t = 3 \\ &= 0 \qquad \text{otherwise;} \\ D_{4t} &= 1 \qquad \text{if } N_t = 4 \\ &= 0 \qquad \text{otherwise.} \end{aligned}$$

Here the binary variables single out those observations that "look like" one of the parent populations.

In the model, Tversky and Kahneman's hypothesis could be interpreted as

$$\beta_3 < 0, \qquad \beta_4 > 0.$$

In this model, unless $\beta_1 < \beta_2$ individuals will be giving "too much" weight to the evidence and too little to the prior. Note that if individuals cue only on the observations that "look like" one of the two parent populations, β_1 and β_2 could be equal, while in the first model $\beta_1 > \beta_2$. To the extent that priors are consistently underweighted, one would expect β_1 to be greater than β_2. In any event both parameters should be positive.

The results of estimating the parameters of (3) are shown in Table V. All estimates reported are based on maximum likelihood logit analysis. For the purposes of the analysis the subjects were divided into four groups, depending upon whether or not there was a monetary incentive to be accurate and whether the subjects were "experienced." A subject was classified as experienced on the jth trial if the subject had previously been exposed to (i.e., had observed) the same prior-outcome combination as occurred on the jth trial. This separation of the observations was done because inspection of the data suggested that subjects were more likely to give the correct response if they had seen the same problem before.

Note that in every case the coefficient on the likelihood ratio exceeds the coefficient of the log of the prior odds, and that the differences are statistically significant. This result is as predicted by our generalization of the representativeness heuristic. Thus, it does appear, as T and K have suggested, that individuals tend to give too little weight to prior information. Note, however, that the prior odds do appear to enter significantly in the equations.

The hypothesis that a single function holds for the several data sets can be tested with a likelihood ratio test. Using the result that asymptotically minus twice the logarithm of the likelihood ratio is distributed as chi squared with degrees of freedom, given by the number of restrictions tested [Kendall and Stuart, 1967, pp. 230–31],

TABLE V

LOGIT RESULTS

$$Y^* = \alpha + \beta_1 \ln LR(A) + \beta_2 \ln P_A/(1 - P_A) + u$$

(numbers in parentheses are t-ratios)

Group[a]	α	β_1	β_2	$\beta_1 - \beta_2$	$-2 \ln L$	n
PF	−0.09	2.01	1.43	0.58	1,589.0	1,747
	(1.4)	(19.9)	(14.2)	(4.9)		
PS	−0.25	2.86	2.34	0.52	996.0	1,170
	(2.8)	(14.0)	(15.9)	(2.8)		
NF	0.17	1.78	1.21	0.57	1,485.1	1,630
	(2.5)	(19.5)	(10.5)	(4.6)		
NS	0.24	2.65	2.17	0.48	874.9	1,061
	(2.8)	(15.3)	(13.6)	(2.9)		
P·	−0.11	2.25	1.82	0.43	2,612.8	2,917
	(2.2)	(24.4)	(20.0)	(4.4)		
N·	0.18	2.02	1.58	0.44	2,393.9	2,691
	(3.5)	(24.7)	(17.3)	(4.5)		
·F	0.04	1.86	1.33	0.53	3,085.8	3,377
	(0.9)	(27.9)	(16.3)	(6.4)		
·S	0.00	2.62	2.20	0.42	1,887.9	2,231
	(0.0)	(20.5)	(20.9)	(3.4)		
··	0.04	2.08	1.69	0.39	5,028.0	5,608
	(1.1)	(34.8)	(26.4)	(5.8)		

a. Key to groups: · = summation; ·· = all subjects; P = monetary incentives were available; N = no monetary incentives were available; F = inexperienced subjects, i.e., first time have seen a particular prior-outcome combination; S = experienced subjects.

the tests can be performed using the figures in the fifth column of Table V. The results show that the same equation can be used to describe the behavior of inexperienced subjects whether or not they are financially motivated. On the other hand, the hypothesis of homogeneity is rejected when one pools experienced and inexperienced subjects or the two groups of experienced subjects.

The results from logit analysis using the extended model (4) are shown in Table VI. The coefficient of the log likelihood ratio exceeds the coefficient of the log prior odds for three of the four groups of subjects, but the differences are not significant at the 0.01 level. For all groups the sign of β_3 is negative as predicted from the representativeness hypothesis, and in three out of four cases the sign of β_4 is positive. The individual coefficients β_3 and β_4 are frequently not significantly different from zero and never significantly differ from each other in absolute value. Comparing the figures in column 8 in Table VI with those in column 5 of Table V, one sees that the pair of

TABLE VI

LOGIT RESULTS

$$Y^* = \alpha + \beta_1 \ln LR(A) + \beta_2 \ln P_A/(1 - P_A) + \beta_3 D_3 + \beta_4 D_4 + u$$

(numbers in parentheses are t-ratios)

Group[a]	α	β_1	β_2	$\beta_1 - \beta_2$	β_3	β_4	$\beta_3 - \beta_4$	$-2 \ln L$	n
PF	−0.09	1.78	1.49	0.29	−0.56	0.56	0.00	1,545.2	1,747
	(0.8)	(17.2)	(12.1)	(2.3)	(3.3)	(3.7)	(0.0)		
PS	0.34	2.69	2.30	0.39	−0.50	−0.69	−1.19	989.5	1,170
	(0.7)	(5.4)	(15.6)	(0.8)	(0.7)	(1.7)	(1.1)		
NF	−0.08	1.54	1.35	0.19	−0.33	0.82	0.49	1,445.0	1,630
	(0.7)	(16.7)	(10.9)	(1.4)	(2.0)	(4.6)	(1.7)		
NS	−0.16	2.31	2.21	−0.12	−0.28	0.78	0.50	861.4	1,061
	(0.8)	(10.8)	(13.2)	(0.5)	(1.0)	(2.7)	(1.0)		
P·	0.04	2.05	1.87	0.18	−0.50	0.07	−0.43	2,594.6	2,917
	(0.4)	(20.7)	(19.9)	(1.6)	(3.3)	(0.6)	(1.8)		
N·	−0.14	1.71	1.74	−0.03	−0.32	0.79	0.47	2,336.2	2,691
	(1.4)	(19.8)	(17.4)	(0.3)	(2.3)	(5.5)	(2.0)		
·F	−0.05	1.65	1.42	0.23	−0.50	0.65	0.15	2,988.1	3,377
	(0.7)	(25.0)	(16.5)	(2.6)	(4.4)	(5.8)	(0.8)		
·S	−0.03	2.59	2.21	0.38	0.06	5.23	5.29	1,887.5	2,231
	(0.3)	(18.4)	(20.5)	(2.6)	(0.5)	(0.1)	(0.1)		
··		1.90	1.78	0.12	−0.47	0.34	−0.13	4,958.2	5,608
		(30.9)	(26.2)	(1.6)	(4.9)	(3.9)	(0.8)		

a. Key to groups: · = summation; ·· = all subjects; P = monetary incentives were available; N = no monetary incentives were available; F = inexperienced subjects, i.e., first time have seen a particular prior-outcome combination; S = experienced subjects.

variables (D_3,D_3) is jointly significant for inexperienced subjects, but not significant or less significant for experienced subjects. Thus, for these data the qualitative predictions of the representativeness hypothesis appear to be borne out.

As before, monetary incentives *do not appear to affect the behavior of inexperienced subjects,* in that the hypothesis that the same functions describe both sets of subjects cannot be rejected at any conventional level of significance. This is *not* true, however, for the experienced subjects. Overall, the specification (4) seems to be superior to (3) in that it generally fits the data better and also eliminates the embarrassingly high t-ratios for the intercepts reported in Table V. In these models, nonzero constant terms do not make any sense, so leaving them in is a kind of test of the specification of the model. Overall, the conclusion seems to be that the representativeness hypothesis as developed here holds. That is, in forming subjective log-odds subjects give relatively too much weight to the evidence and too little weight to the prior odds. This conclusion follows for both forms of the model considered here. When the simpler version (3) is used, the coefficient of the log likelihood ratio is significantly greater than the coefficients of the log prior odds. For those cases for which (4) is the better model, the coefficient of the log likelihood ratio is either greater than or not significantly different from the other coefficient, and the "special event" factors are significant.

The estimates in Tables V and VI all assume that the subjects from several educational institutions make up a homogeneous population. To test this hypothesis, (3) and (4) were reestimated for each institution with the data broken into groups as in Tables V and VI. The results obtained were consistent with those previously reported, that is, generally subjects gave too much weight to the data as described in the previous paragraph. For each of the categories shown in Tables V and VI, the hypothesis of homogeneity across institutions was usually rejected at conventional levels of significance. Since qualitatively the results are similar to those in Tables V and VI, to save space only the aggregate results are reported.

The final set of results is a generalization of the previous models, designed to explore the definition of experience used in the previous estimations. The model used is basically a heteroskedasticity model; the assumption being that the logistic coefficients are the same for both experienced and inexperienced subjects, but that the disturbance distributions differ by a scale factor. The basic idea was that with experience the amount of randomness in subjects' decisions might be reduced, and that this would show up as a decrease in the dispersion of the distributions of the disturbances in (3) and (4).

It should be pointed out that for limited dependent variable models heteroskedasticity leads to inconsistent parameter estimates, though, of course, estimating the equation for each population separately provides consistent but inefficient estimates. The estimates in Table VII are maximum likelihood estimates for a logistic model with heteroskedasticity. The form of the likelihood function is such that no serious computational burdens are introduced by this generalization of the standard model. The primary simplification comes from the cross partials of the likelihood function with respect to the various population scale parameters being zero. The full details of this are beyond the scope of this paper.

Table VII presents the results of refitting the model (4) under the assumption that both "experienced" and "inexperienced" subjects use the same functions (i.e., the same parameter values), but differ only with respect to the dispersion of the distributions of the disturbances. The model (3) was also reestimated, but since the coefficients of the binary variables were jointly significant, only the results from (4) are reported. Note that there was no feedback during the course of the experiment, so any "learning" that might have taken place results from familiarity with a problem or from further reflections on it, etc.

The results of estimating the heteroskedastic model are rather striking. In all but one case (one of the Northridge groups), the experienced subjects showed less random or "more precise" behavior than the inexperienced subjects, though the result is statistically significant for only two cases. Thus, in some sense opinion becomes "firm" or a "consensus" emerges with repetition of a problem.

IV

In this paper some experimental work of Kahneman and Tversky, presenting evidence that individual reasoning processes do not follow the law of mathematical statistics, has been discussed. The results of experiments designed to test the representativeness heuristic in a manner relevant to economics were presented.

In addition to the basic model (1), two generalizations were estimated. The same qualitative results were obtained: individuals tend to give too much weight to the "evidence" and thus too little weight to their prior beliefs, though priors are *not* ignored. In addition, there is some evidence that repetition of a problem or choice task even without feedback leads to more firmly held opinions or less random-

TABLE VII

LOGIT RESULTS HETEROSKEDASTIC MODEL ALL SUBJECTS

$$Y^* = \alpha + \beta_1 \ln LR(A) + \beta_2 \ln P_A/(1 - P_A) + \beta_3 D_3 + \beta_4 D_4 + u$$

(numbers in parentheses are t-ratios)

α	β_1	β_2	$\beta_1 - \beta_2$	β_3	β_4	$\beta_3 + \beta_4$	$-2 \ln L$	n
0.07	3.74	3.28	0.46	−0.77	0.34	−0.43	4,831.62	5,608
(0.5)	(4.8)	(4.8)	(2.6)	(3.2)	(1.9)	(1.3)		

ESTIMATED VALUES OF h[a]

School	Inexperienced	Experienced	Difference
Pasadena City College	0.41	0.65	0.24
	(4.5)	(4.3)	(2.6)
Occidental College	0.48	0.49	0.01
	(4.5)	(4.3)	(0.2)
University of Southern California	0.74	0.94	0.20
	(4.2)	(3.9)	(1.2)
California State University, Los Angeles	0.33	0.37	0.04
	(4.4)	(3.0)	(0.6)
University of California, Los Angeles	0.58	0.80	0.38
	(4.6)	(4.6)	(2.6)
California State University, Northridge 1	0.36	0.51	0.15
	(4.1)	(2.9)	(1.0)
California State University, Northridge 2	1.00	0.71	−0.29
		(2.9)	(1.2)

a. The larger the value of h, the more concentrated is the distribution of the disturbances. h for California State University, Northridge 2, inexperienced, was set equal to unity.

ness in judgment, in the sense that the distribution of the u_i becomes more concentrated. Finally, and to the author the most surprising, the evidence that financial incentives affect the behavior is far from compelling. Responses to unfamiliar problems (that is, problems that had not previously been seen) showed no sensitivity to the presence or absence of monetary incentives for accuracy, though as experience is gained, the picture is not so clear.

Some may ask why we should care about the behavior of individual students in the sorts of environments used in this paper. That is, economic theory is really a theory of market behavior, i.e. of aggregates, and that the repetitive nature of market interactions, together with the reinforcement provided by the profit system (economic agents either learn to process information efficiently or are forced to act as if they have), render single observations on individual behavior irrelevant. Also, a relatively few individuals sensitive to arbitrage possibilities may make markets work as predicted by the theories. Thus, we really do not care much about individual behavior or information processing capacity. At the beginning of the paper it was argued that there are areas of economic research that require economists to be concerned about the nature of individual decision processes. It may be that the behavior of members of dissimilar groups differs systematically, and no claim is made that the results reported here would replicate with qualitatively different subject pools (though this is a testable proposition). However, conventional economic theories as exposited do not discriminate among types of individuals; i.e., they do not contain parameters for students, stock market specialists, housewives, business executives, etc. Thus, as long as individual decision processes are a matter of legitimate concern for economics, the results of the sort presented here are relevant to economics.

Appendix

INSTRUCTIONS

Name ________________________________

Social Security Number ________________________

Address ______________________________

The experimenters are trying to determine how people make decisions. We have designed a simple choice experiment, and we shall ask you to make decisions at various times. The amount of money you make will depend on how good your decisions are. During the experiment you will be asked to make a number of decisions. At the end of the experiment we shall randomly choose one of your decisions and if it is correct, you will receive $15 and if it is incorrect, you will receive $5.

If you look at the person in the front of the room, you will see that he or she has three randomizing devices, otherwise known as bingo cages, which are designated as Cage A, Cage B, and Cage X. Inside both Cage A and Cage B are six balls, some of which are marked with an N and some with a G. Cage A has four N's and two G's and Cage B has three N's and three G's. Inside Cage X there are six balls numbered one, two, three, four, five, and six.

The experiment will proceed as follows. First, we shall ask you to select one individual as a monitor to watch the procedures, to examine the equipment, and to make sure that the experimenters really are doing what they say they are doing. The monitor should check the truthfulness of what the experimenter says, but other than that may not communicate any information to you in any way. If the monitor communicates any other information, he or she will be asked to leave without payment. The monitor will receive $10 for his efforts.

(pick volunteer)

Now Cages A and B are put behind this screen, and we spin Cage X. Before each run we will tell you that if certain numbers come up, we will choose Cage A, and otherwise we will choose Cage B. For example, if 1, 2, 3, or 4 are drawn, we will pick Cage A: if a 5 or 6 is drawn, we will pick Cage B. After drawing from Cage X, the monitor will be asked to choose the appropriate cage (A or B) from behind the screen. Now the experimenter will make six draws from the cage, replacing the drawn ball each time. He will write the results of the draws on the board. You will be asked to indicate on your answer sheet whether you think the draws come from Cage A or Cage B. . . .

The only talking allowed during the course of the experiment will be to clarify questions you may have about the procedure, and these questions should be directed to the experimenter. We will now walk through a complete run of the experiment to make sure everyone understands the procedure.

Cage A has 4 N's and 2 G's
Cage B has 3 N's and 3 G's

Run No. 0. In this run there are —— chances out of 6 for choosing Cage A and —— chances for choosing Cage B.
Record the results for this run: —— —— —— —— —— ——.
Circle the one you think the balls come from. Cage A Cage B

Run No. 1. In this run there are —— chances out of 6 for choosing A and —— chances for choosing Cage B.
Record the results for this run: —— —— —— —— —— ——.
Circle the one you think the balls come from. Cage A Cage B

CALIFORNIA INSTITUTE OF TECHNOLOGY

REFERENCES

Amemiya, Takeshi, "Qualitative Response Models," *Annals of Economic and Social Measurement,* IV (1975), 363–72.
Becker, Gary S., "Crime and Punishment: An Economic Approach," *Journal of Political Economy,* LXXVI (March/April 1968), 169–217.
——, "A Theory of Marriage, Part I," *Journal of Political Economy,* LXXXI (July/Aug. 1973), 813–46.
——, "A Theory of Marriage, Part II," *Journal of Political Economy, Supplement,* LXXXII (March/April 1974), 511–26.
Dhrymes, P. J., *Introductory Econometrics* (New York: Springer-Verlag, 1978).
Ehrlich, Isaac, "The Deterrent Effect of Capital Punishment: A Question of Life and Death," *American Economic Review,* LXV (June 1975), 397–417.
Fair, Ray C., "A Theory of Extramarital Affairs," *Journal of Political Economy,* LXXXVI (Feb. 1978), 45–61.
Fiorina, Morris P., *Representatives, Roll Calls, and Constituencies* (Lexington, MA: D. C. Heath, 1974).
Grether, David M., "Recent Psychological Studies of Behavior under Uncertainty," *American Economic Review, Papers and Proceedings,* LXVIII (May 1978), 70–74.
Hamermesh, D., and N. Soss, "An Economic Theory of Suicide," *Journal of Political Economy,* LXXXII (Jan./Feb. 1974), 83–98.
Hammerton, M., "A Case of Radical Probability Estimation," *Journal of Experimental Psychology,* CI (Dec. 1973), 252–54.
Kahneman, D., and A. Tversky, "Subjective Probability: A Judgment of Representativeness," *Cognitive Psychology,* III (1972), 430–54.
——, and ——, "On the Psychology of Prediction," *Psychological Review,* LXXX (July 1973), 237–51.
Kendall, Maurice G., and A. Stuart, *The Advanced Theory of Statistics,* Vol. 2, *Statistical Inference and Statistical Relationship,* 2d ed. (New York: Hafner Press, 1967).
Maddala, G. S., *Econometrics* (New York: McGraw-Hill, 1977).
McFadden, Daniel, "Quantitative Choice Analysis: A Survey," *Annals of Economic and Social Measurement,* V (1976), 363–90.
Mortensen, D., "Job Matching under Imperfect Information," in *Evaluating the Labor Market Effects of Social Programs,* O. Ashenfelter and J. Blum, eds. (Princeton: Princeton University Press, 1976), pp. 194–232.
Riker, William H., and Peter C. Ordeshook, *Introduction to Positive Political Theory* (Englewood Cliffs, NJ: Prentice-Hall, 1973).
Salop, Steven, and Joseph Stiglitz, "Bargains and Ripoffs: A Model of Monopolistically Competitive Price Dispersion," *Review of Economic Studies,* XLIV (1977), 493–510.
Schwartz, Alan, and Louis L. Wilde, "Intervening in Markets on the Basis of Imperfect Information: A Legal and Economic Analysis," *University of Pennsylvania Law Review,* CXXVII (1979), 630–82.
Slovic, P., B. Fischoff, and S. Lichtenstein, "Behavioral Decision Theory," *Annual Review of Psychology,* XXVIII (1977a), 1–39.
——, ——, ——, B. Corrigan, and B. Combs, "Preference for Insuring Against Probable Small Loss: Implication for the Theory and Practice of Insurance," *Journal of Risk and Insurance,* XLIV (1977b), 237–58.
Tversky, A., and D. Kahneman, "Belief in the Law of Small Numbers," *Psychological Bulletin,* LXXVI (1971), 105–10.
——, and ——, "Availability: A Heuristic for Judging Frequency and Probability," *Cognitive Psychology,* LI (1973), 207–32.
——, and ——, "Judgment under Uncertainty: Heuristics and Biases," *Science,* CLXXXV (1974), 1124–31.
Wilde, Louis L., "Labor Market Equilibrium under Nonsequential Search," *Journal of Economic Theory,* XVI (1977), 373–93.
——, and Alan Schwartz, "Equilibrium Comparative Shopping," *Review of Economic Studies,* XLVI (1979), 543–53.

THE LIMITATIONS OF PIGOUVIAN TAXES AS A LONG-RUN REMEDY FOR EXTERNALITIES*

DENNIS W. CARLTON AND GLENN C. LOURY

I. INTRODUCTION

A central problem of economic policy is to assure efficiency of the competitive process when externalities are present. One traditional method of dealing with an externality is the imposition of a Pigouvian tax (per unit tax) on the externality-generating activity [Pigou, 1927, and Baumol, 1972]. This paper shows that contrary to widely held beliefs use of such a tax will not in general lead to an efficient allocation of resources in the long run. The source of the inefficiency of the tax is really quite simple. A per unit tax uniformly raises a firm's average cost curve, and therefore leads the firm in the long run to minimize average cost at the same output as in the pre-tax situation. In general, however, the output that is socially optimal in the presence of externalities is not the output that minimizes the firm's average production costs.[1] However, if one supplements the Pigouvian tax with a lump sum tax-subsidy scheme for participating firms, then a socially efficient allocation can be achieved.

II. THE MODEL

We present a simple partial-equilibrium model to illustrate our arguments. Imagine a competitive industry consisting of identical firms producing a homogeneous product. Each firm incurs production costs $C(q)$ when producing q units of output. Production in this industry also imposes additional damages on society due to some external effect. We assume these external damages resulting from in-

* This work was initiated while both authors were visiting the Economics group at Bell Laboratories. We thank John Panzar, A. Mitchell Polinsky, and an anonymous referee for helpful comments.

1. An example can illustrate this point simply. Suppose that steel is produced with a technology that generates a U-shaped average cost (AC) curve with the min AC point at output q^*. Suppose that steel production causes pollution damage. This pollution damage need not be constant per unit of steel produced by the firm. For example, starting up the steel furnace may generate pollution damage that is independent of output, in which case average pollution damage per ton of steel produced could fall initially, or alternatively the amount of smoke emitted per ton may depend on how many tons of steel the firm is producing. The minimum average pollution damage per unit of steel output will not in general occur at the output q^* which minimizes average production costs. In this case, Pigouvian taxation alone cannot achieve efficiency.

The Quarterly Journal of Economics, November 1980 0033-5533/80/0095-0559$01.00

dustry production may be written as $D(n,q)$, where n is the number of firms in the industry and q is the output of each firm. Thus, we restrict ourselves to symmetric behavior by active firms, and implicitly assume that external damages are invariant with respect to changes in firms' employment of factors of production that keep output constant. Average production costs $C(q)/q$ are taken to be U-shaped with the minimum average production cost occurring at scale q_s. $P(Q)$ represents the industry's inverse demand function, where $Q = nq$ is total industry output. We assume that the efficient scale of firm production is "small" relative to the size of the market, so that the indivisibility of firms may be neglected and the number of firms n can be taken to be a continuous variable. Finally, we assume interior solutions to all maximum problems.

The welfare criterion is the usual sum of consumer plus producer surplus.[2] The short run is defined as a situation in which the number of firms n is fixed.[3] A Pigouvian tax t is a charge to each firm of $\$t$ for each unit of output produced.

A short-run competitive equilibrium with Pigouvian tax t and number of firms n is a price-quantity pair (p,q) such that supply equals demand and price equals private marginal costs. Using the definition of the inverse demand curve, we can summarize these two conditions by the single condition,

$$P(nq) = C'(q) + t. \tag{1}$$

A short-run social optimum with number of firms n is a price-quantity pair (p,q), which maximizes social welfare. If we again use the inverse demand curve to define p, we can completely characterize the optimal q as the solution to

$$\max_{q \geq 0} \int_0^{nq} P(s)ds - nC(q) - D(n,q).$$

Hence q satisfies the first-order condition,

$$nP(nq) = nC'(q) + \frac{\partial D}{\partial q}(n,q),$$

2. The results of this section are unchanged if instead of using a surplus criterion to measure social welfare, we use a Bergsonian social welfare function. Also, the results are unchanged if the problem is reformulated as one in which the number and output of firms of one industry affect the cost curves of other competitive industries.

3. We assume that in the short run, all n identical firms operate. A rising marginal cost curve guarantees this condition, provided that any output is produced at all. See Polinsky [1977] for a discussion of the short-run effects of taxation when firms differ in their production technology.

or

$$P(nq) = C'(q) + \frac{1}{n}\frac{\partial D}{\partial q}(n,q). \tag{2}$$

The following result provides a frequently used justification for the use of Pigouvian taxation.

THEOREM 1. For the appropriately chosen tax t, the short-run competitive equilibrium coincides with the short-run social optimum.

Proof. It is necessary to show that if q^* satisfies (2), it also satisfies (1) for the appropriately chosen t. Suppose that q^* solves (2) and define $t = (1/n)(\partial D/\partial q)\,(n,q^*)$. Then, it follows immediately from (2) that q^* also satisfies (1).

Q.E.D.

In the long run, entry or exit may occur, so the number of firms n is free to vary. A long-run competitive equilibrium with tax t (LRCE) consists of a price-quantity-number of firms triple such that supply equals demand, price equals private marginal cost, and profits equal zero. Again using the definition of the inverse demand curve, we can completely characterize a LRCE by

$$P(nq) = C'(q) + t, \tag{3}$$

and

$$qP(nq) = C(q) + tq. \tag{4}$$

A long-run social optimum (LRSO) is a price-quantity-number of firms triple that maximizes social welfare. Using the definition of the inverse demand curve, we can completely characterize a LRSO by the q,n that solve

$$\max_{\substack{q \geq 0 \\ n \geq 0}} \int_0^{nq} P(s)ds - nC(q) - D(n,q).$$

The first-order conditions are

$$nP(nq) = nC'(q) + \frac{\partial D}{\partial q}(n,q)$$

or

$$P(nq) = C'(q) + \frac{1}{n}\frac{\partial D}{\partial q}(n,q), \tag{5}$$

and

$$qP(nq) = C(q) + \frac{\partial D}{\partial n}(n,q). \tag{6}$$

Theorem 1 asserts that any short-run social optimum may be attained as a short-run competitive equilibrium with the appropriately chosen Pigouvian tax rate. However, as competitive entry occurs, the tax rate must be adjusted to maintain short-run optimality. That this adjustment process need not result in a long-run social optimum is illustrated by the following result.

THEOREM 2. In general there exists no Pigouvian tax rate t such that the long-run competitive equilibrium (LRCE) coincides with the long-run social optimum (LRSO).

Proof. It is necessary to show that if t is the Pigouvian tax, then if n^*, q^* satisfy (5) and (6) (i.e., n^*, q^* are a LRSO), they will not also satisfy (3) and (4) (i.e., n^*, q^* are not a LRCE). First, notice that if t does not equate social to marginal cost, then it is obvious that (3) cannot be satisfied by q^*, n^*. To complete the proof, we must show that if t is chosen to equate social to marginal cost, then (4) will not be satisfied by n^*, q^*.

Suppose that q^*, n^* satisfy (5) and (6) and let the Pigouvian tax $t^* = (1/n^*)(\partial D/\partial q)\,(n^*,q^*)$. For such a t^*, it is clear from (5) that (n^*,q^*) will also satisfy (3). However, for such a (t^*,n^*), q^* will not in general satisfy (4). To see this, rewrite (6) as

$$q^*P(n^*q^*) = C(q^*) + t^*q^* - t^*q^* + \frac{\partial D}{\partial n}(n^*,q^*),$$

or

$$q^*P(n^*q^*) = C(q^*) + t^*q^* + q^*\left[\frac{1}{q^*}\frac{\partial D}{\partial n}(n^*,q^*) - t^*\right], \tag{7}$$

or

$$q^*P(n^*q^*) = C(q^*) + t^*q^* + F^*,$$

where

$$F^* = q^*\left(\frac{1}{q^*}\frac{\partial D}{\partial n}(n^*,q^*) - t^*\right),$$

or using the definition of t^*,

$$F^* = q^*\left[\frac{1}{q^*}\frac{\partial D}{\partial n}(n^*,q^*) - \frac{1}{n^*}\frac{\partial D}{\partial q}(n^*,q^*)\right]. \tag{8}$$

It is immediately obvious from (7) that t^*, n^*, q^* will satisfy (4) iff $F^* = 0$. But there is no reason why F^* should always equal 0 (e.g., if $D(n,q) = nq^{1/2}$, then $F^* > 0$ for any $q > 0$).

Q.E.D.

The reasons for this failure of a pure Pigouvian tax instrument can be explained intuitively as follows. There are essentially two quantities, number of firms and scale of each firm, which the government is trying to control with just one instrument, the Pigouvian tax. In the short run the structure of the industry (n) is fixed and individual firm output is the only matter of concern. This last quantity can be completely controlled by a Pigouvian tax, which shifts marginal private costs so that they coincide with the marginal social costs at the socially optimal level of industry (and individual firm) production. In the long run, however, the industry structure is flexible and should be adjusted optimally along with individual firms' output. Yet the number of firms and the output of each firm cannot in general be varied independently in the long-run competitive equilibrium with just a Pigouvian tax. This is because the tax shifts the firm's average cost curve upward in a parallel manner. Minimum average tax-inclusive cost always occurs at q_s,[4] regardless of the tax rate t. By varying t, the government affects the number of firms but not their scale in the long run.

Only in the special case where, for any given industry output, externality damage is *independent* of individual firm scale (as occurs when constant returns to scale characterize the externality generation) will q_s be the optimal scale of the firm in the long-run social optimum. In such a case, the scale of an individual firm has no effect on externality damages, and the optimal scale is determined solely by production considerations. In this very special case, Pigouvian taxes can lead to the long-run social optimum.[5] The following theorem illustrates this point.

THEOREM 3. If for any given industry output, externality damages are independent of individual firm output so that $D(n,q) = \overline{D}(nq)$, then with appropriate Pigouvian taxation the long-run competitive equilibrium (LRCE) coincides with the long-run social optimum (LRSO).[6]

4. Recall that q_s is the output at which average production cost is minimized.

5. The intuition underlying this result should be clear. If for any industry output, externality damages are independent of firm scale, then only production cost considerations influence optimal firm scale. Competition takes these production considerations into account. Hence the tax need regulate only the number of firms, since competition takes care of optimal scale. One instrument can regulate one variable perfectly.

6. This result also appears in Schultze and D'Arge [1974].

Proof. Suppose that n^*,q^* are a LRSO and therefore satisfy (5) and (6). If $D(n,q) = \bar{D}(nq)$, then from (8) it is obvious that $F^* = 0$, and hence it follows from (7) that if $t^* = (1/n^*)(\partial D/\partial q)\ (n^*,q^*)$, then n^*, q^*, and t^* will satisfy (4), and it follows from (5) that they satisfy (3). Hence (n^*,q^*) represents a LRCE.

Q.E.D.

If the government can levy a lump sum entry tax-subsidy on active firms in the industry along with the Pigouvian tax, then the long-run social optimum can be attained. Define a long-run competitive equilibrium with Pigouvian tax t and lump sum tax F as the triple (p,q,n), which satisfies supply equals demand, price equals marginal cost, and profits equal zero. Using the inverse demand curve, we can write these conditions as

$$P(nq) = C'(q) + t, \tag{9}$$

and

$$qP(nq) = C(q) + tq + F. \tag{10}$$

We can now prove the following.

THEOREM 4. There is always a tax policy (t,F) such that the long-run competitive equilibrium (LRCE) coincides with the long-run social optimum (LRSO).

Proof. It is necessary to show that if q^*,n^* are a LRSO and hence satisfy (5) and (6), then there is a t^* and F^* such that q^*,n^* are a LRCE and hence satisfy (9) and (10).

Choose $t^* = (1/n^*)(\partial D/\partial q)\ (n^*,q^*)$ and define F^* as in (8). It is obvious from (5) that (9) is satisfied. It follows immediately from (7) that (10) is satisfied. Hence q^*,n^* represent a LRCE.

Q.E.D.

This simple result confirms intuition and assures that a Pigouvian tax supplemented by a lump sum tax can restore full optimality. The optimal lump sum F^* can be either negative, zero, or positive. However, as long as damages depend positively on output, the total tax payment $(F^* + t^*q^*)$ will always be positive. The optimal lump sum tax F^* will be positive (negative) when average pollution damage is falling (rising) at the optimal firm output.[7] Moreover, when payment of a lump sum subsidy is indicated $(F^* < 0)$, it can be effected

7. The proof of these results is available on request.

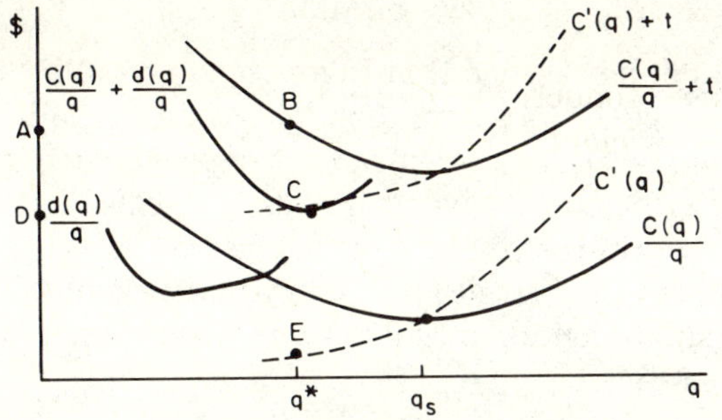

FIGURE I

by exempting the firm from payment of the Pigouvian tax on a certain amount ($-F^*/t^*$) of its output.[8]

IV. A Special Case

The case $D(n,q) = nd(q)$, in which the damage cost from the externality is additive across firms, is of particular interest because of its simplicity. Here the social cost function for the firm is simply $C(q) + d(q)$. The socially efficient solution requires that firms should pay a lump sum tax if the average damage function is falling at the optimal output level ($d'(q^*) > d(q^*)/q^*$). For the case where $d(q) = q^\alpha$, $\alpha > 0$, a lump sum tax or subsidy is required as α is less or greater than one. When $\alpha > 1$, the optimal lump sum subsidy can be determined without further knowledge of demand or technology. For this damage function, the optimal subsidy is equivalent to a tax exemption of $1 - 1/\alpha$ of a firm's output.

Figure I illustrates the determination of the optimal tax rate and subsidy for the case where $d(q)/q$ is rising at the social optimum. As the figure suggests, only if $d(q)/q$ is constant or else just happens to achieve a minimum at the same point as $C(q)/q$, can a simple Pigouvian tax guarantee a long-run social optimum. Here q^* is the socially optimal scale, while q_s is the scale that would prevail under simple Pigouvian taxation. The optimal subsidy is $ABCD$ and the optimal tax is CE.

8. Proof available on request. Notice that this way of distributing the subsidy completely avoids the problem often mentioned with regard to subsidies, that firms will simply collect the subsidy and produce zero output. Since it can be shown in general that total tax payments are always positive, this method of distributing subsidies can always be used. Moreover, if the exemption is interpreted as the property right allocation of the firm to pollute, it follows that only one assignment of property rights will be efficient.

V. Summary

This paper has argued that Pigouvian taxes alone cannot be expected to correct the most common forms of externalities in the long run. Pigouvian taxes alone are incapable of providing firms in long-run equilibrium with an incentive to operate at a scale of plant other than the one that minimizes average private cost. It is only by using lump sum subsidy or entry fees that a policy maker could guarantee that both marginal production incentives *and* incentives for entry into the industry are efficient.

University of Chicago
University of Michigan

References

Baumol, William, "On Taxation and the Control of Externalities," *American Economic Review,* LXII (1972), 307–32.

Pigou, A. C., *The Economics of Welfare,* 4th ed. (London: 1960).

Polinsky, A. M., "Notes on the Symmetry of Taxes and Subsidies in Pollution Control," Harvard Institute of Economic Research, 1977.

Schultze, W., and R. D'Arge, "The Coase Proposition, Information Constraints and Long Run Equilibrium," *American Economic Review,* LXIV (Sept. 1974), 763–72.

RELATIVE DEPRIVATION AND THE GINI COEFFICIENT: COMMENT

JOHN D. HEY AND PETER J. LAMBERT

In a recent issue of this *Journal*, Yitzhaki [1979] showed an important, but hitherto unrealized, connection between the theory of relative deprivation (as propounded by Runciman [1966] and others) and the Gini coefficient. Specifically, Yitzhaki showed that a measure of aggregate relative deprivation (of a society, or indeed of a reference group within a society) could be expressed as the product of the mean income (of that society or reference group) and the Gini coefficient (for that society or reference group).

The purpose of this Comment is to provide an alternative motivation for Yitzhaki's main result. Additionally, we derive a number of extra results which show that various other familiar Lorenz-curve properties have natural interpretations within the framework of relative deprivation theory.

Following Yitzhaki, we denote the cumulative income distribution by $F(\cdot)$: this representation allows for both discrete and continuous distributions of income. A careful reading of Runciman suggests the following alternative approach to the characterization of deprivation. Consider a reference individual with income y, and examine his feelings toward an individual with income z. Define $D(y;z)$, the deprivation felt by y relative to z, as follows:

$$D(y;z) = \begin{cases} z - y & y \leq z \\ 0 & y \geq z \end{cases}. \tag{1}$$

This is motivated by Runciman's remark [1966, p. 10]: "The magnitude of a relative deprivation is the extent of the difference between the desired situation and that of the person desiring it." We now suppose, following Runciman once again [1966, p. 19], that the larger the number of individuals in society with income z, the more our reference individual feels the deprivation $D(y;z)$. Thus to arrive at an overall measure, we simply weight the $D(y;z)$ by $dF(z)$—the "proportion" of society with income z. Our overall measure[1] is therefore

1. Strictly speaking, this is an *average*, rather than an *aggregate* measure; however, the latter can be obtained from the former by multiplying by the number of people in the society (or reference group). For simplicity of exposition we follow Yitzhaki in confining attention to *average* measures.

The Quarterly Journal of Economics, November 1980 0033-5533/80/0095-0567$01.00

$$D(y) = \int_0^{y^*} D(y;z)dF(z), \tag{2}$$

where y^* denotes the highest income in society ($y^* = \inf \{y:F(y) = 1\}$). Finally, if we substitute from (1) into (2), and integrate the resulting expression by parts, we get

$$D(y) = \int_y^{y^*} [1 - F(z)]dz. \tag{3}$$

This expression is identical with Yitzhaki's equation (1), and thus lends support to Yitzhaki's own characterization of relative deprivation.

For mathematical convenience, we follow Yitzhaki in introducing a new function $S(y)$, termed the "relative satisfaction" of an individual with income y, defined by

$$S(y) = \int_0^{y} [1 - F(z)]dz. \tag{4}$$

We note that this can be considered as a complement to the relative deprivation function, since

$$D(y) + S(y) = \mu, \tag{5}$$

and thus, for fixed μ, relative deprivation and relative satisfaction are inversely related.

From (3) and (4), Yitzhaki derives expressions for the overall deprivation and satisfaction felt by a society, and shows in particular that society's relative deprivation can be expressed as the product of mean income and the Gini coefficient. This result enables income distributions to be ranked in terms of relative desirability—at least as far as society's *overall* relative deprivation is concerned. Thus, for example, if we are trying to choose between two income distributions with identical means, then Yitzhaki's result implies that we should choose that distribution with the lower Gini coefficient if we wish to minimize society's overall relative deprivation.[2]

This result, however, says nothing about individual levels of relative deprivation (or satisfaction). Nevertheless, we can exploit Yitzhaki's insight and derive results in this direction, by using well-known theorems concerning Lorenz-curve properties. To keep our analytics simple, we follow Yitzhaki in confining initial attention to the satisfaction function. Consider two alternative income distribu-

2. Connections between relative deprivation and the Gini coefficient are hinted at in Sen [1976]; readers of this will note the obvious link between Sen's "income gap" and our $D(y;z)$ function.

tions $F(\cdot)$ and $G(\cdot)$. From (4), it follows that the difference between the relative satisfactions felt by an individual with income y is given by

$$S_F(y) - S_G(y) = s(y), \tag{6}$$

where

$$s(y) \equiv \int_0^y [G(z) - F(z)]dz.$$

The reader familiar with the literature on stochastic dominance (or with the literature on measuring risk or inequality) will recognize the function $s(y)$. In dominance theory, if $s(y)$ is everywhere nonnegative, then $F(\cdot)$ is said to dominate $G(\cdot)$ stochastically in the second degree. Moreover, if we confine attention to distributions with the same mean income, then $s(y^*) = 0$, and in this case if $s(y)$ is everywhere nonnegative, then $F(\cdot)$ is a less *risky* distribution than $G(\cdot)$ in the sense of Rothschild and Stiglitz [1970]. In such cases, and only in such cases, as Atkinson [1970] has shown, the Lorenz curve for $F(\cdot)$ is everywhere *above* the Lorenz curve for $G(\cdot)$. We immediately have a very important consequence: if two distributions have the same mean, and if their Lorenz curves do not cross, then under the distribution whose Lorenz curve is higher (nearer to the line of complete equality), there is more relative satisfaction at each level of income than there is at the same level under the other distribution. Moreover, it immediately follows from (5) that at all incomes there is less relative deprivation under the distribution with the higher Lorenz curve.[3] Furthermore, as Atkinson [1970, p. 247] points out we can immediately infer that, in such a case, if a dictator with imposed utility function $U(\cdot)$ is making a choice between $F(\cdot)$ and $G(\cdot)$ according to which yields the higher expected utility

$$\int_0^{y^*} U(z)dF(z) \quad \text{or} \quad \int_0^{y^*} U(z)dG(z),$$

then he will choose that distribution with the higher (lower) Lorenz

3. In general, it is impossible to determine what happens to a particular individual under the two distributions, since this depends crucially on how the transformation is effected. However, if under the conditions stated above an individual has income x under $F(\cdot)$ and y under $G(\cdot)$, where $y \leq x$, then the relative deprivation for him is greater under $G(\cdot)$, since

$$S_F(x) - S_G(y) = \int_y^x [1 - F(z)]dz + s(y).$$

This also demonstrates the impossibility of saying anything definite (in the absence of further restrictions) if $y \geq x$.

curve if his utility function is concave (convex). Thus, for example, if at each income level there is less deprivation (and more satisfaction) under $F(\cdot)$ than under $G(\cdot)$, and if society prefers $F(\cdot)$ on this account, then the social preference will be exactly matched by that of a dictator with an "equality-preferring" utility function. Finally, it follows that in such a case, $F(\cdot)$ will be chosen in preference to $G(\cdot)$ if the Rawlsian max-min principle is used (and $G(\cdot)$ chosen if a max-max principle is used); see Lambert and Hey [1979].

The above results have been derived under the assumption of equal means. If the means are not equal, certain modifications are necessary, and the conclusions are not quite so strong. However, the following results can be obtained:[4]

(a) If mean income is greater under F than under G and if the Lorenz curve for F is everywhere above that for G, then
  (i) at each income level, there is more relative satisfaction under F than under G;
  (ii) all "equality-preferring" dictators prefer F to G;
  (iii) F will be chosen under the Rawlsian max-min principle.

(However, we can say nothing about "inequality-preferring" dictators, relative deprivation levels, nor about the result of applying the max-max criterion.)

(b) If mean income is greater under G than under F, and if the reverse[5] Lorenz curve for G is everywhere above that for F, then
  (i) at each income level, there is less deprivation under F than under G;
  (ii) all "inequality-preferring" dictators prefer G to F;
  (iii) G will be chosen under the max-max principle.

(However, we can say nothing about "equality-preferring" dictators, relative satisfaction levels, nor about the result of applying the max-min criterion.)

Before concluding, we note an immediate extension of this approach. This extension takes into account an aspect of Runciman's definition that was ignored by Yitzhaki. According to Runciman [1966, p. 10], ". . . the degree of a relative deprivation is the intensity with which it is felt." In the light of this remark, it would seem reasonable to reformulate the deprivation function (1) as follows:

4. The proofs are fairly transparent and have been omitted. The reader could refer to Atkinson [1970] and to Hadar and Russell [1969].

5. The *reverse* Lorenz curve cumulates from the highest income *downwards*—it lies *above* the 45° line. Clearly, this is the appropriate concept when talking about relative deprivation in cases when deprivation and satisfaction do not add to the same constant.

$$D(y;z) = \begin{cases} u(z) - u(y) & y \leq z \\ 0 & y \geq z \end{cases}, \tag{7}$$

where $u(\cdot)$ is an individual's utility function (assumed here to be the same for all individuals). This reformulation necessitates the reworking of all of the above material in utility space, rather than income space. However, as is probably apparent, most of the results carry over to this more general formulation as long as they are interpreted appropriately. In particular, the Rothschild and Stiglitz risk ordering must be replaced by the Diamond and Stiglitz risk ordering (with respect to the individual u), as developed in Lambert and Hey [1979]; the second-degree stochastic dominance must be replaced by the "second degree stochastic dominance with respect to a function" of Meyer [1977]; and the (income) Lorenz curves must be replaced by utility Lorenz curves.[6] The "equality-preferring" dictator must be replaced by a "more-equality-preferring" dictator; that is, one who has a utility function that is a concave transformation of that of the individuals in society (and thus puts relatively less weight on high incomes than do the members of the society themselves); a similar change is required for the "inequality-preferring" dictator. However, the Rawlsian max-min (and the max-max) results survive unchanged.

To give some flavor of the results obtainable from this general extension, we give one example.

Consider two distributions F and G, and suppose that "total utility" is the same under both (i.e., $\int_0^{y^*} u(z)[dF(z) - dG(z)] = 0$, where $u(\cdot)$ is as defined above). *Then the following statements are equivalent:*

(i) F is less risky than G according to the Diamond and Stiglitz definition with respect to the reference function $u(\cdot)$;

(ii) at all income levels, there is less relative deprivation under F than under G (using the extended definition (7) rather than (1));

(iii) at all income levels, there is more relative satisfaction under F than under G (using the corresponding extension of (2));

(iv) *all* "more-equality-preferring" dictators prefer F to G;

(v) *all* "more-inequality-preferring" dictators prefer G to F;

(vi) the utility-Lorenz curve for F lies everywhere above that for G;

6. Or concentration curves; see Kakwani [1977].

Furthermore, (i) to (vi) imply the following (see Lambert and Hey [1979]):

(vii) the Rawlsian max-min rule yields a preference for F;
(viii) the max-max rule yields a preference for G;
(ix) the Rawlsian difference rule yields a preference for F.

In addition, Yitzhaki's aggregate (society) results carry over to the Gini coefficient as defined for the utility-Lorenz curve.

To conclude, we return briefly to Yitzhaki's relative satisfaction function (4). This function, which has no obvious counterpart in Runciman's work (and which was essentially introduced by Yitzhaki for mathematical convenience in deriving his subsequent results), can be derived from a function,

$$S(y;z) = \min(y,z) \tag{8}$$

(the counterpart to equation (1) for deprivation), averaged in a manner analogous to (2). We can find no obvious intuition behind (8) as a measure of the satisfaction felt by an individual with income y relative to an individual with income z. We tentatively suggest the following alternative formulation[7] (though "gloating" rather than "satisfaction" may be a more appropriate term):

$$S'(y;z) = \begin{cases} 0 & y \leq z \\ y - z & y \geq z. \end{cases} \tag{9}$$

The overall measure corresponding to this is

$$S'(y) = \int_0^y F(z)dz. \tag{10}$$

Clearly, we have

$$D(y) - S'(y) = \mu - y, \tag{11}$$

and thus, for example, if $F(\cdot)$ and $G(\cdot)$ have the same mean, then $D_F(y) - D_G(y) = S'_F(y) - S'_G(y)$; so that relative deprivation and (this alternative) relative satisfaction move *together*—rather than inversely. All of the statements on "satisfaction" above would thereby be reversed!

Whatever the relative merits of the two satisfaction measures, Yitzhaki's insight into the characterization of relative deprivation provides some satisfying conclusions; the economics profession is perhaps the less deprived as a consequence.

UNIVERSITY OF YORK

7. Or the utility reformulation, as in (7).

References

Atkinson, A. B., "On the Measurement of Inequality," *Journal of Economic Theory*, II (1970), 244–63.

Hadar, J., and W. R. Russell, "Rules for Ordering Uncertain Prospects," *American Economic Review*, LIX (March 1969), 25–34.

Kakwani, N. C., "Applications of Lorenz Curves in Economic Analysis," *Econometrica*, XLV (April 1977), 719–27.

Lambert, P. J., and J. D. Hey, "Attitudes to Risk," *Economics Letters*, II (Aug. 1979), 215–18.

Meyer, J., "Second Degree Stochastic Dominance with Respect to a Function," *International Economic Review*, XVIII (June 1977), 477–87.

Rothschild, M., and J. E. Stiglitz, "Increasing Risk, I: A Definition," *Journal of Economic Theory*, II (1970), 225–43.

Runciman, W. G., *Relative Deprivation and Social Justice* (London: Routledge and Kegan Paul, 1966).

Sen, A., "Poverty: An Ordinal Approach to Measurement," *Econometrica*, XLIV (March 1976), 219–31.

Yitzhaki, S., "Relative Deprivation and the Gini Coefficient," this *Journal*, XCIII (May 1979), 321–24.

RELATIVE DEPRIVATION AND THE GINI COEFFICIENT: REPLY

SHLOMO YITZHAKI

In their comment, John Hey and Peter Lambert (henceforth H & L) provide an alternative motivation for the representation of the theory of relative deprivation by the Gini coefficient. They also derive additional results that interpret other familiar Lorenz curve properties within the framework of relative deprivation theory. I would like to comment on three points: the alternative motivation, the extension of the relation into the utility space, and the use of the satisfaction rather than the deprivation function.

First, it should be noted that the motivation of my note and that provided by H & L lead to the same representation, and technically speaking the difference is only in the order of integration. The difference between the two approaches is in the interpretation given to the results.

H & L assume that each individual compares his income with that of each of the other individuals in his reference group. This means that for each pair of incomes, the intervening income distribution is irrelevant. In each comparison, the intensity of deprivation (satisfaction) is the difference in income. Summing the intensities over the entire society gives aggregate deprivation.

According to my approach there are no individual comparisons. Each unit of income represents an ability to consume a bundle of commodities. The value of having a specific bundle (a unit of income) is a function of the scarcity of this bundle in the reference group, and the deprivation felt by an individual is the sum of the values of the bundles in the reference group that he is not able to consume (see Yitzhaki [1979]).

The second point is related to H & L's use of Kakwani's [1977] results in order to define the deprivation function in terms of the utility function. Since the utility function is not known, this extension appears to be of only theoretical value.

On the other hand, if instead of using $1 - F(\ \ )$ as an index of scarcity the index $[1 - F(\ \ )]^{\nu}$, $\nu > 0$ is used, then the satisfaction function would have the following properties:

If $\nu = 0$, then $S = \mu$, where μ is the mean income, and S is the aggregate satisfaction.

If $\nu = 1$, then $S = \mu(1 - G)$, where G is the Gini coefficient.

The Quarterly Journal of Economics, November 1980 0033-5533/80/0095-0575$01.00

If $\nu \rightarrow \infty$, then S is approaching the Rawlsian max-min criteria.

These properties, which are similar to those of Atkinson's index of inequality, enable us to extend this approach without defining the utility function. (For the derivation of these properties see Yitzhaki [1980].)

Lastly, I would like to say that my use of the satisfaction function is not just a mathematical convenience. Economists use the notion of having as a base for utility theory. The utility function is defined on the commodities an individual has. Sociologists approach the same problem by concentrating on the notion of not having (deprivation). As is shown elsewhere [Yitzhaki, 1979], the two approaches are equivalent. The use of the satisfaction function is motivated by the idea of using the same notion as economists do.

HEBREW UNIVERSITY OF JERUSALEM

REFERENCES

Kakwani, N. C., "Applications of Lorenz Curves in Economic Analysis," *Econometrica,* XLV (April 1977), 719–27.

Yitzhaki, Shlomo, "Relative Deprivation: A New Approach to the Social Welfare Function," Discussion Paper No. 798, Jerusalem, Falk Institute, 1979.

——, "On an Extension of the Gini Inequality Index," Discussion Paper No. 8013, Jerusalem, Falk Institute, 1980.

EXCHANGE-RATE VARIABILITY, REAL AND MONETARY SHOCKS, AND THE DEGREE OF CAPITAL MOBILITY UNDER RATIONAL EXPECTATIONS

ROBERT DRISKILL AND STEPHEN MCCAFFERTY

Much of the recent literature on flexible exchange rates has shared two characteristics: first, it has emphasized the critical role of expectations in exchange-rate determination, and second, it has, either explicitly or implicitly, been concerned with exchange-rate volatility or variability.[1] In light of these common threads, it is somewhat surprising that, with the exception of Barro [1978], none of these models has explicitly incorporated uncertainty. Without this, the forecasting problem, which is at the heart of expectations formation, cannot be adequately analyzed, and it is impossible to describe rigorously what is meant by exchange-rate variability. Consequently, comparative-statics results relating changes in structural parameters to changes in exchange-rate variability cannot be rigorously derived.

This paper develops a model of a small, open economy under flexible exchange rates that explicitly incorporates uncertainty. The forecasting problem at the heart of expectational formation can thus be explicitly modeled by assuming that agents make unbiased forecasts based upon knowledge that includes the structure of the model; that is, agents are assumed to have rational expectations in the sense of Muth [1961]. Also, the explicit discrete random process that describes exchange-rate behavior over time is derived, and comparative-statics results about the characteristics of this process are developed. The most interesting result obtained is that increases in the degree of capital mobility, i.e., increases in the degree of portfolio sensitivity to changes in anticipated relative asset yields, decrease that portion of exchange-rate variability attributable to real shocks, but increase that portion attributable to monetary shocks. Another result is that correlations between the trade balance, relative price changes, and spot and forward rates depend on the relative importance of real and monetary shocks.

In a sense, this paper extends the pioneering work of Barro [1978], which also explicitly incorporated uncertainty. Our model, though, focuses on three assumptions not incorporated in Barro's model but

1. A non-exhaustive but representative list of such models includes Barro [1978], Calvo and Rodriguez [1977], Dornbusch [1976a, 1976b], Henderson [1979], Kouri [1976], and Niehans [1975, 1977].

The Quarterly Journal of Economics, November 1980 0033-5533/80/0095-0577$01.00

that have been thought crucial in a number of other models of exchange-rate determination. These three assumptions are that the domestic price of output is "sticky," that asset markets clear every period, and that relative prices are an important determinant of trade flows.[2] And, as already noted, a further distinction between our work and Barro's is that we derive comparative-statics results about exchange-rate variability, one of which addresses the much-debated question of whether capital flows exacerbate or reduce exchange-rate fluctuations.

It is perhaps useful to point out here that some of our comparative-statics results are similar to ones that can be derived from deterministic models. In particular, a fixed-output version of Niehans' [1975] model implies that changes in the degree of capital mobility have differential effects on the current-period exchange rate depending on whether the current-period exogenous shift variable is real or monetary. However, our results go beyond this, since they deal not only with current-period exchange-rate variability but also with asymptotic variability.

I. The Model

In order to analyze explicitly the stochastic properties of the model, the basic structure is kept quite simple. This means, of course, that we abstract from certain important aspects of economic reality. Nonetheless, the model still incorporates the aforementioned three critical assumptions of domestic price-level stickiness, attainment of period-by-period asset-market equilibrium, and responsiveness of trade flows to relative prices. In addition, our major conclusions have plausible intuitive interpretations, and thus seem robust with respect to sensible but complicating alterations of the model.

The model is of a small, open economy, facing a perfectly elastic supply of imports at a fixed world price (set for simplicity at one). Domestic output is produced at a constant rate, sold at a fixed price, and is an imperfect substitute for goods produced in the rest of the world. There are no physical assets, and domestic residents can hold either bonds or domestic money. Foreigners, however, are assumed

2. The importance of a sticky domestic price level is emphasized by Dornbusch [1976b], Henderson [1979], Niehans [1977], and is considered a stylized fact of the U. S. economy by Okun [1975] and Nordhaus [1975]. The assumption that asset markets clear every period is found in a large number of papers including Calvo and Rodriguez [1977], Dornbusch [1976b], Henderson [1979], and Kouri [1976]. Finally, the importance of relative price effects on trade flows is emphasized by Calvo and Rodriguez [1977] and by Niehans [1977].

to hold only their own country's money and bonds.[3] Unless otherwise noted, all variables will be measured as deviations from their equilibrium values.

There are three basic building-blocks in the model: a money-market equilibrium condition; a trade-balance and capital-flow specification coupled with a foreign-exchange market-clearing equation; and an expectational assumption. All behavioral equations are assumed to have specific linear forms, and the model is specified in discrete time.

A. The Money Market

Rather conventionally, money demand is assumed to have the following form:

$$m_t^d = p_t - \lambda r_t, \tag{1}$$

where m is the log of the domestic money supply, p is the log of the domestic price level, and r is the domestic interest rate. Since real income is assumed constant, it is suppressed as a money demand argument. Money supply is assumed to fluctuate around a constant mean $\overline{m}$, set for simplicity at zero:

$$m_t^s = \overline{m} + \epsilon_t = \epsilon_t, \tag{2}$$

where ϵ_t is a serially uncorrelated random variable with zero mean and known variance σ_ϵ^2. This money supply function interjects into the model the simplest possible form of monetary shock. Note that the ensuing analysis is just as applicable if the monetary shocks enter the demand rather than the supply of money. Money-market equilibrium is assumed to hold each period, and the equilibrium condition can thus be written as

$$r_t = -(1/\lambda)\epsilon_t, \tag{3}$$

where for simplicity p_t is set equal to zero.

B. The Foreign Exchange Market

Demands and supplies for foreign exchange arise either from transactions on the trade account or on the capital account. The net supply of foreign exchange arising from the trade balance is assumed to be an increasing function of the log of relative prices:

$$T_t = \alpha(e_t + p_t^f - p_t) + u_t \qquad \alpha > 0, \tag{4}$$

3. Some or all of these assumptions are found in most of the recent exchange-rate literature.

where T is the actual trade balance measured in foreign currency units, e is the log of the exchange rate, p^f and p are the logs of the foreign and domestic goods prices, respectively, and u_t is a serially uncorrelated disturbance with zero mean and known variance σ_u^2. The assumption that $\alpha > 0$ means that the Marshall-Lerner conditions are fulfilled. For ease, p^f is set equal to zero.

Capital flows arise from changes in desired stocks of domestically held foreign assets. The domestic stock demand for foreign assets, B_t, is assumed to be a linear function of the expected relative yield of foreign vis-à-vis domestic assets:

$$(5) \qquad B_t = \eta[E_t e_{t+1} - e_t + r_t^f - r_t] \quad \eta > 0,$$

where $E_t e_{t+1}$ is the expectation of e_{t+1} conditional on all information available at time t, r_t^f is the (fixed) foreign interest rate and η measures the sensitivity of portfolio responsiveness to changes in relative yields, i.e., η is the measure of capital mobility.[4] This specification ignores the role of wealth as an argument in the foreign-asset demand function. Under flexible exchange rates, this wealth effect may have important consequences for exchange-rate determination, since exchange-rate changes themselves lead to wealth changes and consequent capital "reflows." These effects are analyzed in Henderson [1979], but proved to be intractable when added to the present analysis.

The foreign-exchange market-clearing equation is simply

$$(6) \qquad \Delta B_t = T_t,$$

which says that the exchange rate in period t adjusts so that the flow excess supply of foreign exchange from the trade balance just equals the desired change in the stock demand for foreign assets by assetholders. Implicit in this equation is the assumption that portfolios are totally adjusted to their desired levels within each period. The equation also implies that there is no government intervention, i.e., no "managed floating," and also that net international interest payments are small enough to be ignored.

Equations (1) through (6) form a system of equations that can be solved under rational expectations for e_t as a stochastic function

4. Ideally, η should be derived from expected utility maximization, in which case it can be shown to depend negatively on a measure of risk aversion and on the forecast variance of the yield (cf. Muth [1961], p. 324). As demonstrated in McCafferty and Driskill [1980], this dependency of η on the stochastic structure of the system creates a potential problem of non-unique equilibria, a problem we do not want to pursue in this paper. Hence, in this model we take η as parametrically given.

of time. The remainder of this paper is concerned with providing this solution, and interpreting the resulting stochastic properties.

II. The Exchange-Rate Process

Substituting equations (1) through (5) into equation (6), we form the following difference equation in e_t:

$$e_t = \frac{\eta}{\eta + \alpha} e_{t-1} + \frac{\eta}{\eta + \alpha} E_t e_{t+1} \frac{-\eta}{\eta + \alpha} E_{t-1} e_t + \frac{\eta/\lambda}{\eta + \alpha} \epsilon_t - \frac{\eta/\lambda}{\eta + \alpha} \epsilon_{t-1} - \frac{u_t}{\eta + \alpha}. \tag{7}$$

To solve this equation, it is helpful to note that the ultimate solution will have the following form:

$$e_t = \pi_0 e_{t-1} + \pi_1 \epsilon_{t-1} + \pi_2 \epsilon_t + \pi_3 u_t. \tag{8}$$

$E_t e_{t+1}$ and $E_{t-1} e_t$ can then be found by taking expectations of equation (8), updating one period when finding $E_t e_{t+1}$. Substituting the resulting expressions back into (7) yields the following equation:

$$e_t = \frac{\eta(1 - \pi_0)}{\eta(1 - \pi_0) + \alpha} e_{t-1} + \frac{(\eta \pi_1 + 1/\lambda)}{\eta(1 - \pi_0) + \alpha} \epsilon_t + \frac{(-\eta \pi_1 - 1/\lambda)}{\eta(1 - \pi_0) + \alpha} \epsilon_{t-1} - \frac{u_t}{\eta(1 - \pi_0) + \alpha}. \tag{9}$$

Rationality implies that

$$\pi_0 = \frac{\eta(1 - \pi_0)}{\eta(1 - \pi_0) + \alpha} \tag{10}$$

$$\pi_1 = \frac{-\eta(\pi_1 + 1/\lambda)}{\eta(1 - \pi_0) + \alpha} \tag{11}$$

$$\pi_2 = \frac{\eta(\pi_1 + 1/\lambda)}{\eta(1 - \pi_0) + \alpha} \tag{12}$$

$$\pi_3 = \frac{-1}{\eta(1 - \pi_0) + \alpha}. \tag{13}$$

Equation (10) is quadratic in π_0; the roots are real, positive, and occur in reciprocal pairs. The smaller (stable) root is

$$\pi_0 = 1 + \frac{\alpha}{2\eta} - \frac{\alpha}{2\eta} \sqrt{1 + \frac{4\eta}{\alpha}}. \tag{14}$$

It is easily seen that as η ranges from zero to infinity, π_0 ranges from zero to one, and is everywhere increasing over that interval.

To solve for π_1, it is useful to note the following relationship:

$$\eta(1-\pi_0)+\alpha=\frac{\eta(1-\pi_0)}{\pi_0}. \tag{15}$$

Hence, it is readily shown that

$$\pi_1=-\frac{1}{\lambda}\pi_0,\quad \pi_1=-\pi_2,\quad \pi_3=\frac{-\pi_0}{\eta(1-\pi_0)}. \tag{16}$$

Consequently,

$$e_t=\pi_0 e_{t-1}+\frac{\pi_0}{\lambda}\epsilon_t-\frac{\pi_0}{\lambda}\epsilon_{t-1}-\frac{\pi_0}{\eta(1-\pi_0)}u_t, \tag{17}$$

which can be solved iteratively to yield

$$e_t=\frac{\pi_0}{\lambda}\epsilon_t+\frac{\pi_0(\pi_0-1)}{\lambda}\{\epsilon_{t-1}+\pi_0\epsilon_{t-2}+\pi_0^2\epsilon_{t-3}+\cdots\} \times\frac{-\pi_0}{\eta(1-\pi_0)}\{u_t+\pi_0 u_{t-1}+\pi_0^2 u_{t-2}+\cdots\}. \tag{18}$$

Thus, the exchange rate is described by the discrete random process of equation (18), and its unconditional mean and variance can be easily computed as

$$E(e_t)=0 \quad \text{for all } t \tag{19}$$

$$\sigma_e^2=\frac{\sigma_u^2}{(\alpha\eta/\pi_0)(1-\pi_0^2)}+\frac{2\sigma_\epsilon^2\pi_0^2}{\lambda^2(1+\pi_0)}. \tag{20}$$

Further statistical properties of the model can be summarized by some implied covariances. First consider the covariance of the trade balance with relative prices, which in this context are identical to the exchange rate:

$$E(e_tT_t)=\frac{\pi_0^2}{(1+\pi_0)}\left\{\frac{-\sigma_n^2}{\eta(1-\pi_0)}+\frac{2\alpha\sigma_\epsilon^2}{\lambda^2}\right\}. \tag{21}$$

The interesting characteristic here is that the covariance may be positive or negative, depending on the relative magnitudes of the variances of real and monetary shocks.

A second covariance of interest is the one between the spot and forward rate. Denoting the log of the forward rate by f_t, covered interest arbitrage insures that

$$f_t-e_t=r_t-r_t^f. \tag{22}$$

The covariance of e_t and f_t is thus

$$(23)\quad E(e_t f_t) = E(e_t(r_t - r_t^f + e_t)) = \frac{\pi_0 \sigma_u^2}{\alpha\eta(1-\pi_0^2)} - \frac{\pi_0(1-\pi_0)\sigma_\epsilon^2}{\lambda^2(1+\pi_0)}.$$

Again, the sign of the covariance depends upon the relative magnitudes of real and monetary disturbances. Note also that as η goes to infinity (perfect capital mobility), the covariance goes to zero.

III. Comparative Statics

Knowing the explicit expression for the exchange-rate variance, we can derive comparative-statics results about the effects on the variance of changes in structural parameters. First note that, not surprisingly, exchange-rate variance increases with increases in σ_u^2 and σ_ϵ^2, the underlying structural variances. The more interesting comparative-statics results concern the effects of changes in α, the degree of responsiveness of trade flows to relative price changes, and in η, the degree of capital mobility.

First, consider the effects of changes in α:

$$(24)\quad \frac{d\sigma_e^2}{d\alpha} = \frac{2\sigma^2}{\lambda^2}\left[\frac{2\pi_0 + \pi_0{}^2}{(1+\pi_0)^2}\right]\frac{d\pi_0}{d\alpha} - \frac{\sigma_u^2}{\{\alpha^2\sqrt{1+4\eta/\alpha}\}^2}\left\{\frac{2\alpha + 6\eta}{\sqrt{1+4\eta/\alpha}}\right\} < 0,$$

since

$$\frac{d\pi_0}{d\alpha} = \frac{-\pi_0}{\alpha\sqrt{1+4\eta/\alpha}} < 0.$$

An increase in α unambiguously decreases exchange-rate variance. Some intuition can be gained by considering flow demands for and supplies of foreign exchange. First note that an increase in α makes trade flows relatively more important than capital flows in the foreign-exchange market. Consequently, monetary shocks, which have their direct impact on capital flows, will have less of an effect on the exchange rate when α is large. Real shocks, which have their direct impact on the trade balance, will also have less of an effect on the exchange rate when α is large because a larger α requires a smaller change in e_t to equilibrate the trade balance for any given size real shock u_t.

Now consider the effects of changes in η on exchange-rate variability. First note the effect on that part of the exchange-rate variance due to real disturbances, which we shall denote by

$$V_u = \frac{\sigma_u^2}{(\alpha\eta/\pi_0)(1 - \pi_0^2)}. \tag{25}$$

This can be rewritten as

$$V_u = \frac{\sigma_u^2}{\alpha^2\sqrt{1 + 4\eta/\alpha}}. \tag{26}$$

which clearly decreases as η increases. That is, increasing capital mobility decreases that part of exchange-rate variability arising from real stochastic disturbances. Again, this can be interpreted in terms of foreign-exchange net demands and supplies. At time t, and assuming that there are no monetary shocks, the foreign-exchange market-clearing equation is

$$T_t = \alpha e_t + u_t = \Delta B_t = \eta(1 - \pi_0)e_t - \eta(1 - \pi_0)e_{t-1}. \tag{27}$$

Now, for given e_{t-1} and u_t, the effect of an increase in η on e_t is unambiguously negative, since

$$\frac{d(\eta(1 - \pi_0))}{d\eta} > 0.$$

Turning to the effects of changes in the degree of capital mobility on that part of exchange-rate variability due to monetary disturbances, which we denote by

$$V_\epsilon = \frac{2\sigma_\epsilon^2\pi_0^2}{\lambda^2(1 + \pi_0)}, \tag{28}$$

we find that increases in η increase exchange-rate variability:

$$\frac{dV_\epsilon}{d\eta} = \frac{2\sigma_\epsilon^2}{\eta^2}\left\{\frac{\pi_0^2(2 + \pi_0)(1 - \pi_0)}{(1 + \pi_0)^3}\right\} > 0. \tag{29}$$

Intuition for this result can be gained by first considering the case of perfect capital mobility, or *uncovered* interest arbitrage:[5]

$$r_t = r_t^f + E_t e_{t+1} - e_t. \tag{30}$$

Now, since $r_t = -(1/\lambda)\epsilon_t$, and setting $r_t^f = 0$ for simplicity, it is straightforward that

$$e_t = (1/\lambda)\epsilon_t, \quad E_t e_{t+1} = 0, \tag{31}$$

which is also the limiting form of equation (17) as η goes to infinity.

5. This is the definition of perfect capital mobility used by Dornbusch [1976b].

Intuitively, suppose that a monetary increase decreases the domestic interest rate, leading to an incipient capital outflow that depreciates the current exchange rate so much that the expected next-period appreciation just offsets the new interest differential. Now, with less than perfect capital mobility, a given change in the interest differential will not have to be offset exactly by an expected exchange-rate appreciation. Rather, the capital outflow will be less than infinite, the expected next-period appreciation will be less than the new interest differential, and consequently the current exchange-rate will not have to depreciate quite so much.

To reiterate, the effects of an increase in the degree of capital mobility are a decrease in that portion of exchange-rate variability due to real shocks and an increase in that portion due to monetary shocks. In a sense, then, whether or not speculative capital flows are "destabilizing" or "stabilizing" depends on whether the underlying stochastic disturbances are real or monetary.[6]

IV. Concluding Remarks

In this paper we have constructed a rather simple open-economy model that incorporates assumptions of sticky prices, asset markets that clear period by period, and rational expectations. The important innovation is the explicit inclusion of uncertainty, which permits us to trace the sources of exchange-rate variability back to the interaction of real and monetary stochastic shocks with various structural parameters of the model. Perhaps the most interesting result we find is that changes in the degree of capital mobility have asymmetric effects on exchange-rate variability, depending on whether the underlying stochastic disturbances are real or monetary.

It should be noted that a key element of our model was the elimination via various simplifying assumptions of any feedback from the foreign-exchange market to the goods and money markets. While this kept the analysis tractable, it would be useful to extend the model to incorporate this type of feedback.

Another extension of the model would be to incorporate a government policy reaction function in the foreign exchange market, i.e., incorporate "managed floating." Since it is reasonable to assume (as we do in this paper) that the current exchange rate is part of the in-

6. There are other aspects to stability besides the question of exchange rate variability. In particular, the recent literature has paid considerable attention to the question of Walrasian stability in the presence of a trade-balance J-curve effect. For a consideration of these problems, see Driskill and McCafferty [1980].

formation set available to market participants, such government reaction functions would probably have some effect, in contrast to much recent work on policy under rational expectations.

UNIVERSITY OF CALIFORNIA, DAVIS, AND
OHIO STATE UNIVERSITY

REFERENCES

Barro, R. J., "A Stochastic Equilibrium Model of an Open Economy Under Flexible Exchange Rates," this *Journal,* XCII (Feb. 1978), 149–64.
Calvo, G. A., and C. A. Rodriguez, "A Model of Exchange Rate Determination Under Currency Substitution and Rational Expectations," *Journal of Political Economy,* LXXXV (June 1977), 617–25.
Dornbusch, R., "Exchange Rate Expectations and Monetary Policy," *Journal of International Economics,* VI (Aug. 1976a), 231–44.
——, "Expectations and Exchange Rate Dynamics," *Journal of Political Economy,* LXXXIV (Dec. 1976b), 1161–76.
Driskill, R., and S. McCafferty, "Speculation, Rational Expectations, and Stability of the Foreign Exchange Market," *Journal of International Economics,* X (Feb. 1980).
Henderson, D., "The Dynamic Effects of Exchange Market Intervention: Two Extreme Views and a Synthesis," International Finance Discussion Papers, Number 142, June 1979.
Kouri, P. J. K., "The Exchange Rate and the Balance of Payments in the Short Run and in the Long Run: A Monetary Approach," *Scandinavian Journal of Economics,* LXXVIII (1976), 280–304.
McCafferty, S., and R. Driskill, "Problems of Existence and Uniqueness in Non-Linear Models of Rational Expectations," *Econometrica,* XLVIII (July 1980), 1313–17.
Muth, J., "Rational Expectations and the Theory of Price Movements," *Econometrica,* XXIX (July 1961), 315–35.
Niehans, J., "Some Doubts About the Efficacy of Monetary Policy Under Flexible Exchange Rates," *Journal of International Economics,* V (Aug. 1975), 275–81.
——, "Exchange Rate Dynamics with Stock-Flow Interactions," *Journal of Political Economy,* LXXXV (Dec. 1977), 1245–57.
Nordhaus, William, "Discussion," *Brookings Papers on Economic Activity* (1975), 440–43.
Okun, Arthur M., "Inflation: Its Mechanics and Welfare Costs," *Brookings Papers on Economic Activity,* 2 (1975), 351–90.

No. 381

THE QUARTERLY JOURNAL OF ECONOMICS

FOUNDED 1886

Vol. XCV December 1980 No. 4

ARTICLES

Generalized Findlay-Grubert Theorem . . . . *Jitendralal Borkakoti* 587

Unionization and Productivity: Micro-Econometric Evidence . *Kim B. Clark* 613

"Rational" Duopoly Equilibria . . . . *John Laitner* 641

Technology, Entrepreneurs, and Firm Size
. . . . *Guillermo A. Calvo and Stanislaw Wellisz* 663

Public-Private Consumption Tradeoffs and the Balanced Budget Multiplier
. . . . *Uri Possen and Steven Slutsky* 679

Experience, Performance, and Earnings
. . . . *James L. Medoff and Katharine G. Abraham* 703

Technology Transfer to Overseas Subsidiaries by U. S.-Based Firms
. . . . *Edwin Mansfield and Anthony Romeo* 737

Factor Market Dynamics and the Incidence of Taxes and Subsidies
. . . . *Daniel S. Hamermesh* 751

NOTES

The Cost of Capital in Nonmarketed Firms . . . . *Bengt Holmstrom* 765

Dual Markets, Rationing, and Queues
. . . . *Jagdish N. Bhagwati and Balbir S. Sihag* 775

Dividend Policy and Tax Incidence in a Growing Economy
. . . . *J. Gregory Ballentine* 781

PUBLISHED FOR HARVARD UNIVERSITY
BY JOHN WILEY & SONS, NEW YORK

QJECAT 95(4) 587–788 (1980)
ISSN 0033-5533

The Quarterly Journal of Economics

Published eight times in 1980 (February, March, May, June, August, September, November and December), two volumes, four issues per volume, by John Wiley & Sons, Inc. Second class postage paid at New York, New York, and at additional mailing offices.

Subscription price (1981): $30.00 per volume. Postage and handling outside U.S.A.: $8.00 per volume. Please allow four weeks for change of address. Back volumes are available for previous years. Request price list from publisher. Claims for undelivered copies must be made no later than three months following month of publication. Missing copies will be supplied when losses have been sustained in transit and where reserve stock will permit.

Books, periodicals and manuscripts should be addressed to THE QUARTERLY JOURNAL OF ECONOMICS, Littauer Center, Cambridge, Massachusetts 02138. Two copies of manuscripts should be submitted in clear double-spaced typewritten copy. Manuscripts of more than thirty-five double-spaced typed pages in length are not ordinarily considered for publication. After publication, twenty-five complimentary reprints are sent to the author receiving proofs. This journal does not carry a page charge for contributors.

Business correspondence should be addressed to Journals Department, John Wiley & Sons, 605 Third Avenue, New York, New York 10158.

Information for Authors

The provisions of the new copyright law, which went into effect in January 1978, make it advisable for authors to transfer copyrights to publishers explicitly and in writing. Under the old copyright law the transfer implicit in submission gave adequate protection to all concerned. Accordingly, we now require that the following agreement be executed and signed by the author(s) before a manuscript is accepted for publication. The signed agreement is then to be returned to *The Quarterly Journal of Economics*.

Agreement to Transfer Copyright

Name of Article: ____

____

I submit herewith the article named above for publication in *The Quarterly Journal of Economics*. It has not been published before. If and when the article is accepted for publication, I, as the author, hereby agree to transfer (for U.S. Government employees: to the extent transferable) to the President and Fellows of Harvard College all rights under existing copyright laws except for the following, which the author specifically retains:

1. The right to make further copies of all or part of the published article for my use in classroom teaching;
2. The right to reuse all or part of this material in a compilation of my own works or in a textbook of which I am the author;
3. The right to make copies of the published work for internal distribution within the institution that employs me.

I agree that copies made under these circumstances will continue to carry the copyright notice that appeared in the original published work. I agree to inform my coauthors, if any, of the above terms.

____
Signature(s) and date(s)

____

____
Print name(s) and title(s)

____
Institutions or companies (if appropriate)

THE

QUARTERLY JOURNAL OF ECONOMICS

Vol. XCV December 1980 No. 4

ARTICLES

Generalized Findlay-Grubert Theorem .... *Jitendralal Borkakoti* 587

Unionization and Productivity: Micro-Econometric Evidence . *Kim B. Clark* 613

"Rational" Duopoly Equilibria .... *John Laitner* 641

Technology, Entrepreneurs, and Firm Size
.... *Guillermo A. Calvo and Stanislaw Wellisz* 663

Public-Private Consumption Tradeoffs and the Balanced Budget Multiplier
.... *Uri Possen and Steven Slutsky* 679

Experience, Performance, and Earnings
.... *James L. Medoff and Katharine G. Abraham* 703

Technology Transfer to Overseas Subsidiaries by U. S.-Based Firms
.... *Edwin Mansfield and Anthony Romeo* 737

Factor Market Dynamics and the Incidence of Taxes and Subsidies
.... *Daniel S. Hamermesh* 751

NOTES

The Cost of Capital in Nonmarketed Firms .... *Bengt Holmstrom* 765

Dual Markets, Rationing, and Queues
.... *Jagdish N. Bhagwati and Balbir S. Sihag* 775

Dividend Policy and Tax Incidence in a Growing Economy
.... *J. Gregory Ballentine* 781

THE
QUARTERLY JOURNAL
OF ECONOMICS

Vol. XCV December 1980 No. 4

GENERALIZED FINDLAY-GRUBERT THEOREM*

JITENDRALAL BORKAKOTI

This generalization allows the relative price to vary and explicitly considers Hicks-, Harrod-, and Solow-neutrality. Under certain conditions, the Harrod-neutral and the Solow-neutral shifts are equivalent to the Hicks factor-saving shift. If Hicks-Harrod-Solow neutral or the Hicks factor-saving improvement occurs in one of the two sectors, then the relative price of that good falls, and the level of output of that good increases. However, the level of output of the other good remains constant if Hicks-Harrod-Solow-neutral progress occurs, and decreases or increases according to whether the Hicks x-saving or x-using technological progress occurs in the x-intensive sector.

Findlay and Grubert [1959] have analyzed the effects of neutral and factor-saving technological progress on the levels of production in a simple two-good, two-factor model by assuming constant commodity prices. In Part I of their paper they use geometric techniques to establish the change in factor prices (and hence the change in the ratio at which the factors are used in each sector) necessary to keep the commodity prices constant after technological progress has taken place in one sector. In part II they use these results in a standard box diagram to analyze the effects of technological progress, at constant commodity prices, on the levels of sectoral production. Their basic results *strictu sensu* are unsatisfactory general equilibrium results, not only because the demand side is neglected, but also because there is no reasonable justification for holding commodity prices constant

* I am grateful to Professor J. Black, Dr. E. A. Kuska, and Professor Michio Morishima for comments on an earlier draft of this paper. Errors that may remain, however, are my own responsibility. An earlier version of this paper was presented at the International Economics Study Group Seminar at the London School of Economics in January 1978.

The Quarterly Journal of Economics, December 1980 0033-5533/80/0095-0587$02.50

in a closed economy.[1] In general, commodity prices will change, and of course, these prices in the post-technological progress situation will be determined by sectoral demand and supply. This paper generalizes the Findlay-Grubert theorem not only by bringing the demand side explicitly into a full general equilibrium model, but also by explicitly considering the Hicks-neutral, the Harrod-neutral, and the Solow-neutral process technological progress.[2] It should be mentioned that the work of Amano [1964] and Jones [1965] falls short of eradicating the above-mentioned lacunae in the Findlay-Grubert theorem.

THE MODEL

Assume that an economy produces two consumption goods, C and B, by fully employing two factors of production, namely, capital (K) and labor (L). The consumption good C is the numeraire of the system such that p is the price of good B in terms of good C. It is assumed that good C is always relatively K-intensive for all relevant wage-rental ratios. Define the following per capita variables as

$$y = Y/L = \text{per capita national income}$$
$$y_j = Y_j/L = \text{sectoral per capita output,} \quad j = C,B$$
$$k_j = K_j/L_j = \text{sectoral capital-labor ratio,} \quad j = C,B$$
$$l_j = L_j/L = \text{sectoral proportion of labor,} \quad j = C,B$$
$$k = K/L = \text{overall capital-labor ratio.}$$

Defining ω as the wage-rental ratio and allowing technological progress to occur in the K-intensive sector C, we may write the model as

$$(1) \quad y_C = \mu f_C(k_C(\omega))l_C, \quad \text{for Hicks-neutrality}$$

$$(2) \quad y_C = f_C(k_C(\omega),\mu)l_C, \quad \text{for Harrod-neutrality}$$

$$(3) \quad y_C = f_C(\mu k_C(\omega))l_C, \quad \text{for Solow-neutrality}$$

$$(4) \quad y_B = f_B(k_B(\omega))l_B$$

$$(5) \quad p = \mu f'_C(k_C)/f'_B(k_B), \quad \text{for Hicks-neutrality}$$

1. It is necessary to point out that in Part III of their paper, Findlay and Grubert use their results about the changes in the production levels (caused by technological progress) to determine the direction of the movement of the terms of trade in a trading world. This is clearly different from analyzing the autarkic movement of the relative price by using a model that determines sectoral demand and supply simultaneously.

2. Neutrality is a matter of definition. Sato and Beckman [1968] have shown that there could be as many as sixteen definitions of neutral technological progress within the neoclassical framework.

(6) $p = f'_C(k_C,\mu)/f'_B(k_B),$ for Harrod-neutrality

(7) $p = \mu f'_C(\mu k_C)/f'_B(k_B),$ for Solow-neutrality

(8) $\omega = f_C(k_C)/f'_C(k_C) - k_C,$ for Hicks-neutrality

(9) $\omega = f_C(k_C,\mu)/f'_C(k_C,\mu) - k_C,$ for Harrod-neutrality

(10) $\omega = f_C(\mu k_C)/\mu f'_C(\mu k_C) - k_C,$ for Solow-neutrality

(11) $$\omega = f_B(k_B)/f'_B(k_B) - k_B$$

(12) $$k_C l_C + k_B l_B = k$$

(13) $$l_C + l_B = 1$$

(14) $$y = y_C + p y_B$$

(15) $$y_C = ay.$$

Consider only Hicks-, Harrod-, or Solow-neutrality at a time. In each case, there are nine independent equations to solve for nine unknowns, namely, y, y_j, k_j, l_j, ω, and p; while μ is the exogenous technological progress parameter and k is given and fixed. Note that f_j are the standard per capita production functions that exhibit all the well-known neoclassical properties, which need not be repeated here. The per capita production function takes the forms[3] of (1), (2), and (3), respectively, for Hicks-, Harrod-, and Solow-neutral technological progress.[4]

First note that (15) is the Graham type demand function derived from the Cobb-Douglas type of utility function $U = Y_C^a Y_B^b$, where $0 < a < 1$, $0 < b < 1$, $a + b = 1$, and Y_C and Y_B are the quantities of goods C and B. The demand function for good B is $y_B = (b/p)y$, which follows from (14) and (15). These specific-form demand functions, however, do not make our model less general than any other familiar two-sector model. As Inada [1964] has proved,[5] the classical aggregate saving function that is used by Uzawa [1963] does imply that the implicit utility functions are of the Cobb-Douglas type. The rest of the equations of the model are self-explanatory.[6]

Referring to the Hicks-neutral case, it may be noted that μ appears in the production function (1) and in the supply-price relation (5), but not in the wage-rental relation (8). Thus, the factor-intensity

3. See Allen [1968] and Uzawa [1961].
4. This is a once-for-all technological improvement.
5. See also Morishima [1969, pp. 97–99], where he discusses the properties of a homothetic utility function.
6. Readers who are not familiar with the two-sector models should read Uzawa [1963].

curves are not affected by the Hicks-neutral technological progress, although the price-relation curve[7] shifts upward, as is evident from (5). On the other hand, if the Harrod-neutral technological progress occurs, then μ appears in the wage-rental relation (9) in addition to (2) and (6). First, because of the homogeneity property of the production function, the following result may easily be derived:[8]

$$\delta f'_C/\delta\mu = -f''_C[k_C/\mu]. \tag{16}$$

The implicit relation between ω and k_B is not disturbed in sector B, but the implicit relation[9] now in sector C is between ω, k_C, and μ. Partially differentiate (9) with respect to ω and simplify to obtain

$$k'_C = \left.\frac{\delta k_C}{\delta\omega}\right|_{\mu=\text{const.}} = \frac{-[f'_C(k_C,\mu)]^2}{f_C(k_C,\mu)f''_C}. \tag{17}$$

The factor-intensity curve for good C is thus upward sloping. Partially differentiate (9) with respect to μ to obtain

$$\left.\frac{\delta k_C}{\delta\mu}\right|_{\omega=\text{const.}} = \left[\frac{\delta f'_C}{\delta\mu}(\omega + k_C) - \frac{\delta f_C}{\delta\mu}\right] \Big/ -f''_C(\omega + k_C). \tag{18}$$

Equation (18) does not reveal at once whether the factor-intensity curve would remain constant, shift upward, or shift downward as a result of the Harrod-neutral technological progress, since the sign of the numerator of (18) is not immediately determinate without further investigation. The expression of the numerator is crucial, as would soon be apparent, and a detailed discussion of its sign will be carried out shortly. Consider the supply-price equation (6). Partially differentiate (6) with respect to ω, holding μ constant, to obtain

$$\frac{1}{p}\frac{\delta p}{\delta\omega} = \frac{1}{\omega + k_B(\omega)} - \frac{1}{\omega + k_C(\omega,\mu)}. \tag{19}$$

In view of the assumed factor-intensity condition, the price-relation curve is upward sloping. It is not easily verified[10] that the price-relation curve shifts upward as a result of the Harrod-neutral technological progress.

In the traditional literature, for example, Hahn and Matthews [1964], Solow-neutrality is regarded as a mirror-image of Harrod-

7. The price-relation curve is a continuous function that relates commodity prices to factor prices.

8. The detailed derivation is presented in Appendix I. Also note that f'_C and f''_C denote $\delta f_C/\delta k_C$ and $\delta^2 f_C/\delta k_C^2$, respectively.

9. Let this relation be of the form, $k_C = J(\omega,\mu)$.

10. If we differentiate (19) partially with respect to μ, we have an expression where $\delta k_C/\delta\mu$ and $\delta k_B/\delta\mu$ appear. Since the signs of $\delta k_C/\delta\mu$ and $\delta k_B/\delta\mu$ are not immediately clear, therefore, the sign of $\delta p/\delta\mu$ is also not clear.

neutrality, and as a result, some aspects of the Solow-neutral technological progress are not discussed. While the "mirror-image" treatment is mathematically all right, it is far from being so in the economic sense. The "mirror-image" treatment must express the system as a per-unit-of-capital system; and this being so, no appropriate comparisons could be made with either the Hicks or the Harrod neutral case, where the system is a per capita system. It is thus necessary to consider the Solow-neutral technological progress separately, and it will soon be apparent that Solow-neutrality makes a specific contribution to our analysis.

Referring to the Solow-neutral case, we may note that μ appears in the supply-price equation (7) and in the wage-rental equation (10), in addition to the production function (3). The implicit relation between ω and k_B is not disturbed. Partially differentiate (10) with respect to ω to obtain

$$(20) \qquad k_C' = \left.\frac{\delta k_C}{\delta \omega}\right|_{\mu=\text{const.}} = \frac{-[f_C'(\mu k_C)]^2}{f_C(\mu k_C) f_C''(\mu k_C)} > 0.$$

Thus, the factor-intensity curve for good C is upward sloping.[11] Partially differentiate (10) with respect to μ holding ω constant, and simplify to obtain

$$(21) \qquad \left.\frac{\delta k_C}{\delta \mu}\right|_{\omega=\text{const.}} = \frac{k_C}{\mu}\left[\frac{\omega}{k_C}\frac{\delta k_C}{\delta \omega} - 1\right].$$

It is not clear from (21) whether the factor-intensity curve $k_C(\omega,\mu)$ would shift or not. However, it is interesting to note that the factor-intensity curve would remain unchanged if σ_C (the elasticity of substitution between the factors) is unity. This is clear from (21). If $\sigma_C > 1$, then the $k_C(\omega,\mu)$ curve would shift upward; and if $\sigma_C < 1$, then it would shift downward. Now, differentiate (7) partially with respect to ω and simplify to obtain

$$(22) \qquad \left.\frac{\delta p}{\delta \omega}\right|_{\mu=\text{const.}} = \frac{p}{(\omega + k_B)} - \frac{p}{(\omega + k_C)}.$$

Thus, the price-relation curve is upward sloping. It is, however, not clear from (7) that the $p(\omega,\mu)$ curve shifts upward as a result of the Solow-neutral technological progress.

The Hicks-Neutral Case

The purpose here is to find the effect of technological progress in the relatively K-intensive sector C on the relative price p and on

11. Note that in this case, $f_C' = \delta f_C / \delta(\mu k_C)$.

the levels of production of the consumption goods, C and B, by taking into account the supply and demand of both the sectors within the full general equilibrium system. First, consider the Hicks-neutral technological progress. Partially differentiate the system (1), (4), (5), (8), (11)–(15) with respect to μ, holding k constant, to obtain

$$[E_C][W_C] = [N_C]. \tag{23}$$

The actual matrix and vectors are

$$\begin{bmatrix} 0 & 1 & 0 & -\mu f_C' l_C & 0 & -\mu f_C & 0 & 0 & 0 \\ 0 & 0 & 1 & 0 & -\mu f_B' l_B & 0 & -f_B & 0 & 0 \\ 0 & 0 & 0 & \frac{-\mu f_C''}{f_B'} & \frac{\mu f_C' f_B''}{[f_B']^2} & 0 & 0 & 0 & 1 \\ 0 & 0 & 0 & \frac{-1}{k_C'} & 0 & 0 & 0 & 1 & 0 \\ 0 & 0 & 0 & 0 & \frac{-1}{k_B'} & 0 & 0 & 1 & 0 \\ 0 & 0 & 0 & l_C & l_B & k_C & k_B & 0 & 0 \\ 0 & 0 & 0 & 0 & 0 & 1 & 1 & 0 & 0 \\ 1 & -1 & -p & 0 & 0 & 0 & 0 & 0 & -y_B \\ -a & 1 & 0 & 0 & 0 & 0 & 0 & 0 & 0 \end{bmatrix} \begin{bmatrix} \frac{\delta y}{\delta \mu} \\ \frac{\delta y_C}{\delta \mu} \\ \frac{\delta y_B}{\delta \mu} \\ \frac{\delta k_C}{\delta \mu} \\ \frac{\delta k_B}{\delta \mu} \\ \frac{\delta l_C}{\delta \mu} \\ \frac{\delta l_B}{\delta \mu} \\ \frac{\delta \omega}{\delta \mu} \\ \frac{\delta p}{\delta \mu} \end{bmatrix} = \begin{bmatrix} f_C l_C \\ 0 \\ \frac{f_C'}{f_B'} \\ 0 \\ 0 \\ 0 \\ 0 \\ 0 \\ 0 \end{bmatrix}$$

Appropriately substitute vector N_C in matrix E_C by using Cramer's rule to obtain

$$\begin{cases} \frac{\delta p}{\delta \mu} = \frac{|P_C|}{|E_C|} \quad \frac{\delta y_C}{\delta \mu} = \frac{|C_C|}{|E_C|} \quad \frac{\delta y_B}{\delta \mu} = \frac{|B_C|}{|E_C|} \\ \frac{\delta \omega}{\delta \mu} = \frac{|\Omega_C|}{|E_C|} \quad \frac{\delta k_C}{\delta \mu} = \frac{|K_C|}{|E_C|} \quad \frac{\delta k_B}{\delta \mu} = \frac{|R_C|}{|E_C|} \end{cases}. \tag{24}$$

Finding the determinants and simplifying, the following results are obtained:

$$(25)\quad |E_C| = \frac{-\mu f_C'}{k_C' k_B'}\left[\frac{k_C'(\omega + k_B)(k - k_B)}{(k_C - k_B)} + \frac{k_B'(\omega + k_C)(k_C - k)}{(k_C - k_B)} + \frac{a(k_C - k_B)(k_C - k)}{(\omega + k_C)}\right]$$

$$(26)\quad |P_C| = \frac{-\mu [f_C']^2}{k_C' k_B' f_B'}\left[\frac{k_C'(k - k_B)(\omega + k_B)}{(k_C - k_B)} + \frac{k_B'(k_C - k)(\omega + k_C)}{(k_C - k_B)} + \frac{(1 - a)(k_C - k_B)(k - k_B)}{(\omega + k_B)}\right]$$

$$(27)\quad |C_C| = -a\mu [f_C']^2 \left[\frac{(k - k_B)(k_C - k)}{k_C' k_B'} + \frac{(k_C - k)(\omega + k)(\omega + k_C)}{k_C'(k_C - k_B)} + \frac{(k - k_B)(\omega + k)(\omega + k_B)}{k_B'(k_C - k_B)}\right].$$

Therefore,

$$(28)\qquad |E_C| < 0; \quad |P_C| < 0; \quad |C_C| < 0.$$

Furthermore,

$$(29)\qquad |B_C| = 0; \quad |\Omega_C| = 0; \quad |K_C| = 0; \quad |R_C| = 0.$$

In view of (24), (28), and (29),

$$(30)\qquad \begin{cases} \dfrac{\delta p}{\delta \mu} > 0, & \dfrac{\delta y_C}{\delta \mu} > 0, \quad \dfrac{\delta y_B}{\delta \mu} = 0, \\[2ex] \dfrac{\delta \omega}{\delta \mu} = 0, & \dfrac{\delta k_C}{\delta \mu} = 0, \quad \dfrac{\delta k_B}{\delta \mu} = 0. \end{cases}$$

The full general equilibrium effect of the Hicks-neutral technological progress in the relatively K-intensive sector C is to decrease the relative price of good C, to increase the level of output of good C, and to leave the level of output of the other good B unchanged. Furthermore, the wage-rental ratio and the sectoral capital/labor ratios are left unchanged. It is easily verified that the per capita income also increases. At constant commodity prices, Findlay and Grubert [1959] found that the level of output of good C increased and the level of output of good B decreased. In contrast to this, the level of output of good B remains unchanged in our generalized case when the relative commodity price is allowed to vary along with all other variables. The natural extension would be to show that similar conclusions hold if the Hicks-neutral technological progress occurs in the relatively L-intensive sector B. This is done in Appendix II.

THE HARROD-NEUTRAL CASE

Now consider the Harrod-neutral technological progress. Partially differentiate the system (2), (4), (6), (9), (11)–(15) with respect to μ, holding k constant, and simplify to obtain

$$[D_C][V_C] = [M_C]. \tag{31}$$

The actual matrix and vectors are presented in Appendix III. Now appropriately substitute vector M_C in matrix D_C by using Cramer's rule to obtain

$$\begin{cases} \dfrac{\delta p}{\delta \mu} = \dfrac{|P_C|}{|D_C|} & \dfrac{\delta y_C}{\delta \mu} = \dfrac{|C_C|}{|D_C|} & \dfrac{\delta y_B}{\delta \mu} = \dfrac{|B_C|}{|D_C|} \\ \dfrac{\delta \omega}{\delta \mu} = \dfrac{|\Omega_C|}{|D_C|} & \dfrac{\delta k_C}{\delta \mu} = \dfrac{|K_C|}{|D_C|} & \dfrac{\delta k_B}{\delta \mu} = \dfrac{|R_C|}{|D_C|} \end{cases} \tag{32}$$

Finding the determinants and simplifying, we obtain the following results:

$$|D_C| = \frac{-f_C'}{k_C' k_B'}\left[\frac{k_C'(\omega + k_B)(k - k_B)}{(k_C - k_B)} + \frac{k_B'(\omega + k_C)(k_C - k)}{(k_C - k_B)} + \frac{a(k_C - k_B)(k_C - k)}{(\omega + k_C)}\right] \tag{33}$$

$$\therefore |D_C| < 0 \tag{34}$$

$$|P_C| = \frac{f_C'(k - k_B)}{f_B' k_B'(k_C - k_B)}\left[k_C \frac{\delta f_C'}{\delta \mu} - \frac{\delta f_C}{\delta \mu}\right] - \frac{f_C'(k - k_B)k_B}{f_B' k_B'(k_C - k_B)} \frac{\delta f_C'}{\delta \mu} - \frac{f_C'(k_C - k)(k - k_B)}{f_B' k_C' k_B'(\omega + k)(\omega + k_C)} \frac{\delta f_C}{\delta \mu} - \frac{f_C'(k_C - k)}{f_B' k_C'(k_C - k_B)} \frac{\delta f_C}{\delta \mu} \tag{35}$$

$$|C_C| = \frac{a f_C'(k - k_B)(\omega + k_B)}{k_B'(k_C - k_B)}\left[k_C \frac{\delta f_C'}{\delta \mu} - \frac{\delta f_C}{\delta \mu}\right] - \frac{a f_C'(k - k_B)(\omega + k_B)k}{k_B'(k_C - k_B)} \frac{\delta f_C'}{\delta \mu} - \frac{a f_C'(k - k_B)(k_C - k)}{k_C' k_B'(\omega + k_C)} \frac{\delta f_C}{\delta \mu} - \frac{a f_C'(k_C - k)(\omega + k)}{k_C'(k_C - k_B)} \frac{\delta f_C}{\delta \mu} \tag{36}$$

$$(37) \quad |B_C| = \frac{-f_B'(\omega + k_B)(k_C - k)(k - k_B)^2}{k_B'(\omega + k)(k_C - k_B)^2}\left[(\omega + k_C)\frac{\delta f_C'}{\delta\mu} - \frac{\delta f_C}{\delta\mu}\right]$$

$$(38) \quad |\Omega_C| = \frac{(\omega + k_B)(k - k_B)}{k_B'(k_C - k_B)}\left[(\omega + k_C)\frac{\delta f_C'}{\delta\mu} - \frac{\delta f_C}{\delta\mu}\right]$$

$$(39) \quad |K_C| = \frac{-(\omega + k_C)(k_C - k)}{(k_C - k_B)}\left[(\omega + k_C)\frac{\delta f_C'}{\delta\mu} - \frac{\delta f_C}{\delta\mu}\right] - \frac{(k - k_B)(k_C - k)}{k_B'(\omega + k)}\left[(\omega + k_C)\frac{\delta f_C'}{\delta\mu} - \frac{\delta f_C}{\delta\mu}\right]$$

$$(40) \quad |R_C| = \frac{(k - k_B)(\omega + k_B)}{(k_C - k_B)}\left[(\omega + k_C)\frac{\delta f_C'}{\delta\mu} - \frac{\delta f_C}{\delta\mu}\right].$$

It is now certainly clear that the sign of $|B_C|$, $|\Omega_C|$, $|K_C|$, or $|R_C|$ depends on whether $\delta f_C/\delta\mu \gtreqless (\omega + k_C)\,\delta f_C'/\delta\mu$, while the sign of $|P_C|$ and $|C_C|$ depends on whether $\delta f_C/\delta\mu \geqq (\omega + k_C)\,\delta f_C'/\delta\mu$.

A Necessary Digression

Uzawa [1961] has proved that the Hicks-neutral and the Harrod-neutral shifts are similar if and only if the production function takes the Cobb-Douglas form. The economics of this proposition is best explained by quoting the words of Hahn and Matthews:

> Assume given labour force. Hicks-neutral progress retains the same distribution of income in the event that K remains unchanged. Harrod-neutral technical progress retains the same distribution in the event that K rises in the same proportion as Y. For both requirements to be satisfied, the distribution of income must therefore be the same as between two situations that differ only in the level of K. This implies unit elasticity of substitution between L and K. The only production function with this property is the Cobb-Douglas production function [1964, p. 51].

On the other hand, Kennedy [1962a, 1962b] has put forward the stronger proposition that the Hicks-neutral and the Harrod-neutral definitions are the same. Kennedy's argument is best put in his own words:

> Suppose (Harrod's definition) that at constant rate of interest, an improvement leaves K/Y ratio unchanged. This implies that, for a given labour force, the real wage must rise in the same proportion as the rise in output. Equilibrium in the labour market requires that the real wage must also rise in the same proportion as the marginal product of labour. With a constant rate of interest, the cost of a "machine" will rise in the same proportion as the real wage. It follows that if the capital-output ratio is to remain unchanged, the quantity of machines must also be unchanged. Further, if the rate of interest is constant, the marginal product of machines must rise in the same proportion as the cost of machines. But the cost of machines will rise in the same proportion as the marginal product of labour. Therefore, with an unchanged quantity of machines, the marginal product of machines will rise in the same proportion as the marginal product of labour (Hicks's definition) [1962a, p. 249].

Thus, Uzawa and Kennedy hold very different views. Asimakopulos [1963][12] shows that the positions on the similarity between Hicks-neutrality and Harrod-neutrality are different because the implicit economic models are different. The Uzawa model allows accumulation of capital to take place and assumes distinct consumption goods and capital goods. The Kennedy model assumes that the total net output is consumed, and hence that there is no accumulation of capital. It also assumes distinct consumption goods and capital goods. Both of the models assume that the labor force is constant.

Diamond [1965] has developed an index[13] to describe the bias of technological progress. The index is defined as

$$D = \frac{\delta(F_K/F_L)}{\delta t} \Big/ \frac{F_K}{F_L} = \frac{F_{Kt}}{F_K} - \frac{F_{Lt}}{F_L}. \tag{41}$$

In (41), F_K and F_L are the marginal products of capital and labor, respectively, and t is the shift parameter in a twice differentiable production function $F(K,L,t)$ homogeneous of the first degree. D will be referred to as the Diamond-index, which measures the percentage change in the marginal rate of technical substitution between K and L with inputs held constant. D is a measure of the Hicks-bias. Technological change is Hicks L-saving, Hicks-neutral, and Hicks K-saving, respectively, according to whether $D > 0$, $D = 0$, or $D < 0$. Furthermore, Diamond considers Kennedy's theorem by using a two-sector model and finds that, for Hicks-neutrality and Harrod-neutrality to be equivalent, D must equal zero in the sector where technological progress occurs (provided that technological change takes place only in the consumption-good sector).

Now consider the present model, when the Harrod-neutral technological progress takes place in the consumption-good sector C, which has only two consumption-good sectors. There is no accumulation of capital. Consumption goods and capital goods are distinct in the sense that the given endowment of "capital" is taken as the collection of machines, i.e., capital goods, which could be used to produce either good C or good B. This model is thus akin to the Kennedy model. The crucial feature is the fixed endowments of capital and labor. Consider, therefore, the Diamond-index for sector C to obtain

$$D = \frac{1}{(f_C - f_C' k_C)} \left\{ (\omega + k_C) \frac{\delta f_C'}{\delta \mu} - \frac{\delta f_C}{\delta \mu} \right\}. \tag{42}$$

12. For further details see Asimakopulos [1963, pp. 675–77].
13. See also Burmeister and Dobell [1970].

Now note that the expression in the braces in (42) is the crucial expression that appears in (37)–(40). Therefore, the Harrod-neutral technical change is revealed to be equivalent to the Hicks-neutral shift if and only if

(43) $$D = 0, \quad \text{or} \quad (\omega + k_C)(\delta f'_C/\delta\mu) = \delta f_C/\delta\mu.$$

The Harrod-neutral technological change is equivalent to the Hicks K-saving shift if and only if

(44) $$D < 0, \quad \text{or} \quad \delta f_C/\delta\mu > (\omega + k_C)(\delta f'_C/\delta\mu).$$

The Harrod-neutral technological change is equivalent to the Hicks L-saving shift if and only if

(45) $$D > 0, \quad \text{or} \quad \delta f_C/\delta\mu < (\omega + k_C)(\delta f'_C/\delta\mu).$$

The signs of the determinants (35)–(40) are now easily considered.

The alternative procedure is to develop an elasticity condition. Define the following elasticities:

(46) $$\epsilon_A = (\mu/f_C)(\delta f_C/\delta\mu) \quad \epsilon_M = (\mu/f'_C)(\delta f'_C/\delta\mu).$$

ϵ_A is the elasticity of the average product of labor (in sector C) with respect to μ, and ϵ_M is the elasticity of the marginal product of capital (in sector C) with respect to μ. These elasticities are considered because the difference between ϵ_M and ϵ_A provides the crucial expression as shown below:

(47) $$\epsilon_M - \epsilon_A = (\mu/f_C)\{(\omega + k_C)(\delta f'_C/\delta\mu) - (\delta f_C/\delta\mu)\}.$$

Thus, the signs of the determinants (35)–(40) depend on whether $\epsilon_M \gtreqless \epsilon_A$. It is interesting to note that the following results hold for a Cobb-Douglas production function $Y = AK^{\alpha}L^{1-\alpha}$:

(48) $$\begin{cases} \epsilon_M = \epsilon_A = 1, \text{ for Hicks-neutrality (equally } K\text{- and } L\text{-augmenting)} \\ \epsilon_M = \epsilon_A = (1-\alpha), \text{ for Harrod-neutrality (} L\text{-augmenting only)} \\ \epsilon_M = \epsilon_A = \alpha, \text{ for Solow-neutrality (} K\text{-augmenting only).} \end{cases}$$

Thus, Harrod-neutrality and Hicks-neutrality are equivalent if $(\omega + k_C)(\delta f'_C/\delta\mu) = (\delta f_C/\delta\mu)$ or $\epsilon_A = \epsilon_M$. This is another way of arriving at Uzawa's result. Furthermore, Hicks-neutrality and Solow-neutrality are also equivalent iff $\epsilon_A = \epsilon_M$. Consider now the more general ACMS production function, namely, $Y = \gamma[\delta K^{-\theta} + (1-\delta)L^{\theta}]^{-1/\theta}$, where γ, δ, and θ are parameters such that $0 < \delta < \delta\ 1$ and $-1 < \theta <$

∞. The elasticity of factor substitution $\sigma = 1/(1+\theta)$, so that the following may be noted:[14]

$$(49)\qquad \begin{cases} \sigma > 1 & \text{iff} \quad -1 < \theta < 0 \\ \sigma = 1 & \text{iff} \quad \theta = 0 \\ \sigma < 1 & \text{iff} \quad 0 < \theta < \infty. \end{cases}$$

Allow equally K- and L-augmenting (Hicks's definition) technological progress to obtain

$$(50)\qquad \epsilon_M = \epsilon_A = 1.$$

Allow L-augmenting change (Harrod's definition) to obtain

$$\epsilon_A = \frac{\mu^{-\theta}(1-\delta)}{[\delta k^{-\theta} + (1-\delta)\mu^{-\theta}]}, \quad \epsilon_M = \frac{\mu^{-\theta}(1-\delta)(1+\theta)}{[\delta k^{-\theta} + (1-\delta)\mu^{-\theta}]}.$$

$$(51a)\qquad \therefore \epsilon_M \gtreqless \epsilon_A \text{ according to } \theta \gtreqless 0.$$

From (49) and (51a), it is clear that

$$(51b)\qquad \epsilon_M \gtreqless \epsilon_A \quad \text{according to } \sigma \lesseqgtr 1.$$

To the extent that the general-form production function includes the relatively general ACMS function as a special case, (47) and (51b) *mutatis mutandis* imply that

$$(51)\qquad (\omega + k_C)(\delta f'_C/\delta\mu) \gtreqless \delta f_C/\delta\mu \quad \text{according to } \sigma_C \lesseqgtr 1.$$

Now allow K-augmenting change (Solow's definition) to obtain

$$(52)\qquad \begin{cases} \epsilon_A = \dfrac{\delta}{\mu^\theta k^\theta[\delta\mu^{-\theta}k^{-\theta} + (1-\delta)]} \\ \epsilon_M = \dfrac{\delta}{\mu^\theta k^\theta[\delta\mu^{-\theta}k^{-\theta} + (1-\delta)]} - \dfrac{(1-\delta)\theta}{[\delta\mu^{-\theta}k^{-\theta} + (1-\delta)]}. \end{cases}$$

$$(53a)\qquad \therefore \epsilon_A \gtreqless \epsilon_M \quad \text{according to} \quad \theta \gtreqless 0.$$

From (49) and (53a), it is clear that

$$(53b)\qquad \epsilon_A \gtreqless \epsilon_M \quad \text{according to} \quad \sigma \lesseqgtr 1.$$

To the extent that the general-form function includes the ACMS function as a special case, (47) and (53b) *mutatis mutandis* imply

$$(53)\qquad (\omega + k_C)(\delta f'_C/\delta\mu) \lesseqgtr \delta f_C/\delta\mu \quad \text{according to} \quad \sigma_C \lesseqgtr 1.$$

14. See Allen [1968, p. 52].

It is thus clear from the above discussion that both the Harrod-neutral and the Solow-neutral shifts are equivalent to the Hicks-neutral shift if and only if $\epsilon_A = \epsilon_M$. This paper, however, does not use the elasticity procedure.

Continuation of Harrod-Neutrality

If $\delta f_C/\delta\mu = (\omega + k_C)\,(\delta f'_C/\delta\mu)$, then the Harrod-neutral shift is equivalent to the Hicks-neutral shift, so that from (32), (33)–(40), and (43), the following results are obtained:

$$(54)\qquad \begin{cases} \delta p/\delta\mu > 0, & \delta y_C/\delta\mu > 0, \quad \delta y_B/\delta\mu = 0, \\ \delta\omega/\delta\mu = 0, & \delta k_C/\delta\mu = 0, \quad \delta k_B/\delta\mu = 0. \end{cases}$$

It may be noted that the qualitative results (30) and (54) are identical. If $\delta f_C/\delta\mu > (\omega + k_C)(\delta f'_C/\delta\mu)$, then the Harrod-neutral shift is equivalent to the Hicks K-saving shift in the K-intensive good, so that from (32), (33)–(40), and (44), the following results are obtained:

$$(55)\qquad \begin{cases} \delta p/\delta\mu > 0, & \delta y_C/\delta\mu > 0, \quad \delta y_B/\delta\mu < 0 \\ \delta\omega/\delta\mu > 0, & \delta k_C/\delta\mu < 0, \quad \delta k_B/\delta\mu > 0. \end{cases}$$

Therefore, if the Hicks K-saving (L-using) technological progress occurs in the relatively K-intensive sector C, then the full general equilibrium effect reduces the relative price of good C, increases the level of output of good C, and decreases the level of output of good B. Furthermore, it is revealed that the wage-rental ratio increases, while the sectoral capital-labor ratio increases in sector B and decreases in sector C. Now, if $\delta f_C/\delta\mu < (\omega + k_C)(\delta f'_C/\delta\mu)$, then the Harrod-neutral shift is equivalent to the Hicks L-saving (K-using) shift in the K-intensive sector C. From (32), (33)–(40), and (45), the following results are obtained:

$$(56)\qquad \begin{cases} \delta p/\delta\mu = ?, & \delta y_C/\delta\mu = ?, \quad \delta y_B/\delta\mu > 0, \\ \delta\omega/\delta\mu < 0, & \delta k_C/\delta\mu > 0, \quad \delta k_B/\delta\mu < 0. \end{cases}$$

Therefore, if the Hicks L-saving technological progress occurs in the relatively K-intensive sector C, then the full general equilibrium effect increases the level of output of good B, decreases the wage-rental ratio, and increases the sectoral capital-labor ratio in sector C, but decreases the same in sector B. The results for the level of output of good C and for the relative price, however, are not clear. The problem is that the expression $[k_C(\delta f'_C/\delta\mu) - (\delta f_C/\delta\mu)]$, which appears in (35) and (36), cannot be signed from the condition $\delta f_C/\delta\mu < (\omega + k_C)\delta f'_C/\delta\mu$. The natural extension is to prove that similar results are obtained if the

Harrod-neutral technological progress occurs in the relatively L-intensive sector B. These results are presented in Appendix II. In this case (when L-using technological progress occurs in the L-intensive good), it is interesting to note that unambiguous results are obtained for the relative price and the level of production of good B.

THE SOLOW-NEUTRAL CASE

Partially differentiate the Solow-neutral system (3), (4), (7), (10), and (11)–(15) with respect to μ, holding k constant, and simplify to obtain

$$[F_C][G_C] = [H_C]. \tag{57}$$

The actual matrix and vectors are presented in Appendix III. Appropriately substitute vector H_C in matrix F_C by using Cramer's rule, to obtain

$$\begin{cases} \dfrac{\delta p}{\delta \mu} = \dfrac{|P_C|}{|F_C|} & \dfrac{\delta y_C}{\delta \mu} = \dfrac{|C_C|}{|F_C|} \\ \dfrac{\delta y_B}{\delta \mu} = \dfrac{|B_C|}{|F_C|} & \dfrac{\delta k_B}{\delta \mu} = \dfrac{|R_C|}{|F_C|} \end{cases}. \tag{58}$$

Finding the determinants and simplifying obtains the following results:

$$|F_C| = \frac{-\mu f_C'}{k_C' k_B'}\left[\frac{(\omega + k_B)(k - k_B)k_C'}{(k_C - k_B)} + \frac{(\omega + k_C)(k_C - k)k_B'}{(k_C - k_B)} + \frac{(k_C - k)(k - k_B)}{(\omega + k)}\right] \tag{59}$$

$$\therefore |F_C| < 0. \tag{60}$$

$$|P_C| = \frac{-\mu [f_C']^2}{f_B' k_C' k_B'}\left[\frac{k_B(k - k_B)k_C'}{(k_C - k_B)} + \frac{k_C(k_C - k)k_B'}{(k_C - k_B)} + \frac{k_C(k - k_B)}{(\omega + k)}\right] \tag{61}$$

$$\therefore |P_C| < 0. \tag{62}$$

$$|C_C| = \frac{-a\mu [f_C']^2}{k_C' k_B'}\left[\frac{k(\omega + k_B)(k - k_B)k_C'}{(k_C - k_B)} + \frac{k_C(\omega + k)(k_C - k)k_B'}{(k_C - k_B)} + \frac{(k_C - k)(k - k_B)k_C}{(k_C - k_B)}\right] \tag{63}$$

$$(64) \qquad \therefore |C_C| < 0$$

$$(65) \qquad |B_C| = \frac{-af'_C f'_B(\omega + k_B)(k - k_B)(k_C - k)k_C}{k'_C k'_B(k_C - k_B)(\omega + k_C)} \left[\frac{\omega}{k_C}\frac{\delta k_C}{\delta \omega} - 1\right]$$

$$(66) \qquad \therefore |B_C| \lesseqqgtr 0 \quad \text{according to} \quad \sigma_C \gtreqqless 1$$

$$(67) \qquad |R_C| = \frac{f'_C(k - k_B)(\omega + k_B)k_C}{k'_C(k_C - k_B)} \left[\frac{\omega}{k_C}\frac{\delta k_C}{\delta \omega} - 1\right]$$

$$(68) \qquad \therefore |R_C| \gtreqqless 0 \quad \text{according to} \quad \sigma_C \gtreqqless 1.$$

It may be noted immediately that the determinants $|F_C|$, $|P_C|$, and $|C_C|$ have unconditional clear signs, while the signs of the determinants $|B_C|$ and $|R_C|$ depend crucially on whether the value of the elasticity of substitution is greater than, equal to, or less than unity. From (58)–(68), the following results are obtained:

$$(69) \qquad \begin{cases} \delta p/\delta \mu > 0, \quad \delta y_C/\delta \mu > 0 \\ \delta y_B/\delta \mu \gtreqqless 0 \quad \text{according to} \quad \sigma_C \gtreqqless 1 \\ \delta k_B/\delta \mu \gtreqqless 0 \quad \text{according to} \quad \sigma_C \lesseqqgtr 1. \end{cases}$$

Furthermore, the signs of $\delta\omega/\delta\mu$ or $\delta k_B/\delta\mu$ can be determined by considering the appropriate equation in (57). For example, $\delta\omega/\delta\mu = 0$ if $\delta k_B/\delta\mu = 0$. The full general equilibrium effect of the Solow-neutral technological progress in the relatively K-intensive sector C decreases the price of good C and increases the level of output of good C, irrespective of the value of σ_C. However, the level of output of good B remains constant iff $\sigma_C = 1$, and this is equivalent to the Hicks-neutral result. The level of output of good B increases iff $\sigma_C > 1$, and this is equivalent to the Hicks L-saving result. On the other hand, the level of output of good B decreases iff $\sigma_C < 1$, and this is equivalent to the Hicks K-saving result. The natural extension is to consider the Solow-neutral technological progress in the relative L-intensive sector B. This is done in Appendix II. The analysis is now complete. Table I presents a summary of the results.

The generalized Findlay-Grubert theorem may be stated in the following way: For any given fixed quantities of capital and labor, and for given Graham-type demand functions, if Hicks-Harrod-Solow-neutral disembodied process technological progress occurs in one of the two consumption-good sectors, irrespective of the relative sectoral factor intensities, then the relative price of that good must fall and the level of output of that good must increase, while the level of output of the other good must remain constant in a full general equilibrium

TABLE I

Capital-intensive sector C	Hicks-neutral	Harrod-neutral Equivalent to			Solow-neutral Equivalent to		
		Hicks-neutral	Hicks K-saving	Hicks L-saving	Hicks-neutral $\sigma_C = 1$	Hicks K-saving $\sigma_C < 1$	Hicks L-saving $\sigma_C > 1$
$\frac{\delta p}{\delta \mu}$	+	+	+	?	+	+	+
$\frac{\delta y_C}{\delta \mu}$	+	+	+	?	+	+	+
$\frac{\delta y_B}{\delta \mu}$	0	0	–	+	0	–	+
Labor-intensive sector B					$\sigma_j = 1$	$\sigma_j < 1$	$\sigma_j > 1$
$\frac{\delta p}{\delta \mu}$	–	–	–	–	–	?	– $\sigma_C = \sigma_B$
$\frac{\delta y_C}{\delta \mu}$	0	0	+	–	0 $\sigma_B = 1$	+ $\sigma_B < 1$	– $\sigma_B > 1$
$\frac{\delta y_B}{\delta \mu}$	+	+	+	+	+ $\sigma_C = 1$	? $\sigma_C < 1$	+ $\sigma_C > 1$

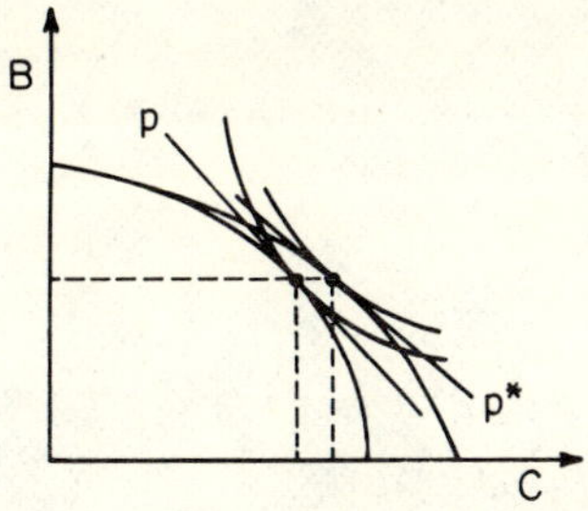

FIGURE I
Hicks-Neutral

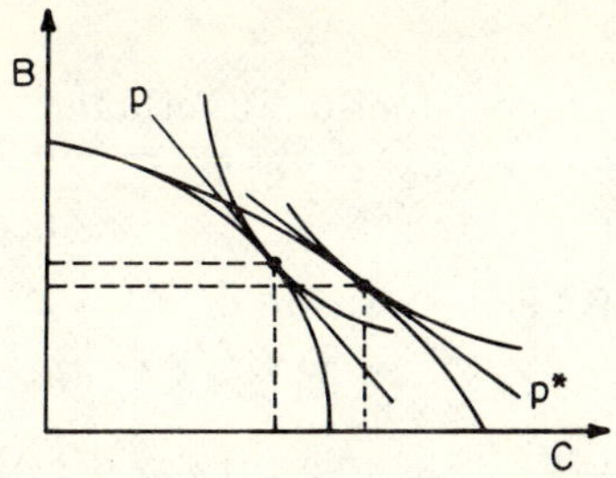

FIGURE II
Hicks K-Saving

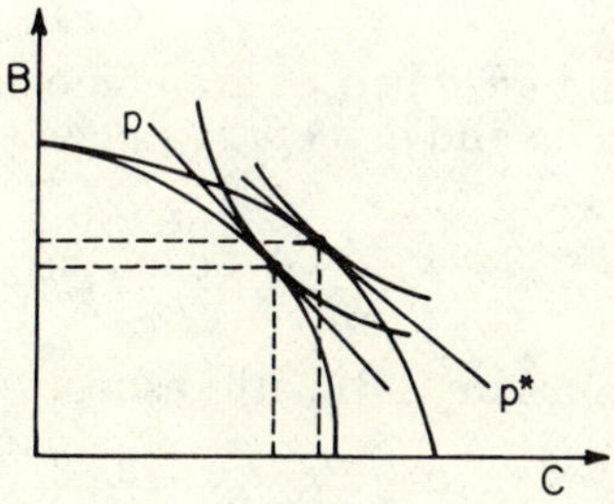

FIGURE III
Hicks K-Using

system. If the Hicks K-saving technological progress occurs in the relatively K-intensive good, and if the Hicks L-saving technological progress occurs in the relative L-intensive good, then in each case the own level of output must increase, the own relative price must fall, and the level of output of the other sector must fall. Last, if the Hicks K-using technological progress occurs in the relatively K-intensive good, and if the Hicks L-using technological progress occurs in the relatively L-intensive good, then in each case the own level of output must increase, the own relative price must fall, and the level of output of the other sector must increase. It may be noted that the last result is derived from the Solow-neutral analysis for the K-intensive good, while the same is derived from the Harrod-neutral analysis for the L-intensive good. These results are illustrated for the K-intensive good C only in Figures I, II, and III, where p^* is the post-technological progress relative price.

APPENDIX I

The production function of good C is $Y_C = F_C(K_C,\mu L_C)$. Since it is homogeneous of degree one, the per capita form is

$$y_C = f_C(k_C,\mu)l_C. \tag{I.1}$$

By Euler's theorem

$$Y_C = (\delta F_C/\delta K_C)K_C + (\delta F_C/\delta(\mu L_C))\mu L_C:$$

$$\therefore y_C = [(\delta F_C/\delta K_C)k_C + (\delta F_C/\delta(\mu L_C))\mu]l_C. \tag{I.2}$$

From (I.1) and (I.2),

$$f_C(k_C,\mu) = \frac{\delta F_C}{\delta K_C}(K_C,\mu L_C)k_C + \frac{\delta F_C}{\delta(\mu L_C)}(K_C,\mu L_C)\mu \tag{I.3}$$

$$\therefore f_C(k_C,\mu) = \frac{\delta F_C}{\delta K_C}(L_C k_C,\mu L_C)k_C + \frac{\delta F_C}{\delta(\mu L_C)}(L_C k_C,\mu L_C)\mu.$$

In (I.3), $\delta F_C/\delta K_C$ and $\delta F_C/\delta(\mu L_C)$ are homogeneous of degree zero in K_C and μL_C or in k_C and μ *keeping* L_C constant. By Euler's theorem,

$$\frac{\delta^2 F_C}{\delta K_C \delta K_C}K_C + \frac{\delta^2 F_C}{\delta K_C \delta(\mu L_C)}\mu L_C = 0. \tag{I.4}$$

Partially differentiate (I.3) with respect to k_C to obtain

$$\frac{\delta f_C}{\delta k_C} = \frac{\delta F_C}{\delta K_C} + \frac{\delta^2 F_C}{\delta K_C \delta k_C}L_C k_C + \frac{\delta^2 F_C}{\delta(\mu L_C)\delta k_C}L_C \mu \tag{I.5}$$

$$\therefore \frac{\delta f_C}{\delta k_C} = \frac{\delta F_C}{\delta K_C} + \frac{\delta^2 F_C}{\delta K_C \delta K_C}K_C + \frac{\delta^2 F_C}{\delta(\mu L_C)\delta K_C}\mu L_C.$$

From (I.4) and (I.5), we get

$$\frac{\delta f_C}{\delta k_C} = \frac{\delta F_C}{\delta K_C}. \tag{I.6}$$

We know that $\delta F_C/\delta K_C$ is homogeneous of degree zero, so that from (I.6) $\delta f_C/\delta k_C$ is homogeneous of degree zero. The left-hand side of (I.6) may be rewritten as

$$\frac{\delta f_C}{\delta k_C}(k_C,\mu) = f'_C(k_C,\mu).$$

By Euler's theorem,

$$\frac{\delta f'_C}{\delta k_C}k_C + \frac{\delta f'_C}{\delta \mu}\mu = 0, \quad \text{or} \quad f''_C k_C = \frac{-\delta f'_C}{\delta \mu}\mu,$$

$$\therefore \frac{\delta f'_C}{\delta \mu} = -f''_C \frac{k_C}{\mu}.$$

Q.E.D.

APPENDIX II

A system of equations *mutatis mutandis* similar to (1)–(15) of the text may be written out by allowing technological progress in the L-intensive sector B. It is not necessary to write out the equations. In this Appendix only the results for the relative price and the levels of production of the two goods are presented. Differentiate the equations for the Hicks-neutral system partially with respect to μ, holding k constant, to obtain

$$[E_B][W_B] = [N_B]. \tag{II.1}$$

The actual matrix and vectors are not written out for the sake of brevity. By using Cramer's rule in (II.1) the following results are obtained:

$$\frac{\delta p}{\delta \mu} = \frac{|P_B|}{|E_B|} < 0; \quad \frac{\delta y_B}{\delta \mu} = \frac{|B_B|}{|E_B|} > 0; \quad \frac{\delta y_C}{\delta \mu} = \frac{|C_B|}{|E_B|} = 0. \tag{II.2}$$

In (II.2) the relevant determinants are

$$|E_B| = \frac{-f_C'}{k_C' k_B'}\left[\frac{k_C'(\omega + k_B)(k - k_B)}{(k_C - k_B)} + \frac{k_B'(\omega + k_C)(k_C - k)}{(k_C - k_B)} + \frac{a(k_C - k_B)(k_C - k)}{\mu(\omega + k_C)}\right] \tag{II.3}$$

$$\therefore |E_B| < 0$$

$$|P_B| = \frac{[f_C']^2}{f_B'}\left[\frac{(\omega + k_C)(k_C - k)}{k_C'(k_C - k_B)} + \frac{(\omega + k_B)(k - k_B)}{k_B'(k_C - k_B)} + \frac{a(k_C - k_B)(k_C - k)}{\mu^2 k_C' k_B'(\omega + k_C)}\right] \tag{II.4}$$

$$\therefore |P_B| > 0.$$

$$|B_B| = \frac{-f_C' f_B(\omega + k_B)^2}{(k_C - k_B)^2}\left[\frac{(k_C - k)(k - k_B)}{k_B'} + \frac{(k_C - k)^2(\omega + k_C)}{k_C'(\omega + k)}\right] \tag{II.5}$$

$$\therefore |B_B| < 0.$$

Furthermore,

$$|C_B| = 0. \tag{II.6}$$

Therefore, if the Hicks-neutral technological progress takes place in the relatively L-intensive sector B, then the full general equilibrium effect lowers the relative price of good B, increases the level of output of good B, and leaves the level of output of good C unchanged. Now differentiate the equations for the Harrod-neutral system partially with respect to μ, holding k constant, to obtain

$$[D_B][V_B] = [M_B]. \tag{II.7}$$

The actual matrix and vectors are not written out. Appropriately substitute vector M_B in the relevant column of the matrix D_B to obtain

$$\text{(II.8)} \qquad \frac{\delta p}{\delta \mu} = \frac{|P_B|}{|D_B|}, \quad \frac{\delta y_B}{\delta \mu} = \frac{|B_B|}{|D_B|}, \quad \frac{\delta y_C}{\delta \mu} = \frac{|C_B|}{|D_B|}.$$

First note that $|D_B|$ is identical to $|D_C|$.

$$\text{(II.9)} \qquad \therefore\ |D_B| < 0.$$

Finding the determinants and then simplifying obtains the following results:

$$\text{(II.10)} \qquad |P_B| = \frac{[f'_C]^2(k_C - k)}{[f'_B]^2(k_C - k_B)k'_C}\left\{\frac{\delta f_B}{\delta \mu} + (k_C - k_B)\frac{\delta f'_B}{\delta \mu}\right\} + \frac{[f'_C]^2(k - k_B)}{[f'_B]^2(k_C - k_B)k'_B}\frac{\delta f_B}{\delta \mu} + \frac{a[f'_C]^2(k_C - k)(k_C - k_B)}{[f'_B]^2(\omega + k_B)(\omega + k_C)k'_C k'_B}\frac{\delta f_B}{\delta \mu}.$$

$$\text{(II.11)} \qquad |B_B| = \frac{-af'_C(k_C - k)^2(\omega + k_B)}{k'_C(k_C - k_B)}\frac{\delta f'_B}{\delta \mu} - \frac{f'_C(\omega + k_C)(k_C - k)^2(k - k_B)}{k'_C(k_C - k_B)^2(\omega + k)}\frac{\delta f_B}{\delta \mu} - \frac{f'_C(\omega + k_B)(k_C - k)(k - k_B)}{k'_B(k_C - k_B)^2}\frac{\delta f_B}{\delta \mu} - \frac{af'_C(k_C - k)^2}{k'_C k'_B(\omega + k_C)}\frac{\delta f_B}{\delta \mu}.$$

$$\text{(II.12)} \qquad |C_B| = \frac{-a[f'_C]^2(k_C - k)^2}{f'_B(k_C - k_B)k'_C}\left\{\frac{\delta f_B}{\delta \mu} - (\omega + k_B)\frac{\delta f'_B}{\delta \mu}\right\}.$$

It may be noted once again that the sign of $|C_B|$ depends crucially on whether $(\omega + k_B)\ \delta f'_B/\delta\mu \gtreqless \delta f_B/\delta\mu$. However, it is interesting to note that, given the factor intensity condition, $|P_B|$ is always positive, and $|B_B|$ is always negative, irrespective of whether $(\omega + k_B)\ \delta f'_B/\delta\mu \gtreqless \delta f_B/\delta\mu$. Therefore, from (II.8)–(II.11) the following results follow:

$$\text{(II.13)} \qquad \delta p/\delta\mu < 0, \quad \delta y_B/\delta\mu > 0.$$

As shown earlier, the Harrod-neutral shift is equivalent to the Hicks-neutral shift if and only if $(\omega + k_B)\ \delta f'_B/\delta\mu = \delta f_B/\delta\mu$. Therefore, from (II.8), (II.9), and (II.12) the following is obtained:

$$\text{(II.14)} \qquad \delta y_C/\delta\mu = 0.$$

The Harrod-neutral shift is equivalent to the Hicks K-saving (L-using) shift if and only if $\delta f_B/\delta\mu > (\omega + k_B)\ \delta f'_B/\delta\mu$ so that

$$\text{(II.15)} \qquad \delta y_C/\delta\mu > 0.$$

The Harrod-neutral shift is equivalent to the Hicks L-saving (K-

using) shift if and only if $\delta f_B/\delta\mu < (\omega + k_B)\,\delta f'_B/\delta\mu$ so that

(II.16) $$\delta y_C/\delta\mu < 0.$$

Now partially differentiate the equations for the Solow-neutral case with respect to μ to obtain

(II.17) $$[F_B][G_B] = [H_B].$$

The actual matrix and vectors are not written out. Appropriate use of Cramer's rule obtains the following:

(II.18) $$\frac{\delta p}{\delta\mu} = \frac{|P_B|}{|F_B|}, \quad \frac{\delta y_B}{\delta\mu} = \frac{|B_B|}{|F_B|}, \quad \frac{\delta y_C}{\delta\mu} = \frac{|C_B|}{|F_B|}.$$

Finding the determinants and simplifying obtains the following results:

(II.19) $$|F_B| = \frac{-f'_C}{k'_C k'_B}\left[\frac{(k-k_B)(\omega+k_B)k'_C}{(k_C-k_B)} + \frac{(k_C-k)(\omega+k_C)k'_B}{(k_C-k_B)} + \frac{a(k_C-k)(k_C-k_B)}{(\omega+k_C)}\right]$$

$$\therefore\ |F_B| < 0.$$

(II.20) $$|P_B| = \frac{\omega[f'_C]^2}{\mu^2 f'_B}\left[\frac{(k-k_B)}{\sigma_B(k_C-k_B)} + \frac{(k_C-k)}{\sigma_C(k_C-k_B)} + \frac{\omega(k_C-k)}{\sigma_C\sigma_B(\omega+k)k_C}\right].$$

The sign of $|P_B|$ is not immediately clear. However, if $\sigma_j = 1$, then (II.20) reduces to

(II.21) $$|P_B| = \frac{\omega[f'_C]^2}{\mu^2 f'_B}\left[1 - \frac{(k_C-k)}{k_C}\frac{\omega}{(\omega+k)}\right]$$

(II.22) $$\therefore\ |P_B| > 0 \quad \text{iff } \sigma_j = 1, \quad j = C,B.$$

If $\sigma_j > 1$, and further if $\sigma_C = \sigma_B$, then it is easily shown from (II.20) that

(II.23) $$|P_B| > 0 \quad \text{iff } \sigma_j > 1, \quad \sigma_C = \sigma_B.$$

If $\sigma_j < 1$ and $\sigma_C = \sigma_B$, then (II.20) may be rewritten as

(II.24) $$|P_B| = \frac{\omega[f'_C]^2}{\mu^2 f'_B\sigma_C\sigma_B}\left[\sigma_C - \frac{(k_C-k)}{k_C}\frac{\omega}{(\omega+k)}\right].$$

(II.25) $$\therefore\ \text{sign of } |P_B| = ? \quad \text{iff } \sigma_j < 1.$$

(II.26) $$|C_B| = \frac{a[f'_C]^2(k_C-k)^2 k_B}{\mu k'_C k'_B(k_C-k_B)}\left[\frac{\omega}{k_B}\frac{\delta k_B}{\delta\mu} - 1\right]$$

$$\text{(II.27)} \quad \begin{cases} \therefore |C_B| = 0 & \text{iff } \sigma_B = 1 \\ \therefore |C_B| > 0 & \text{iff } \sigma_B > 1 \\ \therefore |C_B| < 0 & \text{iff } \sigma_B < 1. \end{cases}$$

$$\text{(II.28)} \quad |B_B| = \frac{-f_C' f_B'(\omega + k_B)(k - k_B)(k_C - k)\omega}{\sigma_B(k_C - k_B)^2} \times \left[1 - \frac{(k_C - k_B)\omega}{\sigma_C(\omega + k)k_C}\right] - \frac{f_C' f_B'(\omega + k_C)(k_C - k)^2\omega}{\sigma_C(k_C - k_B)^2 k_C} - \frac{a f_C' f_B'(k_C - k)^2}{\sigma_C(k_C - k_B)k_C}$$

$$\text{(II.29)} \quad \begin{cases} \therefore |B_B| < 0 & \text{iff } \sigma_C = 1 \\ \therefore |B_B| < 0 & \text{iff } \sigma_C > 1 \\ \therefore |B_B| = ? & \text{iff } \sigma_C < 1. \end{cases}$$

From (II.18)–(II.29) the following results are finally obtained:

$$\text{(II.30)} \quad \delta p/\delta\mu < 0 \quad \text{iff } \sigma_j > 1 \quad \text{and} \quad \sigma_C = \sigma_B \quad \text{or} \quad \sigma_j = 1$$

$$\text{(II.31)} \quad \delta p/\delta\mu = ? \quad \text{iff } \sigma_j < 1 \quad \text{and} \quad \sigma_C = \sigma_B$$

$$\text{(II.32)} \quad \begin{cases} \delta y_C/\delta\mu = 0 & \text{iff } \sigma_B = 1 \\ \delta y_C/\delta\mu < 0 & \text{iff } \sigma_B > 1 \\ \delta y_C/\delta\mu > 0 & \text{iff } \sigma_B < 1 \end{cases}$$

$$\text{(II.33)} \quad \delta y_B/\delta\mu > 0 \quad \text{iff } \sigma_C = 1 \quad \text{or } \sigma_C > 1$$

$$\text{(II.34)} \quad \delta y_B/\delta\mu = ? \quad \text{iff } \sigma_C < 1.$$

It is now revealed that, if the Solow-neutral technological progress occurs in the relatively L-intensive good, then the full general equilibrium effect will lower its price, provided that (a) the value of the elasticity of substitution is the same in both the sectors, and that (b) both the elasticities of subsitution be either equal to or greater than unity. However, nothing specific could be said if the elasticities are less than unity. The level of output of the relatively K-intensive good will increase, decrease, or remain constant according to whether the elasticity of substitution in the L-intensive good is less than, greater than, or equal to unity, respectively. On the other hand, the level of output of the relatively L-intensive good will increase if the elasticity of substitution in the K-intensive good is either equal to or greater than unity, although nothing specific could be said if the same elasticity of substitution is less than unity.

APPENDIX III

The actual matrix and vectors of (31) are shown below. The actual matrix and vectors of (57) are shown on p. 610.

$$\begin{bmatrix} 0 & 1 & 0 & -f'_C l_C & 0 & -f_C & 0 & 0 & 0 \\ 0 & 0 & 1 & 0 & -f'_B l_B & 0 & -f_B & 0 & 0 \\ 0 & 0 & 0 & \frac{-f''_C}{f'_B} & \frac{f'_C f''_B}{[f'_B]^2} & 0 & 0 & 0 & 1 \\ 0 & 0 & 0 & \frac{f_C f''_C}{[f'_C]^2} & 0 & 0 & 0 & 1 & 0 \\ 0 & 0 & 0 & 0 & \frac{f_B f''_B}{[f'_B]^2} & 0 & 0 & 1 & 0 \\ 0 & 0 & 0 & l_C & l_B & k_C & k_B & 0 & 0 \\ 0 & 0 & 0 & 0 & 0 & 1 & 1 & 0 & 0 \\ 1 & -1 & -p & 0 & 0 & 0 & 0 & 0 & -y_B \\ -a & 1 & 0 & 0 & 0 & 0 & 0 & 0 & 0 \end{bmatrix} \begin{bmatrix} \frac{\delta y}{\delta \mu} \\ \frac{\delta y_C}{\delta \mu} \\ \frac{\delta y_B}{\delta \mu} \\ \frac{\delta k_C}{\delta \mu} \\ \frac{\delta k_B}{\delta \mu} \\ \frac{\delta l_C}{\delta \mu} \\ \frac{\delta l_B}{\delta \mu} \\ \frac{\delta \omega}{\delta \mu} \\ \frac{\delta p}{\delta \mu} \end{bmatrix} = \begin{bmatrix} l_C \frac{\delta f_C}{\delta \mu} \\ 0 \\ \frac{1}{f'_B} \frac{\delta f'_C}{\delta \mu} \\ \frac{1}{f'_C} \frac{\delta f_C}{\delta \mu} - \frac{f_C}{[f'_C]^2} \frac{\delta f'_C}{\delta \mu} \\ 0 \\ 0 \\ 0 \\ 0 \\ 0 \end{bmatrix}$$

$$\begin{bmatrix} 0 & 1 & 0 & -\mu f'_C l_C & 0 & -f_C & 0 & 0 & 0 \\ 0 & 0 & 1 & 0 & -f'_B l_B & 0 & -f_B & 0 & 0 \\ 0 & 0 & 0 & \dfrac{-\mu^2 f''_C}{f'_B} & \dfrac{\mu f'_C f''_B}{[f'_B]^2} & 0 & 0 & 0 & 1 \\ 0 & 0 & 0 & \dfrac{-1}{k'_C} & 0 & 0 & 0 & 1 & 0 \\ 0 & 0 & 0 & 0 & \dfrac{-1}{k'_B} & 0 & 0 & 1 & 0 \\ 0 & 0 & 0 & l_C & l_B & k_C & k_B & 0 & 0 \\ 0 & 0 & 0 & 0 & 0 & 1 & 1 & 0 & 0 \\ 1 & -1 & -p & 0 & 0 & 0 & 0 & 0 & -y_B \\ -a & 1 & 0 & 0 & 0 & 0 & 0 & 0 & 0 \end{bmatrix} \begin{bmatrix} \dfrac{\delta y}{\delta \mu} \\ \dfrac{\delta y_C}{\delta \mu} \\ \dfrac{\delta y_B}{\delta \mu} \\ \dfrac{\delta k_C}{\delta \mu} \\ \dfrac{\delta k_B}{\delta \mu} \\ \dfrac{\delta l_C}{\delta \mu} \\ \dfrac{\delta l_B}{\delta \mu} \\ \dfrac{\delta \omega}{\delta \mu} \\ \dfrac{\delta p}{\delta \mu} \end{bmatrix} = \begin{bmatrix} f'_C k_C \\ 0 \\ \dfrac{f'_C}{f'_B} + \dfrac{\mu k_C f''_C}{f'_B} \\ \dfrac{k_C}{\mu} - \dfrac{f_C}{\mu^2 f'_C} - \dfrac{f_C f''_C k_C}{\mu [f'_C]^2} \\ 0 \\ 0 \\ 0 \\ 0 \\ 0 \end{bmatrix}$$

MIDDLESEX POLYTECHNIC

REFERENCES

Allen, R. G. D., *Macroeconomic Theory* (London: Macmillan, 1968).
Amano, A., "Determinants of Comparative Costs: A Theoretical Approach," *Review of Economic Studies,* XXXI (June 1964), 207–20.
Asimakopulos, A., "The Definition of Neutral Inventions," *Economic Journal,* LXXIII (Nov. 1963), 675–80.
Burmeister, E., and A. R. Dobell, *Mathematical Theories of Economic Growth* (London: Macmillan, 1970).
Diamond, P. A., "Disembodied Technical Change in a Two-sector Model," *Review of Economic Studies,* XXXII (April 1965), 161–68.
Findlay, R., and H. Grubert, "Factor Intensities, Technological Progress, and the Terms of Trade," *Oxford Economic Papers,* XI (Feb. 1959), 111–21.
Hahn, F. H., and R. C. O. Matthews, "The Theory of Economic Growth: A Survey," *Economic Journal,* LXXIV (Dec. 1964), 779–902.
Jones, R. W., "The Structure of Simple General Equilibrium Models," *Journal of Political Economy,* LXXIII (Dec. 1965), 557–72.
Inada, K., "On the Stability of Growth Equilibria in Two-sector Models," *Review of Economic Studies,* XXXI (April 1964), 127–42.
Kennedy, C., "Harrod on 'Neutrality,'" *Economic Journal,* LXXII (March 1962a), 249–50.
——, "The Character of Improvements and of Technical Progress," *Economic Journal,* LXXII (Dec. 1962b), 889–911.
Morishima, M., *The Theory of Economic Growth* (Oxford: Clarendon Press, 1969).
Sato, R., and M. J. Beckman, "Neutral Inventions and Production Functions," *Review of Economic Studies,* XXXV (Jan. 1968), 57–66.
Uzawa, H., "Neutral Inventions and the Stability of Growth Equilibrium," *Review of Economic Studies,* XXVIII (Feb. 1961), 117–24.
——, "On a Two-sector Model of Economic Growth II," *Review of Economic Studies,* XXX (June 1963), 105–18.

UNIONIZATION AND PRODUCTIVITY: MICRO-ECONOMETRIC EVIDENCE*

KIM B. CLARK

It is widely agreed that unionization affects the rules and procedures governing the employment relation in organized establishments. The effect of these changes on establishment productivity, however, is unclear. This issue is examined using establishment level data from the U. S. cement industry. A positive union effect on the order of 6–8 percent is found in both cross-section and time series data. Although some caution is in order in interpreting the results, the evidence suggests that unionization can lead to productive changes in the operation of the enterprise.

Trade unions have a perceptible influence on the production process in organized establishments [Slichter, Healy, and Livernash 1960]. Even a cursory glance through a modern labor agreement reveals the depth of union involvement in the operation of the enterprise. Contract provisions extend beyond matters of compensation and promotion to include the introduction of new technology, the assignment of workers to specific tasks, the size of crews, and the amount of work to be performed. Perhaps more important than specific rules, the typical labor agreement establishes a formal system for setting rules and resolving disputes.

With the extent of union interest and involvement in the production process, it seems natural to question the impact of the union on enterprise performance, and in particular on productivity. Yet the question has received little analysis. In the late 1890s and the early 1900s, Marshall and Moore examined the union productivity effect theoretically, but the ideas they advanced were not followed up with empirical analysis [Marshall, 1899, and Bok and Dunlop, 1970]. Without evidence, discussions in the literature rarely rose beyond an inconclusive exchange of opinions.[1] However, in the recent papers by Brown and Medoff [1978], and by Frantz, attempts have been made to provide econometric analysis of the union impact in United States manufacturing.[2] Using value added per manhour to measure pro-

* The research reported here was partially supported by grants from the Department of Labor, the National Science Foundation, and the Wertheim Fund of Harvard University. Helpful comments were received from John T. Dunlop, Richard Freeman, James Medoff, and members of the Labor Workshop at the University of Chicago Business School and the Labor Seminar at Harvard University. Laura Nelson ably assisted with the computations.

1. Bok and Dunlop [1970], pp. 260–61, provide a brief summary of this literature.
2. Pencavel [1975] examines productivity and unionization in British coal mining.

The Quarterly Journal of Economics, December 1980 0033-5533/80/0095-0613$02.70

ductivity, both studies find positive union effects. While the evidence is suggestive, the findings rest on untested assumptions about technology and pricing behavior. Since value added has been used to measure output in these studies, what appears to be an output effect may well be a difference in prices. Moreover, possible differences in technology between union and nonunion establishments are not controlled for in the analysis. Brown and Medoff find the empirical results to be very sensitive to assumptions about differences in the parameters of the production process.[3]

This paper extends previous work by relaxing the technology and value added assumptions. The analysis focuses on the effect of unionization on productivity using establishment level data from the U. S. cement industry. The output of a cement plant is measured in physical terms, and data on both union and nonunion establishments permit estimation of the union effect controlling for differences in technology. Furthermore, the availability of time series data on productivity before and after unionization makes possible estimation of the union impact while controlling for firm-specific effects, as well as changes in labor quality. The paper is divided into five sections. After laying out the analytical framework in Section I, the empirical model and the data are briefly described in the second section. Section III presents the basic empirical results, while Section IV contains an analysis of firm-specific effects and quality adjustments. Conclusions are found in Section V.

I. An Analytical Framework

The theoretical description of the production process used in this paper is quite simple. Output is treated as a function of capital and labor input, where capital is presumably adjusted for the effects of depreciation, and labor is measured to reflect variations in quality. Given the level of inputs, output may also depend on organizational and institutional factors; i.e., methods of organization, effectiveness of management, and the motivation of workers. Within this simple framework, labor productivity, defined as the ratio of output to labor input, depends on the capital-labor ratio, the scale of operations, and the various organizational factors.[4]

3. The same is true of the value added assumption. Indeed, Brown and Medoff show that if unions have a wage effect and relative cost differences are fully reflected in prices, the estimated union coefficient identifies only a price effect. See Brown and Medoff [1978].

4. The analysis would be unchanged if framed in terms of total factor productivity. The only difference lies in the treatment of factor shares. See Jorgenson and Griliches [1965].

Unionization may affect each of these determinants. The traditional channel of influence links the union wage effect to capital-labor substitution.[5] In response to a rise in the relative wage, the firm seeks to raise the marginal product of labor by raising the capital-labor ratio. The net effect, however, is an increase in unit costs and a misallocation of resources. A second channel of influence recognizes that the rules governing the employment relation under trade unions are likely to affect methods of organization and other aspects of the internal operation of the firm.

While the traditional union effect leads to inefficiency, the direction of the organization effect is unclear. If unionization puts pressure on management to improve operations, the production process may yield a larger volume of output for any combination of capital and labor.[6] The opposite conclusion holds if unionization reduces motivation or otherwise impedes the effective operation of the enterprise. Thus, both the sign and magnitude of the organization effect are open to empirical question and analysis. The organization effects must be combined with the traditional substitution effects to assess the overall union impact on efficiency.

The link between unionization and the organizational determinants of productivity depends on changes in the labor contract under unions and on adjustments made by workers and management to new provisions. The distinction between changes in the rules of the employment relation, and the resulting changes in behavior that link the contract to productivity has often been overlooked in discussions of this issue. The existence of a rule, on its face inimical to productivity, has been treated as *prima facie* evidence of a negative organization effect.[7] Yet few contract provisions directly affect the determinants of productivity. Most operate indirectly through changes in incentives that affect the decisions of workers and managers.

Rules, both formal and informal, are common to all work situations. In a nonunion setting, management generally determines the formal rules governing the terms and conditions of employment. Under trade unions, the introduction of a mechanism for collective voice affects both the substantive rules governing the employment relation and the procedures for rule making and dispute settlement.

5. The traditional channel is discussed in Johnson and Miezskowski [1970], and the paper by Lewis in Bradley [1959].

6. This effect assumes the existence of unexploited opportunities to increase profits and is therefore closely related to Leibenstein's X-efficiency; see Leibenstein [1966] for an extended analysis.

7. The most prominent example of featherbedding rules are found in the construction and transportation sectors.

Union influence extends beyond mere codification of existing rules. While workers may affect rules in a nonunion setting through individual mobility, this channel is indirect and depends on management's ability and willingness to make complex inferences relating contract provision to turnover [Freeman, 1976]. Collective bargaining establishes a more powerful, direct means of influence, and may provide a more effective channel of information about worker preferences and potential tradeoffs implicit in alternative contract provisions.

By introducing new procedures and new channels of information, and by altering the substantive rules of the workplace, unionization is likely to lead to changes in the behavior of workers and managers. For workers, perhaps the most significant change is a shift in relative power and increased control over conditions of work. Freeman has argued that the existence of collective voice under unions creates an alternative to "exit" behavior (quitting, absenteeism) and, ceteris paribus, can be expected to reduce turnover, with clear consequences for productivity [Freeman, 1980]. Firms with lower rates of turnover are likely to have a higher level of investment in firm-specific training, and may have more effective work groups. While the relationship between wage adjustments and turnover may be evident to managers in the nonunion setting, the union "voice" effect leads to less turnover for a *given* level of compensation. A similar effect may follow from the use of seniority rules, which tend to be more prevalent in union contracts. In those production processes where skills obtained on the job are important, seniority rules may reduce rivalry among workers and increase incentives for assistance and cooperation.[8] In addition, the arbitrariness inherent in rankings based on management's assessment of ability (or other subjective criteria) may adversely affect workers' perception of their jobs. Introduction of seniority criteria may thus have positive effects on motivation and morale.[9]

For managers, the introduction of a trade union affects the viability of previous methods and procedures. In the face of a rise in the price of labor and union interest in the production process, management has an incentive to increase the effort obtained from a given level of labor input, and to address aspects of the production process that may have been neglected.[10] The upshot is that collective bargaining

8. The effect of seniority on training is discussed in Williamson, Wachter, and Harris [1975].

9. Research in organizational behavior suggests that there is no necessary link between morale and productivity. The link between motivation and productivity is quite strong, however, and is affected by workers' perceptions. See Lawler [1973].

10. The neglect of some aspects of the production process is consistent with behavior characterized by bounded rationality and satisficing, rather than full optimization. For an analytical treatment of several satisficing models, see Radner [1975].

may encourage management to take steps to improve productivity. Management action may be enhanced by collective bargaining. Union leaders and union rules may facilitate the introduction of new methods and techniques that may have been resisted by the employees [Lester and Aronson, 1971]. Yet collective voice contains the potential for reducing productivity. The power inherent in the potential for collective action may be used to protect malfeasance and codify reduced work effort [Slichter *et al.,* 1960]. Management's ability to fire undesirable workers may be reduced and the union contract may advance rules which require that work be done more than once, or that restrict managements' ability to adjust to changing conditions. Thus, seniority rules may hinder the effective matching of workers and jobs, and rules limiting displacement of workers may impede the introduction of new technology. The grievance procedure may be abused with numerous petty issues clogging the channels. Instead of providing useful information, the day-to-day administration of the contract may result in a disruption of the production process.

It seems clear that the ultimate effect of unionization depends on complex union-worker-management interaction, at the bargaining table and on the shop floor. The direction and magnitude of productivity changes will depend on specific policies and adjustments. These considerations underscore the importance of empirical analysis in resolving the unionism-productivity issue.

II. Empirical Analysis of the Cement Industry

The basic problem facing any empirical analysis of the union impact on organizational aspects of the firm is to control for other differences in union and nonunion establishments. Among the many potential differences identified in the literature, two have been singled out as deserving of particular attention. The first is the technology of production; the second is the measurement of output. Brown and Medoff have shown that few conclusions can be drawn when union and nonunion establishments use different technologies, if those differences are not reflected in the analysis. Moreover, unless output is measured in physical terms, the potential effect of unionization on prices clouds the productivity comparison. These considerations justify the empirical focus adopted in this paper. Cement is one of the few industries in which union and nonunion establishments with the same basic technology produce a relatively homogeneous product easily measured in physical units. With data on production in individual cement plants, it is possible to control for technological differences and to compare productivity without invoking assumptions about pricing behavior.

Cement is a fine grey powder produced in a highly capital-intensive process.[11] The basic flow of production in a cement plant consists of three stages. In the first, stone rich in calcium, silicon, aluminum, and iron is extracted, crushed, and ground. The raw material is then fed into a large rotating kiln, fired to about 2,700°F, and partly fused into small pebbles called "clinker." In the final stage clinker is ground and mixed with gypsum and other chemical agents to form cements with various strengths and drying properties. Cement is produced to generally recognized specifications established by the American Society for Testing Materials.[12] The homogeneous nature of the product and the existence of established product specifications facilitates comparison of the output of different establishments.

The physical characteristics of the product have important implications for the structure of the industry and the analysis of productivity. Finished cement has a low value-to-weight ratio and shipping costs are a high proportion of the delivered price. The consequence of high shipping costs is a regional market structure. In 1972, less than 5 percent of industry shipments exceeded 300 miles, while close to 60 percent were less than 100 miles [U. S. Dept. of Commerce, 1976]. While the regional nature of the industry creates conditions of apparent oligopoly, historically the homogeneous nature of the product and the capital intensity of production have led to intense price competition.[13] Overt attempts to limit competition through a basing point pricing system were declared illegal in 1947, and there is substantial evidence of moderately competitive pricing behavior in the 1960s and early 1970s.[14]

The regional character of the cement product markets is reflected in the structure of collective bargaining where single employer agreements with substantial local negotiations are the rule. The dominant union in the industry is the United Cement, Lime and Gypsum Workers International Union, which represents about 75 percent of all cement plants.[15] The UCLGWIU is relatively decen-

11. For information on the cement industry see Loescher [1959]. An informative booklet on the industry is published by the Portland Cement Association [1974].

12. See Loescher [1959], pp. 135–36.

13. Loescher [1959] presents an analysis of pricing practices in the industry.

14. See Clark [1978], pp. 45–48. Beginning in 1960, the industry experienced several years of excess capacity. In the face of increasing supply, the real price of cement fell 25 percent from 1960 to 1970.

15. See Heneghan [1957] for a discussion of the history of the union.

tralized, and local and regional officers play a significant role in shaping the substance of negotiations. Slightly less than 9 percent of the plants in the industry are nonunion, with the remainder divided among the Steelworkers, joint councils, and independent unions. Taken together, the regional nature of markets and the decentralized character of the union suggest that the impact of the union may vary by region. The empirical analysis allows for regional union effects, with primary focus on the South and Southwest where most competition between union and nonunion plants takes place.

The Data

Since 1919 the Portland Cement Association has conducted an annual survey of association members requesting information on the production of clinker, finished cement, cement shipments, and manhours for each of the respondent firm's establishments. This survey constitutes the basic source of data used in the empirical analysis.[16]

The survey provides annual data on tons of finished cement produced, which is the output measure used here. The data on manhours are broken down by department, permitting the construction of variables measuring production and supervisory or nonproduction labor input. The supervisory category includes plant management, supervisors, clerical staff, and laboratory personnel. The production category includes workers in the quarry, the raw grinding and finishing departments, and the general labor group.

Beginning in 1973 information is available on location, plant capacity, fuel usage, and the installation date and "practical" capacity of individual kilns. The location data permit construction of five regional categories: Northeast, North Central, South, Southwest, and West.[17] Total capacity of the plant determines grouping into size categories, which provide an alternative to total manhours as a measure of scale effects. Data on kiln age and capacity have been used to construct a measure of the capital stock in the ith plant in year t given

16. The survey covers about 80 percent of the establishments in the industry. While the composition of the sample varies slightly from year to year, there appears to be no systematic variation in participation by region, union status, size of productivity.

17. The regions were defined as follows: North East—Maine, New Hampshire, Vermont, Massachusetts, Connecticut, Rhode Island, New York, Delaware, New Jersey, Pennsylvania, Maryland, West Virginia; North Central—Ohio, Indiana, Illinois, Michigan, Iowa, Minnesota, Wisconsin, Missouri, Kansas, Nebraska, South Dakota, North Dakota; South—Florida, Georgia, Alabama, South Carolina, North Carolina, Virginia, Kentucky, Tennessee, Mississippi; Southwest—Louisiana, Arkansas, Texas, Oklahoma; West—New Mexico, Arizona, Utah, Idaho, Colorado, Nevada, Montana, Washington, Oregon, California.

by

$$K_{it} = \sum_{j} \lambda^{t-j} C_{ijt} \quad 0 < \lambda < 1, \tag{1}$$

where C_j is the capacity of kilns of the jth vintage.[18] The adjustment parameter reflects the effects of depreciation, obsolescence, and vintage, and is determined empirically by searching for the value that minimizes the error sum of squares in the regression equation.

The data set is completed with information on union status. We initially obtained a record of plants operating under a collective bargaining agreement from the Cement Employers Association. Separate verification of union status was obtained from the staff of the United Cement, Lime and Gypsum Workers International Union. In one situation, the question of union status was answered through direct contact with the plant in question.

Table I presents a summary of the sources and definitions of the variables used in the analysis, and compares the cement industry data set with a hypothetical ideal. The ideal analysis would place establishments in the two sectors on a comparable basis by controlling for differences in the amount and quality of labor and capital, the parameters of the production function, and returns to scale. In general, the cement data set measures up quite well to this standard. The existence of well-known ASTM standards enables us to compare the output of different establishments in physical terms. Productivity and unionization can be examined at the establishment level with controls for possible union/nonunion differences in technology. Reasonably good measures of the vintage of the plant and the operating kilns are available, and we have two measures of establishment size that should provide a reasonably good fix on returns to scale.

The principal weakness in the data is the absence of good measures of labor quality. The regional controls capture structural differences in labor quality, but fail to control for any substitution of higher for lower quality labor induced by the union wage effect. However, the likely effect of quality adjustments on productivity can

18. It is important to note that the assumption that all capital is proportional to kiln capacity could result in a biased estimate of the union effect. If, for example, unionization raises the wage-rental ratio, firms will have incentive to substitute capital for labor. In the case where some part of the capital stock is not proportional to kiln capacity, our measure of the capital-labor ratio will understate the true ratio in union establishments, and so lead to an upward bias in the union coefficient. It is our view that this bias is quite small. Given the nature of the production process, the fraction of the capital stock not proportional to the size of the kiln is likely to be relatively small. If, for example, we set this fraction as high as 0.20, and assume a union wage effect of 15 percent, then with an elasticity of substitution equal to one, and a capital share of 0.4, the bias amounts to a little over one percentage point.

TABLE I

THE CEMENT INDUSTRY DATA SET AND THE IDEAL

Measurement issues	Ideal characteristics	Cement data set: Characteristics	Cement data set: Definitions (and symbols)
1. Measuring output	Output measured in physical units; corrected for quality differences	Production measured in tons; types of cement defined by official standards	Output: tons of finished cement (Q)
2. Labor input adjusted for quality	Hours per worker adjusted for differences in innate ability	Manhours available in unweighted form; no information on personal characteristics of workers; regional differences captured by dummy; check on bias through time series data	Production workers: total manhours by production department (L); supervisory: total manhours of plant management, foreman, clerical, and laboratory staff (S)
3. Capital input adjusted for quality	Capital stock adjusted for depreciation, obsolescence, and vintage effects; utilization of stock	Capital measured by rated capacity adjusted for maintenance; data available on vintage of capacity; no independent measure of utilization	Capital stock in the ith plant: $\sum_j \lambda^{t-j} C_{ijt}$; j indexes vintage (C = kiln capacity)
4. Returns to scale	Measure of size reflecting proportionate change in all inputs	Size measured by total manhours per establishment and plant capacity	Size measures: (1) unadjusted capacity (size categories) (2) total production manhours per establishment (L)
5. Union/nonunion differences in technology	Observations on union and nonunion establishments	Data available on characteristics of union and nonunion plants; number of nonunion plants is small	Age of plant: $\frac{1}{C_{it}} \sum C_{ijt}(t-j)$ Vintage: t-age of plant

be estimated from time series data on plants that change union status. In a time series context, the labor quality effect depends not only on technology and changes in compensation, but on the extent of turnover as well. Together with an estimate of the union wage effect, information on turnover can be used to determine the extent of bias induced by the omission of quality measures.[19]

The Empirical Model

The cement data set provides measures of output (Q) and three inputs: capital (K), production worker hours (L), and the hours of supervisory personnel (S). These data may be summarized, and the effect of unionization measured using standard production function analysis. Output is assumed to depend on the three inputs, and organization factors. Apart from organization effects, labor productivity depends on the capital-labor ratio, the ratio of supervisory to production worker hours, and the scale of operations. Productivity also may differ between union and nonunion establishments because of differences in the parameters of the production function. To control for these possibilities, and thus to identify union/nonunion differences that stem from organization factors, we specify a Cobb-Douglas production function for each sector.[20]

In intensive form, the two production processes may be written as

$$\ln(Q/L)_k = \ln(A_u) + \alpha_u \ln(K/L)_k + \gamma_u \ln(S/L)_k + (\theta_u - 1) \ln L_k \tag{2}$$

and

$$\ln(Q/L)_j = \ln(A_n) + \alpha_n \ln(K/L)_j + \gamma_n \ln(S/L)_j + (\theta_n - 1) \ln L_j, \tag{3}$$

where u and n indicate union and nonunion, respectively, k and j index establishments in the two sectors, and returns to scale is given by $\theta = \alpha + \beta + \gamma$, where β is the elasticity of output with respect to

19. Brown and Medoff found that measured labor quality explained very little of the variation in productivity in aggregate data. In research in progress Chamberlain has used the Brown-Medoff data to estimate the union productivity effect with a model in which both observed and unobserved components of labor quality were introduced. He found that accounting for unobserved quality differences had little impact on the union productivity effect.

20. The Cobb-Douglas form is restrictive, but useful for its simplicity. Other functional forms leave basic conclusions unchanged. Using a CES specification, for example, we obtain a union effect of 0.093 (0.050) in the Southwest region, and an effect of 0.015 (0.100) in the South. These results should be compared with those in line 1 of Table IV.

labor. The parameter A captures the organizational determinants of productivity and is assumed to be invariant across establishments within the sector.

Equations (2) and (3) control for union/nonunion differences in the production parameters, but within the two sectors, technology and productivity may vary because of vintage and region effects. While the basic production process in cement is much the same today as it was in 1920, changes in technology have increased the extent of mechanization and automation, increased the size and speed of machinery, and significantly altered plant layout and design. Not only is the level of productivity likely to be affected by vintage, but the parameters of the production function may change as well. Since nonunion establishments tend to be newer, it is important to control for vintage in identifying the union organization effect. In the empirical work reported below, we begin with a model that allows all parameters to differ by vintage. Successive restrictions on the production function parameters and the union effect by vintage are then tested. In addition to vintage effects, we also allow the union coefficient to vary by region. As noted earlier, cement is priced and sold in regional markets, and the pattern of collective bargaining has a distinctly regional character in which local and regional union officers play key roles in determining the nature of labor-management relations.

If region effects were absent and the union and nonunion sectors were technologically identical except for differences in organizational factors, the union impact could be estimated using a simple dummy variable. The organizational differences could be written as $A_u = A_n(1 + b)$, and the coefficient on the union dummy would provide an estimate of b, the productivity differential. In equations (2) and (3), however, the input ratios have different effects on productivity in the two sectors, so that the estimated union effect not only may vary by region and vintage, but also may depend on parameter differences and the level of the input ratios at which the union/nonunion comparison takes place. To see the implications of differences in technology, we make use of covariance analysis in which all parameters are allowed to vary between the sectors. Ignoring problems of heteroskedasticity, the union and nonunion parameters may be estimated jointly using interaction terms between the basic independent variables and the union dummy.[21] If we confine the analysis to plants of the same vin-

21. The formulation in (4) assumes that the standard deviations of the error terms in the union and nonunion equations are identical. Rerunning the equations separately results in standard errors of estimate not significantly different from one another, and consequently little change in the standard errors of the coefficients.

tage, the most general form of the model is given by

$$\text{(4)} \quad \ln\left(\frac{Q}{L}\right)_i = \ln A_n + bU + (\alpha_u - \alpha_n)\ln\left(\frac{K}{L}\right)_i U + (\gamma_u - \gamma_n)\ln\left(\frac{S}{L}\right)_i U + (\theta_u - \theta_n)\ln L_i U + \alpha_n \ln\left(\frac{K}{L}\right)_i + \gamma_n \ln\left(\frac{S}{L}\right)_i + (\theta_n - 1)\ln L_i + \sum_k^r (\pi_u - \pi_n)_k REG_k U + \sum_k^r \pi_{nk} REG_k,$$

where U takes a value of 1 if the plant is unionized and zero otherwise, and REG indicates the region dummies. By specifying the model at this level of generality, we can assess the implications of constraining the region and production parameters to be identical.

The coefficients on the interaction terms provide estimates of the difference between union and nonunion parameters, while the nonunion parameters are given by the coefficients on the regular independent variables. In this formulation the union impact depends on region, the extent of differences in technology, and the particular value of the independent variables chosen for comparison. The union productivity effect in the kth region is given by

$$\text{(5)} \quad \left[\frac{\partial \ln(Q/L)}{\partial U}\right]_k = b + (\alpha_u - \alpha_n)\ln\left(\frac{K}{L}\right)_i + (\gamma_u - \gamma_n)\ln\left(\frac{S}{L}\right)_i + (\theta_u - \theta_n)\ln L_i + (\pi_u - \pi_n)_k.$$

Equation (5) makes clear that if production parameter differences are large, and we ignore them in estimating $\partial \ln(Q/L)/\partial U$, a substantial bias may be introduced. In addition, the choice of comparison values of the input ratios may be of some consequence. In the work that follows, mean values will be used in calculations of the productivity effect.

III. The Empirical Results

This section summarizes the cement industry data and presents estimates of several variants of the basic model developed in Section II. The means and standard deviations of the variables used in the empirical analysis are presented in Table II. The data cover the period 1973–1976 and include 29 nonunion observations (9 plants) and 436

TABLE II

MEANS AND STANDARD DEVIATIONS OF PRODUCTIVITY AND DETERMINANTS

Basic variables	Complete sample (1) Total (T = 465)	(2) Union (T = 436)	(3) Nonunion (T = 29)	New vintage sample (constructed since 1957) (4) Union (T = 88)	(5) Nonunion (T = 19)
1. Average productivity of production workers (tons per manhour)	2.16	2.13	2.55	3.07	2.96
	(0.82)	(0.81)	(0.80)	(0.86)	(0.78)
2. Capital-labor ratio[a] (adjusted tons of capacity per manhour)	1.91	1.88	2.34	2.88	3.01
	(1.84)	(1.88)	(1.20)	(1.19)	(1.15)
3. Average utilization[b] rate	0.86	0.85	0.94	0.88	0.92
	(0.19)	(0.19)	(0.22)	(0.17)	(0.27)
4. Supervisor-labor[c] ratio	0.31	0.31	0.36	0.41	0.40
	(0.13)	(0.13)	(0.14)	(0.18)	(0.15)
5. Average cement capacity (thousands of tons)	566.9	567.8	555.0	594.2	575.5
	(330.8)	(333.6)	(296.9)	(308.9)	(341.4)
6. Average kiln age[d]	21.09	21.69	13.21	12.16	8.28
	(13.01)	(13.13)	(8.08)	(3.32)	(3.36)

a. The capital measure is calculated according to equation (1) with $\lambda = 0.985$.
b. Utilization is output divided by cement capacity.
c. Measured as ratio of nonproduction manhours to production manhours.
d. Kiln age is defined as $(1/C_{it})\sum_j C_{ijt}(t-j)$, where C is cement capacity, i indexes plants, t is time, and j indexes vintage.

observations (119 plants) in the union sector. Each plant-year has been treated as a separate observation.[22]

Turning first to data from the complete sample (columns 2 and 3), we see that evidence on average productivity (line 1) in Table II reveals that nonunion establishments are 18 percent more productive than establishments that are unionized. Part of the reason for the difference is evident in the higher nonunion capital-labor ratio (22 percent) in line 2, and the higher rate of capacity utilization in line 3. The nonunion sector also has a higher supervisor ratio, but the difference is quite small. Similarly small differences in size are found in line 5, with plants in the union sector about 2 percent larger.

The importance of controlling for vintage in comparing union and nonunion establishments is evident in line 6, which contains data on average kiln age. Unionized establishments are significantly older than the plants in the nonunion sector. The difference primarily reflects the almost complete organization of the industry by 1950, and the entry of new plants in the 1960s, which have remained nonunion. The average kiln age actually understates differences in the vintage of the capital stock. It is common practice in the industry to install new kilns in old plants. Thus, two plants of the same kiln age may have very different grinding and crushing equipment, very different plant designs, and very different manning requirements. The problem is especially acute in the case of union-nonunion comparisons, since most nonunion plants have been constructed since the late 1950s. To correct more fully for differences in the vintage of the plant, we have calculated means and standard deviations for plants built since 1957.[23] The results are presented in columns 4 and 5.

22. The treatment of each plant-year as a separate observation ignores the time series–cross-section nature of the data. The most serious problem with the procedure is the failure to take into account firm-specific effects that may lead to understatement of the standard errors as well as bias in the union effect. Because union status changes in only one establishment in the 1973–1976 period, it is not possible to identify both the effect of unionization and individual firm effects. We have assumed that the average firm effect in the union and nonunion sector is identical, so that firm effects net out union/nonunion comparison. We have examined the impact of entering a time trend in the analysis, and allowing for a time-varying intercept through year dummies. Neither of these adjustments affects the results. With year dummies, for example, the average union effect is 0.068 (0.043) compared with 0.064 (0.045) with a trend term, and 0.070 (0.046) with these terms excluded. In addition to possible bias in the union coefficient, omission of firm effects may lead to biased estimates of the standard errors. The presence of a time-invariant, firm-specific parameter induces a kind of autocorrelation in the errors for a given firm. Failure to account for "within firm" autocorrelation leads to downward bias in the estimates of the standard errors. Standard generalized least squares procedures are not appropriate in the current situation because the sample design is unbalanced. The more complex estimation procedure appropriate for an unbalanced design has not been attempted. A partial check on the validity of the estimates is presented in Clark [1980] and summarized below in Table V. Accounting for firm-specific effects in a smaller sample leads to estimates of the union coefficient and standard error that are comparable to those presented in Table III. Nevertheless, tests of significance reported below should be treated as no more than suggestive of the information in the data.

The contrast between union-nonunion comparisons based on the total sample and those based on the new plants is instructive. Among new plants, unionized establishments are more productive by 3.6 percent. As in the previous comparison, however, nonunion establishments have a higher capital-labor ratio, and operate at higher rates of utilization. The data for newly constructed plants are thus not inconsistent with the existence of a positive union productivity effect. Union establishments are more productive in spite of operating at lower rates of utilization, and with a lower capital-labor ratio. In addition, line 6 reveals that even among plants built since 1957, nonunion establishments are significantly newer. Taken together these patterns suggest the plausibility of a positive union effect.

Estimates with Vintage Effects

The basic model to be estimated has been laid out in equation (4). Several variants of the model are examined in this section, beginning in Table III, which focuses on vintage effects. The assumption that all parameters vary with the vintage of the plant is tested in a relatively crude way by breaking the sample into plants built before ("old") and after ("new") 1957. We first estimate the basic model in each sample and then impose the constraint of a common production function across vintages, but allow the union effect to differ between old and new plants. The final specification in Table III eliminates all vintage interactions. It is important to note that the estimated union effects are average effects across regions under the assumption of a common technology in union and nonunion plants. The equality constraints on the region effects and the parameters of the production process will be examined subsequently.

The results with full vintage interaction in line 1 of Table III provide a reasonable description of the cement production process.[24]

23. Finer vintage distinctions are not possible given the number of nonunion observations. The 1957 break point was chosen after consulting industry experts and after examining the time pattern of new plant construction. While a number of plants were constructed in the early 1950s, the major postwar expansion of new cement capacity began in the mid-to-late 1950s.

24. Since gross output has been used to calculate productivity in Table III, the results rest on an assumed proportionality between materials (including energy) and gross output. The assumption is likely to be reasonably accurate for raw material, but there is evidence that the ratio of energy to output has changed quite substantially over the last ten years. Even if energy use and unionization are uncorrelated, omission of energy may bias the results. As long as energy (or more accurately the ratio of energy to other inputs) is correlated with included variables that are in turn correlated with unionization, the union coefficient will be biased. The size and extent of the bias will depend crucially on the relationship between the union dummy and the capital-labor ratio. For example, a regression of $\ln(K/L)$ on U using the new plant sample and other control variables from line 1a, yields a coefficient of -0.067 (0.080). Assuming that the relationship between energy and capital is positive, as seems likely, the result implies that the omission of energy actually induces a downward bias in the union effect. In any case, given the magnitude of the coefficient, the extent of the bias is likely to be quite small. Similar conclusions apply to the question of bias induced by measurement error in the capital stock.

The coefficients on the capital-labor ratio are consistent with the capital-intensive nature of cement production and the increased level of automation and mechanization in newer plants. Supervisors apparently play a much more crucial role in the older plants, where their effect on labor productivity is almost twice that found in the newer plants. The effect of scale has been captured by size dummies. While they provide significant explanatory power, no clear monotonic relationship between productivity and the scale of operations emerges. An assumption of constant returns cannot be rejected in specifications with total labor hours as the scale variable.[25] The evidence on the union effect reveals a positive impact among the newer plants, while the older union plants appear slightly less productive than their nonunion counterparts.[26] The large standard error on the union coefficient in the older sample may reflect the small number of nonunion observations, and the greater disparity in age between older union and nonunion plants.

Imposing the constraint of a common production function (including size and region effects) in line 2 has little impact on the estimated union effects by vintage. Among newer plants, the union coefficient falls from 0.100 to 0.091, while the standard error rises to 0.055. The older union and nonunion plants are both less productive than the newer plants and, as before, not significantly different from one another; the estimated differential is 0.029, with a standard error more than twice as large. The disparity in the union effect among old and new plants is evident in line 3 where the union impact is assumed to be independent of vintage. The averaging process yields a coefficient on the union dummy that, though positive, is much smaller than estimates with the new plant sample.

There is little evidence in Table III of a significant negative impact of the union on productivity, and the results in the new plant sample, where the union and nonunion establishments are more comparable, suggest that the effect may be positive.[27] Inferences

25. For example, if size dummies are replaced by the log of manhours in line 16, the coefficient is −0.033, with a standard error of 0.050. The union coefficient under that specification is 0.068 (0.046). It appears that the manhours variable fails to capture differences by size which affect inferences about the union effect.

26. There is a potential selectivity bias in the new sample evidence. If new union plants were designed with the expectation that they would be unionized after construction, then unmeasured differences in technology designed to cope with work rules could affect the results. Discussions with a number of leading engineering and design firms suggest that such considerations are likely to be of no practical consequence. The engineers uniformly hold the view that beyond some influence on the size of the workforce, potential unionization played no role in plant design. Technical considerations pertaining to processing efficiency were dominant.

27. The magnitude of the union impact in the new plant sample is roughly comparable to the estimated change in unit costs arising from the union wage effect. Using

clearly depend on the specification of vintage interactions. Likelihood ratio tests provide some insight into the data's information on the appropriate specification. We first test the hypothesis that all parameters vary with vintage (line 1) against the alternative that allows only for union-vintage interaction (line 2). Using an F-test, the restrictions are rejected at better than the 0.005 level (see the notes to Table III). Since the specification in line 3 is nested, it too is rejected. The results thus suggest that the old and new plants are sufficiently different to warrant separate analysis. Since most of the information on the union differential is in the newer sample, the remainder of this section uses data on those plants to test additional hypotheses about the effects of region and technology.

Union Effects by Region and Differences in Technology

The estimates of the basic model in Table III assume no regional differences in the union effect and identical production parameters in the union and nonunion sectors. These assumptions are examined in Table IV by introducing region interaction terms (line 1) and by estimating the full unconstrained model with separate coefficients for the union and nonunion establishments (line 2). The estimates of the union effect by region in line 1 cover the South and Southwest since these are the only regions in which new union and nonunion plants coexist.[28] The evidence clearly suggests a substantial difference between the two regions, with the effect in the Southwest much larger. The union effect in the South is negative in two of the specifications, although the coefficient is small, and about one-fifth the size of its standard error. The imprecision in the estimates reflects the small number of nonunion observations (4) in the South. More information is available in the Southwest, which contains many of the nonunion firms in the industry. The regional pattern evident in Table IV is consistent with one interpretation of the relative prevalence of nonunion firms in the Southwest. Given a union wage effect, and the regional nature of markets, union firms in the Southwest may face greater competitive pressure and a more immediate incentive to improve operations and reduce costs.

---

data on the entry wage in union and nonunion establishments, Clark [1978] finds that compensation in unionized establishments is about 12–18 percent higher than in comparable nonunion establishments. This translates into an effect on cement costs of about 5–8 percent. The evidence thus suggests that unionization has no effect on unit costs.

28. To preserve degrees of freedom, the West and Southwest have been grouped together in Tables III and IV. In separate runs, these regions had almost identical coefficients; combining the two regions has no effect on the results.

TABLE III

ESTIMATES OF THE UNION EFFECT WITH ALTERNATIVE CONTROLS FOR PLANT VINTAGE

Specification	Cons	$\ln\left(\frac{K}{L}\right)$	$\ln\left(\frac{S}{L}\right)$	Union	Union (new)	Union (old)	Non-union (old)	Vintage	Size	Region	R^2	*SEE*
1. Unconstrained model												
(a) Old plant	0.947	0.247)	0.195	−0.040	—	—	—	—	X	X	0.519	0.216
sample	(0.091)	(0.025)	(0.033)	(0.070)								
(b) New plant	0.802	0.442	0.090	0.100	—	—	—	—	X	X	0.702	0.160
sample	(0.133)	(0.068)	(0.042)	(0.047)								
2. Common production	1.035	0.276	0.178	—	0.091	−0.140	−0.111	—	X	X	0.673	0.211
function; union effects by vintage	(0.074)	(0.073)	(0.027)		(0.055)	(0.053)	(0.084)					
3. Common production	0.853	0.277	0.178	0.044	—	—	—	0.221	X	X	0.672	0.211
function; no union effects by vintage	(0.067)	(0.023)	(0.027)	(0.043)				(0.029)				

Note: (1) The capital measure is calculated according to equation (1), with $\lambda = 0.985$.
(2) Regions are defined in footnote 24.
(3) Size categories are based on total cement capacity and breakdown as follows (in 1,000 tons): 0–250, 250–500, 500–750, 750–1,000, 1,000+.
(4) Old and new are defined as before and after 1957, respectively; vintage has the value 1 if new and zero otherwise; the number of observations in each union-vintage cell are as follows:

	Old	New	Total
Union	348	88	436
Non-union	10	19	29
Total	358	107	465

(5) *F*-test of the specifications:

Line #	*SSR*	*k*	*d.f.*	*F*-statistic
1	18.704	22	443	—
2	20.064	13	452	3.579* (1 vs 2)
3	20.150	12	453	3.423 (1 vs 3)

* $F(9,443)\ 0.005 = 2.671$.

The effect of relaxing the technology constraint is examined in line 2 where estimates of the union effect from the full unconstrained model are presented (see equation (4)). The estimates are based on the new plant sample with the addition of older nonunion plants. The use of all available nonunion plants is designed to improve the precision of estimates in the nonunion sector. While the use of older nonunion plants may bias the union effect, our primary interest is not in specific estimates, but in the change in the union effect when the technology constraint is relaxed. Thus, the estimates in line 2 are to be viewed as no more than illustrative of the impact of specification changes.

In order to provide a basis of comparison, line 2a contains estimates of the model without region or technology effects. The assumption of constant returns has been imposed and is maintained when the region and technology constraints are relaxed. The use of older nonunion plants has only minor effects on the results. In comparable specifications with the older nonunion plants excluded, the production function parameters are very similar, and the union effect of 8 percent is of the same order of magnitude. It appears that the larger sample conveys much of the same information as obtained when the older nonunion plants are excluded. A greater measure of divergence is evident in line 2b where estimates are presented with the regional constraints relaxed. The production parameters are similar to those found in line 1, but the union effect shows greater variation across regions. The most striking change is found in the South, where the union effect is much more negative. The effect in the Southwest is quite close to the sample average, while the North Central estimate is large and positive. As with the earlier results, the union effect in the South is based on relatively few observations and there appears to be a good deal of divergence in productivity among the nonunion plants within that region. The result is a large standard error on the Southern effect, so that when the three regions are averaged, the effects in the North Central and Southwest dominate.

In line 2c we present estimates of the model without constraining the production parameters in the union and nonunion sectors to be identical. The results provide evidence of no significant differences in technology between the two sectors. Although the union sector emerges with a lower capital coefficient, and a higher coefficient on the supervisor-worker ratio, the interaction terms have large standard errors.[29] The union effect by region has been calculated using equation

29. The coefficients on the interaction terms are −0.098 (0.108) on the capital-labor ratio and 0.055 (0.111) on the supervisor-worker ratio.

TABLE IV

THE EFFECT OF TECHNOLOGY AND REGION ON THE PRODUCTIVITY EFFECT

Specifications	Cons	$\ln\left(\frac{K}{L}\right)$	$\ln\left(\frac{S}{L}\right)$	$\ln L$	Input-union interaction terms	Size dummies	Region dummies	Region-union interaction terms	Union effect by region: South	Union effect by region: W/Southwest	Union effect by region: North Central	R^2	*SEE*
Specifications													
1. Union effect by region													
(a) Constant returns	0.840	0.429	0.119	—	—	—	X	X	−0.016	0.092	—	0.653	0.170
	(0.169)	(0.060)	(0.044)						(0.103)	(0.052)			
(b) Nonconstant returns—total manhours	1.021	0.431	0.113	−0.036	—	—	X	X	−0.023	0.091	—	0.655	0.170
	(0.306)	(0.060)	(0.045)	(0.050)					(0.104)	(0.052)			
(c) Nonconstant returns—size dummies	0.938	0.427	0.098	—	—	X	X	X	0.001	0.125	—	0.705	0.160
	(0.184)	(0.070)	(0.043)						(0.104)	(0.053)			
2. Union effect with and without region and technology differences													

(a) No region or technology effects; constant returns	0.681 (0.095)	0.474 (0.049)	0.121 (0.043)	—	—	—	X	—	0.081 (0.040)	0.081 (0.040)	0.081 (0.040)	0.681	0.172
(b) Region effects; no union/nonunion differences in technology; constant returns	0.662 (0.117)	0.437 (0.052)	0.135 (0.043)	—	—	—	X	X	−0.078 (0.093)	0.110 (0.049)	0.171 (0.098)	0.692	0.170
(c) Region effects; separate union/nonunion technologies; constant returns	0.510 (0.209)	0.496 (0.080)	0.055 (0.111)	—	X	—	X	X	−0.043 (0.102)	0.111 (0.052)	0.165 (0.106)	0.695	0.171

Note: (1) The sample in line 1 contains plants built since 1957; the sample in line 2 contains all of the plants in line 1, and adds nonunion plants built before 1957.

(2) The number of observations by union-region cell are as follows:

	line 1					line 2				
	South	Southwest	N.C.	N.E.	Total	South	Southwest	N.C.	N.E.	Total
Union	13	38	23	14	88	13	38	23	14	88
Nonunion	4	15	—	—	19	5	20	4	—	29
Total	17	53	23	14	107	18	58	27	14	117

(3) The union effect in 2a is an average over all regions; note that the input coefficients in 2c pertain to the nonunion sector (see equation (4)).

(5) and mean values of (K/L) and (S/L) in each region. The results suggest that technology differences explain little of the union-nonunion productivity differential. The estimated union effects in line 2c are very close to the effects estimated with the technology constraint imposed. The evidence thus suggests that constraining the production functions to be identical in the union and nonunion sectors does not obscure important technological distinctions, and does not affect inferences about the union effect.

IV. Firm Effects and Quality Adjustments

The empirical analysis in Section III found some evidence that unionized establishments are more productive than their nonunion counterparts. However, the implication that unionization leads to productive changes in the operation of the enterprise rests on two assumptions. First, the union coefficient can only be identified as a measure of the productivity effect of unionization if we assume the absence of individual firm effects, or that any effects specific to the enterprise are independent of union status and other determinants. Second, it is necessary to assume that quality adjustments are nonexistent or small. The statistical design in Section III failed to control for union-induced changes in worker quality. The union coefficient, therefore, may capture more than organization effects.

These issues have been examined at length in Clark [1980] and will be addressed only briefly here. To estimate the impact of the union holding constant firm-specific effects, we make use of data on productivity in six establishments that changed union status in the 1953–1976 era. Information on turnover in each establishment sheds light on the extent of quality differences after the union is introduced, and permits a rough calculation of the bias caused by omission of quality measures.

Productivity Before and After Unionization

Empirical analysis of productivity using time series data on a given establishment requires modifications to the basic model developed in Section III. Since the focus is on a change in union status in a specific establishment, controls for region and vintage may be omitted. However, changes in methods of organization and management that improve productivity are likely to occur over time and should be controlled for in estimating the union effect.[30] Assuming

30. In principle, variation in the utilization of the capital stock should also be included. In practice, controlling for utilization rates has only moderate effects on the estimated union coefficient. For example, under constant returns to scale, introduction of the utilization rate yields a union coefficient of 0.100 (0.040); when corrected for autocorrelation, the result is 0.064 (0.040).

that disembodied technological change in the ith firm is of the simple exponential form, the basic model may be rewritten as

$$\text{(6)} \quad \ln(Q/L)_{it} = \ln A_0 + \delta t + bU_{it} + \alpha \ln(K/L)_{it} + \gamma \ln(S/L)_{it} + (\theta - 1) \ln L_{it} + \upsilon_{it},$$

where δ is the rate of technological change, υ is the error term, and all other variables are defined as before.

As specified in (6), the parameters of the production process are assumed to be identical in each firm, but productivity may vary across establishments because of differences in organization factors. It is common in production function analysis, for example, to attribute part of any unexplained variation in output to firm-specific differences in managerial ability. If specific differences in organizational factors exist, ignoring them may lead to biased estimates of production parameters, including the union productivity effect. Firm-specific effects may be held constant by assuming that the error term has the following "fixed effects" structure:

$$\text{(7)} \quad \upsilon_{it} = \mu_i + \epsilon_{it}$$

$$E\upsilon_{it} = \mu_i$$

$$\text{cov}(\upsilon_{it},\upsilon_{is}) = E\epsilon_{it}\epsilon_{is} = \begin{cases} \sigma_\upsilon^2 & \text{when } i = j \text{ and } t = s \\ 0 & \text{otherwise.} \end{cases}$$

Under this specification, consistent estimates can be obtained by introducing individual establishment intercepts.

Time series data from the PCA survey have been developed for six cement plants that were unionized in the 1953–1976 period. Since some of the establishments were constructed after 1953, we do not have data on each plant in each year of the period. There are an average of 17 years of data per establishment.[31] Table V presents a summary of the union coefficients estimated from alternative specifications of equation (6). The sign of the union effect is invariably positive, while the exact order of magnitude and precision of the estimate depends on model specification. The evidence supports the conclusion, however, that unionization leads to gains in productivity within an establishment, with the size of the effect ranging from 8 to 10 percent. These results are not sensitive to adjustments in the model to allow for variation in capacity utilization or other omitted variables.[32]

31. There is an average of 8.7 years of data following unionization.

32. It might be argued that abrupt changes in the firm's environment, which raise productivity, may be correlated with unionization. Using data on plants, which do not change union status, Clark [1980] finds that omitted variable bias of this sort is not important. Controlling for variation in productivity in other plants, the union effect is 0.092 (0.046) under nonconstant returns, and 0.069 (0.043) under constant returns.

TABLE V

ESTIMATES OF THE UNION DIFFERENTIAL CONTROLLING FOR FIRM-SPECIFIC EFFECTS

Specification	Firm intercepts	Union	*SEE*	D.W.	ρ
1. Nonconstant returns to scale	√	0.107	0.179	0.89	—
		(0.064)			
Corrected for autocorrelation	√	0.104	0.147	—	0.576
		(0.070)			(0.091)
2. Constant returns to scale	√	0.084	0.181	0.83	—
		(0.063)			
Corrected for autocorrelation	√	0.103	0.147	—	0.590
		(0.070)			(0.091)

Source. Adapted from Clark [1980], Table 2.
Note. The results corrected for autocorrelation were estimated with input parameters set at cross-section values.

Quality Adjustments

Evidence of a positive union productivity effect has been found in both time series and cross-section data, but no controls for possible changes in labor quality have been introduced. If unionization induces firms to acquire workers of higher quality, the estimated union effect may reflect quality differences as well as changes in organization. While sufficient data are not available to address the extent of union-nonunion differences in quality, it is possible to place an upper bound on the potential bias due to omission of quality measures in the before/after analysis.

The change in productivity that follows from union-induced changes in labor quality depends on technology and the union wage effect. If unionization raises the wage, the firm will attempt to reduce costs by substituting higher for lower quality workers. But a distinction must be made between changing the quality of the workforce and changing workforce productivity. While it is clear that productivity and quality are related positively, the magnitude of productivity change resulting from a change in quality depends on the technology of production. Without precise specification of the way in which workers of different quality interact with each other and with other factors of production, few conclusions can be drawn about the extent to which the firm can recover the incremental cost of an exogenous wage increase by hiring workers of higher quality. It is possible, however, to place an upper bound on the change in productivity. In order for the firm to achieve a stable equilibrium, a given change in quality must lead to a more rapid increase in the wage than in productivity.[33] This condition is intuitively reasonable, since if it were not true, the firm could lower unit costs by raising the wage. The implication is that the effect in quality adjustments on productivity is bounded by the union wage effect.

The stability condition can be used to gauge the effect of omitting quality adjustments in the before/after analysis. Assume that unionization raises the wage by ϕ percent. Because of contract rules and associated legal problems, the firm is not likely to adopt the optimal overall level of worker quality immediately. Until the workforce has turned over completely, the firm will have old and new workers, and the new workers will be of higher quality. The stability condition implies that the efficiency advantage of new workers will be less than ϕ percent. If we assume that unionization does not change the basic technology of production, the effect of unionization on productivity can be written as $b + hD\beta$, where b is the organization effect as before, h is the efficiency advantage of new workers, D is the proportion of new workers in the workforce, and β is the elasticity of output with respect to changes in production labor input.[34] The empirical analysis summarized in Table V implicitly assumed $hD\beta = 0$, so that the union coefficient could be identified as the organization effect. A more realistic upper bound on the quality effect can be estimated from available information on labor's share, the union wage effect, and turnover in the six plants.

Based on the estimation results in Table III, a likely value for β is 0.45. Evidence in Clark [1978] suggests that the union wage effect lies in the range from 12–18 percent. This estimate is based on data on the entry wage, with adjustments for fringe benefits, and changes in job classifications. Since the efficiency advantage of new workers is less than the wage effect, we shall use a value of 15 percent in the calculations that follow. As part of a general case study of the effects of unionization in the six before/after plants, information has been obtained on the percentage of the 1976 workforce employed at the

33. This result holds in a model in which quality augments the efficiency of labor and in which the wage is an increasing function of quality. See Clark [1980]. These results are based on a model that assumes optimizing behavior. If satisficing characterizes decision making, a change in labor quality could exceed the change in the wage over some range of quality. However, it seems reasonable to suppose that as a general rule, unit labor costs are positively correlated with wage rates. This condition is consistent with several modes of decision making and is the essential point in the model of quality adjustments examined here.

34. After unionization, the production process is $Q = AK^{1-\beta}(L_o + (1 + h)L_n)^{\beta}$, where o and n indicate old and new, respectively. We note that $A = A_o(1 + b)$, $L = L_o + L_n$ and $D = (L_n/L)$. Pooling union and nonunion observations we have $\ln(Q/L) = \ln A_o + [b + hD\beta]U + (1 - \beta)\ln(K/L)$, where U is the union dummy.

time the plant was organized (see Clark [1980] for details of the case studies). The average value of D in 1976 was 0.34, with estimates ranging from 0.05 to 0.65. This overstates the proportion of new workers relevant for present purposes, since D should be measured by an average value over the sample period. If the rate of growth of D was constant throughout the union era, then the estimated value at the midpoint of the period would be appropriate. Using the end-point value of D, the estimated quality effect is 0.023, the effect is 0.011 if D is set at its midpoint. Given that these calculations provide upper bounds, the evidence suggests that omission of quality measures introduces at most a small bias into estimates of the union effect in the before/after analysis.

V. Conclusion

The empirical evidence in this paper tends to support the view that unionization increases the productivity of otherwise comparable establishments. We found no strong evidence of a negative effect, and the results among newer plants in the cross section and the evidence from the time series comparisons suggest a positive union impact. Given the small number of observations and the size of the standard errors these results should be interpreted with some caution. It does appear, however, that controls for individual firm effects, technology differences, and changes in labor quality have only moderate effects on the magnitude of the union differential. Since the traditional channels of union influence have been held constant, the results capture the effects of unionization that work through changes in the internal operation of the firm.

The finding of a positive union effect in a particular situation does not warrant the conclusion that unionization raises productivity everywhere, always. Indeed, evidence from the coal industry suggests that the deterioration of industrial relations in that industry in the 1970s led to a significant decline in productivity in unionized establishments.[35] It is evident that the union effect in a particular setting will vary with the character of industrial relations. As Marshall argued long ago, the effect of unionization on productivity depends on union policy as well as management adjustment. Research reported here and elsewhere has uncovered positive union effects, but remains incomplete. The task ahead is to identify the actual channels of union

35. These results are based on work in progress by Margaret Connerton, Richard Freeman, and James Medoff.

influence and those practices and procedures that affect productivity.

HARVARD UNIVERSITY

REFERENCES

Bok, Derek, and John T. Dunlop, *Labor and the American Community* (New York: Simon and Schuster, 1970).
Bradley, Philip P., *The Public Stake in Union Power* (Charlottesville: University of Virginia Press, 1959).
Brown, Charles, and James L. Medoff, "Trade Union in the Production Process," *Journal of Political Economy,* LXXXVI (June 1978), 355–78.
Clark, Kim B., "Unions and Productivity in the Cement Industry," Ph.D. thesis, Harvard University, 1978.
——, "The Impact of Unionization on Productivity: A Case Study," *Industrial and Labor Relations Review,* XXXIII (1980), 451–69.
Freeman, Richard B., "Individual Mobility and Collective Voice in the Labor Market," *American Economic Review,* LXVI (May 1976), 361–68.
——, "The Exit-Voice Tradeoff in the Labor Market: Unionism, Job Tenure, Quits, and Separations," this *Journal,* XCIV (1980), 643–74.
Heneghan, John M., "A History of the United Cement, Lime and Gypsum Workers International Union," processed (1952).
Johnson, Harry, and Peter Mieszkowski, "The Effects of Unionization on the Distribution of Income: A General Equilibrium approach," this *Journal*, LXXXIV (Nov. 1970), 539–61.
Jorgenson, Dale, and Zvi, Griliches, "The Explanation of Productivity Change," *Review of Economic Studies,* XXXIV (July 1967), 249–82.
Lawler, E. E., *Motivation in Work Organizations* (Monteray: Wadsworth Company, 1973).
Leibenstein, Harvey, "Allocative Efficiency Vs. '*X*-Efficiency,' " *American Economic Review,* LVI (June 1966), 392–415.
Lester, R., and R. Aronson, *Job Modification Under Collective Bargaining* (Princeton: Industrial Relations Section, 1971), 57–60.
Loescher, Samuel M., *Imperfect Collusion in the Cement Industry* (Cambridge: Harvard University Press, 1959).
Marshall, Alfred, *Elements of Economics,* Vol. I, 3rd. ed. (London: 1899).
Pencavel, John, "The Distributional and Efficiency Effects of Trade Unions in Britain," *British Journal of Industrial Relations,* XV (July 1977), 137–56.
Portland Cement Association, *The Cement Industry: An Economic Report,* 1974.
Radner, Roy, "A Behavioral Model of Cost Reduction," *Bell Journal of Economics,* VI (Spring 1975), 196–205.
Slichter, Sumner, James Healy, and Robert Livernash, *The Impact of Collective Bargaining on Management* (Washington, D. C.: The Brookings Institution, 1960).
U. S. Department of Commerce, *Construction Review,* XXII (June 1976), 11.
Williamson, Oliver, Jeffrey Harris, and Michael Wachter, "Understanding the Employment Relation: The Analysis of Idiosyncratic Exchange," *Bell Journal of Economics,* VI (Spring 1975), 250–78.

"RATIONAL" DUOPOLY EQUILIBRIA*

JOHN LAITNER

This paper examines duopoly models in which each firm tries to guess the reaction of its rival to a change in its output. We seek equilibria in which the guesses are accurate, or "rational." For static models we discover that many output combinations (X, Y) can fit into such equilibria and that our concept of "rationality" must necessarily be one-sided: if a firm has accurate expectations at (X, Y) about its rival's reactions, the competitor's reactions cannot themselves be based on "rational" calculations. Turning to a dynamic model, we find that an oversupply of solution pairs continues to be a problem.

Consider a simple duopoly problem of the Cournot quantity-adjustment variety. Assume that both firms want to maximize their own profits and that cooperation agreements and side-payment contracts are ruled out. There are then two possible analytical approaches in the static case. One we might label the "nonconjectural" model. In it the duopolists make their output decisions in isolation—locked in separate rooms perhaps. Only after both have fixed their plans does each learn his rival's choice, and at that point no further output changes can take place.[1] The Cournot equilibrium is a natural concept for this type of model: Given sufficiently well-behaved cost and demand functions, each duopolist can develop a "best-reply" function showing his profit-maximizing production level for each fixed output of the other firm. In a "nonconjectural" problem, each firm will want to choose a point on its best-reply function curve. A Cournot equilibrium has the desirable feature that both firms are choosing best-reply output levels at the same time.

We call the second possible model "conjectural." In this model firms make their output decisions simultaneously (as above), but each knows, as it makes its decision, what output its rival will choose.[2] Thus, each firm should take into account the fact that its output decision will affect its rival's behavior. So conjectural variation terms—functions showing the (immediate) reactions from their rivals that firms expect as responses to changes in their outputs—play an important role. We can think of the following story. At time $t - \epsilon$, $\epsilon > 0$, both duopolists announce their output decisions for the period

* I wish to thank Ted Bergstrom, John Cross, Hal Varian, and an anonymous referee for helpful comments on an earlier draft of this paper.

1. Cyert and de Groot [1970] and Friedman [1977, Ch. 5, 1968] deal with sophisticated variants of this model.
2. Marschak and Selten [1974, 1978] work with this type of model. Hahn [1978] uses similar ideas in a different context.

The Quarterly Journal of Economics, December 1980 0033-5533/80/0095-0641$02.20

to begin at time t, each firm attempting to maximize its (one-period) profits in light of its conjectural variation function. After the first announcement, both firms reevaluate their decisions and issue a (simultaneous) announcement of corrections. The time is $t - \delta, \epsilon > \delta > 0$. The process continues until the corrected output bundle satisfies both firms. Each firm's chosen output at time t will reflect, therefore, a knowledge of its rival's output plans. Although most empirical analyses use price in place of quantity as a decision variable for producers, existing data suggest that the conjectural model may be realistic, at least in some cases (see Blair [1972, Ch. 19], and Kaplan, Dirlam, and Lanzillotti [1958, pp 31–36], for example).[3]

In this paper we examine conjectural models. In particular, we study various types of "conjectural equilibria"—stopping points for the iterative process outlined in the preceding paragraph. Such outcomes are Nash equilibria conditional on expectation functions: at equilibrium neither duopolist perceives any advantage to changing his output. In Section I we find, as might be imagined, that if we do not require that expectations correspond to reality, the set of possible "conjectural equilibrium" outcome points may well be enormous.

In Section II we attempt to remedy the overabundance of solutions by requiring that expectations ("conjectural variations") be "rational"—in other words, we try demanding that the reactions each firm expects from its rival be reactions that the rival will actually perceive to be desirable. This constraint seems consistent with the "perfect information assumption" of traditional microeconomic theory. Surprisingly, we can show that the set of output pairs qualifying (with the correct choice of conjectural variation functions) as "rational conjectural equilibria" for a given problem may still be very large.

Section III extends the analysis to a dynamic model, which permits a different type of "rationality" requirement. Although an extreme multiplicity of equilibria continues to prevail, we are able to define "rationality" in a somewhat more satisfactory way than is the case for the static model.

I. Conjectural Equilibria

First, we set up a simple static model. Then we present our definition of a "conjectural equilibrium" and prove that a large set of output combinations can qualify.

3. In order to avoid the complications of having to incorporate product differentiation we work exclusively with quantity-adjustment models.

The model has the following elements. Two firms produce a single homogeneous product that cannot be obtained elsewhere. If $Q = X + Y$ is the sum of their outputs, $P(Q)$ gives the market price. The firm's total cost functions are $C(X)$ and $D(Y)$, respectively. Each firm attempts to maximize its own profits. The profit functions are

$$H(X,Y) = P(X+Y)X - C(X), \tag{1}$$

$$I(X,Y) = P(X+Y)Y - D(Y), \tag{2}$$

respectively. Although the firms make their output decisions simultaneously, plan changes are always possible before production begins. So each firm is aware that its choice of a production level will affect its rival's behavior. If, at any prospective output point (X,Y) with each firm aware of how much its rival plans to produce, the first firm believes that an infinitesimal change Δ in its output level will elicit a reaction $\Delta(\partial Y/\partial X)^e|_{(X,Y)}$ in the planned output of its competitor, we define $F(X,Y) = (\partial Y/\partial X)^e|_{(X,Y)}$. Similarly, we let the second firm's "expectation (or conjectural variation) function" be $G(X,Y) = (\partial X/\partial Y)^e|_{(X,Y)}$.

For Firm 1 to calculate the response that it expects to a noninfinitesimal change in X, it must integrate the differential equation $dY/dX = F(X,Y)$. We shall say "$\phi(\cdot)$ solves $dY/dX = F(X,Y)$" if[4]

$$\phi(X_0,Y_0,X_0) = Y_0 \tag{3}$$

and

$$\frac{\partial\phi(X_0,Y_0,X)}{\partial X} = F(X,\phi(X_0,Y_0,X))$$

$$\text{all } X \geq 0 \quad \text{and} \quad (X_0,Y_0) \geq (0,0).$$

We shall say that "$\psi(\cdot)$ solves $dX/dY = G(X,Y)$" if

$$\psi(X_0,Y_0,Y_0) = X_0 \tag{4}$$

and

$$\frac{\partial\psi(X_0,Y_0,Y)}{\partial Y} = G(\psi(X_0,Y_0,Y),Y)$$

$$\text{all } Y \geq 0 \quad \text{and} \quad (X_0,Y_0) \geq (0,0).$$

For the sake of simplicity, we shall assume that firms' conjectural variation functions always have the property that one and only one

4. Our conventions are $(a',b') > (a,b)$ implies that $a' > a, b' > b$ and $(a',b') \geq (a,b)$ implies that $a' \geq a, b' \geq b$.

$\phi(\cdot)$ satisfies line (3) and one and only one $\psi(\cdot)$ satisfies line (4).[5] If $\phi(\cdot)$ satisfies line (3), then starting from (X_0, Y_0), for each choice of X on the part of the first firm $(X, \phi(X_0, Y_0, X))$ gives the (current) outcome point that the firm will expect.

Given a conjectural variation function $F(\cdot)$ for the first firm, we let the set on which the firm perceives that it is maximizing its own profits be $K(F(\cdot))$:

$$(5) \quad K(F(\cdot)) = \left\{ (X_0, Y_0) \geq (0,0): H(X_0, Y_0) \geq H(X, \phi(X_0, Y_0, X)) \right.$$
$$\left. \text{all } X \geq 0\text{—for } \phi(\cdot) \text{ solving } \frac{dY}{dX} = F(X,Y) \right\}.$$

Similarly, for the second firm

$$(6) \quad L(G(\cdot)) = \left\{ (X_0, Y_0) \geq (0,0): I(X_0, Y_0) \geq I(\psi(X_0, Y_0, Y), Y) \right.$$
$$\left. \text{all } Y \geq 0\text{—for } \psi(\cdot) \text{ solving } \frac{dX}{dY} = G(X,Y) \right\}.$$

We define a "conjectural equilibrium" in terms of these sets:

D1) A "conjectural equilibrium" is a tuple $(X^*, Y^* F^*(\cdot), G^*(\cdot))$, such that
$$(X^*, Y^*) \epsilon K(F^*(\cdot)) \cap L(G^*(\cdot)).$$

Thus, if $F^*(\cdot)$ and $G^*(\cdot)$ give the conjectural variation functions of Firms 1 and 2, respectively, and if $(X^*, Y^*, F^*(\cdot), G^*(\cdot))$ is a conjectural equilibrium, at (X^*, Y^*) neither firm will perceive that it can derive a higher profit by changing its output. Firm 1, for example, will foresee a change from X^* to X^{**} on its part, causing a change from Y^* to $Y^{**} = \phi(X^*, Y^*, X^{**})$ (where $\phi(\cdot)$ solves $dY/dX = F^*(X,Y)$) on the part of Firm 2; and, if $(X^*, Y^*) \epsilon K(F^*(\cdot)) \cap L(G^*(\cdot))$, $H(X^*, Y^*) \geq H(X^{**}, Y^{**})$.

As in the case of a conventional Cournot equilibrium (and note that any tuple satisfying D1 and having $F^*(X,Y) = 0 = G^*(X,Y)$ all (X,Y) will define a Cournot equilibrium), a conjectural equilibrium $(X^*, Y^*, F^*(\cdot), G^*(\cdot))$ will usually not have the attribute "rationality" (see Section II). Definition D1 does not require any correspondence between the reactions the first (second) firm would like to make to changes in $Y(X)$ and the second (first) firm's conjectural variation

5. See Theorems 7.2 and 7.3 of Brauer and Nohel [1967] for one set of sufficiency conditions for the existence and uniqueness of $\phi(\cdot)$ and $\psi(\cdot)$.

function, even at (X^*, Y^*). Yet, without some theory of expectations there seems to be no reason to prefer one equilibrium tuple to another.

What is more, with proper choices of $F^*(\cdot)$ and $G^*(\cdot)$, a great variety of output combinations (X^*, Y^*) can be made to satisfy D1, as the following proposition shows.

PROPOSITION I. Suppose that $C(\cdot)$ and $D(\cdot)$ are nondecreasing and strictly convex, $C(0) = D(0) = 0$, and $C'(0) = D'(0) = 0$. Let the market demand curve be downward sloping. Suppose that $P(Q) > 0$ and $P''(Q) < 0$, all $Q \geq 0$. Then, with the correct choice of $F^*(\cdot)$ and $G^*(\cdot)$ we can incorporate any point $(X^*, Y^*) > (0,0)$ with $P(X^* + Y^*) - C'(X^*) \geq 0$ and $P(X^* + Y^*) - D'(Y^*) \geq 0$ into a conjectural equilibrium tuple $(X^*, Y^*, F^*(\cdot), G^*(\cdot))$.

The Appendix to this paper supplies a proof. The proposition shows that if cost and demand functions meet the specified hypotheses, then any positive output combinations up to and including competitive-market outcomes can be made to constitute conjectural equilibria.[6] For example, fixing $F^*(X,Y) = -1 = G^*(X,Y)$ all (X,Y) any pair of competitive-market outcomes (X^*, Y^*) forms a conjectural equilibrium tuple $(X^*, Y^*, F^*(\cdot), G^*(\cdot))$ (see the proof of Proposition I). Similarly, suppose that $(X^c, Y^c) > (0,0)$ is a cartel outcome. Then setting $F^*(X,Y) = Y^c/X^c$ and $G^*(X,Y) = X^c/Y^c$ all (X,Y), $(X^c, Y^c, F^*(\cdot), G^*(\cdot))$ gives an equilibrium. In each case we have an outcome at which both firms believe they are maximizing their own profits.

II. Rational Expectations

Our conjectural model simultaneously allows equilibrium output pairs as varied as competitive-market and cartel outcomes. In this section we attempt to make the model more selective by requiring rational expectations. We shall say that the first firm's expectations are "rational" at a point (X, Y) if the predictions the firm makes about the responses of its rival to small (but not necessarily infinitesimal) changes in X represent changes in Y with which the second firm would itself be satisfied (in the face of the given changes in X). We can say the same for the second firm's expectations.

6. The hypotheses here provide a sufficient but not necessary set of conditions for our results. They are chosen to make the proofs in the appendix as straightforward as possible. No attempt is made to find the least restrictive set of sufficient conditions for the results of Proposition I (and Proposition II).

The notation of the preceding section enables us to be more precise: We think of the first firm's conjectural variation function, $F(\cdot)$, as being "rational" in the vicinity of a point $(X_0, Y_0)\epsilon L(G(\cdot))$ if $(X,\phi(X_0,Y_0,X))\epsilon L(G(\cdot))$ for all X in some open neighborhood U of X_0, where $\phi(\cdot)$ is the solution to $dY/dX = F(X,Y)$. Note that requiring rationality for the first firm's expectations only makes sense at points $(X_0,Y_0)\epsilon L(G(\cdot))$—if $(X_0,Y_0)\not\epsilon L(G(\cdot))$, the second firm is not maximizing its perceived profits at the point (X_0, Y_0), so it should immediately adjust its output. The first firm should not be required to predict responses on the part of its rival that maximize the rival's profits of the rival initially shows no inclination to act in its own best interests. Similarly, we should care about the rationality of the second firm's expectations only at points $(X_0, Y_0)\epsilon K(F(\cdot))$.

Our new definition of equilibrium is

D2) A "rational conjectural equilibrium" is a tuple $(X^*,Y^*,F^*(\cdot), G^*(\cdot))$ such that (i) $(X^*,Y^*)\epsilon K(F^*(\cdot)) \cap L(G^*(\cdot))$; (ii) for some open neighborhood U of $X^*, X\epsilon U$ implies $(X,\phi(X^*,Y^*,X)) \epsilon L(G^*(\cdot))$ if $\phi(\cdot)$ solves $dY/dX = F^*(X,Y)$; and, (iii) for some open neighborhood V of Y^*, $Y\epsilon V$ implies $(\psi(X^*,Y^*,Y),Y)\epsilon K(F^*(\cdot))$ if $\psi(\cdot)$ solves $dX/dY = G^*(X,Y)$.

If $(X^*,Y^*,F^*(\cdot),G^*(\cdot))$ is to be a rational conjectural equilibrium, this definition requires that the first firm's expectations be "rational" at (X^*,Y^*) for small changes in X, and that the second firm's expectations be "rational" at (X^*,Y^*) for small changes in Y.

Since our solution functions $\phi(\cdot)$ and $\psi(\cdot)$ correspond to Marschak and Selten's [1974, 1978] "response functions," definition D2 is analogous to Marshak and Selten's definition of a "weak convolution." The advantages of our formulation are its tie to the familiar concept of a conjectural variation, and its simplicity, which enables us to characterize a firm's expectations with a bivariate function ($F(\cdot)$ or $G(\cdot)$), rather than with a trivariate response function of Marschak and Selten's form. In any case, since our nonuniqueness results are based on $\phi(\cdot)$ and $\psi(\cdot)$ stemming from $F(\cdot)$ and $G(\cdot)$, multiple equilibria must be at least as great a problem with Marshak and Selten's response functions (of which $\phi(\cdot)$ and $\psi(\cdot)$ are specialized examples) as they are in the present paper.

Definition D2 apparently achieves a greater degree of restrictiveness than D1 only at the expense of assuming away nonrationality. Actually, however, in terms of points (X, Y) that can qualify (with the correct choices of $F^*(\cdot)$ and $G^*(\cdot)$) as equilibria, the new definition does not turn out to be much stronger.

PROPOSITION II. Suppose that $P(\cdot)$, $C(\cdot)$, and $D(\cdot)$ satisfy the hypotheses of Proposition I. Then if (X^*,Y^*) also satisfies the hypotheses, we can construct $F^*(\cdot)$ and $G^*(\cdot)$ such that $(X^*,Y^*,F^*(\cdot),G^*(\cdot))$ satisfies D2, provided that $|Y^*P'(Q^*)/(P(Q^*) - D'(Y^*) + Y^*P'(Q^*))|\ |X^*P'(Q^*)/(P(Q^*) - C'(X^*) + X^*P'(Q^*))| > 1$ and $|Y^*P'(Q^*)/(P(Q^*) - D'(Y^*) + Y^*P'(Q^*))| < \infty$, where $Q^* = X^* + Y^*$.

In the proof, which is given in the Appendix, we construct $K(F^*(\cdot))$ and $L(G^*(\cdot))$ to be straight lines. The new assumption at the end of the proposition requires that the former line be steeper than the latter. This is analogous to requiring "stable" reaction functions in the case of the standard Cournot model. While the new assumption rules out competitive-market outcomes (for which the product of absolute values is 1), it does not exclude some outcomes with $X + Y$ infinitesimally smaller than the market-solution sum. Similarly, it rules out the cartel outcome (for which the product of absolute values is again 1), but it does allow some outcomes for which $X + Y$ is infinitesimally larger than the cartel sum. In fact, if (X^c,Y^c) and (X^m,Y^m) are the cartel and competitive-market outcomes, respectively, the new assumption does not exclude any output point (X^*,Y^*) with $(X^c,Y^c) < (X^*,Y^*) < (X^m,Y^m)$ from being a component of an equilibrium tuple $(X^*,Y^*,F^*(\cdot),G^*(\cdot))$.[7]

Thus, although imposing "rationality" limits the set of equilibrium tuples $(X^*,Y^*,F^*(\cdot),G^*(\cdot))$ a great deal, it leaves a large set of points (X,Y) that can fit into such tuples (at least given the hypotheses of Proposition II). Furthermore, the concept of rationality embodied in definition D2 is far from satisfying. Suppose that $(X^*,Y^*,F^*(\cdot),G^*(\cdot))$ is a rational conjectural equilibrium. Then the first firm's conjectures about its rival's reactions to changes in X are "rational" at (X^*,Y^*). In other words, if Firm 1 varies X slightly from X^*, the response it anticipates from its competitor will coincide with a response the second firm perceives to be desirable (for itself). Yet, the second firm's perceptions depend on its conjectures about the behavior of Firm 1. If the first firm moves X away from X^*, it will not foresee an increase in its profits and, in general, it will foresee a decrease. We have already noted, however, that Firm 2 cannot have sensible conjectures about the first firm's reactions if the first firm is presently acting in a way contrary to its own interests. Thus, Firm

7. For the cartel case, $P(Q) + QP'(Q) - C'(X) = 0 = P(Q) + QP'(Q) - D'(Y)$. Thus, $(X^*,Y^*) > (X^c,Y^c)$ implies that the denominators in the new assumption are less than $-X^*P'(Q^*)$, $-Y^*P'(Q^*)$, respectively. $(X^*,Y^*) < (X^m,Y^m)$ implies that the denominators are greater than $Y^*P'(Q^*),X^*P'(Q^*)$, respectively.

1 is "rational" at (X^*, Y^*), because it can predict responses from Firm 2 that are consistent with the latter's profit goals, but the predicted responses will not normally themselves be based on sensible expectations. In a sense, therefore, we have succeeded in imposing "rationality" at one, and only one, level of sophistication.

III. A Dynamic Model

In this section we stop asking that one firm's expectations about its competitor's behavior be rational even if the competitor's behavior is based on expectations that are themselves unfounded. We switch to a discrete-time dynamic model with a cost-of-adjustment function for each firm (see, for example, Gould [1968]). We assume that each wants to maximize the present value of its future cash flow. Let $(X(t), Y(t))$ be the actual output pair at time t. The adjustment costs make initial conditions, say, $(X(0), Y(0))$, important and the evolution of $(X(t), Y(t)), t > 0$ nontrivial. In place of the concept of rationality from Section II, we require (i) that if $X(t+1) - X(t)$ is a change, the first firm perceives to be profit maximizing (for itself) at time $t+1$, the firm's anticipation about $Y(t+1) - Y(t)$ conditional on $X(t+1) - X(t)$ must be consistent with behavior the second firm perceives to be profit maximizing (for itself); and (ii) that if $Y(t+1) - Y(t)$ is a change the second firm perceives to be in its best interests (with respect to profit maximization), the firm's expectations about $X(t+1) - X(t)$ conditional on $Y(t+1) - Y(t)$ must be consistent with behavior that the first firm perceives to be profit maximizing (for itself). Thus, the dynamic-model analogues of firm's conjectural variation functions must be rational for all profit-maximizing changes between time periods initiated by either firm. Although we shall require such rationality at all points that could be initial conditions for the model, Proposition IV (below) and our examples show that a multiplicity of equilibria continues to be a problem.

In the new model the first firm determines its optimal output time path by solving

$$\sup_{\{X(t+1)\}} \sum_{t=s}^{\infty} (1+r)^{-t}(X(t)P(X(t)+Y(t)) - C(X(t), X(t+1) - X(t))) \tag{7}$$

subject to

$$Y(t+1) = F(X(t), Y(t), X(t+1)), \tag{8}$$

$$Y(s) = y, \quad X(s) = x, \tag{9}$$

where s is the time now, r is the interest rate, $C(\cdot)$ includes costs of adjustment as well as conventional production costs, and (x,y) gives initial conditions. Line (8) replaces the firm's conjectural variation function of earlier sections.[8] The second firm uses a similar setup with $D(\cdot)$ in place of $C(\cdot)$ and $G(X(t),Y(t),Y(t+1)) = X(t+1)$ in place of (8).

Let $H(x,y,F(\cdot))$ be $(1+r)^s$ times the supremum of line (7) subject to lines (8) and (9). Let $I(x,y,G(\cdot))$ give the analogue for the second firm. Then $H(\cdot)$ is independent of s and must satisfy

$$H(x,y,F(\cdot)) = \sup_{\{x'\}} \{xP(x+y) - C(x,x'-x) + (1+r)^{-1}H(x',F(x,y,x'),F(\cdot))\}. \tag{10}$$

So, if $H(\cdot)$ is concave and nondecreasing in x and y, if $C(\cdot)$ is increasing and strictly convex in its second argument, and if $F(\cdot)$ is concave in its third argument, there will be a function $g: R^2 \rightarrow R$ independent of s such that $g(x,y)$ gives the unique x' maximizing the $\{\cdot\}$ expression in line (10).

To make these ideas more precise, let M be the set of functions $F(\cdot)$ of the form of line (8) and concave in their third argument such that for each element of M line (7) defines a nondecreasing, concave $H(x,y,F(\cdot))$. (The proof of Proposition III below will present an example in which M will include all $F(\cdot)$, which are linear.) For any $F(\cdot)\epsilon M$ let

$$\begin{aligned} K(F(\cdot)) = \{(g: R^2 \rightarrow R)\colon & xP(x+y) - C(x,g(x,y)-x) \\ & + (1+r)^{-1}H(g(x,y),F(x,y,g(x,y)); F(\cdot)) \\ & \geq xP(x+y) - C(x,x'-x) \\ & + (1+r)^{-1}H(x',F(x,y,x'); F(\cdot)) \quad \text{all } x'\}. \end{aligned} \tag{11}$$

Then for each $F(\cdot)\epsilon M, K(F(\cdot))$ will contain a single function $g(\cdot)$. Let N and $L(G(\cdot))$ for $G(\cdot)\epsilon N$ be constructed analogously for Firm 2.

To define equilibria for the new model, we need a little additional terminology. First, we shall say that the system of difference equations

8. Note that although we have switched to a dynamic problem, the model is still "conjectural." In other words, given $X(0)$ and $Y(0)$ we think of the point $(X(1),Y(1))$ as being determined as follows: At time $1-\epsilon$, $\epsilon > 0$, each firm selects a tentative output, $X(1)$ or $Y(1)$, for time $t = 1$. If each firm behaves as the other expected, $(X(1),Y(1))$ is the output bundle for time $t = 1$. Otherwise, at time $1-\delta, \epsilon > \delta > 0$, the firms announce a corrected bundle $(X(1),Y(1))$. The "corrections" continue until both firms are satisfied—all changes taking place before time $t = 1$. The process recurs at each time t. In line (8), firm 1 reasons that $Y(t+1)$ depends on $X(t+1)$ because of this tatonnement. When $F^*(\cdot)$ and $G^*(\cdot)$ are part of a dynamic conjectural equilibrium tuple, $(X(1),Y(1)) = (G^*(X(0),Y(0),Y(1)),F^*(X(0),Y(0),X(1)))$ ends the tatonnement for time $t = 1$.

$(F(\cdot),G(\cdot))$ with $F(\cdot)\epsilon M$ and $G(\cdot)\epsilon N$ is "causally determinate" if, for each (x,y), there is one and only one (x',y') with $F(x,y,x') = y'$ and $G(x,y,y') = x'$. Second, if $F(\cdot)\epsilon M, G(\cdot)\epsilon N, (F(\cdot),G(\cdot))$ is causally determinate, $g(\cdot) = K(F(\cdot))$, and $f(\cdot) = L(G(\cdot))$, we shall write $(g(\cdot),f(\cdot)) \sim (G(\cdot),F(\cdot))$ when for any (x,y) pair $(g(x,y),f(x,y)) = (x',y')$ if and only if $(G(x,y,y'),F(x,y,x')) = (x',y')$. In other words, $(g(\cdot),f(\cdot)) \sim (G(\cdot),F(\cdot))$ implies the two systems of difference equations generate coincident time paths from every set of initial conditions (x,y).[9]

Then our definition of an equilibrium for the new model is as follows:

D3) We say that $(f^*(\cdot),g^*(\cdot),F^*(\cdot),G^*(\cdot))$ is a "dynamic conjectural equilibrium" if (i) $F^*(\cdot)\epsilon M$, $G^*(\cdot)\epsilon N$, and $(F^*(\cdot),G^*(\cdot))$ is causally determinate; (ii) $g^*(\cdot) = K(F^*(\cdot))$ and $f^*(\cdot) = L(G^*(\cdot))$; and (iii) $(g^*(\cdot),f^*(\cdot)) \sim (G^*(\cdot),F^*(\cdot))$. For a given dynamic conjectural equilibrium tuple of functions, we say that (X^*,Y^*) is an "equilibrium point" if $g^*(X^*,Y^*) = X^*$ and $f^*(X^*,Y^*) = Y^*$.

Note that equilibrium tuples of functions rather than particular points of R^2 become our main focus of attention.

To understand the new definition, suppose that $(f^*(\cdot),g^*(\cdot), F^*(\cdot),G^*(\cdot))$ is a dynamic conjectural equilibrium for a given duopoly problem. Let $t = 0$ be the initial time for the analysis, and let an initial point $(X(0),Y(0))$ be specified. Then if the first firm believes $F^*(\cdot)$ correctly summarizes its rival's behavior, $g^*(X(0),Y(0)) = X(1)$ describes the first firm's perceived profit-maximizing output (see the right-hand side of line (10)) at time $t = 1$. The same is true for $Y(1) = f^*(X(0),Y(0))$ and Firm 2. However, part (iii) of definition D3 requires that $(G^*(X(0),Y(0),Y(1)),F^*(X(0),Y(0),X(1))) = (X(1),Y(1))$. Therefore, each firm's expectations about its rival's behavior are borne out.[10] The same arguments hold for any initial point $(X(0),Y(0))$, and we can repeat the analysis above at $t = 1$ with $(X(1),Y(1))$ serving as a starting point.

If $(f^*(\cdot),g^*(\cdot),F^*(\cdot),G^*(\cdot))$ is a dynamic conjectural equilibrium tuple and (X^*,Y^*) is a corresponding equilibrium point, when

9. Note that if the systems $(g(\cdot),f(\cdot))$ and $(G(\cdot),F(\cdot))$ always generate the same time paths, then $(g(\cdot),f(\cdot)),(G(\cdot),f(\cdot))$, and $(g(\cdot),F(\cdot))$ must always generate the same paths.

10. See note 8. Note we do not require that if Firm 1, for example, chooses $X^*(1) \neq g^*(X(0),Y(0))$, that it be able to predict the second firm's response accurately—i.e., we do not require that $F^*(X(0),Y(0),X^*(1))$ = the second firm's profit-maximizing choice of $Y(1)$ if $X^*(1) \neq g^*(X(0),Y(0))$: If the first firm chooses $X(1) \neq g^*(X(0),Y(0))$, its behavior is not consistent with profit maximization (given expectation function $F^*(\cdot)$), so the second firm has no sensible response which the first firm, in turn, could "rationally" anticipate.

$(X(0),Y(0)) = (X^*,Y^*),(X(1),Y(1)) = (g^*(X(0),Y(0)),f^*(X(0),Y(0))) = (X^*,Y^*)$. Therefore, if the duopoly starts at (X^*,Y^*) or ever moves to it, neither firm will subsequently have any incentive to be the first to change its output. Thus, (X^*,Y^*) will presumably persist forever after.

In order to be able to establish the existence of a dynamic conjectural equilibrium we make very strong assumptions about functional forms:

$$P(Q) = \alpha + \beta Q, \quad \alpha > 0, \quad \beta < 0; \tag{12}$$

and

$$C(Z,Z^*) = D(Z,Z^*) = \sigma Z^2 + \sigma Z^{*2}, \quad \sigma > 0. \tag{13}$$

(Adding linear or quadratic terms to (13) will not change our proofs below.) This specification can perhaps be viewed as an approximation to a variety of more realistic problems. We have

PROPOSITION III. Suppose that $r > 0$. Fix any d^* with $|d^*| < 1$. There exist a^*, b^*, c^* and A^*,B^*,C^* such that if $Y(t+1) = F(X(t),Y(t),X(t+1)) = a^*X(t) + b^*Y(t) + c^* + d^*X(t+1)$, $X(t+1) = G(X(t),Y(t),Y(t+1)) = a^*Y(t) + b^*X(t) + c^* + d^*Y(t+1)$, $X(t+1) = g(X(t),Y(t)) = A^*Y(t) + B^*X(t) + C^*$, and $Y(t+1) = f(X(t),Y(t)) = A^*X(t) + B^*Y(t) + C^*$, then $(f(\cdot),g(\cdot),F(\cdot),G(\cdot))$ constitutes a "dynamic conjectural equilibrium" for our model. Furthermore, for our solution the linear system $(g(\cdot),f(\cdot))$ has eigenvalues of modulus less than 1.[11]

The proof is in the Appendix.

We can also show that different choices of d^* in Proposition III will yield different equilibrium tuples.

PROPOSITION IV. In the proof of Proposition III, different values of d^* must yield different equilibrium tuples.

Thus, we have a repetition of the multiple-equilibrium phenomenon that Propositions I and II established. Although Proposition IV does not insure that the same wide assortment of equilibria that prevailed in the static model must reappear, the following numerical example shows that great variety may well again be the typical case.

Setting $\alpha = 10, \beta = -1, \sigma = 2$, and $r = 0.1$, we calculated equilibrium tuples for different values of $d^*, |d^*| < 1$. Tables I and II present the results, including the coefficients of $V(X,Y) = V1 \cdot X^2 + V2XY$

11. In fact, we could prove that no solution exists for which the linear system $(g(\cdot),f(\cdot))$ has eigenvalues of modulus greater than or equal to 1.

TABLE I

COEFFICIENTS FOR DYNAMIC EQUILIBRIA OF A SYMMETRIC DUOPOLY PROBLEM*

Trial	V1	V2	V3	V4	V5	V6	a^*	b^*	c^*	d^*
1	−4.31	−1.12	0.00	14.00	−0.23	61.50	−0.03	0.34	0.99	0.00
2	−4.31	−1.11	0.00	14.00	−0.23	61.89	−0.11	0.34	0.72	0.25
3	−4.31	−1.12	0.00	13.98	−0.24	60.94	0.06	0.34	1.26	−0.25
4	−4.32	−1.11	0.00	14.00	−0.22	62.13	−0.19	0.34	0.47	0.50
5	−4.31	−1.12	0.01	13.96	−0.24	60.18	0.14	0.34	1.55	−0.50
6	−4.32	−1.11	0.00	14.00	−0.22	62.24	−0.26	0.34	0.23	0.75
7	−4.32	−1.13	0.01	13.93	−0.25	59.21	0.24	0.34	1.84	−0.75
8	−4.32	−1.11	0.00	14.00	−0.21	62.24	−0.31	0.34	0.09	0.90
9	−4.32	−1.13	0.01	13.91	−0.25	58.51	0.30	0.34	2.04	−0.90

* The figures presented in both Tables I and II are rounded.

TABLE II

COEFFICIENTS, LONG-RUN EQUILIBRIA, AND EIGENVALUES ($E1,E2$) FOR $g^*(\ )$

Trial	A^*	B^*	C^*	X^*	$E1$	$E2$
1	−0.03	0.34	0.99	1.44	0.31	0.37
2	−0.03	0.33	0.97	1.39	0.30	0.36
3	−0.03	0.35	1.01	1.48	0.32	0.38
4	−0.03	0.32	0.94	1.35	0.30	0.35
5	−0.03	0.36	1.04	1.53	0.32	0.39
6	−0.02	0.32	0.92	1.31	0.29	0.34
7	−0.03	0.36	1.06	1.58	0.33	0.40
8	−0.02	0.32	0.91	1.28	0.29	0.34
9	−0.04	0.37	1.07	1.61	0.33	0.40

$+ V3Y^2 + V4X + V5Y + V6$ for Firm 1, the eigenvalues of the system $(g(\cdot),f(\cdot))$ and the (unique) equilibrium point $(X^*,Y^*) = (X^*,X^*)$. Notice that in each case the equilibrium point was globally stable (Proposition III indicated this would be true), and that because of our rationality requirements, the process of convergence from any given initial conditions would be much more credible than, for instance, the usual "dynamic" story for the nonconjectural Cournot model (see Friedman [1977] and Fellner's [1960] comments on the latter).

As we fixed different values of d^*, a familiar train of solutions appeared. As d^* approached $1,X^*$ approached the long-run cartel solution ($X = 1.25$). When d^* equaled $0,X^*$ approximately equaled the long-run Cournot equilibrium outcome ($X = 1.43$). As d^* approached $-1,X^*$ approached the competitive-market long-run equilibrium ($X = 1.67$). Demanding rational expectations for the dynamic model did not, therefore, lead to any more restricted set of equilibria than we observed in Section II.

In closing this section, let us compare our dynamic model with Friedman's [1968] and then ask whether our dynamic conjectural equilibria manifest one of the "perfectness" properties outlined by Selten [1975]. The differences between our model and Friedman's are immediately apparent: Although Friedman's duopoly game is repeated over and over, his model is "nonconjectural" within each time period, because (using our notation) his function $F(\cdot)$ does not depend on $X(t + 1)$ and his function $G(\cdot)$ does not depend on $Y(t + 1)$. At Friedman's equilibrium point (X^*,Y^*), each firm is maximizing its perceived profit function, and each firm's expectations about its rival's reactions after a one-period time lag are rational. On the other hand, firms' expectations are not necessarily rational away from (X^*,Y^*).

Furthermore, because Friedman's firms do not incur adjustment costs, the problem alluded to at the end of Section II reappears: Suppose that Firm 1 varies X infinitesimally starting at (X^*, Y^*). Then Firm 1 will be able to correctly anticipate its rival's response. Firm 1 will not perceive its own change in X to be profit-maximizing, however, so its expectations are not rational about any output adjustment it would actually want to make. The same argument shows that the second firm's response to the first firm's output change cannot be based on rational expectations (see Section II). In this section our model is contemporaneously "conjectural"; rationality prevails everywhere in the sense that, for any initial point $(X(0), Y(0))$, if the first firm perceives a change $X(1) - X(0)$ to be in its interests and expects a reaction $Y(1) - Y(0)$ from its rival, the second firm will, in fact, perceive $Y(1) - Y(0)$ to be a profit-maximizing change (for itself). Rationality is defined only in terms of output changes that both firms perceive to be profit-maximizing.

Turning to the idea of "perfectness," we find that each dynamic conjectural equilibrium has a property corresponding to what Selten [1975] names "subgame perfectness." Suppose that $(f^*(\cdot), g^*(\cdot), F^*(\cdot), G^*(\cdot))$ satisfies D3, and that $(X(0), Y(0))$ is any given initial condition. Then $(X(1), Y(1)) = (g^*(X(0), Y(0)), f^*(X(0), Y(0)))$ is a point at which both firms will perceive themselves to be maximizing their own profits at time $t = 1$. The same is true for $(X(2), Y(2)) = (g^*(X(1), Y(1)), f^*(X(1), Y(1)))$ at time $t = 2$, and so on for $t > 2$. If we disrupt the evolution of the duopoly, however, so that at time $t = 1$ outputs are $(X'(1), Y'(1)) \neq (X(1), Y(1))$, we can treat $(X'(1), Y'(1))$ as an initial condition for time $t = 1$ and, hence, see that $(X'(2), Y'(2)) = (g^*(X'(1), Y'(1)), f^*(X'(1), Y'(1)))$, $(X'(3), Y'(3)) = (g^*(X'(2), Y'(2)), f^*(X'(2), Y'(2)))$, . . . will generate a new sequence of states such that for all $t \geq 2$ both firms feel they are maximizing their profits. In other words, $(g^*(\cdot), f^*(\cdot))$ will induce an equilibrium strategy for both firms from the starting point $(X'(1), Y'(1))$, despite the fact that $(X'(1), Y'(1)) \neq (X(1), Y(1))$. This is true for any disruption.

IV. Conclusion

This paper appraises conjectural duopoly models as an alternative to nonconjectural ones. Working in Cournot's familiar quantity-adjustment framework, we first define the simplest of our equilibrium concepts, the "conjectural equilibrium," and show that many different output combinations can satisfy the definition if we make the correct choice of expectation functions.

We then attempt to require rational expectations for the static model. The results are disappointing for two reasons. First, an enormous variety of output combinations (X^*,Y^*) can still fit into equilibrium tuples $(X^*,Y^*,F^*(\cdot),G^*(\cdot))$ (see Proposition II). Second, our definition of rationality in the static model is not entirely satisfying. Suppose, for example, that at (X^*,Y^*) both firms are maximizing their perceived profit functions and both have rational expectations. Then our definition of rational expectations dictates that if one firm changes its output slightly, it will foresee a response from its rival that the rival will perceive to be profit-maximizing. The initial change away from (X^*,Y^*) by the first firm, however, will not generally be warranted in terms of its profits, given that (X^*,Y^*) is profit-maximizing in both firms' eyes. Thus, in the static model rationality amounts to an ability on the part of a firm to predict sensibly its rival's responses to nonsense behavior on its own behalf.

Section III attempts to rectify the latter problem. We construct a dynamic model with costs of adjustment for firms. The costs give initial conditions an important role. By checking responses to varying initial conditions, we can then define "rationality" without ever considering output adjustments on the part of a firm that the firm perceives to be other than profit-enhancing. Although our definition of rationality is therefore more satisfactory in one sense than it was in the static-model case, Proposition IV and our numerical calculations show that an oversupply of equilibria, and even of equilibrium points, remains a serious issue.

Perhaps the final conclusion that we should draw from this analysis is that, although conjectural duopoly models are interesting, they are troubled with an overabundance of possible equilibria in each case. If we employ such models, therefore, we should not expect particular outcomes in the space of output combinations. Instead, we should concentrate on investigating equilibrium tuples $(X^*,Y^*,F^*(\cdot),G^*(\cdot))$ (or $(f^*(\cdot),g^*(\cdot),F^*(\cdot),G^*(\cdot))$)—assumptions about rationality do imply observable limits on the set of possible equilibria in the space of tuples.

Appendix

Proof of Proposition I

Fix any $(X^*,Y^*) > 0$ with $P(X^* + Y^*) - C'(X^*) \geq 0$ and $P(X^* + Y^*) - D'(Y^*) \geq 0$. Define $F^*(X,Y) = F^*$ and $G^*(X,Y) = G^*$ all (X,Y) with F^* and G^* constants chosen, so that if $Q^* = X^* + Y^*$, then $P(Q^*) + X^*P'(Q^*)(1 + F^*) = C'(X^*)$ and $P(Q^*) + Y^*P'(Q^*)(1 + G^*)$

$= D'(Y^*)$. The last step is possible, since $X^*, Y^*, P'(Q^*) \neq 0$. We have $1 + F^* \geq 0$ and $1 + G^* \geq 0$ because $P'(Q^*) < 0$.

Both firms now satisfy their (perceived) first-order conditions at (X^*, Y^*). We next show that the first firm's second-order conditions hold globally. The argument for the second firm is analogous.

Differentiating the first firm's perceived marginal profit function (using the constraint $(\partial Y/\partial X)|_{(X,Y)} = F^*$), we have $2P'(Q)(1 + F^*) + XP''(Q)(1 + F^*)^2 - C''(X) < 0$ all $(X,Y) \geq 0$, because each term is less than or equal to 0 and $C''(X) > 0$.

Proof of Proposition II

Fix any (X^*, Y^*) satisfying the proposition's hypotheses. Let $T = \{(X,Y) \geq (0,0): P(X + Y) - C'(X) < 0\}$. Let $T\#$ be the complement of T.

Step 1. For constants A, B, A^*, and B^* define $\alpha(X) = A + BX, \beta(Y) = A^* + B^*Y, K = \{(X, \alpha(X)): X > 0, \alpha(X) > 0\}$, and $L = \{(\beta(Y), Y): Y > 0, \beta(Y) > 0\}$. Choose the constants so that $\alpha(X^*) = Y^*, \beta(Y^*) = X^*, P(Q^*) + X^*P'(Q^*)(1 + (1/\beta'(Y^*))) - C'(X^*) = 0$, and $P(Q^*) + Y^*P'(Q^*)(1 + (1/\alpha'(X^*))) - D'(Y^*) = 0$. Then $1 + (1/B^*) \geq 0$ and $1 + (1/B) \geq 0$. Also, $|B||B^*| = |Y^*P'(Q^*)/(P(Q^*) - D'(Y^*) + Y^*P'(Q^*))| \cdot |X^*P'(Q^*)/(P(Q^*) - C'(X^*) + X^*P'(Q^*))| > 1$. So, $|B| = |\text{slope of } K| > |1/B^*| = |\text{slope of } L|$. And, $|B| < \infty$.

Step 2. Consider Firm 1. The firm's perceived marginal profit function is $MP1(X,Y) = P(Q) + XP'(Q)(1 + F(X,Y)) - C'(X)$ where $Q = X + Y$. Along K let $F^*(X,Y)$ be such that $MP1(X,Y) = 0$. Then $1 + F^*(X,Y) \geq 0$ all $(X,Y) \epsilon K \cap T\#$.

$F^*(X^*,Y^*) = 1/B^*$ = the slope of L. Thus, for some open interval U^* containing X^* we have $(X,Y) > (0,0)$ and $|F^*(X,Y)| < |B| = |\text{the slope of } K|$ all $(X,Y) \epsilon K$ and $X \epsilon U^*$. Let $L^* = \{(\beta(Y), Y): Y \geq 0, \beta(Y) \geq 0\}$. Let $L^*(X,Y) = \{(X,Y)\} + (L^* - \{(X^*,Y^*)\})$ all $(X,Y) \epsilon K$. Then for each $(X,Y) \epsilon L^*(X',Y')$ with $(X',Y') \epsilon K$ and $X' \epsilon U^*$ let $F^*(X,Y) = F^*(X',Y')$.

Step 3. Let $(X,Y) \epsilon K$ and $X \epsilon U^*$. Suppose that $P(X,Y)$ is the path of points $(X'Y')$ Firm 1 expects to encounter if, starting from (X,Y), it varies X. Then at (X,Y) the graph of $P(X,Y)$ cuts K and has a smaller absolute slope than K.

Let $S = \{(X,Y): (X,Y) \epsilon L^*(X',Y')$ some $(X',Y') \epsilon K \cap (U^* x(-\infty, \infty))\}$. (Note that $|\text{slope of } K| > |\text{slope of } L| \geq 0$.) We now define $F^*(\cdot)$ on the complement of S. Set $F^*(X,Y) = -1$ all $(X,Y) \epsilon T$. Let (X_L, Y_L) be the lower limit point of $K \cap (U^* x(-\infty, \infty))$ and let (X_U, Y_U) be the upper limit point. To begin, set $F^*(X,Y) = F^*(X',Y')$ all $(X,Y) \epsilon L^*(X',Y')$ where $(X',Y') \epsilon K$ and $(X,Y) \notin T$. If in the case of any of the figures $X_0 > 0$, let $F^*(X',Y') = 1/B^*$ all $(X',Y') \epsilon$ closure (R). (The figures define the set R.)

Case A. Suppose that K has a positive slope.

For $(X,Y) \epsilon K \cap (U^* x(-\infty, \infty))$ consider $P(X,Y)$ to the right of K. In Figure I (i), $F^*(X',Y') = \infty$ on the upper boundary of R. So if $P(X,Y)$ falls as X increases, $P(X,Y)$ must exit into T above the upper

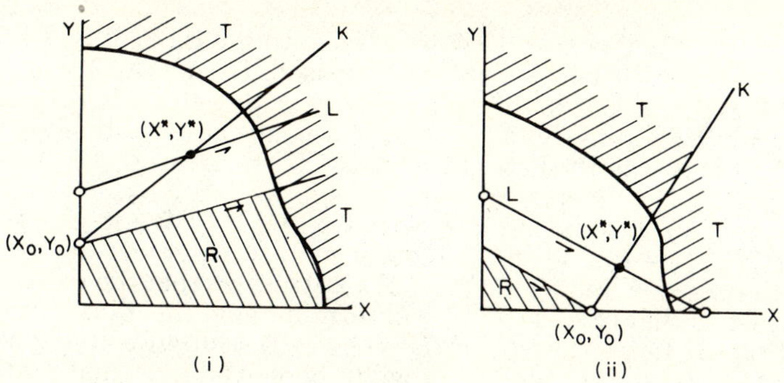

FIGURE I

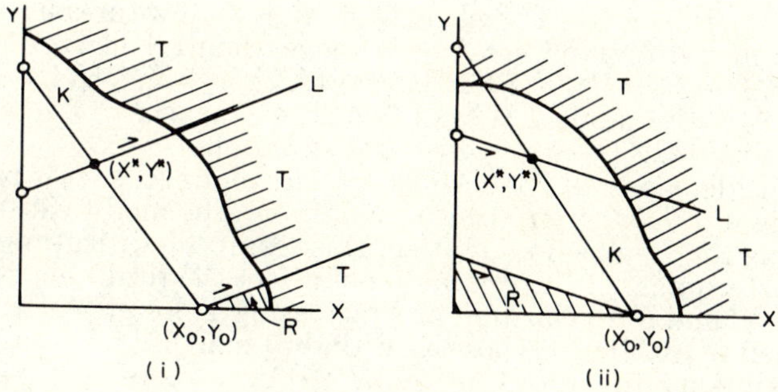

FIGURE II

boundary of R. In Figure I (ii) set $F^*(X,Y) = 0$ along the X-axis to the right of X_0.

Suppose that (X',Y') is to the right of K, $(X',Y') \notin T$, and $(X',Y') \epsilon L^*(X'',Y'')$ with $(X'',Y'') \epsilon K - T$ and $(X'',Y'') \geq (X_U,Y_U)$. Then if $F^*(X',Y') >$ slope of K, change $F^*(\cdot)$ so that $F^*(X',Y') =$ slope of K.

Thus, if $(X,Y) \epsilon K \cap (U^* x(-\infty,\infty))$, $P(X,Y)$ will stay to the right of K as X is increased, finally exiting into T.

Consider (X',Y') to the left of K, $(X',Y') \geq (0,0)$, $(X',Y') \notin T$, and $(X',Y') \epsilon L^*(X'',Y'')$ with $(X'',Y'') \epsilon K - T$, $(X'',Y'') \leq (X_L,Y_L)$. Then if $F^*(X',Y') >$ slope of K, change $F^*(\cdot)$ so that $F^*(X',Y') =$ slope of K. For (X',Y') on the X-axis to the left of any intersection point (X_0,Y_0), let $F^*(X',Y') = 0$.

Thus, if $(X,Y) \epsilon K \cap (U^* x(-\infty,\infty))$, $P(X,Y)$ will stay to the left of K as X is decreased, finally exiting into T or terminating on the Y-axis.

Case B. Suppose that K has a negative slope. Then $1 + (1/B) \geq 0$ and $B < 0$ implies that $B \leq -1$. For $F^*(\cdot)$ unmodified in Case A above, $1 + F^*(X',Y') \geq 0$ all $(X',Y') \epsilon K \cap T\#$, so $F^*(X',Y') \geq -1$ all (X',Y').

Let $(X,Y)\epsilon K \cap (U^*x(-\infty,\infty))$. Then to the right of K, $P(X,Y)$ cannot fall faster than K as X is increased. Let $F^*(X',Y') = 0$ for (X',Y') on the X-axis to the right of (X_0, Y_0). Since $F^*(X',Y') = 1/B^*$ on the upper boundary of R (see the second paragraph of step 3), $P(X,Y)$ must stay to the right of K as X is increased, exiting into T.

For (X',Y') to the left of K with $(X',Y') > (0,0)$ and $(X',Y')\not\epsilon T$, let $F^*(X',Y') = 0$ if $Y' = 0$. No other modifications are needed—if $P(X,Y)$ rises as X falls, $1 + F^*(X',Y') \geq 0$ insures that the rise cannot be as fast as that of K. $P(X,Y)$ will terminate on the Y-axis or in T.

Step 4. Let $(X,Y)\epsilon K \cap (U^*x(-\infty,\infty))$. Suppose that $dMP1/dX|_{L^*(X,Y)}$ gives the rate of change in perceived marginal profit as we move along $L^*(X,Y)$. Then, if $(X',Y')\epsilon L^*(X,Y), dMP1(X',Y')/dX|_{L^*(X,Y)} = P'(Q')(1 + (1/B^*)) + P'(Q')(1 + F^*(X',Y')) + X'P''(Q')(1 + (1/B^*))(1 + F^*(X',Y')) + X'P'(Q')(F^*_X(X',Y') + F^*_Y(X',Y')/B^*)) - C''(X')$, where $Q' = X' + Y'$. If we are on a portion of $F^*(\cdot)$ unmodified in Case A or B above, then $1 + (1/B^*) \geq 0$; $1 + F^*(X',Y') = 1 + F^*(X,Y) \geq 0$; $F^*_X(X',Y') + F^*_Y(X',Y')/B^* = dF^*(X',Y')/dX'$ along $L^*(X,Y)$, which $= 0$; and $C''(X') > 0$. So, $dMR1(X',Y')/dX|_{L^*(X,Y)} < 0$ in that situation.

Consider Case A. Then $MR1(\cdot)$ is zero along K, so it is negative to the right of K where $F^*(\cdot)$ is unmodified. The modifications in R and along the X-axis do not affect this result. Modifications in the northeastern part of the graph do not affect the result either, since holding X' and $F^*(\cdot)$ constant and increasing Y' lowers $MP1(X',Y')$. To the left of K, $MP1(\cdot)$ is positive with the unmodified $F^*(\cdot)$ function. All possible modifications make $MP1(\cdot)$ even more positive by reducing the term multiplying $X'P'(Q')$, a nonpositive number.

Similar arguments hold for Case B. Thus, as Firm 1 considers changing X starting at $(X,Y)\epsilon K \cap (U^*x(-\infty,\infty))$, it perceives that its profit function would fall after any feasible increase or decrease in X. So, $K \cap (U^*x(-\infty,\infty)) \subset K(F^*(\cdot))$.

We can repeat this analysis for Firm 2, letting $MP2(\cdot)$ replace $MP1(\cdot)$, $G^*(\cdot)$ replace $F^*(\cdot)$, and V^* replace U^*. Then $L \cap ((-\infty,\infty)xV^*) \subset L(G^*(\cdot))$.

Step 5. $(X^*,Y^*)\epsilon K(F^*(\cdot)) \cap L(G^*(\cdot))$ by construction.

Since the slope of K is finite, there exists an open interval V such that $Y^*\epsilon V \subset V^*$ and $((-\infty,\infty)xV) \cap K \subset (U^*x(-\infty,\infty)) \cap K$. By construction, if $Y^* + \Delta Y\epsilon V$, Firm 1 will perceive $X^* + \Delta X$ with $(X^* + \Delta X, Y^* + \Delta Y)\epsilon(U^*x(-\infty,\infty)) \cap K$ to be profit-maximizing. That requires $\Delta X = \Delta Y/\alpha'(X) = \Delta Y/B$. But, $G^*(\cdot)$ is level along K with $G^*(X,Y) = G^*(X^*,Y^*) = 1/B$ all $(X,Y)\epsilon K$. So, $Y\epsilon V$ implies $(\psi(X^*,Y^*,Y),Y)\epsilon(U^*x(-\infty,\infty)) \cap K \subset K(F^*(\cdot))$ if $\psi(\cdot)$ solves $dX/dY = G^*(X,Y)$.

We can make a similar argument defining a set U with $X^*\epsilon U \subset U^*$ and $X\epsilon U$ implying $(X,\phi(X^*,Y^*,X))\epsilon((-\infty,\infty)xV^*) \cap L \subset L(G^*(\cdot))$ if $\phi(\cdot)$ solves $dY/dX = F^*(X,Y)$.

Thus, $(X^*,Y^*,F^*(\cdot),G^*(\cdot))$ satisfies D2.

Proof of Proposition III

Let $\pi(X,Y,X^*) = X(\alpha + \beta X + \beta Y) - \sigma X^2 - \sigma(X^* - X)^2$. Form $\pi^*(\cdot)$ from $\pi(\cdot)$ by dropping all nonquadratic terms. Given any A and

B simulate the equation system

$$X(t+1) = AY(t) + BX(t),$$
$$Y(t+1) = AX(t) + BY(t)$$

forward from each $(X(0),Y(0)) = (X,Y)$ to form

$$V^*(X,Y,A,B) = \sum_{t=0}^{\infty} (1+r)^{-t}\pi^*(X(t),Y(t),X(t+1)).$$

Let $S = \{(A,B): |A| + |B| \leq 1\}$. Then for each $(A,B,)\epsilon S$ the equation system above has eigenvalues of modulus less than or equal to 1 and the function $V^*(X,Y,A,B)$ defined from simulations is finite, strictly concave in X, and quadratic (with no linear or constant terms) for each (X,Y).

Step 1. Suppose that

$$\mu(A,B) = \begin{pmatrix} 1 & -d \\ -d & 1 \end{pmatrix} \begin{pmatrix} A \\ B \end{pmatrix}.$$

Then if $(a,b) = \mu(A,B)$,

$$X(t+1) = AY(t) + BX(t),$$
$$Y(t+1) = aX(t) + bY(t) + dX(t+1)$$

will generate the same time path from any initial conditions as the system of the first paragraph. If we choose X^* to maximize

$$\pi^*(X,Y,X^*) + (1+r)^{-1}V^*(X^*,Y^*,A,B)$$

subject to

$$Y^* = aX + bY + dX^*,$$

our control rule will have the form

$$X^* = A^*Y + B^*X,$$

where A^* and B^* are independent of X and Y. The control rule will be unique. Let $\theta(\cdot)$ be such that

$$\theta(A,B) = (A^*,B^*).$$

For each $(X,Y), V^*(X,Y,A,B)$ varies continuously with (A,B). Thus, Berge's [1963] "maximum theorem" shows that $\theta(\cdot)$ is continuous on S. For $(A,B)\epsilon S$ let $\theta^*(A,B) = \theta(A,B)$ if $\theta(A,B)\epsilon S$, and let $\theta^*(A,B) = \gamma\cdot\theta(A,B)$ otherwise with $\gamma < 1$, such that $\gamma\theta(A,B)$ lies on the boundary of S closest to $\theta(A,B)$. Then $\theta^*: S \rightarrow S$ and $\theta^*(\cdot)$ is continuous on S. So Brouwer's fixed-point theorem shows that $\theta^*(\cdot)$ has at least one fixed point on S. Let (A^*,B^*) be any such fixed point.

Step 2. Since the equation system defined at the beginning of Step 1 has a symmetric matrix, its eigenvalues are real. We can thus choose corresponding real eigenvectors. But if $(e1,e2)$ is such a vector, $(e2,e1)$ is a second eigenvector for the same eigenvalue. Let $(e3,e4)$ be an eigenvector for the second eigenvalue. Then $(e4,e3)$ must work as well. Both $(e1,e2)$ and $(e2,e1)$ must be orthogonal to both $(e3,e4)$ and $(e4,e3)$ (see Hadley [1961]). The only way that can be true is if

$|e1| = |e2|$ and $|e3| = |e4|$. In other words, we can assume that $E1 = (e1,e2) = (1,1)$ and $E2 = (e3,e4) = (-1,1)$.

Suppose that $(A^*,B^*)\epsilon S$ is a fixed point for $\theta^*(\cdot)$ but not for $\theta(\cdot)$. Then $\theta(A^*,B^*) = \tau\cdot(A^*,B^*)$, where $\tau > 1$ and $(A^*,B^*)\epsilon\partial S$. Suppose that $A^* + B^* = 1$. Choose a very large $x > 0$, and set $(X,Y) = (x,x)$. Then the definition of $\theta(\cdot)$ shows that the first firm's optimal behavior in the maximization problem outlined in Step 1 is to choose $X^* = \tau(A^*Y + B^*X) = \tau x(A^* + B^*) = \tau x = \tau X$ with $\tau > 1$. The definition of $C(\cdot)$ and a graph of developments after the choice of X^* will show that, for a large enough $x, X^* = \tau X$ cannot be optimal: $X^* = 0$ will dominate. This contradicts the definition of $\theta(\cdot)$.

Other cases are similar. For example, let $A^* > 0$, $B^* < 0$, and $|A^*| + |B^*| = 1$. Suppose that $\theta(A^*,B^*) = \tau(A^*,B^*)$, $\tau > 1$. Then $A^* - B^* = 1$. For large $x > 0$ let $(X,Y) = (-x,x)$. Then $X^* = \tau(A^*Y + B^*X) = \tau(A^* - B^*)x = \tau x$. A diagram will show that for a large enough $x, X^* = 0$ will dominate (from the first firm's point of view) the control rule defined by $\theta(\cdot)$. Again we have a contradiction of the definition of $\theta(\cdot)$.

Thus, we can assume that $\theta^*(A^*,B^*) = (A^*,B^*)\epsilon S$ implies $\theta(A^*,B^*) = (A^*,B^*)\epsilon S$. In fact, the same diagrammatic arguments which work above will show that $\theta(A^*,B^*) = (A^*,B^*)\epsilon\ \mathrm{int}(S)$ in each such case. $(A^*,B^*)\epsilon\ \mathrm{int}(S)$ implies the eigenvalues of our original equation system both have modulus less than one.

Step 3. Let $\theta(A^*,B^*) = (A^*,B^*)\epsilon\ \mathrm{int}(S)$. Then A^* and B^* define an optimal control rule $X^* = A^*Y + B^*X$ for Firm 1, given $Y^* = a^*X + b^*Y + d^*X^*$ with $(a^*,b^*) = \mu(A^*,B^*)$; and $Y^* = A^*X + B^*Y$ defines the same for Firm 2, given $X^* = a^*Y + b^*X + d^*Y^*$.

Now we switch from $\pi^*(\cdot)$ back to $\pi(\cdot)$. Let (A^*,B^*) and (a^*,b^*) be as generated above. For any c^*, the right choice of C will make $X^* = A^*Y + B^*X + C$ give the optimal behavior for Firm 1 given $Y^* = a^*X + b^*Y + c^* + d^*X^*$. (Similarly, $Y^* = A^*X + B^*Y + C$ will be optimal for Firm 2 given $\pi(\cdot)$ and $X^* = a^*Y + b^*X + c^* + d^*Y^*$.) In fact, simple algebra will show the "right" choice of C will be given by

$$C^* = gc^* + h,$$

where g and h depend only on exogenous constants and A^* and B^*, which we are no longer changing.

For a complete equilibrium tuple it remains only to show that

$$c^*/(1 - d) = gc^* + h$$

for some c^*. This will be true unless $g = 1/(1 - d)$ and $h \neq 0$. Suppose that $g = 1/(1 - d)$ and $h \neq 0$. For any $c^* > |h|$ let $c^{**} = (1 - d)(gc^* + h)$. Let $C^* = c^*/(1 - d)$ and $C^{**} = c^{**}/(1 - d)$.

For larger and larger values of c^*, (C^*,C^{**}) will become arbitrarily close in relative terms to the 45-degree ray in the positive orthant. Set $(X,Y) = (0,0)$. Consider the evolution of the system,

$$X(t + 1) = A^*Y(t) + B^*X(t) + C^{**},$$

$$Y(t + 1) = A^*X(t) + B^*Y(t) + C^*$$

from $(X(0),Y(0)) = (X,Y)$, and notice that for Firm 1

$$V(X,Y,A^*,B^*,C^*,C^{**}) = \sum_{t=0}^{\infty} (1+r)^{-t}\pi(X(t),Y(t),X(t+1)).$$

For large enough c^*, a diagram will show that Firm 1 is better off setting $A^* = B^* = C^{**} = 0$ than adopting C^{**}, given $(X,Y) = (0,0)$ and any $(A^*,B^*)\epsilon S$. This contradicts the definition of C^{**}. So if $h \neq 0$, then $g \neq 1/(1-d)$.

Thus, for any $(A^*,B^*) = \theta(A^*,B^*)\epsilon\ \mathrm{int}(S)$, we can find c^* such that $C^* = gc^* + h$ makes

$$X^* = A^*Y + B^*X + C^*$$

optimal for Firm 1 given

$$Y^* = a^*X + b^*Y + c^* + d^*X^*$$

and $(a^*,b^*) = \mu(A^*,B^*)$. And

$$Y^* = A^*X + B^*Y + C^*$$

is optimal for Firm 2, given

$$X^* = a^*Y + b^*X + c^* + d^*Y^*.$$

Proof of Proposition IV

Suppose that $d^* \neq d^{**}$, $|d^*|$ and $|d^{**}| < 1$; yet we have the same equilibrium values A^*,B^*,C^*,a^*,b^*,c^* in both cases. By simulating the system $(g(\cdot),f(\cdot))$ forward from different initial conditions (x,y) and then calculating the present value of each firm's profits in each case, we can determine $V(x,y)$ for each firm. Suppose that we calculate $V(\cdot)$ for the second firm in this way. Then $f(x,y)$ must satisfy $2\sigma(f(x,y) - y) = (1+r)^{-1}\,[V_2(g(x,y),f(x,y)) + d^*V_1(g(x,y),f(x,y))]$. But that cannot be true for both d^* and d^{**} if $d^* \neq d^{**}$, unless $V_1(g(x,y), f(x,y)) = 0$ all (x,y). An examination of $V(x^*,y^*)$ at different points (x^*,y^*) in the extremities of the positive orthant will show that $V_1(x^*,y^*)$ cannot be 0 everywhere. However, the correct choice of (x,y) will yield $(x^*,y^*) = (g(x,y),f(x,y))$ for any (x^*,y^*). So, for $d^{**} \neq d^*$ we must have a different set of parameters A^{**},B^{**},C^{**}, a^{**},b^{**},c^{**}.

THE UNIVERSITY OF MICHIGAN

REFERENCES

Berge, C., *Topological Spaces,* trans. by E. M. Patterson (Edinburgh: Oliver & Boyd, 1963).
Blair, J., *Economic Concentration; Structure, Behavior and Public Policy* (New York: Harcourt Brace Jovanovich, Inc., 1972).
Brauer, F., and J. A. Nohel, *Ordinary Differential Equations* (New York: W. A. Benjamin, Inc., 1967).
Cyert, R. M., and M. de Groot, "Multiperiod Decision Models with Alternating Choice as a Solution to the Duopoly Problem," this *Journal,* LXXXIV (1970), 410–29.

Fellner, W., *Competition Among the Few* (New York: Augustus M. Kelley, 1960).
Friedman, J. W., "Reaction Functions and the Theory of Duopoly," *Review of Economic Studies,* XXXV (1968), 257–72.
——, *Oligopoly and the Theory of Games* (Amsterdam: North-Holland Publishing Company, 1977).
Gould, J., "Adjustment Costs in the Theory of Investment of the Firm," *Review of Economic Studies,* XXXV (1968), 47–55.
Hadley, G., *Linear Algebra* (Reading, MA: Addison-Wesley, 1961).
Hahn, F., "On Non-Walrasian Equilibria," *Review of Economic Studies,* XLV (1978), 1–18.
Kaplan, A. D., J. B. Dirlam, and R. F. Lanzillotti, *Pricing in Big Business: A Case Approach* (Washington, D.C.: The Brookings Institution, 1958).
Marschak, T., and R. Selten, *General Equilibrium with Price-Making Firms* (Berlin: Springer-Verlag, 1974).
——, and ——, "Restabilizing Responses, Inertia Supergames, and Oligopolistic Equilibria," this *Journal,* XCII (1978), 71–94.
Selten, R., "Reexamination of the Perfectness Concept for Equilibrium Points in Extensive Games," *International Journal of Game Theory,* IV (1975), 25–55.

TECHNOLOGY, ENTREPRENEURS, AND FIRM SIZE*

GUILLERMO A. CALVO AND STANISLAW WELLISZ

We analyze Schumpeterian entrepreneurship within a general equilibrium model of a competitive economy patterned after Lucas. All individuals have access to exogenously growing knowledge. Those who acquire sufficient knowledge become entrepreneurs. If learning is only a function of ability, the faster the progress, the fewer the entrepreneurs, and the higher their pay relative to workers' wages. If knowledge is only a function of lifetime, the faster the progress is, the earlier the entry will be into the entrepreneurial group. When age and ability are considered together, the individuals (if any) who become entrepreneurs with faster progress are younger and more able than those (if any) who drop out of the group.

In this paper we explore the role of entrepreneurship by introducing Schumpeterian concepts into the general equilibrium analysis of a competitive economy.[1] We derive the optimal number of entrepreneurs and the characteristics of the marginal members of the entrepreneurial group under alternative assumptions concerning the ability and age structure of the population and the rate of technical progress. We also draw inferences concerning income distribution and the size distribution of firms.[2]

Our analysis is closely related to that of Lucas [1978]. Like him, we are concerned with the problem of efficient allocation of resources within a closed economy with a workforce that is homogeneous with respect to productivity as employees, but heterogeneous with respect to managerial ability.[3] Our model is compatible with his and, to facilitate cross-references, we adopt a similar notation. We differ from Lucas, however, in two important respects. First, while Lucas "does not say anything about the nature of tasks performed by managers, other than that whatever managers do, some do it better than others" [Lucas, 1978, p. 511], we concentrate on specific entrepreneurial functions. Second, in Lucas' model individuals with sufficient inborn ability become managers immediately upon entering the labor force,

*We wish to acknowledge the helpful comments of an anonymous referee. This work was supported by a grant from the National Science Foundation.

1. For an alternative mode of attack on the problem of the firm, more closely related to the Schumpeterian system, see Nelson and Winter [1977, 1978].
2. This problem is the principal focal point of Kaldor [1960], Mayer [1960], and Lucas [1978].
3. However, we omit the problem of allocation of homogeneous capital that enters Lucas' analysis, and focus our attention exclusively on human resources.

The Quarterly Journal of Economics, December 1980 0033-5533/80/0095-0663$1.50

whereas in our model they acquire the necessary knowledge through a learning process.

We model entrepreneurship in the spirit of Schumpeter and of Kaldor. We take from the former the notion that the function of entrepreneurs is to apply general technical knowledge to firm-specific purposes [Schumpeter, 1939, pp. 84–87, 130–31 and passim]. From the latter we borrow the justification of the assumption that every firm has only one entrepreneur. Decisions that affect the firm as a whole "should be made on a comparison with all other decisions already made or likely to be made" and "must therefore pass through a single brain" [Kaldor, 1960, p. 43]. We do not exclude, of course, the possibility of delegation of certain managerial functions, but in this paper we are concerned with the captains, and draw no distinction between the officers and the crews.[4]

We assume that all individuals have access to a common pool of general knowledge. Those who acquire sufficient knowledge become entrepreneurs. As we shall show, the rate of increase of technical knowledge is an important determinant in the selection of entrepreneurs. However, creation of knowledge as such is not a concern of ours. We shall assume that technological knowledge is exogenous, and we shall concentrate on the relation between technology and entrepreneurship.

Individuals may differ as to their ability, which we define as the rate at which they are capable of acquiring new knowledge. We assume that an individual who has an entrepreneurial position applies his knowledge to firm-specific purposes as soon as he acquires it. These assumptions simplify the general equilibrium analysis. Acquisition of specific knowledge through learning-by-doing lends itself more readily to the partial approach (see Prescott and Visscher [1978]).

This paper falls into three parts. In the first we state our model and apply it to the problem of selecting entrepreneurs from among a population with heterogeneous abilities. In the second we concentrate on the age factor in order to study the life cycle problem. Part III is devoted to a discussion of the interaction of age and ability.

I. Ability, Managerial Selection, and Firm Size

In this section we shall explore the consequences of the assumption that individuals vary in terms of ability; that is, in terms

4. For a discussion of problems of managerial hierarchy, see Williamson [1967] and Calvo and Wellisz [1978, 1979]. We shall utilize some of our results to justify "span of control" assumptions made in this paper.

of the rate at which they acquire and apply technical knowledge. We shall show that at steady state the faster the technical progress is, the higher will be the ability required of the marginal entrepreneur. It follows that with a given distribution of abilities, the faster the progress, the smaller the entrepreneurial group, and the larger the average firm size. On the other hand, a single "burst" of progress leads initially to a more stringent entrepreneurial selection (and to greater concentration), followed by a return to the initial situation that occurs when the laggards adopt the new technology. If technology is stationary, and if there are no random shocks, entrepreneurial ability does not determine firm size. If knowledge does not accumulate, everybody eventually acquires it, and nobody has entrepreneurial advantage even if there is a wide dispersion of abilities.[5]

As a framework of our analysis, we shall first present a simplified version of a model recently studied by Lucas [1978]; we shall subsequently expand and adapt the model to suit our needs.

Let x denote an individual's ability. We shall assume, with Lucas, that the distribution of abilities over individuals can be represented by a (continuous) cumulative distribution function that we denote $\Gamma(x)$, $0 \leq x$. Thus, $\Gamma(x)$ is the share of total active population with ability less than or equal to x. We assume that $\Gamma(x)$ is independent of time.

The *productive effectiveness* of a type-x individual is denoted E_x, and is assumed to affect his productivity as entrepreneur in the following manner. Output in a firm run by a type-x individual is given by

$$E_x f(n_x), \tag{1}$$

where n_x is the number of workers employed in his firm, and f is a strictly concave, increasing, and twice differentiable function defined on the nonnegative real line, such that

$$\lim_{n \to 0} [f(n) - (1+n)f'(n)] < 0 \tag{2}$$

$$\lim_{n \to \infty} [f(n) - (1+n)f'(n)] > 0. \tag{3}$$

5. Kaldor conjectured that in a full long-period equilibrium "the task of management is reduced to pure supervision, co-ordinating ability [which corresponds to our definition of entrepreneurship] becomes free good and the optimum size of the individual firm becomes infinite (or indeterminate)" [1960, p. 45]. Supervision per se may, however, set a limit to firm size, as shown by Williamson [1967] and by Calvo and Wellisz [1978].

Notice that conditions (2) and (3) are slightly more general than Inada's conditions.

What (1) is asserting is that productive effectiveness operates as "Hicks-neutral" technical progress. Notice, incidentally, that we are assuming that productive effectiveness is the same for all individuals of type x independent of their age. The case where age is emphasized will be the subject of the next section. The properties of f are essentially those assumed in Lucas [1978], and they could be thought of as reflecting what has been termed "loss of control" [Williamson, 1967, and Calvo and Wellisz, 1978].

Firms are profit-maximizers; hence, in equilibrium,

$$E_x f'(n_x) = w, \tag{4}$$

where w (>0) is the wage rate. Inverting (4), we get

(5) $g(w/E_x)$ = demand for labor by each type-x individual *if* he owns a firm,

where $g \equiv f'^{-1}$. Therefore, the quasi rent of a type-x individual if he owns a firm is

$$E_x f(g(w/E_x)) - wg(w/E_x). \tag{6}$$

In equilibrium, a type-x individual will prefer to be an entrepreneur or a worker depending on whether (6) is greater or less than w, while those for which (6) equals w would be indifferent between the two courses of action. We assume that E_x is a nondecreasing function of x, although this assumption will in fact become an implication of this and the next section.

Let z be a type for which (6) equals w. By (4) and the conditions that quasi rent of a z-type equals the wage, we get

$$E_z \frac{f(n_z)}{1 + n_z} = w = E_z f'(n_z), \tag{7}$$

which, by (2) and (3) and the other assumptions on f, uniquely determines employment in firms run by type-z individuals independently of E_z and z. Let us denote the equilibrium level of employment in a z-type firm by $\bar{n}$. Thus, (7) implies that

$$w = E_z f'(\bar{n}). \tag{8}$$

Therefore, there is a one-to-one correspondence between E_z and w. Thus, recalling (5) and (8), we can compactly characterize a general equilibrium by the condition that demand equals supply in the labor market:

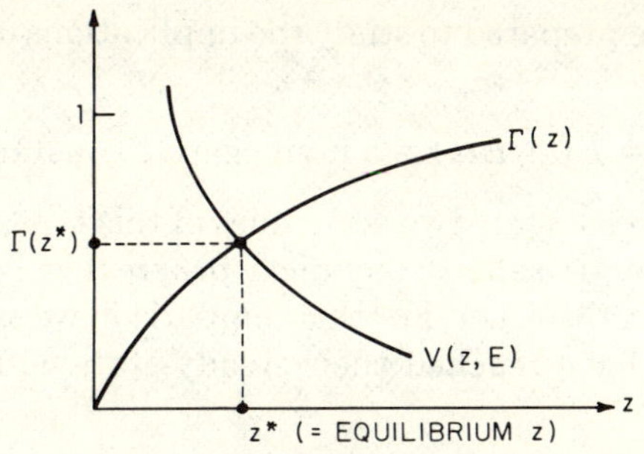

FIGURE I

$$V(z,E) \equiv \int_z^{\infty} g\left(\frac{E_z}{E_x} f'(\bar{n})\right) d\Gamma(x) = \Gamma(z), \tag{9}$$

where E denotes the entire function E_x, $x \geq 0$, and z is the type below which everybody is a worker. (We shall refer to z as the "marginal type.") The determination of equilibrium is shown in Figure I, which is essentially Figure 2 of Lucas [1978]. The equilibrium solution is clearly a function of the distribution of productive effectiveness. A change in the distribution of E that shifts the V-curve to the right, for example, will imply a higher equilibrium z; more people will prefer to become workers in equilibrium, and thus the *average size of firms* (measured by the average number of workers per firm = $\Gamma(z)/(1 - \Gamma(z))$) will increase.

Thus far we have been going over the ground covered by Lucas [1978]. We now depart from him to investigate the dynamic behavior of E_x.

We assume that

$$\dot{E}_x(t) = x[\bar{E}(t) - E_x(t)]. \tag{10}$$

In other words, the productive effectiveness grows in proportion to the gap between an exogenous technological level and the actual productive efficiency.[6] The proportion, in turn, is given by the learning ability of the individual, x. So for the same gap, the higher the abilities, the greater the individual's increase in effectiveness will be. But if the gap becomes zero, productive effectiveness will cease to grow, no matter what the level of ability. In a simple manner, this captures the hypothesis referred to at the outset.

6. Nelson and Phelps [1966] used a formulation similar to (10) to analyze the impact of education on growth.

Now we are prepared to study the implications of the model. Let us assume

$$\alpha = \dot{\bar{E}}(t)/\bar{E}(t) = \text{a nonnegative constant.} \tag{11}$$

Suppose that we compare two economies of this type, identical except that the exogenous rate of technical progress α is greater in one economy than in the other. For this comparison we shall assume that the economies have reached their steady-state equilibria; thus we must have

$$\dot{E}_x(t)/E_x(t) = \alpha, \qquad \text{all } t \text{ and } x. \tag{12}$$

It follows from (10) and (11) that

$$\alpha = x[\bar{E}(t)/E_x(t) - 1]$$

or

$$\bar{E}(t)/E_x(t) = 1 + \alpha/x. \tag{13}$$

So for each t, $E_x(t)$ is a nondecreasing function of x, implying that at each point of the steady-state path (8) is satisfied. Hence, in steady state

$$\frac{E_z(t)}{E_x(t)} = \frac{1 + \alpha/x}{1 + \alpha/z} \le 1 \qquad \text{for } x \ge z. \tag{14}$$

It is easy to verify that (14) decreases with α. Thus, recalling (9) and that $g' < 0$, it follows that an increase in α will produce an outward shift of the V function in Figure I, which, as noted before, implies that the average size of firms will increase. Therefore, the economy with a higher rate of exogenous technical progress will have, on the average, larger firms and more able entrepreneurs.

Convergence to the steady state is no problem here, because the dynamic behavior of the economy is governed by (10). Solving (10), the reader can verify that $\bar{E}(t)/E_x(t)$ approaches the expression given in (13) as t grows large. Hence, $E_z(t)/E_x(t)$ will converge to (14) and, by (9), the average firm size will tend toward that associated with the steady state. It is an open question, although perhaps of rather marginal interest, whether the approach is monotonic or not.

Another experiment in the spirit of Schumpeter is to examine the case where $\bar{E}$ suffers a discontinuous and, say, a once-and-for-all upward jump. Let the initial and new levels of $\bar{E}$ be denoted $\bar{E}_1$ and $\bar{E}_2$, respectively. Suppose that we start from the steady state corresponding to $\bar{E}_1$. Clearly, then, $\bar{E}_x(0) = E_1$ for all $x > 0$, that is to say, everybody (except for $x = 0$) has the same productive efficiency at the start, and equal to the exogenously given technological level of the past $\overline{E}_1$. Suppose that $\overline{E}$ jumps to $\overline{E}_2$ at $t = 0$. Obviously, the distribution of E_x (0) is unaffected, so the size of the firms remains equal to that in the past. In fact, at $t = 0$, every individual with $x > 0$ would be indifferent between being a worker or an entrepreneur, firms would be of identical size $= \overline{n}$, and by (9), z would be determined by the condition

$$g(f(\overline{n})) = \Gamma(z)/(1 - \Gamma(z)). \tag{15}$$

After the technical discovery, however, fast learners will start taking the lead because, by (10),

$$\dot{E}_x(0) = x[\overline{E}_2 - \overline{E}_1]. \tag{16}$$

Consequently,

$$\left.\frac{d}{dt}\frac{E_z(t)}{E_x(t)}\right|_{t=0} < 0, \qquad x > z, \tag{17}$$

which implies an outward shift in the V function in the first stages of the process. In turn, this implies that firms will initially tend to become larger on the average. Eventually, however, everybody (except for $x = 0$) will catch up with the new technology and, except for a higher wage rate, the system will have the same characteristics that it had before the change. Empirical evidence is compatible with this conclusion: Mansfield [1962] found that successful innovators tend to grow faster than other firms, but that their advantage was eroded with time.

Our model can also be used to explore the impact of the rate of technical progress on income distribution. Let us define $D(\alpha)$ as the steady-state *ratio of average entrepreneurial income to the wage rate when the rate of technical progress equals* α. From previous considerations we know that $D(0) = 1$ and $D(\alpha) > 1$ for all $\alpha > 0$. Therefore, it follows that there are instances where an increase in the rate of technical progress leads to greater inequality between entrepreneurs and workers (as measured by D). This proposition can be strengthened if one is ready to make more specific assumptions on $f(\cdot)$. A class of functions that, as shown by Lucas [1978], is of particular interest because it is closely associated with the validity of Gibrat's Law, is characterized as follows:

$$f(n) = An^{\beta}, \qquad A > 0, \qquad 0 < \beta < 1.$$

Let $\pi(x)$ denote the equilibrium profit of a type-x entrepreneur (in general π will be a function of α). Under the above Cobb-Douglas type function we have

$$\frac{\pi(x)}{n_x w} = 1 - \beta$$

and, hence, in equilibrium

$$D(\alpha) = \frac{1}{1 - \Gamma(z)} \int_z^\infty \frac{\pi(x)}{w}\, d\Gamma(x) = \frac{1 - \beta}{1 - \Gamma(z)}\, \Gamma(z).$$

Since we previously showed that steady-state z rises with α, it follows that $D(\alpha)$ increases with α. Thus, more rapid progress brings about a shrinkage of the entrepreneurial group (the less able entrepreneurs become "proletarized"), and increases the relative income of the remaining members of the group. These conclusions, derived within a neoclassical framework, have a slightly Marxian flavor.

In a similar fashion one can show that, for the Cobb-Douglas case, a once-and-for-all jump in the level of technology will initially result in an increase in D, as defined above; however, in the long run D will return to 1. This provides a clue to the Kuznets curve puzzle. When a relatively backward, static society begins to catch up with technologically more advanced systems, there is generation of entrepreneurial profits. As the gap between theoretical knowledge and its applications decreases, and as the laggards catch up with the leaders, the size of the entrepreneurial group grows but unit entrepreneurial profits decrease. Thus, growth in its early phases may be associated with increased income distribution inequality, and in its later phases with a tendency toward income equalization.

II. Age and Learning

In this section we focus our attention on the life cycle problems. We assume that individuals have identical inherent abilities, but at a given point of time their effectiveness is a function of their lifetime learning. More specifically

(18) $A(t,v)$ = productive inefficiency at time t of an individual born at time v,

and we assume (here $\dot{A} \equiv \partial A/\partial t$) that

(19) $$\dot{A}(t,v) = \gamma[\bar{E}(t) - A(t,v)] \qquad \gamma > 0$$

with

(20) $$A(v,v) \equiv 0, \qquad \text{all } v.$$

In other words, individuals are a *tabula rasa* the day they first set foot (head?) on the earth (equation (20)), and steadily learn as the years pass by, at a rate proportional to the gap between the current technological knowledge and their actual productive efficiency (equation (19)). In contrast with the previous section, however, the factor of proportionality is the same for everybody.

We shall first characterize the steady state. Solving (19) for initial condition (20), and taking (11) into account, we get

$$A(t,v) = \overline{E}(0)e^{\alpha t}\gamma/(\gamma + \alpha)[1 - e^{-(\gamma+\alpha)(t-v)}]. \tag{21}$$

In fact, in order to utilize the static portion of the model developed in the previous section, it will be convenient to define

(22) $E_h(t)$ = productive efficiency of an individual of age h at time t.

Thus, by (21) and (22), at the steady state

$$E_h(t) = \overline{E}(t)\gamma/(\gamma + \alpha)[1 - e^{-(\gamma+\alpha)h}]. \tag{21'}$$

Since by (11) and (21′) $E_{h''}(t) > E_{h'}(t)$ if $h'' > h'$, assumption (8) with h substituted for x is satisfied at all times. There, (9)—with h substituted for x—characterizes a general equilibrium if $\Gamma(h)$ is interpreted as the proportion of individuals whose age is less than or equal to h and z is understood to be the age of the youngest entrepreneur. For the present purposes we shall assume, as in the previous section, that $\Gamma(h)$ is constant over time.

By (21′)

$$\frac{E_z(t)}{E_h(t)} = \frac{1 - e^{-(\gamma+\alpha)z}}{1 - e^{-(\gamma+\alpha)h}}, \qquad h > 0. \tag{23}$$

So we are now in the position of comparing average firm size across steady states. In formal terms this involves studying the expression in (23) for $h > z$ as a function of α. As we show in the Appendix, it turns out that the latter increases with α which, by (9), permits us to show that, in contrast with the previous section, z decreases with α. Thus, the age of the youngest entrepreneur, and consequently the average firm size, decreases with the rate of technical progress. The intuition is that a higher rate of technical progress tends to wash out the relative advantage of being older. We shall be able to see this in a more straightforward manner when we study the second experiment of this section.

Convergence to the steady state is again shown very simply, but we shall not take up space to prove it. A much more interesting aspect of the present set of assumptions is the nature of the transition. To facilitate comparison, we shall again study the case where there is a once-and-for-all jump in $\bar{E}$ at $t = 0$, from $\bar{E}_1$ to $\bar{E}_2$ ($>\bar{E}_1$). The economy is assumed to start at the steady state corresponding to $\bar{E}_1$.

By (19) and (20)

$$A(t,v) = \bar{E}_1 e^{-\gamma t}[1 - e^{\gamma v}] + \bar{E}_2[1 - e^{-\gamma t}], \qquad \text{for } v \leq 0 \tag{24a}$$

$$A(t,v) = \bar{E}_2[1 - e^{-\gamma(t-v)}], \qquad \text{for } v \geq 0. \tag{24b}$$

Hence, if we recall (22),

$$E_h(t) = \bar{E}_2 - \bar{E}_1 e^{-\gamma h} - (\bar{E}_2 - \bar{E}_1)e^{-\gamma t}, \qquad \text{for } t - h \leq 0 \tag{25a}$$

$$E_h(t) = \bar{E}_2[1 - e^{-\gamma h}], \qquad \text{for } t - h \geq 0. \tag{25b}$$

As is familiar to us now, the shift in the V-function in Figure I depends on the behavior of $E_z(t)/E_h(t)$. The first simple observation in this respect is that, by (25b), the above ratio equals that of (23) for $\alpha = 0$ if t is sufficiently large so that there is no one alive who was born before time zero. Thus, in normal circumstances the economy will revert back in finite time to the same steady state from which it started.

To study the transition, let us consider the case where $z > t$, i.e., when the youngest entrepreneur was born before $t = 0$. Then, by (25a)

$$\frac{E_z(t)}{E_h(t)} = \frac{\bar{E}_2 - \bar{E}_1 e^{-\gamma z} - (\bar{E}_2 - \bar{E}_1)e^{-\gamma t}}{\bar{E}_2 - \bar{E}_1 e^{-\gamma h} - (\bar{E}_2 - \bar{E}_1)e^{-\gamma t}}. \tag{26}$$

This ratio is less than 1 for $h > z$ and increases over time. This will necessarily be the relevant situation at $t = 0$ and shortly thereafter. So it follows that shortly after the technical change (which occurs at $t = 0$), z will fall below its steady state (and also, by assumption, initial) level. This means that during the early stages of the transition, the age of the youngest entrepreneur will decrease, and also the average firm size will become smaller. This contrasts with the situation in Section I, where we showed that a similar experiment would initially result in a larger, not smaller, average firm size.

Since the economy eventually returns to the steady state, z will necessarily recover its initial level but, as can easily be checked using (25), at no point in time will z overshoot that level.

The intuition behind this result is not difficult to find. By (19) we see that at $t = 0$ the learning of an individual (his $\dot{A}$) will have an exogenous component ($= \gamma(\bar{E}_2 - \bar{E}_1)$), which is the same for all individuals. Thus, it is to be expected that the relative efficiency of two individuals of different ages will initially shift closer to 1, and thus the relative advantage of being older will tend to disappear. For this reason, the minimum age for joining the entrepreneurial ranks initially declines, reducing the average firm size.

The analysis of "learning by aging" yields two conclusions, one trivial and one not so obvious. The trivial conclusion is that, in a society in which all individuals have the same inherent ability, you will get to the top if you live long enough: in time, you will become a village elder. It is less obvious, however, that you will join the top ranks faster if technology grows more quickly, even if you are no more able (and have less accumulated learning) than your elders. Thus, even if we disregard ability, we conclude that youth is favored by progress.

Another conclusion is that in the present model entrepreneurial quasi rents do not tend to disappear even when technology is stationary. This result, an easy implication of our assumptions, acquires greater significance considering the widely accepted view that technological progress is an essential ingredient for the existence of such entrepreneurial income. It also shows that Lucas' [1978] setup is not necessarily inconsistent with a stationary technology.

III. Ability, Age, and Learning

We shall now take a small analytic step, and a giant one in the direction of greater realism: we shall combine our two models and consider the age and ability factors simultaneously.

We shall indicate by $A_x(t,v)$ the productive efficiency at time t of an individual of ability x and who was born at time v. We assume that

$$\dot{A}_x(t,v) = x[\bar{E}(t) - A_x(t,v)]. \tag{27}$$

If we recall (13) and (21′) it is quite obvious that, at a steady state,

$$\frac{E_{xh}(t)}{\bar{E}(t)} = \frac{1 - e^{-(x+\alpha)h}}{1 + \alpha/x} \equiv R(x,h;\alpha) \equiv \text{"relative efficiency" of an } (x,h)\text{-type}, \tag{28}$$

where

$E_{xh}(t)$ = productive efficiency of an individual of quality x and age h at time t.

Figure II depicts a typical map of iso-"relative efficiency" curves for a given α. Letting $\Gamma(x,h)$ denote the (time-independent) cumulative distribution over quality x and age h, we can now express the equilibrium condition (i.e., the analogue of (9)) as follows:

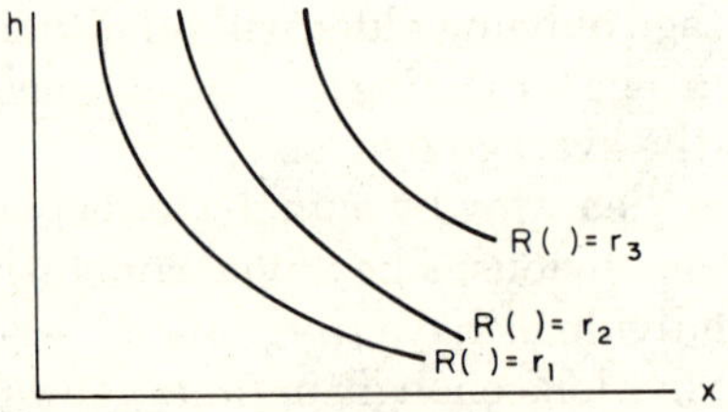

FIGURE II
Isoefficiency Curves ($r_1 < r_2 < r_3$)

$$(9') \quad \int_{B_\alpha(r)} g\left(\frac{r}{R(x,h;\alpha)} f'(\bar{n})\right) d\Gamma(x,h) = 1 - \int_{B_\alpha(r)} d\Gamma(x,h),$$

where

$$(29) \qquad B_\alpha(r) = \{(x,h){:}R(x,h;\alpha) \geq r\}.$$

Thus, r denotes the relative efficiency of the least efficient entrepreneur in equilibrium, and it takes the place of the variable z of our previous analysis. We shall therefore call r the *marginal relative efficiency*.

We shall now show that isoefficiency curves become "steeper" as α increases.

The slope of an isorelative efficiency curve is given by

$$(30) \quad \left.\frac{dh}{dx}\right|_{R=\text{const.}} = -\frac{R_x}{R_h} - \left\{\frac{h}{x+\alpha} + \frac{\alpha}{x(x+\alpha)^2}\left[e^{(x+\alpha)h} - 1\right]\right\} \equiv s(x,h;\alpha).$$

Now,

$$(31) \quad \frac{\partial s}{\partial \alpha} = \frac{h}{(x+\alpha)^2} - \frac{(x+\alpha)^2 - 2(x+\alpha)\alpha}{x(x+\alpha)^4} \times \left[e^{(x+\alpha)h} - 1\right] - \frac{\alpha h}{x(x+\alpha)^2} e^{(x+\alpha)h}$$

$$= \frac{1}{(x+\alpha)^2}\left\{\left[h - \frac{e^{(x+\alpha)h} - 1}{x+\alpha}\right] + \frac{\alpha}{x} h \left[\frac{e^{(x+\alpha)h} - 1}{(x+\alpha)h} - e^{(x+\alpha)h}\right]\right\} < 0$$

when $(x + \alpha) > 0$ and $h > 0$.

Now we can characterize what happens in a steady state with α'' compared to one with α', $\alpha'' > \alpha'$. This is shown in Figure III, where r' and r'' are the marginal relative efficiencies associated with α' and

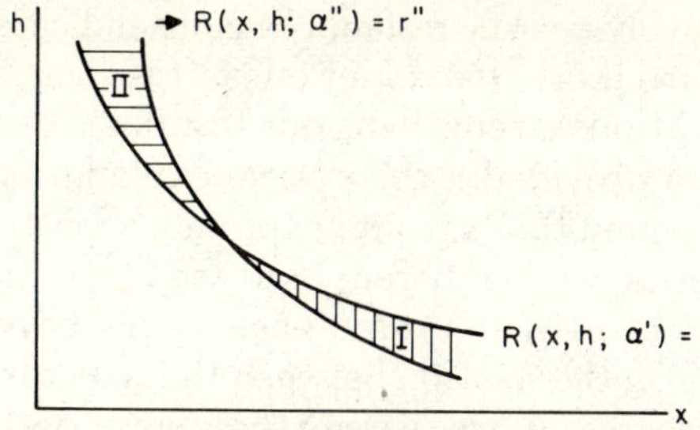

FIGURE III
Effect of Change in α

α'', respectively. Shaded area I indicates the set of (x,h) pairs that become entrepreneurs as α shifts from α' to α''. On the other hand, area II corresponds to the set of pairs that cease to be entrepreneurs under the same circumstances. We have found, therefore, that *as the rate of* (exogenous) *technical progress increases, the quality of the "new" entrepreneurs is higher and their age is lower than those of any individual who ceases to be an entrepreneur in the new equilibrium.*[7] In the present case, however, the effect of the average size of firms cannot be ascertained without further knowledge of the production and distribution functions.

A similar result would obtain during the transition from stationary levels $\overline{E}_1 < \overline{E}_2$. One can easily show (the proof is left for the interested reader) that the steady state is the same for $\overline{E}_1$ as for $\overline{E}_2$ (except for a higher wage in the second situation); however, during the first stages of the transition, entrepreneurs who relinquish their helms will be older and less able than the new entrepreneurs.

Finally, by (30) we see that isoefficiency curves tend to become perfectly vertical as $\alpha \to \infty$, indicating that the ranking of productive efficiencies will tend to depend exclusively on quality, and not on age, as the (exogenous) rate of technical progress becomes very large.

In this section we have shown that the acceleration of technical progress eliminates older, less inherently able individuals from the entrepreneurial ranks, and adds younger, more inherently capable ones to these ranks. This result was obtained without appealing to the argument that ability to learn declines with age. We also dispensed with the cost of acquisition of human capital argument which states

7. Notice that the r' and r'' lines in Figure III do not necessarily intersect, and even if they do, areas I or II could be null according to the probability measure induced by $\Gamma(\cdot,\cdot)$. This implies that as α increases, there may be no "new" entrepreneurs or, alternatively, that no one ceases to be an entrepreneur.

that, if learning involves costs, rational calculus indicates that younger people should learn more than older ones. It is clear that either one of those considerations strengthens our results.

We have also provided a theoretical explanation of the often-observed phenomenon that age and experience matter more in relatively static societies, while inherent ability matters more in societies where technology evolves at a rapid pace. Going beyond the model, we may speculate on the relation between the structure of leadership and the rate of progress. If we assume that power derived from leadership is valued for itself, it seems plausible that elderly leaders are likely to oppose progress which represents a threat to their supremacy for the same reason progress is likely to be championed by younger, more able individuals. This self-interest may provide one explanation for the conservatism of older leaders and the radicalism of the younger challengers.

APPENDIX

Let us define

$$\text{(A1)} \qquad \psi(\alpha) = \frac{1 - e^{-(\gamma+\alpha)z}}{1 - e^{-(\gamma+\alpha)x}}, \qquad 0 < z < x.$$

We shall show that $\psi(\alpha)$ is monotonically increasing for all $\alpha \geq 0$, which is what was asserted in Section II. For present purposes, however, it will be convenient to think of ψ as being defined on the interval $[-\gamma,\infty)$, where

$$\text{(A2)} \qquad \psi(-\gamma) = \lim_{\alpha\downarrow -\gamma} \psi(\alpha) = \frac{z}{x}.$$

We shall show the (stronger) proposition that $\psi(\alpha)$ is monotonically increasing over $[-\psi,\infty)$. The proof is by contradiction.

First note that

$$\text{(A3)} \qquad \lim_{\alpha\to\infty} \psi(\alpha) = 1 > \frac{z}{x}$$

and

$$\text{(A4)} \qquad \psi(\alpha) < 1 \qquad \text{for all } \alpha \geq -\gamma.$$

Furthermore, by (A1),

$$\text{(A5)} \qquad \text{If } \alpha \geq -\gamma \quad \text{and} \quad \psi'(\alpha) = 0, \quad \text{then} \quad \psi(\alpha) = z/x\, e^{(\gamma+\alpha)(x-z)}.$$

One implication of the above is

$$\text{(A6)} \qquad \psi(\alpha) \geq z/x \qquad \text{for all } \alpha \geq -\gamma,$$

because if the latter were contradicted, by (A2) and (A3), there would exist an α such that $\psi(\alpha) < z/x$ and $\psi'(\alpha) = 0$. But this contradicts (A5), according to which

$$\psi(\alpha) = z/x\, e^{(\gamma+\alpha)(x-z)} > z/x$$

[because $\gamma + \alpha > 0$ and $x - z > 0$].

Therefore, by (A2)–(A4) and (A6) if $\psi(\alpha)$ were not monotonically increasing, we should have $\alpha_2 > \alpha_1 > -\gamma$ such that α_1 is a local maximum, α_2 is a local minimum and

$$\psi(\alpha_1) > \psi(\alpha_2); \tag{A7}$$

but, by (A5),

$$\psi(\alpha_1)/\psi(\alpha_2) = e^{(\alpha_1-\alpha_2)(x-z)} < 1,$$

contradicting (A7). This proves the proposition.

COLUMBIA UNIVERSITY

REFERENCES

Calvo, Guillermo A., and Stanislaw Wellisz, "Supervision, Loss of Control, and the Optimum Size of the Firm," *Journal of Political Economy,* LXXXVI (Oct. 1978), 943–52.

——, and ——, "Hierarchy, Ability, and Income Distribution," *Journal of Political Economy,* LXXXVII (Oct. 1979), 991–1010.

Kaldor, Nicholas, "The Equilibrium of the Firm," in *Essays on Value and Distribution* (London: Gerald Duckworth and Co. Ltd., 1960), Ch. 2.

Lucas, Robert E., Jr., "On the Size Distribution of Business Firms," *Bell Journal of Economics,* IX (Autumn 1978), 508–23.

Mayer, Thomas, "The Distribution of Ability and Earnings," *Review of Economics and Statistics,* XLII (May 1960), 189–95.

Nelson, Robert R., and Sidney G. Winter, "Simulation of Schumpeterian Competition," *American Economic Review,* LXVII (Feb. 1977), 271–76.

——, and ——, "Forces Generating and Limiting Concentration under Schumpeterian Competition," *Bell Journal,* IX (Autumn 1978), 524–48.

Prescott, Edward C., and Michael Visscher, "Organization Capital," Carnegie-Mellon University, mimeographed, 1978.

Schumpeter, Joseph A., *Business Cycles* (New York and London: McGraw-Hill Book Co., 1939).

Williamson, Oliver E., "Hierarchical Control and Optimum Firm Size," *Journal of Political Economy,* LXXV (April 1967), 123–38.

PUBLIC-PRIVATE CONSUMPTION TRADEOFFS AND THE BALANCED BUDGET MULTIPLIER*

URI POSSEN AND STEVEN SLUTSKY

This paper considers consumers who have multiperiod utility functions that have private and public goods as arguments. The paper analyzes the effect on private demands of various exogenous balanced budget changes in the path of public expenditure: temporary, permanent, and countercyclical. The effects of temporary and countercyclical changes depend upon whether public and private goods are complements or substitutes and whether public goods are over- or undersupplied. The largest impact comes from countercyclical changes in undersupplied complementary public goods. Permanent changes tend to have a smaller impact but are harder to specify, since the results crucially depend upon the third derivatives of utility functions.

I. INTRODUCTION

A major debate of the post-Keynesian era is whether fiscal policy matters in the determination of the level of aggregate variables. The effectiveness of one fiscal tool, the balanced budget multiplier, has been the subject of much theoretical and empirical scrutiny. For the most part, this work has involved determining whether induced price and interest rate changes cancel out a direct expansionary impact. The general conclusion of these studies is that only in certain limiting cases is the expansionary impact eliminated by these factors. Such other writers as Milton Friedman [1963, pp. 80–81] and Martin Bailey [1970, pp. 154–55], however, have questioned even the existence of a direct expansionary potential from a balanced budget change. They argue that the possibility of consumers reducing their consumption of private goods in response to increased public expenditure may diminish or eliminate the expansionary impact of the multiplier. In fact, Friedman even seems to argue that the balanced budget multiplier can be contractionary.

A simple modification of a standard macro model is sufficient to demonstrate these arguments. The model consists of an IS curve, $Y = C(Y - T,G) + I(r) + G$, an LM curve, $M/P = L(r,Y)$, and an

* We would like to thank Jacques Drèze and Anton Barten for helpful comments. All errors are the responsibility of the authors. This paper was partially written while Steven Slutsky was visiting the C.O.R.E., University of Louvain.

The Quarterly Journal of Economics, December 1980 0033–5533/80/0095-0679$02.40

aggregate supply function, $P = F(Y)$. The only difference with the standard model is that private consumption is a function of the level of public goods as well as of disposable income. The balanced budget multiplier is

$$\frac{dY}{dG} = \frac{1 - C_Y + C_G}{1 \; C_Y + I_r(L_Y + F_Y)/L_r}.$$

Stability implies that the denominator is positive. Therefore, if $1 - C_Y + C_G > 0$, as occurs in the standard model which assumes that $C_G = 0$ and $C_Y < 1$, the multiplier is positive. Only with a vertical LM curve, $L_r = 0$, or a vertical supply curve, $F_Y = \infty$, is the multiplier zero. If C_G is negative, so that the increase in government spending reduces private consumption, $1 - C_Y + C_G$ is smaller than in the standard model, and if the magnitude of C_G is sufficiently large, it may be zero or even negative, implying that an increase in government expenditure could lead to a contraction in the economy. If, on the other hand, C_G is positive, an increase in government expenditures raises private consumption, and the numerator is larger than appears in the standard model.

In the Bailey-Friedman analyses, the sign and magnitude of C_G are arbitrarily specified. Its properties should be determined from an analysis of the intertemporal utility maximization decisions of individuals. The purpose of this paper is to study the properties of C_G and $1 - C_Y + C_G$ through a multiperiod model.[1] In each period the government announces the amount of consumption it will provide and the distribution of taxes (which fully cover government costs) among individuals. Individuals are assumed to believe these announcements. Taking expected future income and prices as given, individuals allocate their wealth to private consumption in the different periods. Private consumption in any period is thus affected by the path of announced government consumption. The standard consumption function is then the sum of individuals' first-period consumption. Note that since income is exogenous, this paper analyzes only consumption behavior and not the full macro economy. Thus, it is concerned with the numerator but not the denominator of the above multiplier.

The derivatives of the consumption function studied here come

1. Note that in this multiperiod context C_y is not just the MPC out of wealth but is the MPC multiplied by the discounted change in taxes. Thus, $1 - C_y$ for a permanent change is smaller than for a temporary one because the discounted tax change is bigger.

not from changes over time along the initially announced path of government expenditures but from changes in the path itself. The time path of the government expenditure change is crucial in determining the sign and magnitude of C_G. This paper studies the impacts of temporary increases in spending in the first period with expenditure unchanged in later periods, announced future increases in spending, permanent increases in all periods, and countercyclical changes that increase spending in one period and decrease it in another. The resulting impacts of these measures are shown to be quite different.

The essential tool used to derive the results of this paper is the analysis of demand functions that contain quantities as well as prices as arguments. In addition to being public goods, these quantities could be in the demand functions because individuals are facing rationing constraints. Therefore, the conclusions derived would also apply to macroeconomic models in which the existence of fixed prices leads to rationing as studied by Barro and Grossman [1976] and Malinvaud [1977]. The results when reinterpreted explain the behavior in unrationed markets as the individuals' perceived constraints in the rationed markets change in current and future periods.

Differentiating these demand functions gives the impact of infinitesimal changes in government policies. However, such changes will often be significant relative to the initial level. Therefore, an alternative method of analyzing consumer demand is also presented that allows for the direct consideration of such finite changes. This method highlights the importance of factors not usually considered in demand analysis. These factors may also be of use in analyzing other situations.

The remainder of the paper has the following organization. Section II presents the basic model and describes the maximization and demand of a representative consumer. The effectiveness of various temporary measures is analyzed in Section III, and that of permanent and countercyclical measures is considered in Section IV. Section V briefly considers modifications due to aggregation of the results for a representative consumer. Some concluding remarks are given in Section VI.

II. Demands of a Representative Consumer

Consider a representative individual living a finite life of n periods who consumes private goods denoted by the n-vector $C = (C_1,$

$\ldots, C_n$) and public goods denoted by the n-vector $G = (G_1, \ldots, G_n)$.[2] The individual is assumed to know the initial vector of public consumption. Preferences of the individual can be represented by a thrice continuously differentiable, monotonic, strictly quasi-concave utility function that has the intertemporally additive form[3]

$$U(C,G) = \sum_1^n \left(\frac{1}{(1+a)^{j-1}}\right)\hat{U}(C_j,G_j).$$

The individual faces a discounted price vector for private goods $p = (p_1, \ldots, p_n)$, where $p_j = \hat{p}_j/(1+r)^{j-1}$ and $\hat{p}_j$ is the current price, which he takes as given, unaffected by his decisions or by the level of government activity. The individual pays for the public goods according to the discounted tax function $t_j(G_j)$, which are known in all periods and are taken as given.[4] Define $t(G) \equiv \Sigma_1^n\, t_j(G_j)$. Since this paper is concerned with balanced budget multipliers, taxes are specified as a function of G and not of income. However, $t_j(G_j)$ could be derived from income, wealth, or sales taxes.[5]

The individual has initial period income Y_1 and discounted future income Y_f which are assumed constant, since multiplier effects on income are not considered in this paper. Moreover, individuals are assumed to face no borrowing constraint, and thus their lifetime budget constraint is $pC + t(G) = Y_1 + Y_f \equiv W$.

The consumption decision of the individual can be summarized as

$$\max_C \sum_1^n \left(\frac{1}{1+a}\right)^{j-1} \hat{U}(C_j,G_j),$$

2. Public and private goods in each period are assumed to be one-dimensional aggregates. Since G is taken as exogenous by the consumer, government consumption in each period can be made multidimensional without any effect on the analysis. Disaggregating private consumption causes more difficulties, complicating the analysis and making it sometimes difficult to interpret results. The basic implications would not be altered, however.

3. First derivatives are denoted as $U_j = \partial U/\partial C_j$ and $U_{n+j} = \partial U/\partial G_j$, and second derivatives as $U_{jj} = \partial U_j/\partial C_j$ and $U_{jn+j} = \partial U_j/\partial G_j$. Third derivatives are similarly defined.

Strict quasi concavity implies that $U_{kk} \geqq 0$ is possible in one period at most. If $U_{kk} > 0$, then private consumption in the kth period is superior, and private consumption in all other periods is inferior. If $U_{kk} = 0$, then demands for C_i, $i \neq k$, are independent of the level of wealth. These results are shown in Green [1961]. Hence, $U_{kk} < 0$, all k, is assumed.

4. t_i need not be proportional to G_i, since the relationship depends upon the technology of producing public goods, on whether the government cost minimizes in production, and on whether the individual's tax is proportional to the total cost.

5. We are disregarding the effect of such taxes on the supply of factors and hence any deadweight losses that might be associated with them. A more complete model would put leisure in the utility function and consider the extra tradeoff that would arise from this extra private decision variable. The effects of such deadweight losses are likely to be more significant in other sectors of a full macro model than in consumption.

subject to $pC = W - t(G)$. With the marginal utility of wealth denoted as λ, the first-order conditions are[6]

$$(1)\quad U_j - \lambda p_j \equiv \hat{U}_j(C_jG_j)/(1+a)^{j-1} - \lambda\, \hat{p}_j/(1+r)^{j-1} = 0, \qquad j = 1, \ldots, n$$

$$pC + t(G) = W.$$

These first-order conditions state that the consumer adjusts private consumption to equate marginal utility per dollar spent on private goods across all periods. The demand functions that arise from solving the maximization are

$$(2)\qquad C_j = C_j(p, W - t(G), G), \qquad j = 1, \ldots, n.$$

From these demand functions one can obtain the total expenditure of the consumer in period j, $E_j = p_jC_j + t_j(G_j)$. After summing over all individuals, the derivative of E_j has macroeconomic implications, since it is the numerator of the multiplier presented in the introduction.

The major building blocks for the analysis of this paper are the derivatives of C_j and E_j with respect to any G_i.[7] Let $\overline{K}(C_j,G_i)$ be the effect on private demand of a change in G_i if total tax payments, hence wealth left to spend on other commodities, are held constant, and let $t_i' = \partial t_i(G_i)/\partial G_i$ be the marginal tax cost to the individual of an increase in G_i. Totally differentiating equation (1) and solving by Cramer's rule yields

$$(3)\qquad \frac{\partial C_j}{\partial W} = \frac{p_j}{U_{jj}}\left(1 \Big/ \sum_{k=1}^{n} \frac{p_k^2}{U_{kk}}\right)$$

(4)

$$\overline{K}(C_i,G_i) = -\frac{U_{in+i}}{U_{ii}}\left(\sum_{k \neq i} \frac{p_k^2}{U_{kk}} \Big/ \sum_{k=1}^{n} \frac{p_k^2}{U_{kk}}\right) = -\frac{U_{in+i}}{U_{ii}}\left(1 - p_i \frac{\partial C_i}{\partial W}\right)$$

$$(5)\quad \overline{K}(C_j,G_i) = \frac{p_ip_j}{U_{ii}U_{jj}}\left(U_{in+i} \Big/ \sum_{k=1}^{n} \frac{p_k^2}{U_{kk}}\right) = \frac{U_{in+i}}{U_{ii}}\, p_i \frac{\partial C_j}{\partial W}.$$

6. These first-order conditions assume that the consumer is at an interior point, $C_j > 0$ all j. The levels of government expenditure must be specified so that this is feasible, and the tax structure must be such that all individuals have positive after-tax wealth. Also it should be observed that these conditions are necessary, since the constraint is linear in C. They are sufficient since $U(C,G)$ is strictly quasi concave in C. Finally, one might note that $U(C,G)$ need not be strictly quasi concave in G or in C and G jointly.

7. These derivatives are obtained in Slutsky [1979]. The analysis is similar in nature to that done for rationed commodities by Tobin and Houthakker [1950–51] or for conditional demands by Pollak [1969]. These works on rationed commodities and conditional demand, generally assume that the constrained commodity is supplied at the desired level of the individual.

Since private consumption in each period is assumed to superior ($0 < p_i\,(\partial C_i/\partial W) < 1$), equations (4) and (5) indicate that $\overline{K}(C_i,G_i)$ and $\overline{K}(C_j,G_i)$ have opposite sign. The derivatives of C_j and E_j obtained by differentiating equation (2) and substituting in equations (3)–(5) giving

$$(6)\quad \frac{\partial C_i}{\partial G_i} = \overline{K}(C_i,G_i) - t_i'\frac{\partial C_i}{\partial W} = -\left(\frac{U_{in+i}}{U_{ii}} - \frac{t_i'}{p_i}\right) p_i \frac{\partial C_i}{\partial W}$$

$$(7)\quad \frac{\partial C_i}{\partial G_i} = \overline{K}(C_j,G_i) - t_i'\frac{\partial C_j}{\partial W} = \left(\frac{\hat{U}_{in+i}}{U_{ii}} - \frac{t_i'}{p_i}\right) p_i \frac{\partial C_j}{\partial W}$$

(8)

$$\frac{\partial E_i}{\partial G_i} = p_i\left[\overline{K}(C_i,G_i) + \frac{t_i'}{p_i} - t_i'\frac{\partial C_i}{\partial W}\right] = p_i\left(\frac{t_i'}{p_i} - \frac{U_{in+i}}{U_{ii}}\right)\left(1 - p_i\frac{\partial C_i}{\partial W}\right).$$

From these equations, it is apparent that the signs and magnitudes of the various terms are not independent. The magnitudes of the various derivatives of C_i and E_i with respect to G_i and G_j are each correlated with the magnitude of $\partial C_i/\partial W$.

In order to enhance understanding of these general equations, it is useful to specify them for a standard special case, the CES utility function. In each period this utility function takes the special form,

$$\hat{U}(C_i,G_i) = 1/\delta\,[\alpha(AC_i)^{-\rho} + (1-\alpha)(BG_i)^{-\rho}]^{-\delta/\rho}.$$

The parameter ρ, running from -1 to $+\infty$, gives the degree of intraperiod substitutability and the parameter δ, running from $+1$ to $-\infty$, is an interperiod factor involving the degree of homogeneity of the utility function used to represent intraperiod preferences. As is apparent from equations (3)–(8), the term (U_{in+i}/U_{ii}) is crucial for determining the signs of the various derivatives. For the CES function this term has the form

$$(9)\quad \frac{U_{in+i}}{U_{ii}} = (\delta+\rho)\Big/(\delta-1)\frac{\alpha}{1-\alpha}\left(\frac{B}{A}\right)^{\rho}\left(\frac{G_i}{C_i^*}\right)^{\rho+1} - (\rho+1)\frac{G_i}{C_i^*},$$

where C_i^* is the utility-maximizing level of C_i and the denominator is negative, since $U_{ii} < 0$ is required.

III. The Effects of Temporary Measures

This section studies the effect on private consumption in the various periods of temporary measures, changes that last for only one period either current or announced for the future. For a particular

i, $\overline{K}(C_i G_i)$, after aggregation across individuals, is the C_G term discussed in the introduction. Commodities C_j and G_i will be defined to be complements if $\overline{K}(C_j,G_i) > 0$, independent if $\overline{K}(C_j,G_i) = 0$, and substitutes if $\overline{K}(C_j,G_i) < 0$.

PROPOSITION I. $\overline{K}(C_j,G_i)$ can be decomposed into two parts, one based upon the Hicksian cross substitution term and the other, positive since C_j is superior, based upon the marginal value of extra public expenditures. Therefore, unlike Hicksian complementarity, there is no priori bias against any C_j being complementary with G_i.[8]

Let $t_i^* \equiv (\partial U/\partial G_i)/\lambda$ be the marginal value of G_i. If the individual faces this tax rate and has his wealth adjusted to $W^* \equiv W + t^*(G) - t(G)$, he would continue to consume the same level of private consumption and would view G_i as his desired level of public consumption. In Slutsky [1979] it is shown that

$$\overline{K}(C_j,G_i) = \frac{K(C_j,t_i^*)}{K(G_i,t_i^*)} + t_i^* \frac{\partial C_i}{\partial W}, \tag{10}$$

where $K(C_j,t_i^*)$ is the utility-compensated change in the demand for C_j with respect to t_i^* when the individual is allowed to choose his level of G_i, and $K(G_i,t_i^*)$ is the utility-compensated change in the desired level of G_i when t_i^* is varied. Since $K(G_i,t_i^*)$ is always negative, the sign of the ratio $K(C_j,t_i^*)/K(G_i,t_i^*)$ is opposite to that of $K(C_j,t_i^*)$. If, in the sense of Hicks, C_j and G_i are substitutes, the ratio will be negative; if they are complements, it will be positive; and if independent, it will be zero. Since $\partial C_j/\partial W > 0$, for Hicksian complementary and independent commodities, $\overline{K}(C_j,G_i)$ will always be positive. It will be negative only if they are Hicksian substitutes of the degree large enough to outweigh the implicit wealth effect term. The extra positive term removes the bias toward substitutability arising under the Hicksian definitions.[9] As follows from equations (4) and (5), G_i is

8. To some extent, government supplied goods are more likely to be complements with, rather than substitutes for, privately supplied goods. For substitutes, there may be opposition to such supply by the existing group of firms and workers who produce the private goods for which the public goods substitute. This group may be more politically powerful than the unknown group who will produce the public goods. This requires somewhat shortsighted behavior by such producers, since an increase in a public good has in general an opposite effect on private consumption in future and current periods.

9. As a definition of complementarity $\overline{K}(C_j,G_i)$ violates some other properties satisfied by the standard Hicksian one. For $\overline{K}(C_j,G_i)$ utility changes as G_i is varied. Also the standard symmetry property is not satisfied by $\overline{K}(C_j,G_i)$ so that C_j could be a complement of G_i but G_i a substitute for C_j. For example, if $K(C_j,G_i) = K(G_i,C_j) = 0$ when C_j is superior and G_i is inferior, $\overline{K}(G_i,C_j) > 0$, and $\overline{K}(G_i,C_j) < 0$.

either complementary with C_i and substitutable with all other C_j or the reverse. No a priori reason exists for one of these situations to predominate over the other. In either case,

$$\sum_{j=1}^{n} p_j \overline{K}(C_j,G_i) = 0,$$

the complementary and substitutable parts in sum cancel out. Therefore, $C_G > 0$ seems as likely to occur as the substitute case studied by Bailey and Friedman.

PROPOSITION II. The sign of $\overline{K}(C_j,G_i)$ is fully intertemporal, depending upon both the intraperiod substitution possibilities and the rate at which the marginal utility of private consumption diminishes in current and future periods.

To see the intertemporal nature of $\overline{K}(C_j,G_i)$, note from equations (4) and (5) that the sign of $\overline{K}(C_1,G_1)$ is the same as that of U_{1n+1}, whereas the sign of $\overline{K}(C_1,G_i)$ is opposite to that of U_{in+i}. Both U_{1n+1} and U_{in+i} may take either sign so that C_1 and G_i can be either complements or substitutes, even though the utility function is additive between periods. The intertemporal nature of U_{1n+1} arises because the consumer's options always involve changing private consumption in period one relative to private consumption in other periods. Thus, the sign of U_{1n+1} is affected not only by the shape of the intraperiod indifference curves for C_1 and G_1 but also by the numerical representation of these intraperiod preferences used to form the multiperiod utility function.

As an example of these propositions, consider the CES case. For the CES utility function the sign of U_{1n+1} is determined by the sign of $\delta + \rho$, the sum of the interperiod and intraperiod parameters. Since the ranges of ρ and δ are the mirror images of each other, there is no a priori bias for $\delta + \rho$ to be either positive or negative as argued in general in Proposition I. Moreover, the standard Keynesian case, $\overline{K}(C_i,G_i) = 0$ and after aggregation $C_G = 0$, does not imply, as is sometimes argued, that public goods provide no utility. It does not even imply that public and private goods have intraperiod additivity. For the CES, the Keynesian case arises if $\delta + \rho = 0$ with the utility function additive within as well as between periods.

An implication of Proposition II for empirical work is that it may be difficult to determine whether complementarity or substitutability holds. It is not sufficient to look at intraperiod substitutability alone, since the interperiod diminishing marginal utility is likely to be just as important. Even if the CES case is utilized, it may be difficult to determine the magnitude of δ.[10] In addition, even the intraperiod effect is not straightforward when private consumption in each period is a vector and not a scalar. A public good may be complementary with one private good, an increase in its level raising expenditure on that good, but still be substitutable with overall private consumption, the increase in its level reducing expenditure on the latter. For example, an increase in government spending that reduces pollution could lower private expenditure on air purifiers but raise it on outdoor activities.

Propositions I and II concern untaxed changes in G_i on private consumption in period one. Next, consider the effect of taxed changes on total expenditure. Note that $\partial E_j/\partial G_i = p_j\, \partial C_j/\partial G_i$ is opposite in sign to $\partial E_i/\partial G_i$. From equation (8), the sign of $\partial E_i/\partial G_i$ is determined by the sign of $(t_i'/p_i - U_{in+i}/U_{ii})$. The following argument explains this term. From an initially given vector of public consumption G_i, consider a change in government consumption and taxes in period i. Assume that total expenditure in each period is held constant so that $\partial C_i/\partial G_i = -t_i'/p_i$ and $\partial C_j/\partial G_i = 0, j \neq i$. This adjustment leaves the budget constraint satisfied and keeps marginal utilities unchanged in all periods but the one in which government expenditure is changed. Let the resulting change in marginal utility in period i be $\partial U_i/\partial G_i)^{E_i=c}$. The first-order conditions in (1) are still satisfied except possibly for the one of period i. If, after the initial change, marginal utility of private consumption in period i declines, C_i must be reduced, and C_j increased to satisfy all the first-order conditions, since $U_{ii} < 0$. Therefore, when private consumption in all periods is optimally readjusted, E_i will have declined. Conversely, if, after the initial change, U_i rises, C_i must be increased, and C_j decreased, leading to an increase in E_i. Hence, the change in $E_i, \partial E_i/\partial G_i$, will be in the same direction as $\partial U_i/\partial G_i)^{E_i=c}$. Differentiating U_i for this type of change yields

(11a) $$\left.\frac{\partial U_i}{\partial G_i}\right)^{E_i = c} = -U_{ii}\frac{t_i'}{p_i} + U_{in+i}.$$

The following proposition then follows immediately from either equation (8) or (11a) and equation (10).

10. In the context of uncertainty it has been argued that utility might be bounded from above in order to avoid situations like the St. Petersburg Paradox. If δ is restricted to being negative in order to do this, substitutability would be more likely, prevented only by a significant degree of intraperiod complementarity. Such an argument for bounded utility, however, does not seem compelling in this context, since boundedness is required for full lifetime utility, not just that of a single period.

PROPOSITION III. $\partial E_i/\partial G_i < 0$ iff $U_{in+i} < U_{ii}(t_i'/p_i)$. Thus, a sufficient condition for $\partial E_i/\partial G_i > 0$ is complementarity or independence as defined here, $\overline{K}(C_i,G_i) \geqq 0$. Hence, a weaker sufficient condition is that C_i and G_i be complements or independent in the Hicksian sense.

Since individuals cannot pick the level of public goods, a second crucial factor in the effectiveness of government policy is whether the individual desires the level of public goods chosen by the government to be increased or decreased, i.e., whether he views public goods as under- or oversupplied.[11] Combining equations (7) and (10) gives

$$(12) \qquad \frac{\partial C_j}{\partial G_i} = \frac{K(C_j,t_i^*)}{K(G_i,t_i^*)} + (t_i^* - t_i')\frac{\partial C_j}{\partial W}$$

as the overall effect on private consumption of a change in G_i. From equation (10) and the definition of E_i, the effect on expenditure in period i of an increase in G_i is

$$(13) \qquad \frac{\partial E_i}{\partial G_i} = \frac{p_i K(C_i,t_i^*)}{K(G_i,t_i^*)} + t_i' + (t_i^* - t_i')p_i\frac{\partial C_i}{\partial W}.$$

These equations would appear to indicate that $\partial C_i/\partial G_i$ and $\partial E_i/\partial G_i$ will tend to be negative when public goods are oversupplied. However, because of the interrelations between terms, this view is somewhat misleading as the following proposition shows.

PROPOSITION IV. A sufficient condition for $\partial E_i/\partial G_i > 0$ is that G_i is oversupplied $(t_i^* - t_i' < 0)$.

To see this, rewrite equation (11a) by adding and subtracting $(t_i^*/p_i)U_{ii}$ to get

$$(11b) \qquad \left.\frac{\partial U_i}{\partial G_i}\right)^{E_i=c} = -\,U_{ii}\frac{t_i^*}{p_i} + U_{in+i} + \left(\frac{t_i^*}{p_i} - \frac{t_i'}{p_i}\right)U_{ii}.$$

If wealth increases but private and public consumptions in all other periods are held fixed, then $\partial G_i/\partial W$, the change in the desired level of G_i due to the change in wealth with t_i^* held fixed, has the same sign as $\partial t_i^*/\partial W$, the change in the marginal value of G_i due to a change in

11. Friedman [1963] argues that the government may be inefficient, its services providing less in value than they cost, and that in this inefficient situation the multiplier will appear expansionary, although not in a very meaningful sense, since government expenditure replaces more desired private consumption. Grossman and Lucas [1974] in a model in which public goods directly enter the private production function show that increased public expenditures is expansionary if and only if it is oversupplied. However, they incorrectly assert that in the case of pure public consumption goods, the "optimal level of government expenditures would not appear to have any macroeconomic implications. . . ."

wealth when G_i is held fixed. Since $\partial t_i^*/\partial W = p_i/U_i\partial C_i/\partial W(-U_{ii}t_i^*/p_i + U_{in+i})$, if $\partial G_i/\partial W > 0$, i.e., G_i is a superior good for this type of change,[12] then $-U_{ii}t_i^*/p_i + U_{in+i} > 0$. Therefore, since $U_{ii} < 0$, a sufficient condition for $\partial U_i/\partial G_i)^{E_i=c} > 0$ and hence, as argued earlier, for $\partial E_i/\partial G_i > 0$, is that $t_i^* - t_i^{'} < 0$. A necessary, but not sufficient, condition for $\partial E_i/\partial G_i < 0$ is that $t_i^* - t_i^{'} > 0$.

The sufficient conditions discussed in Propositions III and IV cannot be treated as completely independent, and may interact in a nonadditive way as is shown in the next proposition. This proposition considers the change in effectiveness of government policies when the degree of under- or oversupply changes. In order to do this in a meaningful fashion it is better to study the effect of a dollar change in government policy as opposed to a change in the physical amount of good being supplied. Increasing the marginal inefficiency directly increases government expenditure for a given physical change in the public good. Thus, Proposition V is concerned with the magnitude and sign of $\partial E_i/\partial t_i$, the effect on total expenditure of a dollar increase in government expenditure, where $\partial E_i/\partial t_i = 1/t_i^{'}\ \partial E_i/\partial G_i$. Multiplying equation (8) by $1/t_i^{'}$ makes $1 - (p_i/t_t^{'})/(U_{in+i}/U_{ii})$, the term determining the sign of $\partial E_i/\partial t_i$.

PROPOSITION V. (1) When C_i and G_i are substitutes, increasing the degree of undersupply can make $\partial E_i/\partial t_i$ less positive or more negative with $\partial E_i/\partial t_i < 0$ occurring only if G_i is greatly undersupplied.
(2) When C_1 and G_i are complements, increasing the degree of undersupply can make $\partial E_i/\partial t_i$ more positive.

This proposition can be shown using the CES utility function. For the CES, using equation (9) and the relationship $t_i^{'}/p_i = (1 - \alpha)/\alpha(A/B)^{\rho}(C_i^*/G_i)^{\rho+1}$ yields

$$(14)\quad 1 - \frac{p_i}{t_i^{'}}\frac{U_{in+i}}{U_{ii}} = 1 - (\delta + \rho)\Bigg/\left[(\delta - 1)\frac{t_i^{'}}{t_i^*} - (\rho + 1)\frac{t_iG_i}{p_iC_i}\right].$$

If one uses equations (14) and (8), it follows directly that for $(\delta + \rho)$ negative increasing $t_i^{'}$ or decreasing t_i^* for C_i^* fixed increases $\partial E_i/\partial t_i$, making it less contractionary and even switching its sign from negative to positive. When $\rho = -1$ so that C_i and G_i are perfect substitutes, the right-hand side of equation (14) reduces to $1 - t_i^*/t_i^{'}$. The sign of $\partial E_i/\partial t_i$ is completely determined by whether public goods are over-

12. This is superiority of desired G_i within the period, other periods' consumptions held fixed. It is not necessarily superiority when consumption in all periods can vary.

or undersupplied. When ρ does not equal -1, a large gap between t_i' and t_i^* may be necessary to make $\partial E_i/\partial t_i$ negative. For example, if $\rho = -2/3$, $\delta = 0$, and $t'G_i/p_iC_i^* = 1/2$, then $t_i^* > 2t_i'$ is necessary for $\partial Ei/\partial t_i < 0$. For $\delta + \rho = 0$, the Keynesian independent case, the right-hand side of equation (14) equals one and whether or by how much the good is under- or oversupplied is irrelevant in determining $\partial E_i/\partial t_i$. When $\delta + \rho > 0$, making G_i more oversupplied reduces the magnitude of $\partial E_i/\partial t_i$ but cannot change its positive sign. If the goods are perfect complements and G_i is oversupplied, an untaxed increase in G_i leads to no change in utility and thus to no change in private consumption. The only effect of the change in G_i is that the tax increase needed to keep the budget in balance causes a fall in C_i, but since the drop in after-tax wealth is spread over all periods, it leads to a rise in E_i. If G_i is undersupplied, an untaxed increase in G_i leads to an increase in C_i to go along with the larger G_i, and the spreading effect of the tax increase causes a further rise in C_i. Thus E_i rises even farther when G_i is undersupplied than when it is oversupplied.[13]

As an example of this proposition, consider the macroeconomic effects of an increase in the marginal efficiency of providing government goods. That is, assume $\bar{t}_i(G_i^0) = t_i(G_i^0)$ but

$$\frac{\partial \bar{t}_i(G_i^0)}{\partial G_i} < \frac{\partial t_i(G_i^0)}{\partial G_i}.$$

If G in all periods is kept at initial levels G^0, every individual will have the same after-tax wealth as before and hence will purchase the same private consumption vector. The comparison between $\partial E_i/\partial t_i$ and $\partial E_i/\partial \bar{t}_i$ is then simplified, since they start from the same initial conditions. From equation (8) one obtains

$$\frac{\partial E_i}{\partial \bar{t}_i} = \frac{1}{\bar{t}_i'}\frac{\partial E_i}{\partial G_i} = \frac{p_i}{\bar{t}_i'}\overline{K}(C_i,G_i) + 1 - p_i\frac{\partial C_i}{\partial W}.$$

The reduction in t_i', which makes $t_i^* - t_i'$ larger, makes $\partial E_i/\partial t_i$ larger if $\overline{K}(C_i,G_i) > 0$ but makes $\partial E_i/\partial t_i$ smaller if $\overline{K}(C_i,G_i) < 0$. The macroeconomic effect of increased efficiency therefore depends in part upon complementarity or substitutability in consumer tastes.

Whether complementarity or substitutability holds has similar implications for other factors. A combined change in G_i and C_i that holds E_i fixed but increases U_i will cause C_i to increase. The degree depends upon how rapidly U_i decreases as C_i increases and on how

13. These examples are presented in more detail in Possen and Slutsky [1980]. Note that the results for the special cases of perfect substitutes, independence, and perfect complements are valid in general and do not require the CES functional form.

rapidly U_j increases as C_j declines in other periods. It is easy to verify that the larger in absolute value any U_{kk}, $k \neq i$, is the smaller $(1 - p_i(\partial C_i/\partial W)$ is and in turn $\partial E_i/\partial G_i$. The larger in absolute value U_{ii} is, the larger $(1 - p_i\partial C_i)/(\partial W)$ is. However, U_{ii} also enters into the other term of (8). The absolute value of U_{in+i}/U_{ii} is smaller if U_{ii} is larger. Hence, if U_{ii} is larger, $t'_i/p_i - U_{in+i}/U_{ii}$ will be bigger if $U_{in+i} < 0$ and will be smaller if $U_{in+i} > 0$. The result if C_i and G_i are substitutes $(U_{in+i} < 0)$ is that unambiguously, if U_{ii} becomes larger in absolute value, $\partial E_i/\partial G_i$ will be larger. If $U_{in+i} > 0$, the situation is ambiguous. In any case, if for some reason U_{ii} is altered, then U_{in+i} is also likely to be affected and definite statements would be difficult to make.

The magnitude of the ratio of public to private consumption can also be important in determining $\overline{K}(C_i,G_i)$ and $\partial E_i/\partial t_i$. This effect is independent of whether G_i is under- or oversupplied. For the CES, since

$$\frac{t'_i}{t^*_i} = \frac{t'_i}{p_i}\left(\frac{\alpha}{1-\alpha}\right)\left(\frac{BG_i}{AC^*_i}\right)^{\rho}\frac{G_i}{C^*_i},$$

t'_i/t^*_i can be held fixed when G_i/C^*_i changes by varying α, A, and B. An increase of G_i/C^*_i raises the absolute value of the denominator of the right-hand side of (14). If $\delta + \rho < 0$, this change increases $\partial E_i/\partial t_i$ and may switch its sign from negative to positive. If $\delta + \rho > 0$, the change decreases the magnitude of $\partial E_i/\partial t_i$. When $\delta = 1$, so that utility in each period is linearly homogeneous in C_i and G_i, $\overline{K}(C_i,G_i)$ is proportional to C^*_i/G_i and the right-hand side of (14) reduces to $1 - p_iC^*_i/t'_iG_i$, regardless of the value of ρ. Since it can be shown that the larger G_i is, the smaller C^*_i/G_i is, increasing G_i in this case reduces $\overline{K}(C_i,G_i)$.

The previous propositions have all been concerned with the effect of infinitesimal changes in G_i. The alternative method of varying consumer demand described below allows results to be obtained directly for finite changes. In addition, it highlights the importance of the relationship between nearby indifference curves in affecting demand. This ordinal factor can be as significant as the more commonly studied curvature properties of a given indifference curve that effectively determines the Slutsky matrix. Thus, three factors are significant: curvature of an indifference curve, the relation of nearby indifference curves, and the utility representation of intraperiod preferences used in the overall lifetime utility function.

To specify this approach formally, consider two points, (C^0_i,G^0_i) and (C'_i,G'_i), with $G^0_i \leq G'_i$, lying on the same period i indifference

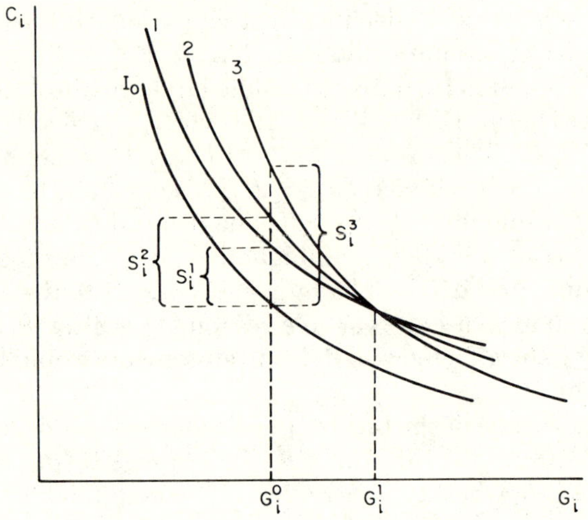

FIGURE I

Vertical, Homothetic, and Horizontal Shifts of Curve I_o

curve, denoted μ under some arbitrary labeling of indifference curves. Let $S_i(G_i^0,G_i^{'},\mu) \equiv [U_i(C_i^{'},G_i^{'})/U_i(C_i^0,G_i^0)]$. $S_i(G_i^0,G_i^{'},\mu)$ tells how much C_i must be increased at point (C_i^0,G_i^0) in order to place the individual on the same indifference curve that he would be placed on by a given increase in C_i at $(C_i^{'},G_i^{'})$. $S_i(G_i^0,G_i^{'},\mu)$ is an ordinal measure independent of the specific labeling of indifference curves. It gives an indication of the degree to which C_i is more desirable at points on the same indifference curve with more G_i and less C_i. By construction, $S_i(G_i^0,G_i^0,\mu) = 1$. Differentiating $S_i(G_i^0,G_i^{'},\mu)$ around $G_i = G_i^0$ gives $\partial S_i/\partial G_i = (-U_{ii}\,(t_i^*/p_i) + U_{in+i})/U_i$, since $-t_i^*/p_i = dC_i/dG_i)^{U=\mu}$ is the slope of the indifference curve. As demonstrated above, if G_i is a superior good, $-U_{ii}(t_i^*/p_i) + U_{in+i} > 0$. If G_i is superior at all points in the interval between G_i^0 and $G_i^{'}$, then $S_i(G_i^0,G_i^{'},\mu) > 1$.

The way indifference curves relate to each other is important in determining the magnitude of $S_i(G_i^0,G_i^{'},\mu)$. To see this, consider an indifference map that can be generated by a shift of a single indifference curve, $U^i(C_i,G_i) = \mu_0$. If there exists some $k(\mu)$ such that for any $(\tilde{C}_i,\tilde{G}_i)$ lying on curve $U^i(C_i,G_i) = \mu$, $U^i(\tilde{C}_i - k(\mu),\tilde{G}_i) = \mu_0$, then $S_i(G_i^0,G_i^{'},\mu) = 1$, regardless of the curvature of the indifference curves. When C_i and G_i are not perfect substitutes, and there exists a $k(\mu)$ such that for any $\tilde{C}_i,\tilde{G}_i$ lying on curve $U^i(C_i,G_i) = \mu$, $U^i(k(\mu)$-

$\tilde{C}_i,k(\mu)\tilde{G}_i) = \mu_0$, $S_i(G_i^0,G_i',\mu) > 1$, and, if under these same conditions, $U^i(\tilde{C}_i,\tilde{G}_i - k(\mu)) = \mu_0$, $S_i(G_i^0,G_i',\mu)$ will be even larger than for the previous case as illustrated in Figure I. In general, an indifference map will not be generated by shifting a single curve in some fashion. Nevertheless, the relation between different indifference curves may have as important effects on demand as the more commonly studied curvature properties.

In the next proposition, this analysis is used to consider finite changes in G_i.

PROPOSITION VI. If an increase in G_i, with E_i constrained to be fixed, lowers utility, then when E_i is unconstrained, ΔE_i must be positive.

Consider ΔU_i, the change in U_i found by moving from an initial point (C_i^0,G_i^0) to point (C_i',G_i') such that $G_i' > G_i^0$ and $p_iC_i^0 + t_i(G_i^0) = p_iC_i' + t_i(G_i') = E_i$. Let $(\overline{C}_i,G_i^0)$ be the point on the same indifference curve μ_1 as (C_i',G_i'). Then

$$(15) \qquad \Delta U_i = S_i(G_i^0,G_i',\mu_1)\, U_i(\overline{C}_i,G_i^0) - U_i(C_i^0,G_i^0).$$

From noninferiority of G_i it follows that $S_i(G_i^0,G_i',\mu_1) \geqq 1$; and from $U_{ii} < 0$, it follows that if $U(\overline{C}_i,G_i^0) < U(C_i^0,G_i^0)$, then $U_i(\overline{C}_i,G_i^0) > U_i(C_i^0,G_i^0)$. Thus, when $U(\overline{C}_i,G_i^0) < U(C_i^0,G_i^0)$, ΔU_i is positive, since $\Delta t_i > 0$ by construction. If one uses an argument similar to that presented earlier, ΔE_i has the same sign as ΔU_i and therefore in this case is positive. This result holds even if the individual locally desires an increase in government spending, $t_i^* > t_i'$. A sufficiently large change in G_i will make welfare lower at (C_i',G_i') and lead to $\Delta E_i > 0$.

When the individual is better off at (C_i',G_i') than at (C_i^0,G_i^0), then $U_i(\overline{C}_i,G_i^0) < U_i(C_i^0,G_i^0)$; and if $S_i(G_i^0,G_i',\mu_1) \geqq 1$, the two factors in the first terms of equation (15) go in opposite directions. In such a case the sign of ΔU_i cannot be determined. It depends upon whether S_i is sufficiently larger than 1 to overcome diminishing marginal utility. Figure II illustrates the case where G_i^A and G_i^B are chosen such that $U^i(C_i^A,G_i^A) > U^i(C_i^0,G_i^0) > U^i(C_i^B,G_i^B)$.

Intuitively, both Propositions IV and VI assert that if increasing public and reducing private consumption just enough to hold total spending in the period constant reduces utility in the period, then the individual will prefer to spread this utility drop throughout his lifetime. To do this, he must raise private consumption in the period and lower it in later periods. Conversely, if the combined change raises utility in the period, he will again desire to spread this change throughout his lifetime by lowering private consumption in the period.

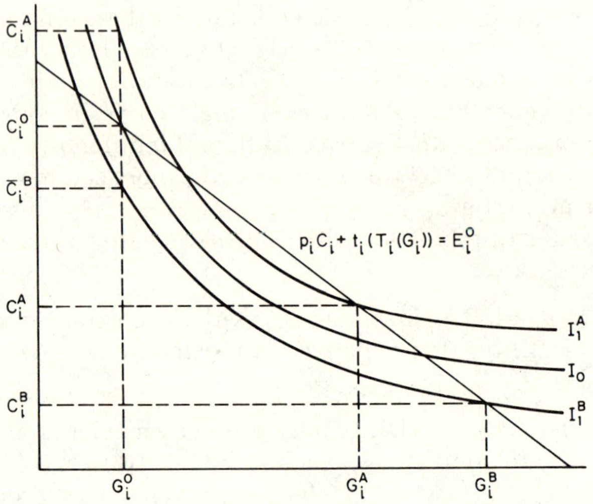

FIGURE II

Changes in G_i from a Point Where $t_i^* > t_i'$

However, the direct increase in G_i and decrease in C_i tends to increase private marginal utility and thus to lead to an increase in private consumption in the period. Therefore, the resulting net effect on E_i is ambiguous.

It is worth emphasizing that Propositions IV and VI are only sufficient conditions for a temporary increase to be expansionary. As shown in Proposition V, it is not necessary for the government to be inefficient to be expansionary, and in some circumstances being efficient is more effective.

IV. The Initial Impact of Permanent and Countercyclical Measures

Let $\overline{K}(C_1,G)$ be the overall effect on first-period private consumption of a permanent change in government expenditures when taxes are held unchanged, let $t' = \Sigma_1^n t_i'$ be the actual discounted change in taxes, and let $\partial E_1/\partial G$ be the effect on first-period total expenditure. Then

$$\overline{K}(C_1,G) = \sum_1^n \overline{K}(C_1,G_i), \quad \frac{\partial C_1}{\partial G} = \overline{K}(C_1,G) - t' \frac{\partial C_1}{\partial W},$$

and

$$\frac{\partial E_1}{\partial G} = p_1 \frac{\partial C_1}{\partial G} + t_1'.$$

PROPOSITION VII. (1). $\overline{K}(C_1,G)$ tends to be smaller in magnitude than $\overline{K}(C_1,G_1)$ and not necessarily of the same sign.

(2) If current prices and the rate of interest are the same in all periods with $p_i = p/(1+r)^{i-1}$, $G_i = G_0$, all i, and $r = a$, then $\overline{K}(C_1,G) = 0$.

From equations (4) and (5),

$$(16)\quad \overline{K}(C_1,G) = \left[-\frac{U_{1n+1}}{U_{11}}\sum_2^n \frac{p_k^2}{U_{kk}} + \frac{p_1}{U_{11}}\sum_2^n p_k \frac{U_{kn+k}}{U_{kk}}\right] \Big/ \sum_1^n \frac{p_k^2}{U_{kk}}.$$

The term $-U_{1n+1}/U_{11}$ gives the direct effect of the change in G_1 and the term $\Sigma_2^n(U_{kn+k}/U_{kk})$ gives the effect on period 1 of changes in future periods. If the utility function is similar in nature in all periods, then U_{in+i} will have the same sign in all periods. Hence $-U_{1n+1}/U_{11}$ will be opposite in sign to U_{kn+k}/U_{kk}. The announced future changes have an effect that counteracts the direct effect from the current action. Whatever their signs, $\overline{K}(C_1,G)$ is likely to be smaller in magnitude than $\overline{K}(C_1,G_1)$. Intuitively, an individual would normally desire to spread the effect of a temporary change in government spending over his entire lifetime. Since government consumption is exogenously fixed, his only response is to alter the path of private consumption as a partial adjustment. A permanent government change is already spread over the individual's lifetime and thus in general less adjustment in the private consumption path is needed.

It might be argued as a behavioral hypothesis that discounted future effects of changes in G_i, $i > 1$, will be less important in period 1 than the effects of changes in G_1 and that $\overline{K}(C_1,G)$ would have the same sign as $\overline{K}(C_1,G_1)$ but would be of smaller magnitude. It must be emphasized, however, that a strong justification for this cannot really be made as a premise about the properties of utility, since as given in equation (16), the current and future effects both depend upon sums of future variables that involve discounting of future prices or utilities.

To be more specific, when $U_{1n+1} \neq 0$, (16) can be written as

$$(17)\quad \overline{K}(C_1,G) = -\frac{U_{1n+1}}{U_{11}}\sum_1^n \left[\frac{p_k}{p_1}\frac{U_{11}}{U_{kk}}\left(\frac{p_k}{p_1}\frac{U_{kn+k}}{U_{1n+1}}\right)\right] \Big/ \left(1 + \sum_1^n \left(\frac{p_k}{p_1}\right)^2 \frac{U_{11}}{U_{kk}}\right).$$

The sign of this expression is determined by the signs of the products of U_{1n+1} and $p_k/p_1 - U_{kn+k}/U_{1n+1} \equiv D_k$. Moreover, the sign of $\overline{K}(C_1,G)$ is the same as (opposite to) the sign of $\overline{K}(C_1,G_1)$ if $D_k > 0$ ($D_k < 0$). The ratios p_k/p_1 involve the nominal rate of interest between periods k and 1 as modified by changes in current costs of private consumption, while the ratios U_{kn+k}/U_{1n+1} involve the pure rate of discount of utility between periods k and 1 modified by effects on the derivatives of utility of differential consumption of public or private goods in the different periods.

Under the condition of part (2) of Proposition VII, to satisfy the first-order conditions (equation (1)), the path of private consumption must be constant over time, that is, $C_i = C_0$ for all i and some C_0. Thus, $D_k = 0$, since $U_{in+i}/U_{1n+1} = (1+a)^{-(i-1)}$ and $p_k/p_1 = (1+r)^{-(i-1)}$, and therefore, from equation (16) $\overline{K}(C_1,G) = 0$. In this case whatever the sign of $\overline{K}(C_1,G_1)$, a permanent untaxed increase in government consumption leads to no change in the path of private consumption.

PROPOSITION VIII. If the assumptions of Proposition VII (2) are not met, the sign of $\overline{K}(C_1,G)$ depends upon the signs and magnitudes of third derivatives of the utility function in addition to the factors affecting the sign of $\overline{K}(C_1,G_1)$. For the CES utility function under certain parameter values, there is some tendency for $\overline{K}(C_1,G)$ to be positive when C_i^*/G_i is declining and for $\overline{K}(C_1,G)$ to be negative when C_i^*/G_i is rising.

Assume that the assumptions of Proposition VII (2) are met except that $a \neq r$. That individual will have a rising path of private consumption if $a < r$ and a declining path if $a > r$. Let $\hat{U}_{kn+k} = (1+a)^{k-1}U_{kn+k}$ be the intraperiod cross derivatives in period k before discounting, so that

$$D_k = \left(\frac{1}{1+a}\right)^{k-1}\left[\left(\frac{1+a}{1+r}\right)^{k-1} - \frac{U_{kn+k}}{U_{1n+1}}\right].$$

The relation of $\hat{U}_{kn+k}$ to U_{1n+1} depends upon the derivative of $\hat{U}_{kn+k}$ with respect to C_k, $\hat{U}_{kkn+k}$. For a $< r$, since $((1+a)/(1+r))^{k-1} < 1$ and $C_k > C_1$, $D_k < 0$ if $\hat{U}_{kn+k}\hat{U}_{kkn+k} \geqq 0$, but the sign of D_k is ambiguous if $\hat{U}_{kn+k}\hat{U}_{kkn+k} < 0$. For $a > r$, since $((1+a)/(1+r))^{k-1} > 1$ and $C_k < C_1$, $D_k > 0$ if $\hat{U}_{kn+k}\hat{U}_{kkn+k} \geqq 0$, but its sign is ambiguous if $\hat{U}_{kn+k}\hat{U}_{kkn+k} < 0$.

As another possibility, assume the basic assumptions except that the initial path of government expenditure is not constant but is either rising, $G_i > G_j$, $i > j$ or is falling, $G_i < G_j$, $i > j$. The time path of private consumption will now also be nonconstant but whether it moves in the same or opposite direction to government consumption depends upon the sign of U_{in+i}. Since $a = r$ is assumed here, $\partial \hat{U}(C_i,G_i)/\partial C_i = \lambda p_1$, all i. Hence $dC_i = -\hat{U}_{in+i}/\hat{U}_{ii}\, dG_i$, where dC_i and dG_1 are deviations of these variables from the first-period levels. The sign of

$$D_k = \left(\frac{1}{1+a}\right)^{k-1}\left[1 - \frac{\hat{U}_{kn+k}}{U_{1n+1}}\right]$$

depends upon the relative magnitude of $\hat{U}_{kn+k}$ and U_{1n+1} which in turn depends upon the third derivatives, $\hat{U}_{kn+kn+k}$ and $\hat{U}_{kkn+k}$. Along the path,

$$d\hat{U}_{kn+k} = \left[\hat{U}_{kn+kn+k} - \frac{\hat{U}_{kn+k}}{\hat{U}_{kk}}\hat{U}_{kkn+k}\right] dG_k$$

with D_k of opposite sign to $\hat{U}_{kn+k} d\hat{U}_{kn+k}$ and hence, $\overline{K}(C_1,G)$ of opposite sign to $d\hat{U}_{kn+k}$ whatever the sign of $\hat{U}_{kn+k}$.

The sign of $\overline{K}(C_1,G)$ thus depends crucially upon the third derivatives of the utility function of which little can be said on the basis of a priori theoretical grounds. Even under special assumptions, ambiguity frequently results. For example, for the CES utility function where $a \neq r$ or $G_i \neq G_j$, the CES leads to ambiguity, unless there is sufficient complementarity, and the ratio of public to private consumption takes on certain values. When $a \neq r$, it can then be shown that $\hat{U}_{kn+k}\hat{U}_{kkn+k} > 0$ so that $\overline{K}(C_1,G) < 0$ for $a < r$, and $\overline{K}(C_1,G) > 0$ for $a > r$. When the path of G_i is nonconstant, C_i^*/G_i is lowest when G_i is largest even if C_i^* increases with G_i. It can be shown that when the initial path of G_i is rising over time, $\overline{K}(C_1,G) > 0$; and if it is declining over time, $\overline{K}(C_1,G) < 0$.[14] Therefore, in both of these cases, the conclusion of the proposition for the CES is obtained.

The properties of $\partial E_1/\partial G$ follow from those of $\overline{K}(C_1,G)$ and the effects of permanent tax increases on C_1.

PROPOSITION IX. $\partial E_1/\partial G$ tends to be smaller than $\partial E_1/\partial G_i$. If, in addition to the assumptions of Proposition VII (2), $t_i' = t_1'/(1+r)^{i-1}$ for all i, then $\partial E_1/\partial G = 0$. If all these assumptions are not met, third derivatives again are crucial for determining the sign of $\partial E_1/\partial G$.

As argued in Proposition VII $\overline{K}(C_1,G)$ tends to be smaller than $\overline{K}(C_1,G_1)$. In addition, the permanent tax increase causes a larger

14. The conditions on third derivatives for the CES are presented in Possen and Slutsky [1980].

reduction in C_1 than does the temporary increase. Under the assumptions that $p_i = p_1/(1+r)^{i-1}$, $a = r$, and $G_i = G_0$, all i, substituting in equation (3) gives

$$\frac{\partial C_1}{\partial W} = \frac{p_1}{U_{11}}\left(1 \Big/ \sum_1^n \left(\frac{p_1{}^2/(1+r)^{2k-2}}{U_{11}/(1+a)^{k-1}}\right)\right) = \frac{1}{p_1}\sum_1^n \frac{1}{(1+r)^{k-1}}.$$

If $t'_i = t'_1/(1+r)^{i-1}$, then

$$t' = t_1 \sum_1^n \frac{1}{(1+r)^{k-1}}.$$

Therefore, $t'\,\partial C_1/\partial W = t'_1/p_1$, and $\partial C_1/\partial G = \overline{K}(C_1,G) - t'\,\partial C_1/\partial W = -t'_1/p_1$. It then follows that $\partial E_1/\partial G = p_1\,\partial C_1/\partial G + t'_1 = 0$. The permanent tax increase reduces private consumption in period 1, by exactly the amount of tax increase in the period, which means that a permanent balanced budget increase in spending causes a dollar-for-dollar reduction in private spending and has no expansionary effect. As before, if the given assumptions are not met, these results are modified. For example, if the path of government spending is not constant,

$$t'\frac{\partial C_1}{\partial W} = \frac{t'_1}{p_1}\frac{\sum_1^n 1/(1+r)^{k-1}}{\sum_1^n (1/(1+r)^{k-1}(U_{11}/\hat{U}_{kk}))}.$$

By similar reasoning to that above,

$$d\hat{U}_{kk} = \left[-\hat{U}_{kkk}\frac{\hat{U}_{kn+k}}{\hat{U}_{kk}} + \hat{U}_{kkn+k}\right]dG_k$$

tells how $\hat{U}_{kk}$ changes along the initially given path of government expenditure. Then $t'(\partial C_1/\partial W) > t'_1/p_1$ if $d\hat{U}_{kk} < 0$ and $t'(\partial C_1/\partial W) < t'_1/p_1$ if $d\hat{U}_{kk} > 0$. For the CES function the sign of $t'(\partial C_1/\partial W) - t'_1/p_1$ is generally ambiguous in those circumstances in which the sign of $\overline{K}(C_1,G)$ is determinate.

If permanent measures seem less effective than temporary ones, countercyclical measures may be more so. Define a countercyclical change dG_c as one in which $dG_1 = dG_c$, $dG_2 = (-t'_1/t'_2)dG_c$, and $dG_j = 0$, $j > 2$. Let

$$\text{(18)} \qquad \overline{K}(C_1,G_c) = \overline{K}(C_1,G_1)\frac{dG_1}{dG_c} + \overline{K}(C_1,G_2)\frac{dG_2}{dG_c} = \overline{K}(C_1,G_1) - \frac{t'_1}{t'_2}\overline{K}(C_1,G_2)$$

and

$$\frac{dE_1}{dG_c} = \frac{\partial E_1}{G_1}\frac{dG_1}{dG_c} + \frac{\partial E_1}{\partial G_2}\frac{dG_2}{dG_c} = \frac{\partial E_1}{\partial G_1} - \frac{t_1'}{t_2'}\frac{\partial E_1}{\partial G_2}. \tag{19}$$

PROPOSITION X. If conditions in periods one and two are roughly the same, $\overline{K}(C_1,G_c)$ and $\partial E_1/\partial G_c$ will have the same sign as $\overline{K}(C_1,G_1)$ and $\partial E_1/\partial G_1$ but will be larger in magnitude. If $\overline{K}(C_1,G_1) > 0$, then $\partial E_1/\partial G_1 > t_1'$.

If conditions in periods one and two are roughly similar, then $\overline{K}(C_1,G_1)$ and $\partial E_1/\partial G_1$ will have the same signs as $\overline{K}(C_2,G_2)$ and $\partial E_2/\partial G_2$. But as shown in equations (4)–(5) and (7)–(8), $\overline{K}(C_1,G_2)$ and $\partial E_1/\partial G_2$ are opposite in sign to $\overline{K}(C_2,G_2)$ and $\partial E_2/\partial G_2$. Therefore, since G_1 and G_2 move in opposite directions, the two terms in equations (18) and (19) reinforce each other making the countercyclical measures larger in magnitude than temporary ones.

Furthermore,

$$\frac{\partial C_1}{\partial G_c} = \frac{\partial C_1}{\partial G_1} - \frac{t_1'}{t_2'}\frac{\partial C_1}{\partial G_2} = \overline{K}(C_1,G_c). \tag{20}$$

The second equality of equation (20) follows directly upon substituting in equations (6) and (7). Since taxes have been changed in opposite directions in the two periods, the wealth terms cancel out. The only effect left is the substitution term $\overline{K}(C_1,G_c)$. Direct differentiation of E yields

$$\frac{\partial E_1}{\partial G_c} = p_1\frac{\partial C_1}{\partial G_c} + t_1' = p_1\overline{K}(C_1,G_c) + t_1'. \tag{21}$$

Therefore, when aggregated to obtain the numerator for the countercyclical measure, equation (21) says that the direct expansionary effect t_1' has no direct wealth effect offset and for complementary goods is further augmented. Under- and oversupply appear to play no role in equation (21). However, from equation (19) $\partial E_1/\partial G_c$ has the same signs as $\partial E_1/\partial G_1$, which is affected by that factor. Thus, the magnitude of $\overline{K}(C_1,G_c)$ is affected by the under- or oversupply. If public goods are oversupplied in both periods, then $\partial E_1/\partial G_c > 0$ even if $\overline{K}(C_1,G_c) < 0$.

V. AGGREGATE BEHAVIOR

The previous sections studied a representative consumer. For macroeconomic analysis, the effect on aggregate variables is what is relevant. It can be shown, however, that even if individuals differ, the essential nature of the previous results remains valid. That is, equations like (12) can be written to have the change in aggregate consumption equaling the sum over individuals of the Hicksian substitution terms plus an unweighted average of the marginal propensities to consume out of wealth times the aggregate net marginal benefit from the public good plus an extra term whose sign is that of the correlation across individuals between their marginal propensities to consume and their net benefits from the government change. Other equations such as (6), (8), and (13) can be similarly aggregated with the addition of correlation terms. These correlation terms will have either the same sign as that for equation (12) or will have a sign opposite to the correlations between the marginal propensities to consume and individual marginal tax costs. Then Proposition IV remains valid with the additional requirement that the correlation term in equation (12) not perversely dominate (be large and negative). Proposition III in terms of aggregate complementarity holds whatever the correlation term.[15]

An interesting special case is the overlapping generations life-cycle model for which marginal propensities to consume are directly correlated with age. As shown in equations (4)–(8), the magnitudes of derivatives of demand with respect to G_i are correlated with the marginal propensity to consume and, therefore, in this model with age. It then follows that a change in government spending is most expansionary when younger generations are taxed and, if there exist age-specific public goods, when the public goods increased are those desired by the younger generation if public and private goods are complements and those desired by the older generation if they are substitutes.

VI. Conclusion

Does a balanced budget change have an expansionary impact? Depending upon the type of action, a potential exists for such an impact from temporary measures and even more so from countercyclical ones. Moreover, the impact of such measures may be even stronger than appears in the standard model, depending upon the degrees of complementarity or substitutability and under- or over-supply. Permanent measures as shown may be less effective.

This analysis is based upon the so called "ultrarationality" postulate of consumer behavior (see David and Scadding [1974]) that consumers take account of future government actions in a consistent way and upon the assumption that perfect lending markets exist. It

15. These results are shown in Possen and Slutsky [1980].

is worth noting that if both of these conditions are satisfied, then the analysis is valid for debt-financed expenditure changes as well as for those financed by current taxes, since consumers will perfectly discount the future taxes needed to pay off the debt. Violations of either of these assumptions would require modification of the results. For example, permanent measures could tend to be more effective than indicated and countercyclical ones less so if people do not fully anticipate their future tax payments. Similarly, in such circumstances debt-financed changes will be more effective than balanced budget changes.

In addition, the above results may be altered if individuals do not believe government announcements completely, as studied in Possen and Slutsky [1980]. Depending on how individuals form expectations, there is a tendency for temporary measures to be less effective than indicated by the analysis here. Countercyclical measures, however, tend to maintain their potency, even under rational expectations and this may be the most desirable policy option.[16]

Furthermore, the potential that may exist for expansionary impact by various policies is only potential. Due to lags in the government's recognition of the need for and its ability to implement action and in consumer's perception and responses to such actions, this potential may not be realizable.

Finally, it should be emphasized that this paper analyzed the direct short-run impact of policy. Nothing could be said about future effects or about welfare without a complete macroeconomic model in which the full multiplier effects of actions can be determined. It does appear that fiscal policy can potentially be used more for short-run than for long-run expansion, since the impact of permanent measures seems minimal. Also, nothing was said about the second-period impact of temporary or countercyclical measures. These might appear to be contractionary. This cannot be determined without a full model, since the induced income generated by the first-period multiplier might be sufficient to raise wealth at the start of the second period negating the contractionary impulse.

CORNELL UNIVERSITY
CORNELL UNIVERSITY AND TULANE UNIVERSITY

16. The countercyclical measures appear similar to increases based upon "pump priming" or balancing the budget over the business cycle. However, unlike pump priming, these measures are expansionary only in the first period and do not have some permanent effect based upon an underlying instability in the economy. Unlike balancing the budget over the cycle, the budget here is always in balance but policy operates in opposite directions at different times through real expenditure changes. Holding expenditures constant but adjusting taxes over the cycle has no effect given the ultrarationality assumptions.

References

Barro, R. J., "Are Government Bonds Net Wealth?" *Journal of Political Economy,* LXXXII (Nov./Dec. 1974), 1095–117.

——, and H. I. Grossman, *Money, Employment and Inflation* (Cambridge: Cambridge University Press, 1976).

Bailey, Martin, *National Income and the Price Level,* 2d ed. (New York: McGraw-Hill, 1971).

David, Paul A., and J. L. Scadding, "Private Savings: Ultrarationality, Aggregation, and 'Denison's Law,'" *Journal of Political Economy,* LXXXII (March/April 1974), 225–50.

Friedman, Milton, *Capitalism and Freedom* (Chicago: University of Chicago Press, 1963).

Green, H. A. J., "Direct Additivity and Consumer Behavior," *Oxford Economic Papers,* XIII (June 1961), 132–36.

Grossman, H. I., and R. F., Lucas, "The Macro-Economic Effects of Productive Public Expenditure," *The Manchester School,* XLII (June 1974), 162–70.

Malinvaud, E., *The Theory of Unemployment Reconsidered* (Oxford: Basil Blackwell, 1977).

Pollak, Robert, "Conditional Demand Functions and Consumption Theory," this *Journal,* LXXXIII (Feb. 1969), 60–78.

Possen, U. M., and S. Slutsky, "The Effect of Government Expenditure on Private Consumption: A Utility Maximization Approach," CORE Discussion Paper No. 8005, 1980.

Slutsky, Steven, "Preferences and Demands in Constrained Situations," Working Paper No. 192, Department of Economics, Cornell University, 1979.

Tobin, James, and H. S. Houthakker, "The Effects of Rationing on Demand Elasticities," *Review of Economic Studies,* XVIII (1950–51), 140–53.

EXPERIENCE, PERFORMANCE, AND EARNINGS*

JAMES L. MEDOFF AND KATHARINE G. ABRAHAM

This study provides direct evidence concerning the relationship between experience and performance among managerial and professional employees doing similar work in two major U. S. corporations. The facts presented indicate that while, within grade levels, there is a strong positive association between experience and relative earnings, there is either no association or a negative association between experience and relative rated performance. If we are correct that the performance ratings given to managerial and professional employees in any grade level adequately reflect those employees' relative productivity in the year of assessment, the results imply that the human capital on-the-job training model cannot explain a substantial part of the observed return to labor market experience.

There is abundant evidence that earnings grow with labor market experience over most of a normal worklife. Since the advent of human capital theory,[1] the vast majority of labor economists have accepted, or at least not openly challenged, this theory's contention that the upward sloping segment of the experience-earnings profile reflects on-the-job training, which causes the relevant underlying experience-productivity profile to slope upwards. However, there are other potential explanations of the relationship between experience and earnings in which productivity growth plays a very minor role. For instance, Mincer [1974, p. 80] recognizes the possibility that the positive association between experience and earnings might only "reflect the prevalence of institutional arrangements such as seniority provisions in employment practices." He then makes the observation that sets the stage for this study: "Such practices, however, do not contradict the productivity-augmenting hypothesis, unless it can be shown that growth of earnings under seniority provisions is largely independent of productivity growth." [2]

Thus, the human capital interpretation of the experience-earnings profile is distinguished from other interpretations by the pre-

* We are most grateful to C. Brown, G. Chamberlain, J. Dunlop, R. Freeman, Z. Griliches, H. Leonard, H. G. Lewis, J. Mincer, A. Rees, S. Rosen, M. Wagner, and participants in seminars at Berkeley, the University of Chicago, Columbia, Harvard, the National Bureau of Economic Research, the University of Pennsylvania, and Princeton for their helpful criticisms and suggestions. We are also indebted to J. Fay and M. Van Denburgh for their invaluable assistance in carrying out the research to be discussed. The study was supported by the National Bureau's program for research on labor economics. Any opinions expressed are not necessarily shared by the individuals who have aided us or by the National Bureau.

1. This event can be marked by the publication of Becker [1964].
2. Mincer has seniority provisions under collective bargaining agreements in mind when he makes this statement, but his logic applies equally well to other institutional settings.

The Quarterly Journal of Economics, December 1980 0033-5533/80/0095-0703$03.40

diction that earnings growth reflects productivity growth.[3] Despite the dominance of human capital theory over labor economics during the past fifteen years, there exists no evidence that corresponding pieces of the experience-earnings and experience-productivity profiles have slopes of the same sign. There is a simple explanation of why this important proposition has not been addressed empirically: it is very difficult to measure an individual worker's productivity in an advanced industrial society. However, if the hypothesis is to be tested, this measurement problem must be addressed.

This study has as its basis the assumption that job performance ratings done by immediate supervisors are valid indicators of the relative current productivity of white male managerial and professional employees engaged in comparable work (i.e., that an employee rated ahead of X percent of his peers is more productive than X percent). Under this assumption, which will be supported at length below, it is possible to compare the relative earnings and relative productivity of employees in similar jobs who have different amounts of experience. The evidence to be presented, drawn from the personnel records of two major U. S. corporations, has as its most important implication that, while greater experience moves white male managerial and professional employees toward the upper tail of the earnings distribution for their grade levels, it does not move them toward the upper tail of the relevant performance distribution. Thus, the primary finding to be discussed appears to be at odds with what would be expected, given the human capital interpretation of the experience-earnings profile.

Section I describes the two company personnel files used in the research and discusses how they were transformed for statistical analysis. Section II demonstrates that, while there is a positive association within grade levels between relative earnings and experience, there is not a positive association between relative performance and experience. Potential criticisms of the way in which we have come to our main conclusion, that a substantial fraction of experience-earnings differentials cannot be explained by experience-productivity differentials, are considered in Section III. Factors that might possibly explain the finding are briefly considered in Section IV.

3. In the human capital model, productivity growth does not necessarily produce earnings growth; if a worker's productivity were enhanced by firm-specific on-the-job training financed solely by the firm, the earnings profile would be flat. However, if growth in earnings is observed, according to the model, either general or specific training (financed partially by the worker) and thus growth in productivity must have occurred.

I. The Company Personnel Files

Company personnel departments are a rich and little-explored source of economic microdata. Most major U. S. corporations collect and computerize extensive information on the demographic characteristics, earnings, and job performance of their employees. Hence, they represent a primary potential supplier of evidence concerning the relationship between experience-earnings and experience-productivity profiles.

The Company A and Company B Personnel Data Files

Two large corporations in the U. S. manufacturing sector, hereafter called Company A and Company B, have provided computerized personnel records for virtually all the members of their exempt workforces.[4] The Company A file contains information computerized (and, thus, roughly current) through March 15, 1977; it has only a limited amount of historical data and only persons active during at least one pay period since mid-1975 are included on the file. The Company B records contain information entered through July 1, 1977, including a complete log of all personnel actions since 1971 for persons active on or after September 1, 1976, and an abbreviated personnel action log for persons active on or after January 1, 1974.

All samples drawn from the Company A data set were limited to employees in jobs categorized as managerial or professional under the Equal Employment Opportunity Commission's job classification scheme. The samples extracted from the B file include only employees in those grade levels into which the Company classifies its managerial and professional jobs. To be included in an analysis, an employee in a selected position or grade level had to be white, male, "active," full time, regular, and domestically based as of the appropriate date(s).

Both the A file and the B file contain data on each employee's education, birth date, service date, and current physical work location. Both files also record each individual's most recent performance rating and current salary. In addition, the Company B file contains usable information on each individual's performance evaluation history and salary history.

Time with the company was calculated for each individual by reference to his service date. The schooling information in each file

4. Both companies deleted information on the name, address, and social security number of each worker to insure employee anonymity. Neither company provided the personnel records for a very small number of their top executives, as the records contained sufficiently detailed information that these individuals might have been identifiable even without name, address, or social security number.

was used to categorize individuals by highest level of educational attainment: less than high school, high school diploma, bachelor's degree, master's or law degree,[5] or doctorate. A pre-company experience variable was computed to equal age minus schooling minus company service minus five. For this purpose, it was assumed that those with less than a high school education had spent 10 years in school, high school graduates 13 years, college graduates 16 years, master's degree holders and lawyers 18 years, and Ph.D.'s 21 years. Dummy variables were created for the Company A and Company B physical work locations which place each site in one of four regions: Northeast, North Central, South, or West.

Performance Ratings at Company A and Company B

One piece of information that distinguishes a typical company personnel file from other sources of economic microdata is the assessment of how well each individual performs his or her job. At both Company A and Company B, supervisors review each managerial and professional employee's performance roughly once a year. Company A's "Employee Assessment" form instructs the reviewer to:

> List the six most important job duties or Areas of Accountability in decreasing order of importance. Next establish standards of performance or Expected Results for each area. Be sure to set your standards and/or objectives so that successful accomplishment falls into the 2 (Good) column. These standards should be discussed with the employee at the *beginning* of the assessment period. At the end of the assessment period, indicate the extent to which the results were obtained. . . .

The reviewer is then instructed to rate the subordinate's overall performance in his or her current job as: outstanding, good, acceptable, not acceptable, or too new to rate. In addition, the reviewer is asked to provide a separate assessment of each employee's potential for advancement, rating each employee as follows: promotable with no apparent limitations, promotable beyond next level, promotable one higher level, not promotable, or too new to rate. After a feedback session, the completed rating form is signed by both the rater and the ratee, and then given to the rater's superior for comments and a signature.

Company B's "Supervisor's Guide for Performance Review and Development Planning," in use from 1970 through the end of 1976, offered the following suggestions to the reviewer:

> The performance review of employees demands care and attention and should be carried on without distractions or interruptions. Before you begin a performance

5. The Company A education coding system does not include a separate law degree category. There are nine lawyers included with those holding master's degrees in the basic Company B regression sample.

review, refresh your knowledge of the content of the employee's position description. If only a generalized description is available, take time to think through the specific components of the job. It is very important that you analyze how the employee is performing in *each* of his areas of major responsibility. The more concrete your thoughts are, the more helpful your suggestions will be. The review should cover a sufficiently long span so that a pattern of performance can be observed. Except for extremely unusual cases, a period of 4 to 6 months experience with the employee should be sufficient to enable you to make objective judgments about him and thus complete a performance review.

Considering the employee's performance over an extended period will aid greatly in minimizing the influence of recent incidents and will help you to be objective and fair minded. Each factor being reviewed should be considered separately and be based on fact rather than opinion.

Reviews should be based on the employee's performance in his present position and only for the period since his last review. Since previous ratings should not be allowed to influence the current reviews, many managers prefer to make their evaluations without having the past records at hand.

The supervisor began the review by listing up to four of his subordinate's strengths ("He is particularly good at:"), and indicating whether "each is (essential, important, supplementary) to his job." The supervisor then indicated up to four areas where there was room for improvement ("He could use help in:") and the relative importance of each to the subordinate's job. Finally, the reviewer was told:

Now that you have completed your analysis of his strengths and opportunities for improvement, check the box opposite the paragraph that most nearly describes your evaluation of his overall performance:

- ☐ EXCELLENT: Consistently exceeds expected performance in accomplishing objectives and position requirements.
- ☐ SUPERIOR: Exceeds expectations and demonstrates high level performance in accomplishing objectives and position requirements.
- ☐ GOOD: Accomplishes objectives and position requirements as originally anticipated and in a manner resulting in expected performance.
- ☐ SATISFACTORY: Acceptable performance of position requirements with indication of ability for improvement.
- ☐ MINIMUM ACCEPTABLE: Probationary performance level for employees in same position for more than twelve months, requiring consultation with the employee and a specified plan for improvement within a designated period of time.
- ☐ UNACCEPTABLE: Unsatisfactory. Does not perform at an acceptable level of accomplishment.

The rating chosen then became the basis of the rater's recommendation for a salary action (which was reviewed by the appropriate group of the rater's superiors). No ratings in the bottom two categories were observed.

At the beginning of 1977, the Company B performance/salary review process was altered. One relevant change was in the number and description of the overall performance rating categories. Under the new program there are only four rating categories. Even though only the first four rating categories were ever used under the old program, the different descriptions under the old and new plans led to different rating distributions in the two regimes. For this reason, the performance ratings done before January 1, 1977, are not comparable to those done after that date.

As both companies' evaluation procedures indicate, a performance rating should be based on how well an individual, in the year of evaluation, is carrying out the responsibilities of his or her job. Thus, a performance rating should reflect an employee's current level of performance relative to the level of performance deemed normal for someone in his or her position. It follows that the ratings of two employees are comparable only if the workers are in similar jobs.

For compensation purposes, companies assess the relative importance and difficulty of their myriad positions and group them in light of these assessments into grade levels. For both companies under analysis, this grading is based on a position description filled out (and kept current) by the supervisor of the job (with the concurrence of higher level supervisors, when necessary). The "Exempt Position Description" form in Company B (which is quite typical) obtains information about the following: the basic purpose of the job, the duties and responsibilities of the position, and the job holder's relationship to others within or outside the organization. In addition, the form elicits:

> Functional Scope Data: A listing of the functional statistics commonly used in the industry and/or profession to indicate scope and size of responsibility, e.g.: a) Sales Volume, b) Total Employment, c) Operating Budget, d) Department Payroll, e) Total Assets, f) Number Supervised—direct and indirect, g) Cost of Rentals, h) Purchasing Volume, i) Other.

and

> Position specifications: The normal knowledge or training required; the normal minimum experience and the required personal characteristics such as level of maturity, tactfulness, judgment, creativity, etc. All of the foregoing should be regarded as being necessary for an average employee in order to attain a satisfactory level of proficiency in the job.

The jobs held by sample members from Company A fall into nineteen grade levels; those held by sample members from B fall into twelve. In light of the way in which jobs are classified into grade levels, it is assumed that positions within a grade level are of equal importance and difficulty.[6] Thus, within a grade level it seems most rea-

6. Interviews with a number of Company B supervisors lent strong support to this assumption.

TABLE I

CHARACTERISTICS OF WHITE MALE MANAGERIAL AND PROFESSIONAL SAMPLES USED IN REGRESSION ANALYSIS

	Mean (standard deviation)	
	Company A (N = 4,788)	Company B (N = 2,841)
Highest level of educational attainment:		
Less than high school diploma (yes = 1)	0.050	0.026
High school diploma (yes = 1)	0.449	0.466
Bachelor's degree (yes = 1)	0.444	0.401
Master's or law degree (yes = 1)	0.049	0.082
Doctorate (yes = 1)	0.007	0.025
Age (years)	43.1	44.1
	(10.5)	(9.9)
Pre-company experience (years)	6.8	9.5
	(6.7)	(7.7)
Company service (years)	16.8	14.9
	(10.4)	(9.6)
Annual salary (dollars)[a]	17,884	20,008
	(3,240)	(4,916)
Performance rating:		
(1) Not acceptable/satisfactory (yes = 1)[b]	0.002	0.012
(2) Acceptable/good (yes = 1)[b]	0.053	0.366
(3) Good/superior (yes = 1)[b]	0.743	0.584
(4) Outstanding/excellent (yes = 1)[b]	0.202	0.038

a. These figures are based on current dollar salaries as of March 15, 1977, for Company A and as of July 1, 1976, for Company B.

b. Performance rating 1 is worst, and performance rating 4 is best. The Company A performance category description precedes the slash and the Company B description follows the slash.

sonable to assume that a higher performance rating implies higher productivity.

A Comparison of the Two Companies' Workforces

Examination of Table I reveals great similarity in the demographic characteristics of the basic Company A and Company B regression samples.[7] In both companies, nearly 50 percent of the sample

7. The basic regression samples consist of all white males who were "active" full-time regular domestically based managerial and professional employees as of March 15, 1977, at Company A and as of July 1, 1976, at Company B for whom valid information on education, birth date, service date, physical work location, most recent performance rating, current salary, and current grade level was available. The requirements that education, birth date, service date, and physical work location be available resulted in the exclusion of 22 Company A employees and 791 Company B employees. At the time we obtained the Company B data, the firm was in the process of adding educational codes to its computerized personnel system. Almost all of the Company B exclusions resulted from not yet complete (and apparently randomly missing) educational information.

did not graduate from college. The Company B sample contains a somewhat higher proportion of people with advanced degrees; this is consistent with the organization's involvement in research and development activities. On average, Company A's employees have somewhat less pre-company experience than Company B's employees (6.8 years versus 9.5 years), but somewhat longer company service (16.8 years versus 14.9 years). The average annual salary at Company B exceeds the average annual salary at Company A by nearly $2,900.[8] There is a larger concentration of people in the top performance categories at Company A than at Company B; this is most likely attributable to the differences in the sets of rating instructions given the supervisors at the two companies.

II. Relative Earnings and Relative Performance

This section offers evidence for three propositions:

1. Managerial and professional employees with more than average pre-company experience and company service have higher than average salaries;

2. About 40 percent of the earnings differentials associated with pre-company experience and with company service occur within grade levels;

3. These within-grade-level earnings differentials cannot be explained by within-grade-level differentials in job performance. The third proposition, which is the study's major finding, is demonstrated both by a test in which performance rating dummies are entered into a within-grade-level human capital earnings function and by estimating and contrasting multinomial logit earnings and performance category equations.

Earnings Function Results

The regression results presented in Table II allow us to compare the earnings of groups of managerial and professional employees stratified by both educational attainment and labor market experience. These findings are based on a standard semi-log earnings function:

$$\ln(y) = \mathbf{x}\beta + \epsilon,$$

8. This figure was produced by inflating the Company B mean salary to March 1977 dollars using the Consumer Price Index to make it comparable to the Company A mean salary, then taking the difference between the two mean salaries.

where y equals annual salary rate, $\mathbf{x}$ is a vector whose elements capture highest level of educational attainment, pre-company experience, company service, and region, β is a vector of parameters to be estimated, and ϵ is an equation error. As stated above, the pre-company experience variable was constructed to equal age minus years assumed spent in school by those with different degrees minus company service minus five. Thus, in the presence of dummy variables capturing highest degree received and a company service variable, differences in pre-company experience will be indistinguishable from differences in age.

Equations (1) and (4) indicate that, with pre-company experience and company service held constant, individuals with advanced degrees receive substantially higher salaries than individuals with less education. The proportional reward to education within the two companies studied appears quite similar, except that, holding experience constant, college graduates are relatively better off at Company B; the percentage earnings differential between those with a high school diploma but not a bachelor's degree and college graduates with comparable labor market experience is only 13 percent at Company A as compared with 22 percent at Company B.

In both companies, controlling for educational attainment and company service, there is a positive association between salary and pre-company experience, and, controlling for schooling and pre-company experience, a positive association between salary and company service, which weakens with length of service but does not vanish within the set of feasible differences in years of service.

Regressions (2) and (5) include grade-level dummies, and hence provide information on within-grade-level earnings differentials. These within-grade-level salary differentials are central to this study, since performance ratings are conditional on the importance and difficulty of an employee's position, and thus, on his grade level. This implies that the performance ratings can at most explain the fraction of a total earnings differential that occurs within grade levels.

As can be seen by comparing regressions (1) and (4) with regressions (2) and (5), relatively little of the return to educational attainment takes the form of higher within-grade-level earnings. Controlling for pre-company experience and company tenure, systematic within-grade-level earnings differences account for an average of only 12 percent in Company A and 10 percent in Company B of the total earnings differential between those with a bachelor's degree and less educated workers and for an average of only 22 percent and 13 percent

TABLE II

EARNINGS FUNCTION ESTIMATES

	Company A: Dependent variable = ln (annual salary as of March 15, 1977)[a] (N = 4,788)			Company B: Dependent variable = ln (annual salary as of July 1, 1976)[a] (N = 2,481)		
	(1)	(2)	(3)	(4)	(5)	(6)
Less than high school diploma (yes = 1)	−0.247	−0.075	−0.077	−0.263	−0.014	−0.016
	(.010)	(.007)	(.007)	(.024)	(.012)	(.012)
High school diploma (yes = 1)	−.131	−.013	−.015	−.221	−.022	−.024
	(.005)	(.003)	(.003)	(.008)	(.005)	(.005)
Master's or law degree (yes = 1)	.104	.022	.020	.099	.011	.015
	(.010)	(.006)	(.006)	(.014)	(.007)	(.007)
Doctorate (yes = 1)	.214	.051	.054	.256	.051	.052
	(.025)	(.016)	(.016)	(.024)	(.012)	(.012)
Years of pre-company experience/10	.043	.023	.027	.070	.026	.028
	(.008)	(.005)	(.005)	(.014)	(.007)	(.007)

(Years of pre-company experience)^2/100	−.003	−.003	−.004	−.001	−.002	−.002
	(.003)	(.002)	(.002)	(.005)	(.002)	(.002)
Years of company service/10	.202	.087	.088	.192	.056	.056
	(.008)	(.006)	(.006)	(.013)	(.007)	(.007)
(Years of company service)^2/100	−.031	−.013	−.013	−.028	−.005	−.005
	(.002)	(.001)	(.001)	(.004)	(.002)	(.002)
Performance rating 1 (worst; yes = 1)	—	—	−.053	—	—	−.036
			(.027)			(.016)
Performance rating 2 (yes = 1)	—	—	−.039	—	—	−.018
			(.006)			(.004)
Performance rating 4 (best; yes = 1)	—	—	.025	—	—	.026
			(.003)			(.009)
Constant	yes	yes	yes	yes	yes	yes
Region dummies (3)	yes	yes	yes	yes	yes	yes
Grade level dummies (18; 11)	no	yes	yes	no	yes	yes
R^2	.356	.741	.747	.335	.849	.851
SEE	.144	.091	.090	.190	.091	.090

a. The mean (standard deviation) of the dependent variable is 9.776 (0.179) at Company A and 9.876 (0.233) at Company B.
Note. Standard errors are in parentheses below coefficient estimates.

of the total earnings differential between advanced degree holders and those with only a bachelor's degree.[9] Thus, college graduates earn more than less educated workers almost entirely because they are assigned to jobs in grade levels with higher mean earnings; the same is somewhat less true of advanced degree holders as compared with those with only a bachelor's degree.

In contrast, a large fraction of the return to pre-company experience and to company service reflects higher within-grade-level earnings. At the appropriate sample mean for pre-company experience, 48 percent (in A) and 34 percent (in B) of the salary differential associated with an additional year of this construct occurs within grade levels. At the appropriate mean for company service, 44 percent (in A) and 38 percent (in B) of the return to an additional year of tenure occurs within grade levels. Thus, a substantial fraction of the observed relationship between experience and earnings cannot be explained by between-grade-level differences in mean salaries.

Why do workers with more education, more pre-company experience, and more company service have higher within-grade-level earnings? One possible explanation would be that such workers have acquired valuable skills during their years in school and in the labor force, and as a result their productivity exceeds that of less educated and less experienced workers in the same grade level. If this explanation were valid, it would be expected that the introduction of performance rating dummies into the ln(earnings) equations which have grade-level controls would move the estimated coefficients of the schooling, pre-company experience, and company tenure variables toward zero. However, comparison of equations (2) and (5) with equations (3) and (6) reveals that, although higher rated performance is associated with significantly and substantially higher earnings, introduction of the rating dummies has virtually no effect on the relevant education and experience coefficients. *Thus, performance does not appear to be a mediating factor in the within-grade-level positive relationship between either education or labor force experience and earnings.* In other words, within groups of similar jobs, despite the positive correlation between "human capital" and earnings, there does not appear to be a positive correlation between "human capital" and performance.

9. These figures are weighted averages. The weights for the first set are the proportions of those with less than a high school education and of high school graduates in the less educated worker group; the weights for the second set are the proportions of master's or law degree holders and of doctorates in the advanced degree group.

Multinomial Logit Results

The multinomial logit models estimated for Table III offer another way of looking at the earnings-performance nexus.[10] In constructing the models, employees rated either "not acceptable" or "acceptable" (in A) or "satisfactory" or "good" (in B) were categorized as below-average performers for their grade level.[11] Employees rated "good" (in A) or "superior" (in B) were categorized as average performers for their grade level. Employees rated "outstanding" (in A) or "excellent" (in B) were categorized as above-average performers for their grade level. Next, employees were categorized as having either a below-average salary, an average salary, or an above-average salary for their grade level. Salary categories were assigned on the basis of each individual's percentile ranking in the relevant within-grade-level salary distribution in such a way as to make the salary and the performance categories comparable. Suppose, for example, that X_1 percent of the individuals in grade level k were in the lowest performance category, X_2 percent were in the middle performance category, and X_3 percent were in the top performance category. An individual in the bottom X_1 percent of the grade level k salary distribution would be assigned to the lowest salary category, an individual in the next X_2 percent of the grade level k salary distribution to the middle salary category, and an individual in the top X_3 percent of the grade level k salary distribution to the top salary category. Assuming that performance ratings accurately reflect relative productivity, if more productive workers were always paid more than less productive workers, the assignment of individuals to salary categories would be identical with the assignment of individuals to performance categories.[12]

A maximum likelihood multinomial logit procedure was used to estimate the effects of education, pre-company experience, and

10. Nerlove and Press [1973] discuss the multinomial logit model.

11. The small number of employees with the lowest observed performance rating, "not acceptable" in Company A and "satisfactory" in Company B, made it seem advisable to combine the bottom two categories at each company to create a "below-average" category.

12. The samples used for constructing the performance and salary categories consisted of all "active" full-time regular domestically based white male managerial and professional employees in each grade level for whom both a valid salary and a valid performance rating were available. There were fewer people in the multinomial logit samples due to the more stringent data availability requirements that had to be satisfied. Thus, unless relative rated performance in the larger sample is perfectly related to relative salary, our procedure need not (and does not) result in the number of logit sample members in each salary category equaling the number of logit sample members in the corresponding performance category.

TABLE IIIA

MULTINOMIAL LOGIT SALARY CATEGORY AND PERFORMANCE CATEGORY EQUATION ESTIMATES

	Company A (N = 4,784)				Company B (N = 2,822)			
	Salary category (1)[a]		Performance category (2)[a]		Salary category (3)[a]		Performance category (4)[a]	
	Category 2[b]	Category 3[b]	Category 2[b]	Category 3[b]	Category 2[b]	Category 3[b]	Category 2[b]	Category 3[b]
Less than high school diploma (yes = 1)	−2.538	−3.036	0.214	0.503	−0.330	−0.054	−0.026	1.774
	(0.287)	(0.342)	(0.308)	(0.367)	(0.288)	(0.553)	(0.271)	(0.585)
High school diploma (yes = 1)	−0.583	−0.571	0.231	0.470	−0.279	−0.848	0.217	0.491
	(0.186)	(0.203)	(0.166)	(0.184)	(0.113)	(0.283)	(0.108)	(0.287)
Master's or law degree (yes = 1)	—	—	—	—	0.265	0.413	−0.665	−0.656
					(0.167)	(0.390)	(0.159)	(0.383)
Doctorate (yes = 1)	—	—	—	—	1.414	0.282	−0.682	−0.332
					(0.341)	(1.076)	(0.287)	(0.524)
Master's degree, law degree or doctorate (yes = 1)[c]	1.156	1.645	0.105	0.238	—	—	—	—
	(0.474)	(0.489)	(0.348)	(0.362)				

Years of pre-company experience/10	0.439	0.834	−0.806	−1.318	0.546	0.441	−0.512	−0.991
	(0.268)	(0.296)	(0.267)	(0.292)	(0.165)	(0.393)	(0.162)	(0.405)
(Years of pre-company experience)^2/100	−0.072	−0.081	0.198	0.273	−0.073	0.078	0.040	0.147
	(0.094)	(0.106)	(0.099)	(0.110)	(0.055)	(0.120)	(0.054)	(0.134)
Years of company service/10	1.122	2.890	0.429	−0.122	1.131	0.928	0.095	−0.582
	(0.280)	(0.322)	(0.261)	(0.290)	(0.164)	(0.402)	(0.153)	(0.408)
(Years of company service)^2/100	−0.133	−0.408	−0.127	−0.060	−0.132	0.035	−0.068	0.014
	(0.070)	(0.078)	(0.063)	(0.070)	(0.046)	(0.100)	(0.042)	(0.117)
Constant	yes	yes	yes	yes	yes	yes	yes	yes
Region dummies (3; 2)[d]	yes	yes	yes	yes	yes	yes	yes	yes
Grade level dummies (15; 8)[e]	yes	yes	yes	yes	yes	yes	yes	yes
χ^2	711.30		351.70		413.37		216.96	
d.f.	50		50		36		36	

a. All equations were estimated using a maximum likelihood multinomial logit procedure.

b. Category 1 represents the lowest level, category 2 the middle level, and category 3 the highest level of salary or performance. The coefficient estimates reported are equal to $\beta_2 - \beta_1$ (under category 2) and $\beta_3 - \beta_1$ (under category 3).

c. Since none of the thirty-five Company A doctorates were in the lowest salary category, individuals at Company A with doctorates were included with the master's or law degree group.

d. In the Company B sample, individuals in the West region were included with the North Central region group.

e. Individuals in grade levels where not all of the salary and performance categories were represented were excluded from the sample.

Note. Standard errors are in parentheses below the coefficient estimates.

company service on the probability of an individual's being in each of the salary categories and in each of the performance categories. The multinomial logit model specifies the probability that an individual is in category i to be of the form, $e^{\mathbf{x}\beta_i}/\sum_{j=1}^{3} e^{\mathbf{x}\beta_j}$, $i = 1, 2, 3$, where $\mathbf{x}$ is a vector of individual characteristics containing education dummies, pre-company experience and company service variables, region dummies, and grade level dummies, and the β_1, β_2, and β_3 are vectors of parameters. The coefficients presented in Table IIIA are estimates of the elements in vectors equal to $\beta_i - \beta_1$, $i = 2, 3$.

If the higher within-grade-level earnings of those with more education, more pre-company experience, and more company service were a reflection solely of the higher relative productivity of such workers, one would expect the estimated coefficients in salary category equations (1) and (3) to equal the estimated coefficients in performance category equations (2) and (4). In fact, the estimated coefficients in the salary category equations are markedly different from the estimated coefficients in the performance category equations. At both Company A and Company B, those with less than a college education appear to have a much lower probability of being in one of the top two salary categories than do those whose highest degree is a bachelor's degree, but an equal or higher probability of being in one of the top two performance categories. Those with advanced degrees, on the other hand, appear to have a substantially higher probability of being in one of the highest two earnings categories than do those whose final degree was a bachelor's degree, without having a substantially higher probability at A and actually having a substantially lower probability at B of being in one of the top two performance categories.

At both Company A and Company B, pre-company experience appears to decrease an individual's chances of being in the bottom salary category, while increasing his chances of being in the bottom performance category. At both companies, additional company service has a significant and strongly positive effect on the probability that an employee will be in one of the top two salary categories; at Company A the incremental effect of an additional year of service falls as the amount of accrued seniority gets larger but does not vanish within the feasible set of values for the variable. While the initial years of service at Company A have a small but significant positive effect on the probability of an individual being in the middle performance category rather than in either the top or the bottom performance category, this effect vanishes in under seventeen years (i.e., within two years beyond the mean amount of company service). At Company

TABLE IIIB

MULTINOMIAL LOGIT SALARY CATEGORY AND PERFORMANCE CATEGORY EQUATION ESTIMATES

	Company A (N = 4,784)			Company B (N = 2,822)		
	Bottom category	Middle category	Top category	Bottom category	Middle category	Top category
Salary categories						
Probability of average sample member being in category (sample means in brackets)	0.030 [0.052]	0.758 [0.748]	0.212 [0.200]	0.330 [0.380]	0.644 [0.582]	0.025 [0.038]
Percentage change in probability attributable to:						
(1) an additional year of pre-company experience	−4.117 (1.536)	0.098 (0.212)	1.027 (0.751)	−2.771 (0.517)	1.319 (0.268)	1.997 (1.898)
(2) an additional year of company service	−8.331 (0.903)	0.184 (0.130)	2.241 (0.465)	−5.028 (0.388)	2.373 (0.208)	3.480 (2.785)
Performance categories						
Probability of average sample member being in category (sample means in brackets)	0.048 [0.055]	0.783 [0.743]	0.169 [0.202]	0.368 [0.381]	0.606 [0.582]	0.026 [0.037]
Percentage change in probability attributable to:						
(1) an additional year of pre-company experience	5.784 (1.427)	−0.270 (0.165)	−1.147 (0.691)	2.827 (0.477)	−1.648 (0.291)	−2.682 (1.846)
(2) an additional year of company service	0.537 (0.760)	0.001 (0.097)	−0.704 (0.414)	0.787 (0.335)	−0.410 (0.205)	−2.103 (1.343)

a. The probability figures reported here were derived using the fitted values of the multinomial logit coefficients reported in Table IIIA. The sample mean values of the education dummies, region dummies, and grade dummies and the mean amount of both pre-company experience and company service were assumed. The standard errors are "back-of-an-envelope" approximations calculated with the probability of an average sample member being in each category treated as known rather than estimated.

Note. Standard errors are in parentheses below the percentage change estimates.

B, length of tenure has no significant effect on a person's performance category.

The point estimates (and approximate standard errors) presented in Table IIIB were calculated using the estimated coefficients from the multinomial logit models (and the variance-covariance matrix of the parameter estimates). In both Company A and Company B, the point estimates of the multinomial logit coefficients imply that for the mean sample member an additional year of either pre-company experience or company service would do the following: (1) substantially reduce the probability of being in the below-average salary category, increase the probability of being in the average salary category, and increase by a larger percentage the probability of being in the above-average salary category; and (2) increase the probability of being in the below-average performance category, reduce or leave unaffected the probability of being in the average performance category, and reduce by a larger percentage the probability of being in the above-average performance category. Thus, the multinomial logit coefficient estimates strongly suggest that while pre-company experience and company service tend to move individuals with average measured characteristics toward the top of the relevant within-grade-level salary distribution, they tend to move them toward the bottom of the relevant within-grade-level performance distribution. It seems clear that at least among the samples of employees at Company A and Company B under analysis, higher relative productivity cannot be offered as a satisfactory explanation of the higher relative within-grade-level salaries associated with additional labor force experience.[13]

III. Potential Criticisms

Our finding that a substantial fraction of the experience-earnings differential among managerial and professional employees in major U. S. corporations cannot be explained by an experience-performance differential is inconsistent with the explanation of the experience-earnings profile associated with human capital theory. Thus, it is likely that this paradigm's adherents will argue that the test which we have conducted was ill-conceived. In this section we attempt to anticipate and address potential criticisms of our approach. We have grouped these criticisms according to whether they question our econometric

13. It is perhaps worth commenting that, although the data used in this study only permit us to conclude that at Companies A and B the within-grade-level portion of the experience-earnings differential cannot be explained by an experience-performance differential, there is no direct evidence on the extent to which the cross-grade-level portion of the experience-earnings differential at Companies A and B reflects higher productivity of more experienced workers.

methods or our key assumption that within similar jobs, rated performance is monotonically related to productivity.[14]

Econometric Issues

As stated above, the key piece of information used in our analysis is the performance rating given to each employee. Since this assessment seems to be conditional on an employee's job assignment and, hence, his grade level, our analysis has focused on whether the within-grade-level portion of the experience-earnings differential (a substantial part of the total experience-earnings differential) could be explained by a within-grade-level experience-performance differential.

A critic might correctly point out that by looking within grade levels at a given firm, we most likely induce a negative partial correlation between experience and unobserved ability. Even if in the whole relevant sample, experience and ability have a zero correlation, within a given grade level, more experienced employees most likely are less able than less experienced employees, since otherwise they probably would have been promoted to jobs in higher grade levels. A critic might also point out that performance ratings are almost surely error-ridden proxies for relative within-grade-level productivity.

With regard to our earnings function results, it can be shown formally that neither the existence of a negative within-grade-level correlation between experience and ability nor random error in the performance ratings we have used to capture relative productivity can explain the failure of the estimated within-grade-level return to labor market experience to move toward zero when performance rating controls are introduced.[15]

14. Another potential criticism might be that our work is flawed because we look at cross-sectional data rather than at changes over time in the relative earnings and relative performance of members of a cohort. This argument is dealt with in Medoff and Abraham [forthcoming]; longitudinal data from another large company yield the result that, for white male managers or professionals remaining in a grade level, relative earnings rise and relative performance falls with the passage of time.

15. For a sample of people in a grade level, let earnings be a function solely of productivity:

$$\ln Y = \alpha_1 C + \epsilon_1, \quad \alpha_1 > 0, \tag{1}$$

and productivity be a function of both experience and ability:

$$C = \alpha_2 X + \alpha_3 A + \epsilon_2,\ \alpha_2,\ \alpha_3 > 0,\ \mathrm{cov}(X,A) < 0. \tag{2}$$

Suppose that we have a variable which captures productivity with error for those in the given grade level:

$$P = C + \epsilon_3. \tag{3}$$

Assume that these three equations accurately describe the relevant relationships and that ϵ_1, ϵ_2, and ϵ_3 are uncorrelated with each other, with X, and with A. Under these conditions, if $\ln Y$ is first regressed on X alone and then regressed on both X and P, the expected value of the experience coefficient falls toward zero when P is added. This model is laid out more fully in Medoff and Abraham [forthcoming].

The conclusions that can be drawn from our multinomial logit results also appear to be unaffected. It is true that if there is a negative within-grade-level correlation between experience and ability, the estimated effect of experience on performance will be biased downward. It should not be forgotten, however, that the estimated effect of experience on earnings will *also* be biased downward. The goal of our multinomial logit analyses is *not* to derive consistent estimates of the effect of experience on either performance or salary. Rather, they are intended to yield an answer to the question: Can the 40 or so percent of the total earnings advantage enjoyed by more experienced managers and professionals at the firms we have studied that occurs within grade levels be explained by the fact that the more experienced employees within these grade levels are better performers? Our answer of "no" does not depend on the consistency of either our estimate of the impact of experience on performance or our estimate of the impact of experience on earnings. All that the response depends on is that the *difference* between these two estimated experience effects be a consistent estimate of the difference between the two "true" experience effects. We know of no reason why it should not be.

It also seems unlikely that classical measurement error in our performance variable should in any way affect the main conclusions derivable from our multinomial logit models. In a linear model, error in the dependent variable of the type under discussion will weaken the equation's overall explanatory power but will not lead to inconsistent estimated coefficients. In the relevant multinomial logit models, the performance ratings form the basis for the dependent variables. We do not see how errors that arise out of random error in the performance ratings would lead to inconsistency in the estimated multinomial logit coefficients. Consistency is all that matters for our purpose.

Use of Performance Ratings

The validity of our analysis depends on the assumption that within a grade level, for the samples studied, performance ratings are valid indicators of relative productivity. There is an extensive literature on white-collar performance evaluations.[16] Since critical articles are more likely to find their way into personnel journals than those that applaud current practices, performance evaluation programs have been subject to a fair amount of criticism.

16. For good general discussions and further references, see Barrett [1966], Bass and Barrett [1972], Landy and Trumbo [1976], and McCormick and Tiffin [1974].

Much of this criticism focuses on the possibility that supervisors may be overly lenient in rating their subordinates. While inflated ratings are a matter of concern for personnel administrators, there is no evidence to suggest that such inflation distorts the relative rankings of employees by true performance. Even if the ratings of all employees are biased upwards, the best employees should be rated above average, and the worst employees below average. This is all that matters for the present study.

A second criticism of performance ratings asserts that since different supervisors may have divergent beliefs about what constitutes good performance, ratings done by different supervisors should not be compared. While it does seem unlikely that any two supervisors would be completely consistent in their ratings, the results of laboratory studies suggest that a high degree of interrater reliability can be expected.[17] In any event, so long as subordinates with particular observed characteristics are not systematically paired with superiors who rate more or less generously, our findings cannot be called into question on account of variation in supervisors' rating standards.

A third potential weakness of performance ratings is that employees' personal characteristics (race, sex, age, time with company) might influence supervisors' performance assessments. Whether race or sex affects ratings is irrelevant in the context of the present study, since we have restricted our analysis to samples of white males. Evidence that supervisors systematically underrate the relative performance of older or more senior workers would be very relevant. However, in our review of the pertinent literature, we have found no such evidence.

One cannot conclude a priori that any systematic bias in performance ratings associated with age or tenure should be in the direction of understating rather than overstating older or more senior workers' relative productivity. While one might argue that the typical supervisor would tend to give a higher than deserved rating to an employee in a given grade level with less than average experience because of, say, lack of familiarity with his or her weaknesses or because of lower performance expectations, it seems equally plausible to argue that the typical supervisor would favor an employee with greater than average experience because of, say, friendship developed over a period of years or because of lower expectations for someone

17. Relevant research includes Borman [1975] and Whitlock [1963]. Lawler [1967, p. 371] refers to Whitlock's work and asserts that "other studies have shown that raters tend to agree upon the weight to be assigned to . . . different behavior specimens; thus, inter-rater reliability is possible." Unfortunately, he does not specify what other studies he has in mind.

who is more likely to be a "stayer" as opposed to a "mover" in the corporate hierarchy. (If the idea that a supervisor would implicitly assume there to be a negative partial correlation between experience and what one can expect from an employee seems implausible, the reader should reassess its plausibility remembering that the relevant partial correlation is with grade level held constant.) In fact, the limited empirical evidence that is available on the issue of age- and seniority-related bias in performance ratings suggests that more experienced employees tend to be rated somewhat *higher* than is warranted by their true relative performance.[18] Thus, it appears that, so long as older or more senior workers are not systematically below superiors who underrate subordinates with these characteristics (which we find most doubtful), unequal treatment in ratings is not an acceptable explanation for more experienced workers in a grade level receiving ratings that are no higher and perhaps somewhat lower than those received by otherwise comparable less experienced workers.

Another related possibility is that perhaps even within grade levels at a company, more experienced workers might tend to be assigned more difficult tasks than less experienced workers (perhaps because more is expected of those with more experience). If this were the case, employees with greater than average experience could have greater productivity than their less experienced peers and still receive no higher or even lower performance ratings. However, since jobs are grouped into grade levels on the basis of the importance and difficulty of the tasks the job holder must perform, any difference in the potential value of the tasks performed by employees in the same grade level should be small. Further, the only evidence we have seen that bears on this point suggests that older workers in a group of employees holding similar jobs tend to be assigned *less* difficult rather than *more* difficult tasks. In an article discussed at greater length in Section IV of this study, Dalton and Thompson [1971] report that among engineers at six companies there was a negative relationship between supervisors' assessment of the complexity of the tasks a subordinate was typically asked to perform and the subordinate's age. (Their finding is illustrated graphically in Figure I in Section IV.)

18. Two studies of blue collar workers, one by Rothe [1949] and one by Rundquist and Bittner [1948], contain some evidence that the ratings of long service laundry workers and of container inspectors tend to be inflated. A study by Ferguson [1949] of ratings given to assistant life insurance sales managers and another study by Stockford and Bissell [1949] of ratings given to first line supervisors at a manufacturing plant suggest that superiors tend to be more lenient in rating those whom they have known for a longer period of time.

An analysis of promotion probabilities and percentage salary increases in Company B can provide two tests of our contention that performance ratings mirror relative true performance. These tests are based on the seemingly reasonable assumptions that, holding educational attainment, experience, and grade level constant, differentials in promotion probabilities reflect differentials in productivity and that, holding the same variables plus ln(salary) constant, differentials in percentage salary increases also reflect productivity differentials.[19] Under these assumptions, a strong positive association between rated performance and probability of promotion or a strong positive association between rated performance and percentage salary increase among employees in the same grade level who have the same amount of schooling and experience can be taken as evidence of a strong association between relative performance rating and relative productivity.

Table IV presents estimates of the effects of educational attainment, experience, and rated performance on promotion probabilities and percentage total salary changes.[20] A maximum likelihood logit procedure was used to estimate the promotion equations; ordinary least squares was used to estimate the percentage salary change equations.

The partial effect of rated performance in 1976 on the probability that a Company B employee received a promotion between July 1, 1976, and July 1, 1977, is estimated in equation (1). The results imply that individuals with either of the bottom two performance ratings were substantially and significantly less likely to have been promoted than otherwise comparable individuals with either of the top two ratings. The equation (2) results support the same conclusion with regard to the effect of rated performance as of July 1, 1974, on the probability of having received a promotion between July 1, 1975, and July 1, 1977.

19. Holding productivity constant, ln(salary) should be negatively related to percentage salary increase if firms tend to increase the relative earnings of those who are paid less and decrease the relative earnings of those who are paid more than they are currently contributing. The assumptions made in the text also permit education, experience, and grade level to have independent effects on probability of promotion and percentage salary increase, although a priori it is not clear in which direction these effects should go.

20. Estimates for Company A are not presented in Table IV because the Company A file does not contain the necessary historical performance rating data. The Company B samples consist of all white males who were "active" full-time regular domestically based managerial and professional employees throughout the relevant periods, for whom education, experience, and physical work location are known, for whom a valid initial performance rating and grade level are available, and, when relevant, for whom the requisite salary data exist.

TABLE IV

ESTIMATES OF THE RELATIONSHIP OF SCHOOLING, EXPERIENCE, AND PERFORMANCE RATING TO THE PROBABILITY OF BEING PROMOTED AND TO PERCENTAGE SALARY INCREASES AT COMPANY B

	Dependent variable = 1 if promoted between July 1, 1976 and July 1, 1977, 0 otherwise (N = 2,728) (1)[b]	Dependent variable = 1 if promoted between July 1, 1975 and July 1, 1977, 0 otherwise (N = 2,491) (2)[b]	Percent salary change July 1, 1976 to July 1, 1977[a] (N = 2,763) (3)[b]	(Percent salary change July 1, 1975 to July 1, 1977)/2[a] (N = 2,491) (4)[b]
Mean (standard deviation) of dependent variable	0.064	0.209	9.712	9.580
	(0.245)	(0.407)	(4.098)	(3.168)
Less than high school diploma (yes = 1)	0.089	−0.072	0.125	0.304
	(0.656)	(0.420)	(0.496)	(0.411)
High school diploma (yes = 1)	−0.390	−0.282	−0.057	−0.317
	(0.229)	(0.143)	(0.194)	(0.158)
Master's or law degree (yes = 1)	0.250	0.045	−0.486	−0.335
	(0.276)	(0.178)	(0.289)	(0.218)
Doctorate (yes = 1)	−0.002	0.169	−0.348	0.321
	(0.488)	(0.314)	(0.504)	(0.395)
Years of pre-company experience/10	−0.711	−0.741	−0.706	−0.743
	(0.318)	(0.220)	(0.287)	(0.249)
(Years of pre-company experience)^2/100	0.083	0.094	0.035	0.051
	(0.112)	(0.083)	(0.096)	(0.090)

Years of company service/10[c]	−1.277	−0.818	−1.517	−0.743
	(0.303)	(0.211)	(0.283)	(0.240)
(Years of company service)^2/100[c]	0.227	0.096	0.256	0.058
	(0.085)	(0.062)	(0.076)	(0.067)
Ln(annual salary)[c]	—	—	−8.296	−9.255
			(0.799)	(0.613)
Performance rating 1 (worst; yes = 1)[c]	—	−1.517	−2.879	−2.155
		(0.743)	(0.684)	(0.488)
Performance rating 2 (yes = 1)[c]	—	−0.631	−1.735	−1.134
		(0.125)	(0.158)	(0.132)
Performance rating 1 or performance rating 2 (worst; yes = 1)[c,d]	−0.992	—	—	—
	(0.205)			
Performance rating 4 (best; yes = 1)[c]	−0.139	0.285	0.991	0.949
	(0.377)	(0.208)	(0.382)	(0.270)
Constant	yes	yes	yes	yes
Region dummies (3)	yes	yes	yes	yes
Grade level dummies (8; 11; 11; 11)[c,e]	yes	yes	yes	yes
χ^2	139.07	225.92	—	—
d.f.	21	25	—	—
R^2	—	—	0.147	0.178
SEE	—	—	3.802	2.888

a. Percent salary change was calculated as the natural logarithm of the annual salary in the ending year minus the natural logarithm of the annual salary in the starting year times 100.
b. Equations (1) and (2) were estimated using a maximum likelihood logit procedure, equations (3) and (4) using ordinary least squares.
c. Years of company service, salary rating, and grade level are as of July 1, 1976, if used in equations (1) and (3) and as of July 1, 1974, if used in equations (2) and (4).
d. Since none of those with the lowest performance rating in 1976 received a promotion between July 1, 1976, and July 1, 1977, the two bottom performance categories were combined in estimating equation (1).
e. Individuals in grade levels where either everyone or no one received a promotion were excluded from the logit samples.
Note. Standard errors are in parentheses below the coefficient estimates.

Promotion-related salary increases are a relatively small part of total salary increases at Company B. Between July 1, 1976, and July 1, 1977, only 9 percent of the total dollar amount of salary increases granted were associated with promotions, while 83 percent were labeled "merit" increases. Regression (3) demonstrates a substantial and significant positive partial correlation between 1976 relative performance rating and 1976–1977 percentage total salary increase. This result suggests that, while a part of so-called "merit" increases is relatively automatic, part does in fact reflect merit. The fourth regression shows that individuals with a given amount of schooling and experience who received higher performance ratings in 1974 received substantially and significantly higher average percentage salary increases between July 1, 1975, and July 1, 1977, than did their lower rated grade-level peers.

Critics of the use of performance ratings in the analysis presented in Section II might make one further argument: since a major use of ratings is to condition decision-making concerning promotions, rated performance is likely to reflect not only a manager's or professional's productivity in his current job but also his supervisor's assessment of his potential for advancement within the company. Holding education constant, more experienced (older) managers and professionals are typically less likely to be promoted out of any given grade level than less experienced (younger) managers and professionals and, hence, apt to be perceived as having limited potential for future advancement.[21] Thus, to the extent that performance ratings are affected by supervisors' assessments of individuals' future potential, more experienced workers might typically receive lower performance ratings than warranted simply on the basis of their current productivity.

The institutional basis for this argument is weak insofar as at both Company A and Company B, the instructions to supervisors preparing ratings clearly ask for an assessment of how well each employee is fulfilling the requirements of his or her current job, not for a forecast of the employee's productivity profile over his or her work life. At Company A supervisors are asked to make entries on a per-

21. Estimation of promotion equations similar to those in Table IV but without performance rating controls yielded education and experience coefficients virtually identical to those reported in Table IV. The coefficients from the equations without rating controls imply that, for a Company B employee with the relevant sample mean characteristics, an additional year of either pre-company experience or company service was associated with a 6 percent lower chance of receiving a promotion between July 1, 1976, and July 1, 1977, and with a 5 percent lower chance of receiving a promotion between July 1, 1975, and July 1, 1977.

formance review worksheet *"during the year* for the purpose of *providing supporting information for the annual employee assessment"* [our italics]; the intent is clearly that each employee's annual performance rating should reflect his or her performance during the appraisal year. At Company B, as seen above, the "Supervisor's Guide for Performance Review and Development Planning" states that "[r]eviews should be based on the employee's performance in his present position and *only for the period* [typically one year] *since his last review"* [our italics].[22]

Finally, it should be noted that at Company A, as at many U. S. corporations, each employee's promotability is formally assessed separately from his performance. A Company A supervisor who believed that a particular employee would do well in a higher level job would not have to convey that information to higher management indirectly by giving the employee a higher than deserved performance rating but could convey his belief directly by awarding the employee an appropriate promotability rating. Statistical results discussed in Medoff and Abraham [forthcoming] based on data from another U. S. manufacturing corporation indicate that the performance ratings and the promotability measure used at that company really do capture different things; while the performance ratings do very much better in explaining current salary, the promotability measure strongly dominates in predicting advancement to a higher grade level.[23]

In light of what we have been able to learn from our review of the relevant personnel literature, from the case studies we have done, and from various analyses with company personnel data, we feel very comfortable in assuming that performance ratings are good indicators of employees' relative productivity in the year of evaluation. Hence, we believe that this diverse evidence strongly supports the interpretation we have given to our results.

22. A small number of Company B supervisors were asked to "list the five most important factors (in order of importance) that you consider when you give a performance rating to a subordinate." Of the thirteen supervisors responding to this question, only one indicated that he considered an employee's potential when awarding a performance rating. For this supervisor, potential was the last factor listed, coming behind "achievement against action plan," "creative element brought to assignments," "need for supervision to complete assignments," and "attitude." All of the thirteen supervisors' responses were consistent with a belief that the actual practices followed by Company B raters closely matched the instructions they were given.

23. The Company A performance measure contributes more to explaining current salary than does the Company A promotability measure. However, we were not able to test whether at Company A the promotability measure dominated the performance measure in predicting promotions because the Company A file did not contain the historical performance rating and promotability rating information such a test would have required.

IV. Toward a Richer Explanation of the Experience-Earnings Relationship

The finding that at least a substantial fraction of the experience-earnings differential cannot be explained by an experience-performance differential among samples of white male managerial and professional employees at Companies A and B does not appear to be an aberration. We observed the same phenomenon in two comparable studies, Medoff [1977] and Medoff and Abraham [forthcoming], of a major airline and of another manufacturing firm. Dalton and Thompson [1971] also obtained similar results in an analysis (supported by the Harvard Business School) of the relative performance and earnings of 2,500 managerial and professional employees of different ages in six technology-based companies. Figure I is based on the information presented by Dalton and Thompson. The average percentile performance ranking of employees in each age group depicted in this figure is determined by supervisors' assessments of the "contribution made to the company during the past year" by their subordinates. Dalton and Thompson's findings imply that although engineers older than thirty five received relatively low performance ratings, they received relatively high earnings. In addition, the Dalton and Thompson results indicate a negative relationship between relative performance and age among first and second level managers after their late thirties.[24] While information on the managers' compensation was not presented, it would be most exceptional if there were a corresponding negative association between relative earnings and age among those past their late thirties. In comparing the relative salaries and performance of older and younger engineers, Dalton and Thompson [p. 59] write:

> While performance rankings begin to fall after the mid-thirties salaries continue to climb until the early forties before leveling off. This increasing discrepancy between a person's performance rankings and his "salary ranking" is one of the factors that makes project leaders reluctant to have older engineers assigned to their projects.

The divergence between experience-earnings and experience-performance differentials among managerial and professional employees in major U. S. firms raises a number of questions: (1) Why might the relative performance of a managerial or professional employee stay constant or decrease over much of his or her worklife? (2) What factors condition the salary determination process such that

24. For a summary of other studies concerning the relationship between experience or age and performance that strongly support the main assertion of this study, see Medoff and Abraham [April 1980].

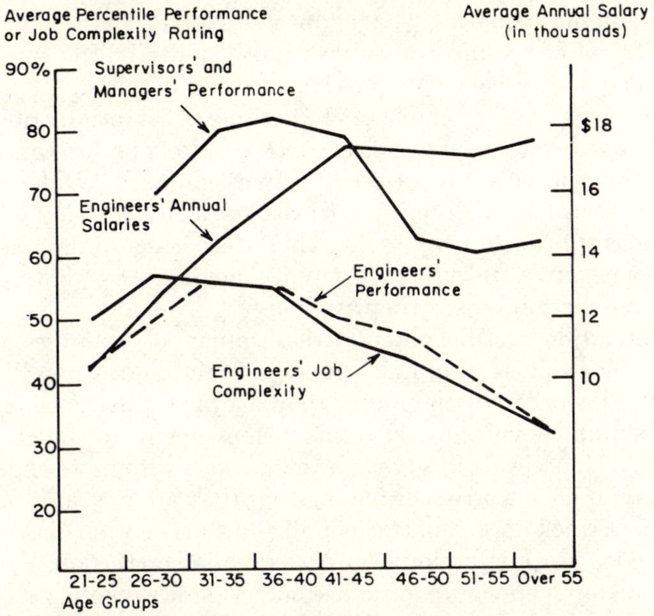

FIGURE I
Age, Performance, and Salary of Engineers; Age and Performance of Supervisors and Managers; Age and Job Complexity of Engineers
(Adapted from Dalton and Thompson [1971])

within grade levels the experience-earnings differential cannot be explained by an experience-performance differential? (3) While the observed divergence between these two differentials appears to be inconsistent with a strictly human capital interpretation of the experience-earnings profile, can the finding be reconciled with competitive theory?

Why Might Relative Performance Not Increase with Experience?

Human capital theory argues that with the passage of time workers accumulate productivity-augmenting skills. While on-the-job learning is undoubtedly of some importance, especially when a person is just beginning a job, other factors change over time in a direction that implies a decrease in workers' capacity for their assignments. Most importantly, during periods of rapid technological change, skills workers acquired during the formal education process may soon become obsolete. Skill obsolescence creates the largest problems for those in technical fields; for instance, revisions in college engineering curricula since the 1950s have given increasing emphasis to basic science and mathematics, which appears to have greatly reduced the "half-life" of an engineering education.[25] Similarly, the recent emphasis on quantitative techniques has most likely caused the business training of many older managers to become substantially obsolete.

A second factor that can be expected to affect performance is the stimulation (or lack of it) offered by an assignment. While learning most likely occurs with doing (at least for a short period of time), boredom is apt to set in eventually. Thus, the passage of time can come to have a negative effect on productivity, mediated by what might be called "on-the-job sensory deprivation."[26]

Motivation is a final potential determinant of within-grade-level performance that is also, most likely, a function of time. Within a grade level, workers with greater than average experience are relatively behind their cohort in terms of movement up the corporate hierarchy. Hence, within a grade level, workers with more experience are likely to have a stronger feeling that they are not on their company's fast track or on any track at all and thus become discouraged. This can lead to a reduction in effort expended on the job, especially since companies appear to avoid discharges (at least among those who are not new hires), demotions, and substantial cuts in relative salaries, fear of which might give employees an incentive to avoid slackening off. Dalton and Thompson [1971, p. 63] observed that the effort of the engineers they studied seemed to decline with age and offered the following explanation of the phenomenon:

> An older engineer often views the future with pessimism. He expects little positive reward, even if he does put forth greater effort.

Further, it has been claimed that older employees value promotions less highly than do younger employees.[27] This suggests that age can be expected to reduce the effort employees expend in trying to advance.

25. See Kaufman [1974].

26. For a discussion of the extensive literature on the importance of boredom in industrial settings, see Maier [1973]. While most of the relevant studies have focused primarily on production jobs, there is no reason why boredom should not have an effect on those who remain in a given nonproduction assignment. Indeed, Kaufman [June 1974, p. 379] argues that, "Although the emphasis on such techniques as job enrichment in recent years has focused mainly on nonprofessional employees, it is the professionals in the organization who are likely to be most affected by the intrinsic motivation of their work."

27. The issue of what rewards are most valued by different groups of employees has received a great deal of attention from industrial psychologists. The study by Hall and Mansfield [1975] lends support to the argument that older workers care less about promotions than younger workers. Their paper also contains references to earlier studies that reached similar conclusions.

Thus, even if obsolescence and encroaching boredom were not a problem for older workers in a job, motivational considerations could explain why, within grade levels, relative performance might not increase with experience. Next, we must address the more difficult question of why within-grade-level earnings do increase with experience.

Why Might Relative Earnings Increase with Experience Even If Relative Productivity Does Not?

At this point in time, neither we nor, to the best of our knowledge, anyone else can provide direct evidence in support of a new interpretation of the experience-earnings relationship; our findings demonstrate only that productivity-augmenting on-the-job training should play a substantially smaller role in any new explanation than it does under human capital theory. Moreover, since we feel that, to be of value, any new interpretation must have an empirical basis, all we wish to do at present is to suggest several alternatives whose validity must be assessed through the collection and analysis of additional information on the origins and functioning of firms' compensation policies.

First, for any of a variety of reasons, employees and employers may enter into implicit contracts that provide for relative earnings growth unrelated to changes in relative productivity over the course of a worker's tenure with the firm.[28] One reason for both firms and workers to prefer such a pay scheme is that deferring part of workers' compensation may deter quitting or behavior that would lead to discharge, increasing the expected present value of each employee's net contribution to the firm and (assuming competition) increasing the expected present value of each employee's lifetime compensation.[29] Moreover, the regular receipt of raises may improve workers' morale, which may in turn increase their productivity and present value of lifetime compensation. Alternatively, steep wage profiles might serve as a self-selection device. For example, workers with high innate quit propensities might be less likely to come to work for a firm that underpaid people at the start of their work lives and made up the difference later on.[30] A different rationale for implicit contracts providing that at least some workers be paid less than they produce

28. For discussion of another type of implicit contract, see Baily [1974] and Azariadis [1975].

29. One implicit contract model that offers a cheating deterrence story is developed in Lazear [1979].

30. See Salop and Salop [1976] for a formal development of this argument.

when young and more than they produce when old might rest on workers being risk-averse and owners of firms being risk-neutral. Not knowing at the beginning of their work lives whether their productivity would grow rapidly or slowly, workers might want a pay scheme that guaranteed annual pay increases of a certain amount independent of whether they turned out to be high-productivity or low-productivity employees. Still another possibility is that workers might prefer deferred compensation if the rate of return on assets the firm can earn exceeds the rate of return on assets accessible to the employee.

While all of the preceding seem at least on the surface to be plausible hypotheses, so far as we know none has any empirical basis. Furthermore, under implicit wage agreements of the sort discussed above, the firm could increase current profits by violating its pledge to pay long-service employees more than their productive value. Thus, some enforcement mechanism must be introduced. One potential *deus ex machina* is the firm's reputation (among present employees, future employees, and the society at large), which is a determinant of its long-run profitability. Whether or not such a mechanism exists is an open question.[31]

A second issue that merits consideration as a factor in the divergence between the earnings and performance of senior employees involves the relationship between a superior and subordinate. It is likely that the disutility from firing or reducing the relative salary of a long-time subordinate employee conditions a supervisor's decisions. This is just an extension of the point that factors other than profits are likely to enter the utility function of a manager.

A third issue which deserves mention is that workers have beliefs concerning "just" relative compensation. These beliefs could stem from certain societal values (e.g., "elders should be respected") and could be quite strong. Thus, a compensation policy which pays each employee his or her value of marginal product at each point in time may not be the policy that would be chosen by the marginal or average employee in the firm.

Each of these points is a member of a larger set that share the realization that individuals are quite likely to prefer a compensation policy which does not relate relative wages only to relative productivity. If any of the points is valid, long-run profit maximization need not imply that when an employee's relative earnings are increasing, the worker's relative performance could not be constant or decreasing. Thus, it is not true that the divergence of experience-earnings and

31. For an empirical analysis of this issue, see Medoff and Abraham [April 1980].

experience-performance profiles must be inconsistent with the tenets of competitive theory. However, whether it is or is not remains to be demonstrated.

V. Conclusion

This study has provided direct evidence concerning the relationship between experience and performance among managerial and professional employees doing similar work at two major U. S. corporations. The facts presented indicate that while, within grade levels, there is a strong positive association between experience and relative earnings, there is either no association or a negative association between experience and relative performance. Since the fraction of the experience-earnings relationship that occurs within grade levels is substantial, at a minimum a substantial portion of this relationship cannot be explained by the human capital model of productivity-augmenting on-the-job training.

An explanation of why in U. S. corporations more experienced workers doing a given job receive higher salaries than their less experienced, but no less productive, peers remains to be documented. At present, there are a number of theories that have been offered as consistent with our findings, but each of them suffers the same deficiency as the human capital theory about the experience-earnings profile: absence of an empirical basis. Nevertheless, we are confident that through future explorations within firms guided by those who administer and those who are affected by corporate compensation policies, the requisite evidence can be obtained. This will represent an important step toward an empirically based interpretation of experience-earnings differentials in particular and earnings differentials in general.

Harvard University
Massachusetts Institute of Technology

References

Azariadis, Costas, "Implicit Contracts and Underemployment Equilibria," *Journal of Political Economy,* LXXXIII, No. 6 (Dec. 1975), 1183–1202.

Baily, Martin, "Wages and Employment Under Uncertain Demand," *Review of Economic Studies,* XLI, No. 125 (Jan. 1974), 37–50.

Barrett, Richard S., *Performance Rating* (Chicago: Science Research Associates, Inc., 1966).

Bass, Bernard M., and Gerald V. Barrett, *Man, Work and Organizations: An Introduction to Industrial and Organizational Psychology* (Boston: Allyn and Bacon, Inc., 1972).

Becker, Gary S., *Human Capital: A Theoretical and Empirical Analysis with Special Reference to Education* (New York: National Bureau of Economic Research, 1964).

Borman, Walter C., "Effect of Instructions to Avoid Halo Error on Reliability and Validity of Performance Evaluation Ratings," *Journal of Applied Psychology,* LX, No. 5 (Oct. 1975), 556–60.

Dalton, Gene W., and Paul H. Thompson, "Accelerating Obsolescence of Older Engineers," *Harvard Business Review,* XLIX, No. 5 (Sept.–Oct. 1971), 57–67.

Ferguson, Leonard W., "The Value of Acquaintance Ratings in Criterion Research," *Personnel Psychology,* II, No. 1 (Spring 1949), 93–102.

Hall, Douglas T., and Roger Mansfield, "Relationships of Age and Seniority with Career Variables of Engineers and Scientists," *Journal of Applied Psychology,* LX, No. 2 (April 1975), 201–10.

Kaufman, H. G., *Obsolescence and Professional Career Development* (New York: Amacon, 1974).

——, "Relationship of Early Work Challenge to Job Performance, Professional Contributions, and Competence of Engineers," *Journal of Applied Psychology,* LIX, No. 3 (June 1974), 377–79.

Landy, Frank J., and Don A. Trumbo, *Psychology of Work Behavior* (Homewood, IL: The Dorsey Press, 1976).

Lawler, Edward E., "The Multitrait-Multirater Approach to Measuring Managerial Job Performance," *Journal of Applied Psychology,* LI, No. 5 (Oct. 1967), 369–81.

Lazear, Edward P., "Why Is There Mandatory Retirement?" *Journal of Political Economy,* LXXXVII, No. 6 (Dec. 1979), 1261–84.

Maier, Norman R. F., *Psychology in Industrial Organizations* (Boston: Houghton Mifflin Company, 1973).

McCormick, Ernest J., and Joseph Tiffin, *Industrial Psychology* (Englewood Cliffs, NJ: Prentice-Hall, Inc., 1974).

Medoff, James L., "The Earnings Function: A Glimpse Inside the Black Box," mimeographed, Dec. 1977.

——, and Katharine G. Abraham, "Are Those Paid More Really More Productive?: The Case of Experience," *Journal of Human Resources,* forthcoming.

——, and ——, "Involuntary Terminations under Explicit, Implicit, and No Employment Contracts," mimeographed, April 1980.

Mincer, Jacob, *Schooling, Experience, and Earnings* (New York: National Bureau of Economic Research, 1974).

Nerlove, Marc, and S. James Press, *Univariate and Multivariate Log-Linear and Logistic Models* (Santa Monica, CA: The Rand Corporation, 1973).

Rothe, H. F., "The Relation of Merit Ratings to Length of Service," *Personnel Psychology,* II, No. 2 (Summer 1949), 237–42.

Rundquist, E. A., and R. H. Bittner, "Using Ratings to Validate Personnel Instruments: A Study in Method," *Personnel Psychology,* I, No. 2 (Summer 1948), 163–84.

Salop, Joanne, and Steven Salop, "Self-Selection and Turnover in the Labor Market," this *Journal,* XC, No. 4 (Nov. 1976), 619–27.

Stockford, Lee, and H. W. Bissell, "Factors Involved in Establishing a Merit-Rating Scale," *Personnel,* XXVI, No. 2 (Sept. 1949), 94–116.

Whitlock, Gerald H., "Application of the Psychophysical Law to Performance Evaluation," *Journal of Applied Psychology,* XXXXVII, No. 1 (Feb. 1963), 15–23.

TECHNOLOGY TRANSFER TO OVERSEAS SUBSIDIARIES BY U. S.-BASED FIRMS*

EDWIN MANSFIELD AND ANTHONY ROMEO

Although economists and policy makers have devoted considerable attention to the transfer of technology by U. S.-based multinational firms to their overseas subsidiaries, very little is known about the nature of the technology that is being transferred overseas in this way, the extent to which it leaks out to non-U. S. competitors, the size of the benefits it confers on the host (and other non-U. S.) countries, and the sorts of non-U. S. firms that receive the largest benefits of this sort. This paper presents findings that shed new light on each of these topics.

I. INTRODUCTION

In recent years, there has been considerable controversy over the transfer of technology by U. S.-based multinational firms to their overseas subsidiaries.[1] Some groups in the United States, feeling that the apparent narrowing of the American technological lead is due in part to such transfers, argue that the technological activities of such firms should be subjected to various new kinds of regulations. Other groups deny that such measures are necessary or desirable. In the countries where the subsidiaries are located, there is sometimes a feeling that the terms on which the transfers occur are inequitable, and that there are dangers in becoming too dependent on outside technology. Despite the enormous amount of attention that has been devoted to this topic, very little is known about the nature of the technology that is being transferred overseas in this way, the extent to which it leaks out to non-U. S. competitors, the size of the benefits it confers on the host (and other non-U. S.) countries, and the sorts of non-U. S. firms that receive the largest benefits of this sort.[2] Our purpose in this paper is to present some findings that shed new light on each of these matters.

* The work on which this paper is based was supported by a grant to Mansfield by the National Science Foundation. Of course, the Foundation is not responsible for the views expressed here. We are grateful for this support, as well as for the cooperation of the many firms in the United States and the United Kingdom that provided us with data. We are also grateful for the comments of Richard Caves, Rolf Piekarz, and Arthur Bloomfield on an earlier draft.

1. For discussions of these controversies, see Biemiller [1971], Caves [1974a], Hufbauer [1974], and Mansfield [1974, 1978]. For present purposes, overseas is defined as outside the United States. (Thus, Canada is "overseas.")

2. For an evaluation of the current state of the art in this area, see Caves [1974a], Hufbauer [1974], and Mansfield [1974, 1978, 1980]. Relevant material is also contained in Baranson [1970, 1976] and Mansfield *et al.* [1977, 1979a, 1979b, 1979c].

The Quarterly Journal of Economics, December 1980 0033-5533/80/0095-0737$01.40

II. Age of Technology Transferred Overseas

Some observers in the United States are concerned that many U. S.-based firms may be transferring their most modern technology overseas. In their view, such a procedure is dangerous because it increases the likelihood that this technology will fall into the hands of non-U. S. firms that will use it to compete more effectively with the U. S.-based firms. Although Baranson [1976] has presented some case studies that suggest that U. S.-based firms are becoming more willing than in the past to transfer their newest technology overseas, there is very little published information on this score. To help fill this gap, we obtained information concerning the age of the technology transferred in a sample of sixty-five cases.

To obtain these cases, we chose a carefully selected sample of thirty-one U. S.-based firms. Twenty-six of these firms were chosen essentially at random from the largest 500 manufacturing firms; two were chosen from the second largest 500 manufacturing firms, and three were chosen from those not in the 1,000 largest manufacturing firms. Once this sample was chosen, one or more of the technologies that each firm had transferred overseas during 1960 to 1978 were selected,[3] also essentially at random. Interviews were carried out with senior executives of each firm, and the firm's internal records were used to determine the year when each technology was first introduced in the United States. The number of years that elapsed between the time when the technology was first introduced in the United States and the year when it was transferred overseas is used as a measure of the age of the technology when it was transferred.

As shown in Table I, the mean age of the technologies transferred to overseas subsidiaries in developed countries was about six years, which was significantly less than the mean age of the technologies transferred to overseas subsidiaries in developing countries (about ten years). This difference is not surprising. Because many newer technologies are inappropriate for developing countries, or are difficult and expensive to transfer there, we would expect the technology transferred to developing countries to be older than that transferred to developed countries. Table I also suggests that the mean age of the technologies transferred through licenses, joint ventures, and channels

3. The sample covers a wide variety of industries, including chemicals, drugs, petroleum, electrical equipment and electronics, machinery, instruments, glass, food and rubber. The number of firms in the sample is divided between the largest 500 firms and the second largest 500 firms in proportion to the total sales in each group. The number of cases obtained from each firm did not vary greatly, and averaged about two. One technology was transferred overseas before 1960.

TABLE I

MEAN AND STANDARD DEVIATION OF NUMBER OF YEARS BETWEEN TECHNOLOGY'S TRANSFER OVERSEAS AND ITS INITIAL INTRODUCTION IN THE UNITED STATES, 65 TECHNOLOGIES

Channel of technology transfer	Mean (years)	Standard deviation (years)	Number of cases
Overseas subsidiary in developed country	5.8	5.5	27
Overseas subsidiary in developing country	9.8	8.4	12
Licensing or joint venture	13.1	13.4	26

other than subsidiaries tends to be higher than the mean age of the technologies transferred to subsidiaries. This is consistent with the finding in Mansfield, Romeo, and Wagner [1979] that firms tend to transfer their newest technology overseas through subsidiaries rather than licensing or joint ventures, but that the latter channels become more important as the technology gets older.[4]

Are the recently transferred technologies newer than those transferred a number of years ago? To find out, we used χ^2 tests to see whether the proportion of transferred technologies that were less than five years old (at the time of transfer) was greater during 1969–1978 than during 1960–1968.[5] For technologies transferred to subsidiaries in developed countries, this was the case, and the increase in this proportion (from 27 percent in 1960–1968 to 75 percent in 1969–1978) was both large and statistically significant. But for technologies transferred to subsidiaries in developing countries or for those transferred through channels other than subsidiaries, there appeared to be no such tendency, at least in this sample. The fact that the technologies licensed to, or jointly exploited with, non-U. S. firms were

4. Based on a t-test, the mean age of the technologies transferred to subsidiaries in developed countries is significantly smaller (at the 0.05 significance level) than the mean age of the technologies transferred to subsidiaries in developing countries. The standard deviation of the ages of the technologies transferred through licensing and joint ventures is significantly greater (at the 0.05 significance level) than that of the ages of the technologies transferred to subsidiaries in developed countries. Thus, the Aspin-Welch or Dixon-Massey test had to be used to test whether the mean age of the technologies transferred to subsidiaries in developed countries is less than the mean age of technologies transferred through licensing and joint ventures. Both tests indicate that this difference is significant at the 0.05 level, which is used throughout this paper.

5. More accurately, this test is carried out for technologies transferred to subsidiaries in developed countries. For technologies transferred to subsidiaries in developing countries, and for technologies transferred through licensing and joint ventures, the observed difference in the proportion is not in accord with this hypothesis, so there is no need for such a test.

no newer in 1969–1978 than in 1960–1968 is worth noting, since some observers worry that U. S. firms may have come to share in this way more and more of their newest technologies with foreigners.[6]

III. Leakage of Technology and Competitive Response by Non-U. S. Firms

As noted above, another major concern of some observers is that the transfer of technology to overseas subsidiaries will hasten the time when non-U. S. producers have access to this technology. Yet no systematic studies have been carried out to determine how rapidly such technology "leaks out" and the extent to which such transfers actually hasten its leaking out. To help fill this void, we obtained estimates of this sort for twenty-six technologies chosen essentially at random from those included in the previous section (which were transferred to subsidiaries).[7] In each case, the U. S.-based firm estimated how soon (after it was transferred) the technology became known to one or more of its non-U. S. competitors. Although it is frequently difficult for firms to make very precise estimates of this sort (since they do not know exactly when their competitors acquire the relevant information), these firms (with all the benefits of hindsight) felt that they could provide reasonably reliable estimates, based on direct knowledge concerning their competitors' information-gathering activities, as well as on data regarding the time when their competitors set in motion relevant investment projects and introduced imitative products or processes. For present purposes, these estimates should be quite adequate.

The results, shown in Table II, indicate that the mean lag between the technology transfer and the time when some non-U. S. competitor had access to the technology was about four years.[8]

6. Davidson and Harrigan [1977] have presented valuable evidence concerning the age of technologies transferred abroad by U. S.-based firms, at the time when they were first transferred abroad. Their results, like ours, suggest that the average age of technology transferred abroad has declined. Note that our data do not pertain only to the initial transfer abroad of a technology.

7. Fifteen firms are included. The technologies span a wide range of American industry, including chemicals, drugs, petroleum, machinery, food, and rubber.

8. One of the simplest models that might be used to represent this leakage process is that the probability of a technology's leaking out between time t and time $t + \Delta$ is proportional to Δ and independent of t. In other words, the Poisson process might be used as a simple model. If this model is applicable, the length of time before a technology leaks out has an exponential probability distribution. In fact, the observed distribution is not very different from such an exponential distribution, but the sample is too small to carry out a goodness-of-fit test. One assumption of this model is that the probability of a technology's leaking out to non-U. S. competitors is zero until it is transferred. This need not be the case, although none of the technologies in our sample leaked out before they were transferred. It is easy to relax this assumption. We are not saying that a model of this sort is the appropriate one; all we are proposing is that it is an interesting hypothesis to test, at least for some kinds of technologies.

TABLE II

NUMBER OF YEARS BETWEEN TECHNOLOGY TRANSFER AND THE TIME WHEN THE TECHNOLOGY BECAME KNOWN TO SOME NON-U. S. COMPETITOR, 26 TECHNOLOGIES

Number of years	Number of technology transfers[a]
Zero and under 0.5	4
0.5 and under 1.5	7
1.5 and under 4.5	5
4.5 and under 6.5	4
6.5 and over	6

a. In some cases, the technology had not become known to non-U. S. competitors at the time the data were collected; thus, we only have lower bounds on the relevant time interval. In these cases, we assume in this table that they would be divided among the class intervals above this lower bound in proportion to the number of cases in each of the relevant class intervals. This assumption is innocuous and is not made in the analysis of the data. See note 10.

However, because non-U. S. firms gained access to many of these technologies relatively soon after they were transferred, one cannot conclude that the transfer of the technology hastened its spread. Even if the technology had not been transferred to an overseas subsidiary, it might have leaked out about as quickly. According to executives of the firms in the sample, in most cases the technology transfer had little or no effect on how quickly the technologies leaked out. However, in about one-fourth of the cases, they felt that the technology transfer probably hastened foreigners' access to these technologies by at least two and one half years. Based on their estimates, there is no indication that the average effect has been greater in one industry than in another, but there is an indication that the transfer of a process technology tends to hasten its spread to a greater degree than does the transfer of a product technology.[9]

To test some of these propositions, we carried out a χ^2 test to determine whether the lag between the time when a technology was first used in the United States and the time when non-U. S. competitors had access to it was affected by how soon after its first use in the United States it was transferred to an overseas subsidiary. The results

9. On the average, according to the executives, these technology transfers hastened non-U. S. competitors' access to the technology by 3.1 years for processes and by 0.4 years for products. Using the Dixon-Massey test, which does not assume that the standard deviations are equal (but does assume normality), this difference is statistically significant. There is no contradiction between the assumption of normality here and the simple model in note 8 (or between the assumption and the data). Whereas we were concerned in note 8 with how rapidly the technology leaked out, here we are concerned with how it leaked out much more quickly because of its being transferred to an overseas subsidiary. Moreover, the simple model in note 8 would be expected to hold for only certain kinds of technologies.

indicate that the latter variable has no statistically significant effect on the lag. Thus, our data seem to bear out the opinions of the firms that, while their transfer to an overseas subsidiary may have hastened substantially the spread of a relatively small number of these technologies, it had little or no impact on the spread of most of them.[10]

The most frequent channel by which the technology "leaked out" was reverse engineering, according to the firms. That is, non-U. S. competitors took apart and analyzed the new or modified product to gain insights into the relevant technology. Also, information provided by patents was judged to play a significant role; and non-U. S. firms sometimes gained access to the technology by hiring away personnel employed by the subsidiary. As pointed out above, non-U. S. firms frequently could have obtained the technology in these or other ways if the transfer had not occurred. (For example, in some cases, they might have hired away personnel employed by U. S. firms, or they might have obtained the technology from the United States or another source in other ways.) However, in those cases where the technology transfer hastened their access to the technology, they often would not have been stimulated to do so, either because they would not have been aware of the technology's existence, or because they would not have felt it was profitable to try to obtain the technology in these ways.[11]

Richard Caves [1974a] has pointed out that "Most of our knowledge about transfers of technology through the multinational firm is anecdotal and incomplete. What has been the experience of foreign subsidiaries of U. S. firms with the successful imitation of their technologies by foreign competitors [pp. 37–38]?" To help answer this question, each firm in our sample estimated the effect of the technology transfer on how rapidly each of its products or processes based on the technologies in the sample was imitated. As would be expected on the basis of this section's previous results, it appears that in most cases there was little or no effect. However, in about one-third of the cases, the product or process was imitated at least two and one-half years earlier than the firms would have expected if the technology had

10. The technologies in the sample were divided into two groups, depending on whether or not they were transferred to an overseas subsidiary within five years of their first use in the United States. They were also divided into two groups, depending on whether or not they became known to some non-U. S. competitor within eight years after their first use in the United States. The value of χ^2 for the resulting 2×2 contingency table (after Yates's correction was applied) was 1.65, which is far from statistically significant. This result indicates that the relationship between these two factors is not very strong.

11. It is worth adding that the non-U. S. competitors that have gained access to the technology often are not headquartered in the country where the overseas subsidiary is located. In this sample, they were headquartered most often in West Germany.

TABLE III

ESTIMATED EFFECT OF TECHNOLOGY TRANSFER ON HOW SOON THE FIRST NON-U. S. COMPETITOR INTRODUCED A COMPETING PRODUCT OR PROCESS, 25 TRANSFERS OF TECHNOLOGY[a]

Acceleration in introduction of competing product or process (years)	Number of technology transfers
Zero and under 0.5	12
0.5 and under 2.5	4
2.5 and under 5.5	7
5.5 and under 10.5	1
10.5 and over	1

a. Data on this score could not be obtained for one technology in the sample; thus, the total number included here is 25.

not been transferred to the overseas subsidiary (Table III). Once again, there is an indication that this effect tended to be greater for processes than for products.

IV. BENEFITS TO NON-U. S. USERS AND SUPPLIERS

As Caves [1974b] and others have pointed out, the transfer of technology by U. S.-based firms to their overseas subsidiaries may result in considerable benefits to the host (and other) countries. Yet despite the importance of measuring the size of these benefits, practically no quantitative information is available on the score.[12] In this section we present some rough estimates of this sort.

The transferred technology can have benefits of various sorts. One type of benefit is a reduction of the costs of non-U. S. *users* of the products or processes based on the transferred technology. For each technology in our sample (described in Section III), data provided by the U. S.-based firm were employed to estimate how much non-U. S. users of the goods produced with, or based on, this technology saved as a result of the technology transfer. These savings measure the cost reductions to non-U. S. users of these goods over and above what would have occurred if the technology had not been transferred (but the relevant technology and goods were perhaps available from the United States or elsewhere). They include savings due to on-the-spot training of users in the utilization of products and processes based on the technology, on-the-spot provision of complementary tech-

12. However, there have been a number of interesting and important studies, notably Brash [1966], Caves [1974b], and Safarian [1966].

nology to users, and lower costs of producing and distributing the goods based on the technology, among other things. Estimates were made for each year subsequent to the transfer of the technology. Since only those savings that could be quantified with reasonable accuracy are included, the estimates are almost certainly conservative. For almost 80 percent of the technologies, savings of this sort occurred; the mean discounted saving (for the twenty-four technologies for which data are available) was about $13 million.[13]

Another way that the transferred technology can benefit non-U. S. economies is by cutting the costs of non-U. S. firms that *supply* inputs used to produce the product or process based on the transferred technology. For each technology in our sample, data provided by the U. S.-based firm were employed to estimate how much non-U. S. suppliers saved each year as a result of the technology transfer. Such savings often resulted from training programs and the transfer to suppliers of know-how that reduced the cost of producing components or other inputs used by the subsidiary in applying the transferred technology. As would be expected, savings to suppliers occurred less frequently than savings to users. For about 40 percent of the technologies, savings of this sort accrued to suppliers, the mean discounted saving (for all twenty-four technologies for which data are available) being about $4 million.[14] These estimates, like those in the previous paragraph, are almost certainly conservative, since only those savings that could be documented and quantified with reasonable accuracy are included.

How large have been the total resource savings per year to non-U. S. users and suppliers due to technology transfer of this sort by the firms in our sample? To obtain a rough lower bound on this amount, we calculated the annual cost reduction (to users and suppliers combined) resulting from each of the jth firm's technology transfers in the sample. For the ith technology transfer by the jth firm, this

13. Throughout this section, when we estimate the savings due to each technology transfer, the comparison is with the costs of the users or suppliers if the transfer had not taken place. In many cases, if the transfer had not occurred, the technology could have been licensed from the U. S.-based firm or provided by other sources, or a different technology could have been used. The discount rate used here (and throughout this section) is 10 percent. Exchange rates were used to convert the savings into U. S. dollars. In five of the cases, the discounted savings to users were zero; in seven cases, they were positive but less than $1 million; in eleven cases, they were between $1 million and $100 million; and in one case, they were over $100 million.

14. In fourteen of the twenty-four cases, the discounted savings to suppliers were zero; in three cases they were positive but less than $1 million; and in seven cases, they were between $1 million and $100 million.

Whether or not the technology transfer resulted in cost reductions to non-U. S. users or suppliers, it may have provided them with significant new information or new production capabilities. According to the U. S.-based firms, significant information of this sort was transmitted to non-U. S. users in about two-thirds of the cases and to non-U. S. suppliers in about one-third of the cases.

annual savings is denoted by c_{ij}, and the number of years this saving continues is denoted by t_{ij}. Then we obtained an estimate from each firm in our sample of the annual number of technology transfers (during 1968–1977) that resulted in total savings to non-U. S. users and suppliers that were at least as large as those resulting from the average technology transfer of this firm included in our sample; the result for the jth firm is denoted by N_j. In a steady-state condition where N_j technology transfers of this sort occur each year in the jth firm, a lower bound on the total savings per year to non-U. S. users and suppliers due to this firm's technology transfer is

$$g_j = \frac{N_j}{m_j} \sum_{i=1}^{m_j} c_{ij} t_{ij}, \tag{1}$$

where m_j is the number of technology transfers by the jth firm included in the sample.[15] Inserting estimates of c_{ij}, N_j, and t_{ij} obtained from these firms into this equation, we find that the sum of g_j for the firms in our sample is about $633 million per year.

Based on this sample, a firm's value of g_j seems, on the average, to be (approximately) proportional to the total annual sales of its overseas subsidiaries, which, of course, is not surprising. If this sample of firms is representative, a lower bound for the total annual savings to non-U. S. users and suppliers due to all technology transfer of this sort by U. S.-based firms can be obtained by dividing $633 million by the proportion of all annual sales of U. S. firms' overseas subsidiaries accounted for by the firms in our sample. The result is approximately $35 billion, or about 1 percent of the total annual output of countries outside the United States.[16] Because it is based on a relatively small

15. The total saving in a particular year (say year T) is equal to the sum of the savings due to each of the technology transfers that still have an effect in year T. Consider a steady-state situation where m_j transfers (with the values of c_{ij} and t_{ij} in the sample) occur each year. For simplicity, assume that t_{ij} always assumes integer values of 1 or more. The total savings in year T due to transfers in year T equals $\sum_{i=1}^{m_j} c_{ij}$, since t_{ij} in all cases is at least 1; the total saving in year T due to transfers in year $T-1$ equals the sum of the c_{ij} for transfers where t_{ij} is 2 or more; the total saving in year T due to transfers in year $T-2$ equals the sum of the c_{ij} for transfers where t_{ij} is 3 or more; and so on. Thus, the total saving in year T due to *all* transfers equals $\sum_{i=1}^{m_j} c_{ij} t_{ij}$. If N_j, rather than m_j, transfers occur per year (but if the values of c_{ij} and t_{ij} remain the same), the total saving in year T would be

$$\frac{N_j}{m_j} \sum_{i=1}^{m_j} c_{ij} t_{ij}.$$

Based on the past history and performance of these firms, the assumption of a steady-state situation of this sort does not seem unrealistic.

16. When g_j is regressed on the jth firm's 1976 sales of its overseas subsidiaries, the slope, but not the constant, of the regression equation is statistically significant.

Based on Kravis, Heston, and Summers [1978], the 1970 aggregate gross domestic product (in noncentrally-planned economies) outside the United States was about $2.4 trillion. Obviously, this figure is crude, but sufficient for present purposes. The figure of 1 percent is obtained by dividing $35 billion by $2.4 trillion.

sample, this result should be treated with a great deal of caution. Moreover, it should be stressed once more that this is a lower bound.[17]

V. Effects on Technological Capabilities and Innovative Performance of British Firms

When U. S.-based firms transfer technology to overseas subsidiaries, there is likely to be an impact on many firms in the host countries (and elsewhere). But very little is known about the kinds of non-U. S. firms that are most affected. To obtain some information on this score, we focused attention on the United Kingdom, the country (outside North America) where direct investment by U. S.-based firms has been greatest. Seventy of the largest firms in the United Kingdom provided an assessment of the extent to which their technological capabilities during 1968–1977 were affected by technological transfers by U. S.-based firms to their overseas subsidiaries. This information was obtained largely through correspondence and interviews.[18] Although we recognize that such assessments may be biased, we feel that the results are of interest.

About two-thirds of these firms felt that their technological capabilities during this period were raised (to some extent at least) by technology transfers of this sort. But only 20 percent felt that this effect was of importance.[19] The proportion regarding it as important was higher in the electrical equipment (including electronics and computers) and general engineering industries than in the others. Technology transfers of this sort seem to have had some effect on the innovative activities of most of these British firms. As shown in Table IV, over half of these firms felt that at least some of their products and processes had been introduced, or introduced more quickly, because

17. Also, these estimates pertain only to the effects on users and suppliers, which are not the only affected parties.

18. The sample of seventy firms was selected from *Jane's Major Companies of Europe*. It included a wide variety of manufacturing industries: chemicals, electrical equipment (including electronics and computers), transportation equipment, general engineering, paper, textiles, food, commodities, building materials, construction, metals, oil and gas, beer, wine, and spirits, and alcohol. Each firm filled out a questionnaire concerning this topic; then interviews were carried out with the managing director (or other major official) of a subsample of these firms. Also, interviews were carried out with officials of overseas subsidiaries of U. S. firms.

19. Initially the firms were permitted to use whatever definition of "important" that they regarded as appropriate. Then they were asked to specify what they meant by this term. Based on the replies, it appears that they generally regarded any benefit that enhanced profits by 1 percent or more as important. Thus, their definition seemed rather liberal. There is no evidence of substantial differences among firms in the definition used.

TABLE IV

PERCENT OF FIRM'S NEW PRODUCTS AND PROCESSES INTRODUCED (OR INTRODUCED MORE QUICKLY) BECAUSE OF THE TRANSFER OF TECHNOLOGY BY A U. S.-BASED FIRM TO AN OVERSEAS SUBSIDIARY, 68 BRITISH FIRMS, 1968–1977

Percent of new products	Number of firms	Percent of new processes	Number of firms
Zero	30	Zero	32
0.1 to 4	28	0.1 to 4	29
5 to 9	8	5 to 9	5
10 to 25	2	10 to 25	2
More than 25	0	More than 25	0
Total[a]	68		68

a. Data on this score could not be obtained from two firms in the sample; thus, the total number included here is 68.

of the transfer of a new product or process by a U. S.-based firm to an overseas subsidiary. But only 10 to 15 percent of these firms felt that 5 percent or more of their new products or new processes were affected in this way. The percent of a firm's new products or processes influenced in this way tended to be larger in the electrical equipment (including electronics and computers) and oil and gas industries than in the others.

These data, despite their obvious imperfections, enable us to test for the first time two hypotheses that are often encountered in this area. The first hypothesis, put forth by Caves [1974b] and others, is that non-U. S. firms in industries where subsidiaries of U. S. firms account for a large share of the local market are affected more by this kind of technology transfer than are non-U. S. firms in industries where such subsidiaries account for a small share of the local market.[20] This hypothesis is by no means trivial, since the amount and importance of technology transferred from the U. S. to the local market may bear little or no relationship to the subsidiaries' share of the local market. The second hypothesis stems from work at OECD and elsewhere which indicates that the U. S. technological lead has tended to be greater in relatively R & D-intensive industries than in others. This hypothesis states that, if the share of the local market held by the subsidiaries of U. S. firms is held constant, the impact tends to be greater on non-U. S. firms in industries where a relatively large

20. Caves [1974b] put forth this hypothesis in connection with Australia and Canada, but it seems applicable to the United Kingdom as well.

TABLE V

REGRESSION COEFFICIENTS OF M_i, R_i, π_i, AND S_i

Dependent variable[a]	Independent variable[b]			
	M_i	R_i	π_i	S_i
p_i	1.051	0.0282	−0.0486	0.000113
	(1.06)	(1.13)	(2.16)	(1.72)
u_i	2.160	0.0773	−0.0177	0.0000296
	(2.44)	(3.46)	(0.88)	(0.50)
v_i	17.62	0.121	−0.0966	0.0000180
	(2.65)	(0.71)	(0.64)	(0.04)
w_i	22.59	0.0893	−0.0392	0.0000813
	(3.67)	(0.57)	(0.28)	(0.20)

a. The definitions of the dependent variables are as follows: p_i equals 1 if the ith firm indicated it received benefits from technology transfer due to purchases from subsidiaries of U. S. firms and zero otherwise; u_i equals 1 if the ith firm indicated it received benefits from technology transfer due to its supply of goods and services to subsidiaries of U. S. firms and zero otherwise; v_i is the percentage of the ith firm's new products that were introduced (or introduced more quickly) because of the transfer of technology by U. S. firms to their overseas subsidiaries; and w_i is the percentage of the ith firm's new processes that were introduced (or introduced more quickly) because of the transfer of technology by U. S. firms to their overseas subsidiaries.

When p_i is the dependent variable, $\bar{R}^2$ is 0.30; when u_i is the dependent variable, it is 0.46; when v_i is the dependent variable, it is 0.46; and when w_i is the dependent variable, it is 0.49.

b. The definitions of the independent variables are as follows: M_i is the proportion of assets in the ith firm's industry held by subsidiaries of U. S. firms; R_i is the percent of sales spent on research and development by the ith firm's industry; π_i is the profit (as a percent of sales) of the ith firm; and S_i is the sales (in millions of pounds) of the ith firm. Besides these independent variables, dummy variables were included to allow the intercept to vary from one broad industry group to another. For details, see note 21. The t-statistics are shown in parentheses under the regression coefficients.

percentage of sales is spent on research and development than in industries where a relatively small percentage of sales is spent for this purpose.

Each of the dependent variables described in Table V is a measure of the extent of the perceived impact on the ith British firm of technology transfer of this sort. To test these hypotheses, we regressed each of these dependent variables on the proportion of assets in the ith industry held by subsidiaries of U. S. firms (M_i) and on the percent of sales spent on research and development by the ith firm's industry (R_i). In addition, since a firm's size and profitability may be associated with its perception of the extent to which it is affected by technology transfer of this sort, we included the ith firm's sales (S_i) and its profit as a percent of sales (π_i) as additional variables in each regression. The signs of all the regression coefficients, shown in Table V, are in accord with both hypotheses, but whereas the coefficients of M_i are almost always statistically significant, this is not true of the coefficients of R_i. (Also, the perceived impact of technology transfers of this sort seems to be greater for larger firms than for smaller ones, and greater for less profitable firms than for more profitable ones, but these differences are seldom statistically significant.) Thus, these results provide much stronger support for the first than for the second hypothesis.[21]

VI. CONCLUSIONS

Despite the enormous amount of controversy over the transfer of technology by U. S.-based multinational firms, very little is known about the nature of the technology that is being transferred, the rate at which it leaks out to non-U. S. competitors, the extent to which it benefits non-U. S. users and suppliers, and the characteristics of the non-U. S. firms that are most affected by it. We believe that this paper, which seems to be one of the first systematic attempts to study these topics, has shed some new light on them. Obviously, however, it is only a beginning. We hope that future studies will go farther in whittling away at the many questions in this area that remain largely untouched.

UNIVERSITY OF PENNSYLVANIA
UNIVERSITY OF CONNECTICUT

REFERENCES

Baranson, J., "Technology Transfer Through the International Firm," *American Economic Review*, LX (May 1970), 435–40.

——, "International Transfers of Industrial Technology by U. S. Firms and Their Implications for the U. S. Economy," Report to the U. S. Department of Labor, 1976.

Biemiller, A., *Testimony on Science, Technology, and the Economy*, Subcommittee on Science, Research, and Development, House of Representatives, July 28, 1971.

Brash, D., *American Investment in Australian Industry* (Cambridge: Harvard University Press, 1966).

Caves, R., "Effect of International Technology Transfers on the U. S. Economy," in National Science Foundation, *The Effects of International Technology Transfers on U. S. Economy* (Washington, D. C.: Government Printing Office, 1974a).

——, "Multinational Firms, Competition, and Productivity in Host-Country Industries," *Economica*, XLI (May 1974b), 176–93.

Davidson, W., and R. Harrigan, "Key Decisions in International Marketing: Introducing New Products Abroad," *Columbia Journal of World Business*, XII (Winter 1977), 15–23.

21. To prevent confusion, note that we are investigating the characteristics of the firms that seem to be most affected by technology transfer of this sort. We are not asserting that these characteristics (measured by the independent variables in Table V) necessarily cause the impact to be greatest among firms possessing them. Also, note that, although there is some positive correlation between M_i and R_i, it is not high enough to bar us from estimating the regression coefficients of both variables. The data regarding S_i and π_i come from *Jane's Major Companies of Europe*. The data regarding M_i pertain to 1965 and come largely from Dunning [1970], and those regarding R_i pertain to 1969 and come from Freeman [1974].

Dunning, J., *Studies in International Investment* (London: George Allen and Unwin, 1970).
Freeman, C., *The Economics of Industrial Innovation* (London: Penguin, 1974).
Hufbauer, G., "Technology Transfers and the American Economy," in National Science Foundation, *The Effects of International Technology Transfers on U. S. Economy* (Washington, D. C.: Government Printing Office, 1974).
Kravis, I., A. Heston, and R. Summers, "Real GDP Per Capita for More than One Hundred Countries," *Economic Journal*, LXXXVIII (June 1978), 215–42.
Mansfield, E., "Technology and Technological Change," in J. Dunning, ed., *Economic Analysis and the Multinational Enterprise* (London: George Allen and Unwin, 1974).
——, "International Technology Transfer and Overseas Research and Development," *Statement to the Subcommittee on International Finance and the Subcommittee on Science, Technology, and Space*, U. S. Senate, May 16, 1978.
——, "Technology and Productivity in the United States," Conference on Postwar Changes in the American Economy, National Bureau of Economic Research, 1980.
——, A. Romeo, and S. Wagner, "Foreign Trade and U. S. Research and Development," *Review of Economics and Statistics*, LXI (Feb. 1979), 49–57.
——, D. Teece, and A. Romeo, "Overseas Research and Development by U. S.-Based Firms," *Economica*, XLVI (May 1979), 187–96.
——, J. Rapoport, A. Romeo, E. Villani, S. Wagner, and F. Husic, *The Production and Application of New Industrial Technology* (New York: W. W. Norton, 1977).
Safarian, A., *Foreign Ownership of Canadian Industry* (Toronto: McGraw-Hill, 1966).

FACTOR MARKET DYNAMICS AND THE INCIDENCE OF TAXES AND SUBSIDIES*

DANIEL S. HAMERMESH

We extend work on payroll tax incidence by recognizing that labor markets adjust slowly because of the slow adjustment of both labor demand and supply to their equilibrium values. We modify the basic model of the incidence of payroll taxes with variable factor supply to include dynamic adjustments. We find that, under reasonable assumptions about the magnitudes of the lags in adjustment, it takes several years before half of the distance to a new equilibrium in wages and employment is reached. Thus, even if payroll taxes are borne by labor in the long run, a large part of any increase in the tax will be borne by capital for some time. For purposes of policy, the effects of payroll tax increases must be analyzed as if part of their effect is on profits, regardless of the long-run distribution of the burden.

The bulk of the huge literature on tax incidence and the somewhat smaller corpus of work on the payroll tax treats factor supplies as fixed (see, e.g., Harberger [1962] and Shoven and Whalley [1972]). Thus, even though the taxes being analyzed are on factors of production, factor markets are included in only the most rudimentary fashion implicit in the assumption of a constant supply. Feldstein [1974] has constructed a model of the incidence of the payroll tax which assumes that the supply of labor is an increasing function of the wage rate and includes growth dynamics through capital accumulation. Once these steps are taken, the model must be expanded further to allow the reflection of the slow adjustment of factor supply and demand to changes in real wages. Labor-market dynamics are relatively unimportant in a model in which supply is assumed fixed because it is likely that labor demand adjusts fairly rapidly toward its long-run value. Once supply is made endogenous, though, its slow adjustment makes the inclusion of dynamics of some importance in examining the incidence of taxes.

In this study we append several equations describing labor market dynamics to the one-product, two-factor static model of tax incidence. Using the best available estimates of the lags implicit in the adjustment processes, we find that, even though payroll tax increases may eventually be borne mostly by labor, it probably takes

* Research for this paper was financed by the Office of Research and Statistics, Social Security Adminstration, under Grant No. 10-P-90313/5. Helpful comments were provided by Ronald Ehrenberg, Paul Menchik, Norman Obst, an anonymous referee, and participants in seminars at the Social Security Administration and the Ohio State University.

The Quarterly Journal of Economics, December 1980 0033-5533/80/0095-0751$01.40

several years before a majority of the tax burden is shifted.[1] The inclusion of factor-market dynamics also leads to an asymmetry in the time path of the tax burden. Actual employment must be the minimum of the amounts supplied and demanded (see Barro and Grossman [1976]). This disequilibrium means that a subsidy—equivalent to a decrease in a tax rate—can have a short-run burden substantially different from a tax increase if the time paths of notional labor demand and supply differ.

Our model implicitly assumes that any change in the payroll tax revenues is offset by equal changes in lump-sum transfers (taxes). Thus we are examining the impact of changes in a tax that affects behavior, but whose changes do not affect the budget balance (tax revenue) of the government. Though this assumption of balanced-budget (differential) incidence is rarely stated in the vast general equilibrium literature on tax incidence (from Harberger [1962] through Feldstein [1974]), it can be assumed to be implicit in those studies. (If the assumption is not made, the literature can be assumed to show only part of the behavioral effects of changes in the taxes analyzed.) Like this literature, then, our results can be assumed to represent either balanced-budget or differential incidence analysis of changes in taxes on factors.

I. Labor-Market Dynamics in the Two-Factor Model

The basic static model, nearly identical to that of Feldstein [1974], contains a production function,

$$Y = F(K,L), \tag{1}$$

assumed to be linear homogeneous, relating output Y to the inputs of capital and labor services (K and L). From this function and from the assumption of profit maximization in competitive markets, we have static demand conditions for labor and capital:

$$F_L(K,L) = w[1 + \tau], \tag{2}$$

and

$$F_K(K,L) = r. \tag{3}$$

1. Break [1974] indicates that the general consensus is that payroll taxes are mostly borne by labor in the long run. This conclusion rests mainly on the assumption that long-run labor supply elasticities to the market are very low. Though Brittain [1971] provides the main empirical support, Feldstein's [1972] criticism of the theoretical underpinnings of Brittain's work, and the empirical work of Hamermesh [1979] and others, cast some doubt upon this supposed consensus.

w is the net real wage paid by employers, τ is the payroll tax rate, and r is the user cost of capital. (The subscripts on F denote partial derivatives with respect to the subscripted argument.) The static model is closed by two factor supply equations:

$$L = L(w[1 - \tau]), \quad L' > 0; \tag{4}$$

and

$$K = K(r), \quad K' > 0. \tag{5}$$

Including $w[1 - \tau]$ as the argument in equation (4) departs from previous static models of the payroll tax; it does, though, reflect the institutional fact that the tax is assessed on both demanders and suppliers of labor. Its inclusion requires us to interpret w also as the gross wage received by employees before the half of the tax levied on them is assessed.[2] Making this assumption in (4) has no impact on the long-run incidence of changes in τ.

While the static model has proved extremely useful in analyzing comparative static, or long-run, effects of changes in the payroll tax, it tells nothing about short-run changes in tax burdens, and nothing about the dynamics of changes in incidence. In order to examine these effects, we append to (1)–(5) a set of equations describing labor-market dynamics. There are good reasons for doing so. A huge literature exists rationalizing the presence of lags in labor demand (see, e.g., Brechling [1975]). It is assumed that there exist costs of adjusting employment demand to equilibrium, and that the marginal cost of adjustment rises with increases in the magnitude of the adjustment made in a given time period. The simplest formulation is the geometric lag,

$$\dot{L}^D = \lambda_1(L^{D*} - L^D), \tag{6}$$

where the asterisk refers to the equilibrium quantity, and the superscript D denotes the quantity demanded.

Much less work has been undertaken on the dynamics of labor supply. (Heckman and Willis [1977] have noted that there is a persistence of behavior in labor supply, in that individuals whose labor supply is higher than expected in one year will show similarly high labor supply in adjacent years.) Despite this paucity of work, one can rationalize the presence of adjustment lags in several ways. First, it

2. The static model could be generalized to include different tax rates levied on employees and employers. Similarly, though our simulations of the dynamics of tax incidence are based on equal changes in tax rates on both sides of the labor market, they could be done under the assumption that these changes differ.

is very likely that there are lags in perceptions of the permanence of wage changes. Since there are fixed costs of entering the labor force, a change in wages that is perceived as transitory will not induce many individuals to enter the labor force or increase their supply of hours. Only after a wage change has persisted for some time will it be perceived as permanent and induce the long-run change in supply that is implicit in equation (4).[3] Since the rate at which individuals perceive the permanence of a change in wages differs, one can justify a distributed lag of actual behind-equilibrium-labor supply analogous to the relation in equation (6). Second, the model in equations (1)–(5) is highly aggregative. When a wage increase occurs that induces increases in the supply of labor, relative wages across occupations change at varying rates. These variations imply that the long-run impact of the wage increase on labor supply will take time to be reached, both because it takes time for new labor force entrants to respond to changes in occupational differentials by acquiring training in the appropriate fields, and because the wage differentials adjust to equilibrium at different rates. All of these considerations suggest that the adjustment of labor supply can be described as

$$\dot{L}^S = \lambda_2(L^{S*} - L^S), \tag{7}$$

where the superscript S denotes the quantity supplied.

Postulating that demand and supply of labor adjust to their equilibrium values with lags necessitates further modifications of the basic model. Because labor demand equals labor supply only in equilibrium, the real wage also adjusts in response to the differences between the amounts demanded and supplied. Without going into the microeconomics underlying this adjustment process, we simply assume that wage adjustment is characterized by

$$\dot{w} = \lambda_3(L^D - L^S). \tag{8}$$

The theoretical basis for the lagged adjustment in (8) is independent of that for (6) and (7).[4] Lagged adjustment in these latter two equations affects the cost of adjusting temporary to permanent notional demand and supply. Even if there were no costs of adjustment in these two equations, some time-consuming process would exist by which notional labor demand and supply are brought into equality by

3. In a model of diffusion of information, a logistic curve rather than a geometric adjustment makes more sense. However, we use the geometric relation because that has become conventional in the literature.

4. This specification of the disequilibrium behavior of wages has most recently been used by Rosen and Quandt [1978] in empirical work.

changes in the real wage rate. This process is reflected in the lag specified in (8).[5]

Once we assume the existence of lagged supply and demand responses, the amount of labor used in production depends on the relation between the amounts supplied and demanded. No more labor can be used in production than is supplied by the population; similarly, if more labor is supplied than is demanded, unemployment will exist in the labor market. This suggests that employment E is determined by

$$E = \min[L^D, L^S], \tag{9}$$

and that equation(1) must be replaced by

$$Y = F(K,E). \tag{1'}$$

Also, the equilibrium factor demand conditions now become

$$F_{L^{D*}}(K, L^{D*}) = w[1+\tau] \tag{2'}$$

5. The local stability of the system of differential equations implied by (1)–(8) can be examined by linearizing them into

$$\dot{L}^D = \lambda_1 \, [l_1 w[1+\tau] - L^D] + C_1;$$
$$\dot{L}^S = \lambda_2 \, [l_2 w[1-\tau] - L^S] + C_2;$$

and

$$\dot{w} = \lambda_3 \, [L^D - L^S],$$

where the C_i do not affect the dynamics of the system;

$$l_1 = \left(\frac{\partial F_K}{\partial K} - \left(\frac{dK(r)}{dr}\right)^{-1}\right) \Bigg/ \begin{vmatrix} \dfrac{\partial F_{L^{D*}}}{\partial L^{D*}} & \dfrac{\partial F_{L^{D*}}}{\partial K} \\ \dfrac{\partial F_K}{\partial K}\dfrac{\partial F_K}{\partial K} & -\left(\dfrac{dK(r)}{dr}\right)^{-1} \end{vmatrix}$$

and

$$l_2 = L'.$$

The system is stable if

$$\lambda_1 + \lambda_2 > 0; \qquad l_1 \, [1+\tau] < l_2 \, [1-\tau];$$

and

$$\lambda_1^2\lambda_2 + \lambda_1\lambda_2^2 + \lambda_2^2\lambda_3 l_2 \, (1-\tau) - (1+\tau) \, l_1\lambda_1^2\lambda_3 > 0.$$

The first condition is implied by the adjustment of demand and supply toward long-run demand and supply. The second and third conditions will be satisfied if $l_1 < 0$ and $l_2 > 0$. That $l_2 > 0$ is given by the assumption that the supply of labor is upward sloping. The numerator in l_1 is negative, since the first term is negative (marginal products diminish with increases in the input) while the second term is positive (the supply of capital is upward sloping). Both diagonal terms in the determinant in the denominator are negative, as is $\partial F_K/\partial K$; in a two-factor function it is usually assumed that $\partial F_{L^{D*}}/\partial K > 0$, so that the denominator is positive. Thus, $l_1 < 0$, and the system of differential equations is locally stable. The simulations of disturbances in the system should produce convergence for all economically reasonable values of the parameters characterizing the system.

and

(3′) $$F_K(K,L^{D*}) = r.$$

Since our interest is in the payroll tax and in labor market issues, we have not appended equations describing capital-market dynamics to the basic model, (1)–(5). Implicitly, and in the interest of simplicity, we assume that firms' demand for capital (described by (3)) is always and instantaneously met by capital suppliers (5). Clearly, these assumptions should be relaxed in work like this that focuses on, for example, the corporate profits tax, or in future work that might examine how the dynamics of *interrelated* factor demand affect the dynamics of tax incidence.

II. A Simulation Model

Since the system of differential equations is at least locally stable, it would be nice to obtain a closed-form solution for it and follow the paths of the variables of interest as they adjust to changes in the payroll tax rate τ. However, even the simplest realistic specifications of the production and factor supply relations make the resulting equations highly nonlinear. More important, the disequilibrium condition embodied in (9) prevents us from using a linearized version of the system in (1′)–(3′) and (4)–(8) to examine the time paths of the variables. Given these problems, we simulate the impact of changes in the payroll tax rate on wages, employment, and the tax burden, using equations (1′)–(3′) and (4)–(9).

The production relation (1′) is specified as a standard CES form. We assume that the elasticity of substitution between capital and labor is $\sigma = 0.75$, following a long literature (see Nerlove [1967]). Further, we assume that the relative constancy of factor shares over time in the United States reflects the underlying parameters in the production function rather than a fortuitous coincidence of biased technical change and changes in relative factor supply. Thus, the distribution parameter for capital α is set at $\alpha = 0.33$ throughout the simulations. The choice of the production function dictates the form of the long-run factor demand equations:

(2″) $$L_t^{D*} = Y_t\ [W_t[1+\tau]/(1-\alpha)]^{-\sigma},$$

and

(3″) $$K_t = Y_t\ [r_t/\alpha]^{-\sigma}.$$

In these equations, we implicitly assume that firms set their *equi-*

librium factor demand by using the production relation and the current period's values of output and factor prices. These same variables determine both equilibrium and actual demand for capital, given our exclusion of adjustment lags in capital markets.

The empirical underpinnings of the remaining equations are less solid, so for each of the parameters specified we choose two or three values that should cover the range in which the true value can be expected to lie. We first assume that the equation describing equilibrium labor supply can be written as

$$L_t^{S*} = [[1 - \tau]w_t]^{\eta}, \tag{4'}$$

where η is the long-run elasticity of labor supply in response to changes in the net wage. Studies of labor supply provide a discouragingly wide range of estimates of this parameter. To cover this range, we assume that η can take the values 0.25, 1, or 3. The first is near what has generally been estimated for adult males, while the last is near the high end of the range of estimates for married women.[6] The capital supply equation is assumed to be of the form

$$r_t = K_t^{1/\nu}, \tag{5'}$$

where ν is the elasticity of the supply of capital. Being forced to rely on guesswork about this, we assume that it can take the values 1 or 5 in the simulations.

Of the three dynamic equations, the one that reflects labor demand has the strongest empirical foundation. We respecify (6) as

$$L_t^D - L_{t-1}^D = \lambda_1(L_t^{D*} - L_{t-1}^D), \tag{6'}$$

to put it in discrete time, and we note the changed meaning of the parameter λ_1. The voluminous empirical literature (summarized in Hamermesh [1976]) suggests that more than half of the gap between equilibrium and actual employment demand is made up within one year, but probably not within one quarter. Accordingly, if we assume that the year is the unit of time in our simulation model, an appropriate range of values for the parameter λ_1 is between 0.9 and 0.5. The first value implies that half of the gap between L_t^{D*} and L_{t-1}^D is made up in one quarter; the second, that half of the gap is removed in one year.

There is less empirical evidence on the dynamics of labor supply. Freeman [1977] has estimated a time-series model of labor demand and supply, with the result that the average lag in the adjustment of

6. See the studies in Cain and Watts [1973] for a sampling of estimated labor supply elasticities.

actual to equilibrium supply is over thirty quarters. Kalachek *et al.* [1979], using a micro data set, find that only two-thirds of any disequilibrium in labor supply is removed in four years. That result is supported by earlier work by Fleisher *et al.* [1973], showing that 31 percent of the gap between actual and equilibrium labor supply is removed each year. Accordingly, if we rewrite (7) as

$$L_t^S - L_{t-1}^S = \lambda_2 \, (L_t^{S*} - L_{t-1}^S), \tag{7'}$$

the values used in the simulation for λ_2 should be below those for λ_1. We choose $\lambda_2 = 0.5$ or 0.1. It is hard to argue that workers' perceptions of permanent and transitory changes in the returns to work adjust so slowly as to produce the half-life of over five years implicit in the value $\lambda_2 = 0.1$. Presumably a lag that is that long must stem from relative wage changes and the need to acquire training that takes substantial amounts of time in specific occupations.

Equation (8) can be put in discrete time as

$$w_t - w_{t-1} = \lambda_3 \, (L_t^D - L_t^S). \tag{8'}$$

There is some empirical basis for the values of λ_3 to be used in the simulations. Ashenfelter *et al.* [1972] provide evidence that the adjustment process has an average lag of at least two years, and this finding is corroborated in Johnson [1977]. Presumably this lag arises because of money illusion on the part of workers and because of labor-market rigidities—long-term union contracts and specific investments that inhibit mobility. In any case available empirical work suggests that $\lambda_3 = 0.5$ and 0.1 bracket the likely values for this parameter.

There are forty-eight possible quintuplets of parameters (η, ν, λ_1, λ_2, λ_3), and for each we simulate the equilibrium values of the nine variables Y, E, L^{D*}, K, L^{S*}, r, L^D, L^S, and w.[7] (Obviously, in equilibrium in this model $E = L^{D*} = L^D = L^{S*} = L^S$.) The equilibrium values were computed under the assumption that $\tau = 0.0585$, to reflect the OASDHI payroll tax rate prevailing between 1973 and 1977. These values were used as initial values for the endogenous variables in the two simulation exercises of interest. First, the tax rate was increased by 0.01, to $\tau = 0.0685$. This provides information on the effect of a higher payroll tax rate on wages and employment and on their time paths, as well as on the share of the change in the payroll tax

7. The model was simulated for three sharply different sets of initial values. In each case it eventually converged to the same set of solution values. Given the choice of initial values of the variables, for each particular set of parameters used, the system was allowed to run until none of the endogenous variables changed by more than a fraction 0.00001 of its value between a particular period $t-1$ and t.

revenue that comes from reduced earnings of labor. In the second simulation the original equilibrium values were again used to examine the effect of a decrease in the payroll tax rate of 0.01, from $\tau = 0.0585$ to $\tau = 0.0485$. This simulates the effect of a wage subsidy; it allows us to examine whether and how the time paths of the endogenous variables of interest (wages and employment) differ from their paths in the simulations of an increase in the tax rate. We can thus consider whether all relevant information about the effects of a wage subsidy is contained (with a change in sign) in information on the effects of a payroll tax increase, or whether the two must be considered separately.

The comparative static changes in employment and the wage rate in response to the simulated increase and decrease in the payroll tax rate simply reinforce the findings of previous work. A higher labor supply elasticity is associated with a smaller decrease in the net wage when the tax rate is increased. Higher supply elasticities for capital imply slightly greater negative impacts of tax increases on wage rates (because of the easier availability of capital to substitute against labor in production). Not surprisingly, too, the equilibrium effects of an increase or decrease in the payroll tax rate on wage rates and employment are essentially the same but of opposite sign.[8]

Much more interesting are the time paths of the endogenous variables, particularly employment and the wage rate. For selected years after the tax rate is changed, for the combination of parameters $\eta = 1$ and $\nu = 1$, Table I shows the fractions of the gaps between initial and final equilibria that are covered by employment and wages.[9] Only if we assume that labor demand, labor supply, and wages adjust very quickly, do employment and wages approach their equilibrium values fairly closely within three years when the payroll tax is increased. Otherwise, it is at least five years before both employment and wages move at least halfway from their initial values to their eventual equilibrium values.

A consideration of polar cases can help to identify the causes of this result. Compare, for example, the time path of w when $\lambda_1 = 0.9$, $\lambda_2 = 0.5$, and $\lambda_3 = 0.5$, to that when $\lambda_1 = 0.9$, $\lambda_2 = 0.1$, and $\lambda_3 = 0.5$. In the former case the wage is within 10 percent of its equilibrium value before three years; in the latter case, it is more than 10 percent from equilibrium after ten years. The length of the lagged adjustment

8. Tables showing the equilibrium changes in employment and wage rates are available upon request from the author, as are tables on these variables' time paths like those in the text, but for different combinations of parameters.

9. Results for $\eta = 0.25$ or 3 and $\nu = 5$ do not differ qualitatively from those presented in Table I.

TABLE I

TIME PATHS OF THE EFFECTS OF A 1 PERCENTAGE POINT INCREASE (DECREASE) IN THE PAYROLL TAX RATE; $\sigma = 0.75$; $\nu = 1$; $\eta = 1$

Adjustment speeds					
Demand	Supply	Wages	Year	Employment	Wage rate
0.9	0.5	0.5	1	0.91 (0.38)	0.65 (0.31)
			3	0.93 (0.76)	1.07 (0.70)
			5	0.97 (0.90)	1.04 (0.88)
			10	1.00 (0.99)	1.00 (0.99)
0.9	0.5	0.1	1	1.23 (0.34)	0.24 (0.08)
			3	1.44 (0.63)	0.69 (0.23)
			5	1.20 (0.73)	0.91 (0.35)
			10	1.01 (0.84)	1.01 (0.58)
0.9	0.1	0.5	1	0.72 (0.08)	0.88 (0.40)
			3	0.39 (0.24)	1.54 (0.93)
			5	0.44 (0.39)	1.49 (1.17)
			10	0.71 (0.68)	1.28 (1.23)
0.9	0.1	0.1	1	1.20 (0.07)	0.31 (0.10)
			3	1.21 (0.20)	0.92 (0.29)
			5	0.82 (0.31)	1.22 (0.45)
			10	0.66 (0.54)	1.31 (0.72)
0.5	0.5	0.5	1	0.36 (0.33)	0.03 (0.03)
			3	0.82 (0.63)	0.39 (0.28)
			5	0.98 (0.79)	0.80 (0.57)
			10	0.99 (0.95)	1.02 (0.91)
0.5	0.5	0.1	1	0.36 (0.33)	0.00 (0.01)
			3	0.89 (0.59)	0.12 (0.08)
			5	1.18 (0.68)	0.36 (0.20)
			10	1.25 (0.80)	0.94 (0.47)
0.5	0.1	0.5	1	0.30 (0.07)	0.31 (0.21)
			3	0.52 (0.22)	1.13 (0.70)
			5	0.49 (0.37)	1.48 (1.01)
			10	0.66 (0.64)	1.19 (1.14)
0.5	0.1	0.1	1	0.35 (0.07)	0.08 (0.05)
			3	0.81 (0.19)	0.38 (0.20)
			5	1.00 (0.30)	0.75 (0.34)
			10	0.85 (0.52)	1.34 (0.63)

in supply is thus important. Comparing the first case with that when $\lambda_1 = 0.5$, $\lambda_2 = 0.5$, and $\lambda_3 = 0.5$, we find that assuming a longer lag in the adjustment of demand (a half-life of one year instead of one quarter) produces markedly slower wage adjustment: in this third case, the wage rate is more than 10 percent away from its equilibrium value after five years. These two examples suggest that both demand

and supply lags are important in determining the time path of the effects of changes in payroll taxes on wage rates.

These simulations suggest the crucial finding of this study: Even in cases when the wage rate eventually decreases by an amount nearly equal to the increase in the payroll tax rate (when η is small), reasonable assumptions about the parameters describing the lags in labor-market behavior produce results that mean that much of the eventual impact is delayed for several years. Past work that relies on the assumption of an inelastic supply of labor for its conclusion that labor bears the payroll tax is of little relevance for analyzing the immediate effects of higher payroll taxes, because the short-run burden is partly on capital and persists over a substantial number of years.

Table I presents the time paths of wages and employment in response to a decrease in the payroll tax in parentheses. Most striking is the much slower response. The reasons for this asymmetry are that employment is the minimum of the amount of labor supplied and demanded, and that the adjustment of actual to desired labor supply is slower than that of actual to desired labor demand. Thus, when the tax rate is increased, employment adjusts rapidly because labor demand, which adjusts relatively rapidly, is the binding constraint. When the tax rate is cut, labor demand rises rapidly, but because labor supply increases only slowly, employment, which is the lesser of actual labor supply and demand, also increases only slowly.[10]

All of the discussion has focused on the effects of tax changes on the individual endogenous variables, employment, and wage rates. Also of interest, though, are the eventual impact and time path of the fraction of the change in tax revenues that is accounted for by changes in labor income. (This is just $-d[wE(1-\tau)]/dT$, where $T = 2\tau wE$.) Following Feldstein [1974], we assume that the loss in earnings resulting from a tax-induced decline in employment is exactly offset by the value of the increased leisure time, so that $d(wE[1-\tau]) = E[1-\tau]dw - Ewd\tau$, the net loss in labor income. We calculate the fraction $-d(wE[1-\tau])/dT$ under the assumption that the endogenous variables are valued at the midpoint between their initial values and their values in period t.

Labor's net loss as a fraction of the change in tax revenue at various time periods is shown in Table II. The results on this measure differ slightly from those on the specific variables, employment and

10. Even where $\lambda_1 = \lambda_2$, the time paths are not the same for increases and decreases in τ. This difference results from the difference between the long-run labor supply and demand elasticities. (λ_1 and λ_2 indicate rates of adjustment toward L^{D*} and L^{S*} that move differing amounts per time period because these elasticities differ.)

TABLE II

LABOR'S NET LOSS (GAIN) AS A FRACTION OF THE CHANGE IN TAX REVENUE OF AN INCREASE (DECREASE) IN THE PAYROLL TAX RATE OF 1 PERCENTAGE POINT

Adjustment speeds			Years after change			
Labor demand	Labor supply	Wages	1	3	5	10
0.9	0.5	0.5	0.75 (0.61)	0.88 (0.75)	0.88 (0.81)	0.87 (0.85)
		0.1	0.65 (0.54)	0.81 (0.60)	0.85 (0.64)	0.87 (0.72)
	0.1	0.5	0.80 (0.61)	0.97 (0.78)	0.97 (0.86)	0.93 (0.90)
		0.1	0.67 (0.53)	0.86 (0.59)	0.92 (0.64)	0.94 (0.74)
0.5	0.5	0.5	0.53 (0.52)	0.66 (0.61)	0.80 (0.71)	0.87 (0.83)
		0.1	0.52 (0.52)	0.58 (0.55)	0.68 (0.59)	0.86 (0.68)
	0.1	0.5	0.60 (0.56)	0.86 (0.71)	0.97 (0.81)	0.90 (0.87)
		0.1	0.54 (0.52)	0.66 (0.56)	0.79 (0.61)	0.96 (0.71)

wage rates, in that the eventual incidence of the tax rise on labor is approached somewhat more rapidly. However, under reasonable assumptions about speeds of adjustment, labor can avoid up to one-third of its eventual burden of the tax increase for several years.

The results of similar calculations for a tax decrease are shown in parentheses in Table II. In this case, the numbers can be interpreted as showing the increase in labor's net earnings as a fraction of the fall in taxes at each time. A comparison of the results here mirrors the comparison made in the discussion of Table I: Because we usually assume that supply adjusts more slowly than demand and is the constraining quantity when the tax rate is decreased, labor's gain as a fraction of the decrease in taxes rises more slowly toward its eventual value. However, the adjustment is again somewhat quicker than is that of either wage rates or employment.

III. CONCLUSIONS

The results of this paper show the importance of thinking about the nature of the labor market when considering the effects of the payroll tax. Once variable labor supply is allowed in response to payroll tax changes, labor-market dynamics and the disequilibrium behavior that they induce become essential for analyzing the effects of the tax. Two major conclusions stem from this extension. First, the nature and probable lengths of lags in labor supply, labor demand, and wage adjustment make it quite likely that it is several years before the general equilibrium impacts of a change in payroll taxes are felt. Thus, regardless of whether labor bears most of a tax increase in the long run, there is a period of at least several years during which labor escapes part of the eventual tax burden and wages fall only part of the way toward their final equilibrium. Second, while the static general equilibrium models that have been used to analyze tax incidence are symmetric with respect to tax increases and decreases, no such symmetry exists in the short run. Instead, because labor supply appears to adjust more slowly than labor demand, a payroll tax cut (subsidy) will cause employment to vary over a longer period of time than a tax increase. This finding also implies that, even though the eventual incidence of a change in the payroll tax is independent of whether it is levied on employees or employers, this will not generally be true in the short run.

MICHIGAN STATE UNIVERSITY AND NBER

REFERENCES

Ashenfelter, O., G. Johnson, and J. Pencavel, "Trade Unions and the Rate of Change of Money Wages in United States Manufacturing Industry," *Review of Economic Studies,* XXXIV (Jan. 1972), 27–54.

Barro, R., and H. Grossman, *Money, Employment and Inflation* (Cambridge, England: Cambridge University Press, 1976).

Break, G., "The Incidence and Economic Effects of Taxation," in G. Break *et al., The Economics of Public Finance* (Washington: The Brookings Institution, 1974).

Brechling, F., *Investment and Employment Decisions* (Manchester, England: Manchester University Press, 1975).

Brittain, J., "The Incidence of Social Security Payroll Taxes," *American Economic Review,* LXI (March 1971), 110–25.

Cain, G., and H. Watts, *Income Maintenance and Labor Supply* (Chicago: Rand McNally, 1973).

Feldstein, M., "The Incidence of the Social Security Payroll Tax: Comment," *American Economic Review,* LXII (Sept. 1972), 735–38.

——, "Tax Incidence with Growth and Variable Factor Supply," this *Journal,* LXXXVII (Nov. 1974), 551–73.

Fleisher, B., D. Parsons, and R. Porter, "Asset Adjustments and the Labor Supply of Older Workers," in Cain and Watts, eds., *Income Maintenance and Labor Supply* (Chicago: Rand McNally, 1973), 279–327.

Freeman, R., "Employment and Wage Adjustment Models in U.S. Manufacturing, 1950–1976," unpublished paper, Harvard University, 1977.

Hamermesh, D., "Econometric Studies of Labor Demand and their Application to Policy Analysis," *Journal of Human Resources,* XI (Fall 1976), 507–25.

——, "New Estimates of the Incidence of the Payroll Tax," *Southern Economic Journal,* XLIV (April 1979), 1208–19.

Harberger, A. C., "The Incidence of the Corporation Income Tax," *Journal of Political Economy,* LXX (June 1962), 215–40.

Heckman, J., and R. Willis, "A Beta-Logistic Model for the Analysis of Sequential Labor Force Participation by Married Women," *Journal of Political Economy,* LXXXV (Feb. 1977), 27–58.

Johnson, G., "The Determination of Wages in the Union and Non-Union Sectors," *British Journal of Industrial Relations,* XV (1977), 211–25.

Kalachek, E., F. Raines, and D. Larson, "The Determination of Labor Supply: A Dynamic Model," *Industrial and Labor Relations Review,* XXXII (April 1979), 367–77.

Nerlove, M., "Recent Empirical Studies of the CES and Related Functions," in M. Brown, ed., *The Theory and Empirical Analysis of Production* (New York: National Bureau of Economic Research, 1967).

Rosen, H., and R. Quandt, "Estimation of a Disequilibrium Aggregate Labor Market," *Review of Economics and Statistics,* LX (Aug. 1978), 371–79.

Shoven, J., and J. Whalley, "A General Equilibrium Calculation of the Effects of Differential Taxation of Income from Capital in the U.S.," *Journal of Public Economics,* I (Nov. 1972), 281–321.

THE COST OF CAPITAL IN NONMARKETED FIRMS

BENGT HOLMSTROM

I. INTRODUCTION

All western economies are mixed in the sense that there is both a marketed and a nonmarketed sector of firms. A natural question then arises: Should unincorporated business use higher or lower discount rates than incorporated business does? The same question has been a source of much controversy in public finance. Some authors, among them Arrow and Lind [1970] and Samuelson [1964], argue that public enterprises should use a lower discount rate because the government is better able to absorb risk and can more effectively diversify investments. Another group, which finds Hirshleifer [1966] and Diamond [1967] among its supporters, maintains that the discount rate should be the same for projects with comparable risk profiles, regardless of who undertakes them. As Diamond states:

> by means of portfolio diversification on the part of consumers, all of the economy's averaging possibilities are brought to bear on each production decision. Thus, . . . , large firms have no pooling advantages over small firms, nor does the government have an advantage over private business [1967, p. 771].

In an accompanying footnote, he further argues convincingly that this conclusion remains intact even when bankruptcy is considered.

Sandmo [1974] takes a consolidated view of the issue. He makes the important observation that market structure is essential for the discussion. If the government firms represent the same risk classes as the private ones and shares of the latter are traded on an efficient market, then Hirshleifer's and Diamond's view appears correct. On the other hand, if no market (or an imperfect market) for private shares exists, then this conclusion is not necessarily valid, though Sandmo does not go for an explicit comparison.

Recently, Stapleton and Subrahmanyam [1978] have provided such an explicit comparison in a highly simplified model, with the rather surprising (at least at first sight) conclusion that the government should use a higher discount rate! Their rationale sounds simple: in a perfect market, risk is distributed more efficiently than in government firms, where the tax system implies a somewhat arbitrary location of "shares." Hence, the market risk premium and, thereby, the cost of capital for marketed firms should be lower than for government. The purpose of this paper is to point out that Stapleton's

The Quarterly Journal of Economics, December 1980 0033-5533/80/0095-0765$01.00

and Subrahmanyam's result follows from an irrelevant comparison that favors the market and that the relevant comparison leads to no unambiguous conclusions about the cost of capital in the two sectors except under the assumption that risk classes in both sectors are identical or that sectors are totally independent.

To explicate: Stapleton and Subrahmanyam compare discount rates in a mixed economy with those in an identical but purely private economy. Why would that be of interest? The pure private economy is a hypothetical point of reference. It seems rather obvious that it will do better, since shares are allocated optimally there, whereas they are not in the mixed economy.[1] In contrast, reality is a single mixed economy with marketed and nonmarketed firms existing side by side. Then, what should be done is a contemporaneous comparison of how these two types of firms react to the same investment opportunity. I shall do this here, using for simplicity and comparison, essentially, the same model as Stapleton and Subrahmanyam.

The outcome of the analysis is that the cost of capital can be either higher or lower in the nonmarketed sector, and this will not depend on simple characteristics that could easily be transformed into explicit rules. The reason is that, even if the capital market is perfect, an imperfect distribution of shares in the nonmarketed sector will induce distortions in share holdings in the marketed sector as investors try to balance their total portfolio. As a consequence, risk can no longer be measured in a single dimension and each sector will price dimensions differently. Furthermore, neither marketed nor nonmarketed firms can look for appropriate discount rates in market data when shares are not correctly distributed, and value-maximization will be an inappropriate decision rule for traded firms.[2]

In the public finance context, these conclusions complement Sandmo's qualifications of Hirshleifer's and Diamond's claim that the cost of capital is equal in the private and public sectors. Sandmo shows that for this to be true, it is essential that the private sector be perfect; this paper shows that it is also essential that all risk classes in the public sector be represented in the private sector.

II. The Model

Consider an economy with two firms, A and B, and two investors

1. This disregards the important possibility that government can incorporate nonlinear sharing rules not available in the private market. In Stapleton and Subrahmanyam's model, it is of no consequence, since they work with exponential utilities.

2. Stiglitz [1972] has shown that even with a competitive capital market in a mean-variance framework, market value maximization will yield a slightly different result than the Pareto optimal decision rule prescribed.

indexed $i = 1,2$. Both investors possess exponential utility functions over wealth:

$$U_i(z) = -\rho_i \cdot e^{-z/\rho_i}, \quad i = 1,2, \tag{1}$$

where ρ_i is the risk tolerance of investor i. The framework is single-period. The uncertain return of firm A is $\tilde{x}_A$, and that of B $\tilde{x}_B$. The distribution of the pair $(\tilde{x}_A, \tilde{x}_B)$ is multivariate normal; the expected values are denoted μ_A, μ_B variances σ_A^2, σ_B^2 and the covariance σ_{AB}. Investor i is endowed with e_i units of money in the first period. He owns initially $\bar{s}_{iA}$ shares in firm A and $\bar{s}_{iB}$ shares in firm B. He can trade shares of A on a perfect market where the only other asset is a riskless one, yielding a certain exogenously given rate of return r. Shares of B cannot be traded.

Investor i's portfolio decision is to determine investment levels in firm A and the riskless asset. Let P be the price of firm A shares. Investor i will then choose s_{iA}, his purchase of shares in firm A, in order to maximize the certainty equivalent:[3]

$$C_i = e_i(1+r) + \bar{s}_{iA}P(1+r) + s_{iA}(\mu_A - P(1+r)) + \bar{s}_{iB}\mu_B - \frac{1}{2\rho_i}(S_{iA}^2\sigma_A^2 + \bar{s}_{iB}^2\sigma_B^2 + 2s_{iA}\bar{s}_{iB}\sigma_{AB}). \tag{2}$$

In (2), the investment in the riskless asset is included indirectly as a function of s_{iA}, determined by the budget constraint. Also, it is assumed that investor i acts as a price taker. Maximizing (2) gives the solution:

$$s_{iA} = \frac{1}{\sigma_A^2}\{\mu_A - P(1+r) - \sigma_{AB}\bar{s}_{iB}\}. \tag{3}$$

Since $s_{1A} + s_{2A} = 1$ in equilibrium, this implies that the equilibrium price is

$$P = \frac{1}{1+r}\left\{\mu_A - \frac{1}{\bar{\rho}}(\sigma_A^2 + \sigma_{AB})\right\}. \tag{4}$$

Here $\bar{\rho} = \rho_1 + \rho_2$ is the risk tolerance for the syndicate of two.[4] Substituting (4) into (3) gives i's purchase of shares in terms of given data:

$$s_{iA} = \frac{\rho_i}{\bar{\rho}} + \frac{\sigma_{AB}}{\sigma_A^2}\left(\frac{\rho_i}{\bar{\rho}} - \bar{s}_{iB}\right). \tag{5}$$

3. The certainty equivalent of a normally distributed variable with mean μ and variance σ^2 is $\mu - (1/2\rho)\sigma^2$ when utility is exponential.

4. General versions of (3) and (4) are given in Mayers [1976].

One notices that the equilibrium price in (4) is just the same as it would be if both firms were marketed. In contrast, share purchases will be different; in particular, the separation theorem does not hold. In a purely private market, agents would purchase shares $s_{iA} = s_{iB} = \rho_i/\bar{\rho}, i = 1,2$. If the fixed allocation of shares in firm B differs from this ideal, investors will seek to counterbalance the bias by purchases in the market. That will be possible if $\sigma_{AB} \neq 0$. For instance, if $\sigma_{AB} > 0$ and investor 1's share is too high in the unincorporated firm ($\bar{s}_{1B} > \rho_1/\bar{\rho}$), (5) says that he will buy correspondingly less than $\rho_1/\bar{\rho}$ shares in firm A to avoid excess unsystematic risk. Looked upon in isolation then, the share distribution in the market will be imperfect as well.

A special case, that deserves to be mentioned, arises when there is perfect correlation (positive or negative) between the marketed and nonmarketed firm. That will enable the investor to offset fully his possibly biased allocation of shares in the nonmarketed sector. For an illustration, let $\tilde{x}_A = b\tilde{x}_B$, b a constant. Investor i's return from shares will then be by (5)

$$(6) \qquad \bar{s}_{iB}\tilde{x}_B + \left[\frac{\rho_i}{\bar{\rho}} + \frac{1}{b}\left(\frac{\rho_i}{\bar{\rho}} - \bar{s}_{iB}\right)\right] b\tilde{x}_B = \frac{\rho_i}{\bar{\rho}}\tilde{x}_B[1 + b],$$

which is the same return he would enjoy if both firms were marketed. The observation suggests that the imperfections in a mixed economy may be smaller than one would at first believe.

III. A Comparison of Cost of Capital

Let the mixed economy be in equilibrium as described in the previous section, that is, shares in firm A are given by (5). Next, for both firms introduce the same opportunity to invest in a new project. Which firm will require a higher expected return from the project before accepting it?

For convenience, assume that the new project yields constant returns to scale, $\tilde{y}$ per unit of investment, and that $\tilde{y}$ is normally distributed with mean μ_y, variance σ_y^2 and covariances $\sigma_{Ay} = \text{cov}(\tilde{x}_A,\tilde{y})$, $\sigma_{By} = \text{cov}(\tilde{x}_B,\tilde{y})$. Thus, if firm A invests an amount I in the project, its return changes to $\tilde{x}_A + I\tilde{y}$ and correspondingly for firm B.

Because shares are not held to minimize risk in the mixed economy, value-maximization cannot be considered the appropriate objective for the marketed firm. Instead, I shall use the Pareto criterion for judging investments in both firms. With exponential utilities the Pareto criterion becomes particularly simple: it is just the maximization of the sum of the investors' certainty equivalents in (2).

Investment in the Marketed Firm

When firm A invests I in the new project, price will change to $P(I)$, share purchases to $s_{iA}(I)$, the return of firm A to $\mu_A(I)$, its variance to $\sigma_A^2(I)$, and the covariance with B to $\sigma_{AB}(I)$. No other variables will change, since $\bar{s}_{iB}$'s were fixed and r was exogenously given. The certainty equivalent of i then becomes

$$(7)\quad C_i(I) = e_i(1+r) + s_{iA}P(I)(1+r) + s_{iA}(I)(\mu_A(I) - P(I)(1+r)) + \bar{s}_{iB}\mu_B - \frac{1}{2\rho_i}\{s_{iA}^2(I)\sigma_A^2(I) + \bar{s}_{iB}^2\sigma_B^2 + 2s_{iA}(I)\bar{s}_{iB}\sigma_{AB}(I)\},$$

where s_{iA} is given by (5). The welfare criterion recommends investment (in some positive amount) if

$$(8)\quad \frac{d}{dI}(C_1(I) + C_2(I))\bigg|_{I=0} > 0.$$

By definition $s_{iA} = s_{iA}(0)$. Hence, using the first-order condition for optimal portfolio choice, which gives $s_{iA}(I)$, one obtains

$$(9)\quad \frac{dC_i}{dI}\bigg|_{I=0} = s_{iA}\mu_y - \frac{1}{2\rho_i}(s_{iA}^2 2\sigma_{Ay} + 2\sigma_{By}s_{iA}\bar{s}_{iB}).$$

Here the following facts are used:

$$(10)\quad \frac{d\mu_A(I)}{dI}\bigg|_{I=0} = \frac{dE(\tilde{x}_A + I\tilde{y})}{dI}\bigg|_{I=0} = \mu_y,$$

$$(11)\quad \frac{d\sigma_A^2(I)}{dI}\bigg|_{I=0} = \frac{dE(\tilde{x}_A + I\tilde{y} - \mu_A - I\mu_y)^2}{dI}\bigg|_{I=0} = 2\sigma_{Ay},$$

$$(12)\quad \frac{d\sigma_{AB}(I)}{dI}\bigg|_{I=0} = \frac{dE(\tilde{x}_A + I\tilde{y} - \mu_A - I\mu_y)(\tilde{x}_B - \mu_B)}{dI}\bigg|_{I=0} = \sigma_{By},$$

where E stands for the expectation operator. One should notice that the variance of $\tilde{y}$ does not enter the expressions. On the margin, when I is small, its effect is negligible. Nor does the change in price affect the certainty equivalent because it was assumed that we started from equilibrium asset holdings. Placing (9) in (8) gives the Pareto improvement criterion:

$$(13)\quad \mu_y - \left(\frac{s_{1A}^2}{\rho_1} + \frac{s_{2A}^2}{\rho_2}\right)\sigma_{Ay} - \left(\frac{s_{1A}\bar{s}_{1B}}{\rho_1} + \frac{s_{2A}\bar{s}_{2B}}{\rho_2}\right)\sigma_{By} > 0.$$

Investment should be undertaken if and only if (13) holds. In comparison, the value-maximizing criterion reads

$$\mu_y - \frac{1}{\bar{\rho}}(\sigma_{Ay} + \sigma_{By}) > 0. \tag{14}$$

Note that if $s_{1A} = \bar{s}_{1B} = \rho_1/\bar{\rho}$ so that $s_{2A} = \bar{s}_{2B} = \rho_2/\bar{\rho}$, then (13) and (14) coincide.[5] Another case of equivalence arises if $\tilde{x}_A = b\tilde{x}_B$, b, a constant (cf (6)).[6] The rationale for both cases is that they enable investors to reach exactly the same position as they would, if both firms were marketed. Except under these special circumstances, however, (13) indicates that, in contrast to standard market models, there is neither a single measure for project risk nor a market price by which the cost of risk can be evaluated.[7] Instead, the risk is measured in as many dimensions as there are firms, and each component is charged with a unique price. For these component prices one has

$$\frac{s_{1A}^2}{\rho_1} + \frac{s_{2A}^2}{\rho_2} \geq \frac{1}{\bar{\rho}}, \tag{15}$$

$$\frac{s_{1A}\bar{s}_{1B}}{\rho_1} + \frac{s_{2A}\bar{s}_{2B}}{\rho_2} \leq \frac{1}{\bar{\rho}}, \quad \text{if } \sigma_{AB} > 0, \tag{16}$$

$$\frac{s_{1A}\bar{s}_{1B}}{\rho_1} + \frac{s_{2A}\bar{s}_{2B}}{\rho_2} \geq \frac{1}{\bar{\rho}}, \quad \text{if } \sigma_{AB} < 0. \tag{17}$$

Equalities hold only if $s_{1A} = \bar{s}_{1B} = \rho_1/\bar{\rho}$. (15) is proved by noting that $s_{2A} = 1 - s_{1A}$, and that the minimum of the left-hand side is achieved for $s_{1A} = \rho_1/\bar{\rho}$. (16) and (17) are proved in a similar way; the left-hand sides can be written as quadratic functions of $\bar{s}_{1B}$ using market-clearing conditions and (5), and optimization yields the result.

Since σ_{AB}, σ_{Ay}, and σ_{By} need not have any particular relationship to each other—they can be chosen independently if desired—(13)–(17) show that the Pareto criterion may be either stricter or more lenient than the value-maximization criterion. In particular, if $\sigma_{AB} > 0$, $\sigma_{Ay} > 0$, and $\sigma_{By} = 0$, then market data give a value too low for the cost of capital; whereas the reverse is true when $\sigma_{AB} > 0$, $\sigma_{By} > 0$, and $\sigma_{Ay} = 0$.

Investment in the Nonmarketed Firm

The analysis for the same investment in the nonmarketed firm

5. This is so because the variance of $\tilde{y}$ dropped out. Otherwise, a difference remained, as Stiglitz [1972] observes.

6. Sandmo's assumption about the same risk classes in both sectors corresponds to this special case.

7. This statement does not, of course, apply to the evaluation of firms in equilibrium; see (4).

B proceeds identically. The acceptance criterion corresponding to (13) becomes

$$\mu_y - \left(\frac{s_{1A}\bar{s}_{1B}}{\rho_1} + \frac{s_{2A}\bar{s}_{2B}}{\rho_2}\right)\sigma_{Ay} - \left(\frac{\bar{s}_{1B}^2}{\rho_1} + \frac{\bar{s}_{2B}^2}{\rho_2}\right)\sigma_{By} > 0. \tag{18}$$

Thus, risk is measured in two dimensions $(\sigma_{Ay},\sigma_{By})$ as before, but prices are changed. Analogously to (15),

$$\frac{\bar{s}_{1B}^2}{\rho_1} + \frac{\bar{s}_{2B}^2}{\rho_2} \geq \frac{1}{\bar{\rho}}, \tag{19}$$

with equality only when shares are efficiently allocated.

The interesting comparison is the one between (18), which gives the cost of capital for the nonmarketed firm, and (13), which gives the cost of capital for the marketed firm. We can immediately see the main conclusion that the cost of capital could in general be either higher or lower in the marketed sector than in the nonmarketed sector contrary to the result of Stapleton and Subrahmanyam [1978]. To be a bit more specific, the following sample relationships can be recorded:

PROPOSITION. Assume that $\sigma_{AB} > 0$ and $\bar{s}_{1B} \neq \rho_1/\bar{\rho}$. Then

a. $\sigma_{Ay} \leq 0$, $\sigma_{By} > 0 \Rightarrow CoC_A < CoC_B$,
b. $\sigma_{By} \leq 0$, $\sigma_{Ay} > 0 \Rightarrow CoC_B < CoC_A$,
c. for any σ_{Ay}, there exists a $\bar{\sigma}_{By}$ such that $\sigma_{By}(\gtrless)\bar{\sigma}_{By} \Rightarrow CoC_A(\lessgtr)CoC_B$,
d. for any σ_{By}, there exists a $\bar{\sigma}_{Ay}$ such that $\sigma_{Ay}(\gtrless)\bar{\sigma}_{Ay} \Rightarrow CoC_A(\gtrless)CoC_B$,
e. if $\sigma_{Ay} > \sigma_{By} > 0$, $\sigma_A^2 > \sigma_{AB}$, then $CoC_A < CoC_B$.

Proof. Straightforward calculations in (13) and (18), using (5).

Statements a and b show that diversification is an essential consideration when there is a nonmarketed sector. In standard versions of the capital asset pricing model (see, for instance, Mossin [1973]), this is not the case, since firms do not face a portfolio choice problem at all. In such models, the acceptance criterion for an investment is independent of which firm undertakes it. This leads Diamond [1967] to conclude that the cost of capital should be the same for government as for private firms, but as we see, explicit consideration of market structure and the type of risk present in different sectors may alter the conclusion. Note, in particular, that even if the nonmarketed firm B contemplates an investment in the same risk class as firm A (so that $\sigma_{Ay} \propto \sigma_A^2$, $\sigma_{By} \propto \sigma_{AB}$), it cannot read the price of risk from (4), nor will it use the same criteria as firm A would use in considering the same project.

This shows that for Diamond's result to be true, it is essential that all risk classes in the public sector should be represented in the private (marketed) sector as well.

Statements c and d show monotonicity properties. The higher σ_{Ay}, ceteris paribus, the more likely the cost of capital for firm A will be higher than for firm B. The reverse is true for increases in σ_{By}. Statement e is included to show that the size of firms also plays a role. If the marketed sector is large, $\sigma_{AB} < \sigma_A^2$, $\sigma_{By} < \sigma_{Ay}$, and this makes the cost of capital in that sector relatively lower.

Finally, one may note that if the return of the new project is uncorrelated with both sectors (i.e., $\sigma_{Ay} = \sigma_{By} = 0$), then the acceptance criterion becomes the same in marketed and unmarketed firms. It is for this case that Arrow and Lind argued that the public discount rate should be lower because they assumed that risk is shared inefficiently in the private sector.

In the preceding, I have used the Pareto criterion as a yardstick for accepting or rejecting projects in both sectors of the economy. Results will be slightly different, of course, if the private sector uses market value maximization. However, the main conclusion remains intact: no unambiguous statements in general can be put forward, as a comparison of (14) and (18) quickly reveals.

IV. Concluding Remarks

The main purpose of the paper has been to show that no unambiguous comparisons of the cost of capital between marketed and nonmarketed firms seem possible when the two sectors are imperfectly correlated. This contrasts with recent results of Stapleton and Subrahmanyam [1978]. Since the conclusions are already negative in a highly stylized example, one should not expect any unambiguous statements in more complex situations either. The explicit comparison that was possible in the example shows that the determinants of differences in the cost of capital are many and hardly easy to use for conditional judgment. Ultimately, this is due to the fact that all firms will face a portfolio problem when a nonmarketed sector is present.

Northwestern University

References

Arrow, K. J., and R. C. Lind, "Uncertainty and the Evaluation of Public Investment Decisions," *American Economic Review,* LX (June 1970), 364–78.

Diamond, P. A., "The Role of a Stock Market in a General Equilibrium Model with Technological Uncertainty," *American Economic Review,* LVIII (Sept. 1967), 759–76.

Hirshleifer, J., "Investment Decisions Under Uncertainty: Applications of the State-Preference Approach," this *Journal,* LXXX (May 1966), 252–77.

Mayers, D., "Nonmarketable Assets, Market Segmentation and the Level of Asset Prices," *Journal of Financial and Quantitative Analysis,* XI (March 1976), 1–12.

Mossin, J., *Theory of Financial Markets* (Englewood Cliffs, NJ: Prentice-Hall, 1973).

Samuelson, P. A., "Discussion," *American Economic Review,* LIV (May 1964), 93–96.

Sandmo, A., "Discount Rates for Public Investment Under Uncertainty," *Allocation Under Uncertainty: Equilibrium and Optimality,* J. H. Drèze, ed. (London: Macmillan, 1974).

Stapleton, R. C., and M. G. Subrahmanyam, "Economy, Optimal Public Sector Investment Decision Rules, and the Social Rate of Discount," this *Journal,* XCII (Aug. 1978), 399–411.

Stiglitz, J., "On the Optimality of the Stock Market Allocation of Investment," this *Journal,* LXXXVI (Feb. 1972), 25–60.

DUAL MARKETS, RATIONING, AND QUEUES*

JAGDISH N. BHAGWATI AND BALBIR S. SIHAG

I. THE PROBLEM

Many developing countries are characterized by dual markets in "essential" commodities such as staple foodgrains. Thus, the government typically *supplements* the open market in such commodities, where the price is left free to vary to any level that will clear the market, with "fair price" shops that allocate to every potential consumer a predetermined ration of the same commodities at a fixed, (subsidized and hence lower) price.[1]

An interesting, but hitherto neglected, implication of such a dual market is the differential cost, in terms of queuing time that access to the two, i.e., open and rationed, markets entails; and, in turn, the consequences that it can have for the actual *utilization* of the ration *entitlement* by the intended beneficiaries of the rationed market.

For, typically, the fair price shops are few in number and access to them entails substantially longer waiting in queues than if the consumer shifts instead to the open market where the shops are considerably greater in number.

It follows therefore that, since time has an opportunity cost for the consumer, we would expect the utilization of the ration entitlement to vary directly with the excess of the (open) market over the (subsidized) ration price of the commodity.

Since the rations are typically allotted without discrimination to the rich, the not-so-poor, and the poor, as long as they reside within the eligible geographical area, presumably to avoid the transaction and policing costs entailed by use of a means test, we may envisage this opportunity cost of the queuing time for the rich as consisting "ideally" in the wage paid to servants for queuing, for the not-so-poor as consisting of the leisure forgone, and for the poor as consisting in the wage income forgone while waiting in the queue. The operation of *any* of these alternative forms of opportunity costs would suffice to create an incentive in the direction of reducing utilization of the

* Thanks are due to National Science Foundation Grant No. SOC 79-07541 for partial financial support of the research underlying this paper. The comments of T. N. Srinivasan, Peter Diamond, and an anonymous referee are gratefully acknowledged.

1. A number of studies of such dual markets in developing countries have recently appeared. For example, see Ahmed [1979], George [1979], and Swamy [1979].

The Quarterly Journal of Economics, December 1980 0033-5533/80/0095-0775$01.00

ration entitlement as the gain from buying at the ration, rather than the market, price reduces.[2]

II. The Evidence

The question then is, does reality conform to our theorizing? As it happens, we have managed to procure a body of data on the rationing system in the area of Metropolitan Delhi, India, over a sufficiently large number of observations to test for our hypothesis.

The rationing system in Metropolitan Delhi, for the period of our statistical analysis, did indeed correspond to the dual-market model outlined in Section I. We managed to procure, for the period April 1975 to October 1977, the primary data on a monthly basis on the ration price (P_R), the market price (P_M), the ration entitlement (E), and the utilization thereof (U), for wheat.

The data were aggregate and therefore the rate of ration utilization (U/E) could not be analyzed by income categories reflecting even the broad classification into the rich, the not-so-poor, and the poor.

However, the monthly breakdown did enable us to check for seasonality in utilization: a possibility that turned out to be actually relevant. As it happens, the seasonality appears to enter the problem because the immediate post-harvest months are characterized by the withdrawal from both the open and the rationed markets of many farmer-consumers, since they tend to satisfy their consumption needs simply by setting aside some of their own harvest for that purpose, while entering the market *qua* consumers in later months much like other non-wheat-producing consumers. Yet another reason, suggested by the referee, may be a *change* in the quality differential between foodgrains supplied in the two markets. This may well be a contributory factor in explaining the seasonal dummy, since in the immediate post-harvest months, the availability of "coarser" foodgrains would increase and their price would fall, thus drawing away some of the

2. To avoid tedious algebra, we do not spell out here a simple allocation-of-time model (or a hired-servants model [for the rich]) that would "formalize" the simple argumentation in the test. Needless to say, we are assuming that leisure is not an inferior good when we take the allocation-of-time model.

Taking the opportunity-cost-of-labor-wages model, however, we can readily show the "crossover" wage such that an increase in the wage from that level would take the consumer out from the rationed market. Thus, assume the ration at α lbs, λ as the price differential in favor of the rationed supply, γ as the fraction of the day used up additionally in queuing, and k as the daily wage. The crossover wage is then evidently $k^* = \lambda\alpha/\gamma$.

poorer people from the queue for the "higher-quality" foodgrain, wheat.[3]

With dummies introduced, therefore, to capture the seasonality factor, the equations that we estimated were as follows:[4]

$$(1)\quad \log\left(\frac{U}{E}\right) = -0.38 - \underset{(2.41)}{1.33}\log\left(\frac{P_R}{P_M}\right) - \underset{(2.79)}{0.21D_5} - \underset{(2.22)}{0.16D_6}$$

$$R^2 = 0.68;\quad D\text{-}W = 1.70;\quad SER = 0.130;\quad e = 0.58$$

$$(2)\quad \log(U) = 7.27 - \underset{(2.24)}{1.34}\log\left(\frac{P_R}{P_M}\right) + \underset{(0.75)}{0.27}\log(E) - \underset{(3.08)}{0.21D_5} - \underset{(2.55)}{0.17D_6}$$

$$R^2 = 0.80;\quad D\text{-}W = 1.60;\quad SER = 0.124;\quad e = 0.72$$

$$(3)\quad \log(U) = 4.17 - \underset{(2.46)}{1.37}\log\left(\frac{P_R}{P_M}\right) + \underset{(1.64)}{0.56}\log(E_{-1}) - \underset{(3.22)}{0.22D_5} - \underset{(2.72)}{0.18D_6}$$

$$R^2 = 0.81;\quad D\text{-}W = 1.52;\quad SER = 0.119;\quad e = 0.67.$$

(U = ration utilization; E = ration entitlement E_{-1} = one-period-lagged ration entitlement; P_R = ration price; P_M = market price; D_5 and D_6 = dummies for the months of May and June; D-W = Durbin-Watson statistic; SER = standard error of regression; e = autocorrelation among residuals; and the values within the parentheses are the t-values.)

Equation (1) regresses the rate of ration utilization on the relative price of wheat in the rationed and open markets. The results are excellent: all the coefficients are of the expected sign and statistically

3. The wheat supplied during the period of our study in Metropolitan Delhi ration shops has generally been itself of the higher indigenous quality rather than the coarser imported variety. It might, however, be mentioned that one post-harvest factor that goes in the reverse direction is the possibility that wages fall after the harvest-induced demand for labor disappears, and hence the opportunity cost of queues may fall for the poor, *or* more people may flow into Metropolitan Delhi looking for urban work. On the other hand, the months of May and June, characterized by heat and holidays, may also imply some outflow of the not-so-poor and the rich from universities, bureacracy, judiciary, parliamentary, and other sectors of employment in the city.

4. We may note that simultaneity is not a problem, since the open market price in the Delhi metropolitan region is determined by the supply and demand situation over a much larger area and therefore can be regarded as independent of local demand within the metropolitan area. Furthermore, we should note that we adopted the Cochrane-Orcutt method to remove autocorrelation among the error terms.

significant at the 5 percent level. The dummy variables show that the fifth and sixth months, i.e., May and June, which are the immediate post-harvest months, have negative signs, conforming to hypotheses such as what the farmer-consumers withdraw from the rationed and open markets during that period, as argued above.

However, the coefficient for ration entitlement is necessarily constrained to unity in equation (1). To relax this requirement, we estimated equation (2): where this coefficient turned out to be substantially lower than unity and also statistically insignificant, suggesting that an increase in the entitlement leads only to a marginal increase in the utilization during the same period. Equation (3) was therefore considered with a time lag of one period, which seemed reasonable on a priori grounds, with the result that the coefficient for ration entitlement became larger and statistically significant at the 10 percent level of significance. Again, the coefficients have the expected signs, as with equation (1). (Again, seasonality shows up here. A decline in utilization occurs up to 20–25 percent in May and at 16–18 percent in June.)

Thus, regardless of whether we choose equation (1) or equation (3)—though, we prefer the latter, for reasons that follow immediately from our discussion above—the hypothesis that we began with is consistent with the statistical evidence. For, in either case, the ration utilized varies inversely with the price of wheat in the rationed relative to the open market.

III. Concluding Remarks

Our analysis evidently has relevance to planning for the governmental procurement policies in dual-market systems, since procurements are determined by the expected utilization of the ration entitlements.

It also has wider ramifications for the welfare implications of rationing systems, since the social opportunity cost of queuing will vary with the value that society may choose to place on *what* is forgone. Thus, if the opportunity cost is in terms of alternative work forgone, this may be valued more highly by a planner than the opportunity cost in terms of the leisure of a *babushka*!

Finally, while we have referred to ration systems in developing countries, and our specific statistical evidence pertains to the Indian wheat ration system, the analysis is equally applicable to developed countries. E.g., the U.K. medical service market is a classic example that would fit readily into our analytical framework, since the National Health Service makes medical services available at a fixed, subsidized price vector, but there are typically queues for high-quality service; whereas the open market makes these services available more quickly at higher prices. There is, of course, also a problem of differential quality between the two markets when a service of a certain quality may simply not be available under the National Health Service.

COLUMBIA UNIVERSITY
MASSACHUSETTS INSTITUTE OF TECHNOLOGY

REFERENCES

Ahmed, Raisuddin, *Foodgrain Supply, Distribution, and Consumption Policies within a Dual Pricing Mechanism: A Case Study of Bangladesh,* IFPRI (International Food Policy Research Institute) Research Report No. 8, Washington, D.C., May 1979.

George, P. S., *Public Distribution of Foodgrains in Kerala—Income Distribution Implication and Effectiveness,* IFPRI Research Report No. 7, Washington, D.C., March 1979.

Swamy, Gurushri, "Public Food Distribution in India," GREP Division Working Paper, I.B.R.D. (World Bank), July 1979.

DIVIDEND POLICY AND TAX INCIDENCE IN A GROWING ECONOMY*

J. GREGORY BALLENTINE

In their recent article, Feldstein, Green, and Sheshinski [1979, hereinafter FGS] demonstrate that the burden of a corporation income tax on equity profits with interest payments deductible is shared by equity holders and debt holders. In the particular context of the FGS model, this result is quite surprising and even counterintuitive. Since the FGS model takes the economy's capital-labor ratio to be fixed and, in the principal case they examine, the fraction of the capital stock financed by equity is fixed independent of the net return on equity, it would seem that a tax on equity income would be borne by stockholders. That is, if when net return falls stockholders do not adjust their equity investments either by saving less or by switching to debt, how are they able to avoid part of the tax burden?

In this note we explore the FGS result more fully in order to determine its source and its generality. We do so by noting how the result changes under two different modifications of the model. The first modification is minor and is actually termed "more natural" than the original model by FGS themselves [FGS, 1979, p. 414, note 4]. With just this modification it is clear that the FGS result lacks generality. Using the second, more substantive, modification, the FGS result is completely reversed, and the more intuitive conclusion that equity holders bear the tax is obtained. Further, the modified model makes it clear that in the FGS analysis the diffusion of the burden from equity to debt holders arises largely from their assumption as to the way in which firms' dividend policies are determined.

The simplest way to begin our discussion is to introduce the FGS notation and sketch their model. i_N and e_N are the rates of return net of all taxes on corporate debt and equity, respectively. The personal tax rate on debt is θ. The personal tax rate on equity depends on the fraction of after-corporate-tax earnings paid out as dividends (written as p), on the personal tax on dividends (which is θ), and on the effective personal tax on retentions (which is $\mu\theta$). $\mu < 1$ indicates that retentions are preferentially taxed. Writing one minus the effective personal tax on equity income as x, we have

$$x = p(1-\theta) + (1-p)(1-\mu\theta).$$

* The author would like to thank Fred Arditti and William Bomberger for their comments on an earlier draft of this paper.

The Quarterly Journal of Economics, December 1980 0033-5533/80/0095-0781$01.00

FGS assume that firms perceive that the returns they must pay on debt and equity are given by the functions

$$i_N = \phi(b, e_N, i_N)$$

and

$$e_N = \psi(b, e_N, i_N),$$

where b is the fraction of capital that is debt financed and $\partial i_N/\partial b$ and $\partial e_N/\partial b$ are both positive.[1]

The cost of capital net of the corporation income tax is given by

$$N = \frac{b(1-\tau)i_N}{1-\theta} + \frac{e_N(1-b)}{x},$$

where τ is the corporation income tax rate. The firm chooses a debt equity ratio and a dividend payout rate to minimize N. With $\mu < 1$, the firm can always lower N by lowering p until $p = 0$. If all earnings are retained, however, the firm's stock of equity capital may grow faster than the rate of growth of the economy as a whole (n), which is inconsistent with long-run equilibrium. Thus, the firm chooses a value of p to minimize N under the constraint $n \geq (1-p)e_N/x$.

The complete system of equations for the model is

$$(1) \qquad 0 = f' - bi_N/(1-\theta) - (1-b)e_N/(1-\tau)x$$

$$(2) \qquad 0 = (1-\mu)\theta xn - (x+\theta-1)e_N$$

$$(3) \qquad 0 = \frac{(1-\tau)}{(1-\theta)}(i_N + b\phi') - \frac{e_N}{x} + \frac{(1-b)\psi'}{1-\theta}.$$

Equation (1) is the profit-maximizing condition that the value of the marginal product of capital (f') is equal to the marginal cost of capital.[2] Equations (2) and (3) are the first-order conditions for minimizing N with respect to p and b, respectively. We shall restrict our analysis to the primary case considered by FGS in which portfolio preferences keep b constant. In that case equations (1)–(3) are sufficient to determine the three variables i_N, e_N, and x.

Before turning to our modification of the model, it must be noted that the solution for $di_N/d\tau$, which FGS report, contains an error. The correct solution is[3]

1. For simplicity we deal only with long-run equilibrium, and thus we can take market variables and firm variables to be equal. See FGS [1979, p. 416].
2. FGS assume that the aggregate savings rate is constant; thus the capital-labor ratio in the economy is constant, and f' is also constant.
3. The derivation is available upon request.

$$\frac{di_N}{d\tau} = \frac{-(1-b)^2}{(1-\tau)^2}\psi'.$$

This is unambiguously negative, so the FGS conclusion that debt holders share the burden is unaffected by their error.

In totally differentiating equations (1)–(3) to solve for $di_N/d\tau$, FGS assume that the derivatives, $\partial i_N/\partial b = \phi'$ and $\partial e_N/\partial b = \psi'$, are independent of i_N and e_N. Our first modification of their analysis is to assume instead that the elasticities, $(\partial i_N/\partial b)(b/i_N) = \epsilon_\phi$ and $(\partial e_N/\partial b)(b/e_N) = \epsilon_\psi$, are independent of i_N and e_N.[4] Using their assumption, FGS find that $di_N/d\tau$ is unambiguously negative. Under our alternative we can derive[5]

$$\frac{di_N}{d\tau} = \left(\frac{e_N}{x(1-\tau)}\right)\left(\frac{b}{1-b}\right)\epsilon_\psi(1-p)\theta(\mu-1)\Big/$$
$$(1-\tau)\left\{(1+\epsilon_\phi)\left(1+\frac{(1-\tau)i_N b}{(1-b)e_N}\right)+\frac{b}{(1-b)}\,\frac{(1-p)\theta(1-\mu)}{x}\right\}.$$

This is negative as long as $\mu < 1$, but if retentions are taxed at the same rate as dividends; that is, if $\mu = 1$, then $di_N/d\tau = 0$. Further, it can also be shown that if $\mu > 1$, $di_N/d\tau = 0$.[6]

The significance of the different assumptions can be explained by using an analogy. Clearly if one assumes that some rate of return is constant net of taxes and then one analyzes the impact of a tax on *that* return, the tax will be found to have nonneutral results; i.e., the tax will lower, or at least change, other rates of return. This is similar to the effect of the FGS assumption. They assumed that the rise in the *net of tax* return to equity induced by a rise in b, ψ', is constant. But, it is the gross of tax rise in the return to equity, $\psi'/(1-\theta)(1-\tau)$, which is relevant for the firm's choice of a debt-equity ratio. (The role of $\psi'/(1-\theta)(1-\tau)$ can be seen by dividing equation (3) by $(1-\tau)$.) Thus, if, by assumption, ψ' is constant, the corresponding cost must rise when τ is increased. This causes the firm to attempt to change its

4. As mentioned above, FGS state that the elasticity assumption used here is more natural than the assumption they used. They contend, however, that the elasticity assumption complicates the algebra without adding much of interest [FGS, 1979, p. 414, note 4]. Our analysis shows that using the elasticity assumption does add interesting results.

5. The derivation is available from the author.

6. Equations (2) and (3) and the equation for $di_N/d\tau$ given in the text are not appropriate when $\mu > 1$. This is because, if $\mu > 1$, the optimal value of p is 1 and the constraint $n \geq (1-p)e$ is strictly nonbinding. In this case x is no longer a variable, it is a constant equal to $1-\theta$. To solve for $di_N/d\tau$ when $\mu > 1$, one uses equation (1) and the first-order condition for an unconstrained minimization of N with respect to b. The resulting solution shows that $di_N/d\tau = 0$. A derivation of that solution is available from the author.

debt-equity ratio leading to changes in i_N. If, on the other hand, the elasticity assumption is used, ψ' may not be constant; it will fall in proportion to any fall in the return on equity e_N. Since the tax does lower e_N, ψ' will fall, which *tends* to keep the relevant cost unchanged, preventing any adjustment that might reduce i_N.

Of course, the elasticity assumption does not guarantee that i_N will not change. As our equation for $di_N/d\tau$ shows, under the elasticity assumption the effect on the interest rate of a corporation income tax applied equally to dividends and retentions depends crucially upon whether retentions receive preferential personal income tax treatment. The reason for this interrelationship is a bit complex and hinges upon the manner in which the dividend payout ratio is determined in the FGS model. To see the source of this interrelationship, we begin by rewriting equation (3) as

$$(3')\qquad \frac{e_N}{x(1-\tau)} = \frac{i_N}{1-\theta} + \frac{i_N\epsilon_\phi}{1-\theta} + \frac{e_N\epsilon_\psi}{(1-\theta)(1-\tau)}\,\frac{(1-b)}{b}.$$

We can refer to the left-hand side of (3′) as the marginal cost of equity finance and the right-hand side as the marginal cost of debt finance.[7] The marginal cost of equity, then, is the return, gross of tax, which must be paid on an extra unit of equity capital. The marginal cost of debt is the return that must be paid on an extra unit of debt capital plus both the marginal rise in the debt risk premium and the marginal rise in the equity risk premium, all gross of the relevant taxes.

Notice that the personal tax rate applied to the marginal cost of an extra unit of equity capital is $1 - x$, while the personal tax applied to the marginal rise in the equity risk premium is θ. If the elasticity assumption is used in the model, then it is entirely due to this simple difference in the tax treatment of equity returns that an increase in τ lowers the interest rate. Further, that difference in personal taxation is due solely to the way in which the dividend payout ratio is determined in the model.

We shall first explain why this difference in tax treatment is so significant. Suppose that when τ is increased, equity holders bear the full burden of the tax increase. This means that i_N does not fall and e_N/x falls in proportion to the fall in $1 - \tau$. We seek to determine why this cannot be a new equilibrium. Clearly, if i_N and $e_N/x(1 - \tau)$ are unchanged, then the marginal cost of a unit of capital financed using

7. This terminology is a bit loose. Equation (3′) describes cost minimization with respect to the fraction of capital financed by debt and not with respect to the level of debt finance and the level of equity finance separately. But this convenient terminology does not introduce any error.

b units of debt capital and $(1 - b)$ units of equity capital is unchanged.[8] This means that equation (1) still holds. If $(1 - p)$ rises in proportion to the fall in $(1 - \tau)$, then with the assumed fall in e_N/x, equation (2) will also still hold.[9]

But equation (3′) will not hold. The gross return to an extra unit of equity capital, the gross return to an extra unit of debt capital, and the gross of tax marginal rise in the debt risk premium are all unchanged. However, the gross of tax marginal rise in the equity risk premium must have risen. Note that x rises because the decline in the equity return after corporate profits, e_N/x, allows firms to retain a higher proportion of that return. If $e_N/x(1 - \tau)$ does not change and x rises, then $e_N/(1 - \theta)(1 - \tau)$ must rise.

What has happened, then, is that the tax increase has raised the marginal cost of debt finance. In order for firms to be willing to use the same amount of debt finance, the interest rate must fall. But why does the marginal cost of debt rise when the interest rate remains unchanged and a tax on equity is increased? The answer is simply that the marginal equity risk premium is taxed at the constant personal rate θ instead of the declining personal rate $1 - x$.

If the personal tax rate applied to the marginal equity risk premium were $1 - x$ instead of θ, all three equations would have held in the example given above and, therefore, a rise in τ would leave i_N unchanged in the new equilibrium. The reason for this difference in personal tax treatment is the way in which the dividend payout ratio is determined. Essentially p is determined by the firm retaining as much profits as it can, subject to the constraint on the rate of growth of equity capital. Changes in equity profits for a given amount of equity capital, that is, changes in the rate of return on equity after corporate taxes, do not induce proportionate changes in retentions and dividends, but are all paid out as dividends.[10] Consequently, the personal tax rate applied to the return on a unit of equity is $1 - x$, but the tax rate applied to the change in that return due to a change in b,

8. Note that here we are referring to the marginal cost of a unit of capital holding b unchanged. On the other hand, the marginal capital cost terms in equation (3′) deal with changes in debt or equity with the attendant change in b.

9. Equation (2) can be rewritten as $n = (1 - p)e_N/x$, which is to say, with $\mu \leq$ the value of p, which minimizes N always just satisfies the constraint. Let primes denote equilibrium values before the tax increase and bars denote the possible values we are considering after the tax increase. Then $n = (1 - p')e_N'/x'$. We are considering the case in which $e_N'/x'(1 - \tau') = \bar{e}_N/\bar{x}(1 - \bar{\tau})$; thus $(1 - \bar{p}) = (1 - p')(1 - \tau')/(1 - \bar{\tau})$ satisfies equation (2).

10. Recall that when we hypothesized that e_N/x fell in proportion to the fall in $(1 - \tau)$, the payout rate rose. This is because the decline in the rate of return after corporate taxes, e_N/x, was entirely a decline in dividends.

the marginal equity risk premium, is the same as the tax on dividends θ.

We can see now why the value of μ is so important in determining whether or not i_N falls when τ rises. If $\mu = 1$, the payout rate is indeterminate and $x = 1 - \theta$. If $\mu > 1$, the payout rate is 1 and again $x = 1 - \theta$. In either case x is constant, and the same personal tax rate is applied to the return on equity and the marginal equity risk premium. Thus, if $\mu \geq 1$, a rise in τ induces a new equilibrium at which i_N is unchanged and $e_N/(1 - \theta)$ falls in proportion to the fall in $(1 - \tau)$.[11] That is, stockholders bear the full burden of a tax on equity.[12]

Up to this point the only change we have made in the FGS model is the assumption that $\psi' b/e_N$ and $\phi' b/i_N$ are constant in place of the assumption that ψ' and ϕ' are constant. We now very briefly consider a more substantial alteration in the model that results in the conclusion that i_N never falls when τ is raised. Suppose that the dividend payout ratio is not determined by minimizing N with respect to p, but instead is determined solely by the cost of paying one dollar of dividends net of all taxes in terms of forgone retentions net of all taxes. That is, let $p = g[(1 - \mu\theta)/(1 - \theta)]$. The theoretical justification for such a relationship is, admittedly, somewhat sketchy. Feldstein [1970] presents a brief intuitive rationale for it, while King [1977, Ch. 6] gives a more detailed but still rather heuristic justification. However, in Feldstein [1970], and King [1971 and 1977], this type of relationship has obtained good empirical results.

The point here is not to argue that one method of determining p is clearly more realistic than the other. Instead the point is that both are plausible alternatives, and it is worthwhile to know whether the effect of the corporation income tax on the interest rate on corporate debt hinges upon the seemingly somewhat unrelated question of the determination of the dividend payout ratio.

In fact, the effect of τ on i_N hinges upon just this question. If $p = g[(1 - \mu\theta)/(1 - \theta)]$, then all equity returns and changes in the return on equity are paid out in the proportion p and, thus, are taxed at the personal tax rate $1 - x$. The three equations of the model for this case are equation (1), $p = g[(1 - \mu\theta)/(1 - \theta)]$, and the first-order condition for an unconstrained minimum of N with respect to b, which can be written as

11. Since θ is constant, the fall is entirely a fall in e_N.

12. We can also now see why, when it is assumed that ψ' is constant instead of $\epsilon_{\psi'}$, i_N must fall no matter what the value of μ is. The third term in equation (3′) can be written as $(1 - b)\psi'/(1 - \theta)(1 - \tau)$. If ψ' is constant, then this term must rise when τ rises, jarring the firm out of equilibrium even if i_N is unchanged, $\mu \geq 1$, and $e_N/(1 - \theta)(1 - \tau)$ is unchanged.

$$\frac{e_N}{x(1-\tau)} = \frac{i_N}{(1-\theta)} + \frac{i_N \epsilon_\phi}{(1-\theta)} + \frac{e_N \epsilon_\psi}{x(1-\tau)} \frac{(1-b)}{b}.$$

Notice that both the return on equity and the marginal equity risk premium receive the same personal tax treatment. Upon differentiating this model with respect to τ, it can be shown that $di_N/d\tau = 0$; the corporation income tax has no effect on the interest rate on corporate debt.[13] Thus, in this model, stockholders bear the full tax burden.[14]

UNIVERSITY OF FLORIDA

REFERENCES

Feldstein, Martin, "Corporate Taxation and Dividend Behavior," *Review of Economic Studies,* XXXVII (1970), 57–72.

——, Jerry Green, and Eytan Sheshinski, "Corporate Financial Policy and Taxation in a Growing Economy," this *Journal,* XCIII (Aug. 1979), 411–32.

King, M. A., "Corporate Taxation and Dividend Behavior—A Comment," *Review of Economic Studies,* XXXVIII (1971), 377–80.

——, *Public Policy and the Corporation* (London: Chapman and Hall Ltd., 1977).

13. The derivation of $di_N/d\tau$ for this case is available from the author. FGS use their model to show that changes in μ have no effect on i_N and that, if their assumption fixing b is relaxed and b is positively related to $i_N - e_N$, then an increase in τ raises b. Both of these conclusions still hold in the modified models discussed in this note.

14. Even if firms do choose p on the basis of $(1 - \mu\theta)/(1 - \theta)$, if the FGS assumption that ψ' and θ' are constant is used instead of the assumption that the corresponding elasticities are constant, then an increase in τ will change i_N. The reason is the same as before; by assuming ψ' to be constant, one is assuming that the rise in net of tax equity returns caused by a change in b is constant. Therefore, changes in the tax on that net return i.e., changes in τ, will cause the marginal cost of debt finance to change, leading firms to adjust their behavior and, in turn, leading to changes in i_N.